In a recent survey, "appreciating human diversity" was rated the *most important* outcome of an introductory anthropology course.

WITHDRAWN

appreciating DIVERSITY

Culturally Appropriate Marketing

Innovation succeeds best when it is culturally appropriate. This axiom of applied anthropology could guide the international spread not only of development projects but also of businesses, such as fast food. Each time McDonald's or Burger King expands to a new nation, it must devise a culturally appropriate strategy for fitting into the new setting.

McDonald's has been successful internationally, with more than a quarter of its sales outside the United States. One place where McDonald's is expanding successfully is Brazil, where more than 50 million middle-class people, most living in densely packed cities, provide a concentrated market for a fast-food chain. Still, it took McDonald's some time to find the right marketing strategy for Brazil.

In 1980 when I visited Brazil after a seven-year absence, I first noticed, as a manifestation of Brazil's growing participation in the world economy, the appearance of two McDonald's restaurants in Rio de Janeiro. There wasn't much difference between Brazilian and North American McDonald's. The restaurants looked alike. The menus were more or less the same, as was the taste of the quarter-pounders. I picked up an artifact, a white paper bag with yellow lettering, exactly like the take-out bags then used in American McDonald's. An advertising device, it carried several messages about how Brazilians could bring McDonald's into their lives. However, it seemed to me that McDonald's Brazilian ad campaign was missing some important points about how fast food should be marketed in a culture that values large, leisurely lunches.

The bag proclaimed, "You're going to enjoy the [McDonald's] difference," and listed several "favorite places where you can enjoy McDonald's products." This list confirmed that the marketing people were trying to adapt to Brazilian middle-class culture, but they were making some mistakes. "When you go out in the car with the kids" transferred the uniquely developed North American cultural combination of highways, affordable cars, and suburban living to the very different context of urban Brazil. A similar suggestion was "traveling to the country place." Even Brazilians who owned country places could not find McDonald's, still confined to the cities, on the road. The ad creator had apparently never attempted to drive up to a fast-food restaurant in a neighborhood with no parking spaces.

Several other suggestions pointed customers toward the beach, where *cariocas* (Rio natives) do spend much of their leisure time. One

> **"Appreciating Diversity"** boxes explore the rich diversity of cultures (past and present) that anthropologists study. These boxes supplement the extensive discussions of cultures around the world presented throughout the text.

 These are just some of the reasons why **three out of four** Kottak adopters report that they will adopt the new edition of the text.

Anthropology

Appreciating Human Diversity

Fourteenth Edition

Conrad Phillip Kottak
University of Michigan

To my mother, Mariana Kottak Roberts

The **McGraw·Hill** Companies

Mc Graw Hill — Connect Learn Succeed™

Published by McGraw-Hill, a business unit of The McGraw-Hill Companies, Inc., 1221 Avenue of the Americas, New York, NY 10020. Copyright © 2011, 2009, 2008, 2006, 2004, 2002, 2000, 1997, 1994, 1991, 1987, 1982, 1978, 1974 by The McGraw-Hill Companies, Inc. All rights reserved. No part of this publication may be reproduced or distributed in any form or by any means, or stored in a database or retrieval system, without the prior written consent of The McGraw-Hill Companies, Inc., including, but not limited to, any network or other electronic storage or transmission, or broadcast for distance learning.

Some ancillaries, including electronic and print components, may not be available to customers outside the United States.

This book is printed on acid-free paper.

2 3 4 5 6 7 8 9 0 DOW/DOW 9 8 7 6 5 4 3 2 1 0

ISBN: 978-0-07-811699-5
MHID: 0-07-811699-6

Vice President, Editorial: *Michael Ryan*
Director, Editorial: *Beth Mejia*
Sponsoring Editor: *Gina Boedeker*
Director of Development: *Rhona Robbin*
Developmental Editor: *Emily Pecora*
Marketing Manager: *Caroline McGillen*
Production Editor: *Leslie Racanelli*
Manuscript Editor: *Patricia Ohlenroth*
Design Manager: *Cassandra Chu*
Interior Designer: *Maureen McCutcheon*
Cover Designer: *Cassandra Chu*
Map Preparations: *Mapping Specialists*
Photo Research Coordinator: *Nora Agbayani*
Photo Researcher: *Barbara Salz*
Production Supervisor: *Louis Swaim*
Media Project Manager: *Jami Woy*
Composition: *9.5/11 Palatino by Aptara®, Inc.*
Printing: *45# New Era Matte by R. R. Donnelley & Sons*

Cover image: *Keren Su/Lonely Planet Images*

The credits for this book begin on page 627 and are considered an extension of the copyright page.

Library of Congress Cataloging-in-Publication Data

Kottak, Conrad Phillip.
  Anthropology: Appreciating human diversity / Conrad Phillip Kottak. — Fourteenth ed.
    p. cm.
  Includes bibliographical references and index.
  ISBN-13: 978-0-07-811699-5 (alk. paper)
  ISBN-10: 0-07-811699-6 (alk. paper)
  1. Anthropology. I. Title.

2009943478

The Internet addresses listed in the text were accurate at the time of publication. The inclusion of a website does not indicate an endorsement by the authors or McGraw-Hill, and McGraw-Hill does not guarantee the accuracy of the information presented at these sites.

www.mhhe.com

Contents in Brief

Contents

1   *What Is Anthropology?*   2

PART 1   INTRODUCTION TO ANTHROPOLOGY

2 *Culture* 24

3 *Applying Anthropology* 48

6   *Human Variation and Adaptation*   *114*

7   *The Primates*   *134*

8 Early Hominins   160

10 *The Origin and Spread of Modern Humans* 206

13   *Method and Theory in Cultural Anthropology*   280

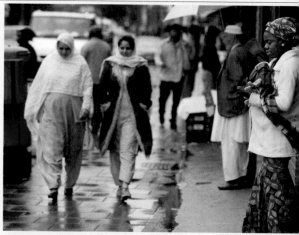

16 *Making a Living* 360

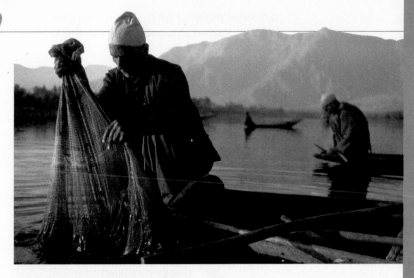

17 *Political Systems* 388

18   *Gender*   416

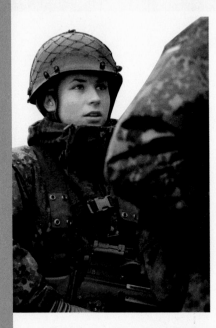

19   *Families, Kinship, and Descent*   444

20   Marriage   466

21   Religion   490

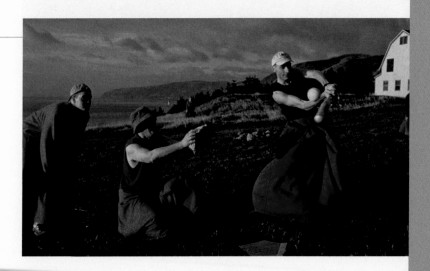

22   *Arts, Media, and Sports*   *516*

List of Boxes

appreciating ANTHROPOLOGY

appreciating DIVERSITY

living anthropology VIDEOS

through the eyes of OTHERS

RECAP

About the Author

Conrad Phillip Kottak

Conrad Phillip Kottak (A.B. Columbia College, 1963; Ph.D. Columbia University, 1966) is the Julian H. Steward Collegiate Professor of Anthropology at the University of Michigan, where he has taught since 1968. He served as anthropology department chair from 1996 to 2006. In 1991 he was honored for his teaching by the university and the state of Michigan. In 1992 he received an excellence in teaching award from the College of Literature, Sciences, and the Arts of the University of Michigan. In 1999 the American Anthropological Association (AAA) awarded Professor Kottak the AAA/Mayfield Award for Excellence in the Undergraduate Teaching of Anthropology. In 2005 he was elected to the American Academy of Arts and Sciences, and in 2008 to the National Academy of Sciences.

Professor Kottak has done ethnographic fieldwork in Brazil (since 1962), Madagascar (since 1966), and the United States. His general interests are in the processes by which local cultures are incorporated—and resist incorporation—into larger systems. This interest links his earlier work on ecology and state formation in Africa and Madagascar to his more recent research on globalization, national and international culture, and the mass media.

The fourth edition of Kottak's popular case study *Assault on Paradise: The Globalization of a Little Community in Brazil,* based on his continuing field work in Arembepe, Bahia, Brazil, was published in 2006 by McGraw-Hill. In a research project during the 1980s, Kottak blended ethnography and survey research in studying "Television's Behavioral Effects in Brazil." That research is the basis of Kottak's book *Prime-Time Society: An Anthropological Analysis of Television and Culture* (revised edition published by Left Coast Press in 2010)—a comparative study of the nature and impact of television in Brazil and the United States.

Kottak's other books include *The Past in the Present: History, Ecology and Cultural Variation in Highland Madagascar* (1980), *Researching American Culture:*

A Guide for Student Anthropologists (edited 1982) (both University of Michigan Press), and *Madagascar: Society and History* (edited 1986) (Carolina Academic Press). The most recent editions (14th) of his texts *Anthropology: Appreciating Human Diversity* (this book) and *Cultural Anthropology: Appreciating Cultural Diversity* were published by McGraw-Hill in 2010. He also is the author of *Mirror for Humanity: A Concise Introduction to Cultural Anthropology* (7th ed., McGraw-Hill, 2009) and *Window on Humanity: A Concise Introduction to Anthropology* (4th ed., McGraw-Hill, 2010). With Kathryn A. Kozaitis, he wrote *On Being Different: Diversity and Multiculturalism in the North American Mainstream* (3rd ed., McGraw-Hill, 2008).

Conrad Kottak's articles have appeared in academic journals, including *American Anthropologist, Journal of Anthropological Research, American Ethnologist, Ethnology, Human Organization,* and *Luso-Brazilian Review.* He also has written for more popular journals, including *Transaction/SOCIETY, Natural History, Psychology Today,* and *General Anthropology.*

In recent research projects, Kottak and his colleagues have investigated the emergence of ecological awareness in Brazil, the social context of deforestation and biodiversity conservation in Madagascar, and popular participation in economic development planning in northeastern Brazil. Professor Kottak has been active in the University of Michigan's Center for the Ethnography of Everyday Life, supported by the Alfred P. Sloan Foundation. In that capacity, for a research project titled "Media, Family, and Work in a Middle-Class Midwestern Town," Kottak and his colleague Lara Descartes have investigated how middle-class families draw on various media in planning, managing, and evaluating their choices and solutions with respect to the competing demands of work and family. That research is the basis of their recent book *Media and Middle Class Moms: Images and Realties of Work and Family* (Descartes and Kottak 2009, Routledge/Taylor and Francis).

Conrad Kottak appreciates comments about his books from professors and students. He can be reached by e-mail at the following Internet address: **ckottak@bellsouth.net.**

When I wrote the first edition of this book in the 1970s, the field of anthropology was changing rapidly. Anthropologists were writing about a "new archaeology" and a "new ethnography." Studies of language as actually used in society were revolutionizing overly formal and static linguistic models. Symbolic and interpretive approaches were joining ecological and materialist ones. I strove to write a book that addressed all these changes, while also providing a solid foundation of core concepts and the basics.

Anthropology continues to be an exciting field. Profound changes—including advances in communication and transportation, the expansion of global capitalism, and the challenges of a changing climate—have affected the people and societies that anthropologists study. While any competent text must present anthropology's core, it must also demonstrate anthropology's relevance to today's world.

Appreciating the Experiences Students Bring to the Classroom

One of my main goals for this edition has been to show students why anthropology should matter to them. Previous editions included short boxed sections titled **"Understanding Ourselves."** For this edition, I've expanded these accounts and moved them to the beginning of each chapter. These introductions, which draw on student experience, using familiar examples, illustrate the relevance of anthropology to everyday life and set the stage for the content that follows.

Another feature that draws on student experience, **"Through the Eyes of Others,"** offers short accounts by foreign students of how they came to perceive and appreciate key differences between their own cultures of origin and contemporary culture in the United States. These accounts point out aspects of U.S. culture that may be invisible to students who are from the United States, because they are understood as being "normal" or "just the way things are." As these examples illustrate, the viewpoint of an outsider can help make visible particular features of one's own culture.

Both the "Understanding Ourselves" introductions and "Through the Eyes of Others" boxes tie into a key theme of this book; namely, that **anthropology helps us understand ourselves.** By studying other cultures, we learn to appreciate, to question, and to reinterpret aspects of our own. As one cultural variant among many, American culture is worthy of anthropological study and analysis. Any adequate study of contemporary American culture must include popular culture. I keep up with developments in American—and, increasingly, international—popular culture, and use popular culture examples to help my students, and my readers, understand and appreciate anthropological concepts and approaches. To cite just a few examples, the anthropology of *Star Wars*, *The Wizard of Oz*, and *Desperate Housewives* are explored in this book, along with more traditional aspects of American culture.

Appreciating Human Diversity

No academic field has a stronger commitment to, or respect for, human diversity than anthropology does. Anthropologists routinely listen to, record, and attempt to represent voices and perspectives from a multitude of times, places, countries, and cultures. Through its various subfields, anthropology brings together biological, social, cultural, linguistic, and historical approaches. Multiple and diverse perspectives provide a fuller appreciation of what it means to be human.

Newly imagined for this edition, chapters now contain boxes titled **"Appreciating Diversity,"** which focus on the various forms of human biological and cultural diversity, in time and space that make anthropology so fascinating. Some of these explorations of diversity, for example the recent popularity of hugging in U.S. high schools, will likely be familiar to students. Others, like the story of a Turkish man with five wives and fifty-five children, will prompt them to consider human societies very different from their own.

A key feature of today's student body that makes anthropology more relevant than ever is its increasing diversity. Anthropologists once were the experts who *introduced* diversity to the students. The tables may have turned. Sometime during the 1990s the most common name in my 101 class shifted from Johnson to Kim. Today's students already know a lot about diversity and cultural differences, often from their own backgrounds as well as from the media. For instructors, knowing one's audience today means appreciating that, compared with us when we first learned anthropology, the undergraduate student body is likely to be (1) more diverse, (2) more familiar with diversity; and (3) more comfortable with diversity. We're very lucky to be able to build on such student experience.

Appreciating the Field of Anthropology

I want students to appreciate the field of anthropology and the various kinds of diversity it studies. How do anthropologists work? How does anthropology contribute to our understanding of the world? To help students answer these questions, chapters now contain boxed sections titled **"Appreciating Anthropology,"** which focus on the value and usefulness of anthropological research and approaches.

At its core, anthropology is grounded in both the sciences and the humanities. As a science, anthropology relies on systematic observation, careful record-keeping, and evidence-based analysis. Anthropologists apply these tools of the scientific method to the study of human cultures. In the words of Clyde Kluckhohn (1944), "Anthropology provides a scientific basis for dealing with the crucial dilemma of the world today: How can peoples of different appearance, mutually unintelligible languages, and dissimilar ways of life get along peaceably together?"

Anthropology reveals its roots in the humanities through the comparative and cross-cultural perspective it brings to bear on the full range of human endeavors and creative expressions. In fact, I see anthropology as one of the most humanistic academic fields because of its fundamental appreciation of human diversity. Anthropologists routinely listen to, record, and attempt to represent voices and perspectives from a multitude of times, places, countries, cultures, and fields. Multiple and diverse perspectives provide a fuller appreciation of what it means to be human.

Appreciating Human Diversity

appreciating DIVERSITY

"Give Me a Hug"

In Winter 2008 I created and taught a course called "Experiencing Culture" to American college students in Italy. Students wrote bi-weekly journals reflecting on the cultural differences they observed between Europeans and Americans. One thing that really struck them was the greater frequency and intensity of PDAs—public displays of affection between romantic couples in Italy, compared with the U.S.

The world's nations and cultures have strikingly different notions about displays of affection and personal space. Cocktail parties in international meeting places such as the United Nations can resemble an elaborate insect mating ritual as diplomats from different countries advance, withdraw, and sidestep. When Americans talk, walk, and dance, they maintain a certain distance from others. Italians or Brazilians, who need less personal space, may interpret such "standoffishness" as a

sign of coldness. In conversational pairs, the Italian or Brazilian typically moves in, while the American "instinctively" retreats from a "close talker."

Such bodily movements illustrate not instinct, but culture—behavior programmed by years of exposure to a particular cultural tradition. Culture, however, is not static, as is suggested by this recent account of hugging behavior in American schools. Appreciate as well that any nation usually contains diverse and even conflicting cultural values. One example is generational diversity, which the famed anthropologist Margaret Mead, one of my teachers, referred to as "the generation gap." Americans (in this case parents and school officials versus teenagers) exhibit generational differences involving the propriety of PDAs and concerns about sexual harassment.

There is so much hugging at Pascack Hills High School in Montvale, N.J., that students have broken down the hugs by type:

There is the basic friend hug, probably the most popular, and the bear hug, of course.

But now there is also the bear claw, when a boy embraces a girl awkwardly with his elbows poking out.

There is the hug that starts with a high-five, then moves into a fist bump, followed by a slap on the back and an embrace.

There's the shake and lean; the hug from behind; and, the newest addition, the triple—any combination of three girls and boys hug-

Ethnicity and Race 15

What is social status, and how does it relate to ethnicity?

How are race and ethnicity socially constructed in various societies?

What are the positive and negative aspects of ethnicity?

This street scene in Birmingham, England shows Asian and Afro-Caribbean women in the Lozells neighborhood, a site of unrest between these two ethnic groups. What national and ethnic identities might these women claim?

Anthropology Atlas

Comprising 18 maps, this atlas presents a global view of
issues important to anthropologists and to the people
they study, such as world forest loss, the origin and
spread of food production, and ancient civilizations.
Cross references in the text tie the
maps to relevant chapter discussions.

MAP 15
World Religions

Because religion is a fundamental characteristic of human culture, a depiction of the spatial distribution of religions comes close to a map of cultural patterns. More than just a set of behavior patterns having to do with worship and ceremony, religion influences the ways in which people deal with one another, with their institutions, and with their environments. An examination of this map in the context of conflict within and among nations also shows that the tension between countries and the internal stability of states are also functions of the spatial distribution of religion.

QUESTIONS

Look at Map 15, "World Religions."

1. Which continent has the most diversity with respect to the major religions?

2. Which continent is most Protestant? Why do you think that is the case?

3. Where in the world are "tribal" religions still practiced?

understanding OURSELVES

"Hey, it's all in the genes." We routinely use assumptions about genetic determination to explain, say, why tall parents have tall kids or why obesity runs in families. But just how much do genes really influence our bodies? The genetics behind some physical traits, e.g., blood types, are clear, but the genetic roots of other traits are less so. For example, can you crease or fold your tongue by raising its sides? (See the photo below.) Some people easily can; some people never can; some people who never thought they could can after practicing. An apparent genetic limitation turns out to be more plastic.

Human biology is plastic, but only to a degree. If you're born with blood group O, you've got it for life. The same is true for hemophilia and sickle cell anemia. Fortunately, cultural (medical) solutions now exist for many genetic disorders. Can you appreciate in yourself or your family

any genetic condition for which there has been a cultural (e.g., medical) intervention? Although modern medical advances usually are viewed favorably, some people worry that culture may be intervening too much with intrinsic biological features. Some members of the hearing-impaired community, for example, spurn cochlear implants, viewing them as a threat to a deaf subculture that they hold dear. Plastic surgery, genetic screening, and the possibility of genetic engineering of infants (e.g. "designer babies") concern those who imagine a future in which physical "perfection" might reduce human diversity and increase socioeconomic inequality.

Even as our culture struggles with issues of medically manipulated biological plasticity, many people still question the long-term plasticity of the human genome, a process known as evolution. Most basically, evolution is the idea that all living organisms come from ancestors that were different in some way. The

Tongue rolling—a genetic trait, at least partially. Some members of this family seem to be better at it than others are.

---

features correlate with social factors, including class and gender differences (Tannen 1990)? One reason for variation is geography, as in regional dialects and accents. Linguistic variation also is expressed in the bilingualism of ethnic groups. Linguistic and cultural anthropologists collaborate in studying links between language and many other aspects of culture, such as how people reckon kinship and how they perceive and classify colors.

ANTHROPOLOGY AND OTHER ACADEMIC FIELDS

As mentioned previously, one of the main differences between anthropology and the other fields that study people is holism, anthropology's unique blend of biological, social, cultural, linguistic, historical, and contemporary perspectives. Paradoxically, while distinguishing anthropology, this breadth is what also links it to many other disciplines. Techniques used to date fossils and artifacts have come to anthropology from physics, chemistry, and geology. Because plant and animal remains often are found with human bones and artifacts, anthropologists collaborate with botanists, zoologists, and paleontologists.

As a discipline that is both scientific and humanistic, anthropology has links with many other academic fields. Anthropology is a **science**—a "systematic field of study or body of knowledge that aims, through experiment, observation, and deduction, to produce reliable explanations of phenomena, with reference to the material and physical world" (*Webster's New World Encyclopedia* 1993, p. 937). The following chapters present anthropology as a humanistic science devoted to discovering, describing, understanding, and explaining similarities and differences in time and space among humans and our ancestors. Clyde Kluckhohn (1944) described anthropology as "the science of human similarities and differences" (p. 9). His statement of the need for such a field still stands: "Anthropology provides a scientific basis for dealing with the crucial dilemma of the world today: how can peoples of different appearance, mutually unintelligible languages, and dissimilar ways of life get along peaceably together?" (p. 9). Anthropology has compiled an impressive body of knowledge that this textbook attempts to encapsulate.

Besides its links to the natural sciences (e.g., geology, zoology) and social sciences (e.g., sociology, psychology), anthropology also has strong links to the humanities. The humanities include English, comparative literature, classics, folklore, philosophy, and the arts. These fields study languages, texts, philosophies, arts, music, performances, and other forms of creative expression. Ethnomusicology, which studies forms of musical expression on a worldwide basis, is especially closely related to anthropology. Also linked to folklore, the systematic

study of tales, myths, and legends from a variety of cultures. One might well argue that anthropology is among the most humanistic of all academic fields because of its fundamental respect for human diversity. Anthropologists listen to, record, and represent voices from a multitude of nations and cultures. Anthropology values local knowledge,

through the eyes of OTHERS

STUDENT: María Alejandra Pérez, Ph.D. Candidate in Cultural Anthropology
COUNTRY OF ORIGIN: Venezuela
SUPERVISING PROFESSORS: Erik Mueggler and Fernando Coronil
SCHOOL: University of Michigan

Changing Places, Changing Identities

I was born and lived in Venezuela's capital, Caracas, for 15 years. Caracas was large and chaotic, but wonderfully cosmopolitan. Years of relatively stable democracy and a state infrastructure fueled by oil made this city attractive to many immigrants, not just from rural areas, but from the rest of South America and Europe as well. While growing up, I never thought much about how the place where we live impacts, often in very small ways, who we are. As I later came to realize, it is amazing how much what is familiar to us comes into focus when we travel and live elsewhere, far from the people and customs we are used to. Elements of our identity change, too, in different situations. In fact, plunging ourselves into a different context and carefully evaluating the complexity of this experience are a fundamental part of anthropological research.

Moving from Caracas as a teenager was bad enough, but when my family and I arrived in Trinidad, a small town in southern Colorado, one blustery November night, I wondered what I had done wrong to deserve such a fate! In Trinidad, my father joked that you'd miss the town limits if you biked too fast. Many of my new high school classmates had never flown on an airplane, much less seen the ocean. Most of them had last names such as Gonzales and Salazar, and their families had lived in the area for several generations. As different as I felt from them, we shared, in the American social context, identifiers such as Hispanic or Latino, terms that never made much sense to me, since they purportedly bundled together people I viewed as not having much in common. Just as I noticed how different my classmates were from me, elements that I felt made my family "distinctly Venezuelan" stood out, both tinted and amplified, no doubt, by my nostalgia for the people and places left behind. We stayed up late, danced to salsa on Christmas Eve and New Year's, lamented the lack of homemade *hallacas* (a traditional Venezuelan Christmas dish) and blabbed and joked in a Spanish that is characteristically *Caraqueño* (from Caracas). These seemingly trivial stereotypes became for me, during that first holiday away from home, the essence of our identity.

Years later, while conducting fieldwork in rural eastern Venezuela, I would again face the challenge of defining my identity both to myself and to local people who viewed me as a foreigner. This time, after several years of graduate school, I could better understand my reactions. I now appreciate what it means to be part of one culture and not another and that what it means to be local is contextual and dynamic.

science
Field of study that seeks reliable explanations, with reference to the material and physical world.

"Understanding Ourselves" Introductions

These chapter introductions (expanded from a feature previously spread throughout the book) prompt students to relate anthropology to their own culture and their own lives. Students learn that anthropology provides insights into nearly every aspect of daily life, from what we eat for breakfast, to how reliant we are on bipedalism (our own two feet), to how often baseball players spit, to cite just a few examples.

"Through the Eyes of Others" Essays

Written by students raised outside the United States, these essays contrast aspects of life in contemporary American culture with similar aspects in the authors' cultures of origin. The observations within these essays show students how cultural practices that seem familiar and natural are not seen as such by others.

Bring to the Classroom

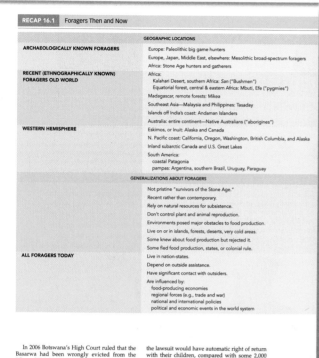

RECAP 16.1 | Foragers Then and Now

	GEOGRAPHIC LOCATIONS
ARCHAEOLOGICALLY KNOWN FORAGERS	Europe: Paleolithic big game hunters
	Europe, Japan, Middle East, elsewhere: Mesolithic broad-spectrum foragers
	Africa: Stone Age hunters and gatherers
RECENT (ETHNOGRAPHICALLY KNOWN) FORAGERS OLD WORLD	Africa: Kalahari Desert, southern Africa: *San* ("Bushmen") Equatorial forest, central & eastern Africa: Mbuti, Efe ("pygmies")
	Madagascar, remote forests: Mikea
	Southeast Asia—Malaysia and Philippines: Tasaday
	Islands off India's coast: Andaman Islanders
	Australia: entire continent—Native Australians ("aborigines")
WESTERN HEMISPHERE	Eskimos, or Inuit: Alaska and Canada
	N. Pacific coast: California, Oregon, Washington, British Columbia, and Alaska
	Inland subarctic Canada and U.S. Great Lakes
	South America: coastal Patagonia pampas: Argentina, southern Brazil, Uruguay, Paraguay
	GENERALIZATIONS ABOUT FORAGERS
	Not pristine "survivors of the Stone Age."
	Recent rather than contemporary.
	Rely on natural resources for subsistence.
	Don't control plant and animal reproduction.
	Environments posed major obstacles to food production.
	Live on or in islands, forests, deserts, very cold areas.
	Some knew about food production but rejected it.
	Some fled food production, states, or colonial rule.
ALL FORAGERS TODAY	Live in nation-states.
	Depend on outside assistance.
	Have significant contact with outsiders.
	Are influenced by: food-producing economies regional forces (e.g., trade and war) national and international policies political and economic events in the world system

In 2006 Botswana's High Court ruled that the Basarwa had been wrongly evicted from the "Central Kalahari Game Reserve." In the context of global political action for cultural rights, this verdict was hailed as a victory for indigenous peoples around the world (Motseta 2006). In December 2006, Botswana's attorney general recognized the court order to allow the Basarwa to return to their ancestral lands, while imposing conditions likely to prevent most of them from doing so. Only the 189 people who actually filed the lawsuit would have automatic right of return with their children, compared with some 2,000 Basarwa wishing to return. The others would have to apply for special permits. Returning Basarwa would be allowed to build only temporary structures and to use enough water for subsistence needs. Water would be a major obstacle since the government shut the main well in 2002, and water is scarce in the Kalahari. Furthermore, anyone wishing to hunt would have to apply for a permit.

Chapter 16 Making a Living **365**

"Recap" Tables

These tables systematically summarize the major points of a section or chapter, giving students an easily accessible studying and learning tool.

rather than mainly for subsistence. Indigenous peoples and traditional cultures have devised various strategies to deal with threats to their autonomy, identity, and livelihood. New forms of political mobilization and cultural expression are emerging from the interplay of local, regional, national, and international cultural forces (see Ong and Collier, eds. 2005).

Acing the COURSE

Summary

1. Culture, which is distinctive to humanity, refers to customary behavior and beliefs that are passed on through enculturation. Culture rests on the human capacity for cultural learning. Culture encompasses rules for conduct internalized in human beings, which lead them to think and act in characteristic ways.

2. Although other animals learn, only humans have cultural learning, dependent on symbols. Humans think symbolically—arbitrarily bestowing meaning on things and events. By convention, a symbol stands for something with which it has no necessary or natural relation. Symbols have special meaning for people who share memories, values, and beliefs because of common enculturation. People absorb cultural lessons consciously and unconsciously.

3. Cultural traditions mold biologically based desires and needs in particular directions. Everyone is cultured, not just people with elite educations. Cultures may be integrated and patterned through economic and social forces, key symbols, and core values. Cultural rules don't rigidly dictate our behavior. There is room for creativity, flexibility, diversity, and disagreement within societies. Cultural means of adaptation have been crucial in human evolution. Aspects of culture also can be maladaptive.

4. The human capacity for culture has an evolutionary basis that extends back at least 2.6 million years—to early tool makers whose products survive in the archaeological record (and most probably even further back—based on observation of tool use and manufacture by apes). Humans share with monkeys and apes such traits as manual dexterity (especially opposable thumbs), depth and color vision, learning ability based on a large brain, substantial parental investment in a limited number of offspring, and tendencies toward sociality and cooperation.

5. Many hominin traits are foreshadowed in other primates, particularly in the African apes, which, like us, belong to the hominid family. The ability to learn, basic to culture, is an adaptive advantage available to monkeys and apes. Chimpanzees make tools for several purposes. They also hunt and share meat. Sharing and cooperation are more developed among humans than among the apes, and only humans have systems of kinship and marriage that permit us to maintain lifelong ties with relatives in different local groups.

6. Using a comparative perspective, anthropology examines biological, psychological, social, and cultural universals and generalities. There also are unique and distinctive aspects of the human condition (cultural particularities). North American cultural traditions are no more natural than any others. Levels of culture can be larger or smaller than a nation. Cultural traits may be shared across national boundaries. Nations also include cultural differences associated with ethnicity, region, and social class.

7. Ethnocentrism describes judging other cultures by using one's own cultural standards. Cultural relativism, which anthropologists may use as a methodological position rather than a moral stance, is the idea of avoiding the use of outside standards to judge behavior in a given society. Human rights are those based on justice and morality beyond and superior to particular countries, cultures, and religions. Cultural rights are vested in religious and ethnic minorities and indigenous societies, and IPR, or intellectual property rights, apply to an indigenous group's collective knowledge and its applications.

8. Diffusion, migration, and colonialism have carried cultural traits and patterns to different world areas. Mechanisms of cultural change include diffusion, acculturation, and independent invention. Globalization describes a series of processes that promote change in a world in which nations and people are interlinked and mutually dependent.

44 PART 1 Introduction to Anthropology

"Acing the Course" Sections

These end-of-chapter sections include summaries, key terms, and self-quizzes that encourage students to review and retain the chapter content. Self-grading quizzes on the book's online learning center (www.mhhe.com/kottak14e) provide further opportunities for practice and review.

"Appreciating Anthropology" Boxes

These accounts explore ways in which anthropologists are actively engaged in some of our most urgent 21st-century concerns. From studying the culture of Hurricane Katrina survivors to observing the habitats and habits of endangered primates, these boxes demonstrate that topics raised in every chapter can be found in today's headlines.

appreciating
ANTHROPOLOGY

Should Anthropologists Study Terrorism?

How and how much should anthropology matter? For decades I've heard anthropologists complain that government officials fail to appreciate, or simply are ignorant of, findings of anthropology that are relevant to making informed policies. The American Anthropological Association deems it of "paramount importance" that anthropologists study the roots of terrorism and violence. How should such studies be conducted? This account describes a Pentagon program, Project Minerva, initiated late in the (George W.) Bush administration, to enlist social science expertise to combat security threats.

Project Minerva has raised concerns among anthropologists. Based on past experience, scholars worry that governments might use anthropological knowledge for goals and in ways that are ethically problematic. Government policies and military operations have the potential to bring harm to the people anthropologists study. Social scientists object especially to the notion that Pentagon officials should determine which projects are worthy of funding. Rather, anthropologists favor a (peer review) system in which panels of their profes-

sional peers (other social scientists) judge the value and propriety of proposed research, including research that might help identify and deter threats to national security.

Can you appreciate anthropology's potential value for national security? Read the Code of Ethics of the American Anthropological Association at www.aaanet.org/committees/ethics/ethcode.htm. In the context of that code, can you also appreciate anthropologists' reluctance to endorse Project Minerva and its procedures?

Eager to embrace eggheads and ideas, the Pentagon has started an ambitious and unusual program to recruit social scientists and direct the nation's brainpower to combating security threats like the Chinese military, Iraq, terrorism and religious fundamentalism.

Defense Secretary Robert M. Gates has compared the initiative—named Minerva, after the Roman goddess

"Living Anthropology" Video Icons

These icons reference a set of videos that show practicing anthropologists at work and that can be viewed on the open-access online learning center (www.mhhe.com/kottak14e). Students hear anthropologists describe the research they are doing and are given a glimpse of the many sites and peoples that anthropologists study.

This diver holds a ceramic vessel uncovered from a ship wrecked in 1025 A.D., in Turkey's Serce Liman Bay, Mugla province. Graduate degrees in underwater, or nautical, archaeology are available at East Carolina University, Florida State University, and Texas A&M University. This growing field of study investigates submerged sites, most often shipwrecks.

A more labor-intensive and refined way of excavating is to dig through the stratigraphy one layer at a time. The strata, which are separated by differences in color and texture, are studied one by one. This technique provides more information about the context of the artifacts, fossils, or features because the scientist works more slowly and in meaningful layers. A given 4-foot (1.2-meter) level may include within it a series of successive house floors, each with artifacts. If this deposit is excavated according to arbitrary levels, all the artifacts are mixed together. But if it is excavated according to the natural stratigraphy, with each house floor excavated separately, the resulting picture is much more detailed. The procedure here is for the archaeologist to remove and bag all the artifacts from each house floor before proceeding to the level below that one.

Any excavation recovers varied material remains, such as ceramics, stone artifacts (lithics), human and animal bones, and plant remains. Such remains may be small and fragmented. To increase the likelihood that small remains will be recovered, the soil is passed through screens. To recover very small remains, such as fish bones and carbonized plant remains, archaeologists use a technique called *flotation*. Soil samples are sorted using water and a series of very fine meshes. When the water dissolves the soil, the carbonized plant remains float to the top. The fish bones and other heavier remains sink to the bottom. Flotation requires considerable time and labor. This makes it inappropriate to use on all the soil that is excavated from a site. Flotation samples are taken from a limited number of deposits, such as house floors, trash pits, and hearths.

KINDS OF ARCHAEOLOGY

Archaeologists pursue diverse research topics, using a wide variety of methods. Experimental archaeologists try to replicate ancient techniques and processes (e.g., tool making) under controlled conditions. Historical archaeologists use written records as guides and supplements to archaeological research. They work with remains more recent—often much more recent—than the advent of writing. Colonial archaeologists, for instance, use historical records as guides to locate and excavate postcontact sites in North and South America,

 living anthropology **VIDEOS**

The Necropolis of Pupput, www.mhhe.com/kottak

When ground was broken for a luxury hotel in Hammamet, Tunisia, no one expected to find remains of what has turned out to be the largest Roman necropolis (funerary site) in North Africa. This clip shows archaeologists excavating wood and bone to reconstruct burial rites in the ancient city of Pupput, where Romans lived for three centuries some 2,000 years ago. The Romans at Pupput had varied funerary practices, including burial and cremation. What happens to bone when it is heated to very high temperatures? What information can archaeologists draw from the study of preserved wood, such as that shown here? At the end of the day, what work do archaeologists do after they have finished that day's digging?

Early Hominins 8

What key traits make us human, and when and how are they revealed in the fossil record?

Who were the australopithecines, and what role did they play in human evolution?

When and where did hominins first make tools?

A reconstruction of Lucy, an early upright biped, aka *Australopithecus afarensis*, in the Senckenberg Museum of Natural History in Frankfurt, Germany. Bipedal locomotion is the most ancient trait that makes us truly human.

CRITICAL THINKING

1. What is culture? How is it distinct from what this chapter describes as a biocultural approach? How do these concepts help us understand the complex ways that human populations adapt to their environments?

2. What themes and interests unify the subdisciplines of anthropology? In your answer, refer to historical reasons for the unity of anthropology. Are these historical reasons similar in all places where anthropology developed as a discipline?

3. If, as Franz Boas illustrated early on in American anthropology, cultures are not isolated, how can ethnography provide an account of a particular community, society, or culture? Note: There is no easy answer to this question! Anthropologists continue to deal with it as they define their research questions and projects.

4. The American Anthropological Association has formally acknowledged a public service role by recognizing that anthropology has two dimensions: (1) academic anthropology and (2) practicing or applied anthropology. What is applied anthropology? Based on your reading of this chapter, identify examples from current events where an anthropologist could help identify, assess, and solve contemporary social problems.

5. In this chapter, we learn that anthropology is a science, although a very humanistic one. What do you think this means? What role does hypothesis testing play in structuring anthropological research? What is the difference between theories, laws, and hypotheses?

Multiple Choice: 1. (D); 2. (D); 3. (C); 4. (D); 5. (A); 6. (A); 7. (E); 8. (C); 9. (A); 10. (D); Fill in the Blank: 1. holistic; cross-cultural, 2. biocultural; 3. Ethnography; 4. Applied anthropology; 5. scientific method

Endicott, K. M., and R. Welsch
  2009 *Taking Sides: Clashing Views on Controversial Issues in Anthropology*, 4th ed. Guilford, CT: McGraw-Hill/Dushkin. Thirty-eight anthropologists offer opposing viewpoints on 19 polarizing issues, including ethical dilemmas.

Fagan, B. M.
  2009 *Archeology: A Brief Introduction*, 10th ed. Upper Saddle River, NJ: Prentice Hall. Introduction to archaeological theory, techniques, and approaches, including field survey, excavation, and analysis of materials.

Geertz, C.
  1995 *After the Fact: Two Countries, Four Decades, One Anthropologist*. Cambridge, MA: Harvard University Press. A prominent cultural anthropologist reflects on his work in Morocco and Indonesia.

Harris, M.
  1989 *Our Kind: Who We Are, Where We Came From, Where We Are Going*. New York: Harper-Collins. Clearly written survey of the origins of humans, culture, and major sociopolitical institutions.

Nash, D.
  1999 *A Little Anthropology*, 3rd ed. Upper Saddle River, NJ: Prentice Hall. Short introduction to societies and cultures, with comments on developing nations and modern America.

Wolf, E. R.
  1982 *Europe and the People without History*. Berkeley: University of California Press. Influential and award-winning study of the relation between Europe and various nonindustrial populations.

Suggested Additional Readings

Go to our Online Learning Center website at **www.mhhe.com/kottak** for Internet exercises directly related to the content of this chapter.

Internet Exercises

Expanded Coverage of Paleoanthropology

There are now three chapters on paleoanthropology rather than two (Chapters 8–10 in this edition). The addition of a chapter enabled the author to break complex material into easier-to-absorb chunks, and allowed him to add new material on the recent "Ardi" skeleton, the settling of Australia and the Pacific, and creative expression.

Additional Readings

These suggestions for further reading guide students toward more detailed and focused explorations of the key topics introduced in the book.

Highlights of the 14th Edition

CHAPTER 1
- New content on the cultural practice of friendly hugging among high school students in America
- New material on Dr. Stanley Ann Dunham Soetoro's work and philosophy, and her influence on her son, Barack Obama

CHAPTER 2
- Updated coverage of the role of individualism in American culture

CHAPTER 3
- Revised discussion of culturally-appropriate marketing

CHAPTER 4
- Updated discussion of humans as social beings

CHAPTER 5
- Updated content on the relative influence of culture and genetics in human physiology
- New content on the spread of the syphilis virus as a result of Columbus's New-World exploration

CHAPTER 6
- Updated discussion of an understanding of diversity that transcends race and ethnicity
- New content on genetic markers and phenotype

CHAPTER 7
- Updated content on the human strengths and weaknesses of the five senses as evidence of evolutionary biology
- New content on the traits of apes and humans as opposed to monkeys and other primates
- Updated discussion of environmental destruction and endangered primates

CHAPTER 8
- Updated content on the importance of bipedalism to human beings
- New coverage of the *Sahelanthropus* fossil
- New coverage of the 2009 *Ardipithecus* find ("Ardi")
- Revised coverage of the Oldowan Tools

CHAPTER 9
- Revised discussion of what the thick, bony walls of *H. erectus* skulls can tell us about their behavior

- Updated coverage of Acheulian tool making
- New content on the first controlled use of fire
- New material on recent fossil finds in Spanish caves
- New material on how *H. floresiensis* walked

CHAPTER 10
- This new chapter focuses on modern humans, the advent of behavioral modernity, advances in technology, glacial retreat, cave art, the settling of Australia and the Americas, and the people of the Pacific.

CHAPTER 11
- Updated discussion of the domestication and spread of agriculture throughout the world

CHAPTER 12
- Revised coverage of stratification and the state

CHAPTER 13
- Revised coverage of cultural anthropologists in a global community
- New material on Clyde Kluckhohn's views on the public service role of anthropology
- New content on anthropologists studying terrorism

CHAPTER 14
- Revised coverage on the relationships between language and culture
- New material on the demand for Web content in local languages

CHAPTER 15
- Updated coverage of ethnicity as a shifting, culturally-determined identity
- New content on the confusion between race and ethnicity in the popular discourse, including a discussion of the Sotomayor confirmation hearings and controversy
- Expanded content on genotype and phenotype in Brazil

CHAPTER 16
- Updated content on the conflict between work and family in American culture

- New content on the impacts of deforestation and climate change on native cultures

CHAPTER 17
- Expanded content on the various levels of political control (local/tribal vs. state/national) that most contemporary peoples live under
- Expanded discussion of diwaniyas of Kuwait

CHAPTER 18
- Updated discussion of gender equality/inequality in America today
- Expanded discussion of gender roles and the division of labor
- New content on women-only commuter trains in major Indian cities
- Expanded discussion of gender alternatives

CHAPTER 19
- Expanded discussion of the definition of family in the contemporary United States

CHAPTER 20
- Updated information on gay-marriage laws in the United States
- Expanded discussion on dowries

CHAPTER 21
- Expanded content on baseball players and magical thinking
- New material on the celebration of Claude Lévi-Strauss's 100th birthday, and an assessment of his life's work

CHAPTER 22
- Expanded discussion of the splintering of U.S. mass media and U.S. culture
- Revised coverage of the departmentalization of art in Western culture
- Updated discussion of class in American and Brazilian mass media

CHAPTER 23
- Updated discussion of the globalization of culture and commerce

CHAPTER 24
- Expanded coverage of the earth as a global unit, rather than a compilation of national units

Support for Students and Instructors

CourseSmart
Learn Smart. Choose Smart.

With the CourseSmart eTextbook version of this title, students can save up to 50 percent off the cost of a print book, reduce their impact on the environment, and access powerful Web tools for learning. Faculty can also review and compare the full text online without having to wait for a print desk copy. CourseSmart is an online eTextbook, which means users need to be connected to the Internet in order to access it. Students can also print sections of the book for maximum portability.

For the Student

The Student Online Learning Center website (www .mhhe.com/kottak14e) is a free Web-based student supplement featuring video clips, self-quizzes, interactive exercises and activities, anthropology web links, and other useful tools. Designed specifically to complement individual chapters of the 14th edition, the Online Learning Center gives students access to material such as the following:

- Video Library
- Appendix: "Ethics and Anthropology"
- Appendix: "American Popular Culture"
- An electronic version of the in-text Anthropology Atlas
- Student Self-Quizzes
- Virtual Exploration Activities
- Interactive Exercises
- Chapter Outlines and Objectives
- Vocabulary Flash Cards
- FAQs

For the Instructor

The Instructor Online Learning Center website (www.mhhe.com/ kottak14e) is a password-protected instructor-only site, which includes the following materials:

- Instructor's Manual
- PowerPoint Lecture Slides
- Computerized Test Bank
- Question Bank for the Classroom Performance System (CPS)
- Image Bank
- Links to Professional Resources
- *Faces of Culture* Video Correlation Guide

Acknowledgments

As always, I'm grateful to many colleagues at McGraw-Hill. I'm lucky to be a McGraw-Hill author. Thanks to Gina Boedeker, Sponsoring Editor for Anthropology, for organizing a very productive revision-planning meeting in May 2009. There I had a chance to meet Emily Pecora, who has been a wonderfully helpful, efficient, and responsive developmental editor. Emily distilled the suggestions by reviewers of the thirteenth edition along with the ideas hatched at our meeting in May. With input from several others, Emily, Gina, and I developed a new theme for this fourteenth edition—**appreciation**—of students, of anthropology, and of human diversity. Over summer 2009 Emily graciously, promptly, and attentively responded to the revision work I was doing, including the new "Understanding Ourselves" essays that now begin each chapter. Her help was tremendously valuable to me as I implemented the new theme and attempted to respond to as many of the reviewers' comments as possible. Demonstrating why she's such a great anthropology editor, Gina Boedeker has remained attentive to the revision process and timing. Marketing Manager Caroline McGillen also attended our May meeting and made helpful suggestions. I thank her and all the McGraw-Hill sales representatives for the work they do on behalf of my books.

I thank Leslie Racanelli once again for her outstanding work as production editor, coordinating and overseeing the process from received manuscript through, and even beyond, pages. Louis Swaim, production supervisor, worked with the printer to make sure everything came out right. It's always a pleasure to plan and choose photos with Barbara Salz, freelance photo researcher, with whom I've worked for about 20 years. Thanks, too, to Susan Mansfield, Barbara's assistant, who also worked on the photo program for this edition. I thank Geoffrey Hughes for his work on the Instructor's Manual and Maria Perez for her work on the Test Bank for this book. Emily McKee and Sara Cooley did an outstanding job updating the online components for the book. Gerry Williams updated the instructor PowerPoint files. Sincere thanks to Patricia Ohlenroth once again for her fine job of copyediting; and George Watson for proofreading. I am grateful to Cassandra Chu and Maureen McCutcheon for working to create and execute the attractive new design.

Nora Agbayani and Toni Michaels, photo research coordinators, also deserve thanks. For creating and updating the attractive maps, I would like to acknowledge the work of Mapping Specialists.

Thanks, as well, to Jami Woy, media project manager, for creating the OLC with video clips and all the other supplements. Once again I thank Wesley Hall, who has handled the literary permissions.

I'm especially indebted to the professors who reviewed the 13th edition of this book and of my *Cultural Anthropology* text in preparation for the 14th editions. They suggested many of the changes I've implemented here in the 14th edition—and others I'll work on for subsequent editions. The names and schools of these reviewers are as follows:

Lisa Gezon, *University of West Georgia*
Brian A. Hoey, *Marshall University*
Charles W. Houck, *University of North Carolina–Charlotte*
Cara Roure Johnson, *University of Connecticut*
Constanza Ocampo-Raeder, *University of Maine (Orono)*
Geoffrey G. Pope, *William Patterson University*
Robert Rubinstein, *Syracuse University*
Richard A. Sattler, *University of Montana*
Michael Simonton, *Northern Kentucky University*
Merrily Stover, *University of Maryland–University College*
Katharine Wiegle, *Northern Illinois University*
Brent Woodfill, *University of Louisiana at Lafayette*

I'm also grateful to the valued reviewers of previous editions of this book and of my *Cultural Anthropology* text. Their names are as follows:

Julianna Acheson, *Green Mountain College*
Stephanie W. Alemán, *Iowa State University*
Mohamad Al-Madani, *Seattle Central Community College*
Douglas J. Anderson, *Front Range Community College*
E. F. Aranyosi, *University of Washington*
Robert Bee, *University of Connecticut*
Joy A. Bilharz, *SUNY at Fredonia*

James R. Bindon, *University of Alabama*
Kira Blaisdell-Sloan, *Louisiana State University*
Kathleen T. Blue, *Minnesota State University*
Daniel Boxberger, *Western Washington University*
Vicki Bradley, *University of Houston*
Lisa Kaye Brandt, *North Dakota State University*
Ethan M. Braunstein, *Northern Arizona University*
Ned Breschel, *Morehead State University*
Peter J. Brown, *Emory University*
Margaret S. Bruchez, *Blinn College*
Vaughn M. Bryant, *Texas A&M University*
Andrew Buckser, *Purdue University*
Richard H. Buonforte, *Brigham Young University*
Karen Burns, *University of Georgia*
Richard Burns, *Arkansas State University*
Mary Cameron, *Auburn University*
Joseph L. Chartkoff, *Michigan State University*
Dianne Chidester, *University of South Dakota*
Stephen Childs, *Valdosta State University*
Inne Choi, *California Polytechnic State University–San Luis Obispo*
Wanda Clark, *South Plains College*
Jeffrey Cohen, *Penn State University*
Fred Conquest, *Community College of Southern Nevada*
Barbara Cook, *California Polytechnic State University–San Luis Obispo*
Maia Greenwell Cunningham, *Citrus College*
Sean M. Daley, *Johnson County Community College*
Karen Dalke, *University of Wisconsin–Green Bay*
Norbert Dannhaeuser, *Texas A&M University*
Michael Davis, *Truman State University*
Hillary DelPrete, *Wagner College*
Darryl de Ruiter, *Texas A&M University*
Paul Demers, *University of Nebraska–Lincoln*
Robert Dirks, *Illinois State University*
William W. Donner, *Kutztown University*
Mary Durocher, *Wayne State University*

Paul Durrenberger, *Pennsylvania State University*

George Esber, *Miami University of Ohio*

Les W. Field, *University of New Mexico*

Grace Fraser, *Plymouth State College*

Todd Jeffrey French, *University of New Hampshire, Durham*

Richard H. Furlow, *College of DuPage*

Vance Geiger, *University of Central Florida*

Laurie Godfrey, *University of Massachusetts–Amherst*

Bob Goodby, *Franklin Pierce College*

Gloria Gozdzik, *West Virginia University*

Tom Greaves, *Bucknell University*

Mark Grey, *University of Northern Iowa*

Sharon Gursky, *Texas A&M University*

John Dwight Hines, *University of California, Santa Barbara*

Homes Hogue, *Mississippi State University*

Kara C. Hoover, *Georgia State University*

Stevan R. Jackson, *Virginia Tech*

Alice James, *Shippensburg University of Pennsylvania*

Richard King, *Drake University*

Christine Kray, *Rochester Institute of Technology*

Eric Lassiter, *Ball State University*

Jill Leonard, *University of Illinois—Urbana–Champaign*

Kenneth Lewis, *Michigan State University*

David Lipset, *University of Minnesota*

Walter E. Little, *University at Albany, SUNY*

Jon K. Loessin, *Wharton County Junior College*

Brian Malley, *University of Michigan*

Jonathan Marks, *University of North Carolina–Charlotte*

H. Lyn Miles, *University of Tennessee at Chattanooga*

Barbara Miller, *George Washington University*

Richard G. Milo, *Chicago State University*

John Nass, Jr., *California University of Pennsylvania*

Frank Ng, *California State University–Fresno*

Divinity B. O'Connor DLR-Roberts, *Des Moines Area Community College*

Martin Ottenheimer, *Kansas State University*

De Ann Pendry, *University of Tennessee–Knoxville*

Leonard Plotnicov, *University of Pittsburgh*

Janet Pollak, *William Patterson College*

Christina Nicole Pomianek, *University of Missouri–Columbia*

Howard Prince, *CUNY–Borough of Manhattan Community College*

Frances E. Purifoy, *University of Louisville*

Asa Randall, *University of Florida*

Mark A. Rees, *University of Louisiana at Lafayette*

Bruce D. Roberts, *Minnesota State University Moorhead*

Rita C. Rodabaugh, *Central Piedmont Community College*

Steven Rubenstein, *Ohio University*

Richard Scaglion, *University of Pittsburgh*

Mary Scott, *San Francisco State University*

James Sewastynowicz, *Jacksonville State University*

Brian Siegel, *Furman University*

Megan Sinnott, *University of Colorado–Boulder*

Esther Skirboll, *Slippery Rock University of Pennsylvania*

Alexia Smith, *University of Connecticut*

Gregory Starrett, *University of North Carolina–Charlotte*

Karl Steinen, *University of West Georgia*

Noelle Stout, *Foothill and Skyline Colleges*

Elizabeth A. Throop, *Eastern Kentucky University*

Ruth Toulson, *Brigham Young University*

Susan Trencher, *George Mason University*

Mark Tromans, *Broward Community College*

Christina Turner, *Virginia Commonwealth University*

Donald Tyler, *University of Idaho*

Daniel Varisco, *Hofstra University*

Albert Wahrhaftig, *Sonoma State University*

Joe Watkins, *University of New Mexico*

David Webb, *Kutztown University of Pennsylvania*

George Westermark, *Santa Clara University*

Donald A. Whatley, *Blinn College*

Nancy White, *University of South Florida*

Mary S. Willis, *University of Nebraska–Lincoln*

I'm grateful for their enthusiasm and their suggestions for changes, additions, and deletions (sometimes in very different directions!).

Students, too, regularly share their insights about this and my other texts via e-mail and so have contributed to this book. Anyone—student or instructor—with access to e-mail can reach me at **ckottak@ bellsouth.net.**

As usual, my family has offered me understanding, support, and inspiration during the preparation of this book. Dr. Nicholas Kottak, who like me holds a doctorate in anthropology, regularly shares his insights with me, as does my daughter, Dr. Juliet Kottak Mavromatis, and my wife, Isabel (Betty) Wagley Kottak. Isabel has been my companion in the field and in life for more than four decades. I renew my dedication of this book to the memory of my mother, Mariana Kottak Roberts, for kindling my interest in the human condition, for reading and commenting on my writing, and for the insights about people and society she provided.

After four decades of teaching, I've benefited from the knowledge, help, and advice of so many friends, colleagues, teaching assistants, graduate student instructors, and students that I can no longer fit their names into a short preface. I hope they know who they are and accept my thanks.

I'm very grateful to my many colleagues at Michigan who regularly share their insights and suggest ways of making my books better. Thanks especially to my fellow 101ers: Kelly Askew, Tom Fricke, Stuart Kirsch, Holly Peters-Golden, and Andrew Shryock. Their questions and suggestions help me keep this book current. Special thanks to Joyce Marcus and Kent Flannery for continuing to nurture the archaeologist in me.

Over my many years of teaching introductory anthropology, feedback from undergraduates and graduate students has kept me up to date on the interests, needs, and views of the people for whom this book is written. I continue to believe that effective textbooks are based in enthusiasm and in the enjoyment of teaching. I hope this product of my experience will be helpful to others.

Conrad Phillip Kottak
Johns Island, SC and Ann Arbor, MI
ckottak@bellsouth.net

Anthropology

Appreciating Human Diversity

What distinguishes anthropology from other fields that study human beings?

How do anthropologists study human diversity in time and space?

Why is anthropology both scientific and humanistic?

Street scene with soccer in Istanbul, Turkey. Culture, including sports, helps shape our bodies, personalities, and personal health.

What Is Anthropology?

1

understanding OURSELVES

When you grew up, which sport did you appreciate the most—soccer, swimming, football, baseball, tennis, golf, or some other sport (or perhaps none at all)? Is this because of "who you are" or because of the opportunities you had as a child to practice and participate in this particular activity? Think about the phrases and sentences you would use to describe yourself in a personal ad or on a networking site—your likes and dislikes, hobbies, and habits. How many of these descriptors would be the same if you had been born in a different place or time?

When you were young, your parents might have told you that drinking milk and eating vegetables would help you grow up "big and strong." They probably didn't as readily recognize the role that *culture* plays in shaping bodies, personalities, and personal health. If nutrition matters in growth, so, too, do cultural guidelines. What is proper behavior for boys and girls? What kinds of work should men and women do? Where should people live? What are proper uses of their leisure time? What role should religion play? How should people relate to their family, friends, and neighbors? Although our genetic attributes provide a foundation for our growth and development, human biology is fairly plastic—that is, it is malleable. Culture is an environmental force that affects our development as much as do nutrition, heat, cold, and altitude. Culture also guides our emotional and cognitive growth and helps determine the kinds of personalities we have as adults.

Among scholarly disciplines, anthropology stands out as the field that provides the cross-cultural test. How much would we know about human behavior, thought, and feeling if we studied only our own kind? What if our entire understanding of human behavior were based on analysis of questionnaires filled out by college students in Oregon? That is a radical question, but one that should make you think about the basis for statements about what humans are like, individually or as a group. A primary reason why anthropology can uncover so much about what it means to be human is that the discipline is based on the cross-cultural perspective. One culture can't tell us everything we need to know about what it means to be human. Often culture is "invisible" (assumed to be normal, or just the way things are) until it is placed in comparison to another culture. For example, to appreciate how watching television affects us, as human beings, we need to study not just North America today but some other place—and perhaps also some other time (such as Brazil in the 1980s; see Kottak 1990*b*). The cross-cultural test is fundamental to the anthropological approach, which orients this textbook.

HUMAN DIVERSITY

Anthropologists study human beings wherever and whenever they find them—in rural Kenya, a Turkish café, a Mesopotamian tomb, or a North American shopping mall. Anthropology is the exploration of human diversity in time and space. Anthropology studies the whole of the human condition: past, present, and future; biology, society, language, and culture. Of particular interest is the diversity that comes through human adaptability.

Humans are among the world's most adaptable animals. In the Andes of South

America, people wake up in villages 16,000 feet above sea level and then trek 1,500 feet higher to work in tin mines. Tribes in the Australian desert worship animals and discuss philosophy. People survive malaria in the tropics. Men have walked on the moon. The model of the *USS Enterprise* in Washington's Smithsonian Institution symbolizes the desire to "seek out new life and civilizations, to boldly go where no one has gone before." Wishes to know the unknown, control the uncontrollable, and create order out of chaos find expression among all peoples. Creativity, adaptability, and flexibility are basic human attributes, and human diversity is the subject matter of anthropology.

Students often are surprised by the breadth of **anthropology,** which is the study of the human species and its immediate ancestors. Anthropology is a uniquely comparative and **holistic** science. Holism refers to the study of the whole of the human condition: past, present, and future; biology, society, language, and culture. Most people think that anthropologists study fossils and nonindustrial, non-Western cultures, and many of them do. But anthropology is much more than the study of nonindustrial peoples: It is a comparative field that examines all societies, ancient and modern, simple and complex. The other social sciences tend to focus on a single society, usually an industrial nation like the United States or Canada. Anthropology, however, offers a unique cross-cultural perspective by constantly comparing the customs of one society with those of others.

People share society—organized life in groups—with other animals, including baboons, wolves, and even ants. Culture, however, is more distinctly human. **Cultures** are traditions and customs, transmitted through learning, that form and guide the beliefs and behavior of the people exposed to them. Children learn such a tradition by growing up in a particular society, through a process called enculturation. Cultural traditions include customs and opinions, developed over the generations, about proper and improper behavior. These traditions answer such questions as: How should we do things? How do we make sense of the world? How do we tell right from wrong? What is right, and what is wrong? A culture produces a degree of consistency in behavior and thought among the people who live in a particular society. (This chapter's "Appreciating Diversity" box on pp. 6–7 discusses how attitudes about displays of affection, which are transmitted culturally, can also change.)

The most critical element of cultural traditions is their transmission through learning rather than through biological inheritance. Culture is not itself biological, but it rests on certain features of human biology. For more than a million years, humans have had at least some of the biological capacities on which culture depends. These abilities are to learn, to think symbolically, to use language, and to employ tools and other products in organizing their lives and adapting to their environments.

Anthropology confronts and ponders major questions of human existence as it explores human biological and cultural diversity in time and space. By examining ancient bones and tools, we unravel the mysteries of human origins. When did our ancestors separate from those remote great-aunts and great-uncles whose descendants are the apes? Where and when did *Homo sapiens* originate? How has our species changed? What are we now, and where are we going? How have changes in culture and society influenced biological change? Our genus, *Homo,* has been changing for more than one million years. Humans continue to adapt and change both biologically and culturally.

Adaptation, Variation, and Change

Adaptation refers to the processes by which organisms cope with environmental forces and stresses, such as those posed by climate and *topography* or terrains, also called landforms. How do organisms change to fit their environments, such as dry climates or high mountain altitudes? Like other animals, humans use biological means of adaptation. But humans are unique in also having cultural means of adaptation. Recap 1.1 summarizes the cultural and biological means that humans use to adapt to high altitudes.

Mountainous terrains pose particular challenges, those associated with high altitude and oxygen deprivation. Consider four ways (one cultural and three biological) in which humans may cope with low oxygen pressure at high altitudes. Illustrating cultural (technological) adaptation would be a pressurized airplane cabin equipped with oxygen masks. There are three ways of adapting biologically to high altitudes: genetic adaptation, long-term physiological adaptation, and short-term physiological adaptation. First, native populations of high-altitude areas, such as the Andes of Peru and the Himalayas of Tibet and Nepal, seem to have acquired certain genetic advantages for life at very high altitudes. The Andean tendency to develop a voluminous chest and lungs probably has a genetic basis. Second, regardless of their genes, people who grow up at a high altitude become physiologically more efficient there than genetically similar people who have grown up at sea level would be. This illustrates long-term physiological adaptation during the body's growth and development. Third, humans also have the capacity for short-term or immediate physiological adaptation. Thus, when lowlanders arrive in the

anthropology
The study of the human species and its immediate ancestors.

holistic
Encompassing past, present, and future; biology, society, language, and culture.

culture
Traditions and customs transmitted through learning.

appreciating

DIVERSITY

"Give Me a Hug"

In Winter 2008 I created and taught a course called "Experiencing Culture" to American college students in Italy. Students wrote bi-weekly journals reflecting on the cultural differences they observed between Europeans and Americans. One thing that really struck them was the greater frequency and intensity of PDAs—public displays of affection between romantic couples in Italy, compared with the U.S.

The world's nations and cultures have strikingly different notions about displays of affection and personal space. Cocktail parties in international meeting places such as the United Nations can resemble an elaborate insect mating ritual as diplomats from different countries advance, withdraw, and sidestep. When Americans talk, walk, and dance, they maintain a certain distance from others. Italians or Brazilians, who need less personal space, may interpret such "standoffishness" as a

sign of coldness. In conversational pairs, the Italian or Brazilian typically moves in, while the American "instinctively" retreats from a "close talker."

Such bodily movements illustrate not instinct, but culture—behavior programmed by years of exposure to a particular cultural tradition. Culture, however, is not static, as is suggested by this recent account of hugging behavior in American schools. Appreciate as well that any nation usually contains diverse and even conflicting cultural values. One example is generational diversity, which the famed anthropologist Margaret Mead, one of my teachers, referred to as "the generation gap." Americans (in this case parents and school officials versus teenagers) exhibit generational differences involving the propriety of PDAs and concerns about sexual harassment.

There is so much hugging at Pascack Hills High School in Montvale, N.J., that students have broken down the hugs by type:

There is the basic friend hug, probably the most popular, and the bear hug, of course.

But now there is also the bear claw, when a boy embraces a girl awkwardly with his elbows poking out.

There is the hug that starts with a high-five, then moves into a fist bump, followed by a slap on the back and an embrace.

There's the shake and lean; the hug from behind; and, the newest addition, the triple—any combination of three girls and boys hugging at once.

"We're not afraid, we just get in and hug," said Danny Schneider, a junior at the school, where hallway hugging began shortly after 7 A.M. on a recent morning as students arrived. "The

Students at Pascack Hills High School in Montvale, New Jersey, hug in the hallway before the start of the school day. Does this behavior seem strange to you?

highlands, they immediately increase their breathing and heart rates. Hyperventilation increases the oxygen in their lungs and arteries. As the pulse also increases, blood reaches their tissues more rapidly. All these varied adaptive responses—cultural and biological—achieve a single goal: maintaining an adequate supply of oxygen to the body. Note that some athletes now are adopting techniques learned from indigenous societies and from scientific experiments to increase their own short-term physiological adaptation for sports success (specifically, using low-oxygen tents to simulate high altitudes).

food production
An economy based on plant cultivation and/or animal domestication.

As human history has unfolded, the social and cultural means of adaptation have become increasingly important. In this process, humans have devised diverse ways of coping with the range of environments they have occupied in time and space. The rate of cultural adaptation and change has accelerated, particularly during the past 10,000 years. For millions of years, hunting and gathering of nature's bounty—*foraging*—was the sole basis of human subsistence. However, it took only a few thousand years for **food production** (the cultivation of plants and domestication of animals), which guy friends, we don't care. You just get right in there and jump in."

There are romantic hugs, too, but that is not what these teenagers are talking about.

Girls embracing girls, girls embracing boys, boys embracing each other—the hug has become the favorite social greeting when teenagers meet or part these days. . . .

A measure of how rapidly the ritual is spreading is that some students complain of peer pressure to hug to fit in. And schools from Hillsdale, N.J., to Bend, Ore., wary in a litigious era about sexual harassment or improper touching—or citing hallway clogging and late arrivals to class—have banned hugging or imposed a three-second rule.

Parents, who grew up in a generation more likely to use the handshake, the low-five or the high-five, are often baffled by the close physical contact. "It's a wordless custom, from what I've observed," wrote Beth J. Harpaz, the mother of two boys, 11 and 16, and a parenting columnist for The Associated Press, in a new book, "13 Is the New 18." . . .

"Witnessing this interaction always makes me feel like I am a tourist in a country where I do not know the customs and cannot speak the language." For teenagers, though, hugging is hip. And not hugging?

"If somebody were to not hug someone, to never hug anybody, people might be just a little wary of them and think they are weird or peculiar," said Gabrielle Brown, a freshman at Fiorello H. LaGuardia High School in Manhattan.

Comforting as the hug may be, principals across the country have clamped down.

"Touching and physical contact is very dangerous territory," said Noreen Hajinlian, the principal of George G. White School, a junior high school in Hillsdale, N.J., who banned hugging two years ago. . . .

Schools that have limited hugging invoked longstanding rules against public displays of affection, meant to maintain an atmosphere of academic seriousness and prevent unwanted touching, or even groping.

But pro-hugging students say it is not a romantic or sexual gesture, simply the "hello" of their generation. . . .

Amy L. Best, a sociologist at George Mason University, said the teenage embrace is more a reflection of the overall evolution of the American greeting, which has become less formal since the 1970s. "Without question, the boundaries of touch have changed in American culture," she said. "We display bodies more readily, there are fewer rules governing body touch and a lot more permissible access to other people's bodies."

Hugging appears to be a grassroots phenomenon and not an imitation of a character or custom on TV or in movies. The prevalence of boys' nonromantic hugging (especially of other boys) is most striking to adults. Experts say that over the last generation, boys have become more comfortable expressing emotion, as embodied by the MTV show "Bromance," which is now a widely used term for affection between straight male friends. . . .

African American boys and men have been hugging as part of their greeting for decades, using the word "dap" to describe a ritual involving handshakes, slaps on the shoulders and, more recently, a hug, also sometimes called the gangsta hug among urban youth. . . .

Some parents find it paradoxical that a generation so steeped in hands-off virtual communication would be so eager to hug.

"Maybe it's because all these kids do is text and go on Facebook so they don't even have human contact anymore," said Dona Eichner, the mother of freshman and junior girls at the high school in Montvale. . . .

Carrie Osbourne, a sixth-grade teacher at Claire Lilienthal Alternative School, said hugging was a powerful and positive sign that children are inclined to nurture one another, breaking down barriers. "And it gets to that core that every person wants to feel cared for, regardless of your age or how cool you are or how cool you think you are," she said.

As much as hugging is a physical gesture, it has migrated online as well. Facebook applications allowing friends to send hugs have tens of thousands of fans.

SOURCE: Sarah Kershaw, "For Teenagers, Hello Means 'How About a Hug?'" From The New York Times, May 28, 2009. © The New York Times. All rights reserved. Used by permission and protected by the Copyright Laws of the United States. The printing, copying, redistribution, or retransmission of the Material without express written permission is prohibited. www.nytimes.com

originated some 12,000–10,000 years ago, to replace foraging in most areas. Between 6000 and 5000 B.P. (before the present), the first civilizations arose. These were large, powerful, and complex societies, such as ancient Egypt, that conquered and governed large geographic areas.

Much more recently, the spread of industrial production has profoundly affected human life. Throughout human history, major innovations have spread at the expense of earlier ones. Each economic revolution has had social and cultural repercussions. Today's global economy and communications link all contemporary people, directly or indirectly, in the modern world system. People must cope with forces generated by progressively larger systems—region, nation, and world. The study of such contemporary adaptations generates new challenges for anthropology: "The cultures of world peoples need to be constantly rediscovered as these people reinvent them in changing historical circumstances" (Marcus and Fischer 1986, p. 24). (The "Appreciating Diversity" box above discusses how American teens have reinvented standards involving bodily contact among generational peers.)

FORM OF ADAPTATION	TYPE OF ADAPTATION	EXAMPLE
Technology	Cultural	Pressurized airplane cabin with oxygen masks
Genetic adaptation (occurs over generations)	Biological	Larger "barrel chests" of native highlanders
Long-term physiological adaptation (occurs during growth and development of the individual organism)	Biological	More efficient respiratory system, to extract oxygen from "thin air"
Short-term physiological adaptation (occurs spontaneously when the individual organism enters a new environment)	Biological	Increased heart rate, hyperventilation

GENERAL ANTHROPOLOGY

general anthropology
Anthropology as a whole: cultural, archaeological, biological, and linguistic anthropology.

anthropology **ATLAS**

See Maps 8 and 9. Map 8 shows the origin and spread of agriculture (food production). Map 9 shows ancient civilizations.

The academic discipline of anthropology, also known as **general anthropology** or "four-field" anthropology, includes four main subdisciplines or subfields. They are sociocultural, archaeological, biological, and linguistic anthropology. (From here on, the shorter term *cultural anthropology* will be used as a synonym for "sociocultural anthropology.") Of the subfields, cultural anthropology has the largest membership. Most departments of anthropology teach courses in all four subfields.

There are historical reasons for the inclusion of four subfields in a single discipline. The origin of anthropology as a scientific field, and of American anthropology in particular, can be traced back to the 19th century. Early American anthropologists were concerned especially with the history and cultures of the native peoples of North America. Interest in the origins and diversity of Native Americans brought together studies of customs, social life, language, and physical traits. Anthropologists still are pondering such questions as: Where did Native Americans come from? How many waves of migration brought them to the New World? What are the linguistic, cultural, and biological links among Native Americans and between them and Asia? Another reason for anthropology's inclusion of four subfields was an interest in the relation between biology (e.g., "race") and culture. More

Early American anthropology was especially concerned with the history and cultures of Native North Americans. Ely S. Parker, or Ha-sa-noan-da, was a Seneca Indian who made important contributions to early anthropology. Parker also served as Commissioner of Indian Affairs for the United States.

than 60 years ago, the anthropologist Ruth Benedict realized that "In World history, those who have helped to build the same culture are not necessarily of one race, and those of the same race have not all participated in one culture. In scientific language, culture is not a function of race" (Benedict 1940, Ch. 2). (Note that a unified four-field anthropology did not develop in Europe, where the subdisciplines tend to exist separately.)

There are also logical reasons for the unity of American anthropology. Each subfield considers variation in time and space (that is, in different geographic areas). Cultural and archaeological anthropologists study (among many other topics) changes in social life and customs. Archaeologists have used studies of living societies and behavior patterns to imagine what life might have been like in the past. Biological anthropologists examine evolutionary changes in physical form, for example, anatomical changes that might have been associated with the origin of tool use or language. Linguistic anthropologists may reconstruct the basics of ancient languages by studying modern ones.

The subdisciplines influence each other as anthropologists talk to each other, read books and journals, and associate in professional organizations. General anthropology explores the basics of human biology, society, and culture and considers their interrelations. Anthropologists share certain key assumptions. Perhaps the most fundamental is the idea that sound conclusions about "human nature" cannot be derived from studying a single nation, society, or cultural tradition. A comparative, cross-cultural approach is essential.

Cultural Forces Shape Human Biology

For example, anthropology's comparative, biocultural perspective recognizes that cultural forces constantly mold human biology. (**Biocultural** refers to the inclusion and combination of both biological and cultural perspectives and approaches to comment on or solve a particular issue or problem.) Culture is a key environmental force in determining how human bodies grow and develop. Cultural traditions promote certain activities and abilities, discourage others, and set standards of physical well-being and attractiveness. Physical activities, including sports, which are influenced by culture, help build the body. For example, North American girls are encouraged to pursue, and therefore do well in, competition involving figure skating, gymnastics, track and field, swimming, diving, and many other sports. Brazilian girls, although excelling in the team sports of basketball and volleyball, haven't fared nearly as well in individual sports as have their American and Canadian counterparts. Why are people encouraged to excel as athletes in some nations but not others? Why do people in some countries invest so much time and effort in competitive sports that their bodies change significantly as a result?

Cultural standards of attractiveness and propriety influence participation and achievement in sports. Americans run or swim not just to compete but to keep trim and fit. Brazil's beauty standards accept more fat, especially in female buttocks and hips. Brazilian men have had some international success in swimming and running, but Brazil rarely sends female swimmers or runners to the Olympics. One reason Brazilian women avoid competitive swimming in particular may be that sport's effects on the body. Years of swimming sculpt a distinctive physique: an enlarged upper torso, a massive neck, and powerful shoulders and back. Successful female swimmers tend to be big, strong, and bulky. The countries that produce them most consistently are the United States, Canada, Australia, Germany, the Scandinavian nations, the Netherlands, and the former Soviet Union, where this body type isn't as stigmatized as it is in Latin countries. Swimmers develop hard bodies, but Brazilian culture says that women should be soft, with big hips and buttocks, not big shoulders. Many young female swimmers in Brazil choose to abandon the sport rather than the "feminine" body ideal.

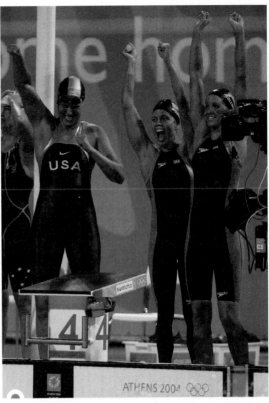

biocultural
Combining biological and cultural approaches to a given problem.

Carly Piper, Natalie Coughlin, and Dana Vollmer, members of the U.S. swimming relay team, from left to right, celebrate after taking the gold medal and setting a new world record in the women's 4 × 2000-meter freestyle relay at the 2004 Olympic Games in Athens, Greece. Years of swimming sculpt a distinctive physique: an enlarged upper torso, a massive neck, and powerful shoulders and back.

THE SUBDISCIPLINES OF ANTHROPOLOGY

Cultural Anthropology

Cultural anthropology is the study of human society and culture, the subfield that describes, analyzes, interprets, and explains social and cultural similarities and differences. To study and interpret cultural diversity, cultural anthropologists engage in two kinds of activity: ethnography (based on field work) and ethnology (based on cross-cultural comparison). **Ethnography** provides an account of a particular community, society, or culture. During ethnographic field work, the ethnographer gathers data that he or she organizes, describes, analyzes, and interprets to build and present that account, which may be in the form of a book, article, or film. Traditionally, ethnographers have lived in small communities and studied local behavior, beliefs, customs, social life, economic activities, politics, and religion.

cultural anthropology
The comparative, cross-cultural, study of human society and culture.

ethnography
Fieldwork in a particular cultural setting.

ETHNOGRAPHY	ETHNOLOGY
Requires field work to collect data	Uses data collected by a series of researchers
Often descriptive	Usually synthetic
Group/community specific	Comparative/cross-cultural

archaeological anthropology
The study of human behavior through material remains.

What kind of experience is ethnography for the ethnographer? The box offers some clues.

The anthropological perspective derived from ethnographic field work often differs radically from that of economics or political science. Those fields focus on national and official organizations and policies and often on elites. However, the groups that anthropologists have traditionally studied usually have been relatively poor and powerless, as are most people in the world today. Ethnographers often observe discriminatory practices directed toward such people, who experience food shortages, dietary deficiencies, and other aspects of poverty. Political scientists tend to study programs that national planners develop, while anthropologists discover how these programs work on the local level.

Cultures are not isolated. As noted by Franz Boas (1940/1966) many years ago, contact between neighboring tribes has always existed and has extended over enormous areas. "Human populations construct their cultures in interaction with one another, and not in isolation" (Wolf 1982, p. ix). Villagers increasingly participate in regional, national, and world events. Exposure to external forces comes through the mass media, migration, and modern transportation. City and nation increasingly invade local communities with the arrival of tourists, development agents, government and religious officials, and political candidates. Such linkages are prominent components of regional, national, and international systems of politics, economics, and information. These larger systems increasingly affect the people and places anthropology traditionally has studied. The study of such linkages and systems is part of the subject matter of modern anthropology.

ethnology
The study of sociocultural differences and similarities.

Ethnology examines, interprets, analyzes, and compares the results of ethnography—the data gathered in different societies. It uses such data to compare and contrast and to make generalizations about society and culture. Looking beyond the particular to the more general, ethnologists attempt to identify and explain cultural differences and similarities, to test hypotheses, and to build theory to enhance our understanding of how social and cultural systems work. (See the section "The Scientific Method" at the end of this chapter.) Ethnology gets its data for comparison not just from ethnography but also from the other

subfields, particularly from archaeology, which reconstructs social systems of the past. (Recap 1.2 summarizes the main contrasts between ethnography and ethnology.)

Archaeological Anthropology

Archaeological anthropology (more simply, "archaeology") reconstructs, describes, and interprets human behavior and cultural patterns through material remains. At sites where people live or have lived, archaeologists find artifacts, material items that humans have made, used, or modified, such as tools, weapons, camp sites, buildings, and garbage. Plant and animal remains and ancient garbage tell stories about consumption and activities. Wild and domesticated grains have different characteristics, which allow archaeologists to distinguish between gathering and cultivation. Examination of animal bones reveals the ages of slaughtered animals and provides other information useful in determining whether species were wild or domesticated.

Analyzing such data, archaeologists answer several questions about ancient economies. Did the group get its meat from hunting, or did it domesticate and breed animals, killing only those of a certain age and sex? Did plant food come from wild plants or from sowing, tending, and harvesting crops? Did the residents make, trade for, or buy particular items? Were raw materials available locally? If not, where did they come from? From such information, archaeologists reconstruct patterns of production, trade, and consumption.

 living anthropology **VIDEOS**

"New" Knowledge among the Batak, www.mhhe.com/kottak

This clip shows Batak women, men, and children at work, making a living. It describes how they grow rice in an environmentally friendly way, unlike the destructive farming techniques of the lowlanders who have invaded their homeland. How have the Batak and conservation agencies worked together to reduce deforestation? Based on the clip, name several ways in which the Batak are influenced by forces beyond their homeland.

Archaeologists have spent much time studying potsherds, fragments of earthenware. Potsherds are more durable than many other artifacts, such as textiles and wood. The quantity of pottery fragments allows estimates of population size and density. The discovery that potters used materials that were not locally available suggests systems of trade. Similarities in manufacture and decoration at different sites may be proof of cultural connections. Groups with similar pots may be historically related. Perhaps they shared common cultural ancestors, traded with each other, or belonged to the same political system.

Many archaeologists examine paleoecology. *Ecology* is the study of interrelations among living things in an environment. The organisms and environment together constitute an ecosystem, a patterned arrangement of energy flows and exchanges. Human ecology studies ecosystems that include people, focusing on the ways in which human use "of nature influences and is influenced by social organization and cultural values" (Bennett 1969, pp. 10–11). *Paleoecology* looks at the ecosystems of the past.

In addition to reconstructing ecological patterns, archaeologists may infer cultural transformations, for example, by observing changes in the size and type of sites and the distance between them. A city develops in a region where only towns, villages, and hamlets existed a few centu-

ries earlier. The number of settlement levels (city, town, village, hamlet) in a society is a measure of social complexity. Buildings offer clues about political and religious features. Temples and pyramids suggest that an ancient society had an authority structure capable of marshaling the labor needed to build such monuments. The presence or absence of certain structures, like the pyramids of ancient Egypt and Mexico, reveals differences in function between settlements. For example, some towns were places where people came to attend ceremonies. Others were burial sites; still others were farming communities.

Archaeologists also reconstruct behavior patterns and lifestyles of the past by excavating. This involves digging through a succession of levels at a particular site. In a given area, through time, settlements may change in form and purpose, as may the connections between settlements. Excavation can document changes in economic, social, and political activities.

Although archaeologists are best known for studying prehistory, that is, the period before the invention of writing, they also study the cultures of historical and even living peoples. Studying sunken ships off the Florida coast, underwater archaeologists have been able to verify the living conditions on the vessels that brought ancestral African Americans to the New World

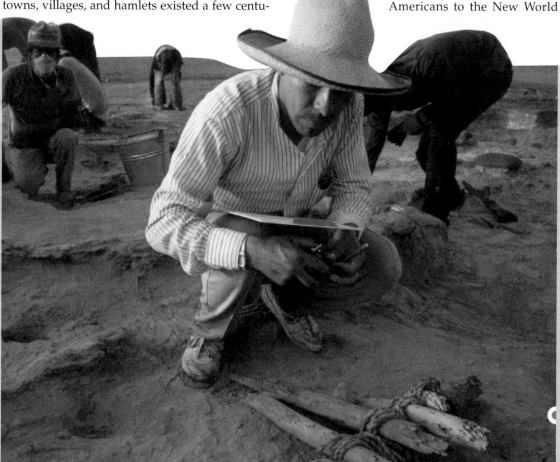

Archaeology in the coastal deserts around Nazca and Ica, Peru.

as enslaved people. In a research project begun in 1973 in Tucson, Arizona, archaeologist William Rathje has learned about contemporary life by studying modern garbage. The value of "garbology," as Rathje calls it, is that it provides "evidence of what people did, not what they think they did, what they think they should have done, or what the interviewer thinks they should have done" (Harrison, Rathje, and Hughes 1994, p. 108). What people report may contrast strongly with their real behavior as revealed by garbology. For example, the garbologists discovered that the three Tucson neighborhoods that reported the lowest beer consumption actually had the highest number of discarded beer cans per household (Podolefsky and Brown 1992, p. 100)! Rathje's garbology also has exposed misconceptions about how much of different kinds of trash are in landfills: While most people thought that fast-food containers and disposable diapers were major waste problems, in fact they were relatively insignificant compared with paper, including environmentally friendly, recyclable paper (Rathje and Murphy 2001).

Biological, or Physical, Anthropology

The subject matter of **biological**, or **physical, anthropology** is human biological diversity in time and space. The focus on biological variation unites five special interests within biological anthropology:

1. Human evolution as revealed by the fossil record (paleoanthropology).

2. Human genetics.

3. Human growth and development.

4. Human biological plasticity (the body's ability to change as it copes with stresses, such as heat, cold, and altitude).

5. The biology, evolution, behavior, and social life of monkeys, apes, and other nonhuman primates.

These interests link physical anthropology to other fields: biology, zoology, geology, anatomy, physiology, medicine, and public health. Osteology—the study of bones—helps paleoanthropologists, who examine skulls, teeth, and bones, to identify human ancestors and to chart changes in anatomy over time. A paleontologist is a scientist who studies fossils. A paleoanthropologist is one sort of paleontologist, one who studies the fossil record of human evolution. Paleoanthropologists often collaborate with archaeologists, who study artifacts, in reconstructing biological and cultural aspects of human evolution. Fossils and tools are often found together. Different types of tools provide informa-

tion about the habits, customs, and lifestyles of the ancestral humans who used them.

More than a century ago, Charles Darwin noticed that the variety that exists within any population permits some individuals (those with the favored characteristics) to do better than others at surviving and reproducing. Genetics, which developed later, enlightens us about the causes and transmission of this variety. However, it isn't just genes that cause variety. During any individual's lifetime, the environment works along with heredity to determine biological features. For example, people with a genetic tendency to be tall will be shorter if they are poorly nourished during childhood. Thus, biological anthropology also investigates the influence of environment on the body as it grows and matures. Among the environmental factors that influence the body as it develops are nutrition, altitude, temperature, and disease, as well as cultural factors, such as the standards of attractiveness we considered previously.

Biological anthropology (along with zoology) also includes primatology. The primates include our closest relatives—apes and monkeys. Primatologists study their biology, evolution, behavior, and social life, often in their natural environments. Primatology assists paleoanthropology, because primate behavior may shed light on early human behavior and human nature.

Linguistic Anthropology

We don't know (and probably never will) when our ancestors acquired the ability to speak, although biological anthropologists have looked to the anatomy of the face and the skull to speculate about the origin of language. And primatologists have described the communication systems of monkeys and apes. We do know that well-developed, grammatically complex languages have existed for thousands of years. Linguistic anthropology offers further illustration of anthropology's interest in comparison, variation, and change. **Linguistic anthropology** studies language in its social and cultural context, across space and over time. Some linguistic anthropologists make inferences about universal features of language, linked perhaps to uniformities in the human brain. Others reconstruct ancient languages by comparing their contemporary descendants and in so doing make discoveries about history. Still others study linguistic differences to discover varied perceptions and patterns of thought in different cultures.

Historical linguistics considers variation in time, such as the changes in sounds, grammar, and vocabulary between Middle English (spoken from approximately A.D. 1050 to 1550) and modern English. **Sociolinguistics** investigates relationships between social and linguistic variation. No language is a homogeneous system in which everyone speaks just like everyone else. How do different speakers use a given language? How do linguistic features correlate with social factors, including class and gender differences (Tannen 1990)? One reason for variation is geography, as in regional dialects and accents. Linguistic variation also is expressed in the bilingualism of ethnic groups. Linguistic and cultural anthropologists collaborate in studying links between language and many other aspects of culture, such as how people reckon kinship and how they perceive and classify colors.

ANTHROPOLOGY AND OTHER ACADEMIC FIELDS

As mentioned previously, one of the main differences between anthropology and the other fields that study people is holism, anthropology's unique blend of biological, social, cultural, linguistic, historical, and contemporary perspectives. Paradoxically, while distinguishing anthropology, this breadth is what also links it to many other disciplines. Techniques used to date fossils and artifacts have come to anthropology from physics, chemistry, and geology. Because plant and animal remains often are found with human bones and artifacts, anthropologists collaborate with botanists, zoologists, and paleontologists.

As a discipline that is both scientific and humanistic, anthropology has links with many other academic fields. Anthropology is a **science**—a "systematic field of study or body of knowledge that aims, through experiment, observation, and deduction, to produce reliable explanations of phenomena, with reference to the material and physical world" (*Webster's New World Encyclopedia* 1993, p. 937). The following chapters present anthropology as a humanistic science devoted to discovering, describing, understanding, and explaining similarities and differences in time and space among humans and our ancestors. Clyde Kluckhohn (1944) described anthropology as "the science of human similarities and differences" (p. 9). His statement of the need for such a field still stands: "Anthropology provides a scientific basis for dealing with the crucial dilemma of the world today: how can peoples of different appearance, mutually unintelligible languages, and dissimilar ways of life get along peaceably together?" (p. 9). Anthropology has compiled an impressive body of knowledge that this textbook attempts to encapsulate.

Besides its links to the natural sciences (e.g., geology, zoology) and social sciences (e.g., sociology, psychology), anthropology also has strong links to the humanities. The humanities include English, comparative literature, classics, folklore, philosophy, and the arts. These fields study languages, texts, philosophies, arts, music, performances, and other forms of creative expression. Ethnomusicology, which studies forms of musical expression on a worldwide basis, is especially closely related to anthropology. Also linked is folklore, the systematic

study of tales, myths, and legends from a variety of cultures. One might well argue that anthropology is among the most humanistic of all academic fields because of its fundamental respect for human diversity. Anthropologists listen to, record, and represent voices from a multitude of nations and cultures. Anthropology values local knowledge,

STUDENT: **María Alejandra Pérez, Ph.D.**
Candidate in Cultural Anthropology
COUNTRY OF ORIGIN: **Venezuela**
SUPERVISING PROFESSORS: **Erik Mueggler and Fernando Coronil**
SCHOOL: **University of Michigan**

Changing Places, Changing Identities

I was born and lived in Venezuela's capital, Caracas, for 15 years. Caracas was large and chaotic, but wonderfully cosmopolitan. Years of relatively stable democracy and a state infrastructure fueled by oil made this city attractive to many immigrants, not just from rural areas, but from the rest of South America and Europe as well. While growing up, I never thought much about how the place where we live impacts, often in very small ways, who we are. As I later came to realize, it is amazing how much what is familiar to us comes into focus when we travel and live elsewhere, far from the people and customs we are used to. Elements of our identity change, too, in different situations. In fact, plunging ourselves into a different context and carefully evaluating the complexity of this experience are a fundamental part of anthropological research.

Moving from Caracas as a teenager was bad enough, but when my family and I arrived in Trinidad, a small town in southern Colorado, one blustery November night, I wondered what I had done wrong to deserve such a fate! In Trinidad, my father joked that you'd miss the town limits if you biked too fast. Many of my new high school classmates had never flown on an airplane, much less seen the ocean. Most of them had last names such as Gonzales and Salazar, and their families had lived in the area for several generations. As different as I felt from them, we shared, in the American social context, identifiers such as Hispanic or Latino, terms that never made much sense to me, since they purportedly bundled together people I viewed as not having much in common. Just as I noticed how different my classmates were from me, elements that I felt made my family "distinctly Venezuelan" stood out, both tinted and amplified, no doubt, by my nostalgia for the people and places left behind. We stayed up late, danced to salsa on Christmas Eve and New Year's, lamented the lack of homemade *hallacas* (a traditional Venezuelan Christmas dish) and blabbed and joked in a Spanish that is characteristically *Caraqueño* (from Caracas). These seemingly trivial stereotypes became for me, during that first holiday away from home, the essence of our identity.

Years later, while conducting fieldwork in rural eastern Venezuela, I would again face the challenge of defining my identity both to myself and to local people who viewed me as a foreigner. This time, after several years of graduate school, I could better understand my reactions. I now appreciate what it means to be part of one culture and not another and that what it means to be local is contextual and dynamic.

science
Field of study that seeks reliable explanations, with reference to the material and physical world.

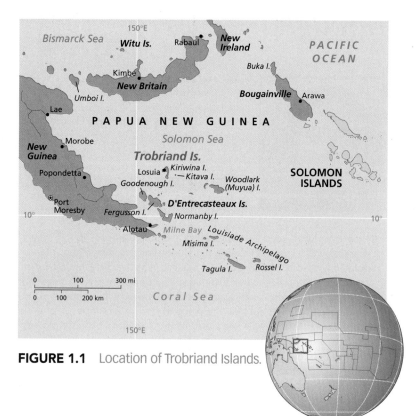

FIGURE 1.1   Location of Trobriand Islands.

diverse worldviews, and alternative philosophies. Cultural anthropology and linguistic anthropology in particular bring a comparative and nonelitist perspective to forms of creative expression, including language, art, narratives, music, and dance, viewed in their social and cultural context.

Cultural Anthropology and Sociology

Cultural anthropology and sociology share an interest in social relations, organization, and behavior. However, important differences between these disciplines arose from the kinds of societies each traditionally studied. Initially sociologists focused on the industrial West; anthropologists, on nonindustrial societies. Different methods of data collection and analysis emerged to deal with those different kinds of societies. To study large-scale, complex nations, sociologists came to rely on questionnaires and other means of gathering masses of quantifiable data. For many years, sampling and statistical techniques have been basic to sociology, whereas statistical training has been less common in anthropology (although this is changing as anthropologists increasingly work in modern nations).

Traditional ethnographers studied small and nonliterate (without writing) populations and relied on methods appropriate to that context. "Ethnography is a research process in which the anthropologist closely observes, records, and engages in the daily life of another culture—an experience labeled as the fieldwork method—and then writes accounts of this culture, emphasizing descriptive detail" (Marcus and Fischer 1986, p. 18). One key method described in this quote is participant observation—taking part in the events one is observing, describing, and analyzing.

In many areas and topics, anthropology and sociology now are converging. As the modern world system grows, sociologists now do research in developing countries and in other places that were once mainly within the anthropological orbit. As industrialization spreads, many anthropologists now work in industrial nations, where they study diverse topics, including rural decline, inner-city life, and the role of the mass media in creating national cultural patterns.

Anthropology and Psychology

Like sociologists, most psychologists do research in their own society. But statements about "human" psychology cannot be based solely on observations made in one society or in a single type of society. The area of cultural anthropology known as psychological anthropology studies cross-cultural variation in psychological traits. Societies instill different values by training children differently. Adult personalities reflect a culture's child-rearing practices.

Bronislaw Malinowski, an early contributor to the cross-cultural study of human psychology, is famous for his field work among the Trobriand Islanders of the South Pacific (Figure 1.1). The Trobrianders reckon kinship matrilineally. They consider themselves related to the mother and her relatives, but not to the father. The relative who disciplines the child is not the father but the mother's brother, the maternal uncle. Trobrianders show a marked respect for the uncle, with whom a boy usually has a cool and distant relationship. In contrast, the Trobriand father–son relationship is friendly and affectionate.

Malinowski's work among the Trobrianders suggested modifications in Sigmund Freud's famous theory of the universality of the Oedipus complex (Malinowski 1927). According to Freud (1918/1950), boys around the age of five become sexually attracted to their mothers. The Oedipus complex is resolved, in Freud's view, when the boy overcomes his sexual jealousy of, and identifies with, his father. Freud lived in patriarchal Austria during the late 19th and early 20th centuries—a social milieu in which the father was a strong authoritarian figure. The Austrian father was the child's primary authority figure and the mother's sexual partner. In the Trobriands, the father had only the sexual role.

If, as Freud contended, the Oedipus complex always creates social distance based on jealousy toward the mother's sexual partner, this would have shown up in Trobriand society. It did not. Malinowski concluded that the authority structure did more to influence the father–son relationship than did sexual jealousy. Although Melford Spiro (1993) has critiqued Malinowski's conclusions (see also Weiner 1988), no contemporary anthropologist would dispute Malinowski's contention that individual psychology is molded in a specific cultural context. Anthropologists continue to provide cross-cultural perspectives on psychoanalytic propositions (Paul 1989) as well as on issues of developmental and cognitive psychology (Shore 1996).

APPLIED ANTHROPOLOGY

Anthropology is not a science of the exotic carried on by quaint scholars in ivory towers. Rather, anthropology has a lot to tell the public. Anthropology's foremost professional organization, the American Anthropological Association (AAA), has formally acknowledged a public service role by recognizing that anthropology has two dimensions: (1) academic anthropology and (2) practicing or **applied anthropology.** The latter refers to the application of anthropological data, perspectives, theory, and methods to identify, assess, and solve contemporary social problems. As Erve Chambers (1987, p. 309) states, applied anthropology is the "field of inquiry concerned with the relationships between anthropological knowledge and the uses of that knowledge in the world beyond anthropology." More and more anthropologists from the four subfields now work in such "applied" areas as public health, family planning, business, economic development, and cultural resource management. (This chapter's "Appreciating Anthropology" box on pp. 16–17 discusses the career of President Barack Obama's mother, a sociocultural and applied anthropologist, who instilled in her son an appreciation of human diversity.)

Because of anthropology's breadth, applied anthropology has many applications. For example, applied medical anthropologists consider both the sociocultural and the biological contexts and implications of disease and illness. Perceptions of good and bad health, along with actual health threats and problems, differ among societies. Various ethnic groups recognize different illnesses, symptoms, and causes and have developed different health-care systems and treatment strategies.

Applied archaeology, usually called *public archaeology*, includes such activities as cultural resource management, contract archaeology, public educational programs, and historic preservation. An important role for public archaeology has been created by legislation requiring evaluation of sites threatened by dams, highways, and other construction activities. To decide what needs saving, and to preserve significant information about the past when sites cannot be saved, is the work of **cultural resource management** (CRM). CRM involves not only preserving sites but allowing their destruction

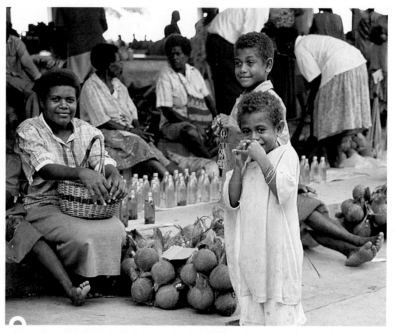

Bronislaw Malinowski is famous for his field work among the matrilineal Trobriand Islanders of the South Pacific. Does this Trobriand market scene suggest anything about the status of Trobriand women?

if they are not significant. The "management" part of the term refers to the evaluation and decision-making process. Cultural resource managers work for federal, state, and county agencies and other clients. Applied cultural anthropologists sometimes work with the public archaeologists, assessing the human problems generated by the proposed change and determining how they can be reduced.

THE SCIENTIFIC METHOD

Anthropology, we have seen, is a science, although a very humanistic one. Within sociocultural anthropology, **ethnology** is the comparative science that attempts to identify and explain cultural differences and similarities, test hypotheses, and build theory to enhance our understanding of how social and cultural systems work. The data for ethnology come from societies located in various times and places and so can come from archaeology as well as from ethnography, their more usual source. Ethnologists compare, contrast, and make generalizations about societies and cultures.

Theories, Associations, and Explanations

A **theory** is a set of ideas formulated to explain something. An effective theory offers an explanatory framework that can be applied to multiple cases. Just as ethnological theories help explain sociocultural differences and similarities, evolutionary theory is used to explain biological associations. An **association** is an observed relationship between two or more variables, such as the length of

applied anthropology
Using anthropology to solve contemporary problems.

theory
A set of ideas formulated to explain something.

association
An observed relationship between two or more variables.

cultural resource management
Deciding what needs saving when entire archaeological sites cannot be saved.

appreciating ANTHROPOLOGY

Anthropologist's Son Elected President

It is widely known that President Barack Obama is the son of a Kenyan father and a White American mother from Kansas. Less recognized is the fact that the 44th president of the United States is the son of an anthropologist—Dr. Stanley Ann Dunham Soetoro (usually called simply Ann Dunham). This account focuses on her life and her appreciation of human diversity, which led her to a career in anthropology and which she inculcated in her son. A sociocultural anthropologist by training, Dunham focused her attention on issues of microfinance and socioeconomic problems faced by Indonesian women. She applied anthropology, using her knowledge to identify and solve contemporary problems. She was both a cultural and an applied anthropologist.

Anthropologists study humanity in varied times and places and in a rapidly changing world. By virtue of his parentage, his enculturation, and his experience abroad, Barack Obama provides an excellent symbol of the diversity and interconnections that characterize such a world. As well, his election is a tribute to an ever more diverse United States and to the ability of the American people to appreciate such a nation.

In the capsule version of the Barack Obama story, his mother is simply the white woman from Kansas. . . . On the campaign trail, he has called her his "single mom." But neither description begins to capture the unconventional life of Stanley Ann Dunham Soetoro, the parent who most shaped Mr. Obama. . . .

In Hawaii, she married an African student at age 18. Then she married an Indonesian, moved to Jakarta, became an anthropologist, wrote an 800-page dissertation on peasant blacksmithing in Java, worked for the Ford Foundation, championed women's work and helped bring microcredit to the world's poor.

She had high expectations for her children. In Indonesia, she would wake her son at 4 A.M. for correspondence courses in English before school; she brought home recordings of Mahalia Jackson, speeches by the Rev. Dr. Martin Luther King Jr., and when Mr. Obama asked to stay in Hawaii for high school rather than return to Asia, she accepted living apart—a decision her daughter says was one of the hardest in Ms. Soetoro's life.

"She felt that somehow, wandering through uncharted territory, we might stumble upon something that will, in an instant, seem to represent who we are at the core," said Maya Soetoro-Ng, Mr. Obama's half-sister. "That was very much her philosophy of life—to not be limited by fear or narrow definitions, to not build walls around ourselves and to do our best to find kinship and beauty in unexpected places." . . .

Mr. Obama . . . barely saw his father after the age of 2. Though it is impossible to pinpoint the imprint of a parent on the life of a grown child, people who knew Ms. Soetoro well say they see her influence unmistakably in Mr. Obama. . . .

"She was a very, very big thinker," said Nancy Barry, a former president of Women's World Banking, an international network of microfinance providers, where Ms. Soetoro worked in New York City in the early 1990s . . .

In a Russian class at the University of Hawaii, she met the college's first African student, Barack Obama. They married and had a son in August 1961, in an era when interracial marriage was rare in the United States . . .

The marriage was brief. In 1963, Mr. Obama left for Harvard, leaving his wife and child. She then married Lolo Soetoro, an Indonesian student. When he was summoned home in 1966 after the turmoil surrounding the rise of Suharto, Ms. Soetoro and Barack followed. . . .

Her second marriage faded, too, in the 1970s. Ms. Soetoro wanted to work, one friend said, and Mr. Soetoro wanted more children. He became more American, she once said, as she became more Javanese. "There's a Javanese belief that if you're married to someone and it doesn't work, it will make you sick," said Alice G. Dewey, an anthropologist and friend. "It's just stupid to stay married." . . .

---

a giraffe's neck and the number of its offspring. Theories, which are more general than associations, suggest or imply multiple associations and attempt to explain them. Something, for example, the giraffe's long neck, is explained if it illustrates a general principle (a law), such as the concepts of adaptive advantage and differential fitness. In evolutionary theory, fitness is measured by reproductive success. In this case, giraffes with longer necks have a feeding advantage compared with their shorter-necked fellows; in times of food scarcity they eat better, live longer, and have more surviving offspring. The truth of a scientific statement (e.g., evolution occurs because of differential repro-

ductive success due to variation within the population) is confirmed by repeated observations.

Any science aims for reliable explanations that predict future occurrences. Accurate predictions stand up to tests designed to disprove (falsify) them. Scientific explanations rely on data, which can come from experiments, observation, and other systematic procedures. Scientific causes are material, physical, or natural (e.g., viruses) rather than supernatural (e.g., ghosts). Science is one way of understanding the world, but not the only way (See "Understanding Ourselves," p. 4).

In their 1997 article "Science in Anthropology," Melvin Ember and Carol R. Ember describe how

By 1974, Ms. Soetoro was back in Honolulu, a graduate student and raising Barack and Maya, nine years younger. . . . When Ms. Soetoro decided to return to Indonesia three years later for her field work, Barack chose not to go . . .

Fluent in Indonesian, Ms. Soetoro moved with Maya first to Yogyakarta, the center of Javanese handicrafts. A weaver in college, she was fascinated with what Ms. Soetoro-Ng calls "life's gorgeous minutiae." That interest inspired her study of village industries, which became the basis of her 1992 doctoral dissertation.

"She loved living in Java," said Dr. Dewey, who recalled accompanying Ms. Soetoro to a metalworking village. "People said: 'Hi! How are you?' She said: 'How's your wife? Did your daughter have the baby?' They were friends. Then she'd whip out her notebook and she'd say: 'How many of you have electricity? Are you having trouble getting iron?'"

She became a consultant for the United States Agency for International Development on setting up a village credit program, then a Ford Foundation program officer in Jakarta specializing in women's work. Later, she was a consultant in Pakistan, then joined Indonesia's oldest bank to work on what is described as the world's largest sustainable microfinance program, creating services like credit and savings for the poor.

Visitors flowed constantly through her Ford Foundation office in downtown Jakarta and through her house in a neighborhood to the

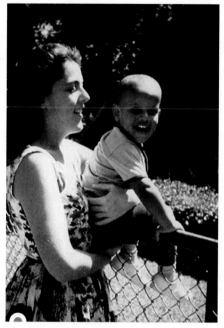

President Barack Obama and his mother, Ann Dunham, who was a cultural and applied anthropologist, in an undated photo from the 1960s. Dunham met Obama's father, Barack Obama Sr. from Kenya, when both were students at the University of Hawaii at Manoa; they married in 1960.

south, where papaya and banana trees grew in the front yard and Javanese dishes . . . were served for dinner. Her guests were leaders in the Indonesian human rights movement, peo-

ple from women's organizations, representatives of community groups doing grass-roots development. . . .

Ms. Soetoro-Ng . . . remembers conversations with her mother about philosophy or politics, books, esoteric Indonesian woodworking motifs. . . .

"She gave us a very broad understanding of the world," her daughter said. "She hated bigotry. She was very determined to be remembered for a life of service and thought that service was really the true measure of a life." Many of her friends see her legacy in Mr. Obama—in his self-assurance and drive, his boundary bridging, even his apparent comfort with strong women.

She died in November 1995, as Mr. Obama was starting his first campaign for public office. After a memorial service at the University of Hawaii, one friend said, a small group of friends drove to the South Shore in Oahu. With the wind whipping the waves onto the rocks, Mr. Obama and Ms. Soetoro-Ng placed their mother's ashes in the Pacific, sending them off in the direction of Indonesia.

scientists strive to improve our understanding of the world by testing **hypotheses**—suggested but as yet unverified explanations. An explanation must show how and why the thing to be understood (the *explicandum* or *dependent variable*) is associated with or related to something else, a *predictor variable*. Associations require covariation; when one thing (a variable) changes, the other one varies as well. Theories provide explanations for associations (Ember and Ember 1997).

One explanation for the occurrence of an association is that it illustrates a general principle. Thus, "water solidifies (freezes) at 32 degrees" states an association between two variables: the state of the water and the air temperature. The truth of the statement is confirmed by repeated observations of freezing and the fact that water does not solidify at higher temperatures. Such general relationships are called laws. Explanations based on such laws allow us to understand the past and predict the future. Yesterday ice formed at 32 degrees, and tomorrow it will still form at 32 degrees.

In the social sciences, associations usually are stated in the form of probability rather than as such absolute laws. The variables of interest are likely to, but don't always, vary as predicted. They *tend* to be related in a predictable way, but there are exceptions (Ember and Ember 1997). For

hypothesis
A suggested but as yet unverified explanation.

The name *kwashiorkor*, for a condition caused by severe protein deficiency, comes from a West African word meaning "one-two." Some cultures abruptly wean one infant when a second one is born. In today's world, refugees from civil wars, including the Angolan girl shown here, are among the most common victims of malnutrition.

consciously, that having another baby too soon would jeopardize the survival of the first one. Thus, they avoid sex for more than a year after the birth of the first baby. When such abstinence becomes institutionalized, everyone is expected to respect the taboo.

Theories suggest patterns, connections, and relationships that may be confirmed by new research. Whiting's theory, for example, suggests hypotheses for future researchers to test. Because his theory proposes that the postpartum taboo is adaptive under certain conditions, one might hypothesize that certain changes would cause the taboo to disappear. By adopting birth control, for instance, families could space births without avoiding intercourse. So, too, might the taboo disappear if babies started receiving protein supplements, which would reduce the threat of kwashiorkor.

What constitutes acceptable evidence that a theory or explanation probably is right? Cases that have been personally selected by a researcher don't provide an acceptable test of a hypothesis or theory. Ideally, hypothesis testing should be done using a sample of cases that have been selected randomly from some statistical universe. (Whiting did this in choosing his cross-cultural sample.) The relevant variables should be measured reliably, and the strength and significance of the results should be evaluated by using legitimate statistical methods (Bernard 2006). Recap 1.3 summarizes the main steps in using the scientific method, as just discussed here.

When Multiple Variables Predict

The scientific method, as shown in Recap 1.3, is not limited to ethnology but applies to any anthropological endeavor that formulates research questions and gathers or uses systematic data to test hypotheses. Nor does there have to be a single research question. Often anthropologists gather data that enable them to pose and test a number of separate hypotheses about attitudes and behavior. For example, in a research project during the 1980s, my associates and I used a combination of ethnography and survey research to study television's behavioral effects in Brazil (see Kottak 1990*a*).

Our most general research question was this: How has variable exposure to television affected Brazilians? We gathered data from more than 1,000 Brazilians living in seven different communities to answer this question. Uniquely, our research design permitted us to distinguish between *two key measures of individual exposure to television*. First was current viewing level (average daily hours spent watching TV). Such a measure is used routinely to assess the impact of television in the United States. Our second, and far more significant, variable was *length of home TV exposure*.

Unlike us, researchers in the United States must rely solely on current viewing level to measure TV's

example, in a worldwide sample of societies, the anthropologist John Whiting (1964) found a strong (but not 100 percent) association or correlation between a sexual custom and a type of diet. A long postpartum sex taboo (a ban on sexual intercourse between husband and wife for a year or more after the birth of a child) tended to be found in societies where the diet was low in protein.

After confirming the association through cross-cultural data (ethnographic information from a sample of several societies), Whiting's job was to formulate a theory that would explain why the dependent variable (in this case the postpartum sex taboo) depended on the predictor variable (a low-protein diet). Why might societies with low-protein diets develop this taboo? Whiting's theory was that the taboo is adaptive; it helps people survive and reproduce in certain environments. (More generally, anthropologists have argued that many cultural practices are adaptive.) In this case, with too little protein in their diets, babies may develop and die from a protein-deficiency disease called kwashiorkor. But if the mother delays her next pregnancy, her current baby, by breast-feeding longer, has a better chance to survive. Whiting suggests that parents are aware, unconsciously or

RECAP 1.3   Steps in the Scientific Method

Have a research question	Why do some societies have long postpartum taboos?
Construct a hypothesis	Delaying marital sex reduces infant mortality when diets are low in protein.
Posit a mechanism	Babies get more protein when they nurse longer; nursing is not a reliable method of contraception.
Get data to test your hypothesis	Use a (random) sample of cross-cultural data (data from several societies; such datasets exist for cross-cultural research).
Devise a way of measuring	Code societies 1 when they have a postpartum taboo of one year or longer, 0 when they do not; code 1 when diet is low protein, 0 when it is not.
Analyze your data	Notice patterns in the data: long postpartum taboos generally are found in societies with low-protein diets, whereas societies with better diets tend to lack those taboos. Use appropriate statistical methods to evaluate the strength of these associations.
Draw a conclusion	In most cases, the hypothesis is confirmed.
Derive implications	Such taboos tend to disappear when diets get better or new reproductive technologies become available.
Contribute to larger theory	Cultural practices can have adaptive value because they can enhance the survival of offspring.

influence, because there is little variation in length of home exposure, except for variation based on age. Americans aged 60 and younger never have known a world without TV. Some American researchers have tried to use age as an *indirect* measure of TV's long-term effects. Their assumption is that viewing has a cumulative effect, its influence increasing (up to a point) with age. However, that approach has difficulty distinguishing between the effects of years of TV exposure and other changes associated with aging. By contrast, our Brazilian sample included people in the same age groups but exposed to TV for different lengths of time—because television had reached their towns at different times. Years of age and years of home exposure were two separate variables.

Having gathered detailed quantitative data, we could use a statistical method that measures the separate (as well as the combined) effects of several "potential predictors" on a dependent variable. To use a more general example, to predict "risk of heart attack" (the dependent variable), potential predictors would include sex (gender), age, family history, weight, blood pressure, cholesterol level, exercise, and cigarette smoking. Each one would make a separate contribution, and some would have more impact than others. However, someone with many "risk factors" (particularly the most significant ones) would have a greater risk of heart attack than someone with few predictors.

Returning to television in Brazil, we used a standard set of nine potential predictor variables and examined their effects on hundreds of dependent variables (Kottak 1990*a*). Our potential predictors included gender, age, skin color, social class, education, income, religious involvement,

years of home TV exposure, and current televiewing level. We could measure the separate (as well as the combined) influence of each predictor on each dependent variable.

One of our strongest statistical measures of television's impact on attitudes was the correlation between TV exposure and liberal views on sex-gender issues. TV exposure had a stronger effect on sex-gender views than did such other predictor variables as gender, education, and income. The heavier and longer-exposed viewers were strikingly more liberal—less traditional in their opinions on such matters as whether women "belong at home," should work when their husbands have good incomes, should work when pregnant, should go to bars, should leave a husband they no longer love, should pursue men they like; whether men should cook and wash clothes; and whether parents should talk to their children about sex. All these questions produced TV-biased answers, in that Brazilian television depicts an urban-modern society in which sex-gender roles are less traditional than in small communities.

Are these effects or just correlations? That is, does Brazilian TV make people more liberal, or do already liberal people, seeking reinforcement for their views, simply watch more television? Do they look to TV and its urban-elite world for moral options that are missing, suppressed, or disapproved in their own, more traditional, towns? We concluded that this liberalization is both a correlation and an effect. There is a strong *correlation* between liberal social views and *current* viewing hours. Liberal small-town Brazilians appear to watch more TV to validate personal views that the local setting suppresses. However, confirming that

Family and friends watching a soccer game on TV in Brazil. Soccer and *telenovelas* are key features of Brazilian popular culture.

long-term TV exposure also has an *effect* on Brazilians' attitudes, there is an even stronger correlation between years of home viewing by individuals and their liberal social views.

It is difficult to separate effects of televiewing from mere correlations when we use current viewing level as a predictor variable. Questions like the following always arise: Does television create fears about the outside world—or do already fearful people tend to stay home and watch more TV? *Effects* are clearer when length of home exposure can be measured. Logically, we can compare this predictor and its influence over time to education and its effects. If the cumulative effects of formal education increase with years of schooling, then it seems

reasonable to assume some similar influence as a result of years of home exposure to television.

Heavy viewers in Brazil probably are predisposed to liberal views. However, content, entering homes each day, reinforces those views over time. TV-biased and TV-reinforced attitudes spread as viewers take courage from the daily validation of their unorthodox (local) views in (national) programming. More and more townsfolk encounter nontraditional views and come to see them as normal.

In this case, we measured and confirmed an association and then offered explanations for why that association is an effect as well as a correlation. Our study suggested hypotheses for future research on how people use television and how it affects them in other ways, places, and times. Indeed, recent research in a Michigan town (Descartes and Kottak 2009) has revealed forms of use and impact similar to those we discovered in Brazil.

Acing the COURSE

Summary

1. Anthropology is the holistic and comparative study of humanity. It is the systematic exploration of human biological and cultural diversity.

Examining the origins of, and changes in, human biology and culture, anthropology provides explanations for similarities and differences. The four subfields of general anthropology are socio-cultural, archaeological, biological, and linguistic. All consider variation in time and space. Each also examines adaptation—the process by which organisms cope with environmental stresses.

2. Cultural forces mold human biology, including our body types and images. Societies have particular standards of physical attractiveness. They also have specific ideas about what activities—for example, various sports—are appropriate for males and females.

3. Cultural anthropology explores the cultural diversity of the present and the recent past. Archaeology reconstructs cultural patterns, often of prehistoric populations. Biological anthropology documents diversity involving fossils, genetics, growth and development, bodily responses, and nonhuman primates. Linguistic anthropology considers diversity among languages. It also studies how speech changes in social situations and over time.

4. Concerns with biology, society, culture, and language link anthropology to many other fields—sciences and humanities. Anthropologists study art, music, and literature across cultures. But their concern is more with the creative expressions of common people than with arts designed for elites.

Anthropologists examine creators and products in their social context. Sociologists traditionally study urban and industrial populations, whereas anthropologists have focused on rural, nonindustrial peoples. Psychological anthropology views human psychology in the context of social and cultural variation.

5. Anthropology has two dimensions: academic and applied. Applied anthropology is the use of anthropological data, perspectives, theory, and methods to identify, assess, and solve contemporary social problems.

6. Ethnologists attempt to identify and explain cultural differences and similarities and to build theories about how social and cultural systems work. Scientists strive to improve understanding by testing hypotheses—suggested explanations. Explanations rely on associations and theories. An association is an observed relationship between variables. A theory is more general, suggesting or implying associations and attempting to explain them. The scientific method characterizes any anthropological endeavor that formulates research questions and gathers or uses systematic data to test hypotheses. Often anthropologists gather data that enable them to pose and test a number of separate hypotheses.

anthropology 5
applied anthropology 15
archaeological anthropology 10
association 15
biocultural 9
biological anthropology 12
cultural anthropology 9
cultural resource management 15
culture 5
ethnography 9

ethnology 10
food production 6
general anthropology 8
holistic 5
hypothesis 17
linguistic anthropology 12
physical anthropology 12
science 13
sociolinguistics 12
theory 15

MULTIPLE CHOICE

1. Which of the following most characterizes anthropology among disciplines that study humans?
   a. It studies foreign places.
   b. It includes biology.
   c. It uses personal interviews of the study population.
   d. It is holistic and comparative.
   e. It studies only groups that are thought to be "dying."

2. What is the most critical element of cultural traditions?
   a. their stability due to the unchanging characteristics of human biology
   b. their tendency to radically change every 15 years
   c. their ability to survive the challenges of modern life
   d. their transmission through learning rather than through biological inheritance
   e. their material manifestations in archaeological sites

3. Over time, how has human reliance on cultural means of adaptation changed?
   a. Humans have become increasingly less dependent on them.
   b. Humans have become entirely reliant on biological means.
   c. Humans have become increasingly more dependent on them.
   d. Humans are just beginning to depend on them.
   e. Humans no longer use them.

4. The fact that anthropology focuses on both culture and biology
   a. is unique to the kind of anthropology found in Europe.
   b. is the reason it has traditionally studied primitive societies.
   c. is a product of the participant observation approach.
   d. allows it to address how culture influences biological traits and vice versa.
   e. is insignificant, since biology is studied by biological anthropologists while culture is studied by cultural anthropologists.

5. In this chapter, what is the point of describing the ways in which humans cope with low oxygen pressure in high altitudes?
   a. to illustrate human capacities of cultural and biological adaptation, variation, and change
   b. to expose the fact that "it is all in the genes"
   c. to show how culture is more important than biology
   d. to describe how humans are among the world's least adaptable animals
   e. to stress the rising popularity of extreme sport anthropology

6. Four-field anthropology
   a. was largely shaped by early American anthropologists' interests in Native Americans.
   b. is unique to Old World anthropology.
   c. stopped being useful when the world became dominated by nation-states.
   d. was replaced in the 1930s by the two-field approach.
   e. originally was practiced in Europe, because of a particularly British interest in military behavior.

7. The study of nonhuman primates is of special interest to which subdiscipline of anthropology?
   a. cultural anthropology
   b. archaeological anthropology
   c. linguistic anthropology
   d. developmental anthropology
   e. biological anthropology

8. All of the following are true about practicing or applied anthropology *except* that
   a. it encompasses any use of the knowledge and/or techniques of the four subfields to identify, assess, and solve practical social problems.
   b. it has been formally acknowledged by the American Anthropological Association as one of the two dimensions of the discipline.
   c. it is less relevant for archaeology since archaeology typically concerns the material culture of societies that no longer exist.
   d. it is a growing aspect of the field, with more and more anthropologists developing applied components of their work.
   e. it has many applications because of anthropology's breadth.

9. Which of the following terms is defined as a suggested but yet unverified explanation for observed things and events?
   a. hypothesis
   b. theory
   c. association
   d. model
   e. law

10. The scientific method
    a. is limited to ethnology since it is the aspect of anthropology that studies sociocultural differences and similarities.
    b. is a powerful tool for understanding ourselves since it guarantees complete objectivity in research.
    c. is the best and only reliable way of understanding the world.
    d. characterizes any anthropological endeavor that formulates research questions and gathers or uses systematic data to test hypotheses.
    e. only applies to the analysis of data that leads to predictions, not associations.

FILL IN THE BLANK

1. Anthropology is unique among other social sciences in its emphasis on both _____ and _____ perspectives.

2. A ___biocultural___ approach refers to the inclusion and combination of both biological and cultural perspectives and approaches to comment on or solve a particular issue or problem.

3. ___ethnography___ provides an account of field work in a particular community, society, or culture.

4. ___applied___ encompasses any use of the knowledge and/or techniques of the four subfields of anthropology to identity, assess, and solve practical problems. More and more anthropologists increasingly work in this dimension of the discipline.

5. The _____ characterizes any anthropological endeavor that formulates research questions and gathers or uses systematic data to test hypotheses.

CRITICAL THINKING

1. What is culture? How is it distinct from what this chapter describes as a biocultural approach? How do these concepts help us understand the complex ways that human populations adapt to their environments?

2. What themes and interests unify the subdisciplines of anthropology? In your answer, refer to historical reasons for the unity of anthropology. Are these historical reasons similar in all places where anthropology developed as a discipline?

3. If, as Franz Boas illustrated early on in American anthropology, cultures are not isolated, how can ethnography provide an account of a particular community, society, or culture? Note: There is no easy answer to this question! Anthropologists continue to deal with it as they define their research questions and projects.

4. The American Anthropological Association has formally acknowledged a public service role by recognizing that anthropology has two dimensions: (1) academic anthropology and (2) practicing or applied anthropology. What is applied anthropology? Based on your reading of this chapter, identify examples from current events where an anthropologist could help identify, assess, and solve contemporary social problems.

5. In this chapter, we learn that anthropology is a science, although a very humanistic one. What do you think this means? What role does hypothesis testing play in structuring anthropological research? What is the difference between theories, laws, and hypotheses?

Multiple Choice: 1. (D); 2. (D); 3. (C); 4. (D); 5. (A); 6. (A); 7. (E); 8. (C); 9. (A); 10. (D); **Fill in the Blank:** 1. holistic, cross-cultural; 2. biocultural; 3. Ethnography; 4. Applied anthropology; 5. scientific method

Endicott, K. M., and R. Welsch
    2009 *Taking Sides: Clashing Views on Controversial Issues in Anthropology,* 4th ed. Guilford, CT: McGraw-Hill/Dushkin. Thirty-eight anthropologists offer opposing viewpoints on 19 polarizing issues, including ethical dilemmas.

Fagan, B. M.
    2009 *Archeology: A Brief Introduction,* 10th ed. Upper Saddle River, NJ: Prentice Hall. Introduction to archaeological theory, techniques, and approaches, including field survey, excavation, and analysis of materials.

Geertz, C.
    1995 *After the Fact: Two Countries, Four Decades, One Anthropologist.* Cambridge, MA: Harvard University Press. A prominent cultural anthropologist reflects on his work in Morocco and Indonesia.

Harris, M.
    1989 *Our Kind: Who We Are, Where We Came From, Where We Are Going.* New York: Harper-Collins. Clearly written survey of the origins of humans, culture, and major sociopolitical institutions.

Nash, D.
    1999 *A Little Anthropology,* 3rd ed. Upper Saddle River, NJ: Prentice Hall. Short introduction to societies and cultures, with comments on developing nations and modern America.

Wolf, E. R.
    1982 *Europe and the People without History.* Berkeley: University of California Press. Influential and award-winning study of the relation between Europe and various nonindustrial populations.

Suggested Additional Readings

Go to our Online Learning Center website at **www.mhhe.com/kottak** for Internet exercises directly related to the content of this chapter.

Internet Exercises

What is culture and why do we study it?

What is the relation between culture and the individual?

How does culture change?

Children and adults praying in Bali, Indonesia. People learn and share beliefs and behavior as members of cultural groups.

Culture

understanding OURSELVES

How special are you? To what extent are you "your own person" and to what extent are you a product of your particular culture? How much does, and should, your cultural background influence your actions and decisions? Americans may not fully appreciate the power of culture because of the value their culture places on "the *individual*." Americans like to regard everyone as unique in some way. Yet individualism itself is a distinctive *shared* value, a feature of American culture, transmitted constantly in our daily lives. In the media, count how many stories focus on individuals versus groups. From the late Mr. (Fred) Rogers of daytime TV to "real-life" parents, grandparents, and teachers, our enculturative agents insist we all are "someone special." That we are individuals first and members of groups second is the opposite of this chapter's lesson about culture. Certainly we have distinctive features because we are individuals, but we have other distinct attributes because we belong to cultural groups.

For example, as we saw in the "Appreciating Diversity" box in Chapter 1 (pp. 6–7), a comparison of the United States with Brazil, Italy, or virtually any Latin nation reveals striking contrasts between a national culture (American) that discourages physical affection and national cultures in which the opposite is true. Brazilians touch, embrace, and kiss one another much more frequently than North Americans do. Such behavior reflects years of exposure to particular cultural traditions. Middle-class Brazilians teach their kids—both boys and girls—to kiss (on the cheek, two or three times, coming and going) every adult relative they ever see. Given the size of Brazilian extended families, this can mean hundreds of people. Women continue kissing all those people throughout their lives. Until they are adolescents, boys kiss all adult relatives. Men typically continue to kiss female relatives and friends, as well as their fathers and uncles throughout their lives.

Do you kiss your father? Your uncle? Your grandfather? How about your mother, aunt, or grandmother? The answer to these questions may differ between men and women, and for male and female relatives. Culture can help us to make sense of these differences. In America, a cultural homophobia (fear of homosexuality) may prevent American men from engaging in displays of affection with other men; similarly, American girls typically are encouraged to show affection, while American boys typically aren't. It's important to note that these cultural explanations rely upon example and expectation, and that no cultural trait exists because it is natural or right. *Ethnocentrism* is the error of viewing one's own culture as superior and applying one's own cultural values in judging people from other cultures. How easy is it for you to see beyond the ethnocentric blinders of your own experience? Do you have an ethnocentric position regarding displays of affection?

WHAT IS CULTURE?

The concept of culture has long been basic to anthropology. Well over a century ago, in his book *Primitive Culture,* the British anthropologist Sir Edward Tylor proposed that cultures—systems of human behavior and thought—obey natural laws and therefore can be studied scientifically. Tylor's definition of culture still offers an overview of the subject matter of anthropology and is widely quoted: "Culture . . . is that complex whole which includes knowledge, belief, arts, morals, law, custom, and any other capabilities and habits acquired by man as a member of society" (Tylor 1871/1958, p. 1). The crucial phrase here is "acquired by man as a member of society." Tylor's definition focuses on attributes that people acquire not through biological inheritance but by growing up in a particular society where they are exposed to a specific cultural tradition. **Enculturation** is the process by which a child learns his or her culture.

Culture Is Learned

The ease with which children absorb any cultural tradition rests on the uniquely elaborated human capacity to learn. Other animals may learn from experience; for example, they avoid fire after discovering that it hurts. Social animals also learn from other members of their group. Wolves, for instance, learn hunting strategies from other pack members. Such social learning is particularly important among monkeys and apes, our closest biological relatives. But our own *cultural learning* depends on the uniquely developed human capacity to use **symbols,** signs that have no necessary or natural connection to the things they signify or for which they stand.

On the basis of cultural learning, people create, remember, and deal with ideas. They grasp and apply specific systems of symbolic meaning. Anthropologist Clifford Geertz defines culture as ideas based on cultural learning and symbols. Cultures have been characterized as sets of "control mechanisms—plans, recipes, rules, instructions, what computer engineers call programs for the governing of behavior" (Geertz 1973, p. 44). These programs are absorbed by people through enculturation in particular traditions. People gradually internalize a previously established system of meanings and symbols. They use this cultural system to define their world, express their feelings, and make their judgments. This system helps guide their behavior and perceptions throughout their lives.

Every person begins immediately, through a process of conscious and unconscious learning and interaction with others, to internalize, or incorporate, a cultural tradition through the process of enculturation. Sometimes culture is taught directly, as when parents tell their children to say "thank you" when someone gives them something or does them a favor.

Culture also is transmitted through observation. Children pay attention to the things that go on around them. They modify their behavior not just because other people tell them to but as a result of their own observations and growing awareness of what their culture considers right and wrong. Culture also is absorbed unconsciously. North Americans acquire their culture's notions about how far apart people should stand when they talk not by being told directly to maintain a certain distance but through a gradual process of observation, experience, and conscious and unconscious behavior modification. No one tells Latins to stand closer together than North Americans do, but they learn to do so anyway as part of their cultural tradition.

Anthropologists agree that cultural learning is uniquely elaborated among humans and that all humans have culture. Anthropologists also accept a doctrine named in the 19th century as "the psychic unity of man." This means that although *individuals* differ in their emotional and intellectual tendencies and capacities, all human *populations* have equivalent capacities for culture. Regardless of their genes or their physical appearance, people can learn any cultural tradition.

To understand this point, consider that contemporary Americans and Canadians are the genetically mixed descendants of people from all over the world. Our ancestors were biologically varied, lived in different countries and continents, and participated in hundreds of cultural traditions. However, early colonists, later immigrants, and their descendants have all become active participants in American and Canadian life. All now share a national culture.

Culture Is Symbolic

Symbolic thought is unique and crucial to humans and to cultural learning. Anthropologist Leslie White defined culture as

> dependent upon symbolling . . . Culture consists of tools, implements, utensils, clothing, ornaments, customs, institutions, beliefs, rituals, games, works of art, language, etc. (White 1959, p. 3)

For White, culture originated when our ancestors acquired the ability to use symbols, that is, to originate and bestow meaning on a thing or event, and, correspondingly, to grasp and appreciate such meanings (White 1959, p. 3).

A symbol is something verbal or nonverbal, within a particular language or culture, that comes to stand for something else. There is no obvious, natural, or necessary connection between the symbol and what it symbolizes. A pet

enculturation
The process by which culture is learned and transmitted across the generations.

symbol
Something, verbal or nonverbal, that stands for something else.

Symbols may be linguistic or nonverbal. The latter include flags, which stand for countries. Here, colorful flags of several nations wave in front of the United Nations building in New York City.

that barks is no more naturally a *dog* than a *chien*, *Hund*, or *mbwa*, to use the words for the animal we call "dog" in French, German, and Swahili. Language is one of the distinctive possessions of *Homo sapiens*. No other animal has developed anything approaching the complexity of language.

Symbols are usually linguistic. But there are also nonverbal symbols, such as flags, that stand for countries, as arches do for a hamburger chain. Holy water is a potent symbol in Roman Catholicism. As is true of all symbols, the association between a symbol (water) and what is symbolized (holiness) is arbitrary and conventional. Water is not intrinsically holier than milk, blood, or other natural liquids. Nor is holy water chemically different from ordinary water. Holy water is a symbol within Roman Catholicism, which is part of an international cultural system. A natural thing has been arbitrarily associated with a particular meaning for Catholics, who share common beliefs and experiences that are based on learning and that are transmitted across the generations.

For hundreds of thousands of years, humans have shared the abilities on which culture rests. These abilities are to learn, to think symbolically, to manipulate language, and to use tools and other cultural products in organizing their lives and coping with their environments. Every contemporary human population has the ability to use symbols and thus to create and maintain culture. Our nearest relatives—chimpanzees and gorillas—have rudimentary cultural abilities. However, no other animal has elaborated cultural abilities—to learn, to communicate, and to store, process, and use information—to the extent that *Homo* has.

Culture Is Shared

Culture is an attribute not of individuals per se but of individuals as members of *groups*. Culture is transmitted in society. Don't we learn our culture by observing, listening, talking, and interacting with many other people? Shared beliefs, values, memories, and expectations link people who grow up in the same culture. Enculturation unifies people by providing us with common experiences.

Today's parents were yesterday's children. If they grew up in North America, they absorbed certain values and beliefs transmitted over the generations. People become agents in the enculturation of their children, just as their parents were for them. Although a culture constantly changes, certain fundamental beliefs, values, worldviews, and child-rearing practices endure. Consider a simple American example of enduring shared enculturation. As children, when we didn't finish a meal, our parents may have reminded us of starving children in some foreign country, just as our grandparents might have done a generation earlier. The specific country changes (China, India, Bangladesh, Ethiopia, Somalia, Rwanda—what was it in your home?). Still, American culture goes on transmitting the idea that by eating all our brussels sprouts or broccoli, we can justify our own good fortune, compared to a hungry child in an impoverished or war-ravaged country.

Despite characteristic American notions that people should "make up their own minds" and "have a right to their opinion," little of what we think is original or unique. We share our opinions and beliefs with many other people. Illustrating the power of shared cultural background, we are most likely to agree with and feel comfortable with people who are socially, economically, and culturally similar to ourselves. This is one reason why Americans abroad tend to socialize with each other, just as French and British colonials did in their overseas empires. Birds of a feather flock together, but for people, the familiar plumage is culture.

Culture and Nature

Culture takes the natural biological urges we share with other animals and teaches us how to express them in particular ways. People have to eat, but culture teaches us what, when, and how. In many cultures people have their main meal at noon, but most North Americans prefer a large dinner. English people may eat fish for breakfast, while North Americans may prefer hot cakes and cold cereals. Brazilians put hot milk into strong coffee, whereas North Americans pour cold milk into a weaker brew. Midwesterners dine at 5 or 6 P.M., Spaniards at 10 P.M.

Cultural habits, perceptions, and inventions mold "human nature" in many directions. People have to eliminate wastes from their bodies. But some cultures teach people to defecate squatting, while others tell them to do it sitting down. A generation ago, in Paris and other French cities, it was customary for men to urinate almost publicly, and seemingly without embarrassment, in barely shielded *pissoirs* located on city streets. Our "bathroom" habits, including waste elimination, bathing, and dental care, are parts of cultural traditions that have converted natural acts into cultural customs.

Our culture—and cultural changes—affect the ways in which we perceive nature, human nature, and "the natural." Through science, invention, and discovery, cultural advances have overcome many "natural" limitations. We prevent and cure diseases such as polio and smallpox that felled our ancestors. We use Viagra to restore and enhance sexual potency. Through cloning, scientists have altered the way we think about biological identity and the meaning of life itself. Culture, of course, has not freed us from natural threats. Hurricanes, floods, earthquakes, and other natural forces regularly challenge our wishes to modify the environment through building, development, and expansion. Can you think of other ways in which nature strikes back at people and their products?

Culture Is All-Encompassing

For anthropologists, culture includes much more than refinement, taste, sophistication, education, and appreciation of the fine arts. Not only college graduates but all people are "cultured." The most interesting and significant cultural forces are those that affect people every day of their lives, particularly those that influence children during enculturation. *Culture,* as defined anthropologically, encompasses features that are sometimes regarded as trivial or unworthy of serious study, such as "popular" culture. To understand contemporary North American culture, we must consider television, fast-food restaurants, sports, and games. As a cultural manifestation, a rock star may be as interesting as a symphony conductor, a comic book as significant as a book-award winner. (Describing the multiple ways in which anthropologists have studied the Ariaal of northern Kenya, this chapter's "Appreciating Anthropology" demonstrates how anthropology, like culture, is all encompassing.)

living anthropology **VIDEOS**

Being Raised Canela, www.mhhe.com/kottak

This clip focuses on Brazil's Canela Indians. One of the key figures in the clip is the boy Carampei, who was four years old in 1975. Another is the "formal friend" of a small boy whose finger has been burned and who has been disciplined by his mother. The clip depicts enculturation among the Canela—various ways in which children learn their culture. How does the footage of Carampei show his learning of the rhythms of Canela life? The clip shows that children start doing useful work at an early age, but that the playfulness and affection of childhood are prolonged into adulthood. How does the behavior of the formal friend illustrate this playfulness? Notice how Canela culture is integrated in that songs, dances, and tales are interwoven with subsistence activity. From an emic perspective, what is the function of the hunters' dance? Think about how the clip shows the formal and informal, the conscious and unconscious aspects of enculturation.

Culture Is Integrated

Cultures are not haphazard collections of customs and beliefs. Cultures are integrated, patterned systems. If one part of the system (e.g., the economy) changes, other parts change as well. For example, during the 1950s, most American women planned domestic careers as homemakers and mothers. Most of today's college women, by contrast, expect to get paid jobs when they graduate.

Cultures are integrated systems. When one behavior pattern changes, others also change. During the 1950s, most American women expected to have careers as wives, mothers, and domestic managers. As more and more women have entered the workforce, attitudes toward work and family have changed. On the left, Mom and kids do the dishes in 1952. On the right (taken in January 2005), nuclear expert and deputy director of ISIS (Institute for Science and International Security) Corey Hinderstein uses her office in Washington, D.C., to monitor nuclear activities all over the globe. What do you imagine she will do when she gets home?

appreciating ANTHROPOLOGY

Remote and Poked, Anthropology's Dream Tribe

Anthropology, remember, is a four subfield discipline that is characteristically comparative, cross-cultural, and biocultural. Anthropologists are known for their close observation of human behavior in natural settings and their focus on human biological and cultural diversity in time and space. It is typical of the anthropological approach to go right to—and live with—the local people, whether in northern Kenya, as described here, or in middle-class America.

Anthropologists study human biology and culture in varied times and places and in a rapidly changing world. This account focuses on a remote population, the Ariaal of northern Kenya, whom anthropologists have been studying since the 1970s. In the account we learn about the multifaceted research interests that anthropologists have. Among the Ariaal, anthropologists have studied a range of topics, including kinship and marriage customs, conflict, and even biomedical issues such as illness and body type and function. As you read this account, consider, too, what anthropologists get from the people being studied and vice versa.

The Ariaal, a nomadic community of about 10,000 people in northern Kenya, have been seized on by researchers since the 1970s, after one anthropologist, Elliot Fratkin—stumbled upon them and began publishing his accounts of their lives. . . .

Other researchers have done studies on everything from their cultural practices to their testosterone levels. *National Geographic* focused on the Ariaal in 1999, in an article on vanishing cultures.

But over the years, more and more Ariaal—like the Masai and the Turkana in Kenya and the Tuaregs and Bedouins elsewhere in Africa—are settling down. Many have emigrated closer to Marsabit, the nearest town, which has cellphone reception and even sporadic Internet access.

The scientists continue to arrive in Ariaal country, with their notebooks, tents, and bizarre queries, but now they document a semi-isolated people straddling modern life and more traditional ways.

For Benjamin C. Campbell, a biological anthropologist at Boston University who was introduced to the Ariaal by Dr. Fratkin, their way of life, diet, and cultural practices make them worthy of study.

Other academics agree. Local residents say they have been asked over the years how many livestock they own (many), how many times they have had diarrhea in the last month (often) and what they ate the day before yesterday (usually meat, milk or blood).

Ariaal women have been asked about the work they do, which seems to exceed that of the men, and about local marriage customs, which compel their prospective husbands to hand over livestock to their parents before the ceremony can take place. . . .

The researchers may not know this, but the Ariaal have been studying them all these years as well.

The Ariaal note that foreigners slather white liquid on their very white skin to protect them

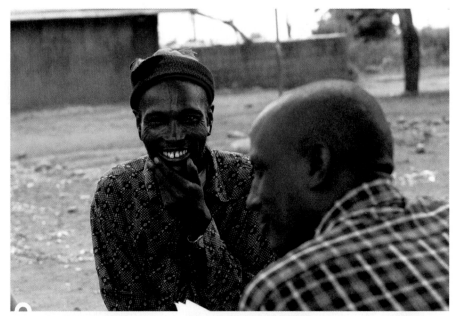

Koitaton Garawale (left) is amused by questions posed by researcher Daniel Lemoille in Songa, Kenya. The Ariaal, a nomadic community of about 10,000 people in northern Kenya, have been studied since the 1970s by Elliot Fratkin and other anthropologists, representing various subfields.

from the sun, and that many favor short pants that show off their legs and the clunky boots on their feet. Foreigners often partake of the local food but drink water out of bottles and munch on strange food in wrappers between meals, the Ariaal observe.

The scientists leave tracks as well as memories behind. For instance, it is not uncommon to see nomads in T-shirts bearing university logos, gifts from departing academics.

In Lewogoso Lukumai, a circle of makeshift huts near the Ndoto Mountains, nomads rushed up to a visitor and asked excitedly in the Samburu language, "Where's Elliot?"

They meant Dr. Fratkin, who describes in his book "Ariaal Pastoralists of Kenya" how in 1974 he stumbled upon the Ariaal, who had been little known until then. With money from the University of London and the Smithsonian Institution, he was traveling north from Nairobi in search of isolated agro-pastoralist groups in Ethiopia. But a coup toppled Haile Selassie, then the emperor, and the border between the countries was closed. So as he sat in a bar in Marsabit, a boy approached and, mistaking him for a tourist, asked if he wanted to see the elephants in a nearby forest. When the aspiring anthropologist declined, the boy asked if he wanted to see a traditional ceremony at a local village instead. That was Dr. Fratkin's introduction to the Ariaal, who share cultural traits with the Samburu and Rendille tribes of Kenya.

Soon after, he was living with the Ariaal, learning their language and customs while fighting off mosquitoes and fleas in his hut of sticks covered with grass.

The Ariaal wear sandals made from old tires and many still rely on their cows, camels and goats to survive. Drought is a regular feature of their world, coming in regular intervals and testing their durability.

"I was young when Elliot first arrived," recalled an Ariaal elder known as Lenampere in Lewogoso Lukumai, a settlement that moves from time to time to a new patch of sand. "He came here and lived with us. He drank milk and blood with us. After him, so many others came." . . .

Not all African tribes are as welcoming to researchers, even those with the necessary permits from government bureaucrats. But the Ariaal have a reputation for cooperating—in exchange, that is, for pocket money. "They think I'm stupid for asking dumb questions," said Daniel Lemoille, headmaster of the school in Songa, a village outside of Marsabit for Ariaal nomads who have settled down, and a frequent research assistant for visiting professors. "You have to try to explain that these same questions are asked to people all over the world and that their answers will help advance science." . . .

The Ariaal have no major gripes about the studies, although the local chief in Songa, Stephen Lesseren, who wore a Boston University T-shirt the other day, said he wished their work would lead to more tangible benefits for his people.

"We don't mind helping people get their Ph.D.'s," he said. "But once they get their Ph.D.'s, many of them go away. They don't send us their reports . . . We want feedback. We want development."

Even when conflicts break out in the area, as happened this year as members of rival tribes slaughtered each other, victimizing the Ariaal, the research does not cease. With tensions still high, John G. Galaty, an anthropologist at McGill University in Montreal who studies ethnic conflicts, arrived in northern Kenya to question them.

In a study in *The International Journal of Impotence Research*, Dr. Campbell found that

Ariaal men with many wives showed less erectile dysfunction than did men of the same age with fewer spouses.

Dr. Campbell's body image study, published in the *Journal of Cross-Cultural Psychology* this year, also found that Ariaal men are much more consistent than men in other parts of the world in their views of the average man's body [one like their own] and what they think women want [one like their own].

Dr. Campbell came across no billboards or international magazines in Ariaal country and only one television in a local restaurant that played CNN, leading him to contend that Ariaal men's views of their bodies were less affected by media images of burly male models with six-pack stomachs and rippling chests.

To test his theories, a nonresearcher without a Ph.D. showed a group of Ariaal men a copy of *Men's Health* magazine full of pictures of impossibly well-sculpted men and women. The men looked on with rapt attention and admired the chiseled forms.

"That one, I like," said one nomad who was up in his years, pointing at a photo of a curvy woman who was clearly a regular at the gym. Another old-timer gazed at the bulging pectoral muscles of a male bodybuilder in the magazine and posed a question that got everybody talking. Was it a man, he asked, or a very, very strong woman?

What are some of the social repercussions of the economic change? Attitudes and behavior regarding marriage, family, and children have changed. Late marriage, "living together," and divorce have become more common. The average age at first marriage for American women rose from 20 in 1955 to 26 in 2007. The comparable figures for men were 23 and 28 (U.S. Census Bureau 2007). The number of currently divorced Americans more than quadrupled from 4 million in 1970 to about 23 million in 2007 (*Statistical Abstract of the United States* 2009). Work competes with marriage and family responsibilities and reduces the time available to invest in child care.

Cultures are integrated not simply by their dominant economic activities and related social patterns but also by sets of values, ideas, symbols, and judgments. Cultures train their individual members to share certain personality traits. A set of characteristic central or **core values** (key, basic, or central values) integrates each culture and helps distinguish it from others. For instance, the work ethic and individualism are core values that have integrated American culture for generations. Different sets of dominant values influence the patterns of other cultures.

Culture Can Be Adaptive and Maladaptive

As we saw in Chapter 1, humans have both biological and cultural ways of coping with environmental stresses. Besides our biological means of adaptation, we also use "cultural adaptive kits," which contain customary activities and tools. Although humans continue to adapt biologically, reliance on social and cultural means of adaptation has increased during human evolution.

In this discussion of the adaptive features of our cultural behavior, let's recognize that what's good for the individual isn't necessarily good for the group. Sometimes adaptive behavior that offers short-term benefits to particular individuals may harm the environment and threaten the group's long-term survival. Economic growth may benefit some people while it also depletes resources needed for society at large or for future generations (Bennett 1969, p. 19). Despite the crucial role of cultural adaptation in human evolution, cultural traits, patterns, and inventions also can be *maladaptive,* threatening the group's continued existence (survival and reproduction). Air conditioners help us deal with heat, as fires and furnaces protect us against the cold. Automobiles permit us to make a living by getting us from home to workplace. But the by-products of such "beneficial" technology often create new problems. Chemical emissions in-

crease air pollution, deplete the ozone layer, and contribute to global warming. Many cultural patterns, such as overconsumption and pollution, appear to be maladaptive in the long run.

CULTURE'S EVOLUTIONARY BASIS

The human capacity for culture has an evolutionary basis that extends back at least 2.6 million years—to early toolmakers whose products survive in the archeological record (and most probably even further back, based on observation of tool use and manufacture by apes).

Similarities between humans and apes, our closest relatives, are evident in anatomy, brain structure, genetics, and biochemistry. Most closely related to us are the African great apes: chimpanzees and gorillas. *Hominidae* is the zoological family that includes fossil and living humans. Also included as **hominids** are chimps and gorillas. The term **hominins** is used for the group that leads to humans but not to chimps and gorillas and that encompasses all the human species that ever have existed.

Many human traits reflect the fact that our primate ancestors lived in the trees. These traits include grasping ability and manual dexterity (especially opposable thumbs), depth and color vision, learning ability based on a large brain, substantial parental investment in a limited number of offspring, and tendencies toward sociality and cooperation. Like other primates, humans have flexible, five-fingered hands and *opposable thumbs:* each thumb can touch all the other fingers on the same hand. Like monkeys and apes, humans also have excellent depth and color vision. Our eyes are placed forward in the skull and look directly ahead, so that their fields of vision overlap. Depth perception, impossible without overlapping visual fields, proved adaptive—e.g., for judging distance—in the trees. Having color and depth vision also facilitates the identification of various food sources, as well as mutual grooming, picking out burrs, insects, and other small objects from hair. Such grooming is one way of forming and maintaining social bonds.

The combination of manual dexterity and depth perception allows monkeys, apes, and humans to pick up small objects, hold them in front of their eyes, and appraise them. Our ability to thread a needle reflects an intricate interplay of hands and eyes that took millions of years of primate evolution to achieve. Such dexterity, including the opposable thumb, confers a tremendous advantage in manipulating objects and is essential to a major human adaptive capacity: tool making. In primates, and especially in humans,

core values
Key, basic, or central values that integrate a culture.

hominid
Member of hominid family; any fossil or living human, chimp, or gorilla.

hominins
Hominids excluding the African apes; all the human species that ever have existed.

the ratio of brain size to body size exceeds that of most mammals. Even more important, the brain's outer layer—concerned with memory, association, and integration—is relatively larger. Monkeys, apes, and humans store an array of images in their memories, which permits them to learn more. Such a capacity for learning is a tremendous adaptive advantage. Like most other primates, humans usually give birth to a single offspring rather than a litter. Receiving more parental attention, that one infant has enhanced learning opportunities. The need for longer and more attentive care of offspring places a selective value on support by a social group. Humans have developed considerably the primate tendency to be social animals, living and interacting regularly with other members of their species.

What We Share with Other Primates

There is a substantial gap between primate *society* (organized life in groups) and fully developed human *culture*, which is based on symbolic thought. Nevertheless, studies of nonhuman primates reveal many similarities with humans, such as the ability to learn from experience and change behavior as a result. Apes and monkeys, like humans, learn throughout their lives. In one group of Japanese macaques (land-dwelling monkeys), for example, a three-year-old female started washing sweet potatoes before she ate them. First her mother, then her age peers, and finally the entire troop began washing sweet potatoes as well. The ability to benefit from experience confers a tremendous adaptive advantage, permitting the avoidance of fatal mistakes. Faced with environmental change, humans and other primates don't have to wait for a genetic or physiological response. They can modify learned behavior and social patterns instead.

Although humans do employ tools much more than any other animal does, tool use also turns up among several nonhuman species, including birds, beavers, sea otters, and especially apes (see Mayell 2003). Nor are humans the only animals that make tools with a specific purpose in mind. Chimpanzees living in the Tai forest of Ivory Coast make and use stone tools to break open hard, golfball-sized nuts (Mercader, Panger, and Boesch 2002). At specific sites, the chimps gather nuts, place them on stumps or flat rocks, which are used as anvils, and pound the nuts with heavy stones. The chimps must select hammer stones suited to smashing the nuts and carry them to where the nut trees grow. Nut cracking is a learned skill, with mothers showing their young how to do it.

In 1960, Jane Goodall (1996) began observing wild chimps—including their tool use and hunt-

STUDENT: **Pavlina Lobb**
COUNTRY OF ORIGIN: **Bulgaria**
SUPERVISING PROFESSOR: **Jennifer Burrell**
SCHOOL: **State University of New York at Albany**

Bulgarian Hospitality

Among those who have visited Bulgaria, discussions about the country and its customs almost always turn to traditional Bulgarian hospitality. Life in Bulgaria is organized around social relations and maintenance of those relations. Hospitality is just one expression of this social dependency. Bulgarians visit regularly with friends and relatives, needing no special occasion or purpose. "Dropping in" is not discouraged or seen as an inconvenience. Guests are always welcomed and accommodated. The idea that a guest is the most important person in the house is deeply rooted in the Bulgarian mentality and is expressed in many folk tales (so children learn the custom at a young age). Once you enter the home of your host, you are immediately invited to the table. No matter the time of day, you will be offered some kind of food and drink. Indeed, refusing to eat or drink may upset the host. In Bulgaria, sharing the bread and salt on the table symbolizes sharing one's fortune and thus establishing a strong social relationship—you will not be left hungry or thirsty as long as you have family and friends. Bulgarian hospitality goes further when it comes to spending the night; no matter how small your host's house or apartment, there will always be a place for you. Accepting hospitality is not seen as taking advantage because giving and sharing are reciprocal—the host will expect to be treated the same way when returning the visit.

Before I came to the United States, I thought that such hospitality was universal. Not until I became acquainted with the American idea of individualism did I begin to appreciate traditional Bulgarian hospitality and what it means to its people. In the United States, independence and individualism are essential parts of the culture. There are unwritten rules when it comes to making social visits. Arriving unannounced is usually frowned upon, and punctuality is also very important. Concern for following these rules and not violating another's personal space means that visits are usually made in response to an invitation or on special occasions.

Although many Americans argue that individualism helps people become more responsible, self-confident, and independent, it is interpreted very differently through the eyes of foreigners. As a primary feature of American society, individualism has affected social relationships between family members and friends to a significant extent—making it possible for individuals to become isolated and lonely. As social contacts are reduced, people become more alienated, turning into strangers to each other.

ing behavior—at Gombe Stream National Park in Tanzania, East Africa. The most studied form of ape tool making involves "termiting," in which chimps make tools to probe termite hills. They

Primates have five-digited feet and hands, well suited for grasping. Flexible hands and feet that could encircle branches were important features in the early primates' arboreal life. In adapting to bipedal (two-footed) locomotion, hominids eliminated most of the foot's grasping ability—illustrated here by the chimpanzee.

choose twigs, which they modify by removing leaves and peeling off bark to expose the sticky surface beneath. They carry the twigs to termite hills, dig holes with their fingers, and insert the twigs. Finally, they pull out the twigs and dine on termites that were attracted to the sticky surface. Given what is known about ape tool use and manufacture, it is almost certain that early hominins shared this ability, although the first evidence for hominin stone tool making dates back only 2.6 million years. Upright bipedalism would have permitted the carrying and use of tools and weapons against predators and competitors.

The apes have other abilities essential to culture. Wild chimps and orangs aim and throw objects. Gorillas build nests, and they throw branches, grass, vines, and other objects. Hominins have elaborated the capacity to aim and throw, without which we never would have developed projectile technology and weaponry—or baseball.

Like tool making, hunting once was cited as a distinctive human activity not shared with the apes. Again, however, primate research shows that other primates, especially chimpanzees, are habitual hunters. For example, in Uganda's Kibale National Park chimps form large hunting parties, including an average of 26 individuals (almost always adult and adolescent males). Most hunts (78 percent) result in at least one prey item being caught—a much higher success rate than that among lions (26 percent), hyenas (34 percent), or cheetahs (30 percent). Chimps' favored prey there is the red colobus monkey (Mitani and Watts 1999).

anthropology **ATLAS**

Map 2 locates major primate groups, including monkeys and apes.

Archaeological evidence suggests that humans hunted by at least 2.6 million years ago, based on stone meat-cutting tools found at Olduvai Gorge in Tanzania.

Given our current understanding of chimp hunting and tool making, we can infer that hominids may have been hunting much earlier than the first archaeological evidence attests. Because chimps typically devour the monkeys they kill, leaving few remains, we may never find archaeological evidence for the first hominin hunt, especially if it was done without stone tools.

How We Differ from Other Primates

Although chimps often share meat from a hunt, apes and monkeys (except for nursing infants) tend to feed themselves individually. Cooperation and sharing are much more developed among humans. Until fairly recently (12,000 to 10,000 years ago), all humans were hunter-gatherers who lived in small social groups called bands. In some world areas, the hunter-gatherer way of life persisted into recent times, permitting study by ethnographers. In such societies, men and women bring resources back to the camp and share them. Everyone shares the meat from a large animal. Nourished and protected by younger band members, elders live past reproductive age and are respected for their knowledge and experience. Humans are among the most cooperative of the primates—in the food quest and other social activities. As well, the amount of information stored in a human band is far greater than that in any other primate group.

Another difference between humans and other primates involves mating. Among baboons and chimps, most mating occurs when females enter estrus, during which they ovulate. In estrus, the vaginal area swells and reddens, and receptive females form temporary bonds with, and mate with, males. Human females, by contrast, lack a visible estrus cycle, and their ovulation is concealed. Not knowing when ovulation is occurring, humans maximize their reproductive success by mating throughout the year. Human pair bonds for mating are more exclusive and more durable than are those of chimps. Related to our more constant sexuality, all human societies have some form of marriage. Marriage gives mating a reliable basis and grants to each spouse special, though not always exclusive, sexual rights in the other.

Marriage creates another major contrast between humans and nonhuman primates: exogamy and kinship systems. Most cultures have rules of exogamy requiring marriage outside one's kin or local group. Coupled with the recognition of kinship, exogamy confers adaptive advantages. It creates ties between the spouses' different groups of origin. Their children have relatives, and therefore allies, in two kin groups rather than just one. The key point here is that ties of affection and mutual support between members of different local groups tend to be absent among primates other than *Homo*. Other primates tend to disperse at adolescence. Among chimps and gorillas, females tend to migrate, seeking mates in other groups. Humans also choose mates from outside the natal group, and usually at least one spouse moves. However, *humans maintain lifelong ties with sons and daughters*. The systems of kinship and marriage that preserve these links provide a major contrast between humans and other primates.

Tool use by chimps. These chimps in Liberia are using stone tools to crack palm nuts, as described in the text.

UNIVERSALITY, GENERALITY, AND PARTICULARITY

In studying human diversity in time and space, anthropologists distinguish among the universal, the generalized, and the particular. Certain biological, psychological, social, and cultural features are **universal**, found in every culture. Others are merely **generalities**, common to several but not all human groups. Still other traits are **particularities**, unique to certain cultural traditions.

Universality

Universal traits are the ones that more or less distinguish *Homo sapiens* from other species (see Brown 1991). Biologically based universals include a long period of infant dependency, year-round (rather than seasonal) sexuality, and a complex brain that enables us to use symbols, languages, and tools. Psychological universals involve common ways in which humans think, feel, and process information. Most such universals probably reflect human biological universals, such as the structure of the human brain or certain physical differences between men and women, or children and adults.

Among the social universals is life in groups and in some kind of family. In all human societies, culture organizes social life and depends on social interactions for its expression and continuation. Family living and food sharing are universals. Among the most significant cultural universals are exogamy and the *incest taboo* (prohibition against marrying or mating with a close relative). All cultures consider some people (various cultures differ about *which* people) too closely related to mate or marry. The violation of this taboo is

incest, which is discouraged and punished in a variety of ways in different cultures. If incest is prohibited, *exogamy*—marriage outside one's group—is inevitable. Because it links human groups together into larger networks, exogamy has been crucial in human evolution.

Generality

Between universals and uniqueness (see the next section) is a middle ground that consists of cultural generalities. These are regularities that occur in different times and places but not in all cultures. Societies can share the same beliefs and customs because of borrowing or through (cultural) inheritance from a common cultural ancestor. Speaking English is a generality shared by North Americans and Australians because both countries had English settlers. Another reason for generalities is domination, as in colonial rule, when customs and procedures are imposed on one culture by another one that is more powerful. In many countries, use of the English language reflects colonial history. More recently, English has spread through diffusion (cultural borrowing) to many other countries, as it has become the world's foremost language for business and travel.

Cultural generalities also can arise through independent invention of the same cultural trait or pattern in two or more different cultures. For example, farming arose through independent invention in the Eastern (e.g., the Middle East) and Western (e.g., Mexico) Hemispheres. Similar needs and circumstances have led people in different lands to innovate in parallel ways. They have independently come up with the same cultural solution to a common problem.

One cultural generality that is present in many but not all societies is the *nuclear family,* a kinship

universal
Something that exists in every culture.

generality
Culture pattern or trait that exists in some but not all societies.

particularity
Distinctive or unique culture trait, pattern, or integration.

Cultures use rituals to mark such universal life-cycle events as birth, puberty, marriage, parenthood, and death. But particular cultures differ as to which events merit special celebration and in the emotions expressed during their rituals. Compare the wedding party (top) in Bali, Indonesia, with the funeral (bottom) among the Tanala of eastern Madagascar. How would you describe the emotions suggested by the photos?

anthropology **ATLAS**

Map 12 shows patterns of world land use around 500 years ago. The different economic types are examples of cultural generalities.

group consisting of parents and children. Although many middle-class Americans ethnocentrically view the nuclear family as a proper and "natural" group, it is not universal. It was absent, for example, among the Nayars, who live on the Malabar Coast of India. Traditionally, the Nayars lived in female-headed households, and husbands and wives did not live together. In many other societies,

the nuclear family is submerged in larger kin groups, such as extended families, lineages, and clans. However, the nuclear family is prominent in many of the technologically simple societies that live by hunting and gathering. It is also a significant kin group among contemporary middle-class North Americans and Western Europeans. Later, an explanation of the nuclear family as a basic kinship unit in specific types of society will be given.

Particularity: Patterns of Culture

A cultural particularity is a trait or feature of culture that is not generalized or widespread; rather, it is confined to a single place, culture, or society. Yet because of cultural borrowing, which has accelerated through modern transportation and communication systems, traits that once were limited in their distribution have become more widespread. Traits that are useful, that have the capacity to please large audiences, and that don't clash with the cultural values of potential adopters are more likely to be borrowed than others are. Still, certain cultural particularities persist. One example would be a particular food dish (e.g., pork barbeque with a mustard-based sauce available only in South Carolina, or the pastie—beef stew baked in pie dough—characteristic of Michigan's upper peninsula). Besides diffusion, which, for example, has spread McDonald's food outlets, once confined to San Bernardino, California, across the globe, there are other reasons why cultural particularities are increasingly rare. Many cultural traits are shared as cultural universals and as a result of independent invention. Facing similar problems, people in different places have come up with similar solutions. Again and again, similar cultural causes have produced similar cultural results.

At the level of the individual cultural trait or element (e.g., bow and arrow, hot dog, MTV), particularities may be getting rarer. But at a higher level, particularity is more obvious. Different cultures emphasize different things. *Cultures are integrated and patterned differently and display tremendous variation and diversity.* When cultural traits are borrowed, they are modified to fit the culture that adopts them. They are reintegrated—patterned anew—to fit their new setting. MTV in Germany or Brazil isn't at all the same thing as MTV in the United States. As was stated in the earlier section "Culture Is Integrated," patterned beliefs, customs, and practices lend distinctiveness to particular cultural traditions.

Consider universal life-cycle events, such as birth, puberty, marriage, parenthood, and death, which many cultures observe and celebrate. The occasions (e.g., marriage, death) may be the same and universal, but the patterns of ceremonial observance may be dramatically different. Cultures vary in just which events merit special celebration. Americans, for example, regard expensive weddings as more socially appropriate than lavish funerals. However, the Betsileo of Madagascar take the opposite view. The marriage ceremony is a minor event that brings together just the couple and a few close relatives. However, a funeral is a measure of the deceased person's social position and lifetime achievement, and it may attract a thousand people. Why use money on a house, the Betsileo say, when one can use it on the tomb where one will spend eternity in the company of dead relatives? How unlike contemporary Americans' dreams of home ownership and preference for quick and inexpensive funerals. Cremation, an increasingly common option in the United States, would horrify the Betsileo, for whom ancestral bones and relics are important ritual objects.

Cultures vary tremendously in their beliefs, practices, integration, and patterning. By focusing on and trying to explain alternative customs, anthropology forces us to reappraise our familiar ways of thinking. In a world full of cultural diversity, contemporary American culture is just one cultural variant, more powerful perhaps, but no more natural, than the others.

individuals and groups in the same culture. Golden arches may cause one person to salivate, while another person plots a vegetarian protest. The same flag may be waved to support or oppose a given war.

Even when they agree about what should and shouldn't be done, people don't always do as their culture directs or as other people expect. Many rules are violated, some very often (e.g., automobile speed limits). Some anthropologists find it useful to distinguish between ideal culture and real culture. The *ideal culture* consists of what people say they should do and what they say they do. *Real culture* refers to their actual behavior as observed by the anthropologist.

Culture is both public and individual, both in the world and in people's minds. Anthropologists are interested not only in public and collective behavior but also in how *individuals* think, feel, and act. The individual and culture are linked because human social life is a process in which individuals internalize the meanings of *public* (i.e., cultural) messages. Then, alone and in groups, people influence culture by converting their private (and often divergent) understandings into public expressions (D'Andrade 1984).

Conventionally, culture has been seen as social glue transmitted across the generations, binding people through their common past, rather than

CULTURE AND THE INDIVIDUAL: AGENCY AND PRACTICE

Generations of anthropologists have theorized about the relationship between the "system," on the one hand, and the "person" or "individual," on the other. The "system" can refer to various concepts, including culture, society, social relations, and social structure. Individual human beings always make up, or constitute, the system. But, living within that system, humans also are constrained (to some extent, at least) by its rules and by the actions of other individuals. Cultural rules provide guidance about what to do and how to do it, but people don't always do what the rules say should be done. People use their culture actively and creatively, rather than blindly following its dictates. Humans aren't passive beings who are doomed to follow their cultural traditions like programmed robots. Instead, people learn, interpret, and manipulate the same rules in different ways—or they emphasize different rules that better suit their interests. Culture is *contested:* Different groups in society struggle with one another over whose ideas, values, goals, and beliefs will prevail. Even common symbols may have radically different *meanings* to different

Illustrating the international level of culture, Roman Catholics in different nations share knowledge, symbols, beliefs, and values transmitted by their church. Shown here is a Catholic seminary in Xian, China. Besides religious conversion, what other forces work to spread international culture?

as something being continually created and reworked in the present. The tendency to view culture as an entity rather than a process is changing. Contemporary anthropologists now emphasize how day-to-day action, practice, or resistance can make and remake culture (Gupta and Ferguson, eds. 1997b). *Agency* refers to the actions that individuals take, both alone and in groups, in forming and transforming cultural identities.

The approach to culture known as *practice theory* (Ortner 1984) recognizes that individuals within a society or culture have diverse motives and intentions and different degrees of power and influence. Such contrasts may be associated with gender, age, ethnicity, class, and other social variables. Practice theory focuses on how such varied individuals—through their ordinary and extraordinary actions and practices—manage to influence, create, and transform the world they live in. Practice theory appropriately recognizes a reciprocal relation between culture (the system—see above) and the individual. The system shapes the way individuals experience and respond to external events, but individuals also play an active role in the way society functions and changes. Practice theory recognizes both constraints on individuals and the flexibility and changeability of cultures and social systems.

Levels of Culture

Of increasing importance in today's world are the distinctions between different levels of culture: national, international, and subcultural. **National culture** refers to those beliefs, learned behavior patterns, values, and institutions that are shared by citizens of the same nation. **International culture** is the term for cultural traditions that extend beyond and across national boundaries. Because culture is transmitted through learning rather than genetically, cultural traits can spread through borrowing or *diffusion* from one group to another.

Because of borrowing, colonialism, migration, and multinational organizations, many cultural traits and patterns have international scope. For example, Roman Catholics in many different countries share beliefs, symbols, experiences, and values transmitted by their church. The contemporary United States, Canada, Great Britain, and Australia share cultural traits they have inherited from their common linguistic and cultural ancestors in Great Britain. The World Cup has become an international cultural event, as people in many countries know the rules of, play, and follow soccer.

Cultures also can be smaller than nations (see Jenks 2004). Although people who live in the same country share a national cultural tradition, all cultures also contain diversity. Individuals, families, communities, regions, classes, and other groups within a culture have different learning experiences as well as shared ones. **Subcultures** are different symbol-based patterns and traditions associated with particular groups in the same complex society. In a large nation like the United States or Canada, subcultures originate in region, ethnicity, language, class, and religion. The religious backgrounds of Jews, Baptists, and Roman Catholics create subcultural differences between them. While sharing a common national culture, U.S. northerners and southerners also differ in aspects of their beliefs, values, and customary behavior as a result of regional variation. French-speaking Canadians contrast with English-speaking people in the same country. Italian Americans have ethnic traditions different from those of Irish, Polish, and African Americans. Using sports and foods, Table 2.1 gives some examples of international, national, and subculture. Soccer and basketball are played internationally. Monster-truck rallies are held throughout the United States. Bocci is a bowling-like sport from Italy still played in some Italian American neighborhoods.

Nowadays, many anthropologists are reluctant to use the term *subculture*. They feel that the prefix "sub-" is offensive because it means "below." "Subcultures" may thus be perceived as "less than" or somehow inferior to a dominant, elite, or national culture. In this discussion of levels of culture, I intend no such implication. My point is simply that nations may contain many different culturally defined groups. As mentioned earlier, culture is contested. Various groups may strive to promote the correctness and value of their own practices, values, and beliefs in comparison with those of other groups or of the nation as a whole. (This chapter's "Appreciating Diversity" demonstrates how contemporary indigenous groups have to grapple with multiple levels of culture, contestation, and political regulation.)

TABLE 2.1 Levels of Culture, with Examples from Sports and Foods

LEVEL OF CULTURE	SPORTS EXAMPLES	FOOD EXAMPLES
International	Soccer, basketball	Pizza
National	Monster-truck rallies	Apple pie
Subculture	Bocci	Big Joe Pork Barbeque (South Carolina)

Ethnocentrism, Cultural Relativism, and Human Rights

Ethnocentrism is the tendency to view one's own culture as superior and to use one's own standards and values in judging outsiders. We witness ethnocentrism when people consider their own cultural beliefs to be truer, more proper, or more moral than those of other groups. However, fundamental to anthropology, as the study of human diversity, is the fact that what is alien (even disgusting) to us may be normal, proper, and prized elsewhere (see the previous discussion of cultural particularities, including burial customs). The fact of cultural diversity calls ethnocentrism into question, as anthropologists have shown all kinds of reasons for unfamiliar practices. During a course like this, anthropology students often reexamine their own ethnocentric beliefs. Sometimes as the strange becomes familiar, the familiar seems a bit stranger and less comfortable. One goal of anthropology is to show the value in the lives of others. But how far is too far? What happens when cultural practices, values, and rights come into conflict with human rights?

Several cultures in Africa and the Middle East have customs requiring female genital modification. *Clitoridectomy* is the removal of a girl's clitoris. *Infibulation* involves sewing the lips (labia) of the vagina to constrict the vaginal opening. Both procedures reduce female sexual pleasure and, it is believed in some societies, the likelihood of adultery. Although traditional in the societies where they occur, such practices, characterized as female genital mutilation (FGM), have been opposed by human rights advocates, especially women's rights groups. The idea is that the custom infringes on a basic human right: disposition over one's body and one's sexuality. Indeed, such practices are fading as a result of worldwide attention to the problem and changing sex-gender roles. Some African countries have banned or otherwise discouraged the procedures, as have Western nations that receive immigration from such cultures. Similar issues arise with circumcision and other male genital operations. Is it right for a baby boy to be circumcised without his permission, as routinely has been done in the United States? Is it proper to require adolescent boys to undergo collective circumcision to fulfill cultural traditions, as is done traditionally in parts of Africa and Australia?

According to an idea known as **cultural relativism,** it is inappropriate to use outside standards to judge behavior in a given society; such behavior should be evaluated in the context of the culture in which it occurs. Anthropologists employ cultural relativism not as a moral belief but as a methodological position: In order to understand another culture fully, we must try to understand how the people in that culture see things. What motivates them—what are they thinking—when they do those things? Such an approach does not preclude making moral judgments. In the FGM example, one can understand the motivations for the practice only by looking at things from the point of view of the people who engage in it. Having done this, one then faces the moral question of what, if anything, to do about it.

We also should recognize that different people and groups within the same society—for example, women versus men or old versus young—can have widely different views about what is proper, necessary, and moral. When there are power differentials in a society, a particular practice may be supported by some people more than others (e.g., old men versus young men). In trying to understand the meaning of a practice or belief within any cultural context, we should ask who is relatively advantaged and disadvantaged by that custom. Can you think of a practice or belief in your own culture that is based on, and serves to maintain, social inequalities?

The idea of **human rights** invokes a realm of justice and morality beyond and superior to particular countries, cultures, and religions. Human rights, usually seen as vested in individuals, include the right to speak freely, to hold religious beliefs without persecution, and not to be murdered, injured, enslaved, or imprisoned without charge. These rights are not ordinary laws that particular governments make and enforce. Human rights are seen as *inalienable* (nations cannot abridge or terminate them) and international (larger than and superior to individual nations and cultures). Four United Nations documents describe nearly all the human rights that have been internationally recognized. Those documents are the UN Charter; the Universal Declaration of Human Rights; the Covenant on Economic, Social and Cultural Rights; and the Covenant on Civil and Political Rights.

Alongside the human rights movement has arisen an awareness of the need to preserve cultural rights. Unlike human rights, **cultural rights** are vested not in individuals but in groups, including indigenous peoples and religious and ethnic minorities. Cultural rights include a group's ability to raise its children in the ways of its forebears, to continue its language, and not to be deprived of its economic base by the nation in which it is located (Greaves 1995). Many countries have signed pacts endorsing, for cultural minorities within nations, such rights as self-determination; some degree of home rule; and the right to practice the group's religion, culture, and language. The related notion of indigenous **intellectual property rights (IPR)** has arisen in an

anthropology **ATLAS**

Map 10 locates classic ethnographic field sites—"cultures" or societies already studied by 1950.

ethnocentrism
Judging other cultures using one's own cultural standards.

human rights
Rights based on justice and morality beyond and superior to particular countries, cultures, and religions.

cultural rights
Rights vested in religious and ethnic minorities and indigenous societies.

cultural relativism
Idea that to know another culture requires full understanding of its members' beliefs and motivations.

IPR
Intellectual property rights; an indigenous group's collective knowledge and its applications.

appreciating

DIVERSITY

Culture Clash: Makah Seek Return to Whaling Past

Cultures are diverse but not isolated. Throughout human history links between groups have been provided by cultural practices such as marriage, kinship, religion, trade, travel, exploration, and conquest. For centuries, indigenous peoples have been exposed to a world system. Contemporary forces and events make even the illusion of autonomy hard to maintain. Nowadays, as is described here, members of local cultures and communities must heed not only their own customs but also agencies, laws, and lawsuits operating at the national and international levels.

As you read this account and this chapter on culture, pay attention to the various kinds of rights being asserted—animal rights, cultural rights, economic rights, legal rights, and human rights—and how those rights might clash. Also consider the different levels of culture and of political representation (local, regional, national, and global) that determine how contemporary people such as the Makah live their lives and maintain their traditions. Think, too, about the minimal impact on whale populations of the Makah hunt compared with commercial whaling. Today, cultural connections come increasingly through the Internet, as indigenous groups, including the Makah, maintain their own websites—forums for discussions of whaling and other issues of interest to them. Check out http://www.makah.com/.

The whaling canoes are stored in a wooden shed, idle for the past six years. They were last used when the Makah Indians were allowed to take their harpoons and a .50-caliber rifle and set out on their first whale hunt since the late 1920s.

There were eight young men in a canoe with a red hummingbird, a symbol of speed, painted on the tip. There were motorboats ferrying other hunters, news helicopters, and animal rights activists in speedboats and even a submarine.

On May 17, 1999, a week into the hunt, the Makah killed a 30-ton gray whale, striking it with harpoons and then killing it with a gunshot to the back of the head.

That rainy spring day remains etched in the minds of many Makah as a defining moment in their efforts to reach back to their cultural and historical roots. It was their first kill in seven decades, and it was their last since they were stopped by court rulings. They have asked the federal government for permission to resume hunting, and public meetings on the request are scheduled for October.

The Makah, a tribe of about 1,500 near the mouth of the Strait of Juan de Fuca on the Olympic Peninsula, see themselves as whalers and continue to identify themselves spiritually with whales.

"Everybody felt like it was a part of making history," Micah L. McCarty, a tribal council member, said of the 1999 hunt. "It's inspired a cultural renaissance, so to speak. It inspired a lot of people to learn artwork and become more active in building canoes; the younger generation took a more keen interest in singing and dancing."

The Makah, a tribe of mostly fishermen that faces serious poverty and high unemployment, were guaranteed the right to hunt whales in an 1855 treaty with the United States, the only tribe with such a treaty provision. Whaling had been the tribe's mainstay for thousands of years.

But the tribe decided to stop hunting whales early in the 20th century, when commercial harvesting had depleted the species. Whale hunting was later strictly regulated nationally and internationally, and the United States listed the Northern Pacific gray whale, the one most available to the Makah, as endangered.

The protections helped the whales rebound, and they were taken off the endangered list in

1994. Several years later, the Makah won permission to hunt again, along with a $100,000 federal grant to set up a whaling commission.

By the time they were ready, none of the Makah had witnessed a whale hunt or even tasted the meat, hearing only stories passed down through the generations. They learned that the whale was a touchstone of Makah culture—the tribe's logo today pictures an eagle perched on a whale—and that the tribe's economy was built around the lucrative trade with Europeans in whale oil, used for heating and lighting, during the 18th and early 19th centuries.

For a year before the 1999 hunt, the new Makah whale hunters prepared for their sacramental pursuit, training in canoes on the cold and choppy waters of the Pacific Ocean, praying on the beach in the mornings and at the dock in the evenings.

Animal rights groups were preparing, too. When the hunt began, the small reservation and its surrounding waters were teeming with news helicopters and protest groups. On that May afternoon, when the protesters were somewhere off the reservation, the Makah killed their whale. They held a huge celebration on the beach, where 15 men were waiting to butcher the animal, its meat later kippered and stewed.

But the protests and the television cameras "took a lot of the spirituality out of it," said Dave Sones, vice chairman of the tribal council.

Mr. McCarty said, "I equate it with interrupting High Mass."

The Makah went whale hunting, largely unnoticed, again in 2000, paddling out on a 32-foot cedar whaling canoe, but they did not catch anything. Soon after, animal rights groups, including the Humane Society of the United States, sued to stop the hunting. In 2002, an appeals court declared the hunting illegal, saying the National Oceanic and Atmospheric Administration had not adequately studied the impact of Makah hunting on the survival of the whale species.

Dewey Johnson and his son Michael (top) show their support for fellow Makah tribe members at Neah Bay, Washington, in their quest to hunt gray whales for the first time in 70 years. *Sea Shepherd* captain Paul Watson stands at Neah Bay beside a 25-foot submarine painted to look like an orca whale (below). This ship emits orca sounds that can scare away gray whales. Watson leads the opposition against Makah whaling, which was declared illegal in 2002.

Despite the strict national and international regulations on whale hunting, several tribes of Alaska Natives, subsistence whale hunters for centuries, are exempt from provisions of the 1972 Marine Mammal Protection Act, allowing them to hunt the bowhead whale. That species, unlike the gray whale, is listed as endangered, said Brian Gorman, a spokesman for the oceanic agency.

Despite their treaty rights, the Makah were not granted an exemption under the 1972 act. Last February, the tribe asked the agency for a waiver that would grant them permanent rights to kill up to 20 gray whales in any five-year period, which they insist they already have under their 1855 treaty.

The Makah's request is "setting a dangerous precedent," said Naomi Rose, a marine mammal scientist for the Humane Society.

The Alaska hunting, Ms. Rose said, "is a true subsistence hunt," whereas the Makah, who view whale hunting mostly as ceremonial, are pursuing "cultural whaling" that is not essential to their diet.

"There are too many other bad actors out there" who might try to apply for waivers too, she said. The Makah "have a treaty right, but we're asking them not to exercise it," she said. But other environmental groups, including Greenpeace, which is adamantly opposed to the commercial harvesting of whales, have remained neutral on the Makah's quest.

"No indigenous hunt has ever destroyed whale populations," said John Hocevar, an oceans specialist with Greenpeace. "And looking at the enormous other threats to whales and putting the Makah whaling in context, it's pretty different."

Mr. Gorman, of the federal fisheries agency, said: "They have a treaty right that the U.S. government signed. It doesn't take an international lawyer to figure out that they do have this treaty."

attempt to conserve each society's cultural base—its core beliefs and principles. IPR are claimed as a cultural right, allowing indigenous groups to control who may know and use their collective knowledge and its applications. Much traditional cultural knowledge has commercial value. Examples include ethnomedicine (traditional medical knowledge and techniques), cosmetics, cultivated plants, foods, folklore, arts, crafts, songs, dances, costumes, and rituals. According to the IPR concept, a particular group may determine how its indigenous knowledge and the products of that knowledge are used and distributed, and the level of compensation required. (This chapter's "Appreciating Diversity" discusses how notions of human, cultural, and animal rights may come into conflict.)

The notion of cultural rights recalls the previous discussion of cultural relativism, and the issue raised there arises again. What does one do about cultural rights that interfere with human rights? I believe that anthropology, as the scientific study of human diversity, should strive to present accurate accounts and explanations of cultural phenomena. Most ethnographers try to be objective, accurate, and sensitive in their accounts of other cultures. However, objectivity, sensitivity, and a cross-cultural perspective don't mean that anthropologists have to ignore international standards of justice and morality. The anthropologist doesn't have to approve customs such as infanticide, cannibalism, and torture to

record their existence and determine their causes and the motivations behind them. Each anthropologist has a choice about where he or she will do field work. Some anthropologists choose not to study a particular culture because they discover in advance or early in field work that behavior they consider morally repugnant is practiced there. When confronted with such behavior, each anthropologist must make a judgment about what, if anything, to do about it. What do you think?

MECHANISMS OF CULTURAL CHANGE

Why and how do cultures change? One way is **diffusion,** or borrowing of traits between cultures. Such exchange of information and products has gone on throughout human history because cultures have never been truly isolated. Contact between neighboring groups has always existed and has extended over vast areas (Boas 1940/1966). Diffusion is *direct* when two cultures trade, intermarry, or wage war on one another. Diffusion is *forced* when one culture subjugates another and imposes its customs on the dominated group. Diffusion is *indirect* when items move from group A to group C via group B without any firsthand contact between A and C. In this case, group B might consist of traders or merchants who take

diffusion
Borrowing of cultural traits between societies.

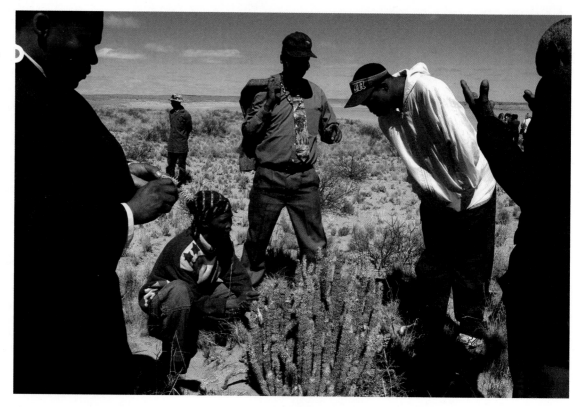

The notion of indigenous intellectual property rights (IPR) has arisen in an attempt to conserve each society's cultural base, including its medicinal plants, which may have commercial value. Shown here is the hoodia plant, a cactus that grows in the Kalahari Desert of southern Africa. Hoodia, which traditionally is used by the San people to stave off hunger, is used now in diet pills marketed on the Internet.

products from a variety of places to new markets. Or group B might be geographically situated between A and C, so that what it gets from A eventually winds up in C, and vice versa. In today's world, much transnational diffusion is due to the spread of the mass media and advanced information technology.

Acculturation, a second mechanism of cultural change, is the exchange of cultural features that results when groups have continuous firsthand contact. The cultures of either group or both groups may be changed by this contact (Redfield, Linton, and Herskovits 1936). With acculturation, parts of the cultures change, but each group remains distinct. In situations of continuous contact, cultures may exchange and blend foods, recipes, music, dances, clothing, tools, technologies, and languages.

One example of acculturation is a *pidgin,* a mixed language that develops to ease communication between members of different societies in contact. This usually happens in situations of trade or colonialism. Pidgin English, for example, is a simplified form of English. It blends English grammar with the grammar of a native language. Pidgin English was first used for commerce in Chinese ports. Similar pidgins developed later in Papua New Guinea and West Africa.

Independent invention—the process by which humans innovate, creatively finding solutions to problems—is a third mechanism of cultural change. Faced with comparable problems and challenges, people in different societies have innovated and changed in similar ways, which is one reason cultural generalities exist. One example is the independent invention of agriculture in the Middle East and Mexico. Over the course of human history, major innovations have spread at the expense of earlier ones. Often a major invention, such as agriculture, triggers a series of subsequent interrelated changes. These economic revolutions have social and cultural repercussions. Thus, in both Mexico and the Middle East, agriculture led to many social, political, and legal changes, including notions of property and distinctions in wealth, class, and power.

GLOBALIZATION

The term **globalization** encompasses a series of processes, including diffusion and acculturation, working to promote change in a world in which nations and people are increasingly interlinked and mutually dependent. Promoting such linkages are economic and political forces, along with modern systems of transportation and communication. The forces of globalization include international commerce, travel and tourism, transnational migration, the media, and various high-tech infor-

Globalization includes the internationalization of people and cultures through transnational migration and developments in commerce, transportation, and communication. This recent photo of Chinese youth in an Internet café was taken in Prato, Tuscany, Italy. For what purposes do you think these teenagers use these computers?

mation flows (see Appadurai, ed. 2001). During the Cold War, which ended with the fall of the Soviet Union, the basis of international alliance was political, ideological, and military. Thereafter, the focus of international pacts shifted to trade and economic issues. New economic unions have been created through NAFTA (the North American Free Trade Agreement), GATT (the General Agreement on Trade and Tariffs), and the EU (the European Union).

Long-distance communication is easier, faster, and cheaper than ever and extends to remote areas. The mass media help propel a globally spreading culture of consumption, stimulating participation in the world cash economy. Within nations and across their borders, the media spread information about threats, products, services, rights, institutions, and lifestyles. Emigrants transmit information and resources transnationally as they maintain their ties with home (phoning, faxing, e-mailing, making visits, sending money). In a sense, such people live multilocally— in different places and cultures at once. They learn to play various social roles and to change behavior and identity depending on the situation (see Cresswell 2006).

Local people must increasingly cope with forces generated by progressively larger systems— region, nation, and world. An army of alien actors and agents now intrudes on people everywhere. Terrorism is a global threat. Tourism has become the world's number one industry (see Holden 2005). Economic development agents and the media promote the idea that work should be for cash

acculturation
An exchange of cultural features between groups in firsthand contact.

independent invention
The independent development of a cultural feature in different societies.

globalization
The accelerating interdependence of nations in the world system today.

rather than mainly for subsistence. Indigenous peoples and traditional cultures have devised various strategies to deal with threats to their autonomy, identity, and livelihood. New forms of political mobilization and cultural expression are emerging from the interplay of local, regional, national, and international cultural forces (see Ong and Collier, eds. 2005).

Acing the
COURSE

Summary

1. Culture, which is distinctive to humanity, refers to customary behavior and beliefs that are passed on through enculturation. Culture rests on the human capacity for cultural learning. Culture encompasses rules for conduct internalized in human beings, which lead them to think and act in characteristic ways.

2. Although other animals learn, only humans have cultural learning, dependent on symbols. Humans think symbolically—arbitrarily bestowing meaning on things and events. By convention, a symbol stands for something with which it has no necessary or natural relation. Symbols have special meaning for people who share memories, values, and beliefs because of common enculturation. People absorb cultural lessons consciously and unconsciously.

3. Cultural traditions mold biologically based desires and needs in particular directions. Everyone is cultured, not just people with elite educations. Cultures may be integrated and patterned through economic and social forces, key symbols, and core values. Cultural rules don't rigidly dictate our behavior. There is room for creativity, flexibility, diversity, and disagreement within societies. Cultural means of adaptation have been crucial in human evolution. Aspects of culture also can be maladaptive.

4. The human capacity for culture has an evolutionary basis that extends back at least 2.6 million years—to early tool makers whose products survive in the archaeological record (and most probably even further back—based on observation of tool use and manufacture by apes). Humans share with monkeys and apes such traits as manual dexterity (especially opposable thumbs), depth and color vision, learning ability based on a large brain, substantial parental investment in a limited number of offspring, and tendencies toward sociality and cooperation.

5. Many hominin traits are foreshadowed in other primates, particularly in the African apes, which, like us, belong to the hominid family. The ability to learn, basic to culture, is an adaptive advantage available to monkeys and apes. Chimpanzees make tools for several purposes. They also hunt and share meat. Sharing and cooperation are more developed among humans than among the apes, and only humans have systems of kinship and marriage that permit us to maintain lifelong ties with relatives in different local groups.

6. Using a comparative perspective, anthropology examines biological, psychological, social, and cultural universals and generalities. There also are unique and distinctive aspects of the human condition (cultural particularities). North American cultural traditions are no more natural than any others. Levels of culture can be larger or smaller than a nation. Cultural traits may be shared across national boundaries. Nations also include cultural differences associated with ethnicity, region, and social class.

7. Ethnocentrism describes judging other cultures by using one's own cultural standards. Cultural relativism, which anthropologists may use as a methodological position rather than a moral stance, is the idea of avoiding the use of outside standards to judge behavior in a given society. Human rights are those based on justice and morality beyond and superior to particular countries, cultures, and religions. Cultural rights are vested in religious and ethnic minorities and indigenous societies, and IPR, or intellectual property rights, apply to an indigenous group's collective knowledge and its applications.

8. Diffusion, migration, and colonialism have carried cultural traits and patterns to different world areas. Mechanisms of cultural change include diffusion, acculturation, and independent invention. Globalization describes a series of processes that promote change in a world in which nations and people are interlinked and mutually dependent.

MULTIPLE CHOICE

Test Yourself!

1. Which of the following is *not* one of the ways in which individuals acquire the culture?
   a. genetic transmission
   b. unconscious acquisition
   c. through observation
   d. through direct instruction
   e. conscious acquisition

2. The "psychic unity" of humans, a doctrine that most anthropologists accept, states that
   a. psychology is the exclusive domain of the academic discipline of psychology.
   b. all humans share the same spiritual ethos.
   c. although individuals differ in their emotional and intellectual tendencies and capacities, all human populations have equivalent capacities for culture.
   d. psychological attributes are determined by our genes.
   e. even psychological attributes must be analyzed through the lens of cultural relativism.

3. Which of the following statements about cultural traits, patterns, and inventions is false?
   a. They mostly are determined genetically.
   b. They can be disadvantageous in the long run.
   c. They can be disadvantageous in the short run.
   d. They can be maladaptive.
   e. They are transmitted through learning.

4. This chapter's description of the similarities and differences between humans and apes, our closest relatives,
   a. explains why all hominids have evolved the same capacities for culture.
   b. emphasizes the need to expand the definition of cultural rights to include not just human individuals but also chimps and gorillas.
   c. explains why genetics has been more important than culture in determining our particular evolutionary path.
   d. illustrates how human females' lack of a visible estrus cycle determined our unique capacity for culture.
   e. emphasizes culture's evolutionary basis, stressing the interaction between biology and culture.

5. Certain biological, psychological, social, and cultural features are universal, found in every culture. All of the following are examples of universal features *except*
   a. a long period of infant dependency.
   b. seasonal (rather than year-round) sexuality.
   c. common ways in which humans think, feel, and process information.
   d. life in groups and in some kind of family.
   e. exogamy and the incest taboo (prohibition against marrying or mating with a close relative).

6. Which of the following statements about culture is *not* true?
   a. All human groups have culture.
   b. Culture is the major reason for human adaptability.
   c. Human groups differ in their capacities for culture.
   d. The capacity for culture is shared by all humans.
   e. Cultural learning is uniquely elaborated among humans.

7. In explaining how anthropologists have theorized the relationship between "system" and "person," this chapter notes that culture is contested. This means that
   a. different groups in society struggle with one another over whose ideas, values, goods, and beliefs will prevail.
   b. while many symbols can have different meanings, most common symbols are agreed upon by everyone in a culture.
   c. humans are passive beings who are doomed to follow their cultural traditions.
   d. genes have programmed humans to manipulate the meanings and cultural symbols to increase our reproductive process.
   e. culture doesn't exist.

8. In anthropology, methodological cultural relativism
   a. is not a moral position, but a methodological one.
   b. is both a moral and methodological stance toward other cultures.
   c. is synonymous to moral relativism.
   d. is another version of ethnocentrism.
   e. is a political position that argues for the defense of human rights, regardless of culture.

9. There were at least seven different regions where agriculture developed. Therefore, agriculture is an example of which of the following mechanisms of cultural change.
   a. acculturation
   b. enculturation
   c. independent invention
   d. colonization
   e. diffusion

10. What is the term for the processes that are making nations and people increasingly interlinked and mutually dependent?
   a. acculturation
   b. independent invention
   c. diffusion
   d. globalization
   e. enculturation

FILL IN THE BLANK

1. Although humans continue to adapt _biological_, reliance on _cultural_ means of adaptation has increased during human evolution.

2. Cultural traits, patterns, and inventions also can be _malad_, threatening the group's continued existence (survival and reproduction).

3. According to Leslie White, culture, and therefore humanity, came into existence when humans began to use _symbols_.

4. The term _homind_ refers to any fossil or living human, chimp, or gorilla, while the term _hominin_ refers only to any fossil or living human.

5. Unlike human rights, _cultural rights_ are vested not in individuals but in groups, including indigenous peoples and religious and ethnic minorities.

CRITICAL THINKING

1. This chapter includes the culture definitions of various authors (Tylor, Geerts, Kottak). How are these definitions similar? How are they different? How has reading this chapter altered your own understanding of what culture is?

2. Our culture—and cultural changes—affect how we perceive nature, human nature, and "the natural." This has been a theme that has and continues to fascinate science fiction writers. Recall the latest science fiction book, movie, or TV program that creatively explores the boundaries between nature and culture. How does the story develop the tension between nature and culture to craft a plot?

3. In American culture today, the term "diversity" is used in many contexts, usually referring to some positive attribute of our human experience, something to appreciate, to maintain, and even to increase. In what contexts have you heard the term used? To what precisely does the term refer?

4. What are some issues about which you find it hard to be culturally relativistic? If you were an anthropologist with the task of investigating these issues in real life, can you think of a series of steps that you would take to design a project that would, to the best of your ability, practice methodological cultural relativism? (You may want to review the use of the scientific method in an anthropological project presented in Chapter 1.)

5. What are the mechanisms of cultural change described in this chapter? Can you come up with additional examples of each mechanism? Also, recall the relationship between culture and individuals. Can individuals be agents of cultural change?

Appadurai, A., ed.
  2001 *Globalization*. Durham, NC: Duke University Press. An anthropological approach to globalization and international relations.
Bohannan, P.
  1995 *How Culture Works*. New York: Free Press. A consideration of the nature of culture.
Brown, D.
  1991 *Human Universals*. New York: McGraw-Hill. Surveys the evidence for "human nature" and explores the roles of culture and biology in human variation.
Geertz, C.
  1973 *The Interpretation of Cultures*. New York: Basic Books. Essays about culture viewed as a system of symbols and meaning.

Hall, E. T.
  1990 *Understanding Cultural Differences*. Yarmouth, ME: Intercultural Press. Focusing on business and industrial management, this book examines the role of national cultural contrasts among France, Germany, and the United States.
Van der Elst, D., and P. Bohannan
  2003 *Culture as Given, Culture as Choice*, 2nd ed. Prospect Heights, IL: Waveland. Culture and individual choices.

Go to our Online Learning Center website at **www.mhhe.com/kottak** for Internet exercises directly related to the content of this chapter.

How can change be bad?

How can anthropology be applied to medicine, education, and business?

How does the study of anthropology fit into a career path?

In Bangladesh, a health worker (dressed in teal) explains how to give oral rehydration fluids to treat childhood diarrhea. Smart planners, including those in public health, pay attention to locally based demand— what the people want—such as ways to reduce infant mortality.

Applying Anthropology 3

understanding OURSELVES

Is change good? The idea that innovation is desirable is almost axiomatic and unquestioned in American culture—especially in advertising. According to poll results, in November 2008 Americans voted for change in record numbers. "New and improved" is a slogan we hear all the time—a lot more often than "old reliable." Which do you think is best—change or the status quo?

That "new" isn't always "improved" is a painful lesson learned by the Coca-Cola Company (TCCC) in 1985 when it changed the formula of its premier soft drink and introduced "New Coke." After a national brouhaha, with hordes of customers protesting, TCCC brought back old, familiar, reliable Coke under the name "Coca-Cola Classic," which thrives today. New Coke, now history, offers a classic case of how not to treat consumers. TCCC tried a *top-down change* (a change initiated at the top of a hierarchy rather than inspired by the people most affected by the change). Customers didn't ask TCCC to change its product; executives made that decision.

Business executives, like public policy makers, run organizations that provide goods and services to people. The field of market research, which employs a good number of anthropologists, is based on the need to appreciate what actual and potential customers do, think, and want. Smart planners study and listen to people to try to determine *locally based demand*. In general, what's working well (assuming it's not discriminatory or illegal) should be maintained, encouraged, tweaked, and strengthened. If something's wrong, how can it best be fixed? What changes do the people—and which people—want? How can conflicting wishes and needs be accommodated? Applied anthropologists help answer these questions, which are crucial in understanding whether change is needed, and how it will work.

Innovation succeeds best when it is culturally appropriate. This axiom of applied anthropology could guide the international spread of programs aimed at social and economic change as well as of businesses. Each time an organization expands to a new nation, it must devise a culturally appropriate strategy for fitting into the new setting. In their international expansion, companies as diverse as McDonald's, Starbucks, and Ford have learned that more money can be made by fitting in with, rather than trying to Americanize, local habits.

Applied anthropology is one of two dimensions of anthropology, the other being theoretical/academic anthropology. Applied, or *practical,* anthropology is the use of anthropological data, perspectives, theory, and methods to identify, assess, and solve contemporary problems involving human behavior and social and cultural forces, conditions, and contexts. For example, medical anthropologists have worked as cultural interpreters in public health programs, so as to facilitate their fit into local culture. Many applied anthropologists have worked for or with international development agencies, such as the World Bank and the U.S. Agency for International Development (USAID). In North America, garbologists help the Environmental Protection Agency, the paper industry, and packaging and trade associations. Archaeology is applied as well in cultural resource management and historic preservation. Biological anthropologists work in public health, nutrition, genetic counseling, substance abuse,

ANTHROPOLOGY'S SUBFIELDS (ACADEMIC ANTHROPOLOGY)	EXAMPLES OF APPLICATION (APPLIED ANTHROPOLOGY)
Cultural anthropology	Development anthropology
Archaeological anthropology	Cultural resource management (CRM)
Biological or physical anthropology	Forensic anthropology
Linguistic anthropology	Study of linguistic diversity in classrooms

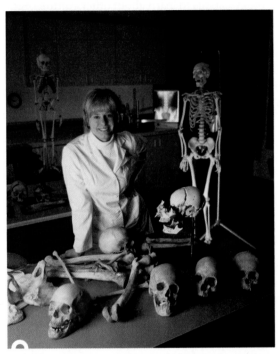

Like other forensic anthropologists, Dr. Kathy Reichs (shown here) and her alter ego, Temperance Brennan, work with the police, medical examiners, the courts, and international organizations to identify victims of crimes, accidents, wars, and terrorism. Brennan is the heroine of several novels by Reichs, as well as of the TV series *Bones*, which debuted on Fox in 2005.

epidemiology, aging, and mental illness. Forensic anthropologists work with the police, medical examiners, the courts, and international organizations to identify victims of crimes, accidents, wars, and terrorism. Linguistic anthropologists study physician–patient interactions and show how dialect differences influence classroom learning. The goal of most applied anthropologists is to find humane and effective ways of helping local people. Recap 3.1 lists the two dimensions and four subfields of anthropology that were first introduced in Chapter 1.

One of the most valuable tools in applying anthropology is the ethnographic method. Ethnographers study societies firsthand, living with and learning from ordinary people. Ethnographers are participant observers, taking part in the events they study in order to understand local thought and behavior. Applied anthropologists use ethnographic techniques in both foreign and domestic settings. Other "expert" participants in social-change programs may be content to converse with officials, read reports, and copy statistics. However, the applied anthropologist's likely early request is some variant of "take me to the local people." We know that people must play an active role in the changes that affect them and that "the people" have information "the experts" lack.

applied anthropology
Using anthropology to solve contemporary problems.

 living anthropology **VIDEOS**

Unearthing Evil: Archaeology in the Cause of Justice, www.mhhe.com/kottak

This clip features archaeologist Richard Wright and his team of 15 forensic archaeologists and anthropologists working "in the cause of justice" in Bosnia-Herzegovina in 1998. The focus of the clip is the excavation of a site of mass burial or reburial of the bodies of some 660 civilians who were murdered during the conflict that followed the dissolution of Yugoslavia. Wright and his colleagues worked with the international community to provide evidence of war crimes. This evidence has led to the convictions of war criminals. Why was Wright nervous about this work? Compare the forensic work shown here with the discussion of forensic anthropology in this chapter.

Anthropological theory, the body of findings and generalizations of the four subfields, also guides applied anthropology. Anthropology's holistic perspective—its interest in biology, society, culture, and language—permits the evaluation of many issues that affect people. Theory aids practice, and application fuels theory. As we compare social-change policy and programs, our understanding of cause and effect increases. We add new generalizations about culture change to those discovered in traditional and ancient cultures.

THE ROLE OF THE APPLIED ANTHROPOLOGIST

Early Applications

Application was a central concern of early anthropology in Great Britain (in the context of colonialism) and the United States (in the context of Native American policy). Before turning to the new, we should consider some dangers of the old. For the British empire, specifically its African colonies, Malinowski (1929a) proposed that "practical anthropology" (his term for colonial applied anthropology) should focus on Westernization, the diffusion of European culture into tribal societies. Malinowski questioned neither the legitimacy of colonialism nor the anthropologist's role in making it work. He saw nothing wrong with aiding colonial regimes by studying land tenure and land use, to recommend how much of their land local people should be allowed to keep and how much Europeans should get. Malinowski's views exemplify a historical association between early anthropology, particularly in Europe, and colonialism (Maquet 1964).

During World War II, American anthropologists studied Japanese and German "culture at a distance" in an attempt to predict the behavior of the enemies of the United States. After that war, applied anthropologists worked on Pacific islands to promote local-level cooperation with American policies in various trust territories.

Academic and Applied Anthropology

Applied anthropology did not disappear during the 1950s and 1960s, but academic anthropology did most of the growing after World War II. The baby boom, which began in 1946 and peaked in 1957, fueled expansion of the American educational system and thus of academic jobs. New junior, community, and four-year colleges opened, and anthropology became a standard part of the college curriculum. During the 1950s and 1960s, most American anthropologists were college professors, although some still worked in agencies and museums.

This era of academic anthropology continued through the early 1970s. Especially during the Vietnam War, undergraduates flocked to anthropology classes to learn about other cultures. Students were especially interested in Southeast Asia, whose indigenous societies were being disrupted by war. Many anthropologists protested the superpowers' apparent disregard for non-Western lives, values, customs, and social systems.

During the 1970s, and increasingly thereafter, although most anthropologists still worked in academia, others found jobs with international organizations, government, business, hospitals, and schools. This shift toward application, though only partial, has benefited the profession. It has forced anthropologists to consider the wider social value and implications of their research.

Applied Anthropology Today

Today, most applied anthropologists see their work as radically removed from the colonial perspective. Modern applied anthropology usually is seen as a helping profession, devoted to assisting local people, as anthropologists speak up for the disenfranchised in the international political arena. However, applied anthropologists also solve problems for clients who are neither poor nor powerless. Applied anthropologists working for businesses try to solve the problem of expanding profits for their employer or client. In market research, ethical issues may arise as anthropologists attempt to help companies operate more efficiently and profitably. Ethical ambiguities are present as well in cultural resource management (CRM), in deciding how to preserve significant remains and information when sites are threatened by development or public works. A CRM firm typically is hired by someone seeking to build a road or a factory. In such cases, the client may have a strong interest in an outcome in

During the Vietnam War, many anthropologists protested the superpowers' disregard for the values, customs, social systems, and lives of indigenous peoples. Several anthropologists (including the author) attended this all-night Columbia University teach-in against the war in 1965.

Supervised by archaeologists from India, with funding from the United Nations, these workers are cleaning and restoring the front facade of Cambodia's historic Angkor Wat temple. To decide what needs saving, and to preserve significant information about the past even when sites cannot be saved, is the work of cultural resource management (CRM).

which no sites are found that need protecting. Contemporary applied anthropologists still face ethical questions: To whom does the researcher owe loyalty? What problems are involved in holding firm to the truth? What happens when applied anthropologists don't make the policies they have to implement? How does one criticize programs in which one has participated (see Escobar 1991, 1994)? Anthropology's professional organizations have addressed such questions by establishing codes of ethics and ethics committees. See www.aaanet.org for the Code of Ethics of the AAA. As Tice (1997) notes, attention to ethical issues is paramount in the teaching of applied anthropology today.

By instilling an appreciation for human diversity, the entire field of anthropology combats *ethnocentrism*—the tendency to view one's own culture as superior and to use one's own cultural values in judging the behavior and beliefs of people raised in other societies. This broadening, educational role affects the knowledge, values, and attitudes of people exposed to anthropology. This chapter focuses specifically on this question: What specific contributions can anthropology make in identifying and solving problems stirred up by contemporary currents of economic, social, and cultural change, including globalization?

Because anthropologists are experts on human problems and social change and because they study, understand, and respect cultural values, they are highly qualified to suggest, plan, and implement policy affecting people. Proper roles for applied anthropologists include (1) identifying needs for change that local people perceive, (2) working with those people to design culturally appropriate and socially sensitive change, and (3) protecting local people from harmful policies and projects that may threaten them. Another role of applied anthropology, as described in this chapter's "Appreciating Anthropology," is to help a community preserve its culture in the face of threat or disaster, such as Hurricane Katrina.

Anthropology's systemic perspective recognizes that changes don't occur in a vacuum. A program or project always has multiple effects, some of which are unforeseen. In an American example of unintended consequences, a program aimed at enhancing teachers' appreciation of cultural differences led to ethnic stereotyping (Kleinfield 1975). Specifically, Native American students did not welcome teachers' frequent comments about their Indian heritage. The students felt set apart from their classmates and saw this attention to their ethnicity as patronizing and demeaning. Internationally, dozens of economic development projects intended to increase productivity through irrigation have worsened public health by creating waterways where diseases thrive.

appreciating ANTHROPOLOGY

Archaeologist in New Orleans Finds a Way to Help the Living

Anthropology is applied in identifying and solving various kinds of problems involving social conditions and human behavior, such as helping a community preserve its culture in the face of threat or disaster. Among the clients of applied anthropologists are governments, agencies, local communities, and businesses. This account describes the work of an anthropologist doing public archaeology in New Orleans in the wake of Hurricane Katrina. Cultural resource management, as discussed here, is one form of applied anthropology: the application of anthropological perspectives, theory, methods, and data to identify, assess, and solve social problems.

"That's a finger bone."

Shannon Lee Dawdy kneeled in the forlorn Holt graveyard to touch a thimble-size bone poking up out of the cracked dirt. She examined it without revulsion, with the fascination of a scientist and with the sadness of someone who loves New Orleans.

Dr. Dawdy, a 38-year-old assistant professor of anthropology at the University of Chicago, is one of the more unusual relief workers among the thousands who have come to the devastated expanses of Louisiana, Mississippi, and Texas in the aftermath of Hurricanes Katrina and Rita. She is officially embedded with the Federal Emergency Management Agency [FEMA] as a liaison to the state's historic preservation office.

Her mission is to try to keep the rebuilding of New Orleans from destroying what is left of its past treasures and current culture.

While much of the restoration of the battered Gulf Coast is the effort of engineers and machines, the work of Dr. Dawdy, trained as an archaeologist, an anthropologist and a historian, shows that the social sciences have a role

to play as well. "It's a way that archaeology can contribute back to the living," she said, "which it doesn't often get to do."

Holt cemetery, a final resting place for the city's poor, is just one example of what she wants to preserve and protect.

Other New Orleans graveyards have gleaming mausoleums that keep the coffins above the marshy soil. But the coffins of Holt are buried, and the ground covering many of them is bordered with wooden frames marked with makeshift headstones.

Mourners decorate the graves with votive objects: teddy bears for children and an agglom-

Archaeologist Shannon Dawdy of the University of Chicago at work in New Orleans, post-Katrina.

DEVELOPMENT ANTHROPOLOGY

Development anthropology is the branch of applied anthropology that focuses on social issues in, and the cultural dimension of, economic development. Development anthropologists do not just carry out development policies planned by others; they also plan and guide policy. (For more detailed discussions of issues in development anthropology, see Edelman and Haugerud 2004; Escobar 1995; Ferguson 1995; Nolan 2002; and Robertson 1995.)

However, ethical dilemmas often confront development anthropologists (Escobar 1991, 1995). Our respect for cultural diversity often is offended because efforts to extend industry and technology may entail profound cultural changes. Foreign aid usually doesn't go where need and suffering are greatest. It is spent on political, economic, and strategic priorities as international donors, politieration of objects, including ice chests, plastic jack-o'-lanterns and chairs, on the graves of adults. There is the occasional liquor bottle. . . .

Many of the objects on the graves were washed away by the storm, or shifted from one part of the graveyard to another. Dr. Dawdy has proposed treating the site as archaeologists would an ancient site in which objects have been exposed on the surface by erosion.

Before the hurricanes, the cemetery was often busy, a hub of activity on All Souls' Day, when people came to freshen the grave decorations.

"The saddest thing to me now was how few people we see," she said, looking at the empty expanse and the scarred live oaks. "I realize we're having enough trouble taking care of the living," she added, but the lack of activity in a city normally so close to the spirits of the past "drove home how far out of whack things are." . . .

Treating Holt as an archaeological site means the government should not treat the votive artifacts as debris, she said, but as the religious artifacts that they are, with some effort to restore the damaged site, to find the objects and at least record where they came from.

FEMA simply tries to clean up damaged areas, and its Disaster Mortuary Operational Response Teams—called Dmort—deal with the bodies of the dead and address problems in cemeteries that might lead to disease.

If such places are destroyed, Dr. Dawdy said, "then people don't feel as connected here." She added that they might be more willing to come back to a damaged city if they felt they were returning to a recognizable home.

Though she has deep emotional ties to New Orleans, Dr. Dawdy was born in Northern California. She came here in 1994 to write her master's thesis for the College of William & Mary, and, "I wrote it all day," she said. "If I had written a minimum of five pages, I could come out for a parade at night." Over the eight weeks it took to finish the project, she said: "I fell in love with New Orleans. I really consider it the home of my heart."

She started a pilot program at the University of New Orleans, working with city planners and grants for research projects that involved excavation, oral history and hands-on work with the city to safeguard its buried treasures.

She left that job to earn a double doctorate at the University of Michigan in anthropology and history that focused on French colonial times in New Orleans, then landed a coveted faculty position at the University of Chicago. . . .

Even before Hurricane Katrina, Dr. Dawdy had found ways to return to New Orleans. In 2004, she made an intriguing discovery while researching a possible archaeological site under an old French Quarter parking garage slated for demolition. Property records and advertisements from the 1820's said that the site had been the location of a hotel with an enticing name: the Rising Sun Hotel.

Dr. Dawdy found a January 1821 newspaper advertisement for the hotel in which its owners promised to "maintain the character of giving the best entertainment, which this house has enjoyed for twenty years past."

It went on: "Gentlemen may here rely upon finding attentive Servants. The bar will be supplied with genuine good Liquors; and at the Table, the fare will be of the best the market or the season will afford." . . .

New Orleans, she noted, has always been known for its libertine lifestyle. The French all but abandoned the city as its colony around 1735 as being unworthy of the nation's support as a colony. Novels like "Manon Lescaut" portrayed the city as a den of iniquity and corruption, and across Europe, "they thought the locals were basically a bunch of rogues, immoral and corrupt," Dr. Dawdy said.

She added that she saw parallels to today, as some skepticism emerges about rebuilding the city. Dr. Dawdy characterized that posture as, "Those people in New Orleans aren't worth saving, because they're all criminals anyway." But even if the devastation makes it hard to envision the road back, the city, she said, is worth fighting for.

"The thing about New Orleans that gives me hope is they are so tied to family, place, history," Dr. Dawdy said. "If anyone is going to stick it out, out of a sense of history, out of a sense of tradition, it is New Orleans."

cal leaders, and powerful interest groups perceive them. Planners' interests don't always coincide with the best interests of the local people. Although the aim of most development projects is to enhance the quality of life, living standards often decline in the target area (Bodley, ed. 1988).

Equity

A commonly stated goal of recent development policy is to promote equity. **Increased equity** means reduced poverty and a more even distribution of wealth. However, if projects are to increase equity, they must have the support of reform-minded governments. Wealthy and powerful people typically resist projects that threaten their vested interests.

Some types of development projects, particularly irrigation schemes, are more likely than others to widen wealth disparities, that is, to have a negative equity impact. An initial uneven

equity, increased
Reduction in absolute poverty, with a more even distribution of wealth.

A mix of boats harbored at Dai-Lanh fishing village in Vietnam. A boat owner gets a loan to buy a motor. To repay it, he increases the share of the catch he takes from his crew. Later, he uses his rising profits to buy a more expensive boat and takes even more from his crew. Can a more equitable solution be found?

overinnovation
Trying to achieve too much change.

distribution of resources (particularly land) often becomes the basis for greater skewing after the project. The social impact of new technology tends to be more severe, contributing negatively to quality of life and to equity, when inputs are channeled to or through the rich.

Many fisheries projects also have had negative equity results (see Durrenberger and King, eds. 2000). In Bahia, Brazil (Kottak 2006), sailboat owners (but not nonowners) got loans to buy motors for their boats. To repay the loans, the owners increased the percentage of the catch they took from the men who fished in their boats. Over the years, they used their rising profits to buy larger and more expensive boats. The result was stratification—the creation of a group of wealthy people within a formerly egalitarian community. These events hampered individual initiative and interfered with further development of the fishing industry. With new boats so expensive, ambitious young men who once would have sought careers in fishing no longer had any way to obtain their own boats. They sought wage labor on land instead. To avoid such results, credit-granting agencies must seek out enterprising young fishers rather than give loans only to owners and established businesspeople.

STRATEGIES FOR INNOVATION

Development anthropologists, who are concerned with social issues in, and the cultural dimension of, economic development, must work closely with local people to assess and help them realize their own wishes and needs for change. Too many true local needs cry out for a solution to waste money funding development projects in area A that are inappropriate there but needed in area B, or that are unnecessary anywhere. Development anthropology can help sort out the needs of the As and Bs and fit projects accordingly. Projects that put people first by consulting with them and responding to their expressed needs must be identified (Cernea, ed. 1991). Thereafter, development anthropologists can work to ensure socially compatible ways of implementing a good project.

In a comparative study of 68 rural development projects from all around the world, I found the *culturally compatible* economic development projects to be twice as successful financially as the incompatible ones (Kottak 1990b , 1991). This finding shows that using anthropological expertise in planning to ensure cultural compatibility is cost-effective. To maximize social and economic benefits, projects must (1) be culturally compatible, (2) respond to locally perceived needs, (3) involve men and women in planning and carrying out the changes that affect them, (4) harness traditional organizations, and (5) be flexible.

Overinnovation

In my comparative study, the compatible and successful projects avoided the fallacy of **overinnovation** (too much change). We would expect people to resist development projects that require major changes in their daily lives. People usually want to change just enough to keep what they have. Motives for modifying behavior come from the traditional culture and the small concerns of ordinary life. Peasants' values are not such abstract ones as "learning a better way," "progressing," "increasing technical know-how," "improving efficiency," or "adopting modern techniques."

Instead, their objectives are down-to-earth and specific ones. People want to improve yields in a rice field, amass resources for a ceremony, get a child through school, or have enough cash to pay the tax bill. The goals and values of subsistence producers differ from those of people who produce for cash, just as they differ from those of development planners. Different value systems must be considered during planning.

In the comparative study, the projects that failed were usually both economically and culturally incompatible. For example, one South Asian project promoted the cultivation of onions and peppers, expecting this practice to fit into a preexisting labor-intensive system of rice-growing. Cultivation of these cash crops wasn't traditional in the area. It conflicted with existing crop priorities and other interests of farmers. Also, the labor peaks for pepper and onion production coincided with those for rice, to which the farmers gave priority.

Throughout the world, project problems have arisen from inadequate attention to, and consequent lack of fit with, local culture. Another naive and incompatible project was an overinnovative scheme in Ethiopia. Its major fallacy was to try to convert nomadic herders into sedentary cultivators. It ignored traditional land rights. Outsiders—commercial farmers—were to get much of the herders' territory. The herders were expected to settle down and start farming. This project helped wealthy outsiders instead of the local people. The planners naively expected free-ranging herders to give up a generations-old way of life to work three times harder growing rice and picking cotton for bosses.

Underdifferentiation

The fallacy of **underdifferentiation** is the tendency to view "the less-developed countries" as more alike than they are. Development agencies have often ignored cultural diversity (e.g., between Brazil and Burundi) and adopted a uniform approach to deal with very different sets of people. Neglecting cultural diversity, many projects also have tried to impose incompatible property notions and social units. Most often, the faulty social design assumes either (1) individualistic productive units that are privately owned by an individual or couple and worked by a nuclear family or (2) cooperatives that are at least partially based on models from the former Eastern bloc and Socialist countries.

One example of faulty Euro-American models (the individual and the nuclear family) was a West African project designed for an area where the extended family was the basic social unit. The project succeeded despite its faulty social design because the participants used their traditional extended family networks to attract additional settlers. Eventually, twice as many people as planned benefited as extended family members flocked to the project area. Here, settlers modified the project design that had been imposed on them by following the principles of their traditional society.

The second dubious foreign social model that is common in development strategy is the cooperative. In the comparative study of rural development projects, new cooperatives fared badly. Cooperatives succeeded only when they harnessed preexisting local-level communal institutions. This is a corollary of a more general rule: Participants' groups are most effective when they are based on traditional social organization or on a socioeconomic similarity among members.

Neither foreign social model—the nuclear family farm nor the cooperative—has an unblemished record in development. An alternative is needed: greater use of indigenous social models for indig-

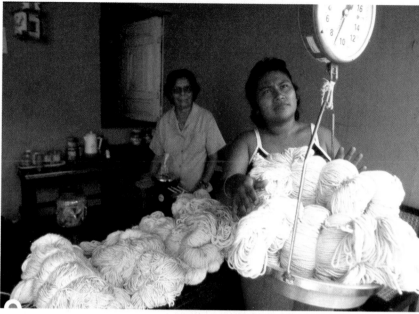

To maximize benefits, development projects should respond to locally perceived needs. Shown here (foreground) is the president of a Nicaraguan cooperative that makes and markets hammocks. This cooperative has been assisted by a nongovernmental organization (NGO) whose goals include increasing the benefits that women derive from economic development.

enous development. These are traditional social units, such as the clans, lineages, and other extended kin groups of Africa, Oceania, and many other nations, with their communally held estates and resources. The most humane and productive strategy for change is to base the social design for innovation on traditional social forms in each target area.

underdifferentiation
Seeing less-developed countries as all the same; ignoring cultural diversity.

Indigenous Models

Many governments are not genuinely, or realistically, committed to improving the lives of their citizens. Interference by major powers also has kept governments from enacting needed reforms. In some nations, however, the government acts more as an agent of the people. Madagascar provides an example. The people of Madagascar, the Malagasy, had been organized into descent groups before the origin of the state. A *descent group* is a kin group composed of people whose social solidarity is based on their belief that they share common ancestry. The Merina, creators of the major precolonial state of Madagascar, wove descent groups into its structure, making members of important groups advisers to the king and thus giving them authority in government. The Merina state made provisions for the people it ruled. It collected taxes and organized labor for public works projects. In return, it redistributed resources to peasants in need. It also granted them some protection against war and slave raids and allowed them to cultivate their rice fields in peace. The government maintained the waterworks for rice cultivation. It opened to ambitious peasant boys the chance of becoming, through hard work and study, state bureaucrats.

Throughout the history of the Merina state—and continuing in modern Madagascar—there have been strong relationships between the individual, the descent group, and the state. Local Malagasy communities, where residence is based on descent, are more cohesive and homogeneous than are communities in Latin America or North America. Madagascar gained political independence from France in 1960. Although it still was economically dependent on France when I first did research there in 1966–1967, the new government had an economic development policy aimed at increasing the ability of the Malagasy to feed themselves. Government policy emphasized increased production of rice, a subsistence crop, rather than cash crops. Furthermore, local communities, with their traditional cooperative patterns and solidarity based on kinship and descent, were treated as partners in, not obstacles to, the development process.

In a sense, the descent group (clan or lineage) is preadapted to equitable national development. In Madagascar, members of local descent groups have customarily pooled their resources to educate their ambitious members. Once educated, these men and women gain economically secure positions in the nation. They then share the advantages of their new positions with their kin. For example, they give room and board to rural cousins attending school and help them find jobs.

anthropology and education
Study of students in the context of their family, peers, and enculturation.

Malagasy administrations appear generally to have shared a commitment to democratic economic development. Perhaps this is because government officials are of the peasantry or have strong personal ties to it. By contrast, in Latin American countries, the elites and the lower class have different origins and no strong connections through kinship, descent, or marriage.

Furthermore, societies with descent-group organization contradict an assumption that many social scientists and economists seem to make. It is not inevitable that as nations become more tied to the world economy, indigenous forms of social organization will break down into nuclear family organization, impersonality, and alienation. Descent groups, with their traditional communalism and corporate solidarity, have important roles to play in economic development.

Realistic development promotes change but not overinnovation. Many changes are possible if the aim is to preserve local systems while making them work better. Successful economic development projects respect, or at least don't attack, local cultural patterns. Effective development draws on indigenous cultural practices and social structures.

ANTHROPOLOGY AND EDUCATION

Attention to culture also is fundamental to **anthropology and education,** involving research that extends from classrooms into homes, neighborhoods, and communities (see Spindler, ed. 2000, 2005). In classrooms, anthropologists have observed interactions among teachers, students, parents, and visitors. Jules Henry's classic account of the American elementary school classroom (1955) shows how students learn to conform to and compete with their peers. Anthropologists view children as total cultural creatures whose enculturation and attitudes toward education belong to a context that includes family and peers.

Sociolinguists and cultural anthropologists work side by side in education research. For example, in a study of Puerto Rican seventh-graders in the urban Midwest (Hill-Burnett 1978), anthropologists uncovered some misconceptions held by teachers. The teachers mistakenly had assumed that Puerto Rican parents valued education less than did non-Hispanics, but in-depth interviews revealed that the Puerto Rican parents valued it more.

The anthropologists also found that certain practices were preventing Hispanics from being adequately educated. For example, the teachers' union and the board of education had agreed to teach "English as a foreign language." However, they had provided no bilingual teachers to work

A Hispanic girl and an Asian girl read a book written in Spanish together in a bilingual elementary school classroom. In such classrooms, and extending out into the community, anthropologists of education study the backgrounds, behavior, beliefs, and attitudes of teachers, students, parents, and families in their (multi)cultural context.

with Spanish-speaking students. The school was assigning all students (including non-Hispanics) with low reading scores and behavior problems to the English-as-a-foreign-language classroom. This educational disaster brought together in the classroom a teacher who spoke no Spanish, children who barely spoke English, and a group of English-speaking students with reading and behavior problems. The Spanish speakers were falling behind not just in reading but in all subjects. They could at least have kept up in the other subjects if a Spanish speaker had been teaching them science, social studies, and math until they were ready for English-language instruction in those areas.

URBAN ANTHROPOLOGY

Alan and Josephine Smart (2003) note that cities have long been influenced by global forces, including world capitalism and colonialism. However, the roles of cities in the world system have changed recently as a result of the time-space compression made possible by modern transportation and communication systems. That is, everything appears closer today because contact and movement are so much easier.

In the context of contemporary globalization, the mass media can become as important as local factors in guiding daily routines, dreams, and aspirations. People live in particular places, but their imaginations and attachments don't have to be locally confined (Appadurai 1996). People migrate to cities partly for economic reasons, but also to be where the action is. People seek experiences available only in cities, such as live theater or busy streets. Rural Brazilians routinely cite *movimento*, urban movement and excitement, as something to be valued. International migrants tend to settle in the largest cities, where the most is happening. For example, in Canada, which, after Australia, has the highest percentage of foreign-born population, 71.2 percent of immigrants settled in Toronto, Vancouver, or Montreal. Nearly half of Toronto's citizens were born outside Canada (Smart and Smart 2003).

The proportion of the world's population living in cities has been increasing ever since the Industrial Revolution. Only about 3 percent of people were city dwellers in 1800, compared with 13 percent in 1900, over 40 percent in 1980, and about 50 percent today (see Smart and Smart 2003). The more-developed countries (MDCs) were 76 percent urbanized in 1999, compared with 39 percent for the less-developed countries (LDCs). However, the urbanization growth rate is much faster in the LDCs (Smart and Smart 2003). The world had only 16 cities with more than a million people in 1900, but there were 314

such cities in 2005. By 2025, 60 percent of the global population will be urban (Butler 2005; Stevens 1992).

About one billion people, one-sixth of Earth's population, live in urban slums, mostly without water, sanitation, public services, and legal security (Vidal 2003). If current trends continue, urban population increase and the concentration of people in slums will be accompanied by rising rates of crime, along with water, air, and noise pollution. These problems will be most severe in the LDCs.

As industrialization and urbanization spread globally, anthropologists increasingly study these processes and the social problems they create. **Urban anthropology,** which has theoretical (basic research) and applied dimensions, is the cross-cultural and ethnographic study of global urbanization and life in cities (see Aoyagi, Nas, and Traphagan, eds. 1998; Gmelch and Zenner, eds. 2002; Smart and Smart 2003; Stevenson 2003). The United States and Canada have become popular arenas for urban anthropological research on topics such as immigration, ethnicity, poverty, class, and urban violence (Mullings, ed. 1987; Vigil 2003).

Urban versus Rural

Recognizing that a city is a social context that is very different from a tribal or peasant village, an early student of urbanization, the anthropologist Robert Redfield, focused on contrasts between rural and urban life. He contrasted rural communities, whose social relations are on a face-to-face basis, with cities, where impersonality characterizes many aspects of life. Redfield (1941) proposed that urbanization be studied along a rural–urban continuum. He described differences in values and social relations in four sites that spanned such a continuum. In Mexico's Yucatán peninsula, Redfield compared an isolated Maya-speaking Indian community, a rural peasant village, a small provincial city, and a large capital. Several studies in Africa (Little 1971) and Asia were influenced by Redfield's view that cities are centers through which cultural innovations spread to rural and tribal areas.

In any nation, urban and rural represent different social systems. However, cultural diffusion or borrowing occurs as people, products, images, and messages move from one to the other. Migrants bring rural practices and beliefs to cities and take urban patterns back home. The experiences and social forms of the rural area affect adaptation to city life. City folk also develop new institutions to meet specific urban needs (Mitchell 1966).

An applied anthropology approach to urban planning would start by identifying key social groups in the urban context. After identifying

urban anthropology
Anthropological study of cities and urban life.

those groups, the anthropologist might elicit their wishes for change, convey those needs to funding agencies, and work with agencies and local people to realize those goals. In Africa relevant groups might include ethnic associations, occupational groups, social clubs, religious groups, and burial societies. Through membership in such groups, urban Africans maintain wide networks of personal contacts and support (Banton 1957; Little 1965). These groups also have links with, and provide cash support and urban lodging for, their rural relatives. Sometimes such groups think of themselves as a gigantic kin group, a clan that includes urban and rural members. Members may call one another "brother" and "sister." As in an extended family, rich members help their poor relatives. A member's improper behavior can lead to expulsion—an unhappy fate for a migrant in a large ethnically heterogeneous city.

One role for the urban applied anthropologist is to help relevant social groups deal with urban institutions, such as legal and social services, with which recent migrants may be unfamiliar. In certain North American cities, as in Africa, kin-based ethnic associations are relevant urban groups. One example comes from Los Angeles, which has the largest Samoan immigrant community (over 12,000 people) in the United States. Samoans in Los Angeles draw on their traditional system of

matai (*matai* means "chief"; the matai system now refers to respect for elders) to deal with modern urban problems. One example: In 1992, a white police officer shot and killed two unarmed Samoan brothers. When a judge dismissed charges against the officer, local leaders used the matai system to calm angry youths (who have formed gangs, like other ethnic groups in the Los Angeles area). Clan leaders and elders organized a well-attended community meeting, in which they urged young members to be patient. The Samoans then used the American judicial system. They brought a civil case against the officer in question and pressed the U.S. Justice Department to initiate a civil rights case in the matter (Mydans 1992*b*). Not all conflicts involving gangs and law enforcement end so peacefully.

James Vigil (2003) examines gang violence in the context of large-scale immigrant adaptation to American cities. He notes that most gangs prior to the 1970s were located in white ethnic enclaves in Eastern and Midwestern cities. Back then, gang incidents typically were brawls involving fists, sticks, and knives. Today, gangs more often are composed of nonwhite ethnic groups, and handguns have replaced the less lethal weapons of the past. Gangs still consist mostly of male adolescents who have grown up together, usually in a low-income neighborhood, where it's estimated

Anthropologists have noted the significance of urban youth groups, including gangs, which now have transnational scope. Here a gang member deported from California to San Salvador makes the hand sign to represent the 18th Street gang. That gang, which originated in California, has spread throughout Central America via mass deportations of ethnic Salvadorans from the U.S. Separated from their families, thousands of these former Californians look to gangs for social support and physical protection.

that about 10 percent of young men join gangs. Female gang members are much rarer—from 4 to 15 percent of gang members. With gangs organized hierarchically by age, older members push younger ones (usually 14- to 18-year-olds) to carry out violent acts against rivals (Vigil 2003).

The populations that include most of today's gang members settled originally in poorer urban areas. On the East Coast these usually were rundown neighborhoods where a criminal lifestyle already was present. Around Los Angeles, urban migrants created squatterlike settlements in previously empty spaces. Immigrants tend to reside in neighborhoods apart from middle-class people, thus limiting their opportunities for integration. Confined in this manner, and facing residential overcrowding, poor people often experience frustration, which can lead to aggressive acts (Vigil 2003). As well, industries and jobs have moved from inner cities to distant suburbs and foreign nations. Urban minority youth have limited access to entry-level jobs; often they receive harsh treatment from authorities, especially law enforcement. Frustration and competition over resources can spark aggressive incidents, fueling urban violence. For survival, many residents of abandoned neighborhoods have turned to informal and illegal economic arrangements, of which drug trafficking in particular has heightened gang violence (Vigil 2003). How might an applied anthropologist approach the problem of urban violence? Which groups would need to be involved in the study?

MEDICAL ANTHROPOLOGY

Medical anthropology is both academic/theoretical and applied/practical and includes anthropologists from all four subfields (see Anderson 1996; Briggs 2005; Brown 1998; Dressler et al. 2005; Joralemon 2006; Singer and Baer 2007). Medical anthropologists examine such questions as which diseases and health conditions affect particular populations (and why) and how illness is socially constructed, diagnosed, managed, and treated in various societies.

Disease refers to a scientifically identified health threat caused genetically or by a bacterium, virus, fungus, parasite, or other pathogen. **Illness** is a condition of poor health perceived or felt by an individual (Inhorn and Brown 1990). Perceptions of good and bad health, along with health threats and problems, are culturally constructed. Various ethnic groups and cultures recognize different illnesses, symptoms, and causes and have developed different health-care systems and treatment strategies.

The incidence and severity of *disease* vary as well (see Barnes 2005; Baer, Singer, and Susser 2003). Group differences are evident in the United States. Keppel, Pearch, and Wagener (2002) examined data between 1990 and 1998 using 10 health status indicators in relation to racial and ethnic categories used in the U.S. census: non-Hispanic white, non-Hispanic black, Hispanic, American Indian or Alaskan Native, and Asian or Pacific Islander. Black Americans' rates for six measures (total mortality, heart disease, lung cancer, breast cancer, stroke, and homicide) exceeded those of other groups by a factor ranging from 2.5 to almost 10. Other ethnic groups had higher rates for suicide (white Americans) and motor vehicle accidents (American Indians and Alaskan Natives). Overall, Asians had the longest life spans (see Dressler et al. 2005).

Hurtado and colleagues (2005) note the prevalence of poor health and unusually high rates of early mortality among indigenous populations in South America. Life expectancy at birth is at least 20 years shorter among indigenous groups compared with other South Americans. In 2000, the life expectancy of indigenous peoples in Brazil and Venezuela was lower than that in Sierra Leone, which had the lowest reported national life expectancy in the world (Hurtado et al. 2005).

How can applied anthropologists help ameliorate the large health disparity between indigenous peoples and other populations? Hurtado and colleagues (2005) suggest three steps: (1) identify the most pressing health problems that indigenous

medical anthropology
The comparative, biocultural study of disease, health problems, and health-care systems.

disease
A scientifically identified health threat caused by a known pathogen.

illness
A condition of poor health perceived or felt by an individual.

Merina women plant paddy rice in the highlands south of Antsirabe, Madagascar. Schistosomiasis, of which all known varieties are found in Madagascar, is among the fastest-spreading and most dangerous parasitic infections now known. It is propagated by snails that live in ponds, lakes, and waterways (often ones created by irrigation systems, such as those associated with paddy rice cultivation).

communities face; (2) gather information on solutions to those problems; and (3) implement solutions in partnership with the agencies and organizations that are in charge of public health programs for indigenous populations.

In many areas, the world system and colonialism worsened the health of indigenous peoples by spreading diseases, warfare, servitude, and other stressors. Traditionally and in ancient times, hunter-gatherers, because of their small numbers, mobility, and relative isolation from other groups, lacked most of the epidemic infectious diseases that affect agrarian and urban societies (Cohen and Armelagos, eds. 1984; Inhorn and Brown 1990). Epidemic diseases such as cholera, typhoid, and bubonic plague thrive in dense populations, and thus among farmers and city dwellers. The spread of malaria has been linked to population growth and deforestation associated with food production.

Certain diseases, and physical conditions, such as obesity, have spread with economic development and globalization (Ulijaszek and Lofink 2006). *Schistosomiasis* or bilharzia (liver flukes) is probably the fastest-spreading and most dangerous parasitic infection now known. It is propagated by snails that live in ponds, lakes, and waterways, usually ones created by irrigation projects. A study done in a Nile Delta village in Egypt (Farooq 1966) illustrated the role of culture (religion) in the spread of schistosomiasis. The disease was more common among Muslims than among Christians because of an Islamic practice called *wudu*, ritual ablution (bathing) before prayer. The applied anthropology approach to reducing such diseases is to see if local people perceive a connection between the vector (e.g., snails in the water) and the disease. If not, such information may be provided by enlisting active local groups, schools, and the media.

The highest global rates of HIV infection and AIDS-related deaths are in Africa, especially southern Africa. As it kills productive adults, AIDS leaves behind children and seniors who have difficulty replacing the lost labor force (Baro and Deubel 2006). In southern and eastern Africa, AIDS and other sexually transmitted diseases (STDs) have spread along highways, via encounters between male truckers and female prostitutes. STDs also are spread through prostitution, as young men from rural areas seek wage work in cities, labor camps, and mines. When the men return to their natal villages,

they infect their wives (Larson 1989; Miller and Rockwell, eds. 1988). Cities also are prime sites of STD transmission in Europe, Asia, and North and South America (see Baer, Singer, and Susser 2003; French 2002). Cultural factors also affect the spread of HIV, which is less likely to be transmitted when men are circumcised than when they are not.

The kinds of and incidence of disease vary among societies, and cultures interpret and treat illness differently. Standards for sick and healthy bodies are cultural constructions that vary in time and space (Martin 1992). Still, all societies have what George Foster and Barbara Anderson call "disease-theory systems" to identify, classify, and explain illness. According to Foster and Anderson (1978), there are three basic theories about the causes of illness: personalistic, naturalistic, and emotionalistic. *Personalistic disease theories* blame illness on agents, such as sorcerers, witches, ghosts, or ancestral spirits. *Naturalistic disease theories* explain illness in impersonal terms. One example is Western medicine or *biomedicine*, which aims to link illness to scientifically demonstrated agents that bear no personal malice toward their victims. Thus Western medicine attributes illness to organisms (e.g., bacteria, viruses, fungi, or parasites), accidents, toxic materials, or genes.

Other naturalistic ethnomedical systems blame poor health on unbalanced body fluids. Many Latin societies classify food, drink, and environmental conditions as "hot" or "cold." People believe their health suffers when they eat or drink hot or cold substances together or under inappropriate conditions. For example, one shouldn't drink something cold after a hot bath or eat a pineapple (a "cold" fruit) when one is menstruating (a "hot" condition).

Emotionalistic disease theories assume that emotional experiences cause illness. For example, Latin Americans may develop *susto*, an illness caused by anxiety or fright (Bolton 1981; Finkler 1985). Its symptoms (lethargy, vagueness, distraction) are similar to those of "soul loss," a diagnosis of similar symptoms made by people in Madagascar. Modern psychoanalysis also focuses on the role of the emotions in physical and psychological well-being.

All societies have **health-care systems** consisting of beliefs, customs, specialists, and techniques aimed at ensuring health and at preventing, diagnosing, and curing illness. A society's illness-causation theory is important for treatment.

A traditional healer at work in Malaysia. Shown here, mugwort, a small, spongy herb, is burned to facilitate healing. The healer lights one end of a moxa stick, roughly the shape and size of a cigar, and attaches it, or holds it close, to the area being treated for several minutes until the area turns red. The purpose of moxibustion is to strengthen the blood, stimulate spiritual energy, and maintain general health.

health-care systems Beliefs, customs, and specialists concerned with preventing and curing illness.

When illness has a personalistic cause, magicoreligious specialists may be good curers. They draw on varied techniques (occult and practical), which comprise their special expertise. A shaman may cure soul loss by enticing the spirit back into the body. Shamans may ease difficult childbirths by asking spirits to travel up the birth canal to guide the baby out (Lévi-Strauss 1967). A shaman may cure a cough by counteracting a curse or removing a substance introduced by a sorcerer.

If there is a "world's oldest profession" besides hunter and gatherer, it is **curer,** often a shaman. The curer's role has some universal features (Foster and Anderson 1978). Thus curers emerge through a culturally defined process of selection (parental prodding, inheritance, visions, dream instructions) and training (apprentice shamanship, medical school). Eventually, the curer is certified by older practitioners and acquires a professional image. Patients believe in the skills of the curer, whom they consult and compensate.

We should not lose sight, ethnocentrically, of the difference between **scientific medicine** and Western medicine per se. Despite advances in technology, genomics, molecular biology, pathology, surgery, diagnostics, and applications, many Western medical procedures have little justification in logic or fact. Overprescription of drugs, unnecessary surgery, and the impersonality and inequality of the physician–patient relationship are questionable features of Western medical systems (see Briggs 2005 for linguistic aspects of this inequality). Also, overuse of antibiotics, not just for people but also in animal feed, seems to be triggering an explosion of resistant microorganisms, which may pose a long-term global public health hazard.

Still, biomedicine surpasses tribal treatment in many ways. Although medicines such as quinine, coca, opium, ephedrine, and rauwolfia were discovered in nonindustrial societies, thousands of effective drugs are available today to treat myriad diseases. Preventive health care improved during the twentieth century. Today's surgical procedures are much safer and more effective than those of traditional societies.

But industrialization and globalization have spawned their own health problems. Modern stressors include poor nutrition, dangerous machinery, impersonal work, isolation, poverty, homelessness, substance abuse, and noise, air, and water pollution (see McElroy and Townsend 2003). Health problems in industrial nations are caused as much by economic, social, political, and cultural factors as by pathogens. In modern North America, for example, poverty contributes to many illnesses, including arthritis, heart conditions, back problems, and hearing and vision impairment (see Bailey 2000). Poverty also is a factor in the differential spread of infectious diseases.

In the United States and other developed countries today, good health has become something of an ethical imperative (Foucault 1990). Individuals are expected to regulate their behavior and shape themselves in keeping with new medical knowledge. Those who do so acquire the status of sanitary citizens—people with modern understanding of the body, health, and illness, who practice hygiene and depend on doctors and nurses when they are sick. People who act differently (e.g., smokers, overeaters, those who avoid doctors) are stigmatized as unsanitary and blamed for their own health problems (Briggs 2005; Foucault 1990).

Even getting an epidemic disease such as cholera or living in an infected neighborhood may be interpreted today as a moral failure. It's assumed that people who are properly informed and act rationally can avoid such "preventable" diseases. Individuals are expected to follow scientifically based imperatives (e.g., "boil water," "don't smoke"). People can become objects of avoidance and discrimination simply by belonging to a group (e.g., gay men, Haitians, smokers, veterans) seen as having a greater risk of getting a particular disease (Briggs 2005).

Medical anthropologists have served as cultural interpreters in public health programs, which must pay attention to local theories about the nature, causes, and treatment of illness. Health interventions cannot simply be forced on communities. They must fit into local cultures and be accepted by local people. When Western medicine is introduced, people usually retain many of their old methods while also accepting new ones (see Green 1987/1992). Native curers may go on treating certain conditions (spirit possession), whereas doctors may deal with others. If both modern and traditional specialists are consulted and the patient is cured, the native curer may get as much or more credit than the physician.

A more personal treatment of illness that emulates the non-Western curer-patient-community relationship could probably benefit Western systems. Western medicine tends to draw a rigid line between biological and psychological causation. Non-Western theories usually lack this sharp distinction, recognizing that poor health has intertwined physical, emotional, and social causes. The mind–body opposition is part of Western folk taxonomy, not of science (see also Brown 1998; Helman 2001; Joralemon 2006; Strathern and Stewart 1999).

Medical anthropologists increasingly are examining the impact of new scientific and medical techniques on ideas about life, death, and *personhood*

curer
One who diagnoses and treats illness.

scientific medicine
A health-care system based on scientific knowledge and procedures.

At a major information technology company, Marietta Baba examines one of the world's fastest supercomputers. She is studying that firm's adaptation to the rise of the service economy. Professor Baba, a prominent applied anthropologist and dean of the College of Social Science at Michigan State University, also has studied Michigan's automobile industry.

appreciating DIVERSITY

Culturally Appropriate Marketing

Innovation succeeds best when it is culturally appropriate. This axiom of applied anthropology could guide the international spread not only of development projects but also of businesses, such as fast food. Each time McDonald's or Burger King expands to a new nation, it must devise a culturally appropriate strategy for fitting into the new setting.

McDonald's has been successful internationally, with more than a quarter of its sales outside the United States. One place where McDonald's is expanding successfully is Brazil, where more than 50 million middle-class people, most living in densely packed cities, provide a concentrated market for a fast-food chain. Still, it took McDonald's some time to find the right marketing strategy for Brazil.

In 1980 when I visited Brazil after a seven-year absence, I first noticed, as a manifestation of Brazil's growing participation in the world economy, the appearance of two McDonald's restaurants in Rio de Janeiro. There wasn't much difference between Brazilian and North American McDonald's. The restaurants looked alike. The menus were more or less the same, as was the taste of the quarter-pounders. I picked up an artifact, a white paper bag with yellow lettering, exactly like the take-out bags then used in American McDonald's. An advertising device, it carried several messages about how Brazilians could bring McDonald's into their lives. However, it seemed to me that McDonald's Brazilian ad campaign was missing some important points about how fast food

should be marketed in a culture that values large, leisurely lunches.

The bag proclaimed, "You're going to enjoy the [McDonald's] difference," and listed several "favorite places where you can enjoy McDonald's products." This list confirmed that the marketing people were trying to adapt to Brazilian middle-class culture, but they were making some mistakes. "When you go out in the car with the kids" transferred the uniquely developed North American cultural combination of highways, affordable cars, and suburban living to the very different context of urban Brazil. A similar suggestion was "traveling to the country place." Even Brazilians who owned country places could not find McDonald's, still confined to the cities, on the road. The ad creator had apparently never attempted to drive up to a fast-food restaurant in a neighborhood with no parking spaces.

Several other suggestions pointed customers toward the beach, where *cariocas* (Rio natives) do spend much of their leisure time. One

---

(what is and is not a person). For decades, disagreements about personhood—about when life begins and ends—have been part of political and religious discussions of contraception, abortion, assisted suicide, and euthanasia (mercy killing). More recent additions to such discussions include stem cell research, frozen embryos, assisted reproduction, genetic screening, cloning, and life-prolonging medical treatments. Ideas about what it means to be human and to be alive or dead are being reformulated. In the United States, the controversy surrounding the death of Terri Schiavo in 2005 brought such questions into public debate. Kaufman and Morgan (2005) emphasize the contrast between what they call low-tech and high-tech births and deaths in today's world. A desperately poor young mother dies of AIDS in Africa while half a world away an American child of privilege is born as the result of a $50,000 in-vitro fertilization procedure. Medical anthropologists increasingly are concerned with new and contrasting conditions that allow humans to enter, live, and depart life, and with how the boundaries of life and death are being questioned and negotiated in the 21st century.

ANTHROPOLOGY AND BUSINESS

Carol Taylor (1987) discusses the value of an "anthropologist-in-residence" in a large, complex organization, such as a hospital or a business. A free-ranging ethnographer can be a perceptive oddball when information and decisions usually move through a rigid hierarchy. If allowed to observe and converse freely with all types and levels of personnel, the anthropologist may acquire a unique perspective on organizational conditions and problems. Also, high-tech companies, such as Xerox, IBM, and Apple, have employed anthropologists in various roles. Closely observing how people actually use computer products, anthropologists work with engineers to design products that are more user-friendly.

For many years anthropologists have used ethnography to study business settings (Arensberg 1987; Jordan 2003). For example, ethnographic research in an auto factory may view workers, managers, and executives as different social categories participating in a common social system. Each group has characteristic attitudes, values, and be-could eat McDonald's products "after a dip in the ocean," "at a picnic at the beach," or "watching the surfers." These suggestions ignored the Brazilian custom of consuming cold things, such as beer, soft drinks, ice cream, and ham and cheese sandwiches, at the beach. Brazilians don't consider a hot, greasy hamburger proper beach food. They view the sea as "cold" and hamburgers as "hot"; they avoid "hot" foods at the beach.

Also culturally dubious was the suggestion to eat McDonald's hamburgers "lunching at the office." Brazilians prefer their main meal at midday, often eating at a leisurely pace with business associates. Many firms serve ample lunches to their employees. Other workers take advantage of a two-hour lunch break to go home to eat with the spouse and children. Nor did it make sense to suggest that children should eat hamburgers for lunch, since most kids attend school for half-day sessions and have lunch at home. Two other suggestions—"waiting for the bus" and "in the

beauty parlor"—did describe common aspects of daily life in a Brazilian city. However, these settings have not proved especially inviting to hamburgers or fish filets.

The homes of Brazilians who can afford McDonald's products have cooks and maids to do many of the things that fast-food restaurants do in the United States. The suggestion that McDonald's products be eaten "while watching your favorite television program" is culturally appropriate, because Brazilians watch TV a lot. However, Brazil's consuming classes can ask the cook to make a snack when hunger strikes. Indeed, much televiewing occurs during the light dinner served when the husband gets home from the office.

Most appropriate to the Brazilian lifestyle was the suggestion to enjoy McDonald's "on the cook's day off." Throughout Brazil, Sunday is that day. The Sunday pattern for middle-class families is a trip to the beach, liters of beer, a full midday meal around 3 P.M., and a light evening

snack. McDonald's found its niche in the Sunday evening meal, when families flock to the fast-food restaurant, and it is to this market that its advertising is now appropriately geared.

McDonald's is expanding rapidly in Brazilian cities, and in Brazil as in North America, teenage appetites are fueling the fast-food explosion. As McDonald's outlets appeared in urban neighborhoods, Brazilian teenagers used them for after-school snacks, while families had evening meals there. As an anthropologist could have predicted, the fast-food industry has not revolutionized Brazilian food and meal customs. Rather, McDonald's is succeeding because it has adapted to preexisting Brazilian cultural patterns.

The main contrast with North America is that the Brazilian evening meal is lighter. McDonald's now caters to the evening meal rather than to lunch. Once McDonald's realized that more money could be made by fitting in with, rather than trying to Americanize, Brazilian meal habits, it started aiming its advertising at that goal.

---

havior patterns. These are transmitted through *microenculturation,* the process by which people learn particular roles in a limited social system. The free-ranging nature of ethnography takes the anthropologist back and forth from worker to executive. Each is an individual with a personal viewpoint and a cultural creature whose perspective is, to some extent, shared with other members of a group. Applied anthropologists have acted as "cultural brokers," translating managers' goals or workers' concerns to the other group (see Ferraro 2006).

For business, key features of anthropology include (1) ethnography and observation as ways of gathering data, (2) cross-cultural expertise, and (3) focus on cultural diversity. An important business application of anthropology has to do with knowledge of how consumers use products. This chapter's "Appreciating Diversity" provides an example of this and shows how innovation succeeds best when it is culturally appropriate. Businesses hire anthropologists because of the importance of observation in natural settings and the focus on cultural diversity. Thus, Hallmark Cards has hired anthropologists to observe par-

ties, holidays, and celebrations of ethnic groups to improve its ability to design cards for targeted audiences. Anthropologists go into people's homes to see how they actually use products.

CAREERS AND ANTHROPOLOGY

Many college students find anthropology interesting and consider majoring in it. However, their parents or friends may discourage them by asking, "What kind of job are you going to get with an anthropology major?" The first step in answering this question is to consider the more general question, "What do you do with any college major?" The answer is "Not much, without a good bit of effort, thought, and planning." A survey of graduates of the literary college of the University of Michigan showed that few had jobs that were clearly linked to their majors. Medicine, law, and many other professions require advanced degrees. Although many colleges offer bachelor's degrees in engineering, business, accounting, and social work, master's degrees often are needed to get the best jobs in those fields. Anthropologists, too, need an advanced degree, almost always a Ph.D., to find gainful employment in academic, museum, or applied anthropology.

A broad college education, and even a major in anthropology, can be an excellent foundation for success in many fields. A recent survey of women executives showed that most had majored not in business but in the social sciences or humanities. Only after graduating did they study business, obtaining a master's degree in business administration. These executives felt that the breadth of their college educations had contributed to their business careers. Anthropology majors go on to medical, law, and business schools and find success in many professions that often have little explicit connection to anthropology.

Anthropology's breadth provides knowledge and an outlook on the world that are useful in many kinds of work. For example, an anthropology major combined with a master's degree in business is excellent preparation for work in international business. Breadth is anthropology's hallmark. Anthropologists study people biologically, culturally, socially, and linguistically, across time and space, in developed and underdeveloped nations, in simple and complex settings. Most colleges have anthropology courses that compare cultures and others that focus on particular world areas, such as Latin America, Asia, and Native North America. The knowledge of foreign areas acquired in such courses can be useful in many jobs. Anthropology's comparative outlook, its long-standing indigenous focus, and its appreciation of diverse lifestyles combine to provide an excellent foundation for overseas employment (see Omohundro 2001).

Even for work in North America, the focus on culture is valuable. Every day we hear about cultural differences and about social problems whose solutions require a multicultural viewpoint—an ability to recognize and reconcile ethnic differences. Government, schools, and private firms constantly deal with people from different social classes, ethnic groups, and tribal backgrounds. Physicians, attorneys, social workers, police officers, judges, teachers, and students can all do a better job if they understand social differences in a part of the world such as ours that is one of the most ethnically diverse in history.

Knowledge about the traditions and beliefs of the many social groups within a modern nation is important in planning and carrying out programs that affect those groups. Attention to social background and cultural categories helps ensure the welfare of affected ethnic groups, communities, and neighborhoods. Experience in planned social change—whether community organization in North America or economic development overseas—shows that a proper social study should be done before a project or policy is implemented. When local people want the change and it fits their lifestyle and traditions, it will be more successful, beneficial, and cost-effective. There will be not only a more humane but also a more economical solution to a real social problem.

People with anthropology backgrounds are doing well in many fields. Even if one's job has little or nothing to do with anthropology in a formal or obvious sense, a background in anthropology provides a useful orientation when we work with our fellow human beings. For most of us, this means every day of our lives.

Acing the COURSE

Summary

1. Anthropology has two dimensions: academic and applied. Applied anthropology uses anthropological perspectives, theory, methods, and data to identify, assess, and solve problems. Applied anthropologists have a range of employers. Examples are government agencies; development organizations; NGOs; tribal, ethnic, and interest groups; businesses; social services and educational agencies. Applied anthropologists come from all four subfields. Ethnography is one of applied anthropology's most valuable research tools. A systemic perspective recognizes that changes have multiple consequences, some unintended.

2. Development anthropology focuses on social issues in, and the cultural dimension of, economic development. Development projects typically promote cash employment and new technology at the expense of subsistence economies. Not all governments seek to increase equality and end poverty. Resistance by elites to reform is typical and hard to combat. At the same time, local peo-

ple rarely cooperate with projects requiring major and risky changes in their daily lives. Many projects seek to impose inappropriate property notions and incompatible social units on their intended beneficiaries. The best strategy for change is to base the social design for innovation on traditional social forms in each target area.

3. Anthropology and education researchers work in classrooms, homes, and other settings relevant to education. Such studies may lead to policy recommendations. Both academic and applied anthropologists study migration from rural areas to cities and across national boundaries. North America has become a popular arena for urban anthropological research on migration, ethnicity, poverty, and related topics. Although rural and urban are different social systems, there is cultural diffusion from one to the other.

4. Medical anthropology is the cross-cultural, biocultural study of health problems and conditions, disease, illness, disease theories, and health-care systems. Medical anthropology includes anthropologists from all four subfields and has theoretical (academic) and applied dimensions. In a given setting, the characteristic diseases reflect diet, population density, the economy, and social complexity. Native theories of illness may be personalistic, naturalistic, or emotionalistic. In applying anthropology to business, the key features are (1) ethnography and observation as ways of gathering data, (2) cross-cultural expertise, and (3) a focus on cultural diversity.

5. A broad college education, including anthropology and foreign-area courses, offers excellent background for many fields. Anthropology's comparative outlook and cultural relativism provide an excellent basis for overseas employment. Even for work in North America, a focus on culture and cultural diversity is valuable. Anthropology majors attend medical, law, and business schools and succeed in many fields, some of which have little explicit connection with anthropology.

Key Terms

anthropology and education 58
applied anthropology 50
curer 63
development anthropology 54
disease 61
equity, increased 55
health-care systems 62

illness 61
medical anthropology 61
overinnovation 56
scientific medicine 63
underdifferentiation 57
urban anthropology 59

Test Yourself!

MULTIPLE CHOICE

1. The use of anthropological data, perspectives, theory, and methods to identify, assess, and solve contemporary social problems is known as
   a. economic anthropology.
   b. conceptual anthropology.
   c. applied anthropology.
   d. sociobiology.
   e. participant observation.

2. What is one of the most valuable and distinctive tools of the applied anthropologist?
   a. knowledge of genetics
   b. familiarity with farming techniques
   c. statistical expertise
   d. teaching ability
   e. the ethnographic research method

3. Which of the following is an example of cultural resource management?
   a. any archaeological work done in an urban setting
   b. any archaeology implemented by the World Bank
   c. the emergency excavation and cataloging of a site that is about to be destroyed by a new highway
   d. archaeology sponsored by indigenous peoples
   e. a museum returning archaeological finds to the indigenous peoples whose ancestors produced the artifacts

4. What case does this chapter use to illustrate some of the dangers of the old applied anthropology?
   a. anthropologists' collaboration with NGOs in the 1920s
   b. the American Anthropological Association's drafting of the ethics guidelines
   c. Robert Redfield's work on the contrasts between urban and rural communities
   d. Malinowski's view that anthropologists should focus on Westernization and aid colonial regimes in their expansion
   e. the correlation between the increase of undergraduates interested in anthropology and the Vietnam War

5. Which of the following should *not* be one of the goals of an applied anthropological approach to urban programs?
   a. work with the community to ensure that the change is implemented correctly
   b. create a single universal policy to be applied to all urban communities
   c. identify key social groups in the urban context

d. translate the needs and desires of the community to funding agencies

e. elicit wishes from the target community

6. In 1992 a Los Angeles policeman shot and killed two unarmed Samoan brothers. When a judge dismissed charges against the officer, local Samoan leaders used the traditional matai system to calm angry youths and organize community meetings that eventually led to a just resolution. This example illustrates

a. how an immigrant community can draw from its traditions (in this case kin-based ethnic associations) to adapt to urban life.

b. that anthropology has little application in urban settings.

c. that non-Western immigrants have difficulty adjusting to modern city life, unless they give up their traditions.

d. how some traditional systems contribute disproportionately to homelessness.

e. that "clan mentality" is excessively violent in urban settings.

7. What is medical anthropology?

a. the field that has proved that indigenous peoples do not give up their indigenous ways, even in modern cities with technologically advanced health-care programs

b. the application of non-Western health knowledge to a troubled industrialized medical system

c. a growing field that considers the biocultural context and implications of disease and illness

d. typically in cooperation with pharmaceutical companies, a field that does market research on the use of health products around the world

e. the application of Western medicine to solve health problems around the world

8. What term refers most generally to beliefs, customs, specialists, and techniques aimed at ensuring health and curing illness?

a. a disease theory

b. medical anthropology

c. shamanism

d. health-care system

e. overinnovation

9. Why would companies designing and marketing products hire an anthropologist?

a. to pretend they care about customers' cultural preferences

b. to provide jobs for the growing number of unemployed academics

c. to make sure that they are abiding by the American Anthropological Association's code of ethics

d. to gain a better understanding of their customers in an increasingly multicultural world

e. to fulfill the requirements to become a nonprofit organization

10. What best describes the breadth of applied anthropology?

a. any use of the knowledge and/or techniques of the four subfields, with a special emphasis on forensics and biological anthropology, given the rise of deaths due to the so-called War on Terror

b. the use of anthropological knowledge to increase the size of anthropology departments nationwide

c. the hiring of anthropologists by the armed forces interested in improving secret intelligence

d. any use of the knowledge and/or techniques of the four subfields to identify, assess, and solve practical problems

e. the hiring practices of nongovernmental organizations interested in culture

FILL IN THE BLANK

1. _____ examines the sociocultural dimensions of economic development.

2. The term _____ describes the consequence of development programs that try to achieve too much change.

3. Increased _____ describes the goal of reducing absolute poverty, with a more even distribution of wealth.

4. Medical anthropologists use the term _____ to refer to a scientifically identified health threat caused by a known pathogen, while the term _____ refers to a condition of poor health perceived or felt by an individual.

5. A _____ is one who diagnoses and treats illness.

CRITICAL THINKING

1. This chapter uses the association between early anthropology and colonialism to illustrate some of the dangers of early applied anthropology. We also learn how American anthropologists studied Japanese and German "culture at a distance" in an attempt to predict the behavior of the enemies of the United States during World War II. Political and military conflicts with other nations and cultures continue today. What role could and/or should applied anthropologists play in these conflicts, if any?

2. What roles could applied anthropologists play in the design and implementation of development projects? Based on past experience and research on this topic, what could an applied anthropologist focus on avoiding and/or promoting?

3. This chapter describes some of the applications of anthropology in educational settings. Think back to your grade school or high school classroom. Were there any social issues that might have interested an anthropologist? Were there any problems that an applied anthropologist might have been able to solve? How so?

4. In Chapter 2 we learned how our culture—and cultural changes—affect how we perceive nature, human nature, and the "natural." Give examples of how medical anthropologists examine the shifting boundaries between culture and nature.

5. Indicate your career plans if known, and describe how you might apply the knowledge learned through introductory anthropology in your future vocation. If you have not yet chosen a career, pick one of the following: economist, engineer, diplomat, architect, or elementary schoolteacher. Why is it important to understand the culture and social organization of the people who will be affected by your work?

Chambers, E.
1985 *Applied Anthropology: A Practical Guide.* Upper Saddle River, NJ: Prentice Hall. How to do applied anthropology, by a leader in the field.

Ervin, A. M.
2005 *Applied Anthropology: Tools and Perspectives for Contemporary Practice,* 2nd ed. Boston: Pearson/ Allyn & Bacon. Up-to-date treatment of applied anthropology.

Ferraro, G. P.
2010 *The Cultural Dimension of International Business,* 6th ed. Upper Saddle River, NJ: Prentice Hall. How the theory and insights of cultural anthropology can influence the conduct of international business.

Joralemon, D.
2010 *Exploring Medical Anthropology,* 3rd ed. Boston: Pearson. Recent introduction to a growing field.

Omohundro, J. T.
2001 *Careers in Anthropology,* 2nd ed. Boston: McGraw-Hill. Offers some vocational guidance.

Spindler, G. D., ed.
2000 *Fifty Years of Anthropology and Education, 1950–2000: A Spindler Anthology.* Mahwah, NJ: Erlbaum. Survey of the field of educational anthropology by two prominent contributors, George and Louise Spindler.

Suggested Additional Readings

Go to our Online Learning Center website at **www.mhhe.com/kottak** for Internet exercises directly related to the content of this chapter.

Internet Exercises

What ethical
concerns and issues
affect physical
anthropology and
archaeology?

How do physical
anthropologists and
archaeologists
study the past?

How do
anthropologists
determine the dates
of sites, remains,
and evolutionary
events?

Excavations at Gran Dolina,
Atapuerca, Spain, where
hominin fossils and stone
tools date back 800,000 years.
Physical anthropologists and
archeologists typically
cooperate and collaborate as
members of field teams.

understanding OURSELVES

Take a quiz on Facebook, a *social* networking website that "helps you connect and share with the people in your life." Notice the many questions that get at how social (or not) you are. For example, do you prefer to: chill with friends, attend family events, take a nature hike, or be alone and concentrate on work or study? Anthropology studies people as members of groups—societies and cultures. Compared with our primate relatives, humans are unusually social. Even chimpanzees, our closest relatives, don't cooperate nearly as much as we do. There's reason to believe our urge to cooperate emerged early in human evolution. We'll never know all the causes of human sociality, and there is substantial cross-cultural variation in preferences for social contact versus solitude. In some societies sick people say "I want to be alone" while in others it's "Please don't leave me." Which would it be for you?

Regardless of cultural variation, a human appreciation of the social appears to be based in features of human anatomy—from the brain to the pelvis. Consider the female pelvis, whose evolution has been guided by these facts: (1) Humans walk upright; (2) babies are born with big brains; and (3) babies have to negotiate a complicated birth canal during childbirth. There are striking contrasts between humans and other primates in anatomy and in the birthing process. Nonhuman primates aren't bipedal; they use four limbs rather than two to move about. Compared with humans, they have smaller brains, simpler birth canals, and more independent infants.

Human babies, in moving through the birth canal, must make several turns. Their heads and shoulders, the two body parts with the largest dimensions, must be aligned consistently with the widest parts of that canal. Monkeys and apes don't have this problem; their birth canals have a constant shape. Also, the primate infant emerges facing forward. The mother can grasp it, even pull it straight to her nipple. Human babies are born facing backward, away from the mother, so she has trouble assisting in the birth. The presence of someone else (e.g., a midwife or doctor) to help with delivery reduces the mortality risk for human infants and their mothers.

Birthing assistance is almost universal among human societies. The characteristic human wish to have supportive, familiar people around at childbirth probably goes way back. Based on pelvic openings and estimated infant skull sizes of fossilized human precursors, anthropologists Karen Rosenberg and Wenda Trevathan surmise that such assistance may date back millions of years. Nonhuman primate mothers seek seclusion when they give birth and act as their own midwives in the birthing process. Not so humans, who are as social as ever. Midwives, obstetricians, baby showers are all manifestations of human sociality. The next time you encounter one, appreciate that such manifestations of human sociality have deep evolutionary roots.

ETHICS

This chapter is about how anthropologists (physical anthropologists and archaeologists) conduct scientific studies of the past. However, science, we cannot forget, exists in society and also in the context of law, values, and ethics. Anthropologists can't study things simply because they happen to be interesting or of value to science. Anthropologists are increasingly aware of the ethical and legal contexts in which their work unfolds. Problems involving contrasting systems of ethics and values are especially likely to occur when anthropologists work outside their country or culture of origin.

Anthropologists frequently do research outside their own nations. Physical anthropologists and archaeologists often work as members of international teams. These teams include researchers from several countries, including the *host country*—the place where the research takes place. In **paleoanthropology** (aka *human paleontology*)—the study of human evolution through the fossil record—physical anthropologists and archaeologists often work together. Much of our knowledge of early human evolution comes from Africa, where international collaboration is common (see Dalton 2006).

International work exposes physical anthropologists and archaeologists to varying national and cultural procedures, value systems, and ethical and legal codes. In such contexts, the American Anthropological Association (AAA) advises anthropologists to be guided by its Code of Ethics (see http://www.aaanet.org/committees/ethics/ethcode.htm). To gain permission and collaboration in the host country, anthropologists need to inform officials and colleagues there about the purpose, funding, and likely results of their research. They need to negotiate the matter of where the materials produced by the research will be analyzed and stored—in the host country or in the anthropologists' country—and for how long. To whom do research materials, such as bones, artifacts, and blood samples, belong? What kinds of restrictions will apply to their use? (See "Appreciating Anthropology.")

Recalling the discussion of IPR (Intellectual Property Rights) in Chapter 2, an international movement now advocates on behalf of indigenous peoples and formerly colonized areas. The archaeologist David Hurst Thomas (2000) faults some early anthropologists for robbing Native Americans not only of their history and dignity but also of their bodies. Thomas cites the aftermath of a massacre in 1864 of hundreds of Cheyenne Indians. After removal of the skin from their corpses, their skeletons were shipped to the Army Medical Museum in Washington, D.C. Their bones were exhibited at the Smithsonian and elsewhere (Thomas 2000; Rothstein 2006).

Lawsuits against museums by groups seeking the repatriation of remains and artifacts are now common. Peru, for instance, recently sued Yale University to recover objects removed during the exploration of Machu Picchu (an important Peruvian archaeological site) by Yale explorer Hiram Bingham in 1912. Native Australians have argued that images of native Australian fauna, such as the emu and kangaroo, belong exclusively to the Aboriginal people (Brown 2003). Some female curators in Australia have been banned from handling Aboriginal objects (Rothstein 2006). Michael F. Brown (2003) describes efforts by Hopi Indians to control and restrict historic photos of secret religious ceremonies. A Mennonite missionary, Heinrich R. Voth, who had been granted access to the rites, took the photos around 1900. The work of Frances Densmore, an ethnomusicologist who worked for the Smithsonian Institution's Bureau of American Ethnology, has been compared to stealing. In 1907 Densmore recorded some 3,000 wax cylinders of songs from 30 Indian tribes (Rothstein 2006).

Who should own and distribute what? How can the truth be known? These questions, like so many others of our time, have entered the domain of legal wrangling and formal adjudication. Inevitably, anthropology is involved when science confronts religion, whether Western or non-Western. According to Edward Rothstein (2006), when tribal leaders insist on the absolute truth of their traditions, regardless of evidence, it smacks of other forms of religious fundamentalism. An Umatilla elder, for example, defended their claim to Kennewick Man (see "Appreciating Anthropology") by insisting that Umatilla oral history goes back 10,000 years—a claim that neither the judge, nor most scientists, find convincing.

Along with the dubious or unethical actions of some anthropologists in the past, such debates can pit anthropologists against local communities. This is a serious dilemma for anthropologists, who usually rely on the goodwill and cooperation of local communities to do their work. It's crucial for anthropologists to establish and maintain proper relations between themselves as guests and the host nations and communities where they work. Government agencies, tribal councils, local boards, and nongovernmental organizations (NGOs) are some of the entities that may be in charge of protecting sites or granting permissions. The anthropologist will need their agreement and informed consent to conduct research. (**Informed consent** refers to people's agreement to take part in research after they have been fully informed about its purpose, nature, funding, procedures, and potential impact on them.) With living humans, informed consent is a necessity—for example, in obtaining biological samples, such as blood or urine. The research subjects must be told how

(text continues on p. 76)

paleoanthropology
Study of hominid, hominin, and human life through the fossil record.

informed consent
Agreement to take part in research, after being fully informed about it.

appreciating ANTHROPOLOGY

The Kennewick Conundrum

Many of these "Appreciating Anthropology" boxes describe how anthropologists work to represent or assist indigenous groups in various situations, for example, when disasters strike or when disputes arise with external agents. Sometimes, however, questions of ownership of and access to physical and archaeological remains place anthropologists and indigenous people in opposed camps. Not everyone appreciates anthropology all the time.

The Native American Graves Protection and Repatriation Act (NAGPRA) gives ownership of Native American remains to Indians (Native Americans). Hundreds of thousands of Indian remains are said to be in American museums. NAGPRA requires museums to return remains and artifacts to any tribe that requests them and can prove a "cultural affiliation" between itself and the remains or artifact. The 1996 discovery in Washington state (on federal land) of a skeleton dubbed "Kennewick Man" led to a legal case between anthropologists and five Indian tribes with ancestral homelands in the area where Kennewick Man was discovered. The anthropologists wanted to conduct a thorough scientific study of the 9,000-year-old skeleton. What might its anatomy and DNA reveal about the early settlement of the Americas? The Umatilla Indians and their allies in four other Indian Nations believe they have always occupied the region where the skeleton was found. In their view, Kennewick Man was an ancestor, whom they wanted to rebury with dignity and without contamination from scientific testing. On August 30, 2002, U.S. Magistrate Judge John Jelderks ruled that the Kennewick remains could be subjected to scientific study—the results of which are described below.

The bones, more than 350 pieces, were laid out on a bed of sand, a human jigsaw with ancient resonance. Head to toe, one of the oldest and best-preserved sets of remains ever discovered in North America was ready to give up its secrets.

After waiting 9 years to get a close look at Kennewick Man, the 9,000-year-old skeleton that was found on the banks of the Columbia River in 1996 and quickly became a fossil celebrity, a team of scientists spent 10 days this month examining it.

They looked at teeth, bones and plaque to determine how he lived, what he ate and how he died. They studied soil sedimentation and bone calcium for clues to whether he was ritually buried, or died in the place where he was found. They measured the skull, and produced a new model that looks vastly different from an earlier version.

And while they were cautious about announcing any sweeping conclusions regarding a set of remains that has already prompted much new thinking on the origins of the first Americans, the team members said the skeleton was proving to be even more of a scientific find than they had expected.

"I have looked at thousands of skeletons and this is one of the most intact, most fascinating, most important I have ever seen," said Douglas W. Owsley, a forensic anthropologist from the Smithsonian Institution's National Museum of Natural History. "It's the type of skeleton that comes along once in a lifetime."

He said the initial job of the team was to "listen to the bones," and the atmosphere, judging from the excitement of the scientists as they discussed their work, was electric.

Dr. Owsley said answers to the big questions about Kennewick Man—where he fits in the migratory patterns of early Americans, his age at the time of death, what type of culture he belonged to—will come in time, after future examinations.

"But based on what we've seen so far, this has exceeded my expectations," said Dr. Owsley, leader of the 11-member team and one of the scientists who sued the government for access to the bones. "This will continue to change and enhance our view of early Americans."

In preparation for the initial examination, the hip and skull were flown to Chicago, where they went through high-resolution CT scans, much more detailed than hospital scans. Those three-dimensional pictures were used to produce casts and replicas of the bones.

For now, the team has finished what amounts to a sort of autopsy, with added value. To that end the examination, which took place under extraordinary circumstances at the Burke Museum of Natural History and Culture at the University of Washington, was aided by a forensic anthropologist, Hugh Berryman of Nashville, who often assists in criminal investigations.

"This is real old C.S.I.," said Dr. Berryman, referring to the crime scene investigations that inspired the hit television shows.

The skeleton caused a furor from the time of discovery, making waves far beyond the academic realm, after an examining anthropologist said it appeared to have "Caucasoid" features. One reconstruction made Kennewick Man look like Patrick Stewart, the actor who played Capt. Jean-Luc Picard in *Star Trek: The Next Generation*.

American Indian tribes in the desert of the Columbia River Basin claimed the man as one of their own, calling him the Ancient One. The tribes planned to close off further examination and to bury the remains, in accordance with a federal law that says the government must turn over Indian remains to native groups that can claim affiliation with them.

A Seattle radio reporter examines plastic re-creations of Kennewick Man's pelvis and skull made using CT scans of the bones (left). At right is a clear image of the skull reconstruction.

A group of scientists sued, setting off a legal battle, while the bones remained in the custody of the Army Corps of Engineers.

In 2002, a federal magistrate, John Jelderks of Portland, Ore., ruled that there was little evidence to support the idea that Kennewick "is related to any identifiable group or culture, and the culture to which he belonged may have died out thousands of years ago."

The ruling, backed by a federal appeals court last year, cleared the way for the scientists to begin their study.

After being dragged into the culture wars, Kennewick Man remains a delicate subject—something that was clear in how the examining scientists parsed their descriptions of the skull at the end of 10 days of study.

David Hunt, an anthropologist at the Smithsonian who was instrumental in remodeling the skull, said he was sure there would be criticism of his reproduction, but he said it was based on the latest and most precise measurements of the head. He said it was accurate to within less than a hundredth of an inch.

Standing by the translucent model inside the Burke, Dr. Hunt said, "I see features that are similar to other Paleo Indians," referring to remains older than 7,000 years that have been found in North America.

But his colleague at the Smithsonian Dr. Owsley said that term was imprecise. "It should be Paleo-American," Dr. Owsley said. "These bones are very different from what you see in Native American skeletons."

Earlier, other anthropologists said that Kennewick Man most resembled the Ainu, aboriginal people from northern Japan. The scientists who examined Kennewick Man this month did not dispute that designation, but they said fresh DNA testing, carbon dating ,and further examinations would give them more accurate information.

Earlier DNA testing, done during the court cases, failed to turn up matches with contemporary cultures.

One key to Kennewick Man's life and times will be the stone spear point that was found embedded in his hip bone. Dr. Owsley said it

was clear that the man did not die of the projectile, which had been snapped off.

"This was a healed-over wound," he said.

But the spear point, which was made of basalt, will be the guiding clue as anthropologists seek a match to other cultures.

Kennewick Man's discovery brought fresh vigor to the discussion over how the Americas were inhabited. Earlier theories held that people crossed a land bridge between Siberia and Alaska. But Kennewick Man, along with a few other findings, suggested that there were waves of migration by different people, some possibly by boat. . . .

(continued from p. 73)

the samples will be collected, used, and identified, and about the potential costs and benefits to them. Informed consent is needed from anyone providing data or information, owning materials being studied, or otherwise having an interest that might be affected by the research.

The AAA Code says that anthropologists should not exploit individuals, groups, animals, or cultural or biological materials. They should recognize their debt to the people with whom they work and should reciprocate in appropriate ways. For example, it is highly appropriate for North American anthropologists working in another country to (1) include host country colleagues in their research planning and requests for funding, (2) establish truly collaborative relationships with those colleagues and their institutions before, during, and after field work, (3) include host country colleagues in dissemination, including publication, of the research results, and (4) ensure that something is "given back" to host country colleagues. For example, research equipment and technology are allowed to remain in the host country. Or funding is provided for host country colleagues to do research, attend international meetings, or visit foreign institutions—especially those where their international collaborators work.

Physical anthropologists and archaeologists, more often than cultural anthropologists, work as members of teams. Teams include host country collaborators; typically, they also include students—graduate and undergraduate. Training students in the value of long-term collaboration is one way of preserving opportunities for future field workers to follow current researchers to the field.

METHODS

As they study the past, physical anthropologists and archaeologists often collaborate. In the study of human evolution, the physical anthropologists focus on the fossil remains—and what they tell us

about ancient human biology. The archaeologists focus on the artifacts—and what they tell us about past cultures. Often their work proceeds jointly as they try to infer the relation between the physical features and cultural features of the remains they are examining. What are some of the methods and techniques used by physical anthropologists and archaeologists to study the past?

Multidisciplinary Approaches

Scientists from diverse fields, for example, soil science and **paleontology** (the study of ancient life through the fossil record), using varied techniques, collaborate with physical anthropologists and archaeologists in the study of sites where fossils and/or artifacts have been found. **Palynology,** the study of ancient plants through pollen samples taken from such sites, is used to determine a site's environment at the time of occupation. Physical anthropologists and archaeologists turn to physicists and chemists for help with dating techniques. Physical anthropologists representing a subspecialty known as *bioarchaeology* may complement the picture of ancient life at a particular site by examining human skeletons to reconstruct their physical traits, health status, and diet (Larsen 2000). Evidence for social status may endure in hard materials—bones, jewels, buildings—through the ages. During life, bone growth and stature are influenced by diet. Genetic differences aside, taller people are often that way because they eat better than shorter people do. Differences in the chemical composition of groups of bones at a site may help distinguish privileged nobles from less fortunate commoners. To reconstruct ancient biology and ways of life, physical anthropologists, archaeologists, and their collaborators analyze the remains of humans, plants, and animals, as well as such artifacts (manufactured items) as ceramics, tiles, casts, and metals.

Visible remains found at archaeological sites include animal and human bones, rocks, charcoal from ancient fires, remains in burials and storage pits, and worked stone and bone. Archaeologists

---

paleontology
Study of ancient life through the fossil record.

palynology
Study of ancient plants and environments through pollen samples.

These photos illustrate three kinds of microscopic evidence of plant characteristics, including domestication. The photo on the left shows a phytolith from domesticated squash, dated to 10,000 B.P., found in the soil at Ecuador's Vegas site. The middle photo shows reserve starch grains from the root of a modern manioc plant. The photo on the right shows maize pollen grain dated to 5,000 B.P. from the Kob site in Belize.

today also can draw on microscopic evidence, such as fossil pollen, phytoliths (plant crystals), and starch grains. A *phytolith* ("plant stone") is a microscopic crystal found in many plants, including wheat, maize, rice, beans, squash, manioc (cassava), and other early domesticates. Because phytoliths are inorganic and do not decay, they can reveal which plants were present at a given site even when no other plant remains survive. Phytoliths can be recovered from teeth, tools, containers, ritual objects, and garden plots. Starch grain analysis, another useful technique, recovers microfossils of food plants from the stone tools used to process them. Starch grains preserve well in areas, e.g., the humid tropics, where other organic remains typically decay. These grains have been recovered from stone cutting and grinding tools, attached to pottery fragments and basketry, and in human coprolites (ancient feces) (Bryant 2003, 2007a, 2007b).

Vaughn Bryant (2007b) presents a strong case for the importance of such microscopic evidence in studying the past. As one example, he cites Bonnie Williamson's analysis of Middle to Late Stone Age tools found at the Rose Cottage cave site in South Africa. Examining hundreds of stone tools, Williamson found that many of them still had residues stuck to their cutting edges. Contradicting the prevailing assumption that such tools were used mainly to hunt and butcher game animals, Williamson found that over 50 percent of all the residues were from plants. The blood (animal) residues on the tools were few compared with the starch grain evidence for plant usage. This study and a later one by Williamson suggested an important role for women (in gathering and processing plant foods) in early cultures. As we'll see in Chapter 10, microscopic techniques also have revealed that plant domestication first occurred not in the highlands of the New World (as previously was thought) but in the tropical lowlands. Starch grains recovered from soils in Oceania have been used to date the early settlement of the Polynesian islands (Bryant 2007b).

Physical anthropologists and archaeologists draw on low-tech as well as high-tech tools and methods. Small hand-held tools are used at excavation sites, where photos, maps, drawings, and measurements record where every find stands in relation to the site as a whole. Data are entered in field notebooks and computers.

Illustrating more sophisticated technology, sites, such as a system of ancient canals, may be located and defined from the air. Aerial photos (taken from airplanes) and satellite images are forms of **remote sensing** used in site location. For example, ancient buried footpaths visible not to the naked eye but only in satellite imagery have been studied in Costa Rica by University of Colorado and National Aeronautics and Space Administration (NASA) archaeologists (Scott 2002).

Up to six feet of volcanic ash, sediment, and vegetation had covered and obscured the footpaths. Images of the paths, some dating to 2,500 years ago, were first made in 1984 by a NASA aircraft using instruments that could "see" in the electromagnetic spectrum invisible to humans. In 2001 a commercial satellite took additional images of the buried footpaths, which showed up as thin red lines, reflecting the dense vegetation growing over them. The footpaths were dated on the basis of the stratigraphy (layers of geological deposits) of the Arenal volcano, which has erupted 10 times in the last 4,000 years.

Village life was established around Arenal some 4,000 years ago and endured through the Spanish Conquest some 500 years ago. Villagers periodically fled volcanic eruptions, returning when it was safe to resume farming of corn and beans in the nutrient-rich volcanic soil. According to team leader Payson Sheets of the University of Colorado, "they inhabited a very large region and seemed to avoid conflict, conquest and serious disease . . . They led comfortable lives, relying on an abundance of natural resources and a stable culture" (quoted in Scott 2002).

Excavation of the footpaths uncovered stone tools, pottery, and floors of ancient houses. The paths once linked a cemetery to a spring and quarries where

remote sensing
Use of aerial photos and satellite images to locate sites on the ground.

anthropology **ATLAS**

Map 1 documents deforestation by showing annual percent of forest loss worldwide, 1990–2000.

Archaeological sites can be located and defined from the air. These aerial photos show Peru's Nazca lines, which are visible only from the air. The lines form massive geometric and animal shapes. They probably were made between 900 B.C.E. and 600 C.E., perhaps as an astronomical calendar for agriculture.

anthropometry
Measurement of human body parts and dimensions.

bone biology
Study of bone as a biological tissue.

paleopathology
Study of disease and injury in skeletons from archaeological sites.

molecular anthropology
DNA comparisons used to determine evolutionary links and distances.

construction stone was mined. A primary goal of a 2002 field team led by Sheets was to understand ancient activities at the cemetery, where bodies were laid to rest in stone coffins. Funerary ceramics and meal vessels, plus cooking stones, indicate that people camped, cooked, and feasted at the cemetery for long time periods (Scott 2002).

Anthropologists work with geologists, geographers, and other scientists in using satellite images to find not just ancient footpaths, roads, canals, and irrigation systems but also patterns and sites of, say, flooding or deforestation, which can then be investigated on the ground. Anthropologists have used satellite imagery to identify, and then investigate on the ground, regions where deforestation is especially severe and where people and biodiversity, including nonhuman primates, may be at risk (Green and Sussman 1990; Kottak 1999b; Kottak, Gezon, and Green 1994).

Bone Biology

Physical anthropologists use various techniques to study nutrition, growth, and development in living and fossil organisms. **Anthropometry** is the measurement of human body parts and dimensions, including skeletal parts *(osteometry)*. Central to physical anthropology is **bone biology** (or skeletal biology)—the study of bone as a biological tissue, including its genetics; cell structure; growth, development, and decay; and patterns of movement *(biomechanics)* (Katzenberg and Saunders, eds. 2000). Within bone biology, *osteology* is the study of skeletal variation and its biological and social causes. Osteologists study such variables as stature in living and ancient populations (White and Folkens 2000). The interpretation of fossil remains relies on understanding the structure and function of the skeleton. **Paleopathology** is the study of disease and injury in skeletons from archaeological sites. Some forms of cancer leave evidence in the bone. Breast cancer, for example, may spread (metastasize) skeletally, leaving holes or lesions in bones and skulls. Certain infectious diseases (e.g., syphilis and tuberculosis) also mark bone, as do injuries and nutritional deficiencies (e.g., rickets, a vitamin D deficiency that deforms the bones).

In forensic anthropology, physical anthropologists and archaeologists work in a legal context, assisting coroners, medical examiners, and law enforcement agencies in recovering, analyzing, and identifying human remains and determining the cause of death (Nafte 2000; Prag and Neave 1997). For example, when unknown skeletal remains are found, the police and the Delaware Medical Examiner's Office call on University of Delaware physical anthropologist Karen Rosenberg to help identify the body. By examining the bones, Rosenberg can determine characteristics, such as the height, age, and sex of the person. She notes that "the police authorities always ask for the race of an unidentified person. But racial categories are, in part, culturally defined and in any case are not closed biological 'types.' Recently I identified a skeleton as possibly being Caucasian, then on subsequent examinations thought he might be African American. In actuality, when the identification was made, he turned out to be Hispanic" (Rosenberg, quoted in Moncure 1998).

Molecular Anthropology

Molecular anthropology uses genetic analysis (of DNA sequences) to assess evolutionary links. Through molecular comparison, evolutionary distance among living species, along with dates of most recent common ancestry, can be estimated. Molecular studies also have been used to assess and date the origins of modern humans and examine their relation to extinct human groups such as the Neandertals, which thrived in Europe between 130,000 and 28,000 years ago.

In 1997, ancient DNA was extracted from a Neandertal bone originally found in Germany's

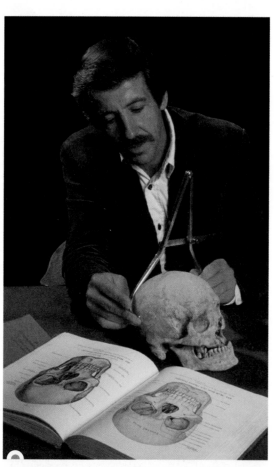

Joe Zias, a curator at Rockefeller Museum, measures an ancient skull. Anthropometry is done on skeletal remains from sites as well as on living people. Has anyone ever done anthropometry on you?

Neander Valley in 1856. This was the first time the DNA of a premodern human had been recovered. This DNA, from an upper arm bone (humerus), was compared with the DNA of modern humans. There were 27 differences between the Neandertal DNA and modern DNA; by contrast, samples of modern DNA show only 5 to 8 differences among the samples.

Molecular anthropologists examine relationships among ancient and contemporary populations and among species. It's well established, for example, that humans and chimpanzees have more than 98 percent of their DNA in common. Molecular anthropologists also reconstruct waves and patterns of migration and settlement. A *haplogroup* is a biological lineage (a large group of related people) defined by a specific cluster of genetic traits that occur together. Native Americans have four major haplogroups, which are also linked to East Asia. Among the many sorts of questions that molecular anthropology may answer: How can DNA sequences be used to trace migration routes during the peopling of North America or the Pacific?

We'll see later that molecular anthropologists also use "genetic clocks" to estimate divergence time (date of most recent common ancestry) among species (e.g., humans, chimps, and gorillas—five million to eight million years ago) and of various human groups (e.g., Neandertals and modern humans).

Paleoanthropology

Paleoanthropologists study early hominids and hominins through fossil remains. **Fossils** are remains (e.g., bones), traces, or impressions (e.g., footprints) of ancient life. Typically, a team composed of scientists, students, and local workers, representing diverse backgrounds and academic fields, participates in a paleoanthropological study. Such teams may include physical anthropologists, archaeologists, paleontologists, geologists, palynologists, paleoecologists, physicists, and chemists. Their common goal is to date and reconstruct the structure, behavior, and ecology of early hominins. The geologists and paleontologists may be called in during early surveying— perhaps using remote sensing—to locate potential early hominin sites. Paleontologists help locate fossil beds containing remains of animals that can be dated and that are known to have coexisted with hominins at various time periods. Good preservation of faunal remains may suggest that hominin fossils have survived as well. Sometimes it's impossible to date the hominin fossils and artifacts found at a given site by using the most accurate and direct (radiometric) methods. In this case, comparison of the faunal remains at that site with similar, but more securely dated, fauna at another site may suggest a date for those animal fossils and the hominins and artifacts associated with them (see Gugliotta 2005b).

Two adult femora. The top one is normal in size and shape. The bottom one shows swelling and a ragged surface resulting from the chronic bacterial infection called osteomyelitis. These thigh bones are from the Mississippian-period Hazel site in Arkansas.

fossils
Remains of ancient life.

Once potential sites have been identified, more intensive surveying begins. Archaeologists take over and search for hominin traces—bones or tools. Only hominins work rock to make tools and move rock fragments over long distances (see Watzman 2006). Some early hominin sites are strewn with thousands of tools. If a site is shown to be a hominin site, much more concentrated work begins. Financial support may come from private donations and government agencies. The research project usually is headed by an archaeologist or a physical anthropologist. The field crew will continue to survey and map the area and start searching carefully for bones and artifacts eroding out of the soil. Also, they will take pollen and soil samples for ecological analysis and rock samples for use in various dating techniques. Analysis is done in laboratories, where specimens are cleaned, sorted, labeled, and identified.

Consideration of the animal habitats suggested by the site (e.g., forest, woodland, or open country) will assist in the reconstruction of the paleoecological settings in which early hominins lived. Pollen samples help reveal diet. Sediments and other geological samples will suggest climatic conditions at the time of deposition. Sometimes fossils are embedded in rock, from which they must be extracted carefully. Once recovered and cleaned, fossils may be made into casts to permit wider study.

SURVEY AND EXCAVATION

Archaeologists and paleoanthropologists typically work in teams and across time and space. Typically, archaeologists, paleoanthropologists, and paleontologists combine both local and regional perspectives. The most common local approach is to excavate, or dig, through layers in a site. Regional approaches include remote sensing, for example, the discovery of ancient Costa Rican footpaths from space that was described earlier, and systematic survey on the ground.

appreciating DIVERSITY

Urge to Cooperate Appears to be Innate and Basic to Human Society and Culture

The study of ancient human, or hominin, diversity involves reconstructions based on collecting, analyzing, and dating physical and archaeological remains. Actual human behavior does not fossilize, except in the form of its material products—such as tools. Students of the human past use varied approaches to reconstruct how early abso lived. Archaeologists examine settlement sites and patterns to see how ancient humans grouped themselves. Anthropologists have approached the evolution of human cooperation, which is basic to group formation, society, and culture, in several ways, including comparative studies of nonhuman primates. Although cooperation is more valued in some cultures than in others, the urge to cooperate appears to be, to some extent at least, innate among humans—lodged in the human brain. Anthropologists generally assume that it took teamwork and altruism for our ancestors to

hunt large game, share food, and engage in other social activities, including raising children. A neural tendency to cooperate and to share would have conferred a survival advantage on our ancestors.

Using a novel method of scanning neural activity in people playing games, scientists have discovered that cooperation triggers pleasure in the brain.

Anthropologist James Rilling and five other scientists monitored brain activity in young women playing a laboratory game called Prisoner's Dilemma. Players select greedy or cooperative strategies as they pursue financial gain. The researchers found that the choice to cooperate stimulated areas of the brain associated with pleasure and reward-seeking behavior—the same areas that respond to desserts, pic-

tures of pretty faces, money, and cocaine (Angier 2002; Rilling et al. 2002). According to coauthor Gregory S. Berns, "In some ways, it says that we're wired to cooperate with each other" (quoted in Angier 2002).

The researchers studied 36 women age 20 to 60. Why women? Some previous studies had found male–male pairs to be more cooperative than female–female pairs, and others had found the opposite. Rilling and his colleagues didn't want to mix more cooperative and less cooperative pairs, and so they restricted their sample to one gender to control for possible differences in tendencies toward cooperation. The choice to use women rather than men was an arbitrary one.

In the experiment two women would meet each other briefly ahead of time. One was then placed in the scanner, while the other remained outside the scanning room. The two interacted by computer, playing about 20 rounds of the game. In every round, each player pressed a

Archaeologists recognize that sites aren't usually discrete and isolated but are parts of larger (regional) social systems, such as a series of villages that offered tribute to the same chief, or bands of hunter-gatherers who once got together for annual ceremonies at a particular place.

Let's examine some of the main techniques that anthropologists use to study patterns of behavior in ancient societies, based on their material remains. Archaeologists recover remains from a series of contexts, such as pits, sites, and regions. The archaeologist also integrates data about different social units of the past, such as the household, the band, the village, and the regional system.

Systematic Survey

Archaeologists and paleoanthropologists have two basic field-work strategies: systematic survey and excavation. **Systematic survey** provides a regional perspective by gathering information on settlement patterns over a large area. *Settlement pattern* refers to the distribution of sites within a particular region—how people grouped themselves and interacted spatially. (See this chapter's

"Appreciating Diversity" for more on the human urge to cooperate that underlies group formation and that has been basic to human adaptation and survival). Regional surveys reconstruct settlement patterns by addressing several questions: Where were sites located? How big were they? What kinds of buildings did they have? How old are the sites? Ideally, a systematic survey involves walking over the entire survey area and recording the location and size of all sites. From artifacts found on the surface, the surveyor estimates when each site was occupied. A full-coverage survey isn't always possible. The ground cover may be impenetrable (e.g., thick jungle), or certain parts of the survey area may be inaccessible. Permission to survey may be denied by landowners. Surveyors may have to rely on remote sensing to help locate and map sites.

With regional data, scientists can address many questions about the prehistoric communities that lived in a given area. Archaeologists use settlement pattern information to make population estimates and to assess levels of social complexity. Among hunter-gatherers and simple farmers, there are generally low numbers of people living button to indicate whether she would "cooperate" or "defect." Her answer would be shown on-screen to the other player. Money was awarded after each round. When one player defected and the other cooperated, the defector earned $3, and the cooperator earned nothing. When both cooperated, each earned $2. If both defected, each earned $1. Mutual cooperation from start to finish was a more profitable strategy, at $40 a woman, than complete mutual defection, which yielded only $20 to each woman.

If one woman got greedy, she took the risk that the cooperative strategy might fall apart and that both players would lose money as a result. Most of the time, the women cooperated. Even occasional defections weren't always fatal to an alliance, although the woman who had been "betrayed" once might be suspicious after that. Because of occasional defections, the average per-experiment take for the participants was in the range of $30.

The scans showed that two broad areas of the brain were activated by cooperation. Both areas are rich in neurons that respond to dopamine, a brain chemical that plays a well-known role in addictive behaviors. One is the anteroventral striatum in the midbrain, just above the spinal cord. Experiments have shown that when electrodes are placed in this area, rats will repeatedly press a bar to stimulate the electrodes. They apparently receive such pleasurable feedback that they will starve to death rather than stop pressing the bar (Angier 2002).

Another brain region activated during cooperation was the orbitofrontal cortex, just above the eyes. Besides being part of the reward-processing system, this area is involved in impulse control. According to Rilling, "Every round, you're confronted with the possibility of getting an extra dollar by defecting. The choice to cooperate requires impulse control" (quoted in Angier 2002).

In some cases, the woman in the scanner played a computer and knew her partner was a machine. In other tests, women played a computer but thought it was a human. The reward circuitry of the women was considerably less responsive when they knew they were playing against a computer. The thought of a human bond, not mere monetary gain, was the source of contentment. Also, the women were asked afterward to summarize their feelings during the games. They often described feeling good when they cooperated and expressed feelings of camaraderie toward their playing partners.

SOURCE: Information from N. Angier, "Why We're So Nice: We're Wired to Cooperate," *New York Times*, July 23, 2002. http://www.nytimes.com/2002/ 07/23/ health/psychology/23COOP.html; J. K. Rilling et al., "A Neural Basis for Social Cooperation," *Neuron* 35:395–405; J. K. Rilling, personal communication.

in small camp sites or hamlets with little variation in the architecture. Such sites are scattered fairly evenly across the landscape. With increasing social complexity, the settlement patterns become more elaborate. Population levels rise. Such social factors as trade and warfare have played a more important role in determining the location of sites (on hilltops, waterways, trade routes). In complex societies, a settlement hierarchy of sites emerges. Certain sites are larger, with greater architectural differentiation, than others. Large sites with specialized architecture (elite residences, temples, administrative buildings, meeting places) are generally interpreted as regional centers that exerted control over the smaller sites with less architectural differentiation.

Excavation

Archaeologists also gather information about the past by excavating sites. During an **excavation,** scientists recover remains by digging through the cultural and natural *stratigraphy*—the layers of deposits that make up a site. These layers, or strata, are used to establish the relative time order of the materials encountered during the dig. This relative chronology is based on the principle of *superposition:* In an undisturbed sequence of strata, the oldest layer is on the bottom. Each successive layer above is younger than the one below. Thus, artifacts and fossils from lower strata are older than those recovered from higher strata in the same deposit. This relative time ordering of material remains lies at the heart of archaeological, paleoanthropological, and paleontological research.

The archaeological and fossil records are so rich, and excavation is so labor-intensive and expensive, that nobody digs a site without a good reason. Sites are excavated because they are endangered, or because they answer specific research questions. Cultural resource management (CRM), as discussed in Chapter 3, focuses on managing the preservation of archaeological sites that are threatened by modern development. Many countries require archaeological impact studies before construction can take place. If a site is at risk and the development cannot be stopped, CRM archaeologists are called in to salvage what information they can from the site.

excavation
Digging through layers at a site.

Another reason a site may be chosen for excavation is that it is well suited to answer specific research questions. For example, an archaeologist studying the origins of agriculture wouldn't want to excavate a large, fortified hilltop city with a series of buildings dating to a period well after the first appearance of farming communities. Rather, he or she would look for a small hamlet-size site located on or near good farmland and near a water source. Such a site would have evidence of an early occupation dating to the period when farming communities first appeared in that region.

Before a site is excavated, it is mapped and surface collected so that the researchers can make an informed decision about where exactly to dig. The collecting of surface materials at a given site is similar to what is done over a much larger area in a regional survey. A grid is drawn to represent and subdivide the site. Then collection units, which are equal-size sections of the grid,

Many dating methods are based on the geological study of stratigraphy, the science that examines how earth sediments accumulate in layers known as *strata*, such as those shown here through archaeological excavations at Nippur, Iraq.

are marked off on the actual site. This grid enables the researchers to record the exact location of any artifact, fossil, or feature found at the site. By examining all the materials on the surface of the site, archaeologists can direct their excavations toward the areas of the site that are most likely to yield information that will address their research interests. Once an area is selected, digging begins, and the location of every artifact or feature is recorded in three dimensions.

Digging may be done according to arbitrary levels. Thus, starting from the surface, consistent amounts of soil (usually 4 to 8 feet [1.2 to 2.4 meters]) are systematically removed from the excavation unit. This technique of excavation is a quick way of digging, since everything within a certain depth is removed at once. This kind of excavation usually is done in test pits, which are used to determine how deep the deposits of a site go and to establish a rough chronology for that site.

An archaeologist drives in another stake for a large grid at an excavation site in Teotihuacán, Mexico. Such a grid enables the researchers to record the exact location of any artifact or feature found at the site.

This diver holds a ceramic vessel uncovered from a ship wrecked in 1025 A.D., in Turkey's Serce Liman Bay, Mugla province. Graduate degrees in underwater, or nautical, archaeology are available at East Carolina University, Florida State University, and Texas A&M University. This growing field of study investigates submerged sites, most often shipwrecks.

A more labor-intensive and refined way of excavating is to dig through the stratigraphy one layer at a time. The strata, which are separated by differences in color and texture, are studied one by one. This technique provides more information about the context of the artifacts, fossils, or features because the scientist works more slowly and in meaningful layers. A given 4-foot (1.2-meter) level may include within it a series of successive house floors, each with artifacts. If this deposit is excavated according to arbitrary levels, all the artifacts are mixed together. But if it is excavated according to the natural stratigraphy, with each house floor excavated separately, the resulting picture is much more detailed. The procedure here is for the archaeologist to remove and bag all the artifacts from each house floor before proceeding to the level below that one.

Any excavation recovers varied material remains, such as ceramics, stone artifacts (lithics), human and animal bones, and plant remains. Such remains may be small and fragmented. To increase the likelihood that small remains will be recovered, the soil is passed through screens. To recover very small remains, such as fish bones and carbonized plant remains, archaeologists use a technique called *flotation*. Soil samples are sorted using water and a series of very fine meshes. When the water dissolves the soil, the carbonized plant remains float to the top. The fish bones and other heavier remains sink to the bottom. Flotation requires considerable time and labor. This makes it inappropriate to use on all the soil that is excavated from a site. Flotation samples are taken from a limited number of deposits, such as house floors, trash pits, and hearths.

KINDS OF ARCHAEOLOGY

Archaeologists pursue diverse research topics, using a wide variety of methods. Experimental archaeologists try to replicate ancient techniques and processes (e.g., tool making) under controlled conditions. Historical archaeologists use written records as guides and supplements to archaeological research. They work with remains more recent—often much more recent—than the advent of writing. Colonial archaeologists, for instance, use historical records as guides to locate and excavate postcontact sites in North and South America,

living anthropology **VIDEOS**

The Necropolis of Pupput, www.mhhe.com/kottak

When ground was broken for a luxury hotel in Hammamet, Tunisia, no one expected to find remains of what has turned out to be the largest Roman necropolis (funerary site) in North Africa. This clip shows archaeologists excavating wood and bone to reconstruct burial rites in the ancient city of Pupput, where Romans lived for three centuries some 2,000 years ago. The Romans at Pupput had varied funerary practices, including burial and cremation. What happens to bone when it is heated to very high temperatures? What information can archaeologists draw from the study of preserved wood, such as that shown here? At the end of the day, what work do archaeologists do after they have finished that day's digging?

A swamp is a good place for bones to be buried in sediments. Here a female mammoth is represented sinking into the La Brea Tar Pits in Los Angeles, California. What other locales and conditions favor fossilization?

taphonomy
Study of processes affecting remains of dead animals.

and to verify or question written accounts. Classical archaeologists usually are affiliated with university departments of classics or the history of art, rather than with anthropology departments. These classical scholars focus on the literate civilizations of the Old World, such as Greece, Rome, and Egypt. Classical archaeologists are often as (or more) interested in art—styles of architecture and sculpture—as in the social, political, and economic variables that typically interest the anthropologist. Underwater archaeology is a growing field that investigates submerged sites, most often shipwrecks. Special techniques, including remotely operated vehicles like the one shown in the movie *Titanic,* are used, but divers also do underwater survey and excavation.

In Chapter 3, cultural resource management was discussed as a form of applied (or public) anthropology, as archaeologists apply their techniques of data gathering and analysis to manage sites that are threatened by development, public works, and road building. Some CRM archaeologists are *contract archaeologists,* who typically negotiate specific contracts (rather than applying for research grants) for their studies, which often must be done rapidly, for example, when an immediate threat to archaeological materials becomes known. Based on a membership study done for the Society of American Archaeology, Melinda Zeder (1997) found that 40 percent of the respondents worked as contract archaeologists—for firms in the private sector, state and federal agencies, and educational institutions. An equivalent 40 percent held academic positions.

DATING THE PAST

The archaeological record hasn't revealed every ancient society that has existed on earth; nor is the fossil record a representative sample of all the plants and animals that have ever lived. Some species and body parts are better represented than others are, for many reasons. Hard parts, such as bones and teeth, preserve better than do soft parts, such as flesh and skin. The chances of fossilization increase when remains are buried in a newly forming sediment, such as silt, gravel, or sand. Good places for bones to be buried in sediments include swamps, floodplains, river deltas, lakes, and caves. The species that inhabit such areas have a better chance to be preserved than do animals that live in other habitats. Fossilization is also favored in areas with volcanic ash, or in areas where rock fragments eroding from rising highlands are accumulating in valleys or lake basins. Once remains do get buried, chemical conditions must be right for fossilization to occur. If the sediment is too acidic, even bone and teeth will dissolve. The study of the processes that affect the remains of dead animals is called **taphonomy,** from the Greek *taphos,* which means "tomb." Such processes include scattering by carnivores and scavengers, distortion by various forces, and the possible fossilization of the remains.

The conditions under which fossils are found also influence the fossil record. For example, fossils are more likely to be uncovered through erosion in arid areas than in wet areas. Sparse vegetation allows wind to scour the landscape and uncover fossils. The fossil record has been accumulating longer and is more extensive in Europe than in Africa because civil engineering projects and fossil hunting have been going on longer in Europe than in Africa.

A world map showing where fossils have been found does not indicate the true range of ancient animals. Such a map tells us more about ancient geological activity, modern erosion, or recent human activity—such as paleontological research or road building. In considering the primate and hominin fossil records in later chapters, we'll see that different areas provide more abundant fossil evidence for particular time periods. This doesn't necessarily mean that primates or hominins were not living elsewhere at the same time. Nor does failure to find a fossil species in a particular place always mean that species did not live there. In the words of paleoanthropologist Christopher Stringer, "absence of evidence does not necessarily prove evidence of absence" (quoted in Gugliotta 2005*b*). What dating techniques are used to determine *when* animals that have been fossilized actually lived?

We've seen that *paleontology* is the study of ancient life through the fossil record and that *paleoanthropology* is the study of ancient humans and their immediate ancestors. These fields have established a time frame, or *chronology,* for the evolution of life. Scientists use several techniques to date fossils. These methods offer different degrees of precision and are applicable to different periods of the past.

Relative Dating

Chronology is established by assigning dates to geologic layers (strata) and to the material remains, such as fossils and artifacts, within them. Dating may be relative or absolute. **Relative dating** establishes a time frame in relation to other strata or materials rather than absolute dates in numbers. Many dating methods are based on the geological study of **stratigraphy,** the science that examines the ways in which earth sediments accumulate in layers known as *strata* (singular, *stratum*). As was noted previously, in an undisturbed sequence of strata, age increases with depth. Soil that erodes from a hillside into a valley covers, and is younger than, the soil deposited there previously. Stratigraphy permits relative dating. That is, the fossils in a given stratum are younger than those in the layers below and older than those in the layers above. We may not know the exact or absolute dates of the fossils, but we can place them in time relative to remains in other layers. Changing environmental forces, such as lava flows and the alternation of land and sea, cause different materials to be deposited in a given sequence of strata; this allows scientists to distinguish between the strata.

Remains of animals and plants that lived at the same time are found in the same stratum. When fossils are found within a stratigraphic sequence, scientists know their dates relative to fossils in other strata; this is relative dating. When fossils are found in a particular stratum, the associated geological features (such as frost patterning) and remains of particular plants and animals offer clues about the climate at the time of deposition.

Besides stratigraphic placement, another technique of relative dating is fluorine absorption analysis. Bones fossilizing in the same ground for the same length of time absorb the same proportion of fluorine from the local groundwater. Fluorine analysis uncovered a famous hoax involving the so-called Piltdown man, once considered an unusual and perplexing human ancestor (Winslow and Meyer 1983). The Piltdown "find," from England, turned out to be the jaw of a young orangutan attached to a *Homo sapiens* skull. Fluorine analysis showed the association to be false. The skull had much more flu-

orine than the jaw—impossible if they had come from the same individual and had been deposited in the same place at the same time. Someone had fabricated Piltdown man in an attempt to muddle the interpretation of the fossil record. (The attempt was partially successful—it did fool some scientists.)

Absolute Dating: Radiometric Techniques

The previous section reviewed relative dating based on stratigraphy and fluorine absorption analysis. Fossils also can be dated more precisely, with dates in numbers (**absolute dating**), by using several methods. For example, the ^{14}C, or carbon-14, technique is used to date organic remains. This is a *radiometric* technique (so called because it measures radioactive decay). ^{14}C is an unstable radioactive isotope of normal carbon, ^{12}C. Cosmic radiation entering the Earth's atmosphere produces ^{14}C, and plants take in ^{14}C as they absorb carbon dioxide. ^{14}C moves up the food chain as animals eat plants and as predators eat other animals.

With death, the absorption of ^{14}C stops. This unstable isotope starts to break down into nitrogen (^{14}N). It takes 5,730 years for half the ^{14}C to change to nitrogen; this is the half-life of ^{14}C. After another 5,730 years only one-quarter of the original ^{14}C will remain. After yet another 5,730 years only one-eighth will be left. By measuring the proportion of ^{14}C in organic material, scientists can determine a fossil's date of death, or the date of an ancient campfire. However, because the half-life of ^{14}C is short, this dating technique is less dependable for specimens older than 40,000 years than it is for more recent remains.

Fortunately, other radiometric dating techniques are available for earlier periods. One of the most widely used is the potassium-argon (K/A) technique. ^{40}K is a radioactive isotope of potassium that breaks down into argon-40, a gas. The half-life of ^{40}K is far longer than that of ^{14}C—1.3 *billion* years. With this method, the *older* the specimen, the more reliable the dating. Furthermore, whereas ^{14}C dating can be done only on organic remains, K/A dating can be used only for inorganic substances: rocks and minerals.

^{40}K in rocks gradually breaks down into argon-40. That gas is trapped in the rock until the rock is heated intensely (as with volcanic activity), at which point it may escape. When the rock cools, the breakdown of potassium into argon resumes. Dating is done by reheating the rock and measuring the escaping gas.

In Africa's Great Rift Valley, which runs down eastern Africa and in which early hominin fossils abound, past volcanic activity permits K/A dating. In studies of strata containing fossils, scientists find out how much argon has accumulated in rocks since they were last heated. They

absolute dating
Establishing dates in numbers or ranges of numbers.

relative dating
Establishing a time frame in relation to other strata or materials.

stratigraphy
Study of earth sediments deposited in demarcated layers (strata).

Early hominin fossils abound in Africa's Great Rift Valley, a vista of which is shown on the left. Past volcanic activity permits K/A dating in the Valley, including at Olduvai Gorge, Tanzania, whose centerpiece is the rock formation on the right.

dendrochronology
Tree-ring dating; a form of absolute dating.

anthropology **ATLAS**

See Map 4 for the locations of sites in the Great Rift Valley.

then determine, using the standard ^{40}K half-life, the date of that heating. Considering volcanic rocks at the top of a stratum with fossil remains, scientists establish that the fossils are *older than,* say, 1.8 million years. By dating the volcanic rocks below the fossil remains, they determine that the fossils are *younger than,* say, 2 million years. Thus, the age of the fossils and of associated material is set at between 2 million and 1.8 million years. Note that absolute dating is that in name only; it may give ranges of numbers rather than exact dates.

Many fossils were discovered before the advent of modern stratigraphy. Often we can no longer determine their original stratigraphic placement. Furthermore, fossils aren't always discovered in volcanic layers. Like ^{14}C dating, the K/A technique applies to a limited period of the fossil record. Because the half-life of ^{40}K is so long, the technique cannot be used with materials less than 500,000 years old.

Other radiometric dating techniques can be used to cross-check K/A dates, again by using minerals surrounding the fossils. One such method, *uranium series dating,* measures fission tracks produced during the decay of radioactive uranium (^{238}U) into lead. Two other radiometric techniques are especially useful for fossils that cannot be dated by ^{14}C (up to 40,000 B.P.) or ^{40}K (more than 500,000 B.P.). These methods are *thermoluminescence (TL)* and *electron spin resonance (ESR).* Both TL and ESR measure the electrons that are constantly being trapped in rocks and minerals (Shreeve 1992). Once a date is obtained for a rock found associated with a fossil, that date also can be applied to that fossil. The time spans

for which the various absolute dating techniques are applicable are summarized in Recap 4.1.

Absolute Dating: Dendrochronology

Dendrochronology, or tree-ring dating, is a method of absolute dating that is based on the study and comparison of patterns of tree-ring growth. Such dating is based on the fact that trees grow by adding one ring every year. Counting the rings reveals the age of a tree. Around 1920, A. E. Douglass of the University of Arizona noticed that wide rings grew during wet years, while narrow rings grew during dry years. Climatic variation, for example, moisture, cold, or drought, produces a distinctive year-by-year ring pattern—observable in all the trees that have grown over the same time period in a given region. Ring patterns of trees can be compared and matched ring for ring. Charting such patterns back through time, scientists can compare wood from ancient buildings to known tree-ring chronologies, match the ring patterns, and determine precisely—to the year—the age of the wood used by the historic or prehistoric builder (see Kuniholm 1995; Miller 2004; Schweingruber 1988).

Crossdating is the process of matching ring patterns among trees and assigning rings to specific calendar years. Both visual and statistical techniques are used to make the matches. Wood or charcoal samples from buildings and archaeological sites are crossdated with each other and with wood from living trees to extend the tree-ring chronology beyond the date of the oldest ring of the oldest living tree in the region (Kuniholm 1995).

TECHNIQUE	ABBREVIATION	MATERIALS DATED	EFFECTIVE TIME RANGE
Carbon-14	^{14}C	Organic materials	Up to 40,000 years
Potassium-argon	K/A and ^{40}K	Volcanic rock	Older than 500,000 years
Uranium series	^{238}U	Minerals	Between 1,000 and 1,000,000 years
Thermoluminescence	TL	Rocks and minerals	Between 5,000 and 1,000,000 years
Electron spin resonance	ESR	Rocks and minerals	Between 1,000 and 1,000,000 years
Dendrochronology	Dendro	Wood and charcoal	Up to 11,000 years

Tree-ring dating was first used in the southwestern United States for Native American communities and historical settlements. The bristlecone pine chronology of the American Southwest now exceeds 8,500 years (see Miller 2004). A northern European chronology based on the study of oak and pine is over 11,000 years long. The objective of Cornell University's Aegean dendrochronology project (www.arts.cornell.edu/dendro/), directed by Peter Kuniholm, is to build a master chronology for the region of the Aegean Sea and the Middle East. So far this project has established over 6,000 years of tree-ring chronologies covering much of the period back to about 9,500 years ago for portions of the Aegean, the Balkans, and the Middle East, including Turkey, Cyprus, Greece, parts of Bulgaria and the former Yugoslavia, and some of Italy. (There is one major gap, for which matches have not yet been made, between about 1,500 and 2,500 years ago.) The goal is to extend the chronology back to the period in which prehistoric peoples first started using significant amounts of wood in construction (Kuniholm 1995, 2004).

Dendrochronology is limited to certain tree species—those growing in a climate with marked seasons. The technique works with oak, pine, juniper, fir, boxwood, yew, spruce, and occasionally chestnut. Trees that can't be used include olive, willow, poplar, fruit trees, and cypress. The trees must come from the same region—thus having been exposed to the same environmental patterns—and long ring sequences are needed. Some junipers have as many as 918 rings. Some charcoal fragments from the Neolithic site of Çatal Hüyük in Turkey (see Chapter 11), where dendrochronology has established a 700-year sequence, have as many as 250 rings preserved (Kuniholm 1995). Not only do tree rings permit absolute dating; they also provide information about climatic patterns in specific regions.

Molecular Dating

In 1987, in a very influential study, researchers at the University of California at Berkeley used DNA analysis to advance the idea that anatomically modern humans (AMHs) arose fairly recently (around 130,000 years ago) in Africa. Rebecca Cann, Mark Stoneking, and Allan C. Wilson (1987) analyzed genetic traits in placentas donated by 147 women whose ancestors came from various parts of the world. The researchers focused on mitochondrial DNA (mtDNA), which only the mother contributes to the fertilized egg, and thus to the child. To establish a "genetic clock," the researchers measured the variation in mtDNA in their 147 tissue samples. They cut each sample into segments to compare with the others. By estimating the number of mutations (spontaneous changes in DNA) that had taken place in each sample

anthropology **ATLAS**

Map 8 shows the spread of agriculture during and after the Neolithic, in the Aegean region and elsewhere.

Dr. Tom Sweatnam of the University of Arizona displays tree samples from a Giant Sequoia. What kinds of information can you get from studying tree rings?

since its common origin with the 146 others, the researchers drew an evolutionary tree with the help of a computer. That tree started in Africa, then branched in two. One group stayed in Africa. The other one left Africa and carried its mtDNA to the rest of the world. Assuming a constant mutation rate (e.g., one mutation per 25,000 years), and counting the number of mutations in each sample, molecular anthropologists estimate the time period of the most recent common ancestor. Note that such estimates of divergence dates based on a constant mutation rate are not as widely accepted as are radiometric dating and dendrochronology.

Acing the COURSE

Summary

1. Because science exists in society and also in the context of law and ethics, anthropologists can't study things simply because they happen to be interesting or of scientific value. Anthropologists have obligations to their scholarly field, to the wider society and culture (including that of the host country), and to the human species, other species, and the environment. The anthropologist's primary ethical obligation is to the people, species, and materials he or she studies.

2. In studying the past, physical anthropologists and archaeologists pursue diverse research topics, using varied methods and often working together. At an archaeological site, physical anthropologists may complement the picture of ancient life by examining skeletons to reconstruct their physical traits, health status, and diet. Remote sensing may be used to locate ancient footpaths, roads, canals, and irrigation systems, which can then be investigated on the ground.

3. Central to physical anthropology is bone biology—the study of bone genetics; cell structure; growth, development, and decay; and patterns of movement. Osteologists study skeletal variation and its biological and social causes. Paleopathology is the study of disease and injury in skeletons from archaeological sites. Molecular anthropology uses genetic analysis (of DNA sequences) to assess evolutionary relationships among ancient and contemporary populations and among species.

4. Archaeologists, who typically work in teams and across time and space, combine both local (excavation) and regional (systematic survey) perspectives. Archaeologists use settlement pattern information to make population estimates and to assess levels of social complexity. Sites are excavated because they are in danger of being destroyed or because they address specific research interests. There are many kinds of archaeology, such as historical, classical, and underwater archaeology.

5. The fossil record is not a representative sample of all the plants and animals that ever lived. Hard parts, such as bones and teeth, preserve better than soft parts, such as flesh and skin, do. Anthropologists and paleontologists use stratigraphy and radiometric techniques to date fossils. Carbon-14 (^{14}C) dating is most effective with fossils less than 40,000 years old. Potassium-argon (K/A) dating can be used for fossils older than 500,000 years. ^{14}C dating is done on organic matter, whereas the K/A, ^{238}U, TL, and ESR dating techniques are used to analyze minerals that lie below and above fossils. Dendrochronology, or tree-ring dating, is a method of absolute dating based on the study and comparison of patterns of tree-ring growth. Molecular anthropology has also been used as a dating technique, based on the assumption of a constant mutation rate.

Key Terms

absolute dating 85
anthropometry 78
bone biology 78
dendrochronology 86

excavation 81
fossils 79
informed consent 73
molecular anthropology 78

MULTIPLE CHOICE

1. The American Anthropological Association's Code of Ethics is
   a. designed to protect anthropologists who conduct fieldwork in remote places and are subject to potentially hazardous working conditions.
   b. designed to ensure that anthropologists are aware of their obligations to the field of anthropology, to the host communities that allow them to conduct their research, and to society in general.
   c. applicable only to research being conducted in the United States.
   d. mostly lip service, as most researchers disregard most of its main points.
   e. too broad and too encompassing for most anthropologists to find it useful.

2. All of the following are true about informed consent *except* that
   a. it refers to people's agreement to take part in research, after they have been fully informed about its purpose, nature, procedures, and potential impact on them.
   b. it is required when working with living humans.
   c. it is consistent with the American Anthropological Association's Code of Ethics concern that anthropologists should not exploit individuals.
   d. it must be obtained from anyone providing information or data.
   e. it is applicable only to research being conducted in the United States.

3. In this chapter, what is the main point of describing the University of Colorado and NASA archaeological research project in Costa Rica?
   a. to illustrate how scientists from diverse fields work as a team, often with technologically sophisticated tools, to make sense of the human past
   b. to criticize collaborative efforts between universities and governmental agencies that impose their will on Latin American countries
   c. to illustrate the use of remote sensing when stratigraphic methods cannot be used
   d. to show the impact of the downsizing of NASA

   e. to emphasize the fact that the United States government supports anthropological research

4. Fossil pollen, phytoliths, and starch grains are all examples of
   a. microscopic evidence that archaeologists are using increasingly to study the past.
   b. palynology.
   c. remote sensing techniques increasingly used in multidisciplinary projects.
   d. taphonomic processes.
   e. dendrochronological techniques used to study agricultural remains.

5. What is anthropometry?
   a. the measurement of human linguistic variability
   b. the use of remote sensing to measure the carrying capacity of human populations in a given region
   c. the measurement of human body parts and dimensions
   d. the study of ancient plants used by humans through pollen samples collected from archaeological sites
   e. the study of the ways in which cultural sediments accumulate over time

6. What do molecular anthropologists study?
   a. human body size and dimensions, using an extensive series of measurements of the human form
   b. the relationships among ancient and contemporary populations and among species using DNA comparisons
   c. the biological and geological processes by which dead animals become fossils
   d. the diffusion of languages between communities
   e. how prestige is passed between generations

7. What are the two major components of fieldwork in archaeological anthropology?
   a. the genealogical method and excavation
   b. excavation and participant observation
   c. systematic survey and the emic perspective
   d. systematic survey and excavation
   e. stratigraphy and taphonomy

8. Why do archaeologists use relative dating?
   a. to create precise dates in numbers
   b. to create a relative chronology for the materials uncovered during excavation

c. to overlay various maps of a site to produce a composite map
d. to superimpose motifs from one site onto designs found at another site
e. to locate sites during a systematic survey

9. What does the principle of superposition state?
   a. In an undisturbed sequence of strata, the oldest layer is on the top.
   b. In an undisturbed sequence of strata, the youngest layer is on the bottom.
   c. In an undisturbed sequence of strata, the youngest layer is the deepest in the sequence.
   d. In an undisturbed sequence of strata, the oldest layer is the shallowest in the sequence.
   e. In an undisturbed sequence of strata, the oldest layer is on the bottom.

10. What point is this chapter emphasizing when quoting paleoanthropologist Christopher Stringer stating that, "absence of evidence does not necessarily prove evidence of absence?"
    a. that taphonomy is not a true science because it lacks accuracy
    b. that the fields of paleontology and paleoanthropology have established a chronology of the evolution of life
    c. that even paleontology and paleoanthropology are humanistic disciplines
    d. that the failure to find a fossil species in a particular place does not necessarily mean that it did not live there
    e. that the fossil record is a representative sample of all the plants and animals that ever lived

FILL IN THE BLANK

1. _____ refers to people's agreement to take part in research after they have been fully informed about its purpose, nature, funding, procedures, and potential impact on them.

2. _____ are microscopic crystals found in many plants. Because they are inorganic and do not decay, they can be a great source of information for archaeologists studying sites in which the plants were present.

3. _____ is the study of disease and injury in skeletons from archaeological sites.

4. _____ are remains (e.g., bones), traces, or impressions (e.g., footprints) of ancient life.

5. Many dating methods are based on the geological study of _____, the science that examines the ways in which earth sediments accumulate in layers known as strata.

CRITICAL THINKING

1. This chapter is about how physical anthropologists and archaeologists conduct scientific studies of the past. Science, however, exists in society and also in the context of law, values, and ethics. What are some examples of how this fact affects the work of physical anthropologists and archaeologists?

2. Along with the dubious actions of some anthropologists in the past (recall anthropology's previous cooperation with colonial authorities), debates such as the one about the proper handling of the Kennewick Man (see this chapter's "Appreciating Anthropology") can pit anthropologists against local communities. What is this debate about? Why do cases like this one pose a serious dilemma for anthropologists? Can you think of other cases that would pose similar dilemmas?

3. As this chapter illustrates, many of the ethical issues that affect the work of anthropologists have some legal dimension, whether in their own country, in another country, or even among several nations. Have you thought about law as a possible future career? (If not, think of a friend that has!) Write a convincing argument of why anthropology could be a valuable tool for a lawyer.

4. Imagine yourself to be a physical anthropologist working as part of an international team at an African site where early human fossils have been found. What other academic disciplines might be represented on your team? What kinds of jobs would there be for team members, and where would the members be recruited? What might happen to the fossils and other materials that were recovered? Who would be the authors of the scientific papers describing any discovery made by the team?

5. How can fossils be dated when radiometric dating is impossible?

Feder, K. L.
    2008 *Linking to the Past: A Brief Introduction to Archaeology,* 2nd ed. New York: Oxford University Press. Includes a discussion of field methods in archaeology.

Nafte, M.
    2009 *Flesh and Bone: An Introduction to Forensic Anthropology,* 2nd ed. Durham, NC: Carolina Academic Press. Methods and procedures, avoiding technical terminology.

Park, M. A.
    2010 *Biological Anthropology,* 6th ed. Boston: McGraw-Hill. A concise introduction, with a focus on scientific inquiry.

Renfrew, C., and P. Bahn
    2007 *Archaeology Essentials: Theories, Methods, and Practice.* London: Thames and Hudson.

Most useful treatment of methods in archaeological anthropology.

Turnbaugh, W. A., R. Jurmain, L. Kilgore, and H. Nelson
    2002 *Understanding Physical Anthropology and Archaeology,* 8th ed. Belmont, CA: Wadsworth. Introduction to these two subfields, with a discussion of methods in each.

White, T. D., and P. A. Folkens
    2000 *Human Osteology,* 2nd ed. San Diego: Academic Press. Includes case studies and discussion of molecular osteology, with life-size photos of skeletal parts.

Suggested Additional Readings

Go to our Online Learning Center website at **www.mhhe.com/kottak** for Internet exercises directly related to the content of this chapter.

Internet Exercises

What is evolution, and how does it occur?

How does heredity work, and how is it studied?

What forces contribute to genetic evolution?

Famed biologist E.O. Wilson enjoys a Darwin exhibition in New York's American Museum of Natural History. Wilson has been an effective defender of Darwinian evolution against attacks by nonscientists. In science, evolution is both a theory— that is, an interpretive framework—and a fact.

understanding OURSELVES

H ey, it's all in the genes." We routinely use assumptions about genetic determination to explain, say, why tall parents have tall kids or why obesity runs in families. But just how much do genes really influence our bodies? The genetics behind some physical traits, e.g., blood types, are clear, but the genetic roots of other traits are less so. For example, can you crease or fold your tongue by raising its sides? (See the photo below.) Some people easily can; some people never can; some people who never thought they could can after practicing. An apparent genetic limitation turns out to be more plastic.

Human biology is plastic, but only to a degree. If you're born with blood group O, you've got it for life. The same is true for hemophilia and sickle cell anemia. Fortunately, cultural (medical) solutions now exist for many genetic disorders. Can you appreciate in yourself or your family any genetic condition for which there has been a cultural (e.g., medical) intervention? Although modern medical advances usually are viewed favorably, some people worry that culture may be intervening too much with intrinsic biological features. Some members of the hearing-impaired community, for example, spurn cochlear implants, viewing them as a threat to a deaf subculture that they hold dear. Plastic surgery, genetic screening, and the possibility of genetic engineering of infants (e.g. "designer babies") concern those who imagine a future in which physical "perfection" might reduce human diversity and increase socioeconomic inequality.

Even as our culture struggles with issues of medically manipulated biological plasticity, many people still question the long-term plasticity of the human genome, a process known as evolution. Most basically, evolution is the idea that all living organisms come from ancestors that were different in some way. The

Tongue rolling—a genetic trait, at least partially. Some members of this family seem to be better at it than others are.

oft-heard statement "evolution is only a theory" suggests to the nonscientist that evolution hasn't been proven. Scientists, however, use the term *theory* differently—to refer to an interpretive framework that helps us understand the natural world. In science, evolution is both a theory and a fact. As a *scientific theory* evolution is a central organizing principle of modern biology and anthropology. Evolution also is a fact. The following are examples of evolutionary facts: (1) All living forms come from older or previous living forms. (2) Birds arose from nonbirds; humans arose from nonhumans, and neither birds nor humans existed 250 million years ago. (3) Major ancient life forms, e.g., dinosaurs, are no longer around. (4) New life forms, such as viruses, are evolving right now. (5) Natural processes help us understand the origins and history of plants and animals, including humans and diseases.

What alternatives to evolution have you heard about? Are those scientific theories? Should they be taught in science classes? Do people who reject evolution still get flu shots?

EVOLUTION

Compared with other animals, humans have uniquely varied ways—cultural and biological—of adapting to environmental stresses. Exemplifying cultural adaptation, we manipulate our artifacts and behavior in response to environmental conditions. Contemporary North Americans turn up thermostats or travel to Florida in the winter. We turn on fire hydrants, swim, or ride in air-conditioned cars from New York City to Maine to escape the summer's heat. Although such reliance on culture has increased in the course of human evolution, people haven't stopped adapting biologically. As in other species, human populations adapt genetically in response to environmental forces, and individuals react physiologically to stresses. Thus, when we work in the midday sun, sweating occurs spontaneously, cooling the skin and reducing the temperature of subsurface blood vessels.

We are ready now for a more detailed look at the principles that determine human biological adaptation, variation, and change.

During the 18th century, many scholars became interested in biological diversity, human origins, and our position within the classification of plants and animals. At that time, the commonly accepted explanation for the origin of species came from Genesis, the first book of the Bible: God had created all life during six days of Creation. According to *creationism*, biological similarities and differences originated at the Creation. Characteristics of life forms were seen as immutable; they could not change. Through calculations based on genealogies in the Bible, the biblical scholars James Ussher and John Lightfoot even claimed to trace the Creation to a very specific time: October 23, 4004 B.C., at 9 A.M.

Carolus Linnaeus (1707–1778) developed the first comprehensive and still influential classification, or taxonomy, of plants and animals. He grouped life forms on the basis of similarities and differences in their physical characteristics. He used traits such as the presence of a backbone to distinguish vertebrates from invertebrates and the presence of mammary glands to distinguish mammals from birds. Linnaeus viewed the differences between life forms as part of the Creator's orderly plan. Biological similarities and differences, he thought, had been established at the time of Creation and had not changed.

Fossil discoveries during the 18th and 19th centuries raised doubts about creationism. Fossils showed that different kinds of life had once existed. If all life had originated at the same time, why weren't ancient species still around? Why

According to creationism, all life originated during the six days of Creation described in the Bible. Catastrophism proposed that fires and floods, including the biblical deluge involving Noah's ark (depicted in this painting by the American artist Edward Hicks), destroyed certain species. Note that creationism is not a scientific theory.

weren't contemporary plants and animals found in the fossil record? A modified explanation combining creationism with *catastrophism* arose to replace the original doctrine. In this view, fires, floods, and other catastrophes, including the biblical flood involving Noah's ark, had destroyed ancient species. After each destructive event, God had created again, leading to contemporary species. How did the catastrophists explain certain clear similarities between fossils and modern animals? They argued that some ancient species had managed to survive in isolated areas. For example, after the biblical flood, the progeny of the animals saved on Noah's ark spread throughout the world. (This chapter's "Appreciating Diversity" discusses a recent approach called "Intelligent Design," which has been judged to be a secular repackaging of old-time "creationism.")

Theory and Fact

The alternative to creationism and catastrophism was *transformism,* also called **evolution.** Evolutionists believe that species arise from others through a long and gradual process of transformation, or descent with modification. Charles Darwin became the best known of the evolutionists. However, he was influenced by earlier scholars, including his own grandfather. In a book called *Zoonomia* published in 1794, Erasmus Darwin had proclaimed the common ancestry of all animal species.

Charles Darwin also was influenced by Sir Charles Lyell, the father of geology. During Darwin's famous voyage to South America aboard the *Beagle,* he read Lyell's influential book *Principles of Geology* (1837/1969), which exposed him to Lyell's principle of **uniformitarianism.** Uniformitarianism states that the present is the key to the past. Explanations for past events should be sought in the long-term action of ordinary forces that still operate today. Thus, natural forces (rainfall, soil deposition, earthquakes, and volcanic action) gradually have built and modified geological features such as mountain ranges. The earth's structure has been transformed gradually through natural forces operating for millions of years (see Weiner 1994).

Uniformitarianism was a necessary building block for evolutionary theory. It cast serious doubt on the belief that the world was only 6,000 years old. It would take much longer for such ordinary forces as rain and wind to produce major geological changes. The longer time span also allowed enough time for the biological changes that fossil discoveries were revealing. Darwin applied the ideas of uniformitarianism and long-term transformation to living things. He argued that all life forms are ultimately related and that the number of species has increased over time. (For more on science, evolution, and creationism, see Futuyma 1995; Gould 1999; Wilson 2002.)

Charles Darwin provided a theoretical framework for understanding evolution. He offered natural selection as a powerful evolutionary mechanism that could explain the origin of species, biological diversity, and similarities among related life forms. Darwin proposed a *theory of evolution* in the strict sense. A *theory* is a set of ideas formulated (by reasoning from known facts) to explain something. The main value of a theory is to promote new understanding. A theory suggests patterns, connections, and relationships that may be confirmed by new research. The *fact* of evolution (that evolution has occurred) was known earlier, for example, by Erasmus Darwin. The *theory* of evolution, through natural selection (*how* evolution occurred), was Darwin's major contribution. Actually, natural selection wasn't Darwin's unique discovery. Working independently, the naturalist Alfred Russel Wallace had reached a similar conclusion (Shermer 2002). In a joint paper read to London's Linnaean Society in 1858, Darwin and Wallace made their discovery public. Darwin's book *On the Origin of Species* (1859/1958) offered much fuller documentation.

Natural selection is the process by which the forms most fit to survive and reproduce in a given environment do so in greater numbers than others in the same population. More than survival of the fittest, natural selection is differential reproductive success. Natural selection is a natural process that leads to a result. Natural selection operates when there is competition for strategic resources (those necessary for life) such as food and space between members of the population. There is also the matter of finding mates. You can win the competition for food and space and have no mate and thus have no impact on the future of the species. For natural selection to work on a particular population, there must be variety within that population, as there always is.

 living anthropology **VIDEOS**

Theory of Evolution and Darwin, www.mhhe.com/kottak

Charles Darwin introduced the ideas of natural selection and survival of the fittest to explain evolution. Fossils offer one line of evidence for evolutionary changes. Observation of differences and similarities among living species provides additional support. The variety Darwin observed among domestic birds (English pigeons) and wild birds (finches in the Galápagos Islands) led him to believe that comparable processes of selection were at work. In the first case the selection was artificial, the result of animal domestication and breeding experiments. In the second case the selection was natural, having to do with impersonal environmental forces. For scientists, what is a "theory"?

evolution
Transformation of species; descent with modification.

natural selection
Selection of favored forms through differential reproductive success.

uniformitarianism
Natural forces at work today also explain past events.

The giraffe's neck can illustrate how natural selection works on variety within a population. In any group of giraffes, there is always variation in neck length. When food is adequate, the animals have no problem feeding themselves. But when there is pressure on strategic resources, so that dietary foliage is not as abundant as usual, giraffes with longer necks have an advantage. They can feed off the higher branches. If this feeding advantage permits longer-necked giraffes to survive and reproduce even slightly more effectively than shorter-necked ones, giraffes with longer necks will transmit more of their genetic material to future generations than will giraffes with shorter necks.

An incorrect alternative to this (Darwinian) explanation would be the inheritance of acquired characteristics. That is the idea that in each generation, individual giraffes strain their necks to reach just a bit higher. This straining somehow modifies their genetic material. Over generations of strain, the average neck gradually gets longer through the accumulation of small increments of neck length acquired during the lifetime of each generation of giraffes. This is not how evolution works. If it did work in this way, weight lifters could expect to produce especially muscular babies. Workouts that promise no gain without the pain apply to the physical development of individuals, not species. Instead, evolution works as the process of natural selection takes advantage of the variety that is already present in a population. That's how giraffes got their necks.

Evolution through natural selection continues today. For example, in human populations there is differential resistance to disease, as we'll see in the discussion of sickle-cell anemia below. One classic recent example of natural selection is the peppered moth, which can be light or dark (in either case with black speckles, thus the name "peppered"). A change in this species illustrates recent natural selection (in our own industrial age) through what has been called *industrial melanism*. Great Britain's industrialization changed the environment to favor darker moths (those with more melanin) rather than the lighter-colored ones that were favored previously. During the 1800s industrial pollution increased; soot coated buildings and trees, turning them a darker color. The previously typical peppered moth, which had a light color, now stood out against the dark backgrounds of sooty buildings and trees. Such light-colored moths were easily visible to their predators. Through mutations (see p. 101), a new strain of peppered moth, with a darker phenotype, was favored. Because these darker moths were fitter—that is, harder to detect—in polluted environments, they survived and reproduced in greater numbers than lighter moths did. We see how natural selection may favor darker moths in polluted environments and lighter-colored moths in nonindustrial or less polluted environments

A speckled peppered moth and a black one alight on a soot-blackened tree. Which phenotype is favored in this environment? How could this adaptive advantage change?

because of their variant abilities to merge in with their environmental colors and thus avoid predators.

Evolutionary theory is used to explain. Remember from Chapter 1 that the goal of science is to increase understanding through explanation: showing how and why the thing (or class of things) to be understood (e.g., the variation within species, the geographic distribution of species, the fossil record) depends on other things. Explanations rely on associations and theories. An association is an observed relationship between two or more variables, such as the length of a giraffe's neck and the number of its offspring, or an increase in the frequency of dark moths as industrial pollution spreads. A theory is more general, suggesting or implying associations and attempting to explain them. A thing or event—for example, the giraffe's long neck—is explained if it illustrates a general principle or association, such as the concept of adaptive advantage. The truth of a scientific statement (e.g., evolution occurs because of differential reproductive success due to variation within the population) is confirmed by repeated observations. (See "Appreciating Diversity" for a discussion of differences between evolutionary theory and intelligent design.)

GENETICS

Charles Darwin recognized that for natural selection to operate, there must be variety in the population undergoing selection. Documenting and explaining such variety among humans—human biological diversity—is one of anthropology's major concerns. Genetics, a science that emerged after Darwin, helps us understand the causes of biological

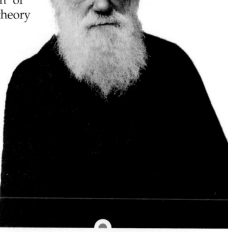

Charles Darwin, around 1880.

appreciating

DIVERSITY

Intelligent Design versus Evolutionary Theory

Evolutionary theory is basic to understanding and appreciating human diversity. Contemporary humans, members of the species *Homo sapiens* represent one branch in the tree of life. Scientists, who seek natural rather than supernatural explanations, use evolutionary theory to explain how humans evolved from ancestors that were not human. Evolutionary theory also is used to explain biological diversity among contemporary and recent human beings. "Intelligent design" (ID), which is not a scientific theory, no longer can be mentioned in biology classes in a Pennsylvania public school district, a federal district judge ruled on December 20, 2005. Dover Area School Board members had violated the Constitution when they ordered that its biology curriculum had to include the notion that life on earth was produced by an unspecified intelligent designer.

Administrators had been required to read a statement in biology classes asserting that evolution was a theory, not a fact; that the evidence for evolution had gaps; and that ID offered an alternative explanation laid out in a book (purchased by church funds) in the school library. According to the judge (a Republican appointed by President George W. Bush), that statement amounted to an endorsement of religion. It could cause students to doubt a generally accepted scientific theory by presenting a religious alternative masquerading as a scientific theory (see *New York Times* 2005, p. A32).

The Dover school board policy, adopted in October 2004, was believed to have been the first of its kind in the United States. Their attorneys claimed that school board members were seeking to improve science education by exposing students to alternatives to Charles Darwin's theory that evolution occurs through natural selection. ID proponents argued that evolutionary theory can't fully explain complex life forms. Their opponents contended that ID amounts to a secular repackaging of creationism, which courts have ruled cannot be taught in public schools. The Pennsylvania judge agreed: The secular purposes claimed by the board were a pretext for the board's real purpose—to promote religion in public schools.

ID advocates have since been voted off the Dover school board. Although the new board planned to remove ID from science classes, interested students could still learn about ID in an elective course on comparative religion. ID did not belong in the *science* curriculum, the judge ruled, because it is "a religious view, a mere relabeling of creationism and not a scientific theory" (*New York Times* 2005, p. A32).

The ID movement asserts that life forms are too complex to have been formed by natural processes and must have been created by a higher intelligence. The fundamental claim of

---

population genetics
Field that studies genetics of breeding populations.

dominant
Allele that masks another allele in a heterozygote.

recessive
Genetic trait masked by a dominant trait.

chromosomes
Paired lengths of DNA, composed of multiple genes.

gene
Place (locus) on a chromosome that determines a particular trait.

allele
A variant of a particular gene.

variation. We now know that DNA (deoxyribonucleic acid) molecules make up genes and chromosomes, which are the basic hereditary units. Biochemical changes (mutations) in DNA provide much of the variety on which natural selection operates. Through sexual reproduction, recombination of the genetic traits of mother and father in each generation leads to new arrangements of the hereditary units received from each parent. Such genetic recombination also adds variety on which natural selection may operate.

Mendelian genetics studies the ways in which chromosomes transmit genes across the generations. *Biochemical genetics* examines structure, function, and changes in DNA. **Population genetics** investigates natural selection and other causes of genetic variation, stability, and change in breeding populations.

Mendel's Experiments

In 1856, in a monastery garden, the Austrian monk Gregor Mendel began a series of experiments that were to reveal the basic principles of genetics.

Mendel studied the inheritance of seven contrasting traits in pea plants. For each trait there were only two forms. For example, plants were either tall (6 to 7 feet [1.8 to 2.1 meters]) or short (9 to 18 inches [23 to 46 centimeters]), with no intermediate forms. The ripe seeds could be either smooth and round or wrinkled. The peas could be either yellow or green, again with no intermediate colors.

When Mendel began his experiments, one of the prevailing beliefs about heredity was what has been called the "paint-pot" theory. According to this theory, the traits of the two parents blended in their children much as two pigments are blended in a can of paint. Children were therefore a unique mixture of their parents, and when these children married and reproduced, their traits would inextricably blend with those of their spouses. However, prevailing notions about heredity also recognized that occasionally the traits of one parent might swamp those of the other. If children looked far more like their mother than their father, people might say that her "blood" was stronger than his. Occasionally, too, there would be a "throwback," a child who was the image of his or her grandparent

Evolutionary theory is basic to understanding and appreciating human diversity. Contemporary humans, members of the species *Homo sapiens* represent one branch in the tree of life...

intelligent design proponents, such as William A. Dembski, is that "there are natural systems that cannot be adequately explained in terms of undirected natural forces and that exhibit features which in any other circumstance we would attribute to intelligence" (Demski 2004). The source of this intelligence never is identified officially. But since the naturalness of the design is denied, its supernaturalness would seem to be assumed. By injecting ID into the science curriculum, the judge ruled, Dover's board was unconstitutionally endorsing a religious view that advances "a particular version of Christianity" (*New York Times* 2005, p. A32). Attempts, of variable success and spurring ongoing legal challenges, have been made to teach ID in biology classes in several other states.

The Pennsylvania court case thoroughly examined the claim that ID was science. After a six-week trial featuring hours of expert testimony, that claim was rejected. The judge found that ID violated the ground rules of science by invoking supernatural causation and by making assertions that could not be tested or proved wrong (falsified). Nor has ID gained acceptance in the scientific community. It lacks a research and testing program and is unsupported by peer-reviewed research (*New York Times* 2005).

Evolution as a *scientific theory* (as defined in the text) is a central organizing principle of modern biology and anthropology. Evolution also is a *fact*. There is absolutely no doubt that biological evolution has occurred and is occurring still. What is at issue in biology are questions of details of the process and the relative importance of different evolutionary mechanisms. "It is a *fact* that the earth with liquid water is more than 3.6 billion years old. It is a *fact* that cellular life has been around for at least half of that period and that organized multicellular life is at least 800 million years old. It is a *fact* that major life forms now on earth were not at all represented in the past. There were no birds or mammals 250 million years ago. It is a *fact* that major life forms of the past are no longer living. There used to be dinosaurs . . . and there are none now. It is a *fact* that all living forms come from previous living forms. Therefore, all present forms of life arose from ancestral forms that were different. Birds arose from nonbirds and humans from nonhumans. No person who pretends to any understanding of the natural world can deny these facts any more than she or he can deny that the earth is round, rotates on its axis, and revolves around the sun" (Lewontin 1981, quoted in Moran 1993).

One key feature of science, as we saw in Chapter 1 (pp. 15–20), is to recognize the tentativeness and uncertainty of knowledge and understanding, which scientists try to improve. As they work to refine theories and to provide accurate explanations, scientists strive for objectivity and impartiality (trying to reduce the influence of the scientist, including his or her personal beliefs and actions). Science has many limitations and is not the only way we have of understanding. Certainly, the study of religion is another path to understanding. But the goals of objectivity and impartiality do help distinguish science from ways of knowing that are more biased, more rigid, and more dogmatic.

---

or who possessed a distinctive chin or nose characteristic of a whole line of descent.

Through his experiments with pea plants, Mendel discovered that heredity is determined by discrete particles or units. Although traits could disappear in one generation, they reemerged in their original form in later generations. For example, Mendel crossbred pure strains of tall and short plants. Their offspring were all tall. This was the first descending, or first filial, generation, designated F_1. Mendel then interbred the plants of the F_1 generation to produce a generation of grandchildren, the F_2 generation (Figure 5.1). In this generation, short plants reappeared. Among thousands of plants in the F_2 generation, there was approximately one short plant for every three tall ones.

From similar results with the other six traits, Mendel concluded that although a **dominant** form could mask the other form in *hybrid,* or mixed, individuals, the dominated trait—the **recessive**—was not destroyed; it wasn't even changed. Recessive traits would appear in unaltered form in later generations because genetic traits were inherited as discrete units.

These basic genetic units that Mendel described were factors (now called genes or alleles) located on **chromosomes.** Chromosomes are arranged in matching (homologous) pairs. Humans have 46 chromosomes, arranged in 23 pairs, one in each pair from the father and the other from the mother.

For simplicity, a chromosome may be pictured as a surface (see Figure 5.2) with several positions, to each of which we assign a lowercase letter. Each position is a **gene.** Each gene determines, wholly or partially, a particular biological trait, such as whether one's blood is A, B, or O. **Alleles** (for example, b^1 and b^2 in Figure 5.2) are biochemically different forms of a given gene. In humans, A, B, AB, and O blood types reflect different combinations of alleles of a particular gene.

In Mendel's experiments, the seven contrasting traits were determined by genes on seven different pairs of chromosomes. The gene for

Gregor Mendel, the father of genetics.

FIGURE 5.1 Mendel's Second Set of Experiments with Pea Plants.

Trait Exhibited by F₁ Hybrids	F₂ Generation (produced by crossbreeding F₁ hybrids)	
	Exhibit Dominant Trait	Exhibit Recessive Trait
Smooth seed shape	Smooth 3	Wrinkled 1
Yellow seed interior	Yellow 3	Green 1
Gray seed coat	Gray 3	White 1
Inflated pod	Inflated 3	Pinched 1
Green pod	Green 3	Yellow 1
Axial pod	Axial 3	Terminal 1
Tall stem	Tall 3	Short 1
	Offspring exhibit dominant or recessive traits in ratio of 3:1.	

Dominant colors are shown unless otherwise indicated.

FIGURE 5.2 Simplified Representation of a Normal Chromosome Pair.

Letters indicate genes; superscripts indicate alleles.

	F1		F2	
	t	t	T	t
T	Tt	Tt	TT	Tt
(T/t)	Tt	Tt	tT	tt
Genotypic ratio	0:4:0		1:2:1	
Phenotypic ratio	4:0		3:1	

FIGURE 5.3 Punnett Squares of a Homozygous Cross and a Heterozygous Cross.

These squares show how phenotypic ratios of the F₁ and F₂ generation are generated. Colors show genotypes.

heterozygous
Having dissimilar alleles of a given gene.

homozygous
Having identical alleles of a given gene.

genotype
An organism's hereditary makeup.

phenotype
An organism's evident biological traits.

height occurred in one of the seven pairs. When Mendel crossbred pure tall and pure short plants to produce his F₁ generation, each of the offspring received an allele for tallness (T) from one parent and one for shortness (t) from the other. These offspring were mixed, or **heterozygous,** with respect to height; each had two dissimilar alleles of that gene. Their parents, in contrast, had been **homozygous,** possessing two identical alleles of that gene (see Hartl and Jones 2002).

In the next generation (F₂), after the mixed plants were interbred, short plants reappeared in the ratio of one short to three talls. Knowing that shorts only produced shorts, Mendel could assume that they were genetically pure. Another fourth of the F₂ plants produced only talls. The remaining half, like the F₁ generation, were heterozygous; when interbred, they produced three talls for each short. (See Figure 5.3.)

Dominance produces a distinction between **genotype,** or hereditary makeup, and **phenotype,** or expressed physical characteristics. Genotype is what you really are genetically; phenotype is what you appear as. Mendel's peas had three genotypes—TT, Tt, and tt—but only two phenotypes—tall and short. Because of dominance, the heterozygous plants were just as tall as the genetically pure tall ones. How do Mendel's discoveries apply to humans? Although some of our genetic traits follow Mendelian laws, with only two forms—dominant and recessive—other traits are determined differently. For instance, three alleles determine whether our blood type is A, B, AB, or O. People with two alleles for type O have that blood type. However, if they received a gene for either A or B from one parent and one for O from the other, they will have blood type A or B. In other words, A and B are both dominant over O. A and B are said to be *codominant.* If people inherit a gene for A from one parent and one for B from the other, they will have type AB blood, which is chemically different from the other varieties, A, B, and O.

FIGURE 5.4 Determinants of Phenotypes (Blood Groups) in the ABO System.

The four phenotypes—A, B, AB, and O—are indicated in parentheses and by color.

These three alleles produce four phenotypes—A, B, AB, and O—and six different genotypes—OO, AO, BO, AA, BB, and AB (Figure 5.4). There are fewer phenotypes than genotypes because O is recessive to both A and B.

Independent Assortment and Recombination

Through additional experiments, Mendel also formulated his law of **independent assortment.** He discovered that traits are inherited independently of one another. For example, he bred pure round yellow peas with pure wrinkled green ones. All the F_1 generation peas were round and yellow, the dominant forms. But when Mendel interbred the F_1 generation to produce the F_2, four phenotypes turned up. Round greens and wrinkled yellows had been added to the original round yellows and wrinkled greens.

The independent assortment and recombination of genetic traits provide one of the main ways by which variety is produced in any population. *Recombination* is important in biological evolution because it creates new types on which natural selection can operate.

BIOCHEMICAL, OR MOLECULAR, GENETICS

If, as in Mendel's experiments, the same genetic traits always appeared in predictable ratios across the generations, there would be continuity rather than change. There would be no evolution. Various kinds of mutations produce the variety on which natural selection depends. Since Mendel's time, scientists have learned about **mutations**—changes in the DNA molecules of which genes and chromosomes are built. Mendel demonstrated that variety is produced by genetic recombination. Mutation, however, is even more

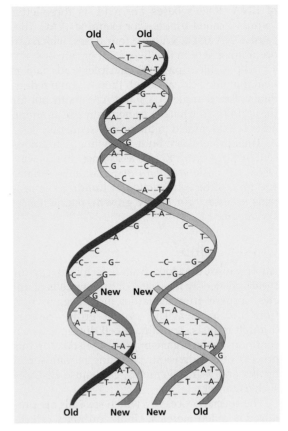

FIGURE 5.5

A double-stranded DNA molecule "unzips," and a new strand forms on each of the old ones, producing two molecules, and eventually two cells, each identical to the first.

important as a source of new biochemical forms on which natural selection may operate.

DNA does several things basic to life. DNA can copy itself, forming new cells, replacing old ones, and producing the sex cells, or *gametes*, that make new generations. DNA's chemical structure also guides the body's production of proteins—enzymes, antigens, antibodies, hormones, and hundreds of others.

The DNA molecule is a double helix (Crick 1962/1968; Watson 1970). Imagine it as a small rubber ladder that you can twist into a spiral. Its sides are held together by chemical bonds between four bases: thymine (T), adenine (A), cytosine (C), and guanine (G). DNA's duplication leads to ordinary cell division, as shown in Figure 5.5.

In protein building, another molecule, RNA, carries DNA's message from the cell's nucleus to its *cytoplasm* (outer area). The structure of RNA, with paired bases, matches that of DNA. This permits RNA to carry a message from DNA in the cell nucleus to guide the construction of proteins in the cytoplasm. A protein, which is a chain of amino acids, is constructed by "reading" a length

independent assortment Chromosomes inherited independently of one another.

mutation Change in DNA molecules.

of RNA. RNA's bases are read as three-letter "words," called *triplets*—for example, AAG. (Because DNA and RNA have four bases, which can occur anywhere in the "word," there are $4 \times 4 \times 4 = 64$ possible triplets.) Each triplet "calls" a particular amino acid, although there is some redundancy; for example, AAA and AAG both call for the amino acid lysine. A protein is made as amino acids are assembled in the proper sequence.

Thus proteins are built following instructions sent by DNA, with RNA's assistance. In this way, DNA, the basic *hereditary* material, also initiates and guides the construction of hundreds of proteins necessary for bodily growth, maintenance, and repair.

Cell Division

An organism develops from a fertilized egg, or *zygote*, created by the union of two sex cells (gametes), a sperm from the father and an egg (ovum) from the mother. The zygote grows rapidly through **mitosis,** or ordinary cell division, which continues as the organism grows. Mistakes in this process of cell division, including chromosomal breaks and rearrangements, can cause diseases such as cancer.

The special process by which sex cells are produced is called **meiosis.** Unlike ordinary cell division, in which two cells emerge from one, in meiosis four cells are produced from one. Each has half the genetic material of the original cell. In human meiosis, four cells, each with 23 individual chromosomes, are produced from an original cell with 23 pairs.

With fertilization of egg by sperm, the father's 23 chromosomes combine with the mother's 23 to re-create the pairs in every generation. However, the chromosomes sort independently, so that a

mitosis
Ordinary cell division.

meiosis
Process by which sex cells are produced.

crossing over
Homologous chromosomes intertwine and exchange DNA.

The chromosomes that determine sex in humans. The X chromosome (left) is clearly larger than the Y chromosome (right). What are the genotypes of males and females in terms of these chromosomes?

child's genotype is a random combination of the DNA of its four grandparents. It is conceivable that one grandparent will contribute very little to his or her grandchild's heredity. Independent assortment of chromosomes is a major source of variety, because the parents' genotypes can be assorted in 2^{23}, or more than 8 million, different ways.

Crossing Over

Another source of variety is **crossing over.** Before fertilization, early in meiosis, as a sperm or egg is being formed, paired chromosomes temporarily intertwine as they duplicate themselves. As they do this, they often exchange lengths of their DNA (Figure 5.6). Crossovers are the sites where homologous chromosomes have exchanged segments by breakage and recombination.

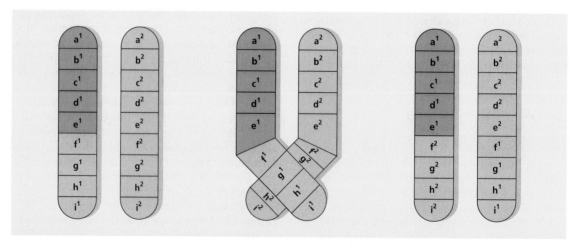

FIGURE 5.6 Crossing Over.

In the first phase of meiosis, homologous chromosomes intertwine as they duplicate themselves. As they do this, they often exchange lengths of their DNA, as shown here. This is known as crossing over. Note that the lower lengths of the original pair now differ. Each chromosome is therefore chemically different from either member of the original pair.

Because of crossing over, each new chromosome is partially different from either member of the original pair. As a person produces sex cells, replacing, say, part of a chromosome one has received from one's mother with a corresponding section of the homologous chromosome from one's father, crossing over partially contradicts Mendel's law of independent assortment and makes a new combination of genetic material available to the offspring. Because crossing over can occur with any chromosome pair, it is an important source of variety.

Mutation

Mutations are the most important source of variety on which natural selection depends and operates. The simplest mutation results from substitution of just one base in a triplet by another. (This is called a *base substitution mutation.*) If such a mutation occurs in a sex cell that joins with another in a fertilized egg, the new organism will carry the mutation in every cell. As DNA directs protein building, a protein different from that produced by the nonmutant parent *may* be produced in the child. The child's protein building will differ from the parent's only if the new base codes for a different amino acid. Because the same amino acid can be coded by more than one triplet, a base substitution mutation doesn't always produce a different protein. However, the abnormal protein associated with the hereditary disease sickle-cell anemia, described below, is caused by just such a difference in a single base between normal individuals and those afflicted with the disease.

Another form of mutation is *chromosomal rearrangement.* Pieces of a chromosome can break off, turn around and reattach, or migrate someplace else on that chromosome. This can occur in the sex cell, or in the fertilized egg or the growing organism, during mitosis. A mismatch of chromosomes resulting from rearrangement can lead to speciation (the formation of new species). Scientists often find that separate but closely related species living in overlapping ranges cannot interbreed because their chromosomes, due to rearrangement, no longer match. Chromosome rearrangements in a fertilized egg can lead to congenital disorders. Cancer cells undergo large-scale chromosome rearrangements. Chromosomes also may fuse. When the ancestors of humans split off from those of chimpanzees around six million years ago, two ancestral chromosomes fused together in the human line. Humans have 23 chromosome pairs, versus 24 for chimps.

Mutation rates vary, but for base substitution mutations, the likely average is 10^{-9} mutations per DNA base per generation. This means that approximately three mutations will occur in every sex cell (Strachan and Read 2004). Many geneticists believe that most mutations are neutral, conferring neither advantage nor disadvantage.

Others argue that most mutations are harmful and will be weeded out because they deviate from types that have been selected over the generations. However, if the selective forces affecting a population change, mutations in its gene pool may acquire an adaptive advantage they lacked in the old environment.

Evolution depends on mutations as a major source of genetically transmitted variety, raw material on which natural selection can work. (Crossing over, independent assortment, and chromosomal recombination are other sources.) Alterations in genes and chromosomes may result in entirely new types of organisms, which may demonstrate some new selective advantage. Variants produced through mutation can be especially significant if there is a change in the environment. They may prove to have an advantage they lacked in the old environment. The spread of the allele that determines sickle-cell anemia, to be examined below, provides one example.

POPULATION GENETICS AND MECHANISMS OF GENETIC EVOLUTION

Population genetics studies the stable and changing populations in which most breeding normally takes place (see Gillespie 2004; Hartl 2000). The term **gene pool** refers to all the alleles, genes, chromosomes, and genotypes within a breeding population—the "pool" of genetic material available. When population geneticists use the term *evolution,* they have a more specific definition in mind than the one given earlier ("descent with modification over the generations"). For geneticists, **genetic evolution** is defined as a change in gene frequency, that is, in the frequency of alleles in a breeding population from generation to generation. Any factor that contributes to such a change can be considered a mechanism of genetic evolution. Those mechanisms include natural selection, mutation (already examined), random genetic drift, and gene flow (see Mayr 2001).

Natural Selection

Natural selection remains the best explanation for (genetic) evolution. Essential to understanding evolution through natural selection is the distinction between genotype and phenotype. Genotype refers just to hereditary factors—genes and chromosomes. Phenotype—the organism's evident biological characteristics—develops over the years as the organism is influenced by particular environmental forces. (See the photo of the identical twins. Identical twins have exactly the same genotype, but their actual biology, their phenotypes, may differ as a result of variation in

gene pool
All the genetic material in a breeding population.

genetic evolution
Change in gene (allele) frequency in a breeding population.

A group of multi-ethnic and multi-aged identical twins attend the Twins & Multiples Day at Coney Island, New York. Even identical twins, who have exactly the same genotype, can vary in phenotype (e.g., in height or weight) depending on their environment and events during growth and development.

adaptive
Favored by natural selection.

the environments in which they have been raised.) Also, because of dominance, individuals with different genotypes may have identical phenotypes (like Mendel's tall pea plants). Natural selection can operate only on phenotype—on what is exposed, not on what is hidden. For example, a harmful recessive gene can't be eliminated from the gene pool if it is masked by a favored dominant.

Phenotype includes not only outward physical appearance but also internal organs, tissues and cells, and physiological processes and systems. Many biological reactions to foods, disease, heat, cold, sunlight, and other environmental factors are not automatic, genetically programmed responses but the product of years of exposure to particular environmental stresses. Human biology is not set at birth but has considerable *plasticity*. That is, it is changeable, being affected by the environmental forces, such as diet and altitude, that we experience as we grow up (see Bogin 2001).

The environment works on the genotype to build the phenotype, and certain phenotypes do better in some environments than other phenotypes do. However, remember that favored phenotypes can be produced by different genotypes. Because natural selection works only on genes that are expressed, maladaptive recessives can be removed only when they occur in homozygous form. When a heterozygote carries a maladaptive recessive, its effects are masked by the favored dominant. The process of perfecting the fit between organisms and their environment is gradual.

Directional Selection

After several generations of selection, gene frequencies will change. Adaptation through natural selection will have occurred. Once that happens, those traits that have proved to be the most **adaptive** (favored by natural selection) in that environment will be selected again and again from generation to generation. Given such *directional selection,* or long-term selection of the same trait(s), maladaptive recessive alleles will be removed from the gene pool.

Directional selection will continue as long as environmental forces stay the same. However, if the environment changes, new selective forces start working, favoring different phenotypes. This also happens when part of the population -colonizes a new environment. Selection in the changed, or new, environment continues until a new equilibrium is reached. Then there is directional selection until another environmental change or migration takes place. Over millions of years, such a process of successive adaptation to a series of environments has led to biological modification and branching. The process of natural selection has led to the tremendous array of plant and animal forms found in the world today.

Selection operates *only* on traits that are present in a population. A favorable mutation *may* occur, but a population doesn't normally come up with a new genotype or phenotype just because one is needed or desirable. Many species have become extinct because they weren't sufficiently varied to adapt to environmental shifts.

There are also differences in the amount of environmental stress that organisms' genetic potential enables them to tolerate. Some species are adapted to a narrow range of environments. They are especially endangered by environmental fluctuation. Others—*Homo sapiens* among them—tolerate much more environmental variation because their genetic potential permits many adaptive possibilities. Humans can adapt rapidly to changing conditions by modifying both biological responses and learned behavior. We don't have to delay adaptation until a favorable mutation appears.

Sexual Selection

Selection also operates through competition for mates in a breeding population. Males may openly compete for females, or females may choose to mate with particular males because they have desirable traits. Obviously, such traits vary from species to species. Familiar examples include color in birds; male birds, such as cardinals, tend to be more brightly colored than females are. Colorful males have a selective advantage because females like them better. As, over the generations, females have opted for colorful mates, the alleles responsible for color have built up in the species. **Sexual selection,** based on differential success in mating, is the term for this process in which certain traits of one sex are selected because of advantages they confer in winning mates.

Stabilizing Selection

We have seen that natural selection reduces variety in a population through directional selection—by favoring one trait or allele over another. Selective forces can also work to *maintain* variety through *stabilizing selection,* by favoring a **balanced polymorphism,** in which the frequencies of two or more alleles of a gene remain constant from generation to generation. This may be because the phenotypes they produce are neutral, or equally favored, or equally opposed by selective forces. Sometimes a particular force favors (or opposes) one allele while a different but equally effective force favors (or opposes) the other allele.

One well-studied example of a balanced polymorphism involves two alleles, Hb^A and Hb^S, that affect the production of the beta strain (Hb) of human hemoglobin. Hemoglobin, which is located in our red blood cells, carries oxygen from the lungs to the rest of the body via the circulatory system. The allele that produces normal hemoglobin is Hb^A. Another allele, Hb^S, produces a different hemoglobin. Individuals who are homozygous for Hb^S suffer from *sickle-cell anemia.* Such anemia, in which the red blood cells are shaped like crescents or sickles, is associated with a disease that is usually fatal. This condition interferes with the blood's ability to store oxygen.

Sexual selection: In many bird species, colorful males have a selective advantage because females are more likely to mate with them than with less colorful males. The male in this pair of painted buntings (how accurate and sexist is that name?), photographed in Texas, is much brighter than the female.

It increases the heart's burden by clogging the small blood vessels.

Given the fatal disease associated with Hb^S, geneticists were surprised to discover that certain populations in Africa, India, and the Mediterranean had very high frequencies of Hb^S (Figure 5.7). In some West African populations, that frequency

sexual selection
Selection of traits that enhance mating success.

balanced polymorphism
Alleles maintain a constant frequency in a population over time.

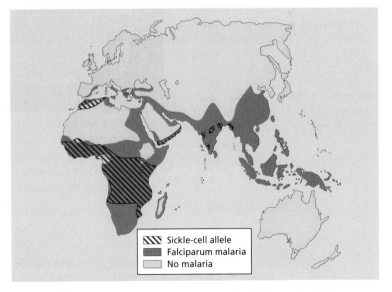

FIGURE 5.7 Distribution of Sickle-Cell Allele and Falciparum Malaria in the Old World.

SOURCE: Adapted from Joseph B. Birdsell, *Human Evolution: An Introduction to the New Physical Anthropology,* 3rd ed., © 1981. Reproduced in print and electronic formats by permission of Pearson Education, Inc., Upper Saddle River, New Jersey.

appreciating ANTHROPOLOGY

H1N1 Anyone?

Anthropology is noteworthy for its holistic and biocultural approaches and its relevance to understanding historic as well as contemporary processes and events. The anthropologists described below view the evolution of disease not just biologically but in the context of social and political history.

Known to us as a dreaded venereal—aka sexually transmitted—disease (STD), syphilis apparently originated in the Americas as a nonvenereal bacterium. It spread to the Old World as part of the Columbian exchange, an early form of globalization, in which products, populations, and pathogens of the Old World and the New World became forever linked after 1492. Once in Europe the bacterium mutated into venereal syphilis, which became a major killer during the Renaissance. The same evolutionary principles and mechanisms (e.g., adaptation to new environments and mutation) that operate in the evolution of life in general, also apply specifically to the evolution of pathogens that cause disease.

Globalization remains an important factor in the spread and mutation of diseases in today's world. The title above suggests one example, the H1N1 virus, which gained attention as a pandemic in 2009. Known originally as swine flu, the virus illustrates the spread of pathogens from animals to humans. Anthropologists appreciate that such transmission became more common after humans had domesticated animals and began to live in close proximity to such animals as pigs, poultry, sheep, and cattle.

Columbus, it seems, made another discovery of something that he was not looking for.

In a comprehensive genetic study, scientists have found what they say is the strongest evidence yet linking the first European explorers of the New World to the origin of sexually transmitted syphilis.

The research, they say, supports the hypothesis that returning explorers introduced organisms leading, in probably modified forms, to the first recorded syphilis epidemic, beginning in Europe in 1493.

The so-called Columbus hypothesis had previously rested on circumstantial evidence, mainly the timing of the epidemic. . . .

Earlier traces of syphilis or related diseases had been few and inconclusive in Europe. Yet nonvenereal forms of the diseases were widespread in the American tropics.

Leaders of the new study said the most telling results were that the bacterium causing sexually transmitted syphilis arose relatively recently in humans and was closely related to

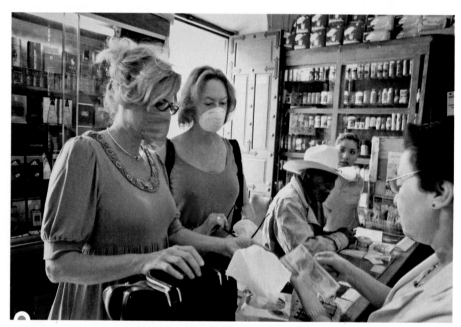

Like earlier diseases, the H1N1 virus spread (rapidly) within the world system. In spring-summer 2009, people in Mexico bought masks and used hand sanitizers to fend off the flu. About 8,000 foreigners live in the Mexican town of San Miguel Allende shown here. In this photo two expatriate women carefully purchase items in a local pharmacy. What precautions do they appear to be taking?

is around 20 percent. Researchers eventually discovered that both Hb^A and Hb^S are maintained because selective forces in certain environments favor the heterozygote over either homozygote.

Initially, scientists wondered why, if most Hb^S homozygotes died before they reached reproductive age, the harmful allele hadn't been eliminated. Why was its frequency so high? The answer turned out to lie in the *heterozygote's* greater fitness. Only people who were homozygous for Hb^S died from sickle-cell anemia. Heterozygotes suffered very mild anemia, if any. On the other hand, although people homozygous for Hb^A did not suffer from anemia, they were much more susceptible to *malaria*—a killer disease that continues to plague *Homo sapiens* in the tropics.

a strain responsible for the nonvenereal infection known as yaws. The similarity was especially evident, the researchers said, in a variation of the yaws pathogen isolated recently among afflicted children in a remote region of Guyana in South America . . .

The findings suggested Columbus and his men could have carried the nonvenereal tropical bacteria home, where the organisms may have mutated into a more deadly form in the different conditions of Europe.

In the New World, the infecting organisms for nonvenereal syphilis, known as bejel, and yaws were transmitted by skin-to-skin and oral contact, more often in children. The symptoms are lesions primarily on the legs, not on or near the genitals.

Kristin N. Harper, a researcher in molecular genetics at Emory University who was the principal investigator in the study, said the findings supported "the hypothesis that syphilis, or some progenitor, came from the New World.". . . Her co-authors included George J. Armelagos, an Emory anthropologist who has studied the origins of syphilis for more than 30 years, and Dr. Michael S. Silverman, a Canadian infectious diseases physician who collected and tested specimens from yaws lesions in Guyana, the only known site today of yaws infections in the Western Hemisphere. The researchers said their study "represents the first attempt to address the problem of the origin of syphilis using molecular genetics, as well as the first source of information regarding the genetic makeup of nonvenereal strains from the Western Hemisphere."

They applied phylogenetics, the study of evolutionary relationships between organisms, in examining 26 geographically disparate strains in the family of Treponema bacteria. Treponema pallidum subspecies pallidum is the agent for the scourge of venereal syphilis. The subspecies endemicum causes bejel, usually in hot, arid climates. . . .

John W. Verano, an anthropologist at Tulane, said the findings would "probably not settle the debate" over the origins of venereal syphilis, though most scientists had become convinced that the disease was not transmitted sexually before Europeans made contact with the New World.

Donald J. Ortner, an anthropologist at the Smithsonian Institution, questioned whether the organisms causing the first European epidemic were actually distinct from others in the treponemal family. "What we are seeing is an organism with a long history, and it is very adaptable to different modes of transmission that produce different manifestations," Dr. Ortner said. . . .

Paleopathologists . . . have for years analyzed skeletons for the bone scars from lesions produced by treponemal diseases, except for the mild form called pinta. In this way, they traced the existence of these infections in the New World back at least 7,000 years. But it has often been difficult to determine the age of the bones and distinguish the different diseases that share symptoms but have different modes of transmission. . . .

In her investigation, Ms. Harper studied 22 human Treponemal pallidum strains. The DNA in their genes was sequenced in nearly all cases, examined for changes and eventually

used in constructing phylogenetic trees incorporating all variations in the strains.

An Old World yaws subspecies was found to occupy the base of the tree, indicating its ancestral position in the treponemal family, she said. The terminal position of the venereal syphilis subspecies on the tree showed it had diverged most recently from the rest of the bacterial family.

Specimens from two Guyana yaws cases were included in the study, after they were collected and processed by Dr. Silverman. Genetic analysis showed that this yaws strain was the closest known relative to venereal syphilis.

If this seemed to solidify the Columbus hypothesis, the researchers cautioned that a "transfer agent between humans and nonhuman primates cannot be ruled out.

Dr. Armelagos said research into the origins of syphilis would continue, because "understanding its evolution is important not just for biology, but for understanding social and political history."

Noting that the disease was a major killer in Renaissance Europe, he said, "It could be argued that syphilis is one of the important early examples of globalization and disease, and globalization remains an important factor in emerging diseases."

The heterozygote, with one sickle-cell allele and one normal one, was the fittest phenotype for a malarial environment. Heterozygotes have enough abnormal hemoglobin, in which malaria parasites cannot thrive, to protect against malaria. They also have enough normal hemoglobin to fend off sickle-cell anemia. The Hb^S allele has been maintained in these populations because the heterozygotes survived and reproduced in greater numbers than did people with any other phenotype.

The example of the sickle-cell allele demonstrates the relativity of evolution through natural selection: Adaptation and fitness are in relation to specific environments. Traits are not adaptive or maladaptive for all times and places. Even harmful alleles can be selected if heterozygotes

Beware the *Anopheles* mosquito, vector of malaria. An adult female is shown here.

random genetic drift
Genetic change due to chance.

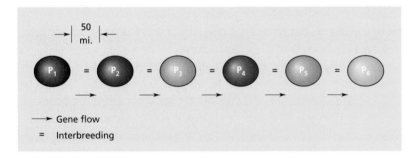

→ Gene flow
= Interbreeding

FIGURE 5.8   Gene Flow between Local Populations.

P₁–P₆ are six local populations of the same species. Each interbreeds (=) only with its neighbor(s). Although members of P₆ never interbreed with P₁, P₆ and P₁ are linked through gene flow. Genetic material that originates in P₁ eventually will reach P₆, and vice versa, as it is passed from one neighboring population to the next. Because they share genetic material in this way, P₁–P₆ remain members of the same species. In many species, local populations distributed throughout a larger territory than the 250 miles depicted here are linked through gene flow.

gene flow
Exchange of genetic material through interbreeding.

species
Members can interbreed to produce offspring that live and reproduce.

speciation
Formation of new species.

have an advantage. Moreover, as the environment changes, favored phenotypes and gene frequencies can change. In malaria-free environments, normal-hemoglobin homozygotes reproduce more effectively than heterozygotes do. With no malaria, the frequency of Hb^S declines because Hb^S homozygotes can't compete in survival and reproduction with the other types. This has happened in areas of West Africa where malaria has been reduced through drainage programs and in-

secticides. Selection against Hb^S also has occurred in the United States among Americans descended from West Africans (Diamond 1997).

Random Genetic Drift

A second mechanism of genetic evolution is **random genetic drift.** This is a change in allele frequency that results not from natural selection but from chance. To understand why, compare the sorting of alleles to a game involving a bag of 12 marbles, 6 red and 6 blue. In step 1, you draw six marbles from the bag. Statistically, your chances of drawing three reds and three blues are less than those of getting four of one color and two of the other. Step 2 is to fill a new bag with 12 marbles on the basis of the ratio of marbles you drew in step 1. Assume that you drew four reds and two blues: The new bag will have eight red marbles and four blue ones. Step 3 is to draw six marbles from the new bag. Your chances of drawing blues in step 3 are lower than they were in step 1, and the probability of drawing all reds increases. If you do draw all reds, the next bag (step 4) will have only red marbles.

This game is analogous to random genetic drift operating over the generations. The blue marbles were lost purely by chance. Alleles, too, can be lost by chance rather than because of any disadvantage they confer. Lost alleles can reappear in a gene pool only through mutation.

Although genetic drift can operate in any population, large or small, *fixation* due to drift is more rapid in small populations. Fixation refers to the total replacement of blue marbles by red marbles—or, to use a human example, of blue eyes by brown eyes. The history of the human line is characterized by a series of small populations, migrations, and fixation due to genetic drift. One cannot understand human origins, human genetic variation, and a host of other important anthropological topics without recognizing the importance of genetic drift.

Gene Flow

A third mechanism of genetic evolution is **gene flow,** the exchange of genetic material between populations of the same species. Gene flow, like mutation, works in conjunction with natural selection by providing variety on which selection can work. Gene flow may consist of direct interbreeding between formerly separated populations of the same species (e.g., Europeans, Africans, and Native Americans in the United States), or it may be indirect.

Consider the following hypothetical case (Figure 5.8). In a certain part of the world live six local populations of a certain species. P₁ is the westernmost of these populations. P₂, which interbreeds with P_1, is located 50 miles to the east. P_2 also interbreeds with P_3, located 50 miles east of P_2. Assume that each population interbreeds with, and only with, the adjacent populations. P_6 is located 250 miles from P_1 and does not directly interbreed with P_1, but it is tied to P_1 through the chain of interbreeding that ultimately links all six populations.

Assume further that some allele exists in P_1 that isn't particularly advantageous in its environment. Because of gene flow, this allele may be passed on to P_2, by it to P_3, and so on, until it eventually reaches P_6. In P_6 or along the way, the allele may encounter an environment in which it does have a selective advantage. If this happens, it may serve, like a new mutation, as raw material on which natural selection can operate.

Alleles are spread through gene flow even when selection is not operating on the allele. In the long run, natural selection works on the variety within a population, whatever its source. Selection and gene flow have worked together to spread the Hb^S allele in Central Africa. Frequencies of Hb^S in Africa reflect not only the intensity of malaria but also the length of time gene flow has been going on (Livingstone 1969).

Gene flow is important in the study of the origin of species. A **species** is a group of related organisms whose members can interbreed to produce offspring that can live and reproduce. A species has to be able to reproduce itself through time. We know that horses and donkeys belong to different species because their offspring cannot meet the test of long-term survival. A horse and a donkey may breed to produce a mule, but mules are sterile. So are the offspring of lions with tigers. Gene flow tends to prevent **speciation**—the formation of new species—unless subgroups of the same species are separated for a sufficient length of time.

When gene flow is interrupted, and isolated subgroups are maintained, new species may arise. Imagine that an environmental barrier arises between P_3 and P_4, so that they no longer interbreed. If over time, as a result of isolation, P_1, P_2, and P_3 become incapable of interbreeding with the other three populations, speciation will have occurred.

THE MODERN SYNTHESIS

The currently accepted view of evolution is known as the "modern synthesis." This refers to the synthesis or combination of Darwin's theory of evolution by natural selection and Mendel's genetic discoveries. The modern synthesis also explains what Mendel could not—the inheritance of multifactorial or complex traits (e.g., height; see the next chapter). According to the modern

STUDENT: Maryna Yevhenivna Bazylevych, Ph.D. Candidate
COUNTRY OF ORIGIN: Ukraine
SUPERVISING PROFESSOR: Dr. Gail H. Landsman
SCHOOL: State University of New York at Albany

Adoption in Ukraine and the United States (a Ukrainian Student's View)

Before arriving in the United States as graduate student in anthropology, I had lived in Ukraine all my life. I remember how surprised I was when an American friend working in Ukraine disclosed that he had been adopted from a foreign country as a baby. In Ukraine, adoption is still a taboo topic. A childless family is considered to be extremely unfortunate, and if a couple decides to adopt, the baby's origin usually remains hidden from the child and the community. Ukrainians often say that good parents would never give up their child, that those who do must have either psychological or substance abuse problems, and that an adopted child could inherit these negative traits. Childless couples are often apprehensive about the adoption process.

In the United States, however, I was struck by the positive attitude toward adoption. Adoptive parents and their children often talk openly about their family history. If children are adopted internationally, their parents often encourage them to learn their home country's culture and language. It was in the United States that I first heard about an open adoption, in which parents who decide to give their baby up for adoption can choose the family who will receive the child. I would say that adoption in general and international adoption in particular became a "fashionable" and socially acceptable act in American society. Newspapers and TV shows highlight the stories of celebrities who adopt children from all over the world. Some social critics talk about the commoditization of children, who may be turning into yet another good in the global economic flow.

We need to be careful in drawing conclusions about the delicate issue of adoption in these two countries. Ukrainian society emphasizes family relationships and blood ties and therefore sometimes displays prejudice toward a child who does not have a biological connection to the family. Because Ukraine was part of the Soviet Union until 1991, people were raised under the Communist ethos that emphasized natural science and evolution over religion and social sciences. In the nature versus nurture debate, biological explanations were preferred. Therefore, adopted children are sometimes assumed to be a copy of their biological parents, rather than a product of their upbringing in a new family. Biological connections receive special significance in the Ukrainian society today, when it is struggling to revive its national identity. In contrast, American society values the spirit of independence and personal achievement. Being from a "good" family does not matter as much as being a successful individual. In the United States, therefore, whether a child is biological or adopted has little significance.

punctuated
equilibrium

Long periods of
stability, with occasional
evolutionary leaps.

synthesis, speciation (the formation of new species) occurs when they become reproductively isolated from one another. How does genetic evolution lead, or not, to new species?

Microevolution refers to genetic changes in a population or species over a few, several, or many generations, but without speciation. *Macroevolution* refers to larger-scale or more significant genetic changes in a population or species, usually over a longer time period, which result in speciation. Indeed, macroevolution is defined as speciation, the divergence of one ancestral species into two (or more) descendant species. Most biologists assume that species develop gradually as successive mutations accumulate in isolated populations, so that eventually the populations are too different to interbreed. But the time and the number of generations required for microevolution to become macroevolution are highly variable.

Modern-day creationists sometimes use a misunderstanding of the contrast between microevolution and macroevolution to comment on evolution. They may say they accept microevolution, such as a change in a species' size or coloring, or as demonstrated in the laboratory or through studies of such traits as the sickle-cell allele. Macroevolution, they claim, by contrast, can't be demonstrated, only inferred from the fossil record.

Note, however, that no degree of phenotypical difference is implied by the term *macroevolution*. A simple chromosomal rearrangement can be sufficient to separate two closely related species whose ranges overlap. They belong to different species not because they are isolated from each other in space but because they cannot hybridize. Although no phenotypic difference is visible between these reproductively isolated species, this is a case of macroevolution rather than microevolution.

To exaggerate the contrast between microevolution and macroevolution would imply, incorrectly, that there are two fundamentally distinct evolutionary processes. Scientists see no such contrast: Microevolution and macroevolution happen in the same way and for the same reasons, reflecting the mechanisms of genetic evolution discussed in this chapter. The modern synthesis recognizes that microevolutionary processes are sufficient to explain macroevolution.

Punctuated Equilibrium

Charles Darwin saw species as arising from others over time, in a gradual and orderly fashion. Microevolutionary changes would accumulate over the generations to eventually produce macroevolution. In other words, minor alterations in the gene pool, accumulating generation after generation, would add up to major changes, including speciation, after thousands of years.

The **punctuated equilibrium** model of evolution (see Eldredge 1985; Gould 2002) points to the fact that long periods of stasis (stability), during which species change little, may be interrupted (punctuated) by evolutionary leaps. One reason for such apparent jumps (which are revealed by the fossil record) may be extinction of one species followed by invasion by a closely related species. For example, a sea species may die out when a shallow body of water dries up, while a closely related species survives in deeper waters. Later, when the sea reinvades the first locale, the protected species will extend its range to the first area. Another possibility is that when barriers are removed, a group may replace, rather than succeed, a related one because it has a trait that makes it adaptively fitter in the environment they now share.

When there is a sudden environmental change, rather than such extinction and replacement, another possibility is for the pace of evolution to speed up. Some highly significant mutation(s) or combination of genetic changes may permit the survival of a radically altered species in a new and very different environmental niche. Many scientists believe that the evolution of our hominin ancestors was marked by one or more such evolutionary leaps.

Although species can survive radical environmental shifts, a more common fate is extinction. The earth has witnessed several mass extinctions—worldwide catastrophes affecting multiple species. The biggest one divided the era of "ancient life" (the Paleozoic) from the era of "middle life" (the Mesozoic). This mass extinction occurred 245 million years ago, when 4.5 million of the earth's estimated 5 million species (mostly invertebrates) were wiped out. The second-biggest extinction, around 65 million years ago, destroyed the dinosaurs. One explanation for the extinction of the dinosaurs is that a massive, long-lasting cloud of gas and dust arose from the impact of a giant meteorite at the end of the Mesozoic. The cloud blocked solar radiation and therefore photosynthesis, ultimately destroying most plants and the chain of animals that fed on them.

From the fossil record, including the hominin fossil record to be discussed in Chapters 8 to 10, we know there are periods of more intense evolutionary change. At the end of the Mesozoic, the extinction of the dinosaurs was accompanied by the rapid spread and speciation of mammals and birds. Speciation responds to many factors, including the rate of environmental change, the speed with which geographic barriers rise or fall, the degree of competition with other species, and the effectiveness of the group's adaptive response.

Acing the COURSE

Summary

1. In the 18th century, Carolus Linnaeus developed biological taxonomy. He viewed differences and similarities among organisms as part of God's orderly plan rather than as evidence for evolution. Charles Darwin and Alfred Russel Wallace proposed that natural selection could explain the origin of species, biological diversity, and similarities among related life forms. Natural selection requires variety in the population undergoing selection.

2. Through breeding experiments with peas in 1856, Gregor Mendel discovered that genetic traits pass on as units. These are now known to be chromosomes, which occur in homologous pairs. Alleles, some dominant, some recessive, are the chemically different forms that occur at a given genetic locus. Mendel also formulated the law of independent assortment. Each of the seven traits he studied in peas was inherited independently of all the others. Independent assortment of chromosomes and their recombination provide some of the variety needed for natural selection. But the major source of such variety is mutation, an alteration in the DNA molecules of which genes are made.

3. Biochemical, or molecular, genetics studies structure, function, and changes in genetic material—DNA. Genetic changes that provide variety within a population include base substitution mutations, chromosomal rearrangements, and genetic recombination. Population genetics studies gene frequencies in stable and changing populations. Natural selection is the most important mechanism of evolutionary change. Others include random genetic drift and gene flow. Natural selection works with traits already present in the population. If variety is insufficient to permit adaptation to environmental change, extinction is likely. New types don't appear just because they are needed.

4. One well-documented case of natural selection in contemporary human populations is that of the sickle-cell allele. In homozygous form, the sickle-cell allele, Hb^S, produces an abnormal hemoglobin. This clogs the small blood vessels, impairing the blood's capacity to store oxygen. The result is sickle-cell anemia, which is usually fatal. The distribution of Hb^S has been linked to that of malaria. Homozygotes for normal hemoglobin are susceptible to malaria and die in great numbers. Homozygotes for the sickle-cell allele die from anemia. Heterozygotes get only mild anemia and are resistant to malaria. In a malarial environment, the heterozygote has the advantage. This explains why an apparently maladaptive allele is preserved. The preservation of Hb^A and Hb^S alleles within a breeding population is an example of a balanced polymorphism, in which the heterozygote has greater fitness than does either homozygote.

5. Other mechanisms of genetic evolution complement natural selection. Random genetic drift operates most obviously in small populations, where pure chance can easily change allele frequencies. Gene flow and interbreeding keep subgroups of the same species genetically connected and thus impede speciation.

6. The modern synthetic theory of evolution (the modern synthesis) blends the Darwin and Wallace theory of evolution through natural selection with Mendel's discovery of the gene. Microevolution and macroevolution are two ends (short-term and long-term) of a continuum of evolutionary change in which gradually changing allele frequencies in a population eventually can lead to the formation of new species. Punctuated equilibrium theory states that long periods of stasis (stability), during which species change little, are interrupted (punctuated) by evolutionary leaps.

Key Terms

adaptive 104
allele 98
balanced polymorphism 105

chromosomes 98
crossing over 102
dominant 98

Test Yourself!

MULTIPLE CHOICE

1. The *fact* of evolution was known prior to Charles Darwin. The *theory* of evolution, through natural selection (*how* evolution occurred), was
   a. Linnaeus's major contribution.
   b. actually the idea of Darwin's grandfather, Erasmus Darwin.
   c. Charles Darwin's major contribution.
   d. compatible with theories of biblical scholars.
   e. at odds with the fossil record.

2. Which of the following is *not* part of Darwin's theory of evolution?
   a. competition for resources
   b. variety in a population
   c. change in form over generations
   d. natural selection
   e. catastrophism

3. Sir Charles Lyell, the father of geology, influenced Darwin with which principle?
   a. catastrophism, the view that extinct species were destroyed by fires, floods, and other catastrophes
   b. uniformitarianism, the view that the present is the key to the past
   c. culpability, the view that the soul is a victim of the flesh
   d. creationism, the explanation for the origin of species given in Genesis
   e. macroevolution, the explanation of large-scale changes in allele frequencies in a population over a long time period

4. What are the two other mechanisms of genetic evolution that complement natural selection?
   a. random genetic drift and gene flow
   b. mutation and Lamarckism
   c. directed genetic drift and genetic engineering
   d. microdrift and macrodrift
   e. mutation and drift

5. Mutations
   a. were discovered by Mendel.
   b. only occur during the development of an individual.
   c. always result in phenotypic change.
   d. occur in 50 percent of sex cells.
   e. are the major source of genetic variation.

6. Evolution can be most simply defined as
   a. natural selection.
   b. mutations in a breeding population.
   c. the process of achieving a perfect fit to the environment.
   d. descent with modification.
   e. competition over strategic resources.

7. Natural selection
   a. is unique to flowering plants.
   b. remains the best explanation for genetic evolution.
   c. is the driving principle behind creationism.
   d. was discovered by Gregor Mendel.
   e. operates only on single-celled animals, since their genotypes are readily accessible to specific environments.

8. What does natural selection directly act on?
   a. heterozygous individuals
   b. the genotypes of organisms
   c. the phenotypes of organisms
   d. DNA
   e. mitochondrial DNA

9. The allele Hb^S, which codes for the type of hemoglobin associated with sickle-cell anemia,
   a. is evenly distributed throughout all human populations.
   b. is always lethal.
   c. has no effect on the viability of a population.
   d. is never expressed in the phenotype when present in a heterozygous state.
   e. confers resistance to malaria.

10. What is the term for the exchange of genetic material between populations of the same species through direct or indirect interbreeding?
    a. gene pool
    b. gene flow
    c. mutation
    d. genetic drift
    e. genetic evolution

FILL IN THE BLANK

1. _Linnaeus_ (1707–1778) developed the first comprehensive and still influential classification, or taxonomy, of plants and animals. He believed, as did many scholars at the time, that biological similarities and differences had been established at the time of Creation and had not changed.

2. A _balanced polymorphism_ occurs when alleles maintain a constant frequency in a population over time.

3. Mendel discovered that traits are inherited independently of one another. This is called _independent assortment_

4. Gene _flow_ refers to the exchange of genetic material through interbreeding, while gene _pool_ refers to all the genetic material in a breeding population.

5. The term _punctuated equilibrium_ refers to long periods of stability, with occasional evolutionary steps.

CRITICAL THINKING

1. During the 18th century, many scholars became interested in biological diversity, human origins, and our position within the classification of plants and animals. Why do you think that this interest arose at this time, at least in Europe? Think of historical events that led to the realization that the world is much larger and also much more diverse than previously thought.

2. In the context of understanding evolution, why is it important to distinguish between a theory and a fact?

3. Also in the context of understanding evolution, why is it important to distinguish between phenotype and genotype?

4. The strange consequences of mutations have been featured in science fiction books and movies. What is a mutation? What role do they play in evolution? Are they always bad?

Multiple Choice: 1. (C); 2. (E); 3. (B); 4. (A); 5. (E); 6. (D); 7. (B); 8. (C); 9. (E); 10. (B); **Fill in the Blank:** 1. Carolus Linnaeus; 2. balanced polymorphism; 3. independent assortment; 4. flow, pool; 5. punctuated equilibrium

Eiseley, L.
   1961   *Darwin's Century.* Garden City, NY: Doubleday, Anchor Books. Discussion of Lyell, Darwin, Wallace, and other major contributors to natural selection and transformation.

Gillespie, J. H.
   2004   *Population Genetics: A Concise Guide,* 2nd ed. Baltimore: Johns Hopkins University Press. Good introduction to population genetics.

Hartl, D. L., and E. W. Jones
   2011   *Essential Genetics: A Genomics Perspective,* 5th ed. Boston: Jones and Bartlett. Basic introduction to genetics.

Mayr, E.
   2001   *What Evolution Is.* New York: Basic Books. A master scholar sums it all up.

Weiner, J.
   1994   *The Beak of the Finch: A Story of Evolution in Our Time.* New York: Alfred A. Knopf. An excellent introduction to Darwin and to evolutionary theory.

Weiss, K. M., and A. Buchanan
   2004   *Genetics and the Logic of Evolution.* Hoboken, NJ: Wiley-Liss. How life develops and changes.

Suggested Additional Readings

Go to our Online Learning Center website at **www.mhhe.com/kottak** for Internet exercises directly related to the content of this chapter.

Internet Exercises

What is the race concept, and why have anthropologists rejected it?

How does natural selection work on contemporary and recent human populations?

Does biological adaptation occur during an individual's lifetime?

A father gives a piggyback ride to his son and daughter. Physical contrasts are evident to anyone. Anthropology's job is to explain them.

Human Variation and Adaptation

understanding OURSELVES

How do you imagine human "diversity"? Maybe you associate that word with "race" or "ethnicity." Perhaps you think of differences in skin or eye color, or something like height, which can be observed by the naked eye. In fact, human biological diversity encompasses much more than observable physical differences. It includes our abilities to digest various foods. It also includes our innate resistance or susceptibility to particular diseases. Consider smallpox, a virus that once plagued humankind. When I was a child, everyone was vaccinated against smallpox. Were you? Probably not, because smallpox has been eradicated in nature since 1979. The virus is preserved only in labs. In the context of the anthrax scare following the Sept. 11, 2001, attacks, fears arose that evildoers might find a way to access lab samples and unleash a smallpox epidemic. In anticipation of such an attack, the government planned to increase the supply and availability of smallpox vaccine. Who, however, would and should receive that vaccine, a highly effective but potentially lethal one? At one time, when smallpox was nearing extinction, more people were dying from the cure than from the disease. Anthropologists know that people with certain blood types seem to be more at risk from smallpox and its vaccine than are people

with other blood types. This type of knowledge about biological diversity can help us make important decisions about public policy and public safety in a society as diverse as our own.

Contemporary North America is strikingly rich in human biological diversity. The photos in this chapter and throughout this book illustrate just a fraction of the world's biological variation. Additional illustration comes from your own experience. Look around you in your classroom or at the mall or multiplex. Inevitably you'll see people whose ancestors lived in many lands. The first (Native) Americans had to cross a land bridge that once linked Siberia to North America. For later immigrants, perhaps including your own parents or grandparents, the voyage may have been across the sea, or overland from nations to the south. They came for many reasons; some came voluntarily, while others were brought in chains. The scale of migration in today's world is so vast that millions of people routinely cross national borders or live far from the homelands of their grandparents. Now meeting every day are diverse human beings whose biological features reflect adaptation to a wide range of environments other than the ones they now inhabit. Physical contrasts are evident to anyone. Anthropology's job is to explain them.

RACE: A DISCREDITED CONCEPT IN BIOLOGY

Historically, scientists have approached the study of human biological diversity in two main ways: (1) racial classification (now largely abandoned) versus (2) the current explanatory approach, which focuses on understanding specific differences. First

we'll consider problems with **racial classification** (the attempt to assign humans to discrete categories [purportedly] based on common ancestry). Then we'll offer some explanations for specific aspects of human biological diversity. *Biological differences are real, important, and apparent to us all.* Modern scientists find it most productive to seek explanations for this diversity, rather than trying to pigeonhole people into categories called races. Certainly, human groups do vary biologically—for example, in their genetic attributes. But often we observe gradual, rather than abrupt, shifts in gene frequencies between neighboring groups. Such gradual genetic shifts are called **clines,** and they are incompatible with discrete and separate races.

What is race anyway? In theory, a biological race would be a geographically isolated subdivision of a species. Such a *subspecies* would be capable of interbreeding with other subspecies of the same species, but it would not actually do so because of its geographic isolation. Some biologists also use "race" to refer to "breeds," as of dogs or roses. Thus, a pit bull and a chihuahua would be different races of dogs. Such domesticated "races" have been bred by humans for generations. Humanity (*Homo sapiens*) lacks such races because human populations have not been isolated enough from one another to develop into such discrete groups. Nor have humans experienced controlled breeding like that which has created the various kinds of dogs and roses.

A race is supposed to reflect shared genetic material (inherited from a common ancestor), but early scholars instead used phenotypical traits (usually skin color) for racial classification. Phenotype refers to an organism's evident traits, its "manifest biology"—anatomy and physiology. Humans display hundreds of evident (detectable) physical traits. They range from skin color, hair form, eye color, and facial features (which are visible) to blood groups, color blindness, and enzyme production (which become evident through testing).

Racial classifications based on phenotype raise the problem of deciding which trait(s) should be primary. Should races be defined by height,

The photos in this chapter illustrate only a small part of the range of human biological diversity. Shown here is a Bai minority woman, from Shapin, in China's Yunnan province.

living anthropology VIDEOS

Origins of the Modern Concepts of Race, www.mhhe.com/kottak

This clip features Dr. Jonathan Marks, a prominent biological anthropologist, discussing the origin and development of the problematic concept of race. As Marks points out, racial classification rests on the universal human tendency to classify. According to the clip, what historical political development also contributed to the race concept? Besides arbitrary physical characteristics, what are other ways of classifying human beings? How many human races did Linnaeus recognize? What, according to the clip, is the proper number of races into which humans should be categorized?

weight, body shape, facial features, teeth, skull form, or skin color? Like their fellow citizens, early European and American scientists gave priority to skin color. Many schoolbooks and encyclopedias still proclaim the existence of three great races: the white, the black, and the yellow. This overly simplistic classification was compatible with the political use of race during the colonial period of the late 19th and early 20th centuries. Such a tripartite scheme kept white Europeans neatly separate from their African, Asian, and Native American subjects. Colonial empires began to break up, and scientists began to question established racial categories, after World War II.

Races Are Not Biologically Distinct

History and politics aside, one obvious problem with "color-based" racial labels is that the terms don't accurately describe skin color. "White" people are more pink, beige, or tan than white. "Black" people are various shades of brown, and "yellow" people are tan or beige. But these terms have also been dignified by more scientific-*sounding* synonyms: Caucasoid, Negroid, and Mongoloid. This chapter's "Appreciating Diversity" discusses how racial contrasts, including skin color, are perceived in, and vary with, specific cultural contexts.

(*text continues on p. 120*)

racial classification Assigning organisms to categories (purportedly) based on common ancestry.

cline Gradual shift in gene (allele) frequencies between neighboring populations.

appreciating DIVERSITY

Ghana's Uneasy Embrace of Slavery's Diaspora

Human diversity is perceived and classified in specific cultural contexts. This account describes efforts by Ghana to attract African Americans to that country as tourists, retirees, and permanent residents. Also discussed are identity issues that African Americans face in Ghana, where often—no matter how dark their skin color may be—they are equated with white foreign tourists. Ghanaians apparently focus more on nationality and class than on skin color in classifying African Americans. We see how racial and ethnic classification can depend on sociocultural factors such as class and nationality as well as on biological factors such as skin color. Our common racial-ethnic labels such as "black" or "white" also encompass a range of gradations in skin color. Think of the variable skin shades of people you know within each of the following categories: "white," "black," "African American," and "persons of color."

CAPE COAST, Ghana—For centuries, Africans walked through the infamous "door of no return" at Cape Coast Castle directly into slave ships, never to set foot in their homelands again. These days, the portal of this massive fort so central to one of history's greatest crimes has a new name, hung on a sign leading back in from the roaring Atlantic Ocean: "The door of return." . . .

Taking Israel as its model, Ghana hopes to persuade the descendants of enslaved Africans to think of Africa as their homeland—to visit, invest, send their children to be educated and even retire here. . . .

In many ways it is a quixotic goal. Ghana is doing well by West African standards—with steady economic growth, a stable, democratic government and broad support from the West, making it a favored place for wealthy countries to give aid.

But it remains a very poor, struggling country where a third of the population lives on less than a dollar a day, life expectancy tops out at 59 and basic services like electricity and water are sometimes scarce. Nevertheless, thousands of

African-Americans already live here at least part of the year, said Valerie Papaya Mann, president of the African American Association of Ghana.

To encourage still more to come, or at least visit, Ghana plans to offer a special lifetime visa for members of the diaspora and will relax citizenship requirements so that descendants of slaves can receive Ghanaian passports. The government is also starting an advertising campaign to persuade Ghanaians to treat African-Americans more like long-lost relatives than as rich tourists.

That is harder than it sounds.

Many African-Americans who visit Africa are unsettled to find that Africans treat them—even refer to them—the same way as white tourists. The term "obruni," or "white foreigner," is applied regardless of skin color.

To African-Americans who come here seeking their roots, the term is a sign of the chasm between Africans and African-Americans. Though they share a legacy, they experience it entirely differently.

"It is a shock for any black person to be called white," said Ms. Mann, who moved here two years ago. "But it is really tough to hear it when you come with your heart to seek your roots in Africa."

The advertising campaign urges Ghanaians to drop "obruni" in favor of "akwaaba anyemi," a slightly awkward phrase fashioned from two tribal languages meaning "welcome, sister or brother." . . .

The government plans to hold a huge event in 2007 to commemorate the 200th anniversary of the end of the trans-Atlantic trade by Britain and the 50th anniversary of Ghana's independence. The ceremonies will include traditional African burial rituals for the millions who died as a result of slavery. Estimates of the trade vary widely . . .

Some perished on the long march from the inland villages where they were captured to seaports. Others died in the dungeons of slave castles and forts, where they were sometimes kept for months, until enough were gathered to pack the hold of a ship. Still others died in the middle passage, the longest leg of the triangular journey between Europe, Africa and the Americas. Of the estimated 11 million who crossed the sea, most went to South America and the Caribbean. About 500,000 are believed to have ended up in the United States.

The mass deportations and the divisions the slave trade wrought are wounds from which Africa still struggles to recover.

Ghana was the first sub-Saharan African nation to shake off its colonial rulers, winning its independence from Britain in 1957. Its founding father, Kwame Nkrumah, attended Lincoln University, a historically black college in Pennsylvania, and saw in African-Americans a key to developing the new nation. "Nkrumah saw the American Negro as the vanguard of the African people," said Henry Louis Gates Jr., chairman of the African and African-American studies department at Harvard. . . .

To Nkrumah, the struggle for civil rights in the diaspora and the struggles for independence from colonial rule in Africa were inextricably linked, both being expressions of the desire of black people everywhere to regain their freedom.

But Nkrumah was ousted in a coup in 1966, and by then Pan-Africanism had already given way to nationalism and cold war politics, sending much of the continent down a trail of autocracy, civil war and heartbreak. Still, African-Americans are drawn to Ghana's rich culture, and the history of slavery.

Ghana still has dozens of slave forts, each a chilling reminder of the brutality of the trade. At Elmina Castle, built by the Portuguese in 1482 and taken over by the Dutch 150 years later, visitors are guided through a Christian chapel built adjacent to the hall where slaves were auctioned, and the balcony over the women's

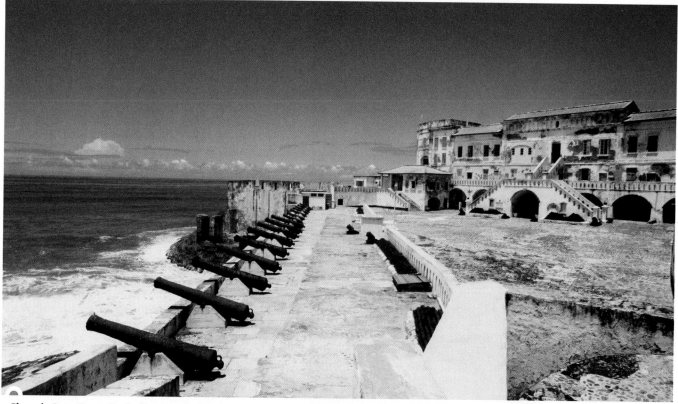

Ghana's Cape Coast Castle (Fort Carolusborg). For centuries, Africans walked through this castle's infamous "door of no return" directly into slave ships. Today, that door has been renamed "the door of return." Ghana hopes to persuade the descendants of enslaved Africans to visit, invest, send their children to be educated, and even retire here.

dungeons from which the fort's governor would choose a concubine from the chattel below.

The room through which slaves passed into waiting ships is the emotional climax of the tour, a suffocating dungeon dimly lit by sunlight pouring through a narrow portal leading to the churning sea. . . .

For African-Americans and others in the African diaspora, there is lingering hostility and confusion about the role Africans played in the slave trade.

"The myth was our African ancestors were out on a walk one day and some bad white dude threw a net over them," Mr. Gates said. "But that wasn't the way it happened. It wouldn't have been possible without the help of Africans." Many Africans, meanwhile, often fail to see any connection at all between them and African-Americans, or feel African-Americans are better

off for having been taken to the United States. Many Africans strive to emigrate; for the past 15 years, the number of Africans moving to the United States has surpassed estimates of the number forced there during any of the peak years of the slave trade. The number of immigrants from Ghana in the United States is larger than that of any other African country except Nigeria, according to the 2000 census.

"So many Africans want to go to America, so they can't understand why Americans would want to come here," said Philip Amoa-Mensah, a guide at Elmina Castle . . .

The relationship is clearly a work in progress. Ghanaians are still learning of their ancestors' pivotal roles in the slave trade, and slave forts on the coast, long used to thousands of foreign visitors, have in recent years become sites for school field trips. . . .

A recent African-American visitor to Cape Coast castle took the emotionally charged step through the door of no return, only to be greeted by a pair of toddlers playing in a fishing boat on the other side, pointing and shouting, "obruni, obruni!"

William Kwaku Moses, 71, a retired security guard who sells shells to tourists on the other side of the door of no return, shushed the children.

"We are trying," he said, with a shrug.

A Native American: a Chiquitanos Indian woman from Bolivia.

A young man from the Marquesas Islands in Polynesia.

A young Australian cowboy in Australia's Simpson Desert.

(continued from p. 117)

Another problem with the tripartite scheme is that many populations don't fit neatly into any one of the three "great races." For example, where would one put the Polynesians? *Polynesia* is a triangle of South Pacific islands formed by Hawaii to the north, Easter Island to the east, and New Zealand to the southwest. Does the "bronze" skin color of Polynesians connect them to the Caucasoids or to the Mongoloids? Some scientists, recognizing this problem, enlarged the original tripartite scheme to include the Polynesian "race." Native Americans presented a similar problem. Were they red or yellow? Some scientists added a fifth race—the "red," or Amerindian—to the major racial groups.

Many people in southern India have dark skins, but scientists have been reluctant to classify them with "black" Africans because of their Caucasoid facial features and hair form. Some, therefore, have created a separate race for these people. What about the Australian aborigines, hunters and gatherers native to what has been, throughout human history, the most isolated continent? By skin color, one might place some Native Australians in the same race as tropical Africans. However, similarities to Europeans in hair color (light or reddish) and facial features have led some scientists to classify them as Caucasoids. But there is no evidence that Australians are closer genetically or historically to either of these groups than they are to Asians. Recognizing this problem, scientists often regard Native Australians as a separate race.

Finally, consider the San ("Bushmen") of the Kalahari Desert in southern Africa. Scientists have perceived their skin color as varying from brown to yellow. Some who regard San skin as "yellow" have placed them in the same category as Asians. In theory, people of the same race share more recent common ancestry with each other than they do with any others. But there is no evidence for recent common ancestry between San and Asians. Somewhat more reasonably, some scholars assign the San to the Capoid race (from the Cape of Good Hope), which is seen as being different from other groups inhabiting tropical Africa.

Similar problems arise when any single trait is used as a basis for racial classification. An attempt to use facial features, height, weight, or any other phenotypical trait is fraught with difficulties. For example, consider the *Nilotes,* natives of the upper Nile region of Uganda and Sudan. Nilotes tend to be tall and to have long, narrow noses. Certain Scandinavians are also tall, with similar noses. Given the distance between their homelands, to classify them as members of the same race makes little sense. There is no reason to assume that Nilotes and Scandinavians are more closely related to each other than either is to shorter and nearer populations with different kinds of noses.

Would it be better to base racial classifications on a combination of physical traits? This would avoid some of the problems mentioned above, but others would arise. First, skin color, stature, skull form, and facial features (nose form, eye shape, lip thickness) don't go together as a unit. For example, people with dark skin may be tall or short and have hair ranging from straight to very curly. Dark-haired populations may have light or dark skin, along with various skull forms, facial features, and body sizes and shapes. The number of combinations is very large, and the amount that heredity (versus environment) contributes to such phenotypical traits is often unclear.

Genetic Markers Don't Correlate with Phenotype

The analysis of human DNA indicates that fully 94 percent of human genetic variation occurs within so-called "races." Considering conventional geographic "racial" groupings such as Africans, Asians, and Europeans, there is only about 6 percent variation in genes from one group to the other. In other words, there is much greater variation within each of the traditional "races" than between them. Humans are much more alike genetically than are other hominoids (the living apes). This suggests a recently shared common ancestor (perhaps as recent as 70,000 to 50,000 years) for all members of modern *Homo sapiens*. Sampling the mitochondrial DNA (mtDNA) of various populations, Rebecca Cann, Mark Stoneking, and Allan C. Wilson (1987) concluded that humans are genetically uniform overall, suggesting recent common ancestry. The fact that African populations are the most diverse genetically provides evidence that Africa was the site where the human diaspora originated.

Contemporary work in genomics has allowed scientists to construct regional and global phylogenetic trees based on shared genetic markers. Such trees are based on mitochondrial DNA (mtDNA) (sampling females) and the Y chromosome (sampling males). As the human genome gets better known, molecular anthropologists refine their models of actual genetic relationships among humans and how they dispersed. A **haplogroup** is a lineage or branch of such a genetic tree marked by one or more specific genetic mutations. For example, the

global mtDNA tree includes branches known as M and N (among others). The Y chromosome tree includes branches known as C and F (among others). Those four branches (either M or N for mtDNA and either C or F for the Y chromosome) are known to be associated with the spread of modern humans out of Africa between 70,000 and 50,000 B.P. Because Native Australians share those four branches, they are known to be part of that diaspora. The Americas were settled (from Asia) much later than Australia by multiple haplogroups, which probably arrived at different times and came by different routes.

Although long-term genetic markers do exist, they don't correlate neatly with phenotype. Phenotypical similarities and differences aren't precisely or even necessarily correlated with genetic relationships. Because of changes in the environment that affect individuals during growth and development, the range of phenotypes characteristic of a population may change without any genetic change whatsoever. There are several examples. In the early 20th century, the anthropologist Franz Boas (1940/1966) described changes in skull form (e.g., toward rounder heads) among the children of Europeans who had migrated to North America. The reason for this was not a change in genes, for the European immigrants tended to marry among themselves. Also, some of their children had been born in Europe and merely raised in the United States. Something in the environment, probably in the diet, was producing this change. We know now that changes in average height and weight produced by dietary differences in a few generations are common and may have nothing to do with race or genetics.

Explaining Skin Color

Traditional racial classification assumed that biological characteristics such as skin color were determined by heredity and that they were stable (immutable) over many generations. We now know that a biological similarity doesn't necessarily indicate recent common ancestry. Dark skin color, for example, can be shared by tropical Africans and indigenous Australians for reasons other than common heredity. Scientists have made considerable

An Afghan woman.

haplogroup
Lineage or branch of a genetic tree marked by one or more specific genetic mutations.

through the eyes of OTHERS

NAME: Natasha Musalem-Perez
COUNTRY OF ORIGIN: Dominican Republic
SUPERVISING PROFESSOR: Timothy McAndrews
SCHOOL: University of Wisconsin–La Crosse

Thinking about Race

Until I moved to the United States, I never thought to question my race. I never identified myself with a standard race nor tried to label others as belonging to a specific race. I never thought that an insignificant aspect of my life could have such an impact in a society until I began studying here. In the Dominican Republic and Puerto Rico, as in the United States, the historic events of discovery, conquest, colonialism, and slavery brought together in the islands, and in all of Latin America, people from three different continents: the white Europeans, the Native Americans (the Taino Indians), and later the black Africans brought as slaves. The people who live on these islands today are interracial—a mixture of these three genetic and cultural heritages, forming a population in which most people cannot be identified as belonging to a standard race. Even when their physical appearance points to a defined race, their genes tell another story. Furthermore, genetic mingling is not the only obvious characteristic of this historical process, for the culture—food, language, and folklore—is also a fusion. This is not to say that these are egalitarian societies; on the contrary, stratification by social class manifests itself in an immense gap between wealthy and poor people. This stratification may reflect a race bias due to the way history developed, since the black slaves remained poor when they were freed while the Spanish colonizers remained wealthy.

As a result of these historical developments, racism and the idea of race are not as central to social life in Puerto Rico and the Dominican Republic as they are in the United States, where racial and ethnic groups have not mixed to the point of being unidentifiable and a clear segregation still exists, rendering racial-ethnic prejudice a factor in social issues. The effect of racial-ethnic prejudice can be seen in the structure of U.S. society and government in programs like affirmative action that are considered necessary to prevent discrimination. At the same time, a person has to identify race or ethnicity on a typical application, especially one related to government affairs. It seems like society is trying to both integrate and segregate at the same time.

It is true that in the Caribbean Islands racial-ethnic groups have been intermingling longer than they have in the United States, where prejudice against interracial marriage still remains. Nevertheless, the great emphasis given to diversity in the United States and the immense efforts to educate people about others and to integrate people's differences shocked me when I began to live here. I had to reevaluate my identity, having become confused about what I thought was clear.

melanin
"Natural sunscreen" produced by skin cells responsible for pigmentation.

progress in explaining variation in human skin color, along with many other features of human biological diversity. We shift now from classification to explanation, in which natural selection plays a key role.

Natural selection is the process by which the forms most fit to survive and reproduce in a given environment do so. Over the generations, the less fit organisms die out, and the favored types survive by producing more offspring. The role of natural selection in producing variation in skin color will illustrate the explanatory approach to human biological diversity. Comparable explanations have been provided for many other aspects of human biological variation, as we'll see later in this chapter.

Skin color is a complex biological trait—influenced by several genes. Just how many genes is not known. **Melanin,** the primary determinant of human skin color, is a chemical substance manufactured in the epidermis, or outer skin layer. The melanin cells of darker-skinned people produce more and larger granules of melanin than do those of lighter-skinned people. By screening out ultraviolet (UV) radiation from the sun, melanin offers protection against a variety of maladies, including sunburn and skin cancer.

Prior to the 16th century, most of the world's very dark-skinned peoples lived in the **tropics,** a belt extending about 23 degrees north and south of the equator, between the Tropic of Cancer and the Tropic of Capricorn. The association between dark skin color and a tropical habitat existed throughout the Old World, where humans and their ancestors have lived for millions of years. The darkest populations of Africa evolved not in shady equatorial forests but in sunny open grassland, or savanna, country.

Outside the tropics, skin color tends to be lighter. Moving north in Africa, for example, there is a gradual transition from dark brown to medium brown. Average skin color continues to lighten as one moves through the Middle East, into southern Europe, through central Europe, and to the north. South of the tropics skin color also is lighter. In the Americas, by contrast, tropical populations don't have very dark skin. This is the case because the settlement of the New World by light-skinned Asian ancestors of Native Americans was relatively recent, probably dating back no more than 20,000 years.

How, aside from migrations, can we explain the geographic distribution of human skin color? Natural selection provides an answer. In the tropics, intense UV radiation poses a series of threats, including severe sunburn, that make light skin color an adaptive disadvantage (Recap 6.1 summarizes those threats). By damaging sweat glands sunburn reduces the body's ability to perspire and thus to regulate its own temperature (thermoregulation). Sunburn also can increase susceptibility to disease. Melanin, nature's own sunscreen, confers a selective advantage (i.e., a better chance to survive and reproduce) on darker-skinned people living in the tropics. (Today, light-skinned people manage to survive in the tropics by staying indoors

Also shown are cultural alternatives that can make up for biological disadvantages and examples of natural selection (NS) operating today in relation to skin color

		CULTURAL ALTERNATIVES	NS IN ACTION TODAY
DARK SKIN COLOR	Melanin is natural sunscreen		
Advantage	In tropics: screens out UV Reduces susceptibility to folate destruction and thus to NTDs, including spina bifida Prevents sunburn and thus enhances sweating and thermoregulation Reduces disease susceptibility Reduces risk of skin cancer		
Disadvantage	Outside tropics: Reduces UV absorption		
	Increases susceptibility to rickets, osteoporosis	Foods, vitamin D supplements	East Asians in northern UK Inuit with modern diets
LIGHT SKIN COLOR	No natural sunscreen		
Advantage	Outside tropics: Admits UV Body manufactures vitamin D and thus prevents rickets, and osteoporosis		
Disadvantage	Increases susceptibility to folate destruction and thus to NTDs, including spina bifida Impaired spermatogenesis	Folic acid/folate supplements	Whites still have more NTDs
	Increases susceptibility to sunburn and thus to impaired sweating and poor thermoregulation Increases disease susceptibility Increases susceptibility to skin cancer	Shelter, sunscreens, lotions, etc.	

and by using cultural products, such as umbrellas and lotions, to screen sunlight). Yet another disadvantage of having light skin color in the tropics is that exposure to UV radiation can cause skin cancer (Blum 1961).

Years ago, W. F. Loomis (1967) focused on the role of UV radiation in stimulating the manufacture (synthesis) of vitamin D by the human body. The unclothed human body can produce its own vitamin D when exposed to sufficient sunlight. However, in a cloudy environment that also is so cold that people have to dress themselves much of the year (such as northern Europe, where very light skin color evolved), clothing interferes with the body's manufacture of vitamin D. The ensuing shortage of vitamin D diminishes the absorption of calcium in the intestines. A nutritional disease known as **rickets,** which softens and deforms the bones, may develop. In women, deformation of the pelvic bones from rickets can interfere with childbirth. In cold northern areas, light skin color maximizes the absorption of UV radiation and the synthesis of vitamin D by the few parts of the body that are exposed to direct sunlight. There has been selection against dark skin color in northern areas because melanin screens out UV radiation.

This natural selection continues today: East Asians who have migrated recently from India and Pakistan to northern areas of the United Kingdom have a higher incidence of rickets and osteoporosis (also related to vitamin D and calcium deficiency) than the general British population. A related illustration involves Eskimos (Inuit) and other indigenous inhabitants of northern Alaska and northern Canada. According to Nina Jablonski (quoted in Iqbal 2002), "Looking at Alaska, one would think that the native people should be pale as ghosts." One reason they aren't is that they haven't inhabited this region very long in terms of geological time. Even more important, their traditional diet, which is rich in seafood, including fish oils, supplies sufficient vitamin D so as to make a reduction in pigmentation unnecessary. However, and again illustrating natural selection at work today, "when these people don't eat their aboriginal diets of fish and marine mammals, they suffer tremendously high rates of vitamin

anthropology **ATLAS**

See Map 7, which plots the distribution of human skin color in relation to ultraviolet variation from the sun.

tropics
Zone between 23 degrees north (Tropic of Cancer) and 23 degrees south (Tropic of Capricorn) of the equator.

rickets
Vitamin D deficiency marked by bone deformation.

D-deficiency diseases such as rickets in children and osteoporosis in adults" (Jablonski quoted in Iqbal 2002). Far from being immutable, skin color can become an evolutionary liability very quickly.

According to Jablonski and George Chaplin (2000), another key factor explaining the geographic distribution of skin color involves the effects of UV on folate, an essential nutrient that the human body manufactures from folic acid. Folate is needed for cell division and the production of new DNA. Pregnant women require large amounts of folate to support rapid cell division in the embryo, and there is a direct connection between folate and individual reproductive success. Folate deficiency causes neural tube defects (NTDs) in human embryos. NTDs are marked by the incomplete closure of the neural tube, so the spine and spinal cord fail to develop completely. One NTD, anencephaly (with the brain an exposed mass), results in stillbirth or death soon after delivery. With spina bifida, another NTD, survival rates are higher, but babies have severe disabilities, including paralysis. NTDs are the second-most-common human birth defect after cardiac abnormalities. Today, women of reproductive age are advised to take folate supplements to prevent serious birth defects such as spina bifida.

Natural sunlight and UV radiation destroy folate in the human body. Because melanin, as we have seen, protects against UV hazards, such as

sunburn and its consequences, dark skin coloration is adaptive in the tropics. Now we see that melanin also is adaptive because it conserves folate in the human body and thus protects against NTDs, which are much more common in light-skinned than in darker-skinned populations (Jablonski and Chaplin 2000). Studies confirm that Africans and African Americans have a low incidence of severe folate deficiency, even among individuals with marginal nutritional status. Folate also plays a role in another process that is central to reproduction, spermatogenesis—the production of sperm. In mice and rats, folate deficiency can cause male sterility; it may well play a similar role in humans.

Today, of course, cultural alternatives to biological adaptation permit light-skinned people to survive in the tropics and darker-skinned people to live in the far north. People can clothe themselves and seek shelter from the sun; they can use artificial sunscreens if they lack the natural protection that melanin provides. Dark-skinned people living in the north can, indeed must, get vitamin D from their diet or take supplements. Today, pregnant women are routinely advised to take folic acid or folate supplements as a hedge against NTDs. Even so, light skin color still is correlated with a higher incidence of spina bifida.

Jablonski and Chaplin (2000) explain variation in human skin color as resulting from a balancing act between the evolutionary needs to (1) protect against all UV hazards (dark skin in the tropics) and (2) have an adequate supply of vitamin D (lighter skin outside the tropics). This discussion of skin color shows that common ancestry, the presumed basis of race, is not the only reason for biological similarities. Natural selection, still at work today, makes a major contribution to variations in human skin color, as well as to many other human biological differences and similarities.

HUMAN BIOLOGICAL ADAPTATION

This section considers several additional examples of human biological diversity that reflect adaptation to environmental stresses, such as disease, diet, and climate. There is abundant evidence for human genetic adaptation and thus for evolution (change in gene frequency) through selection working in specific environments. One example is the adaptive value of the Hb^S heterozygote and its spread in malarial environments, which was discussed in Chapter 5. Adaptation and evolution go on in specific environments. There is no generally or ideally adaptive allele and no perfect phenotype. Nor can an allele be assumed to be maladaptive for all times and all places. We have seen that even Hb^S, which produces a lethal anemia, has a

Spina bifida is a congenital (birth) disorder that leaves a portion of the spinal cord exposed. Treatments include surgery and physiotherapy, but those with the condition, like the girl shown here in Arkansas, often need wheelchairs. Why is light skin color correlated with a higher incidence of spina bifida?

selective advantage in the heterozygous form in malarial environments.

Also, alleles that were once maladaptive may lose their disadvantage if the environment shifts. Color blindness (disadvantageous for hunters and forest dwellers) and a form of genetically determined diabetes are examples. Today's environment contains medical techniques that allow people with such conditions to live fairly normal lives. Formerly maladaptive alleles have thus become neutral with respect to selection. With thousands of human genes now known, new genetic traits are discovered almost every day. Such studies tend to focus on genetic abnormalities, because of their medical and treatment implications.

Genes and Disease

According to the *World Health Report*, published by the World Health Organization (WHO) in Geneva, Switzerland, tropical diseases affect more than 10 percent of the world's population. Malaria, the most widespread of these diseases, afflicts between 350 million and 500 million people annually (World Malaria Report 2005). Schistosomiasis (snail fever), a waterborne parasitic disease, affects more than 200 million. Some 120 million people have filariasis, which causes elephantiasis—lymphatic obstruction leading to the enlargement of body parts, particularly the legs and scrotum (check out the website of the World Health Organization at www.who.int/home/).

The malaria threat has been spreading. Brazil had 560,000 cases in 1988, versus 100,000 in 1977. Worldwide, the number of malaria cases rose from 270 million in 1990 to over 350 million today. Contributing to this rise is the increasing resistance of parasites to drugs used to treat malaria (World Malaria Report 2005). However, hundreds of millions of people are genetically resistant. Sickle-cell hemoglobin is the best known of the genetic antimalarials (Diamond 1997).

Microbes have been major selective agents for humans, particularly before the arrival of modern medicine. Some people are genetically more susceptible to certain diseases than others are, and the distribution of human blood types continues to change in response to natural selection.

After food production emerged around 10,000 years ago, infectious diseases posed a mounting risk and eventually became the foremost cause of human mortality. Food production favors infection for several reasons. Cultivation sustains larger, denser populations and a more sedentary lifestyle than does hunting and gathering. People live closer to each other and to their own wastes, making it easier for microbes to survive and to find hosts. Domesticated animals also transmit diseases to people.

Until 1977, when the last case of smallpox was reported, smallpox had been a major threat to

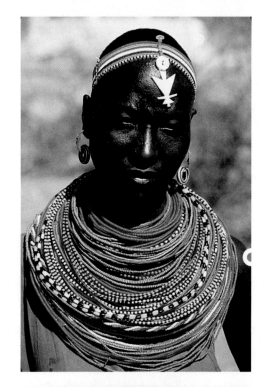

Before the 16th century, almost all the very dark-skinned populations of the world lived in the tropics, as does this Samburu woman from Kenya.

Very light skin color, illustrated in this photo of a mature blond, blue-eyed man, maximizes absorption of ultraviolet radiation by those few parts of the body exposed to direct sunlight during northern winters. This helps prevent rickets.

humans and a determinant of blood group frequencies (Diamond 1990, 1997). The smallpox virus is a mutation from one of the pox viruses that plague such domesticated animals as cows, sheep, goats, horses, and pigs. Smallpox appeared in human beings after people and animals started living together. Smallpox epidemics have played important roles in world history, often killing one-fourth to one-half of the affected populations. Smallpox contributed to Sparta's defeat of Athens in 430 B.C. and to the decline of the Roman empire after A.B. 160.

The ABO blood groups have figured in human resistance to smallpox. Blood is typed according to the protein and sugar compounds on the

In New York City in 1947, the appearance of nine cases of smallpox, including two deaths, spurred a very successful mass vaccination program. Shown here, lines of people wait to be vaccinated at the New York Health Department on April 14, 1947. The threat made the cover of *Cosmopolitan* magazine.

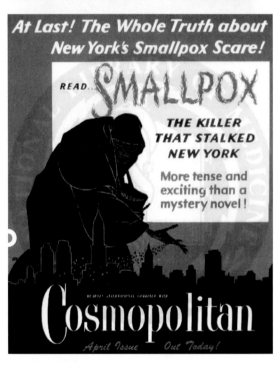

At Last! The Whole Truth about New York's Smallpox Scare!

READ... **SMALLPOX**

THE KILLER THAT STALKED NEW YORK

More tense and exciting than a mystery novel!

Cosmopolitan

April Issue   Out Today!

surface of the red blood cells. Different substances (compounds) distinguish between type A and type B blood. Type A cells trigger the production of *antibodies* in B blood, so that A cells clot in B blood. The different substances work like chemical passwords; they help us distinguish our own cells from invading cells, including microbes, we ought to destroy. The surfaces of some microbes have substances similar to ABO blood group substances. We don't produce antibodies to substances similar to those on our own blood cells. We can think of this as a clever evolutionary trick by the microbes to deceive their hosts, because we don't normally develop antibodies against our own biochemistry.

People with A or AB blood are more susceptible to smallpox than are people with type B or type O. Presumably this is because a substance on the smallpox virus mimics the type A substance, permitting the virus to slip by the defenses of the type A individual. By contrast, type B and type O individuals produce antibodies against smallpox because they recognize it as a foreign substance.

The relation between type A blood and susceptibility to smallpox was first suggested by the low frequencies of the A allele in areas of India and Africa where smallpox had been endemic. A comparative study done in rural India in 1965–1966, during a virulent smallpox epidemic, did much to confirm this relationship. Drs. F. Vogel and M. R. Chakravartti analyzed blood samples from smallpox victims and their uninfected siblings (Diamond 1990). The researchers found 415 infected children, none ever vaccinated against smallpox. All but eight of the infected children had an uninfected (also unvaccinated) sibling.

The results of the study were clear: Susceptibility to smallpox varied with ABO type. Of the 415 infected children, 261 had the A allele; 154 lacked it. Among their 407 uninfected siblings, the ratio was reversed. Only 80 had the A allele; 327 lacked it. The researchers calculated that a type A or type AB person had a seven times greater chance of getting smallpox than did an O or B person.

In most human populations, the O allele is more common than A and B combined. A is most common in Europe; B frequencies are highest in Asia. Since smallpox was once widespread in the Old World, we might wonder why natural selection didn't eliminate the A allele entirely. The answer appears to be this: Other diseases spared the type A people and penalized those with other blood groups.

For example, type O people seem to be especially susceptible to the bubonic plague—the "Black Death" that killed a third of the population of medieval Europe. Type O people are also more likely to get cholera, which has killed as many people in India as smallpox has. On the other hand, blood group O may increase resistance to syphilis. The ravages of that sexually transmitted disease, which may have originated in the New World, may explain the very high frequency of type O blood among the native populations of Central and South America. The distribution of human blood groups appears to represent a compromise among the selective effects of many diseases.

Associations between ABO blood type and noninfectious disorders also have been noted. Type O individuals are most susceptible to duodenal and gastric ulcers. Type A individuals seem most prone to stomach and cervical cancer and ovarian tumors. However, since these noninfectious disorders tend to occur after reproduction has ended, their relevance to adaptation and evolution through natural selection is doubtful (see also Weiss 1993).

In the case of diseases for which there are no cures, genetic resistance maintains its significance. There is genetic variation in susceptibility to the HIV virus, for example. We know that people exposed to HIV vary in their risk of developing AIDS and in the rate at which the disease progresses. AIDS is widespread in many African nations (and in the United States, France, and Brazil). Particularly in Africa, where treatment strategies now used in the industrial nations are not widely available, the death rate from AIDS could eventually (let us hope it does not) rival that of past epidemics of smallpox and plague. If so, AIDS could cause large shifts in human gene frequencies—again illustrating the ongoing operation of natural selection.

Facial Features

Natural selection also affects facial features. For instance, long noses seem to be adaptive in arid areas (Brace 1964; Weiner 1954), because membranes and blood vessels inside the nose moisten the air as it is breathed in. Long noses are also adaptive in cold environments, because blood vessels warm the air as it is breathed in. This nose form distances the brain, which is sensitive to bitter cold, from raw outer air. These were adaptive biological features for humans who lived in cold climates before the invention of central heating.

The association between nose form and temperature is recognized as **Thomson's nose rule** (Thomson and Buxton 1923), which shows up statistically. In plotting the geographic distribution of nose length among human populations who have lived for many generations in the areas they now inhabit, the average nose does tend to be longer in areas with lower mean annual temperatures.

Other facial features also illustrate adaptation to selective forces. Among contemporary humans, average tooth size is largest among Native Australian hunters and gatherers, for whom large teeth had an adaptive advantage, given a diet based on foods with a considerable amount of sand and grit. People with small teeth—if false teeth and sand-free foods are unavailable—can't feed themselves as effectively as people with more massive dentition can (see Brace 2000).

Size and Body Build

Certain body builds have adaptive advantages for particular environments. In 1847, the German (*text continues on p. 130*)

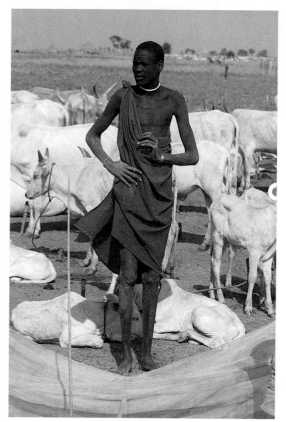

This Nilotic man, a Nuer herder from Sudan, has a tall linear body with elongated extremities (note his fingers). Such proportioning increases the surface area relative to mass and thus dissipates heat (Allen's rule). What other body form can achieve the same result?

Thomson's nose rule Average nose length increases in cold areas.

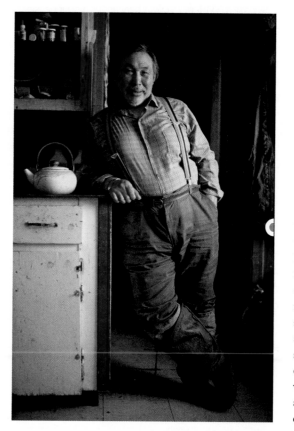

Tatigat, an Inuk man, shown inside his home at Igloolik, Nunavut, Canada. Compact stockiness, fur coats, well-sealed dwellings, and indoor heating systems are biological and cultural ways of adapting to a very cold environment.

Adapting to Thin Air

Anthropologists study the varied ways in which humans adapt, biologically and culturally, to environmental stresses, including disease, temperature, humidity, sunlight, and altitude—as described here. This account describes how anthropologists are studying the dramatically different ways in which three populations have adapted to high altitudes. Working with these populations, in Tibet, Ethiopia, and the Andes, anthropologists follow many lines of evidence—archaeological, biological, and climatological—to answer questions about social, cultural, and biological adaptations. Anthropologists know that the biological diversity we observe among contemporary and prehistoric humans has many causes. This chapter examines those causes, while rejecting attempts to pigeonhole humans into discrete biological categories called races.

Prehistoric and contemporary human populations living at altitudes of at least 8,000 feet (2,500 meters) above sea level may provide unique insights into human evolution, reports an interdisciplinary group of scientists.

Indigenous highlanders living in the Andean Altiplano in South America, in the Tibetan Plateau in Asia, and at the highest elevations of the Ethiopian Highlands in east Africa have evolved three distinctly different biological adaptations for surviving in the oxygen-thin air found at high altitude.

"To have examples of three geographically dispersed populations adapting in different ways to the same stress is very unusual," said Cynthia Beall, a physical anthropologist at Case Western Reserve University in Cleveland, Ohio. "From an evolutionary standpoint the question becomes, Why do these differences exist? . . ."

"High-altitude populations offer a unique natural lab that allows us to follow [many] lines of evidence—archaeological, biological, climatological—to answer intriguing questions about social, cultural, and biological adaptations," said Mark Aldenderfer, an archaeologist at the University of California, Santa Barbara. . . .

The Andean and Tibetan plateaus rise some 13,000 feet (4 kilometers) above sea level. As prehistoric hunter-gatherers moved into these environments, they . . . likely suffered acute hypoxia, a condition created by a diminished supply of oxygen to body tissues. At high altitudes the air is much thinner than at sea level. As a result, a person inhales fewer oxygen molecules with each breath. Symptoms of hypoxia, sometimes known as mountain sickness, include headaches, vomiting, sleeplessness, impaired thinking, and an inability to sustain long periods of physical activity. At elevations above 25,000 feet (7,600 meters), hypoxia can kill.

The Andeans adapted to the thin air by developing an ability to carry more oxygen in each red blood cell. That is: They breathe at the same rate as people who live at sea level, but the Andeans have the ability to deliver oxygen throughout their bodies more effectively than people at sea level do.

"Andeans counter having less oxygen in every breath by having higher hemoglobin concentrations in their blood," Beall said. Hemoglobin is the protein in red blood cells that ferries oxygen through the blood system. Having more hemoglobin to carry oxygen through the blood system than people at sea level counterbalances the effects of hypoxia.

Tibetans compensate for low oxygen content much differently. They increase their oxygen intake by taking more breaths per minute than people who live at sea level.

"Andeans go the hematological route, Tibetans the respiratory route," Beall said.

In addition, Tibetans may have a second biological adaptation, which expands their blood vessels, allowing them to deliver oxygen throughout their bodies more effectively than sea-level people do.

Tibetans' lungs synthesize larger amounts of a gas called nitric oxide from the air they breathe. "One effect of nitric oxide is to increase the diameter of blood vessels, which suggests that Tibetans may offset low oxygen content in their blood with increased blood flow," Beall said.

A pilot study Beall conducted of Ethiopian highlanders living at 11,580 feet (3,530 meters) suggests that—unlike the Tibetans—they don't breathe more rapidly than people at sea level and aren't able to more effectively synthesize nitric oxide. Nor do the Ethiopians have higher hemoglobin counts than sea-level people, as the Andeans do.

Yet despite living at elevations with low oxygen content, "the Ethiopian highlanders were hardly hypoxic at all," Beall said. "I was genuinely surprised."

So what adaptation have the Ethiopian highlanders' bodies evolved to survive at high altitude? "Right now we have no clue how they do it," Beall said. . . .

Knowing how long the populations have been living at the top of the world is crucial to answering the evolutionary question of whether these adaptations are the result of differences in the founding populations, random genetic mutations, or the passage of time.

Archaeologists, paleontologists, and climatologists are pooling their knowledge to pinpoint when some of these early migrations to the high plateaus occurred.

Aldenderfer . . . says cultural adaptations would have to occur first.

"The ability to survive in such harsh environments required control of fire, an expanded tool kit that included bone needles to make complicated clothing that protected the body in a significant way, and the cultural flexibility to change subsistence practices," he said.

Climatologists' changing understanding of the nature of the last ice age is contributing to archaeological efforts.

Ice-core and other evidence show that, rather than being a monolithic period lasting 100,000 years with frigid temperatures and glacial landscapes, the Ice Age included long periods of relatively mild weather.

"Through most of the 20th century it was thought that the Tibetan Plateau was covered by a monstrous ice sheet during the last glacial maximum, about 21,000 years ago," Aldenderfer said. "People couldn't live on an ice sheet. So archaeologists wouldn't even bother to look for sites from that time period."

[Now] knowing the Tibetan Plateau more closely resembled Arctic tundra has led to the discovery of new sites. Archaeological evidence suggests hunter-gatherers occupied the Tibetan Plateau some 25,000 to 20,000 years ago. People began moving into the Andean Altiplano around 11,500 to 11,000 years ago.

What motivated prehistoric people to move into the harsh and challenging conditions presented by high altitude?

"The highlands offered an attractive option with a landscape that was open and pristine," Aldenderfer said. "People probably started out moving up and down for short terms, and then gradually settled at the higher elevations."

A Peruvian man and his adult daughter stand outside their thatch-roofed house in Orouille, Peru. Andeans have adapted to thin air by developing an ability to carry more oxygen in each red blood cell—that is, they breathe at the same rate as people who live at sea level, but they have the ability to deliver oxygen throughout their bodies more effectively than people at sea level do.

Changing environmental conditions also created "new opportunities and new constraints," he said.

In South America, for example, the maritime environment began transforming as temperatures warmed, glaciers retreated, and sea levels rose. Large mammals such as mammoths and mastodons gradually went extinct, as did other herbivores. Warmer temperatures allowed plants and animals to move to higher elevations, creating resource-rich patches of habitat in highland areas. . . .

Similar processes likely occurred in Tibet. Prehistoric people occupied the landscape during the interglacial process, when conditions were relatively benign and hunting was plentiful, Aldenderfer said.

"Suddenly [thereafter] it gets really cold. Biomass declined precipitously. It becomes very arid because of wind-flow patterns. The landscape becomes one of very patchy vegetation, rocky. And the huge herds of gazelle, antelope, and sheep wax and wane," Aldenderfer said. "What happens? . . . Finding biological differences suggests they toughed it out and adapted."

SOURCE: Hillary Mayell, "Three High-Altitude Peoples, Three Adaptations to Thin Air," *National Geographic News*, February 25, 2004. http://news.nationalgeographic.com. © 2004 National Geographic Society. Reprinted with permission.

(*continued from p. 127*)

biologist Karl Christian Bergmann observed that within the same species of warm-blooded animals, populations with smaller individuals are more often found in warm climates, while those with greater bulk, or mass, are found in colder regions. The relation between body weight and temperature is summarized in **Bergmann's rule:** The smaller of two bodies similar in shape has more surface area per unit of weight. Therefore, it sheds heat more efficiently. (Heat loss occurs on the body's surface—the skin perspires.) Average body size tends to increase in cold areas and to decrease in hot ones because big bodies hold heat better than small ones do. To be more precise, in a large sample of native populations, average adult male weight increased by 0.66 pound (0.3 kilogram) for every 1 degree Fahrenheit fall in mean annual temperature (Roberts 1953; Steegman 1975). The "pygmies" and the San, who live in hot climates and weigh only 90 pounds on the average, illustrate this relation in reverse.

Body shape differences also reflect adaptation to temperature through natural selection. The relationship between temperature and body shape in animals and birds was first recognized in 1877 by the zoologist J. A. Allen. **Allen's rule** states that the relative size of protruding body parts—ears, tails, bills, fingers, toes, limbs, and so on—increases with temperature. Among humans, slender bodies with long digits and limbs are advantageous in tropical climates. Such bodies increase body surface relative to mass and allow for more efficient heat dissipation. Among the cold-adapted Eskimos, the opposite phenotype is found. Short limbs and stocky bodies serve to conserve heat. Cold-area populations tend to have larger chests and shorter arms than do people from warm areas (Roberts 1953).

This discussion of adaptive relationships between climate and body size and shape illustrates that natural selection may achieve the same effect in different ways. East African Nilotes, who live in a hot area, have tall, linear bodies with elongated extremities that increase surface area relative to mass and thus maximize heat dissipation (illustrating Allen's rule). Among the "pygmies," the reduction of body size achieves the same result (illustrating Bergmann's rule). Similarly, the large bodies of northern Europeans and the compact stockiness of the Eskimos serve the same function of heat conservation.

Similarly, as we see in "Appreciating Anthropology," human populations use different, but equally effective, biological means of adapting to the environmental stresses associated with high altitudes. Andeans have adapted to thin air by developing the ability to carry more oxygen in each red blood cell, compared with people who live at sea level. Having more hemoglobin

to carry oxygen counterbalances the effects of hypoxia. Tibetans, in contrast, increase their oxygen intake by taking more breaths per minute than do people who live at sea level. Also, their lungs synthesize large amounts of nitric oxide from the air they breathe. The nitric oxide works to expand the diameter of their blood vessels, so that Tibetans offset low oxygen content in their blood with increased blood flow. Ethiopian highlanders, by contrast, use none of these mechanisms. Compared with sea-level peoples, they don't breathe more rapidly, synthesize nitric oxide more effectively, or have a higher hemoglobin count. The exact biological mechanisms that enable Ethiopians to survive at high altitudes are being investigated.

Lactose Tolerance

Many biological traits that illustrate human adaptation are not under simple genetic control. Genetic determination of such traits may be likely but unconfirmed, or several genes may interact to influence the trait in question. Sometimes there is a genetic component, but the trait also responds to stresses encountered during growth. We speak of **phenotypical adaptation** when adaptive changes occur during an individual's lifetime. Phenotypical adaptation is made possible by biological plasticity—our ability to change in response to the environments we encounter as we grow (see Bogin 2001; Frisancho 1993).

Genes and phenotypical adaptation work together to produce a biochemical difference between human groups in the ability to digest large amounts of milk—an adaptive advantage when other foods are scarce and milk is available, as it is in dairying societies. All milk, whatever its source, contains a complex sugar called *lactose*. The digestion of milk depends on an enzyme called *lactase,* which works in the small intestine. Among all mammals except humans and some of their pets, lactase production ceases after weaning, so that these animals can no longer digest milk.

Lactase production and the ability to tolerate milk vary between populations. About 90 percent of northern Europeans and their descendants are lactose tolerant; they can digest several glasses of milk with no difficulty. Similarly, about 80 percent of two African populations, the Tutsi of Rwanda and Burundi in East Africa and the Fulani of Nigeria in West Africa, produce lactase and digest milk easily. Both of these groups traditionally have been herders. However, such nonherders as the Yoruba and the Igbo in Nigeria, the Baganda in Uganda, the Japanese and other Asians, Eskimos, South American Indians, and many Israelis cannot digest lactose (Kretchmer 1972/1975).

However, the variable human ability to digest milk seems to be a difference of degree. Some

---

Bergmann's rule
Larger bodies found in colder areas and smaller bodies in warmer ones.

Allen's rule
Protruding body parts are bigger in warmer areas.

phenotypical adaptation
Adaptive biological changes during an individual's lifetime.

populations can tolerate very little or no milk, but others are able to metabolize much greater quantities. Studies show that people who move from no-milk or low-milk diets to high-milk diets increase their lactose tolerance; this suggests some phenotypical adaptation. We can conclude that no simple genetic trait accounts for the ability to digest milk. Lactose tolerance appears to be one of many aspects of human biology governed both by genes and by phenotypical adaptation to environmental conditions.

We see that human biology changes constantly, even without genetic change. In this chapter we've considered ways in which humans adapt biologically to their environments, and the effects of such adaptation on human biological diversity. Modern biological anthropology seeks to explain specific aspects of human biological variation. The explanatory framework encompasses the same mechanisms —selection, mutation, drift, gene flow, and plasticity—that govern adaptation, variation, and evolution among other life forms (see Futuyma 1998; Mayr 2001).

Acing the
COURSE

Summary

1. Humans have access to varied ways—biological and cultural—of adapting to environmental stresses, such as disease, heat, cold, humidity, sunlight, and altitude. Biological diversity among contemporary and prehistoric humans has many causes. This chapter examines those causes, while rejecting attempts to pigeonhole humans into discrete biological categories called races.

2. How do scientists approach the study of human biological diversity? Because of a range of problems involved in classifying humans into racial categories, contemporary biologists focus on specific differences and try to explain them. Because of extensive gene flow and interbreeding, *Homo sapiens* has not evolved subspecies or distinct races. The genetic breaks that do exist among human populations have not led to the formation of discrete races.

3. Biological similarities between groups may reflect—rather than common ancestry—similar but independent adaptations to similar natural selective forces, such as degrees of ultraviolet radiation from the sun in the case of skin color.

4. Differential resistance to infectious diseases such as smallpox has influenced the distribution of human blood groups. There are genetic antimalarials, such as the sickle-cell allele discussed in Chapter 5. Natural selection also has operated on facial features and body size and shape.

5. Phenotypical adaptation refers to adaptive changes that occur in an individual's lifetime in response to the environment the organism encounters as it grows. Lactose tolerance is due partly to phenotypical adaptation. Biological similarities between geographically distant populations may be due to similar but independent genetic changes, rather than to common ancestry. Or they may reflect similar physiological responses to common stresses during growth. Also, human populations have developed different but equally effective ways of adapting to environmental conditions such as heat, cold, and high altitudes.

Key Terms

Allen's rule 130
Bergmann's rule 130
cline 117
haplogroup 121
melanin 122

phenotypical adaptation 130
racial classification 116
rickets 123
Thomson's nose rule 127
tropics 122

Test Yourself!

MULTIPLE CHOICE

1. It is important to understand that human racial categories are based upon *perceptions* of phenotypic features, and not on genotypes, because
   a. racial categories are internationally standardized.
   b. race should be determined by skeletal measurements, especially cranial capacity.
   c. you are in a place that does not use genealogy.
   d. racial categories are socially defined, not biologically determined.
   e. racial genotypes are more accurate.

2. Which of the following statements about human racial categories is true?
   a. They are applied to endogamous breeding populations.
   b. They are culturally arbitrary, even though most people assume them to be based in biology.
   c. They are biologically valid.
   d. They are based on global racial categories that vary little among societies.
   e. They are only valid when defined by haplogroups.

3. Some biologists use "race" to refer to "breeds," as of dogs or roses. Such domesticated "races" have been bred by humans for generations. Humanity (*Homo sapiens*) lacks such races because
   a. they are politically incorrect.
   b. humans are superior to dogs and roses.
   c. human populations have experienced a type of controlled breeding distinct from that experienced by dogs and roses.
   d. humans are less genetically predictable than dogs and roses.
   e. human populations have not been isolated enough from one another to develop such discrete groups.

4. Rather than attempting to classify humans into racial categories, biologists and anthropologists are
   a. increasingly focusing their attention on explaining why specific biological variations occur.
   b. denying the existence of any biological variation among humankind.
   c. attempting to create new categories based on blood type only.
   d. confident that earlier notions of racial categories are valid.
   e. trying to verify the anthropometric data from the turn of the century.

5. Which of the following has played an evolutionary role in determining skin color?
   a. Hb^S allele
   b. Allen's rule
   c. Bergmann's rule
   d. Thompson's rule
   e. ultraviolet radiation

6. Which of the following is the most likely reason for the dark skin color shared by tropical Africans and southern Indians?
   a. dietary adaptation
   b. prevention of hypervitaminosis D
   c. reducing the frequency of rickets
   d. recent common ancestry
   e. malarial resistance

7. By acting as a natural sunscreen, melanin confers a selective advantage on darker-skinned people living in the tropics. In this part of the world, darker skin
   a. reduces the susceptibility to folate destruction, and thus helps prevent folate deficiencies such as neural tube defects (in the case of pregnant women).
   b. diminishes the production of sperm.
   c. confers an advantage by increasing human mating success.
   d. stimulates the production of folic acid in pregnant women, and thus helps prevent premature births.
   e. limits sweat production and helps keep the body cool.

8. In the early 20th century, anthropologist Franz Boas described changes in skull form among the children of Europeans who had migrated to North America. He found that these changes could not be explained by genetics. His findings underscore the fact that
   a. although the environment influences phenotype, genetics are a more powerful determinant of racial differences.
   b. the politics of migration only get worse with the input of science.
   c. describing changes in skull form is the most accurate way to study the impact of migration on traveling populations.
   d. phenotypical similarities and differences don't necessarily have a genetic basis.
   e. even well-intentioned science can be used for racist ends.

9. What is the term for adaptive biological changes that take place during an individual's lifetime?
   a. genotypical adaptation
   b. cultural adaptation
   c. linguistic adaptation
   d. species-level adaptation
   e. phenotypical adaptation

10. What does Thomson's nose rule state?
   a. Short noses are adaptive in cold environments.
   b. Nose size is causally linked to skin color.
   c. Long noses are adaptive in cold environments.
   d. Nose size is causally linked to cranial capacity.
   e. Long noses are adaptive in hot environments.

FILL IN THE BLANK

1. Modern scientists find it most productive to use an _explanatory_ approach to studying human biological diversity.

2. A _cline_ is a gradual shift in gene frequencies between neighboring populations.

3. The vitamin D deficiency marked by bone deformation is called _rickets_.

4. _Phenotype_ refers to an organism's evident traits, its "manifest biology."

5. Considering conventional geographic "racial" groupings such as Africans, Asians, and Europeans, there is only about a ____6____ percent variation in genes from one group to another. This means that there is much greater variation _within_ each of the traditional "races" than _between_ them.

CRITICAL THINKING

1. What are the problems with human racial classification?

2. What explains skin color in humans? Are the processes that determined skin color in humans still continuing today? If so, what are some examples of this?

3. Read the American Anthropological Association's Statement on "race." What is its main argument? Why was such a public statement by this institution necessary?

4. If "race" is a discredited concept when applied to humans, what has replaced it?

5. Choose five people in your classroom who illustrate a range of phenotypical diversity. Which of their features vary most evidently? How do you explain this variation? Is some of the variation due to culture rather than to biology?

Multiple Choice: 1. (D); 2. (B); 3. (E); 4. (A); 5. (E); 6. (B); 7. (A); 8. (D); 9. (E); 10. (C); **Fill in the Blank:** 1. explanatory; 2. cline; 3. rickets; 4. Phenotype; 5. 6, within, between

Bogin, B.
  2001 *The Growth of Humanity.* New York: Wiley-Liss. Up-to-date perspective on human growth and development.

Diamond, J. M.
  2005 *Guns, Germs, and Steel: The Fates of Human Societies.* New York: W.W. Norton. An ecological approach to expansion and conquest in world history by a nonanthropologist.

Frisancho, A. R.
  1993 *Human Adaptation and Accommodation.* Ann Arbor: University of Michigan Press. Influence of the environment on phenotype, particularly during growth and development; a basic text.

Molnar, S.
  2006 *Human Variation: Races, Types, and Ethnic Groups,* 6th ed. Upper Saddle River, NJ: Prentice Hall. Links between biological and social diversity.

Mukhopadhyay, C. C., R. Henze, and Y. T. Moses
  2007 *How Real Is Race? A Sourcebook on Race, Culture, and Biology.* Lanham, MD: AltaMira. A broad consideration of the issues raised in this chapter and Chapter 14.

Wade, P.
  2002 *Race, Nature, and Culture: An Anthropological Perspective.* Sterling, VA: Pluto Press. A processual approach to human biology and race.

Suggested
Additional
Readings

Go to our Online Learning Center website at **www.mhhe.com/kottak** for Internet exercises directly related to the content of this chapter.

Internet
Exercises

How and why are monkeys and apes similar to humans?

When, where, and how did the first primates, monkeys, apes, and hominids evolve?

How did diversity among Miocene proto-apes figure in hominid origins?

An infant mountain gorilla shows affection to a silverback male. Apes fascinate us because of their humanlike qualities. Zoo gorillas are especially popular when they are displayed in "family" groups.

The Primates 7

understanding OURSELVES

Think about our senses—vision, hearing, touch, taste, and smell. Which are you using right now? Which do you most depend upon to navigate the world? Like almost all other anthropoids—a group that includes monkeys, humans, and apes—humans are diurnal, active during the day. As animals, we are programmed to rise at dawn and to sleep when the sun goes down. As cultural creatures, we venture into the night with torches, lanterns, and flashlights, and shut the dark out of our dwellings with artificial light. If we were night animals, we'd sense things differently. Our eyes might be bigger, like those of an owl or a tarsier. Maybe we'd have biological radar systems, as bats do. Perhaps we'd develop a more acute sense of hearing or smell to penetrate the dark.

Many animals rely upon scents and odors to help them interpret the world. Humans, by contrast, use an array of products to cover up or eliminate even the faint odors our limited olfactory apparatus permits us to smell. *Blindness* and *deafness* are common words that indicate the senses whose loss we deem most significant. The rarity of the word *anosmia,* the inability to smell, tells us something about our senses and our values. The sensory shifts that occurred in primate evolution, especially the one from smell to sight, explain something fundamental about ourselves.

How different are we from other primates? No human looks much like a lemur or a tarsier. That's understandable; our ancestries diverged maybe 50 million years ago. We're much more closely related to, and look more like, our fellow anthropoids--monkeys and apes. Within this group, we are much more similar to apes than to monkeys. Likewise, apes are more similar to humans than to monkeys. Still, in the popular imagination, humans group apes with monkeys, rather than with themselves. At zoos human parents say to their kids "look at the monkey" when they are seeing a chimp, gorilla, or orangantun. The national tabloids use phrases like "monkeying around" or "monkey see, monkey do" when reporting on stories that involve apes. We easily appreciate the monkey in the ape but not the ape in ourselves.

Still, the apes do fascinate us to some degree because of their humanlike qualities. Zoo gorillas are especially popular when they are displayed in "family" groups. The antics of orangutans and especially of chimps have been featured in movies and TV shows. The film *Planet of the Apes* is an example of a movie that recognizes both that apes are not monkeys, and that apes are quite similar to us. Imagine a live-action film called *Planet of the Monkeys.* Where could a director find human actors who could locomote on four legs for an entire movie?

Primatology is the study of nonhuman primates—fossil and living apes, monkeys, and prosimians—including behavior and social life. Fascinating in itself, primatology also helps anthropologists make inferences about the early social organization of *hominids* (members of the family that includes fossil and living humans). Of particular relevance are two kinds of primates:

1. Those whose ecological adaptations are similar to our own: **terrestrial** monkeys and apes—that is, primates that live on the ground rather than in the trees.

2. Those that are most closely related to us: the great apes, specifically the chimpanzees and gorillas.

OUR PLACE AMONG PRIMATES

Similarities between humans and apes are evident in anatomy, brain structure, genetics, and biochemistry. The physical similarities between humans and apes are recognized in zoological **taxonomy**—the assignment of organisms to categories (*taxa*; singular, *taxon*) according to their relationship and resemblance. Many similarities between organisms reflect their common *phylogeny*—their genetic relatedness based on common ancestry. In other words, organisms share features they have inherited from the same ancestor. Humans and apes belong to the same taxonomic superfamily Hominoidea (hominoids). Monkeys are placed in two others (Ceboidea and Cercopithecoidea). This means that humans and apes are more closely related to each other than either is to monkeys.

Figure 7.1 summarizes the various levels of classification used in zoological taxonomy. Each lower-level unit belongs to the higher-level unit above it. Thus, looking toward the bottom of Figure 7.1, similar species belong to the same genus (plural, *genera*). Similar genera make up the same family, and so on through the top of Figure 7.1, where similar phyla (plural of *phylum*) are included in the same kingdom. The highest (most inclusive) taxonomic level is the *kingdom*. At that level, animals are distinguished from plants.

At the lowest level of taxonomy, a species may have subspecies. These are its more or less—but not yet totally—isolated subgroups. Subspecies can coexist in time and space. For example, the Neandertals, who thrived between 130,000 and

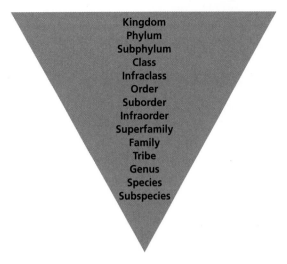

FIGURE 7.1 The Principal Classificatory Units of Zoological Taxonomy.

Moving down the figure, the classificatory units become more exclusive, so that "Kingdom" at the top is the most inclusive unit and "Subspecies" at the bottom is the most exclusive.

28,000 years ago, often are assigned not to a separate species but merely to a different subspecies of *Homo sapiens*. Just one subspecies of *Homo sapiens* survives today.

The similarities used to assign organisms to the same taxon are called **homologies,** similarities they have jointly inherited from a common ancestor. Table 7.1 summarizes the place of humans in zoological taxonomy. We see in Table 7.1 that we are mammals, members of the class

primatology
The study of apes, monkeys, and prosimians.

terrestrial
Ground-dwelling.

taxonomy
Classification scheme; assignment to categories (taxa; singular, taxon).

homologies
Traits inherited from a common ancestor.

TABLE 7.1 The Place of Humans (*Homo sapiens*) in Zoological Taxonomy

Homo sapiens *is an Animal, Chordate, Vertebrate, Mammal, Eutherian, Primate, Anthropoid, Catarrhine, Hominoid, Hominid, and Hominin. (Table 7.2 shows the taxonomic placement of the other primates.)*

TAXON	SCIENTIFIC (LATIN) NAME	COMMON (ENGLISH) NAME
Kingdom	Animalia	Animals
Phylum	Chordata	Chordates
Subphylum	Vertebrata	Vertebrates
Class	Mammalia	Mammals
Infraclass	Eutheria	Eutherians
Order	Primates	Primates
Suborder	Anthropoidea	Anthropoids
Infraorder	Catarrhini	Catarrhines
Superfamily	Hominoidea	Hominoids
Family	Hominidae	Hominids
Tribe	Hominini	Hominins
Genus	*Homo*	Humans
Species	*Homo sapiens*	Recent humans
Subspecies	*Homo sapiens sapiens*	Anatomically modern humans

TABLE 7.2 Primate Taxonomy

Major subdivisions of the two primate suborders: Prosimii and Anthropoidea. Humans are anthropoids who belong to the superfamily Hominoidea, along with the apes.

SUBORDER	INFRAORDER	SUPERFAMILY	FAMILY
Prosimii (Prosimians)	Lemuriformes (Lemurs)	Lemuroidea	Daubentoniidae (Aye-ayes), Indridae (Indri), Lemuridae (Lemurs)
	Lorisiformes (Lorises)	Lorisoidea	Lorisidae
	Tarsiiformes (Tarsiers)	Tarsioidea	Tarsiidae
Anthropoidea (Anthropoids)	Platyrrhini (Platyrrhines—New World monkeys)	Ceboidea	Callitrichidae (Tamarins and marmosets), Cebidae
	Catarrhini (Catarrhines—Old World monkeys, apes, and humans)	Cercopithecoidea	Cercopithecidae (Old World monkeys)
		Hominoidea) (Hominoids)	Hylobatidae (Gibbons and siamangs), Pongidae (Pongids—orangutans), Hominidae (Hominids—gorillas, chimpanzees, and humans)

SOURCE: Adapted from Robert Martin, "Classification of Primates," in Steve Jones, Robert Martin, and David Pilbeam, eds., *The Cambridge Encyclopedia of Human Evolution*, pp. 20–21. © Cambridge University Press, 1992. Reprinted with permission of Cambridge University Press.

analogies
Adaptive traits due to convergent evolution.

convergent evolution
Similar selective forces produce similar adaptive traits.

anthropology **ATLAS**

Map 2 locates the major primate groups. Orangutans and the African apes are part of the primate group most closely related to us: the great apes.

Mammalia. This is a major subdivision of the kingdom Animalia. Mammals share certain traits, including mammary glands, that set them apart from other taxa, such as birds, reptiles, amphibians, and insects. Mammalian homologies indicate that all mammals share more recent common ancestry with each other than they do with any bird, reptile, or insect.

Humans are mammals that, at a lower taxonomic level, belong to the *order* Primates. Another mammalian order is Carnivora: the carnivores (dogs, cats, foxes, wolves, badgers, weasels). Rodentia (rats, mice, beavers, squirrels) form yet another mammalian order. The primates share structural and biochemical homologies that distinguish them from other mammals. These resemblances were inherited from their common early primate ancestors after those early primates became reproductively isolated from the ancestors of the other mammals.

HOMOLOGIES AND ANALOGIES

Organisms should be assigned to the same taxon on the basis of homologies. The extensive biochemical homologies between apes and humans

confirm our common ancestry and support our traditional joint classification as hominoids (see Table 7.2). For example, it is estimated that humans, chimpanzees, and gorillas have more than 97 percent of their DNA in common.

However, common ancestry isn't the only reason for similarities between species. Similar traits also can arise if species experience similar selective forces and adapt to them in similar ways. We call such similarities **analogies.** The process by which analogies are produced is called **convergent evolution.** For example, fish and porpoises share many analogies resulting from convergent evolution to life in the water. Like fish, porpoises, which are mammals, have fins. They are also hairless and streamlined for efficient locomotion. Analogies between birds and bats (wings, small size, light bones) illustrate convergent evolution to flying (see Angier 1998).

In theory, only homologies should be used in taxonomy. With reference to the hominoids, there is no doubt that humans, gorillas, and chimpanzees are more closely related to each other than any of the three is to orangutans, which are Asiatic apes (Ciochon 1983). *Hominidae* is the name of the zoological family that includes hominids—fossil and living humans. Because chimps and gorillas share a more recent common ancestor with humans than they do with the orangutan, many scientists now also place gorillas and chimps in

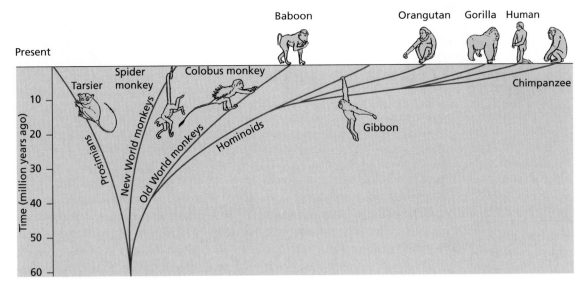

FIGURE 7.2 Primate Family Tree.

When did the common ancestors of all the primates live?

SOURCE: From Roger Lewin, *Human Evolution: An Illustrated Introduction*, 3rd ed., p. 44. Copyright © 1993 by Blackwell Publishing Ltd. Reprinted by permission of Blackwell Publishing Ltd., Oxford, UK.

the hominid family. *Hominid* would then refer to the zoological family that includes fossil and living humans, chimpanzees, gorillas, and their common ancestors. This leaves the orangutan (genus *Pongo*) as the only member of the pongid family (*Pongidae*). If chimps and gorillas are classified as hominids, what do we call the group that leads to humans but not to chimps and gorillas? For that, some scientists insert a taxonomic level called *tribe* between family and genus. The tribe *hominini* describes all the human species that ever have existed (including the extinct ones) and excludes chimps and gorillas. When scientists use the word *hominin* today, they mean pretty much the same thing as when they used the word *hominid* 20 years ago (Greiner 2003). Table 7.2 and Figure 7.2 illustrate our degree of relatedness to other primates.

PRIMATE TENDENCIES

Primates are varied because they have adapted to diverse ecological niches. Some primates are active during the day; others, at night. Some eat insects; others, fruits; others, shoots, leaves, and bulk vegetation; and others, seeds or roots. Some primates live on the ground, others live in trees, and there are intermediate adaptations. However, because the earliest primates were tree dwellers, modern primates share homologies reflecting their common **arboreal** heritage.

Many trends in primate evolution are best exemplified by the **anthropoids**: monkeys, apes,

and humans, which constitute the suborder *Anthropoidea*. The other primate suborder, *Prosimii*, includes lemurs, lorises, and tarsiers. These **prosimians** are more distant relatives of humans than are monkeys and apes. The primate trends—most developed in the anthropoids—can be summarized briefly. Together they constitute an anthropoid heritage that humans share with monkeys and apes.

1. **Grasping.** Primates have five-digited feet and hands that are suited for grasping. Certain features of hands and feet that were originally adaptive for arboreal life have been transmitted across the generations to contemporary primates. Flexible hands and feet that could encircle branches were important features in the early primates' arboreal life. Thumb opposability might have been favored by the inclusion of insects in the early primate diet. Manual dexterity makes it easier to catch insects attracted to abundant arboreal flowers and fruits. Humans and many other primates have **opposable thumbs:** The thumb can touch the other fingers. Some primates also have grasping feet. However, in adapting to **bipedal** (two-footed) locomotion, humans eliminated most of the foot's grasping ability.

2. **Smell to Sight.** Several anatomical changes reflect the shift from smell to sight as the primates' most important means of obtaining information. Monkeys, apes, and humans

prosimians
The primate suborder that includes lemurs, lorises, and tarsiers.

opposable thumb
A thumb that can touch all the other fingers.

bipedal
Two-footed; upright locomotion (of hominins).

arboreal
Living in the trees.

anthropoids
Monkeys, apes, and humans.

Wild Orangutans Learn Tool Use

Humans are much more numerous and diverse than our nearest relatives, the apes. The study of monkeys and apes is of particular interest to anthropology because their attributes and behavior can suggest things about human nature and origins. Of particular relevance to humans are two kinds of primates: (1) those that spend much of their time on the ground, including baboons, gorillas, chimpanzees, and, to some extent, the orangutans described here, and (2) those that are most closely related to us: the great apes, which include the orangs (although chimps and gorillas are much closer relatives).

Here the Dutch primatologist Carel von Schaik discusses his book Among Orangutans: Red Apes and The Rise of Human Culture *(2004). Humans share many features of anatomy, temperament, and behavior, including the sociability described here, with our primate relatives. As we see here as well, the great apes share a learned ability—reliance on tools—with humans. The use and even the manufacture of crude tools by chimpanzees has been known for many years. Observation of tool use by gorillas and orangs is more recent. Interesting, too, is that cultural diversity (e.g., in learned patterns of tool use) exists among apes as well as among humans. Knowing now that all the great apes can learn how to use tools, we can speculate that the common ancestor of apes and humans also had at least a rudimentary capacity for cultural learning.*

People keep asking Carel van Schaik if there is anything left to discover in fieldwork.

"I tell them, 'A lot,'" said Dr. van Schaik, the Dutch primatologist. "Look at gorillas. We've been studying them for decades, and we just now have discovered that they use tools. The same is true for orangutans."

In 1992, when Dr. van Schaik began his research in Suaq, a swamp forest in northern Sumatra, orangutans were believed to be the only great ape that lived a largely solitary life foraging for hard-to-find fruit thinly distributed over a large area.

Researchers thought they were slow-moving creatures—some even called them boring—that didn't have time to do much but eat.

But the orangutans Dr. van Schaik found in Suaq turned all that on its head. More than 100 were gathered together doing things the researchers had never seen in the wild.

Dr. van Schaik worked there for seven years and came to the radical conclusion that orangutans were "every bit as sociable, as technically adept and as culturally capable" as chimpanzees.

His new conclusions about how apes—and humans—got to be so smart are detailed in his latest book, "Among Orangutans: Red Apes and the Rise of Human Culture."

Now a professor of anthropology at the University of Zurich and the director of its Anthropological Institute and Museum, Dr. van Schaik discussed his findings in a recent telephone interview from his office there.

Q. What were you looking for in the Suaq swamp?

A. We'd been working in a mountainous area in northern Sumatra, and it felt as if we were missing the full picture of orangutan social organization. All higher primates—all of them—live in distinct social units except for the orangutan. That's a strong anomaly, and I wanted to solve it.

Q. How was Suaq different from other orangutan habitats?

A. It was an extraordinarily productive swamp forest with by far the highest density of orangutans—over twice the record number. The animals were the most sociable we'd ever seen: they hang out together, they're nice to each other, they even share food.

Q. But you almost left this orangutan habitat after a year?

A. We'd never worked in a place like this, and it was exhausting. To get into the swamp where they were we would wade through water—sometimes chest deep, two hours in, two hours out every day. There were countless species of mosquitoes.

It was what I call orangutan heaven and human hell. But then someone noticed that they were poking sticks into tree holes. It sounded like tool use, so we decided to build boardwalks in the swamp, and things got a lot easier.

have excellent *stereoscopic* (able to see in depth) and color vision. The portion of the brain devoted to vision expanded, while the area concerned with smell shrank.

3. **Nose to Hand.** Sensations of touch, conveyed by *tactile organs*, also provide information. The tactile skin on a dog's or cat's nose transmits information. Cats' tactile hairs, or whiskers, also serve this function. In primates, however, the main touch organ is the hand, specifically the sensitive pads of the "fingerprint" region.

4. **Brain Complexity.** The proportion of brain tissue concerned with memory, thought, and association has increased in primates. The primate ratio of brain size to body size exceeds that of most mammals.

5. **Parental Investment.** Most primates give birth to a single offspring rather than a litter. Because of this, growing primates receive more attention and have more learning opportunities than do other mammals. Learned behavior is an important part of primate adaptation.

Q. Were orangutans using tools?

A. It turned out Suaq had an amazing repertoire of tool use. They shape sticks to get at honey and insects. Then they pick another kind of stick to go after the scrumptious fat-packed seeds of the neesia fruit. One of them figured out that you could unleash the seeds with a stick and that was a big improvement in their diet.

Lean times are rare at Suaq, not only because the forest is productive, but because the orangutans can get to so much more food by using tools. So they can afford to be more sociable.

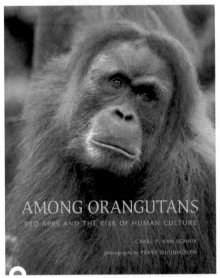

The cover of Carel van Schaik's 2004 book *Among Orangutans: Red Apes and the Rise of Human Culture*, which is described in this account.

Q. How did you discover that the tool use is socially transmitted?

A. Well, one way to prove it is to see if the orangutans use tools everywhere the neesia tree exists. This was in the late 90's. Swamps were being clear-cut and drained everywhere, and the civil war in Aceh was spreading.

I felt like an anthropologist trying to document a vanishing tribe. It turned out that in the big swamps on one side of a river, the orangutans do use tools, and in the small swamp on the other side, they don't. Neesia trees and orangutans exist in both places. But the animals can't cross the river, so the knowledge hadn't spread. At that point, the penny dropped and I realized their tool use was cultural.

Q. So your discovery that the orangutans learned tool use from one another explains "the rise of human culture" part of your book's subtitle?

A. Well, yes. Orangutans split off from the African lineage some 14 million years ago. If both chimps and orangutans make tools, our common great ape ancestor probably had the capacity for culture.

Q. I always thought we got smart after we came down from the trees.

A. Actually orangutans are the largest arboreal mammal and have no predators up in the trees so they live a very long time—up to 60 years in the wild—and have the slowest life history of any nonhuman mammal including elephants and whales.

A slow life history is key to growing a large brain. The other key to intelligence is sociability.

Q. Were orangutans more social in the past?

A. I guess the rich forest areas that allowed them to live in groups were much more common in the past—they're the ones that are best for rice growing and farming—but there's no way of knowing for sure. . . .

Q. You end your book with a bleak picture of the future of orangutans because of habitat conversion and illegal logging. Since then there's been a devastating tsunami and people need to cut down even more trees to put roofs over their heads. What does the future look like now?

A. One way to help people in Sumatra would be to donate wood on a large scale. But things may be better in Borneo.

There's a new Indonesian president, and in the last few months it looks as if the government is serious about cracking down on illegal logging. That leaves me more hopeful.

6. **Sociality.** Primates tend to be social animals that live with others of their species (see "Appreciating Diversity" above). The need for longer and more attentive care of offspring places a selective value on support by a social group.

PROSIMIANS

The primate order has two suborders: prosimians and anthropoids. The early history of the primates is limited to prosimianlike animals known through the fossil record. The first anthropoids, ancestral to monkeys, apes, and humans, appeared more than 40 million years ago. Some prosimians managed to survive in Africa and Asia because they were adapted to nocturnal life. As such, they did not compete with anthropoids, which are active during the day. Prosimians (lemurs) in Madagascar had no anthropoid competitors until people colonized that island some 1,500 years ago.

In their behavior and biology, Madagascar's *lemurs*, with 33 species, show adaptations to an

Compare this line drawing reconstruction of Shoshonius, a tarsierlike Eocene primate, with a modern tarsier from Mindanao in the Philippines. What similarities and differences do you notice?

FIGURE 7.3 Nostril Structure of Catarrhines and Platyrrhines.

Above: narrow septum and "sharp nose" of a guenon, a catarrhine (Old World monkey). Below: broad septum and "flat nose" of Humboldt's woolly monkey, a platyrrhine (New World monkey). Which nose is more like your own? What does that similarity suggest?

array of environments or ecological niches. Their diets and times of activity differ. Lemurs eat fruits, other plant foods, eggs, and insects. Some are nocturnal; others are active during the day. Some are totally arboreal; others spend some time in the trees and some on the ground. Another kind of prosimian is the *tarsier*, today confined to Indonesia, Malaysia, and the Philippines. From the fossil record, we know that 50 million years ago, several genera of tarsierlike prosimians lived in North America and Europe, which were much warmer then than they are now (Boaz 1997). The one genus of tarsier that survived is totally nocturnal. Active at night, tarsiers don't directly compete with anthropoids, which are active during the day. Lorises are other nocturnal prosimians found in Africa and Asia.

MONKEYS

All anthropoids share resemblances that can be considered trends in primate evolution in the sense that these traits are fully developed neither in the

fossils of primates that lived prior to 50 million years ago nor among contemporary prosimians.

The anthropoid suborder has two infraorders: *platyrrhines* (New World monkeys) and *catarrhines* (Old World monkeys, apes, and humans). The catarrhines (sharp-nosed) and platyrrhines (flat-nosed) take their names from Latin terms that describe the placement of the nostrils (see Figure 7.3). Old World monkeys, apes, and humans are all catarrhines. Being placed in the same taxon (infraorder in this case) means that Old World monkeys, apes, and humans are more closely related to each other than to New World monkeys. In other words, one kind of monkey (Old World) is more like a human than it is like another kind of monkey (New World). The New World monkeys were reproductively isolated from the catarrhines before the latter diverged

A woolly spider monkey, aka *muriqui*, from Monte Clares, Brazil. The long arms and elongated prehensile tail create a spiderlike image for this New World monkey.

into the Old World monkeys, apes, and humans. This is why New World monkeys are assigned to a different infraorder.

All New World monkeys and many Old World monkeys are arboreal. Whether in the trees or on the ground, however, monkeys move differently from apes and humans. Their arms and legs move parallel to one another, as dogs' legs do. This contrasts with the tendency toward *orthograde posture,* the straight and upright stance of apes and humans. Unlike apes, which have longer arms than legs, and humans, who have longer legs than arms, monkeys have arms and legs of about the same length. Most monkeys also have tails, which help them maintain balance in the trees. Apes and humans lack tails. The apes' tendency toward orthograde posture is most evident when they sit down. When they move about, chimps, gorillas, and orangutans habitually use all four limbs.

New World Monkeys

New World monkeys live in the forests of Central and South America. Unlike Old World monkeys, many New World monkeys have *prehensile,* or grasping, tails. Sometimes the prehensile tail has tactile skin, which permits it to work like a hand, for instance, in conveying food to the mouth. Old World monkeys, however, have developed their own characteristic anatomic specializations. They have rough patches of skin on the buttocks, adapted to sitting on hard rocky ground and rough branches. If the primate you see in the zoo has such patches, it's from the Old World. If it has a prehensile tail, it's a New World monkey. Among the anthropoids, there's only one nocturnal animal, a New World monkey called the night monkey or owl monkey. All other monkeys and apes, and humans, too, of course, are diurnal—active during the day.

Old World Monkeys

The Old World monkeys have both terrestrial and arboreal species. Baboons and many macaques are terrestrial monkeys. Certain traits differentiate terrestrial and arboreal primates. Arboreal primates tend to be smaller. Smaller animals can reach a greater variety of foods in trees and shrubs, where the most abundant foods are located at the ends of branches. Arboreal monkeys typically are lithe and agile. They escape from the few predators in their environment—snakes and monkey-eating eagles—through alertness and speed. Large size, by contrast, is advantageous for terrestrial primates in dealing with their predators, which are more numerous on the ground.

Another contrast between arboreal and terrestrial primates is in **sexual dimorphism**—marked differences in male and female anatomy and temperament (see Fedigan 1992). Sexual dimorphism tends to be more marked in terrestrial than in arboreal species. Baboon and macaque males are larger and fiercer than are females of the same species. However, it's hard to tell, without close inspection, the sex of an arboreal monkey.

sexual dimorphism Marked differences in male and female anatomy and temperament.

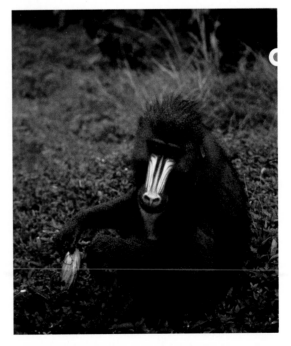

This mandrill (*Papio sphinx*) is a brightly colored terrestrial Old World (African) monkey. Related to the baboon, which shares the same genus name (*Papio*), mandrills live in family groups consisting of an adult male, several females, and their young. Illustrating sexual dimorphism, female color is drabber and size smaller than in the male.

Of the terrestrial monkeys, the baboons of Africa and the (mainly Asiatic) macaques have been the subjects of many studies. Terrestrial monkeys have specializations in anatomy, psychology, and social behavior that enable them to cope with terrestrial life. Adult male baboons, for example, are fierce-looking animals that can weigh 100 pounds (45 kilograms). They display their long, projecting canines to intimidate predators and when confronting other baboons. Faced with a predator, a male baboon can puff up his ample mane of shoulder hair, so that the would-be aggressor perceives the baboon as larger than he actually is.

Longitudinal field research shows that, near the time of puberty, baboon and macaque males typically leave their home troop for another. Because males move in and out, females form the stable core of the terrestrial monkey troop (Cheney and Seyfarth 1990; Hinde 1983). By contrast, among chimpanzees and gorillas, females are more likely to emigrate and seek mates outside their natal social groups (Bradley et al. 2004; Rodseth et al. 1991; Wilson and Wrangham 2003). Among terrestrial monkeys, then, the core group consists of females; among apes it is made up of males.

APES

The Old World monkeys have their own separate superfamily (Cercopithecoidea), while humans and the apes together compose the hominoid superfamily (Hominoidea). Among the hominoids, the so-called great apes are orangutans, gorillas, and chimpanzees. Humans could be included here, too; sometimes we are called "the third African ape." The lesser (smaller) apes are the gibbons and siamangs of Southeast Asia and Indonesia.

Several traits are shared by apes (and humans) as distinct from monkeys and other primates. Body size tends to be larger. The life span in longer. There is a longer interval between births of infants, which depend longer on their parent(s). There is a tendency toward upright posture, although habitual upright bipedalism is only characteristic of hominins. The brain is larger, the muzzle or face shorter and less projecting, and no hominoid has a tail.

Apes live in forests and woodlands. The light and agile **gibbons,** which are skilled brachiators, are completely arboreal. (**Brachiation** is hand-over-hand movement through the trees.) The heavier gorillas, chimpanzees, and adult male orangutans spend considerable time on the ground. Nevertheless, ape behavior and anatomy reveal past and present adaptation to arboreal life. For example, apes still build nests to sleep in trees. Apes have longer arms than legs, which is adaptive for brachiation (see Figure 7.4). The structure of the shoulder and clavicle (collarbone) of the apes and humans suggests that we had a brachiating ancestor. In fact, young apes still do brachiate. Adult apes tend to be too heavy to brachiate safely. Their weight is more than many branches can withstand. Gorillas and chimps now use the long arms they have inherited from their more arboreal ancestors for life on the ground. The terrestrial locomotion of chimps and gorillas is called *knuckle-walking*. In it, long arms and callused knuckles support the trunk as the apes amble around, leaning forward.

gibbons
Small, arboreal, Asiatic apes.

brachiation
Under-the-branch swinging.

FIGURE 7.4 The Limb Ratio of the Arboreal Gibbon and Terrestrial *Homo.*

How does this anatomical difference fit the modes of locomotion used by gibbons and humans?

Gibbons

Gibbons are widespread in the forests of Southeast Asia, especially in Malaysia. Smallest of the apes, male and female gibbons have about the same average height (3 feet, or 1 meter) and weight (12–25 pounds, or 5–10 kilograms). Gibbons spend most of their time just below the forest canopy (treetops). For efficient brachiation, gibbons have long arms and fingers, with short thumbs. Slenderly built, gibbons are the most agile apes. They use their long arms for balance when they occasionally walk erect on the ground or along a branch. Gibbons are the preeminent arboreal specialists among the apes. They subsist on a diet mainly of fruits, with occasional insects and small animals. Gibbons and siamangs, their slightly larger relatives, tend to live in *primary groups,* which are composed of a permanently bonded male and female and their preadolescent offspring.

Orangutans

There are two existing species of orangutan, Asiatic apes that belong to the genus *Pongo.* Highly endangered, contemporary orangs are confined to two Indonesian islands (Dreifus 2000; Mayell 2004*a*). Sexual dimorphism is marked, with the adult male weighing more than twice as much as the female. The orangutan male, like his human counterpart, is intermediate in size between chimps and gorillas. Some orang males exceed 200 pounds (90 kilograms). With only half the

With long arms and fingers, the gibbon is the most agile of the apes. Gibbons occasionally walk upright on the ground, using their long arms as balancers. Shown here, a white-handed gibbon strolls through the forest.

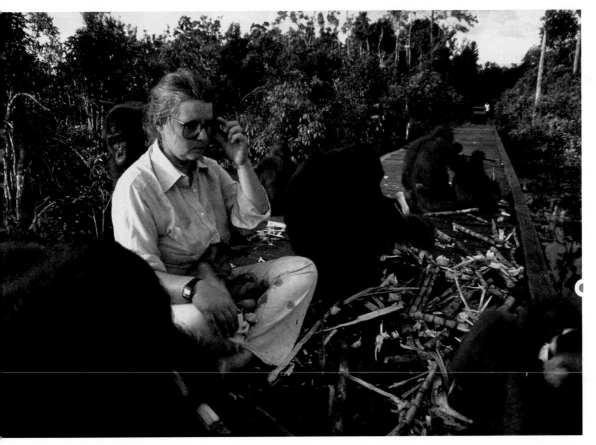

Dr. Biruté Galdikas has studied orangutans in Indonesia for more than a generation. Here she is shown among a group of active orangs at Borneo's Orangutan Rehab Center.

gorilla's bulk, male orangs can be more arboreal, although they typically climb, rather than swing through, the trees. The smaller size of females and young permits them to make fuller use of the trees. Orangutans have a varied diet of fruit, bark, leaves, and insects. Because orangutans live in jungles and feed in trees, they are especially difficult to study. However, field reports about orangutans in their natural setting (MacKinnon 1974; Schaik 2004) have clarified their behavior and social organization. Orangs can be sociable (see "Appreciating Diversity" on pp. 140–141), but others are more solitary—their tightest social units formed by females and preadolescent young, with males foraging alone.

Gorillas

With just one species, *Gorilla gorilla*, there are three subspecies of gorillas. The western lowland gorilla is the animal you normally see in zoos. This, the smallest subspecies of gorilla, lives mainly in forests in the Central African Republic, Congo, Cameroon, Gabon, Equatorial Guinea, and Nigeria. The eastern lowland gorilla, of which there are only four in captivity, is slightly larger and lives in eastern Congo. There are no mountain gorillas, the third subspecies, in captivity, and it's estimated that no more than 650 of these animals survive in the wild. These are the largest gorillas with the longest hair (to keep them warm in their mountainous habitat). They are also the rarest gorillas, which Dian Fossey (1983) and other scientists have studied in Rwanda, Uganda, and eastern Congo. This chapter's "Appreciating Anthropology" on pp. 148–149 discusses threats to gorillas and other primates and how anthropologists have worked to save them.

Full-grown male gorillas may weigh 400 pounds (180 kilograms) and stand 6 feet tall (183 centimeters). Like most terrestrial primates, gorillas show marked sexual dimorphism. The average adult female weighs half as much as the male. Gorillas spend little time in the trees. It's hard for an adult male to move his bulk about in a tree. When gorillas sleep in trees, they build nests, which are usually no more than 10 feet (3 meters) off the ground. By contrast, the nests of chimps and female orangs may be 100 feet (30 meters) above the ground.

Most of the gorilla's day is spent feeding. Gorillas move through jungle undergrowth eating ground plants, leaves, bark, fruits, and other vegetation. Like most primates, gorillas live in social groups. The troop is a common unit of primate social organization, consisting of multiple males

Mountain gorillas are the rarest and most endangered kind of gorilla. Dian Fossey and other scientists have studied them in Rwanda, Uganda, and eastern Congo. Shown here, Fossey (now deceased) plays with a group of young gorillas in Rwanda's Virunga Mountains.

and females and their offspring. Although troops with up to 30 gorillas have been observed, most gorillas live in groups of from 10 to 20. Gorilla troops tend to have fairly stable memberships, with little shifting between troops (Fossey 1983). Each troop has a silverback male, so designated because of the strip of white hair that extends down his back. This is the physical sign of full maturity among the male gorillas. The silverback is usually the only breeding male in the troop, which is why gorilla troops are sometimes called "one-male groups." However, a few younger, subordinate males may also adhere to such a one-male group (Harcourt, Fossey, and Sabater-Pi 1981; Schaller 1963).

Chimpanzees

Chimpanzees belong to the genus *Pan*, which has two species: *Pan troglodytes* (the common chimpanzee) and *Pan paniscus* (the bonobo or "pygmy" chimpanzee) (de Waal 1997; Susman 1987). Like humans, chimps are closely related to the gorilla, although there are some obvious differences. Like gorillas, chimps live in tropical Africa, but they range over a larger area and more varied environments than gorillas do. The common chimp, *Pan troglodytes,* lives in western central Africa (Gabon, Congo, Cameroon), as well as in western Africa (Sierra Leone, Liberia, Gambia) and eastern Africa (Congo, Uganda, and Tanzania). Bonobos live in remote and densely forested areas of just one country—the Democratic Republic of Congo (DRC). Common chimps live mainly in tropical rain forests but also in woodlands and mixed forest-woodland-grassland areas, such as the Gombe Stream National Park, Tanzania, where Jane Goodall (1996) and other researchers began to study them in 1960.

There are dietary differences between chimps and gorillas. Gorillas eat large quantities of green bulk vegetation, but chimps, like orangutans and gibbons, prefer fruits. Chimps are actually omnivorous, adding animal protein to their diet by capturing small mammals, birds' eggs, and insects.

Chimps are lighter and more arboreal than gorillas are. The adult male's weight—between 100 and 200 pounds (45–90 kilograms)—is about a third that of the male gorilla. There is much less sexual dimorphism among chimps than among gorillas. Females approximate 88 percent of the average male height. This is similar to the ratio of sexual dimorphism in *Homo sapiens.*

Several scientists have studied wild chimps, and we know more about the full range of their

anthropology ATLAS

Map 1 shows annual percent of forest loss worldwide.

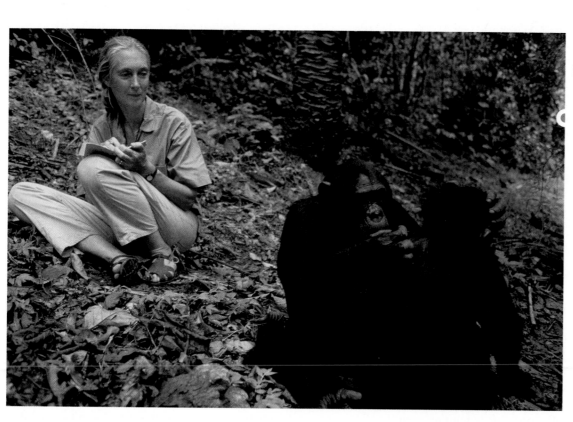

Chimpanzees live mainly in tropical rain forests but also in woodlands and mixed forest-woodland-grassland areas, such as the Gombe Stream National Park, Tanzania, where Jane Goodall began to study them in 1960. Shown here 30 years after her first visit to Gombe, Goodall continues her lifelong commitment to these endangered animals.

appreciating ANTHROPOLOGY

Endangered Primates

Primates are among the most endangered of earth's creatures, and the anthropologists who study them have played key roles in efforts to save them. One of the best examples is Dian Fossey, well-known for her study of mountain gorillas. Portrayed by Sigourney Weaver in the 1988 film Gorillas in the Mist, Fossey was murdered at her cabin near her research site in Rwanda in 1985. Her work lives on in the Gorilla Fund she established. See http://www.gorillafund.org/.

Deforestation poses a special risk for the primates because 90 percent of the 190 living primate species live in tropical forests—in Africa, Asia, South America, and Central America. As the earth's human population swells,

the populations of the nonhuman primates are shrinking. According to the Convention on International Trade in Endangered Species (ratified in 1973), all nonhuman primates are now endangered or soon to be endangered. The apes (gibbons, gorillas, orangutans, and chimps) are in the "most endangered" category. Mountain gorillas, which once ranged widely in the forested mountains of East Africa, are now limited to a small area near the war-ravaged borders of Rwanda, the DRC, and Uganda. Other severely threatened species include the golden lion tamarin monkey of southeastern Brazil, the cotton-top tamarin of Colombia, the lion-tailed macaque of southern

India, the woolly monkeys of Amazonia, and the orangutan of Southeast Asia.

A combination of forest clearing and forest fires has been deadly to orangutans in Sumatra and Borneo in Indonesia (see Dreifus 2000). Sumatra, which is losing 1,000 orangs a year, has an estimated population of fewer than 6,000 left. A road for loggers and miners that penetrated the orangutan range in Sumatra led to contact with humans that proved fatal to hundreds of the animals. Borneo has been devastated by fires in recent years, leaving some 10,000–15,000 orangs, compared with 60,000 in 1980.

In a recent study reported by Carroll (2008), West African chimpanzees were found to have declined by 90 percent over the last 18 years in Côte d'Ivoire (Ivory Coast), a country previously viewed as home to about half of all West African chimps (Carroll 2008). In 2008 in Côte d'Ivoire scientists found just 800 to 1,200

behavior and social organization than we do about the other apes (see Wrangham et al., eds. 1994; Wilson and Wrangham 2003). The long-term research of Jane Goodall and others at Gombe provides especially useful information. Approximately 150 chimpanzees range over Gombe's 30 square miles (80 square kilometers). Goodall (1986, 1996) has described communities of about 50 chimps, all of which know one another and interact from time to time. Communities regularly split up into smaller groups: a mother and her offspring; a few males; males, females, and young; and occasionally solitary animals. The social networks of males are more closed than are those of females, which are more likely to migrate and mate outside their natal group than males are (Wrangham et al., eds. 1994).

When chimps, which are very vocal, meet, they greet one another with gestures, facial expressions, and calls. They hoot to maintain contact during their daily rounds. Like baboons and macaques, chimps exhibit dominance relationships through attacks and displacement. Some adult females outrank younger males, although females do not display as strong dominance relationships among themselves as males do. Males occasionally cooperate in hunting parties.

Bonobos

Ancestral chimps, and especially humans, eventually spread out of the forests and into woodlands and more open habitats. Bonobos, which belong to the species *Pan paniscus,* apparently never left the protection of the trees. Up to 10,000 bonobos survive in the humid forests south of the Zaire River, in the Democratic Republic of Congo. Despite their common name—the *pygmy* chimpanzee—bonobos can't be distinguished from chimpanzees by size. Adult males of the smallest subspecies of chimpanzee average 95 pounds (43 kilograms), and females average 73 pounds (33 kilograms). These figures are about the same for bonobos (de Waal 1995, 1997).

Although much smaller than the males, female bonobos seem to rule. De Waal (1995, 1997) characterizes bonobo communities as female-centered, peace-loving, and egalitarian. The strongest social bonds are among females, although females also bond with males. The male bonobo's status reflects that of his mother, to whom he remains closely bonded for life.

The frequency with which bonobos have sex—and use it to avoid conflict—makes them exceptional among the primates. Despite frequent sex, the bonobo reproductive rate doesn't exceed that chimps, compared with 8,000 to 12,000 in 1989–1990. The 1989–1990 survey itself had confirmed a significant decline from 1960s estimates of about a hundred thousand chimps in Côte d'Ivoire. In all but three of the 11 sites surveyed, researchers found significantly fewer chimp nests than had been found in 1989–1990. In one National Park, only one nest was found, compared with 234 there in 1989–1990. Between 1990 and 2008 the human population of Côte d'Ivoire rose about 50 percent, resulting in more hunting and deforestation, particularly since 2002, when a coup attempt sparked continuning civil unrest.

Habitat destruction and fragmentation can isolate small groups of animals, leaving them vulnerable to extinction due to loss of genetic diversity. Primate populations are slow to recover from such threats. Ape species, for example, are slow reproducers, rarely having more than three to four offspring over a lifetime (Stern 2000).

Although the destruction of their forest habitats is the main reason the primates are disappearing, it isn't the only reason. Another threat is human hunting of primates for bush meat (Viegas 2000). In Amazonia, West Africa, and Central Africa, primates are a major source of food. People kill thousands of monkeys each year. Human hunters are less of a threat to primates in Asia. In India, Hindus avoid monkey meat because the monkey is sacred, while Moslems avoid it because monkeys are considered unclean and not fit for human consumption.

People also hunt primates for their skins and pelts; poachers sell their body parts as trophies and ornaments. Africans use the skins of black-and-white colobus monkeys for cloaks and headdresses, and American and European tourists buy coats and rugs made from colobus pelts. In Amazonia, ocelot and jaguar hunters shoot monkeys to bait the traps they set for the cats.

Primates also are killed when they are agricultural pests. In some areas of Africa and Asia, baboons and macaques raid the crops on which people depend for subsistence. Between 1947 and 1962, the government of Sierra Leone held annual drives to rid farm areas of monkeys, and between 15,000 and 20,000 primates perished each year.

A final reason for the demise of the primates is the capture of animals for use in labs or as pets. Although this threat is minor compared with deforestation and the hunting of primates for food, it does pose a serious risk to certain endangered species in heavy demand. One of the species most hurt by this trade is the chimpanzee, which has been widely used in biomedical research.

of the chimpanzee. A female bonobo gives birth every 5 or 6 years. Then, like chimps, female bonobos nurse and carry around their young for up to 5 years. Bonobos reach adolescence around 7 years of age. Females, which first give birth at age 13 or 14, are full grown by 15 years.

How do we know that bonobos use sexual activity to avoid conflict? According to de Waal:

First, anything, including food, that arouses the interest of more than one bonobo at a time tends to result in sexual contact. If two bonobos approach a cardboard box thrown into their enclosure, they will briefly mount each other before playing with the box. Such situations lead to squabbles in most other species. But bonobos are quite tolerant, perhaps because they use sex to divert attention and to diffuse tension. Second, bonobo sex often occurs in aggressive contexts totally unrelated to food. A jealous male might chase another away from a female, after which the two males reunite and engage in scrotal rubbing. Or after a female hits a juvenile, the latter's mother may lunge at the aggressor, an action that is immediately followed by genital rubbing between the two adults. (De Waal 1995, p. 87)

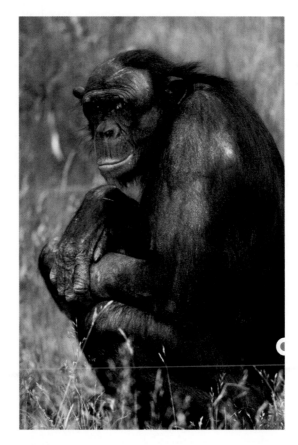

A male bonobo (pygmy chimpanzee) from the Democratic Republic of Congo. Are bonobos smaller than chimps?

BEHAVIORAL ECOLOGY AND FITNESS

According to evolutionary theory, when the environment changes, natural selection starts to modify the *population*'s pool of genetic material. Natural selection has another key feature: the differential reproductive success of *individuals* within the population. **Behavioral ecology** studies the evolutionary basis of social behavior. It assumes that the genetic features of any species reflect a long history of differential reproductive success (that is, natural selection). In other words, biological traits of contemporary organisms have been transmitted across the generations because those traits enabled their ancestors to survive and reproduce more effectively than their competition.

Natural selection is based on *differential* reproduction. Members of the same species may compete to maximize their reproductive fitness—their genetic contribution to future generations. *Individual fitness* is measured by the number of direct descendants an individual has. Illustrating a primate strategy that may enhance individual fitness are cases in which male monkeys kill infants after entering a new troop. Destroying the offspring of other males, they clear a place for their own progeny (Hausfater and Hrdy, eds. 1984).

Besides competition, one's genetic contribution to future generations also can be enhanced by cooperation, sharing, and other apparently unselfish behavior. This is because of *inclusive fitness*—reproductive success measured by the genes one shares with relatives. By sacrificing for their kin—even if this means limiting their own direct reproduction—individuals actually may increase their genetic contributions (their shared genes) to the future. Inclusive fitness helps us understand why a female might invest in her sister's offspring, or why a male might risk his life to defend his brothers. If self-sacrifice perpetuates more of their genes than direct reproduction

behavioral ecology
Study of the evolutionary basis of social behavior.

does, it makes sense in terms of behavioral ecology. Such a view can help us understand aspects of primate behavior and social organization.

Maternal care always makes sense in terms of reproductive fitness theory because females know their offspring are their own. But it's harder for males to be sure about paternity. Inclusive fitness theory predicts that males will invest most in offspring when they are surest the offspring are theirs. Gibbons, for example, have strict male–female pair bonding, which makes it almost certain that the offspring are those of both members of the pair. Thus we expect male gibbons to offer care and protection to their young, and they do. However, among species and in situations in which a male can't be sure about his paternity, it may make more sense to invest in a sister's offspring than in a mate's because the niece or nephew definitely shares some of that male's genes.

PRIMATE EVOLUTION

The fossil record offers evidence for no more than 5 percent of extinct types of primates. Such small numbers provide the merest glimpse of the diverse bioforms—living beings—that have existed on earth.

With reference to the primate fossil record, we'll see that different geographic areas provide more abundant fossil evidence for different time periods. This doesn't necessarily mean that primates were not living elsewhere at the same time. Discussions of primate and human evolution must be tentative because the fossil record is limited and spotty. Much is subject to change as knowledge increases. A key feature of science is to recognize the tentativeness and uncertainty of knowledge. Scientists, including fossil hunters, constantly seek out new evidence and devise new methods, such as DNA comparison, to improve their understanding, in this case of primate and human evolution.

CHRONOLOGY

We learned in Chapter 4 that the remains of animals and plants that lived at the same time are found in the same stratum. Based on fossils found in stratigraphic sequences, the history of vertebrate life has been divided into three main eras. The *Paleozoic* was the era of ancient life—fishes, amphibians, and primitive reptiles. The *Mesozoic* was the era of middle life—reptiles, including the dinosaurs. The *Cenozoic* is the era of recent life—birds and mammals. Each era is divided into periods, and the periods are divided into epochs. (See Figure 7.5a.)

Era	Period	
Cenozoic	Quaternary	
		1.8 m.y.a.
	Tertiary	
		65 m.y.a.
Mesozoic	Cretaceous	
		146 m.y.a.
	Jurassic	
		208 m.y.a.
	Triassic	
		245 m.y.a.
Paleozoic	Permian	
		286 m.y.a.
	Carboniferous	
		360 m.y.a.
	Devonian	
		410 m.y.a.
	Silurian	
		440 m.y.a.
	Ordovician	
		505 m.y.a.
	Cambrian	
		544 m.y.a.
Proterozoic	Neoproterozoic	
		900 m.y.a.
	Mesoproterozoic	
		1,600 m.y.a.
	Paleoproterozoic	
		2,500 m.y.a.
Archaean		
		3,800 m.y.a.
Hadean		
		4,500 m.y.a.

FIGURE 7.5a Geological Time Scales.

The geological time scale, based on stratigraphy. Eras are subdivided into periods, and periods into epochs. In what era, period, and epoch did Homo originate?

Anthropologists are concerned with the Cenozoic *era*, which includes two *periods*: Tertiary and Quaternary. Each of these periods is subdivided into *epochs*. The Tertiary had five epochs: Paleocene, Eocene, Oligocene, Miocene, and Pliocene. The Quaternary includes just two epochs: Pleistocene and Holocene, or Recent. Figure 7.5b gives the approximate dates of these

epochs. Sediments from the Paleocene epoch (65 to 54 **m.y.a.**—million years ago) have yielded fossil remains of diverse small mammals, some probably ancestral to the primates. Prosimian-like fossils abound in strata dating from the Eocene (54 to 36 m.y.a.). The first anthropoid fossils date to the Eocene and the early Oligocene (36 to 23 m.y.a.). Hominoids became widespread during the Miocene (23 to 5 m.y.a.). Hominins first appeared in the late Miocene, just before the Pliocene (5 to 2 m.y.a.) (Figure 7.5b).

m.y.a.
Million years ago.

EARLY PRIMATES

When the Mesozoic era ended, and the Cenozoic era began, some 65 million years ago, North America was connected to Europe but not to South America. (The Americas joined around 20 million years ago.) Over millions of years, the continents have "drifted" to their present locations, carried along by the gradually shifting plates of the Earth's surface (Figure 7.6).

During the Cenozoic, most landmasses had tropical or subtropical climates. The Mesozoic era had ended with a massive worldwide extinction of plants and animals, including the dinosaurs. Thereafter, mammals replaced reptiles as the dominant large land animals. Trees and flowering plants soon proliferated, supplying arboreal foods for the primates that eventually evolved to fill the new niches.

According to the *arboreal theory*, primates became primates by adapting to arboreal life. The primate traits and trends discussed previously developed as adaptations to life high up in the trees. A key feature was the importance of sight over smell. Changes in the visual apparatus were adaptive in the trees, where depth perception facilitated leaping. Grasping hands and feet were used to crawl along slender branches. Grasping feet anchored the body as the primate reached for foods at the ends of branches. Early primates probably had omnivorous diets based on foods available in the trees, such as flowers, fruits, berries, gums, leaves, and insects. The early Cenozoic era witnessed a proliferation of flowering plants, attracting insects that were to figure prominently in many primate diets.

Early Cenozoic Primates

There is considerable fossil evidence that a diversified group of primates lived, mainly in Europe and North America, during the second epoch of the Cenozoic, the Eocene. On that basis it is likely that the earliest primates lived during the first epoch of the Cenozoic, the Paleocene (65–54 m.y.a.). The status of several fossils as possible Paleocene

anthropology **ATLAS**

Map 3 indicates where various fossil primates lived during the Eocene, Oligocene, and Miocene epochs.

Era	Period	Epoch	Climate and Life Forms
Cenozoic	Quaternary	Holocene 11,000 B.P.	Transition to agriculture; emergence of states
		Pleistocene 128 m.y.a.	Climatic fluctuations, glaciation; *Homo, A. boisei*
	Tertiary	Pliocene 5 m.y.a.	*A. robustus, a. africanus, A. afarensis, A. anamensis, Ardipithecus ramidus*
		Miocene 23 m.y.a.	*Sahelanthropus tchadensis, Orrorin tugenensis, Ardipithecus kadabba* Cooler and drier grasslands spread in middle latitudes; Africa collides with Eurasia (16 m.y.a.)
		Oligocene 38 m.y.a.	Cooler and drier in the north; anthropoids in Africa (Fayum); separation of catarrhines and platyrrhines; separation of hylobatids from pongids and hominids
		Eocene 54 m.y.a	Warm tropical climates become widespread; modern orders of mammals appear; prosimianlike primates abundant; anthropoids appear
		Paleocene 65 m.y.a	First major mammal radiation

FIGURE 7.5b Geological Time Scales.

Periods and epochs of the Cenozoic era.

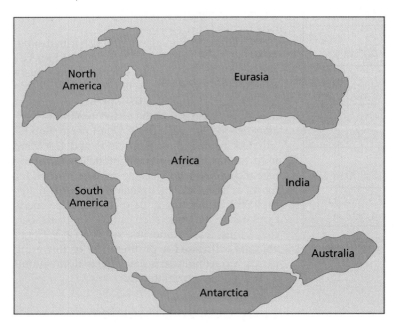

FIGURE 7.6 Placement of Continents at the End of the Mesozoic.

When the Mesozoic era ended, and the Cenozoic began, some 65 million years ago, North America was connected to Europe but not to South America.

primates has been debated. Because there is no consensus on this matter, such fossils are not discussed here.

A tiny primate skull found recently in China (Malkin 2004; Ni et al. 2004) confirms that early primates lived in Asia near the start of the Eocene. A team of Chinese paleontologists led by Xijun Ni found the new primate species, *Teilhardina asiatica*, in China's Hunan Province. The tiny 55-million-year-old skull, with most of its teeth intact, is the most complete skull ever found of a euprimate. (The term *euprimate* refers to the first mammals that shared characteristics such as forward-facing eyes and a relatively large braincase with modern primates.) Fragments of euprimates, all dating to around 55 m.y.a., have been found in Europe and North America. The discovery of a euprimate in Asia means that primates were already widespread by then and that their common ancestor must have evolved even earlier.

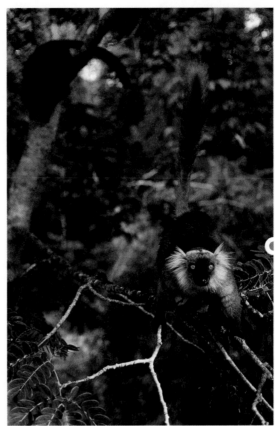

Smilodectes was a lemurlike primate that lived during the Eocene. Compare this drawing reconstructing a *Smilodectes* from Wyoming (left) with a modern black lemur (*Eulemur macaco*) from Madagascar.

In primate evolution, the Eocene (54–38 m.y.a.) was the age of the prosimians, with at least 60 genera in two main families. They lived in North America, Europe, Africa, and Asia. Ancestral lemurs reached Madagascar from Africa late in the Eocene. They must have traveled across the Mozambique Channel, which was narrower then than it is now, on thick mats of vegetation. Such naturally formed "rafts" have been observed forming in East African rivers, then floating out to sea.

Sometime during the Eocene, ancestral anthropoids branched off from the prosimians by becoming more diurnal (active during the day) and by strengthening the trend favoring vision over smell. Some Eocene prosimians had larger brains and eyes, and smaller snouts, than others did. These were the ancestors of the anthropoids. Anthropoid eyes are rotated more forward when compared with lemurs and lorises. Also, anthropoids have a fully enclosed bony eye socket, which lemurs and lorises lack. And unlike lemurs and lorises, anthropoids lack a rhinarium, a moist nose continuous with the upper lip. Anthropoids have a dry nose, separate from the upper lip. By the end of the Eocene, many prosimian species had become extinct, reflecting competition from the first anthropoids.

Oligocene Anthropoids

During the Oligocene epoch (38–23 m.y.a.), anthropoids became the most numerous primates. Most of our knowledge of early anthropoids is based on fossils from Egypt's Fayum deposits. This area is a desert today, but 36–31 million years ago it was a tropical rain forest.

The anthropoids of the Fayum lived in trees and ate fruits and seeds. Compared with prosimians, they had fewer teeth, reduced snouts, larger brains, and increasingly forward-looking eyes. Of the Fayum anthropoid fossils, the *parapithecid* family is the more primitive and is perhaps ancestral to the New World monkeys. The parapithecids were very small (2–3 pounds, 0.9–1.4 kilograms), with similarities to living marmosets and tamarins, small South American monkeys.

The *propliopithecid* family seems ancestral to the catarrhines—Old World monkeys, apes, and humans. The propliopithecids share with the later catarrhines a distinctive dental formula: 2.1.2.3, meaning two incisors, one canine, two premolars, and three molars. (The formula is based on one-fourth of the mouth, either the right or left side of the upper or lower jaw.) The more primitive primate dental formula is 2.1.3.3. Most other primates, including prosimians and New World monkeys, have the second formula, with

hominoid
Superfamily that includes humans and all the apes.

three premolars instead of two. Besides the Fayum, Oligocene deposits with primate bones have been found in North and West Africa, southern Arabia, China, Southeast Asia, and North and South America.

The Oligocene was a time of major geological and climatic change: North America and Europe separated and became distinct continents; the Great Rift Valley system of East Africa formed; India drifted into Asia; and a cooling trend began, especially in the Northern Hemisphere, where primates disappeared.

MIOCENE HOMINOIDS

The earliest hominoid fossils date to the Miocene epoch (23–5 m.y.a.), which is divided into three parts: lower, middle, and upper or late. The early Miocene (23–16 m.y.a.) was a warm and wet period, when forests covered East Africa. Recall that Hominoidea is the superfamily that includes fossil and living apes and humans. For simplicity's sake, the earliest **hominoids** are here called proto-apes, or simply apes. Although some of these may be ancestral to living apes, none is identical, or often even very similar, to modern apes.

Proconsul

The *Proconsul* group represents the most abundant and successful anthropoids of the early Miocene. This group lived in Africa and includes three species. These early Miocene proto-apes had teeth with similarities to those of living apes. But their skeleton below the neck was more monkey-like. Some *Proconsul* species were the size of a small monkey; others, the size of a chimpanzee, usually with marked sexual dimorphism. Their dentition suggests they ate fruits and leaves. *Proconsul* probably contained the last common ancestor shared by the Old World monkeys and the apes. By the middle Miocene, *Proconsul* had been replaced by Old World monkeys and apes.

Later Miocene Apes

During the early Miocene (23–16 m.y.a.), Africa had been cut off by water from Europe and Asia. But during the middle Miocene, Arabia drifted into Eurasia, providing a land connection between Africa, Europe, and Asia. Migrating both ways—out of and into Africa—about 16 m.y.a. were various animals, including hominoids. Proto-apes were the most common primates of the middle Miocene (16–10 m.y.a.). Over 20 species have been discovered. (See Figure 7.7.)

Perhaps the most remarkable Miocene ape was *Gigantopithecus*—almost certainly the largest primate that ever lived. Confined to Asia, it persisted for millions of years, from the Miocene until 400,000 years ago, when it coexisted with members of our own genus, *Homo erectus*. Some people think *Gigantopithecus* is not extinct yet, and that we know it today as the yeti and bigfoot (Sasquatch).

With a fossil record consisting of nothing more than jawbones and teeth, it is difficult to say for sure just how big *Gigantopithecus* was. Based on ratios

FIGURE 7.7 The Geographic Distribution of Known Miocene Apes.

SOURCE: From Robert Jurmain and Harry Nelson, *Introduction to Physical Anthropology*, 6th ed., p. 302. Copyright © 1994 Wadsworth, a part of Cengage Learning, Inc. Reproduced by permission. www.cengage.com/permissions

ecus combines part of the village's name with the Greek word for "ape," while *catalaunicus* commemorates Catalonia, the province where both the village and Barcelona are located.

The *Pierolapithecus* bones include much of the skull, hand and foot bones, three vertebrae, two complete ribs, and large pieces of a dozen others. The find appears to represent a single adult male that weighed about 75 pounds (34 kilograms). Like chimps and gorillas, *Pierolapithecus* was well adapted for tree climbing and knuckle-walking on the ground. Based on the shape of the single surviving tooth, it was probably a fruit eater. Several features distinguished *Pierolapithecus* from the lesser apes (gibbons and siamangs) and monkeys. Its rib cage, lower spine, and wrist suggest it climbed the way modern great apes do. The ape's chest, or thorax, is wider and flatter than that of monkeys and is the earliest modern apelike thorax yet found in the fossil record.

In the current timetable of primate evolution, the lineage of monkeys split off some 25 m.y.a. from the hominoid line, which led to apes and humans. The ancestors of the lesser apes separated from those of the great apes some 16–14 m.y.a.

A reconstruction of *Gigantopithecus* by Russell Ciochon and Bill Munns. Munns is shown here with "Giganto." What would be the likely environmental effects of a population of such large opes?

of jaw and tooth size to body size in other apes, various reconstructions have been made. One has *Gigantopithecus* weighing 1,200 pounds (544 kilograms) and standing 10 feet (3 meters) tall (Ciochon, Olsen, and James 1990). Another puts the height at 9 feet (2.7 meters) and cuts the weight in half (Simons and Ettel 1970). All agree, however, that *Gigantopithecus* was the largest ape that ever lived. There have been at least two species of *Gigantopithecus:* one coexisted with *H. erectus* in China and Vietnam, and the other, much earlier (5 m.y.a.), lived in northern India.

Pierolapithecus catalaunicus

In November 2004, Spanish anthropologists announced their discovery of what may be the last common ancestor of humans, chimpanzees, gorillas, and orangutans (Moyà-Solà et al. 2004). The new ape species, named *Pierolapithecus catalaunicus,* lived around 13 million years ago, during the middle Miocene. The find comes from a new and rich fossil site, near the village of Hostalets de Pierola in Catalonia, Spain. The name *Pierolapith-*

Pierolapithecus catalaunicus. The *Pierolapithecus* bones discovered so far include much of the skull, hand, and foot bones, including toe and finger fragments, three vertebrae, two complete ribs, and large pieces of a dozen others. This Miocene ape, first described in 2004, may be the last common ancestor of all the world's living great apes, including the human family.

Then, around 11–10 m.y.a., the orangutan line diverged from that leading to the African apes and humans. Yet another split took place when the gorilla line branched off from the line leading to chimpanzees and hominins. Around 7–6 m.y.a., another split in the lineage led to the various early hominins, to be examined in the next chapter. Some intriguing fossils dating from that critical time period have been discovered recently.

Acing the COURSE

Summary

1. Humans, apes, monkeys, and prosimians are primates. The primate order is subdivided into suborders, superfamilies, families, tribes, genera, species, and subspecies. Organisms in any subdivision (taxon) of a taxonomy are assumed to share more recent ancestry with each other than they do with organisms in other taxa. But it's sometimes hard to tell the difference between homologies, which reflect common ancestry, and analogies, biological similarities that develop through convergent evolution.

2. Prosimians are the older of the two primate suborders. Some 40 million years ago, anthropoids displaced prosimians from niches their ancestors once occupied. Tarsiers and lorises are prosimians that survived by adapting to nocturnal life. Lemurs survived on the island of Madagascar.

3. Anthropoids include humans, apes, and monkeys. All share fully developed primate trends, such as depth and color vision. Other anthropoid traits include a shift in tactile areas to the fingers. The New World monkeys are all arboreal. Old World monkeys include both terrestrial species (e.g., baboons and macaques) and arboreal ones. The great apes are orangutans, gorillas, chimpanzees, and bonobos. The lesser apes are gibbons and siamangs.

4. Gibbons and siamangs live in Southeast Asian forests. These apes are slight, arboreal animals whose mode of locomotion is brachiation. Sexual dimorphism, slight among gibbons, is marked among orangutans, which are confined to two Indonesian islands. Sexually dimorphic gorillas, the most terrestrial apes, are vegetarians confined to equatorial Africa. Two species of chimpanzees live in the forests and woodlands of tropical Africa. Chimps are less sexually dimorphic, more numerous, and more omnivorous than gorillas are.

5. From the perspective of behavioral ecology, individuals in a population compete to increase their genetic contribution to future generations. Maternal care makes sense from this perspective because females can be sure their offspring are their own. Because it's harder for males to be sure about paternity, evolutionary theory predicts they will invest most in offspring when they are surest the offspring are theirs.

6. Primates have lived during the past 65 million years, the Cenozoic era, with seven epochs: Paleocene, Eocene, Oligocene, Miocene, Pliocene, Pleistocene, and Holocene, or Recent. The arboreal theory states that primates evolved by adapting to life high up in the trees.

7. The first (prosimianlike) fossils clearly identified as primates lived during the Eocene (54–38 m.y.a.), mainly in North America and Europe. During the Oligocene (38–23 m.y.a.), anthropoids became the most numerous primates. The parapithecid family may be ancestral to the New World monkeys. The propliopithecid family seems ancestral to the catarrhines—Old World monkeys, apes, and humans.

8. The earliest hominoid fossils are from the Miocene (23–5 m.y.a.). Africa's *Proconsul* group contained the last common ancestor shared by the Old World monkeys and the apes. Since the middle Miocene (16–10 m.y.a.), Africa, Europe, and Asia have been connected. Proto-apes spread beyond Africa and became the most common primates of the middle Miocene. Asia's *Gigantopithecus*, the largest primate ever to live,

persisted for millions of years, finally coexisting with *Homo erectus*. *Pieropithecus catalaunicus*, which lived around 13 million years ago, could be the last common ancestor of humans, chimpanzees, gorillas, and orangutans.

Test Yourself!

MULTIPLE CHOICE

1. What is the relevance of primatology to anthropology?
   a. Primatology is relevant only to applied anthropologists concerned about deforestation and poaching.
   b. It is central to anthropologists who work in forensics.
   c. It provides evidence for a newly revised description of the Great Chain of Being.
   d. It helps anthropologists make inferences about the early social organization of hominids and untangle issues of human nature and the origins of culture.
   e. There is no longer any relevance of primatology to anthropology because the most important research in the field has already been done.

2. Which of the following is (are) used for putting organisms in the same taxon (zoological category)?
   a. homologies
   b. anthropometrics
   c. only similarities that have evolved since the time of their common ancestor
   d. analogies
   e. all phenotypic similarities

3. What is the term for the evolutionary process by which organisms as unrelated as birds and butterflies develop similar characteristics because of adaptations to similar environments?
   a. inclusive fitness
   b. convergent evolution
   c. brachiation
   d. genetic drift
   e. gene flow

4. If chimps and gorillas are classified as hominids, what do some scientists call the group that leads to humans but not to chimps and gorillas?
   a. the tribe *humanity*
   b. the subtaxa *hominoid*
   c. siamang *humanoids*
   d. the tribe *hominini*
   e. no scientist makes this taxonomic distinction

5. What do the trends that *all* primates share (five fingers, opposable thumbs, stereoscopic vision) indicate?
   a. a common ancestral terrestrial heritage
   b. an ancestral culturally complex environment
   c. a common ancestral arboreal heritage
   d. the primitive "sexual division of labor," in which females gathered seeds while males hunted insects and small animals
   e. a common ancestral frugivorous heritage

6. Which of the following traits is *not* associated with primates?
   a. stereoscopic vision
   b. social groupings
   c. grasping adaptations
   d. reliance on smell as the main sense
   e. brain complexity

7. According to behavioral ecologists, what is inclusive fitness?
   a. reproductive success measured by the representation of genes one shares with other, related individuals
   b. the number of direct descendents an individual organism has
   c. the idea that human behavior is unconnected to genetics because of the existence of culture
   d. the degree to which anaerobic fitness is included in certain behaviors
   e. the ability of an individual to reproduce

8. Rough patches of skin on the buttocks and non-prehensile tails are characteristic traits of
   a. pongids.
   b. prosimians.
   c. Old World monkeys.
   d. New World monkeys.
   e. tarsiers.

9. Sexual dimorphism refers to
   a. marked differences between terrestrial and arboreal mating patterns.
   b. marked differences in male and female anatomy and temperament.
   c. marked differences between Old World and New World monkeys.
   d. continued sexual discrimination in anthropology departments.
   e. sexual maturation rates of prosimian.

10. What makes bonobos exceptional among primates?
   a. their ability to withstand the pressures of deforestation
   b. their degree of sociality
   c. their marked sexual dimorphism
   d. the frequency with which they have sex, a behavior associated with conflict avoidance
   e. their cannibalism

FILL IN THE BLANK

1. A __homology__ is a trait that organisms have jointly inherited from a common ancestor.

2. Based on primate taxonomy, lemurs, lorises, and tarsiers are part of the __Prosimian__ primate suborder.

3. The process by which analogies are produced (resulting, for example, in fins both in fish and porpoises) is called __convergent evolution__.

4. The first anthropoids, ancestral to monkeys, apes, and humans, appeared more than __40__ million years ago, which, according to the geological time scale, corresponds to the __tertiary__ period and the __cenozoic__ era.

5. The __proconsul__ group represents most abundant and successful anthropoids of the early Miocene. It also probably contained the last common ancestor shared by the Old World monkeys and apes.

CRITICAL THINKING

1. How does social organization vary among primates?

2. What is behavioral ecology? How would a behavioral ecologist explain parental investment in their offspring? Can you think of any other theoretical frameworks that could be used to explain these cases?

3. What are some unanswered questions about early primate evolution? What kinds of information would help provide answers? What are some of the difficulties that investigators face in solving these questions?

4. There have been reported sightings of "Big Foot" in the Pacific Northwest of North America and of the yeti (abominable snowman) in the Himalayas. What facts about apes lead you to question such reports?

5. In Chapter 2 you were introduced to how our culture—and cultural changes—affect the ways in which we perceive nature, human nature, and "the natural." Can you think of aspects of your culture that have affected the way you think about humans' relationship to other primates?

Multiple Choice: 1. (D); 2. (A); 3. (B); 4. (D); 5. (C); 6. (D); 7. (A); 8. (C); 9. (B); 10. (D); **Fill in the Blank:** 1. homology; 2. prosimian; 3. convergent evolution; 4. 40; Tertiary, Cenozoic; 5. *Proconsul*

Suggested Additional Readings

Cachel, S.
   2006 *Primate and Human Evolution.* New York: Cambridge University Press. Human and primate evolution, behavior, and the fossil record.
De Waal, F. B. M.
   2001 *The Ape and the Sushi Master: Cultural Reflections by a Primatologist.* New York: Basic Books. Behavior of humans and apes.

Hart, D., and R. W. Sussman
   2009 *Man the Hunted: Primates, Predators, and Human Evolution,* expanded ed. Boulder, CO: Westview. The role of predation in human evolution; unique and readable examination of humans not as hunters but as prey.

Montgomery, S.
  1991 *Walking with the Great Apes: Jane Goodall, Dian Fossey, Biruté Galdikas.* Boston: Houghton Mifflin. The stories of three primatologists who have worked with, and to preserve, chimpanzees, gorillas, and orangutans.

Strier, K. B.
  2007 *Primate Behavioral Ecology,* 3rd ed. Boston: Allyn & Bacon. Behavior and reproductive strategies among primates.

Swindler, D. R.
  1998 *Introduction to the Primates.* Seattle: University of Washington Press. Up-to-date survey.

Go to our Online Learning Center website at **www.mhhe.com/kottak** for Internet exercises directly related to the content of this chapter.

Internet
Exercises

- What key traits make us human, and when and how are they revealed in the fossil record?

- Who were the australopithecines, and what role did they play in human evolution?

- When and where did hominins first make tools?

A reconstruction of Lucy, an early upright biped, aka *Australopithecus afarensis*, in the Senckenberg Museum of Natural History in Frankfurt, Germany. Bipedal locomotion is the most ancient trait that makes us truly human.

understanding OURSELVES

Do you remember the "monkey bars" in your playground? How did you use them? It sure wasn't like a monkey. The human shoulder bone, like that of the apes, is adapted for brachiation—swinging hand over hand through the trees. Monkeys, by contrast, move about on four limbs. Apes can stand and walk on two feet, as humans habitually do, but in the trees, and otherwise when climbing, apes and humans don't leap around as monkeys do. In climbing we extend our arms and pull up. When we use "monkey bars," we hang and move hand over hand rather than getting on top and running across, as a monkey would do. For most contemporary humans, the ability to use "monkey bars" declines long before our ability to walk. Humans have the shoulder of a brachiator because we share a distant brachiating ancestor with the apes. Bipedal locomotion, on the other hand, is the most ancient trait that makes us truly human.

Only when we lose it do we appreciate fully the supreme significance of bipedalism. I know this from personal experience. On September 11, 2005, the day before her 99th birthday, my mother broke her hip. She survived a hip replacement operation, spent a week in the hospital, then entered a rehab center, where she had to rely on staff for much of what previously she had done on her own. She couldn't climb in and out of bed, nor could she bathe herself or attend to personal functions.

Watching my mother endure weeks of indignity, I became acutely aware of what bipedalism means to humans. Younger people with greater upper body strength often can move about independently without using their legs. Not so a very old woman who over the years had suffered several fractures (along with arthritis) affecting wrists, arms, and shoulders. All those had been painful reminders of the aging process. None, however, was as devastating as her hip break. Unable to walk and debilitated by an infection she contracted in the hospital, my mother gradually lost her interests and her will to live. She stopped following the news, abandoning TV and any attempt to read. Her rehabilitation wasn't succeeding; she hated relying on others for her personal functions. She died less than two months after her fall. My mother's longevity illustrates how cultural advances (e.g., medicine, nutrition, operations) have extended the human lifespan—but only to a point. Certainly no Ice Age hominin lived for a century; however, images of the future in the movie *Wall-E* notwithstanding, humans today are no less bipedal than our ancestors were 5 million years ago. Bipedalism is an integral and enduring feature of human adaptation.

WHAT MAKES US HUMAN?

In trying to determine whether a fossil is a human ancestor, should we look for traits that make us human today? Sometimes yes; sometimes no. We do look for similarities in DNA, including mutations shared by certain lineages but not others. But what about such key human attributes as bipedal locomotion, a long period of childhood dependency, big brains, and the use of tools and language? Some of these key markers of humanity are fairly recent—or have origins that are impossible to date. And ironically, some of the physical markers that have led scientists to identify certain fossils as early hominins rather than apes are features that have been lost during subsequent human evolution.

Bipedalism

As is true of all subsequent hominins, postcranial material from **Ardipithecus**, the earliest widely accepted hominin genus (5.8–4.4 m.y.a.), indicates a capacity—albeit an imperfect one—for upright bipedal locomotion. The *Ardipithecus* pelvis appears to be transitional between one suited for arboreal climbing and one modified for bipedalism. Reliance on bipedalism—upright two-legged locomotion—is the key feature differentiating early hominins from the apes. This way of moving around eventually led to the distinctive hominin way of life. Based on African fossil discoveries, such as Ethiopia's *Ardipithecus*, hominin bipedalism is more than five million years old. Some scientists see even earlier evidence of bipedalism in two other fossil finds described below—one from Chad (*Sahelanthropus tchadensis*) and one from Kenya (*Orrorin tugenensis*).

Bipedalism traditionally has been viewed as an adaptation to open grassland or savanna country, although *Ardipithecus* lived in a humid woodland habitat. Adaptation to the savanna occurred later in hominin evolution. Perhaps bipedalism developed in the woodlands but became even more adaptive in a savanna habitat. Scientists have suggested several advantages of bipedalism: the ability to see over long grass and scrub, to carry items back to a home base, and to reduce the body's exposure to solar radiation. Studies with scale models of primates suggest that quadrupedalism exposes the body to 60 percent more solar radiation than does bipedalism. The fossil and archaeological records confirm that upright bipedal locomotion preceded stone tool manufacture and the expansion of the hominin brain. However, although early hominins could move bipedally on the ground, they also preserved enough of an apelike anatomy to make them good climbers (see the description of *Ardipithecus* on pp. 164–165 as well as of "Lucy's baby" in this chapter's "Appreciating Anthropology"). They could take to the trees to sleep and to escape terrestrial predators.

Brains, Skulls, and Childhood Dependency

Compared with contemporary humans, early hominins had very small brains. *Australopithecus afarensis,* a bipedal hominin that lived more than three million years ago, had a cranial capacity (430 cm^3—cubic centimeters) that barely surpassed the chimp average (390 cm^3). The form of the *afarensis* skull also is like that of the chimpanzee, although the brain-to-body size ratio may have been larger. Brain size has increased during hominin

Reconstruction of *Australopithecus* running bipedally with a pebble tool in hand. Along with tool use and manufacture, bipedalism is a key part of being human.

Ardipithecus Earliest recognized hominin genus (5.8–4.4 m.y.a.), Ethiopia.

evolution, especially with the advent of the genus *Homo*. But this increase had to overcome some obstacles. Compared with the young of other primates, human children have a long period of childhood dependency, during which their brains and skulls grow dramatically. Larger skulls demand larger birth canals, but the requirements of upright bipedalism impose limits on the expansion of the human pelvic opening. If the opening is too large, the pelvis doesn't provide sufficient support for the trunk. Locomotion suffers, and posture problems develop. If, by contrast, the birth canal is too narrow, mother and child (without the modern option of Caesarean section) may die. Natural selection has struck a balance between the structural demands of upright posture and the tendency toward increased brain size—the birth of immature and dependent children whose brains and skulls grow dramatically after birth. As the information in "Appreciating Anthropology" suggests, this shift had not yet taken place in *A. afarensis*, at least as represented by "Lucy's baby."

Tools

Given what is known (see Chapter 2) about tool use and manufacture by the great apes, it is likely that early hominins shared this ability as a homology with the apes. We'll see later that the first evidence for hominin stone tool manufacture is dated to 2.6 m.y.a. Upright bipedalism would have permitted the use of tools and weapons against predators and competitors. Bipedal locomotion

appreciating ANTHROPOLOGY

Ethiopian Paleontologist Discovers "Lucy's Baby"

Anthropologists have discovered some of the earliest hominin fossils at the northern end of Africa's Great Rift Valley. When these early hominins thrived more than three million years ago, this region was less arid than it is today. Anthropologists know this because similarly-dated remains of other animals, including hippos, crocodiles, and otters, have been found in the same geological layers. Described here is the recent discovery by an Ethiopian paleoanthropologist of the world's oldest child. She has been dubbed "Lucy's baby" because she was discovered in the same general area as Lucy, a famous early hominin whose remains recently have toured museums in the United States. This parentage, however, could not be, because the baby dates to an earlier geologic time than Lucy. This infant find is amazingly complete, with a full face and much more skeletal material than exists for Lucy. Like Lucy, the child is a member of Australopithecus afarensis, a species that many anthropologists consider ancestral to humans. Analysis of the infant's lower body confirms bipedalism, which already had been the characteristic hominin mode of locomotion for more than a million years before A. afarensis. By comparing this ancient child's maturation with that of modern humans and chimps, anthropologists hope to understand the social implications of variation in the development process.

September 20, 2006—The world's oldest known child has been discovered in East Africa in an area known appropriately as the Cradle of Humanity.

The 3.3-million-year-old fossilized toddler was uncovered in north Ethiopia's badlands along the Great Rift Valley.

The skeleton, belonging to the primitive human species *Australopithecus afarensis,* is remarkable for its age and completeness. . . .

The new find may even trump the superstar fossil of the same species: "Lucy," a 3.2-million-year-old adult female discovered nearby in 1974 that reshaped theories of human evolution.

Some experts have taken to calling the baby skeleton "Lucy's baby" because of the proximity of the discoveries, despite the fact that the baby is tens of thousands of years older.

"This is something you find once in a lifetime," said Zeresenay Alemseged of the Max Planck Institute for Evolutionary Anthropology in Leipzig, Germany, who led the team that made the discovery.

The child was probably female and about three years old when she died, according to the researchers.

Found in sandstone in the Dikika area, the remains include a remarkably well preserved skull, milk teeth, tiny fingers, a torso, a foot, and a kneecap no bigger than a dried pea.

Archaeologists hope that the baby skeleton, because of its completeness, can provide a wealth of details that Lucy and similar fossils couldn't.

The age of death makes the find especially useful, scientists say, providing insights into the growth and development of human ancestors.

"Visually speaking, the Dikika child is definitely more complete [than Lucy]," team member Fred Spoor of University College London (UCL) said.

"It has the complete skull, the mandible, and the whole brain case. Lucy doesn't have much of a head."

"The most impressive difference between them is that this baby has a face," Zeresenay added.

That face, no bigger than a monkey's, was spotted peering from a dusty slope in Decem-

---

also allowed early hominins to carry things, perhaps including scavenged parts of carnivore kills. We know that primates have generalized abilities to adapt through learning. It would be amazing if early hominins, who are much more closely related to us than the apes are, didn't have even greater cultural abilities than contemporary apes have.

Teeth

One example of an early hominin trait that has been lost during subsequent human evolution is big back teeth. (Indeed a pattern of overall dental reduction has characterized human evolution.) Once they adapted to the savanna, with its gritty, tough, and fibrous vegetation, it was adaptively advantageous for early hominins to have large back teeth and thick tooth enamel. This permitted thorough chewing of tough, fibrous vegetation and mixture with salivary enzymes to permit digestion of foods that otherwise would not have been digestible. The churning, rotary motion associated with such chewing also favored reduction of the canines and first premolars (bicuspids). These front teeth are much sharper and longer in the apes than in early hominins. The apes use their sharp self-honing teeth to pierce fruits. Males also flash their big sharp canines to intimidate and impress others, including potential mates. Although bipedalism seems to have characterized the human lineage since it split from the line ber 2000. Its smooth brow and short canine teeth identified it as a hominin, a group that encompasses humans and their ancestors . . .

The fossil child, who died at nursing age, offers important clues to the development of early humans. . . .

For instance, a prolonged, dependent childhood allowed later human species to grow larger brains, which need more time to develop after birth.

At a September 2006 press conference in Addis Ababa, the Ethiopian paleoanthropologist Zeresenay Alemseged displays the newly discovered skull of the oldest known hominin child. Alemseged headed the team that made the find, dating to 3.3 m.y.a. Dubbed "Lucy's baby," despite having lived before that famous fossil, the child also belonged to the species *A. afarensis*. Probably a female, the child died around the age of 3.

"As far as we can tell, it is not yet happening [with Lucy's baby]," Spoor said.

While the adult *A. afarensis* is thought to have had a brain slightly larger than a chimpanzee's, the hominin child's brain appears to have been smaller than an average chimp brain of the same age. . . .

The new fossil also supports the theory that *A. afarensis* walked upright on two legs, but it hints that human ancestors hadn't completely left the trees by that time.

The skeleton's ape-like upper body includes two complete shoulder blades similar to a gorilla's, so it could have been better at climbing than humans are . . .

Louise Humphrey, a paleontologist at the Natural History Museum in London who wasn't part of Zeresenay's team, describes the find as "an extremely valuable addition to the hominin fossil record.

"The fossil also preserves parts of the skeleton not previously documented for *A. afarensis*," she added.

These included a hyoid bone in the throat area that later went on to form part of the human voice box. . . .

How the child died is unclear, though it appears the body was rapidly covered by sand and gravel during a flood.

"It was buried just after it died," Zeresenay said. "That's why we found an almost complete skeleton, so maybe [drowning] could be the cause of its demise."

Like Lucy and many other hominin fossils, the child was uncovered in the low-lying northern end of Africa's Great Rift Valley.

Researchers say the region was once much less arid. Hominins shared the area's lush woods and grasslands with extinct species of elephants, hippos, crocodiles, otters, antelopes, and other animals whose fossils have been found nearby.

For these remains to be preserved and discovered, Zeresenay says, they needed to be covered in sediments and then exposed by tectonic activity, as has happened in the Great Rift Valley.

"These deposited environments were subsequently exposed by tectonics for us to go there and find the hominins," he added.

The Ethiopian paleoanthropologist says several more years of painstaking work will be needed to remove the remaining hard sandstone encasing much of the fossil child's skeleton.

SOURCE: James Owen, "'Lucy's Baby'—World's Oldest Child—Found by Fossil Hunters." *National Geographic News*, September 20, 2006. Reprinted by permission of National Geographic.

leading to the African apes, many other "human" features came later. Yet other early hominin features, such as large back teeth and thick enamel—which we don't have now—offer clues about who was a human ancestor back then.

CHRONOLOGY OF HOMININ EVOLUTION

Recall that the term *hominin* is used to designate the human line after its split from ancestral chimps. *Hominid* refers to the taxonomic family that includes humans and the African apes and their immediate ancestors. In this book *hominid* is used when there is doubt about the hominin status of the fossil. Although recent fossil discoveries have pushed the hominin lineage back to almost six million years, humans actually haven't been around too long when the age of the Earth is considered. If we compare Earth's history to a 24-hour day (with one second equaling 50,000 years),

Earth originates at midnight.
The earliest fossils were deposited at 5:45 A.M.
The first vertebrates appeared at 9:02 P.M.
The earliest mammals, at 10:45 P.M.
The earliest primates, at 11:43 P.M.
The earliest hominins, at 11:57 P.M.
And *Homo sapiens* arrives 36 seconds before midnight. (Wolpoff 1999, p. 10)

Although the first hominins appeared late in the Miocene epoch, for the study of hominin evolution, the Pliocene (5 to 2 m.y.a.), Pleistocene (2 m.y.a. to 10,000 B.P.), and Recent (10,000 B.P. to the present) epochs are most important. Until the end of the Pliocene, the main hominin genus was *Australopithecus*, which lived in sub-Saharan Africa. By the start of the Pleistocene, *Australopithecus* had evolved into *Homo*.

WHO WERE THE EARLIEST HOMININS?

Recent discoveries of fossils and tools have increased our knowledge of hominid and hominin evolution. The most significant recent discoveries have been made in Africa—Kenya, Tanzania, Ethiopia, and Chad. These finds come from different sites and may be the remains of individuals that lived hundreds of thousands of years apart. Furthermore, geological processes operating over thousands or millions of years inevitably distort fossil remains. Table 8.1 summarizes the major events in hominid and hominin evolution. You should consult it throughout this chapter and the next one.

Sahelanthropus tchadensis

In July 2001 anthropologists working in Central Africa—in northern Chad's Djurab Desert—unearthed the 6-to-7-million-year-old skull of the

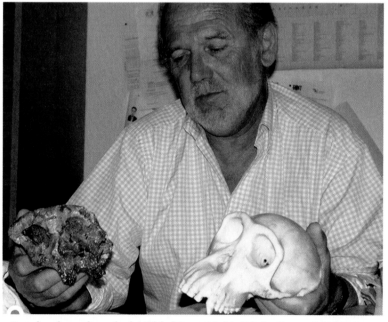

French paleoanthropologist Michel Brunet holds *Sahelanthropus tchadensis*, nicknamed "Toumai" (on the left), and a modern chimpanzee skull (on the right). If Toumai isn't a human ancestor, what else might it be?

oldest possible human ancestor yet found. This discovery consists of a nearly complete skull, two lower jaw fragments, and three teeth. It dates to the time period when humans and chimps would have been diverging from a common ancestor. "It takes us into another world, of creatures that include the common ancestor, the ancestral human and the ancestral chimp," George Washington University paleobiologist Bernard Wood said (quoted in Gugliotta 2002). The discovery was made by a 40-member multinational team led by the French paleoanthropologist Michel Brunet. The actual discoverer was the university undergraduate Ahounta Djimdoumalbaye, who spied the skull embedded in sandstone. The new fossil was dubbed *Sahelanthropus tchadensis*, referring to the northern Sahel region of Chad where it was found. The fossil is also known as "Toumai," a local name meaning "hope of life."

The discovery team identified the skull as that of an adult male with a chimp-sized brain (320–380 cubic centimeters), heavy brow ridges, and a relatively flat, humanlike face. Toumai's habitat included savanna, forests, rivers, and lakes—and abundant animal life such as elephants, antelope, horses, giraffes, hyenas, hippopotamuses, wild boars, crocodiles, fish, and rodents. The animal species enabled the team to date the site where Toumai was found (by comparison with radiometrically dated sites with similar fauna).

The discovery of Toumai moves scientists close to the time when humans and the African apes diverged from a common ancestor (see Weiss 2005). As we would expect in a fossil so close to the common ancestor, Toumai blends apelike and human characteristics. Although the brain was chimp-sized, the tooth enamel was thicker than a chimp's enamel, suggesting a diet that included not just fruits but also tougher vegetation of a sort typically found in the savanna. Also, Toumai's snout did not protrude as far as a chimp's, making it more humanlike, and the canine tooth was shorter than those of other apes. "The fossil is showing the first glimmerings of evolution in our direction," according to University of California at Berkeley anthropologist Tim White (quoted in Gugliotta 2002).

Sahelanthropus is a nearly complete, although distorted, skull. The placement of its *foramen magnum* (the "big hole" through which the spinal cord joins the brain) farther forward than in apes suggests that *Sahelanthropus* moved bipedally. Its discovery in Chad indicates that hominin evolution was not confined to East Africa's Rift Valley. The Rift Valley's abundant fossil record (see below) may well reflect geology, preservation, and modern exposure of fossils rather than the actual geographic distribution of species in the past. The discovery of *Sahelanthropus* in Chad is the first proof of a more widespread distribution of early hominins.

TABLE 8.1 Dates and Geographic Distribution of Major Hominoid, Hominid, and Hominin Fossil Groups

FOSSIL GROUP	DATES, m.y.a.	KNOWN DISTRIBUTION
Hominoid		
Pierolapithecus catalaunicus	13	Spain
Hominid		
Common ancestor of hominids	8?	East Africa
Sahelanthropus tchadensis	7–6	Chad
Orrorin tugenensis	6	Kenya
Hominins		
Ardipithecus kadabba	5.8–5.5	Ethiopia
Ardipithecus ramidus	4.4	Ethiopia
Kenyanthropus platyops	3.5	Kenya
Australopithecines		
A. anamensis	4.2–3.9	Kenya
A. afarensis	3.8–3.0	East Africa (Laetoli, Hadar)
A. garhi	2.5	Ethiopia
Robusts	2.6–1.2	East and South Africa
A. robustus (aka *Paranthropus*)	2.0?–1.0?	South Africa
A. boisei	2.6?–1.2	East Africa
Graciles		
A. africanus	3.0?–2.0?	South Africa
Homo		
H. habilis/H. rudolfensis	2.4?–1.4?	East Africa
H. erectus	1.9?–0.3?	Africa, Asia, Europe
Homo sapiens	0.3–present	
Archaic H. sapiens	0.3–0.28 (300,000–28,000)	Africa, Asia, Europe
Neandertals	0.13–0.28 (130,000–28,000)	Europe, Middle East, North Africa
Anatomically Modern Humans (AMHs)	0.15?–present (150,000–present)	Worldwide (after 20,000 B.P.)

Orrorin tugenensis

In January 2001 Brigitte Senut, Martin Pickford, and others reported the discovery, near the village of Tugen in Kenya's Baringo district, of possible early hominin fossils they called *Orrorin tugenensis* (Aiello and Collard 2001; Senut et al. 2001). The find consisted of 13 fossils from at least 5 individuals. The fossils include pieces of jaw with teeth, isolated upper and lower teeth, arm bones, and a finger bone. *Orrorin* appears to have been a chimp-sized creature that climbed easily and walked on two legs when on the ground. Its date of 6 million years is close to the time of the common ancestor of humans and chimps. The fossilized left femur (thigh bone) suggests upright bipedalism (walking with two feet), while the thick right humerus (upper arm bone) suggests tree-climbing skills. Animal fossils found in the same rocks indicate *Orrorin* lived in a wooded environment.

Orrorin's upper incisor, upper canine, and lower premolar are more like the teeth of a female chimpanzee than like human teeth. But other dental and skeletal features, especially bipedalism, led the discoverers to assign *Orrorin* to the hominin lineage. *Orrorin* lived after *Sahelanthropus tchadensis* but before *Ardipithecus kadabba*, discovered in Ethiopia, also in 2001, and dated to 5.8–5.5 m.y.a. The hominin status of *Ardipithecus* is more generally accepted than is that of either *Sahelanthropus tchadensis* or *Orrorin tugenensis*.

Ardipithecus

Early hominins assigned to *Ardipithecus kadabba* lived during the late Miocene, between 5.8 and 5.5 million years ago. *Ardipithecus* (*ramidus*) fossils were first discovered at Aramis in Ethiopia by Berhane Asfaw, Gen Suwa, and Tim White. Dating to 4.4 m.y.a., these *Ardipithecus ramidus* fossils consisted of the remains of some 17 individuals, with cranial, facial, dental, and upper limb bones. Subsequently, much older *Ardipithecus* (*kadabba*) fossils, dating back to 5.8 m.y.a., very near the time of the common ancestor of humans and the

anthropology **ATLAS**

Map 4 shows the sites where the earliest hominid and hominin fossils have been found, along with a timeline for hominid and hominin evolution.

African apes, were found in Ethiopia. The *kadabba* find consists of 11 specimens, including a jawbone with teeth, hand and foot bones, fragments of arm bones, and a piece of collarbone. At least five individuals are represented. These creatures were apelike in size, anatomy, and habitat. They lived in a wooded area rather than the open grassland or savanna habitat where later hominins proliferated. As of this writing, because of its probable bipedalism, *Ardipithecus kadabba* is recognized as

In October 2009, a newly reported *Ardipithecus* find—a fairly complete skeleton of *Ardipithecus ramidus*, dubbed "Ardi" was heralded throughout the media.

the earliest known hominin, with the *Sahelanthropus tchadensis* find from Chad, dated to 7–6 m.y.a., and *Orrorin tugenensis* from Kenya, dated to 6 m.y.a. possibly even older hominins.

In October 2009, a newly reported *Ardipithecus* find—a fairly complete skeleton of *Ardipithecus ramidus*, dubbed "Ardi"—was heralded on the front page of the *New York Times* and throughout the media (Wilford 2009). Ardi (4.4 m.y.a.) replaces Lucy (3.2 m.y.a.—see below) as the earliest known hominin skeleton. The Ethiopian discovery site lies on what is now an arid floodplain of the Awash River, 45 miles south of Hadar, where Lucy was found. Scientists infer that Ardi was female, based on its small and lightly built (gracile) skull and its small canine teeth compared with others at the site. At four feet tall and 120 pounds, Ardi stood about a foot taller and weighed twice as much as Lucy.

The *Ardipithecus* pelvis appears to be transitional between one suited for arboreal climbing and one modified for bipedal locomotion. The pelvis of later hominins such as Lucy shows nearly all the adaptations needed for full bipedalism. Although Ardi's lower pelvis remains primitive, the structure of her upper pelvis allowed her to walk on two legs with a straightened hip. Still, she probably could neither walk nor run as well as later hominins. Her feet lacked the archlike structure of later hominin feet. Ardi's apelike lower pelvis indicates retention of powerful hamstring muscles for climbing. Her hands, very long arms, and short legs all recall those of extinct apes, and her brain was no larger than that of a modern chimp.

Based on associated animal and plant remains, *Ardipithecus* lived in a humid woodland habitat. More than 145 teeth have been collected at the site. Their size, shape, and wear patterns suggest an omnivorous diet of plants, nuts, and small mammals. Although *Ardipithecus* probably fed both in trees and on the ground, the canines suggest less of a fruit diet than is characteristic of living apes. With reduced sexual dimorphism, *Ardipithecus* canines resemble modern human canines more than the tusklike piercing upper canines of chimps and gorillas.

The first comprehensive reports describing Ardi and related findings, the result of 17 years of study, were published on October 2, 2009, in the journal *Science*, including 11 papers by 47 authors from 10 countries. They analyzed more than 110 *Ardipithecus* specimens from at least 36 different individuals, including Ardi. The ancestral relationship of *Ardipithecus* to *Australopithecus* has not been determined, but Ardi has been called a plausible ancestor for *Australopithecus* (see Wilford 2009).

Kenyanthropus

Complicating the picture is another discovery, which Maeve Leakey has named *Kenyanthropus*

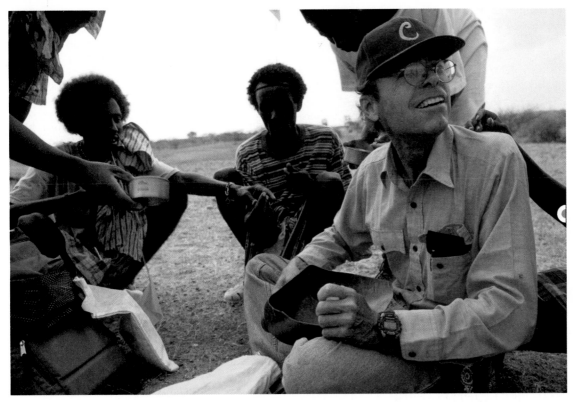

Shown here are three members of the international team responsible for Ardi's discovery and reconstruction. On the left is American Tim White. Below are Ethiopians Johannes Haile-Selassie and Berhane Asfaw.

platyops, or flat-faced "man" of Kenya. (Actually, the sex hasn't been determined.) This 1999 fossil find—of a nearly complete skull and partial jawbone—was made by a research team led by Leakey, excavating on the western side of Lake Turkana in northern Kenya. They consider this 3.5-million-year-old find to represent an entirely new branch of the early human family tree.

Leakey views *Kenyanthropus* as showing that at least two hominin lineages existed as far back as 3.5 million years. One was the well-established fossil species *Australopithecus afarensis* (see below), best known from the celebrated Lucy skeleton. With the discovery of *Kenyanthropus* it would seem that Lucy and her kind weren't alone on the African plain. The hominin family tree, once drawn with a straight trunk, now looks more like a bush, with branches leading in many directions (Wilford 2001*a*).

Kenyanthropus has a flattened face and small molars that are strikingly different from those of *afarensis*. Ever since its discovery in Ethiopia in 1974 by Donald Johanson, *afarensis* has been regarded as the most likely common ancestor of all subsequent hominins, including humans. With no other hominin fossils dated to the period between 3.8 million and 3.0 million years ago, this was the most reasonable conclusion scientists could draw. As a result of the *Kenyanthropus* discovery, however, the place of *afarensis* in human ancestry has been and will be debated. Taxonomic

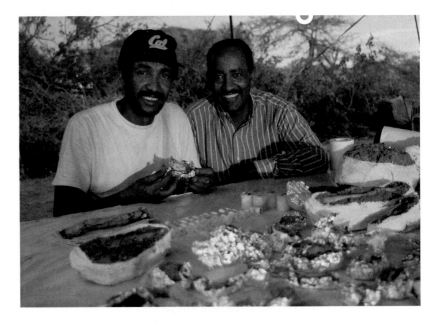

"splitters" (those who stress diversity and divergence) will focus on the differences between *afarensis* and *Kenyanthropus* and see it as representing a new taxon (genus and/or species), as Maeve Leakey has done. Taxonomic "lumpers" will focus on the similarities between *Kenyanthropus* and *afarensis* and may try to place them both in the same taxon—probably *Australopithecus*, which is well established.

Maeve Leakey and *Kenyanthropus platyops*, which she discovered in 1999 by Lake Turkana in northern Kenya. What's the significance of *Kenyanthropus*?

THE VARIED AUSTRALOPITHECINES

Some Miocene hominins eventually evolved into a varied group of Pliocene–Pleistocene hominins known as the **australopithecines**—for which we have an abundant fossil record. This term reflects their one-time classification as members of a distinct taxonomic subfamily, the "Australopithecinae." We now know that the various species of *Australopithecus* discussed in this chapter do not form a distinct subfamily within the order Primates, but the name "australopithecine" has stuck to describe them. Today the distinction between the australopithecines and later hominins is made on the genus level. The australopithecines are assigned to the genus *Australopithecus* (*A.*); later humans, to *Homo* (*H.*).

In the scheme followed here, *Australopithecus* had at least six species:

1. *A. anamensis* (4.2 to 3.9 m.y.a.)

2. *A. afarensis* (3.8 to 3.0 m.y.a.)

3. *A. africanus* (3.0? to 2.0? m.y.a.)

4. *A. garhi* (2.5 m.y.a.)

5. *A. robustus* (2.0? to 1.0? m.y.a.)

6. *A. boisei* (2.6? to 1.2 m.y.a.)

The dates given for each species are approximate because an organism isn't a member of one species one day and a member of another species the next day. Nor could the same dating techniques be used for all the finds. The South African australopithecine fossils (*A. africanus* and *A. robustus*), for example, come from a nonvolcanic

area where radiometric dating could not be done. Dating of those fossils has been based mainly on stratigraphy. The hominin fossils from the volcanic regions of East Africa usually have radiometric dates.

Australopithecus anamensis

Ardipithecus ramidus may (or may not) have evolved into *A. anamensis*, a bipedal hominin from northern Kenya, whose fossil remains were reported first by Maeve Leakey and Alan Walker in 1995 (Leakey et al. 1995; Rice 2002). ***A. anamensis*** consists of 78 fragments from two sites: Kanapoi and Allia Bay. The fossils include upper and lower jaws, cranial fragments, and the upper and lower parts of a leg bone (tibia). The Kanapoi fossils date to 4.2 m.y.a., and those at Allia Bay to 3.9 m.y.a. The molars have thick enamel, and the apelike canines are large. Based on the tibia, *anamensis* weighed about 110 pounds (50 kg.). This would have made it larger than either the earlier *Ardipithecus* or the later *A. afarensis*. Its anatomy implies that anamensis was bipedal. Because of its date and its location in the East African Rift Valley, *A. anamensis* may be ancestral to *A. afarensis* (3.8–3.0 m.y.a.), which usually is considered ancestral to all the later australopithecines (*garhi, africanus, robustus,* and *boisei*) as well as to *Homo* (Figure 8.1).

Australopithecus afarensis

The hominin species known as ***A. afarensis*** includes fossils found at two sites, Laetoli in northern Tanzania and Hadar in the Afar region of Ethiopia. Laetoli is earlier (3.8–3.6 m.y.a.). The Hadar fossils probably date to between 3.3 and 3.0 m.y.a. Thus, based on the current evidence, *A. afarensis* lived between about 3.8 and 3.0 m.y.a. Research directed by Mary Leakey was responsible for the Laetoli finds. The Hadar discoveries resulted from an international expedition directed by D. C. Johanson and M. Taieb. The two sites have yielded significant samples of early hominin fossils. There are two dozen specimens from Laetoli, and the Hadar finds include the remains of between 35 and 65 individuals. The Laetoli remains are mainly teeth and jaw fragments, along with some very informative fossilized footprints. The Hadar sample includes skull fragments and postcranial material, most notably 40 percent of the complete skeleton of a tiny hominin female, dubbed "Lucy," who lived around 3 m.y.a.

Although the hominin remains at Laetoli and Hadar were deposited half a million years apart, their many resemblances explain their placement in the same species, *A. afarensis*. These fossils forced a reinterpretation of the early hominin fossil record. *A. afarensis,* although clearly a hominin, was so similar in many ways to chimps and gorillas that our common ancestry with the African apes must be very recent, certainly no more than

australopithecines
Common term for all members of the genus *Australopithecus*.

A. anamensis
Earliest known *Australopithecus* species (4.2–3.9 m.y.a.), Kenya.

Australopithecus (A.) afarensis
Early *Australopithecus* species (3.8–3.0 m.y.a.), Ethiopia ("Lucy"), Tanzania.

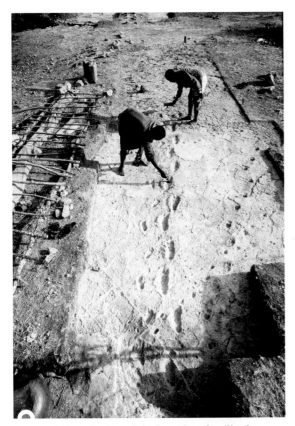

An ancient trail of hominin footprints fossilized in volcanic ash. Mary Leakey found this 230-foot (70-meter) trail at Laetoli, Tanzania, in 1979. It dates from 3.6 m.y.a. and confirms that A. *afarensis* was a striding biped.

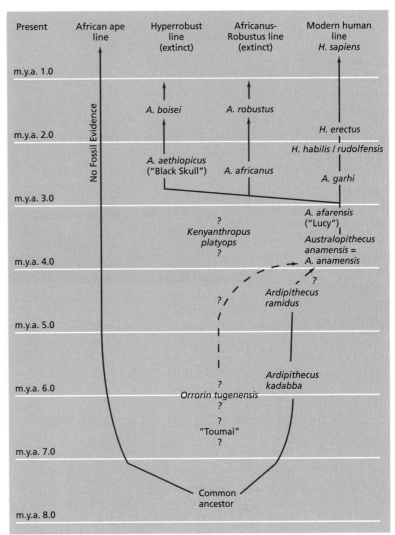

FIGURE 8.1 Phylogenetic Tree for African Apes, Hominids, and Hominins.

The presumed divergence date for ancestral chimps and hominins was between 6 and 8 m.y.a. Branching in later hominin evolution is also shown. For more exact dates, see the text and Table 8.1.

8 m.y.a. *Ardipithecus* and *A. anamensis* are even more apelike. These discoveries show that hominins are much closer to the apes than the previously known fossil record had suggested. Studies of the learning abilities and biochemistry of chimps and gorillas have taught a valuable lesson about homologies that the fossil record is now confirming.

The *A. afarensis* finds make this clear. The many apelike features are surprising in definite hominins that lived as recently as 3 m.y.a. Discussion of hominin fossils requires a brief review of dentition. Moving from front to back, on either side of the upper or lower jaw, humans (and apes) have two incisors, one canine, two premolars, and three molars. Our dental formula is 2.1.2.3, for a total of 8 teeth on each side, upper and lower—32 teeth in all—if we have all our "wisdom teeth" (our third molars). Now back to the australopithecines. Compared with *Homo*, *A. afarensis* had larger and sharper canine teeth that projected beyond the other teeth. The canines, however, were reduced compared with an ape's tusklike canines. The *afarensis* lower premolar was pointed and projecting to sharpen the upper canine. It had one long cusp

and one tiny bump that hints at the bicuspid premolar that eventually developed in hominin evolution.

There is, however, evidence that powerful chewing associated with savanna vegetation was entering the *A. afarensis* feeding pattern. When the coarse, gritty, fibrous vegetation of grasslands and semidesert enters the diet, the back teeth change to accommodate heavy chewing stresses. Massive back teeth, jaws, and facial and cranial structures suggest a diet demanding extensive grinding and powerful crushing. *A. afarensis* molars are large (see Figure 8.2). The lower jaw (mandible) is thick and is buttressed with a bony ridge behind the front teeth. The cheekbones are large

On the left, two sections of a tibia (dating back 4 million years) from A. anamensis, a bipedal hominin from northern Kenya. The tibia is the larger bone of the lower leg. Features of these bone fragments provide evidence that A. anamensis walked upright. To the right, an A. anamensis lower jaw and an upper jaw fragment. The molars have thick enamel, and the apelike canines are large.

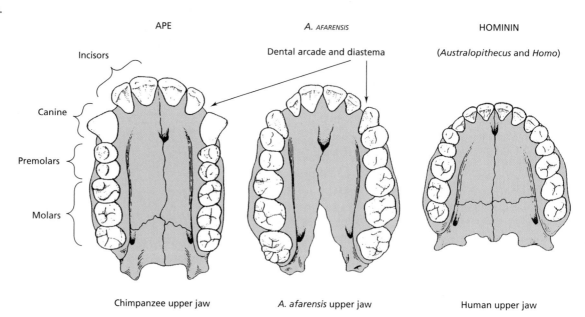

FIGURE 8.2 Comparison of Dentition in Ape, Human, and *A. afarensis* Palates.

SOURCE: © 1981 Luba Dmytryk Gudz/Brill Atlanta.

and flare out to the side for the attachment of powerful chewing muscles.

The skull of *A. afarensis* contrasts with those of later hominins. The cranial capacity of 430 cm^3 (cubic centimeters) barely surpasses the chimp average (390 cm^3). Below the neck, however—particularly in regard to locomotion—*A. afarensis* was unquestionably human. Early evidence of striding bipedalism comes from Laetoli, where volcanic ash, which can be directly dated by the K/A technique, covered a trail of footprints of two or three hominins walking to a water hole. These prints leave no doubt that a small striding biped lived in Tanzania by 3.6 m.y.a. The structure of the pelvic, hip, leg, and foot bones also confirms that upright bipedalism was *A. afarensis*'s mode of locomotion.

More recent finds show that bipedalism predated *A. afarensis*. *A. anamensis* (4.2 m.y.a.) was bipedal, as was the even older *Ardipithecus* (5.8–4.4 m.y.a.). Although bidepal, *A. afarensis* still contrasts in many ways with later hominins. Sexual dimorphism is especially marked. The male–female contrast in jaw size in *A. afarensis* was more marked than in the orangutan. There was a similar contrast in body size. *A. afarensis* females, such

SPECIES	DATES (m.y.a.)	KNOWN DISTRIBUTION	IMPORTANT SITES	BODY WEIGHT (MID-SEX)	BRAIN SIZE (MID-SEX) (cm³)
Anatomically modern humans (AMHs)	195,000 to present			132 lb/60 kg	1,350
Pan troglodytes (chimpanzee)	Modern			93 lb/42 kg	390
A. boisei	2.6? to 1.2	E. Africa	Olduvai, East Turkana	86 lb/39 kg	490
A. robustus	2.0? to 1.0?	S. Africa	Kromdraai, Swartkrans	81 lb/37 kg	540
A. africanus	3.0? to 2.0?	S. Africa	Taung, Sterkfontein, Makapansqat	79 lb/36 kg	490
A. afarensis	3.8 to 3.0	E. Africa	Hadar, Laetoli	77 lb/35 kg	430
A. anamensis	4.2 to 3.9	Kenya	Kanapoi Allia Bay	Insufficient data	No published skulls
Ardipithecus	5.8 to 4.4	Ethiopia	Aramis	Insufficient data	No published skulls

as Lucy, stood between 3 and 4 feet (0.9 and 1.2 meters) tall; males might have reached 5 feet (1.5 meters). *A. afarensis* males weighed perhaps twice as much as the females did (Wolpoff 1999). Recap 8.1 summarizes data on the various australopithecines, including mid-sex body weight and brain size. Mid-sex means midway between the male average and the female average.

Lucy and her kind were far from dainty. Lucy's muscle-engraved bones are much more robust than ours are. With only rudimentary tools and weapons, early hominins needed powerful and resistant bones and muscles. Lucy's arms are longer relative to her legs than are those of later hominins. Here again her proportions are more apelike than ours are. Although Lucy neither brachiated nor knuckle-walked, she was probably a much better climber than modern people are, and she spent some of her day in the trees.

The *A. afarensis* fossils show that as recently as 3 m.y.a., our ancestors had a mixture of apelike and hominin features. Canines, premolars, and skulls were more apelike than most scholars had imagined would exist in such a recent ancestor. On the other hand, the molars, chewing apparatus, and cheekbones foreshadowed later hominin trends, and the pelvic and limb bones were indisputably hominin (Figure 8.3 on page 174). The hominin pattern was being built from the ground up.

Hominins walk with a striding gait that consists of alternating swing and stance phases for each leg and foot. As one leg is pushed off by the big toe and goes into the swing phase, the heel of the other leg is touching the ground and entering the stance phase. Four-footed locomotors such as

Illustration of female *Australopithecus afarensis* "Lucy," discovered in Ethiopia's Omo Valley in 1974.

Old World monkeys are always supported by two limbs. Bipeds, by contrast, are supported by one limb at a time.

The pelvis, the lower spine, the hip joint, and the thigh bone change in accordance with the stresses of bipedal locomotion. Australopithecine

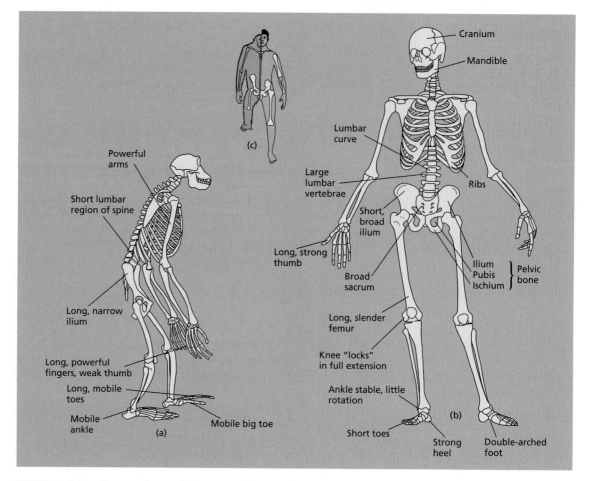

FIGURE 8.3 Comparison of *Homo sapiens* and *Pan troglodytes* (the Common Chimp).

(a) Skeleton of chimpanzee in bipedal position; (b) skeleton of modern human; (c) chimpanzee and human "bisected" and drawn to the same trunk length for comparison of limb proportions. The contrast in leg length is largely responsible for the proportional difference between humans and apes.

pelvises are much more similar (although far from identical) to *Homo*'s than to apes' and show adaptation to bipedalism (Figure 8.4 on page 175). The blades of the australopithecine pelvis (iliac blades) are shorter and broader than are those of the ape. The sacrum, which anchors the pelvis's two side bones, is larger, as in *Homo*. With bipedalism, the pelvis forms a sort of basket that balances the weight of the trunk and supports this weight with less stress. Fossilized spinal bones (vertebrae) show that the australopithecine spine had the lower spine (lumbar) curve characteristic of *Homo*. This curvature helps transmit the weight of the upper body to the pelvis and the legs. Placement of the *foramen magnum* (the "big hole" through which the spinal cord joins the brain) farther forward in *Australopithecus* and *Homo* than in the ape also represents an adaptation to upright bipedalism (Figure 8.5).

 living anthropology **VIDEOS**

Lucy, www.mhhe.com/kottak

This clip describes the discovery and characteristics of Lucy, the first member of *Australopithecus afarensis* to enter the fossil record. On her discovery in 1974, Lucy became the most ancient hominin and hominid in the fossil record at that time. Today that record includes several older probable or possible hominin ancestors, identified as such—like Lucy—by their upright bipedalism. The clip supplies answers to the following questions: Which of Lucy's anatomical traits were similar to those of chimpanzees? Which were similar to those of modern humans? How did Lucy's pelvis differ from an ape's pelvis? What is the explanation for this difference?

In apes, the thigh bone (femur) extends straight down from the hip to the knees. In *Australopithecus* and *Homo*, however, the thigh bone angles into the hip, permitting the space between the knees to be narrower than the pelvis during walking. The pelvises of the australopithecines were similar but not identical to those of *Homo*. The most significant contrast is a narrower australopithecine birth canal (Tague and Lovejoy 1986).

Expansion of the birth canal is a trend in hominin evolution. The width of the birth canal is related to the size of the skull and brain. *A. afarensis* had a small cranial capacity. Even in later australopithecines, brain size did not exceed 600 cubic centimeters. Undoubtedly, the australopithecine skull grew after birth to accommodate a growing brain, as it does (much more) in *Homo*. However, the brains of the australopithecines expanded less than ours do. In the australopithecines, the cranial sutures (the lines where the bones of the skull eventually come together) fused relatively earlier in life.

Young australopithecines must have depended on their parents and kin for nurturance and protection. Those years of childhood dependency would have provided time for observation, teaching, and learning. This may provide indirect evidence for a rudimentary cultural life.

Gracile and Robust Australopithecines

The fossils of *A. africanus* and *A. robustus* come from South Africa. In 1924, the anatomist Raymond Dart coined the term ***Australopithecus africanus*** to describe the first fossil representative of this species, the skull of a juvenile that was found accidentally in a quarry at Taung, South Africa. Radiometric dates are lacking for this nonvolcanic region, but the fossil hominins found at the five main South African sites appear (from stratigraphy) to have lived between 3 and 1 m.y.a.

A. africanus
Gracile *Australopithecus* species (3.0?–2.0? m.y.a.), South Africa.

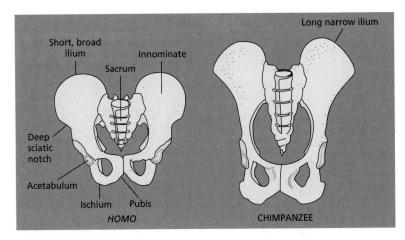

FIGURE 8.4   A Comparison of Human and Chimpanzee Pelvises.

The human pelvis has been modified to meet the demands of upright bipedalism. The blades (ilia; singular, ilium) of the human pelvis are shorter and broader than those of the ape. The sacrum, which anchors the side bones, is wider. The australopithecine pelvis is far more similar to that of Homo than to that of the chimpanzee, as we would expect in an upright biped.

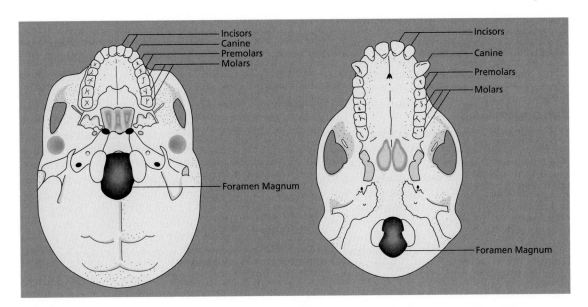

FIGURE 8.5   A Comparison of the Skull and Dentition (Upper Jaw) of *Homo* and the Chimpanzee.

The foramen magnum, through which the spinal cord joins the brain, is located farther forward in Homo than in the ape. This permits the head to balance atop the spine with upright bipedalism. The molars and premolars of the ape form parallel rows. Human teeth, by contrast, are arranged in rounded, parabolic form. What differences do you note between human and ape canines? Canine reduction has been an important trend in hominin evolution.

There were two groups of South African australopithecines: **gracile** (*A. africanus*) and **robust** (*A. robustus*). "Gracile" indicates that members of *A. africanus* were smaller and slighter, less robust, than were members of **A. robustus.** There were also very robust—*hyperrobust*—australopithecines in East Africa. In the classification scheme used here, these have been assigned to **A. boisei.** However, some scholars consider *A. robustus* and *A. boisei* to be regional variants of just one species, usually called *robustus* (sometimes given its own genus, *Paranthropus*).

The relationship between the graciles and the robusts has been debated for generations but has not been resolved. Graciles and robusts probably descend from *A. afarensis*, which itself was gracile in form, or from a South African version of *A. afarensis*. Some scholars have argued that the graciles lived before (3 to 2? m.y.a.) and were ancestral to the robusts (2? to 1? m.y.a.). Others contend that the graciles and the robusts were separate species that may have overlapped in time. (Classifying them as members of different species implies they were reproductively isolated from each other in time or space.) The range of *Australopithecus* sites in East and South Africa is shown on Map 4 in the Map Atlas.

The trend toward enlarged back teeth, chewing muscles, and facial buttressing, which already is noticeable in *A. afarensis*, continues in the South African australopithecines. However, the canines are reduced, and the premolars are fully bicuspid. Dental form and function changed as dietary needs shifted from cutting and slashing to chewing and grinding.

The mainstay of the australopithecine diet was the vegetation of the savanna, although these early hominins also might have hunted small and slow-moving game. As well, they may have scavenged, bringing home parts of kills made by large cats and other carnivores. The ability to hunt large animals was probably an achievement of *Homo* and is discussed later.

The skulls, jaws, and teeth of the australopithecines leave no doubt that their diet was mainly vegetarian. Natural selection modifies the teeth to conform to the stresses associated with a particular diet. Massive back teeth, jaws, and associated facial and cranial structures confirm that the australopithecine diet required extensive grinding and powerful crushing.

In the South African australopithecines, both deciduous ("baby") and permanent molars and premolars are massive, with multiple cusps. The later australopithecines had bigger back teeth than did the earlier ones. However, this evolutionary trend ended with early *Homo,* which had much smaller back teeth, reflecting a dietary change that will be described later.

Contrasts with *Homo* in the front teeth are less marked. But they are still of interest because of what they tell us about sexual dimorphism. *A. africanus's* canines were more pointed, with larger roots, than *Homo's* are. Still, the *A. africanus* canines were only 75 percent the size of the canines of *A. afarensis*. Despite this canine reduction, there was just as much canine sexual dimorphism in *A. africanus* as there had been in *A. afarensis* (Wolpoff 1999). Sexual dimorphism in general was much more pronounced among the early hominins than it is among *Homo sapiens*. *A. africanus* females were about 4 feet (1.2 meters), and males 5 feet (1.5 meters), tall. The average female probably had no more than 60 percent the weight of the average male (Wolpoff 1980a). (That figure contrasts with today's average female-to-male weight ratio of about 88 percent.)

Teeth, jaw, face, and skull changed to fit a diet based on tough, gritty, fibrous grasslands vegetation. A massive face housed large upper teeth and provided a base for the attachment of powerful chewing muscles. Australopithecine cheekbones were elongated and massive structures (Figure 8.6) that anchored large chewing muscles running up the jaw. Another set of robust chewing muscles extended from the back of the jaw to the sides of the skull.

In the more robust australopithecines (*A. robustus* in South Africa and *A. boisei* in East Africa), these muscles were strong enough to produce a *sagittal crest,* a bony ridge on the top of the skull. Such a crest forms as the bone grows. It develops from the pull of the chewing muscles as they meet at the midline of the skull.

In 1985, the paleoanthropologist Alan Walker made a significant find near Lake Turkana in northern Kenya. Called the "black skull" because of the blue-black sheen it bore from the minerals surrounding it, the fossil displayed a "baffling combination of features" (Fisher 1988*a*). The jaw was apelike and the brain was small (as in *A. afarensis*), but there was a massive bony crest atop the skull (as in *A. boisei*). Walker and Richard Leakey (Walker's associate on the 1985 expedition) view the black skull (dated to 2.6 m.y.a.) as a very early hyperrobust *A. boisei*. Others (e.g., Jolly and White 1995) assign the black skull to its own species, *A. aethiopicus*. The black skull shows that some of the anatomical features of the hyperrobust australopithecines (2.6?–1.0 m.y.a.) did not change very much during more than one million years.

A. boisei survived through 1.2 m.y.a in East Africa. Compared with their predecessors, the later australopithecines tended to have larger overall size, skulls, and back teeth. They also had thicker faces, more prominent crests, and more rugged muscle markings on the skeleton. By contrast, the front teeth stayed the same size.

Brain size (measured as cranial capacity, in cubic centimeters—cm^3) increased only slightly between *A. afarensis* (430 cm^3), *A. africanus* (490 cm^3), and *A. robustus* (540 cm^3) (Wolpoff 1999). These

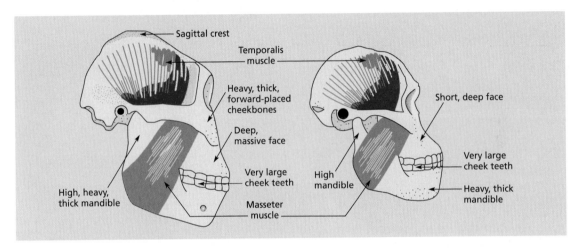

FIGURE 8.6 Skulls of Robust (Left) and Gracile (Right) Australopithecines, Showing Chewing Muscles.

Flaring cheek arches and, in some robusts, a sagittal crest supported this massive musculature. The early hominin diet—coarse, gritty vegetation of the savanna—demanded such structures. These features were most pronounced in A. boisei.

figures can be compared with an average cranial capacity of 1,350 cm^3 in *Homo sapiens*. The modern range goes from less than 1,000 cm^3 to more than 2,000 cm^3 in normal adults. The cranial capacity of chimps (*Pan troglodytes*) averages 390 cm^3 (see Recap 8.1). The brains of gorillas (*Gorilla gorilla*) average around 500 cm^3, which is within the australopithecine range, but gorilla body weight is much greater.

THE AUSTRALOPITHECINES AND EARLY *HOMO*

Between 3 and 2 m.y.a., the ancestors of *Homo* became reproductively isolated from the later australopithecines, such as *A. robustus* and *A. boisei*. The earliest (very fragmentary) evidence for the genus *Homo* (2.5 m.y.a.) comes from the Chemeron formation in Kenya's Baringo Basin (Sherwood, Ward, and Hill 2002). This is a skull fragment, an isolated right temporal bone, known as the Chemeron temporal. By 2 m.y.a. the fossil sample of hominin teeth from East Africa has two clearly different sizes. One set is huge, the largest molars and premolars in hominin evolution; those teeth belonged to *A. boisei*. The other group of (smaller) teeth belonged to members of the genus *Homo*.

By 1.9 m.y.a., there is fossil evidence that different hominin groups occupied different ecological niches in Africa. One of them, *Homo*—by then *Homo erectus*—had a larger brain and a reproportioned skull; it had increased the areas of the brain that regulate higher mental functions. These were our ancestors, hominins with greater capacities for culture than the australopithecines had. *H. erectus* hunted and gathered, made sophisticated tools, and eventually displaced its cousin species, *A. boisei*.

A. boisei of East Africa, the hyperrobust australopithecines, had mammoth back teeth. Their

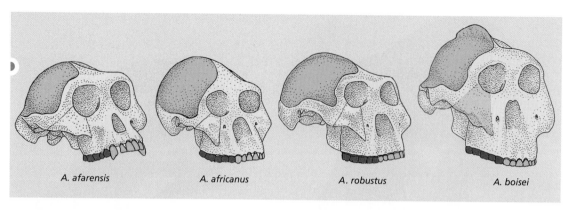

Shown from left to right are A. *afarensis*, A. *africanus*, A. *robustus*, and A. *boisei*. What are the main differences you notice among these four types of early hominins?

A. afarensis   A. africanus   A. robustus   A. boisei

Palates of *Homo sapiens* (left) and A. *boisei* (right), a late, hyperrobust australopithecine. In comparing them, note the australopithecine's huge molars and premolars. What other contrasts do you notice? The large back teeth represent an extreme adaptation to a diet based on coarse, gritty savanna vegetation. Reduction in tooth size during human evolution applied to the back teeth much more than to the front.

Homo habilis
Earliest (2.4?–1.4? m.y.a.) member of genus *Homo*.

females had bigger back teeth than did earlier australopithecine males. A. *boisei* became ever more specialized with respect to one part of the traditional australopithecine diet, concentrating on coarse vegetation with a high grit content.

We still don't know why, how, and exactly when the split between *Australopithecus* and *Homo* took place. Scholars have defended many different models, or theoretical schemes, to interpret the early hominin fossil record. Because new finds so often have forced reappraisals, most scientists are willing to modify their interpretation when given new evidence.

The model of Johanson and White (1979), who coined the term A. *afarensis*, proposes that A. *afarensis* split into two groups. One group, the ancestors of *Homo*, became reproductively isolated from the australopithecines between 3 and 2 m.y.a. Within this group was **Homo habilis,** a term coined by L. S. B. and Mary Leakey to describe the earliest members of the genus *Homo*. Another form of early *Homo* was *H. erectus*, which appears to have lived contemporaneously with *H. habilis* between around 1.9 and 1.4 m.y.a. (Spoor et al. 2007). Other members of A. *afarensis* evolved into the various kinds of later australopithecines (A. *africanus*, A. *robustus*, and hyperrobust A. *boisei*, the last member to become extinct).

There is good fossil evidence that *Homo* and A. *boisei* coexisted in East Africa. A. *boisei* seems to have lived in very arid areas, feeding on harder-to-chew vegetation than had any previous hominin. This diet would explain the hyperrobusts' huge back teeth, jaws, and associated areas of the face and skull.

OLDOWAN TOOLS

The simplest obviously manufactured tools were discovered in 1931 by L. S. B. and Mary Leakey at Olduvai Gorge, Tanzania. That locale gave the tools their name—Oldowan pebble tools. The oldest tools from Olduvai are about 1.8 million years old. Still older (2.6–2.0 m.y.a.) Oldowan implements have been found in Ethiopia, Congo, and Malawi.

Stone tools consist of flakes and cores. The *core* is the piece of rock, in the Oldowan case about the size of a tennis ball, from which flakes are struck. Once flakes have been removed, the core can become a tool itself. A *chopper* is a tool made by flaking the edge of such a core on one side and thus forming a cutting edge.

Oldowan pebble tools represent the world's oldest formally recognized stone tools. Core tools are not the most common Oldowan tools; flakes are. The purpose of flaking stone in the Oldowan tradition was not to create pebble tools or choppers but to create the sharp stone flakes that made up the mainstay of the Oldowan tool kit (Toth 1985). Choppers were a convenient byproduct of flaking and were used as well. However, hominins most likely did not have a preconceived tool form in mind while making them.

Oldowan choppers could have been used for food processing—by pounding, breaking, or bashing. Flakes probably were used mainly as cutters, for example, to dismember game carcasses. Crushed fossil animal bones indicate that stones were used to break open marrow cavities. Also, Oldowan deposits include pieces of bone or horn with scratch marks suggesting they were used to dig up tubers or insects. Oldowan core and flake tools are shown in the photos on this page. The flake tool in the lower photo is made of chert. Most Oldowan tools at Olduvai Gorge were made from basalt, which is locally more common and coarser.

For decades anthropologists have debated the identity of the earliest stone tool makers. The first *Homo habilis* find got its name (*habilis* is Latin for "able") for its presumed status as the first hominin tool maker. Recently the story has grown more complicated, with a discovery making it very likely that one kind of australopithecine also made and habitually used stone tools.

A. garhi and Early Stone Tools

In 1999 an international team reported the discovery, in Ethiopia, of a new species of hominin, along with the earliest traces of animal butchery (Asfaw, White, and Lovejoy 1999). These new fossils, dating to 2.5 m.y.a., may be the remains of a direct human ancestor and an evolutionary link between *Australopithecus* and the genus *Homo*. At the same site was evidence that antelopes and

horses had been butchered with the world's earliest stone tools. When scientists excavated these hominin fossils, they were shocked to find a combination of unforeseen skeletal and dental features. They named the specimen ***Australopithecus garhi***. The word *garhi* means "surprise" in the Afar language.

Tim White, coleader of the research team, viewed the discoveries as important for three reasons. First, they add a new potential ancestor to the human family tree. Second, they show that the thigh bone (femur) had elongated by 2.5 million years ago, a million years before the forearm shortened—to create our current human limb proportions. Third, evidence that large mammals were being butchered shows that early stone technologies were aimed at getting meat and marrow from big game. This signals a dietary revolution that eventually may have allowed an invasion of new habitats and continents (*Berkleyan* 1999).

In 1997 the Ethiopian archaeologist Sileshi Semaw announced he had found the world's earliest stone tools, dating to 2.6 m.y.a., at the nearby Ethiopian site of Gona. But which human ancestor had made these tools, he wondered, and what

A. garhi
Tool-making *Australopithecus* species (2.6 m.y.a.), Ethiopia.

Oldowan
Earliest (2.6–1.2 m.y.a.) stone tools; sharp flakes struck from cores (choppers).

Above, an Oldowan chopper core; below, an Oldowan flake tool. The purpose of flaking stone in the Oldowan tradition was not to create pebble tools or choppers but to create the sharp stone flakes that made up the mainstay of the Oldowan tool kit.

were they used for? The 1999 discoveries by Asfaw, White, and their colleagues provided answers, identifying *A. garhi* as the best candidate for toolmaker (*Berkleyan* 1999).

The association, in the same area at the same time, of *A. garhi*, animal butchery, and the earliest stone tools suggests that the australopithecines were toolmakers, with some capacity for culture. Nevertheless, cultural abilities developed exponentially with *Homo*'s appearance and expansion. With increasing reliance on hunting, tool making, and other cultural abilities, *Homo* eventually became the most efficient exploiter of the savanna niche. The last surviving members of *A. boisei* may have been forced into ever-more-marginal areas. They eventually became extinct. By 1 m.y.a., a single species of hominin, *H. erectus*, not only had rendered other hominin forms extinct but also had expanded the hominin range to Asia and Europe. An essentially human strategy of adaptation, incorporating hunting as a fundamental ingredient of a generalized foraging economy, had emerged. Despite regional variation, it was to be the basic economy for our genus until 11,000 years ago. We turn now to the fossils, tools, and life patterns of the various forms of *Homo*.

Acing the COURSE

Summary

1. A skull found in 2001 in northern Chad, dated at 6–7 million years old, officially named *Sahelanthropus tchadensis,* more commonly called "Toumai," may or may not be the earliest hominin yet known, as may the somewhat less ancient *Orrorin tugenensis,* found in Kenya in 2001.

2. Hominins lived during the late Miocene, Pliocene (5.0 to 2.0 m.y.a.), and Pleistocene (2.0 m.y.a. to 10,000 B.P.) epochs. The australopithecines had appeared by 4.2 m.y.a. The six species of *Australopithecus* were *A. anamensis* (4.2 to 3.9 m.y.a.), *A. afarensis* (3.8 to 3.0 m.y.a.), *A. africanus* (3.0? to 2.0? m.y.a.), *A. garhi* (2.5 m.y.a.), *A. robustus* (2.0? to 1.0? m.y.a.), and *A. boisei* (2.6? to 1.2 m.y.a.). The earliest identifiable hominin remains date to between 7.0 m.y.a. and 5.8 m.y.a. The *Sahelanthropus tchadensis* find from northern Chad is a possible early hominin, as is *Orrorin tugenensis* from Kenya. More generally accepted hominin remains from Ethiopia are classified as *Ardipithecus kadabba* (5.8–5.5 m.y.a.) and *ramidus* (4.4 m.y.a.). Next comes *A. anamensis*, then a group of fossils from Hadar, Ethiopia, and Laetoli, Tanzania, classified as *A. afarensis*.

3. These earliest hominins shared many primitive features, including slashing canines, elongated premolars, a small apelike skull, and marked sexual dimorphism. Still, *A. afarensis* and its recently discovered predecessors were definite hominins. In *A. afarensis* this is confirmed by large molars and, more important, by skeletal evidence (e.g., in Lucy) for upright bipedalism.

4. Remains of two later groups, *A. africanus* (graciles) and *A. robustus* (robusts), were found in South Africa. Both groups show the australopithecine trend toward a powerful chewing apparatus. They had large molars and premolars and large and robust faces, skulls, and muscle markings. All these features are more pronounced in the robusts than they are in the graciles. The basis of the australopithecine diet was savanna vegetation.

5. By 2.0 m.y.a. there is ample evidence for two distinct hominin groups: early *Homo* and *A. boisei*, the hyperrobust australopithecines. The latter eventually became extinct around 1.2 m.y.a. *A. boisei* became increasingly specialized, dependent on tough, coarse, gritty, fibrous savanna vegetation. The australopithecine trend toward dental, facial, and cranial robustness continued with *A. boisei*, but these structures were reduced in *H. habilis* (2.4?–1.4? m.y.a.) and *H. erectus* (1.9–0.3? m.y.a).

6. Pebble tools dating to between 2.6 and 2.0 m.y.a. have been found in Ethiopia, Congo, and Malawi. Scientists have disagreed about their maker, some arguing that only early *Homo* could have made them. Evidence has been presented that *A. garhi* made pebble tools around 2.6 m.y.a. Cultural abilities developed exponentially with *Homo*'s appearance and evolution.

MULTIPLE CHOICE

1. Bipedalism traditionally has been viewed as an adaptation to open grassland or savanna country. However,
   a. the fossils of *Sahelanthropus tchadensis* and *Orrorin tugenensis* establish beyond doubt that bipedalism emerged over 7 million years ago, while these hominins still lived in trees.
   b. the recent Ardi find suggests that bipedalism was an adaptation to mountain trekking.
   c. adaptation to the savanna occurred later in hominin evolution, after the emergence of bipedalism, as the evidence of *Ardipithecus*, which lived in a humid woodland habitat, suggests.
   d. recent DNA evidence suggests that the main cause of bipedalism was a mutation that occurred 7 million years ago.
   e. the fossils of *Orrorin tugenensis* suggest that bipedalism was an adaptation to river wading, an activity that provided key nutrients from fish.

2. The term *hominin* is used to refer to the human line after its split from ancestral chimps. *Hominid* is used
   a. to refer to the taxonomic family that includes humans and the African apes and their immediate ancestors.
   b. in cases where the brain cavity of fossils equals or exceeds that of anatomically modern humans.
   c. by scientists who do not view "Ardi" as a hominin.
   d. by Asian scientists who disagree with the rest of the scientific community's use of the term *hominin*.
   e. to refer to the human line after its split from ancestral tarsiers.

3. If we compare Earth's history to a 24-hour day (with one second equaling 50,000 years),
   a. the first vertebrates arrive 36 seconds before midnight.
   b. the latest dinosaurs die out at midnight.
   c. the ocean levels increase twofold at 1 A.M.
   d. *Homo sapiens* arrives 36 seconds before midnight.
   e. the earliest hominins arrive at mid-day.

4. What do researchers know about *Ardipithecus ramidus*?
   a. It was a knuckle-walking proto chimpanzee.
   b. It was really a male *Australopithecus anamensis*.
   c. It evolved into *Ardipithecus kadabba*.
   d. It is ancestral to Neandertals, but not to anatomically modern humans.
   e. It was a bipedal hominin with strongly apelike characteristics.

5. As a result of the *Kenyanthropus* discovery in 1999,
   a. the debate over the place of *afarensis* in human ancestry has been won by the taxonomic "splitters."
   b. the place of *afarensis* in human ancestry has been and will be debated between taxonomic "splitters" and "lumpers."
   c. Oldowan stone tools are no longer considered the oldest tools.
   d. the hominin family tree, once drawn with branches leading in many directions, now looks more like straight trunk.
   e. the chronology of the emergence of human culture is no longer debated.

6. "Lucy" is the nickname of
   a. Timothy White's favorite fossil.
   b. Mary Leakey
   c. an *Ardipithecus ramidus* found in Ethiopia.
   d. a small female member of *A. afarensis*.
   e. an *A. anamensis*, 80 percent of whose skeleton was found in Tanzania.

7. Which of the following most clearly identifies *Australopithecus afarensis* as a hominin?
   a. pointed canines that project beyond the other teeth
   b. stereoscopic vision
   c. postcranial (below the head) remains that confirm upright bipedalism
   d. curved or parabolic dental arcade
   e. molars larger than those of later *Australopithecus* remains

8. The presence of very large molars and a sagittal crest on the top of the skull is evidence of
   a. the more robust australopithecines' adaptation to food sources dominated by hard-shelled seeds and grasses.
   b. a probable adaptation to a cold weather climate exhibited by Neandertals.

c. the earliest hominin use of domesticated plants.

d. the earliest australopithecine evidence of humanlike brain organization.

e. the dramatic increase in hunting activity starting with the earliest members of the genus *Homo*.

9. What is the significance of the discovery of *Australopithecus afarensis*?

a. It showed that humans evolved in Asia rather than in Africa.

b. It is the oldest hominin fossil yet found in the New World.

c. *Afarensis* remains are the oldest to be found in association with evidence of both stone tools and fire use.

d. It shows that the gracile australopithecines were not hominins after all.

e. It provided fossil evidence that bipedalism preceded the evolution of a humanlike brain.

10. How were Oldowan tools, the oldest recognized stone tools, manufactured?

a. by chipping blades off a metal core

b. using deer antlers to pressure flake a chert core

c. by chipping flakes, the mainstay of the Oldowan toolkit, off a core

d. by striking steel against a stone core

e. by grinding a coarser stone against a softer one

FILL IN THE BLANK

1. _Bipedalism_ refers to upright two-legged locomotion, and it is considered the key feature differentiating early hominins from the apes.

2. The fossil and archaeological records confirm that upright bipedal locomotion _preceded_ stone tool manufacture and the expansion of the hominin brain.

3. The average cranial capacity in *Homo sapiens* is _1,350_ cm³. The cranial capacity of chimps (*Pan troglodytes*) averages _390_ cm³. The brains of gorillas (*Gorilla gorilla*) average _500_ cm³, which is within the australopithecine range.

4. Between 3 and 2 m.y.a., the ancestors of *Homo* became reproductively isolated from the later australopithecines, such as *A. robustus* and *A. boisei*, the latter of which coexisted with *Homo* until around _1.2_ m.y.a.

5. _Oldowan_ pebble tools represent the world's oldest formally recognized stone tools.

CRITICAL THINKING

1. If you found a new hominid fossil in East Africa, dated to five million years ago, would it most likely be an ape ancestor or a human ancestor? How would you tell the difference?

2. In trying to determine whether a fossil is a human ancestor, researchers sometimes look for traits that have been lost during subsequent human evolution. What is an example of this? How could humans come to lose a trait that is used to determine ancestry in the past?

3. In human evolution, what is the relationship between brains, skulls, and childhood dependency? Thinking back to Chapter 1, how does the study of this relationship illustrate anthropology's biocultural approach?

4. In October 2009, a newly reported *Ardipithecus* fossil was heralded in the news as a very important find. What new light did it shed on the understanding of human evolution?

5. The fossil remains found in Laetoli and Hadar forced a reinterpretation of the early hominin record. How so? What does this reinterpretation suggest about hominins' relation to apes?

Campbell, B. G., J. D. Loy, and K. Cruz-Uribe
2006 *Humankind Emerging,* 9th ed. Boston: Pearson Allyn & Bacon. Well-illustrated survey of physical anthropology, particularly the fossil record.

Johanson, D. C., and B. Edgar
2006 *From Lucy to Language,* rev. ed. New York: Simon & Schuster. Popular account of human evolution by a prominent contributor to understanding the fossil record.

Lewin, R.
2005 *Human Evolution: An Illustrated Introduction,* 5th ed. Malden, MA: Blackwell. Readable and well-illustrated introduction.

McKee, J. K., F. E. Poirier, and W. S. McGraw
2005 *Understanding Human Evolution,* 5th ed. Upper Saddle River, NJ: Prentice Hall. Principles of human evolution.

Park, M. A.
2010 *Biological Anthropology,* 6th ed. New York: McGraw-Hill. A concise introduction, with a focus on scientific inquiry.

Relethford, J. H.
2010 *The Human Species: An Introduction to Biological Anthropology,* 8th ed. New York: McGraw-Hill. Up-to-date text in biological anthropology.

Suggested Additional Readings

Go to our Online Learning Center website at **www.mhhe.com/kottak** for Internet exercises directly related to the content of this chapter.

Internet Exercises

What were the earliest forms of *Homo*, and where did they originate and eventually migrate?

What were the major tool-making traditions and adaptive strategies of archaic *Homo*?

What were the Neandertals like, and how did they differ from earlier and later forms of *Homo*?

How much did the Neandertals resemble modern humans? Here a scientist grafts images of living humans onto Neandertal skulls in a lab at the University of Zurich, Switzerland.

understanding OURSELVES

Fred Flintstone was the only caveman (the only cave person, for that matter) to appear on a VH1 list of the "200 Greatest Pop Culture Icons." He ranked number 42, between Cher and Martha Stewart. The Flintstones and their neighbors the Rubbles don't look much like Neanderthals (which anthropologists spell Neandertal, without the *h*). Real Neandertals had heavy brow ridges and slanting foreheads and lacked chins. The Flintstones and the Rubbles didn't act much like Neandertals either. *The Flintstones* transposed a 20th century American blue-collar lifestyle back to prehistoric times—Fred and Barney worked in factories, "drove" stone cars, and used dinosaurs as construction cranes and can openers. While it is certainly ridiculous to imagine that Neandertals used dinosaurs as tools, it is equally ridiculous to imagine dinosaurs and Neandertals coexisting at all. Dinosaurs were extinct long before humans, hominins, or hominids ever walked the earth. Just as American popular culture never tires of calling apes "monkeys," it can't seem to resist mixing dinosaurs and ancient humans.

Decades after Fred first appeared on TV, Geico commercials introduced new cavemen, along with the slogan "So easy a caveman can do it." Geico's cavemen live in a modern world of bowling alleys, cell phones, airports, and tennis courts. They have another modern trait—a sense of outrage over the insult implied in Geico's slogan. Should it be insulting to call someone "a Neandertal"? Their average cranial capacity, exceeding 1,400 cubic centimeters, actually was larger than the modern average. What that says about intelligence isn't clear. One fossil in particular helped create the enduring popular stereotype of the slouching, inferior, Neandertal caveman. This was the skeleton discovered a century ago at La Chapelle-aux-Saints in southwestern France. The original assessment of this fossil created an inaccurate image of Neandertals as apelike brutes who had trouble walking upright. Closer analysis revealed that La Chapelle was an aging man whose bones were distorted by osteoarthritis. This story illustrates the danger of attempting to reach broad conclusions based upon a small sample size.

Actually, as one would expect, Neandertals were a variable population. Some fossil hominins even combine Neandertal robustness with modern features. For example, the remains of a four-year-old boy found in Portugal, dating back some 24,000 years, show mixed Neandertal and modern features. This find and others have raised the question as to whether Neandertals and anatomically modern humans could have mated. Another modern activity in which the Geico cavemen engage is dating anatomically modern women. Whether similar attractions are part of history, or are as unrealistic as Fred using a dinosaur to open a can of creamed corn, is one more subject for scientific debate.

EARLY *HOMO*

As we saw in Chapter 8, at two million years ago, there is East African evidence for two distinct hominin groups: early *Homo* and *A. boisei*, the hyperrobust australopithecines, which became extinct around 1.2 m.y.a. *A. boisei* became increasingly specialized, dependent on tough, coarse, gritty, fibrous savanna vegetation. The australopithecine trend toward dental, facial, and cranial robustness continued with *A. boisei*. However, these structures were reduced as early forms of *Homo* evolved into early *H. erectus* by 1.9 m.y.a. By that date *Homo* was generalizing the subsistence quest to the hunting of large animals to supplement the gathering of vegetation and scavenging.

H. rudolfensis and *H. habilis*

In 1972, in an expedition led by Richard Leakey, Bernard Ngeneo unearthed a skull designated KNM-ER 1470. The name comes from its catalog number in the Kenya National Museum (KNM) and its discovery location (East Rudolph—ER)—east of Lake Rudolph, at a site called Koobi Fora. The 1470 skull attracted immediate attention because of its unusual combination of a large brain (775 cm³) and very large molars. Its brain size was more human than that of the australopithecine, but its molars recalled those of the hyperrobust australopithecine. Some paleoanthropologists attributed the large skull and teeth to a very large body, assuming that this had been one *big hominin*. But no postcranial remains were found with 1470, nor have they been found with any later discovery of a 1470-like specimen.

How to interpret KNM-ER 1470? On the basis of its brain size, it seemed to belong in *Homo*. On the basis of its back teeth, it seemed more like *Australopithecus*. There also are problems with dating. The best dating guess is 1.8 m.y.a., but another estimate suggests that 1470 may be as old as 2.4 m.y.a. Originally, some paleoanthropologists assigned 1470 to *H. habilis*, while others saw it as an unusual australopithecine. In 1986, it received its own species name, *Homo rudolfensis*, from the lake near which it was found. This label has stuck—although it isn't accepted by all paleoanthropologists. Those who find *H. rudolfensis* to be a valid species emphasize its contrasts with *H. habilis*. Note the contrasts in the two skulls in the photo above. KNM-ER 1813, on the left, is considered *H. habilis*; KNM-ER 1470, on the right, is *H. rudolfensis*. The *habilis* skull has a more marked brow ridge and a depression behind it, whereas 1470 has a less pronounced brow ridge and a longer, flatter face. Some think that *rudolfensis* lived earlier than and is ancestral to *habilis*. Some think that *rudolfensis* and *habilis* are simply male and female members of the same species—*H. habilis*. Some think they are separate species that coexisted in time and space (from about 2.4 m.y.a. to about 1.7 m.y.a.). Some think that one or the other gave rise to *H. erectus*. The debate continues. The only sure conclusion is that several different kinds of hominin lived in Africa before and after the advent of *Homo*.

H. habilis and *H. erectus*

A team headed by L. S. B. and Mary Leakey found the first representative of *Homo habilis* (OH7—Olduvai Hominid 7) at Olduvai Gorge in Tanzania in 1960. Olduvai's oldest layer, Bed I, dates to 1.8 m.y.a. This layer has yielded both small-brained *A. boisei* (average 490 cm³) fossils and *H. habilis* skulls, with cranial capacities between 600 and 700 cm³.

Meet two kinds of early *Homo*. On the left KNM-ER 1813. On the right KNM-ER 1470. The latter (1470) has been classified as *H. rudolfensis*. What's the classification of 1813?

Another important *habilis* find was made in 1986 by Tim White of the University of California, Berkeley. OH62 is the partial skeleton of a female *H. habilis* from Olduvai Bed I. This was the first find of an *H. habilis* skull with a significant amount of skeletal material. OH62, dating to 1.8 m.y.a., consists of parts of the skull, the right arm, and both legs. Because scientists had assumed that *H. habilis* would be taller than tiny Lucy (*A. afarensis*), OH62 was surprising because of its small size and apelike limb bones. Not only was OH62 just as tiny as Lucy (3 feet, or 0.9 meter), its arms were longer and more apelike than expected. The limb proportions suggested greater tree-climbing ability than later hominins had. *H. habilis* may still have sought occasional refuge in the trees.

The small size and primitive proportions of *H. habilis* were unexpected given what was known about early *H. erectus* in East Africa. In deposits near Lake Turkana, Kenya, Richard Leakey had uncovered two *H. erectus* skulls dating to 1.6 m.y.a. By that date, *H. erectus* (males at least) had already attained a cranial capacity of 900 cm^3, along with a modern body shape and height. An amazingly complete young male *H. erectus* fossil (WT15,000) found at West Turkana in 1984 by Kimoya Kimeu, a collaborator of the Leakeys, has confirmed this. WT15,000, also known as the Nariokotome boy, was a 12-year-old male who had already reached 5 feet 5 inches (1.67 meters). He might have grown to 6 feet had he lived.

Sister species

Two recent hominin fossil finds from Ileret, Kenya (east of Lake Turkana), are very significant for two main reasons; they show that (1) *H. habilis* and *H. erectus* overlapped in time rather than being ancestor and descendant, as had been thought; (2) sexual dimorphism in *H. erectus* was much greater than expected (see Spoor et al. 2007; Wilford 2007a).

One of these finds (KNM-ER 42703) is the upper jawbone of a 1.44-million-year-old *H. habilis*. The other (KNM-ER 42700) is the almost complete but faceless skull of a 1.55-million-year-old *H. erectus*. Their names come from their catalog numbers in the Kenya National Museum–East Rudolph, and their dates were determined from volcanic ash deposits.

These Ileret finds negated the conventional view (held since the Leakeys described the first *habilis* in 1960) that *habilis* and then *erectus* evolved one after the other. Instead, they apparently split from a common ancestor prior to 2 m.y.a. Then they lived side by side in eastern Africa for perhaps half a million years. According to Maeve Leakey, one of the authors of the report (Spoor et al. 2007), the fact that they remained separate species for so long "suggests that they had their own ecological niche, thus avoiding direct competition" (quoted in Wilford 2007a, p. A6). They lived in the same general area (an ancient lake basin), much as gorillas and chimpanzees do today.

Given these finds, the fossil record for early *Homo* in East Africa can be revised as follows: *H. habilis* (1.9–1.44 m.y.a) and *H. erectus* (1.9–1.0 m.y.a). The oldest definite *H. habilis* (OH24) dates to 1.9 m.y.a. although some fossil fragments with

THE FAR SIDE® By GARY LARSON

"What a find, Williams! The fossilized footprint of a brachiosaurus! ... And a *Homo habilis* thrown in to boot!"

What's wrong with this picture?

A. boisei (left) and *H. habilis* (right). Both OH5 (L) and OH24 (R) were found in Bed I at Olduvai Gorge, Tanzania, and were probable contemporaries.

habilis attributes have been dated as early as 2.33 m.y.a. The oldest *erectus* may date back to 1.9 m.y.a. as well.

What about sexual dimorphism in *H. erectus*? As the smallest *erectus* find ever, KNM-ER 42700 also may be the first female *erectus* yet found, most probably a young adult or late subadult. The small skull suggests that the range in overall body size among *H. erectus* was much greater than previously had been imagined, with greater sexual dimorphism than among chimps or contemporary humans. Human and chimp males are about 15 percent larger than females, but dimorphism is much greater in gorillas, and apparently also in *erectus*. Another possibility is that the (as yet undiscovered) *H. erectus* males that inhabited this lake basin along with this female at that time also were smaller than the typical *erectus* male.

The Significance of Hunting

The ecological niche that separated *H. erectus* from both *H. habilis* and *A. boisei* probably involved greater reliance on hunting, along with improved cultural means of adaptation, including better tools. Significant changes in technology occurred during the 200,000-year period between Bed I (1.8 m.y.a.) and Lower Bed II (1.6 m.y.a) at Olduvai. Tool making got more sophisticated soon after the advent of *H. erectus.* Out of the crude tools in Bed I evolved better-made and more varied tools. Edges were straighter, for example, and differences in form suggest functional differentiation—that is, the tools were being made and used for different jobs, such as smashing bones or digging for tubers. The more sophisticated tools aided in hunting and gathering. With such tools, *Homo* could obtain meat on a more regular basis and dig and process tubers, roots, nuts, and seeds more efficiently. New tools that could batter, crush, and pulp coarse vegetation also reduced chewing demands.

With changes in the types of foods consumed, the burden on the chewing apparatus eased. Chewing muscles developed less, and supporting structures, such as jaws and cranial crests, also were reduced. With less chewing, jaws developed less, and so there was no place to put large teeth. The size of teeth, which form before they erupt, is under stricter genetic control than jaw size and bone size are. Natural selection began to operate against the genes that caused large teeth. In smaller jaws, large teeth now caused dental crowding, impaction, pain, sickness, fever, and sometimes death (there were no dentists). *H. erectus* back teeth are smaller, and the front teeth are relatively larger than australopithecine teeth. *H. erectus* used its front teeth to pull, twist, and grip objects. A massive ridge over the eyebrows (a superorbital torus) provided buttressing against the forces exerted in these activities. It also provided protection, as we see in "Appreciating Diversity" on pp. 190–191.

As hunting became more important, encounters with large animals increased. Individuals with stronger skulls had better-protected brains and better survival rates. Given the dangers associated with larger prey, and without sophisticated spear or arrow technology, which developed later, natural selection favored the thickening of certain areas for better protection against blows and falls. The base of the skull expanded dramatically, with a ridge of spongy bone (an occipital bun) across the back, for the attachment of massive neck muscles. The frontal and parietal (side) areas of the skull also increased, indicating expansion in those areas of the brain. Finally, average cranial capacity expanded from about 500 cm^3 in the australopithecines to 1,000 cm^3 in *H. erectus*, which is within the modern range of variation.

anthropology **ATLAS**

Map 4 shows the origins and diffusion of early hominins and hominids. Pinnacle Point and many other African sites discussed here are located.

OUT OF AFRICA I: *H. ERECTUS*

Biological and cultural changes enabled *H. erectus* to exploit a new adaptive strategy—gathering and hunting. *H. erectus* pushed the hominin range beyond Africa—to Asia and Europe. Small groups broke off from larger ones and moved a few miles away. They foraged new tracts of edible vegetation and carved out new hunting territories. Through population growth and dispersal, *H. erectus* gradually spread and changed. Hominins

This photo shows the early (1.6 m.y.a) *Homo erectus* WT15,000, or Nariokotome boy, found in 1984 near Lake Turkana, Kenya. This is the most complete *Homo erectus* ever found.

appreciating DIVERSITY

Headstrong Hominins

On the evolutionary timeline of hominin biological diversity, the anatomical contrasts between *Homo erectus* and modern humans are clear. There must have been behavioral differences as well. How did anatomy and behavior fit together in *H. erectus* populations? Noel Boaz and Russell Ciochon (2004) have proposed that several protective features of the *H. erectus* skull evolved in response to behavior, specifically interpersonal violence—fighting among those thick-skulled hominins. Ever since the discovery of the first *H. erectus* skull, scholars have been struck by the unusual cranial anatomy. The top and sides of the skull have thick, bony walls (see the photos). The *H. erectus* skullcap resembles a cyclist's helmet—low and streamlined, so as to protect the brain, ears, and eyes from impact. "In contrast, we modern humans hold our enormous, easily injured, semiliquid brains in relatively thin-walled bony globes. We have to buy our bicycle helmets" (Boaz and Ciochon 2004, p. 29). In other words, a cultural adaptation (plastic) has replaced a biological one (bone).

Based on these and other cranial features, Boaz and Ciochon speculate that *H. erectus* needed sturdy anatomical headgear to protect against life-threatening breaks. Even today, with modern medicine, skull fractures can be fatal. An apparently minor fracture can rip blood vessels inside the skull. Blood builds up under the skull. Such a hematoma pushing on the brain can cause a coma and, eventually, death.

For *H. erectus* this bleeding would have been much more problematic than for people with access to modern medicine. The neurological damage caused by such a hematoma can lead to partial paralysis, locomotion problems, poor hand-eye coordination, difficulties in speaking, and cognitive disruptions. Boaz and Ciochon note that "any traits that reduced the chances of cranial fracture would have given a substantial evolutionary advantage to the individuals who possessed them" (Boaz and Ciochon 2004, p. 30).

The authors contend that the blows delivered in a fight are more likely to land at eye level than on the top of the head. Although modern human skulls have some degree of eye-level bony armor, the thicker ring of bone in the *H. erectus* skull would have provided much more protection. The thick brow ridge protected the eye sockets, while bony bulges on each side of the skull shielded the sinus where blood flows into the internal jugular vein. This buttressing also protected the ear region. Finally, the bony ridge at the back of the skull protected several sinuses that carried blood within the rearmost brain lobes.

The thick jaws of *H. erectus* also would have been adaptive. Today, a broken jaw makes

were following an essentially human lifestyle based on hunting and gathering. This basic pattern survived until recently in marginal areas of the world, although it is now fading rapidly. We focus in this chapter on the biological and cultural changes that led from early *Homo*, through intermediate forms, to anatomically modern humans (AMHs).

Paleolithic Tools

The stone-tool-making techniques that evolved out of the Oldowan, or pebble tool, tradition and that lasted until about 15,000 years ago are described by the term **Paleolithic** (from Greek roots meaning "old" and "stone"). The Paleolithic has three divisions: Lower (early), Middle, and Upper (late). Each part is roughly associated with a particular stage in human evolution. The Lower Paleolithic is roughly associated with *H. erectus*; the Middle Paleolithic with archaic *H. sapiens*, including the Neandertals of Western Europe and the Middle East; and the Upper Paleolithic with anatomically modern humans.

The best stone tools are made from rocks such as flint that fracture sharply and in predictable ways when hammered. Quartz, quartzite, chert, and obsidian also are suitable. Each of the three main divisions of the Paleolithic had its typical *tool-making traditions*—coherent patterns of tool manufacture. The main Lower Paleolithic tool-making tradition used by *H. erectus* was the **Acheulian**, named after the French village of St. Acheul, where it was first identified.

As we saw in Chapter 8, Oldowan flaking wasn't done to make choppers (according to a predetermined form). It was done simply to produce sharp flakes. A fundamental difference shows up in the Acheulian tool-making tradition. The Acheulian technique involved chipping the core bilaterally and symmetrically. The core was converted from a round piece of rock into a flattish oval hand ax about 6 inches (15 centimeters) long. Its cutting edge was far superior to that of the

Acheulian
Lower Paleolithic tool tradition associated with *H. erectus*.

Paleolithic
Old Stone Age, including Lower (early), Middle, and Upper (late).

it painful, difficult, and sometimes impossible to chew. Surgical wiring of the broken sections is required. For *H. erectus*, such a break could have been life-threatening. There was an inside thickening of the jaw, just behind the chin, to protect against breaks.

Among the dozens of *H. erectus* fossils found near Beijing, China, the anthropologist/anatomist Franz Weidenreich detected several fractures that had subsequently healed. The fact that the trauma victims survived offers confirmation of the protective value of their skulls. Boaz and Ciochon believe that the thick skulls and healed fractures of *H. erectus* provide a record of violence within the species.

This defensive armor—the anatomical headgear—was reduced once *H. sapiens* evolved a larger, more globular, thin-walled skull. Although human violence didn't end, other means of protection, or avoidance of conflict, or both, evolved among the descendants of *H. erectus*. Boaz and Ciochon think those new protective mechanisms belong to the realm of cultural rather than biological diversity.

Homo erectus skullcaps have been likened to a bicycle helmet because of their protective properties. These three skulls show dramatic similarities despite different ages. The skull shown in the top photo is a cast of skull XII from the "Peking Man" collection and dates to 670,000 to 410,000 years ago. The two other skulls are much older. Sangiran 2 from Java (middle photo) may be as old as 1.6 m.y.a., while OH9 from Olduvai Gorge, Tanzania (bottom photo), may date back 1.4 million years. What similarities do you note among the three skulls?

Oldowan chopper (see Figure 9.1). The Acheulian hand ax, shaped like a tear drop, represents a predetermined shape based on a template in the mind of the toolmaker. Evidence for such a mental template in the archaeological record suggests a cognitive leap between earlier hominins and *H. erectus*.

Acheulian hand axes, routinely carried over long distances, were used in varied cutting and butchering tasks, including gutting, skinning, and dismembering animals. Analysis of their wear patterns suggests that hand axes were versatile tools used for many tasks, including wood working and vegetable preparation. Cleavers—core tools with a straight edge at one end—were used for heavy chopping and hacking at the sinews of larger animals. Stone picks, which were heavier than the hand ax, probably were used for digging. Hand axes, cleavers, and picks were heavy-duty tools, used for cutting and digging. Acheulian toolmakers also used flakes, with finer edges, for light-duty tools—to make incisions and for finer

FIGURE 9.1 Evolution in Tool Making.

Finds at Olduvai Gorge and elsewhere show how pebble tools (the first tool at the left) evolved into the Acheulian hand ax of H. erectus. *This drawing begins with an Oldowan pebble tool and moves through crude hand axes to fully developed Acheulian tools associated with* H. erectus.

work. Flakes became progressively more important in human evolution, particularly in Middle and Upper Paleolithic tool making.

The Acheulian tradition illustrates trends in the evolution of technology: greater efficiency, manufacture of tools with predetermined forms and for specific tasks, and an increasingly complex technology. These trends became even more obvious with the advent of *H. sapiens.*

Adaptive Strategies of *H. erectus*

Interrelated changes in biology and culture have increased human adaptability—the capacity to live in and modify an ever-wider range of environments. Improved tools helped *H. erectus* increase its range. Biological changes also increased hunting efficiency. *H. erectus* had a rugged but essentially modern skeleton that permitted long-distance stalking and endurance during the hunt. The *H. erectus* body was much larger and longer-legged than those of previous hominins, permitting longer-distance hunting of large prey. There is archaeological evidence of *H. erectus*'s success in hunting elephants, horses, rhinos, and giant baboons.

An increase in cranial capacity has been a trend in human evolution. The average *H. erectus* brain (about 1,000 cm^3) doubled the australopithecine average. The capacities of *H. erectus* skulls range from 800 to 1,250 cm^3, well above the modern minimum.

H. erectus had an essentially modern, though very robust, skeleton with a brain and body closer in size to *H. sapiens* than to *Australopithecus.* Still, several anatomical contrasts, particularly in the cranium, distinguish *H. erectus* from modern

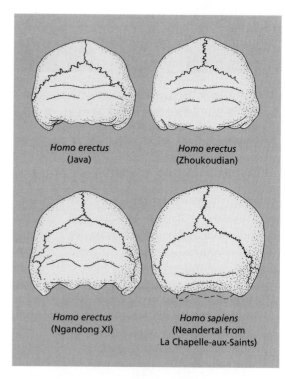

FIGURE 9.2 Rear Views of Three Skulls of *H. erectus* and One of "Archaic" *Homo sapiens* (a Neandertal).

Note the more angular shape of the H. erectus *skulls, with the maximum breadth low down, near the base.*

SOURCE: Clifford J. Jolly and Randall White, *Physical Anthropology and Archaeology*, 5th ed., p. 271. Copyright © 1995 by The McGraw-Hill Companies, Inc. Reprinted with permission.

humans. Compared with moderns, *H. erectus* had a lower and more sloping forehead accentuated by a large brow ridge above the eyes (see "Appreciating Diversity" on pp. 190–191). Skull bones were thicker, and, as noted, average cranial capacity was smaller. The brain case was lower and flatter than in *H. sapiens*, with spongy bone development at the lower rear of the skull. Seen from behind, the *H. erectus* skull has a broad-based angular shape that has been compared to a half-inflated football and a hamburger bun (Figure 9.2). The *H. erectus* face, teeth, and jaws were larger than those in contemporary humans but smaller than those in *Australopithecus.* The front teeth were especially large, but molar size was well below the australopithecine average. Presumably, this reduction reflected changes in diet or food processing.

Taken together, the *H. erectus* skeleton and chewing apparatus provide biological evidence of a fuller commitment to hunting and gathering, which was *Homo*'s only adaptive strategy until plant cultivation and animal domestication emerged some 10,000 to 12,000 years ago. Archaeologists have found and studied several sites of *H. erectus* activity, including cooperative hunting.

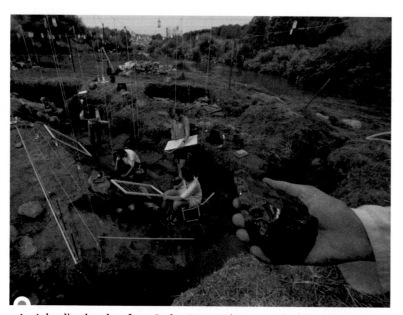

An Acheulian hand ax from Gesher Benot Ya'aqov, Israel, Jordan River. This site, shown here under excavation, dates back to 750,000 B.P. Which hominin might have made the ax?

Hearths at various sites confirm that fire was part of the human adaptive kit by this time. Earlier evidence for human control over fire has been found in Israel, dating back to almost 800,000 years ago (Gugliotta 2004). Sites with even earlier claims for fire (around 1.5 m.y.a.) include Koobi Fora, Kenya; Baringo, Kenya; and Middle Awash, Ethiopia. However, none of these early claims has unequivocal evidence for the controlled use of fire. Definitive evidence of human control of fire by 500,000 B.P. has been demonstrated at Cave of Hearths, South Africa; Montagu Cave, South Africa; Kalambo Falls, Zambia; and Kabwe in Zimbabwe. Fire provided protection against cave bears and saber-toothed tigers. It permitted *H. erectus* to occupy cave sites, including Zhoukoudian, near Beijing, in China, which has yielded the remains of more than 40 specimens of *H. erectus.* Fire widened the range of climates open to human colonization. It may have played a role in the expansion out of Africa. Its warmth enabled people to survive winter cold in temperate regions. Human control over fire offered other advantages, such as cooking, which breaks down vegetable fibers and tenderizes meat. Cooking kills parasites and makes meat more digestible, thus reducing strain on the chewing apparatus.

Could language (fireside chats, perhaps) have been an additional advantage available to *H. erectus?* Archaeological evidence confirms the cooperative hunting of large animals and the manufacture of complicated tools. These activities might have been too complex to have gone on without some kind of language. Speech would have aided coordination, cooperation, and the learning of traditions, including tool making. Words, of course, aren't preserved until the advent of writing. However, given the potential for language-based communication—which even chimps and gorillas share with *H. sapiens*—and given brain size within the low *H. sapiens* range, it seems plausible to assume that *H. erectus* had rudimentary speech. For contrary views, see Binford (1981), Fisher (1988*b*), and Wade (2002).

The Evolution and Expansion of *H. erectus*

The archaeological record of *H. erectus* activities can be combined with the fossil evidence to provide a more complete picture of our Lower Paleolithic ancestors. We now consider some of the fossil data, whose geographic distribution is shown in Figure 9.3. Early *H. erectus* remains, found by Richard Leakey's team at East and West Turkana, Kenya, and dated to around 1.6 m.y.a., including the Nariokotome boy, were discussed previously.

One fairly complete skull, one large mandible, and two partial skulls—one of a young adult male (780 cm^3) and one of an adolescent female

(650 cm^3)—were found in the 1990s at the Dmanisi site in the former Soviet Republic of Georgia. They have been assigned a date of 1.7–1.77 m.y.a. There are notable similarities between the two partial skulls and that of the Nariokotome boy (1.6 m.y.a.). Chopping tools of comparable age associated with the Kenyan and Georgian fossils also are similar. The more complete and more recent (2001) skull find is more primitive, with a stronger resemblance to *H. habilis* than is the case with the other Dmanisi fossils. Primitive characteristics of this skull include its large canine teeth and small cranial capacity (Vekua, Lordkipanidze, and Rightmire 2002). This specimen may be that of a teenage girl whose skull had not yet reached full size, but whose canines had. The simplest explanation for the anatomical diversity observed at Dmanisi is that *H. erectus* was at least as variable a species as is *H. sapiens.* The Dmanisi finds suggest a rapid spread, by 1.77 m.y.a., of early *Homo* out of Africa and into Eurasia (see Figure 9.3).

The Dmanisi fossils are the most ancient undisputed human fossils outside Africa. How did those hominins get to Georgia? The most probable answer is in pursuit of meat. As hominins became more carnivorous, they expanded their home ranges in accordance with those of the animals they hunted. Meat-rich diets provided higher-quality protein as fuel. The australopithecines, with smaller bodies and brains, could survive mainly on

anthropology **ATLAS**

Map 5 locates these and other sites where fossil representatives of the genus *Homo* have been found. Early migration patterns indicate movement out of Africa into Europe and Asia. Numerous site locations illustrate the extensive range covered.

FIGURE 9.3 The Sites of Discovery of *Homo erectus* and Its Probable Maximum Distribution.

SOURCE: Clifford J. Jolly and Randall White, *Physical Anthropology and Archaeology,* 5th ed., p. 268. Copyright © 1995 by The McGraw-Hill Companies, Inc. Reprinted with permission.

plants. They probably used a limited range at the edge of forests, not too deep in or too exposed far out on the savanna. Once hominins developed stronger bodies and high-protein meat diets, they could—indeed had to—spread out. They ranged farther to find meat, and this expansion eventually led them out of Africa, into Eurasia (Georgia) and eventually Asia (see Wilford 2000).

More recent skeletal finds from Dmanisi suggest how this expansion might have taken place (Wilford 2007b). (Previously only skulls had been found there.) Four new fossil skeletons show that the ancient Dmanisi population combined primitive skulls and upper bodies with more advanced spines and lower limbs for greater mobility. These evolved limb proportions enabled early *Homo* to expand beyond Africa.

In 1891, the Indonesian island of Java yielded the first *H. erectus* fossil find, popularly known as "Java man." Eugene Dubois, a Dutch army surgeon, had gone to Java to discover a transitional form between apes and humans. Of course, we now know that the transition to hominin had taken place much earlier than the *H. erectus* period and occurred in Africa. However, Dubois's good luck did lead him to the most ancient human fossils discovered at that time. Excavating near the village of Trinil, Dubois found parts of an *H. erectus* skull and a thigh bone. During the 1930s and 1940s, excavations in Java uncovered additional remains. The various Indonesian *H. erectus* fossils date back at least 700,000, and perhaps as much as 1.6 million, years. Fragments of a skull and a lower jaw found in northern China at Lantian may be as old as the oldest Indonesian fossils. Other *H. erectus* remains, of uncertain date, have been found in Algeria and Morocco in North Africa.

H. erectus remains also have been found in Upper Bed II at Olduvai, Tanzania, in association with Acheulian tools. In "Appreciating Diversity" on pp. 190–191, you will find a photo of one such find, OH9, which dates back perhaps 1.4 million years, along with a photo of a Javanese find, Sangiran 2, which may be a bit older. African *H. erectus* fossils also have been found in Ethiopia, Eritrea, and South Africa (in addition to Kenya and Tanzania). The time span of *H. erectus* in East Africa was long. *H. erectus* fossils have been found in Bed IV at Olduvai, dating to 500,000 B.P., about the same age as the Beijing fossils, described below as well as in "Appreciating Diversity."

The largest group of *H. erectus* fossils was found in the Zhoukoudian cave in China. The Zhoukoudian ("Peking"—now Beijing—"man") site, excavated from the late 1920s to the late 1930s, was a major find for the human fossil record. Zhoukoudian yielded remains of tools, hearths, animal bones, and more than 40 hominins, including five skulls. The analysis of these remains led to the conclusion that the Java and Zhoukoudian fossils were examples of the same broad stage of human evolution. Today they are commonly classified together as *H. erectus*.

A skull of one of these Beijing fossils, Skull XII, is shown in "Appreciating Diversity" on pp. 190–191. The four-stage photo spread (to the left) shows a reconstruction of *H. erectus* based on the Javanese find Sangiran 17, the most complete *H. erectus* skull found in Indonesia. The Zhoukoudian individuals lived more recently than did the Javanese *H. erectus*, between 670,000 and 410,000 years ago, when the climate in China was colder and moister than it is today. The inference about the climate has been made on the basis of the animal remains found with the human fossils. The people at Zhoukoudian ate venison, and seed and plant remains suggest they were both gatherers and hunters.

What about Europe? A cranial fragment found at Ceprano, Italy, in 1994 has been assigned a date of 800,000 B.P. Other probable *H. erectus* remains have been found in Europe, but their dates are uncertain. All are later than the Ceprano skull, and they usually are classified as late *H. erectus*, or transitional between *H. erectus* and early *H. sapiens*.

ARCHAIC *H. SAPIENS*

Africa, which was center stage during the australopithecine period, is joined by Asia and Europe during the *H. erectus* and *H. sapiens* periods of hominin evolution. European fossils and tools have contributed disproportionately to our knowledge and interpretation of early (archaic) *H. sapiens*. This doesn't mean that *H. sapiens* evolved in Europe or that most early *H. sapiens* lived in Europe. Indeed, the fossil evidence suggests that *H. sapiens*, like *H. erectus* before it, originated in Africa. *H. sapiens* lived in Africa for more than 100,000 years before starting the settlement of Europe around 50,000 B.P. There were probably many more humans in the tropics than in Europe during the ice ages. We merely *know more* about recent human evolution in Europe because archaeology and

Meet *Homo erectus*. Sangiran 17 is the most complete *H. erectus* skull from Java. In this process of reconstruction, a cast of the fossil (a) was rounded out with teeth, lower jaw, and chewing muscles (b). Additional soft tissues (c) and then the skin (d) were added. Given the robust features of this fossil, it is assumed to be male.

Fossil representatives of the genus Homo, compared with anatomically modern humans (AMHs) and chimps (Pan troglodytes).

SPECIES	DATES	KNOWN DISTRIBUTION	IMPORTANT SITES	BRAIN SIZE (IN cm³)
Anatomically modern humans (AMHs)	195,000 B.P. to present	Worldwide	Omo Kibish, Herto, Border Cave, Klasies River, Skhūl, Qafzeh, Cro-Magnon	1,350
Neandertals	130,000 to 28,000 B.P.	Europe, southwestern Asia	La Chapelle-aux-Saints	1,430
Archaic *Homo sapiens*	300,000 to 28,000 B.P.	Africa, Europe, Asia	Kabwe, Arago, Dali, Mount Carmel caves	1,135
Homo erectus	1.7 m.y.a. to 300,000 B.P.	Africa, Asia, Europe	East + West Turkana, Olduvai, Ileret, Dmanisi, Zhoukoudian, Java, Ceprano	900
Pan troglodytes	Modern	Central Africa	Gombe, Mahale	390

fossil hunting—not human evolution—have been going on longer there than in Africa and Asia.

Recent discoveries, along with reinterpretation of the dating and the anatomical relevance of some earlier finds, are filling in the gap between *H. erectus* and archaic *H. sapiens*. **Archaic *H. sapiens*** (300,000? to 28,000 B.P.) encompasses the earliest members of our species, along with the **Neandertals** (*H. sapiens neanderthalensis*—130,000 to 28,000 B.P.) of Europe and the Middle East and their Neandertal-like contemporaries in Africa and Asia. Brain size in archaic *H. sapiens* was within the modern human range. (The modern average, remember, is about 1,350 cm³.) (See Recap 9.1 for a summary of the major groups.) A rounding out of the brain case was associated with the increased brain size. As Jolly and White (1995) put it, evolution was pumping more brain into the *H. sapiens* cranium—like filling a football with air.

Ice Ages of the Pleistocene

Traditionally and correctly, the geological epoch known as the **Pleistocene** has been considered the epoch of early human life. Its subdivisions are the Lower Pleistocene (2 to 1 m.y.a.), the Middle Pleistocene (1 m.y.a. to 130,000 B.P.), and the Upper Pleistocene (130,000 to 11,000 B.P.). These subdivisions refer to the placement of geological strata containing, respectively, older, intermediate, and younger fossils. The Lower Pleistocene extends from the start of the Pleistocene to the advent of the ice ages in the Northern Hemisphere around one million years ago.

Each subdivision of the Pleistocene is associated with a particular group of hominins. Late *Australopithecus* and early *Homo* lived during the Lower Pleistocene. *Homo erectus* spanned most of the Middle Pleistocene. *Homo sapiens* appeared late in the Middle Pleistocene and was the sole hominin of the Upper Pleistocene.

During the second million years of the Pleistocene, there were several ice ages, or **glacials,** major advances of continental ice sheets in Europe and North America. These periods were separated by **interglacials,** long warm periods between the major glacials. (Scientists used to think there were four main glacial advances, but the picture has grown more complex.) With each advance, the world climate cooled and continental ice sheets—massive glaciers—covered the northern parts of Europe and North America. Climates that are temperate today were arctic during the glacials.

During the interglacials, the climate warmed up and the *tundra*—the cold, treeless plain—retreated north with the ice sheets. Forests returned to areas, such as southwestern France, that once had tundra vegetation. The ice sheets advanced and receded several times during the last glacial, the *Würm* (75,000 to 12,000 B.P.). Brief periods of relative warmth during the Würm (and other glacials) are called *interstadials*, in contrast to the longer interglacials. Hominin fossils found in association with animals known to occur in cold or warm climates, respectively, permit us to date them to glacial or interglacial (or interstadial) periods.

H. antecessor and *H. heidelbergensis*

In northern Spain's Atapuerca mountains, the site of Gran Dolina has yielded the remains of 780,000-year-old hominins that Spanish researchers call *H. antecessor* and see as a possible common ancestor of the Neandertals and anatomically modern humans. At the nearby cave of Sima dos Huesos a team led by Juan Luis Arsuaga has found thousands of fossils representing at least 33 hominins of all ages. Almost 300,000 years old, they may represent an early stage of Neandertal evolution (Lemonick and Dorfman 1999).

archaic *H. sapiens*
Early *H. sapiens* (300,000 to 28,000 B.P.); includes Neandertals.

Neandertals
Archaic *H. sapiens* group inhabiting Europe and the Middle East from 130,000 to 28,000 B.P.

Pleistocene
Main epoch (1.8 m.y.a.– 11,000 B.P.) of evolution of *Homo*.

glacials
Major advances of continental ice sheets in Europe and North America.

interglacials
Extended warm periods between glacials.

appreciating ANTHROPOLOGY

Fossils in Spain Are Treasure-Trove for Scientists

Described here is one of the richest hominin fossil sites in the world, certainly the most important one in Europe. In these Spanish caves, anthropologists have found the oldest jawbone fragment in western Europe, dating to 1.2 m.y.a., along with many other hominin fossils.

Human fossils have been found from the Ethiopian highlands to the Indonesian island of Java. However, the single site with the biggest deposits is located in northern Spain.

About 150 miles north of Madrid, a jeep pulls up to a clump of trees in the Sierra de Atapuerca, a collection of hills that are rich with caves.

A man with a helmet and a miner's headlamp gets out. He looks more like a mountain guide than a scientist. He's Juan Luis Arsuaga, Spain's best-known paleontologist [and paleoanthropologist].

He walks into a large cave, which is marked by a pirate flag. "This is the entrance to the site that has produced the most human fossils in history," Arsuaga says. "What better way to mark it?"

The Atapuerca hills are made of what's called karstic limestone, which means they're riddled with subterranean tunnels and caverns. In the 19th century, a British mining company discovered them when it blasted through a hill to lay down a railway.

At first, only animal bones were found. Then in 1976, a paleontology student found the first human remains. Since then, an abundance of human fossils and stone tools have been found.

Inside the cave, a group of scientists prepares to go even deeper underground. One of them is Rolf Quam, a paleoanthropologist from Binghamton University in New York.

"In the field of human evolution, which is what I'm in, Atapuerca is a world reference site," Quam says. "This is the richest fossil bearing deposit in the world. And every single site in Atapuerca that has been excavated has yielded human remains, which is something that is very unusual."

Last year, the team uncovered a 1.2 million-year-old jawbone fragment from a species

known as *Homo antecessor*. It's the oldest hominid fossil ever found in western Europe.

Near the railway trench, another site yielded human remains of 28 individuals, dating back at least half a million years. The Spanish paleontologist believes it's a mass grave.

"This was a collective act, something a group did with its dead," Arsuaga says.

The American member of the team says scientists are trying to solve another riddle.

"Why did humans live here continually for a million years? That's one of the big questions we're trying to answer," Quam asks. "What is it about the Sierra that makes it so inviting for human occupation?"

One theory is that the fauna was particularly rich in the Sierra de Atapuerca hills, which lie at the confluence of several geological systems.

Others believe the abundance of caves made it a desirable place to live.

But as the recent find of two more skull fragments demonstrates, there's still a lot to be learned from what lies buried in the hills.

SOURCE: © 2009, NPR®, News report by NPR's Jerome Socolovsky was originally broadcast on NPR's *Morning Edition®* on August 3, 2009, and is used with the permission of NPR. Any unauthorized duplication is strictly prohibited.

"Appreciating Anthropology" reports on an early hominin jaw fragment found recently in these Spanish hills.

A massive hominin jaw was discovered in 1907 in a gravel pit at Mauer near Heidelberg, Germany. Originally called "Heidelberg man" or *Homo heidelbergensis,* the jaw appears to be around 500,000 years old. The deposits that yielded this jaw also contained fossil remains of several animals, including bear, bison, deer, elephant, horse, and rhinoceros. Recently, some anthropologists have revived the species name *H. heidelbergensis* to refer to a group of fossil hominins that in this text are described as either late *H. erectus* or archaic *H. sapiens.* This group would include hominins dated (very roughly) between 700,000 and

200,000 years ago and found in different parts of the world including Europe, Africa, and Asia. Such fossils, here assigned to either *H. erectus* or archaic *H. sapiens,* would be transitional between *H. erectus* and later hominin forms such as the Neandertals and anatomically modern humans.

Besides the hominin *fossils* found in Europe, there is archaeological—including abundant stone tool—evidence for the presence and behavior of late *H. erectus* and then archaic *H. sapiens* in Europe. A recent chance discovery on England's Suffolk seacoast shows that humans reached northern Europe 700,000 years ago (Gugliotta 2005). Several stone flakes were recovered from seashore sediment bordering the North Sea. These archaic humans crossed the Alps into northern

Most of Europe's earliest known hominins have been found in northern Spain's Atapuerca mountains. They have been assigned to the species *Homo antecessor*. Here an archaeologist sets up pieces of an 800,000 year-old human skull from Atapuerca for a 2009 exhibition in Paris.

Europe more than 200,000 years earlier than previously imagined—during an interglacial period. At that time, the fertile lowlands they inhabited were part of a land bridge connecting what is now Britain to the rest of Europe. They lived in a large delta with several rivers and a dry, mild Mediterranean climate. Various animals were among its abundant resources. It is not known whether the descendants of these settlers remained in England. The next glacial period may have been too extreme for human habitation so far back. Members of the excavating team, including anthropologist Christopher Stringer, eventually found 32 flakes, made by striking a flint stone core with another stone. One flake had been retouched to sharpen its edges, while another was a sharpened flint

stone core. The razor-sharp flakes, 1 to 2 inches long, had probably been used as knife or spear points.

At the site of Terra Amata, which overlooks Nice in southern France, archaeologists have documented human activity dating back some 300,000 years. Small bands of hunters and gatherers consisting of 15 to 25 people made regular visits during the late spring and early summer to Terra Amata, a sandy cove on the coast of the Mediterranean. Archaeologists determined the season of occupation by examining fossilized human excrement, which contained pollen from flowers that are known to bloom in late spring. There is evidence for 21 such visits. Four groups camped on a sand bar, 6 on the beach, and 11 on a

Reconstruction of a hut made from saplings about 300,000 years ago at the Terra Amata site in Nice, France. The Terra Amata Museum, whose diorama is shown here, was built on the archaeological site, which was visited annually by ancient foragers. What foods did they eat?

sand dune. Archaeologists surmise that the 11 dune sites represent that number of annual visits by the same band (deLumley 1969/1976).

From a camp atop the dune, these people looked down on a river valley where animals were abundant. Bones found at Terra Amata show that their diet included red deer, young elephants, wild boars, wild mountain goats, an extinct variety of rhinoceros, and wild oxen. The Terra Amata people also hunted turtles and birds and collected oysters and mussels. Fish bones also were found at the site. The arrangement of postholes shows that these people used saplings to support temporary huts. There were hearths—sunken pits and piled stone fireplaces—within the shelters. Stone chips inside the borders of the huts show that tools were made from locally available rocks and beach pebbles. Thus, at Terra Amata, hundreds of thousands of years ago, people were already pursuing an essentially human lifestyle, one that survived in certain coastal regions into the 20th century.

Archaic *H. sapiens* lived during the last part of the *Middle Pleistocene*—during the *Mindel* (second) glacial, the interglacial that followed it, and the following *Riss* (third) glacial. The distribution of the fossils and tools of archaic *H. sapiens*, which have been found in Europe, Africa, and Asia, shows that *Homo*'s tolerance of environmental diversity had increased. For example, the Neandertals and their immediate ancestors managed to survive extreme cold in Europe. Archaic *H. sapiens* occupied the Arago cave in southeastern

France at a time when Europe was bitterly cold. The only Riss glacial site with facial material, Arago, was excavated in 1971. It produced a partially intact skull, two jawbones, and teeth from a dozen individuals. With an apparent date of about 200,000 B.P., the Arago fossils have mixed features that seem transitional between *H. erectus* and the Neandertals.

THE NEANDERTALS

Neandertals were first discovered in Western Europe. The first one was found in 1856 in a German valley called Neander Valley—*tal* is the German word for a valley. Scientists had trouble interpreting the discovery. It was clearly human and similar to modern Europeans in many ways, yet different enough to be considered strange and abnormal. This was, after all, 35 years before Dubois discovered the first *H. erectus* fossils in Java and almost 70 years before the first australopithecine was found in South Africa. Darwin's *On the Origin of Species,* published in 1859, had not yet appeared to offer a theory of evolution through natural selection. There was no framework for understanding human evolution. Over time, the fossil record filled in, along with evolutionary theory. There have been numerous subsequent discoveries of Neandertals in Europe and the Middle East and of archaic human fossils with similar features in Africa and Asia. The similarities and differences between Neandertals and other relatively recent hominins have become clearer.

Fossils that are not Neandertals but that have similar features (such as large faces and brow ridges) have been found in Africa and Asia The Kabwe skull from Zambia (130,000 B.P.), is an archaic *H. sapiens* with a Neandertal-like brow ridge. Archaic Chinese fossils with Neandertal-like features have been found at Maba and Dali. Neandertals have been found in Central Europe and the Middle East. For example, Neandertal fossils found at the Shanidar cave in northern Iraq date to around 60,000 B.P., as does a Neandertal skeleton found at Israel's Kebara cave (Shreeve 1992). At the Israeli site of Tabun on Mount Carmel, a Neandertal female skeleton was excavated in 1932. She was a contemporary of the Shanidar Neandertals, and her brow ridges, face, and teeth show typical Neandertal robustness.

In 2007 Svante Pääbo and his colleagues at Germany's Max Planck Institute for Evolutionary Anthropology announced their identification of Neandertal mitochondrial DNA (mtDNA) in bones found at two sites in central Asia and Siberia. One of them, Teshik Tash, in Uzbekistan, previously had been seen as the easternmost limit of Neandertal territory. However, bones from the second site, the Okladnikov cave in the Altai mountains, place the Neandertals much farther (1,250 miles) east, in southern Siberia. The mtDNA sequence at these sites differs only slightly from that of European Neandertals. The Neandertals may have reached these areas around 127,000 years ago, when a warm period made Siberia more accessible than it is today (see Wade 2007).

Cold-Adapted Neandertals

By 75,000 B.P., after an interglacial interlude, Western Europe's hominins (Neandertals, by then) again faced extreme cold as the Würm glacial began. To deal with this environment, they wore clothes, made more elaborate tools (see the photo on page 201), and hunted reindeer, mammoths, and woolly rhinos.

The Neandertals were stocky, with large trunks relative to limb length—a phenotype that minimizes surface area and thus conserves heat. Another adaptation to extreme cold was the Neandertal face, which has been likened to a *H. erectus* face that has been pulled forward by the nose. Illustrating Thomson's rule (see Chapter 6), this extension increased the distance between outside air and the arteries that carry blood to the brain and was adaptive in a cold climate. The brain is sensitive to temperature changes and must be kept warm. The massive nasal cavities of Neandertal fossils suggest long, broad noses. This would expand the area for warming and moistening air.

Neandertal characteristics also include huge front teeth, broad faces, and large brow ridges,

A Neandertal skeleton (right) and a modern human skeleton (left and behind) displayed at New York's American Museum of Natural History. The Neandertal skeleton, reconstructed from casts of more than 200 fossil bones, was part of the museum's 2003 exhibit titled "The First Europeans: Treasures from the Hills of Atapuerca." Where is Atapuerca, and what kind of hominin lived there?

and ruggedness of the skeleton and musculature. What activities were associated with these anatomical traits? Neandertal teeth probably did many jobs later done by tools (Brace 1995; Rak 1986). The front teeth show heavy wear, suggesting that they were used for varied purposes, including chewing animal hides to make soft winter clothing out of them. The massive Neandertal face showed the stresses of constantly using the front teeth for holding and pulling.

Comparison of early and later Neandertals shows a trend toward reduction of their robust features.

Reconstruction of a Neandertal woman from skull and skeletal evidence found at Tabun in Israel. She lived about 100,000 years ago.

Mousterian
Middle Paleolithic tool
tradition associated with
Neandertals.

AMHs
Anatomically modern
humans; e.g., Cro
Magnon, Skhūl, Qafzeh,
Herto.

Neandertal technology, a Middle Paleolithic tradition called **Mousterian,** improved considerably during the Würm glacial. Although the Neandertals are remembered more for their physiques than for their manufacturing abilities, their tool kits were sophisticated. Mousterian technology included at least 14 categories of tools designed for different jobs. The Neandertals elaborated on a revolutionary technique of flake-tool manufacture (the *Levallois* technique) invented in southern Africa around 200,000 years ago, which spread widely throughout the Old World. Uniform flakes were chipped off a specially prepared core of rock. Additional work on the flakes produced such special-purpose tools as those shown in Figure 9.4. Scrapers were used to prepare animal hides for clothing. And special tools also were designed for sawing, gouging, and piercing (Binford and Binford 1979).

Tools assumed many burdens formerly placed on the anatomy. For example, tools took over jobs once done by the front teeth. Through a still imperfectly understood mechanism, facial muscles and supporting structures developed less. Smaller front teeth—perhaps because of dental crowding—were favored. The projecting face reduced, as did the brow ridge, which had provided buttressing against the forces generated when the large front teeth were used for environmental manipulation.

The Neandertals and Modern People

Generations of scientists have debated whether the Neandertals were ancestral to modern Europeans. The current prevailing view, denying this ancestry, proposes that *H. erectus* split into separate groups, one ancestral to the Neandertals, the other ancestral to *anatomically modern humans* **(AMHs),** who first reached Europe around 50,000 B.P. (Early AMHs in Western Europe often are referred to as *Cro Magnon,* after the earliest fossil find of an anatomically modern human, in France's Les Eyzies region, Dordogne Valley, in 1868.) The current predominant view is that modern humans evolved in Africa and eventually colonized Europe, displacing the Neandertals there.

Consider the contrasts between the Neandertals and AMHs. Like *H. erectus* before them, the Neandertals had heavy brow ridges and slanting foreheads. However, average Neandertal cranial capacity (more than 1,400 cm^3) exceeded the modern average. Neandertal jaws were large, providing support for huge front teeth, and their faces were massive. The bones and skull were generally more rugged and had greater sexual dimorphism—particularly in the face and skull—than do those of AMHs. In some Western European fossils, these contrasts between Neandertals and AMHs are accentuated—giving a stereotyped, or

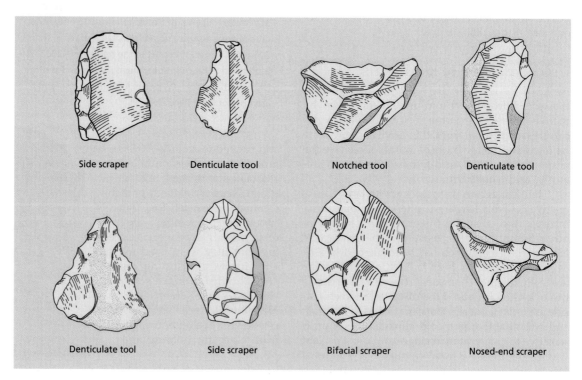

Side scraper   Denticulate tool   Notched tool   Denticulate tool

Denticulate tool   Side scraper   Bifacial scraper   Nosed-end scraper

FIGURE 9.4 Middle Paleolithic Tools of the Mousterian Tool-Making Tradition.

The manufacture of diverse tool types for special purposes confirms Neandertal sophistication.

classic Neandertal, appearance. The interpretation of one fossil in particular helped create the popular stereotype of the slouching cave dweller. This was the complete human skeleton discovered in 1908 at La Chapelle-aux-Saints in southwestern France, in a layer containing the characteristic Mousterian tools made by Neandertals. It was the first Neandertal to be discovered with the whole skull, including the face, preserved.

The La Chapelle skeleton was given for study to the French paleontologist Marcellin Boule. His analysis of the fossil helped create an inaccurate stereotype of Neandertals as brutes who had trouble walking upright. Boule argued that La Chapelle's brain, although larger than the modern average, was inferior to modern brains. Further, he suggested that the Neandertal head was slung forward like an ape's. To round out the primitive image, Boule proclaimed that the Neandertals were incapable of straightening their legs for fully erect locomotion. However, later fossil finds show that the La Chapelle fossil wasn't a typical Neandertal but an extreme one. Also, this much-publicized "classic" Neandertal turned out to be an aging man whose skeleton had been distorted by osteoarthritis. Hominins, after all, have been erect bipeds for millions of years. European Neandertals were a variable population. Other Neandertal finds lack La Chapelle's combination of extreme features and are more acceptable ancestors for AMHs.

Those scientists who still believe that Neandertals could have contributed to the ancestry of modern Europeans cite certain fossils to support their view. For example, the Central European site of Mladeč (31,000 to 33,000 B.P.) has yielded remains of several hominins that combine Neandertal robustness with modern features. Wolpoff (1999) also notes modern features in the late Neandertals found at l'Hortus in France and Vindija in Croatia. The fossil remains of a four-year-old boy discovered at Largo Velho in Portugal in 1999 and dated to 24,000 B.P. also shows mixed Neandertal and modern features.

HOMO FLORESIENSIS

In 2004 news reports trumpeted the discovery of bones and tools of a group of tiny humans who inhabited Flores, an Indonesian island 370 miles east of Bali, until fairly recent times (see Wade 2004; Roach 2007). Early in hominin evolution, as we saw in the last chapter, it wasn't unusual for different species, even genera, of hominins, to live at the same time. But until the 2003–2004 discoveries on Flores, few scientists imagined that a different human species had survived through 12,000 B.P., and possibly even later. These tiny people lived, hunted, and gathered on Flores from about 95,000 B.P. until at least 13,000 B.P. One of their

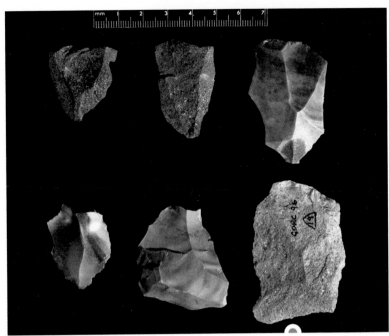

Neandertal technology, a Middle Paleolithic tradition called Mousterian, improved considerably during the Würm glacial. These Mousterian flake tools were found at Gorham's Cave, Gibraltar.

most surprising features is the very small skull, about 370 cm^3—slightly smaller than the chimpanzee average.

A skull and several skeletons of these miniature people were found in a limestone cave on Flores by a team of Australian and Indonesian archaeologists, who assigned them to a new human species, *H. floresiensis.* (Additional specimens have been found and described subsequently; see Gugliotta 2005; Roach 2007.) The discovery of *H. floresiensis,* described as a downsized version of *H. erectus,* shows that archaic humans survived much later than had been thought. Before modern people reached Flores, which is very isolated, the island was inhabited only by a select group of animals that had managed to reach it. These animals, including *H. floresiensis,* faced unusual evolutionary forces that pushed some toward gigantism and some toward dwarfism. The carnivorous lizards that reached Flores, perhaps on natural rafts, became giants. These Komodo dragons now are confined mainly to the nearby island of Komodo. Elephants, which are excellent swimmers, reached Flores, where they evolved to a dwarf form the size of an ox.

Previous excavations by Michael Morwood, one of the discoverers of *H. floresiensis,* estimated that

A cast of the anatomically extreme classic Neandertal skull found at La Chapelle-aux-Saints, France.

The skull of *Homo floresiensis* (left; modern human, right), a miniature hominid that inhabited Middle Earth, or at least the Indonesian island of Flores, between 95,000 and 13,000 years ago.

H. erectus had reached Flores by 840,000 years ago, based on crude stone tools found there. This *H. erectus* population and its descendants are assumed to have been influenced by the same evolutionary forces that reduced the size of the elephants. The first specimen of *H. floresiensis,* an adult female, was uncovered in 2003, from beneath 20 feet (6.1 meters) of silt coating the floor of the Liang Bua cave. Paleoanthropologists identified her as a very small but otherwise normal individual—a diminutive version of *H. erectus.* Because the downsizing was so extreme, smaller than that in modern human pygmies, she and her fellows were assigned to a new species. Her skeleton is estimated to date back some 18,000 years. Remains of six additional individuals found in the cave date from 95,000 to 13,000 B.P. The cave also has yielded bones of giant lizards, giant rats, pygmy elephants, fish, and birds.

H. floresiensis apparently controlled fire, and the stone tools found with them are more sophisticated than any known to have been made by *H. erectus.* Among the tools were small blades that might have been mounted on wooden shafts. Hunting elephants—probably cooperatively—and making complex tools, the Floresians may (or may not) have had some form of language. The suggestion of such cultural abilities is surprising for a hominin with a chimplike brain. The small cranium has raised some doubt that *H. floresiensis* actually made the tools. The ancestors of the anatomically modern people who colonized Australia more than 40,000 years ago may have traveled through this area, and it is possible that they made the stone tools. On the other hand, there is no evidence that modern humans reached Flores prior to 11,000 years ago.

The *H. floresiensis* population of the Liang Bua cave region appears to have been wiped out by a volcanic eruption around 12,000 B.P., but they may have survived until much later elsewhere on Flores. The Ngadha people of central Flores and the Manggarai people of West Flores still tell stories about little people who lived in caves until the arrival of the Dutch traders in the 16th century (Wade 2004).

As reported in 2009, an analysis of the lower limbs and especially an almost complete left foot and parts of the right shows that *H. floresiensis* walked upright, but possessed apelike features (Wilford 2009). The big toe, for example, was stubby, like a chimp's. The feet were large, more than seven and a half inches long, out of proportion to the short lower limbs. These proportions, similar to those of some African apes, have never before been seen in hominins. The feet were flat. The navicular bone, which helps form the arch in modern human feet, was more like one in the great apes. Without a strong arch *H. floresiensis* could have walked but not run like humans.

William Jungers, the anthropologist who led the analytic team, raised the possibility that the ancestor of *H. floresiensis* was not *H. erectus,* as originally had been assumed, but possibly another, more primitive, hominin ancestor (see Wilford 2009).

Acing the
COURSE

Summary

1. Compared with late *Australopithecus,* dental, facial, and cranial robustness was reduced in early *Homo, habilis* (1.9–1.44 m.y.a.) and *erectus* (1.9–0.3 m.y.a.). *H. erectus* extended the hominin food quest to the hunting of large animals. *H. erectus,* with a much larger body, had smaller back teeth than *Australopithecus* but larger front teeth and supporting structures, including a massive eyebrow ridge. The Lower Paleolithic Acheulian tradition provided *H. erectus* with better tools. *H. erectus*'s average cranial capacity doubled the australopithecine average. Tool complexity and archaeological evidence for cooperative hunting suggest a long period of enculturation and learning. *H. erectus* extended the hominin range beyond Africa to Asia and Europe.

2. Ancient *H. erectus* skulls have been found in Kenya and Georgia (in Eurasia), dating back some 1.77–1.6 million years. At Olduvai Gorge, Tanzania, geological strata spanning more than a million years demonstrate a transition from Oldowan tools to the Acheulian implements of *H. erectus*. *H. erectus* persisted for more than a million years, evolving into archaic *H. sapiens* by the Middle Pleistocene epoch, some 300,000 years ago. Fire allowed *H. erectus* to expand into cooler areas, to cook, and to live in caves.

3. The classic Neandertals, who inhabited Western Europe during the early part of the Würm glacial, were among the first hominin fossils found. With no examples of *Australopithecus* or *H. erectus* yet discovered, the differences between them and modern humans were accentuated. Even today, anthropologists tend to exclude the classic Neandertals from the ancestry of Western Europeans.

4. The classic Neandertals adapted physically and culturally to bitter cold. Their tool kits were much more complex than those of preceding humans. Their front teeth were among the largest to appear in human evolution. The Neandertals manufactured Mousterian flake tools. The changeover from Neandertal to modern appears to have occurred in Western Europe by 28,000 B.P.

5. In 2004 and 2005 scientists reported discoveries of bones and tools of a new hominin species they called *H. floresiensis*. This population of tiny humans lived on the isolated island of Flores in Indonesia. A probable descendant of *H. erectus*, which had settled Flores by 840,000 B.P., *H. floresiensis* is marked by the unusually small size of its body and its chimp-sized skull. There is debate about whether *H. floresiensis* was smart enough to have made the stone tools found in association with the skeletal remains, though there is no evidence that AMHs reached Flores before 11,000 B.P. The *H. floresiensis* remains have been assigned dates ranging from 95,000 to 13,000 B.P.

Test Yourself!

MULTIPLE CHOICE

1. Despite the continued debate surrounding *H. rudolfensis* and *H. habilis* there is a sure conclusion:
   a. that a seafood diet made *Homo*'s success in Africa possible.
   b. that several different kinds of hominins lived in Africa before and after the advent of *Homo*.
   c. that *rudolfensis* and *habilis* are simply male and female members of the same species.
   d. that *H. erectus* descended from one of the two.
   e. the debate will probably never be settled because all of the potential fossil sites in Africa have been dug.

2. Which of the following factors definitely is *not* related to the development of larger brains among *H. erectus* populations?
   a. neotony
   b. greater reliance on hunting
   c. more complex social environment
   d. animal domestication
   e. bipedalism

3. Which of the following is a trend in hominin evolution since the australopithecines?
   a. Sexual dimorphism has disappeared.
   b. Population numbers have remained stable.
   c. Bipedalism has appeared.
   d. The geographic range of the hominins has decreased.
   e. Molar size has decreased.

4. Which of the following traits did *not* contribute to the increasing adaptability of *H. erectus*?
   a. a varied tool kit that facilitated cooperative hunting
   b. microlithic stone tools
   c. an essentially modern postcranial skeleton, permitting long-distance stalking and endurance during a hunt
   d. an average brain size that was double that of the australopithecines
   e. a period of childhood dependency that exceeded that of australopithecines

5. What is the most likely explanation for why early *Homo* left Africa and spread into Eurasia?
   a. the hyperspecialization on vegetarian diets
   b. *Homo*'s smaller bodies, in relation to australopithecines', made them more nimble and fit for long-distance travel
   c. the need to find meat
   d. overpopulation in Africa
   e. the maladaptation to more energy-inefficient system of locomotion

6. What species is associated with Zhoukoudian, a site in China that has yielded the most specimens of this species?
   a. *H. habilis*
   b. archaic *Homo sapiens*
   c. Neandertals
   d. *H. erectus*
   e. anatomically modern humans

7. The Dmanisi fossils (1.77–1.7 m.y.a.) found in the former Soviet Republic of Georgia
   a. suggest a very slow spread of early *Homo* out of Africa and into Eurasia.
   b. exhibit no anatomical diversity, unlike the variable anatomically modern humans.
   c. establish the undisputed new species, *H. ergaster*.
   d. are older than the fossils of the Nariokotome boy found in Kenya.
   e. are the most ancient undisputed human fossils found outside of Africa.

8. Why are there such a high number of European archaic *H. sapiens* finds?
   a. Anatomically modern humans evolved in France.
   b. The richness of data from the Zhoukoudian site.
   c. Archaic *H. sapiens* were driven there by the more aggressive Cro Magnons.
   d. There is a long history of Paleolithic archaeology in Europe relative to other regions in the world.
   e. Glaciers caused stratigraphic disturbances.

9. What does the debate about Neandertals' relation to anatomically modern humans focus on?
   a. whether Neandertals are directly in anatomically modern humans evolutionary line, or whether they constitute an extinct offshoot
   b. whether Neandertals were human or a *H. erectus* hybrid
   c. whether Neandertals made microlithic tools
   d. whether Neandertals are the isolated ancestors of the Caucasian race or more general ancestors
   e. whether Neandertals are the founders of the Native American population

10. What is one of the most surprising aspects of the recent discovery of *H. floresiensis*?
   a. the suggestion that this species had developed capacities for language despite their small brains, as is evidence in their cave art
   b. the suggestion of sophisticated cultural abilities typically associated with anatomically modern humans, and not with a hominin with a chimplike brain
   c. the evidence that this new species may have replace Neandertals in the Middle East later than expected
   d. the clear evidence that this species evolved from *H. erectus*
   e. the suggestion that anatomically modern humans may have reached the Americas much earlier than expected

FILL IN THE BLANK

1. _Paleolithic_ toolmaking evolved out of the Oldowan, or pebble tool, tradition and lasted until about 15,000 years ago.

2. Two recent hominin fossil finds from Ileret, Kenya, are very significant because they show that *H. habilis* and *H. erectus* overlapped in time rather than being ancestor and descendant, as had been thought.

3. The _Acheulian hand ax_, shaped like a tear drop, represents a predetermined shape based on a template in the mind of the tool-maker. Evidence for such a mental template in the archaeological record suggests a cognitive leap between earlier hominins and *H. erectus*.

4. Although there are African sites with early claims for fire (around 1.5 m.y.a.), definitive evidence of human control of fire dates to _500,000 BC_.

5. Although the Neandertals are remembered more for their physiques than for their manufacturing abilities, their tool kits were sophisticated. Their technology, a Middle Paleolithic tradition, is called _Mousterian_.

CRITICAL THINKING

1. As anatomically modern humans we make up a variable population and yet we are all one species. When looking at the fossil record, how have scientists confronted the issue of variability and speciation?

2. *H. erectus* persisted for more than a million years. What were its key adaptation strategies? In particular, what does its tool-making abilities suggest about its evolving cognitive capacities?

3. The classic Neandertals, who inhabited Western Europe during the early part of the Würm glacial, were among the first hominin fossils found. Why did scientists have trouble interpreting these early discoveries? How have early misinterpretations of Neandertals persisted in our culture? Do these persistent misinterpretations matter?

4. Paleoanthropology is an exciting and constantly changing field! What is the significance of two recent hominin fossil finds from Ileret, Kenya? Also, what are some explanations that researchers have recently offered to explain the surprising *Homo floresiensis* discoveries in Indonesia?

Multiple Choice: 1. (B); 2. (D); 3. (E); 4. (B); 5. (C); 6. (D); 7. (E); 8. (D); 9. (A); 10. (B); **Fill in the Blank:** 1. Paleolithic; 2. *habilis* and *erectus*; 3. Acheulian hand ax; 4. 500,000 B.P.; 5. Mousterian

Suggested Additional Readings

Fagan, B. M.
  2010 *People of the Earth: A Brief Introduction to World Prehistory,* 13th ed. Upper Saddle River, NJ: Prentice Hall. Prehistoric peoples and civilizations.
  2008 *World Prehistory: A Brief Introduction,* 7th ed. New York: Longman. From the Paleolithic to the Neolithic around the world.

Gamble, C.
  1999 *The Palaeolithic Societies of Europe.* New York: Cambridge University Press. Survey mainly of the Middle and Upper Paleolithic in Europe.

Shipman, P.
  2001 *The Man Who Found the Missing Link.* New York: Simon & Schuster. Eugene Dubois discovers "Java Man" (*H. erectus*).

Wenke, R. J., and D. I. Olszewski
  2007 *Patterns in Prehistory: Mankind's First Three Million Years,* 5th ed. New York: Oxford University Press. Very thorough survey of fossil and archaeological reconstruction of human evolution.

Internet Exercises

Go to our Online Learning Center website at **www.mhhe.com/kottak** for Internet exercises directly related to the content of this chapter.

When and where did modern human anatomy and behavior originate?

What major changes took place in human lifestyles and adaptive strategies as the Ice Age ended?

When and how did modern humans settle Australia, the Americas, and the Pacific?

There is abundant evidence for expressive culture, including art and music, in Europe by 35,000 years ago. The animals shown here, from a mural in France's Lascaux cave, may have had both social and economic significance.

The Origin and Spread of Modern Humans

understanding OURSELVES

Our choices about how, and to whom, we display aspects of ourselves say something about us not only as individuals but also as social and cultural beings. Think about your appearance right now. What does your clothing say about you—implicitly or explicitly, intentionally or unintentionally? Does your cap, shirt, or jacket display the name of your school, a brand, or a favorite sports team? Do or don't you—and why do you or don't you—have tattoos or piercings? What does facial hair, or its absence, say about you or someone else? Why is your hair long or short? Why did you choose any makeup you are wearing? How about any jewelry? If you're male, why are you, or are you not, circumcised? The way that we present our bodies reflects both on (1) who and what we're trying to look like and (2) what sort of person we're trying *not* to resemble.

Body decoration is a cultural universal, as are other forms of creative expression, including the arts and language, and all say something about us. Expressive culture rests on symbolic thought. As is true generally of symbols (remember Chapter 2), the relation between a symbol and what it stands for is arbitrary. Nike shoes are no more intrinsically swooshlike than Adidas are. Michigan Wolverines are no more like wolverines than Florida Gators are, and vice versa. For archaeologists,

evidence for symbolic thought, as manifested materially in patterned or decorated artifacts, strongly suggests modern behavior. Consider the pigment red ochre, a natural iron oxide that modern hunter-gatherers use to create body paint for ritual occasions. Archaeologists suspect that ochre was used similarly in the past. Traces of red ochre have been found on carefully worked stone and bone artifacts, dating back 100,000 years, in South Africa's Blombos Cave. One piece has a carved crosshatch design—three straight lines with another set of three at a diagonal to them—offering the world's earliest evidence for intentional patterning with symbolic meaning.

There is abundant evidence for expressive culture, including art and music, in Europe by 35,000 years ago. At this point, humans were decorating themselves with paints and jewelry and making flutes and figurines. It's likely that linguistic ability was part of this expressive package. Linguist Merritt Ruhlen speculates that all the world's languages descend from a common one spoken 40,000 to 50,000 years ago by anatomically modern humans who originated in Africa. Did a "creative" gene emerge in Africa and fuel human colonization of the rest of the world? Although anthropologists don't have a definitive answer to this question, we do agree about the key role that expressive culture plays in human life.

MODERN HUMANS

Anatomically modern humans (AMHs) evolved from an archaic *H. sapiens* African ancestor. Eventually, AMHs spread to other areas, including Western Europe, where they replaced, or interbred with, the Neandertals, whose robust traits eventually disappeared.

Out of Africa II

Recent Fossil and Archaeological Evidence Fossil and archaeological evidence has been accumulating to support the African origin of AMHs. A major find was announced in 2003: the 1997 discovery in an Ethiopian valley of three anatomically modern skulls—two adults and a child. When found, the fossils had been fragmented so badly that their reconstruction took several years. Tim White and Berhane Asfaw were coleaders of the international team that made the find near the village of Herto, 140 miles northeast of Addis Ababa. All three skulls were missing the lower jaw. The skulls showed evidence of cutting and handling, suggesting they had been detached from their bodies and used—perhaps ritually—after death. A few teeth, but no other bones, were found with the skulls, again suggesting their deliberate removal from the body. Layers of volcanic ash allowed geologists to date them to 154,000–160,000 B.P. The people represented by the skulls had lived on the shore of an ancient lake, where they hunted and fished. The skulls were found along with hippopotamus and antelope bones and some 600 tools, including blades and hand axes.

Except for a few archaic characteristics, the **Herto** skulls are anatomically modern—long with broad midfaces, featuring tall, narrow nasal bones. The cranial vaults are high, falling within modern dimensions. These finds provide additional support for the view that modern humans originated in Africa and then spread into Europe and Asia (Wilford 2003).

Omo Kibish is one of several sites along the Omo River in southwestern Ethiopia. Between 1967 and 1974 Richard Leakey and his colleagues

from the Kenya National Museum recovered AMH remains originally considered to be about 125,000 years old. The specimens now appear to be much older. Indeed, with an estimated date of 195,000 B.P., they appear to be the earliest AMH fossils yet found (McDougall, Brown and Fleagle 2005). The Omo remains include two partial skulls (Omo 1 and Omo 2), four jaws, a leg bone, about 200 teeth, and several other parts. One site, Omo Kibish I, contained a nearly complete skeleton of an adult male. Middle Stone Age tools have been found in the same stratigraphic layers. Studies of the Omo 1 skull and skeleton indicate an overall modern human morphology with some primitive features. The Omo 2 skull is more archaic. (See the illustration below for cranial contrasts between *H. erectus*, archaic *H. sapiens*, Neandertals, and AMHs.)

From sites in South Africa comes further evidence of early African AMHs. One such site, Pinnacle Point cave, is described in this chapter's "Appreciating Diversity" on pp. 218–219. At Border Cave, a remote rock shelter in South Africa, fossil remains dating back perhaps 150,000 years are believed to be those of early modern humans. The remains of at least five AMHs have been discovered, including the nearly complete skeleton of a four- to six-month-old infant buried in a shallow grave. Excavations at Border Cave also have produced some 70,000 stone tools, along with the remains of several mammal species,

Herto
Very early (160,000–154,000 B.P.) AMHs found in Ethiopia.

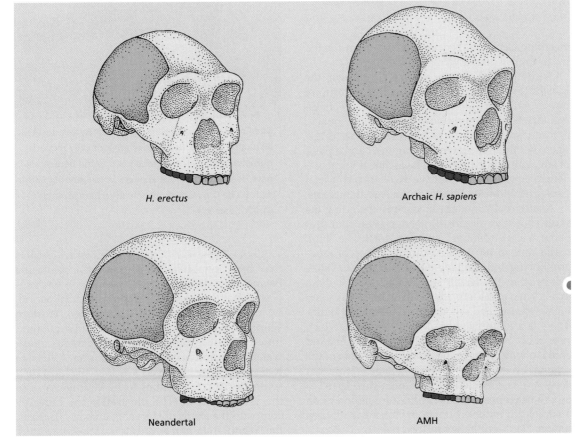

H. erectus

Archaic H. sapiens

Neandertal

AMH

Compare these drawings of *H. erectus*, archaic *H. sapiens*, Neandertal, and AMH. What are the main differences you notice? Is the Neandertal more like *H. erectus* or AMH?

0 cm.   5 cm.

FIGURE 10.1 Skhūl V.

This anatomically modern human with some archaic fea-tures dates to 100,000 B.P. This is one of several fossils found at Skhūl, Israel.

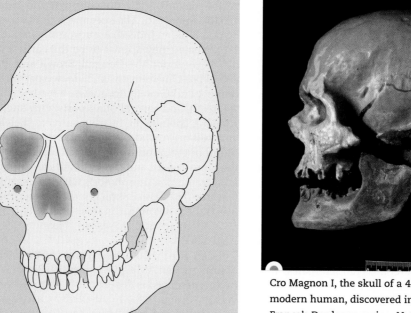

Cro Magnon I, the skull of a 45 year-old anatomically modern human, discovered in 1868 near Les Eyzies in France's Dordogne region. Note the distinct chin.

The Cro Magnon rock shelter near Les Eyzies-de-Tayac, Dordogne, France. Remains of anatomically modern humans, such as the famous fossil found here in 1868, have been found in rock shelters from France to South Africa. The Cro Magnon people lived here around 31,000 years ago.

including elephants, believed to have been hunted by the ancient people who lived there.

A complex of South African caves near the Klasies River Mouth was occupied by a group of hunter-gatherers some 120,000 years ago. Frag-mentary bones suggest how those people looked. A forehead fragment has a modern brow ridge. There is a thin-boned cranial fragment and a piece of jaw with a modern chin. The archaeological evi-dence suggests that these cave dwellers did coastal gathering and used Middle Stone Age stone tools.

Anatomically modern specimens, including the skull shown in Figure 10.1, have been found at Skhūl, a site on Mount Carmel in Israel. The Skhūl fossils date to 100,000 B.P. Another group of mod-ern-looking and similarly dated (92,000 B.P.) skulls comes from the Israeli site of Qafzeh. All these skulls have a modern shape; their brain cases are higher, shorter, and rounder than Neandertal skulls. There is a more filled-out forehead region, which rises more vertically above the brows. A marked chin is another modern feature (see the photo of the original Cro Magnon find on this page.) (Note that early AMHs in Western Europe often are referred to as **Cro Magnons,** after the earliest fossil find of an anatomically modern human, in France's Les Eyzies region, Dordogne Valley, in 1868.)

Cro Magnon
The first fossil find (1868) of an AMH, from France's Dordogne Valley.

Given these early dates from Israel, AMHs may have inhabited the Middle East before the Neandertals did. Ofer Bar-Yosef (1987) has sug-gested that during the last (Würm) glacial period, which began around 75,000 years ago, Western European Neandertals spread east and south (and into the Middle East) as part of a general south-ward expansion of cold-adapted fauna. AMHs, in turn, may have followed warmer-climate fauna south into Africa, returning to the Middle East once the Würm ended. (The illustration on page 209 compares the skulls of *H. erectus,* archaic *H. sapiens,* the Neandertals, and AMHs.)

Genetic Evidence for Out of Africa II

In 1987 a group of molecular geneticists at the University of California at Berkeley offered support for the idea that modern humans (AMHs) arose fairly recently in Africa, then spread out and colonized the world. Rebecca Cann, Mark Stoneking, and Allan C. Wilson (1987) analyzed genetic markers in placentas donated by 147 women whose ancestors came from Africa, Europe, the Middle East, Asia, New Guinea, and Australia.

The researchers focused on mitochondrial DNA (mtDNA). This genetic material is located in the cytoplasm (the outer part of a cell—not the nucleus) of cells. Ordinary DNA, which makes up the genes that determine most physical traits, is found in the nucleus and comes from both parents. But only the mother contributes mitochondrial DNA to the fertilized egg. The father plays no part in mtDNA transmission, just as the mother has nothing to do with the transmission of the Y chromosome, which comes from the father and determines the sex of the child.

living anthropology VIDEOS

Origins of the World's Languages, www.mhhe.com/kottak

Linguist Merritt Ruhlen attempts to uncover "fossil words" that have been passed down from a single original language to the 5,000 or so languages of today. Ruhlen reduces those 5,000 languages to 420 families, then to 12 groups, and finally into universal word roots such as those for "one" and "water." He speculates that all the world's languages descend from a common language spoken perhaps 40,000 to 50,000 years ago by anatomically modern humans who originated in Africa, eventually spreading out to colonize the world.

To establish a "genetic clock," the Berkeley researchers measured the variation in mtDNA in their 147 tissue samples. They cut each sample into segments to compare with the others. By estimating the number of mutations that had taken place in each sample since its common origin with the 146 others, the researchers drew an evolutionary tree with the help of a computer.

That tree started in Africa and then branched in two. One group remained in Africa, while the other one split off, carrying its mtDNA to the rest of the world. The variation in mtDNA was greatest among Africans. This suggests they have been evolving the longest. The Berkeley researchers concluded that everyone alive today has mtDNA that descends from a woman (dubbed "Eve") who lived in sub-Saharan Africa around 200,000 years ago. Eve was not the only woman alive then; she was just the only one whose descendants have included a daughter in each generation up to the present. Because mtDNA passes exclusively through females, mtDNA lines disappear whenever a woman has no children or has only sons. The details of the Eve theory suggest that her descendants left Africa no more than 135,000 years ago. They eventually displaced the Neandertals in Europe and went on to colonize the rest of the world.

In 1997, ancient DNA was extracted from one of the Neandertal bones originally found in Germany's Neander Valley in 1856. This DNA, from an upper arm bone (humerus), has been compared with the DNA of modern humans. The kinds of matches we would expect in closely related humans did not occur. Thus, there were 27 differences between the Neandertal DNA and a reference sample of modern DNA. By contrast, samples of DNA from modern populations worldwide show only five to eight differences with the reference sample. This was the first time that DNA of a premodern human had been recovered. The original analysis was done by Svante Pääbo. The findings then were duplicated by Mark Stoneking and Anne Stone at Pennsylvania State University.

In 2006, Pääbo reported on the first sequencing of nuclear DNA (in addition to mtDNA) extracted from a Neandertal. This genetic material came from a 45,000-year-old Neandertal fossil from Vindija Cave, outside Zagreb, Croatia. As of 2006, Pääbo and his colleagues (Green et al. 2006) had sequenced about a million base-pairs, comprising 0.03 percent of the Neandertal genome. One particularly interesting finding is that the Neandertal Y chromosome differs significantly from that of modern humans. This may mean there was little interbreeding between the two groups. The DNA extracted so far suggest that Neandertals diverged from the evolutionary line leading to AMHs between 315,000 and 500,000 years ago (see Green et al. 2006).

The Neandertals may (or may not) have coexisted with modern humans in the Middle East for thousands of years. The overlap in Europe, and especially in Western Europe, appears to have been much shorter (see "Appreciating Anthropology"). At certain Israeli and African sites, modern humans date back 100,000 years or more. Middle Eastern Neandertals date back 40,000 to 60,000 years. In Western Europe, Neandertals may have survived until about 28,000 years ago.

To what extent did Neandertals and AMHs interact? Did they trade or interbreed (Wilford 2005)? Were the Neandertals outcompeted by modern humans or killed off by them? Future discoveries will continue to provide answers to such questions, which have engaged paleoanthropologists for decades.

appreciating

ANTHROPOLOGY

Improved Science Puts Modern Humans in Europe Earlier

For more than a century anthropologists have known of the overlap between archaic (Neandertal) and anatomically modern humans (AMHs) in Europe. This account describes how anthropologists have recently recalibrated the radiocarbon dating of Neandertals and AMHs in Europe. Radiocarbon (C^{14}) dating is most useful for remains that are 50,000 years old or less. The revised dating described here suggests that modern humans have been in Europe longer than previously thought—perhaps for 50,000 years—and that their time of overlap with the Neandertals was less than previously thought, perhaps no more than 2,000 years in western Europe.

New advances in radiocarbon dating are threatening to upend old theories about when modern humans migrated to Europe from Africa and how rapidly they advanced. The research casts new light on significant patterns of human migration into Central and Western Europe in the crucial period from 50,000 to 35,000 years ago,

scientists say. It suggests that the dispersal of anatomically modern *Homo sapiens* into Europe was more rapid than previously thought.

That, in turn, would mean that their coexistence with Neanderthals was briefer and that their introduction of cave art, symbolic artifacts and personal ornamentation occurred much earlier.

"Evidently the native Neanderthal populations of Europe succumbed much more rapidly to competition from the expanding biologically modern populations than previous estimates have generally assumed," Paul Mellars, an archaeologist at the University of Cambridge in England, wrote in an article appearing today in the journal *Nature*.

Although other scientists have for several years been pondering the implications of the revised radiocarbon dating for archaeological research throughout the world, Dr. Mellars's

description of the new techniques and their significance is the first comprehensive review of the subject in a major journal. The most pronounced discrepancies between radiocarbon and actual ages coincide with the fateful epoch when modern people first made themselves at home in Europe.

For years, it had been thought that modern humans from Africa began arriving in Western Europe at least 40,000 years ago, and so could have competed and mingled with the local population for at least 12,000 years. The revised dating of fossils and artifacts leaves much less time for two species to have been in close contact.

Dr. Mellars concludes from the revised chronology that the overlap between Neanderthals and new arrivals must be shortened to about 6,000 years in Central and Northern Europe, perhaps only 1,000 to 2,000 years in regions like western France.

Katerina Harvati, a paleontologist at the Max-Planck Institute for Evolutionary Anthropology in Leipzig, Germany, said these advances "can potentially lead to a breakthrough in our understanding of this critical time period in European prehistory."

THE ADVENT OF BEHAVIORAL MODERNITY

Scientists agree that (1) around six million years ago, our hominin ancestors originated in Africa, and as apelike creatures they became habitual bipeds; (2) by 2.6 million years ago, still in Africa, hominins were making crude stone tools; (3) by 1.7 million years ago, hominins had spread from Africa to Asia and eventually Europe; and (4) sometime around 200,000 years ago, anatomically modern humans (AMHs) evolved from ancestors who had remained in Africa. Like earlier hominins (*Homo erectus*), AMHs spread out from Africa. Eventually they replaced nonmodern human types, such as the Neandertals in Europe and the successors of *Homo erectus* in the Far East.

There is disagreement, however, about when, where, and how early AMHs achieved **behavioral modernity**—relying on symbolic thought, elaborating cultural creativity, and as a result

behavioral modernity
Fully human behavior based on symbolic thought and cultural creativity.

becoming fully human in behavior as well as in anatomy. Was it as much as 165,000 or as little as 45,000 years ago? Was it in Africa, the Middle East, or Europe? What triggered the change: a genetic mutation, population increase, competition with nonmodern humans, or some other cause? The traditional view has been that modern behavior originated fairly recently, perhaps 45,000–40,000 years ago, and only after *Homo sapiens* pushed into Europe. This theory of a "creative explosion" is based on finds such as the impressive cave paintings at Lascaux, Chauvet Cave, and other sites in France and Spain (Wilford 2002*b*). However, recent discoveries outside Europe suggest a much older, more gradual evolution of modern behavior.

Anthropologist Richard G. Klein of Stanford University is a leading advocate for the idea that human creativity dawned suddenly, in Europe around 45,000 years ago. Prior to this time, Klein thinks *Homo* had changed very slowly in anatomy

Dr. Harvati agreed that the new chronology suggested "an earlier appearance of early modern human complex behaviors and an earlier Neanderthal extinction and also suggests a shorter coexistence interval of the two species."

Radiocarbon dating, introduced shortly after World War II, has been widely used in measuring time in prehistory, back to the method's effective limit of 50,000 years ago. It assumes that the proportion of radioactively unstable carbon 14 to stable carbon 12 has remained virtually constant in Earth's atmosphere through this time period. It works by measuring the rate of decay of carbon 14 in once living materials, like plant and animal remains.

Although scientists once estimated the dating uncertainty to be no more than several hundred years, they came to suspect two potential sources of greater error. One was contamination of test samples by intrusions of more recent carbon. The other was fluctuations in proportions of carbon 14 to carbon 12, which scientists came to recognize as a consequence to variations in cosmic radiation reaching the upper atmosphere.

Recent research at the University of Oxford, Dr. Mellars said, has led to a more effective filtration process to reduce contamination in test samples. Other investigations of deep-sea sediments off Venezuela and ice-core records from Greenland yielded evidence of carbon variation problems, which turned out to be especially pronounced between 30,000 and 40,000 years ago. Accordingly, radio carbon dates were recalibrated.

The revised dates, for example, show that a standard radiocarbon reading of 40,000 years translated into a calendar age of 43,000. Even more consequential, a date of 35,000 years is revised to an actual age of 40,500, Dr. Mellars reported.

If correct, the new chronology means that fossil and archaeological evidence, especially in the crucial 30,000-to-40,000 year period, is much older than once estimated. Modern people may have arrived in Europe slightly earlier, but the extinction of the Neanderthals, previously thought to have occurred around 30,000 years ago, is now subject to greater revision because the standard dating yielded the most serious underestimates of true ages.

The degree of age discrepancies is also illustrated by the revised date for the splendid wall art in Chauvet cave in southern France. The charcoal used to produce the Chauvet drawings was originally dated around 31,000 to 32,000 years ago. A team of scientists reported in 2004 in the journal *Science* a revised date closer to 36,000.

In previous estimates, the modern human dispersal through Europe occurred 43,000 to 36,000 years ago. The 7,000-year period implies an overall dispersal rate of a about 0.3 kilometer a year, less than two-tenths of a mile. Starting somewhat earlier, the faster dispersal over 5,000 years is now clocked at 0.4 kilometer a year.

Dr. Mellars cautioned that the revised dating based on new research must be viewed as provisional, concluding that the implications of the new studies "will need to be kept under active and vigilant review."

and behavior. After this "dawn of culture," human anatomy changed little, but behavior started changing dramatically (Klein with Edgar 2002). Indeed, by 40,000 years ago AMHs in Europe were making varied tools that display a pattern of abstract and symbolic thought. Their modern behavior included burying their dead with ceremonies, adorning their bodies with paints and jewelry, and making figurine images of fertile females. Their cave paintings displayed images from their minds, as they remembered the hunt, and events and symbols associated with it.

To explain such a flowering of creativity, Klein proposes a neurological hypothesis. About 50,000 years ago, he thinks, a genetic mutation acted to rewire the human brain, possibly allowing for an advance in language. Improved communication, in Klein's view, could have given people "the fully modern ability to invent and manipulate culture" (quoted in Wilford 2002*b*).

Klein thinks this genetic change probably happened in Africa and then allowed "human populations to colonize new and challenging environments" (quoted in Wilford 2002*b*). Reaching Europe, the rewired modern humans met and replaced the resident Neandertals. Klein recognizes that his genetic hypothesis "fails one important measure of a proper scientific hypothesis—it cannot be tested or falsified by experiment or by examination of relevant human fossils" (quoted in Wilford 2002*b*). AMH skulls from the time period in question show no change at all in brain size or function.

Questioning Klein's views are discoveries made in Africa and the Middle East during the last 30 years. These finds provide substantial evidence for earlier (than in Europe) modern behavior, in the form of finely made stone and bone tools, self-ornamentation, and abstract carvings. Surveying African archaeological sites dating to between 300,000 and 30,000 years ago, Sally

McBrearty and Alison Brooks (2000) conclude that what might appear to be a sudden event in Europe actually rested on a slow process of cultural accumulation within Africa, where *Homo sapiens* became fully human long before 40,000 years ago. At South Africa's Blombos Cave, for example, an archaeological team led by Christopher Henshilwood found evidence that AMHs were making bone awls and weapon points more than 70,000 years ago. Three points had been shaped with a stone blade and then finely polished. Henshilwood thinks these artifacts indicate symbolic behavior and artistic creativity—people trying to make beautiful objects (Wilford 2002b).

Earlier excavations in Congo's Katanda region had uncovered barbed bone harpoon points dating back 90,000 to 80,000 years (Yellen, Brooks, and Cornelissen 1995). Anthropologists Brooks and John Yellen contend that these ancient people "not only possessed considerable technological capabilities at this time, but also incorporated symbolic or stylistic content into their projectile forms" (quoted in Wilford 2002b).

In 2007 anthropologists reported the discovery of even earlier evidence (dating back to 164,000 B.P.) for behavioral modernity in a cave site at Pinnacle Point, South Africa (see "Appreciating Diversity on pp. 218–219). The cave yielded small stone bladelets, which could be attached to wood to make spears, as well as red ochre, a pigment often used for body paint. Also significant is the ancient diet revealed by remains from this seaside site. For the first time, we see early representatives of *H. sapiens* subsisting on a variety of shellfish and other marine resources. According to paleoanthropologist Curtis Marean, who led the discovery team, once early humans knew how to make a living from the sea, they could use coastlines as productive home ranges and move long distances (Guyot and Hughes 2007).

anthropology ATLAS

Map 4 shows the cave site of Pinnacle Point, South Africa.

Recent discoveries by the Mossel Bay Archaeology Project, South Africa, include the large blade at the bottom, along with several other blades. Ochre specimens with scrape marks, such as the blades shown here, are believed to have been made by early humans who used this red pigment in symbolic behavior.

Cultural advances would have facilitated the spread of AMHs out of Africa. Such advances had reached the Middle East by 43,000 years ago, where, in Turkey and Lebanon, Steven Kuhn, Mary Stiner, and David Reese (2001) found evidence that coastal people made and wore beads and shell ornaments (see also Mayell 2004b). Some of the shells were rare varieties, white or brightly colored. These authors suggest that population increase could have caused changes in the living conditions of these AMHs—putting pressure on their resources and forcing experimentation with new strategies for survival (Kuhn, Stiner, and Reese 2001).

Even a modest increase in the population growth rate could double or triple the numbers and populations of small AMH bands. People would be living nearer to one another with more opportunities to interact. Body ornaments could have been part of a system of communication, signaling group identity and social status. Such communication through ornamentation implies "the existence of certain [modern] cognitive capacities" (Stiner and Kuhn, quoted in Wilford 2002b; Kuhn, Stiner, and Reese 2001).

Clive Gamble attributes the rise of modern human behavior more to increasing social competition than to population increase. Competition with neighboring populations, including the Neandertals in Europe, could have produced new subsistence strategies along with new ways of sharing ideas and organizing society. Such innovations would have advantaged AMH bands as they occupied new lands and faced new circumstances, including contact with nonmodern humans.

According to archaeologist Randall White, early personal adornment in Africa and the Middle East shows that human creativity capacity existed among AMHs long before they reached Europe (Wilford 2002b). Facing new circumstances, including competition, AMHs honed their cultural abilities, which enabled them to maintain a common identity, communicate ideas, and organize their societies into "stable, enduring regional groups" (quoted in Wilford 2002b). Symbolic thought and cultural advances, expressed most enduringly in artifacts, ornamentation, and art, gave them the edge over the Neandertals, whom they eventually replaced in Europe.

The origin of behavioral modernity continues to be debated. We see, however, that archaeological work in many world areas suggests strongly that neither anatomical modernity nor behavioral modernity was a European invention. Africa's role in the origin and development of humanity has been prominent for millions of years of hominin evolution.

Body ornamentation, a sign of behavioral modernity. On the left, a man from Papua Barat, Indonesia (island of New Guinea—see map atlas 10). On the right, a man photographed at Finsbury Park, England. What are the social functions of such ornamentation?

ADVANCES IN TECHNOLOGY

In Europe, Upper Paleolithic tool making is associated with AMHs. In Africa, earlier AMHs made varied tools. The terms *Lower*, *Middle*, and *Upper Paleolithic* are applied to stone tools from Europe. The terms *Early*, *Middle*, and *Late Stone Age* are applied to materials from Africa. The people who lived at the Klasies River Mouth cave sites in South Africa made Middle Stone Age tools. However, some of the early African tool finds at Blombos Cave and in Katanda are reminiscent of the European Upper Paleolithic. AMHs in Europe made tools in a variety of traditions, collectively known as Upper Paleolithic because of the tools' location in the upper, or more recent, layers of sedimentary deposits. Some cave deposits have Middle Paleolithic Mousterian tools (made by Neandertals) at lower levels and increasing numbers of Upper Paleolithic tools at higher levels.

The **Upper Paleolithic** traditions all emphasized **blade tools.** Blades were hammered off a prepared core, as in Mousterian technology, but a blade is longer than a flake—its length is more than twice its width. Blades were chipped off cores 4 to 6 inches (10 to 15 centimeters) high by hitting a punch made of bone or antler with a hammerstone (Figure 10.2). Blades were then modified to produce a variety of special-purpose

implements. Some were composite tools that were made by joining reworked blades to other materials.

The blade-core method was faster than the Mousterian and produced 15 times as much cutting edge from the same amount of material. More efficient tool production might have been especially valued by people whose economy depended on cooperative hunting of mammoths, woolly rhinoceroses, bison, wild horses, bears, wild cattle, wild boars, and—principally—reindeer. It has been estimated that approximately 90 percent of the meat eaten by Western Europeans between 25,000 and 15,000 B.P. came from reindeer.

Trends observable throughout the archaeological record also mark the changeover from the Mousterian to the Upper Paleolithic. First, the number of distinct tool types increased. This trend reflected functional specialization—the manufacture of special tools for particular jobs. A second trend was increasing standardization in tool

The Venus of Willendorf, on display in Vienna's Natural History Museum, dates back some 27,000–30,000 years. Notice the apparent fertility symbolism.

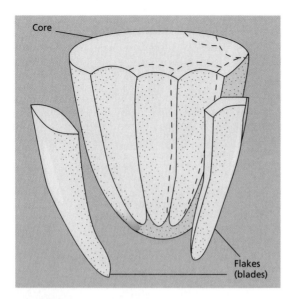

FIGURE 10.2 Upper Paleolithic Blade-Tool Making.

Blades are flakes that are detached from a specially prepared core. A punch (usually a piece of bone or antler) and a hammerstone (not shown here) were used to knock the blade off the core.

Upper Paleolithic
Blade-tool-making traditions of early AMHs.

blade tool
Basic Upper Paleolithic tool, hammered off a prepared core.

anthropology **ATLAS**

Map 6 charts migrations of *Homo sapiens* out of Africa to other world areas, including Europe, Asia, Australia, and the Americas. For the peopling of the Americas, see Chapter 10. For "the peopling of the Pacific," read the essay with that name on our Online Learning Center website at **www .mhhe.com/kottak.**

manufacture. The form and inventory of tools reflect several factors: the jobs tools are intended to perform, the physical properties of the raw materials from which they are made, and distinctive cultural traditions about how to make tools. Furthermore, accidental or random factors also influenced tool forms and the proportions of particular tool types (Isaac 1972). However, Mousterian and Upper Paleolithic tools were more standardized than those of *H. erectus* were.

Other trends include growth in *Homo*'s total population and geographic range and increasing local cultural diversity as people specialized in particular economic activities. Illustrating increasing economic diversity are the varied special-purpose tools made by Upper Paleolithic populations. Scrapers were used to hollow out wood and bone, scrape animal hides, and remove bark from trees. Burins, the first chisels, were used to make slots in bone and wood and to engrave designs on bone. Awls, which were drills with sharp points, were used to make holes in wood, bone, shell, and skin.

Upper Paleolithic bone tools have survived: knives, pins, needles with eyes, and fishhooks. The needles suggest that clothes sewn with thread—made from the sinews of animals—were being worn. Fishhooks and harpoons confirm an increased emphasis on fishing. This chapter's "Appreciating Diversity" discusses very early evi-

dence for a diet based on marine resources, along with small stone blade tools (bladelets) and red ochre used as body paint.

Different tool types may represent culturally distinct populations that made their tools differently because of different ancestral traditions. Archaeological sites also may represent different activities carried out at different times of the year by a single population. Some sites, for example, are obviously butchering stations, where prehistoric people hunted, made their kills, and carved them up. Others are residential sites, where a wider range of activities was carried out.

With increasing technological differentiation, specialization, and efficiency, humans have become increasingly adaptable. Through heavy reliance on cultural means of adaptation, *Homo* has become (in numbers and range) the most successful primate by far. The hominin range expanded significantly in Upper Paleolithic times.

GLACIAL RETREAT

Consider now one regional example, Western Europe, of the consequences of glacial retreat. The Würm glacial ended in Europe between 17,000 and 12,000 years ago, with the melting of the ice sheet in northern Europe (Scotland, Scandinavia, northern Germany, and Russia). As the ice retreated, the tundra and steppe vegetation grazed by reindeer and other large herbivores gradually moved north. Some people moved north, too, following their prey.

Shrubs, forests, and more solitary animals appeared in southwestern Europe. With most of the big-game animals gone, Western Europeans were forced to use a greater variety of foods. To replace specialized economies based on big game, more generalized adaptations developed during the 5,000 years of glacial retreat.

As water flowed from melting glacial ice, sea levels all over the world started rising. Today, off most coasts, there is a shallow-water zone called the *continental shelf*, over which the sea gradually deepens until the abrupt fall to deep water, which is known as the *continental slope*. During the ice ages, so much water was frozen in glaciers that most continental shelves were exposed. Dry land extended right up to the slope's edge. The waters right offshore were deep, cold, and dark. Few species of marine life could thrive in this environment.

How did people adapt to the postglacial environment? As seas rose, conditions more encouraging to marine life developed in the shallower, warmer offshore waters. The quantity and variety of edible species increased tremendously in waters over the shelf. Furthermore, because rivers now flowed more gently into the oceans, fish such

Vivid Upper Paleolithic cave paintings from Lascaux, Dordogne, France. How might you explain what you see depicted here?

as salmon could ascend rivers to spawn. Flocks of birds that nested in seaside marshes migrated across Europe during the winter. Even inland Europeans could take advantage of new resources, such as migratory birds and springtime fish runs, which filled the rivers of southwestern France.

Although hunting remained important, southwestern European economies became less specialized. A wider range, or broader spectrum, of plant and animal life was being hunted, gathered, collected, caught, and fished. This was the beginning of what anthropologist Kent Flannery (1969) has called the *broad-spectrum revolution.* It was revolutionary because, in the Middle East, it led to food production—human control over the reproduction of plants and animals, a process to be examined in Chapter 11. In a mere 10,000 years—after more than a million years during which hominins had subsisted by foraging for natural resources—food production based on plant cultivation and animal domestication replaced hunting and gathering in most areas.

CAVE ART

It isn't the tools or the skeletons of Upper Paleolithic people but their art that has made them most familiar to us. Most extraordinary are the cave paintings, the earliest of which dates back some 36,000 years. More than a hundred cave painting sites are known, mainly from a limited area of southwestern France and adjacent northeastern Spain. The most famous site is Lascaux, found in 1940 in southwestern France by a dog and his young human companions.

The paintings adorn limestone walls of caves located deep in the earth. Over time, the paintings have been absorbed by the limestone and thus preserved. Prehistoric big-game hunters painted their prey: woolly mammoths, wild cattle and horses, deer, and reindeer. The largest animal image is 18 feet (5.5 meters) long.

Most interpretations associate cave painting with magic and ritual surrounding the hunt. For example, because animals are sometimes depicted with spears in their bodies, the paintings might have been attempts to ensure success in hunting. Artists might have believed that by capturing the animal's image in paint and predicting the kill, they could influence the hunt's outcome.

Another interpretation sees cave painting as a magical human attempt to control animal reproduction. Something analogous was done by Native Australian (Australian aboriginal) hunters and gatherers, who held annual *ceremonies of increase* to honor and to promote, magically, the fertility of the plants and animals that shared their homeland. Australians believed that ceremonies were necessary to perpetuate the species on which humans depended. Similarly, cave paintings might have been part of annual ceremonies of increase. Some of the animals in the cave murals are pregnant, and some are copulating. Did

South African Cave Provides Earliest Evidence for Modern Behavior

Cultural variation is based on diversity in behavior patterns and beliefs. Recent discoveries in Africa suggest that modern ways of acting and thinking (as well as anatomically modern bodies) are much older—indeed more than 100,000 years older–than anthropologists imagined just a generation ago. Described here is the recent discovery of very early evidence (164,000 B.P.) for behavioral modernity in a cave at Pinnacle Point, South Africa. We learn as well that the early modern diet was more diverse than previously thought; we can add seafood to the land animals and plants that were hunted and gathered by our forebears.

Evidence of early humans living on the coast in South Africa 164,000 years ago, far earlier than previously documented, is being reported in the Oct. 18 issue of the journal *Nature*.

The international team of researchers reporting the findings include Curtis Marean, a paleoanthropologist with the Institute of Human Origins at Arizona State University and three graduate students in the School of Human Evolution and Social Change.

"Our findings show that at 164,000 years ago in coastal South Africa humans expanded

Looking out of Pinnacle Point Cave, South Africa. This seaside site has provided very early evidence (164,000 B.P.) for human behavioral modernity. The cave has yielded stone spear points as well as red ochre, a pigment often used for body paint. The cave's inhabitants ate shellfish and other marine resources.

their diet to include shellfish and other marine resources, perhaps as a response to harsh environmental conditions," notes Marean . . . This is the earliest dated observation of this behavior.

Further, the researchers report that co-occurring with this diet expansion is a very early use of pigment, likely for symbolic behavior, as well as the use of bladelet stone tool technology, previously dating to 70,000 years ago.

These new findings not only move back the timeline for the evolution of modern humans, they show that lifestyles focused on coastal habitats and resources may have been crucial to the evolution and survival of these early humans.

After decades of debate, paleoanthropologists now agree the genetic and fossil evidence suggests that the modern human species, *Homo sapiens*, evolved in Africa between 100,000 and 200,000 years ago.

Yet, archaeological sites during that time period are rare in Africa. And, given the enormous expanse of the continent, where in Africa did this crucial step to modern humans occur?

Upper Paleolithic people believe they could influence the sexual behavior or reproduction of their prey by drawing them? Or did they perhaps think that animals would return each year to the place where their souls had been captured pictorially?

Paintings often occur in clusters. In some caves, as many as three paintings have been drawn over the original, yet next to these superimposed paintings stand blank walls never used for painting. It seems reasonable to speculate that an event in the outside world sometimes reinforced a painter's choice of a given spot. Perhaps there was an especially successful hunt soon after the painting had been done. Perhaps members of a social subdivision significant in Upper Paleo-

lithic society customarily used a given area of wall for their drawings.

Cave paintings also might have been a kind of pictorial history. Perhaps Upper Paleolithic people, through their drawings, were reenacting the hunt after it took place, as hunters of the Kalahari Desert in southern Africa still do today. Designs and markings on animal bones may indicate that Upper Paleolithic people had developed a calendar based on the phases of the moon (Marshack 1972). If this is so, it seems possible that Upper Paleolithic hunters, who were certainly as intelligent as we are, would have been interested in recording important events in their lives.

It is worth noting that the *late* Upper Paleolithic, when many of the most spectacular multi-

"Archaeologists have had a hard time finding material residues of these earliest modern humans," Marean says. "The world was in a glacial stage 125,000 to 195,000 years ago, and much of Africa was dry to mostly desert; in many areas food would have been difficult to acquire. The paleoenvironmental data indicate there are only five or six places in all of Africa where humans could have survived these harsh conditions."

In seeking the "perfect site" to explore, Marean analyzed ocean currents, climate data, geological formations and other data to pin down a location where he felt sure to find one of these progenitor populations: the Cape of South Africa at Pinnacle Point. "It was important that we knew exactly where to look and what we were looking for," says Marean. . . .

The Middle Stone Age, dated between 35,000 and 300,000 years ago, is the technological stage when anatomically modern humans emerged in Africa, along with modern cognitive behavior, says Marean. When, however, within that stage modern human behavior arose is currently debated. . . .

"Generally speaking, coastal areas were of no use to early humans—unless they knew how to use the sea as a food source," says Marean. "For millions of years, our earliest hunter-gatherer relatives only ate terrestrial plants and animals. Shellfish was one of the last additions to the human diet before domesticated plants and animals were introduced."

Before, the earliest evidence for human use of marine resources and coastal habitats was dated about 125,000 years ago. "Our research shows that humans started doing this at least 40,000 years earlier. This could have very well been a response to the extreme environmental conditions they were experiencing."

"We also found what archaeologists call bladelets—little blades less than 10 millimeters in width, about the size of your little finger," Marean says. "These could be attached to the end of a stick to form a point for a spear, or lined up like barbs on a dart—which shows they were already using complex compound tools. And, we found evidence that they were using pigments, especially red ochre, in ways that we believe were symbolic," he describes.

Archaeologists view symbolic behavior as one of the clues that modern language may have been present. The earliest bladelet technology was previously dated to 70,000 years ago, near the end of the Middle Stone Age, and the modified pigments are the earliest securely dated and published evidence for pigment use.

"Coastlines generally make great migration routes," Marean says. "Knowing how to exploit the sea for food meant these early humans could now use coastlines as productive home ranges and move long distances."

Results reporting early use of coastlines are especially significant to scientists interested in the migration of humans out of Africa. Physical evidence that this coastal population was practicing modern human behavior is particularly important to geneticists and physical anthropologists seeking to identify the progenitor population for modern humans.

"This evidence shows that Africa, and particularly southern Africa, was precocious in the development of modern human biology and behavior. We believe that on the far southern shore of Africa there was a small population of modern humans who struggled through this glacial period using shellfish and advanced technologies, and symbolism was important to their social relations. It is possible that this population could be the progenitor population for all modern humans," Marean says.

SOURCE: Judi Guyot and Carol Hughes, "ASU Team Detects Earliest Modern Humans," *ASUNews*, October 17, 2007. Reprinted by permission of *ASUNews*, Arizona State University.

colored cave paintings were done and Paleolithic artistic techniques were perfected, coincides with the period of glacial retreat. An intensification of cave painting for any of the reasons connected with hunting magic could have been caused by concern about decreases in herds as the open lands of southwestern Europe were being replaced by forests.

THE SETTLING OF AUSTRALIA

As continental glaciers ebbed and flowed, modern humans took advantage of global climate change to expand their range. During the major glacial phases, with so much water frozen in ice, land bridges formed, aiding human colonization of new areas. People spread from Africa into Europe and Asia, eventually reaching Australia and, much later, the Americas and the Pacific islands.

When and how was Australia settled? At times of major glacial advance, such as 50,000 years ago, dry land connected Australia, New Guinea, and Tasmania. *Sahul* is the name for the larger continent thus formed (O'Connell and Allen 2004). At its largest, Sahul was separated from Asia only by narrow straits (Figure 10.3). Humans somehow made the crossing, perhaps in primitive watercraft, from Asia into Sahul, perhaps around 50,000 B.P. Genetic markers, fossils, and archaeological sites help us understand that settlement.

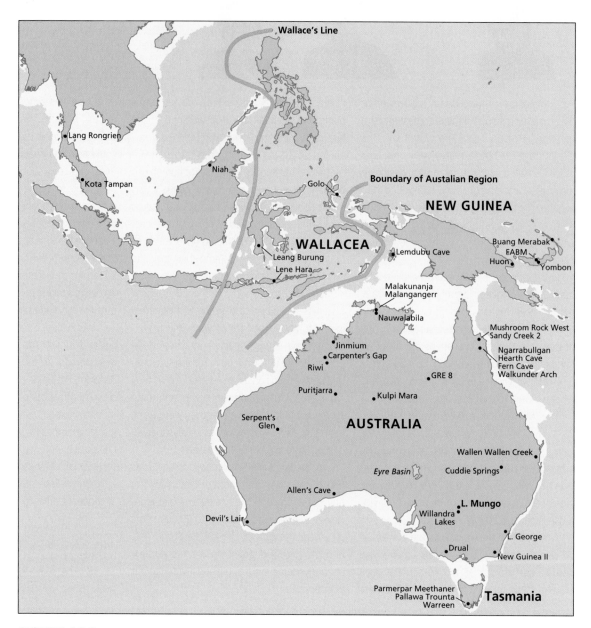

FIGURE 10.3

At times of major glacial advance, such as 50,000 years ago, dry land connected Australia, New Guinea, and Tasmania. Sahul is the name for the larger continent thus formed. At its largest, Sahul was separated from Asia only by narrow straits. Shaded on this map is the continent formed by a 200 meter fall in sea level. Wallacea is a transitional zoogeographic zone between Asia and Australia. The map also locates major archaeological sites, including Lake Mungo.

SOURCE: Reprinted from *Journal of Archaeological Science*, Vol. 31, No. 6, O'Connell, J. F., and J. Allen, "Dating the Colonization of Sahul (Pleistocene Australia–New Guinea): A Review of Recent Research," pp. 835–853, copyright 2004, with permission from Elsevier. http://www.sciencedirect.com/science/journal03054403

Georgi Hudjashov and his colleagues (2007) analyzed genetic samples from Native Australians and New Guineans/Melanesians. They looked at both mitochondrial DNA (mtDNA) (n = 172 samples) and Y chromosomes (n = 522). They compared those samples with known branches of global phylogenetic trees. The global mtDNA tree includes branches known as M and N (among others). The Y chromosome tree includes branches known as C and F (among oth-

ers). All the Australian/New Guinean samples fit into one of those four branches (either M or N for mtDNA and either C or F for the Y chromosome). Those four branches are known to be associated with the spread of modern humans out of Africa between 70,000 and 50,000 B.P.

Not surprisingly (given their geographical proximity), Native Australians are closely related to New Guineans and Melanesians. This close genetic relationship suggested there was only one initial

The earliest Australian skeletons, including this one, come from Lake Mungo in New South Wales. The world's oldest human mtDNA (dating back 46,000 years) has been extracted from this fossil. When was Australia first settled?

colonization of Sahul. Genetic dating (ca. 50,000 B.P.) agrees more or less with archaeological evidence for early Australian settlement by 46,000 B.P. After that, prehistoric Australia and New Guinea appear to have been cut off genetically from the rest of the world. Between them, however, there was some gene flow until the land bridge that once connected Australia and New Guinea was submerged around 8,000 B.P. Long-time isolation explains the marked genetic contrasts between Australia/New Guinea, on the one hand, and Eurasia on the other.

In terms of the fossil record, Australia has given us a few of the oldest (ca. 46,000 B.P.) modern human skeletons known outside Africa. The earliest Australian skeletons come from Lake Mungo in New South Wales (Figure 10.3). One of these finds (Mungo III) is of the world's oldest ritual ochre burial. The body was intentionally buried and decorated with ochre, a natural pigment (Bowler et al. 2003). The world's oldest human mtDNA was extracted from this fossil. The same stratum at Mungo contains evidence for the first recorded cremation of a human being (Mungo I). Radiometric dating places humans, including these specimens, at Lake Mungo by 46,000 B.P. O'Connell and Allen (2004) reviewed data from more than 30 Australian archaeological sites older than 20,000 B.P. They concluded that Australia was occupied by 46,000 B.P.—but not much earlier. Dating based on genetic markers, on the other hand, has not ruled out earlier colonization. Northern and western Australia, closer to the rest of Sahul, may have been settled by 50,000 years ago.

SETTLING THE AMERICAS

Another effect of continental glaciation was to expose—during several periods of glacial advance—*Beringia,* the Bering land bridge that once connected North America and Siberia. Submerged today under the Bering Sea, Beringia was once a vast area of dry land, several hundred miles wide. The original settlers of the Americas came from Northeast Asia. Living in Beringia thousands of years ago, these ancestors of Native Americans didn't realize they were embarking on the colonization of a new continent. They were merely big-game hunters who, over the generations, moved gradually eastward as they spread their camps and followed their prey—woolly mammoths and other tundra-adapted herbivores. Other ancient hunters entered North America along the shore by boat, fishing and hunting sea animals.

This was truly a "new world" to its earliest colonists, as it would be to the European voyagers who rediscovered it thousands of years later. Its natural resources, particularly its big game, never before had been exploited by humans. Early bands followed the game south. Although ice sheets covered most of what is now Canada, colonization gradually penetrated the heartland of what is now the United States. Successive generations of hunters followed game through unglaciated corridors, breaks in the continental ice sheets (see Figure 10.4). Other colonists spread by boat down the Pacific coast.

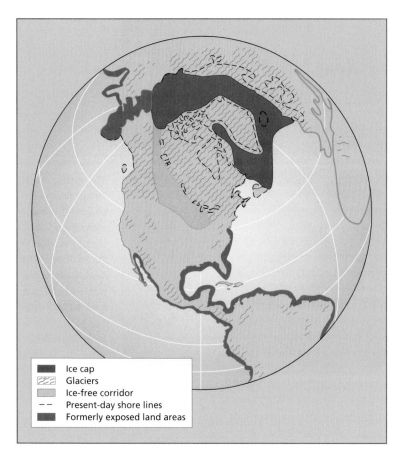

FIGURE 10.4 The Ancestors of Native Americans Came to North America as Migrants from Asia.

They followed big-game herds across Beringia, an immense stretch of land exposed during the Ice Ages. Was their settlement of the Americas intentional? When did it probably happen? Other migrants reached North America along the shore by boat, fishing and hunting sea animals.

Legend:
- Ice cap
- Glaciers
- Ice-free corridor
- – – Present-day shore lines
- Formerly exposed land areas

Clovis tradition
Early American tool tradition; projectile point attached to hunting spear.

haplogroup
A lineage marked by one or more specific genetic mutations.

On North America's rolling grasslands, early American Indians, *Paleoindians,* hunted horses, camels, bison, elephants, mammoths, and giant sloths. The **Clovis tradition**—a sophisticated stone technology based on a point that was fastened to the end of a hunting spear (Figure 10.5)—flourished, widely but very briefly, in the Central Plains, on their western margins, and in what is now the eastern United States (Green 2006; Largent 2007*a*, 2007*b*). Non-Clovis sites dating to the Clovis period also exist, in both North and South America.

Using C^{14} (radiocarbon) dates, where available, for all known Clovis sites, Michael Waters and Thomas Stafford (2007) conclude that the Clovis tradition lasted no more than 450 years (13,250–12,800 B.P.) and perhaps only 200 years (13,125–12,925 B.P.). During this short time span, Clovis technology originated and spread throughout North America. Unknown is whether this spread involved the actual movement of big-game hunters, or the very rapid diffusion of a superior technology from group to group (Largent 2007*b*).

Waters and Stafford (2007) also calculate that it would have taken from 600 to 1,000 years for the first Americans and their descendants to travel by land from the southern part of the Canadian ice-free corridor to Tierra del Fuego at the southern tip of South America—a distance of more than 8,680 miles (14,000 km). At least four sites in southern South America have C^{14} dates about the same as the Clovis C^{14} dates. No more than 350 years separate the youngest possible date of those sites from the oldest possible date for Clovis. This would be insufficient time (10–18 human generations) for people to enter North America; adapt to environments ranging from arctic tundra to grasslands, deserts, and rain forests; increase in population; and reach southern South America.

Waters and Stafford conclude there must have been people in the Americas before Clovis. Indeed, an emerging archaeological record supports a pre-Clovis occupation of the New World. For example, non-Clovis tools and butchered mammoth remains dating to 13,500 B.P. and 12,500 B.P. have been found at sites in Wisconsin. People also appear to have been living in South America as much as 1,500 years before Clovis at Monte Verde, Chile (Largent 2007*a*).

Thus, the Clovis people were not the first settlers of the Americas. Evidence for the early occupation of southern South America (along with other lines of evidence) suggests that the first migration(s) of people into the Americas may date back 18,000 years. Analysis of DNA—bolstered, some anthropologists believe, by anatomical evidence—suggests that the Americas were settled by more than one **haplogroup**—a lineage

FIGURE 10.5 A Clovis Spear Point.

Such points were attached to spears used by Paleoindians of the North American plains between 12,000 and 11,000 B.P. Are there sites with comparable ages in South America?

This mural of early Americans crossing over Beringia is from the National Museum of Anthropology in Mexico City. Beringia was a vast stretch of land exposed during the Ice Ages. The settlement of North America was not as intentional as this mural suggests.

marked by one or more specific genetic mutations. The various early colonists (as many as four or five haplogroups, according to some anthropologists) came at different times, perhaps by different routes, and had different physiques and genetic markers, which continue to be discovered and debated (see Bonnichsen and Schneider 2000).

THE PEOPLING OF THE PACIFIC

Who settled the vast Pacific? Today, when archaeologists dig in Australia, Papua New Guinea, and the neighboring islands of the southwest Pacific (consult the map on page 224 throughout this discussion), they find traces of humankind more than 30,000 years old. Humans reached northern Australia around 50,000 years ago. People even reached the islands north of Australia, as far as the Solomon Islands, more than 30,000 years ago (Terrell 1998).

And there they stayed. Based on current evidence, people waited thousands of years before they risked sailing farther eastward on the open sea. Until 3000 B.P., the Solomon Islands formed the eastern edge of the inhabited Pacific. The deep-sea crossings and colonization that began around 3000 B.P. were linked to the rapid spread of the earliest pottery found in Oceania, an ornately decorated ware with geometric designs called Lapita.

The first Lapita potsherds were excavated in 1952. The name comes from the discovery site on the Melanesian island of New Caledonia. (Locate New Caledonia on the map (Figure 10.6) on

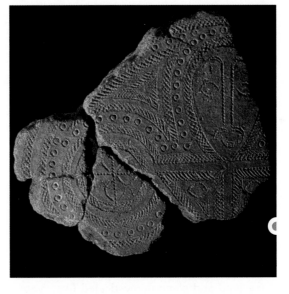

Lapita pottery fragments from the Solomon Islands, dated to 3000 B.P.

page 224.) Many scholars see this ornate ware as the product of an ethnically distinct people, and think the Lapita "cultural complex" was carried into the Pacific by a migration of racially distinct newcomers from Asia.

No one knows why people with Lapita pottery left home and risked sailing in deeper waters. Was it for reasons of wanderlust, a pioneering spirit, or improvements in canoe building and navigation? Some experts think the domestication of certain plants and animals thought to be of Asian origin— such as dogs, pigs, and chickens—somehow fueled Lapita's expansion (Terrell 1998).

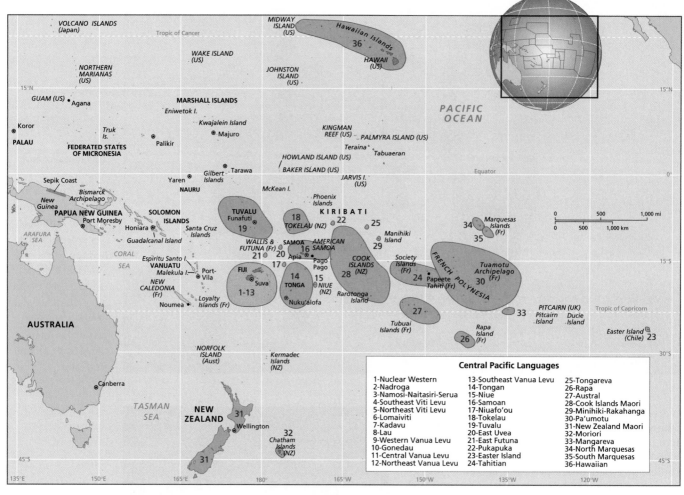

FIGURE 10.6 Oceania.

Polynesian islands are shaded khaki. Other Central Pacific languages outside of Polynesia are spoken in the area shaded orange, which includes Fiji.

Central Pacific Languages

1-Nuclear Western	13-Southeast Vanua Levu	25-Tongareva
2-Nadroga	14-Tongan	26-Rapa
3-Namosi-Naitasiri-Serua	15-Niue	27-Austral
4-Southeast Viti Levu	16-Samoan	28-Cook Islands Maori
5-Northeast Viti Levu	17-Niuafo'ou	29-Minihiki-Rakahanga
6-Lomaiviti	18-Tokelau	30-Pa'umotu
7-Kadavu	19-Tuvalu	31-New Zealand Maori
8-Lau	20-East Uvea	32-Moriori
9-Western Vanua Levu	21-East Futuna	33-Mangareva
10-Gonedau	22-Pukapuka	34-North Marquesas
11-Central Vanua Levu	23-Easter Island	35-South Marquesas
12-Northeast Vanua Levu	24-Tahitian	36-Hawaiian

Archaeologist John Terrell has excavated a site dated to 3000 B.P. on the Sepik (midnorthern) coast of Papua New Guinea. At that time, according to Terrell (1998), newly stabilized coastal lagoons were producing an abundance of (mainly wild) foods, fueling human population growth. The resource base of the early Lapita pottery makers included diverse foods, some wild and some domesticated (e.g., yams, taro, pigs, chickens).

Archaeologist David Burley uncovered early Lapita shards (potsherds) at Fanga'uta lagoon on the island of Tongatapu in the Polynesian kingdom of Tonga. Early outrigger canoes reached that lagoon after traveling hundreds, and perhaps more than a thousand, miles from the west. Radiocarbon dating of charcoal among the shards showed that seafarers reached Tonga between 2,950 and 2,850 years ago. *This is the earliest known settlement in Polynesia.* Burley thinks that Tongatapu "probably served as the initial staging point for population expansion" to other islands of

Tonga, then to Samoa, and then on to the rest of Polynesia (quoted in Wilford 2002a).

Improvements in their outrigger canoes allowed Lapita navigators to sail across large stretches of open sea, thus propelling the Polynesian diaspora. The larger canoes could have carried dozens of people, plus pigs and other cargo. Polynesian seafarers eventually reached Tahiti to the east, and Hawaii—located more than 2,500 miles northeast of Tonga and Samoa. Later voyages carried the Polynesian diaspora south to New Zealand, and farther east to Easter Island. Covering one-fourth of the Pacific, Polynesia became the last large area of the world to be settled by humans.

The Lapita pottery found at Tongatapu offered clues about where the seafarers originated. Analyzing bits of the shards, William Dickinson, a University of Arizona geologist, found sandy minerals from outside Tonga. Some of the pots had been brought there from elsewhere. It turned out that the artifacts were made of minerals found only on the Santa Cruz Islands in Melanesia, some

This print from 1811 shows a traditional (New Zealand) Maori war canoe Earlier, the Lapita people had reached and colonized vast areas of the Pacific, including New Zealand, in their outrigger canoes.

1,200 miles to the west of Tonga, and just east of the Solomon Islands. (Burley and Dickinson 2001). The shards from Tongatapu provided the first physical evidence linking the voyages of the Lapita people between the western and eastern parts of the Pacific. This evidence may mean that Tonga was first settled by people who came directly from central Melanesia (Wilford 2002a).

Anthropologists from all four subfields— archaeologists and physical, cultural, and linguistic anthropologists—have considered questions about Polynesian origins. Who made Lapita pottery, along with the distinctive stone tools, beads, rings, and shell ornaments often found with it? Did the Lapita complex originate with indigenous dark-skinned Melanesians, assumed to descend from the first settlers of the Pacific? Or was it introduced by new, lighter-skinned arrivals from Southeast Asia? Did lighter- and darker-skinned groups intermarry in Melanesia, forming a hybrid population that created the Lapita complex and eventually colonized Polynesia?

In the 18th century, the explorer Captain James Cook was struck by how similar were the appearance and customs of light-skinned Polynesians living on islands thousands of miles apart, such as Tonga, Hawaii, New Zealand, and Easter Island. Cook thought that the Polynesians originally had come from Malaysia. French navigators stressed the physical and cultural differences between the Polynesians and the darker-skinned Melanesians who lived near New Guinea, and who resembled the indigenous peoples of Papua New Guinea.

Until recently, anthropologists supposed that the ancestors of the Polynesians originated in mainland China and/or Taiwan, which they left between 3,600 and 6,000 years ago. They were seen as spreading rapidly through the Pacific, largely bypassing Melanesia. This would explain why the Polynesians are not dark-skinned and why they speak Austronesian languages, rooted in Taiwan, rather than Papuan languages, spoken in parts of Melanesia. This view now seems discredited by the fact that nothing resembling Lapita pottery has ever been found in Taiwan or southern China. Lapita features first show up in Melanesia, on islands of the Bismarck Archipelago. Recent genetic studies also suggest that ancestral Polynesians stopped off in Melanesia. Interbreeding between early Polynesians and Melanesians has left clear genetic markers in today's Polynesians, The debate now focuses on where the interbreeding took place and how extensive it was.

DNA evidence has convinced Mark Stoneking, a molecular anthropologist, that the ancestors of the Polynesians were indeed Austronesians. (The Austronesian, or Malayo-Polynesian, language family covers a large area of the world. Austronesian

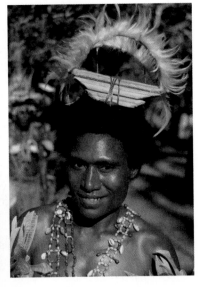

On the left, a Polynesian woman from Tahiti, Society Islands, French Polynesia. On the right, a Melanesian woman from Madang, Papua New Guinea. What differences and similarities do you notice between these two women?

languages are the main languages of Polynesia [e.g., Hawaiian], Indonesia, and Malaysia, and even of Madagascar, located just off the African coast.) Stoneking thinks that the ancestral Polynesians left Southeast Asia and sailed to, then expanded along, the coast of New Guinea. They intermingled with Melanesians there and then started voyaging eastward into the Pacific. Interacting with other human groups, ancestral Polynesians exchanged genes and cultural traits (Gibbons 2001; Wilford 2002a).

Excavating in Melanesia's Bismarck Archipelago, archaeologist Patrick Kirch found evidence that newcomers from the islands of southeast Asia had reached Melanesia by 3500 B.P. They built their houses on stilts, as in houses still found in Southeast Asia. They sailed in outrigger canoes and brought agricultural plants along with them. There was mixing between the newcomers and the Melanesians. *Out of their contact and interaction emerged the Lapita pottery style* (see Kirch 2000).

Why don't Polynesians resemble their presumed Melanesian cousins? Can we explain the physical differences between Polynesians and Melanesians? Might the Polynesian population have originated in what geneticists call a founder event? In such an event, just a few people, whose physical traits do not randomly sample the larger population from which they came, happen to give rise to a very large diaspora. A very small number of people, say, a few canoeloads, reaching Tonga's Fanga'uta lagoon, may have given rise to the entire, geographically dispersed Polynesian population. The physical traits of such a small founding group could not fully represent the population from which they came. Whatever traits the founders happened to have, such as light skin color, would be transmitted to their descendants. This may explain why the Polynesians look so different from Melanesians, even though they have DNA in common.

By 2000 B.P., according to Patrick Kirch (2000), the people of Tonga had developed a significant new technology: the double-hull sailing canoe. Even though they could not spot other islands on the distant horizon, as their ancestors had been able to do in the Southwestern Pacific, the notion that the ocean was full of islands endured. Once they could more securely travel long distances—with the new canoe—they set forth. These weren't all accidental voyages and discoveries, as once was thought. These ancient sailors tacked against the prevailing east-to-west winds, knowing that, if necessary, they could ride a following wind back home.

Long ago, the anthropologist Alexander Lesser disputed what he saw as the "myth of the primitive isolate" (quoted in Terrell 1998)—the idea that ancient peoples lived in closed societies, each one out of contact with others. It is doubtful that the human world has ever been one of distinct societies, sealed cultures, or isolated ethnic groups. Even on the small islands and atolls of the vast Pacific Ocean lived societies that contradicted the "primitive isolate." The adventurous and interconnected peoples of the Pacific and their prehistoric past reveal that human diversity is as much a product of contact as of isolation (Terrell 1998).

Acing the
COURSE

Summary

1. The ancestors of AMHs (anatomically modern humans) were archaic *H. sapiens* groups, most probably those in Africa. Early AMH fossil finds include Skhūl (100,000 B.P.), Qafzeh (92,000 B.P.), Herto (160,000–154,000 B.P.), Omo Kibish (195,000 B.P.), and various South African sites. The Neandertals (130,000–28,000 B.P.) and AMHs were contemporaries, rather than ancestor and descendant.

AMHs made Upper Paleolithic blade tools in Europe and Middle and Late Stone Age flake tools in Africa.

2. As glacial ice melted, foraging patterns were generalized, adding fish, fowl, and plant foods to the diminishing big-game supply. The beginning of a broad-spectrum economy in Western Europe coincided with an intensification of Upper Paleolithic cave art. On limestone cave walls, prehistoric hunters painted images of animals important in their lives. Explanations of cave paintings link them to hunting magic, ceremonies of increase, and initiation rites.

3. During the major glacial phases, land bridges formed, aiding human colonization of new areas, including Australia and the Americas. Around 50,000 years ago, dry land connected Australia, New Guinea, and Tasmania, forming the large continent of Sahul, separated from Asia only by narrow straits, which humans somehow crossed. The close genetic relationship between Native Australians, New Guineans, and Melanesians suggests a single initial colonization of Sahul from Asia. Genetic dating (ca. 50,000 B.P.) agrees more or less with archaeological evidence for early Australian settlement by 46,000 B.P. Australia has yielded a few of the oldest (ca. 46,000 B.P.) modern human skeletons known outside Africa, including the Lake Mungo finds.

4. Humans probably entered the Americas no more than 18,000 years ago. Pursuing big game or moving by boat along the North Pacific Coast, they gradually moved into North America. Adapting to different environments, Native Americans developed a variety of cultures. Some continued to rely on big game. Others became broad-spectrum foragers.

5. Papua New Guinea and the neighboring islands of the southwest Pacific have been settled for at least 30,000 years. Only around 3,000 B.P. did people start sailing further eastward, carrying the earliest Oceanian pottery, called Lapita. Seafarers reached Tonga between 2,950 and 2,850 years ago—the earliest known settlement in Polynesia. Tonga appears to have served as the initial point of expansion, via outrigger canoe, to Samoa and eventually Tahiti, Hawaii, New Zealand, and Easter Island. The ancestral Polynesians probably left Southeast Asia, sailed to, and then expanded along the coast of New Guinea. They intermingled with Melanesians there, then started voyaging eastward. The light skin color of Polynesians, which contrasts with the darker skin color of Melanesians, may have originated as an instance of the founder effect.

Key Terms

behavioral modernity 212
blade tool 215
Clovis tradition 222
Cro Magnon 210

haplogroup 222
Herto 209
Upper Paleolithic 215

Test Yourself!

MULTIPLE CHOICE

1. Fossil and archaeological evidence has been accumulating to support the African origin of anatomically modern humans. Sometimes this evidence results from reanalyzing fossils years after their discovery, as in the case of
   a. the Herto remains found in South Africa's Blombos Cave which have an estimated date of 100,000 B.P.
   b. the Omo remains from southwestern Ethiopia, which now appear to be the earliest AMH fossils yet found, with an estimated date of 195,000 B.P.
   c. Neandertal remains found in 1967 in the Neader Valley, Kenya, now believed to be twice as old as originally estimated.
   d. the Skhūl remains found in South Africa's Pinnacle Point Cave, dating back to 200,000 B.P.
   e. *H. erectus* fossils found in southern Ethiopia, originally thought to date to 150,000 B.P. are now believed to be twice as old.

2. All of the following are characteristic of AMH skulls *except*
   a. narrow nasal bones.
   b. a long skull with broad midfaces.
   c. a more filled-out forehead region, which rises more vertically above the brows.
   d. a marked chin.
   e. a pronounced occipital bun.

3. What does the Eve theory suggest?
   a. Everyone alive today has the mtDNA from a woman (dubbed "Eve") who lived in Australia around 40,000 years ago.
   b. There are serious limits to the use of genetic evidence in studies of human evolution.
   c. "Eve's" descendants left Africa no more than 135,000 years ago, and eventually displaced the Neandertals in Europe, and went on to colonize the rest of the world.
   d. There is more than one "Eden," with AMHs originating simultaneously in Africa, Australia, and Europe.
   e. Fossils of a woman dubbed "Eve" establish that AMHs left Africa 50,000 years ago, and eventually colonized Europe.

4. Scientists disagree most about
   a. when, where, and how early anatomically modern humans achieved behavioral modernity.
   b. when and where our hominin ancestors became habitual bipeds.
   c. when and where hominins began making crude stone tools.
   d. when anatomically modern humans evolved from ancestors who remained in Africa.
   e. by when hominins spread from Africa to Asia and eventually Europe.

5. In 2007 anthropologists reported evidence of behavioral modernity dating back to 164,000 B.P. in a cave site at Pinnacle Point, South Africa. Among the finds at this site was evidence of an ancient diet containing a variety of shellfish and other marine sources. Why is this significant?
   a. It suggests early humans' capacity to make a living from the sea, and thus use coastlines as productive home ranges and move long distances.
   b. It suggests humans' capacity to make fire used to soften the shells of crustaceans.
   c. Such foods point to a diet rich in essential fatty acids.
   d. It suggests early humans' difficulty digesting red meats.
   e. It suggests early humans' capacity to share food.

6. All of the following are trends that mark the changeover from the Mousterian to the Upper Paleolithic *except*
   a. an increase in the number of distinct tool types, reflecting functional specialization.
   b. increasing standardization in tool manufacture.
   c. growth in Homo's total population and geographic range.
   d. rudimentary cultivation techniques to grow medicinal herbs.
   e. increasing local cultural diversity as people specialized in particular economic activities.

7. The broad-spectrum revolution was a significant event in human evolution because
   a. it led to the extinction of the Neandertals, who had survived by eating big game animals.
   b. it marked the sudden advent of behavioral modernity.
   c. it brought about a new tool tradition based on flaked tools.
   d. it provided new environmental circumstances that made important socio-cultural adaptations, like the development of plant cultivation more likely.
   e. it made possible AMHs' colonization of Africa.

8. The geographic expansion of the hominin range
   a. reached its territorial maximum by 50,000 B.P.
   b. reflects the evolutionary success of increasing reliance on tools, language, and culture.
   c. is limited to Europe and Africa prior to the anatomically modern human's stage of human evolution.
   d. usually involved large migrations over long distances, triggered by natural disasters like flood and drought.
   e. was completed when Neandertal foragers entered the New World.

9. The spread of AMHs to Australia by 46,000 B.P. and into the Americas perhaps by 18,000 B.P. illustrate
   a. AMHs' capacity to cross, directly from southern Africa, large and deep bodies of water with rudimentary sailing rafts.
   b. the problem of over-population and disease that pushed AMHs to unpopulated regions.
   c. the role of mutations that predisposed some groups of AMHs to take greater risks and explore the unknown.
   d. the impact that the discovery of the wheel had on human mobility.
   e. the importance of understanding the effects of major glacial phases on the reduction of water levels and the narrowing of straits and the exposure of land bridges connecting otherwise separate land masses.

10. All of the following are true about the peopling of the Pacific *except*:
   a. Humans may have reached as far as the Solomon Islands more than 30,000 years ago.
   b. Once humans reached the Pacific, they did not settle there but moved on to the western coast of South America.
   c. The earliest known settlement in Polynesia occurred sometimes between 2,950 and 2,850 years ago.
   d. Navigation skills played an important role in the peopling of the Pacific.
   e. Tonga appears to have served as an initial point of expansion, via outrigger canoe, to Samoa and eventually Tahiti, Hawaii, New Zealand, and Easter Island.

FILL IN THE BLANK

1. Hominins burying their dead with ceremonies, adorning their bodies with paints and jewelry, and making figurine images of fertile females are all evidence of _____, fully human behavior based on symbolic thought and cultural activity.

  behavioral modernity

2. The *Upper Paleolithic* traditions, associated with AMHs in Europe, all emphasized *blade* tools.

3. *AMH* are the hominins associated with cave paintings, among the earliest evidence of human art.

4. At times of major glacial advance, such as 50,000 years ago, dry land connected Australia, New Guinea, and Tasmania, thus forming the *Sahul* continent.

5. The *Clovis* tradition—a sophisticated stone technology based on a point that was fastened to the end of a hunting spear—flourished in the Central Plains, on their western margins, and in what is now the eastern United States, approximately 13,000 B.P.

CRITICAL THINKING

1. In 1997, ancient DNA was extracted from one of the Neandertal bones originally found in Germany in 1856. This was the first time that DNA of a premodern human had been recovered. What does the analysis of this DNA suggest about Neandertals' relation to AMHs? What other evidence have scientists presented regarding Neandertals' place in the modern human's evolutionary line?

2. What does behavioral modernity mean? What are the competing theories that attempt to explain the advent of behavioral modernity in AMHs? Is behavioral modernity a quality of individual humans or humans as part of a social group? (Perhaps the answer is not one or the other but an interaction between the two, which some anthropologists might argue are inseparable.)

3. What cultural advances facilitated the spread of AMHs out of Africa?

4. What cultural changes accompanied glacial retreat in Europe during the late Upper Paleolithic?

5. It isn't the tools or the skeletons of Upper Paleolithic people but their art that has made them most familiar to us. What are some of the interpretations of cave art that researchers have proposed?

Multiple Choice: 1. (B); 2. (E); 3. (C); 4. (A); 5. (A); 6. (D); 7. (D); 8. (B); 9. (E); 10. (B); Fill in the Blank: 1. behavioral modernity; 2. Upper Paleolithic; blade; 3. Anatomically modern humans; 4. Sahul; 5. Clovis

Fagan, B. M.
  2010 *People of the Earth: A Brief Introduction to World Prehistory,* 13th ed. Upper Saddle River, NJ: Prentice Hall. Prehistoric peoples and civilizations.
  2008 *World Prehistory: A Brief Introduction,* 7th ed. New York: Longman. From the Paleolithic to the Neolithic around the world.

Gamble, C.
  1999 *The Palaeolithic Societies of Europe.* New York: Cambridge University Press. Survey mainly of the Middle and Upper Paleolithic in Europe.

Klein, R. G., with B. Edgar
  2002 *The Dawn of Human Culture.* New York: Wiley. Becoming modern, physically and culturally.

Shipman, P.
  2001 *The Man Who Found the Missing Link.* New York: Simon & Schuster. Eugene Dubois discovers "Java Man" (*H. erectus*).

Wenke, R. J., and D. I. Olszewski
  2007 *Patterns in Prehistory: Mankind's First Three Million Years,* 5th ed. New York: Oxford University Press. Very thorough survey of fossil and archaeological reconstruction of human evolution.

Suggested Additional Readings

Internet Exercises

Go to our Online Learning Center website at **www.mhhe.com/kottak** for Internet exercises directly related to the content of this chapter.

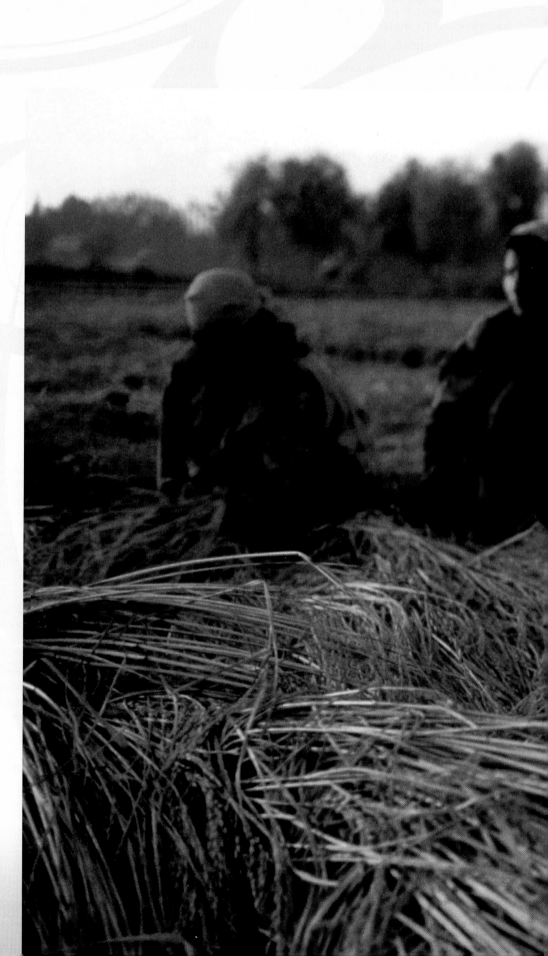

- When and where did the Neolithic originate, and what were its main features?

- What similarities and differences marked the Neolithic economies of the Old World and the New World?

- What costs and benefits are associated with food production?

Harvesting rice in India's Kashmir valley. Rice, another Old World crop, was domesticated in China more than 8,000 years ago.

The First Farmers

understanding OURSELVES

What could be more American than McDonald's, hamburgers, hot dogs, or apple pie? More American, in other words, than a now global fast-food chain, a sandwich and sausage named for German cities, or a fruit first grown in the Middle East baked in a pastry crust from wheat, domesticated there as well. What we think of as truly American usually has foreign roots. Consider just McDonald's Big Mac as a world system in miniature. It consists of two all-beef patties (from cattle, an Old World domesticate), special sauce (similar to mayonnaise, invented in France), lettuce (Egypt), cheese (from cow's milk—Old World), pickles (India), onions (Iran and West Pakistan), and it comes on a sesame-seed (India) bun (wheat—Middle East). The breakfast Egg McMuffin is only slightly less cosmopolitan. Eggs are from chickens, domesticated in Southeast Asia. Cheese comes from cow's milk (cows were domesticated in India, the Middle East, and Africa's eastern Sahara). Canadian bacon is from pork (western Asia), and the muffin is made of wheat (Middle East). If you crave "real American," i.e., New World origin, food, have some turkey or beans on a taco or tortilla (from maize or corn) and chocolate for dessert.

The domestication of plants and animals for food occurred, independently, in both the Old World and in the Americas around 11,000 years ago. Animals and crops thrived together in the Middle East, Africa, Europe, and Asia. Not so in the Americas, where wild oxen, horses, pigs, and camels went extinct long before crops were ever cultivated. Key differences in early food production between the hemispheres help us to understand their subsequent histories. A mutually supportive relationship developed between farming and herding in the Old World, where crops sustained sheep, goats, and eventually cattle, pigs, horses, and donkeys.

What, again deceptively, could be more American than the habit of using your own wheels to get you to your favorite restaurant? Wheels? Only in Old World prehistory were animals harnessed to pull wheeled vehicles. Ancient Mexicans did also invent the wheel, but only for toys. Their homeland lacked the appropriate animals to pull plows, oxcarts, chariots, and carriages. How could a dog, turkey, or duck match a horse, donkey, or ox as a beast of burden? The absence of large animal domestication in ancient Mexico is a key factor in world history, helping us understand the divergent development of societies on different sides of the oceans. Wheels fueled the growth of transport, trade, and travel in the Old World. Thousands of years after the origin of food production, advantages in transport would fuel an "age of discovery" and enable the European conquest of the Americas. Again, a key feature of contemporary American life turns out to have foreign roots.

In Chapter 10, we considered some of the economic implications of the end of the Ice Age in Europe. With glacial retreat, foragers pursued a more generalized economy, focusing less on large animals. This was the beginning of what Kent Flannery (1969) has called the **broad-spectrum revolution.** This refers to the period beginning around 15,000 B.P. in the Middle East and 12,000 B.P. in Europe, during which a wider range, or broader spectrum, of plant and animal life was hunted, gathered, collected, caught, and fished. It was revolutionary because in the Middle East it led to food production—human control over the reproduction of plants and animals.

THE MESOLITHIC

The broad-spectrum revolution in Europe includes the late Upper Paleolithic and the **Mesolithic,** which followed it. Again, because of the long history of European archaeology, our knowledge of the Mesolithic (particularly in southwestern Europe and the British Isles) is extensive. The Mesolithic had a characteristic tool type—the *microlith* (Greek for "small stone"). Of interest to us is what an abundant inventory of small and delicately shaped stone tools can tell us about the total economy and way of life of the people who made them.

By 12,000 B.P., subarctic animals no longer lived in southwestern Europe. By 10,000 B.P. the glaciers had retreated to such a point that the range of hunting, gathering, and fishing populations in Europe extended to the formerly glaciated British Isles and Scandinavia. The reindeer herds had gradually retreated to the far north, with some human groups following (and ultimately domesticating) them. Europe around 10,000 B.P. was forest rather than treeless steppe and tundra—as it had been during the Upper Paleolithic. Europeans were exploiting a wider variety of resources and gearing their lives to the seasonal appearance of particular plants and animals.

People still hunted, but their prey were solitary forest animals, such as the roe deer, the wild ox, and the wild pig, rather than herd species. This led to new hunting techniques: solitary stalking and trapping. The coasts and lakes of Europe and the Middle East were fished intensively. Some important Mesolithic sites are Scandinavian shell mounds—the garbage dumps of prehistoric oyster collectors. Microliths were used as fishhooks and in harpoons. Dugout canoes were used for fishing and travel. The process of preserving meat and fish by smoking and salting grew increasingly important. (Meat preservation had been less of a problem in a subarctic environment since winter snow and ice, often on the ground nine months of the year, offered convenient refrigeration.) The bow and arrow became essential for hunting water fowl in swamps and marshes. Dogs were domesticated as retrievers by Mesolithic people (Champion and Gamble 1984). Woodworking was important in the forested environment of northern and Western Europe. Tools used by Mesolithic carpenters appear in the archaeological record: new kinds of axes, chisels, and gouges.

Big-game hunting and, thereafter, Mesolithic hunting and fishing were important in Europe,

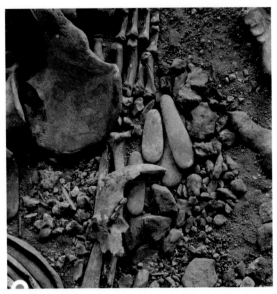

Evidence of the Mesolithic occupation of Italy. Displayed here are a beaver jaw, ochre, stone tools, and assorted bones, just as they were found (in situ) at a Mesolithic cave burial in Arene Candide grotto, near Savona, Italian Riviera.

but other foraging strategies were used by prehistoric humans in Africa and Asia. Among contemporary foragers in the tropics, gathering is the dietary mainstay (Lee 1968/1974). Although herds of big game animals were more abundant in the tropics in prehistory than they are today, gathering probably always has been at least as important as hunting for tropical foragers (Draper 1975).

Generalized, broad-spectrum economies lasted about 5,000 years longer in Europe than in the Middle East. Whereas Middle Easterners had begun to cultivate plants and breed animals by 10,000 B.P., food production reached Western Europe only around 5000 B.P. (3000 B.C.E.) and northern Europe 500 years later.

After 15,000 B.P., throughout the inhabited world, as the big-game supply diminished, foragers had to pursue new resources. Human attention shifted from large-bodied, slow reproducers (such as mammoths) to species such as fish, mollusks, and rabbits that reproduce quickly and prolifically (Hayden 1981). This happened with the European Mesolithic. It also happened at the Japanese site of Nittano (Akazawa 1980), located on an inlet near Tokyo. Nittano was occupied several times between 6000 and 5000 B.P. by members of the *Jomon* culture, for which 30,000 sites are known in Japan. These broad-spectrum foragers hunted deer, pigs, bears, and antelope. They also ate fish, shellfish, and plants. Jomon sites have yielded the remains of 300 species of shellfish and 180 species of edible plants (including berries, nuts, and tubers) (Akazawa and Aikens 1986).

broad-spectrum revolution
Foraging varied plant and animal foods at end of Ice Age; prelude to Neolithic.

Mesolithic
Stone tool making, emphasizing microliths within broad-spectrum economies.

THE NEOLITHIC

The archaeologist V. Gordon Childe (1951) used the term *Neolithic Revolution* to describe the origin and impact of food production—plant cultivation and animal domestication. **Neolithic** was coined to refer to new techniques of grinding and polishing stone tools. However, the primary significance of the Neolithic was the new total economy rather than just its characteristic artifacts, which also included pottery.

The transition from Mesolithic to Neolithic occurs when groups become dependent on domesticated foods (more than 50 percent of the diet). Usually this happens after a very long period of experimenting with and using domesticates as supplements to broad-spectrum foraging. The archaeological signature of Neolithic cultures (which are called *Formative* in the Americas) includes dependence on cultivation, sedentary (settled) life, and the use of ceramic vessels.

Neolithic economies based on food production were associated with substantial changes in human lifestyles. By 12,000 B.P., the shift toward the Neolithic was under way in the Middle East (Turkey, Iraq, Iran, Syria, Jordan, and Israel). People started intervening in the reproductive cycles of plants and animals. No longer simply harvesting nature's bounty, they grew their own food and modified the biological characteristics of the plants and animals in their diet. By 10,000 B.P., domesticated plants and animals were part of the broad spectrum of resources used by Middle Easterners. By 7500 B.P., most Middle Easterners had moved away from the broad-spectrum foraging pattern toward more specialized, Neolithic, economies based on fewer species, which were domesticates.

They had become committed farmers and herders. Kent Flannery (1969) has proposed a series of eras during which the Middle Eastern transition to farming and herding took place. The era of seminomadic hunting and gathering (12,000–10,000 B.P.) encompasses the last stages of broad-spectrum foraging. This was the period just before the first domesticated plants (wheat and barley) and animals (goats and sheep) were added to the diet. Next came the era of early dry farming (of wheat and barley) and caprine domestication (10,000–7500 B.P.). *Dry farming* refers to farming without irrigation; such farming depended on rainfall. *Caprine* (from *capra,* Latin for "goat") refers to goats and sheep, which were domesticated during this era.

During the era of increased specialization in food production (7500–5500 B.P.), new crops were added to the diet, along with more productive varieties of wheat and barley. Cattle and pigs were domesticated. By 5500 B.P., agriculture extended to the alluvial plain of the Tigris and Euphrates rivers (Figure 11.1), where early Mesopotamians lived in walled towns, some of which grew into cities. (Recap 11.1 highlights these stages or eras in the transition to food production in the ancient Middle East.) After two million years of stone-tool making, *H. sapiens* was living in the Bronze Age, when metallurgy and the wheel were invented.

Neolithic
Economies based on food production (cultivated crops and domesticated animals).

Neolithic was coined to refer to techniques of grinding and polishing stone tools, like these axes and hammers from Austria, Hungary, and the Czech Republic. Was the new toolmaking style the most significant thing about the Neolithic?

RECAP 11.1	The Transition to Food Production in the Middle East

ERA	DATES (B.P.)
Origin of state (Sumer)	5500 B.P.
Increased specialization in food production	7500–5500 B.P.
Early dry farming and caprine domestication	10,000–7500 B.P.
Seminomadic hunting and gathering (e.g., Natufians)	12,000–10,000 B.P.

THE FIRST FARMERS AND HERDERS IN THE MIDDLE EAST

Middle Eastern food production arose in the context of four environmental zones. From highest to lowest, they are high plateau (5,000 feet, or 1,500 meters), Hilly Flanks, piedmont steppe (treeless plain), and alluvial desert—the area watered by the Tigris and Euphrates rivers (100–500 feet, or 30–150 meters). The **Hilly Flanks** is a subtropical woodland zone that flanks those rivers to the north (Figure 11.1).

It was once thought that food production began in oases in the alluvial desert. (*Alluvial* describes rich, fertile soil deposited by rivers and streams.) This arid region was where Mesopotamian civilization arose later. Today, we know that although the world's first civilization (Mesopotamian) did indeed develop in this zone, irrigation, a late (7000 B.P.) invention, was necessary to farm the alluvial desert. Plant cultivation and animal domestication started not in the dry river zone but in areas with reliable rainfall.

The archaeologist Robert J. Braidwood (1975) proposed instead that food production started in the Hilly Flanks, or subtropical woodland zone, where wild wheat and barley would have been most abundant (see Figure 11.1). In 1948, a team headed by Braidwood started excavations at Jarmo, an early food-producing village inhabited between 9000 and 8500 B.P., located in the Hilly Flanks. We now know, however, that there were farming villages earlier than Jarmo in zones adjacent to the Hilly Flanks. One example is Ali Kosh (Figure 11.1), a village in the foothills (piedmont steppe) of the Zagros mountains. By 9000 B.P., the people of Ali Kosh were herding goats, intensively collecting various wild plants, and harvesting wheat during the late winter and early spring (Hole, Flannery, and Neely 1969).

Climate change played a role in the origin of food production (Smith 1995). The end of the Ice Age brought greater regional and local variation in climatic conditions. Lewis Binford (1968) proposed that in certain areas of the Middle East (such as the Hilly Flanks), local environments were so rich in resources that foragers could adopt **sedentism**—sedentary (settled) life in villages. Binford's prime example is the widespread Natufian culture (12,500–10,500 B.P.), based on broad-spectrum foraging. The **Natufians,** who collected wild cereals and hunted gazelles, had year-round villages. They were able to stay in the same place (early villages) because they could harvest nearby wild cereals for six months.

Donald Henry (1989, 1995) documented a climate change toward warmer, more humid conditions just before the Natufian period. This expanded the altitude range of wild wheat and

FIGURE 11.1 The Vertical Economy of the Ancient Middle East.

Geographically close but contrasting environments were linked by seasonal movements and trade among broad-spectrum foragers. As people traveled and traded, they removed plants from the zones where they grew wild in the Hilly Flanks into adjacent zones where humans became agents of selection. Food production emerged on the margins of the Hilly Flanks, at places such as Ali Kosh, rather than within that area, at places such as Jarmo.

barley, thus enlarging the available foraging area and allowing a longer harvest season. Wheat and barley ripened in the spring at low altitudes, in the summer at middle altitudes, and in the fall at high altitudes. As locations for their villages, the Natufians chose central places where they could harvest wild cereals in all three zones.

Around 11,000 B.P., this favorable foraging pattern was threatened by a second climate change—to drier conditions. As many wild cereal habitats dried up, the optimal zone for foraging shrank. Natufian villages were now restricted to areas with permanent water. As population continued to grow, some Natufians attempted to maintain productivity by transferring wild cereals to well-watered areas, where they started cultivating.

In the view of many scholars, the people most likely to adopt a new subsistence strategy, such as food production, would be those having the most trouble in following their traditional subsistence strategy (Binford 1968; Flannery 1973; Wenke 1996).

Hilly Flanks
Woodland zone just north of Tigris and Euphrates rivers.

sedentism
Settled (sedentary) life.

Natufians
Widespread Middle Eastern foraging culture (12,500–10,500 B.P.).

Some 12,000 to 10,000 years ago, ancient Middle Easterners followed the availability of plants and animals, from lower to higher zones. With domestication, this pattern evolved into nomadic herding (pastoralism). Contemporary Middle Eastern herders still take their flocks to grazing areas at different elevations. This 1997 photo shows a Bedouin shepherd in the hills near Bethlehem, West Bank, Israel.

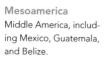

Mesoamerica
Middle America, including Mexico, Guatemala, and Belize.

Thus, those ancient Middle Easterners living outside the area where wild foods were most abundant would be the most likely to experiment and to adopt new subsistence strategies. This would have been especially true as the climate dried up. Recent archaeological finds support this hypothesis that food production began in *marginal areas,* such as the piedmont steppe, rather than in the optimal zones, such as the Hilly Flanks, where traditional foods were most abundant.

Even today, wild wheat grows so densely in the Hilly Flanks that one person working just an hour with Neolithic tools can easily harvest a kilogram of wheat (Harlan and Zohary 1966). People would have had no reason to invent cultivation when wild grain was ample to feed them. Wild wheat ripens rapidly and can be harvested over a three-week period. According to Flannery, over that time period, a family of experienced plant collectors could harvest enough grain—2,200 pounds (1,000 kilograms)—to feed themselves for a year. But after harvesting all that wheat, they'd need a place to put it. They could no longer maintain a nomadic lifestyle, since they'd need to stay close to their wheat.

Sedentary village life thus developed before farming and herding in the Middle East. The Natufians and other Hilly Flanks foragers had no choice but to build villages near the densest stands of wild grains. They needed a place to keep their grain. Furthermore, sheep and goats came to graze on the stubble that remained after humans had harvested the grain. The fact that basic plants and animals were available in the same area also favored village life. Hilly Flanks foragers built houses, dug storage pits for grain, and made ovens to roast it.

Natufian settlements, occupied year-round, show permanent architectural features and evidence for the processing and storage of wild grains. One such site is Abu Hureyra, Syria (see Figure 11.1), which was initially occupied by Natufian foragers around 11,000 to 10,500 B.P. Then it was abandoned—to be reoccupied later by food producers, between 9500 and 8000 B.P. From the Natufian period, Abu Hureyra has yielded the remains of grinding stones, wild plants, and 50,000 gazelle bones, which represent 80 percent of all the bones recovered at the site (Jolly and White 1995).

Prior to domestication, the favored Hilly Flanks zone had the densest human population. Eventually, its excess population started to spill over into adjacent areas. Colonists from the Flanks tried to maintain their traditional broad-spectrum foraging in these marginal zones. But with sparser wild foods available, they had to experiment with new subsistence strategies. Eventually, population pressure on more limited resources forced people in the marginal zones to become the first food producers (Binford 1968; Flannery 1969). *Early cultivation began as an attempt to copy, in a less favorable environment, the dense stands of wheat and barley that grew wild in the Hilly Flanks.*

The Middle East, along with certain other world areas where food production originated, is a region that for thousands of years has had a *vertical economy.* (Other examples include Peru and **Mesoamerica**—Middle America, including Mexico, Guatemala, and Belize.) A vertical economy exploits environmental zones that, although close together in space, contrast with one another in altitude, rainfall, overall climate, and vegetation (Figure 11.1). Such a close juxtaposition of varied environments allowed broad-spectrum foragers to use different resources in different seasons.

Early seminomadic foragers in the Middle East had followed game from zone to zone. In winter they hunted in the piedmont steppe region, which had winter rains rather than snow and provided winter pasture for game animals 12,000 years ago. (Indeed it is still used for winter grazing by herders today.) When winter ended, the steppe dried up. Game moved up to the Hilly Flanks and high plateau country as the snow melted. Pastureland became available at higher elevations. Foragers gathered as they climbed, harvesting wild grains that ripened later at higher altitudes. Sheep and goats followed the stubble in the wheat and barley fields after people had harvested the grain.

The four Middle Eastern environmental zones shown in Figure 11.1 also were tied together through trade. Certain resources were confined to specific zones. Asphalt, used as an adhesive in the manufacture of sickles, came from the steppe. Copper and turquoise sources were located in the high plateau. Contrasting environments were linked in two ways: by foragers' seasonal migration and by trade.

The movement of people, animals, and products between zones—plus population increase supported by highly productive broad-spectrum foraging—was a precondition for the emergence of food production. As they traveled between zones, people carried seeds into new habitats. Mutations, genetic recombinations, and human selection led to new kinds of wheat and barley. Some of the new varieties were better adapted to the steppe and, eventually, the alluvial desert than the wild forms had been.

Genetic Changes and Domestication

What are the main differences between wild and domesticated plants? The seeds of domesticated cereals, and often the entire plant, are larger. Compared with wild plants, crops produce a higher yield per unit of area. Domesticated plants also lose their natural seed dispersal mechanisms. Cultivated beans, for example, have pods that hold together, rather than shattering as they do in the wild. Domesticated cereals have tougher connective tissue holding the seedpods to the stem.

Grains of wheat, barley, and other cereals occur in bunches at the end of a stalk (Figure 11.2). The grains are attached to the stalk by an *axis*, plural *axes*. In wild cereals, this axis is brittle. Sections of the axis break off one by one, and a seed attached to each section falls to the ground. This is how wild cereals spread their seeds and propagate their species. But a brittle axis is a problem for people. Imagine the annoyance experienced by broad-spectrum foragers as they tried to harvest wild wheat, only to have the grain fall off or be blown away.

In very dry weather, wild wheat and barley ripen—their axes totally disintegrating—in just three days (Flannery 1973). The brittle axis must have been even more irritating to people who planted the seeds and waited for the harvest. But fortunately, certain stalks of wild wheat and barley happened to have tough axes. These were the ones whose seeds people saved to plant the following year.

Another problem with wild cereals is that the edible portion is enclosed in a tough husk. This husk was too tough to remove with a pounding stone. Foragers had to roast the grain to make the husk brittle enough to come off. However, some

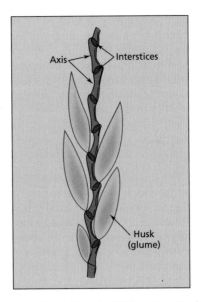

FIGURE 11.2 A Head of Wheat or Barley.

In the wild, the axis comes apart as its parts fall off one by one. The connecting parts (interstices) are tough and don't come apart in domesticated grains. In wild grains, the husks are hard. In domestic plants, they are brittle, which permits easy access to the grain. How did people deal with hard husks before domestication?

wild plants happened to have genes for brittle husks. Humans chose the seeds of these plants (which would have germinated prematurely in nature) because they could be more effectively prepared for eating.

People also selected certain features in animals (Smith 1995). Some time after sheep were domesticated, advantageous new phenotypes arose. Wild sheep aren't woolly; wool coats were products of domestication. Although it's hard to imagine, a wool coat offers protection against extreme heat. Skin temperatures of sheep living in very hot areas are much lower than temperatures on the surface of their wool. Woolly sheep, but not their wild ancestors, could survive in hot, dry alluvial lowlands. Wool had an additional advantage: its use for clothing.

What are some of the differences between wild and domesticated animals? Plants got larger with domestication, while animals got smaller, probably because smaller animals are easier to control. Middle Eastern sites document changes in the horns of domesticated goats. Such change may have been genetically linked to some other desirable trait that has left no skeletal evidence behind.

We've seen that sheep and goats were the first animals to be domesticated in the ancient Middle East, where the domestication of cattle, pigs, and other animals came later. Domestication was an ongoing process, as people kept refining and changing the traits they considered desirable in plants and animals—as they still do today through bioengineering. Different animals were domesticated at different times and in different regions. The factors that govern animal domestication are discussed further in the section "Explaining the Neolithic" later in this chapter.

Food Production and the State

The shift from foraging to food production was gradual. The knowledge of how to grow crops and breed livestock didn't immediately convert Middle Easterners into full-time farmers and herders. Domesticated plants and animals began as minor parts of a broad-spectrum economy. Foraging for fruits, nuts, grasses, grains, snails, and insects continued.

Over time, Middle Eastern economies grew more specialized, geared more exclusively toward crops and herds. The former marginal zones became centers of the new economy and of population increase and emigration. Some of the increasing population spilled back into the Hilly Flanks, where people eventually had to intensify production by cultivating. Domesticated crops could now provide a bigger harvest than could the grains that grew wild there. Thus, in the Hilly Flanks, too, farming eventually replaced foraging as the economic mainstay.

Farming colonies spread down into drier areas. By 7000 B.P., simple irrigation systems had developed, tapping springs in the foothills. By 6000 B.P., more complex irrigation techniques

made agriculture possible in the arid lowlands of southern Mesopotamia. In the alluvial desert plain of the Tigris and Euphrates rivers, a new economy based on irrigation and trade fueled the growth of an entirely new form of society. This was the *state*, a social and political unit featuring a central government, extreme contrasts of wealth, and social classes. The process of state formation is examined in the next chapter.

We now understand why the first farmers lived neither in the alluvial lowlands, where the Mesopotamian state arose around 5500 B.P., nor in the Hilly Flanks, where wild plants and animals abounded. Food production began in marginal zones, such as the piedmont steppe, where people experimented at reproducing, artificially, the dense grain stands that grew wild in the Hilly Flanks. As seeds were taken to new environments, new phenotypes were favored by a combination of natural and human selection. The spread of cereal grains outside their natural habitats was part of a system of migration and trade between zones, which had developed in the Middle East during the broad-spectrum period. Food production also owed its origin to the need to intensify production to feed an increasing human population—the legacy of thousands of years of productive foraging.

OTHER OLD WORLD FOOD PRODUCERS

The path from foraging to food production was one that people followed independently in at least seven world areas. As we'll see later in this chapter, at least three were in the Americas. At least four were in the Old World. In each of these centers, people independently invented domestication, although of different sets of crops and animals.

As we'll see in more detail later in this chapter, food production also spread from the Middle East. This happened through trade; through diffusion of plants, animals, products, and information; and through the actual migration of farmers. Middle Eastern domesticates spread westward to northern Africa, including Egypt's Nile Valley, and into Europe (Price 2000). Trade also extended eastward from the Middle East to India and Pakistan. In Egypt, an agricultural economy based on plants and animals originally domesticated in the Middle East led to a pharaonic civilization.

The African Neolithic

Excavations in southern Egypt have revealed considerable complexity in its Neolithic economy

Simple irrigation systems were being used in the Middle East by 7000 B.P. By 6000 B.P., complex irrigation techniques made agriculture possible in the arid lowlands of southern Mesopotamia. Simple irrigation systems continue to be used in many world areas, including the rural area shown here near Cairo, Egypt.

and social system, along with very early pottery and cattle, which may have been domesticated locally rather than imported from the Fertile Crescent. Located in the eastern Sahara and southern Egypt, Nabta Playa is a basin that, during prehistoric summers, filled with water. Over several millennia this temporary lake attracted people who used it for social and ceremonial activities (Wendorf and Schild 2000). Nabta Playa was first occupied around 12,000 B.P., as Africa's summer rains moved northward, providing moisture for grasses, trees, bushes, hares, and gazelle, along with humans. The earliest settlements (11,000–9300 B.P.) at Nabta were small seasonal camps of herders of domesticated cattle. (Note the very early, and perhaps independent, domestication of cattle here.) According to Wendorf and Schild (2000), Nabta Playa provides early evidence for what anthropologists have called the "African cattle complex," in which cattle are used economically for their milk and blood, rather than killed for their meat (except on ceremonial occasions). Nabta was occupied only seasonally, as people came over from the Nile or from better-watered areas to the south. They returned to those areas in the fall.

By 9000 B.P. people were living at Nabta Playa year-round. To survive in the desert, they dug large, deep wells and lived in well-organized villages, with small huts arranged in straight lines. Plant remains show they collected sorghum, millet, legumes (peas and beans), tubers, and fruits. These were wild plants, and so the economy was not fully Neolithic. By 8800 B.P. these people were making their own pottery, possibly the earliest pottery in Egypt. By 8100 B.P. sheep and goats had diffused in from the Middle East.

Around 7500 B.P. new settlers occupied Nabta, whose previous inhabitants had been forced away by a major drought. The newcomers brought a more sophisticated social and ceremonial system. They sacrificed young cattle, which they buried in clay-lined and roofed chambers covered with rough stone slabs. They lined up large, unshaped stones. They also built Egypt's earliest astronomical measuring device: a "calendar circle" used to mark the summer solstice. Nabta Playa had become a regional ceremonial center: a place where various groups gathered seasonally or occasionally to conduct ceremonies and to socialize. The existence of such centers, as well as their religious, political, and social functions, is familiar to ethnographers who have worked in Africa. Nabta seems to have been such a center for prehistoric herders who lived in southern Egypt. It probably began to function as a regional ceremonial center around 8100–7600 B.P., when various groups gathered there for ceremonial and other purposes during the summer wet season.

Gathering on the northwestern shores of the summer lake, those ancient people left debris, including numerous cattle bones. At other African Neolithic sites (Edwards 2004), cattle bones are rarely numerous, which suggests that the cattle were being tapped "on the hoof" for their milk and blood, rather than being slaughtered and eaten. The numerous cattle bones at Nabta Playa, however, suggest that its people killed cattle seasonally for ceremonial purposes. Among modern African herders, cattle, which represent wealth and political power, are rarely killed except on important ceremonial or social occasions.

Nabta's role as a regional ceremonial center is also suggested by an alignment of nine large upright stone slabs near the place where people gathered, along the northwest margin of the seasonal lake. This formation, probably dating between 7500 and 5500 B.P., recalls similarly dated large stone alignments found in Western Europe, which were built during the late Neolithic and early Bronze Age.

Construction of large, complex megalithic structures requires well-organized work parties and a major effort. This suggests that some authority (religious or civil) may have been managing resources and human labor over time. The findings at Nabta Playa represent an elaborate and previously unsuspected ceremonialism, as well as social complexity, during the African Neolithic.

The Neolithic in Europe and Asia

Around 8000 B.P., communities on Europe's Mediterranean shores, in Greece, Italy, and France, started shifting from foraging to farming, using imported species. By 7000 B.P., there were fully sedentary farming villages in Greece and Italy. By 6000 B.P., there were thousands of farming villages as far east as Russia and as far west as northern France (see Bogaard 2004).

Domestication and Neolithic economies spread rapidly across Eurasia. Archaeological research confirms the early (8000 B.P.) presence of domesticated goats, sheep, cattle, wheat, and barley in Pakistan (Meadow 1991). In that country's Indus River Valley, ancient cities (Harappa and Mohenjodaro) emerged slightly later than did the first Mesopotamian city-states. Domestication and state formation in the Indus Valley were influenced by developments in, and trade with, the Middle East.

China was also one of the first world areas to develop farming, based on millet and rice. Millet is a tall, coarse cereal grass still grown in northern China. This grain, which today feeds a third of the world's population, is used in contemporary North America mainly as birdseed. By 7500 B.P., two varieties of millet supported early farming

Millet, being harvested here on a Chinese plateau, was grown in the Hwang-He (Yellow River) Valley by 7000 B.P. This grain supported early farming communities in northern China. What was being grown in southern China at the same time?

living anthropology **VIDEOS**

Agriculture and Change, www.mhhe.com/kottak

This clip focuses on early food production and its implications. According to the clip, humans started managing the reproduction of plants and animals around 12,000 years ago. The clip suggests that food production enabled nomadic humans to settle down and live in permanent villages near their fields and water sources. Food production eventually led to towns, cities, and states. Compare the discussion of sedentism in the ancient Middle East in the text with the contention that food production caused sedentary life in the clip. Did food production in the Middle East precede or follow sedentism? According to the clip, what role did women play in the origin of food production?

communities in northern China, along the Yellow River. Millet cultivation paved the way for widespread village life and eventually for Shang dynasty civilization, based on irrigated agriculture, between 3600 and 3100 B.P. (See Chapter 12.) The northern Chinese also had domesticated dogs, pigs, and possibly cattle, goats, and sheep by 7000 B.P. (Chang 1977).

Discoveries by Chinese archaeologists suggest that rice was domesticated in the Yangtze River corridor of southern China as early as 8400 B.P. (Smith 1995). Other early rice comes from the 7,000-year-old site Hemudu, on Lake Dongting in

southern China. The people of Hemudu used both wild and domesticated rice, along with domesticated water buffalo, dogs, and pigs. They also hunted wild game (Jolly and White 1995).

China seems to have been the scene of two independent transitions to food production, based on different crops grown in strikingly different climates. Southern Chinese farming was rice aquaculture in rich subtropical wetlands. Southern winters were mild; and summer rains, reliable. Northern China, by contrast, had harsh winters, with unreliable rainfall during the summer growing season. This was an area of grasslands and temperate forests. Still, in both areas by 7500 B.P., food production supported large and stable villages. Based on the archaeological evidence, early Chinese villagers had architectural expertise. They lived in substantial houses, made elaborate ceramic vessels, and had rich burials.

At Nok Nok Tha in central Thailand, pottery made more than 5,000 years ago has imprints of husks and grains of domesticated rice (Solheim 1972/1976). Animal bones show that the people of Nok Nok Tha also had humped zebu cattle similar to those of contemporary India. Rice might have been cultivated at about the same time in the Indus River Valley of Pakistan and adjacent western India.

It appears that food production arose independently at least seven times in different world areas. Figure 11.3 is a map highlighting those seven areas: the Middle East, northern China, southern China, sub-Saharan Africa, central Mexico, the south central Andes, and the eastern United States. A different set of major foods was domesticated, at different times, in each area, as is shown in Recap 11.2. Some grains, such as millet and rice, were domesticated more than once. Millet grows wild in China and Africa, where it became an important food crop, as well as in Mexico, where it did not. Indigenous African rice, grown only in West Africa, belongs to the same genus as Asian rice. Pigs and probably cattle were independently domesticated in the Middle East, China, and sub-Saharan Africa. Independent domestication of the dog was virtually a worldwide phenomenon, including the Western Hemisphere. We turn now to archaeological sequences in the Americas.

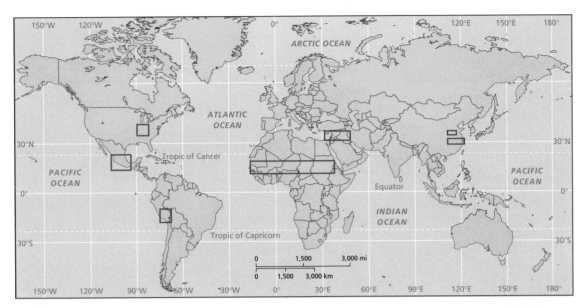

FIGURE 11.3 Seven World Areas Where Food Production Was Independently Invented.

Do any of these areas surprise you?

SOURCE: Bruce D. Smith, *The Emergence of Agriculture* (New York: Scientific American Library, 1995), p. 12. Reprinted by permission of the author. smith.bruce@nmnh.si.edu

RECAP 11.2	Seven World Areas Where Food Production Was Independently Invented

WORLD AREA	MAJOR DOMESTICATED PLANTS/ANIMALS	EARLIEST DATE (B.P.)
Middle East	Wheat, barley Sheep, goats, cattle, pigs	10,000
Andean region	Squash, potato, quinoa, beans Camelids (llama, alpaca), guinea pigs	10,000–5000
Southern China (Yangtze River corridor)	Rice Water buffalo, dogs, pigs	8500–6500
Mesoamerica	Maize, beans, squash Dogs, turkeys	8000–4700
Northern China (Yellow River)	Millet Dogs, pigs, chickens	7500
Sub-Saharan Africa	Sorghum, pearl millet, African rice	4000
Eastern United States	Goosefoot, marsh elder, sunflower, squash	4500

SOURCE: Data compiled from Bruce D. Smith, *The Emergence of Agriculture* (New York: Scientific American Library, W. H. Freeman, 1995).

THE FIRST AMERICAN FARMERS

As hunters benefiting from the abundance of big game, bands of foragers gradually spread through the Americas. As they moved, these early Americans learned to cope with a great diversity of environments. Eventually their descendants would independently invent food production, paving the way for the emergence of states based on agriculture and trade in Mexico and Peru.

The most significant contrast between Old and New World food production involved animal domestication, which was much more important in the Old World than in the New World. The animals that had been hunted during the early American big-game tradition either became extinct before people could domesticate them or were not domesticable. The largest animal ever domesticated in the New World (in Peru, around 4500 B.P.) was the llama. Early Peruvians and Bolivians ate llama meat and used that animal as a beast of burden (Flannery, Marcus, and Reynolds 1989). They

Early Peruvians and Bolivians ate llama meat, harnessed llamas as beasts of burden, and used llama dung to fertilize their fields. What was the largest animal domesticated in the New World?

By diffusion, manioc or cassava, originally domesticated in lowland South America, has become a caloric staple in the tropics worldwide. This young Thai farmer displays his manioc crop.

maize
Corn; first domesticated in tropical southwestern Mexico around 8000 B.P.

manioc
Cassava; tuber domesticated in the South American lowlands.

bred the llama's relative, the alpaca, for its wool. Peruvians also added animal protein to their diet by raising and eating guinea pigs and ducks.

The turkey was domesticated in Mesoamerica and in the southwestern United States. Lowland South Americans domesticated a type of duck. The dog is the only animal that was domesticated throughout the New World. There were no cattle, sheep, or goats in the areas where food production arose. As a result, neither herding nor the kinds of relationships that developed between herders and farmers in many parts of the Middle East, Europe,

Asia, and Africa emerged in the precolonial Americas. The New World crops were different, although staples as nutritious as those of the Old World were domesticated from native wild plants.

Three key caloric staples, major sources of carbohydrates, were domesticated by Native American farmers. **Maize**, or corn, first domesticated in the tropical lowlands of southwestern Mexico, became the caloric staple in Mesoamerica and Central America and eventually reached coastal Peru. The other two staples were root crops: white ("Irish") potatoes, first domesticated in the Andes, and **manioc**, or cassava, a tuber first cultivated in the South American lowlands, where other root crops such as yams and sweet potatoes also were important. Other crops added variety to New World diets and made them nutritious. Beans and squash provided essential proteins, vitamins, and minerals. Maize, beans, and squash were the basis of the Mesoamerican diet. This chapter's "Appreciating Anthropology" discusses how anthropologists recently have confirmed that the earliest domesticates, including squash, in the Americas are about as old as the first Old World domesticates.

Food production was independently invented in at least three areas of the Americas: Mesoamerica, the eastern United States, and the south central Andes. Mesoamerica is discussed in detail below. Food plants known as goosefoot and marsh elder, along with the sunflower and a species of squash, were domesticated by Native Americans in the eastern United States by 4500 B.P. Those crops supplemented a diet based mainly on hunting and gathering. They never became caloric staples like maize, wheat, rice, millet, manioc, and potatoes. Eventually, maize diffused from Mesoamerica into what is now the United States, reaching both the Southwest and the eastern area just mentioned. Maize provided a more reliable caloric staple for native North American farming. Domestication of several species was under way in the south central Andes of Peru and Bolivia by 5,000 B.P. They were the potato, quinoa (a cereal grain), beans, llamas, alpacas, and guinea pigs (Smith 1995). This chapter's "Appreciating Anthropology" discusses how anthropologists recently have confirmed the very early domestication of squash, cotton, and peanuts in Peru.

The Tropical Origins of New World Domestication

Based on microscopic evidence from early cultivated plants, New World farming began in the lowlands of South America and then spread to Central America, Mexico, and the Caribbean islands. In Chapter 4 we learned about new techniques that allow archaeologists and botanists to recover and analyze microscopic evidence from pollens, starch grains, and phytoliths (plant crystals) (Bryant 2003, 2007a). This evidence has forced revision of old assumptions, most prominently the idea that New World farming originated in upland areas, such as the highlands of Mexico and Peru. This chapter's "Appreciating Anthropology" reports that domesticated squash seeds from Peru date back 10,000 years. Although found in the highlands (western Andes), those seeds, along with other domesticates from that site, were not domesticated there originally. This means that domestication must have occurred even earlier, most probably in South America's tropical lowlands.

Dolores Piperno and Karen Stothert (2003) found that phytoliths from cultivated squashes and gourds are substantially larger than those from wild species. They then used phytolith size to confirm that domesticated squash and gourds (*Cucurbita*) were grown in coastal Ecuador between 9,000 and 10,000 years ago.

According to Piperno and Deborah Pearsall (1998), farming in the tropical lowlands of Central and South America began at about the same time as food production arose in the Middle East—around 10,000 years ago. By that time, cultural groups in Panama, Peru, Ecuador, and Colombia

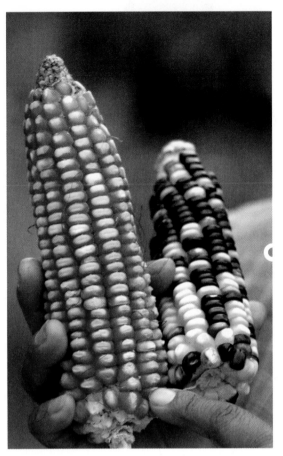

Two different types of corn (maize) from among the many varieties grown in Oaxaca, Mexico, where archaeologists have studied early highland maize cultivation. Do the earliest Mesoamerican domesticates come from the Mexican highlands?

were cultivating plants in garden plots near their homes. Between 9000 and 8000 B.P., changes in seed form and phytolith size suggest that farmers were selecting certain characteristics in their cultivated plants. By 7,000 years ago, farmers had expanded their plots into nearby forests, which they cleared using slash-and-burn techniques. By that time also, early farming ideas and techniques were diffusing from tropical lowlands into drier regions at higher elevations (Piperno and Pearsall 1998; Bryant 1999, 2003).

What about maize (corn), a major New World crop, long thought to have been domesticated in the Mexican highlands? Recent molecular and genetic studies indicate that maize domestication actually took place in the lowlands of southwestern Mexico. The wild ancestor of maize is a species of **teosinte** (a wild grain) native to the Rio Balsas watershed of tropical southwestern Mexico (Holst, Moreno, and Piperno 2007). Evidence for the evolution of maize from its wild ancestor has yet to be found in that poorly studied region. Still, we can infer some of the likely steps in maize domestication.

Such a process would have included increases in the number of kernels per cob, cob size, and the number of cobs per stalk (Flannery 1973). These changes would make it increasingly profitable to collect wild teosinte and eventually to plant

teosinte
Wild ancestor of maize; grows wild in southwestern Mexico.

The Early Origin of New World Domestication

New dating techniques applied to plant remains found in northern Peru have pushed back the origin of domestication in the New World to about the same time that food production arose in the Old World. Previously anthropologists had believed that Old World (Middle Eastern) farming predated the earliest cultivation in the Americas by three or four millennia. Peruvian squash seeds dating back 10,000 years show there was no such time lag between the first farming in the New World and in the Old. Other sites and dates discussed in this chapter support this finding.

Seeds of domesticated squash found by scientists on the western slopes of the Andes in northern Peru are almost 10,000 years old, about twice the age of previously discovered cultivated crops in the region, new, more precise dating techniques have revealed.

The findings about Peru and recent research in Mexico, anthropologists say, are evidence that some farming developed in parts of the Americas nearly as early as in the Middle East, which is considered the birthplace of the earliest agriculture.

Digging under house floors and grinding stones and in stone-lined storage bins, the archaeologist Tom D. Dillehay of Vanderbilt University, in Nashville, uncovered the squash seeds at several places in the Ñanchoc Valley, near the Pacific coast about 400 miles north of Lima. The excavations also yielded peanut hulls and cotton fibers—about 8,500 and 6,000 years old, respectively.

The new, more precise dating of the plant remains, some of which were collected two decades ago, is being reported by Dr. Dillehay and colleagues in today's issue of the journal *Science*.

Their research also turned up traces of other domesticated plants, including a grain, manioc and unidentified fruits, and stone hoes, furrowed garden plots and small-scale irrigation canals from approximately the same period of time.

The researchers concluded that these beginnings in plant domestication "served as catalysts for rapid social changes that eventually contributed to the development of intensified agriculture, institutionalized political power and towns in both the Andean highlands and on the coast between 5,000 and 4,000 years ago."

The evidence at Ñanchoc, Dr. Dillehay's team wrote, indicated that "agriculture played a more important and earlier role in the development of Andean civilization than previously understood."

In an accompanying article on early agriculture, Eve Emshwiller, an ethnobotanist at the University of Wisconsin, Madison, was quoted as saying that the reports of early dates for plant domestication in the New World were remarkable because this appeared to have occurred not long after humans colonized the Americas, now thought to be at least 13,000 years ago.

The article also noted that 10,000-year-old cultivated squash seeds had recently been reported in Mexico, along with evidence of domesticated corn there by 9,000 years ago . . .

In the Fertile Crescent of the Middle East, an arc from modern-day Israel through Syria and Turkey to Iraq, wheat and barley were domesticated by 10,000 years ago, and possibly rye by 13,000 years ago. . . .

Dr. Dillehay has devoted several decades of research to ancient cultures in South America. His most notable previous achievement was the discovery of a campsite of hunter-gatherers at Monte Verde, in Chile, which dates to 13,000 years ago. Most archaeologists recognize this as the earliest

maize. Undoubtedly, some of the mutations necessary for domesticated maize had occurred in wild teosinte before people started growing it. However, since teosinte was well adapted to its natural niche, the mutations offered no advantage and didn't spread. But once people started harvesting wild maize intensively, they became selective agents, taking back to camp a greater proportion of plants with tough axes and cobs. These were the plants most likely to hold together during harvesting and least likely to disintegrate on the way back home. Eventually, teosinte became dependent on humans for its survival because maize lacks a natural means of dispersal—a brittle axis or cob. If humans chose plants with tough axes inadvertently, their selection of plants with soft husks must have been intentional, as was their selection of larger cobs, more kernels per cob, and more cobs per plant.

A phytolith analysis of sediments from San Andrés, in the Mexican state of Tabasco, confirms the spread of maize cultivation eastward to the tropical Mexican Gulf Coast by 7300 B.P. Data from many sites now confirm that maize spread rapidly from its domestication cradle in tropical southwestern Mexico during the eighth millennium B.P. (8000–7001) (Bryant 2007*b*; Piperno 2001; Pohl et al. 2007). For example, analysis of starch grains from stone tools in Panama's tropical lowlands confirms that maize was grown there by 7800–7000 B.P. (Dickau, Ranere, and Cooke 2007).

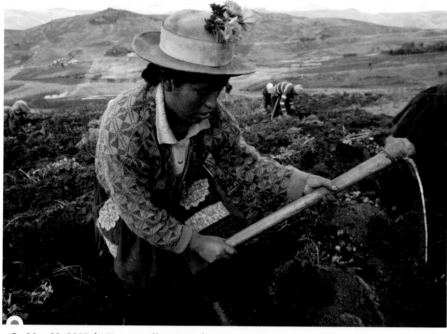

On May 29, 2007, in Huancavelica, Peru, farmers harvest native potatoes at the International Potato Centre (CIP) experimental station in the Andean highlands. The CIP conserves genetic samples of most of the potatoes native to Peru, the birthplace of the potato with more than three thousand varieties. New dating techniques applied to plant remains (squash seeds) found in Peru have pushed back the origin of domestication in the New World to about the same time that food production arose in the Old World, around 10,000 years ago.

Initial radiocarbon dating of the plant remains from Ñanchoc was based on wood charcoal buried at the sites, but the results varied widely and were considered unreliable. More recent radiocarbon dating, with a technique called accelerator mass spectrometry, relied on measurements from undisturbed buried charcoal and an analysis of the actual plant remains.

The distribution of building structures, canals and furrowed fields, Dr. Dillehay said, indicated that the Andean culture was moving beyond cultivation limited to individual households toward an organized agricultural society. Botanists studying the squash, peanut, and cotton remains determined that the specific strains did not grow naturally in the Ñanchoc area. The peanut, in particular, was thought to be better suited to cultivation in tropical forests and savannas elsewhere in South America.

SOURCE: John Noble Wilford, "Squash Seeds Show Andean Cultivation Is 10,000 Years Old, Twice as Old as Thought." From *The New York Times*, June 29, 2007. © 2007 The New York Times. All rights reserved. Used by permission and protected by the Copyright Laws of the United States. The printing, copying, redistribution, or retransmission of the Material without express written permission is prohibited. www.nytimes.com

well-documented human occupation site uncovered so far in the New World.

Other explorations in recent years have yielded increasing evidence of settlements and organized political societies that flourished in the coastal valleys of northern Peru possibly as early as 5,000 years ago. Until now, the record of earlier farming in the region had been sparse.

During the last century, for reasons enumerated by Vaughn Bryant (2003), archaeologists tended to seek evidence for early New World farming in the highlands of Mexico and Peru. These upland areas were easy to reach and had caves and rock shelters with preserved plant remains. They also were in the vicinity of the centers of major civilizations that would eventually develop in the Mexican highlands (see Chapter 12). Decades ago, excavations in the Mexican Valleys of Tehuacan and Oaxaca (see the next section) yielded well-preserved seeds and fruits, maize kernels and cobs, fibers, and rinds. Few archaeologists sought the origin of domestication in lowland and jungle regions, which were wrongly assumed to be infertile and where plants did not preserve well (Bryant 2003). Today, the microscopic evidence says otherwise and reveals the key role of tropical lowland regions in early New World farming.

The Mexican Highlands

Long before Mexican highlanders developed a taste for maize, beans, and squash, they hunted as part of a pattern of broad-spectrum foraging. Mammoth remains dated to 11,000 B.P. have been found along with spear points in the basin that surrounds Mexico City. However, small animals were more important than big game, as were the grains, pods, fruits, and leaves of wild plants.

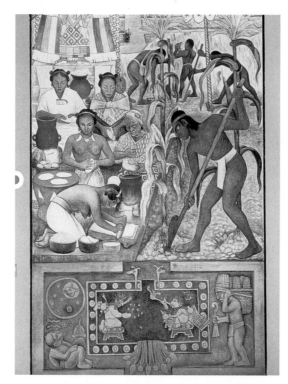

As maize cultivation spread, genetic changes led to higher yields and more productive farming. Pressures to intensify cultivation helped improve water-control systems, such as the canal irrigation shown in this mural by Diego Rivera.

In the Valley of Oaxaca, in Mexico's southern highlands, between 10,000 and 4000 B.P., foragers concentrated on certain wild animals—deer and rabbits—and plants—cactus leaves and fruits, and tree pods, especially mesquite (Flannery 1986). Those early Oaxacans dispersed to hunt and gather in fall and winter. But they came together in late spring and summer, forming larger groups to harvest seasonally available plants. Cactus fruits appeared in the spring. Since summer rains would reduce the fruits to mush and since birds, bats, and rodents competed for them, cactus collection required hard work by large groups of people. The edible pods of the mesquite, available in June, also required intensive gathering.

Eventually, people started planting maize in the alluvial soils of valley floors. This was the zone where foragers traditionally had congregated for the annual spring/summer harvest of cactus fruits and mesquite pods. By 4000 B.P., a type of maize was available that provided more food than the mesquite pods did. Once that happened, people started cutting down mesquite trees and replacing them with corn fields.

By 3500 B.P. in the Valley of Oaxaca, where winter frosts are absent, simple irrigation permitted the establishment of permanent villages based on maize farming. Water close to the surface allowed early farmers to dig wells right in their corn fields. Using pots, they dipped water out of these wells and poured it on their growing plants, a technique known as pot irrigation. Early permanent villages supported by farming appeared in areas of Mesoamerica where there was

reliable rainfall, pot irrigation, or access to humid river bottomlands.

The spread of maize farming resulted in further genetic changes, higher yields, higher human populations, and more intensive farming. Pressures to intensify cultivation led to improvements in water-control systems. New varieties of fast-growing maize eventually appeared, expanding the range of areas that could be cultivated. Increasing population and irrigation also helped spread maize farming. The advent of intensive cultivation laid the foundation for the emergence of the state in Mesoamerica—some 3,000 years later than in the Middle East, a process examined in the next chapter.

EXPLAINING THE NEOLITHIC

This section focuses on the factors that influenced the origin and spread of Neolithic economies in various world areas. (Much of this section is based on observations in Chapters 8 through 10 of Jared Diamond's influential book *Guns, Germs, and Steel: The Fates of Human Societies* [1997]).

Several factors had to converge to make domestication happen and to promote its spread. Most plants, and especially animals, aren't easy—or particularly valuable—to domesticate. Thus, of some 148 large animal species that seem potentially domesticable, only 14 actually have been domesticated. And a mere dozen among 200,000 known plant species account for 80 percent of the world's farm production. Those 12 caloric staples are wheat, corn (maize), rice, barley, sorghum (millet), soybeans, potatoes, cassava (manioc), sweet potatoes, sugarcane, sugar beets, and bananas.

Domestication rested on a combination of conditions and resources that had not come together previously. The development of a full-fledged Neolithic economy required settling down. Sedentism, such as that adopted by ancient Natufian hunter-gatherers, was especially attractive when several species of plants and animals were available locally for foraging and eventual domestication. The Fertile Crescent area of the Middle East had such species, along with a Mediterranean climate favorable to the origin and spread of the Neolithic economy. Among those species were several self-pollinating plants, the easiest wild plants to domesticate, including wheat, which required few genetic changes for domestication. We've seen that the Natufians adopted sedentism prior to farming. They lived off abundant wild grain and the animals attracted to the stubble left after the harvest. Eventually, with climate change, population growth, and the need for people to sustain themselves in the marginal zones, hunter-gatherers started cultivating.

Compared with other world areas, the Fertile Crescent region had the largest area with a

Mediterranean climate, with the highest species diversity. As we saw previously, this was an area of vertical economy and closely packed microenvironments. Such diverse terrains and habitats concentrated in a limited area offered a multiplicity of plant species, as well as goats, sheep, pigs, and cattle. The first farmers eventually domesticated several crops: two kinds of wheat, barley, lentils, peas, and chickpeas (garbanzo beans). As in Mesoamerica, where corn (supplying carbohydrate) was supplemented by squash and beans (supplying protein), the Neolithic diet of the Middle East combined caloric staples such as wheat and barley with protein-rich pulses such as lentils, peas, and chickpeas.

Anthropologists once thought, erroneously, that domestication would happen almost automatically once people gained sufficient knowledge of plants and animals and their reproductive habits to figure out how to make domestication work. Anthropologists now realize that foragers have an excellent knowledge of plants, animals, and their reproductive characteristics, and that some other trigger is needed to start and sustain the process of domestication. A full-fledged Neolithic economy requires a minimal set of nutritious domesticates. Some world areas, for example, North America (north of Mesoamerica), managed independently to invent domestication, but the inventory of available plants and animals was too meager to maintain a Neolithic economy. The early domesticates—squash, sunflower, marsh elder, and goosefoot—had to be supplemented by hunting and gathering. A full Neolithic economy and sedentism did not develop in the east, southeast, and southwest of what is now the United States until maize diffused in from Mesoamerica—more than 3,000 years after the first domestication in the eastern United States.

We've seen how the presence or absence of domesticable animals helps explain the divergent trajectories of the Eastern and Western hemispheres in that the mixed economies that developed in Eurasia and Africa never emerged in Mesoamerica. Of the world's 14 large (over 100 pounds) successful domesticated animal species, 13 are from Eurasia, and only 1 (the llama) is from South America. Ancient Mexicans domesticated dogs and turkeys and created toy wheels, but they lacked sheep, goats, and pigs as well as the oxen or horses needed to make the wheel a viable transport option. Once the big five Eurasian animal domesticates (cow, sheep, goat, pig, horse) were introduced into Africa and the Americas, they spread rapidly.

We've seen that detailed knowledge of plants and their reproduction is not a sufficient condition for domestication to occur. Similarly, the knowledge that animals can be tamed or kept as pets isn't enough to produce animal domestication, because not all tamed animals can be domesticated. Just as some plants (e.g., self-pollinating annuals) are easier to domesticate than others are, so are some animals. Cattle, dogs, and pigs were so easy to domesticate that they were domesticated independently in multiple world areas.

Consider some reasons why most large animal species (134 out of 148 big species) have not been domesticated. Some are finicky eaters (e.g., koalas). Others refuse to breed in captivity (e.g., vicunas). Some animals are just too nasty to domesticate (e.g., grizzly bears), and others have a tendency to panic (e.g., deer and gazelles).

Perhaps the key factor in domestication is animal social structure. The easiest wild animals to domesticate live in hierarchical herds. Accustomed to dominance relations, they allow humans to assume superior positions in the hierarchy. Herd animals are easier to domesticate than solitary ones are. Among the latter, only cats and ferrets have been domesticated, and there's some question about the completeness of domestication of those animals (hence the expression "It's like herding cats"). A final factor in ease of domestication is whether a wild animal typically shares its range with others. Animals with exclusive territories (e.g., rhinoceros, African antelope) are harder to pen up with others than are animals that share their territories with other species.

Geography and the Spread of Food Production

As Jared Diamond (1997, Chapter 10) observes convincingly, the geography of the Old World facilitated the diffusion of plants, animals, technology (e.g., wheels and vehicles), and information (e.g., writing). Most crops in Eurasia were domesticated just once and spread rapidly in an east–west direction. The first domesticates spread from the Middle East to Egypt, Northern Africa, Europe, India, and eventually China (which, however, also had its own domesticates, as we have seen). By contrast, there was less diffusion of American domesticates.

Look at Figure 11.4 to see that Eurasia has a much broader east–west spread than does Africa or does either of the Americas, which are arranged north–south. This is important because climates are more likely to be similar moving across thousands of miles east–west than north–south. In Eurasia, plants and animals could spread more easily east–west than north–south because of common day lengths and similar seasonal variations. More radical climatic contrasts have hindered north–south diffusion. In the Americas, for example, although the distance between the cool Mexican highlands and the South American highlands is just 1,200 miles, those two similar zones are separated by a low, hot, tropical region, which supports very different plant species than the highlands. Such environmental barriers to diffusion kept the

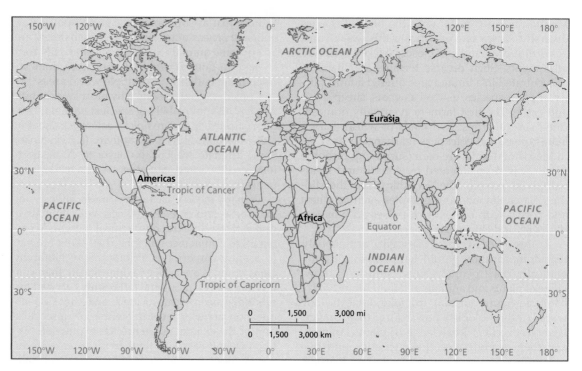

FIGURE 11.4 Major Axes of the Continents.

Note the breadth of the east–west axis in Eurasia, compared with the much narrower east–west spreads in Africa, North America, and South America. Those three continents have north–south as their major axes.

SOURCE: "Figure 10.1: Major Axes of the Continents" from *Guns, Germs, and Steel: The Fates of Human Societies* by Jared Diamond. Published by W. W. Norton & Company, Inc., and Jonathan Cape. Copyright © 1997 by Jared Diamond. Used by permission of W. W. Norton & Company, Inc., The Random House Group Ltd., and the author.

Neolithic societies of Mesoamerica and South America more separate and independent in the Americas than they were in Eurasia. It took some 3,000 years for maize to reach what is now the United States, where productive Neolithic economies eventually did develop. They were based on the cultivation of new varieties of maize adapted to a colder climate and different day lengths.

In the Old World, the spread of Middle Eastern crops southward into Africa eventually was halted by climatic contrasts as well. Certain tropical crops did spread west–east in Africa, but they did not reach Southern Africa because of climatic barriers. Again and again, the geographic and climatic barriers posed by high mountains and broad deserts have slowed the spread of domesticates. In what is now the United States, for example, the east–west spread of farming from the southeast to the southwest was slowed by the dry climates of Texas and the southern great plains.

This section has examined the factors that favored and retarded the origin and spread of Neolithic economies in various world areas. Several factors combined to promote early domestication in the ancient Middle East. The first domesticates spread rapidly across Eurasia, facilitated by climatic similarities across a broad territorial expanse. In the Americas, food production spread

less rapidly because of north–south contrasts. Another factor that slowed the Neolithic transition in the Americas was the lack of large animals suitable for domestication. Factors that explain the origin and diffusion of food production involve climate, economic adaptation, demography, and the specific attributes of plants and animals.

COSTS AND BENEFITS

Food production brought advantages and disadvantages. Among the advantages were discoveries and inventions. People eventually learned to spin and weave; to make pottery, bricks, and arched masonry; and to smelt and cast metals. They developed trade and commerce by land and sea. By 5500 B.P., Middle Easterners were living in vibrant cities with markets, streets, temples, and palaces. They created sculpture, mural art, writing systems, weights, measures, mathematics, and new forms of political and social organization (Jolly and White 1995).

Because it increased economic production and led to new social, scientific, and creative forms, food production is often considered an evolutionary advance. But the new economy also brought hardships. For example, food producers typically

The labor demands of food production far exceed those associated with foraging. Here, in India's Andra Pradesh, these Banjara women are pounding grain. Such processing of food is just one step in getting the grain from the fields into people's mouths. What are some of the other steps?

work harder than foragers do—and for a less adequate diet. Because of their extensive leisure time, foragers have been characterized as living in "the original affluent society" (Sahlins 1972). Certain foragers have survived into recent times and have been studied by anthropologists. Among foragers living in the Kalahari Desert of southern Africa, for example, only part of the group needed to hunt and gather, maybe 20 hours a week, to provide an adequate diet for the entire group. Women gathered, and adult men hunted. Their labor supported older people and children. Early retirement from the food quest was possible, and forced child labor was unknown.

With food production, yields are more reliable, but people work much harder. Herds, fields, and irrigation systems need care. Weeding can require hours of arduous bending. No one has to worry about where to keep a giraffe or a gazelle, but pens and corrals are built and maintained for livestock. Trade takes men, and sometimes women, away from home, leaving burdens for those who stay behind. For several reasons, food producers tend to have more children than foragers do. This means greater child care demands, but child labor also tends to be more needed and valued than it is among foragers. Many tasks in farming and herd-

ing can be done by children. The division of economic labor grows more complex, so that children and older people have assigned economic roles.

And public health declines. Diets based on crops and dairy products tend to be less varied, less nutritious, and less healthful than foragers' diets, which are usually higher in proteins and lower in fats and carbohydrates. With the shift to food production, the physical well-being of the population often declines. Communicable diseases, protein deficiency, and dental caries increase (Cohen and Armelagos 1984). Greater exposure to pathogens comes with food production.

Compared with a seminomadic foraging band, food producers tend to be sedentary. Their populations are denser, which makes it easier to transmit and maintain diseases. We saw in Chapter 5 that malaria and sickle-cell anemia spread along with food production. Population concentrations, especially cities, are breeding grounds for epidemic diseases. People live nearer to other people and animals and their wastes, which also affect public health (Diamond 1997). Compared with farmers, herders, and city dwellers, foragers were relatively disease-free, stress-free, and well nourished.

Other hardships and stresses accompanied food production and the state. Social inequality and poverty increased. Elaborate systems of social stratification eventually replaced the egalitarianism of the past. Resources were no longer common goods, open to all, as they tend to be among foragers. Property distinctions proliferated. Slavery and other forms of human bondage eventually were invented. Crime, war, and human sacrifice became widespread.

The rate at which human beings degraded their environments also increased with food production. The environmental degradation in today's world, including air and water pollution and deforestation, is on a much larger scale, compared with early villages and cities, but modern trends are foreshadowed. After food production, population increase and the need to expand farming led to deforestation in the Middle East. Even today, many farmers think of trees as giant weeds to be cut down to make way for productive fields. Previously, we saw how early Mesoamerican farmers cut down mesquite trees for maize cultivation in the Valley of Oaxaca.

Many farmers and herders burn trees, brush, and pasture. Farmers burn to remove weeds; they also use the ashes for fertilizer. Herders burn to promote the growth of new tender shoots for their livestock. But such practices do have environmental costs, including air pollution. Smelting and other chemical processes basic to the manufacture of metal tools also have environmental costs. As modern industrial pollution has harmful effluents, early chemical processes had byproducts that polluted air, soils, and waters. Salts,

DO THE COSTS OUTWEIGH THE BENEFITS?

BENEFITS	COSTS
Discoveries and inventions	Harder work
New social, political, scientific, and creative forms (e.g., spinning, weaving, pottery, bricks, metallurgy)	Less nutritious diets
	Child labor and child care demands
Monumental architecture, arched masonry, sculpture	Taxes and military drafts
	Public health declines (e.g., more exposure to pathogens, including communicable and epidemic diseases)
Writing	
Mathematics, weights, and measures	Rise in protein deficiency and dental caries
Trade and markets	Greater stress
	Social inequality and poverty
Urban life	Slavery and other forms of human bondage
Increased economic production	Rise in crime, war, and human sacrifice
More reliable crop yields	Increased environmental degradation (e.g., air and water pollution, deforestation)

chemicals, and microorganisms accumulate in irrigated fields. These and other pathogens and pollutants, which were by and large nonissues during the Paleolithic, endanger growing human populations. To be sure, food production had benefits. But its costs are just as evident. Recap 11.3 summarizes the costs and benefits of food production. We see that *progress* is much too optimistic a word to describe food production, the state, and many other aspects of the evolution of society.

Acing the COURSE

Summary

1. By 10,000 B.P., people were pursuing broad-spectrum economies in the British Isles and Scandinavia. Tool kits adapted to a forested environment included small, delicately shaped stone tools called microliths. The Mesolithic had begun. The broad-spectrum revolution, based on a wide variety of dietary resources, began in the Middle East somewhat earlier than in Europe. It culminated in the first food-producing economies in the Middle East around 10,000 B.P.

2. After 15,000 B.P., as the big-game supply diminished, foragers sought out new foods. By 10,000 B.P., domesticated plants and animals were part of a broad spectrum of resources used by Middle Easterners. By 7500 B.P., most Middle Easterners were moving away from broad-spectrum foraging toward more specialized food-producing economies. *Neolithic* refers to the period when the first signs of domestication appeared.

3. Braidwood proposed that food production started in the Hilly Flanks zone, where wheat and barley grew wild. Others questioned this: The wild grain supply in that zone already provided an excellent diet for the Natufians and other ancient Middle Easterners. There would have been no incentive to domesticate. Other scholars view the origin of food production in the context of increasing population and climate changes.

4. Ancient Middle Eastern foragers migrated seasonally in pursuit of game. They also collected wild plant foods as the plants ripened at different altitudes. As they moved about, these foragers took grains from the Hilly Flanks zone, where they grew wild, to adjacent areas. Population spilled over from the Hilly Flanks into areas like the piedmont steppe. In such marginal zones, people started cultivating plants. They were trying to duplicate the dense wild grains of the Hilly Flanks.

5. After the harvest, sheep and goats fed off the stubble of these wild plants. Animal domestication occurred as people started selecting certain features and behavior and guiding the reproduction of goats, sheep, cattle, and pigs. Gradually, food production spread into the Hilly Flanks. Later, with irrigation it spread down into Mesopotamia's alluvial desert, where the first cities, states, and civilizations developed by 5500 B.P. Food production then spread west from the Middle East into North Africa and Europe and east to India and Pakistan.

6. There were at least seven independent inventions of food production: in the Middle East, sub-Saharan Africa, northern and southern China, Mesoamerica, the south central Andes, and the eastern United States. Millet was domesticated by 7000 B.P. in northern China; and rice, by 8000 B.P. in southern China.

7. In the New World the most important domesticates were maize, potatoes, and manioc. The llama of the central Andes was the largest animal domesticated in the New World, where herding traditions analogous to those of the Old World did not develop. Economic similarities between the hemispheres must be sought in foraging and farming.

8. New World farming started in the lowlands of South America, then spread to Central America, Mexico, and the Caribbean islands. Tropical lowland cultivation in Central and South America began at about the same time as food production arose in the Middle East—around 10,000 years ago. By 7000 B.P., farming was diffusing from tropical lowlands into drier regions at higher elevations. The specific ancestor of maize, teosinte, grows wild in tropical southwestern Mexico, where maize probably was domesticated around 8000 B.P. At Oaxaca, in Mexico's southern highlands, maize was gradually added to a broad-spectrum diet by 4000 B.P. Permanent villages supported by maize cultivation arose in the lowlands and in a few frost-free areas of the highlands.

9. Several factors, including a diversity of useful plant and animal species and early sedentism, combined to promote domestication in the ancient Middle East. Domesticates spread rapidly across Eurasia, facilitated by climatic similarities across a broad territorial expanse. In the Americas, food production spread less rapidly because of north–south contrasts. Another factor that slowed the Neolithic transition in the Americas was the lack of large animals suitable for domestication. Factors that explain the origin and diffusion of food production involve climate, economic adaptation, demography, and the specific attributes of plants and animals.

10. Food production and the social and political system it supported brought advantages and disadvantages. The advantages included discoveries and inventions. The disadvantages included harder work, poorer health, crime, war, social inequality, and environmental degradation.

Key Terms

broad-spectrum revolution 233, 234
Hilly Flanks 235
maize 242
manioc 242
Mesoamerica 236

Mesolithic 233
Natufians 235
Neolithic 234
sedentism 235
teosinte 243

Test Yourself!

MULTIPLE CHOICE

1. The Mesolithic refers to
   a. stone-tool making emphasizing microliths within broad-spectrum economies.
   b. the period between 15,000 B.P. in the Middle East and 12,000 B.P. in Europe, during which foragers focused on hunting a limited range of big game.
   c. the technique of cutting and smoking meats to preserve them through the long winters.
   d. the last major glaciation that covered most of Europe with ice.
   e. Scandinavian shell mounds—the garbage dumps of prehistoric oyster collectors.

2. With glacial retreat, foragers pursued a more generalized economy, focusing less on large animals. This was the beginning of what Kent Flannery (1969) has called the
   a. Upper Paleolithic.
   b. Jomon Revolution.
   c. vertical economy revolution.
   d. Neolithic revolution.
   e. broad-spectrum revolution.

3. Why were the Natufians able to live in year-round villages prior to the emergence of domestication?
   a. Because their diet became hyperspecialized to the locally grown foods.
   b. Because they could exploit their rich local environment with broad-spectrum foraging.
   c. Because they had a low-calorie diet relative to the average caloric intake of foragers.
   d. Because they traded with nearby populations that did develop domestication.
   e. Because they reduced the population size of their villages.

4. Early cultivation in the Middle East began as an attempt to
   a. improve, in a more favorable environment, the foraging techniques of villagers living in the Hilly Flanks.
   b. improve the supply of animal feed for the already domesticated cattle.
   c. win a war against nomads encroaching on Natufian territory.
   d. copy, in a less favorable environment, the dense stands of wheat and barley that grew wild in the Hilly Flanks.
   e. impose a social hierarchy among the Natufian commoners.

5. Why do most domesticated grains (such as wheat and barley) have a tougher axis and more brittle husk than wild grains?
   a. Grains with a weak axis and husk could not survive in the wild.
   b. They get better nutrients through being domesticated.
   c. The practices of harvesting and processing grain gradually selected for these features.
   d. The first domesticated grains were from the alluvial plains, where caprine influences strengthened the axis and husk.
   e. B and D only

6. In the alluvial desert plain of the Tigris and Euphrates rivers, a new economy based on irrigation and trade fueled the growth of an entirely new form of society:
   a. the Jomon, a social and political unit with roots in East Asia.
   b. the state, a social and political unit featuring a central government, extreme contrasts of wealth, and social classes.
   c. the city-state, a social and political unit featuring egalitarianism.
   d. the state, featuring what Marshall Sahlins called "the original affluent society."
   e. the village.

7. Food production spread out from the Middle East through trade, diffusion of domesticated species, and actual migration of farmers, to northern Africa, Europe, India, and Pakistan. However, archeological evidence suggests that
   a. in southern Egypt, cattle may have been domesticated locally rather than imported from the Fertile Crescent.
   b. in Oaxaca, llama may have been domesticated locally rather than imported from the Fertile Crescent.
   c. in certain regions of Pakistan sheep may have been domesticated independently.
   d. in southern France barley may have been domesticated locally rather than imported from the Fertile Crescent.
   e. in northern India wheat may have been domesticated earlier than in the Fertile Crescent.

8. The findings of Nabta Playa, located in the eastern Sahara and southern Egypt,
   a. represent an elaborate and previously unsuspected ceremonialism, as well as social complexity during the African Neolithic.
   b. suggest that it was a ceremonial site where the economy was fully Neolithic by 10,000 B.P.
   c. provide evidence for the "African sheep complex."
   d. suggest it was entirely isolated from Middle Eastern influence until 5,000 B.P.
   e. represent a case of sheep and goat domestication unlike the one that occurred in the Middle East.

9. Which of the following statements about life in the Valley of Oaxaca prior to cultivation is *not* true?
   a. People ate maguey, cactus, tree pods, deer, and rabbit.
   b. The populations shifted seasonally between bands and microbands.
   c. People lived in sedentary villages.
   d. The people periodically harvested the wild grass, teosinte.
   e. The inhabitants were foragers.

10. Which of the following is correct about the food-producing traditions of Mesopotamia and Mesoamerica?
   a. Food production occurred as a gradual process in Mesoamerica but was revolutionary in Mesopotamia.
   b. In Mesoamerica, goats, sheep, and pigs were domesticated; while in Mesopotamia, only dogs were domesticated.
   c. Food production emerged in Mesoamerica thousands of years prior to Mesopotamia.
   d. Maize was the staple grain in Mesopotamia, while the primary grain in Mesoamerica was wheat.
   e. Large domesticated animals played an important role Mesopotamia, but were absent from Mesoamerica.

FILL IN THE BLANK

1. _Neolithic_ refers to the first cultural period in a given region in which the first signs of domestication are present.

2. A _vertical economy_ is a system that exploits environmental zones that contrast with one another in altitude, rainfall, overall climate, and vegetation.

3. The practice of using cattle for their milk and blood rather than killing them for their meat (except on ceremonial occasions) is called _African cattle complex_

4. In contrast to the sequence of events in Mesopotamia, food production _led_ to the early village farming community (around 3500 B.P.) in _Mesoamerica_

5. Recent evidence has forced the revision of old assumptions in archaeology, most prominently the idea that New World farming originated in upland areas, such as the highlands of Mexico and Peru. Researchers now suggest that farming in the tropical lowlands of Central and South America began around _10,000_ years ago, about the same time as food production in _The Middle East_

CRITICAL THINKING

1. What is revolutionary about what Kent Flannery (1969) called the "broad-spectrum revolution"? What other more recent events in history do you consider revolutionary? Why?

2. Why is the lack of animal domestication in Mesoamerica considered a key factor in world history?

3. Previously anthropologists had believed that Old World (Middle Eastern) farming predated the earliest cultivation in the Americas by three or four millennia. How have new dating techniques pushed back the origin or domestication in the New World?

4. In this chapter, what are some examples of the role geography plays in key events in human history? Geography also affects how we come to know about the past. How so?

5. Was the origin of food production good or bad. Why?

Bellwood, P. S.
2005   *The First Farmers: Origins of Agricultural Societies.* Malden, MA: Blackwell. Origins and spread of agriculture in various world areas.

Diamond, J. M.
2005   *Guns, Germs, and Steel: The Fates of Human Societies.* New York: W. W. Norton. Disease, tools, and environmental forces and effects throughout human history.

Gamble, C.
2008   *Archaeology, the Basics,* 2nd ed. New York: Routledge. The title says it all.

Price, T. D., and G. M. Feinman
2010   *Images of the Past,* 6th ed. Boston: McGraw-Hill. Introduction to prehistory, including the origin of food production.

Renfrew, C., and P. Bahn
2007   *Archaeology: Theories, Methods, and Practice.* New York: Thames and Hudson. Basic text.

Wenke, R. J., and D. I. Olszewski
2007   *Patterns in Prehistory: Humankind's First Three Million Years,* 5th ed. New York: Oxford University Press. Rise of food production and the state throughout the world; thorough, useful text.

Suggested
Additional
Readings

Go to our Online Learning Center website at **www.mhhe.com/kottak** for Internet exercises directly related to the content of this chapter.

Internet
Exercises

When, where, and
why did early states
originate, and what
were their key
attributes?

How do
archaeologists
distinguish between
chiefdoms and
states?

What similarities
and differences
marked the origin of
early states in the
Old World and the
New World?

Overview of terraced royal
Inca ruins at Machu Picchu,
Peru. The elites of ancient
states used involuntary mass
labor to move stone for
enduring monuments.

The First Cities and States

understanding OURSELVES

You're not the boss of me." Have you ever heard or uttered those words? Who might say them to whom? Certainly you would not be likely to say this to a real employer, or to a police officer who just pulled you over, or to someone judging you in a court of law. We resent it when our siblings, cousins, or friends tell us what to do. But we learn to call judges "Your Honor," police officers "Officer," "Detective," "Lieutenant," "Captain," or "Chief," and employers Ms. or Mr. (as in "Mr. Trump"). Such titles (honorifics) mark differences in status and authority. Generally, we learn to respect and obey such people ("the authorities"). That is, we follow their orders or instructions, as people in the military routinely do with their superiors.

Marked contrasts in status, power, wealth, and privilege distinguish cities and states from the societies that came before them. Everyone reading this book lives in a state-organized society. Our lives differ dramatically from those of our Paleolithic ancestors, or those of more recent foragers. The state has a lot to do with these differences. The demand for labor (human, animal, etc.) increased in Neolithic economies compared with Paleolithic times. This trend continued in states, whose economies and political systems place even greater demands on ordinary people.

Perhaps you've seen a museum display depicting an early state society (e.g., Egypt, Mesopotamia, Maya). Such exhibits tend to highlight the artistic, architectural, literary, and scientific achievements of those civilizations. Ancient Sumerians (in Mesopotamia), Egyptians, Mexicans, and Peruvians had their artists, architects, mathematicians, astronomers, priests, and rulers—just as we do. However (but depicted more rarely), their ordinary citizens had to sweat in the fields to grow food for landlords, specialists, and elites. Unlike hunter-gatherers, residents of states must deal with bosses, despots, and commanders. The elites of ancient states could summon involuntary labor to build temples and pyramids, and to move stone for enduring monuments. In all states, people must pay taxes; in many states, citizens are drafted for work or war. Ordinary people no longer set their own priorities.

How do modern state-organized societies mirror those of the past? Ordinary people no longer may be drafted for work or war, but we do have to work to pay the taxes that pay for wars and public works. Our society is still stratified. Perks still go with wealth, fame, and power. Most of us still work much harder (usually for bosses) than foragers ever did. It's a myth that leisure time has increased with civilization. For a few, there is leisure and privilege; for most, there is work and obligation. And that's not because of human nature; it's because of the state.

THE ORIGIN OF THE STATE

As food-producing economies spread and became more productive, chiefdoms, and eventually states, developed in many parts of the world. A **state** is a form of social and political organization that has a formal, central government and a division of society into classes. The first states developed in Mesopotamia by 5500 B.P. and in Mesoamerica some 3,000 years later.

Chiefdoms were precursors to states, with privileged and effective leaders—chiefs—but lacking the sharp class divisions that characterize states. By 7000 B.P. in the Middle East and 3200 B.P. in Mesoamerica, there is evidence for what archaeologists call the elite level, indicating a chiefdom or a state.

How and why did chiefdoms and states originate? Compared with foraging, food production could support larger and denser populations. Also, the complexity of the division of social and economic labor tended to grow as food production spread and intensified. Systems of political authority and control typically develop to handle regulatory problems encountered as the population grows and/or the economy increases in scale and diversity. Competition, including warfare, among chiefdoms for territory and resources also can stimulate state formation. Anthropologists have identified the causes of state formation and reconstructed the rise of several states. A systemic perspective recognizes that multiple factors always contribute to state formation, with the effects of one magnifying those of the others. Although some contributing factors have appeared again and again, no single one is always present. In other words, state formation has generalized rather than universal causes.

Furthermore, because state formation may take centuries, people experiencing the process at any time rarely perceive the significance of the long-term changes. Later generations find themselves dependent on government institutions that took generations to develop.

Hydraulic Systems

One suggested cause of state formation is the need to regulate *hydraulic* (water-based) agricultural economies (Wittfogel 1957). In certain arid areas, such as ancient Egypt and Mesopotamia, states have emerged to manage systems of irrigation, drainage, and flood control. However, hydraulic agriculture is neither a sufficient nor a necessary condition for the rise of the state. That is, many societies with irrigation never experienced state formation, and states have developed without hydraulic systems.

But hydraulic agriculture does have certain implications for state formation. Water control increases production in arid lands. Because of its labor demands and its ability to feed more people, irrigated agriculture fuels population growth. This in turn leads to enlargement of the system. The expanding hydraulic system supports larger and denser concentrations of people. Interpersonal problems increase, and conflicts over access to water and irrigated land become more frequent. Political authorities may arise to regulate production as well as interpersonal and intergroup relations.

Large hydraulic works can sustain towns and cities and become essential to their subsistence. Regulators protect the economy by mobilizing crews to maintain and repair the hydraulic system. These life-and-death functions enhance the authority of state officials. Thus, growth in hydraulic systems is often (as in Mesopotamia, Egypt, and the Valley of Mexico), but not always, associated with state formation.

Long-Distance Trade Routes

Another theory is that states arise at strategic locations in regional trade networks. These sites include points of supply or exchange, such as crossroads of caravan routes, and places (e.g., mountain passes and river narrows) situated so as to threaten or halt trade between centers. Here again, however, the cause is generalized but neither necessary nor sufficient. Long-distance trade has been important in the evolution of many states, including those in Mesopotamia and Mesoamerica. Such exchange does eventually develop in all states, but it can follow rather than precede state formation. Furthermore, long-distance trade also occurs in societies such as those of Papua New Guinea, where no states developed.

Population, War, and Circumscription

Robert Carneiro (1970) put forth an influential theory that incorporates three factors working together instead of a single cause of state formation. (We call a theory involving multiple factors or variables a **multivariate** theory.) Wherever and whenever *environmental circumscription (or resource concentration), increasing population, and warfare exist,* suggested Carneiro, state formation will begin (Figure 12.1). Environmental circumscription may be physical or social. Physically circumscribed environments include small islands and, in arid areas, river plains, oases, and valleys with streams. Social circumscription exists when neighboring societies block expansion, emigration, or access to resources. When strategic resources are concentrated in limited areas—even when no obstacles to migration exist—the effects are similar to those of circumscription.

Coastal Peru, one of the world's most arid areas, illustrates the interaction of environmental circumscription, warfare, and population increase. The earliest cultivation there was limited to valleys with springs. Each valley was circumscribed by the Andes Mountains to the east, the Pacific Ocean to the west, and desert regions to the north and south. The advent of food production triggered a population increase. In each valley, villages got bigger. Colonists split off from the old villages and founded new ones. With more villages and people, a scarcity of land developed.

state
Society with central government, administrative specialization, and social classes.

multivariate
Involving multiple factors, causes, or variables.

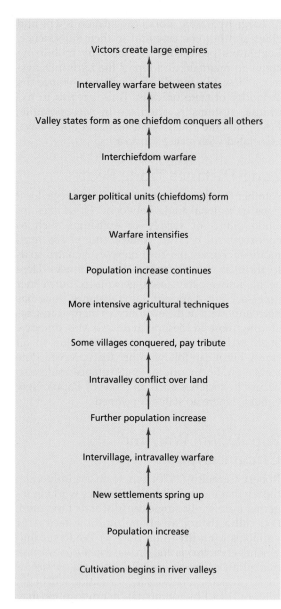

Victors create large empires

↑

Intervalley warfare between states

↑

Valley states form as one chiefdom conquers all others

↑

Interchiefdom warfare

↑

Larger political units (chiefdoms) form

↑

Warfare intensifies

↑

Population increase continues

↑

More intensive agricultural techniques

↑

Some villages conquered, pay tribute

↑

Intravalley conflict over land

↑

Further population increase

↑

Intervillage, intravalley warfare

↑

New settlements spring up

↑

Population increase

↑

Cultivation begins in river valleys

FIGURE 12.1 Carneiro's Multivariate Approach to the Origin of the State as Applied to Coastal Peru.

In this very arid area, food production developed in narrow river valleys where water for cultivation was available (resource concentration). With cultivation, the population increased. Population pressure on land led to warfare, and some villages conquered others. Physical circumscription meant that the losers had no way to escape. The process accelerated as the population grew and as warfare and cultivation intensified. Chiefdoms, states, and empires eventually developed.

empire
Mature state that is large, multiethnic, milita-ristic, and expansive.

Rivalries and raiding developed between villages in the same valley.

Population pressure and land shortages were developing in all the valleys. Because the valleys were circumscribed, when one village conquered another, the losers had to submit to the winners—they had nowhere else to go. Conquered villagers could keep their land only if they agreed to pay tribute to their conquerors. To do this, they had to intensify production, using new techniques to produce more food. By working harder, they managed to pay tribute while meeting their own subsistence needs. Villagers brought new areas under cultivation by means of irrigation and terracing.

Those early inhabitants of the Andes didn't work harder because they chose to do so. They were *forced* to pay tribute, accept political domination, and intensify production by factors beyond their control. Once established, all these trends accelerated. Population grew, warfare in-tensified, and villages eventually were united in chiefdoms. The first states developed when one chiefdom in a valley conquered the others (Carneiro 1990). Eventually, different valleys began to fight. The winners brought the losers into growing states and **empires**—mature, territorially larger, and expansive systems—which eventually expanded from the coast to the highlands. By the 16th century, from their capital, Cuzco, in the high Andes, the Inca ruled one of the major empires in the tropics.

Carneiro's theory is very useful, but again, the association between population density and state organization is generalized rather than universal. States do tend to have large and dense populations (Stevenson 1968). However, population increase and warfare within a circumscribed environment did not trigger state formation in highland Papua New Guinea. Certain valleys there are socially or physically circumscribed and have population densities similar to those of many states. Warfare also was present, but no states emerged. Again, we are dealing with an important theory that explains many but not all cases of state formation.

Whatever their deficiencies may be, all these theories properly look to environmental, demographic, economic, and other down-to-earth factors in particular areas to explain the origin of early states and civilizations. Some theories for the origin of the state are not nearly as plausible. This chapter's "Appreciating Anthropology" casts doubts on certain pseudo-archaeological theories about the emergence of civilizations, especially those in the Americas.

Early states arose in different places, and for many reasons. In each case, interacting causes (often comparable ones) magnified each other's effects. To explain any instance of state formation, we must search for the specific changes in access to resources and in regulatory problems that fostered stratification and state machinery. We also must remember that chiefdoms and states don't inevitably arise from food production.

Anthropologists know of, and have studied, many societies that maintained Neolithic economies without ever developing chiefdoms or states. Similarly, there are chiefdoms that never developed into states, just as there are foragers who never adopted food production, even when they knew about it. Recall from the last chapter those early food producers in what is now the eastern United States who had to keep hunting and gathering for the bulk of their subsistence because the foods they had domesticated (e.g., sunflower, marsh elder) could not supply a complete diet.

ATTRIBUTES OF STATES

Certain attributes distinguished states from earlier forms of society:

1. A state controls a specific regional territory, such as the Nile Valley or the Valley of Mexico. The regional expanse of a state contrasts with the much smaller territories controlled by kin groups and villages in prestate societies. Early states were expansionist; they arose from competition among chiefdoms, as the most powerful chiefdom conquered others, extended its rule over a larger territory, and managed to hold on to, and rule, the land and people acquired through conquest.

2. Early states had productive farming economies, supporting dense populations, often in cities. The agricultural economies of early states usually involved some form of water control or irrigation.

3. Early states used tribute and taxation to accumulate, at a central place, resources needed to support hundreds, or thousands, of specialists. These states had rulers, a military, and control over human labor.

4. States are stratified into social classes. In the first states, the non-food-producing population consisted of a tiny elite, plus artisans, officials, priests, and other specialists. Most people were commoners. Slaves and prisoners constituted the lowest rung of the social ladder. Rulers stayed in power by combining personal ability, religious authority, economic control, and force.

5. Early states had imposing public buildings and monumental architecture, including temples, palaces, and storehouses.

6. Early states developed some form of record-keeping system, usually a written script (Fagan 1996).

Early states had hereditary rulers and a military, with the rulers often playing a military role. Rulers stayed in power by combining personal ability, religious authority, economic control, and the privileged use of force. Shown here is a detail from the painted casket of Egypt's Tutankhamun, the famous "King Tut," who ruled between 1347 and 1337 B.C.E.

ANTHROPOLOGY

Pseudo-Archaeology

The study of prehistory has spawned popular-culture creations, including movies, TV programs, and books. In these fictional works, the anthropologists (and the natives as well) usually don't bear much resemblance to their real-life counterparts. Unlike Indiana Jones, normal and reputable archaeologists don't have nonstop adventures—fighting Nazis, lashing whips, or rescuing antiquities. The archaeologist's profession isn't a matter of raiding lost arks or of going on crusades but of reconstructing lifeways through the analysis of material remains, in order to understand culture and human behavior.

Much of the popular nonfiction dealing with prehistory is also suspect. Through books and the mass media, we have been exposed to the ideas of popular writers such as Thor Heyerdahl and Erich von Daniken. Heyerdahl, a well-known diffusionist, believed that developments in one world area were usually based on ideas borrowed from another. Von Daniken carried diffusionism one step further, proposing that major human achievements had been borrowed from beings from space who visited us at various periods of our past. Heyerdahl and

von Daniken seemed to share (with some science fiction writers) a certain contempt for human inventiveness and originality. They took the position that major changes in ancient human lifestyles were the results of outside instruction or interference rather than the achievements of the natives of the places where the changes took place.

In *The Ra Expeditions* (Heyerdahl 1971), for example, world traveler and adventurer Heyerdahl argued that his voyage in a papyrus boat from the Mediterranean to the Caribbean demonstrated that ancient Egyptians could have navigated to the New World. (The boat was modeled on an ancient Egyptian vessel, but Heyerdahl and his crew took along such modern conveniences as a radio and canned goods.) Heyerdahl maintained that given the possibility of ancient transatlantic voyages, Old World people could have influenced the emergence of civilization in the Americas.

What is the scientific evaluation of Heyerdahl's contention? Even if Old World ancients had reached the New World, they couldn't have done much to propel Native Americans toward state organization because the New World

wasn't yet ready for the state. When Egypt became a major power capable of sending scouts across the seas, around 5,000 years ago, Mexicans were broad-spectrum foragers. The gradual nature of the Mesoamerican transition from foraging to food production is clearly demonstrated by archaeological sequences in such sites as Oaxaca and the Valley of Mexico. Had foreign inputs been important, they would have shown up in the material remains that constitute the archaeological record.

Beginning some 2,000 years ago, states comparable to those of Mesopotamia and Egypt began to rise and fall in the Mexican highlands. This occurred more than 1,000 years after the height of ancient Egyptian influence, between 3600 and 3400 B.P. Had Egypt or any other ancient Old World state contributed to the rise or the fall of Mesoamerican civilization, we would expect this influence to have been exerted during Egypt's heyday as an ancient power—not 1,500 years later.

There is abundant archaeological evidence for the gradual, evolutionary emergence of food production and the state in the Middle East, in Mesoamerica, and in Peru. This evidence effectively counters the diffusionist theories about how and why human achievements, including farming and the state, began. Popular theories to the contrary, changes, advances, and setbacks in ancient American social life

STATE FORMATION IN THE MIDDLE EAST

In the last chapter we saw that food production arose in the ancient Middle East around 10,000 B.P. In the ensuing process of change, the center of population growth shifted from the zone where wheat and barley grew wild (Hilly Flanks) to adjacent areas (piedmont steppe) where those grains were first domesticated. By 6000 B.P., population was increasing most rapidly in the alluvial plain of southern Mesopotamia. (**Mesopotamia** refers to the area between the Tigris and Euphrates rivers in what is now southern Iraq and southwestern Iran.) This growing population supported

Mesopotamia
Area where earliest states developed, between Tigris and Euphrates rivers.

itself through irrigation and intensive river valley agriculture. By 5500 B.P. towns had grown into cities (Gates 2003). The earliest city-states were Sumer (southern Iraq) and Elam (southwestern Iran), with their capitals at Uruk (Warka) and Susa, respectively.

Urban Life

The first towns arose around 10,000 years ago in the Middle East. Over the generations houses of mud brick were built and rebuilt in the same place. Substantial tells or mounds arose from the debris of a succession of such houses. The Middle East and Asia have hundreds or thousands of were the products of the ideas and activities of the Native Americans themselves.

There is simply no valid evidence for Old World interference before the European Age of Discovery, which began late in the 15th century. Francisco Pizzaro conquered Peru's Inca state in 1532, 11 years after its Meso-american counterpart, Tenochtitlán, the Aztec capital, fell to Spanish conquistadors in 1521. (We do have abundant archaeological, as well as written, evidence for this recent, histori-cally known contact between Europeans and Native Americans.)

The archaeological record also casts doubt on contentions that the advances of earthlings came with extraterrestrial help, as Erich von Daniken argued in his book *Chariots of the Gods* (1971), and as Discovery-type TV some-times suggests. Abundant, well-analyzed ar-chaeological data from the Middle East, Mesoamerica, and Peru tell a clear story. Plant and animal domestication, the state, and city life were not brilliant discoveries, inventions, or secrets that humans needed to borrow from extraterrestrials. They were long-term, gradual processes, developments with down-to-earth causes and effects. They required thousands of years of orderly change, not some chance meeting in the high Andes between an ancient Inca chief and a beneficent Johnny Appleseed from Aldebaran.

How much does Indiana Jones tell us about real archaeologists? Shown here is a scene from *Indiana Jones and the Kingdom of the Crystal Skull*, which opened May 22, 2008, 27 years after the opening of *Raiders of the Lost Ark*, the first Indiana Jones movie.

This is not to deny, by the way, that intelli-gent life and civilizations at a variety of techno-logical levels—some more, some less advanced than Earth's—may exist throughout the galaxy or even that extraterrestrials may have occa-sionally ventured into this relatively isolated outer spiral arm of the Milky Way galaxy and even visited Earth itself. However, even if extra-terrestrials have been on Earth, archaeological evidence suggests that their starship com-manders observed a prime directive of nonin-terference in the affairs of less-advanced planets. There is no scientifically valid evidence for the rapid kind of change that sustained ex-traterrestrial intervention would have pro-duced. What would constitute such evidence?

such mounds, only a few of which have been ex-cavated. These sites have yielded remains of an-cient community life, including streets, buildings, terraces, courtyards, wells, and other artifacts.

The earliest known town was Jericho, located in what is now Israel, below sea level at a well-watered oasis a few miles northwest of the Dead Sea (Figure 12.2). From the lowest (oldest) level, we know that around 11,000 years ago, Jericho was first settled by Natufian foragers. Occupation continued thereafter, through and beyond biblical times, when "Joshua fit the battle of Jericho, and the walls came tumbling down" (Laughlin 2006).

During the phase just after the Natufians, the earliest known town appeared. It was an un-planned, densely populated settlement with round houses and some 2,000 people. At this time, well before the invention of pottery, Jericho was sur-rounded by a sturdy wall with a massive tower. The wall may have been built initially as a flood barrier rather than for defense. Around 9000 B.P. Jericho was destroyed, to be rebuilt later. The new occupants lived in square houses with finished plaster floors. They buried their dead beneath their homes, a pattern seen at other sites, such as Çatal Hüyük in Turkey (see on page 262). Pottery reached Jericho around 8000 B.P. (Gowlett 1993).

Long-distance trade, especially of obsidian, a volcanic glass used to make tools and ornaments, became important in the Middle East between

FIGURE 12.2 Sites in Middle Eastern State Formation.

9500 and 7000 B.P. One town that prospered from this trade was Çatal Hüyük in Anatolia, Turkey (DeMarco 1997). A grassy mound 65 feet high holds the remains of this 9,000-year-old town, probably the largest settlement of the Neolithic age. Çatal Hüyük was located on a river, which deposited rich soil for crops, created a lush environment for animals, and was harnessed for irrigation by 7000 B.P. Over the mound's 32 acres (12.9 hectares), up to 10,000 people once lived in crowded mud-brick houses packed so tight that residents entered from their roofs.

Shielded by a defensive wall, Çatal Hüyük flourished between 8000 and 7000 B.P. Its individual mud-brick dwellings, rarely larger than a suburban American bedroom, had separate areas reserved for ritual and secular uses. In a given house, the ritual images (wall paintings) were placed along the walls that faced north, east, or west, but never south. That area was reserved for cooking and other domestic tasks.

The ritual spaces were decorated with wall paintings, sculpted ox heads, bull horns, and relief models of bulls and rams. The paintings showed bulls surrounded by stick figures running, dancing, and sometimes throwing stones. Vultures attacked headless humans. One frieze had human hand prints painted below mounted bull horns. These images and their placement are reminiscent of Paleolithic cave art. The dwellings at Çatal Hüyük were entered through the roof, and people had to crawl through holes from room to room, somewhat like moving between chambers in a cave. The deeper down one went, the richer the art became. The town's spiritual life seems to have revolved around a preoccupation with animals, danger, and death, perhaps related to the site's recent hunter-gatherer past.

Two or three generations of a family were buried beneath their homes. In one dwelling, archaeologists found remains of 17 individuals, mostly children. After two or three generations of family burials, the dwelling was burned. The site was then covered with fine dirt, and a floor laid for a new dwelling.

Çatal Hüyük's residents, though living in a town, acted independently in family groups without any apparent control by a priestly or political elite. The town never became a full-fledged city with centralized organization. Just as it lacked priests, Çatal Hüyük never had leaders who controlled or managed trade and production (Fagan 1996). Food was stored and processed not collectively but on a smaller, domestic scale (DeMarco 1997).

The Elite Level

The first pottery (ceramics) dates back a bit more than 8,000 years, when it first reached Jericho. Before that date, the Neolithic is called the prepottery Neolithic. By 7000 B.P., pottery had become widespread in the Middle East. Archaeologists consider pottery shape, finishing, decoration, and type of clay as features used for dating. The geographic distribution of a given pottery style may indicate trade or alliance spanning a large area at a particular time.

An early and widespread pottery style, the **Halafian,** was first found at Tell Halaf in the mountains of northern Syria. Halafian (7500–6500 B.P.) refers to a delicate ceramic style. It also describes the period during which the elite level and the first chiefdoms emerged. The low number of Halafian ceramics suggests they were luxury goods associated with a social hierarchy.

By 7000 B.P. chiefdoms had emerged in the Middle East. The Ubaid period (7000–6000 B.P.) is named for a southern Mesopotamian pottery type first discovered at a small site, Tell el-Ubaid, located near the major city of Ur in southern Iraq. Similar pottery has been discovered in the deep levels of the Mesopotamian cities of Ur, Uruk, and Eridu. Ubaid pottery is associated with advanced chiefdoms and perhaps the earliest states. It diffused rapidly over a large area, becoming more widespread than earlier ceramic styles such as the Halafian.

Social Ranking and Chiefdoms

It is easy for archaeologists to identify early states. Evidence for state organization includes monumental architecture, central storehouses, irrigation systems, and written records. In Mesoamerica, even chiefdoms are easy to detect archaeologically. Ancient Mexican chiefdoms left behind stone works, such as temple complexes and the huge carved Olmec heads (see page 272). Mesoamericans also had a penchant for marking their elites with durable ornaments and prestige goods, including those buried with chiefs and their families. Early Middle Eastern chiefs were less ostentatious in their use of material markers of prestige, making their chiefdoms somewhat harder to detect archaeologically (Flannery 1999).

On the basis of the kinds of status distinctions within society, the anthropologist Morton Fried (1960) divided societies into three types: egalitarian, ranked, and stratified. An **egalitarian society,**

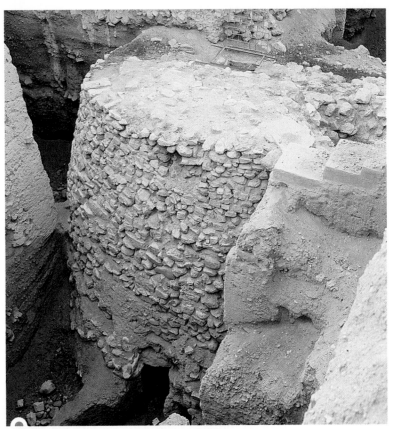

The world's earliest known town was Jericho, located in what is now Israel. Jericho was first settled by Natufian foragers around 11,000 B.P. This round tower dates back 8,000 years.

most typically found among foragers, lacks status distinctions except for those based on age, gender, and individual qualities, talents, and achievements. Thus, depending on the society, adult men, elder women, talented musicians, or ritual specialists might receive special respect for their activities or knowledge. In egalitarian societies, status distinctions are not usually inherited. The child of a respected person will not receive special recognition because of his or her parent but must earn such respect.

Ranked societies, in contrast, do have hereditary inequality. But they lack **stratification** (sharp social divisions—*strata*—based on unequal access to wealth and power) into noble and commoner classes. In ranked societies, individuals tend to be ranked in terms of their genealogical distance from the chief. Closer relatives of the chief have higher rank or social status than more distant ones do. But there is a continuum of status, with many individuals and kin groups ranked about equally, which can lead to competition for positions of leadership. Recap 12.1 lists key features and examples of egalitarian, ranked, and stratified societies.

Not all ranked societies are chiefdoms. Robert Carneiro (1991) has distinguished between two kinds of ranked societies, only the second of

Halafian
Early (7500–6500 B.P.) widespread Mesopotamian pottery style.

ranked society
Society with hereditary inequality but lacking social stratification.

stratification
Presence of social divisions—strata—with unequal wealth and power.

egalitarian society
Society with rudimentary status distinctions.

KIND OF STATUS DISTINCTION	NATURE OF STATUS	COMMON FORM OF SUBSISTENCE ECONOMY	COMMON FORMS OF SOCIAL ORGANIZATION	EXAMPLES
Egalitarian	Status differences are not inherited. All status is based on age, gender, and individual qualities, talents, and achievements.	Foraging	Bands and tribes	Inuit, Ju/'hoansi San, and Yanomami
Ranked	Status differences are inherited and distributed along a continuum from the highest-ranking member (chief) to the lowest without any breaks.	Horticulture, pastoralism, and some foraging groups	Chiefdoms and some tribes	Native American groups of the Pacific Northwest (for example, Salish and Kwakiutl), Natchez, Halaf and Ubaid period polities, Olmec
Stratified	Status differences are inherited and divided sharply between distinct noble and commoner classes.	Agriculture	States	Teotihuacán, Uruk period states, Inca, Shang dynasty, Rome, United States, Great Britain

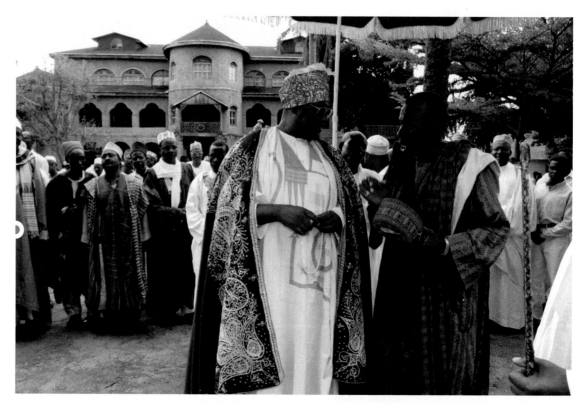

Unlike states such as Cameroon, whose King Njoya is shown here, egalitarian societies lack inherited wealth and status and succession to political office. How are inherited status distinctions marked in your society?

chiefdom
Ranked society with two- or three-level settlement hierarchy.

which is a chiefdom. In the first type, exemplified by some Indians of North America's Pacific Northwest, there were hereditary differences in rank among individuals, but villages were independent of one another and not ranked in relation to each other. Exemplifying the second type were the Cauca of Colombia and the Natchez of the eastern United States. These ranked societies had become **chiefdoms,** societies in which relations among villages as well as among individuals were unequal. The smaller villages had lost their autonomy and were under the authority of leaders who lived at larger villages. According to Kent Flannery (1999), *only those ranked societies with such loss of village autonomy should be called chiefdoms.* In chiefdoms, there is always inequality—differences in rank—among both individuals and communities.

In Mesopotamia, Mesoamerica, and Peru, chiefdoms were precursors to **primary states** (states that arose on their own, not through contact with other state societies—see Wright 1994). Primary states emerged from competition among chiefdoms, as one chiefdom managed to conquer its neighbors and to make them part of a larger political unit (Flannery 1995).

Archaeological evidence for chiefdoms in Mesoamerica dates back more than 3,000 years. Mesoamerican chiefdoms are easy to detect archaeologically because they were flamboyant in the way they marked their aristocracy. High-status families deformed the heads of their infants and buried them with special symbols and grave goods. In burials, prestige goods show a continuum from graves with many, to less, to no precious materials, such as jade and turquoise (Flannery 1999).

The first Middle Eastern states developed between 6000 and 5500 B.P. The first societies based on rank, including the first chiefdoms, emerged during the preceding 1,500 years. In the Middle East, the archaeological record of the period after 7300 B.P. reveals behavior typical of chiefdoms, including exotic goods used as markers of status, along with raiding and political instability. Early Middle Eastern chiefdoms included both the Halafian culture of northern Iraq and the Ubaid

This funerary chamber from Sipan, Peru (a Moche site), contains gold jewelry, pottery, and other artifacts. In chiefdoms and states, high-status families often bury their dead with distinctive symbols and grave goods.

culture of southern Iraq, which eventually spread north.

As in Mesoamerica, ancient Middle Eastern chiefdoms had cemeteries where chiefly relatives were buried with distinctive items: vessels, statuettes, necklaces, and high-quality ceramics. Such goods were buried with children too young to have earned prestige on their own, who happened to be born into elite families. In the ancient village of Tell es-Sawwan, infant graves show a continuum of richness from six statuettes, to three statuettes, to one statuette, to none. Such signs of slight gradations in social status are exactly what one expects in ranked societies (Flannery 1999).

Such burials convince Flannery (1999) that hereditary status differences were present in the Middle East by 7000 B.P. But had the leaders of large villages extended their authority to the smaller villages nearby? Is there evidence for the loss of village autonomy, converting simple ranked societies into chiefdoms? One clue that villages were linked in political units is the use of a common canal to irrigate several villages. This suggests a way of resolving disputes among farmers over access to water, for example, by appeal to a strong leader. By later Halafian times in northern Mesopotamia, there is evidence for such multivillage alliances (Flannery 1999). Another clue to the loss of village autonomy is the emergence of a two-tier settlement hierarchy, with small villages clustering around a large village, especially one with public buildings. There is evidence for this pattern in northern Mesopotamia during the Halafian (Watson 1983).

primary states
States arising through competition among chiefdoms.

Illustrating pictographic writing is this limestone tablet from the proto-urban period of lower Mesopotamia. This Sumerian script records proper names, including that of a landowner—symbolized by the hand—who commissioned the tablet.

anthropology **ATLAS**

Map 13 shows organized states and chiefdoms. The Inca in the Peruvian Andes and the Aztecs in the Valley of Mexico are among the earliest states shown in the New World.

Advanced Chiefdoms

In northeastern Syria, near the border with Iraq, archaeologists have been excavating an ancient settlement that once lay on a major trade route. This large site, Tell Hamoukar, dates back more than 5,500 years (Wilford 2000). Its remains suggest that advanced chiefdoms arose in northern areas of the Middle East independently of the better-known city-states of southern Mesopotamia, in southern Iraq (Wilford 2000).

The oldest layer yet uncovered at Tell Hamoukar contains traces of villages dating back 6,000 years. By 5700 B.P. the settlement was a prosperous town of 32 acres, enclosed by a defensive wall 10 feet (3 meters) high and 13 feet (3.9 meters) wide. The site had fine pottery and large ovens—evidence of food preparation on an institutional scale. The site has yielded pieces of large cooking pots, animal bones, and traces of wheat, barley, and oats for baking and brewing. The archaeologist McGuire Gibson, one of the excavators, believes that food preparation on this scale is evidence of a ranked society in which elites were organizing people and resources (Wilford 2000). Most likely they were hosting and entertaining in a chiefly manner.

Also providing evidence for social ranking are the seals used to mark containers of food and other goods. Some of the seals are small, with only simple incisions or cross-hatching. Others are larger and more elaborate, presumably for higher officials to stamp more valuable goods. Gibson suspects the larger seals with figurative scenes were held by the few people who had greater authority. The smaller, simply incised seals were used by many more people with less authority (Wilford 2000).

cuneiform
Early Mesopotamian wedge-shaped writing, using stylus on clay.

living anthropology **VIDEOS**

The First States, www.mhhe.com/kottak

The clip offers brief views of Mesopotamia and Egypt, plus commentary by a Canadian professor. The clip poses the contrast between the "city-states" of Mesopotamia and the Egyptian "empire," implying a difference in the scale of political organization, with the Egyptian state controlling a much larger territory than did the rulers of Mesopotamia. What was the key factor in Egyptian territorial expansion? Besides the pharaoh, ancient Egypt had a vizier, who administered state officials and oversaw the royal treasury. What kind of role did rulers and temple officials play, according to the clip and the text, in the Mesopotamian city-states? Based on the clip and the text, what kind of association existed between religion and political control in the two areas?

The Rise of the State

In southern Mesopotamia at this time (5700 B.P.), an expanding population and increased food production from irrigation were changing the social landscape even more drastically than in the north. Irrigation had allowed Ubaid communities to spread along the Euphrates River. Travel and trade were expanding, with water serving as the highway system. Such raw materials as hardwood and stone, which southern Mesopotamia lacked, were imported via river routes. Population density increased as new settlements appeared. Social and economic networks now linked communities on the rivers in the south and in the foothills to the north. Settlements spread north into what is now Syria. Social differentials also increased. Priests and political leaders joined expert potters and other specialists. These non-food producers were supported by the larger population of farmers and herders (Gilmore-Lehne 2000).

Economies were being managed by central leadership. Agricultural villages had grown into cities, some of which were ruled by local kings. The Uruk period (6000–5200 B.P.), which succeeded the Ubaid period, takes its name from a prominent southern city-state located more than 400 miles south of Tell Hamoukar (Recap 12.2). The Uruk period established Mesopotamia as "the cradle of civilization" (see Pollock 1999). Recap 12.2 highlights archaeological periods in the process of state formation in the ancient Middle East.

There is no evidence of Uruk influence at Tell Hamoukar until 5200 B.P., when some Uruk pottery showed up. When southern Mesopotamians expanded north, they found advanced chiefdoms, which were not yet states. The fact that writing originated in Sumer, in southern Mesopotamia, indicates a more advanced, state-organized society there. The first writing presumably developed to handle record keeping for a centralized economy.

Writing was initially used to keep accounts, reflecting the needs of trade. Rulers, nobles, priests, and merchants were the first to benefit from it. Writing had reached Egypt by 5200 B.P., probably from Mesopotamia. The earliest writing was pictographic, for example, with pictorial symbols of horses used to represent them.

Early Mesopotamian scribes used a stylus (writing implement) to scrawl symbols on raw clay. This writing left a wedge-shaped impression on the clay, called **cuneiform** writing, from the Latin word for wedge. Both the Sumerian (southern Mesopotamia) and Akkadian (northern Mesopotamia) languages were written in cuneiform (Gowlett 1993).

Writing and temples played key roles in the Mesopotamian economy. For the historic period after 5600 B.P., when writing was invented, there are temple records of economic activities. States can exist without writing, but literacy facilitates

DATES	PERIOD	AGE
3000–2539 B.P.	Neo-Babylonian	Iron Age
3600–3000 B.P.	Kassite	
4000–3600 B.P.	Old Babylonian	Bronze Age
4150–4000 B.P.	Third Dynasty of Ur	
4350–4150 B.P.	Akkadian	
4600–4350 B.P.	Early Dynastic III	
4750–4600 B.P.	Early Dynastic II	
5000–4750 B.P.	Early Dynastic I	
5200–5000 B.P.	Jemdet Nasr	
6000–5200 B.P.	Uruk	Chalcolithic (Copper/Stone)
7500–6000 B.P.	Ubaid (southern Mesopotamia)– Halaf (northern Mesopotamia)	
10,000–7000 B.P.		Neolithic

Early Mesopotamian scribes used a stylus to scrawl symbols on raw clay. This writing, called *cuneiform*, left a wedge-shaped impression on the clay. What languages were written in cuneiform?

the flow and storage of information. We know that Mesopotamian priests managed herding, farming, manufacture, and trade. Temple officials allotted fodder and pastureland for cattle and donkeys, which were used as plow and cart animals.

As the economy expanded, trade, manufacture, and grain storage were centrally managed. Temples collected and distributed meat, dairy products, crops, fish, clothing, tools, and trade items. Potters, metalworkers, weavers, sculptors, and other artisans perfected their crafts.

Prior to the invention of **metallurgy** (knowledge of the properties of metals, including their extraction and processing and the manufacture of metal tools), raw copper was shaped by hammering. If copper is hammered too long, it hardens and becomes brittle, with a risk of cracking. But once heated (annealed) in a fire, copper becomes malleable again. Such annealing of copper was an early form of metallurgy. A vital step for metallurgy was the discovery of **smelting**, the high-temperature process by which pure metal is produced from an ore. Ores, including copper ore, have a much wider distribution than does native copper, which was initially traded as a luxury good because of its rarity (Gowlett 1993).

When and how smelting was discovered is unknown. But after 5000 B.P., metallurgy evolved rapidly. The Bronze Age began when alloys of arsenic and copper, or tin and copper (in both cases known as **bronze**), became common and greatly extended the use of metals. Bronze flows more easily than copper does when heated to a similar temperature, so bronze was more convenient for metal casting. Early molds were carved in stone, as shaped depressions to be filled with molten metal. A copper ax cast from such a mold has been found in northern Mesopotamia and predates 5000 B.P. Thereafter, other metals came into common use. By 4500 B.P., golden objects were found in royal burials at Ur.

Iron ore is distributed more widely than is copper ore. Iron, when smelted, can be used on its own; there is no need for tin or arsenic to make a

metallurgy Extraction and processing of metals to make tools.

smelting High-temperature extraction of metal from ore.

bronze Alloy of copper and arsenic or tin.

This ziggurat, or temple tower, at Ur, Iraq, dates back to 4100 B.P. (2100 B.C.E.). Temples and their officials played key roles in the Mesopotamian economy. Who handles such duties in our society?

fields. By 4600 B.P., Mesopotamia had a well-defined class structure, with complex stratification into nobles, commoners, and slaves.

OTHER EARLY STATES

In northwestern India and Pakistan, the Indus River Valley (or *Harappan*) state, with major cities at Harappa and Mohenjo-daro, takes its name from the river valley along which it extended. (Figure 12.3 maps the four great early river valley states of the Old World: Mesopotamia, Egypt, India/Pakistan, and northern China.) Trade and the spread of writing from Mesopotamia may have played a role in the emergence of the Harappan state around 4600 B.P. Located in Pakistan's Punjab Province, the ruins of Harappa were the first to be identified as part of the Indus River Valley civilization. At its peak, the Indus River Valley state incorporated 1,000 cities, towns, and villages, spanning 280,000 square miles (725,000 square kilometers). This state flourished between 4600 and 3900 B.P. It displayed such features of state organization as urban planning, social stratification, and an early writing system, which remains undeciphered. The Harappans maintained a uniform system of weights, and their cites had carefully planned residential areas with wastewater systems. An array of products from sophisticated craft industries included ceramic vessels made on potter's wheels (Meadow and Kenoyer 2000).

The Indus River Valley state collapsed, apparently through warfare, around 3900 B.P. Its cities became largely depopulated. Skeletons of massacre victims have been found in the streets of Mohenjo-daro. Harappa continued to be occupied, but on a much smaller scale than previously (Meadow and Kenoyer 2000). (For more on the ongoing Harappa Archaeological Research Project, visit http://www.harappa.com.)

The first Chinese state, dating to 3750 B.P., was that of the Shang dynasty. It arose in the Huang He (Yellow) River area of northern China, where wheat, rather than rice, was the dietary staple. This state was characterized by urbanism, palatial (as well as domestic) architecture, human sacrifice, and a sharp division between social classes. Burials of the aristocracy were marked by ornaments of stone, including jade. The Shang had bronze metallurgy and an elaborate writing system. In warfare they used chariots and took prisoners (Gowlett 1993).

Like Mesopotamia and China, many early civilizations came to rely on metallurgy. At Nok Nok Tha in northern Thailand, metalworking goes back 6,000 years. In Peru's Andes, whose astonishing system of suspension bridges is described in this chapter's "Appreciating Diversity," metalworking appeared around 4000 B.P. Ancient

metal alloy (bronze). The Iron Age began once high-temperature iron smelting was mastered. In the Old World after 3200 B.P., iron spread rapidly. Formerly valued as highly as gold, iron crashed in value when it became plentiful (Gowlett 1993).

The Mesopotamian economy, based on craft production, trade, and intensive agriculture, spurred population growth and an increase in urbanism. Sumerian cities were protected by a fortress wall and surrounded by a farming area. By 4800 B.P., Uruk, the largest early Mesopotamian city, had a population of 50,000. As irrigation and the population expanded, communities fought over water. People sought protection in the fortified cities (Adams 1981), which defended themselves when neighbors or invaders threatened.

By 4600 B.P., secular authority had replaced temple rule. The office of military coordinator developed into kingship. This change shows up architecturally in palaces and royal tombs. The palace raised armies and supplied them with armor, chariots, and metal armaments. At Ur's royal cemetery, by 4600 B.P. monarchs were being buried with soldiers, charioteers, and ladies in waiting. These subordinates were killed at the time of a royal burial to accompany the monarch to the afterworld.

Agricultural intensification made it possible for the number of people supported by a given area to increase. Population pressure on irrigated fields helped create a stratified society. Land became scarce private property that was bought and sold. Some people amassed large estates, and their wealth set them off from ordinary farmers. These landlords joined the urban elite, while sharecroppers and serfs toiled in the

anthropology **ATLAS**

Maps 9 and 13 locate the archaic states that developed in the Middle East, Asia, Africa, Europe, and the Americas.

FIGURE 12.3 The Four Great Early River Valley States of the Old World.

By approximately 4000 B.P. urban life had been established along the Tigris and Euphrates rivers in Mesopotamia, the Nile River in Egypt, the Indus and Ganges rivers in India/Pakistan, and the Yellow River in China.

SOURCE: Based on Map 1-1 from Craig, Albert M.; Graham, William A.; Kagan, Donald; Ozment, Steven; and Turner, Frank M. *Heritage of World Civilizations. Vol. I to 1650*, 4th ed. © 1997. Reproduced in print and electronic formats by permission of Pearson Education, Inc., Upper Saddle River, New Jersey.

Andeans were skilled not only in using natural fibers to make bridges but also in working with bronze, copper, and gold. They are well known, too, for their techniques of pottery manufacture. Their arts, crafts, and agricultural knowledge compared well with those of Mesoamerica at its height, to which we turn after a discussion of African states. Note that both Mesoamerican and Andean state formation were truncated by Spanish conquest. The Aztecs of Mexico were conquered in 1519 C.E., and the Inca of Peru in 1532 C.E.

African States

Egypt, a major ancient civilization, developed in northern Africa, as one of the world's first states (Morkot 2005). Egyptian influence extended southward along the Nile into what is now Sudan. Sub-Saharan Africa witnessed the emergence of several states (Hooker 1996), only a few of which can be described here.

As in the other world areas just discussed, metallurgy (especially iron and gold) played a role in the eventual rise of African states (Connah 2004). About 2,000 years ago, iron smelting began to diffuse rapidly throughout the continent. That spread was aided by the migrations of Bantu speakers. (Bantu is Africa's largest linguistic family.) The Bantu migrations, launched from north-central Africa around 2100 B.P., continued for more than a thousand years. Bantu speakers migrated south into the rain forests of the Congo River and east into the African highlands. Along with their language and iron-smelting techniques, they also spread farming, particularly of high-yielding crops such as yams, bananas, and plantains.

One crowning achievement of the Bantu migrations was the Mwenemutapa empire. The southeast-moving ancestors of the

This bronze vessel was commissioned during China's Shang dynasty. The small elephant on top forms the handle of the lid. Wine was poured through the spout formed by the big elephant's trunk. Three notable features of the Shang dynasty were bronze, writing, and social stratification.

appreciating DIVERSITY

The Hanging Roadways of Ancient Peru

Cultures differ widely in their engineering skills. Chapter 6 considered varied human biological adaptations to high altitudes, including the mountainous terrain of the Himalayas and the Andes. Here we focus on cultural rather than biological diversity—how the Incas devised a system of hanging bridges that enabled them to navigate their Andean habitat—and thus maintain their empire.

Conquistadors from Spain came, they saw and they were astonished. They had never seen anything in Europe like the bridges of Peru. Chroniclers wrote that the Spanish soldiers stood in awe and fear before the spans of braided fiber cables suspended across deep gorges in the Andes, narrow walkways sagging and swaying and looking so frail. Yet the suspension bridges were familiar and vital links in the vast empire of the Inca, as they had been to Andean cultures for hundreds of years before the arrival of the Spanish in 1532. The people had not developed the stone arch or wheeled vehicles, but they were accomplished in the use of natural fibers for textiles, boats, sling weapons—even keeping inventories by a prewriting system of knots.

So bridges made of fiber ropes, some as thick as a man's torso, were the technological solution to the problem of road building in rugged terrain. By some estimates, at least 200 such suspension bridges spanned river gorges in the 16th century. One of the last of these, over the Apurímac River, inspired Thornton Wilder's novel "The Bridge of San Luis Rey."

Although scholars have studied the Inca road system's importance in forging and controlling the pre-Columbian empire, John A. Ochsendorf of the Massachusetts Institute of Technology here said, "Historians and archaeologists have neglected the role of bridges."

Dr. Ochsendorf's research on Inca suspension bridges, begun while he was an undergraduate at Cornell University, illustrates an engineering university's approach to archaeology, combining materials science and experimentation with the traditional fieldwork of observing and dating artifacts. Other universities conduct research in archaeological materials, but it has long been a specialty at M.I.T.

Students here are introduced to the multidisciplinary investigation of ancient technologies as applied in transforming resources into cultural hallmarks from household pottery to grand pyramids. In a course called "materials in human experience," students are making a 60-foot-long fiber bridge in the Peruvian style. On Saturday, they plan to stretch the bridge across a dry basin between two campus buildings. . . .

In the case of the Peruvian bridges, the builders relied on a technology well suited to

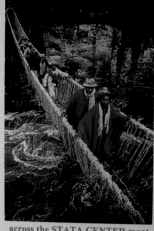

Build an INKA FIBER SUSPENSION BRIDGE

across the STATA CENTER moat
a class lab project in 3.094 [2-3-4 HASS]
Materials in Human Experience

3.094 is a follow-on to 3.091. Class size is limited to 36. First year students are given preference.

This poster (May 2007) celebrates the bridge-making accomplishments of ancient Peruvians and archaeologists' attempts to replicate those skills in the classroom.

---

anthropology **ATLAS**

Map 13 shows states that developed in Africa, Asia, and the Americas. The kingdoms of Ghana, Mali, Songhay, Kanem-Bornu, and Great Zimbabwe (Monomatapa) arose in Africa.

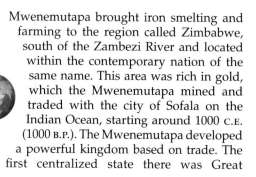

Mwenemutapa brought iron smelting and farming to the region called Zimbabwe, south of the Zambezi River and located within the contemporary nation of the same name. This area was rich in gold, which the Mwenemutapa mined and traded with the city of Sofala on the Indian Ocean, starting around 1000 C.E. (1000 B.P.). The Mwenemutapa developed a powerful kingdom based on trade. The first centralized state there was Great Zimbabwe (*zimbabwe* means "stone enclosure"— the capital was protected by huge stone walls), which arose around 1300 C.E. (700 B.P.). By 1500, Great Zimbabwe dominated the Zambezi Valley militarily and commercially as the seat of the Mwenemutapa empire.

Another African region where states arose, also abetted by trade, was the Sahel, the area just south of the Sahara in western Africa. Farming towns started appearing in the Sahel around 2600 B.P. One such town, Kumbi Saleh, eventually became the problem and their resources. The Spanish themselves demonstrated how appropriate the Peruvian technique was.

Dr. Ochsendorf, a specialist in early architecture and engineering, said the colonial government tried many times to erect European arch bridges across the canyons, and each attempt ended in fiasco until iron and steel were applied to bridge building. The Peruvians, knowing nothing of the arch or iron metallurgy, instead relied on what they knew best, fibers from cotton, grasses and saplings, and llama and alpaca wool.

The Inca suspension bridges achieved clear spans of at least 150 feet, probably much greater. This was a longer span than any European masonry bridges at the time. The longest Roman bridge in Spain had a maximum span between supports of 95 feet. And none of these European bridges had to stretch across deep canyons. . . .

In a recent research paper, Dr. Ochsendorf wrote: "The Inca were the only ancient American civilization to develop suspension bridges. Similar bridges existed in other mountainous regions of the world, most notably in the Himalayas and in ancient China, where iron chain suspension bridges existed in the third century B.C." The first of the modern versions was erected in Britain in the late 18th century, the beginning of the Industrial Revolution. The longest one today connects two islands in Japan, with a span of more than 6,000 feet from tower to supporting tower. These bridges are really "hanging roadways," Dr. Ochsendorf said, to provide a fairly level surface for wheeled traffic.

In his authoritative 1984 book, "The Inka Road System," John Hyslop, who was an official of the Institute of Andean Research and associated with the American Museum of Natural History, compiled descriptions of the Inca bridges recorded by early travelers.

Garcilasco de la Vega, in 1604, reported on the cable-making techniques. The fibers, he wrote, were braided into ropes of the length necessary for the bridge. Three of these ropes were woven together to make a larger rope, and three of them were again braided to make a still larger rope, and so on. The thick cables were pulled across the river with small ropes and attached to stone abutments on each side.

Three of the big cables served as the floor of the bridge, which often was at least four to five feet wide, and two others served as handrails. Pieces of wood were tied to the cable floor. Finally, the floor was strewn with branches to give firm footing for beasts of burden.

More branches and pieces of wood were strung to make walls along the entire length of the bridge. The side covering, one chronicler said, was such that "if a horse fell on all fours, it could not fall off the bridge."

Still, it took a while for the Spanish to adjust to the bridges and to coax their horses to cross them. The bridges trembled underfoot and swayed dangerously in stiff winds.

Ephraim G. Squier, a visitor to Peru from the United States in the 1870s, said of the Apurimac River bridge: "It is usual for the traveler to time his day's journey so as to reach the bridge in the morning, before the strong wind sets in; for, during the greater part of the day, it sweeps up the Canyon of the Apurimac with great force, and then the bridge sways like a gigantic hammock, and crossing is next to impossible."

Other travelers noted that in many cases, two suspension bridges stood side by side. Some said that one was for the lords and gentry, the other for commoners; or one for men, the other for women.

Recent scholars have suggested that it was more likely that one bridge served as a backup for the other, considering the need for frequent repairs of frayed and worn ropes.

The last existing Inca suspension bridge, at Huinchiri, near Cuzco, is virtually rebuilt each year. People from the villages on either side hold a three-day festival and gather stiff grasses for producing more than 50,000 feet of cord. Finally, the cord is braided into 150-foot replacement cables. . . .

the capital of the ancient kingdom of Ghana. West Africa was rich in gold, precious metals, ivory, and other resources, which after 750 C.E. (1250 B.P.) were traded (thanks to the camel) across the Sahara to North Africa, Egypt, and the Middle East. Cities in the Sahel served as southern terminal points for the trans-Saharan trade (e.g., of gold for salt). Several kingdoms developed in this area: Ghana, Mali, Songhay, and Kanem-Bornu, together known as the Sahelian kingdoms, of which Ghana was the first. By 1000 B.P. Ghana's economic vitality, based on the trans-Saharan trade, was supporting an empire formed through the conquest of local chiefdoms, from which tribute was extracted.

States also arose in the forested region of western Africa south of the Sahel. Between 1000 and 1500 C.E., local farming villages started consolidating into larger units, which eventually became centralized states. The largest and most enduring of these states was Benin, in what is now southern Nigeria. Benin, which thrived in the 15th

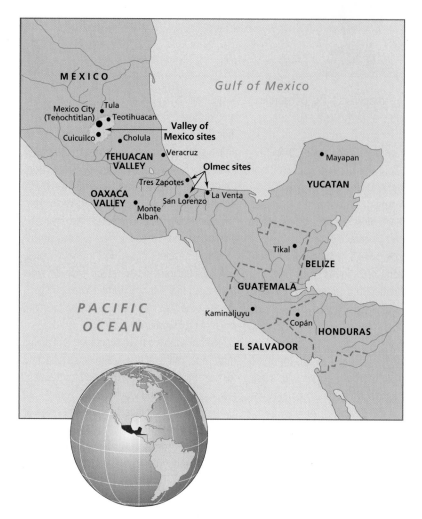

FIGURE 12.4 Major Sites in the Emergence of Food Production and the State in Mesoamerica.

SOURCE: From Clifford J. Jolly and Fred Plog, *Physical Anthropology and Archaeology*, 4th ed., p. 115. Copyright © 1986 by The McGraw-Hill Companies, Inc. Reprinted with permission.

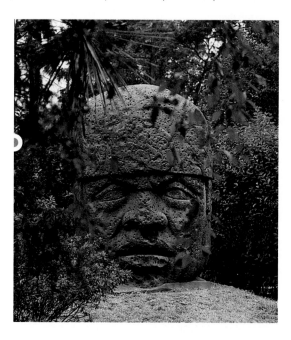

This colossal Olmec head, carved from basalt, is displayed at the La Venta Archaeology Museum in Tabasco state, Mexico, in a setting designed to recall its original site. What is the significance of such a massive artifact?

century C.E. (600–500 B.P.), is known for its artistic creativity, expressed in terra-cotta, ivory, and brass sculpture. Benin art became one of the most influential African art traditions.

STATE FORMATION IN MESOAMERICA

In the last chapter we examined the independent inventions of farming in the Middle East and Mesoamerica. The processes of state formation that took place in these areas were also comparable, beginning with ranked societies and chiefdoms, and ending with fully formed states and empires.

The first monumental buildings (temple complexes) in the Western Hemisphere were constructed by Mesoamerican chiefdoms in many areas, from the Valley of Mexico to Guatemala. These chiefdoms influenced one another as they traded materials, such as obsidian, shells, jade, and pottery. (Figure 12.4 maps major sites in the emergence of Mesoamerican food production, chiefdoms, and states.)

Early Chiefdoms and Elites

The Olmec built a series of ritual centers on Mexico's southern Gulf Coast between 3,200 and 2,500 years ago. Three of these centers, each from a different century, are known. Earthen mounds were grouped into plaza complexes, presumably for religious use. Such centers show that Olmec chiefs could marshal human labor to construct such mounds. The Olmec were also master sculptors; they carved massive stone heads, perhaps as images of their chiefs or their ancestors.

There is evidence, too, that trade routes linked the Olmec with other parts of Mesoamerica, such as the Oaxaca Valley in the southern highlands and the Valley of Mexico (see Figure 12.4). By 3000 B.P. a ruling elite had emerged in Oaxaca. The items traded at that time between Oaxaca and the Olmec were for elite consumption. High-status Oaxacans wore ornaments made of mussel shells from the coast. In return, the Olmec elite imported mirrors and jade made by Oaxacan artisans. Chiefdoms in Oaxaca developed canal and well irrigation, exported magnetite mirrors, and were precocious in their use of adobes (mud bricks), stucco, stone masonry, and architecture. Chiefdoms in the Olmec area farmed river levees, built mounds of earth, and carved colossal stone heads.

The Olmec are famous for their huge carved stone heads, but other early Mexican chiefdoms also had accomplished artists and builders, using adobes and lime plaster and constructing stone buildings, precisely oriented 8 degrees north of east.

The period between 3200 and 3000 B.P. was one of rapid social change in Mexico. All or almost all of Mesoamerica's chiefdoms were linked by trade and exchange. Many competing chiefly centers were concentrating labor power, intensifying agriculture, exchanging trade goods, and borrowing ideas, including art motifs and styles, from each other. Archaeologists now believe it was the *intensity of competitive interaction*—rather than the supremacy of any one chiefdom—that made social change so rapid. The social and political landscape of Mexico around 3000 B.P. was one in which 25 or so chiefly centers were (1) sufficiently separate and autonomous to adapt to local zones and conditions and (2) sufficiently interactive and competitive to borrow and incorporate new ideas and innovations as they arose in other regions (Flannery and Marcus 2000).

It used to be thought that a single chiefdom could become a state on its own. Archaeologists know now that state formation involves one chiefdom's incorporating several others into the emerging state it controls, and making changes in its own infrastructure as it acquires and holds on to new territories, followers, and goods. Warfare and attracting followers are two key elements in state formation. Recall that this chapter's "Appreciating Anthropology" on pp. 260–261 debunks popular pseudo-archaeological theories about the origin of Mesoamerican civilization.

Many chiefdoms have dense populations, intensive agriculture, and settlement hierarchies that include hamlets, villages, and perhaps towns. These factors pave the way for greater social and political complexity. Political leaders emerge, and military success (in raiding) often solidifies their position. Such figures attract lots of followers, who are loyal to their leader. Warfare enables leaders to incorporate new lands and people. Success in warfare leads to states' becoming even more densely occupied and in control of new lands. States, in contrast to chiefdoms, can acquire labor and land and hold on to them. States have armies, warfare, developed political hierarchies, law codes, and military force, which can be used in fact or as a threat.

Olmec and Oaxaca were just two among many flamboyant early Mexican chiefdoms that once thrived in the area from the Valley of Mexico to Guatemala. Oaxaca went on to develop a state a bit earlier than the Teotihuacán state in the Valley of Mexico. Oaxaca and other highland areas came to overshadow the Olmec area and the Mesoamerican lowlands in general. By 2500 B.P., Oaxaca's Zapotec people had developed a distinctive art style, perfected at their capital city of Monte Albán (see Blanton 1999; Marcus and Flannery 1996).

Warfare and State Formation: The Zapotec Case

Warfare often plays a key role in primary state formation. The first Mesoamerican state, **Zapotec** had developed in Mexico's Valley of Oaxaca by

the start of the Common Era (C.E.—formerly A.D.). The city of Monte Albán served as capital of this Zapotec *polity* (political unit, such as a chiefdom or a state) for *twelve hundred years*, between 500 B.C.E. and 700 C.E. (The Zapotec polity was a chiefdom from ca. 500 B.C.E. to 100 B.C.E., and after that a state). Kent Flannery and Joyce Marcus (2003b) describe the archaeological evidence for changing warfare patterns in Oaxaca—from early raiding among sedentary villages to warfare aimed at conquest between 330 and 20 B.C.E. (formerly B.C.).

The oldest defensive palisade in the Valley of Oaxaca dates to 3260–3160 B.P., just a few centuries after village life was established there (see Chapter 11). Over the next millennium, raiding evolved into war, with homes and temples burned, captives killed, and populations relocating to defensible hills. A monument from the site of San José Mogote, dating no later than 2510 B.P. (560 B.C.E.), is the earliest reliably dated monument with writing in Mesoamerica. It depicts a named, sacrificed captive, likely a rival chief and a probable victim of intervillage raiding. Armed conflict in Oaxaca thus began as raiding, with killing, burning, and captive taking but no permanent acquisition of territory. By the time the Spanish conquistadors arrived in the 16th century, the Zapotec-speaking inhabitants of the Valley of Oaxaca (no longer centered at Monte Albán) had armies with noble officers and commoner foot soldiers. They waged wars

Zapotec state
First Mesoamerican state, in the Valley of Oaxaca.

Three of more than 300 carved stones depicting slain war captives at the important archaeological site of Monte Albán, Oaxaca, Mexico. Dated to 500–400 B.C.E., these images originally were set in the Prisoner Gallery of Monte Albán's Building L. This huge display of slain enemies was a form of political and military propaganda. The carved stones warned potential rivals what would happen if they defied Monte Albán.

that exacted tribute from conquered territories (Flannery and Marcus 2003*b*).

The shift from raiding to warfare aimed at territorial conquest occurred prior to 300 B.C.E. This shift is documented not only by hieroglyphs but also by survey and excavation in areas that were targets of Monte Albán's expansionistic designs. As Charles Spencer (2003) notes of Oaxaca, evidence for the earliest conquest warfare occurs simultaneously with evidence for emerging state organization. This correlation supports the idea of a causal link between conquest warfare and state formation.

Long ago, Henry Wright (1977) described the state as a society with not only a centralized but also an internally specialized, administrative organization—a bureaucracy. Chiefdoms, by contrast, lack administrative specialization. States have at least four levels of decision making (Wright 1977). The center or capital establishes subsidiary administrative centers. The result is a nested lattice of secondary, tertiary, and even quaternary centers. Population size tends to follow this administrative structure: States typically have at least a four-level hierarchy of settlements according to both administrative functions and population size. Chiefdoms have no more than three levels (Spencer 2003).

To expand, a state must send delegates, such as soldiers, governors, and other officials, to subjugate and rule in distant territories. Lacking a group of bureaucrats, chiefdoms can't do this, which means that the geographic range of chiefly authority is smaller than in a state. According to Spencer (2003), the limit of a chiefdom's range is half a day's travel from its center. States, however, can transcend such limits and carry out long-distance conquests. Archaeological evidence for conquest warfare includes burned and abandoned villages, specialized forts and administrative outposts, and forced changes in the economic, social, and religious behaviors of subjugated peoples.

Expansion through conquest can play a key role in the formation of a primary state by building the administrative hierarchy. Subjugation of polities in other regions, coupled with regularized tribute exaction, can bring about a transition from chiefdom to state (Spencer 2003). For such a strategy to succeed (especially when the conquered polities lie more than a half-day's trip away), the leadership will have to dispatch agents to the conquered areas. Generals and bureaucrats are needed not only to carry out the subjugation but also to maintain long-term control and to manage tribute collection. Given its need to rely on distant representatives, the central leadership promotes internal administrative specialization and loyalty (and thus bureaucratic proliferation). Tribute provides new resources to support this administrative transformation. Archaeological data from Oaxaca confirm that the conquest of distant polities and bureaucratic

growth were integral parts of the process of Zapotec primary state formation.

Typically, state bureaucracies occupy a group of administrative buildings, especially at the capital. Surrounding the Main Plaza at Monte Albán were specialized buildings, including palaces, temples, and ball courts. Of these, the palace is an especially useful diagnostic of state organization. Hieroglyphs on a building in Monte Albán's Main Plaza record the bringing of outlying areas under Monte Albán's control, often by conquest. There is archaeological evidence at Cañada de Cuicatlán (a two-day walk north of Monte Albán) for Zapotec conquest around 300 B.C.E. Evidence of outright colonization has been found in the Sola Valley, a two-day walk southwest of Monte Albán. The Zapotec also claimed control of the Tututepec area on Oaxaca's Pacific coast.

Monte Albán did not expand its rule in a gradual, concentric fashion. Although it managed to subjugate distant regions to the north, west, and southwest by approximately 300 B.C.E., certain areas to the east and south managed to resist for centuries. For example, Monte Albán attacked and burned its chief local rival, San Martín Tilcajete, only a day's travel to the south, around 330 B.C.E., but the local inhabitants refused to capitulate. They rebuilt their community and constructed defensive walls at a higher location, El Palenque. These people continued to resist Monte Albán until roughly 20 B.C.E., when they finally were conquered.

Evidence for co-occurrence of Monte Albán's conquest strategy with the emerging Zapotec state offers strong support for the expansionist model of primary state formation. That state had formed by 30–20 B.C.E., with a four-tier, site-size settlement hierarchy: royal palaces and two-room state temples. Monte Albán built its own secondary administrative center on a hilltop above the ruins of El Palenque (Elson 2007). After centuries of dominating the region, Monte Albán eventually lost its central role as capital. After 700 C.E., the Zapotec state dissolved into a series of smaller centers or principalities—alternately vying for supremacy through continued warfare and forming peaceful alliances through marriage (Flannery and Marcus 2003*a*; Marcus 1989). (Figure 12.5 locates the Valley of Oaxaca and the sites discussed here.)

States in the Valley of Mexico

During the first century C.E., the Valley of Mexico, located in the highlands where Mexico City now stands, came to prominence in Mesoamerican state formation. In this large valley, **Teotihuacán** flourished between 1900 and 1300 B.P. (100 and 700 C.E.).

The Valley of Mexico is a large basin surrounded by mountains. The valley has rich volcanic soils, but rainfall isn't always reliable. The northern part of the valley, where the huge city and state of Teotihuacán eventually arose, is

Teotihuacán
First valley of Mexico state (100–700 C.E.); earliest Mesoamerican empire.

The Pyramid of the Sun, Teotihuacán's largest structure, is shown in the upper part of the photo. At its height around A.D. 500, Teotihuacán was larger than imperial Rome. The mobilization of manual labor to build such structures is one of the costs of state organization.

FIGURE 12.5 The Oaxaca region, Mexico, showing places mentioned.

colder and drier than the south. Frosts there limited farming until quick-growing varieties of maize were developed. Until 2500 B.P., most people lived in the warmer and wetter southern part of the valley, where rainfall made farming possible. After 2500 B.P., new maize varieties and small-scale irrigation appeared. Population increased and began to spread north.

By 1 C.E. Teotihuacán was a town of 10,000 people. It governed a territory of a few thousand square kilometers and perhaps 50,000 people (Parsons 1974). Teotihuacán's growth reflected its agricultural potential. Perpetual springs permitted irrigation of a large alluvial plain. Rural farmers supplied food for the growing urban population.

By this time, a clear **settlement hierarchy** had emerged. This is a ranked series of communities that differ in size, function, and building types. The settlements at the top of the hierarchy were political and religious centers. Those at the bottom were rural villages. We have seen that a four-level settlement hierarchy provides archaeological evidence of state organization (Wright and Johnson 1975).

Along with state organization at Teotihuacán went large-scale irrigation, status differentiation, and complex architecture. Teotihuacán thrived between 100 and 700 C.E.. It grew as a planned city built on a grid pattern, with the Pyramid of the Sun at its center. By 500 C.E. the population of Teotihuacán had reached 130,000, making it larger than imperial Rome. Farmers were one of its diverse specialized groups, along with artisans, merchants, and political, religious, and military personnel.

After 700 C.E. Teotihuacán declined in size and power. By 900 C.E. its population had shrunk to 30,000. Between 900 and 1200 C.E., the Toltec period, the population scattered, and small cities

The Aztecs played the board game of patolli, as represented here in the Codex Magliabecchiano, housed in the National Library in Florence, Italy.

and towns sprang up throughout the valley. People also left the Valley of Mexico to live in larger cities—like Tula, the Toltec capital—on its edge (see Figure 12.4).

Population increase (including immigration by the ancestors of the Aztecs) and urban growth returned to the Valley of Mexico between 1200 and 1520 C.E. During the **Aztec** period (1325–1520 C.E.) there were several cities, the largest of which—Tenochtitlán, the capital—may have surpassed Teotihuacán at its height. A dozen Aztec towns had more than 10,000 people. Fueling this population growth was intensification of agriculture, particularly in the southern part of the valley, where the drainage of lake bottoms and swamps added new cultivable land (Parsons 1976).

Another factor in the renaissance of the Valley of Mexico was trade. Local manufacture created

settlement hierarchy
Communities with varying size, function, and building types.

Aztec
Last independent Valley of Mexico state (1325 through 1520 C.E.– Spanish Conquest).

products for a series of markets. The major towns and markets were located on the lake shores, with easy access to canoe traffic. The Aztec capital stood on an island in the lake. In Tenochtitlán, the production of luxury goods was more prestigious and more highly organized than that of pottery making, basket making, and weaving. Luxury producers, such as stone workers, feather workers, and gold- and silversmiths, occupied a special position in Aztec society. The manufacture of luxury goods for export was an important part of the economy of the Aztec capital (Hassig 1985; Santley 1985).

WHY STATES COLLAPSE

States can be fragile and decomposable, falling apart along the same cleavage lines (e.g., regional political units) that were forged together to form the state originally. Various factors could threaten their economies and political institutions. Invasion, disease, famine, or prolonged drought could upset the balance. A state's citizens might harm the environment, usually with economic costs. For example, farmers and smelters might cut down trees. Such deforestation promotes erosion and leads to a decline in the water supply. Overuse of land may deplete the soil of the nutrients needed to grow crops.

If factors such as irrigation help create states to begin with, does their decline or failure explain the fall of the state? Irrigation does have costs as well as benefits. In ancient Mesopotamia, irrigation water came from the Tigris and Euphrates rivers. Because sediment (silt) had accumulated in those rivers, their beds were higher than the alluvial plain and fields they irrigated. Canals channeled river water as it flowed down into the fields by gravity. As the water evaporated, water-borne mineral salts remained in the fields, eventually creating a poisonous environment for plants.

Ruins at Copán, a center of classic Maya royalty in western Honduras.

Mashkan-shapir, for example, was a Mesopotamian city located about 20 miles from the Tigris, to which it was connected by a network of canals. This city was abandoned just 20 years after it was settled. Destruction of its fields by mineral salts seems to have been a prime factor in its collapse (see Annenberg/CPB Exhibits 2000 at http://www.learner.org/exhibits/collapse/mesopotamia.html).

The Maya Decline

Generations of scholars have debated the decline of classic Maya civilization around 900 C.E. Classic Maya culture, featuring several competing states, flourished between 300 and 900 C.E. (1700–1100 B.P.) in parts of what are now Mexico, Honduras, El Salvador, Guatemala, and Belize. The ancient Maya are known for their monuments (temples and pyramids), calendars, mathematics, and hieroglyphic writing.

Archaeological clues to Maya decline have been found at Copán, in western Honduras. This classic Maya royal center, the largest site in the southeastern part of the Maya area, covered 29 acres (11.7 hectares). It was built on an artificial terrace overlooking the Copán River. Its rulers inscribed their monuments with accounts of their coronation, their lineage history, and reports of important battles. The Maya dated their monuments with the names of kings and when they reigned. One monument at Copán was intended to be the ruler's throne platform, but only one side had been finished. The monument bears a date, 822 C.E., in a section of unfinished text. Copán has no monuments with later dates. The site probably was abandoned by 830 C.E.

Environmental factors implicated in Copán's demise may have included erosion and soil exhaustion due to overpopulation and overfarming. Overfarming contributes to deforestation and erosion. Hillside farmhouses in particular had debris from erosion—probably caused by overfarming of the hillsides. This erosion began as early as 750 C.E.—until these farm sites were abandoned, with some eventually buried by erosion debris. For the classic Maya in general, William Sanders (1972, 1973) has attributed state decline to overfarming, leading to environmental degradation through grass invasion and erosion.

Food stress and malnutrition were clearly present at Copán, where 80 percent of the buried skeletons display signs of anemia, due to iron deficiency. One skull shows anemia severe enough to have been the cause of death. Even the nobility were malnourished. One noble skull, known to be such from its carved teeth and cosmetic deformation, also has telltale signs of anemia: spongy areas at its rear (Annenberg/CPB Exhibits 2000).

Just as the origins of states, and their causes, are diverse, so are the reasons for state decline.

The Maya state was not as powerful as was once assumed; it was fragile and vulnerable. Increased warfare and political competition destabilized many of its dynasties and governments. Archaeologists now stress the role of warfare in Maya state decline. Hieroglyphic texts document increased warfare among many Maya cities. From the period just before the collapse, there is archaeological evidence for increased concern with fortifications (moats, ditches, walls, and palisades) and moving to defensible locations. Archaeologists have evidence of the burning of structures, the projectile points from spears, and some of the bodies of those killed. Some sites were abandoned, with the people fleeing into the forests to occupy perishable huts. (Copán, as we have seen, was depopulated after 822 C.E.) Archaeologists now believe that social, political, and military upheaval and competition had as much as or more

to do with the Maya decline and abandonment of cities as did natural environmental factors (Marcus, personal communication).

Formerly archaeologists tended to explain state origin and decline mainly in terms of natural environmental factors, such as climate change, habitat destruction, and demographic pressure (see Weiss 2005). Archaeologists now see state origins and declines more fully—in social and political terms—because we can read the texts. And the Maya texts document competition and warfare between dynasties jockeying for position and power. Warfare was indeed a creator and a destroyer of ancient chiefdoms and states. What's its role in our own?

Acing the COURSE

Summary

1. States develop to handle regulatory problems as the population grows and the economy gets more complex. Multiple factors contribute to state formation. Some appear repeatedly, but no single factor is always present. Among the most important factors are irrigation and long-distance trade. Coastal Peru, a very arid area, illustrates how environmental circumscription, population growth, and warfare may contribute to state formation.

2. A state is a society with a formal, central government and a division of society into classes. The first cities and states, supported by irrigated farming, developed in southern Mesopotamia between 6000 and 5500 B.P. Evidence for early state organization includes monumental architecture, central storehouses, irrigation systems, and written records.

3. Towns predate pottery in the Middle East. The first towns grew up 10,000 to 9,000 years ago. The first pottery dates back just over 8,000 years. Halafian (7500–6500 B.P.) refers to a pottery style and to the period when the first chiefdoms emerged. Ubaid pottery (7000–6000 B.P.) is associated with advanced chiefdoms and perhaps the earliest states. Most state formation occurred during the Uruk period (6100–5100 B.P.).

4. Based on the status distinctions they include, societies may be divided into egalitarian, ranked, and stratified. In egalitarian societies, status distinctions are not usually inherited. Ranked societ-

ies have hereditary inequality, but they lack stratification. Stratified societies have sharp social divisions—social classes or *strata*—based on unequal access to wealth and power. Ranked societies with loss of village autonomy are chiefdoms.

5. Mesopotamia's economy was based on craft production, trade, and intensive agriculture. Writing, invented by 5600 B.P., was first used to keep accounts for trade. With the invention of smelting, the Bronze Age began just after 5000 B.P.

6. In northwestern India and Pakistan, the Indus River Valley state flourished from 4600 to 3900 B.P. The first Chinese state, dating to 3750 B.P., was that of the Shang dynasty in northern China. Various states developed in sub-Saharan Africa. The major early states of the Western Hemisphere were in Mesoamerica and Peru.

7. Between 3200 and 3000 B.P., intense competitive interaction among the many chiefdoms in Mesoamerica at that time fueled rapid social change. Some chiefdoms would develop into states (e.g., Oaxaca, Valley of Mexico). Others (e.g., Olmec) would not. In the Valley of Oaxaca, changing patterns of warfare—from village raiding to conquest warfare to gain territory and tribute—played a prominent role in the formation of Mesoamerica's earliest state, the Zapotec state, whose capital was Monte Albán. This city served as the Zapotec capital for one thousand years, from 300 B.C.E. to 700 C.E. After that, the Zapotec state continued, but in the

form of small principalities that fought among themselves until Spanish conquest in the early 16th century C.E. By 1 C.E. (2000 B.P.), the Valley of Mexico had come to prominence. In this large valley in the highlands, Teotihuacán thrived between 100 and 700 C.E. Tenochtitlán, the capital of the Aztec state (1325 to 1520 C.E.), may have surpassed Teotihuacán at its height.

8. Early states faced various threats: invasion, disease, famine, drought, soil exhaustion, erosion, and the buildup of irrigation salts. States may collapse when they fail to keep social and economic order or to protect themselves against outsiders. The Maya state fell in the face of increased warfare among competing dynasties.

Key Terms

Aztec 275
bronze 267
chiefdom 257
cuneiform 266
egalitarian society 263
empire 258
Halafian 263
Mesopotamia 260
metallurgy 267

multivariate 257
primary states 265
ranked society 266
settlement hierarchy 275
smelting 267
state 273
stratification 277
Teotihuacán 274
Zapotec state 274

Test Yourself!

MULTIPLE CHOICE

1. Chiefdoms
   a. are never sedentary.
   b. always led to the formation of states.
   c. require elaborate hydraulic systems if they are to grow into states.
   d. are the most common social arrangement of human populations.
   e. were precursors to states, with privileged and effective leaders—chiefs—but lacking the sharp class divisions that characterize states.

2. Which variable does *not* enter into Carneiro's multivariate theory of state formation?
   a. warfare
   b. population growth
   c. long-distance trade
   d. environmental circumscription
   e. resource concentration

3. Which of the following did *not* distinguish states from earlier forms of society?
   a. control over a specific regional territory
   b. productive farming, supporting dense populations
   c. social stratification
   d. the development of some form of record-keeping system
   e. burials

4. Which of the following statements about egalitarian society is *not* true?
   a. They often are found among foragers.
   b. Everybody has equal status.
   c. There are no social classes.
   d. There is no hereditary inequality.
   e. A person's status is based on his or her age, gender, and individual qualities, talents, and achievements.

5. Which term refers to a ranked society in which villages are *not* autonomous?
   a. chiefdom
   b. primary state
   c. archaic state
   d. tribe
   e. band

6. Which of the following did *not* accompany primary state formation in southern Mesopotamia?
   a. an expanding population
   b. increasing specialization
   c. a growing central leadership
   d. increasing isolation of communities
   e. increasing trade

7. Which of the following statements about the earliest writing is *not* true?
   a. It was syllabic.
   b. It was developed as a form of record keeping.
   c. It spread from Mesopotamia to Egypt.
   d. It played no role in the development of Mesoamerican writing systems.
   e. It was scrawled on wet clay with a stylus.

8. What was the vital step for the development of metallurgy and the wider and rapid distribution of metals evident after 5,000 B.P.?
   a. smelting
   b. copper hammering
   c. heating copper at low temperatures
   d. finding richer veins of copper
   e. investing more labor into mining

9. Which of the following is true about the emergence of states in Africa?
   a. Egypt was the only place in Africa where early states arose.
   b. Iron smelting was unknown in Africa until European colonial expansion.
   c. States arose only along the Nile Valley.

d. Southward Bantu migrations resulted in the emergence of the Mwenemutapa empire.

e. No early states emerged in Africa.

10. Which of the following statements about the collapse of Copán is *not* true?
a. It led to its abandonment around 830 C.E.
b. It was linked to soil exhaustion.

c. It was linked to overpopulation and malnutrition.
d. It was linked to erosion.
e. It was precipitated by an Olmec invasion.

FILL IN THE BLANK

1. A(n) _ranked society_ is a society with hereditary inequality but lacking social stratification.

2. A(n) _egalitarian_ society lacks status distinctions except those based on age, gender, and individual qualities, talents, and achievements.

3. _Cuneiform_ is the name for the early writing in Mesopotamia.

4. _Teotihuacán_ was the capital of the first state to develop in the Valley of Mexico (100–700 C.E.).

5. First settled by Natufian foragers in what is now Israel, _Jericho_ is considered the earliest known town.

CRITICAL THINKING

1. This chapter describes Robert Carneiro's (1970) multivariate theory of state formation. What does it state? How is it representative of a systemic perspective?

2. Imagine yourself an archaeologist trying to identify ancient chiefdoms in the Middle East after excavating Mesoamerican chiefdom sites. What similar and different lines of evidence for ranking and political alliance might you find in the two contexts?

3. How could reviewing the history of state formation prompt us to reexamine our assumptions about what is natural or universal about social organization?

4. Only those ranked societies with loss of village autonomy should be called chiefdoms. What kinds of evidence could archaeologists search for as clues of this loss of autonomy?

5. Based on the evidence from coastal Peru (near the beginning of the chapter) and Oaxaca (near the end of the chapter), what role did warfare play in early state formation?

Multiple Choice: 1. (E); 2. (C); 3. (E); 4. (B); 5. (A); 6. (D); 7. (A); 8. (A); 9. (D); 10. (E); **Fill in the Blank:** 1. ranked society; 2. egalitarian; 3. Cuneiform; 4. Teotihuacán; 5. Jericho

Fagan, B. M.
2008 *World Prehistory: A Brief Introduction*, 7th ed. Upper Saddle River, NJ: Pearson/Prentice Hall. Major events in human prehistory, including the emergence of the state in various locales.

Feinman, G. M., and J. Marcus, eds.
1998 *Archaic States*. Santa Fe, NM: School of American Research Press. Features of early states, in general and in particular world areas.

Joyce, R. A.
2000 *Gender and Power in Prehispanic Mesoamerica*. Austin: University of Texas Press. Issues of gender and power in Mesoamerica before the Spanish Conquest.

Pollock, S.
1999 *Ancient Mesopotamia: The Eden That Never Was*. Cambridge, England: Cambridge University Press. Mesopotamia state formation—a new synthesis.

Trigger, B. G.
2003 *Understanding Early Civilizations: A Comparative Study*. Cambridge, England: Cambridge University Press. A comparative study of seven archaic states: ancient Egypt and Mesopotamia, Shang dynasty China, Aztec, Maya, Inca, and Yoruba.

Wenke, R., and D. I. Olszewski
2007 *Patterns in Prehistory: Humankind's First Three Million Years*, 5th ed. New York: Oxford University Press. Rise of food production and the state throughout the world; thorough, useful text.

Suggested Additional Readings

Internet Exercises

Go to our Online Learning Center website **www.mhhe.com/kottak** for Internet exercises directly related to the content of this chapter.

Where and how do cultural anthropologists do field work?

What are some ways of studying modern societies?

What theories have guided anthropologists over the years?

In Mozambique's Gaza province, the Dutch ethnographer Janine van Vugt (red hair) sits on mats near reed houses, talking to local women.

understanding OURSELVES

"Been on any digs lately?" Ask your professor how many times she or he has been asked this question. Then ask how often he or she actually has been on a dig. Remember that anthropology has four subfields, only two of which (archaeology and biological anthropology) require much digging—in the ground at least. Even among biological anthropologists it's mainly paleoanthropologists (those concerned with the hominid fossil record) who must dig. Students of primate behavior in the wild, such as Jane Goodall, don't do it. Nor, most of the time, is it done by forensic anthropologists, including the title character in the TV show *Bones*.

To be sure, cultural anthropologists "dig out" information about varied lifestyles, as linguistic anthropologists do about the features of unwritten languages. Traditionally cultural anthropologists have done a variant on the *Star Trek* theme of seeking out, if not new at least different, "life" and "civilizations," sometimes boldly going where no scientist has gone before.

Despite globalization, the cultural diversity under anthropological scrutiny right now may be as great as ever before, because the anthropological universe has expanded to modern nations. Today's cultural anthropologists are as likely to be studying artists in Miami or bankers in Beirut as Trobriand sailors in the South Pacific. Still, we can't forget that anthropology did originate in non-Western, nonindustrial societies. Its research techniques, especially those subsumed under the label "ethnography," were developed to deal with small populations. Even when working in modern nations, anthropologists still consider ethnography with small groups to be an excellent way of learning about how people live their lives and make decisions.

Before this course, did you know the names of any anthropologists? If so, which ones? For the general public, biological anthropologists tend to be better known than cultural anthropologists because of what they study. You're more likely to have seen a film of Jane Goodall with chimps or a paleoanthropologist holding a hominid skull than a linguistic or cultural anthropologist at work. Archaeologists occasionally appear in the media to describe a new discovery or to debunk pseudo-archaeological arguments about how visitors from space have left traces on earth. One cultural anthropologist was an important public figure when (and before and after) I was in college. Margaret Mead, famed for her work on teen sexuality in Samoa and gender roles in New Guinea, may well be the most famous anthropologist who ever lived. Mead, one of my own professors at Columbia University, appeared regularly on NBC's *Tonight Show*. In all her venues, including teaching, museum work, TV, anthropological films, popular books, and magazines, Mead helped Americans appreciate the relevance of anthropology to understanding their daily lives. Her work is featured here and elsewhere in this book.

ETHNOGRAPHY: ANTHROPOLOGY'S DISTINCTIVE STRATEGY

Anthropology developed into a separate field as early scholars worked on Indian (Native American) reservations and traveled to distant lands to study small groups of foragers (hunters and gatherers) and cultivators. Traditionally, the process of becoming a cultural anthropologist has required a field experience in another society. Early ethnographers lived in small-scale, relatively isolated societies with simple technologies and economies.

Ethnography thus emerged as a research strategy in societies with greater cultural uniformity and less social differentiation than are found in large, modern, industrial nations. Traditionally, ethnographers have tried to understand the whole of a particular culture (or, more realistically, as much as they can, given limitations of time and perception). To pursue this goal, ethnographers adopt a free-ranging strategy for gathering information. In a given society or community, the ethnographer moves from setting to setting, place to place, and subject to subject to discover the totality and interconnectedness of social life. By expanding our knowledge of the range of human diversity, ethnography provides a foundation for generalizations about human behavior and social life. Ethnographers draw on varied techniques to piece together a picture of otherwise alien lifestyles. Anthropologists usually employ several (but rarely all) of the techniques discussed below (see also Bernard 2006).

ETHNOGRAPHIC TECHNIQUES

The characteristic *field techniques* of the ethnographer include the following:

1. Direct, firsthand observation of behavior, including *participant observation*.

2. Conversation with varying degrees of formality, from the daily chitchat that helps maintain rapport and provides knowledge about what is going on, to prolonged *interviews*, which can be unstructured or structured.

3. The *genealogical method*.

4. Detailed work with *key consultants*, or *informants*, about particular areas of community life.

5. In-depth interviewing, often leading to the collection of *life histories* of particular people (narrators).

6. Discovery of local (native) beliefs and perceptions, which may be compared with the ethnographer's own observations and conclusions.

7. Problem-oriented research of many sorts.

8. Longitudinal research—the continuous long-term study of an area or site.

9. Team research—coordinated research by multiple ethnographers.

Observation and Participant Observation

Ethnographers must pay attention to hundreds of details of daily life, seasonal events, and unusual happenings. They should record what they see as they see it. Things never will seem quite as strange as they do during the first few weeks in the field. Often anthropologists experience culture shock—a creepy and profound feeling of alienation—on arrival at a new field site. Although anthropologists study human diversity, the actual field experience of diversity takes some getting used to, as we see in this chapter's "Appreciating Diversity." The ethnographer eventually grows accustomed to, and accepts as normal, cultural patterns that initially were alien. Staying a bit more than a year in the field allows the ethnographer to repeat the season of his or her arrival, when certain events and processes may have been missed because of initial unfamiliarity and culture shock.

Many ethnographers record their impressions in a personal *diary*, which is kept separate from more formal *field notes*. Later, this record of early impressions will help point out some of the most basic aspects of cultural diversity. Such aspects include distinctive smells, noises people make, how they cover their mouths when they eat, and how they gaze at others. These patterns, which are so basic as to seem almost trivial, are part of what Bronislaw Malinowski called "the imponderabilia of native life and of typical behavior" (Malinowski 1922/1961, p. 20). These features of culture are so fundamental that natives take them for granted. They are too basic even to talk about, but the unaccustomed eye of the fledgling ethnographer picks them up. Thereafter, becoming familiar, they fade to the edge of consciousness. I mention my initial impressions of some such imponderabilia of northeastern Brazilian culture in this chapter's "Appreciating Diversity." Initial impressions are valuable and should be recorded. First and foremost, ethnographers should try to be accurate observers, recorders, and reporters of what they see in the field.

Ethnographers strive to establish *rapport*, a good, friendly working relationship based on personal contact, with their hosts. One of ethnography's most characteristic procedures is participant observation, which means that we take part in community life as we study it. As human beings living among others, we cannot be totally impartial and detached observers. We

appreciating DIVERSITY

Even Anthropologists Get Culture Shock

I first lived in Arembepe (Brazil) during the (North American) summer of 1962. That was between my junior and senior years at New York City's Columbia College, where I was majoring in anthropology. I went to Arembepe as a participant in a now defunct program designed to provide undergraduates with experience doing ethnography—firsthand study of an alien society's culture and social life.

Brought up in one culture, intensely curious about others, anthropologists nevertheless experience culture shock, particularly on their first field trip. Culture shock refers to the whole set of feelings about being in an alien setting, and the ensuing reactions. It is a chilly, creepy feeling of alienation, of being without some of the most ordinary, trivial (and therefore basic) cues of one's culture of origin.

As I planned my departure for Brazil in 1962, I could not know just how naked I would feel without the cloak of my own language and culture. My sojourn in Arembepe would be my first trip outside the United States. I was an urban boy who had grown up in Atlanta, Georgia, and New York City. I had little experience with rural life in my own country, none with Latin America, and I had received only minimal training in the Portuguese language.

New York City direct to Salvador, Bahia, Brazil. Just a brief stopover in Rio de Janeiro; a longer visit would be a reward at the end of field work. As our prop jet approached tropical Salvador, I couldn't believe the whiteness of

the sand. "That's not snow, is it?" I remarked to a fellow field team member. . . .

My first impressions of Bahia were of smells—alien odors of ripe and decaying mangoes, bananas, and passion fruit—and of swatting the ubiquitous fruit flies I had never seen before, although I had read extensively about their reproductive behavior in genetics classes. There were strange concoctions of rice, black beans, and gelatinous gobs of unidentifiable

FIGURE 13.1 Location of Arembepe, Bahia, Brazil.

take part in many events and processes we are observing and trying to comprehend. By participating, we may learn why people find such events meaningful, as we see how they are organized and conducted.

In Arembepe, Brazil, I learned about fishing by sailing on the Atlantic with local fishers. I gave Jeep rides to malnourished babies, to pregnant mothers, and once to a teenage girl possessed by a spirit. All those people needed to consult specialists outside the village. I danced on Arembepe's festive occasions, drank libations commemorating new births, and became a

godfather to a village girl. Most anthropologists have similar field experiences. The common humanity of the student and the studied, the ethnographer and the research community, makes participant observation inevitable.

Conversation, Interviewing, and Interview Schedules

Participating in local life means that ethnographers constantly talk to people and ask questions. As their knowledge of the local language and culture increases, they understand more. There

Conrad Kottak, with his Brazilian nephew Guilherme Roxo, on a revisit to Arembepe in 2004.

passed previously. A crowd of children had heard us coming, and they pursued our car through the village streets until we parked in front of our house, near the central square. Our first few days in Arembepe were spent with children following us everywhere. For weeks we had few moments of privacy. Children watched our every move through our living room window. Occasionally one made an incomprehensible remark. Usually they just stood there . . .

The sounds, sensations, sights, smells, and tastes of life in northeastern Brazil, and in Arembepe, slowly grew familiar . . . I grew accustomed to this world without Kleenex, in which globs of mucus habitually drooped from the noses of village children whenever a cold passed through Arembepe. A world where, seemingly without effort, women . . . carried 18-liter kerosene cans of water on their heads, where boys sailed kites and sported at catching houseflies in their bare hands, where old women smoked pipes, storekeepers offered cachaça (common rum) at nine in the morning, and men played dominoes on lazy afternoons when there was no fishing. I was visiting a world where human life was oriented toward water—the sea, where men fished, and the lagoon, where women communally washed clothing, dishes, and their own bodies.

This description is adapted from my ethnographic study *Assault on Paradise: The Globalization of a Little Community in Brazil*, 4th ed. (New York: McGraw-Hill, 2006).

meats and floating pieces of skin. Coffee was strong and sugar crude, and every tabletop had containers for toothpicks and for manioc (cassava) flour to sprinkle, like Parmesan cheese, on anything one might eat. I remember oatmeal soup and a slimy stew of beef tongue in tomatoes. At one meal a disintegrating fish head, eyes still attached, but barely, stared up at me as the rest of its body floated in a bowl of bright orange palm oil. . . .

I only vaguely remember my first day in Arembepe (Figure 13.1). Unlike ethnographers who have studied remote tribes in the tropical forests of interior South America or the highlands of Papua New Guinea, I did not have to hike or ride a canoe for days to arrive at my field site. Arembepe was not isolated relative to such places, only relative to every other place I had ever been. . . .

I do recall what happened when we arrived. There was no formal road into the village. Entering through southern Arembepe, vehicles simply threaded their way around coconut trees, following tracks left by automobiles that had

are several stages in learning a field language. First is the naming phase—asking name after name of the objects around us. Later we are able to pose more complex questions and understand the replies. We begin to understand simple conversations between two villagers. If our language expertise proceeds far enough, we eventually become able to comprehend rapid-fire public discussions and group conversations.

One data-gathering technique I have used in both Arembepe and Madagascar involves an ethnographic survey that includes an interview schedule. In 1964, my fellow field workers and

I attempted to complete an interview schedule in each of Arembepe's 160 households. We entered almost every household (fewer than 5 percent refused to participate) to ask a set of questions on a printed form. Our results provided us with a census and basic information about the village. We wrote down the name, age, and gender of each household member. We gathered data on family type, religion, present and previous jobs, income, expenditures, diet, possessions, and many other items on our eight-page form.

Although we were doing a survey, our approach differed from the survey research design routinely used by sociologists and other social scientists working in large, industrial nations. That survey research, discussed below, involves sampling (choosing a small, manageable study group from a larger population). We did not select a partial sample from the total population. Instead, we tried to interview in all households in the community (that is, to have a total sample). We used an interview schedule rather than a questionnaire. With the **interview schedule,** the ethnographer talks face-to-face with people, asks the questions, and writes down the answers. **Questionnaire** procedures tend to be more indirect and impersonal; often the respondent fills in the form.

Our goal of getting a total sample allowed us to meet almost everyone in the village and helped us establish rapport. Decades later, Arembepeiros still talk warmly about how we were interested enough in them to visit their homes and ask them questions. We stood in sharp contrast to the other outsiders the villagers had known, who considered them too poor and backward to be taken seriously.

Like other survey research, however, our interview schedule did gather comparable quantifiable information. It gave us a basis for assessing patterns and exceptions in village life. Our schedules included a core set of questions that were posed to everyone. However, some interesting side issues often came up during the interview, which we would pursue then or later. We followed such leads into many dimensions of village life. One woman, for instance, a midwife, became the key cultural consultant we sought out later when we wanted detailed information about local childbirth. Another woman had done an internship in an Afro-Brazilian cult (*candomblé*) in the city. She still went there regularly to study, dance, and get possessed. She became our candomblé expert.

Thus, our interview schedule provided a structure that *directed but did not confine* us as researchers. It enabled our ethnography to be both quantitative and qualitative. The quantitative part consisted of the basic information we gathered and later analyzed statistically. The qualitative dimension came from our follow-up questions, open-ended discussions, pauses for gossip, and work with key consultants.

The Genealogical Method

As ordinary people, many of us learn about our own ancestry and relatives by tracing our genealogies. Various computer programs now allow us to trace our "family tree" and degrees of relationship. The **genealogical method** is a well-established ethnographic technique. Early ethnographers developed notation and symbols to deal with kinship, descent, and marriage. Genealogy is a prominent building block in the social organization of nonindustrial societies, where people live and work each day with their close kin. Anthropologists need to collect genealogical data to understand current social relations and to reconstruct history. In many nonindustrial societies, kin links are basic to social life. Anthropologists even call such cultures "kin-based societies." Everyone is related and spends most of his or her time with relatives. Rules of behavior attached to particular kin relations are basic to everyday life (see Carsten 2004). Marriage also is crucial in organizing nonindustrial societies because strategic marriages between villages, tribes, and clans create political alliances.

Key Cultural Consultants

Every community has people who by accident, experience, talent, or training can provide the most complete or useful information about particular aspects of life. These people are **key cultural consultants,** also called *key informants*. In Ivato, the Betsileo village in Madagascar where I spent most of my time, a man named Rakoto was particularly knowledgeable about village history. However, when I asked him to work with me on a genealogy of the fifty to sixty people buried in the village tomb, he called in his cousin Tuesdaysfather, who knew more about that subject. Tuesdaysfather had survived an epidemic of influenza that ravaged Madagascar, along with much of the world, around 1919. Immune to the disease himself, Tuesdaysfather had the grim job of burying his kin as they died. He kept track of everyone buried in the tomb. Tuesdaysfather

interview schedule
Form (guide) used to structure a formal, but personal, interview.

questionnaire
Form used by sociologists to obtain comparable information from respondents.

genealogical method
Using diagrams and symbols to record kin connections.

key cultural consultant
Expert on a particular aspect of local life.

Kinship and descent are vital social building blocks in nonindustrial cultures. Without writing, genealogical information may be preserved in material culture, such as this totem pole being raised in Metlakatla, Alaska.

helped me with the tomb genealogy. Rakoto joined him in telling me personal details about the deceased villagers.

Life Histories

In nonindustrial societies as in our own, individual personalities, interests, and abilities vary. Some villagers prove to be more interested in the ethnographer's work and are more helpful, interesting, and pleasant than others are. Anthropologists develop likes and dislikes in the field as we do at home. Often, when we find someone unusually interesting, we collect his or her **life history.** This recollection of a lifetime of experiences provides a more intimate and personal cultural portrait than would be possible otherwise. Life histories, which may be recorded or videotaped for later review and analysis, reveal how specific people perceive, react to, and contribute to changes that affect their lives. Such accounts can illustrate diversity, which exists within any community, since the focus is on how different people interpret and deal with some of the same problems. Many ethnographers include the collection of life histories as an important part of their research strategy.

Local Beliefs and Perceptions, and the Ethnographer's

One goal of ethnography is to discover local (native) views, beliefs, and perceptions, which may be compared with the ethnographer's own observations and conclusions. In the field, ethnographers typically combine two research strategies, the emic (native-oriented) and the etic (scientist-oriented). These terms, derived from linguistics, have been applied to ethnography by various anthropologists. Marvin Harris (1968/2001) popularized the following meanings of the terms: An **emic** approach investigates how local people think. How do they perceive and categorize the world? What are their rules for behavior? What has meaning for them? How do they imagine and explain things? Operating emically, the ethnographer seeks the "native viewpoint," relying on local people to explain things and to say whether something is significant or not. The term **cultural consultant,** or *informant,* refers to individuals the ethnographer gets to know in the field, the people who teach him or her about their culture, who provide the emic perspective.

The **etic** (scientist-oriented) approach shifts the focus from local observations, categories, explanations, and interpretations to those of the anthropologist. The etic approach realizes that members of a culture often are too involved in what they are doing to interpret their cultures impartially. Operating etically, the ethnographer emphasizes what he or she (the observer) notices

Anthropologists such as Christie Kiefer typically form personal relationships with their cultural consultants, such as this Guatemalan weaver.

and considers important. As a trained scientist, the ethnographer should try to bring an objective and comprehensive viewpoint to the study of other cultures. Of course, the ethnographer, like any other scientist, is also a human being with cultural blinders that prevent complete objectivity. As in other sciences, proper training can reduce, but not totally eliminate, the observer's bias. But anthropologists do have special training to compare behavior between different societies.

What are some examples of emic versus etic perspectives? Consider our holidays. For North Americans, Thanksgiving Day has special significance. In our view (emically) it is a unique cultural celebration that commemorates particular historical themes. But a wider, etic, perspective sees Thanksgiving as just one more example of the postharvest festivals held in many societies. Another example: Local people (including many Americans) may believe that chills and drafts cause colds, which scientists know are caused by germs. In cultures that lack the germ theory of disease, illnesses are emically explained by various causes, ranging from spirits to ancestors to witches. *Illness* refers to a culture's (emic) perception and explanation of bad health, whereas *disease* refers to the scientific (etic) explanation of poor health, involving known pathogens.

Ethnographers typically combine emic and etic strategies in their field work. The statements, perceptions, categories, and opinions of local people help ethnographers understand how cultures work. Local beliefs are also interesting and valuable in themselves. However, people often fail to admit, or even recognize, certain causes and consequences of their behavior. This is as true of North Americans as it is of people in other societies.

life history
Of a key consultant; a personal portrait of someone's life in a culture.

emic
Research strategy focusing on local explanations and meanings.

cultural consultants
People who teach an ethnographer about their culture.

etic
Research strategy emphasizing the ethnographer's explanations and categories.

Problem-Oriented Ethnography

Although anthropologists are interested in the whole context of human behavior, it is impossible to study everything. Most ethnographers now enter the field with a specific problem to investigate, and they collect data relevant to that problem (see Chiseri-Strater and Sunstein 2007; Kutsche 1998). Local people's answers to questions are not the only data source. Anthropologists also gather information on factors such as population density, environmental quality, climate, physical geography, diet, and land use. Sometimes this involves direct measurement—of rainfall, temperature, fields, yields, dietary quantities, or time allocation (Bailey 1990; Johnson 1978). Often it means that we consult government records or archives.

The information of interest to ethnographers is not limited to what local people can and do tell us. In an increasingly interconnected and complicated world, local people lack knowledge about many factors that affect their lives. Our local consultants may be as mystified as we are by the exercise of power from regional, national, and international centers.

longitudinal research Long-term study, usually based on repeated visits.

Longitudinal Research

Geography limits anthropologists less now than in the past, when it could take months to reach a field site and return visits were rare. New systems of transportation allow anthropologists to widen the area of their research and to return repeatedly. Ethnographic reports now routinely include data from two or more field stays. **Longitudinal research** is the long-term study of a community, region, society, culture, or other unit, usually based on repeated visits.

One example of such research is the longitudinal study of Gwembe District, Zambia (see Figure 13.2). This study, planned in 1956 as a longitudinal project by Elizabeth Colson and Thayer Scudder, continues with Colson, Scudder, and their associates of various nationalities. Thus, as is often the case with longitudinal research, the Gwembe study also illustrates team research—coordinated research by multiple ethnographers (Colson and Scudder 1975; Scudder and Colson 1980). Four villages, in different areas, have been followed for more than five decades. Periodic village censuses provide basic data on population, economy, kinship, and religious behavior. Censused people who have moved are traced and interviewed to see how their lives compare with those of people who have stayed in the villages.

A series of different research questions has emerged, while basic data on communities and individuals continue to be collected. The first focus of study was the impact of a large hydroelectric dam, which subjected the Gwembe people to forced resettlement. The dam also spurred road building and other activities that brought the

FIGURE 13.2 Location of Gwembe in Zambia

living anthropology **VIDEOS**

Adoption into the Canela, www.mhhe.com/kottak

The anthropologist Bill Crocker, as shown in this clip, has been studying the Canela Indians of Brazil since 1957. The clip interweaves photos and footage from his various visits to the field. Crocker has been able to make his research longitudinal and ongoing because the limitations on travel and communication are much less severe now than they were in the past. Compare the time it took to reach the field in 1957 with the more recent trip shown in the clip. There is evidence in the clip that the Canela live in a kinbased society. Crocker gained an entry to Canela society by assuming a kinship status. What was it? Did this status turn out to be a good thing? Why did Crocker hesitate when this connection was first proposed?

people of Gwembe more closely in touch with the rest of Zambia. In subsequent research Scudder and Colson (1980) examined how education provided access to new opportunities as it also widened a social gap between people with different educational levels. A third study then examined a change in brewing and drinking patterns, including a rise in alcoholism, in relation to changing markets, transportation, and exposure to town values (Colson and Scudder 1988).

Team Research

As mentioned, longitudinal research often is team research. My own field site of Arembepe, Brazil, for example, first entered the world of anthropology as a field-team village in the 1960s. It was one of four sites for the now defunct Columbia-Cornell-Harvard-Illinois Summer Field Studies Program in Anthropology. For at least three years, that program sent a total of about twenty undergraduates annually, the author included, to do brief summer research abroad. We were stationed in rural communities in four countries: Brazil, Ecuador, Mexico, and Peru. See this chapter's "Appreciating Diversity" on pp. 284–285 for information on how a novice undergraduate ethnographer perceived Arembepe.

Since my wife, Isabel Wagley-Kottak, and I began studying it in 1962, Arembepe has become a longitudinal field site. Three generations of researchers have monitored various aspects of change and development. The community has changed from a village into a town and illustrates the process of globalization at the local level. Its economy, religion, and social life have been transformed (see Kottak 2006).

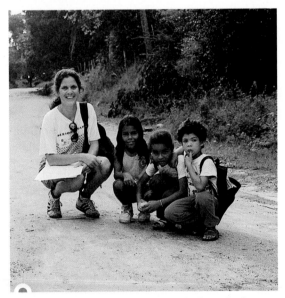

Janet Dunn, one of many anthropologists who have worked in Arembepe. Where is Arembepe, and what kinds of research have been done there?

Brazilian and American researchers worked with us on team research projects during the 1980s (on television's impact) and the 1990s (on ecological awareness and environmental risk perception). Graduate students from the University of Michigan have drawn on our baseline information from the 1960s as they have studied various topics in Arembepe. In 1990 Doug Jones, a Michigan student doing biocultural research, used Arembepe as a field site to investigate standards of physical attractiveness. In 1996–1997, Janet Dunn studied family planning and changing female reproductive strategies. Chris O'Leary, who first visited Arembepe in summer 1997, investigated a striking aspect of religious change there—the arrival of Protestantism; his dissertation (O'Leary 2002) research then examined changing food habits and nutrition in relation to globalization. Arembepe is thus a site where various field workers have worked as members of a longitudinal team. The more recent researchers have built on prior contacts and findings to increase knowledge about how local people meet and manage new circumstances.

Culture, Space, and Scale

The previous sections on longitudinal and team research illustrate an important shift in cultural anthropology. Traditional ethnographic research focused on a single community or "culture," which was treated as more or less isolated and unique in time and space. The shift has been toward recognition of ongoing and inescapable flows of people, technology, images, and information. The study of such flows and linkages is now part of the anthropological analysis. And, reflecting today's world—in which people, images, and information move about as never before—field work must be more flexible and on a larger scale. Ethnography is increasingly multitimed and multisited. Malinowski could focus on Trobriand culture and spend most of his field time in a particular community. Nowadays we cannot afford to ignore, as Malinowski did, the "outsiders" who increasingly impinge on the places we study (e.g., migrants, refugees, terrorists, warriors, tourists, developers). Integral to our analyses now are the external organizations and forces (e.g., governments, businesses, nongovernmental organizations) laying claim to land, people, and resources throughout the world. Also important is increased recognition of power differentials and how they affect cultures, and of the importance of diversity within culture and societies.

The anthropologist Clyde Kluckhohn (1944) saw a key public service role for anthropology. It could provide a "scientific basis for dealing with the crucial dilemma of the world today: how can peoples of different appearance, mutually unintelligible languages, and dissimilar ways of life get along peaceably together." Many anthropologists never would have chosen their profession had they doubted that anthropology had the capacity to enhance human welfare. Because we live in a world full of failed states, war, and terrorism, we must consider the proper role of anthropologists in studying such phenomena. As we see in this chapter's "Appreciating Anthropology," the American Anthropological Association deems it of "paramount importance" that anthropologists study the roots of terrorism and violence. How exactly should this be done, and what are potential risks to anthropologists and the people they study? Read "Appreciating Anthropology" for some answers and for a discussion of the complexity of these questions.

Like many other topics addressed by contemporary anthropology, war and terrorism would require multiple levels of analysis—local, regional, and international. It is virtually impossible in today's world to find local phenomena that are isolated from global forces.

In two volumes of essays edited by Akhil Gupta and James Ferguson (1997*a* and 1997*b*), several anthropologists describe problems in trying to locate cultures in bounded spaces. John Durham Peters (1997), for example, notes that, particularly because of the mass media, contemporary people simultaneously experience the local and the global. He describes those people as culturally "bifocal"—both "near-sighted" (seeing local events) and "far-sighted" (seeing images from far away). Given their "bifocality," their interpretations of the local are always influenced by information from outside. Thus, their attitude about a clear blue sky at home is tinged by their knowledge, through weather reports, that a hurricane may be approaching. The national news may not at all fit opinions voiced in local conversations, but national opinions find their way into local discourse.

The mass media, which anthropologists increasingly study, are oddities in terms of culture and space. Whose image and opinions are these? What culture or community do they represent? They certainly aren't local. Media images and messages flow electronically. TV brings them right to you. The Internet lets you discover new cultural possibilities at the click of a mouse. The Internet takes us to virtual places, but in truth, the electronic mass media are placeless phenomena, which are transnational in scope and play a role in forming and maintaining cultural identities.

Anthropological research today may take us traveling along with the people we study, as they move from village to city, cross the border, or travel internationally on business. As we'll see in the chapter "Global Issues Today," ethnographers increasingly follow the people and images they study. As field work changes, with less and less of a spatially set field, what can we take from traditional ethnography? Gupta and Ferguson

correctly cite the "characteristically anthropological emphasis on daily routine and lived experience" (1997*a*, p. 5). The treatment of communities as discrete entities may be a thing of the past. However, "anthropology's traditional attention to the close observation of particular lives in particular places" (Gupta and Ferguson 1997*b*, p. 25) has an enduring importance. The method of close observation helps distinguish cultural anthropology from sociology and survey research, to which we now turn.

SURVEY RESEARCH

As anthropologists work increasingly in large-scale societies, they have developed innovative ways of blending ethnography and survey research (Fricke 1994). Before examining such combinations of field methods, let's consider survey research and the main differences between survey research and ethnography. Working mainly in large, populous nations, sociologists, political scientists, and economists have developed and refined the **survey research** design, which involves sampling, impersonal data collection, and statistical analysis. Survey research usually draws a **sample** (a manageable study group) from a much larger population. By studying a properly selected and representative sample, social scientists can make accurate inferences about the larger population.

In smaller-scale societies and communities, ethnographers get to know most of the people. Given the greater size and complexity of nations, survey research cannot help being more impersonal. Survey researchers call the people they study *respondents*. These are people who respond to questions during a survey. Sometimes survey researchers interview them personally. Sometimes, after an initial meeting, they ask respondents to fill out a questionnaire. In other cases researchers mail or e-mail questionnaires to randomly selected sample members or have paid assistants interview or telephone them. In a **random sample,** all members of the population have an equal statistical chance of being chosen for inclusion. A random sample is selected by randomizing procedures, such as tables of random numbers, which are found in many statistics textbooks.

Probably the most familiar example of sampling is the polling used to predict political races. The media hire agencies to estimate outcomes and do exit polls to find out what kinds of people voted for which candidates. During sampling, researchers gather information about age, gender, religion, occupation, income, and political party preference. These characteristics (**variables**—attributes that vary among members of a sample or population) are known to influence political decisions.

Many more variables affect social identities, experiences, and activities in a modern nation

survey research
The study of society through sampling, statistical analysis, and impersonal data collection.

sample
A smaller study group chosen to represent a larger population.

random sample
A sample in which all population members have an equal chance of inclusion.

variables
Attributes that differ from one person or case to the next.

ETHNOGRAPHY (TRADITIONAL)	SURVEY RESEARCH
Studies whole, functioning communities	Studies a small sample of a larger population
Usually is based on firsthand field work, during which information is collected after rapport, based on personal contact, is established between researcher and hosts	Often is conducted with little or no personal contact between study subjects and researchers, as interviews are frequently conducted by assistants over the phone or in printed form
Traditionally is interested in all aspects of local life (holistic)	Usually focuses on a small number of variables (e.g., factors that influence voting) rather than on the totality of people's lives
Traditionally has been conducted in nonindustrial, small-scale societies, where people often do not read and write	Normally is carried out in modern nations, where most people are literate, permitting respondents to fill in their own questionnaires
Makes little use of statistics, because the communities being studied tend to be small, with little diversity besides that based on age, gender, and individual personality variation	Depends heavily on statistical analyses to make inferences regarding a large and diverse population, based on data collected from a small subset of that population

A population census taker surrounded by villagers in Paro, Bhutan. Is the technique of gathering information illustrated here more like ethnography or survey research?

than in the small communities where ethnography grew up. In contemporary North America hundreds of factors influence our behavior and attitudes. These social predictors include our religion; the region of the country we grew up in; whether we come from a town, suburb, or city; and our parents' professions, ethnic origins, and income levels.

Ethnography can be used to supplement and fine-tune survey research. Anthropologists can transfer the personal, firsthand techniques of ethnography to virtually any setting that includes human beings. A combination of survey research and ethnography can provide new perspectives on life in **complex societies** (large and populous societies with social stratification and central governments). Preliminary ethnography also can help develop culturally appropriate questions for inclusion in surveys. Recap 13.1 contrasts traditional ethnography with elements of survey research.

complex societies
Large, populous societies (e.g., nations) with stratification and a government.

appreciating ANTHROPOLOGY

Should Anthropologists Study Terrorism?

How and how much should anthropology matter? For decades I've heard anthropologists complain that government officials fail to appreciate, or simply are ignorant of, findings of anthropology that are relevant to making informed policies. The American Anthropological Association deems it of "paramount importance" that anthropologists study the roots of terrorism and violence. How should such studies be conducted? This account describes a Pentagon program, Project Minerva, initiated late in the (George W.) Bush administration, to enlist social science expertise to combat security threats.

Project Minerva has raised concerns among anthropologists. Based on past experience, scholars worry that governments might use anthropological knowledge for goals and in ways that are ethically problematic. Government policies and military operations have the potential to bring harm to the people anthropologists study. Social scientists object especially to the notion that Pentagon officials should determine which projects are worthy of funding. Rather, anthropologists favor a (peer review) system in which panels of their professional peers (other social scientists) judge the value and propriety of proposed research, including research that might help identify and deter threats to national security.

Can you appreciate anthropology's potential value for national security? Read the Code of Ethics of the American Anthropological Association at www.aaanet.org/committees/ethics/ethcode.htm. In the context of that code, can you also appreciate anthropologists' reluctance to endorse Project Minerva and its procedures?

Eager to embrace eggheads and ideas, the Pentagon has started an ambitious and unusual program to recruit social scientists and direct the nation's brainpower to combating security threats like the Chinese military, Iraq, terrorism and religious fundamentalism.

Defense Secretary Robert M. Gates has compared the initiative—named Minerva, after the Roman goddess

Project Minerva, described here, has raised ethical concerns among anthropologists, as has the U. S. military's controversial Human Terrain Team program. This counter-insurgency effort embeds anthropologists and other social scientists with combat brigades in Iraq and Afghanistan to help tacticians in the field understand local cultures. Shown here, a U. S. Army Major takes notes as he talks and drinks tea with local school administrators in Nani, Afghanistan. The Major is attached to a Human Terrain Team.

of wisdom (and warriors)—to the government's effort to pump up its intellectual capital during the cold war after the Soviet Union launched Sputnik in 1957.

Although the Pentagon regularly finances science and engineering research, systematic support for the social sciences and humanities has been rare. Minerva is the first systematic effort in this area since the Vietnam War, said Thomas G. Mahnken, deputy assistant secretary of defense for policy planning, whose office will be overseeing the project.

But if the uncustomary push to engage the nation's evolutionary psychologists, demographers, sociologists, historians and anthropologists in security research—as well as the prospect of new financial support in lean times—has generated excitement among some scholars, it has also aroused opposition from others, who worry that the Defense Department and the academy are getting too cozy . . .

Cooperation between universities and the Pentagon has long been a contentious issue. . . .

"I am all in favor of having lots of researchers trying to figure out why terrorists want to kill Americans," said Hugh Gusterson, an anthropologist at George Mason University. "But how can you make sure you get a broad spectrum of opinion and find the best people? On both counts, I don't think the Pentagon is the way to go."

Mr. Gusterson is a founder of the Network of Concerned Anthropologists, which was created because of a growing unease among scholars about cooperating with the Defense Department.

The American Anthropological Association, an 11,000-member organization, has also told administration officials that while research on these issues is essential, Defense Department money could compromise quality and independence because of the department's inexperience with social science. "There was pretty general agreement that this was an issue we should weigh in on," said Setha M. Low, the or-

ganization's president, who contacted dozens of anthropologists about it.

In its written call for proposals, the department said Minerva was seeking scholars who can, for example, translate original documents, including those captured in Iraq; study changes in the People's Liberation Army as China shifts to a more open political system; and explain the resurgence of the Taliban. The department is also looking for computational models that could illuminate how groups make what seem to be irrational decisions, and decipher the way the brain processes social and cultural norms.

Mr. Gates has stressed the importance of devoting resources to what he calls "'soft power', the elements of national power beyond the guns and steel of the military."

Toward that end, he contacted Robert M. Berdahl, the president of the Association of American Universities—which represents 60 of the top research universities in the country—in December to help design Minerva. A former chancellor of the University of California, Berkeley, and a past president of the University of Texas at Austin, Mr. Berdahl knew Mr. Gates from when the defense secretary served on the association's board.

In January Mr. Berdahl and a small group of senior scholars and university administrators met in Washington with Defense Department officials. Also there was Graham Spanier, the president of Penn State University and the association's chairman. He said the scholars helped refine the guidelines, advising that the research be open and unclassified.

Mr. Berdahl said some participants favored having the National Science Foundation or a similar nonmilitary federal organization, rather than the Pentagon, distribute Minerva money. "It would be a good way to proceed, because they've had a lot of experience with social science," he said.

In a speech to the Association of American Universities in April, Mr. Gates said, "The key principle of all components of the Minerva Consortia will be complete openness and rigid adherence to academic freedom and integrity." At a time when political campaigns have treated the word elitist as an epithet, he quoted the historian Arthur Schlesinger Jr.'s statement that the United States "must return to the acceptance of eggheads and ideas" to meet national security threats.

"We are interested in furthering our knowledge of these issues and in soliciting diverse points of view, regardless of whether those views are critical of the department's efforts," Mr. Gates added.

In response to Mr. Gates's speech, the American Anthropological Association sent a letter to administration officials saying that it is of "paramount importance" that anthropologists study the roots of terrorism and violence, but adding, "We are deeply concerned that funding such research through the Pentagon may pose a potential conflict of interest and undermine the practices of peer review." . . .

Anthropologists have been especially outspoken about the Pentagon's Human Terrain Teams, a two-year-old program that pairs anthropologists and other social scientists with combat units in Afghanistan and Iraq. . . .

As for Minerva, many scholars said routing the money through the National Science Foundation or a similar institution would go a long way toward easing most of their concerns. . . .

In any complex society, many predictor variables (*social indicators*) influence behavior and opinions. Because we must be able to detect, measure, and compare the influence of social indicators, many contemporary anthropological studies have a statistical foundation. Even in rural field work, more anthropologists now draw samples, gather quantitative data, and use statistics to interpret them (see Bernard 2006; Bernard, ed. 1998). Quantifiable information may permit a more precise assessment of similarities and differences among communities. Statistical analysis can support and round out an ethnographic account of local social life.

However, in the best studies, the hallmark of ethnography remains: Anthropologists enter the community and get to know the people. They participate in local activities, networks, and associations in the city, town, or countryside. They observe and experience social conditions and problems. They watch the effects of national and international policies and programs on local life. The ethnographic method and the emphasis on personal relationships in social research are valuable gifts that cultural anthropology brings to the study of any society.

THEORY IN ANTHROPOLOGY OVER TIME

Anthropology has various fathers and mothers. The fathers include Lewis Henry Morgan, Sir Edward Burnett Tylor, Franz Boas, and Bronislaw Malinowski. The mothers include Ruth Benedict and especially Margaret Mead. Some of the fathers might be classified better as grandfathers, since one, Franz Boas, was the intellectual father of Mead and Benedict, and since what is known now as Boasian anthropology arose mainly in opposition to the 19th-century evolutionism of Morgan and Tylor.

My goal in the remainder of this chapter is to survey the major theoretical perspectives that have characterized anthropology since its emergence in the second half of the 19th century. Evolutionary perspectives, especially those associated with Morgan and Tylor, dominated early anthropology. The early 20th century witnessed various reactions to 19th-century evolutionism. In Great Britain, functionalists such as Malinowski and Alfred Reginald Radcliffe-Brown abandoned the speculative historicism of the evolutionists in favor of studies of present-day living societies. In the United States, Boas and his followers rejected the search for evolutionary stages in favor of a historical approach that traced borrowing between cultures and the spread of culture traits across geographic areas. Functionalists and Boasians alike saw cultures as integrated and patterned.

The functionalists especially viewed societies as systems in which various parts worked together to maintain the whole.

By the mid-20th century, following World War II and the collapse of colonialism, there was a revived interest in change, including new evolutionary approaches. Other anthropologists concentrated on the symbolic basis and nature of culture, using symbolic and interpretive approaches to uncover patterned symbols and meanings. By the 1980s anthropologists had grown more interested in the relation between culture and the individual, and the role of human action (agency) in transforming culture. There was also a resurgence of historical approaches, including those that viewed local cultures in relation to colonialism and the world system. Contemporary anthropology is marked by increasing specialization, based on special topics and identities. Reflecting this specialization, some universities have moved away from the holistic, biocultural view of anthropology that is reflected in this book. However, the Boasian view of anthropology as a four-subfield discipline—including biological, archaeological, cultural, and linguistic anthropology—continues to thrive at many universities as well.

Evolutionism

Both Tylor and Morgan wrote classic books during the 19th century. Tylor (1871/1958) offered a definition of culture and proposed it as a topic that could be studied scientifically. Morgan's influential books included *Ancient Society* (1877/1963), *The League of the Ho-dé-no-sau-nee or Iroquois* (1851/1966), and *Systems of Consanguinity and Affinity of the Human Family* (1870/1997). The first was a key work in cultural evolution. The second was an early ethnography. The third was the first systematic compendium of cross-cultural data on systems of kinship terminology.

Ancient Society is a key example of 19th-century evolutionism applied to society. Morgan assumed that human society had evolved through a series of stages, which he called savagery, barbarism, and civilization. He subdivided savagery and barbarism into three substages each: lower, middle, and upper savagery and lower, middle, and upper barbarism. In Morgan's scheme, the earliest humans lived in lower savagery, with a subsistence based on fruits and nuts. In middle savagery people started fishing and gained control over fire. The invention of the bow and arrow ushered in upper savagery. Lower barbarism began when humans started making pottery. Middle barbarism in the Old World depended on the domestication of plants and animals, and in the Americas on irrigated agriculture. Iron smelting and the use of iron tools ushered in upper barbarism. Civilization, finally, came about with the invention of writing.

Morgan's brand of evolutionism is known as **unilinear evolutionism,** because he assumed there was one line or path through which all societies had to evolve. Any society in upper barbarism, for example, had to include in its history, in order, periods of lower, middle, and upper savagery, and then lower and middle barbarism. Stages could not be skipped. Furthermore, Morgan believed that the societies of his time could be placed in the various stages. Some had not advanced beyond upper savagery. Others had made it to middle barbarism, while others had attained civilization.

Critics of Morgan disputed various elements of his scheme, particularly such terms as "savagery" and "barbarism" and the criteria he used for progress. Thus, because Polynesians never developed pottery, they were frozen, in Morgan's scheme, in upper savagery. In fact, in sociopolitical terms, Polynesia was an advanced region, with many complex societies, including the ancient Hawaiian state. We know now, too, that Morgan was wrong in assuming that societies pursued only one evolutionary path. Societies have followed different paths to civilization, based on very different economies.

In his book *Primitive Culture* (1871/1958), Tylor developed his own evolutionary approach to the anthropology of religion. Like Morgan, Tylor proposed a unilinear path—from animism to polytheism, then monotheism, and finally science. In Tylor's view, religion would retreat as science provided better and better explanations. Both Tylor and Morgan were interested in *survivals*, practices that survived in contemporary society from earlier evolutionary stages. The belief in ghosts today, for example, would represent a survival from the stage of animism—the belief in spiritual beings. Survivals were taken as evidence that a particular society had passed through earlier evolutionary stages.

Morgan is well known also for *The League of the Iroquois*, anthropology's earliest ethnography. It was based on occasional rather than protracted field work. Morgan, although one of anthropology's founders, was not himself a professionally trained anthropologist. He was a lawyer in upper New York state who was fond of visiting a nearby Seneca reservation and learning about their history and customs. The Seneca were one of six Iroquois tribes. Through his field work, and his friendship with Ely Parker (see Chapter 1), an educated Iroquois man, Morgan was able to describe the social, political, religious, and economic principles of Iroquois life, including the history of their confederation. He laid out the structural principles on which Iroquois society was based. Morgan also used his skills as a lawyer to help the Iroquois in their fight with the Ogden Land Company, which was attempting to seize their lands.

Ernest Smith's 1936 watercolor depicts a bitterly fought game between Native American rivals. The early American anthropologist Lewis Henry Morgan described lacrosse (shown here) as one of the six games played by the tribes of the Iroquois nation, whose League he described in a famous book (1851).

The Boasians

Four-Field Anthropology

Indisputably, Boas is the father of American four-field anthropology. His book *Race, Language, and Culture* (1940/1966) is a collection of essays on those key topics. Boas contributed to cultural, biological, and linguistic anthropology. His biological studies of European immigrants to the United States revealed and measured phenotypical plasticity. The children of immigrants differed physically from their parents not because of genetic change but because they had grown up in a different environment. Boas showed that human biology was plastic. It could be changed by the environment, including cultural forces. Boas and his students worked hard to demonstrate that biology (including race) did not determine culture. In an important book, Ruth Benedict (1940) stressed the idea that people of many races have contributed to major historical advances and that civilization is the achievement of no single race.

As was mentioned in Chapter 1, the four subfields of anthropology initially formed around interests in Native Americans—their cultures, histories, languages, and physical characteristics. Boas himself studied language and culture among Native Americans, most notably the Kwakiutl of the North Pacific coast of the United States and Canada.

Historical Particularism

Boas and his many influential followers, who studied with him at Columbia University in New

unilinear evolutionism Idea (19th century) of a single line or path of cultural development.

Franz Boas, founder of American four-field anthropology, studied the Kwakwaka' wakw, or Kwakiutl, in British Columbia (BC), Canada. The photo above shows Boas posing for a museum model of a Kwakiutl dancer. The photo on the right is a still from a film by anthropologist Aaron Glass titled *In Search of the Hamat'sa: A Tale of Headhunting* (DER distributor). It shows a real Kwakiutl dancer, Marcus Alfred, performing the same Hamat'sa (or "Cannibal Dance"), which is a vital part of an important Kwakiutl ceremony. The U'mista Cultural Centre in Alert Bay, BC, (www.international.gc.ca/culture/arts/ss_umista-en. asp) owns the rights to the video clip of the Hamat'sa featuring Marcus Alfred.

historical
particularism
Idea (Boas) that histories
are not comparable;
diverse paths can lead to
the same cultural result.

York City, took issue with Morgan on many counts. They disputed the criteria he used to define his stages. They disputed the idea of one evolutionary path. They argued that the same cultural result, for example, totemism, could not have a single explanation, because there were many paths to totemism. Their position was one of **historical particularism**. Because the particular histories of totemism in societies A, B, and C had all been different, those forms of totemism had different causes, which made them incomparable. They might seem to be the same, but they were really different because they had different histories. Any cultural form, from totemism to clans, could develop, they believed, for all sorts of reasons. Boasian historical particularism rejected what those scholars called the *comparative method*, which was associated not only with Morgan and Tylor but with any anthropologist interested in cross-cultural comparison. The evolutionists had compared societies in attempting to reconstruct the evolutionary history of *Homo sapiens*. Later anthropologists, such as Émile Durkheim and Claude Lévi-Strauss (see below), also compared societies in attempting to explain cultural phenomena such as totemism. As is demonstrated throughout this text, cross-cultural comparison is alive and well in contemporary anthropology.

Independent Invention versus Diffusion

Remember from the chapter "Culture" that *cultural generalities* are shared by some but not all societies. To explain cultural generalities, such as totemism and the clan, the evolutionists had stressed independent invention: Eventually people in many areas (as they evolved along a preordained evolutionary path) had come up with the same cultural solution to a common problem. Agriculture, for example, was invented several times. The Boasians, while not denying independent invention, stressed the importance of diffusion, or borrowing, from other cultures. The analytic units they used to study diffusion were the culture trait, the trait complex, and the culture area. A culture trait was something like a bow and arrow. A trait complex was the hunting pattern that went along with it. A culture area was based on the diffusion of traits and trait complexes across a particular geographic area, such as the Plains, the Southwest, or the North Pacific coast of North America. Such areas usually had environmental boundaries that could limit the spread of culture traits outside that area. For the Boasians, historical particularism and diffusion were complementary. As culture traits diffused, they developed their particular histories as they entered and moved through particular societies. Boasians such as Alfred Kroeber, Clark Wissler, and Melville Herskovits studied the distribution of traits and developed culture area classifications for Native North America (Wissler and Kroeber) and Africa (Herskovits).

Historical particularism was based on the idea that each element of culture, such as the culture trait or trait complex, had its own distinctive history and that social forms (such as totemism in different societies) that might look similar were far from identical because of their different histories. Historical particularism rejected comparison and generalization in favor of an individuating historical approach. In this rejection, historical particularism stands in contrast to most of the approaches that have followed it.

Functionalism

Another challenge to evolutionism (and to historical particularism) came from Great Britain. *Functionalism* postponed the search for origins (through evolution or diffusion) and instead focused on the role of culture traits and practices in contemporary society. The two main strands of **functionalism** are associated with Alfred Reginald Radcliffe-Brown and Bronislaw Malinowski, a Polish anthropologist who taught mainly in Great Britain.

Malinowski

Both Malinowski and Radcliffe-Brown focused on the present rather than on historical reconstruction. Malinowski did pioneering field work among living people. Usually considered the father of ethnography by virtue of his years of field work in the Trobriand Islands, Malinowski was a functionalist in two senses. In the first, rooted in his ethnography, he believed that all customs and institutions in society were integrated and interrelated, so that if one changed, others would change as well. Each, then, was a *function* of the others. A corollary of this belief was that the ethnography could begin anywhere and eventually get at the rest of the culture. Thus, a study of Trobriand fishing eventually would lead the ethnographer to study the entire economic system, the role of magic and religion, myth, trade, and kinship. The second strand of Malinowski's functionalism is known as *needs functionalism*. Malinowski (1944) believed that humans had a set of universal biological needs, and that customs developed to fulfill those needs. The function of any practice was the role it played in satisfying those universal biological needs, such as the need for food, sex, shelter, and so on.

Conjectural History

According to Radcliffe-Brown (1962/1965), although history is important, social anthropology could never hope to discover the histories of people without writing. (*Social anthropology* is what cultural anthropology is called in Great Britain.) He trusted neither evolutionary nor diffusionist reconstructions. Since all history was conjectural, Radcliffe-Brown urged social anthropologists to focus on the role that particular practices play in the life of societies today. In a famous essay Radcliffe-Brown (1962/1965) examined the prom-

Bronislaw Malinowski (1884–1942), who was born in Poland but spent most of his professional life in England, did field work in the Trobriand Islands from 1914 to 1918. Malinowski is generally considered to be the father of ethnography. Does this photo suggest anything about his relationship with Trobriand villagers?

inent role of the mother's brother among the Ba Thonga of Mozambique. An evolutionist priest working in Mozambique previously had explained the special role of the mother's brother in this patrilineal society as a survival from a time when the descent rule had been matrilineal. (The unilinear evolutionists believed all human societies had passed through a matrilineal stage.) Since Radcliffe-Brown believed that the history of Ba Thonga society could only be conjectural, he explained the special role of the mother's brother with reference to the institutions of present rather than past Ba Thonga society. Radcliffe-Brown advocated that social anthropology be a **synchronic** rather than a **diachronic** science, that is, that it study societies as they exist today (synchronic, at one time) rather than across time (diachronic).

Structural Functionalism

The term *structural functionalism* is associated with Radcliffe-Brown and Edward Evan Evans-Pritchard, another prominent British social anthropologist. The latter is famous for many books, including *The Nuer* (1940), an ethnographic classic that laid out very clearly the structural principles that organized Nuer society in Sudan. According to functionalism and structural functionalism, customs (social practices) function to preserve the social structure. In Radcliffe-Brown's view, the *function* of any practice is what it does to maintain the system of which it is a part. That system has a structure whose parts work or function to maintain the whole. Radcliffe-Brown saw social systems as comparable to anatomical and physiological systems. The function of organs and physiological processes is their role in keeping the body running smoothly. So, too, he thought, did customs, practices, social roles, and behavior function to keep the social system running smoothly.

functionalism
Approach focusing on the role (function) of sociocultural practices in social systems.

synchronic
(Studying societies) at one time.

diachronic
(Studying societies) across time.

The University of Manchester was developed by bringing together the Victoria University of Manchester (shown here) and the University of Manchester Institute of Science and Technology. Max Gluckman, one of the founders of anthropology's "Manchester school," taught here from 1949 until his death in 1975.

Dr. Pangloss versus Conflict

Given this suggestion of harmony, some functionalist models have been criticized as Panglossian, after Dr. Pangloss, a character in Voltaire's *Candide* who was fond of proclaiming this "the best of all possible worlds." Panglossian functionalism means a tendency to see things as functioning not just to maintain the system but to do so in the most optimal way possible, so that any deviation from the norm would only damage the system. A group of British social anthropologists working at the University of Manchester, dubbed the Manchester school, are well known for their research in African societies and their departure from a Panglossian view of social harmony. Manchester anthropologists Max Gluckman and Victor Turner made conflict an important part of their analysis, such as when Gluckman wrote about rituals of rebellion. However, the Manchester school did not abandon functionalism totally. Its members examined how rebellion and conflict were regulated and dissipated, thus maintaining the system.

Functionalism Persists

A form of functionalism persists in the widely accepted view that there are social and cultural systems and that their elements, or constituent parts, are functionally related (are functions of each other) so that they covary: when one part changes, others also change. Also enduring is the idea that some elements—often the economic ones—are more important than others are. Few would deny, for example, that significant economic changes, such as the increasing cash employment of

women, have led to changes in family and household organization and in related variables such as age at marriage and frequency of divorce. Changes in work and family arrangements then affect other variables, such as frequency of church attendance, which has declined in the United States and Canada.

Configurationalism

Two of Boas's students, Benedict and Mead, developed an approach to culture that has been called **configurationalism.** This is related to functionalism in the sense that culture is seen as integrated. We've seen that the Boasians traced the geographic distribution of culture traits. But Boas recognized that diffusion wasn't automatic. Traits might not spread if they met environmental barriers, or if they were not accepted by a particular culture. There had to be a fit between the culture and the trait diffusing in, and borrowed traits would be reworked to fit the culture adopting them. The chapter "Global Issues Today" examines how borrowed traits are indigenized—modified to fit the existing culture. Although traits may diffuse in from various directions, Benedict stressed that culture traits—indeed, whole cultures—are uniquely patterned or integrated. Her best-selling book *Patterns of Culture* (1934/1959) described such culture patterns.

Mead also found patterns in the cultures she studied, including Samoa, Bali, and Papua New Guinea. Mead was particularly interested in how

configurationalism
View of culture as integrated and patterned.

This 1995 stamp honors Ruth Fulton Benedict (1887–1948), a major figure in American anthropology, most famous for her widely read book *Patterns of Culture*.

cultures varied in their patterns of enculturation. Stressing the plasticity of human nature, she saw culture as a powerful force that created almost endless possibilities. Even among neighboring societies, different enculturation patterns could produce very different personality types and cultural configurations. Mead's best-known—albeit controversial—book is *Coming of Age in Samoa* (1928/1961). Mead traveled to Samoa to study female adolescence there in order to compare it with the same period of life in the United States. Suspicious of biologically determined universals, she assumed that Samoan adolescence would differ from the same period in the United States and that this would affect adult personality. Using her Samoan ethnographic findings, Mead contrasted the apparent sexual freedom and experimentation there with the repression of adolescent sexuality in the United States. Her findings supported the Boasian view that culture, not biology or race, determines variation in human behavior and personality. Mead's later field work among the Arapesh, Mundugumor, and Tchambuli of New Guinea resulted in *Sex and Temperament in Three Primitive Societies* (1935/1950). That book documented variation in male and female personality traits and behavior across cultures. She offered it as further support for cultural determinism. Like Benedict, Mead was more interested in describing how cultures were uniquely patterned or configured than in explaining how they got to be that way.

Neoevolutionism

Around 1950, with the end of World War II and a growing anticolonial movement, anthropologists renewed their interest in culture change and even evolution. The American anthropologists Leslie White and Julian Steward complained that the Boasians had thrown the baby (evolution) out with the bath water (the particular flaws of 19th-century evolutionary schemes). There was a need, the neoevolutionists contended, to reintroduce within the study of culture a powerful concept—evolution itself. This concept, after all, remains basic to biology. Why should it not apply to culture as well?

In his book *The Evolution of Culture* (1959), White claimed to be returning to the same concept of cultural evolution used by Tylor and Morgan, but now informed by a century of archaeological discoveries and a much larger ethnographic record. White's approach has been called *general evolution*, the idea that over time and through the archaeological, historical, and ethnographic records, we can see the evolution of culture as a whole. For example, human economies have evolved from Paleolithic foraging, through early farming and herding, to intensive forms of agriculture, and to industrialism. Socio-

World-famous anthropologist Margaret Mead (1901–1979) in the field in Bali, Indonesia, in 1957.

politically, too, there has been evolution, from bands and tribes to chiefdoms and states. There can be no doubt, White argued, that culture has evolved. But unlike the unilinear evolutionists of the 19th century, White realized that particular cultures might not evolve in the same direction.

Julian Steward, in his influential book *Theory of Culture Change* (1955), proposed a different evolutionary model, which he called *multilinear evolution*. He showed how cultures had evolved along several different lines. For example, he recognized different paths to statehood (e.g., those followed by irrigated versus nonirrigated societies). Steward was also a pioneer in a field of anthropology he called *cultural ecology*, today generally known as *ecological anthropology*, which considers the relationships between cultures and environmental variables.

Unlike Mead and Benedict, who were not interested in causes, White and Steward were. For White, energy capture was the main measure and cause of cultural advance: Cultures advanced in proportion to the amount of energy harnessed per capita per year. In this view, the United States is one of the world's most advanced societies because of all the energy it harnesses and uses. White's formulation is ironic in viewing societies that deplete nature's bounty as being more advanced than those that conserve it.

Steward was equally interested in causality, and he looked to technology and the environment as the main causes of culture change. The environment and the technology available to exploit it were seen as part of what he called the *culture core*—the combination of subsistence and

anthropology **ATLAS**

Map 10 shows ethnographic study sites prior to 1950, including the Trobriand Islands, Samoa, Arapesh, Mundugumor, and Tchambuli.

economic activities that determined the social order and the configuration of that culture in general.

Cultural Materialism

In proposing **cultural materialism** as a theoretical paradigm, Marvin Harris adapted multilayered models of determinism associated with White and Steward. For Harris (1979/2001) all societies had an *infrastructure*, corresponding to Steward's culture core, consisting of technology, economics, and demography—the systems of production and reproduction without which societies could not survive. Growing out of infrastructure was *structure*—social relations, forms of kinship and descent, patterns of distribution and consumption. The third layer was *superstructure*: religion, ideology, play—aspects of culture furthest away from the meat and bones that enable cultures to survive. Harris's key belief, shared with White, Steward, and Karl Marx, was that in the final analysis infrastructure determines structure and superstructure.

Harris therefore took issue with theorists (he called them "idealists") such as Max Weber who argued for the prominent role of religion (the Protestant ethic, as discussed in the chapter "Religion") in changing society. Weber didn't argue that Protestantism had caused capitalism. He merely contended that the individualism and other traits associated with early Protestantism were especially compatible with capitalism and therefore aided its spread. One could infer from Weber's argument that without Protestantism, the rise and spread of capitalism would have been much slower. Harris probably would counter that given the change in economy, some new religion compatible with the new economy would appear and spread with that economy, since infrastructure (what Karl Marx called the base) always determines in the final analysis.

Marvin Harris (1927–2001), chief advocate of the approach known as cultural materialism. Harris taught anthropology at Columbia University and the University of Florida.

Science and Determinism

Harris's influential books include *The Rise of Anthropological Theory* (1968/2001) and *Cultural Materialism: The Struggle for a Science of Culture* (1979/2001). Like most of the anthropologists discussed so far, Harris insisted that anthropology is a *science;* that science is based on explanation, which uncovers relations of cause and effect; and that the role of science is to discover causes, to find determinants. One of White's two influential books was *The Science of Culture* (1949). Malinowski set forth his theory of needs functionalism in a book titled *A Scientific Theory of Culture, and Other Essays* (1944). Mead viewed anthropology as a humanistic science of unique value in understanding and improving the human condition.

Like Harris, White, and Steward, all of whom looked to infrastructural factors as determinants, Mead was a determinist, but of a very different sort. Mead's cultural determinism viewed human nature as more or less a blank slate on which culture could write almost any lesson. Culture was so powerful that it could change drastically the expression of a biological stage—adolescence—in Samoa and the United States. Mead stressed the role of culture rather than economy, environment, or material factors in this difference.

Culture and the Individual

Culturology

Interestingly, Leslie White, the avowed evolutionist and champion of energy as a measure of cultural progress, was, like Mead, a strong advocate of the importance of culture. White saw cultural anthropology as a science, and he named that science *culturology*. Cultural forces, which rested on the unique human capacity for symbolic thought, were so powerful, White believed, that individuals made little difference. White disputed what was then called the "great man theory of history," the idea that particular individuals were responsible for great discoveries and epochal changes. White looked instead to the constellation of cultural forces that produced great individuals. During certain historical periods, such as the Renaissance, conditions were right for the expression of creativity and greatness, and individual genius blossomed. At other times and places, there may have been just as many great minds, but the culture did not encourage their expression. As proof of this theory, White pointed to the simultaneity of discovery. Several times in human history, when culture was ready, people working independently in different places have come up with the same revolutionary idea or achievement. Examples include the formulation of the theory of evolution through natural selection by Charles Darwin and Alfred Russel Wallace, the independent rediscovery of Mendelian genetics by three separate scientists in 1917, and the independent invention of flight by the Wright brothers in the United States and Santos Dumont in Brazil.

The Superorganic

Much of the history of anthropology has been about the roles and relative prominence of culture and the individual. Like White, the prolific Boasian anthropologist Alfred Kroeber stressed the power of culture. Kroeber (1952/1987) called the cultural realm, whose origin converted an ape into an early hominin, the **superorganic.** The superorganic opened up a new domain of analysis separable from, but comparable in importance to, the organic (life—without which there could be no superorganic) and the inorganic (chemistry and physics—the basis of the organic). Like White (and long before him Tylor, who first proposed a science of culture), Kroeber saw culture as the basis of a new science, which became cultural anthropology. Kroeber (1923) laid out the basis of this science in anthropology's first textbook. He attempted to demonstrate the power of culture over the individual by focusing on particular styles and fashions, such as those involving women's hem lengths. According to Kroeber (1944), hordes of individuals were carried along helplessly by the alternating trends of various times, swept up in the undulation of styles. Unlike White, Steward, and Harris, Kroeber did not attempt to explain such shifts; he simply used them to show the power of culture over the individual. Like Mead, he was a cultural determinist.

Durkheim

In France, Émile Durkheim had taken a similar approach, calling for a new social science to be based in what he called, in French, the *conscience collectif*. The usual translation of this as "collective consciousness" does not convey adequately the similarity of this notion to Kroeber's superorganic and White's culturology. This new science, Durkheim proposed, would be based on the study of *social facts*, analytically distinct from the individuals from whose behavior those facts were inferred. Many anthropologists agree with the central premise that the role of the anthropologist is to study something larger than the individual. Psychologists study individuals; anthropologists study individuals as representative of something more. It is those larger systems, which consist of social positions—statuses and roles—and which are perpetuated across the generations through enculturation, that anthropologists should study.

Of course sociologists also study such social systems, and Durkheim, as has been discussed previously, is a common father of anthropology and sociology. Durkheim wrote of religion in Native Australia as readily as of suicide rates in modern societies. As analyzed by Durkheim,

suicide rates (1897/1951) and religion (1912/2001) are collective phenomena. Individuals commit suicide for all sorts of reasons, but the variation in rates (which apply only to collectivities) can and should be linked to social phenomena, such as a sense of anomie, malaise, or alienation at particular times and in particular places.

Symbolic and Interpretive Anthropology

Victor Turner was a colleague of Max Gluckman in the Department of Social Anthropology at the University of Manchester, and thus a member of the Manchester school, previously described, before moving to the United States, where he taught at the University of Chicago and the University of Virginia. Turner wrote several important books and essays on ritual and symbols. His monograph *Schism and Continuity in an African Society* (1957/1996) illustrates the interest in conflict and its resolution previously mentioned as characteristic of the Manchester school. *The Forest of Symbols* (1967) is a collection of essays about symbols and rituals among the Nbembu of Zambia, where Turner did his major field work. In *The Forest of Symbols* Turner examines how symbols and rituals are used to redress, regulate, anticipate, and

superorganic (Kroeber) The special domain of culture, beyond the organic and inorganic realms.

Mary Douglas (1921–2007), a prominent symbolic anthropologist, who taught at University College, London, England, and Northwestern University, Evanston, Illinois. This photo shows her at an awards ceremony celebrating her receipt in 2003 of an honorary degree from Oxford.

(a)

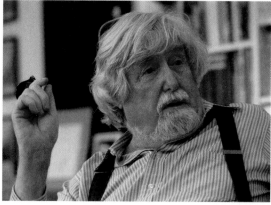

(b)

(a) Three books by the prominent and prolific anthropologist Clifford Geertz (1926–2006): *The Interpretation of Cultures* (the book that established the field of interpretive anthropology); *After the Fact: Two Countries, Four Decades, One Anthropologist*; and *Islam Observed: Religious Development in Morocco and Indonesia*. (b) Geertz himself in 1998.

symbolic anthropology
The study of symbols in their social and cultural context.

interpretive anthropology
(Geertz) The study of a culture as a system of meaning.

avoid conflict. He also examines a hierarchy of meanings of symbols, from their social meanings and functions to their internalization within individuals.

Turner recognized links between **symbolic anthropology** (the study of symbols in their social and cultural context), a school he pioneered along with Mary Douglas (1970), and such other fields as social psychology, psychology, and psychoanalysis. The study of symbols is all-important in psychoanalysis, whose founder, Sigmund Freud, also recognized a hierarchy of symbols, from potentially universal ones to those that had meaning for particular individuals and emerged during the analysis and interpretation of their dreams. Turner's symbolic anthropology flourished at the University of Chicago, where another major advocate, David Schneider (1968), developed a symbolic approach to American culture in his book *American Kinship: A Cultural Account* (1968).

Related to symbolic anthropology, and also associated with the University of Chicago (and later with Princeton University), is **interpretive anthropology,** whose main advocate has been Clifford Geertz. As mentioned in the chapter "Culture," Geertz defined culture as ideas based on cultural learning and symbols. During enculturation, individuals internalize a previously established system of meanings and symbols. They use this cultural system to define their world, express their feelings, and make their judgments.

Interpretive anthropology (Geertz 1973, 1983) approaches cultures as texts whose forms and, especially, meanings must be deciphered in particular cultural and historical contexts. Geertz's approach recalls Malinowski's belief that the ethnographer's primary task is "to grasp the native's point of view, his relation to life, to realize *his* vision of *his* world" (1922/1961, p. 25—Malinowski's italics). Since the 1970s, interpretive anthropology has considered the task of describing and interpreting that which is meaningful to natives. Cultures are texts that natives constantly "read" and ethnographers must deci-

pher. According to Geertz (1973), anthropologists may choose anything in a culture that interests or engages them (such as a Balinese cockfight he interprets in a famous essay), fill in details, and elaborate to inform their readers about meanings in that culture. Meanings are carried by public symbolic forms, including words, rituals, and customs.

Structuralism

In anthropology, structuralism mainly is associated with Claude Lévi-Strauss, a prolific and long-lived French anthropologist. Lévi-Strauss's structuralism evolved over time, from his early interest in the structures of kinship and marriage systems to his later interest in the structure of the human mind. In this latter sense, Lévi-Straussian structuralism (1967) aims not at explaining relations, themes, and connections among aspects of culture but at discovering them.

Structuralism rests on Lévi-Strauss's belief that human minds have certain universal characteristics, which originate in common features of the *Homo sapiens* brain. These common mental structures lead people everywhere to think similarly regardless of their society or cultural background. Among these universal mental characteristics are the need to classify: to impose order on aspects of nature, on people's relation to nature, and on relations between people.

According to Lévi-Strauss, a universal aspect of classification is opposition, or contrast. Although many phenomena are continuous rather than discrete, the mind, because of its need to impose order, treats them as being more different than they are. One of the most common means of classifying is by using binary opposition. Good and evil, white and black, old and young, high and low are oppositions that, according to Lévi-Strauss, reflect the universal human need to convert differences of degree into differences of kind.

Lévi-Strauss applied his assumptions about classification and binary opposition to myths and folk tales. He showed that these narratives have simple building blocks—elementary structures or "mythemes." Examining the myths of different cultures, Lévi-Strauss shows that one tale can be converted into another through a series of simple operations, for example, by doing the following:

1. Converting the positive element of a myth into its negative

2. Reversing the order of the elements

3. Replacing a male hero with a female hero

4. Preserving or repeating certain key elements

Through such operations, two apparently dissimilar myths can be shown to be variations on a common structure, that is, to be transformations of each other. One example is Lévi-Strauss's (1967) analysis of "Cinderella," a widespread tale whose elements vary between neighboring cultures. Through reversals, oppositions, and negations, as the tale is told, retold, diffused, and incorporated within the traditions of successive societies, "Cinderella" becomes "Ash Boy," along with a series of other oppositions (e.g., stepfather versus stepmother) related to the change in gender from female to male.

Processual Approaches

Agency

Structuralism has been faulted for being overly formal and for ignoring social process. We saw in the chapter "Culture" that culture conventionally has been seen as social glue transmitted across the generations, binding people through their common past. More recently, anthropologists have come to see culture as something continually created and reworked in the present. The tendency to view culture as an entity rather than a process is changing. Contemporary anthropologists now emphasize how day-to-day action, practice, or resistance can make and remake culture (Gupta and Ferguson, eds. 1997b). **Agency** refers to the actions that individuals take, both alone and in groups, in forming and transforming cultural identities.

Practice Theory

The approach to culture known as *practice theory* (Ortner 1984) recognizes that individuals within a society or culture have diverse motives and intentions and different degrees of power and influence. Such contrasts may be associated with gender, age, ethnicity, class, and other social variables. Practice theory focuses on how such varied individuals—through their actions and practices—influence and transform the world they live in. Practice theory appropriately recognizes a reciprocal relation between culture and the individual.

Culture shapes how individuals experience and respond to external events, but individuals also play an active role in how society functions and changes. Practice theory recognizes both constraints on individuals and the flexibility and changeability of cultures and social systems. Well-known practice theorists include Sherry Ortner, an American anthropologist, and Pierre Bourdieu and Anthony Giddens, French and British social theorists, respectively.

Leach

Some of the germs of practice theory, sometimes also called action theory (Vincent 1990), can be traced to the British anthropologist Edmund Leach, who wrote the influential book *Political Systems of Highland Burma* (1954/1970). Influenced by the Italian social theorist Vilfredo Pareto, Leach focused on how individuals work to achieve power and how their actions can transform society. In the Kachin Hills of Burma, now Myanmar, Leach identified three forms of sociopolitical organization, which he called *gumlao*, *gumsa*, and Shan. Leach made a tremendously important point by taking a regional rather than a local perspective. The Kachins participated in a regional system that included all three forms of organization. Leach showed how they coexist and interact, as forms and possibilities known to everyone, in the same region. He also showed how Kachins creatively use power struggles, for example, to convert *gumlao* into *gumsa* organization, and how they negotiate their own identities within the regional system. Leach brought process to the formal models of structural functionalism. By focusing on power and how individuals get and use it, he showed the creative role of the individual in transforming culture.

World-System Theory and Political Economy

Leach's regional perspective was not all that different from another development at the same time. Julian Steward, discussed previously as a neoevolutionist, joined the faculty of Columbia University in 1946, where he worked with several graduate students, including Eric Wolf and Sidney Mintz. Steward, Mintz, Wolf, and others planned and conducted a team research project in Puerto Rico, described in Steward's volume *The People of Puerto Rico* (1956). This project exemplified a post–World War II turn of anthropology away from "primitive" and nonindustrial societies, assumed to be somewhat isolated and autonomous, to contemporary societies recognized as forged by colonialism and participating fully in the modern world system. The team studied communities in different parts of Puerto Rico. The field sites were chosen to sample major events and adaptations, such as the sugar

agency
The actions of individuals, alone and in groups, that create and transform culture.

plantation, in the island's history. The approach emphasized economics, politics, and history.

Wolf and Mintz retained their interest in history throughout their careers. Wolf wrote the modern classic *Europe and the People without History* (1982), which viewed local people, such as Native Americans, in the context of world-system events, such as the fur trade in North America. Wolf focused on how such "people without history"—that is, nonliterate people, those who lacked written histories of their own—participated in and were transformed by the world system and the spread of capitalism. Mintz's *Sweetness and Power* (1985) is another example of historical anthropology focusing on **political economy** (the web of interrelated economic and power relations). Mintz traces the domestication and spread of sugar, its transformative role in England, and its impact on the New World, where it became the basis for slave-based plantation economies in the Caribbean and Brazil. Such works in political economy illustrate a movement of anthropology toward interdisciplinarity, drawing on other academic fields, such as history and sociology. Any world-system approach in anthropology would have to pay attention to sociologist Immanuel Wallerstein's writing on world-system theory, including his model of core, periphery, and semiperiphery, as discussed in the chapter "The World System and Colonialism." However, world-system approaches in anthropology have been criticized for overstressing the influence of outsiders, and for paying insufficient attention to the transformative actions of "the people without history" themselves. Recap 13.2 summarizes this and other major theoretical perspectives and identifies the key works associated with them.

political economy
The web of interrelated economic and power relations in society.

Culture, History, Power

More recent approaches in historical anthropology, while sharing an interest in power with the world-system theorists, have focused more on local agency, the transformative actions of individuals and groups within colonized societies. Archival work has been prominent in recent historical anthropology, particularly on areas, such as Indonesia, for which colonial and postcolonial archives contain valuable information on relations between colonizers and colonized and the actions of various actors in the colonial context. Studies of culture, history, and power have drawn heavily on the work of European social theorists such as Antonio Gramsci and Michel Foucault.

Gramsci (1971) developed the concept of *hegemony* for a stratified social order in which subordinates comply with domination by internalizing their rulers' values and accepting domination as "natural." Both Pierre Bourdieu (1977) and Fou-

cault (1979) contend that it is easier to dominate people in their minds than to try to control their bodies. Contemporary societies have devised various forms of social control in addition to physical violence. These include techniques of persuading, coercing, and managing people and of monitoring and recording their beliefs, behavior, movements, and contacts. Anthropologists interested in culture, history and power, such as Ann Stoler (1995, 2002), have examined systems of power, domination, accommodation, and resistance in various contexts, including colonies, postcolonies, and other stratified contexts.

ANTHROPOLOGY TODAY

Early American anthropologists, such as Morgan, Boas, and Kroeber, were interested in, and made contributions to, more than a single subfield. If there has been a single dominant trend in anthropology since the 1960s, it has been one of increasing specialization. During the 1960s, when this author attended graduate school at Columbia University, I had to study and take qualifying exams in all four subfields. This has changed. There are still strong four-field anthropology departments, but many excellent departments lack one or more of the subfields. Four-field departments such as the University of Michigan's still require courses and teaching expertise across the subfields, but graduate students must choose to specialize in a particular subfield and take qualifying exams only in that subfield. In Boasian anthropology, all four subfields shared a single theoretical assumption about human plasticity. Today, following specialization, the theories that guide the subfields differ. Evolutionary paradigms of various sorts still dominate biological anthropology and remain strong in archaeology as well. Within cultural anthropology, it has been decades since evolutionary approaches thrived.

Ethnography, too, has grown more specialized. Cultural anthropologists now head for the field with a specific problem in mind, rather than with the goal of producing a holistic ethnography—a complete account of a given culture—as Morgan and Malinowski intended when they studied, respectively, the Iroquois and the people of the Trobriand Islands. Boas, Malinowski, and Mead went somewhere and stayed there for a while, studying the local culture. Today the field has expanded to include regional and national systems and the movement of people, such as immigrants and diasporas, across national boundaries. Many anthropologists now follow the flows of people, information, finance, and media to multiple sites. Such movement has been made possible by advances in transportation and communication.

THEORETICAL APPROACH	KEY AUTHORS AND WORKS
Culture, history, power	Ann Stoler, *Carnal Knowledge and Imperial Power* (2002); Frederick Cooper and Ann Stoler, *Tensions of Empire* (1997)
Crisis of representation/ postmodernism	Jean François Lyotard, *The Postmodern Explained* (1993); George Marcus and Michael Fischer, *Anthropology as Cultural Critique* (1986)
Practice theory	Sherry Ortner, "Theory in Anthropology since the Sixties" (1984); Pierre Bourdieu, *Outline of a Theory of Practice* (1977)
World-system theory/ political economy	Sidney Mintz, *Sweetness and Power* (1985); Eric Wolf, *Europe and the People without History* (1982)
Feminist anthropology	Rayna Reiter, *Toward an Anthropology of Women* (1975); Michelle Rosaldo and Louise Lamphere, *Women, Culture, and Society* (1974)
Cultural materialism	Marvin Harris, *Cultural Materialism* (1979), *Rise of Anthropological Theory* (1968)
Interpretive anthropology	Clifford Geertz, *Interpretation of Cultures* (1973)*
Symbolic anthropology	Mary Douglas, *Purity and Danger* (1970); Victor Turner, *Forest of Symbols* (1967)*
Structuralism	Claude Lévi-Strauss, *Structural Anthropology* (1967)*
Neoevolutionism	Leslie White, *Evolution of Culture* (1959); Julian Steward, *Theory of Culture Change* (1955)
Manchester school and Leach	Victor Turner, *Schism and Continuity in an African Society* (1957); Edmund Leach, *Political Systems of Highland Burma* (1954)
Culturology	Leslie White, *Science of Culture* (1949)*
Configurationalism	Alfred Kroeber, *Configurations of Cultural Growth* (1944); Margaret Mead, *Sex and Temperament in Three Primitive Societies* (1935); Ruth Benedict, *Patterns of Culture* (1934)
Structural functionalism	A. R. Radcliffe-Brown, *Structure and Function in Primitive Society* (1962)*; E. E. Evans-Pritchard, *The Nuer* (1940)
Functionalism	Bronislaw Malinowski, *A Scientific Theory of Culture* (1944)*, *Argonauts of the Western Pacific* (1922)
Historical particularism	Franz Boas, *Race, Language, and Culture* (1940)*
Unilinear evolutionism	Lewis Henry Morgan, *Ancient Society* (1877); Sir Edward Burnett Tylor, *Primitive Culture*, (1871)

*Includes essays written at earlier dates.

However, with so much time in motion and with the need to adjust to various field sites and contexts, the richness of traditional ethnography may diminish.

Anthropology also has witnessed a crisis in representation—questions about the role of the ethnographer and the nature of ethnographic authority. What right do ethnographers have to represent a people or culture to which they don't belong? Some argue that insiders' accounts are more valuable and appropriate than are studies by outsiders, because native anthropologists not only know the culture better but also should be in charge of representing their culture to the public.

Reflecting the trends just described, the AAA (American Anthropological Association) now has all sorts of subgroups. At its beginning, there were just anthropologists within the AAA. Now there are groups representing biological anthropology, archaeology, and linguistic, cultural, and applied anthropology, as well as dozens of groups formed around particular interests and identities. These groups represent psychological anthropology, urban anthropology, culture and agriculture, anthropologists in small colleges, midwestern anthropologists, senior anthropologists, lesbian and gay anthropologists, Latino/a anthropologists, and so on. Many of the identity-based groups accept the premise that group members are better qualified to study issues and topics involving that group than outsiders are.

Science itself may be challenged. Doubters argue that science can't be trusted because it is carried out by scientists. All scientists, the doubters contend, come from particular individual or cultural backgrounds that pre-vent objectivity, leading to artificial and biased accounts that have no more value than do those of insiders who are nonscientists.

What are we to do if we, as I do, continue to share Mead's view of anthropology as a humanistic science of unique value in understanding and improving the human condition? We must try to stay aware of our biases and our inability totally to escape them. The best scientific choice would seem to be to combine the perpetual goal of objectivity with skepticism about our capacity to achieve it.

Acing the COURSE

Summary

1. Ethnographic methods include observation, rapport building, participant observation, interviewing, genealogies, work with key consultants, life histories, and longitudinal research. Ethnographers do not systematically manipulate their subjects or conduct experiments. Rather, they work in actual communities and form personal relationships with local people as they study their lives.

2. An interview schedule is a form that an ethnographer completes as he or she visits a series of households. The schedule organizes and guides each interview, ensuring that comparable information is collected from everyone. Key cultural consultants teach about particular areas of local life. Life histories dramatize the fact that culture bearers are individuals. Such case studies document personal experiences with culture and culture change. Genealogical information is particularly useful in societies in which principles of kinship and marriage organize social and political life. Emic approaches focus on native perceptions and explanations. Etic approaches give priority to the ethnographer's own observations and conclusions. Longitudinal research is the systematic study of an area or site over time. Forces of change are often too pervasive and complex to be understood by a lone ethnographer. Anthropological research may be done by teams and at multiple sites. Outsiders, flows, linkages, and people in motion are now included in ethnographic analyses.

3. Traditionally, anthropologists worked in small-scale societies; sociologists, in modern nations. Different techniques were developed to study such different kinds of societies. Social scientists working in complex societies use survey research to sample variation. Anthropologists do their field work in communities and study the totality of social life. Sociologists study samples to make inferences about a larger population. Sociologists often are interested in causal relations among a very small number of variables. Anthropologists more typically are concerned with the interconnectedness of all aspects of social life. The diversity of social life in modern nations and cities requires social survey procedures. However, anthropologists add the intimacy and direct investigation characteristic of ethnography.

4. Evolutionary perspectives, especially those of Morgan and Tylor, dominated early anthropology, which emerged during the latter half of the 19th century. The early 20th century witnessed various reactions to 19th-century evolutionism. In the United States, Boas and his followers rejected the search for evolutionary stages in favor of a historical approach that traced borrowing between cultures and the spread of culture traits across geographic areas. In Great Britain, functionalists such as Malinowski and Radcliffe-Brown abandoned conjectural history in favor of studies of present-day living societies. Functionalists and Boasians alike saw cultures as integrated and patterned. The functionalists especially viewed societies as systems in which various parts worked together to maintain the whole. A form of functionalism persists in the widely accepted view that there are social and cultural systems whose constituent parts are functionally related, so that when one part changes, others change as well.

5. In the mid-20th century, following World War II and as colonialism was ending, there was a revived interest in change, including new evolutionary

approaches. Some anthropologists developed symbolic and interpretive approaches to uncover patterned symbols and meanings within cultures. By the 1980s, anthropologists had grown more interested in the relation between culture and the individual, and the role of human action (agency) in transforming culture. There also was a resurgence of historical approaches, including those that viewed local cultures in relation to colonialism and the world system.

6. Contemporary anthropology is marked by increasing specialization, based on special topics and identities. Reflecting this specialization, some universities have moved away from the holistic, biocultural view of anthropology that is reflected in this book. However, this Boasian view of anthropology as a four-subfield discipline—including biological, archaeological, cultural, and linguistic anthropology—continues to thrive at many universities as well.

Test Yourself!

MULTIPLE CHOICE

1. Which of the following statements about ethnography is *not* true?
   a. It may involve participant observation and survey research.
   b. Bronislaw Malinowski was one of its earliest influential practitioners.
   c. It was traditionally practiced in non-Western and small-scale societies.
   d. Contemporary anthropologists have rejected it as overly formal and for ignoring social process.
   e. It is anthropology's distinctive strategy.

2. In the field, ethnographers strive to establish rapport,
   a. and if that fails, the next option is to pay people so they will talk about their culture.
   b. a timeline that states when every member of the community will be interviewed.
   c. a respectful and formal working relationship with the political leaders of the community.
   d. also known as a cultural relativist attitude.
   e. a good, friendly working relationship based on personal contact.

3. Which influential anthropologist referred to everyday cultural patterns as "the imponderabilia of native life and of typical behavior"?
   a. Franz Boas
   b. Marvin Harris
   c. Clifford Geertz
   d. Bronislaw Malinowski
   e. Margaret Mead

4. Which of the following techniques was developed specifically because of the importance of kinship and marriage relationships in nonindustrial societies?
   a. the life history
   b. participant observation
   c. the interview schedule
   d. network analysis
   e. the genealogical method

5. Which of the following is a significant change in the history of ethnography?
   a. Larger numbers of ethnographies are being done about people in Western, industrialized nations.
   b. Ethnographers now use only quantitative techniques.
   c. Ethnographers have begun to work for colonial governments.
   d. Ethnographers have stopped using the standard four-member format, because it disturbs the informants.
   e. There are now fewer native ethnographers.

6. All of the following are true about ethnography *except*:
   a. it traditionally studies entire communities.
   b. it usually focuses on a small number of variables within a sample population.

c. it is based on firsthand fieldwork.
d. it is more personal than survey research.
e. it traditionally has been conducted in non-industrial, small-scale societies.

7. Which of the following is one of the advantages an interview schedule has over a questionnaire-based survey?
a. Interview schedules rely on very short responses, and therefore are more useful when you have less time.
b. Questionnaires are completely unstructured, so your informants might deviate from the subject you want them to talk about.
c. Interview schedules allow informants to talk about what *they* see as important.
d. Interview schedules are better suited to urban, complex societies where most people can read.
e. Questionnaires are emic, and interview schedules are etic.

8. Reflecting today's world in which people, images, and information move as never before, ethnography is
a. becoming increasingly difficult for anthropologists concerned with salvaging isolated and untouched cultures around the world.
b. becoming less useful and valuable to understanding culture.
c. becoming more traditional, given anthropologists concerns of defending the field's roots.
d. requiring that researchers stay in the same site for over three years.
e. increasingly multisited and multitimed, integrating analyses of external organizations and forces to understand local phenomena.

9. All of the following are true about anthropology's four-field approach *except:*
a. Boas is the father of four-field American anthropology.
b. It initially formed around interests in Native Americans—their cultures, histories, languages, and physical characteristics.
c. There are many strong four-field anthropology departments in the United States, but some respected programs lack one or more of the subfields.
d. Four-field anthropology has become substantially less historically oriented.
e. It has rejected the idea of unilinear evolution, which assumed that there was one line or path through which all societies had to evolve.

10. In anthropology, the crisis in representation refers to
a. the study of symbols in their social and cultural context.
b. questions about the role of the ethnographer and the nature of ethnographic authority.
c. Durkheim's critique of symbolic anthropology.
d. the ethnographic technique that Malinowski developed during his fieldwork in the Trobriand Islands.
e. the discipline's branding problem that has made it less popular among college students.

FILL IN THE BLANK

1. A _____ is an expert who teaches an ethnographer about a particular aspect of local life.

2. As one of the ethnographer's characteristic field research practices, the _____ method is a technique that uses diagrams and symbols to record kin connections.

3. A _____ approach studies societies as they exist at one point in time, while a _____ approach studies societies across time.

4. At the beginning of the 20th century, the influential French sociologist _____ proposed a new social science that would be based on the study of _____, analytically distinct from the individuals from whose behavior those facts were inferred.

5. _____, a theoretical approach that aims to discover relations, themes, and connections among aspects of culture, has been faulted for being overly formal and for ignoring social process. Contemporary anthropologists now emphasize how day-to-day action, practice, or resistance can make and remake culture. _____ refers to the actions that individuals take, both alone and in groups, in forming and transforming cultural identities.

CRITICAL THINKING

1. What do you see as the strengths and weaknesses of ethnography compared with survey research? Which provides more accurate data? Might one be better for finding questions, while the other is better for finding answers? Or does it depend on the context of research?

2. In what sense is anthropological research comparative? How have anthropologists approached the issue of comparison? What do they compare (what are their units of analysis)?

3. In your view, is anthropology a science? How have anthropologists historically addressed this question?

4. Historically, how have anthropologists studied culture? What are some contemporary trends in the study of culture, and how have they changed the way anthropologists carry out their research?

5. Do the theories examined in this chapter relate to ones you have studied in other courses? Which courses and theories? Are those theories more scientific or humanistic, or somewhere in between?

Multiple Choice: 1. (D); 2. (E); 3. (D); 4. (E); 5. (A); 6. (B); 7. (C); 8. (E); 9. (D); 10. (B); **Fill in the Blank:** 1. key cultural consultant; 2. genealogical; 3. synchronic, diachronic; 4. Emile Durkheim, social facts; 5. Structuralism, Agency

Angrosino, M. V., ed.
  2007 *Doing Cultural Anthropology: Projects for Ethnographic Data Collection,* 2nd ed. Long Grove, IL: Waveland. How to get ethnographic data.

Bernard, H. R.
  2006 *Research Methods in Anthropology: Qualitative and Quantitative Methods,* 4th ed. Walnut Creek, CA: AltaMira. Expansion of a classic text on research methods in cultural anthropology.

Chiseri-Strater, E., and B. S. Sunstein
  2007 *Fieldworking: Reading and Writing Research,* 3rd ed. Upper Saddle River, NJ: Prentice Hall. Ways of evaluating and presenting research data.

Harris, M.
  2001 *The Rise of Anthropological Theory: A History of Theories of Culture.* Walnut Creek, CA: AltaMira.

A cultural materialist examines the development of anthropological theory.

McGee, R. J., and R. L. Warms
  2008 *Anthropological Theory: An Introductory History,* 4th ed. Boston: McGraw-Hill. Compiles classic articles on anthropological theory since the 19th century.

Spradley, J. P.
  1979 *The Ethnographic Interview.* New York: Harcourt Brace Jovanovich. Discussion of the ethnographic method, with emphasis on discovering locally significant categories, meanings, and understandings.

Suggested Additional Readings

Go to our Online Learning Center website at **www.mhhe.com/kottak** for Internet exercises directly related to the content of this chapter.

Internet Exercises

What makes language different from other forms of communication?

How do anthropologists and linguists study language in general and specific languages in particular?

How does language change over short and long time periods?

Linguistic variation is associated with social and cultural diversity, including ethnicity and gender. These Maya girls speak one of several Mayan languages in Guatemala.

understanding OURSELVES

Can you appreciate anything distinctive or unusual in the way you talk? If you're from Canada, Virginia, or Savannah, you may say "oot" instead of "out." A southerner may request a "soft drink" rather than the New Yorker's "soda." How might a "Valley Girl" or "surfer dude" talk? Usually when we pay attention to how we talk, it's because someone comments on our speech. It may be only when students move from one state or region to another that they appreciate how much of a regional accent they have. I moved as a teenager from Atlanta to New York City. Previously I hadn't realized I had a southern accent, but some guardian of linguistic correctness in my new high school did. They put me in a speech class, pointing out linguistic flaws I never knew I had. One was my "dull s," particularly in terminal consonant clusters, as in the words "tusks" and "breakfasts." Apparently I didn't pronounce all three consonants at the ends of those words. Later it occurred to me that these weren't words I used very often. As far as I know, I've never conversed about tusks or proclaimed "I ate seven breakfasts last week."

Unlike grammarians, linguists and anthropologists are interested in what people do say, rather than what they should say. Speech differences are associated with, and tell us a lot about, social variation, such as region, education, ethnic background, and gender. Men and women talk differently. I'm sure you can think of examples based on your own experience, although you probably never realized that women tend to peripheralize their vowels (think of "aiiee"), whereas men tend to centralize them (think of "uh" and "ugh"). Men are more likely to speak "ungrammatically" than women are. Men and women also show differences in their sports and color terminologies. Men typically know more terms related to sports, make more distinctions among them (e.g., runs versus points), and try to use the terms more precisely than women do. Correspondingly, influenced more by the fashion and cosmetics industries than men are, women use more color terms and attempt to use them more specifically than men do. To make this point when I lecture, I bring an off-purple shirt to class. Holding it up, I first ask women to say aloud what color the shirt is. The women rarely answer with a uniform voice, as they try to distinguish the actual shade (mauve, lilac, lavender, wisteria, or some other purplish hue). I then ask the men, who consistently answer as one, "PURPLE." Rare is the man who on the spur of the moment can imagine the difference between fuchsia and magenta or grape and aubergine.

WHAT IS LANGUAGE?

Language, which may be spoken (*speech*) or written (*writing*), is our primary means of communication. Writing has existed for about 6,000 years. Language originated thousands of years before that, but no one can say exactly when. Like culture in general, of which language is a part, language is transmitted through learning, as part of enculturation. Language is based on arbitrary, learned associations between words and the things for which they stand. The complexity of language—absent in the communication systems of other animals—allows humans to conjure up elaborate images, to discuss the past and the future, to share our experiences with others, and to benefit from their experiences.

Apes, such as these Congo chimpanzees, use call systems to communicate in the wild. Their vocal systems consist of a limited number of sounds—*calls*—that are produced only when particular environmental stimuli are encountered.

Anthropologists study language in its social and cultural context. Linguistic anthropology illustrates anthropology's characteristic interest in comparison, variation, and change. A key feature of language is that it is always changing. Some linguistic anthropologists reconstruct ancient languages by comparing their contemporary descendants and in so doing make discoveries about history. Others study linguistic differences to discover the varied worldviews and patterns of thought in a multitude of cultures. Sociolinguists examine linguistic diversity in nation-states, ranging from multilingualism to the varied dialects and styles used in a single language, to show how speech reflects social differences (Fasold 1990; Labov 1972*a*, 1972*b*). Linguistic anthropologists also explore the role of language in colonization and in the expansion of the world economy (Geis 1987).

NONHUMAN PRIMATE COMMUNICATION

Call Systems

Only humans speak. No other animal has anything approaching the complexity of language.

The natural communication systems of other primates (monkeys and apes) are **call systems.** These vocal systems consist of a limited number of sounds—*calls*—that are produced only when particular environmental stimuli are encountered. Such calls may be varied in intensity and duration, but they are much less flexible than language because they are automatic and can't be combined. When primates encounter food and danger simultaneously, they can make only one call. They can't combine the calls for food and danger into a single utterance, indicating that both are present. At some point in human evolution, however, our ancestors began to combine calls and to understand the combinations. The number of calls also expanded, eventually becoming too great to be transmitted even partly through the genes. Communication came to rely almost totally on learning.

Although wild primates use call systems, the vocal tract of apes is not suitable for speech. Until the 1960s, attempts to teach spoken language to apes suggested that they lack linguistic abilities. In the 1950s, a couple raised a chimpanzee, Viki, as a member of their family and systematically tried to teach her to speak. However, Viki learned only four words ("mama," "papa," "up," and "cup").

Sign Language

More recent experiments have shown that apes can learn to use, if not speak, true language (Miles 1983). Several apes have learned to converse with people through means other than speech. One such communication system is American Sign Language, or ASL, which is widely used by hearing-impaired Americans. ASL employs a limited number of basic gesture units that are analogous to sounds in spoken language. These units combine to form words and larger units of meaning.

The first chimpanzee to learn ASL was Washoe, a female who died in 2007 at the age of 42. Captured in West Africa, Washoe was acquired by R. Allen Gardner and Beatrice Gardner, scientists at the University of Nevada in Reno, in 1966, when she was a year old. Four years later, she moved to Norman, Oklahoma, to a converted farm that had become the Institute for Primate Studies. Washoe revolutionized the discussion of the language-learning abilities of apes (Carey 2007). At first she lived in a trailer and heard no spoken language. The researchers always used ASL to communicate with each other in her presence. The chimp gradually acquired a vocabulary of more than 100 signs representing English words (Gardner, Gardner, and Van Cantfort, eds. 1989). At the age of two, Washoe began to combine as many as five signs into rudimentary sentences such as "you, me, go out, hurry."

The second chimp to learn ASL was Lucy, Washoe's junior by one year. Lucy died, or was

language
Primary means of human communication, spoken and written.

call systems
Communication systems of nonhuman primates.

murdered by poachers, in 1986, after having been introduced to "the wild" in Africa in 1979 (Carter 1988). From her second day of life until her move to Africa, Lucy lived with a family in Norman, Oklahoma. Roger Fouts, a researcher from the nearby Institute for Primate Studies, came two days a week to test and improve Lucy's knowledge of ASL. During the rest of the week, Lucy used ASL to converse with her foster parents. After acquiring language, Washoe and Lucy exhibited several human traits: swearing, joking, telling lies, and trying to teach language to others (Fouts 1997).

When irritated, Washoe called her monkey neighbors at the institute "dirty monkeys." Lucy insulted her "dirty cat." On arrival at Lucy's place, Fouts once found a pile of excrement on the floor. When he asked the chimp what it was, she replied, "dirty, dirty," her expression for feces. Asked whose "dirty, dirty" it was, Lucy named Fouts's coworker, Sue. When Fouts refused to believe her about Sue, the chimp blamed the excrement on Fouts himself.

cultural transmission
Transmission through learning, basic to language.

Cultural transmission of a communication system through learning is a fundamental attribute of language. Washoe, Lucy, and other chimps have tried to teach ASL to other animals, including their own offspring. Washoe taught gestures to other institute chimps, including her son Sequoia, who died in infancy (Fouts, Fouts, and Van Cantfort 1989).

productivity
Creating new expressions that are comprehensible to other speakers.

Because of their size and strength as adults, gorillas are less likely subjects than chimps for such experiments. Lean adult male gorillas in the wild weigh 400 pounds (180 kilograms), and full-grown females can easily reach 250 pounds

"He says he wants a lawyer."

© Tom Chalkley/Condé Nast Publications/cartoonbank.com

(110 kilograms). Because of this, psychologist Penny Patterson's work with gorillas at Stanford University seems more daring than the chimp experiments. Patterson raised her now full-grown female gorilla, Koko, in a trailer next to a Stanford museum. Koko's vocabulary surpasses that of any chimp. She regularly employs 400 ASL signs and has used about 700 at least once.

Koko and the chimps also show that apes share still another linguistic ability with humans: **productivity.** Speakers routinely use the rules of their language to produce entirely new expressions that are comprehensible to other native speakers. I can, for example, create "baboonlet" to refer to a baboon infant. I do this by analogy with English words in which the suffix *-let* designates the young of a species. Anyone who speaks English immediately understands the meaning of my new word. Koko, Washoe, Lucy, and others have shown that apes also are able to use language productively. Lucy used gestures she already knew to create "drinkfruit" for watermelon. Washoe, seeing a swan for the first time, coined "waterbird." Koko, who knew the gestures for "finger" and "bracelet," formed "finger bracelet" when she was given a ring.

Chimps and gorillas have a rudimentary capacity for language. They may never have invented a meaningful gesture system in the wild. However, given such a system, they show many humanlike abilities in learning and using it. Of course, language use by apes is a product of human intervention and teaching. The experiments mentioned here do not suggest that apes can invent language (nor are human children ever faced with that task). However, young apes have managed to learn the basics of gestural language. They can employ it productively and creatively, although not with the sophistication of human ASL users.

Kanzi, a male bonobo, identifies an object he has just heard named through headphone speakers. At a young age, Kanzi learned to understand simple human speech and to communicate by using lexigrams, abstract symbols that represent objects and actions. A keyboard of lexigrams is pictured in the background.

HUMAN LANGUAGE	PRIMATE CALL SYSTEMS
Has the capacity to speak of things and events that are not present (displacement)	Are stimuli-dependent; the food call will be made only in the presence of food; it cannot be faked
Has the capacity to generate new expressions by combining other expressions (productivity)	Consist of a limited number of calls that cannot be combined to produce new calls
Is group specific in that all humans have the capacity for language, but each linguistic community has its own language, which is culturally transmitted	Tend to be species specific, with little variation among communities of the same species for each call

Apes, like humans, also may try to teach their language to others. Lucy, not fully realizing the difference between primate hands and feline paws, once tried to mold her pet cat's paw into ASL signs. Koko taught gestures to Michael, a male gorilla six years her junior.

Apes also have demonstrated linguistic **displacement.** Absent in call systems, this is a key ingredient in language. Normally, each call is tied to an environmental stimulus such as food. Calls are uttered only when that stimulus is present. Displacement means that humans can talk about things that are not present. We don't have to see the objects before we say the words. Human conversations are not limited by place. We can discuss the past and future, share our experiences with others, and benefit from theirs.

Patterson has described several examples of Koko's capacity for displacement (Patterson 1978). The gorilla once expressed sorrow about having bitten Penny three days earlier. Koko has used the sign "later" to postpone doing things she doesn't want to do. Recap 14.1 summarizes the contrasts between language, whether sign or spoken, and the call systems that primates use in the wild.

Certain scholars doubt the linguistic abilities of chimps and gorillas (Sebeok and Umiker-Sebeok, eds. 1980; Terrace 1979). These people contend that Koko and the chimps are comparable to trained circus animals and don't really have linguistic ability. However, in defense of Patterson and the other researchers (Hill 1978; Van Cantfort and Rimpau 1982), only one of their critics has worked with an ape. This was Herbert Terrace, whose experience teaching a chimp sign language lacked the continuity and personal involvement that have contributed so much to Patterson's success with Koko.

No one denies the huge difference between human language and gorilla signs. There is a major gap between the ability to write a book or say a prayer and the few hundred gestures employed by a well-trained chimp. Apes aren't people, but they aren't just animals either. Let Koko express it: When asked by a reporter whether she was a person or an animal, Koko chose neither. Instead, she signed "fine animal gorilla" (Patterson 1978).

The Origin of Language

Although the capacity to remember and combine linguistic symbols may be latent in the apes (Miles 1983), human evolution was needed for this seed to flower into language. A mutated gene known as FOXP2 helps explain why humans speak and chimps don't (Paulson 2005). The key role of FOXP2 in speech came to light in a study of a British family, identified only as KE, half of whose members had an inherited, severe deficit in speech (Trivedi 2001). The same variant form of FOXP2 that is found in chimpanzees causes this disorder. Those who have the nonspeech version of the gene cannot make the fine tongue and lip movements that are necessary for clear speech, and their speech is unintelligible—even to other members of the KE family (Trivedi 2001). Chimps have the same (genetic) sequence as the KE family members with the speech deficit. Comparing chimp and human genomes, it appears that the speech-friendly form of FOXP2 took hold in humans around 150,000 years ago. This mutation conferred selective advantages (linguistic and cultural abilities) that allowed those who had it to spread at the expense of those who did not (Paulson 2005).

Language offered a tremendous adaptive advantage to *Homo sapiens.* Language permits the information stored by a human society to exceed by far that of any nonhuman group. Language is a uniquely effective vehicle for learning. Because we can speak of things we have never experienced, we can anticipate responses before we encounter the stimuli. Adaptation can occur more rapidly in *Homo* than in the other primates because our adaptive means are more flexible.

NONVERBAL COMMUNICATION

Language is our principal means of communicating, but it isn't the only one we use. We communicate when we transmit information about ourselves to others and receive such information

displacement
Describing things and events that are not present; basic to language.

How do American men and women differ as they communicate and interact socially? Is this likely to be true cross-culturally? What do you notice about the interactions pictured in this open-air café in Kraków, Poland?

municating our moods: enthusiasm, sadness, joy, regret. We vary our intonation and the pitch or loudness of our voices. We communicate through strategic pauses, and even by being silent. An effective communication strategy may be to alter pitch, voice level, and grammatical forms, such as declaratives ("I am . . ."), imperatives ("Go forth . . ."), and questions ("Are you . . . ?"). Culture teaches us that certain manners and styles should accompany certain kinds of speech. Our demeanor, verbal and nonverbal, when our favorite team is winning would be out of place at a funeral, or when a somber subject is being discussed.

Culture always plays a role in shaping the "natural." Animals communicate through odors, using scent to mark territories, a chemical means of communication. Among modern North Americans, the perfume, mouthwash, and deodorant industries are based on the idea that the sense of smell plays a role in communication and social interaction. But different cultures are more tolerant of "natural" odors than ours is. Cross-culturally, nodding does not always mean affirmative, nor does head shaking from side to side always mean negative. Brazilians wag a finger to mean no. Americans say "uh huh" to affirm, whereas in Madagascar a similar sound is made to deny. Americans point with their fingers; the people of Madagascar point with their lips. Patterns of "lounging around" vary, too. Outside, when resting, some people may sit or lie on the ground; others squat; others lean against a tree.

Body movements communicate social differences. Lower-class Brazilians, especially women, offer limp handshakes to their social superiors. In many cultures, men have firmer handshakes than women do. In Japan, bowing is a regular part of social interaction, but different bows are used depending on the social status of the people who are interacting. In Madagascar and Polynesia, people of lower status should not hold their heads above those of people of higher status. When one approaches someone older or of higher status, one bends one's knees and lowers one's head as a sign of respect. In Madagascar, one always does this, for politeness, when passing between two people. Although our gestures, facial expressions, and body stances have roots in our primate heritage, and can be seen in the monkeys and the apes, they have not escaped the cultural shaping described in previous chapters. Language, which is so highly dependent on the use of symbols, is the domain of communication, in which culture plays the strongest role.

from them. Our facial expressions, bodily stances, gestures, and movements, even if unconscious, convey information and are part of our communication styles. Deborah Tannen (1990) discusses differences in the communication styles of American men and women, and her comments go beyond language. She notes that American girls and women tend to look directly at each other when they talk, whereas American boys and men do not. Males are more likely to look straight ahead rather than turn and make eye contact with someone, especially another man, seated beside them. Also, in conversational groups, American men tend to relax and sprawl out. American women may adopt a similar relaxed posture in all-female groups, but when they are with men, they tend to draw in their limbs and adopt a tighter stance.

Kinesics is the study of communication through body movements, stances, gestures, and facial expressions. Related to kinesics is the examination of cultural differences in personal space and displays of affection discussed in the chapter "Culture." Linguists pay attention not only to what is said but to how it is said, and to features besides language itself that convey meaning. A speaker's enthusiasm is conveyed not only through words but also through facial expressions, gestures, and other signs of animation. We use gestures, such as a jab of the hand, for emphasis. We use verbal and nonverbal ways of com-

kinesics
Study of communication through body movements and facial expressions.

THE STRUCTURE OF LANGUAGE

The scientific study of a spoken language (*descriptive linguistics*) involves several interrelated areas of analysis: phonology, morphology, lexicon, and syntax. **Phonology,** the study of speech sounds, considers which sounds are present and significant in a given language. **Morphology** studies the forms in which sounds combine to form *morphemes*—words and their meaningful parts. Thus, the word *cats* would be analyzed as containing two morphemes: *cat,* the name for a kind of animal, and *-s,* a morpheme indicating plurality. A language's **lexicon** is a dictionary containing all its morphemes and their meanings. **Syntax** refers to the arrangement and order of words in phrases and sentences. Syntactic questions include whether nouns usually come before or after verbs, or whether adjectives normally precede or follow the nouns they modify.

Speech Sounds

From the movies and TV, and from actually meeting foreigners, we know something about foreign accents and mispronunciations. We know that someone with a marked French accent doesn't pronounce *r* the same way an American does. But at least someone from France can distinguish between "craw" and "claw," which someone from Japan may not be able to do. The difference between *r* and *l* makes a difference in English and in French, but it doesn't in Japanese. In linguistics, we say that the difference between *r* and *l* is *phonemic* in English and French but not in Japanese; that is, *r* and *l* are phonemes in English and French but not in Japanese. A **phoneme** is a sound contrast that makes a difference, that differentiates meaning.

We find the phonemes in a given language by comparing *minimal pairs,* words that resemble each other in all but one sound. The words have totally different meanings, but they differ in just one sound. The contrasting sounds are therefore phonemes in that language. An example in English is the minimal pair *pit/bit.* These two words are distinguished by a single sound contrast between /p/ and /b/ (we enclose phonemes in slashes). Thus /p/ and /b/ are phonemes in English. Another example is the different vowel sound of *bit* and *beat* (see Figure 13.1). This contrast serves to distinguish these two words and the two vowel phonemes written /I/ and /i/ in English.

Standard (American) English (SE), the "region-free" dialect of TV network newscasters, has about 35 phonemes: at least 11 vowels and 24 consonants. The number of phonemes varies from language to language—from 15 to 60, averaging between 30 and 40. The number of phonemes also varies between dialects of a given language. In American English, for example, vowel phonemes vary noticeably from dialect to dialect. Readers should pronounce the words in Figure 14.1, paying attention to (or asking someone else) whether they distinguish each of the vowel sounds. Most Americans don't pronounce them all.

Phonetics is the study of speech sounds in general, what people actually say in various languages. **Phonemics** studies only the *significant* sound contrasts (phonemes) of a given language. In English, like /r/ and /l/ (remember *craw* and *claw*), /b/ and /v/ are also phonemes, occurring in minimal pairs like *bat* and *vat*. In Spanish, however, the contrast between [b] and [v] doesn't distinguish meaning, and they are therefore not phonemes (we enclose sounds that are not phonemic in brackets). Spanish speakers normally use the [b] sound to pronounce words spelled with either *b* or *v.*

In any language, a given phoneme extends over a phonetic range. In English, the phoneme /p/ ignores the phonetic contrast between the

High front (spread)	[i]	as in *beat*
Lower high front (spread)	[I]	as in *bit*
Mid front (spread)	[e]	as in *bait*
Lower mid front (spread)	[ɛ]	as in *bet*
Low front	[æ]	as in *bat*
Central	[ə]	as in *butt*
Low back	[a]	as in *pot*
Lower mid back (rounded)	[ɔ]	as in *bought*
Mid back (rounded)	[o]	as in *boat*
Lower high back (rounded)	[ʊ]	as in *put*
High back (rounded)	[u]	as in *boot*

FIGURE 14.1 Vowel Phonemes in Standard American English.

The phonemes are shown according to height of tongue and tongue position at front, center, or back of mouth. Phonetic symbols are identified by English words that include them; note that most are minimal pairs.

SOURCE: Adaptation of excerpt and Figure 2-1 from Dwight Bolinger and Donald A. Sears, *Aspects of Language*, 3rd ed. © 1981 Heinle/Arts & Sciences, a part of Cengage Learning, Inc. Reproduced by permission. www.cengage.com/permissions

phonology
Study of a language's phonemics and phonetics.

morphology
(Linguistic) study of morphemes and word construction.

lexicon
Vocabulary; all the morphemes in a language and their meanings.

syntax
Arrangement of words in phrases and sentences.

phoneme
Smallest sound contrast that distinguishes meaning.

phonetics
Study of speech sounds—what people actually say.

phonemics
Study of sound contrasts (phonemes) in a language.

[pʰ] in *pin* and the [p] in *spin*. Most English speakers don't even notice that there is a phonetic difference: [pʰ] is aspirated, so that a puff of air follows the [p]; the [p] in *spin* is not. (To see the difference, light a match, hold it in front of your mouth, and watch the flame as you pronounce the two words.) The contrast between [pʰ] and [p] is phonemic in some languages, such as Hindi (spoken in India). That is, there are words whose meaning is distinguished only by the contrast between an aspirated and an unaspirated [p].

Native speakers vary in their pronunciation of certain phonemes. This variation is important in

Sapir-Whorf hypothesis
Idea that different languages produce different patterns of thought.

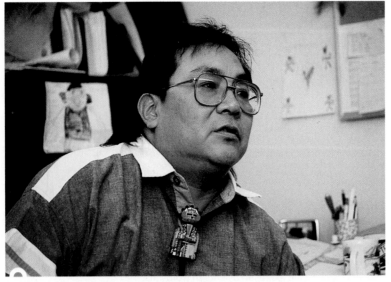

Shown here (in 1995) is Leigh Jenkins, who was or is director of cultural preservation for the Hopi tribal council. The Hopi language would not distinguish between *was* and *is* in the previous sentence. For the Hopi, present and past are real and are expressed grammatically in the same way, while the future remains hypothetical and has a different grammatical expression.

the evolution of language. With no shifts in pronunciation, there can be no linguistic change. The section on sociolinguistics below considers phonetic variation and its relationship to social divisions and the evolution of language.

LANGUAGE, THOUGHT, AND CULTURE

The well-known linguist Noam Chomsky (1955) has argued that the human brain contains a limited set of rules for organizing language, so that all languages have a common structural basis. (Chomsky calls this set of rules *universal grammar*.) The fact that people can learn foreign languages and that words and ideas can be translated from one language into another tends to support Chomsky's position that all humans have similar linguistic abilities and thought processes. Another line of support comes from creole languages. Such languages develop from pidgins, languages that form in situations of acculturation, when different societies come into contact and must devise a system of communication. As mentioned in the "Culture" chapter, pidgins based on English and native languages developed in the context of trade and colonialism in China, Papua New Guinea, and West Africa. Eventually, after generations of being spoken, pidgins may develop into *creole languages*. These are more mature languages, with developed grammatical rules and native speakers (that is, people who learn the language as their primary means of communication during enculturation). Creoles are spoken in several Caribbean societies. Gullah, which is spoken by African Americans on coastal islands in South Carolina and Georgia, is also a creole language. Supporting the idea that creoles are based on universal grammar is the fact that such languages all share certain features. Syntactically, all use particles (e.g., will, was) to form future and past tenses and multiple negation to deny or negate (e.g., he don't got none). Also, all form questions by changing inflection rather than by changing word order. For example, "You're going home for the holidays?" (with a rising tone at the end) rather than "Are you going home for the holidays?"

The Sapir-Whorf Hypothesis

Other linguists and anthropologists take a different approach to the relation between language and thought. Rather than seeking universal linguistic structures and processes, they believe that different languages produce different ways of thinking. This position is sometimes known as the **Sapir-Whorf hypothesis** after Edward Sapir (1931) and his student Benjamin Lee Whorf (1956), its prominent early advocates. Sapir and Whorf argued that the grammatical categories of different languages lead their speakers to think about things in particular ways. For example, the third-person singular pronouns of English (*he, she; him, her; his, hers*) distinguish gender, whereas those of the Palaung, a small tribe in Burma, do not (Burling 1970). Gender exists in English, although a fully developed noun-gender and adjective-agreement system, as in French and other Romance languages (*la belle fille, le beau fils*), does not. The Sapir-Whorf hypothesis therefore might suggest that English speakers can't help paying more attention to differences between males and females than do the Palaung and less than do French or Spanish speakers.

English divides time into past, present, and future. Hopi, a language of the Pueblo region of the Native American Southwest, does not. Rather, Hopi distinguishes between events that exist or have existed (what we use present and past to discuss) and those that don't or don't yet (our future events, along with imaginary and hypothetical events). Whorf argued that this difference leads Hopi speakers to think about time and reality in different ways than English speakers do. A similar example comes from Portuguese, which employs a future subjunctive verb form, introducing a degree of uncertainty into discussions of the future. In English, we routinely use the future tense to talk about something we think will happen. We don't feel the need to qualify "The sun'll come out tomorrow" by adding "if it doesn't go supernova." We don't hesitate to proclaim "I'll see you next year," even when we can't be absolutely sure we will. The Portuguese future subjunctive qualifies the future event, recognizing that the future can't be certain. Our way of expressing the future as certain is so ingrained that we don't even think about it, just as the Hopi don't see the need to distinguish between present and past, both of which are real, while the future remains hypothetical. It would seem, however, that language does not tightly restrict thought, because cultural changes can produce changes in thought and in language, as we shall see in the next section.

Focal Vocabulary

A *lexicon* (or vocabulary) is a language's dictionary, its set of names for things, events, and ideas. Lexicon influences perception. Thus, Eskimos have several distinct words for different types of snow that in English are all called *snow*. Most English speakers never notice the differences between these types of snow and might have trouble seeing them even if someone pointed them out. Eskimos recognize and think about differences in snow that English speakers don't see because our language provides us with just one word.

Similarly, the Nuer of Sudan have an elaborate vocabulary to describe cattle. Eskimos have several

Olives, but what kinds? Undoubtedly the olive vendor has a more elaborate focal vocabulary for what he sells than you or I do.

words for snow and Nuer have dozens for cattle because of their particular histories, economies, and environments. When the need arises, English speakers also can elaborate their snow and cattle vocabularies. For example, skiers name varieties of snow with words that are missing from the lexicons of Florida retirees. Similarly, the cattle vocabulary of a Texas rancher is much ampler than that of a salesperson in a New York City department store. Such specialized sets of terms and distinctions that are particularly important to certain groups (those with particular foci of experience or activity) are known as **focal vocabulary.**

Vocabulary is the area of language that changes most readily. New words and distinctions, when needed, appear and spread. For example, who would have faxed or e-mailed anything a generation ago? Names for items get simpler as they become common and important. A television has become a *TV,* an automobile a *car,* and a digital video disc a *DVD.*

Language, culture, and thought are interrelated. However, and in opposition to the Sapir-Whorf hypothesis, it might be more reasonable to say that changes in culture produce changes in language and thought than the reverse. Consider differences between female and male Americans in regard to the color terms they use (Lakoff 2004). Distinctions implied by such terms as *salmon, rust, peach, beige, teal, mauve, cranberry,* and *dusky orange* aren't in the vocabularies of most American men. However, many of them weren't even in American women's lexicons 50 years ago. These changes reflect changes in American economy, society, and culture. Color terms and distinctions have increased with the growth of the fashion and cosmetic industries. A similar contrast (and growth)

focal vocabulary
Set of words describing particular domains (foci) of experience.

ethnosemantics
Study of lexical (vocabulary) categories and contrasts.

semantics
A language's meaning system.

in Americans' lexicons shows up in football, basketball, and hockey vocabularies. Sports fans, more often males than females, use more terms in reference to, and make more elaborate distinctions between, the games they watch, such as hockey (see Table 14.1). Thus, cultural contrasts and changes affect lexical distinctions (for instance, peach versus salmon) within semantic domains (for instance, color terminology). **Semantics** refers to a language's meaning system.

TABLE 14.1 Focal Vocabulary for Hockey

Insiders have special terms for the major elements of the game.

ELEMENT OF HOCKEY	INSIDERS' TERM
puck	biscuit
goal/net	pipes
penalty box	sin bin
hockey stick	twig
helmet	bucket
space between a goalie's leg pads	five hole

How would a hockey insider use focal vocabulary to describe the items shown in this photo of a Stanley Cup final? How would you describe them?

Meaning

Speakers of particular languages use sets of terms to organize, or categorize, their experiences and perceptions. Linguistic terms and contrasts encode (embody) differences in meaning that people perceive. **Ethnosemantics** studies such classification systems in various languages. Well-studied ethnosemantic *domains* (sets of related things, perceptions, or concepts named in a language) include kinship terminology and color terminology. When we study such domains, we are examining how those people perceive and distinguish between kin relationships or colors. Other such domains include ethnomedicine—the terminology for the causes, symptoms, and cures of disease (Frake 1961); ethnobotany—native classification of plant life (Berlin, Breedlove, and Raven 1974; Carlson and Maffi 2004; Conklin 1954); and ethnoastronomy (Goodenough 1953).

The ways in which people divide up the world—the contrasts they perceive as meaningful or significant—reflect their experiences (see Bicker, Sillitoe, and Pottier, eds. 2004). Anthropologists have discovered that certain lexical domains and vocabulary items evolve in a determined order. For example, after studying color terminology in more than 100 languages, Berlin and Kay (1991, 1999) discovered 10 basic color terms: *white, black, red, yellow, blue, green, brown, pink, orange,* and *purple* (they evolved in more or less that order). The number of terms varied with cultural complexity. Representing one extreme were Papua New Guinea cultivators and Australian hunters and gatherers, who used only two basic terms, which translate as *black* and *white* or *dark* and *light*. At the other end of the continuum were European and Asian languages with all the color terms. Color terminology was most developed in areas with a history of using dyes and artificial coloring.

SOCIOLINGUISTICS

No language is a uniform system in which everyone talks just like everyone else. Linguistic *performance* (what people actually say) is the concern of sociolinguists. The field of sociolinguistics investigates relationships between social and linguistic variation, or language in its social context (Eckert and Rickford, eds. 2001). How do different speakers use a given language? How do linguistic features correlate with social stratification, including class, ethnic, and gender differences (Tannen 1990; Tannen, ed. 1993)? How is language used to express, reinforce, or resist power (Geis 1987; Thomas 1999)?

Sociolinguists don't deny that the people who speak a given language share knowledge of its basic rules. Such common knowledge is the basis of mutually intelligible communication. However, sociolinguists focus on features that vary systematically with social position and situation. To study variation, sociolinguists must do field work. They must observe, define, and measure variable use of language in real-world situations. To show that linguistic features correlate with social, economic, and political differences, the social attributes of speakers also must be measured and related to speech (Fasold 1990; Labov 1972a; Trudgill 2000).

Variation within a language at a given time is historic change in progress. The same forces that, working gradually, have produced large-scale linguistic change over the centuries are still at work today. Linguistic change doesn't occur in a vacuum but in society. When new ways of speaking are associated with social factors, they are imitated, and they spread. In this way, a language changes.

Linguistic Diversity

As an illustration of the linguistic variation that is encountered in all nations, consider the contemporary United States. Ethnic diversity is revealed by the fact that millions of Americans learn first languages other than English. Spanish is the most common. Most of those people eventually become

STUDENT: Laura Macía, Ph.D. Candidate
COUNTRY OF ORIGIN: Colombia
SUPERVISING PROFESSOR: Richard Scaglion
SCHOOL: University of Pittsburgh

It's All in the Nickname

Flaca (Skinny), *Negro* (Black), *Gordo* (Fat), and *Mono* (Blond)—these are names that I would call some of my family members and friends. These are also some of the most popular nicknames in my home country, Colombia. Families in Colombia commonly call the darkest-skinned sibling *Negro* or *Negra* and the one with the lightest complexion *Mono* or *Mona*, while favorite nicknames among couples include *Gordo/a* and *Flaco/a*. These nicknames usually are used among family members and good friends. However, sometimes, people comfortable with their nicknames even use them in introductions, often adding their last names for differentiation purposes, as in *"Soy el Gordo Ramírez, no el Gordo Rodríguez"* (I'm Fat Ramírez, not Fat Rodríguez).

In the United States, labels based on physical attributes are considered politically incorrect. The use of terms such as "black," "fat," or "blond" is often considered insulting. Only under very specific circumstances can these terms be used, usually with strong restrictions regarding when, where, and to whom the name can be attached. Such descriptive appellations are being replaced by more acceptable words such as "African American" or "overweight." Of course, none of these replacements are appropriate as nicknames.

The way in which Colombians and many other Latin Americans use physical characteristics to identify each other could be seen in the United States as offensive and inconsiderate. But to many Latin Americans the care exercised in the United States to avoid references to such physical attributes seems excessive and indicates ignorance of the context in which they are used. Colombians display a wider physical variation within families or close social groups than do most U.S. families. It is in this context that these nicknames are used, usually underscoring differences within one's own family or groups of friends. Because virtually every family has its own *Negro, Gordo,* or *Mono,* these nicknames are not likely to become labels for wider subgroups of society, a context in which they could be considered derogatory or offensive.

bilinguals, adding English as a second language. In many multilingual (including colonized) nations, people use two languages on different occasions: one in the home, for example, and the other on the job or in public. This chapter's "Appreciating Diversity" focuses on India, a multilingual, formerly colonized, nation. Only about one tenth of India's population speaks English, the colonial language. In "Appreciating Diversity" we see how even those English speakers appreciate being able to read, and to find Internet content in, their own regional languages.

appreciating

D I V E R S I T Y

Googling Locally

Cultural, including linguistic, diversity is alive, well, and thriving in many countries, including India, as described here. Despite that nation's colonial history, only about a tenth of the Indian population speaks English. However, even many of those English speakers appreciate being able to read, and to seek out Internet content in, their own regional languages. In this account we see how local entrepreneurs and international companies such as Google, Yahoo, and Microsoft are rushing to meet the demand for Web content in local languages. This example illustrates one of the main lessons of applied anthropology, that external inputs fit in best when they are tailored properly to local settings. Yet another expression of diversity is when Indians shift their linguistic styles—even languages—as they interact with friends, family, coworkers, and Internet sources in their daily lives.

Asia already has twice as many Internet users as North America, and by 2012 it will have three times as many. Already, more than half of the search queries on Google come from outside the United States.

The globalization of the Web has inspired entrepreneurs like Ram Prakash Hanumanthappa, an engineer from outside Bangalore, India. Mr. Ram Prakash learned English as a teenager, but he still prefers to express himself to friends and family members in his native Kannada. But using Kannada on the Web in-

volves computer keyboard maps that even Mr. Ram Prakash finds challenging to learn.

So in 2006 he developed Quillpad, an online service for typing in 10 South Asian languages. Users spell out words of local languages phonetically in Roman letters, and Quillpad's predictive engine converts them into local-language script. Bloggers and authors rave about the service, which has attracted interest from the cellphone maker Nokia and the attention of Google Inc., which has since introduced its own transliteration tool.

Mr. Ram Prakash said Western technology companies have misunderstood the linguistic landscape of India, where English is spoken proficiently by only about a tenth of the population and even many college-educated Indians prefer the contours of their native tongues for everyday speech. "You've got to give them an opportunity to express themselves correctly, rather than make a fool out of themselves and forcing them to use English," he said.

Only there is a shortage of non-English content and applications. So, American technology giants are spending hundreds of millions of dollars each year to build and develop foreign-language Web sites and services—before local companies like Quillpad beat them to the punch and the profits . . .

Nowhere are the obstacles, or the potential rewards, more apparent than in India, whose online population . . . is poised to become the third largest in the world after China and the United States by 2012. Indians may speak one language to their boss, another to their spouse and a third to a parent. In casual speech, words can be drawn from a grab bag of tongues.

In the last two years, Yahoo and Google have introduced more than a dozen services to encourage India's Web users to search, blog, chat and learn in their mother tongues. Microsoft has built its Windows Live bundle of online consumer services in seven Indian languages. Facebook has enlisted hundreds of volunteers to translate its social networking site into Hindi and other regional languages, and Wikipedia now has more entries in Indian local languages than in Korean. Google's search service has lagged behind the local competition in China, and that has made providing locally flavored services a priority for the company in India. Google's initiatives in India are aimed at opening the country's historically slow-growing personal computer market, and at developing expertise that Google will be able to apply to building services for emerging markets worldwide.

"India is a microcosm of the world," said Dr. Prasad Bhaarat Ram, Google India's head of research and development. "Having 22 languages creates a new level of complexity in which you can't take the same approach that you would if

style shifts
Varying one's speech in different social contexts.

diglossia
Language with "high" (formal) and "low" (informal, familial) dialects.

Whether bilingual or not, we all vary our speech in different contexts; we engage in **style shifts** (see Eckert and Rickford, eds. 2001). In certain parts of Europe, people regularly switch dialects. This phenomenon, known as **diglossia,** applies to "high" and "low" variants of the same language, for example, in German and Flemish (spoken in Belgium). People employ the "high" variant at universities and in writing, professions, and the mass media. They use the "low" variant for ordinary conversation with family members and friends.

Just as social situations influence our speech, so do geographic, cultural, and socioeconomic differences. Many dialects coexist in the United States with Standard (American) English (SE). SE itself is a dialect that differs, say, from "BBC English," which is the preferred dialect in Great Britain. According to the principle of *linguistic relativity,* all dialects are equally effective as systems of communication, which is language's main job. Our tendency to think of particular dialects as cruder or more sophisticated than others is a social rather than a linguistic judgment. We rank

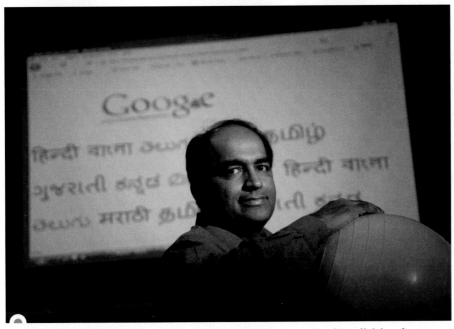

Google's Dr. Prasad Ram, based in Bangalore, India, heads a technology division that uses the English language keyboard to expand in regional languages, including Hindi, Gujarati, Tamil, and several others.

you had one predominant language and applied it 22 times."

Global businesses are spending hundreds of millions of dollars a year working their way down a list of languages into which to translate their Web sites, said Donald A. DePalma, the chief research officer of Common Sense Advisory, a consulting business in Lowell, Mass., that specializes in localizing Web sites. India—with relatively undeveloped e-commerce and online advertising markets—is actually lower on the list than Russia, Brazil and South Korea, Mr. DePalma said . . .

English simply will not suffice for connecting with India's growing online market, a lesson already learned by Western television producers and consumer products makers . . .

Even among the largely English-speaking base of around 50 million Web users in India today, nearly three-quarters prefer to read in a local language, according to a survey by JuxtConsult, an Indian market research company.

Many cannot find the content they are seeking. "There is a huge shortage of local language content," said Sanjay Tiwari, the chief executive of JuxtConsult. A Microsoft initiative, Project Bhasha, coordinates the efforts of Indian academics, local businesses and solo software developers to expand computing in regional languages. The project's Web site, which counts thousands of registered members, refers to language as "one of the main contributors to the digital divide" in India.

The company is also seeing growing demand from Indian government agencies and companies creating online public services in local languages.

"As many of these companies want to push their services into rural India or tier-two towns or smaller towns, then it becomes essential they communicate with their customers in the local language," said Pradeep Parappil, a Microsoft program manager.

"Localization is the key to success in countries like India," said Gopal Krishna, who oversees consumer services at Yahoo India.

certain speech patterns as better or worse because we recognize that they are used by groups that we also rank. People who say *dese, dem,* and *dere* instead of *these, them,* and *there* communicate perfectly well with anyone who recognizes that the *d* sound systematically replaces the *th* sound in their speech. However, this form of speech has become an indicator of low social rank. We call it, like the use of *ain't,* "uneducated speech." The use of *dem, dese,* and *dere* is one of many phonological differences that Americans recognize and look down on.

Gender Speech Contrasts

Comparing men and women, there are differences in phonology, grammar, and vocabulary as well as in the body stances and movements that accompany speech (Baron 1986; Eckert and McConnell-Ginet 2003; Lakoff 2004; Tannen 1990). In public contexts, Japanese women tend to adopt an artificially high voice, for the sake of politeness, according to their traditional culture. In North America and Great Britain, women's speech tends to be more similar to the standard dialect than men's is. Consider the data in Table 14.2,

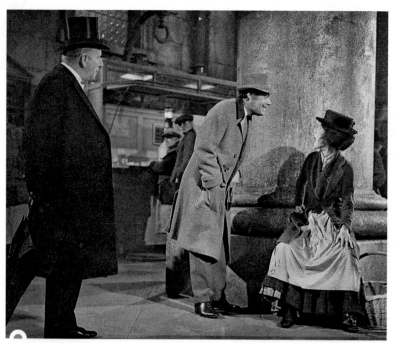

Certain dialects are stigmatized, not because of actual linguistic deficiencies, but because of a symbolic association between a certain way of talking and low social status. In this scene from *My Fair Lady*, Professor Henry Higgins (Rex Harrison) encounters Eliza Doolittle (Audrey Hepburn), a Cockney flower girl. Higgins will teach Doolittle how to speak like an English aristocrat.

honorifics
Terms of respect; used to honor people.

hood he's saying "Phooey on you"? Women are more likely to use such adjectives as *adorable, charming, sweet, cute, lovely,* and *divine* than men are.

Language and Status Position

Honorifics are terms used with people, often by being added to their names, to "honor" them. Such terms may convey or imply a status difference between the speaker and the person being referred to ("the good doctor") or addressed ("Professor Dumbledore"). Although Americans tend to be less formal than other nationalities, American English still has its honorifics. They include such terms as *Mr., Mrs., Ms., Dr., Professor, Dean, Senator, Reverend, Honorable,* and *President.* Often these terms are attached to names, as in "Dr. Wilson," "President Obama," and "Senator McCain," but some of them can be used to address someone without using his or her name, such as "Dr.," "Mr. President," "Senator," and "Miss." The British have a more developed set of honorifics, corresponding to status distinctions based in class, nobility (e.g., Lord and Lady Trumble), and special recognition (e.g., knighthood—"Sir Elton" or "Dame Maggie").

The Japanese language has several honorifics, some of which convey more respect than others do. The suffix *-sama* (added to a name), showing great respect, is used to address someone of higher social status, such as a lord or a respected teacher. Women can use it to demonstrate love or respect for their husbands. The most common Japanese honorific, *-san,* attached to the last name, is respectful, but less formal than "Mr.," "Mrs.," or "Ms." in American English. Attached to a first name, *-san* denotes more familiarity. The honorific *-dono* shows more respect and is intermediate between *-san* and *-sama.*

Other Japanese honorifics don't necessarily honor the person being addressed. The term *-kun,* for example, conveys familiarity when addressing friends, like using *-san* attached to the first name. The term *-kun* is used also with younger or lower-ranking people. A boss might use *-kun* with employees, especially females. Here the honorific works in reverse; the speaker uses the term (somewhat like "boy" or "girl" in English)

gathered in Detroit. In all social classes, but particularly in the working class, men were more apt to use double negatives (e.g., "I don't want none"). Women tend to be more careful about "uneducated speech." This trend shows up in both the United States and England. Men may adopt working-class speech because they associate it with masculinity. Perhaps women pay more attention to the media, where standard dialects are employed.

According to Robin Lakoff (2004), the use of certain types of words and expressions has been associated with women's traditional lesser power in American society (see also Coates 1986; Tannen 1990). For example, *Oh dear, Oh fudge,* and *Goodness!* are less forceful than *Hell* and *Damn.* Watch the lips of a disgruntled athlete in a televised competition, such as a football game. What's the likeli-

TABLE 14.2 Multiple Negation ("I don't want none")
According to Gender and Class (in Percentages)

	UPPER MIDDLE CLASS	LOWER MIDDLE CLASS	UPPER WORKING CLASS	LOWER WORKING CLASS
Male	6.3	32.4	40.0	90.1
Female	0.0	1.4	35.6	58.9

SOURCE: Peter Trudgill, *Sociolinguistics: An Introduction to Language and Society,* 4th ed. (London: Penguin Books, 1974, revised editions 1983, 1995, 2000), p. 70. Copyright © Peter Trudgill, 1974, 1983, 1995, 2000. Reproduced by permission of Penguin Books Ltd.

to address someone he or she perceives as having lower status. Japanese speakers use the very friendly and familiar term *-chan* with someone of the same age or younger, including close friends, siblings, and children (*Free Dictionary* 2004; Loveday 1986, 2001).

Kin terms also can be associated with gradations in rank and familiarity. *Dad* is a more familiar, less formal kin term than *Father*, but it still shows more respect than would using the father's first name. Outranking their children, parents routinely use their kids' first names, nicknames, or baby names, rather than addressing them as "son" and "daughter." American English terms like *bro*, *man*, *dude*, and *girl* (in some contexts) seem similar to the informal/familiar honorifics in Japanese. Southerners up to (and sometimes long past) a certain age routinely use "ma'am" and "sir" for older or higher-status women and men.

Stratification

We use and evaluate speech in the context of *extralinguistic* forces—social, political, and economic. Mainstream Americans evaluate the speech of low-status groups negatively, calling it "uneducated." This is not because these ways of speaking are bad in themselves but because they have come to symbolize low status. Consider variation in the pronunciation of *r*. In some parts of the United States, *r* is regularly pronounced, and in other (*r*less) areas, it is not. Originally, American *r*less speech was modeled on the fashionable speech of England. Because of its prestige, *r*lessness was adopted in many areas and continues as the norm around Boston and in the South.

New Yorkers sought prestige by dropping their *r*'s in the 19th century, after having pronounced them in the 18th. However, contemporary New Yorkers are going back to the 18th-century pattern of pronouncing *r*'s. What matters, and what governs linguistic change, is not the reverberation of a strong midwestern *r* but *social* evaluation, whether *r*'s happen to be "in" or "out."

Studies of *r* pronunciation in New York City have clarified the mechanisms of phonological change. William Labov (1972*b*) focused on whether *r* was pronounced after vowels in such words as *car*, *floor*, *card*, and *fourth*. To get data on how this linguistic variation correlated with social class, he used a series of rapid encounters with employees in three New York City department stores, each of whose prices and locations attracted a different socioeconomic group. Saks Fifth Avenue (68 encounters) catered to the upper middle class, Macy's (125) attracted middle-class shoppers, and S. Klein's (71) had predominantly lower-middle-class and working-class customers. The class origins of store personnel tended to reflect those of their customers.

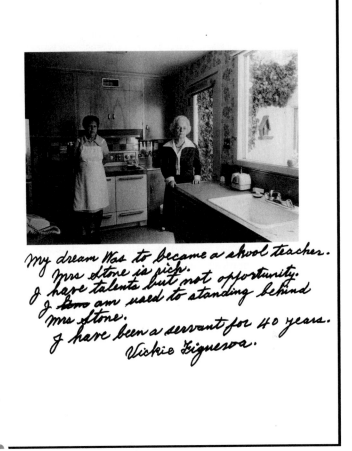

"Proper language" is a strategic resource, correlated with wealth, prestige, and power. How is linguistic (and social) stratification illustrated in the photo above, including the handwritten comments below it?

Having already determined that a certain department was on the fourth floor, Labov approached ground-floor salespeople and asked where that department was. After the salesperson had answered, "Fourth floor," Labov repeated his "Where?" in order to get a second response. The second reply was more formal and emphatic, the salesperson presumably thinking that Labov hadn't heard or understood the first answer. For each salesperson, therefore, Labov had two samples of /r/ pronunciation in two words.

Labov calculated the percentages of workers who pronounced /r/ at least once during the interview. These were 62 percent at Saks, 51 percent at Macy's, but only 20 percent at S. Klein's. He also found that personnel on upper floors, where he asked "What floor is this?" (and where more expensive items were sold), pronounced /r/ more often than ground-floor salespeople did.

In Labov's study, summarized in Table 14.3, /r/ pronunciation was clearly associated with prestige. Certainly the job interviewers who had hired the salespeople never counted *r*'s before

TABLE 14.3 Pronunciation of *r* in New York City Department Stores

STORE	NUMBER OF ENCOUNTERS	% r PRONUNCIATION
Saks Fifth Avenue	68	62
Macy's	125	51
S. Klein's	71	20

Black English Vernacular (BEV) Rule-governed dialect spoken by some African Americans.

offering employment. However, they did use speech evaluations to make judgments about how effective certain people would be in selling particular kinds of merchandise. In other words, they practiced sociolinguistic discrimination, using linguistic features in deciding who got certain jobs.

Our speech habits help determine our access to employment and other material resources. Because of this, "proper language" itself becomes a strategic resource—and a path to wealth, prestige, and power (Gal 1989; Thomas and Wareing, eds. 2004). Illustrating this, many ethnographers have described the importance of verbal skill and oratory in politics (Beeman 1986; Bloch, ed. 1975; Brenneis 1988; Geis 1987). Ronald Reagan, known as a "great communicator," dominated American society in the 1980s as a two-term president. Another twice-elected president, Bill Clinton, despite his southern accent, was known for his verbal skills in certain contexts (e.g., televised debates and town-hall meetings). Communications flaws may have helped doom the presidencies of Gerald Ford, Jimmy Carter, and George Bush (the elder). How do you evaluate the linguistic skills of the current president or prime minister of your country?

The French anthropologist Pierre Bourdieu views linguistic practices as *symbolic capital* that properly trained people may convert into economic and social capital. The value of a dialect—its standing in a "linguistic market"—depends on the extent to which it provides access to desired positions in the labor market. In turn, this reflects its legitimation by formal institutions: educational institutions, state, church, and prestige media. Even people who don't use the prestige dialect accept its authority and correctness, its "symbolic domination" (Bourdieu 1982, 1984). Thus, linguistic forms, which lack power in themselves, take on the power of the groups they symbolize. The education system, however (defending its own worth), denies linguistic relativity, misrepresenting prestige speech as being inherently better. The linguistic insecurity often felt by lower-class and minority speakers is a result of this symbolic domination.

Black English Vernacular (BEV)

No one pays much attention when someone says "runt" instead of "rent." But some nonstandard speech carries more of a stigma. Sometimes stigmatized speech is linked to region, class, or educational background; sometimes it is associated with ethnicity or "race."

The sociolinguist William Labov and several associates, both white and black, have conducted detailed studies of what they call **Black English Vernacular (BEV).** (*Vernacular* means ordinary, casual speech.) BEV is the "relatively uniform dialect spoken by the majority of black youth in most parts of the United States today, especially in the inner city areas of New York, Boston, Detroit, Philadelphia, Washington, Cleveland, . . . and other urban centers. It is also spoken in most rural areas and used in the casual, intimate speech of many adults" (Labov 1972a, p. xiii). This does not imply that all, or even most, African Americans speak BEV.

BEV isn't an ungrammatical hodgepodge. Rather, BEV is a complex linguistic system with its own rules, which linguists have described. The phonology and syntax of BEV are similar to those of southern dialects. This reflects generations of contact between southern whites and blacks, with mutual influence on each other's speech patterns. Many features that distinguish BEV from SE (Standard English) also show up in southern white speech, but less frequently than in BEV.

Linguists disagree about exactly how BEV originated (Rickford 1997). Smitherman (1986) calls it an Africanized form of English reflecting both an African heritage and the conditions of servitude, oppression, and life in America. She notes certain structural similarities between West African languages and BEV. African linguistic backgrounds no doubt influenced how early African Americans learned English. Did they restructure English to fit African linguistic patterns? Or did they quickly learn English from whites, with little continuing influence from the African linguistic heritage? Or, possibly, in acquiring English, did African slaves fuse English with African languages to make a pidgin or creole, which influenced the subsequent development of BEV? Creole speech may have been brought to the American colonies by the many slaves who were imported from the Caribbean during the 17th and 18th centuries. Some slaves may even have learned, while still in Africa, the pidgins or creoles spoken in West African trading forts (Rickford 1997).

Origins aside, there are phonological and grammatical differences between BEV and SE. One phonological difference between BEV and SE is that BEV speakers are less likely to pronounce *r* than SE speakers are. Actually, many SE speakers don't pronounce *r*'s that come right before a consonant (ca*r*d) or at the end of a word (ca*r*). But SE speakers do usually pronounce an *r* that comes right before a vowel, either at the end of a word (fou*r* o'clock) or within a word (Ca*r*ol). BEV speakers, by contrast, are much more likely to

Rap and hip-hop weave BEV into musical expression. Shown here, Nipsey Hussle, Snoop Dogg, Soulja Boy, The Dream, and Dorrough perform at the annual BET Hip Hop Awards ceremony in Atlanta, Georgia, on October 10, 2009.

omit such intervocalic (between vowels) *r*'s. The result is that speakers of the two dialects have different *homonyms* (words that sound the same but have different meanings). BEV speakers who don't pronounce intervocalic *r*'s have the following homonyms: Carol/Cal; Paris/pass.

Observing different phonological rules, BEV speakers pronounce certain words differently than SE speakers do. Particularly in the elementary school context, the homonyms of BEV-speaking students typically differ from those of their SE-speaking teachers. To evaluate reading accuracy, teachers should determine whether students are recognizing the different meanings of such BEV homonyms as *passed, past,* and *pass.* Teachers need to make sure students understand what they are reading, which is probably more important than whether they are pronouncing words correctly according to the SE norm.

The phonological contrasts between BEV and SE speakers often have grammatical consequences. One of these is *copula deletion,* which means the absence of SE forms of the copula—the verb *to be.* For example, SE and BEV may contrast as follows:

SE	SE CONTRACTION	BEV
you are tired	you're tired	you tired
he is tired	he's tired	he tired
we are tired	we're tired	we tired
they are tired	they're tired	they tired

In its deletion of the present tense of the verb *to be,* BEV is similar to many languages, including Russian, Hungarian, and Hebrew. BEV's copula deletion is simply a grammatical result of its phonological rules. Notice that BEV deletes the copula where SE has contractions. BEV's phonological rules dictate that *r*'s (as in *you're, we're,* and *they're*) and word-final *s*'s (as in *he's*) be dropped. However, BEV speakers do pronounce *m,* so that the BEV first-person singular is "I'm tired," just as in SE. Thus, when BEV omits the copula, it merely carries contraction one step further, as a result of its phonological rules.

Also, phonological rules may lead BEV speakers to omit *-ed* as a past-tense marker and *-s* as a marker of plurality. However, other speech contexts demonstrate that BEV speakers do understand the difference between past and present verbs, and between singular and plural nouns. Confirming this are irregular verbs (e.g., *tell, told*) and irregular plurals (e.g., *child, children*), in which BEV works the same as SE.

SE is not superior to BEV as a linguistic system, but it does happen to be the prestige dialect—the one used in the mass media, in writing, and in most public and professional contexts. SE is the dialect that has the most "symbolic capital." In areas of Germany where there is diglossia, speakers of Plattdeusch (Low German) learn the High German dialect to communicate appropriately in the national context. Similarly, upwardly mobile BEV-speaking students learn SE.

HISTORICAL LINGUISTICS

Sociolinguists study contemporary variation in speech—language change in progress. **Historical linguistics** deals with longer-term change. Historical linguists can reconstruct many features of past languages by studying contemporary **daughter languages.** These are languages that descend from the same parent language and that have been changing separately for hundreds or even thousands of years. We call the original language from which they diverge the **protolanguage.** Romance languages such as French and Spanish, for example, are daughter languages of Latin, their common protolanguage. German, English, Dutch,

and the Scandinavian languages are daughter languages of proto-Germanic. Latin and proto-Germanic were both Indo-European languages. Historical linguists classify languages according to their degree of relationship (see Figure 14.2).

Language changes over time. It evolves—varies, spreads, divides into **subgroups** (languages within a taxonomy of related languages that are most closely related). Dialects of a single parent language become distinct daughter languages, especially if they are isolated from one another. Some of them split, and new "granddaughter" languages develop. If people remain in the ancestral homeland, their speech patterns also change. The evolving speech in the ancestral homeland should be considered a daughter language like the others.

A close relationship between languages does not necessarily mean that their speakers are closely related biologically or culturally, because people can adopt new languages. In the equatorial forests of Africa, "pygmy" hunters have discarded their ancestral languages and now speak those of the cultivators who have migrated to the area. Immigrants to the United States and Canada spoke many different languages on arrival, but their descendants now speak fluent English.

Knowledge of linguistic relationships is often valuable to anthropologists interested in history, particularly events during the past 5,000 years. Cultural features may (or may not) correlate with the distribution of language families. Groups that speak related languages may (or may not) be more culturally similar to each other than they are to groups whose speech derives from different linguistic ancestors. Of course, cultural similarities aren't limited to speakers of related languages. Even groups whose members speak unrelated languages have contact through trade, intermarriage, and warfare. Ideas and inventions diffuse widely among human groups. Many items of vocabulary in contemporary English come from French. Even without written documentation of France's influence after the Norman Conquest of England in 1066, linguistic evidence in contemporary English would reveal a long period of important firsthand contact with France. Similarly, linguistic evidence may confirm cultural contact and borrowing when written history is lacking. By considering which words have been borrowed, we also can make inferences about the nature of the contact.

Language Loss

One aspect of linguistic history is language loss. When languages disappear, cultural diversity is reduced as well. According to linguist K. David Harrison, "When we lose a language, we lose centuries of thinking about time, seasons, sea creatures, reindeer, edible flowers, mathematics, landscapes, myths, music, the unknown and the everyday"

subgroups
(Linguistic) closely related languages.

historical linguistics
Study of languages over time.

daughter languages
Languages sharing a common parent language, e.g., Latin.

protolanguage
Language ancestral to several daughter languages.

The *Book of Kells*, an illustrated manuscript, was created at Kells, an ancient Irish monastery. Shown here is the title page of the book, which now resides in the Trinity College library in Dublin, Ireland. Such documents provide historical linguists with information on how languages change.

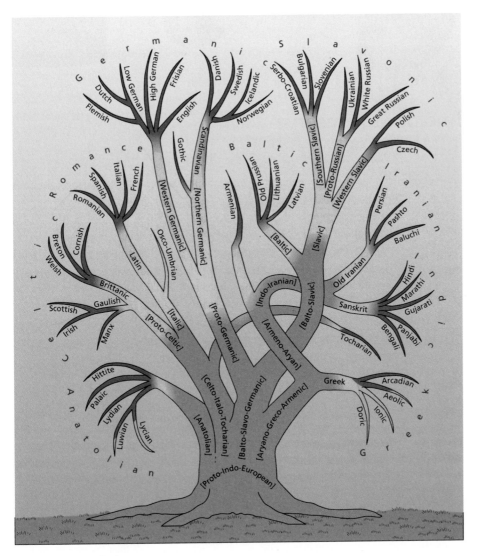

FIGURE 14.2 PIE Family Tree.

This is a family tree of the Indo-European languages. All can be traced back to a protolanguage, Proto-Indo-European (PIE), spoken more than 6,000 years ago. PIE split into dialects that eventually evolved into separate languages, which, in turn, evolved into languages such as Latin and proto-Germanic, which are ancestral to dozens of modern daughter languages.

(quoted in Maugh 2007). Harrison's recent book, *When Languages Die* (2007), notes that an indigenous language goes extinct every two weeks, as its last speakers die. The world's linguistic diversity has been cut in half (measured by number of distinct languages) in the past 500 years, and half of the remaining languages are predicted to disappear during this century. Colonial languages (e.g., English, Spanish, Portuguese, French, Dutch, Russian) have expanded at the expense of indigenous ones. Of approximately 7,000 remaining languages, about 20 percent are endangered, compared with 18 percent of mammals, 8 percent of plants, and 5 percent of birds (Maugh 2007).

Harrison, who teaches at Swarthmore College, is director of research for the Living Tongues Institute for Endangered Languages (http://www.livingtongues.org), which works to maintain, preserve, and revitalize endangered languages through multimedia documentation projects. Researchers from the institute use digital audio and video equipment to record the last speakers of the most endangered languages. *National Geographic*'s Enduring Voices Project (http://languagehotspots.org) strives to preserve endangered languages by identifying the geographic areas with unique, poorly understood, or threatened languages and by documenting those languages and cultures.

The website shows various language hot spots where the endangerment rate ranges from low to severe. The rate is high in an area encompassing Oklahoma, Texas, and New Mexico, where 40

anthropology **ATLAS**

Map 11 plots the distribution of the world's major language families, including Indo-European, whose languages are spoken now in areas far from its geographic origin.

appreciating
ANTHROPOLOGY

Using Modern Technology to Preserve Linguistic and Cultural Diversity

Although some see modern technology as a threat to cultural diversity, others see a role for this technology in allowing social groups to express themselves. The anthropologist H. Russell Bernard has been a pioneer in teaching speakers of endangered languages how to write their language using a computer. Bernard's work permits the preservation of languages and cultural memories. Native peoples from Mexico to Cameroon are using their mother tongue to express themselves as individuals and to provide insiders' accounts of different cultures.

Jesús Salinas Pedraza, a rural schoolteacher in the Mexican state of Hidalgo, sat down to a word processor a few years back and produced a monumental book, a 250,000-word description of his own Indian culture written in the Nähñu language. Nothing seems to be left out: folktales and traditional religious beliefs, the practical uses of plants and minerals and the daily flow of life in field and village . . .

Mr. Salinas is neither a professional anthropologist nor a literary stylist. He is, though, the first person to write a book in Nähñu (NYAW-hnyu), the native tongue of several hundred thousand Indians but a previously unwritten language.

Such a use of microcomputers and desktop publishing for languages with no literary tradition is now being encouraged by anthropologists for recording ethnographies from an insider's perspective. They see this as a means of preserving cultural diversity and a wealth of human knowledge. With even greater urgency,

linguists are promoting the techniques as a way of saving some of the world's languages from imminent extinction.

Half of the world's 6,000 languages are considered by linguists to be endangered. These are the languages spoken by small societies that are dwindling with the encroachment of larger, more dynamic cultures. Young people feel economic pressure to learn only the language of the dominant culture, and as the older people die, the non-written language vanishes, unlike languages with a history of writing, like Latin.

Dr. H. Russell Bernard, the anthropologist at the University of Florida at Gainesville who taught Mr. Salinas to read and write his native language, said: "Languages have always come and gone . . . But languages seem to be disappearing faster than ever before." . . .

Dr. Michael E. Krauss, the director of the Alaska Native Language Center at the University of Alaska in Fairbanks, estimates that 300 of the 900 indigenous languages in the Americas are moribund. That is, they are no longer being spoken by children, and so could disappear in a generation or two. Only two of the 20 native languages in Alaska are still being learned by children . . .

In an effort to preserve language diversity in Mexico, Dr. Bernard and Mr. Salinas decided in 1987 on a plan to teach the Indian people to read and write their own language using microcomputers. They established a native liter-

acy center in Oaxaca, Mexico, where others could follow in the footsteps of Mr. Salinas and write books in other Indian languages.

The Oaxaca center goes beyond most bilingual education programs, which concentrate on teaching people to speak and read their native languages. Instead, it operates on the premise that, as Dr. Bernard decided, what most native languages lack is native authors who write books in their own languages . . .

The Oaxaca project's influence is spreading. Impressed by the work of Mr. Salinas and others, Dr. Norman Whitten, an anthropologist at the University of Illinois, arranged for schoolteachers from Ecuador to visit Oaxaca and learn the techniques.

Now Ecuadorian Indians have begun writing about their cultures in the Quechua and Shwara languages. Others from Bolivia and Peru are learning to use the computers to write their languages, including Quechua, the tongue of the ancient Incas, still spoken by about 12 million Andean Indians . . .

Dr. Bernard emphasized that these native literacy programs are not intended to discourage people from learning the dominant language of their country as well. "I see nothing useful or charming about remaining monolingual in any Indian language if that results in being shut out of the national economy," he said.

Native American languages are at risk. The top hot spot is northern Australia, where 153 Aboriginal languages are endangered (Maugh 2007). Other hot spots are in central South America, the Pacific Northwest of North America, and eastern Siberia. In all these areas indigenous tongues have yielded, either voluntarily or through coercion, to a colonial language. This chapter's "Appreciating Anthropology" discusses how anthropologists are teaching speakers of endangered languages to preserve them by writing their own creative works using computers.

Acing the COURSE

Summary

1. Wild primates use call systems to communicate. Environmental stimuli trigger calls, which cannot be combined when multiple stimuli are present. Contrasts between language and call systems include displacement, productivity, and cultural transmission. Over time, our ancestral call systems grew too complex for genetic transmission, and hominid communication began to rely on learning. Humans still use nonverbal communication, such as facial expressions, gestures, and body stances and movements. But language is the main system humans use to communicate. Chimps and gorillas can understand and manipulate nonverbal symbols based on language.

2. No language uses all the sounds the human vocal tract can make. Phonology—the study of speech sounds—focuses on sound contrasts (phonemes) that distinguish meaning. The grammars and lexicons of particular languages can lead their speakers to perceive and think in certain ways. Studies of domains such as kinship, color terminologies, and pronouns show that speakers of different languages categorize their experiences differently.

3. Linguistic anthropologists share anthropology's general interest in diversity in time and space. Sociolinguistics investigates relationships between social and linguistic variation by focusing on the actual use of language. Only when features of speech acquire social meaning are they imitated. If they are valued, they will spread. People vary their speech, shifting styles, dialects, and languages. As linguistic systems, all languages and dialects are equally complex, rule-governed, and effective for communication. However, speech is used, is evaluated, and changes in the context of political, economic, and social forces. Often the linguistic traits of a low-status group are negatively evaluated. This devaluation is not because of *linguistic* features per se. Rather, it reflects the association of such features with low *social* status. One dialect, supported by the dominant institutions of the state, exercises symbolic domination over the others.

4. Historical linguistics is useful for anthropologists interested in historic relationships among populations. Cultural similarities and differences often correlate with linguistic ones. Linguistic clues can suggest past contacts between cultures. Related languages—members of the same language family—descend from an original protolanguage. Relationships between languages don't necessarily mean that there are biological ties between their speakers, because people can learn new languages.

5. One aspect of linguistic history is language loss. The world's linguistic diversity has been cut in half in the past 500 years, and half of the remaining 7,000 languages are predicted to disappear during this century.

Key Terms

Test Yourself!

MULTIPLE CHOICE

1. Research on communication skills of nonhuman primates reveals that
   a. they, too, possess a universal grammar.
   b. they can't combine the calls for food and danger into a single utterance.
   c. female nonhuman primates are more sensitive to different shades of green than their male counterparts are.
   d. they can construct elaborate call systems, often indicating several messages simultaneously.
   e. Australopithecines also communicated using call systems.

2. When Washoe and Lucy tried to teach sign language to other chimpanzees, this was an example of
   a. displacement.
   b. call systems.
   c. productivity.
   d. cultural transmission.
   e. estrus.

3. Recent research on the origin of language suggests that
   a. the capacity to remember and combine linguistic symbols is latent in all mammals.
   b. a mutation in humans (which happened 150,000 years ago) may have conferred selective advantages (linguistic and cultural abilities).
   c. fine tongue and lip movements that are necessary for clear speech are passed on through enculturation.
   d. it was a sudden event that made tool making among *Homo* possible.
   e. call systems evolved into complex languages 50,000 years ago.

4. What is the study of communication through body movements, stances, gestures, and facial expressions?
   a. ethnosemantics
   b. kinesics
   c. biosemantics
   d. protolinguistics
   e. diglossia

5. The scientific study of a spoken language involves several interrelated areas of analysis. Which area refers to all of a language's morphemes and their meanings?
   a. syntax
   b. ethnosemantics
   c. ethnoscience
   d. phonology
   e. lexicon

6. What does the Sapir-Whorf hypothesis state?
   a. The degree of cultural complexity is associated with the effectiveness of languages as systems of communication.
   b. The Hopi do not use three verb tenses; they have no concept of time.
   c. Different languages produce different ways of thinking.
   d. Culture and language are transmitted independently.
   e. Dialect variation is the result of toilet-training practices.

7. Studies on the differences between female and male Americans in regard to the color terms they use suggest that
   a. in opposition to the Sapir-Whorf hypothesis, it might be more reasonable to say that changes in culture produce changes in language and thought rather than the reverse.
   b. changes in American economy, society, and culture have had no impact on the use of color terms, or any terms, for that matter.
   c. in support of the Sapir-Whorf hypothesis, different languages produce different ways of thinking.
   d. women and men are equally sensitive to marketing tactics of the cosmetic industry.
   e. women spend more money on status goods than men do.

8. Which of the following statements about sociolinguists is *not* true?
   a. They are concerned more with performance than with competence.
   b. They look at society and at language.
   c. They are concerned with linguistic change.
   d. They focus on surface structure.
   e. They investigate the diffusion of genes between populations.

9. Honorifics are terms used with people, often being added to their names, to "honor" them. Why would sociolinguists be interested in studying the use of honorifics?
   a. They enable sociolinguists to study language and culture outside of its context because the same honorifics are used everywhere and they mean the same thing.
   b. Since honorifics always honor the person they are addressed to, sociolinguists can study the positive side of language and culture.
   c. They may convey or imply a status difference between the speaker and the person being referred to or addressed.
   d. They provide data about how different languages are related to one another, which

is what sociolinguists are primarily interested in.

e. There is no reason for contemporary sociolinguists to be interested in honorifics because people don't use these terms anymore.

10. Which of the following statements about Black English Vernacular (BEV) is *not* true?

a. BEV lacks the required linguistic depth to fully express thoughts.

b. Many aspects of BEV are also present in southern white speech.

c. BEV is not inferior to SE.

d. Linguists view BEV as a dialect of SE, not a different language.

e. BEV is not an ungrammatical collection of SE expressions.

FILL IN THE BLANK

1. _____ refers to the ability to create new expressions by combining other expressions, while _____ is the ability to describe things and events that are not present.

2. Variation in speech due to different contexts or situations is known as _____.

3. _____ refers to the existence of "high" and "low" dialects within a single language.

4. In a stratified society, even people who do not speak the prestige dialect tend to accept it as "standard" or superior. In Pierre Bourdieu's term, this is an instance of _____.

5. The world's linguistic diversity has been cut in half in the past _____ years, and half of the remaining _____ languages are predicted to disappear during this century.

CRITICAL THINKING

1. Do you agree with the principle of linguistic relativity? If not, why not? What dialects and languages do you speak? Do you tend to use different dialects, languages, or speech styles in different contexts? Why?

2. Culture always plays a role in shaping what we understand as "natural." What does this mean? Provide three examples of the relevance of this fact in the context of human language and communication.

3. Consider how changing technologies are altering the ways you communicate with family, friends, and even strangers. Suppose your best friend decides to study sociolinguistics in graduate school. What ideas about the relationship between changing technologies, language, and social relations could you suggest to her as worth studying?

4. List some stereotypes about how different people speak. Are those real differences, or just stereotypes? Are the stereotypes positive or negative? Why do you think those stereotypes exist?

5. What is language loss? Why are some researchers and communities worldwide so concerned by this growing phenomenon?

Multiple Choice: 1. (B); 2. (D); 3. (B); 4. (B); 5. (E); 6. (C); 7. (A); 8. (E); 9. (C); 10. (A). **Fill in the Blank:** 1. Productivity, displacement; 2. style shifting; 3. Diglossia; 4. symbolic domination; 5. 500, 7,000

Bonvillain, N.

2008 *Language, Culture, and Communication: The Meaning of Messages,* 5th ed. Upper Saddle River, NJ: Prentice Hall. Up-to-date text on language and communication in cultural context.

Eckert, P., and S. McConnell-Ginet

2003 *Language and Gender.* New York: Cambridge University Press. The sociolinguistics of male and female speech.

Lakoff, R. T.

2004 Language and Woman's Place, rev. ed. (M. Bucholtz, ed.). New York: Oxford University Press. Influential nontechnical discussion of how women use and are treated in Standard American English.

Rickford, J. R., and R. J. Rickford

2000 *Spoken Soul: The Story of Black English.* New York: Wiley. Readable account of the history and social meaning of BEV.

Salzmann, Z.

2007 *Language, Culture, and Society: An Introduction to Linguistic Anthropology,* 4th ed. Boulder, CO: Westview. The function of language in culture and society.

Thomas, L., and S. Wareing, eds.

2004 *Language, Society and Power,* 2nd ed. New York: Routledge. Political dimensions and use of language.

Suggested Additional Readings

Go to our Online Learning Center website at **www.mhhe.com/kottak** for Internet exercises directly related to the content of this chapter.

Internet Exercises

Chapter 14 Language and Communication **333**

What is social status, and how does it relate to ethnicity?

How are race and ethnicity socially constructed in various societies?

What are the positive and negative aspects of ethnicity?

This street scene in Birmingham, England shows Asian and Afro-Caribbean women in the Lozells neighborhood, a site of unrest between these two ethnic groups. What national and ethnic identities might these women claim?

understanding OURSELVES

When asked "who are you?" what first comes to mind? Think of the last person you met, or the person sitting nearest you. What labels pop into your head to describe that person? What kinds of identity cues and clues do people use to figure out the kinds of people they are dealing with, and how to act in various social situations? Part of human adaptive flexibility is our ability to shift self presentation in response to context. Italians, for example, maintain separate sets of clothing to be worn inside and outside the home. They invest much more in their outside wardrobe (thus supporting a vibrant Italian fashion industry)—and what it says about their public persona—than in indoor garb, which is for family and intimates to see. Identities and behavior change with context. "I may be a Neandertal at the office, but I'm all *Homo sapiens* at home." Many of the social statuses we occupy, the "hats" we wear, depend on the situation. People can be both black and Hispanic, or both a father and a ballplayer. One identity is claimed or perceived in certain settings, another in different ones. Among African Americans a "Hispanic" baseball player might be black; among Hispanics, Hispanic.

When our claimed or perceived identity varies depending on the context, this is called the *situational negotiation of social identity*. Depending on the situation, the same man might declare: "I'm Jimmy's father." "I'm your boss." "I'm African American." "I'm your professor." In face-to-face encounters, other people see who we are—actually, who they perceive us to be. They may expect us to think and act in certain (stereotypical) ways based on their perception of our identity (e.g., Latina woman, older white male golfer). Although we can't know which aspect of identity they'll focus on (e.g., ethnicity, gender, age, or political affiliation), face-to-face it's hard to be anonymous or to be someone else entirely. That's what masks, costumes, disguises, and hiding are for. Who's that little man behind the curtain?

Unlike our early ancestors, people today don't just interact face-to-face. We routinely give our money and our trust to individuals and institutions we've never laid eyes on. We phone, write, and—more than ever—use the Internet, where we must choose which aspects of ourselves to reveal. The Internet allows myriad forms of cybersocial interaction, and people can create new personas by using different "handles," including fictitious names and identities. In anonymous regions of cyberspace, people can manipulate ("lie about") their ages, genders, and physical attributes and create their own cyberfantasies. In psychology, multiple personalities are abnormal, but for anthropologists, multiple identities are more and more the norm.

Ethnicity is based on cultural similarities and differences in a society or nation. The similarities are with members of the same ethnic group; the differences are between that group and others. Ethnic groups must deal with other such groups in the nation or region they inhabit, so that interethnic relations are important in the study of that nation or region. (Table 15.1 lists American ethnic groups, based on 2007 figures.)

TABLE 15.1 Racial/Ethnic Identification in the United States, 2007 (Estimated by U.S. Census Bureau)

CLAIMED IDENTITY	NUMBER (MILLIONS)	PERCENTAGE
White (non-Hispanic)	199.1	66.1
Hispanic	45.4	15.1
Black	38.8	12.9
Asian	13.4	4.5
American Indian	2.9	1.0
Pacific Islander	.5	.2
Total population	301.1	99.8

SOURCE: Statistical Abstract of the United States, 2009, Table 6, p. 9.

ETHNIC GROUPS AND ETHNICITY

As with any culture, members of an **ethnic group** *share* certain beliefs, values, habits, customs, and norms because of their common background. They define themselves as different and special because of cultural features. This distinction may arise from language, religion, historical experience, geographic placement, kinship, or "race" (see Spickard, ed. 2004). Markers of an ethnic group may include a collective name, belief in common descent, a sense of solidarity, and an association with a specific territory, which the group may or may not hold (Ryan 1990, pp. xiii, xiv).

According to Fredrik Barth (1969), ethnicity can be said to exist when people claim a certain ethnic identity for themselves and are defined by others as having that identity. **Ethnicity** means identification with, and feeling part of, an ethnic group and exclusion from certain other groups because of this affiliation. But issues of ethnicity can be complex. Ethnic feelings and associated behavior vary in intensity within ethnic groups and countries and over time. A change in the degree of importance attached to an ethnic identity may reflect political changes (Soviet rule ends—ethnic feeling rises) or individual life-cycle changes (young people relinquish, or old people reclaim, an ethnic background).

Cultural differences may be associated with ethnicity, class, region, or religion. Individuals often have more than one group identity. People may be loyal (depending on circumstances) to their neighborhood, school, town, state or province, region, nation, continent, religion, ethnic group, or interest group (Ryan 1990, p. xxii). In a complex society such as the United States or Canada, people constantly negotiate their social identities. All of us "wear different hats," presenting ourselves sometimes as one thing, sometimes as another.

In daily conversation, we hear the term *status* used as a synonym for *prestige*. In this context,

"She's got a lot of status" means she's got a lot of prestige; people look up to her. Among social scientists, that's not the primary meaning of "*status.*" Social scientists use *status* more neutrally—for any position, no matter what the prestige, that someone occupies in society. In this sense, **status** encompasses the various positions that people occupy in society. Parent is a social status. So are professor, student, factory worker, Democrat, shoe salesperson, homeless person, labor leader, ethnic-group member, and thousands of others. People always occupy multiple statuses (e.g., Hispanic, Catholic, infant, brother). Among the statuses we occupy, particular ones dominate in particular settings, such as son or daughter at home and student in the classroom.

Some statuses are **ascribed:** People have little or no choice about occupying them. Age is an ascribed status; we can't choose not to age. Race and gender usually are ascribed; people are born members of a certain group and remain so all their lives. **Achieved statuses,** by contrast, aren't automatic; they come through choices, actions, efforts, talents, or accomplishments and may be positive or negative (Figure 15.1). Examples of achieved statuses include physician, senator, convicted felon, salesperson, union member, father, and college student.

Status Shifting

Sometimes statuses, particularly ascribed ones, are mutually exclusive. It's hard to bridge the gap between black and white, or male and female. Sometimes, taking a status or joining a group requires a conversion experience, acquiring a new and overwhelming primary identity, such as becoming a "born again" Christian.

Some statuses aren't mutually exclusive, but contextual. People can be both black and Hispanic, or both a mother and a senator. One identity is used in certain settings, another in different ones. We call this the *situational negotiation of social*

ethnic group
One among several culturally distinct groups in a society or region.

ethnicity
Identification with an ethnic group.

status
Any position that determines where someone fits in society.

ascribed status
Social status based on little or no choice.

achieved status
Social status based on choices or accomplishments.

identity. When ethnic identity is flexible and situational, it can become an achieved status (Leman 2001).

Hispanics, for example, may move through levels of culture (shifting ethnic affiliations) as they negotiate their identities. "Hispanic" is an ethnic category based mainly on language. It includes whites, blacks, and "racially" mixed Spanish speakers and their ethnically conscious descendants. (There are also "Native American," and even "Asian," Hispanics.) "Hispanic," representing the fastest-growing ethnic group in the United States, lumps together millions of people of diverse geographic origin—Puerto Rico, Mexico, Cuba, El Salvador, Guatemala, the Dominican Republic, and other Spanish-speaking countries of Central and South America and the Caribbean. "Latino" is a broader category, which can also include Brazilians (who speak Portuguese). The national origins of American Hispanics/Latinos in 2007 were as shown in Table 15.2.

Mexican Americans (Chicanos), Cuban Americans, and Puerto Ricans may mobilize to promote general Hispanic issues (e.g., opposition to "English-only" laws) but act as three separate interest groups in other contexts. Cuban Americans are richer on average than Chicanos and Puerto Ricans are, and their class interests and voting patterns differ. Cubans often vote Republican, but Puerto Ricans and Chicanos are more likely to favor Democrats. Some Mexican Americans whose families have lived in the United States for generations have little in common with new Hispanic immigrants, such as those from Central America. Many Americans (especially those fluent in English) claim Hispanic ethnicity in some contexts but shift to a general "American" identity in others.

In many societies an ascribed status is associated with a position in the social-political hierarchy. Certain groups, called *minority groups*, are subordinate. They have inferior power and less secure access to resources than do *majority groups* (which are superordinate, dominant, or controlling). Often ethnic groups are minorities. When an ethnic group is assumed to have a biological basis (distinctively shared "blood" or genes), it is called a **race**. Discrimination against such a group is called **racism** (Cohen 1998; Kuper 2006; Montagu 1997; Scupin 2003; Shanklin 1994).

race
Ethnic group assumed to have a biological basis.

racism
Discrimination against an ethnic group assumed to have a biological basis.

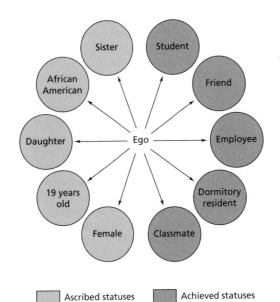

FIGURE 15.1 Social Statuses.

The person in this figure—"ego," or "I"—occupies many social statuses. The green circles indicate ascribed statuses; the purple circles represent achieved statuses.

RACE AND ETHNICITY

Race, like ethnicity in general, is a cultural category rather than a biological reality. That is, ethnic groups, including "races," derive from contrasts perceived and perpetuated in particular societies, rather than from scientific classifications based on common genes (see Wade 2002).

TABLE 15.2 American Hispanics, Latinos, 2007

NATIONAL ORIGIN	PERCENTAGE
Mexican American	64.4%
Puerto Rican	9.1
Cuban	3.5
Central and South American	13.3
Other Hispanic/Latino origin	9.8
Total	100.0%

SOURCE: Pew Hispanic Center, Statistical Portrait of Hispanics in the United States, 2007, Table 5: Detailed Hispanic Origin. http://pewhispanic.org/files/factsheets/hispanics2007/Table-5.pdf.

It is not possible to define human races biologically. Only cultural constructions of race are possible—even though the average person conceptualizes "race" in biological terms. The belief that human races exist and are important is much more common among the public than it is among scientists. Most Americans, for example, believe that their population includes biologically based races to which various labels have been applied. These labels include "white," "black," "yellow," "red," "Caucasoid," "Negroid," "Mongoloid," "Amerindian," "Euro-American," "African American," "Asian American," and "Native American."

This chapter's "Appreciating Anthropology" is a statement on race issued by the American Anthropological Association (AAA). It discusses how races have been socially constructed, for example under colonialism. The statement also stresses that inequalities among "racial" groups are not consequences of their biological inheritance but products of social, economic, educational, and political circumstances.

We hear the words *ethnicity* and *race* frequently, but American culture doesn't draw a very clear line between them. Consider a *New York Times* article published on May 29, 1992.

Discussing the changing ethnic composition of the United States, the article explained (correctly) that Hispanics "can be of any race" (Barringer 1992, p. A12). In other words, "Hispanic" is an ethnic category that crosscuts racial contrasts such as that between "black" and "white." Another *Times* article published that same day reported that during Los Angeles riots in spring 1992, "hundreds of Hispanic residents were interrogated about their immigration status on the basis of their *race* alone [emphasis added]" (Mydans 1992a, p. A8). Use of "race" here seems inappropriate because "Hispanic" usually is perceived as referring to a linguistically based (Spanish-speaking) ethnic group, rather than a biologically based race. Since these Los Angeles residents were being interrogated because they were Hispanic, the article is actually reporting on ethnic, not racial, discrimination.

In a more recent case, consider a speech delivered by then Appeals Court Judge Sonia Sotomayor, newly nominated (in May 2009; confirmed in August 2009) for the U.S. Supreme Court by President Barack Obama. In a 2001 lecture titled "A Latina Judge's Voice," delivered as the "Judge Mario G. Olmos Memorial Lecture" at the University of California, Berkeley, School of

"Hispanic" and "Latino" are ethnic categories that crosscut "racial" contrasts such as that between "black" and "white." Note the physical diversity among these multiracial schoolchildren in Havana, Cuba.

appreciating ANTHROPOLOGY

What's Wrong with Race?

Anthropologists have a lot to say about the race concept. There is considerable public confusion about the meaning and relevance of "race," and false claims about biological differences among "races" continue to be advanced. Stemming from previous actions by the American Anthropological Association (AAA) designed to address public misconceptions about race and intelligence, the need was apparent for a clear AAA statement on the biology and politics of race that would be educational and informational.

The following statement was adopted by the AAA Executive Board, based on a draft prepared by a committee of representative anthropologists. This statement represents the thinking and scholarly positions of most anthropologists, including me—your textbook author.

In the United States both scholars and the general public have been conditioned to viewing human races as natural and separate divisions within the human species based on visible physical differences. With the vast expansion of scientific knowledge in this century, however, it has become clear that human populations are not unambiguous, clearly demarcated, biologically distinct groups. Evidence from the analysis of genetics (e.g., DNA) indicates that most physical variation, about 94%, lies within so-called racial groups. Conventional geographic "racial" groupings differ from one another only in about 6% of their genes. This means that there is greater variation within "racial" groups than between them. In neigh-

boring populations there is much overlapping of genes and their phenotypic (physical) expressions. Throughout history whenever different groups have come into contact, they have interbred. The continued sharing of genetic materials has maintained all of humankind as a single species.

Physical variations in any given trait tend to occur gradually rather than abruptly over geographic areas. And because physical traits are inherited independently of one another, knowing the range of one trait does not predict the presence of others. For example, skin color varies largely from light in the temperate areas in the north to dark in the tropical areas in the south; its intensity is not related to nose shape or hair texture. Dark skin may be associated with frizzy or kinky hair or curly or wavy or straight hair, all of which are found among different indigenous peoples in tropical regions. These facts render any attempt to establish lines of division among biological populations both arbitrary and subjective.

Historical research has shown that the idea of "race" has always carried more meanings than mere physical differences; indeed, physical variations in the human species have no meaning except the social ones that humans put on them. Today scholars in many fields argue that "race" as it is understood in the United States of America was a social mechanism

invented during the 18th century to refer to those populations brought together in colonial America: the English and other European settlers, the conquered Indian peoples, and those peoples of Africa brought in to provide slave labor.

From its inception, this modern concept of "race" was modeled after an ancient theorem of the Great Chain of Being, which posited natural categories on a hierarchy established by God or nature. Thus "race" was a mode of classification linked specifically to peoples in the colonial situation. It subsumed a growing ideology of inequality devised to rationalize European attitudes and treatment of the conquered and enslaved peoples. Proponents of slavery in particular during the 19th century used "race" to justify the retention of slavery. The ideology magnified the differences among Europeans, Africans, and Indians, established a rigid hierarchy of socially exclusive categories, underscored and bolstered unequal rank and status differences, and provided the rationalization that the inequality was natural or God-given. The different physical traits of African-Americans and Indians became markers or symbols of their status differences.

As they were constructing US society, leaders among European-Americans fabricated the cultural/behavioral characteristics associated with each "race," linking superior traits with Europeans and negative and inferior ones to blacks and Indians. Numerous arbitrary and fictitious beliefs about the different peoples were institutionalized and deeply embedded in American thought. . . .

Law, Sotomayor declared (as part of a much longer speech):

> I would hope that a wise Latina woman with the richness of her experiences would more often than not reach a better conclusion than a white male who hasn't lived that life (Sotomayor 2001/2009).

Conservatives, including former House speaker Newt Gingrich and radio talk show host Rush Limbaugh, seized on this declaration as evidence that Sotomayor was a "racist" or a "reverse racist." Again, however, "Latina" is an ethnic (and gendered–female) rather than a racial category. I suspect that Sotomayor also was using "white male" as an ethnic-gender category, to refer to

Ultimately "race" as an ideology about human differences was subsequently spread to other areas of the world. It became a strategy for dividing, ranking, and controlling colonized people used by colonial powers everywhere. But it was not limited to the colonial situation. In the latter part of the 19th century it was employed by Europeans to rank one another and to justify social, economic, and political inequalities among their peoples. During World War II, the Nazis under Adolf Hitler enjoined the expanded ideology of "race" and "racial" differences and took them to a logical end: the extermination of 11 million people of "inferior races" (e.g., Jews, Gypsies, Africans, homosexuals, and so forth) and other unspeakable brutalities of the Holocaust.

"Race" thus evolved as a world view, a body of prejudgments that distorts our ideas about human differences and group behavior. Racial beliefs constitute myths about the diversity in the human species and about the abilities and behavior of people homogenized into " racial" categories. The myths fused behavior and physical features together in the public mind, impeding our comprehension of both biological variations and cultural behavior, implying that

both are genetically determined. Racial myths bear no relationship to the reality of human capabilities or behavior . . .

We now understand that human cultural behavior is learned, conditioned into infants beginning at birth, and always subject to modification. No human is born with a built-in culture or language. Our temperaments, dispositions, and personalities, regardless of genetic propensities, are developed within sets of meanings and values that we call "culture" . . .

It is a basic tenet of anthropological knowledge that all normal human beings have the capacity to learn any cultural behavior.

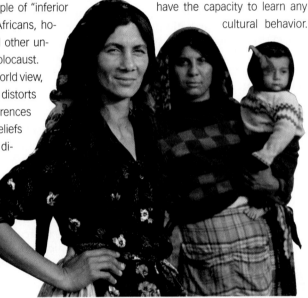

This photo, taken near Bucharest, Romania, shows a Rom (Gypsy) woman standing in front of another woman as she holds her baby daughter. Gypsies (Rom or Roma) have faced discrimination in many nations. During World War II, the Nazis led by Adolf Hitler murdered 11 million Jews, Gypsies, Africans, homosexuals, and others.

The American experience with immigrants from hundreds of different language and cultural backgrounds who have acquired some version of American culture traits and behavior is the clearest evidence of this fact. Moreover, people of all physical variations have learned different cultural behaviors and continue to do so as modern transportation moves millions of immigrants around the world.

How people have been accepted and treated within the context of a given society or culture has a direct impact on how they perform in that society. The "racial" world view was invented to assign some groups to perpetual low status, while others were permitted access to privilege, power, and wealth. The tragedy in the United States has been that the policies and practices stemming from this world view succeeded all too well in constructing unequal populations among Europeans, Native Americans, and peoples of African descent. Given what we know about the capacity of normal humans to achieve and function within any culture, we conclude that present-day inequalities between so-called "racial" groups are not consequences of their biological inheritance but products of historical and contemporary social, economic, educational, and political circumstances.

SOURCE: From the American Anthropological Association (AAA) Statement on "Race" (May 1998). http://www.aaanet.org/stmts/racepp.htm. Reprinted with permission of the American Anthropological Association.

nonminority men. These examples from our everyday experience illustrate the difficulties in drawing a precise distinction between race and ethnicity. It probably is better to use the term *ethnic group* rather than *race* to describe *any* such social group, for example, African Americans, Asian Americans, Anglo Americans, Hispanics, Latinos, Latinas, and even non-Hispanic whites.

THE SOCIAL CONSTRUCTION OF RACE

Races are ethnic groups assumed (by members of a particular culture) to have a biological basis, but actually race is socially constructed. The "races" we hear about every day are cultural, or social, rather than biological categories. Many

descent
Social identity based on ancestry.

hypodescent
Children assigned to same group as minority parent.

Americans mistakenly assume that whites and blacks, for example, are biologically distinct and that these terms stand for discrete races. But these labels, like racial terms used in other societies, really designate culturally perceived rather than biologically based groups.

Hypodescent: Race in the United States

How is race culturally constructed in the United States? In American culture, one acquires his or her racial identity at birth, as an ascribed status, but race isn't based on biology or on simple ancestry. Take the case of the child of a "racially mixed" marriage involving one black and one white parent. We know that 50 percent of the child's genes come from one parent and 50 percent from the other. Still, American culture overlooks heredity and classifies this child as black. This rule is arbitrary. On the basis of genotype (genetic composition), it would be just as logical to classify the child as white.

American rules for assigning racial status can be even more arbitrary. In some states, anyone known to have any black ancestor, no matter how remote, is classified as a member of the black race. This is a rule of **descent** (it assigns social identity on the basis of ancestry), but of a sort that is rare outside the contemporary United States. It is called **hypodescent** (Harris and Kottak 1963) because it automatically places the children of a

anthropology **ATLAS**

Map 7 plots the distribution of human skin color in relation to ultraviolet radiation from the sun before C.E. 1400.

union between members of different groups in the minority group (*hypo* means "lower"). Hypodescent divides American society into groups that have been unequal in their access to wealth, power, and prestige.

The following case from Louisiana is an excellent illustration of the arbitrariness of the hypodescent rule and of the role that governments (federal or, in this case, state) play in legalizing, inventing, or eradicating race and ethnicity (B. Williams 1989). Susie Guillory Phipps, a light-skinned woman with Caucasian features and straight black hair, discovered as an adult that she was black. When Phipps ordered a copy of her birth certificate, she found her race listed as "colored." Since she had been "brought up white and married white twice," Phipps challenged a 1970 Louisiana law declaring anyone with at least one-thirty-second "Negro blood" to be legally black. Although the state's lawyer admitted that Phipps "looks like a white person," the state of Louisiana insisted that her racial classification was proper (Yetman, ed. 1991, pp. 3–4).

Cases like Phipps's are rare because racial identity usually is ascribed at birth and doesn't change. The rule of hypodescent affects blacks, Asians, Native Americans, and Hispanics differently (see Hunter 2005). It's easier to negotiate Indian or Hispanic identity than black identity. The ascription rule isn't as definite, and the assumption of a biological basis isn't as strong.

To be considered Native American, one ancestor out of eight (great-grandparents) or out of four (grandparents) may suffice. This depends on whether the assignment is by federal or state law or by an Indian tribal council. The child of a Hispanic may (or may not, depending on context) claim Hispanic identity. Many Americans with an Indian or Latino grandparent consider themselves white and lay no claim to minority group status.

Race in the Census

The U.S. Census Bureau has gathered data by race since 1790. Initially this was done because the Constitution specified that a slave counted as three-fifths of a white person, and because Indians were not taxed. The racial categories included in the 1990 census were "White," "Black or Negro," "Indian (American)," "Eskimo," "Aleut or Pacific Islander," and "Other." A separate question was asked about Spanish–Hispanic heritage. Check out Figure 15.2 for the racial categories in the 2000 census.

Attempts by social scientists and interested citizens to add a "multiracial" census category have been opposed by the National Association for the Advancement of Colored People (NAACP) and the National Council of La Raza (a Hispanic

A biracial American, Halle Berry, with her mother. What is Halle Berry's race?

advocacy group). Racial classification is a political issue involving access to resources, including jobs, voting districts, and federal funding of programs aimed at minorities. The hypodescent rule results in all the population growth being attributed to the minority category. Minorities fear their political clout will decline if their numbers go down.

But things are changing. Choice of "some other race" in the U.S. Census more than doubled from 1980 (6.8 million) to 2000 (over 15 million)—suggesting imprecision in and dissatisfaction with the existing categories (Mar 1997). In the 2000 census, 2.4 percent of Americans, or 6.8 million people, chose a first-ever option of identifying themselves as belonging to more than one race. The number of interracial marriages and children is increasing, with implications for the traditional system of American racial classification. "Interracial," "biracial," or "multiracial" children who grow up with both parents undoubtedly identify with particular qualities of either parent. It is troubling for many of them to have so important an identity as race dictated by the arbitrary rule of hypodescent. It may be especially discordant when racial identity doesn't parallel gender identity, for instance, a boy with a white father and a black mother, or a girl with a white mother and a black father.

How does the Canadian census compare with the American census in its treatment of race? Rather than race, the Canadian census asks about "visible minorities." That country's Employment Equity Act defines such groups as "persons, other than Aboriginal peoples [aka First Nations in Canada, Native Americans in the United States], who are non-Caucasian in race or non-white in colour" (Statistics Canada 2001a). Table 15.3 shows that "South Asian" and "Chinese" are Canada's largest visible minorities. Note that Canada's total visible minority population of 16.2 percent (up from 11.2 percent in 1996) contrasts with a figure of about 25 percent for the United States in the 2000 census and over 33 percent in 2006. In particular, Canada's black population of 2.5 percent contrasts with the American figure of 13.2 percent (2006) for African Americans, while Canada's Asian population is significantly higher than the U.S. figure of 4.9 percent (2006) on a percentage basis. Only a tiny fraction of the Canadian population (0.4 percent) claimed multiple visible minority affiliation, compared with 2.4 percent claiming "more than one race" in the United States in 2000.

Canada's visible minority population has been increasing steadily. In 1981, 1.1 million visible minorities accounted for 4.7 percent of the total population, versus 16.2 percent today. Visible minorities are growing much faster than

is Canada's total population. Between 2001 and 2006, the total population increased 5 percent, while visible minorities rose 27 percent. If recent immigration trends continue, by 2016, visible minorities will account for 20 percent of the Canadian population.

Not Us: Race in Japan

American culture ignores considerable diversity in biology, language, and geographic origin as it socially constructs race in the United States. North Americans also overlook diversity by seeing Japan as a nation that is homogeneous in race, ethnicity, language, and culture—an image the Japanese themselves cultivate. Thus in 1986 Prime Minister Nakasone created an international furor by contrasting his country's supposed homogeneity (responsible, he suggested, for Japan's success at that time in international business) with the ethnically mixed United States.

Japan is hardly the uniform entity Nakasone described. Scholars estimate that 10 percent of Japan's national population are minorities of various sorts. These include aboriginal Ainu, annexed

NOTE: Please answer BOTH Questions 5 and 6.

5. Is this person Spanish/Hispanic/Latino? *Mark* ☒ *the* **"No"** *box if not Spanish/Hispanic/Latino.*

☐ **No,** not Spanish/Hispanic/Latino
☐ Yes, Mexican, Mexican Am., Chicano
☐ Yes, other Spanish/Hispanic/Latino — *Print group.*
☐ Yes, Puerto Rican
☐ Yes, Cuban

5. What is this person's race? *Mark* ☒ *one or more races to indicate what this person considers himself/herself to be.*

☐ White
☐ Black, African Am., or Negro
☐ American Indian or Alaska Native — *Print name of enrolled or principal tribe.*

☐ Asian Indian ☐ Japanese ☐ Native Hawaiian
☐ Chinese ☐ Korean ☐ Guamanian or Chamorro
☐ Filipino ☐ Vietnamese ☐ Samoan
☐ Other Asian — *Print race.* ☐ Other Pacific Islander — *Print race.*

☐ Some other race — *Print race.*

FIGURE 15.2 Reproduction of Questions on Race and Hispanic Origin from Census 2000.

SOURCE: U.S. Census Bureau, Census 2000 questionnaire.

TABLE 15.3 Visible Minority Population of Canada, 2006 Census

TOTAL POPULATION	NUMBER 31,241,030	PERCENT 100.0
Total visible minority population	5,068,090	16.2
South Asian	1,262,865	4.0
Chinese	1,216,515	3.9
Black	783,795	2.5
Filipino	410,695	1.3
Arab/West Asian	374,835	1.2
Latin American	304,245	1.0
Southeast Asian	239,935	0.8
Korean	141,890	0.5
Japanese	83,300	0.3
Other visible minority	116,895	0.4
Multiple visible minority	133,120	0.4
Nonvisible minority	26,172,940	83.8

SOURCE: From Statistics Canada, 2006 Census, http://www12.statcan.ca/english/census06/data/highlights/ethnic.

Okinawans, outcast *burakumin,* children of mixed marriages, and immigrant nationalities, especially Koreans, who number more than 700,000 (De Vos, Wetherall, and Stearman 1983; Lie 2001).

To describe racial attitudes in Japan, Jennifer Robertson (1992) uses Kwame Anthony Appiah's (1990) term "intrinsic racism"—the belief that a (perceived) racial difference is a sufficient reason to value one person less than another. In Japan the valued group is majority ("pure") Japanese, who are believed to share "the same blood." Thus, the caption to a printed photo of a Japanese American model reads: "She was born in Japan but raised in Hawaii. Her nationality is American but no foreign blood flows in her veins" (Robertson 1992, p. 5). Something like hypodescent also operates in Japan, but less precisely than in the United States, where mixed offspring automatically become members of the minority group. The children of mixed marriages between majority Japanese and others (including Euro-Americans) may not get the same "racial" label as their minority parent, but they are still stigmatized for their non-Japanese ancestry (De Vos and Wagatsuma 1966).

How is race culturally constructed in Japan? The (majority) Japanese define themselves by opposition to others, whether minority groups in their own nation or outsiders—anyone who is "not us." The "not us" should stay that way; assimilation generally is discouraged. Cultural mechanisms, especially residential segregation and taboos on "interracial" marriage, work to keep minorities "in their place."

In its construction of race, Japanese culture regards certain ethnic groups as having a biological basis, when there is no evidence that they do. The best example is the burakumin, a stigmatized group of at least 4 million outcasts, sometimes compared to India's untouchables. The burakumin are physically and genetically indistinguishable from other Japanese. Many of them "pass" as (and marry) majority Japanese, but a deceptive marriage can end in divorce if burakumin identity is discovered (Aoki and Dardess, eds. 1981).

Burakumin are perceived as standing apart from majority Japanese. Through ancestry, descent (and thus, it is assumed, "blood," or genetics) burakumin are "not us." Majority Japanese try to keep their lineage pure by discouraging mixing. The burakumin are residentially segregated in neighborhoods (rural or urban) called *buraku,* from which the racial label is derived. Compared with majority Japanese, the burakumin are less likely to attend high school and college. When burakumin attend the same schools as majority Japanese, they face discrimination. Majority children and teachers may refuse to eat with them because burakumin are considered unclean.

In applying for university admission or a job and in dealing with the government, Japanese must list their address, which becomes part of a household or family registry. This list makes residence in a buraku, and likely burakumin social status, evident. Schools and companies use this information to discriminate. (The best way to pass is to move so often that the buraku address eventually disappears from the registry.) Majority Japanese also limit "race" mixture by hiring marriage mediators to check out the family histories of prospective spouses. They are especially careful to check for burakumin ancestry (De Vos et al. 1983).

The origin of the burakumin lies in a historical tiered system of stratification (from the Tokugawa period—1603–1868). The top four ranked categories were warrior-administrators (*samurai*), farmers, artisans, and merchants. The ancestors of the burakumin were below this hierarchy, an outcast group who did unclean jobs such as animal slaughter and disposal of the dead. Burakumin still do similar jobs, including work with leather and other animal products. The burakumin are more likely than majority Japanese to do manual labor (including farm work) and to belong to the national lower class. Burakumin and other Japanese minorities are also more likely to have careers in crime, prostitution, entertainment, and sports (De Vos et al. 1983).

Like blacks in the United States, the burakumin are **stratified,** or class-stratified. Because certain jobs are reserved for the burakumin, people who are successful in those occupations (e.g., shoe factory owners) can be wealthy. Burakumin also have found jobs as government bureaucrats. Financially successful burakumin can temporarily escape their stigmatized status by travel, including foreign travel.

Discrimination against the burakumin is strikingly like the discrimination that blacks have experienced in the United States. The burakumin often live in villages and neighborhoods with poor housing and sanitation. They have limited access to education, jobs, amenities, and health facilities. In response to burakumin political mobilization, Japan has dismantled the legal structure of discrimination against burakumin and has worked to improve conditions in the buraku. (The Web site http://blhrri.org/index_e.htm is sponsored by the Buraku Liberation and Human Rights Research Institute and includes the most recent information about the burakumin liberation movement.) Still Japan has yet to institute American-style affirmative action programs for education and jobs. Discrimination against nonmajority Japanese is still the rule in companies. Some employers say that hiring burakumin would give their company an unclean image and thus create a disadvantage in competing with other businesses (De Vos et al. 1983).

Phenotype and Fluidity: Race in Brazil

There are more flexible, less exclusionary ways of constructing social race than those used in the United States and Japan. Along with the rest of Latin America, Brazil has less exclusionary categories, which permit individuals to change their racial classification. Brazil shares a history of slavery with the United States, but it lacks the hypodescent rule. Nor does Brazil have racial aversion of the sort found in Japan.

Japan's stigmatized burakumin are physically and genetically indistinguishable from other Japanese. In response to burakumin political mobilization, Japan has dismantled the legal structure of discrimination against burakumin. This Sports Day for burakumin children is one kind of mobilization.

Brazilians use many more racial labels—over 500 were once reported (Harris 1970)—than Americans or Japanese do. In northeastern Brazil, I found 40 different racial terms in use in Arembepe, a village of only 750 people (Kottak 2006). Through their traditional classification system Brazilians recognize and attempt to describe the physical variation that exists in their population. The system used in the United States, by recognizing only three or four races, blinds Americans to an equivalent range of evident physical contrasts. The system Brazilians use to construct social race has other special features. In the United States one's race is an ascribed status; it is assigned automatically by hypodescent and usually doesn't change. In Brazil racial identity is more flexible, more of an achieved status.

Brazilian racial classification pays attention to **phenotype.** Scientists distinguish between *genotype*, or hereditary makeup, and **phenotype**—expressed physical characteristics. Genotype is what you are genetically; phenotype is what you appear as. Identical twins and clones have the same genotype, but their phenotypes vary if they have been raised in different environments. Phenotype describes an organism's evident traits, its "manifest biology"—physiology and anatomy, including skin color, hair form, facial features, and eye color. A Brazilian's phenotype and racial label may change because of environmental factors, such as the tanning rays of the sun or the effects of humidity on the hair.

A Brazilian can change his or her "race" (say from "Indian" to "mixed") by changing his or her manner of dress, language, location (e.g., rural to urban), and even attitude (e.g., by adopting urban

stratified
Class-structured, with differences in wealth, prestige, and power.

Phenotype
Expressed physical characteristics of an organism.

These photos, taken in Brazil by the author in 2003 and 2004, give just a glimpse of the spectrum of phenotypical diversity encountered among contemporary Brazilians.

behavior). Two racial/ethic labels used in Brazil are *indio* (Indian) and *cabôclo.* (someone who "looks Indian" but wears modern clothing and participates in Brazilian culture, rather than living in an Indian community). Similar shifts in racial/ethnic classification occur in other parts of Latin America, e.g., Guatemala. The perception of biological race is influenced not just by the physical phenotype but by how one dresses and behaves.

Furthermore, racial differences in Brazil may be so insignificant in structuring community life that people may forget the terms they have applied to others. Sometimes they even forget the ones they've used for themselves. In Arembepe, I made it a habit to ask the same person on different days to tell me the races of others in the village (and my own). In the United States I am always "white" or "Euro-American," but in Arembepe I got lots of terms besides *branco* ("white"). I could be *claro* ("light"), *louro* ("blond"), *sarará* ("light-skinned redhead"), *mulato claro* ("light mulatto"), or *mulato* ("mulatto"). The racial term used to describe me or anyone else varied from person to person, week to week, even day to day. My best informant, a man with very

dark skin color, changed the term he used for himself all the time—from *escuro* ("dark") to *preto* ("black") to *moreno escuro* ("dark brunet").

The American and Japanese racial systems are creations of particular cultures, rather than scientific—or even accurate—descriptions of human biological differences. Brazilian racial classification also is a cultural construction, but Brazilians have developed a way of describing human biological diversity that is more detailed, fluid, and flexible than the systems used in most cultures. Brazil lacks Japan's racial aversion, and it also lacks a rule of descent like that which ascribes racial status in the United States (Degler 1970; Harris 1964).

For centuries the United States and Brazil have had mixed populations, with ancestors from Native America, Europe, Africa, and Asia. Although races have mixed in both countries, Brazilian and American cultures have constructed the results differently. The historical reasons for this contrast lie mainly in the different characteristics of the settlers of the two countries. The mainly English early settlers of the United States came as women, men, and families, but Brazil's Portuguese colonizers were mainly men—merchants and adventurers. Many of these Portuguese men married Native American women and recognized their racially mixed children as their heirs. Like their North American counterparts, Brazilian plantation owners had sexual relations with their slaves. But the Brazilian landlords more often freed the children that resulted—for demographic and economic reasons. (Sometimes these were their only children.) Freed offspring of master and slave became plantation overseers and foremen and filled many intermediate positions in the emerging Brazilian economy. They were not classed with the slaves but were allowed to join a new intermediate category. No hypodescent rule developed in Brazil to ensure that whites and blacks remained separate (see Degler 1970; Harris 1964).

ETHNIC GROUPS, NATIONS, AND NATIONALITIES

The term **nation** once was synonymous with *tribe* or *ethnic group.* All three of these terms have been used to refer to a single culture sharing a single language, religion, history, territory, ancestry, and kinship. Thus one could speak interchangeably of the Seneca (American Indian) nation, tribe, or ethnic group. Now *nation* has come to mean **state**—an independent, centrally organized political unit, or a government. *Nation* and *state* have become synonymous. Combined in **nation-state** they refer to an autonomous political entity, a country—like the United States, "one nation, indivisible" (see Farner, ed. 2004; Gellner 1997; Hastings 1997).

Because of migration, conquest, and colonialism, most nation-states are not ethnically homogeneous. Of 132 nation-states existing in 1971, Connor (1972) found just 12 (9 percent) to be ethnically homogeneous. In another 25 (19 percent) a single ethnic group accounted for more than 90 percent of the population. Forty percent of the countries contained more than five significant ethnic groups. In a later study, Nielsson (1985) found that in only 45 of 164 states did one ethnic group account for more than 95 percent of the population.

Nationalities and Imagined Communities

Ethnic groups that once had, or wish to have or regain, autonomous political status (their own country) are called **nationalities.** In the words of Benedict Anderson (1991), they are "imagined communities." Even when they become nation-states, they remain imagined communities because most of their members, though feeling comradeship, will never meet (Anderson 1991, pp. 6–10). They can only imagine they all participate in the same unit.

Anderson traces Western European nationalism, which arose in imperial powers such as England, France, and Spain, back to the 18th century. He stresses that language and print played a crucial role in the growth of European national consciousness. The novel and the newspaper were "two forms of imagining" communities (consisting of all the people who read the same sources and thus witnessed the same events) that flowered in the 18th century (Anderson 1991, pp. 24–25).

Over time, political upheavals, wars, and migration have divided many imagined national communities that arose in the 18th and 19th centuries. The German and Korean homelands were artificially divided after wars, according to communist and capitalist ideologies. World War I split the Kurds, who remain an imagined community, forming a majority in no state. Kurds are a minority group in Turkey, Iran, Iraq, and Syria.

In creating multitribal and multiethnic states, **colonialism,** the foreign domination of a territory, often erected boundaries that corresponded poorly with preexisting cultural divisions. But colonial institutions also helped create new "imagined communities" beyond nations. A good example is the idea of *négritude* ("Black identity") developed by African intellectuals in Francophone (French-speaking) West Africa. Négritude can be traced to the association and common experience in colonial times of youths from Guinea, Mali, the Ivory Coast, and Senegal at the William Ponty school in Dakar, Senegal (Anderson 1991, pp. 123–124).

ETHNIC TOLERANCE AND ACCOMMODATION

Ethnic diversity may be associated with positive group interaction and coexistence or with conflict (discussed shortly). There are nation-states in which multiple cultural groups live together in reasonable harmony, including some less developed countries.

Assimilation

Assimilation describes the process of change that a minority ethnic group may experience when it moves to a country where another culture dominates. By assimilating, the minority adopts the patterns and norms of its host culture. It is incorporated into the dominant culture to the point that it no longer exists as a separate cultural unit. Some countries, such as Brazil, are more assimilationist than others. Germans, Italians, Japanese, Middle Easterners, and Eastern Europeans started migrating to Brazil late in the 19th century. These immigrants have assimilated to a common Brazilian culture, which has Portuguese, African, and Native American roots. The descendants of these

nation
Society sharing a language, religion, history, territory, ancestry, and kinship.

state
Stratified society with formal, central government.

nation-state
An autonomous political entity; a country.

colonialism
Long-term foreign domination of a territory and its people.

assimilation
Absorption of minorities within a dominant culture.

nationalities
Ethnic groups that have, once had, or want their own country.

German, Italian, Japanese, Middle Eastern, and Eastern European immigrants have assimilated, culturally and linguistically, to a common Brazilian culture. More than 220,000 people of Japanese descent live in Brazil, mostly in and around the city of São Paulo, Brazil's largest. Shown here, a Sunday morning street scene in Sao Paulo's Liberdade district, home to many of that city's assimilated Japanese Brazilians.

immigrants speak the national language (Portuguese) and participate in the national culture. (During World War II, Brazil, which was on the Allied side, forced assimilation by banning instruction in any language other than Portuguese—especially in German.)

The Plural Society

Assimilation isn't inevitable, and there can be ethnic harmony without it. Ethnic distinctions can persist despite generations of interethnic contact. Through a study of three ethnic groups in Swat, Pakistan, Fredrik Barth (1958/1968) challenged an old idea that interaction always leads to assimilation. He showed that ethnic groups can be in contact for generations without assimilating and can live in peaceful coexistence.

Barth (1958/1968, p. 324) defines **plural society** (an idea he extended from Pakistan to the entire Middle East) as a society combining ethnic contrasts, ecological specialization (i.e., use of different environmental resources by each ethnic group), and the economic interdependence of those groups. Consider his description of the Middle East (in the 1950s): "The 'environment' of any one ethnic group is not only defined by natural conditions, but also by the presence and activities of the

plural society
Society with economically interdependent ethnic groups.

other ethnic groups on which it depends. Each group exploits only part of the total environment, and leaves large parts of it open for other groups to exploit." The ecological interdependence (or, at least, the lack of competition) between ethnic groups may be based on different activities in the same region or on long-term occupation of different regions in the same nation-state.

In Barth's view, ethnic boundaries are most stable and enduring when the groups occupy different ecological niches. That is, they make their living in different ways and don't compete. Ideally, they should depend on each other's activities and exchange with one another. When different ethnic groups exploit the *same* ecological niche, the militarily more powerful group will normally replace the weaker one. If they exploit more or less the same niche, but the weaker group is better able to use marginal environments, they also may coexist (Barth 1958/1968, p. 331). Given niche specialization, ethnic boundaries and interdependence can be maintained, although the specific cultural features of each group may change. By shifting the analytic focus from individual cultures or ethnic groups to *relationships* between cultures or ethnic groups, Barth (1958/1968, 1969) has made important contributions to ethnic studies.

Multiculturalism and Ethnic Identity

The view of cultural diversity in a country as something good and desirable is called **multiculturalism** (see Kottak and Kozaitis 2008). The multicultural model is the opposite of the assimilationist model, in which minorities are expected to abandon their cultural traditions and values, replacing them with those of the majority population. The multicultural view encourages the practice of cultural–ethnic traditions. A multicultural society socializes individuals not only into the dominant (national) culture but also into an ethnic culture. Thus in the United States millions of people speak both English and another language, eat both "American" (apple pie, steak, hamburgers) and "ethnic" foods, and celebrate both national (July 4, Thanksgiving) and ethnic–religious holidays.

In the United States and Canada multiculturalism is of growing importance. This reflects an awareness that the number and size of ethnic groups have grown dramatically in recent years. If this trend continues, the ethnic composition of the United States will change dramatically. (See Figure 15.3.)

Even now, because of immigration and differential population growth, whites are outnumbered by minorities in many urban areas. For example, of the 8,085,742 people living in New York City in 2003, 27 percent were black, 27 percent Hispanic, 10 percent Asian, and 36 percent other—including non-Hispanic whites. The comparable figures for Los Angeles (which had 3,819,951 people) were 11 percent black, 46 percent Hispanic, 10 percent Asian, and 33 percent other, including non-Hispanic whites (U.S. Census Bureau 2006).

In October 2006, the population of the United States reached 300 million people, just 39 years after reaching 200 million and 91 years after reaching the 100 million mark (in 1915). The country's ethnic composition has changed dramatically in the past 40 years. The 1970 census, the first to attempt an official count of Hispanics, found they represented no more than 4.7 percent of the American population, compared with 14.9 percent in 2006. The number of African Americans increased from 11.1 percent in 1967 to 13.2 percent in 2006, while (non-Hispanic) whites ("Anglos") declined from 83 to 65.4 percent. In 1967 fewer than 10 million people in the United States (5 percent of the population) had been born elsewhere, compared with more than 36 million immigrants (12 percent) today (Ohlemacher 2006).

In 1973, 78 percent of the students in American public schools were white, and 22 percent were minorities: blacks, Hispanics, Asians, Pacific Islanders, and "others." By 2004, only 57 percent of public school students were white, and 43 percent were minorities. If current trends continue, minority students will outnumber (non-Hispanic) white students by 2015. They already do in California, Hawaii, Mississippi, New Mexico, and Texas (Dillon 2006).

Immigration, mainly from southern and eastern Europe, had a similar effect on classroom diversity, at least in the largest American cities, a century ago. A study of American public schools in 1908–1909 found that only 42 percent of those urban students were native-born, while 58 percent were immigrants. In a very different (multicultural now versus assimilationist then) context, today's American classrooms have regained the ethnic diversity they demonstrated in the early 1900s, when this author's German-speaking Austro-Hungarian-born father and grandparents immigrated to the United States.

One response to ethnic diversification and awareness has been for many whites to reclaim ethnic identities (Italian, Albanian, Serbian, Lithuanian, etc.) and to joint ethnic associations (clubs, gangs). Some such groups are new. Others have existed for decades, although they lost members during the assimilationist years of the 1920s through the 1950s.

multiculturalism
View of cultural diversity as valuable and worth maintaining.

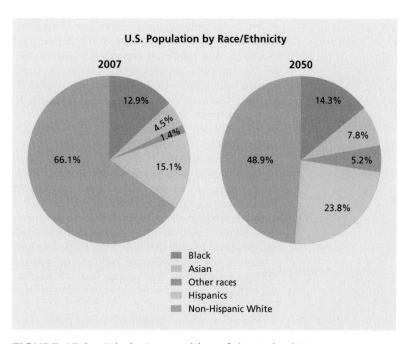

FIGURE 15.3 Ethnic Composition of the United States.

The proportion of the American population that is white and non-Hispanic is declining. The projection for 2050 shown here comes from a U.S. Census Bureau report issued in March 2004. Note especially the dramatic rise in the Hispanic portion of the American population between 2007 and 2050.

SOURCE: Based on data from U.S. Census Bureau, International Data Base, Table 094, http://www.census.gov/ipc/www.idbprint.html; Files 2005 and http://www.census.gov/Press-Release/www/releases/archives/population/010048.html; and *Statistical Abstract of the United States*, 2009, Table 6, p. 9.

In the United States and Canada, multiculturalism is of growing importance. Especially in large cities like Toronto (shown here), people of diverse backgrounds attend ethnic fairs and festivals and feast on ethnic foods. What are some other expressions of multiculturalism in your society?

Multiculturalism seeks ways for people to understand and interact that don't depend on sameness but rather on respect for differences. Multiculturalism stresses the interaction of ethnic groups and their contribution to the country. It assumes that each group has something to offer to and learn from the others. Several forces have propelled North America away from the assimilationist model toward multiculturalism. First, multiculturalism reflects the fact of recent large-scale migration, particularly from the "less developed countries" to the "developed" nations of North America and Western Europe. The global scale of modern migration introduces unparalleled ethnic variety to host nations. Multiculturalism is related to globalization: People use modern means of transportation to migrate to nations whose lifestyles they learn about through the media and from tourists who increasingly visit their own countries.

Migration also is fueled by rapid population growth, coupled with insufficient jobs (both for educated and uneducated people), in the less developed countries. As traditional rural economies decline or mechanize, displaced farmers move to cities, where they and their children often are unable to find jobs. As people in the less developed countries get better educations, they seek more skilled employment. They hope to partake of an international culture of consumption that includes such modern amenities as refrigerators, televisions, and automobiles (Ahmed 2004).

In a world with growing rural–urban and transnational migration, ethnic identities are used increasingly to form self-help organizations focused mainly on enhancing the group's economic competitiveness (Williams 1989). People claim and express ethnic identities for political and economic reasons. Michel Laguerre's (1984, 1998) studies of Haitian immigrants in the United States show that they mobilize to deal with the discriminatory structure (racist in this case, since Haitians tend to be black) of American society. Ethnicity (their common Haitian creole language and cultural background) is a basis for their mobilization. Haitian ethnicity helps distinguish them from African Americans and other ethnic groups.

In the face of globalization, much of the world, including the entire "democratic West," is experiencing an "ethnic revival." The new assertiveness of long-resident ethnic groups extends to the Basques and Catalans in Spain, the Bretons and Corsicans in France, and the Welsh and Scots in the United Kingdom. (See this chapter's "Appreciating Diversity" on pp. 352–353 for more on the Basques). The United States and Canada are becoming increasingly multicultural, focusing on their internal diversity (see Laguerre 1999). "Melting pots" no longer, they are better described as ethnic "salads" (each ingredient remains distinct, although in the same bowl, with the same dressing).

ROOTS OF ETHNIC CONFLICT

Ethnicity, based on perceived cultural similarities and differences in a society or nation, can be expressed in peaceful multiculturalism or in discrimination or violent interethnic confrontation. Culture can be both adaptive and maladaptive. The perception of cultural differences can have disastrous effects on social interaction.

The roots of ethnic differentiation—and therefore, potentially, of ethnic conflict—can be political, economic, religious, linguistic, cultural, or racial (see Kuper 2006). Why do ethnic differences often lead to conflict and violence? The causes include a sense of injustice because of resource distribution, economic or political competition, and reaction to discrimination, prejudice, and other expressions of devalued identity (see Friedman 2003; Ryan 1990, p. xxvii).

In Iraq, under the dictator Saddam Hussein, there was discrimination by one Muslim group (Sunnis) against others (Shiites and Kurds). Sunnis, although a numeric minority within Iraq's population, enjoyed privileged access to power, prestige, and position. After the elections of 2005, which many Sunnis chose to boycott, Shiites gained political control. A civil war developed out of "sectarian violence" (conflicts among sects of the same religion) as Sunnis (and their foreign supporters) fueled an insurgency against the new government and its foreign supporters, including the United States. The civil war was evident by 2006. Shiites retaliated against Sunni attacks and a history of Sunni privilege and perceived discrimination against Shiites, as Shiite militias engaged in ethnic (sectarian) cleansing of their own. The situation remains unresolved as of this writing.

Prejudice and Discrimination

Ethnic conflict often arises in reaction to prejudice (attitudes and judgments) or discrimination (action). **Prejudice** means devaluing (looking down on) a group because of its assumed behavior, values, capabilities, or attributes. People are prejudiced when they hold stereotypes about groups and apply them to individuals. (**Stereotypes** are fixed ideas—often unfavorable—about what the members of a group are like.) Prejudiced people assume that members of the group will act as they are "supposed to act" (according to the stereotype) and interpret a wide range of individual behaviors as evidence of the stereotype. They use this behavior to confirm their stereotype (and low opinion) of the group.

Discrimination refers to policies and practices that harm a group and its members. Discrimination may be *de facto* (practiced, but not legally sanctioned) or *de jure* (part of the law). An example of de facto discrimination is the harsher treatment that American minorities (compared with other Americans) tend to get from the police and the judicial system. This unequal treatment isn't legal, but it happens anyway. Segregation in the southern United States and *apartheid* in South Africa provide two examples of de jure discrimination, which no longer are in existence. In both systems, by law, blacks and whites had different rights and privileges. Their social interaction ("mixing") was legally curtailed.

living anthropology **VIDEOS**

The Return Home, www.mhhe.com/kottak

This clip focuses on ethnic diversity in Bosnia. The war of the early 1990s may have ended, but ethnic animosity remains. In discussing the living arrangements of Croats and Muslims, the narrator of the clip describes a "checkerboard" settlement pattern that existed before the war. What does he mean by this? The clip shows that both Muslims and Croats were displaced by the war. Was the village of Bukovica, where the clip is mainly set, originally a Muslim or a Croat village? How is ethnic difference marked in everyday life, in such routine activities as buying things, talking on the phone, and driving an automobile?

prejudice
Devaluing a group because of its assumed attributes.

stereotypes
Fixed ideas—often unfavorable—about what members of a group are like.

discrimination
Policies and practices that harm a group and its members.

Discrimination refers to policies and practices that harm a group and its members. This protest sign, hoisted in New Orleans' lower 9th ward, shows that at least some community residents see ethnic and racial bias in the fact that African Americans in that city bore the brunt of Hurricane Katrina's devastation.

appreciating
DIVERSITY

The Basques

In the realms of linguistic and cultural diversity, the Basques are distinctive. Having maintained a strong ethnic identity, perhaps for millennia, the Basques of France and Spain are linguistically unique; their language is unrelated to any other known language. Their homeland lies in the western Pyrenees Mountains, straddling the French–Spanish border (Figure 15.4). Of the seven Basque provinces, three are in France and four are in Spain. Although these provinces have not been unified politically for nearly a millennium, the Basques remain one of Europe's most distinctive ethnic groups.

The French Revolution of 1789 ended the political autonomy of the three Basque provinces in France. During the 19th century in Spain the Basques fought on the losing side in two internal wars, yielding much of their political autonomy in defeat. When the Spanish Civil War broke out in 1936, the Basques remained loyal to the republic, opposing the Spanish dictator Francisco Franco, who eventually defeated them. Under Franco's rule (1936–1975), Basques were executed, imprisoned, and exiled, and Basque culture was systematically repressed.

In the late 1950s disaffected Basque youths founded ETA (*Euskadi Ta Azkatasuna*, or "Basque Country and Freedom"). Its goal was complete independence from Spain (Zulaika 1988). The ETA's opposition to Franco escalated into violence, which continued thereafter, diminishing in recent years. Effective March 24, 2006, the leaders of ETA announced a ceasefire, which held for 15 months through June 2007. The group continues its quest for full Basque independence.

Franco's death in 1975 had ushered in an era of democracy in Spain. Mainline Basque nationalists collaborated in framing a new constitution, which gave considerable autonomy to the Basque regions (Trask 1996).

Since 1979 three Spanish Basque provinces have been united as the more or less self-governing Basque Autonomous Region. The Basque language is co-official with Spanish in this territory. Spain's fourth Basque province, Navarra, formed its own autonomous region, where the Basque language has a degree of official standing. In France, like other regional languages, Basque has been victimized for centuries by laws hostile to languages other than French (Trask 1996). After generations of decline, the number of Basque speakers is increasing today. Much education, publishing, and broadcasting now proceed in Basque in the Autonomous Region. Still, Basque faces the same pressures that all other minority languages do: Knowledge of the national language (Spanish or French) is essential, and most education, publishing, and broadcasting is in the national language (Trask 1996).

How long have the Basques been in their homeland? Archaeological evidence suggests

FIGURE 15.4 Location of the Basque homeland.

that a single group of people lived in the Basque country continuously from late Paleolithic times through the Bronze Age (about 3,000 years ago). There is no evidence to suggest that any new population entered the area after that (La Fraugh n.d.).

Historically the Basques have been farmers, herders, and fishers. (Today most of them work in business and industry.) The Basque *basseria* (family farm) once thrived as a mixed-farming unit emphasizing self-sufficiency. The farm family grew wheat, corn, vegetables, fruits, and nuts and raised poultry, rabbits, pigs, cows, and sheep. Subsistence pursuits increasingly have been commercialized, with the production of vegetables, dairy products, and fish aimed at urban markets (Greenwood 1976).

Basque immigrants originally entered North America as either Spanish or French nationals. Basque Americans, numbering some 50,000, now invoke Basqueness as their primary ethnic identity. They are concentrated in California, Idaho, and Nevada. First-generation immigrants usually are fluent in Basque. They are more likely to be bilingual in Basque and English than to have their parents' fluency in Spanish or French (Douglass 1992).

Building on a traditional occupation in Basque country, Basques in the United States are notable for their identification with sheepherding (see Ott 1981). Most of them settled and worked in the open-range livestock districts of the 13 states of the American West. Basques were among the Spanish soldiers, explorers, missionaries, and administrators in the American Southwest and Spanish California. More Basques came during the California gold rush, many from southern South America,

The herding of sheep, shown here in the Basque homeland (Pyrenees), remained a primary occupation of Basque men who started migrating to the American West in the 19th century.

where they were established sheepherders (Douglass 1992).

Restrictive immigration laws enacted in the 1920s, which had an anti-southern European bias, limited Basque immigration to the United States. During World War II, with the country in need of shepherds, the U.S. government exempted Basque herders from immigration quotas. Between 1950 and 1975, several thousand Basques entered the United States on three-year contracts. Later, the decline of the U.S. sheep industry would slow Basque immigration dramatically (Douglass 1992).

Catering to Basque sheepherders, western towns had one or more Basque boardinghouses. The typical one had a bar and a dining room, where meals were served family-style at long tables. A second floor of sleeping rooms was reserved for permanent boarders. Also lodged were herders in town for a brief visit,

vacation, or employment layoff or in transit to an employer (Echeverria 1999).

Initially, few Basques came to the United States intending to stay. Most early immigrants were young, unmarried men. Their herding pattern, with solitary summers in the mountains, did not fit well with family life. Eventually, Basque men came with the intent to stay. They either sent back or went back to Europe for brides (few married non-Basques). Many brides, of the "mail order" sort, were sisters or cousins of an acquaintance made in the United States. Basque boardinghouses also became a source of spouses. The boardinghouse owners sent back to Europe for women willing to come to America as domestics. Few remained single for long (Douglass 1992). In these ways Basque Americans drew on their homeland society and culture in establishing the basis of their family and community life in North America.

Basques have not escaped discrimination in the United States. In the American West, sheepherding is an occupation that carries some stigma. Mobile sheepherders competed with settled livestock interests for access to the range. These were some of the sources of anti-Basque sentiment and even legislation. More recently, newspaper coverage of enduring conflict in the Basque country, particularly the activities of the ETA, has made Basque Americans sensitive to the possible charge of being terrorist sympathizers (Douglass 1992; see also Zulaika 1988).

Chips in the Mosaic

Although the multicultural model is increasingly prominent in North America, ethnic competition and conflict also are evident. There is conflict between newer arrivals, for instance, Central Americans and Koreans, and longer-established ethnic groups, such as African Americans. Ethnic antagonism flared in South-Central Los Angeles in spring 1992 in rioting that followed the acquittal of four white police officers who were tried for the videotaped beating of Rodney King (see Abelmann and Lie 1995).

Angry blacks attacked whites, Koreans, and Latinos. This violence expressed frustration by African Americans about their prospects in an increasingly multicultural society. A *New York Times* CBS News Poll conducted May 8, 1992, just after the Los Angeles riots, found that blacks had a bleaker outlook than whites about the effects of immigration on their lives. Only 23 percent of the blacks felt they had more opportunities than recent immigrants, compared with twice that many whites (Toner 1992).

Korean stores were hard hit during the 1992 riots, and more than a third of the businesses destroyed were Latino-owned. A third of those who died in the riots were Latinos. These mainly recent migrants lacked deep roots to the neighborhood and, as Spanish speakers, faced language barriers (Newman 1992). Many Koreans also had trouble with English.

Koreans interviewed on ABC's *Nightline* on May 6, 1992, recognized that blacks resented them and considered them unfriendly. One man explained, "It's not part of our culture to smile." African Americans interviewed on the same program did complain about Korean unfriendliness. "They come into our neighborhoods and treat us like dirt." These comments suggest a shortcoming of the multicultural perspective: Ethnic groups (blacks here) expect other ethnic groups in the same nation-state to assimilate to some extent to a shared (national) culture. The African Americans' comments invoked a general American value system that includes friendliness, openness, mutual respect, community participation, and "fair play."

Arab militias, called the *Janjaweed*, have forced black Africans off their land in the Darfur region of western Sudan (shown here) through a campaign of killing, rape, and pillage. The Arab militias, equipped by the Sudanese government, are accused of killing up to 30,000 darker-skinned Africans in a campaign that United National officials say constitutes ethnic cleansing and that the United States calls genocide. Since the violence began in March 2003, more than one million people have fled to refugee camps in Sudan and Chad. In this photo, children play among thousands of makeshift huts in the El-Geneina camp.

Two faces of ethnic difference in the former Soviet empire. A propaganda poster depicts a happy mix of nationalities that make up the population of Kyrgyzstan, Central Asia (left). On the right, in August 2008, ethnic Georgians in a refugee camp near Tblissi, Georgia. They fled Georgia's breakaway province, the self-proclaimed new republic, of South Ossetia, where Russians were fighting the Georgian army. A cease fire did not end the tension; Georgia still views South Ossetia as a Russian occupied territory.

Los Angeles blacks wanted their Korean neighbors to act more like generalized Americans—and good neighbors.

Aftermaths of Oppression

Fueling ethnic conflict are such forms of discrimination as genocide, forced assimilation, ethnocide, and cultural colonialism. The most extreme form of ethnic discrimination is **genocide,** the deliberate elimination of a group (such as Jews in Nazi Germany, Muslims in Bosnia, or Tutsi in Rwanda) through mass murder. A dominant group may try to destroy the cultures of certain ethnic groups (**ethnocide**) or force them to adopt the dominant culture (*forced assimilation*). Many countries have penalized or banned the language and customs of an ethnic group (including its religious observances). One example of forced assimilation is the anti-Basque campaign that the dictator Francisco Franco (who ruled between 1939 and 1975) waged in Spain. Franco banned Basque books, journals, newspapers, signs, sermons, and tombstones and imposed fines for using the Basque language in schools. His policies led to the formation of a Basque terrorist group and spurred strong nationalist sentiment in the Basque region (Ryan 1990). This chapter's "Appreciating Diversity" focuses on the Basques, who are unique linguistically and culturally. The Basques of France and Spain have maintained a strong ethnic identity, perhaps for millennia, and their language has no known relatives.

A policy of *ethnic expulsion* aims at removing groups who are culturally different from a country. There are many examples, including Bosnia-Herzegovina in the 1990s. Uganda expelled 74,000 Asians in 1972. The neofascist parties of contemporary Western Europe advocate repatriation (expulsion) of immigrant workers (West Indians in England, Algerians in France, and Turks in Germany) (see Friedman 2003; Ryan 1990, p. 9). A policy of expulsion may create **refugees**—people who have been forced (involuntary refugees) or who have chosen (voluntary refugees) to flee a country, to escape persecution or war.

In many countries, colonial nation-building left ethnic strife in its wake. Thus, over a million Hindus and Muslims were killed in the violence that accompanied the division of the Indian subcontinent into India and Pakistan. Problems between Arabs and Jews in Palestine began during the British mandate period.

Multiculturalism may be growing in the United States and Canada, but the opposite is happening in the former Soviet Union, where ethnic groups (nationalities) want their own nation-states. The flowering of ethnic feeling and conflict as the Soviet empire disintegrated illustrates that years of political repression and ideology provide insufficient common ground for lasting unity. **Cultural colonialism** refers to internal domination—by one group and its culture or ideology over others. One example is the domination over the former Soviet empire by Russian people, language, and culture, and by communist ideology. The dominant culture makes itself the official culture. This is reflected in schools, the media, and public interaction. Under Soviet rule ethnic minorities had very limited self-rule in republics and regions controlled by Moscow. All the republics and their peoples were to be united by the oneness of "socialist internationalism." One common technique in cultural colonialism is to flood ethnic areas

refugees
People who flee a country to escape persecution or war.

genocide
Deliberate elimination of a group through mass murder.

ethnocide
Destruction of cultures of certain ethnic groups.

cultural colonialism
Internal domination by one group and its culture or ideology over others.

TYPE	NATURE OF INTERACTION	EXAMPLES
POSITIVE		
Assimilation	Ethnic groups absorbed within dominant culture	Brazil; United States in early, mid-20th century
Plural Society	Society or region contains economically interdependent ethnic groups	Areas of Middle East with farmers/herders; Swat, Pakistan
Multiculturalism	Cultural diversity valued; ethnic cultures coexist with dominant culture	Canada; United States in 21st century
NEGATIVE		
Prejudice	Devaluing a group based on assumed attributes	Worldwide
Discrimination De Jure	Legal policies and practices harm ethnic group	South African apartheid; former segregation in southern U.S.
Discrimination De Facto	Not legally sanctioned, but practiced	Worldwide
Genocide	Deliberate elimination of ethnic group through mass murder	Nazi Germany; Bosnia; Rwanda; Cambodia; Darfur
Ethnocide	Cultural practices attacked by dominant culture or colonial power	Spanish Basques under Franco
Ethnic Expulsion	Forcing ethnic group(s) out of a country or region	Ugandan Asians; Serbia; Bosnia; Kosovo

with members of the dominant ethnic group. Thus, in the former Soviet Union, ethnic Russian colonists were sent to many areas, to diminish the cohesion and clout of the local people.

The Commonwealth of Independent States (CIS), founded in 1991 and headquartered in Minsk, Belarus, is what remains of the once-powerful Soviet Union (see Yurchak 2005). In Russia and other formerly Soviet nations, ethnic groups (nationalities) have sought, and continue to seek, to forge separate and viable nation-states based on cultural boundaries. This celebration of ethnic autonomy is part of an ethnic florescence that—as surely as globalization and transnationalism—is a trend of the late 20th and early 21st centuries.

Recap 15.1 summarizes the various types of ethnic interaction—positive and negative—that have been discussed.

Acing the
COURSE

Summary

1. An ethnic group refers to members of a particular culture in a nation or region that contains others. Ethnicity is based on actual, perceived, or assumed cultural similarities (among members of the same ethnic group) and differences (between that group and others). Ethnic distinctions can be based on language, religion, history, geography, kinship, or race. A race is an ethnic group assumed to have a biological basis. Usually race and ethnicity are ascribed statuses; people are born members of a group and remain so all their lives.

2. Human races are cultural rather than biological categories. Such races derive from contrasts perceived in particular societies, rather than from scientific classifications based on common genes. In the United States, racial labels such as "white" and "black" designate socially constructed races—categories defined by American culture. American racial classification, governed by the rule of hypodescent, is based neither on phenotype nor on genes. Children of mixed unions, no matter what their appearance, are classified with the minority group parent.

3. Racial attitudes in Japan illustrate intrinsic racism—the belief that a perceived racial difference is a sufficient reason to value one person less than another. The valued group is majority (pure) Japanese, who are believed to share the same blood. Majority Japanese define themselves by opposition to others, such as Koreans and burakumin. These may be minority groups in Japan or outsiders—anyone who is "not us."

4. Such exclusionary racial systems are not inevitable. Although Brazil shares a history of slavery with the United States, it lacks the hypodescent rule. Brazilian racial identity is more of an achieved status. It can change during someone's lifetime, reflecting phenotypical changes.

5. The term *nation* once was synonymous with *ethnic group*. Now nation has come to mean a state—a centrally organized political unit. Because of migration, conquest, and colonialism, most nation-states are not ethnically homogeneous. Ethnic groups that seek autonomous political status (their own country) are nationalities. Political upheavals, wars, and migrations have divided many imagined national communities.

6. Assimilation describes the process of change an ethnic group may experience when it moves to a country where another culture dominates. By assimilating, the minority adopts the patterns and norms of its host culture. Assimilation isn't inevitable, and there can be ethnic harmony without it. A plural society combines ethnic contrasts and economic interdependence between ethnic groups. The view of cultural diversity in a nation-state as good and desirable is multiculturalism. A multicultural society socializes individuals not only into the dominant (national) culture but also into an ethnic one.

7. Ethnicity can be expressed in peaceful multiculturalism, or in discrimination or violent confrontation. Ethnic conflict often arises in reaction to prejudice (attitudes and judgments) or discrimination (action). The most extreme form of ethnic discrimination is genocide, the deliberate elimination of a group through mass murder. A dominant group may try to destroy certain ethnic practices (ethnocide), or to force ethnic group members to adopt the dominant culture (forced assimilation). A policy of ethnic expulsion may create refugees. Cultural colonialism refers to internal domination—by one group and its culture or ideology over others.

Key Terms

Test Yourself!

MULTIPLE CHOICE

1. What is the term for the identification with, and feeling part of, an ethnic tradition and exclusion from other ethnic traditions?
   a. culture shock
   b. cultural relativism
   c. ethnicity
   d. assimilation
   e. ethnocentrism

2. What is the term for a social status that is not automatic; that comes through choices, actions, effects, talents, or accomplishments; and that may be positive or negative?
   a. ascribed status
   b. situational status
   c. negotiated status
   d. ethnicity
   e. achieved status

3. People may occupy a variety of different social statuses during their lives, or even during the course of a day. When claimed or perceived identity varies depending on the audience, this is called
   a. ethnic identity.
   b. racial substitution.
   c. discourse analysis.
   d. rotating core personality traits.
   e. situational negotiation of social identity.

4. Human races, like ethnicities in general, are
   a. cultural rather than biological categories.
   b. a biological reality as much as a cultural one.
   c. used by social scientists to classify humans based on genes and shared blood.
   d. poorly understood by geneticists and therefore considered a cultural category.
   e. a meaningless concept to people living day-to-day.

5. What is the term for the belief that a perceived racial difference is a sufficient reason to value one person less than another (such as in the case of burakumin in Japan)?
   a. extrinsic racism
   b. hypodescent
   c. intrinsic racism
   d. hyperdescent
   e. de jure discrimination

6. Which of the following helps explain the differences between American and Brazilian social constructions of race?
   a. Brazilian plantation landlords had sexual relations with their slaves.
   b. The lack of large native populations in Brazil.
   c. The Portuguese language has a greater number of intermediate color terms than the English language.
   d. Historically in Brazil, freed offspring of master and slave filled many intermediate positions in the emerging Brazilian economy.
   e. English concepts of race were very different from those of the Portuguese.

7. Which of the following statements about ethnic groups that once had, or wish to have or

regain, autonomous political status is *not* true?
   a. They often are minorities in the nation in which they live.
   b. They have been called "imagined communities."
   c. They include or have included the Kurds and Germans.
   d. They are called nationalities.
   e. All or most of their members usually meet regularly face to face.

8. Which of the following statements about nation-states is true?
   a. Nation-states sometimes encourage ethnic divisions for political and economic ends.
   b. Nation-states are ethnically homogeneous.
   c. Nation-states are defined by their lack of ethnic identity.
   d. *Nation-state* is a synonym for *tribe* and *ethnic group*.
   e. Nation-states are parts of other states.

9. What does Benedict Anderson's term "imagined communities" refer to?
   a. postcolonial states, because these did not exist until colonialists thought them up
   b. communities that do not exist in real terms, but are the fictional and temporary products of the ruling intelligentsia
   c. communities composed of many different ethnic groups and subcultures, which therefore will fall apart at any moment
   d. communities in which identity is not established by direct social interaction with other members but through interaction with public media, like a national print media
   e. tribal states in which all members enjoy equal rights, regardless of their ethnicity or religion

10. What is the term for the physical destruction of an ethnic or religious group through mass murder?
   a. ethnic expulsion
   b. forced assimilation
   c. ethnocentrism
   d. racist expulsion
   e. genocide

FILL IN THE BLANK

1. Given the lack of distinction between race and ethnicity, this chapter suggests the term _____ instead of "race" to describe any such social group.

2. _____ is the term for the arbitrary rule that automatically places the children of a union between members of different socioeconomic groups in the less-privileged group.

3. _____ is the view of cultural diversity as valuable and worth maintaining.

4. _____ is the internal domination by one group and its culture/ideology over others.

5. _____ refers to the devaluing of a group because of its assumed behavior, values, abilities, or attributes.

CRITICAL THINKING

1. What's the difference between a culture and an ethnic group? In what culture(s) do you participate? To what ethnic group(s) do you belong? What is the basis of your primary cultural identity? Do others readily recognize this basis and identity? Why or why not?

2. Name five social statuses you currently occupy. Which of those statuses are ascribed, and which ones are achieved? Are any of these statuses mutually exclusive? Which are contextual?

3. In describing the recent history of the census in the United States, this chapter notes how the National Association for the Advancement of Colored People and the National Council of La Raza (a Hispanic advocacy group) have opposed adding a "multiracial" census category. What does this suggest about racial categories?

4. If *race* is a discredited concept when applied to humans, what has replaced it?

5. This chapter describes different types of ethnic interaction. What are they? Are they positive or negative? Anthropologists have and continue to make important contributions to understanding past and ongoing cases of ethnic conflict. What are some examples of this?

3. Multiculturalism; 4. Cultural colonialism; 5. Prejudice

Multiple Choice: 1. (C); 2. (E); 3. (E); 4. (A); 5. (A); 6. (C); 7. (D); 8. (A); 9. (D); 10. (E); **Fill in the Blank:** 1. *ethnic group;* 2. *Hypodescent;*

Friedman, J., ed.
2003 *Globalization, the State, and Violence.* Walnut Creek, CA: AltaMira. Essays by prominent anthropologists focusing on violence in the context of globalization.

Kottak, C. P., and K. A. Kozaitis
2008 *On Being Different: Diversity and Multiculturalism in the North American Mainstream,* 3rd ed. New York: McGraw-Hill. Aspects of diversity in the United States and Canada, plus an original theory of multiculturalism.

Molnar, S.
2006 *Human Variation: Races, types, and Ethnic Groups,* 6th ed. Upper Saddle River, NJ: Prentice Hall. Links between biological and social diversity.

Mukhopadhyay, C. C., R. Henze, and Y. T. Moses
2007 *How Real Is Race: A Sourcebook on Race, Culture, and Biology.* Lanham, MD: Rowman and Littlefield Education. Valuable four-field collection of works by anthropologists on varied dimensions—biological, social, and cultural—of race, racism, and discrimination.

Scupin, R.
2003 *Race and Ethnicity: An Anthropological Focus on the United States and the World.* Upper Saddle River, NJ: Prentice Hall. Broad survey of race and ethnic relations.

Wade, P.
2002 *Race, Nature, and Culture: An Anthropological Perspective.* Sterling, VA: Pluto Press. A processual approach to human biology and race.

Suggested Additional Readings

Internet Exercises

Go to our Online Learning Center website at **www.mhhe.com/kottak** for Internet exercises directly related to the content of this chapter.

What are the major adaptive strategies found in nonindustrial societies?

What is an economy, and what is economizing behavior?

What principles regulate the exchange of goods and services in various societies?

In traditional societies, one's work mates usually are also one's kin. Kin ties link village net fishers who live and work along Dal Lake in India's Kashmir province.

understanding OURSELVES

The necessities of work, marriage, and raising children are fundamental. However, in the non-Western societies where the study of anthropology originated, the need to balance work (economy) and family (society) wasn't as stark as it is for us. In traditional societies, one's workmates usually were also one's kin. There was no need for a "take your child to work" day because most women did that every day. People didn't work with strangers. Home and office, society and economy, were intertwined.

The fact that subsistence and sociality are both basic human needs creates conflicts in modern society. People have to make choices about allocating their time and energy between work and family. Parents in dual-earner and single-parent households always have faced a work-family time bind, and the number of Americans living in such households has almost doubled in recent decades. Fewer than one third of American wives worked outside the home in 1960, compared with almost two-thirds today. That same year, only one fifth of married women with children under age six were in the work force, versus three-fifths today. With women increasingly able to make it "on their own," the economic importance of marriage has declined. In 2007, for the first time ever, the percentage of adult American women who were then unmarried exceeded 50.

Think about the choices your parents have made in terms of economic versus social goals. Have their decisions maximized their incomes, their lifestyles, their individual happiness, family benefits, or what? What about you? What factors motivated you when you chose to apply to and attend college? Did you want to stay close to home, to attend college with friends, or to maintain a romantic attachment (all social reasons)? Did you seek the lowest tuition and college costs—or get a generous scholarship (economic decisions)? Did you choose prestige, or perhaps the likelihood that one day you would earn more money because of the reputation of your alma mater (maximizing prestige and future wealth)? Economists tend to assume that the profit motive rules in contemporary society. However, different individuals, like different cultures, may choose to pursue goals other than monetary gain.

Studies show that most American women now expect to join the paid labor force, just as men do. But the family remains attractive. Most young women also plan to stay home with small children and return to the work force once their children enter school. How about you? If you have definite career plans, how do you imagine your work will fit in with your future family life—if you have one planned? What do your parents want most for you—a successful career or a happy family life with children? Probably both. Will it be easy to fulfill such expectations?

ADAPTIVE STRATEGIES

Compared with hunting and gathering (foraging), the advent of *food production* (plant cultivation and animal domestication) fueled major changes in human life, such as the formation of larger social and political systems—eventually states. The pace of cultural transformation increased enormously. This chapter provides a framework for understanding a variety of human adaptive strategies and economic systems—ranging from hunting and gathering to farming and herding.

The anthropologist Yehudi Cohen (1974*b*) used the term **adaptive strategy** to describe a group's system of economic production. Cohen argued that the most important reason for similarities between two (or more) unrelated societies is their possession of a similar adaptive strategy. For example, there are clear similarities among societies that have a foraging (hunting and gathering) strategy. Cohen developed a typology of societies based on correlations between their economies and their social features. His typology includes these five adaptive strategies: foraging, horticulture, agriculture, pastoralism, and industrialism. Industrialism is discussed in the chapter "The World System and Colonialism." The present chapter focuses on the first four adaptive strategies.

FORAGING

Until 10,000 years ago, people everywhere were foragers, also known as hunter-gatherers. However, environmental differences did create substantial contrasts among the world's foragers. Some, such as the people who lived in Europe during the ice ages, were big-game hunters. Today, hunters in the Arctic still focus on large animals and herd animals; they have much less vegetation and variety in their diets than do tropical foragers. In general, as one moves from colder to warmer areas, there is an increase in the number of species. The tropics contain tremendous biodiversity, a great variety of plant and animal species, many of which have been used by human foragers. Tropical foragers typically hunt and gather a wide range of plant and animal life. The same may be true in temperate areas, such as the North Pacific Coast of North America, where Native American foragers could draw on a rich variety of land and sea resources, including salmon, other fish species, berries, mountain goats, seals, and sea mammals. Nevertheless, despite differences due to environmental variation, all foraging economies have shared one essential feature: People rely on available natural resources for their subsistence, rather than controlling the reproduction of plants and animals.

Such control came with the advent of animal domestication (initially of sheep and goats) and plant cultivation (of wheat and barley), which began 10,000 to 12,000 years ago in the Middle East. Cultivation based on different crops, such as maize, manioc (cassava), and potatoes, arose independently in the Americas. In both hemispheres the new economy spread rapidly. Today, almost all foragers have at least some dependence on food production or on food producers (Kent 1992).

The foraging way of life survived into modern times in certain environments (see Figure 16.1), including a few islands and forests, along with deserts and very cold areas—places where food production was not practicable with simple technology (see Lee and Daly 1999). In many areas, foragers had been exposed to the "idea" of food production but never adopted it because their own economies provided a perfectly adequate and nutritious diet—with a lot less work. In some areas, people reverted to foraging after trying food production and abandoning it. In most areas where hunter-gatherers did survive, foraging should be described as "recent" rather than "contemporary." All modern foragers live in nation-states, depend to some extent on government assistance, and have contacts with food-producing neighbors as well as missionaries and other outsiders. We should not view contemporary foragers as isolated or pristine survivors of the Stone Age. Modern foragers are influenced by regional forces (e.g., trade and war), national and international policies, and political and economic events in the world system.

Although foraging is disappearing as a way of life, the outlines of Africa's two broad belts of recent foraging remain evident. One is the Kalahari Desert of southern Africa. This is the home of the *San* ("Bushmen"), who include the *Ju/'hoansi* (see Kent 1996; Lee 2003). The other main African foraging area is the equatorial forest of central and eastern Africa, home of the Mbuti, Efe, and other "pygmies" (Bailey et al. 1989; Turnbull 1965).

People still do, or until recently did, subsistence foraging in certain remote forests in Madagascar; in Southeast Asia, including Malaysia and the Philippines; and on certain islands off the Indian coast (Lee and Daly 1999). Some of the best-known recent foragers are the aborigines of Australia. Those Native Australians lived on their island continent for more than 50,000 years without developing food production.

The Western Hemisphere also had recent foragers. The Eskimos, or Inuit, of Alaska and Canada are well-known hunters. These (and other) northern foragers now use modern technology, including rifles and snowmobiles, in their subsistence activities (Pelto 1973). The native populations of California, Oregon, Washington, British Columbia, and Alaska all were foragers, as were those of inland subarctic Canada and the Great Lakes. For many Native Americans, fishing, hunting, and gathering remain important subsistence (and sometimes commercial) activities.

Coastal foragers also lived near the southern tip of South America, in Patagonia. On the grassy plains of Argentina, southern Brazil, Uruguay, and Paraguay, there were other hunter-gatherers. The contemporary Aché of Paraguay are usually called "hunter-gatherers" even though they get just a third of their livelihood from foraging. The

adaptive strategy
Means of making a living; productive system.

anthropology **ATLAS**

Map 12 displays the kinds of self-sustaining economies that existed throughout the world in C.E. 1500. In North America, biodiversity allowed various forms of foraging (hunting and gathering) as well as plant cultivation.

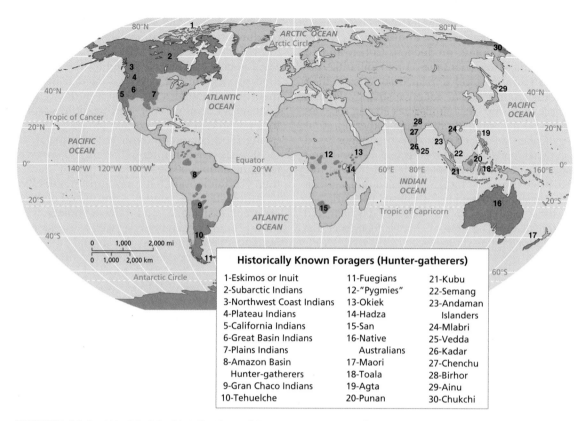

FIGURE 16.1 Worldwide Distribution of Recent Hunter-Gatherers.

SOURCE: Adapted of map and key by Ray Sim, in Göran Burenhult, ed., *Encyclopedia of Humankind: People of the Stone Age* (McMahons Point, NSW, Australia: Weldon Owen, 1993), p. 193. © Weldon Owen Pty. Ltd. Used with permission.

Aché also grow crops, have domesticated animals, and live in or near mission posts, where they receive food from missionaries (Hawkes, O'Connell, and Hill 1982; Hill et al. 1987).

The hunter-gatherer way of life did persist in a few areas that could be cultivated, even after contact with cultivators. Those tenacious foragers, such as indigenous foragers in what is now California, Oregon, Washington, and British Columbia, did not turn to food production because they were supporting themselves very adequately by hunting and gathering (see the section on the potlatch at the end of this chapter). As the modern world system spreads, the number of foragers continues to decline. Recap 16.1 summarizes locations and attributes of foragers.

San: Then and Now

Throughout the world, foraging survived in environments that posed major obstacles to food production. (Some foragers took refuge in such areas after the rise of food production, the state, colonialism, or the modern world system.) The difficulties of cultivating at the North Pole are obvious. In southern Africa, the Dobe Ju/'hoansi San area studied by Richard Lee is surrounded by a waterless

belt 45 to 125 miles (70 to 200 kilometers) in breadth. The Dobe area is hard to reach even today, and there is no archaeological evidence of occupation of this area by food producers before the 20th century (Solway and Lee 1990). However, environmental limits to other adaptive strategies aren't the only reason foragers survived. Their niches had one thing in common: their marginality. Their environments were not of immediate interest to groups with other adaptive strategies.

Most of the estimated 100,000 San who survive today live in poverty on society's fringes. Each year, more and more foragers come under the control of nation-states and are influenced by forces of globalization. As described by Motseta (2006), between 1997 and 2002, the government of Botswana in southern Africa relocated about 3,000 Basarwa San Bushmen outside their ancestral territory, which was converted into a reserve for wildlife protection. The Basarwa received some compensation for their land, along with access to schools, medical facilities, and job training in resettlement centers. However, critics claim this resettlement turned a society of free hunter-gatherers into communities dependent on food aid and government handouts (Motseta 2006).

GEOGRAPHIC LOCATIONS	
ARCHAEOLOGICALLY KNOWN FORAGERS	Europe: Paleolithic big game hunters
	Europe, Japan, Middle East, elsewhere: Mesolithic broad-spectrum foragers
	Africa: Stone Age hunters and gatherers

RECENT (ETHNOGRAPHICALLY KNOWN) FORAGERS OLD WORLD	Africa:
	  Kalahari Desert, southern Africa: *San* ("Bushmen")
	  Equatorial forest, central & eastern Africa: Mbuti, Efe ("pygmies")

	Madagascar, remote forests: Mikea
	Southeast Asia—Malaysia and Philippines: Tasaday
	Islands off India's coast: Andaman Islanders
	Australia: entire continent—Native Australians ("aborigines")
WESTERN HEMISPHERE	Eskimos, or Inuit: Alaska and Canada
	N. Pacific coast: California, Oregon, Washington, British Columbia, and Alaska
	Inland subarctic Canada and U.S. Great Lakes

	South America:
	  coastal Patagonia
	  pampas: Argentina, southern Brazil, Uruguay, Paraguay

GENERALIZATIONS ABOUT FORAGERS	
	Not pristine "survivors of the Stone Age."
	Recent rather than contemporary.
	Rely on natural resources for subsistence.
	Don't control plant and animal reproduction.
	Environments posed major obstacles to food production.
	Live on or in islands, forests, deserts, very cold areas.
	Some knew about food production but rejected it.
	Some fled food production, states, or colonial rule.
ALL FORAGERS TODAY	Live in nation-states.
	Depend on outside assistance.
	Have significant contact with outsiders.

	Are influenced by:
	  food-producing economies
	  regional forces (e.g., trade and war)
	  national and international policies
	  political and economic events in the world system

In 2006 Botswana's High Court ruled that the Basarwa had been wrongly evicted from the "Central Kalahari Game Reserve." In the context of global political action for cultural rights, this verdict was hailed as a victory for indigenous peoples around the world (Motseta 2006). In December 2006, Botswana's attorney general recognized the court order to allow the Basarwa to return to their ancestral lands, while imposing conditions likely to prevent most of them from doing so. Only the 189 people who actually filed the lawsuit would have automatic right of return with their children, compared with some 2,000 Basarwa wishing to return. The others would have to apply for special permits. Returning Basarwa would be allowed to build only temporary structures and to use enough water for subsistence needs. Water would be a major obstacle since the government shut the main well in 2002, and water is scarce in the Kalahari. Furthermore, anyone wishing to hunt would have to apply for a permit.

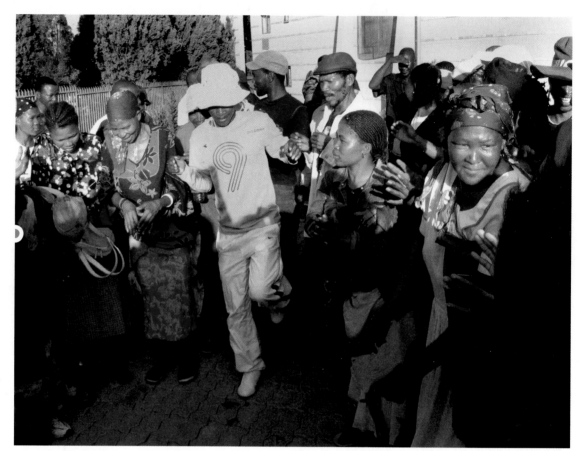

On December 13, 2006, San men and women celebrate outside court in Lobatse, Botswana. The court had just ruled that the plaintiffs could return to live and hunt on their ancestral lands, which had been enclosed within a game reserve.

Correlates of Foraging

correlation
Association; when one variable changes, another does, too.

Typologies, including Cohen's adaptive strategies, are useful because they suggest **correlations**—that is, association or covariation between two or more variables. (Correlated variables are factors that are linked and interrelated, such as food intake and body weight, such that when one increases or decreases, the other tends to change, too.) Ethnographic studies in hundreds of societies have revealed many correlations between the economy and social life. Associated (correlated) with each adaptive strategy is a bundle of particular cultural features. Correlations, however, are rarely perfect. Some foragers lacked cultural features usually associated with foraging, while some of those features were present in groups with other adaptive strategies.

What, then, are some correlates of foraging? People who subsisted by hunting, gathering, and fishing often lived in band-organized societies. Their basic social unit, the **band,** was a small group of fewer than a hundred people, all related by kinship or marriage. Band size varied among cultures and often from one season to the next in a given culture. In some foraging societies, band size stayed the same year-round. In others, the band split up for part of the year. Families left to gather resources better exploited by just a few

band
Basic social unit among foragers; fewer than 100 people; may split seasonally.

people. Later, they regrouped for cooperative work and ceremonies.

Several examples of seasonal splits and reunions are known from ethnography and archaeology. In southern Africa, some San aggregated around waterholes in the dry season and split up in the wet season, whereas other bands dispersed in the dry season (Barnard 1979; Kent 1992). This reflected environmental variation. San who lacked permanent water had to disperse and forage widely for moisture-filled plants. In ancient Oaxaca, Mexico, before the advent of plant cultivation there around 4,000 years ago, foragers assembled in large bands in summer. They collectively harvested tree pods and cactus fruits. Then, in fall, they split into much smaller family groups to hunt deer and gather grasses and plants that were effectively foraged by small teams.

One typical characteristic of the foraging life is mobility. In many San groups, as among the Mbuti of Congo, people shifted band membership several times in a lifetime. One might be born, for example, in a band where one's mother had kin. Later, one's family might move to a band where the father had relatives. Because bands were exogamous (people married outside their own band), one's parents came from two different bands, and one's grandparents might have come from four. People could join any band to which they had kinship or marriage links. A couple could live in, or shift between, the husband's band and the wife's band.

One also could affiliate with a band through fictive kinship—personal relationships modeled on kinship, such as that between godparents and godchildren. San, for example, have a limited number of personal names. People with the same name have a special relationship; they treat each other like siblings. San expected the same hospitality in bands where they had namesakes as they did in a band where a real sibling lived. Kinship, marriage, and fictive kinship permitted San to join several bands. Nomadic (regularly on-the-move) foragers changed bands often, so that band membership could vary substantially from year to year.

Human societies have tended to encourage a division of labor based on gender (see the chapter on gender for much more on this). Among foragers, men typically hunted and fished while women gathered and collected, but the specific nature of the work varied among cultures. Sometimes women's work contributed most to the diet. Sometimes male hunting and fishing predominated. Among foragers in tropical and semitropical areas, gathering often contributed more to the diet than hunting and fishing did—even though the labor costs of gathering were much higher than those of hunting and fishing.

All foragers have maintained social distinctions based on age. Often old people received great respect as guardians of myths, legends, stories, and traditions. Younger people valued the elders' special knowledge of ritual and practical matters. Most foraging societies were egalitarian, with contrasts in prestige minor and based on age and gender.

When considering issues of "human nature," we should remember that the egalitarian band was a basic form of human social life for most of our history. Food production has existed less than 1 percent of the time *Homo* has been on Earth. However, it has produced huge social differences. We now consider the main economic features of food-producing strategies.

CULTIVATION

In Cohen's typology, the three adaptive strategies based on food production in nonindustrial societies are horticulture, agriculture, and pastoralism. In non-Western cultures, as is also true in modern nations, people carry out a variety of economic activities. Each adaptive strategy refers to the main economic activity. Pastoralists (herders), for example, consume milk, butter, blood, and meat from their animals as mainstays of their diet. However, they also add grain to the diet by doing

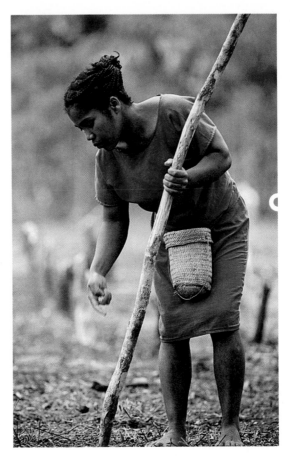

In slash-and-burn horticulture, the land is cleared by cutting down (slashing) and burning trees and bush, using simple technology. After such clearing this woman uses a digging stick to plant mountain rice in Madagascar. What might be the environmental effects of slash-and-burn cultivation?

some cultivating or by trading with neighbors. Food producers also may hunt or gather to supplement a diet based on domesticated species.

Horticulture

Horticulture and agriculture are two types of cultivation found in nonindustrial societies. Both differ from the farming systems of industrial nations like the United States and Canada, which use large land areas, machinery, and petrochemicals. According to Cohen, **horticulture** is cultivation that makes intensive use of *none* of the factors of production: land, labor, capital, and machinery. Horticulturalists use simple tools such as hoes and digging sticks to grow their crops. Their fields are not permanently cultivated and lie fallow for varying lengths of time.

Horticulture often involves *slash-and-burn techniques*. Here, horticulturalists clear land by cutting down (slashing) and burning forest or bush or by setting fire to the grass covering a plot. The vegetation is broken down, pests are killed, and the ashes remain to fertilize the soil. Crops are then sown, tended, and harvested. Use of the plot is not continuous. Often it is cultivated for only a year. This depends, however, on soil fertility and weeds, which compete with cultivated plants for nutrients.

horticulture
Nonindustrial plant cultivation with fallowing.

When horticulturalists abandon a plot because of soil exhaustion or a thick weed cover, they clear another piece of land, and the original plot reverts to forest. After several years of fallowing (the duration varies in different societies), the cultivator returns to farm the original plot again. Horticulture is also called *shifting cultivation*. Such shifts from plot to plot do not mean that whole villages must move when plots are abandoned. Horticulture can support large permanent villages. Among the Kuikuru of the South American tropical forest, for example, one village of 150 people remained in the same place for 90 years (Carneiro 1956). Kuikuru houses are large and well made. Because the work involved in building them is great, the Kuikuru would rather walk farther to their fields than construct a new village. They shift their plots rather than their settlements. On the other hand, horticulturalists in the montaña (Andean foothills) of Peru live in small villages of about 30 people (Carneiro 1961/1968). Their houses are small and simple. After a few years in one place, these people build new villages near virgin land. Because their houses are so simple, they prefer rebuilding to walking even a half-mile to their fields.

This chapter's "Appreciating Anthropology" describes "A World on Fire," the impacts of deforestation and climate change on Native Americans living in Brazil's Xingu National Park. Traditionally the Kamayurá Indians described in "Appreciating Anthropology" relied on a combination of fishing, hunting, and horticulture (mainly based on manioc or cassava) for their livelihood. The

Kamayurá knew how to control their own slash-and-burn cultivation. Now, due to drier weather, forest fires are out of hand. Once too moist to ignite, the forest has become flammable. In 2007, Xingu National Park burned for the first time, and thousands of acres were destroyed.

Agriculture

Agriculture is cultivation that requires more labor than horticulture does, because it uses land intensively and continuously. The greater labor demands associated with agriculture reflect its common use of domesticated animals, irrigation, or terracing.

Domesticated Animals

Many agriculturalists use animals as means of production—for transport, as cultivating machines, and for their manure. Asian farmers typically incorporate cattle and/or water buffalo into agricultural economies based on rice production. Rice farmers may use cattle to trample pretilled flooded fields, thus mixing soil and water, prior to transplanting. Many agriculturalists attach animals to plows and harrows for field preparation before planting or transplanting. Also, agriculturalists typically collect manure from their animals, using it to fertilize their plots, thus increasing yields. Animals are attached to carts for transport as well as to implements of cultivation.

Irrigation

While horticulturalists must await the rainy season, agriculturalists can schedule their planting in advance, because they control water. Like other irrigation experts in the Philippines, the Ifugao (Figure 16.2) irrigate their fields with canals from rivers, streams, springs, and ponds. Irrigation makes it possible to cultivate a plot year after year. Irrigation enriches the soil because the irrigated field is a unique ecosystem with several species of plants and animals, many of them minute organisms, whose wastes fertilize the land.

An irrigated field is a capital investment that usually increases in value. It takes time for a field to start yielding; it reaches full productivity only after several years of cultivation. The Ifugao, like other irrigators, have farmed the same fields for generations. In some agricultural areas, including the Middle East, however, salts carried in the irrigation water can make fields unusable after 50 or 60 years.

Terracing

Terracing is another agricultural technique the Ifugao have mastered. Their homeland has small valleys separated by steep hillsides. Because the population is dense, people need to farm the hills. However, if they simply planted on the steep hillsides, fertile soil and crops would be washed

FIGURE 16.2 Location of the Ifugao.

away during the rainy season. To prevent this, the Ifugao cut into the hillside and build stage after stage of terraced fields rising above the valley floor. Springs located above the terraces supply their irrigation water. The labor necessary to build and maintain a system of terraces is great. Terrace walls crumble each year and must be partially rebuilt. The canals that bring water down through the terraces also demand attention.

Costs and Benefits of Agriculture

Agriculture requires human labor to build and maintain irrigation systems, terraces, and other works. People must feed, water, and care for their animals. Given sufficient labor input and management, agricultural land can yield one or two crops annually for years or even generations. An agricultural field does not necessarily produce a higher single-year yield than does a horticultural plot. The first crop grown by horticulturalists on long-idle land may be larger than that from an agricultural plot of the same size. Furthermore, because agriculturalists work harder than horticulturalists do, agriculture's yield relative to the labor invested is also lower. Agriculture's main advantage is that the long-term yield per area is far greater and more dependable. Because a single field sustains its owners year after year, there is no need to maintain a reserve of uncultivated land as horticulturalists do. This is why agricultural societies tend to be more densely populated than are horticultural ones.

The Cultivation Continuum

Because nonindustrial economies can have features of both horticulture and agriculture, it is useful to discuss cultivators as being arranged along a **cultivation continuum**. Horticultural systems stand at one end—the "low-labor, shifting-plot" end. Agriculturalists are at the other—the "labor-intensive, permanent-plot" end.

We speak of a continuum because there are today intermediate economies, combining horticultural and agricultural features—more intensive than annually shifting horticulture but less intensive than agriculture. Unlike nonintensive horticulturalists, who farm a plot just once before fallowing it, the South American Kuikuru grow two or three crops of *manioc*, or cassava—an edible tuber—before abandoning their plots. Cultivation is even more intense in certain densely populated areas of Papua New Guinea, where plots are planted for two or three years, allowed to rest for three to five, and then recultivated. After several of these cycles, the plots are abandoned for a longer fallow period. Such a pattern is called *sectorial fallowing* (Wolf 1966). Besides Papua New Guinea, such systems occur in places as distant as

Agriculture requires more labor than horticulture does and uses land intensively and continuously. Labor demands associated with agriculture reflect its use of domesticated animals, irrigation, and terracing. The rice farmers of Luzon in the Philippines, such as the Ifugao, are famous for their irrigated and terraced fields.

West Africa and highland Mexico. Sectorial fallowing is associated with denser populations than is simple horticulture.

The key difference between horticulture and agriculture is that horticulture always uses a fallow period whereas agriculture does not. The earliest cultivators in the Middle East and in Mexico were rainfall-dependent horticulturalists. Until recently, horticulture was the main form of cultivation in several areas, including parts of Africa, Southeast Asia, the Pacific islands, Mexico, Central America, and the South American tropical forest.

Intensification: People and the Environment

The range of environments available for food production has widened as people have increased their control over nature. For example, in arid areas of California, where Native Americans once foraged, modern irrigation technology now sustains rich agricultural estates. Agriculturalists live in many areas that are too arid for nonirrigators or too hilly for nonterracers. Many ancient civilizations in arid lands arose on an agricultural base. Increasing labor intensity and permanent land use have major demographic, social, political, and environmental consequences.

cultivation continuum
Continuum of land and labor use.

anthropology **ATLAS**

Map 12 displays the kinds of economies that existed throughout the world at the start of the European age of discovery and conquest—250 years before the Industrial Revolution.

appreciating ANTHROPOLOGY

A World on Fire

Anthropologists were instrumental in pushing the Brazilian government to establish the Xingu National Park. Created in 1961, the park encompasses about 8,530 square miles. It is home to indigenous peoples representing Brazil's four major indigenous language families: Tupi, Arawak, Carib, and Gê. The people and cultures of the Xingu Park have been studied by generations of anthropologists. Now, however, the park and its people are threatened by deforestation and climate change.

XINGU NATIONAL PARK, Brazil—As the naked, painted young men of the Kamayurá tribe prepare for the ritualized war games of a festival, they end their haunting fireside chant with a blowing sound—"whoosh, whoosh"—a symbolic attempt to eliminate the scent of fish so they will not be detected by enemies. For centuries, fish from jungle lakes and rivers have been a staple of the Kamayurá diet, the tribe's primary source of protein.

But fish smells are not a problem for the warriors anymore. Deforestation and, some scientists contend, global climate change are making the Amazon region drier and hotter, decimating fish stocks in this area and imperil-

ing the Kamayurá's very existence. Like other small indigenous cultures around the world with little money or capacity to move, they are struggling to adapt to the changes.

"Us old monkeys can take the hunger, but the little ones suffer—they're always asking for fish," said Kotok, the tribe's chief, who stood in front of a hut containing the tribe's sacred flutes on a recent evening. He wore a white T-shirt over the tribe's traditional dress, which is basically nothing.

Chief Kotok, who like all of the Kamayurá people goes by only one name, said that men can now fish all night without a bite in streams where fish used to be abundant; they safely swim in lakes previously teeming with piranhas. Responsible for 3 wives, 24 children and hundreds of other tribe members, he said his once-idyllic existence had turned into a kind of bad dream . . .

The Intergovernmental Panel on Climate Change says that up to 30 percent of animals and plants face an increased risk of extinction if global temperatures rise 2 degrees Celsius (3.6 degrees Fahrenheit) in coming decades.

But anthropologists also fear a wave of cultural extinction for dozens of small indigenous groups—the loss of their traditions, their arts, their languages . . .

To make do without fish, Kamayurá children are eating ants on their traditional spongy flatbread, made from tropical cassava flour. "There aren't as many around because the kids have eaten them," Chief Kotok said of the ants. Sometimes members of the tribe kill monkeys for their meat, but, the chief said, "You have to eat 30 monkeys to fill your stomach."

Living deep in the forest with no transportation and little money, he noted, "We don't have a way to go to the grocery store for rice and beans to supplement what is missing."

Tacuma, the tribe's wizened senior shaman, said that the only threat he could remember rivaling climate change was a measles virus that arrived deep in the Amazon in 1954, killing more than 90 percent of the Kamayurá. . . .

Many indigenous people depend intimately on the cycles of nature and have had to adapt to climate variations—a season of drought, for example, or a hurricane that kills animals. . . .

The Kamayurá live in the middle of Xingu National Park, a vast territory that was once deep in the Amazon but is now surrounded by farms and ranches. About 5,000 square miles of Amazon forest are being cut down

Thus, because of their permanent fields, intensive cultivators are sedentary. People live in larger and more permanent communities located closer to other settlements. Growth in population size and density increases contact between individuals and groups. There is more need to regulate interpersonal relations, including conflicts of interest. Economies that support more people usually require more coordination in the use of land, labor, and other resources.

Intensive agriculture has significant environmental effects. Irrigation ditches and paddies (fields with irrigated rice) become repositories for organic wastes, chemicals (such as salts), and disease microorganisms. Intensive agriculture typically spreads at the expense of trees and for-

ests, which are cut down to be replaced by fields. Accompanying such deforestation is loss of environmental diversity (see Srivastava, Smith, and Forno 1999). Agricultural economies grow increasingly specialized—focusing on one or a few caloric staples, such as rice, and on the animals that are raised and tended to aid the agricultural economy. Because tropical horticulturalists typically cultivate dozens of plant species simultaneously, a horticultural plot tends to mirror the botanical diversity that is found in a tropical forest. Agricultural plots, by contrast, reduce ecological diversity by cutting down trees and concentrating on just a few staple foods. Such crop specialization is true of agriculturalists both in the tropics (e.g., Indonesian paddy farmers)

Deforestation in the Amazon basin and the resulting climate change have had a profound impact on the Kamayurá tribe who inhabit the Xingu National Park in Mato Grosso, Brazil. Shown here, Kamayurá men in ceremonial dress walk through the central courtyard of their village in June 2009.

ity of fish farming, in which fish would be fed in a penned area of a lake. With hotter temperatures as well as less rain and humidity in the region, water levels in rivers are extremely low. Fish cannot get to their spawning grounds . . .

The tribe's agriculture has suffered, too . . . Last year, families had to plant their cassava four times—it died in September, October and November because there was not enough moisture in the ground. It was not until December that the planting took . . .

But perhaps the Kamayurá's greatest fear are the new summer forest fires. Once too moist to ignite, the forest here is now flammable because of the drier weather. In 2007, Xingu National Park burned for the first time, and thousands of acres were destroyed.

"The whole Xingu was burning—it stung our lungs and our eyes," Chief Kotok said. "We had nowhere to escape. We suffered along with the animals."

SOURCE: Elisabeth Rosenthal, "An Amazon Culture Withers as Food Dries Up." From *The New York Times*, July 25, 2009. © 2009 The New York Times. All rights reserved. Used by permission and protected by the Copyright Laws of the United States. The printing, copying, redistribution, or retransmission of the Material without express written permission is prohibited. www.nytimes.com

annually in recent years, according to the Brazilian government. And with far less foliage, there is less moisture in the regional water cycle, lending unpredictability to seasonal rains and leaving the climate drier and hotter.

That has upended the cycles of nature that long regulated Kamayurá life. They wake with the sun and have no set meals, eating whenever they are hungry. Fish stocks began to dwindle in the 1990s and "have just collapsed" since 2006, said Chief Kotok, who is considering the possibil-

and outside the tropics (e.g., Middle Eastern irrigated farmers).

At least in the tropics, the diets of both foragers and horticulturalists are typically more diverse, although under less secure human control, than the diets of agriculturalists. Agriculturists attempt to reduce risk in production by favoring stability in the form of a reliable annual harvest and long-term production. Tropical foragers and horticulturalists, by contrast, attempt to reduce risk by relying on multiple species and benefiting from ecological diversity. The agricultural strategy is to put all one's eggs in one big and very dependable basket. Of course, even with agriculture, there is a possibility that the single staple crop may fail, and famine may result. The

strategy of tropical foragers and horticulturalists is to have several smaller baskets, a few of which may fail without endangering subsistence. The agricultural strategy makes sense when there are lots of children to raise and adults to be fed. Foraging and horticulture, of course, are associated with smaller, sparser, and more mobile populations.

Agricultural economies also pose a series of regulatory problems—which central governments often have arisen to solve. How is water to be managed—along with disputes about access to and distribution of water? With more people living closer together on more valuable land, agriculturalists are more likely to come into conflict than foragers and horticulturalists

NAME: Dejene Negassa Debsu, Ph.D.
COUNTRY OF ORIGIN: Ethiopia
SUPERVISING PROFESSOR: Peter D. Little
SCHOOL: University of Kentucky

Children, Parents, and Family Economics

Children in my country, Ethiopia, live very different lives than do children in the United States. Poverty deprives children in Ethiopia of adequate food, clean water, and medicine. It also makes them part of the family struggle for survival, necessitating that they contribute to the family's subsistence. Children in rural areas often herd the animals and fetch water and wood for fuel. They help with farming, harvesting, transporting, and other tasks in farming areas. In urban areas, children, especially girls, are hired for domestic service. Others engage in petty activities such as hawking, shoe polishing, and carrying. The expectation that children will contribute to the family economy leaves little time or energy for them to participate in activities that enhance their intellectual development. Children also have no access to school in many parts of the country. Where there is access, many children do not attend. And if they do go, they often drop out before completing primary school in order to support themselves and their parents. Although children in both rural and urban areas make important contributions to the household economy, parents believe that children are not mature enough to participate in family discussions and decision making. Ethiopians belong to kinship groups, in which cooperation is emphasized and elders are valued for their experience. As a result, children are not encouraged to speak in public or in the presence of adults.

In the United States, however, children are raised to become independent members of society. They are not expected to contribute to the household economy; indeed, the law usually prevents them from working for wages until they are teenagers. Because raising children costs so much, many families keep the number of children to one or two whereas Ethiopian parents have six to seven children on the average. Parents in the United States invest in children and expect them to be successful in their education. Parents advise their children, guide them, and take their opinion seriously. Children are encouraged to converse with adults and express their views. They have the opportunity to enhance intellectual development beyond formal education by reading newspapers, television, museums, and movies.

Although Americans might consider their children to be coddled and immature, especially in comparison to children in developing nations, they can be quite mature. Their opportunities for education and intellectual growth allow them to be responsible and independent members of society at a relatively early age. In contrast, Ethiopians seem to assume that children are powerless and immature beings, even though economic needs force them to engage in arduous activities. The difference is not just the family's part in a kinship system, but also the minor role education plays in Ethiopian society due mostly to economic necessity.

are. Agriculture paved the way for the origin of the state, and most agriculturalists live in *states:* complex sociopolitical systems that administer a territory and populace with substantial contrasts in occupation, wealth, prestige, and power. In such societies, cultivators play their role as one part of a differentiated, functionally specialized, and tightly integrated sociopolitical system. The social and political implications of food production and intensification are examined more fully in the next chapter, "Political Systems."

PASTORALISM

Pastoralists live in North Africa, the Middle East, Europe, Asia, and sub-Saharan Africa. These herders are people whose activities focus on such domesticated animals as cattle, sheep, goats, camels, and yak. East African pastoralists, like many others, live in symbiosis with their herds. (*Symbiosis* is an obligatory interaction between groups—here humans and animals—that is beneficial to each.) Herders attempt to protect their animals and to ensure their reproduction in return for food and other products, such as leather. Herds provide dairy products, meat, and blood. Animals are killed at ceremonies, which occur throughout the year, and so meat is available regularly.

People use livestock in a variety of ways. Natives of North America's Great Plains, for example, didn't eat, but only rode, their horses. (Europeans reintroduced horses to the Western Hemisphere; the native American horse had become extinct thousands of years earlier.) For Plains Indians, horses served as "tools of the trade," means of production used to hunt buffalo, a main target of their economies. So the Plains Indians were not true pastoralists but *hunters* who used horses—as many agriculturalists use animals—as means of production.

Unlike the use of animals merely as productive machines, pastoralists typically make direct use of their herds for food. They consume their meat, blood, and milk, from which they make animals' yogurt, butter, and cheese. Although some pastoralists rely on their herds more completely than others do, it is impossible to base subsistence solely on animals. Most pastoralists therefore supplement their diet by hunting, gathering, fishing, cultivating, or trading. To get crops, pastoralists either trade with cultivators or do some cultivating or gathering themselves.

Unlike foraging and cultivation, which existed throughout the world before the Industrial Revolution, pastoralism was confined almost totally to the Old World. Before European conquest, the only pastoralists in the Americas lived in the Andean region of South America. They

ADAPTIVE STRATEGY	ALSO KNOWN AS	KEY FEATURES/VARIETIES
Foraging	Hunting-gathering	Mobility, use of nature's resources
Horticulture	Slash-and-burn, shifting cultivation, swiddening, dry farming	Fallow period
Agriculture	Intensive farming	Continuous use of land, intensive use of labor
Pastoralism	Herding	Nomadism and transhumance
Industrialism	Industrial production	Factory production, capitalism, socialist production

pastoralists
Herders of domesticated animals.

nomadism, pastoral
Annual movement of entire pastoral group with herds.

transhumance
Only part of population moves seasonally with herds.

used their llamas and alpacas for food and wool and in agriculture and transport. Much more recently, Navajo of the southwestern United States developed a pastoral economy based on sheep, which were brought to North America by Europeans. The populous Navajo became the major pastoral population in the Western Hemisphere.

Two patterns of movement occur with pastoralism: nomadism and transhumance. Both are based on the fact that herds must move to use pasture available in particular places in different seasons. In **pastoral nomadism,** the entire group—women, men, and children—moves with the animals throughout the year. The Middle East and North Africa provide numerous examples of pastoral nomads. In Iran, for example, the Basseri and the Qashqai ethnic groups traditionally followed a nomadic route more than 300 miles (480 kilometers) long. Starting each year near the coast, they took their animals to grazing land 17,000 feet (5,400 meters) above sea level (see Salzman 2004).

With **transhumance,** part of the group moves with the herds, but most people stay in the home village. There are examples from Europe and Africa. In Europe's Alps, it is just the shepherds and goatherds—not the whole village—who accompany the flocks to highland meadows in summer. Among the Turkana of Uganda, men and boys accompany the herds to distant pastures, while much of the village stays put and does some horticultural farming. Villages tend to be located in the best-watered areas, which have the longest pasture season. This permits the village population to stay together during a large chunk of the year.

During their annual trek, pastoral nomads trade for crops and other products with more sedentary people. Transhumants don't have to trade for crops. Because only part of the population accompanies the herds, transhumants can maintain year-round villages and grow their own crops. Recap 16.2 lists the main features of Cohen's adaptive strategies.

Pastoralists may be nomadic or transhumant, but they don't typically live off their herds alone. They either trade or cultivate. The photo at the top shows Shasavan tribespeople milking their sheep, east of Tabriz, Iran. Today, rugs made from their sheep wool are marketed on the Internet. Google "Shasavan" and see what comes up. The photo at the bottom shows a male Alpine shepherd in Germany. This man accompanies his flocks to highland meadows each year.

MODES OF PRODUCTION

An **economy** is a system of production, distribution, and consumption of resources; *economics* is the study of such systems. Economists tend to focus on modern nations and capitalist systems, while anthropologists have broadened understanding of economic principles by gathering data on nonindustrial economies. Economic anthropology studies economics in a comparative perspective (see Gudeman, ed. 1998; Plattner, ed. 1989; Sahlins 2004; Wilk 1996).

A **mode of production** is a way of organizing production—"a set of social relations through which labor is deployed to wrest energy from nature by means of tools, skills, organization, and knowledge" (Wolf 1982, p. 75). In the capitalist mode of production, money buys labor power, and there is a social gap between the people (bosses and workers) involved in the production process. By contrast, in nonindustrial societies, labor is not usually bought but is given as a social obligation. In such a *kin-based* mode of production, mutual aid in production is one among many expressions of a larger web of social relations.

Societies representing each of the adaptive strategies just discussed (e.g., foraging) tend to have a similar mode of production. Differences in the mode of production within a given strategy may reflect the differences in environments, target resources, or cultural traditions (Kelly 1995). Thus, a foraging mode of production may be based on individual hunters or teams, depending on whether the game is a solitary or a herd animal. Gathering is usually more individualistic than hunting, although collecting teams may assemble when abundant resources ripen and must be harvested quickly. Fishing may be done alone (as in ice fishing or spearfishing) or in crews (as with open-sea fishing and hunting of sea mammals).

Production in Nonindustrial Societies

Although some kind of division of economic labor related to age and gender is a cultural universal, the specific tasks assigned to each sex and to people of different ages vary. Many horticultural societies assign a major productive role to women, but some make men's work primary (see the chapter on gender for more on this). Similarly, among pastoralists, men generally tend large animals, but in some cultures women do the milking. Jobs accomplished through teamwork in some cultivating societies are done by smaller groups or individuals working over a longer period of time in others.

The Betsileo of Madagascar have two stages of teamwork in rice cultivation: transplanting and harvesting. Team size varies with the size of the field. Both transplanting and harvesting feature a traditional division of labor by age and gender that is well known to all Betsileo and is repeated across the generations. The first job in transplanting is the trampling of a previously tilled flooded field by young men driving cattle, in order to mix earth and water. They bring cattle to trample the fields just before transplanting. The young men yell at and beat the cattle, striving to drive them

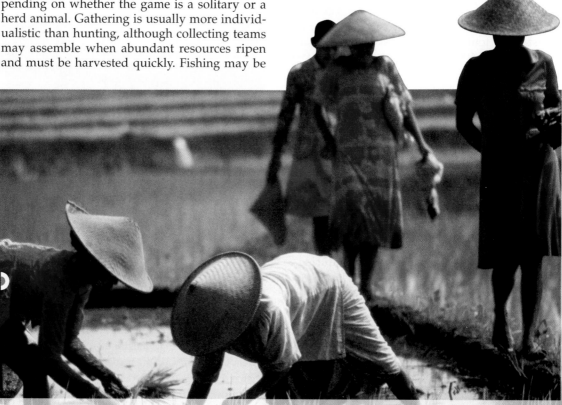

Women transplant rice seedlings in Banjar Negara, Indonesia. Transplanting and weeding are arduous tasks that especially strain the back.

into a frenzy so that they will trample the fields properly. Trampling breaks up clumps of earth and mixes irrigation water with soil to form a smooth mud into which women transplant seedlings. Once the tramplers leave the field, older men arrive. With their spades, they break up the clumps that the cattle missed. Meanwhile, the owner and other adults uproot rice seedlings and bring them to the field.

At harvest time, four or five months later, young men cut the rice off the stalks. Young women carry it to the clearing above the field. Older women arrange and stack it. The oldest men and women then stand on the stack, stomping and compacting it. Three days later, young men thresh the rice, beating the stalks against a rock to remove the grain. Older men then attack the stalks with sticks to make sure all the grains have fallen off.

Most of the other tasks in Betsileo rice cultivation are done by individual owners and their immediate families. All household members help weed the rice field. It's a man's job to till the fields with a spade or a plow. Individual men repair the irrigation and drainage systems and the earth walls that separate one plot from the next. Among other agriculturalists, however, repairing the irrigation system is a task involving teamwork and communal labor.

Means of Production

In nonindustrial societies, there is a more intimate relationship between the worker and the means of production than there is in industrial nations. **Means, or factors, of production** include land (territory), labor, and technology.

Land

Among foragers, ties between people and land were less permanent than among food producers. Although many bands had territories, the boundaries usually were not marked, and there was no way they could be enforced. The hunter's stake in an animal being stalked or hit with a poisoned arrow was more important than where the animal finally died. A person acquired the rights to use a band's territory by being born in the band or by joining it through a tie of kinship, marriage, or fictive kinship. In Botswana in southern Africa, Ju/'hoansi San women, whose work provided over half the food, habitually used specific tracts of berry-bearing trees. However, when a woman changed bands, she immediately acquired a new gathering area.

Among food producers, rights to the means of production also come through kinship and marriage. Descent groups (groups whose members claim common ancestry) are common among nonindustrial food producers, and those who descend from the founder share the group's territory

and resources. If the adaptive strategy is horticulture, the estate includes garden and fallow land for shifting cultivation. As members of a descent group, pastoralists have access to animals to start their own herds, to grazing land, to garden land, and to other means of production.

Labor, Tools, and Specialization

Like land, labor is a means of production. In nonindustrial societies, access to both land and labor comes through social links such as kinship, marriage, and descent. Mutual aid in production is merely one aspect of ongoing social relations that are expressed on many other occasions.

Nonindustrial societies contrast with industrial nations in regard to another means of production: technology. Manufacturing is often linked to age and gender. Women may weave and men may make pottery or vice versa. Most people of a particular age and gender share the technical knowledge associated with that age and gender. If married women customarily make baskets, all or most married women know how to make baskets. Neither technology nor technical knowledge is as specialized as it is in states.

However, some tribal societies do promote specialization. Among the Yanomami of Venezuela and Brazil (Figure 16.3), for instance, certain villages manufacture clay pots and others make hammocks. They don't specialize, as one might suppose, because certain raw materials happen to be available near particular villages. Clay suitable

means (or factors) of production Major productive resource, e.g., land, labor, technology, capital.

FIGURE 16.3 Location of the Yanomami.

for pots is widely available. Everyone knows how to make pots, but not everybody does so. Craft specialization reflects the social and political environment rather than the natural environment. Such specialization promotes trade, which is the first step in creating an alliance with enemy villages (Chagnon 1997). Specialization contributes to keeping the peace, although it has not prevented intervillage warfare.

Alienation in Industrial Economies

There are some significant contrasts between industrial and nonindustrial economies. When factory workers produce for sale and for their employer's profit, rather than for their own use, they may be alienated from the items they make. Such alienation means they don't feel strong pride in or personal identification with their products. They see their product as belonging to someone else, not to the man or woman whose labor actually produced it. In nonindustrial societies, by contrast, people usually see their work through from start to finish and have a sense of accomplishment in the product. The fruits of their labor are their own, rather than someone else's.

In nonindustrial societies, the economic relation between coworkers is just one aspect of a more general social relation. They aren't just coworkers but kin, in-laws, or celebrants in the same ritual. In industrial nations, people don't usually work with relatives and neighbors. If coworkers are friends, the personal relationship usually develops out of their common employment rather than being based on a previous association.

Thus, industrial workers have impersonal relations with their products, coworkers, and employers. People sell their labor for cash, and the economic domain stands apart from ordinary social life. In nonindustrial societies, however, the relations of production, distribution, and consumption are *social relations with economic aspects*. Economy is not a separate entity but is *embedded* in the society.

A Case of Industrial Alienation

For decades, the government of Malaysia has promoted export-oriented industry, allowing transnational companies to install labor-intensive manufacturing operations in rural Malaysia. The industrialization of Malaysia is part of a global strategy. In search of cheaper labor, corporations headquartered in Japan, Western Europe, and the United States have been moving labor-intensive factories to developing countries. Malaysia has hundreds of Japanese and American subsidiaries, which mainly produce garments, foodstuffs, and electronics components. In electronics plants in rural Malaysia, thousands of young women from peasant families now assemble microchips and microcomponents for transistors and capacitors.

Aihwa Ong (1987) did a study of electronics assembly workers in an area where 85 percent of the workers were young unmarried females from nearby villages.

Ong found that, unlike village women, female factory workers had to cope with a rigid work routine and constant supervision by men. The discipline that factories value was being taught in local schools, where uniforms helped prepare girls for the factory dress code. Village women wear loose, flowing tunics, sarongs, and sandals, but factory workers had to don tight overalls and heavy rubber gloves, in which they felt constrained. Assembling electronics components requires precise, concentrated labor. Demanding and depleting, labor in these factories illustrates the separation of intellectual and manual activity—the alienation that Karl Marx considered the defining feature of industrial work. One woman said about her bosses, "They exhaust us very much, as if they do not think that we too are human beings" (Ong 1987, p. 202). Nor does factory work bring women a substantial financial reward, given low wages, job uncertainty, and family claims on wages. Young women typically work just a few years. Production quotas, three daily shifts, overtime, and surveillance take their toll in mental and physical exhaustion.

One response to factory relations of production has been spirit possession (factory women are possessed by spirits). Ong interprets this phenomenon as the women's unconscious protest against labor discipline and male control of the industrial setting. Sometimes possession takes the form of mass hysteria. Spirits have simultaneously invaded as many as 120 factory workers. Weretigers (the Malay equivalent of the werewolf) arrive to avenge the construction of a factory on aboriginal burial grounds. Disturbed earth and grave spirits swarm on the shop floor. First the women see the spirits; then their bodies are invaded. The women become violent and scream abuses. The weretigers send the women into sobbing, laughing, and shrieking fits. To deal with possession, factories employ local medicine men, who sacrifice chickens and goats to fend off the spirits. This solution works only some of the time; possession still goes on. Factory women continue to act as vehicles to express their own frustrations and the anger of avenging ghosts.

Ong argues that spirit possession expresses anguish at, and resistance to, capitalist relations of production. By engaging in this form of rebellion, however, factory women avoid a direct confrontation with the source of their distress. Ong concludes that spirit possession, while expressing repressed resentment, doesn't do much to modify factory conditions. (Other tactics, such as unionization, would do more.) Spirit possession may even help maintain the current system by operating as a safety valve for accumulated tensions.

In Viet Nam, Malaysia, and other parts of Southeast Asia, hundreds of thousands of young women from peasant families now work in factories. With about 50,000 employees, Nike is Vietnam's largest private employer, exporting 22 million pairs of shoes annually. Shown here, a few of Nike's employees in Cu Chi, Viet Nam.

ECONOMIZING AND MAXIMIZATION

Economic anthropologists have been concerned with two main questions:

1. How are production, distribution, and consumption organized in different societies? This question focuses on *systems* of human behavior and their organization.

2. What motivates people in different cultures to produce, distribute or exchange, and consume? Here the focus is not on systems of behavior but on the motives of the *individuals* who participate in those systems.

Anthropologists view both economic systems and motivations in a cross-cultural perspective. Motivation is a concern of psychologists, but it also has been, implicitly or explicitly, a concern of economists and anthropologists. Economists tend to assume that producers and distributors make decisions rationally by using the *profit motive*, as do consumers when they shop around for the best value. Although anthropologists know that the profit motive is not universal, the assumption that individuals try to maximize profits is basic to the capitalist world economy and to much of Western economic theory. In fact, the subject matter of economics is often defined as **economizing,** or the rational allocation of scarce means (or resources) to alternative ends (or uses).

What does that mean? Classical economic theory assumes that our wants are infinite and that our means are limited. Since means are limited, people must make choices about how to use their scarce resources: their time, labor, money, and capital. (This chapter's "Appreciating Diversity" disputes the idea that people always make economic choices based on scarcity.) Economists assume that when confronted with choices and decisions, people tend to make the one that maximizes profit. This is assumed to be the most rational (reasonable) choice.

The idea that individuals choose to maximize profit was a basic assumption of the classical economists of the 19th century and one that is held by many contemporary economists. However, certain economists now recognize that individuals in Western cultures, as in others, may be motivated by many other goals. Depending on the society and the situation, people may try to maximize profit, wealth, prestige, pleasure, comfort, or social harmony. Individuals may want to realize their personal or family ambitions or those of another group to which they belong (see Sahlins 2004).

Alternative Ends

To what uses do people in various societies put their scarce resources? Throughout the world, people devote some of their time and energy to building up a *subsistence fund* (Wolf 1966). In other

economizing
Allocation of scarce means among alternative ends.

appreciating DIVERSITY

Scarcity and the Betsileo

In the realm of cultural diversity, perceptions and motivations vary in both place and time. Consider some changes I've observed among the Betsileo of Madagascar during the decades I've been studying them. Initially, compared with modern consumers, the Betsileo had little perception of scarcity. Now, with population increase and the spread of a cash-oriented economy, perceived wants and needs have increased relative to means. Motivations have changed, too, as people increasingly seek profits, even if it means stealing from their neighbors or destroying ancestral farms.

In the late 1960s my wife and I lived among the Betsileo people of Madagascar, studying their economy and social life (Kottak 1980). Soon after our arrival we met two well-educated schoolteachers (first cousins) who were interested in our research. The woman's father was a congressional representative who became a cabinet minister during our stay. Their family came from a historically important and typical Betsileo village called Ivato, which they invited us to visit with them.

We had traveled to many other Betsileo villages, where often we were displeased with our reception. As we drove up, children would run away screaming. Women would hurry inside. Men would retreat to doorways, where they lurked bashfully. This behavior expressed the Betsileo's great fear of the *mpakafo*. Believed to cut out and devour his victim's heart and liver, the mpakafo is the Malagasy vampire. These cannibals are said to have fair skin and to be very tall. Because I have light skin and stand over six feet tall, I was a natural suspect. The fact that such creatures were not known to travel with their wives helped convince the Betsileo that I wasn't really a mpakafo.

When we visited Ivato, its people were different—friendly and hospitable. Our very first day there we did a brief census and found out who lived in which households. We learned people's names and their relationships to our schoolteacher friends and to each other. We met an excellent informant who knew all about the local history. In a few afternoons I learned much more than I had in the other villages in several sessions.

Ivatans were so willing to talk because we had powerful sponsors, village natives who had made it in the outside world, people the Ivatans knew would protect them. The schoolteachers vouched for us, but even more significant was the cabinet minister, who was like a grandfather and benefactor to everyone in town. The Ivatans had no reason to fear us because their more influential native son had asked them to answer our questions.

Once we moved to Ivato, the elders established a pattern of visiting us every evening. They came to talk, attracted by the inquisitive

foreigners but also by the wine, tobacco, and food we offered. I asked questions about their customs and beliefs. I eventually developed interview schedules about various subjects, including rice production. I used these forms in Ivato and in two other villages I was studying less intensively. Never have I interviewed as easily as I did in Ivato.

As our stay neared its end, our Ivatan friends lamented, saying, "We'll miss you. When you leave, there won't be any more cigarettes, any more wine, or any more questions." They wondered what it would be like for us back in the United States. They knew we had an automobile and that we regularly purchased things, including the wine, cigarettes, and food we shared with them. We could afford to buy products they never would have. They commented, "When you go back to your country, you'll need a lot of money for things like cars, clothes, and food. We don't need to buy those things. We make almost everything we use. We don't need as much money as you, because we produce for ourselves."

The Betsileo weren't unusual for nonindustrial people. Strange as it may seem to an American consumer, those rice farmers actually believed *they had all they needed*. The lesson from the Betsileo of the 1960s is that scarcity, which economists view as universal, is variable. Although shortages do arise in nonindustrial societies, the concept of scarcity (insufficient means) is much less developed in stable subsistence-oriented societies than in the societies characterized by industrialism, particularly as the reliance on consumer goods increases.

words, they have to work to eat, to replace the calories they use in their daily activity. People also must invest in a *replacement fund*. They must maintain their technology and other items essential to production. If a hoe or plow breaks, they must repair or replace it. They also must obtain and replace items that are essential not to

production but to everyday life, such as clothing and shelter.

People also have to invest in a *social fund*. They have to help their friends, relatives, in-laws, and neighbors. It is useful to distinguish between a social fund and a *ceremonial fund*. The latter term refers to expenditures on ceremonies or rituals. To

But, with globalization over the past few decades, significant changes have affected the Betsileo—and most nonindustrial peoples. On my last visit to Ivato, in 2006, the effects of cash and of rapid population increase were evident there—and throughout Madagascar—where the national growth rate has been about 3 percent per year. Madagascar's population doubled between 1966 and 1991—from 6 to 12 million people. Today it stands near 18 million (Kottak 2004). One result of population pressure has been agricultural intensification. In Ivato, farmers who formerly had grown only rice in their rice fields now were using the same land for commercial crops, such as carrots, after the annual rice harvest. Another change affecting Ivato in recent years has been the breakdown of social and political order, fueled by increasing demand for cash.

Cattle rustling has become a growing threat. Cattle thieves (sometimes from neighboring villages) have terrorized peasants who previously felt secure in their villages. Some of the rustled cattle are driven to the coasts for commercial export to nearby islands. Prominent among the rustlers are relatively well-educated young men who have studied long enough to be comfortable negotiating with outsiders, but who have been unable to find formal work, and who are unwilling to work the rice fields like their peasant ancestors. The formal education system has familiarized them with external institutions and norms, including the need for cash. The concepts of scarcity, commerce, and negative reciprocity now thrive among the Betsileo.

Women hull rice in a Betsileo village. In the village of Ivato, farmers who traditionally grew only rice in their rice fields now use the same land for commercial crops, such as carrots, after the annual rice harvest.

I have witnessed other striking evidence of the new addiction to cash during my most recent visits to Betsileo country. Near Ivato's county seat, people now sell precious stones—tourmalines, which were found by chance in local rice fields. We saw an amazing sight: dozens of villagers destroying an ancestral resource, digging up a large rice field, seeking tourmalines—clear evidence of the encroachment of cash on the local subsistence economy.

Throughout the Betsileo homeland, population growth and density are propelling emigration. Locally, land, jobs, and money are all scarce. One woman with ancestors from Ivato, herself now a resident of the national capital (Antananarivo), remarked that half the children of Ivato now lived in that city. Although she was exaggerating, a census of all the descendants of Ivato reveals a substantial emigrant and urban population.

Ivato's recent history is one of increasing participation in a cash economy. That history, combined with the pressure of a growing population on local resources, has made scarcity not just a concept but a reality for Ivatans and their neighbors.

prepare a festival honoring one's ancestors, for example, requires time and the outlay of wealth.

Citizens of nonindustrial states also must allocate scarce resources to a *rent fund*. We think of rent as payment for the use of property. However, rent fund has a wider meaning. It refers to resources that people must render to an individual or agency that is superior politically or economically. Tenant farmers and sharecroppers, for example, either pay rent or give some of their produce to their landlords, as peasants did under feudalism.

Peasants are small-scale agriculturalists who live in nonindustrial states and have rent fund obligations (see Kearney 1996). They produce to

peasant
Small-scale farmer with rent fund obligations.

feed themselves, to sell their produce, and to pay rent. All peasants have two things in common:

1. They live in state-organized societies.

2. They produce food without the elaborate technology—chemical fertilizers, tractors, airplanes to spray crops, and so on—of modern farming or agribusiness.

In addition to paying rent to landlords, peasants must satisfy government obligations, paying taxes in the form of money, produce, or labor. The rent fund is not simply an *additional* obligation for peasants. Often it becomes their foremost and unavoidable duty. Sometimes, to meet the obligation to pay rent, their own diets suffer. The demands of paying rent may divert resources from subsistence, replacement, social, and ceremonial funds.

Motivations vary from society to society, and people often lack freedom of choice in allocating their resources. Because of obligations to pay rent, peasants may allocate their scarce means toward ends that are not their own but those of government officials. Thus, even in societies where there is a profit motive, people are often prevented from rationally maximizing self-interest by factors beyond their control.

DISTRIBUTION, EXCHANGE

The economist Karl Polanyi (1968) stimulated the comparative study of exchange, and several anthropologists followed his lead. To study exchange cross-culturally, Polanyi defined three principles orienting exchanges: the market principle, redistribution, and reciprocity. These principles can all be present in the same society, but in that case they govern different kinds of transactions. In any society, one of them usually dominates. The principle of exchange that dominates in a given society is the one that allocates the means of production.

The Market Principle

In today's world capitalist economy, the **market principle** dominates. It governs the distribution of the means of production: land, labor, natural resources, technology, and capital. "Market exchange refers to the organizational process of purchase and sale at money price" (Dalton, ed. 1967; Madra 2004). With market exchange, items are bought and sold, using money, with an eye to maximizing profit, and value is determined by the *law of supply and demand* (things cost more the scarcer they are and the more people want them).

Bargaining is characteristic of market-principle exchanges. The buyer and seller strive to maximize—to get their "money's worth." In bargaining, buyers and sellers don't need to meet personally. But their offers and counteroffers do need to be open for negotiation over a fairly short time period.

Redistribution

Redistribution operates when goods, services, or their equivalent move from the local level to a center. The center may be a capital, a regional collection point, or a storehouse near a chief's residence. Products often move through a hierarchy of officials for storage at the center. Along the way, officials and their dependents may consume some of them, but the exchange principle here is *re*distribution. The flow of goods eventually reverses direction—out from the center, down through the hierarchy, and back to the common people.

One example of a redistributive system comes from the Cherokee, the original owners of the Tennessee Valley. Productive farmers who subsisted on maize, beans, and squash, supplemented by hunting and fishing, the Cherokee had chiefs. Each of their main villages had a central plaza, where meetings of the chief's council took place, and where redistributive feasts were held. According to Cherokee custom, each family farm had an area where the family could set aside a portion of its annual harvest for the chief. This supply of corn was used to feed the needy, as well as travelers and warriors journeying through friendly territory. This store of food was available to all who needed it, with the understanding that it "belonged" to the chief and was dispersed through his generosity. The chief also hosted the redistributive feasts held in the main settlements (Harris 1978).

Reciprocity

Reciprocity is exchange between social equals, who are normally related by kinship, marriage, or another close personal tie. Because it occurs between social equals, it is dominant in the more egalitarian societies—among foragers, cultivators, and pastoralists. There are three degrees of reciprocity: generalized, balanced, and negative (Sahlins 1968, 2004; Service 1966). These may be imagined as areas of a continuum defined by these questions:

1. How closely related are the parties to the exchange?

2. How quickly and unselfishly are gifts reciprocated?

Generalized reciprocity, the purest form of reciprocity, is characteristic of exchanges between closely related people. In *balanced reciprocity*, social

redistribution
Flow of goods into center, then back out; characteristic of chiefdoms.

reciprocity
Principle governing exchanges among social equals.

market principle
Buying, selling, and valuation based on supply and demand.

distance increases, as does the need to reciprocate. In *negative reciprocity,* social distance is greatest and reciprocation is most calculated. This range, from generalized to negative, is called the **reciprocity continuum.**

living anthropology **VIDEOS**

Insurance Policies for Hunter-Gatherers?
www.mhhe.com/kottak

This clip features Polly Wiesnner, an ethnologist (cultural anthropologist) who has worked among the San ("Bushmen") for 25 years. The clip contrasts the foraging way of life with other economies in terms of storage, risk, and insurance against lean times. Industrial nations have banks, refrigerators, and insurance policies. Pastoralists have herds, which store meat and wealth on the hoof. Farmers have larders and granaries. How do the San anticipate and deal with hard times? What form of insurance do they have? What was it, according to Wiesnner, that allowed *Homo sapiens* to "colonize so many niches in this world"?

With **generalized reciprocity,** someone gives to another person and expects nothing concrete or immediate in return. Such exchanges (including parental gift giving in contemporary North America) are not primarily economic transactions but expressions of personal relationships. Most parents don't keep accounts of every penny they spend on their children. They merely hope that the children will respect their culture's customs involving love, honor, loyalty, and other obligations to parents.

Among foragers, generalized reciprocity has usually governed exchanges. People have routinely shared with other band members (Bird-David 1992; Kent 1992). A study of the Ju/'hoansi San (Figure 16.4) found that 40 percent of the population contributed little to the food supply (Lee 1968/1974). Children, teenagers, and people over 60 depended on other people for their food. Despite the high proportion of dependents, the average worker hunted or gathered less than half as much (12 to 19 hours a week) as the average American works. Nonetheless, there was always food because different people worked on different days.

So strong is the ethic of reciprocal sharing that most foragers have lacked an expression for "thank you." To offer thanks would be impolite because it would imply that a particular act of sharing, which is the keystone of egalitarian society, was unusual. Among the Semai, foragers of central Malaysia (Dentan 1979), to express gratitude would suggest

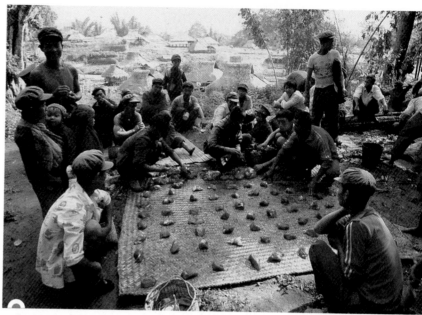

Sharing the fruits of production, a keystone of many nonindustrial societies, also has been a goal of socialist nations, such as China. These workers in Yunnan province strive for an equal distribution of meat.

surprise at the hunter's generosity or success (Harris 1974).

Balanced reciprocity applies to exchanges between people who are more distantly related than are members of the same band or household. In a horticultural society, for example, a man presents a gift to someone in another village. The recipient may be a cousin, a trading partner, or a brother's fictive kinsman. The giver expects something in return. This may not come immediately, but the social relationship will be strained if there is no reciprocation.

Exchanges in nonindustrial societies also may illustrate **negative reciprocity,** mainly in dealing with people outside or on the fringes of their social systems. To people who live in a world of close personal relations, exchanges with outsiders are full of ambiguity and distrust. Exchange is one way of establishing friendly relations with outsiders, but especially when trade begins, the relationship is still tentative. Often, the initial exchange is close to being purely economic; people want to get something back immediately. Just as in market economies, but without using money, they try to get the best possible immediate return for their investment.

Generalized and balanced reciprocity are based on trust and a social tie. But negative reciprocity involves the attempt to get something for as little as possible, even if it means being cagey or deceitful or cheating. Among the most extreme and "negative" examples of negative reciprocity was 19th-century horse thievery by North American Plains Indians. Men would sneak into camps

reciprocity continuum
Runs from generalized (closely related/deferred return) to negative (strangers/immediate return) reciprocity.

generalized reciprocity
Exchanges among closely related individuals.

balanced reciprocity
Midpoint on *reciprocity continuum,* between generalized and negative.

negative reciprocity
Potentially hostile exchanges among strangers.

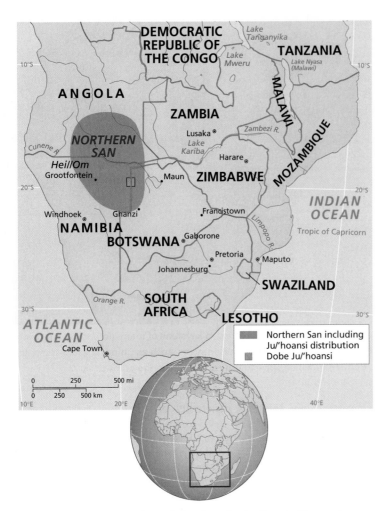

FIGURE 16.4 Location of the San, Including Ju/'hoansi.

Coexistence of Exchange Principles

In today's North America, the market principle governs most exchanges, from the sale of the means of production to the sale of consumer goods. We also have redistribution. Some of our tax money goes to support the government, but some of it also comes back to us in the form of social services, education, health care, and road building. We also have reciprocal exchanges. Generalized reciprocity characterizes the relationship between parents and children. However, even here the dominant market mentality surfaces in comments about the high cost of raising children and in the stereotypical statement of the disappointed parent: "We gave you everything money could buy."

Exchanges of gifts, cards, and invitations exemplify reciprocity, usually balanced. Everyone has heard remarks like "They invited us to their daughter's wedding, so when ours gets married, we'll have to invite them" and "They've been here for dinner three times and haven't invited us yet. I don't think we should ask them back until they do." Such precise balancing of reciprocity would be out of place in a foraging band, where resources are communal (common to all) and daily sharing based on generalized reciprocity is an essential ingredient of social life and survival.

POTLATCHING

One of the most thoroughly studied cultural practices known to ethnography is the **potlatch,** a festive event within a regional exchange system among tribes of the North Pacific Coast of North America, including the Salish and Kwakiutl of Washington and British Columbia and the Tsimshian of Alaska (Figure 16.5). Some tribes still practice the potlatch, sometimes as a memorial to the dead (Kan 1986, 1989). At each such event, assisted by members of their communities, potlatch sponsors traditionally gave away food, blankets, pieces of copper, or other items. In return for this, they got prestige. To give a potlatch enhanced one's reputation. Prestige increased with the lavishness of the potlatch, the value of the goods given away in it.

The potlatching tribes were foragers, but atypical ones. They were sedentary and had chiefs. They had access to a wide variety of land and sea resources. Among their most important foods were salmon, herring, candlefish, berries, mountain goats, seals, and porpoises (Piddocke 1969).

According to classical economic theory, the profit motive is universal, with the goal of maxi-

potlatch
Competitive feast on North Pacific Coast of North America.

and villages of neighboring tribes to steal horses. A similar pattern of cattle raiding continues today in East Africa, among tribes like the Kuria (Fleisher 2000). In these cases, the party that starts the raiding can expect reciprocity—a raid on their own village—or worse. The Kuria hunt down cattle thieves and kill them. It's still reciprocity, governed by "Do unto others as they have done unto you."

One way of reducing the tension in situations of potential negative reciprocity is to engage in "silent trade." One example is the silent trade of the Mbuti "pygmy" foragers of the African equatorial forest and their neighboring horticultural villagers. There is no personal contact during their exchanges. A Mbuti hunter leaves game, honey, or another forest product at a customary site. Villagers collect it and leave crops in exchange. Often the parties bargain silently. If one feels the return is insufficient, he or she simply leaves it at the trading site. If the other party wants to continue trade, it will be increased.

mizing material benefits. How then does one explain the potlatch, in which substantial wealth is given away (and even destroyed—see below)? Christian missionaries considered potlatching to be wasteful and antithetical to the Protestant work ethic. By 1885, under pressure from Indian Agents, missionaries, and Indian converts to Christianity, both Canada and the United States had outlawed potlatching. Between 1885 and 1951 the custom went underground. By 1951 both countries had discreetly dropped the antipotlatching laws from the books (Miller n.d.).

Some scholars seized on this view of the potlatch as a classic case of economically wasteful behavior. The economist and social commentator Thorstein Veblen cited potlatching as an example of conspicuous consumption in his influential book *The Theory of the Leisure Class* (1934), claiming that potlatching was based on an economically irrational drive for prestige. This interpretation stressed the lavishness and supposed wastefulness, especially of the Kwakiutl displays, to support the contention that in some societies people strive to maximize prestige at the expense of their material well-being. This interpretation has been challenged.

Ecological anthropology, also known as *cultural ecology*, is a theoretical school in anthropology that attempts to interpret cultural practices, such as the potlatch, in terms of their long-term role in helping humans adapt to their environments. A different interpretation of the potlatch has been offered by the ecological anthropologists Wayne Suttles (1960) and Andrew Vayda (1961/1968). These scholars see potlatching not in terms of its apparent wastefulness but in terms of its long-term role as a cultural adaptive mechanism. This view not only helps us understand potlatching; it also has comparative value because it helps us understand similar patterns of lavish feasting in many other parts of the world. Here is the ecological interpretation: *Customs like the potlatch are cultural adaptations to alternating periods of local abundance and shortage.*

How does this work? The overall natural environment of the North Pacific Coast is favorable, but resources fluctuate from year to year and place to place. Salmon and herring aren't equally abundant every year in a given locality. One village can have a good year while another is experiencing a bad one. Later their fortunes reverse. In this context, the potlatch cycle of the Kwakiutl and Salish had adaptive value, and the potlatch was not a competitive display that brought no material benefit.

A village enjoying an especially good year had a surplus of subsistence items, which it could trade for more durable wealth items, like blankets, canoes, or pieces of copper. Wealth, in turn, by being distributed, could be converted into

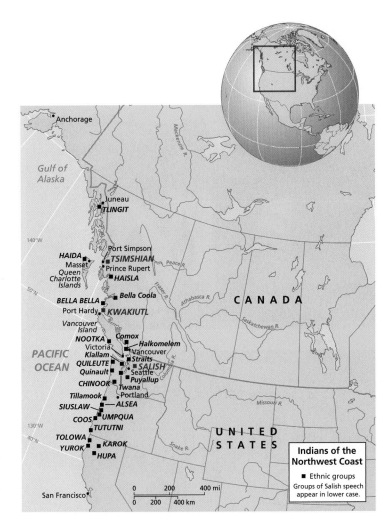

FIGURE 16.5 Location of Potlatching Groups.

prestige. Members of several villages were invited to any potlatch and got to take home the resources that were given away. In this way, potlatching linked villages together in a regional economy—an exchange system that distributed food and wealth from wealthy to needy communities. In return, the potlatch sponsors and their villages got prestige. The decision to potlatch was determined by the health of the local economy. If there had been subsistence surpluses, and thus a buildup of wealth over several good years, a village could afford a potlatch to convert its food and wealth into prestige.

The long-term adaptive value of intercommunity feasting becomes clear when we consider what happened when a formerly prosperous village had a run of bad luck. Its people started accepting invitations to potlatches in villages that were doing better. The tables were turned as the temporarily rich became temporarily poor and vice versa. The

The historic photo (above) shows the amassing of blankets to be given away at a Kwakiutl potlatch. The man in the foreground is making a speech praising the generosity of the potlatch host. In the context of a modern-day potlatch, the Canoe Journey (shown below) has been incorporated as a celebration of healing, hope, happiness, and hospitality. The annual Journey began with nine canoes paddling to Seattle in 1989. It continues today with more than 60 canoes and over 40,000 participants. The Journey honors a long history of transport and trade by the Coast Salish tribes, whose potlatch is discussed in the text.

newly needy accepted food and wealth items. They were willing to receive rather than bestow gifts and thus to relinquish some of their stored-up prestige. They hoped their luck would eventually improve so that resources could be recouped and prestige regained.

The potlatch linked local groups along the North Pacific Coast into a regional alliance and exchange network. Potlatching and intervillage exchange had adaptive functions, regardless of the motivations of the individual participants. The anthropologists who stressed rivalry for prestige were not wrong. They were merely emphasizing motivations at the expense of an analysis of economic and ecological systems.

The use of feasts to enhance individual and community reputations and to redistribute wealth is not peculiar to populations of the North Pacific Coast. Competitive feasting is widely characteristic of nonindustrial food producers. But among most foragers, who live, remember, in marginal areas, resources are too meager to support feasting on such a level. In such societies, sharing rather than competition prevails.

Like many other cultural practices that have attracted considerable anthropological attention, the potlatch does not, and did not, exist apart from larger world events. For example, within the spreading world capitalist economy of the 19th century, the potlatching tribes, particularly the Kwakiutl, began to trade with Europeans (fur for blankets, for example). Their wealth increased as a result. Simultaneously, a huge proportion of the Kwakiutl population died from previously unknown diseases brought by the Europeans. As a result, the increased wealth from trade flowed into a drastically reduced population. With many of the traditional sponsors dead (such as chiefs and their families), the Kwakiutl extended the right to give a potlatch to the entire population. This stimulated very intense competition for prestige. Given trade, increased wealth, and a decreased population, the Kwakiutl also started converting wealth into prestige by destroying wealth items such as blankets, pieces of copper, and houses (Vayda 1961/1968). Blankets and houses could be burned, and coppers could be buried at sea. Here, with dramatically increased wealth and a drastically reduced population, Kwakiutl potlatching changed its nature. It became much more destructive than it had been previously and than potlatching continued to be among tribes that were less affected by trade and disease.

In any case, note that potlatching also served to prevent the development of socioeconomic stratification, a system of social classes. Wealth relinquished or destroyed was converted into a nonmaterial item: prestige. Under capitalism, we reinvest our profits (rather than burning our cash), with the hope of making an additional profit. However, the potlatching tribes were content to relinquish their surpluses rather than use them to widen the social distance between themselves and their fellow tribe members.

Acing the COURSE

Summary

1. Cohen's adaptive strategies include foraging (hunting and gathering), horticulture, agriculture, pastoralism, and industrialism. Foraging was the only human adaptive strategy until the advent of food production (farming and herding) 10,000 years ago. Food production eventually replaced foraging in most places. Almost all modern foragers have at least some dependence on food production or food producers.

2. Horticulture and agriculture stand at opposite ends of a continuum based on labor intensity and continuity and land use. Horticulture doesn't use land or labor intensively. Horticulturalists cultivate a plot for one or two years and then abandon it. Further along the continuum, horticulture becomes more intensive, but there is always a fallow period. Agriculturalists farm the same plot of land continuously and use labor intensively. They use one or more of the following: irrigation, terracing, domesticated animals as means of production and manuring.

3. The pastoral strategy is mixed. Nomadic pastoralists trade with cultivators. Part of a transhumant pastoral population cultivates while another part takes the herds to pasture. Except for some Peruvians and the Navajo, who are recent herders, the New World lacks native pastoralists.

4. Economic anthropology is the cross-cultural study of systems of production, distribution, and consumption. In nonindustrial societies, a kin-based mode of production prevails. One acquires rights to resources and labor through membership in social groups, not impersonally through purchase and sale. Work is just one aspect of social relations expressed in varied contexts.

5. Economics has been defined as the science of allocating scarce means to alternative ends. Western economists assume that the notion of scarcity is universal—which it isn't—and that in making choices, people strive to maximize personal profit. In nonindustrial societies, indeed as in our own, people often maximize values other than individual profit.

6. In nonindustrial societies, people invest in subsistence, replacement, social, and ceremonial funds. States add a rent fund: People must share their output with social superiors. In states, the obligation to pay rent often becomes primary.

7. Besides production, economic anthropologists study and compare exchange systems. The three principles of exchange are the market principle, redistribution, and reciprocity. The market principle, based on supply and demand and the profit motive, dominates in states. With redistribution, goods are collected at a central place, but some of them are eventually given back, or redistributed, to the people. Reciprocity governs exchanges between social equals. It is the characteristic mode of exchange among foragers and horticulturists. Reciprocity, redistribution, and the market principle may coexist in a society, but the primary exchange mode is the one that allocates the means of production.

8. Patterns of feasting and exchanges of wealth among villages are common among nonindustrial food producers, as among the potlatching cultures of North America's North Pacific Coast. Such systems help even out the availability of resources over time.

Test Yourself!

MULTIPLE CHOICE

1. Typologies, such as Yehudi Cohen's *adaptive strategies,* are useful tools of analysis because
   a. they prove that there are causal relationships between economic and cultural variables.
   b. they suggest correlations—that is, association or covariation between two or more variables, such as economic and cultural variables.
   c. they suggest that economic systems are a better way of categorizing societies than relying on cultural patterns.
   d. they are strong predictive powers when analyzed in computer models.
   e. they have become common language among all anthropologists.

2. Which of the following statements about foraging societies is *not* true?
   a. Foraging societies are characterized by large-scale farming.
   b. All modern foraging societies depend to some extent on government assistance.
   c. All modern foraging societies have contact with other, nonforaging societies.
   d. Many foragers have easily incorporated modern technology, such as rifles and snowmobiles, into their subsistence activities.
   e. All modern foraging societies live in nation-states.

3. Which of the following is associated with horticultural systems of cultivation?
   a. intensive use of land and human labor
   b. use of irrigation and terracing
   c. use of draft animals
   d. periodic cycles of cultivation and fallowing
   e. location in arid areas

4. Which of the following statements about horticulture is true?
   a. It typically supports life in cities.
   b. It usually leads to the destruction of the soil through overuse.
   c. It can support permanent villages.
   d. It requires more labor than agriculture.
   e. It is usually associated with state-level societies.

5. Which of the following is the key factor that distinguishes agriculturalists from horticulturalists? Agriculturalists
   a. clear a tract of land they wish to use by cutting down trees and setting fire to the grass.
   b. use their land intensively and continuously.
   c. generally have much more leisure time at their disposal than do foragers.
   d. must be nomadic to take full advantage of their land.
   e. subsist on a more nutritious diet than do horticulturalists.

6. Which of the following is *not* one of the basic economic types found in nonindustrial societies?
   a. foraging
   b. agriculture
   c. horticulture
   d. hydroponics
   e. pastoralism

7. Which of the following is found in all adaptive strategies?
   a. transhumance
   b. a division of labor based on gender
   c. an emphasis on technology
   d. domestication of animals for food
   e. a strong positive correlation between the importance of kinship and complexity of subsistence technology

8. Economic alienation in industrial societies comes about as a result of
   a. separation from the product of one's labor.
   b. loss of land.
   c. a subculture of poverty.
   d. negative reciprocity.
   e. discontent due to low pay.

9. Which of the following statements about generalized reciprocity is true?
   a. It is characterized by the immediate return of the object exchanged.
   b. It usually develops after redistribution but before the market principle.
   c. It is the characteristic form of exchange in egalitarian societies.

d. It disappears with the origin of the state.
e. It is exemplified by silent trade.

10. Which of the following inhibits stratification?
    a. class endogamy
    b. caste notions of purity and pollution

c. monopoly on the legitimate use of force
d. ceremonial redistribution of material goods
e. control over ideology by elites

FILL IN THE BLANK

1. In nonindustrial societies, a _____ mode of production prevails.

2. The way a society's social relations are organized to produce the labor necessary for generating the society's subsistence and energy needs is known as the _____. _____ refer to society's major productive resources, such as land, labor, technology, and capital.

3. Economists tend to assume that producers and distributors make decisions rationally by using the _____ motive. Anthropologists, however, know that this motive is not universal.

4. When a farmer gives 20 percent of his crop to a landlord, he is contributing to his _____ fund.

5. The _____ is a festive event within a regional exchange system among tribes of the North Pacific Coast of North America. _____ anthropologists interpret this event as a cultural adaptation to alternating periods of local abundance and shortage, rejecting the belief that it illustrates economically wasteful and irrational behavior.

CRITICAL THINKING

1. When considering issues of "human nature," why should we remember that the egalitarian band was a basic form of human social life for most of our history?

2. Intensive agriculture has significant effects on social and environmental relations. What are some of these effects? Are they good or bad?

3. What does it mean when anthropologists describe nonindustrial economic systems as "embedded" in society?

4. What are your scarce means? How do you make decisions about allocating them?

5. Give examples from your own exchanges of different degrees of reciprocity. Why are anthropologists interested in studying exchange across cultures?

Means of production; 3. profit; 4. rent; 5. potlatch, Ecological

Multiple Choice: 1. (B); 2. (A); 3. (D); 4. (C); 5. (B); 6. (D); 7. (B); 8. (A); 9. (C); 10. (D); **Fill in the Blank:** 1. kin-based; 2. mode of production,

Bates, D. G.
    2005 *Human Adaptive Strategies: Ecology, Culture, and Politics*, 3rd ed. Boston: Pearson/Allyn & Bacon. Recent discussion of the different adaptive strategies and their political correlates.

Cohen, Y.
    1974 *Man in Adaptation: The Cultural Present*, 2nd ed. Chicago: Aldine. Presents Cohen's economic typology of adaptive strategies and uses it to organize a valuable set of essays on culture and adaptation.

Lee, R. B.
    2003 *The Dobe Ju/'hoansi*, 3rd ed. Belmont, CA: Wadsworth. Account of well-known San foragers, by one of their principal ethnographers.

Lee, R. B., and R. H. Daly
    1999 *The Cambridge Encyclopedia of Hunters and Gatherers*. New York: Cambridge University Press. Indispensable reference work on foragers.

Sahlins, M. D.
    2004 *Stone Age Economics*. New York: Routledge. A reprinted classic, with a new preface.

Salzman, P. C.
    2004 *Pastoralists: Equality, Hierarchy, and the State*. Boulder, CO: Westview. What we can learn from pastoralists about equality, freedom, and democracy.

Suggested Additional Readings

Go to our Online Learning Center website at **www.mhhe.com/kottak** for Internet exercises directly related to the content of this chapter.

Internet Exercises

- What kinds of political systems have existed worldwide, and what are their social and economic correlates?

- How does the state differ from other forms of political organization?

- What is social control, and how is it established and maintained in various societies?

State organized societies have formal governmental institutions, such as the German Reichstag (Parliament) in Berlin, shown here on a typical work day.

Political Systems

understanding OURSELVES

You've probably heard the expression "Big Man on Campus" used to describe a collegian who is very well-known and/or popular. One website (www.ehow.com/how_2112834_be-big-man-campus.html) offers advice about how to become a BMOC. According to that site, helpful attributes include lots of friends, a cool car, a hip wardrobe, a nice smile, a sports connection, and a sense of humor. "Big man" has a different but related meaning in anthropology. Many indigenous cultures of the South Pacific had a kind of political figure that anthropologists call the "big man." Such a leader achieved his status through hard work, amassing wealth in the form of pigs and other native riches. Characteristics that distinguished the big man from his fellows, enabling him to attract loyal supporters (aka lots of friends), included wealth, generosity, eloquence, physical fitness, bravery, and supernatural powers. Those who became big men did so because of their personalities rather than by inheriting their wealth or position.

Do any of the factors that make for a successful big man (or BMOC, for that matter) contribute to political success in a modern nation such as the United States? Although American politicians often use their own wealth, inherited or created, to finance campaigns, they also solicit labor and monetary contributions (rather than pigs) from supporters. And, like big men, successful American politicians try to be gen-

erous with their supporters. Payback may take the form of a night in the Lincoln bedroom, an invitation to a strategic dinner, an ambassadorship, or largesse to a particular area of the country. Tribal big men amass wealth and then give away pigs. Successful American politicians also dish out "pork."

As with the big man, eloquence and communication skills contribute to political success (e.g., Barack Obama, Bill Clinton, and Ronald Reagan), although lack of such skills isn't necessarily fatal (e.g., either President Bush). What about physical fitness? Hair, height, health (and even a nice smile) are certainly political advantages. Bravery, as demonstrated through distinguished military service, may help political careers, but it certainly isn't required. Nor does it guarantee success. Just ask John McCain, John Kerry, or Wesley Clark. Supernatural powers? Candidates who proclaim themselves atheists are as rare as self-identified witches. Almost all political candidates claim to belong to a mainstream religion. Some even present their policies as promoting God's will.

However, contemporary politics isn't just about personality, as it is in big man systems. We live in a state-organized, stratified society with inherited wealth, power, and privilege, all of which have political implications. As is typical of states, inheritance and kin connections play a role in political success. Just think of Kennedys, Bushes, Gores, Clintons, and Doles.

WHAT IS "THE POLITICAL"?

Anthropologists and political scientists share an interest in political systems and organization, but the anthropological approach is global and comparative, and in-

cludes nonstates as well as the states and nation-states usually studied by political scientists. Anthropological studies have revealed substantial variation in power (formal and informal), authority, and legal

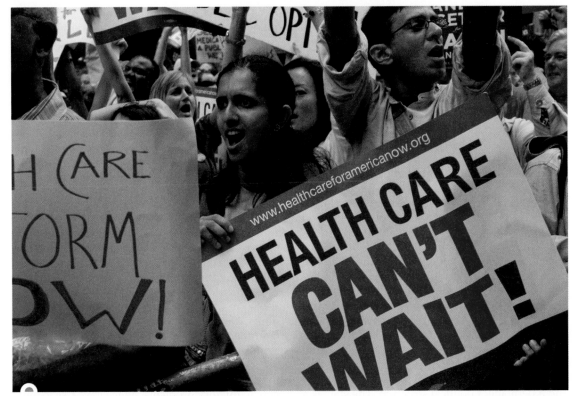

On August 29, 2009 in New York City, supporters of Health Care Reform demonstrate for a public option. Citizens routinely use collective action to influence public policy. Have your own actions ever influenced public policy?

systems in different societies and communities. (Power is the ability to exercise one's will over others; authority is the socially approved use of power.) (See Cheater, ed. 1999; Gledhill 2000; Kurtz 2001; Wolf with Silverman 2001.)

Recognizing that political organization is sometimes just an aspect of social organization, Morton Fried offered this definition:

> Political Organization comprises those portions of social organization that specifically relate to the individuals or groups that manage the affairs of public policy or seek to control the appointment or activities of those individuals or groups. (Fried 1967, pp. 20–21)

This definition certainly fits contemporary North America. Under "individuals or groups that manage the affairs of public policy" come federal, state (provincial), and local (municipal) governments. Those who seek to control the activities of the groups that manage public policy include such interest groups as political parties, unions, corporations, consumers, activists, action committees, religious groups, and nongovernmental organizations (NGOs).

Fried's definition is much less applicable to nonstates, where it was often difficult to detect any "public policy." For this reason, I prefer to speak of *socio*political organization in discussing

the regulation or management of interrelations among groups and their representatives. In a general sense, regulation is the process that ensures that variables stay within their normal ranges, corrects deviations from the norm, and thus maintains a system's integrity. In the case of political regulation, this includes such things as decision making, social control, and conflict resolution. The study of political regulation draws our attention to those who make decisions and resolve conflicts (are there formal leaders?).

Ethnographic and archaeological studies in hundreds of places have revealed many correlations between economy and social and political organization.

TYPES AND TRENDS

Decades ago, the anthropologist Elman Service (1962) listed four types, or levels, of political organization: band, tribe, chiefdom, and state. Today, none of these political entities (*polities*) can be studied as a self-contained form of political organization, since all exist within nation-states and are subject to state control. There is archaeological evidence for early bands, tribes, and chiefdoms that existed before the first states appeared. However, since anthropology came into being long after the origin of the state, anthropologists have never been able to observe "in the flesh" a band, tribe, or chiefdom outside the influence of some state. All the bands, tribes, and chiefdoms known to ethnography have been within the borders of a state. There still may be local political leaders (e.g., village heads) and regional figures (e.g., chiefs) of the sort discussed in this chapter, but all exist and function within the context of state organization.

A *band* refers to a small *kin-based* group (all the members are related to each other by kinship or marriage ties) found among foragers. **Tribes** had economies based on nonintensive food production (horticulture and pastoralism). Living in villages and organized into kin groups based on common descent (clans and lineages), tribes lacked a formal government and had no reliable means of enforcing political decisions. *Chiefdom* refers to a form of sociopolitical organization intermediate between the tribe and the state. In chiefdoms, social relations were based mainly on kinship, marriage, descent, age, generation, and gender—just as they were in bands and tribes. Although chiefdoms were kin-based, they featured differential access to resources (some people had more wealth, prestige, and power than others) and a permanent political structure. The state is a form of sociopolitical organization based on a formal government structure and socioeconomic stratification.

The four labels in Service's typology are much too simple to account for the full range of political diversity and complexity known to archaeology and ethnography. We'll see, for instance, that tribes have varied widely in their political sys-

tribe
Food-producing society with rudimentary political structure.

tems and institutions. Nevertheless, Service's typology does highlight some significant contrasts in political organization, especially those between states and nonstates. For example, in bands and tribes—unlike states, which have clearly visible governments—political organization did not stand out as separate and distinct from the total social order. In bands and tribes, it was difficult to characterize an act or event as political rather than merely social.

Service's labels "band," "tribe," "chiefdom," and "state" are categories or types within a *sociopolitical typology*. These types are correlated with the adaptive strategies (economic typology) discussed in the chapter "Making a Living." Thus, foragers (an economic type) tended to have band organization (a sociopolitical type). Similarly, many horticulturalists and pastoralists lived in tribal societies (or, more simply, tribes). Although most chiefdoms had farming economies, herding was important in some Middle Eastern chiefdoms. Nonindustrial states usually had an agricultural base.

With food production came larger, denser populations and more complex economies than was the case among foragers. These features posed new regulatory problems, which gave rise to more complex relations and linkages. Many sociopolitical trends reflect the increased regulatory demands associated with food production. Archaeologists have studied these trends through time, and cultural anthropologists have observed them among contemporary groups.

BANDS AND TRIBES

This chapter examines a series of societies with different political systems. A common set of questions will be addressed for each one. What kinds of social groups does the society have? How do people affiliate with those groups? How do the groups link up with larger ones? How do the groups represent themselves to each other? How are their internal and external relations regulated? To answer these questions, we begin with bands and tribes and then move on to chiefdoms and states.

Foraging Bands

Modern hunter-gatherers should not be seen as representative of Stone Age peoples, all of whom also were foragers. Just how much can contemporary and recent foragers tell us about the economic and social relations that characterized humanity before food production? Modern foragers, after all, live in nation-states and an interlinked world. For generations, the pygmies of Congo have shared a social world and economic exchanges with their neighbors who are cultivators. All foragers now trade with food producers. Most

Among tropical foragers, women make an important economic contribution through gathering, as is true among the San shown here in Namibia. What evidence do you see in this photo that contemporary foragers participate in the modern world system?

contemporary hunter-gatherers rely on governments and on missionaries for at least part of what they consume.

The San

In the chapter "Making a Living," we saw how the Basarwa San are affected by policies of the government of Botswana, which relocated them after converting their ancestral lands into a wildlife reserve (Motseta 2006). The government of Botswana is not the first to implement policies and systems that affect the Basarwa San. San speakers ("Bushmen") of southern Africa have been influenced by Bantu speakers (farmers and herders) for 2,000 years and by Europeans for centuries. Edwin Wilmsen (1989) argues that many San descend from herders who were pushed into the desert by poverty or oppression. He sees the San today as a rural underclass in a larger political and economic system dominated by Europeans and Bantu food producers. As a result of this system, many San now tend cattle for wealthier Bantu rather than foraging independently. They also have domesticated animals, indicating their movement away from their foraging lifestyle.

Susan Kent (1992, 1996) notes a tendency to stereotype foragers, to treat them all as alike. They used to be stereotyped as isolated, primitive survivors of the Stone Age. A new stereotype sees them as culturally deprived people forced by states, colonialism, or world events into marginal environments. Although this view often is exaggerated, it probably is more accurate than the former one. Modern foragers differ substantially from Stone Age hunter-gatherers.

Kent (1996) stresses variation among foragers, focusing on diversity in time and space among the San. The nature of San life has changed considerably since the 1950s and 1960s, when a series of anthropologists from Harvard University, including Richard Lee, embarked on a systematic study of life in the Kalahari. Lee and others have documented many of the changes in various publications (Lee 1979, 1984, 2003; Silberbauer 1981; Tanaka 1980). Such longitudinal research monitors variation in time, while field work in many San areas has revealed variation in space. One of the most important contrasts was found to be that between settled (sedentary) and nomadic groups (Kent and Vierich 1989). Although sedentism has increased substantially in recent years, some San groups (along rivers) have been sedentary for generations. Others, including the Dobe Ju/'hoansi San studied by Lee (1984, 2003) and the Kutse San that Kent studied, have retained more of the hunter-gatherer lifestyle.

Modern foragers are not Stone Age relics, living fossils, lost tribes, or noble savages. Still, to the extent that foraging has been the basis of their subsistence, contemporary and recent hunter-gatherers can illustrate links between a foraging economy and other aspects of society and culture. For example, San groups that still are mobile, or that were so until recently, emphasize social, political, and gender equality. A social system based on kinship, reciprocity, and sharing is appropriate for an economy with few people and limited resources. The nomadic pursuit of wild plants and animals tends to discourage permanent settlement, wealth accumulation, and status distinctions. In this context, families and bands have been adaptive social units. People have to share meat when they get it; otherwise it rots.

Foraging *bands*, small, nomadic or seminomadic social units, formed seasonally when component nuclear families got together. The particular families in a band varied from year to year. Marriage and kinship created ties between members of different bands. Trade and visiting also linked them. Band leaders were leaders in name only. In such an egalitarian society, they were first among equals. Sometimes they gave advice or made decisions, but they had no way to enforce their decisions.

The Inuit

The aboriginal Inuit (Hoebel 1954, 1954/1968), another group of foragers, provide a good example of methods of settling disputes—**conflict resolution**—in stateless societies. All societies have ways of settling disputes (of variable effectiveness) along with cultural rules or norms about proper and improper behavior. *Norms* are cultural standards or guidelines that enable individuals to distinguish between appropriate and inappropriate behavior in a given society (N. Kottak 2002). While rules and norms are cultural universals, only state societies, those with established governments, have formal laws that are formulated, proclaimed, and enforced.

Foragers lacked formal **law** in the sense of a legal code with trial and enforcement. The absence of law did not entail total anarchy. As described by E. A. Hoebel (1954) in a study of Inuit conflict resolution, a sparse population of some 20,000 Inuit spanned 6,000 miles (9,500 kilometers) of the Arctic region (Figure 17.1). The most significant social groups were the nuclear family and the band. Personal relationships linked the families and bands. Some bands had headmen. There were also shamans (part-time religious specialists). However, these positions conferred little power on those who occupied them.

Hunting and fishing by men were the primary Inuit subsistence activities. The diverse and abundant plant foods available in warmer areas, where female labor in gathering is important, were absent in the Arctic. Traveling on land and sea in a bitter environment, Inuit men faced more dangers than women did. The traditional male role took its toll in lives. Adult women would have outnumbered men substantially without

conflict resolution
Means of settling disputes.

law
Legal code of a state society, with trial and enforcement.

FIGURE 17.1 Location of the Inuit.

occasional female infanticide (killing of a baby), which Inuit culture permitted.

Despite this crude (and to us unthinkable) means of population regulation, there were still more adult women than men. This permitted some men to have two or three wives. The ability to support more than one wife conferred a certain amount of prestige, but it also encouraged envy. (*Prestige* is esteem, respect, or approval for culturally valued acts or qualities.) If a man seemed to be taking additional wives just to enhance his reputation, a rival was likely to steal one of them. Most disputes were between men and originated over women, caused by wife stealing or adultery. If a man discovered that his wife had been having sexual relations without his permission, he considered himself wronged.

Although public opinion would not let the husband ignore the matter, he had several options. He could try to kill the wife stealer. However, if he succeeded, one of his rival's kinsmen would surely try to kill him in retaliation. One dispute could escalate into several deaths as relatives avenged a succession of murders. No government existed to intervene and stop such a *blood feud* (a murderous feud between families). However, one also could challenge a rival to a song battle. In a public setting, contestants made up insulting songs about each other. At the end of the match, the audience judged one of them the winner. However, if a man whose wife had been stolen won, there was no guarantee she would return. Often she would decide to stay with her abductor.

Thefts are common in societies with marked property differentials, like our own, but thefts are uncommon among foragers. Each Inuit had access to the resources needed to sustain life. Every man could hunt, fish, and make the tools necessary for subsistence. Every woman could obtain the materials needed to make clothing, prepare food, and do domestic work. Inuit men could even hunt and fish in the territories of other local groups. There was no notion of private ownership of territory or animals. However, certain minor personal items were associated with a specific person. In various societies, such items include things such as arrows, a tobacco pouch, clothing, and personal ornaments. One of the most basic Inuit beliefs was that "all natural resources are free or common goods" (Hoebel 1954/1968). Band-organized societies usually lack differential access to strategic resources. If people want something from someone else, they ask for it, and usually it is given.

Tribal Cultivators

As is true with foraging bands, there are no totally autonomous tribes in today's world. Still, there are societies, for example, in Papua New Guinea and in South America's tropical forests, in which tribal principles still operate. Tribes typically have a horticultural or pastoral economy and are organized by village life and/or membership in *descent groups* (kin groups whose members trace descent from a common ancestor). Tribes lack socioeconomic stratification (i.e., a class structure) and a formal government of their own. A few tribes still conduct small-scale warfare, in the form of intervillage raiding. Tribes have more effective regulatory mechanisms than foragers do, but tribal societies have no sure means of enforcing political decisions. The main regulatory officials are village heads, "big men," descent-group leaders, village councils, and leaders of pantribal associations. All these figures and groups have limited authority.

Like foragers, horticulturalists tend to be egalitarian, although some have marked gender stratification: an unequal distribution of resources, power, prestige, and personal freedom between men and women. Horticultural villages are usually small, with low population density and open access to strategic resources. Age, gender, and personal traits determine how much respect people receive and how much support they get from others. Egalitarianism diminishes, however, as village size and population density increase. Horticultural villages usually have headmen—rarely, if ever, headwomen.

The Village Head

The Yanomami (Chagnon 1997) are Native Americans who live in southern Venezuela and the adjacent part of Brazil. Their tribal society has about 20,000 people living in 200 to 250 widely scattered villages, each with a population between 40 and 250. The Yanomami are horticulturalists who also hunt and gather. Their staple crops are bananas and plantains (a bananalike crop). There are more significant social groups among the Yanomami than exist in a foraging society. The Yanomami have families, villages, and descent groups. Their

descent groups, which span more than one village, are patrilineal (ancestry is traced back through males only) and exogamous (people must marry outside their own descent group). However, local branches of two different descent groups may live in the same village and intermarry.

As has been true in many village-based tribal societies, the only leadership position among the Yanomami is that of **village head** (always a man). His authority, like that of a foraging band's leader, is severely limited. If a headman wants something done, he must lead by example and persuasion. The headman lacks the right to issue orders. He can only persuade, harangue, and try to influence public opinion. For example, if he wants people to clean up the central plaza in preparation for a feast, he must start sweeping it himself, hoping that his covillagers will take the hint and relieve him.

 living anthropology **VIDEOS**

Leadership among the Canela, www. mhhe.com/kottak

This clip features ethnographer Bill Crocker, who has worked among the Canela for more than 40 years, and Raimundo Roberto, a respected ceremonial chief, who has been Crocker's key cultural consultant during that entire time. Raimundo discusses his role in Canela society, mentioning the values of generosity, sharing, and comforting words. How does this clip illustrate differences between leadership in a tribal society and leadership in our own? Does Raimundo have formal authority? Compare him to the Yanomami village head and the band leader discussed in this chapter. The clip also shows a mending ceremony celebrating the healing of a rift that once threatened Canela society.

When conflict erupts within the village, the headman may be called on as a mediator who listens to both sides. He will give an opinion and advice. If a disputant is unsatisfied, the headman can do nothing. He has no power to back his decisions and no way to impose punishments. Like the band leader, he is first among equals.

A Yanomami village headman also must lead in generosity. Because he must be more generous than any other villager, he cultivates more land. His garden provides much of the food consumed when his village holds a feast for another village. The headman represents the village in its dealings with outsiders. Sometimes he visits other villages to invite people to a feast. The way a person acts as headman depends on his personal traits and the number of supporters he can muster. One village headman, Kaobawa, intervened in a dispute between a husband and a wife and kept him from killing her (Chagnon 1968). He also guaranteed

head, village
Local tribal leader with limited authority.

Yanomami Update: Venezuela Takes Charge, Problems Arise

Appreciating the complexity of culture means recognizing that human beings never have lived in isolation from other groups. The cultural practices that link people include marriage, religion (e.g., the missionization described here), trade, travel, exploration, warfare, and conquest. As we see in this account, local people today must heed not only their own customs but also a diversity of laws, policies, and decisions made by outsiders. As you read this account, pay attention to the various interest groups involved and how their goals and wishes might clash. Also consider the various levels of political regulation (local, regional, national, and international) that determine how contemporary people such as the Yanomami live their lives and strive to maintain their health, autonomy, and cultural traditions. Consider as well the effectiveness of Yanomami leaders in dealing with agents of the Venezuelan state.

PUERTO AYACUCHO, Venezuela—Three years after President Hugo Chávez expelled American missionaries from the Venezuelan Amazon, accusing them of using proselytism of remote tribes as a cover for espionage, resentment is festering here over what some tribal leaders say was official negligence. . . .

Some leaders of the Yanomami, one of South America's largest forest-dwelling tribes, say that 50 people in their communities in the southern rain forest have died since the expulsion of the missionaries in 2005 because of recurring shortages of medicine and fuel, and unreliable transportation out of the jungle to medical facilities.

Mr. Chávez's government disputes the claims and points to more spending than ever on social welfare programs for the Yanomami. The spending is part of a broader plan to assert greater military and social control over expanses of rain forest that are viewed as essential for Venezuela's sovereignty . . .

In recent interviews here, government officials contended that the Yanomami could be exaggerating their claims to win more resources from the government and undercut its authority in the Amazon. . . .

The Yanomami claims come amid growing concern in Venezuela over indigenous health care after a scandal erupted in August over a tepid official response to a mystery disease that killed 38 Warao Indians in the country's northeast.

"This government makes a big show of helping the Yanomami, but rhetoric is one thing and reality another," said Ramón González, 49, a Yanomami leader from the village of Yajanamateli who traveled recently to Puerto Ayacucho, the capital of Amazonas State, to ask military officials and civilian doctors for improved health care.

"The truth is that Yanomami lives are still considered worthless," said Mr. González. "The boats, the planes, the money, it's all for the criollos, not for us," he said, using a term for nonindigenous Venezuelans. . . .

There are about 26,000 Yanomami in the Amazon rain forest, in Venezuela and Brazil, where they subsist as seminomadic hunters and cultivators of crops like manioc and bananas.

They remain susceptible to ailments for which they have weak defenses, including respiratory diseases and drug-resistant strains of malaria. In Puerto Ayacucho, they can be seen wandering through the traffic-clogged streets, clad in the modern uniform of T-shirts and baggy pants, toting cellphones. . . .

Mr. González and other Yanomami leaders provided the names of 50 people, including 22 children, who they said died from ailments like malaria and pneumonia after the military limited civilian and missionary flights to their villages in 2005. The military replaced the missionaries' operations with its own fleet of small planes and helicopters, but critics say the missions were infrequent or unresponsive.

The Yanomami leaders said they made the list public after showing it to health and military safety to a delegation from a village with which a covillager of his wanted to start a war. Kaobawa was a particularly effective headman. He had demonstrated his fierceness in battle, but he also knew how to use diplomacy to avoid offending other villagers. No one in the village had a better personality for the headmanship. Nor (because Kaobawa had many brothers) did anyone have more supporters. Among the Yanomami, when a group is dissatisfied with a village headman, its members can leave and found a new village; this is done from time to time.

Yanomami society, with its many villages and descent groups, is more complex than a band-organized society. The Yanomami also face more regulatory problems. A headman sometimes can prevent a specific violent act, but there is no government to maintain order. In fact, intervillage raiding in which men are killed and women are captured has been a feature of some areas of Yanomami territory, particularly those studied by Chagnon (1997).

We also must stress that the Yanomami are not isolated from outside events, including missionization (although there still may be uncontacted villages). The Yanomami live in two nation-states, Venezuela and Brazil, and external warfare waged by Brazilian ranchers and miners increasingly has officials and receiving a cold response. "They told us we should be grateful for the help we're already being given," said Eduardo Mejía, 24, a Yanomami leader from the village of El Cejal.

"The missionaries were in Amazonas for 50 years, creating dependent indigenous populations in some places, so their withdrawal was bound to have positive and negative effects," said Carlos Botto, a senior official with Caicet, a government research institute that focuses on tropical diseases.

"But one cannot forget that the Yanomami and other indigenous groups have learned how to exert pressure on the government in order to receive food or other benefits," he said. "This does not mean there aren't challenges in providing them with health care, but caution is necessary with claims like these."

The dispute has also focused attention on an innovative government project created in late 2005, the Yanomami Health Plan. With a staff of 46, it trains some Yanomami to be health workers in their villages while sending doctors into the jungle to provide health care to remote communities.

"We have 14 doctors in our team, with 11 trained in Cuba for work in jungle areas," said Meydell Simancas, 32, a tropical disease specialist who directs the project from a compound here once owned by New Tribes Mission.

Dr. Simancas said that more than 20 Yanomami had been trained as paramedics,

Shown here, as part of a public health outreach program, Julio Guzman, an indigenous Yanomami, has his eyes checked by a Venezuelan government doctor.

and that statistics showed that doctors had increased immunizations and programs to control malaria and river blindness across Amazonas.

The Yanomami leaders complaining of negligence acknowledged Dr. Simancas's good intentions. But they said serious problems persisted in coordinating access to doctors and medicine with the military, which the Yanomami and government doctors both rely on for travel in and out of the rain forest. . . .

Yanomami leaders point to what they consider to be a broad pattern of neglect and condescension from public officials . . .

threatened them (Chagnon 1997; *Cultural Survival Quarterly* 1989; Ferguson 1995). During a Brazilian gold rush between 1987 and 1991, one Yanomami died each day, on average, from external attacks (including biological warfare—introduced diseases to which the Indians lack resistance). By 1991, there were some 40,000 Brazilian miners in the Yanomami homeland. Some Indians were killed outright. The miners introduced new diseases, and the swollen population ensured that old diseases became epidemic. In 1991, a commission of the American Anthropological Association reported on the plight of the Yanomami. Brazilian Yanomami were dying at a rate of 10 percent an-

nually, and their fertility rate had dropped to zero. Since then, both the Brazilian and the Venezuelan governments have intervened to protect the Yanomami. One Brazilian president declared a huge Yanomami territory off-limits to outsiders. Unfortunately, since then local politicians, miners, and ranchers often have managed to evade the ban. The future of the Brazilian Yanomami remains uncertain.

As we see in this chapter's "Appreciating Diversity," the Venezuelan Yanomami today must heed not only their own customs but also laws, policies, and decisions made by outsiders. Various levels of political regulation (local, regional, national, and international) now determine how contemporary people such as the Yanomami live their lives.

The "Big Man"

In many areas of the South Pacific, particularly the Melanesian Islands and Papua New Guinea, native cultures had a kind of political leader that we call the "big man." The **big man** (almost always a male) was an elaborate version of the village head, but with one significant difference. The village head's leadership is within one village; the big man had supporters in several villages. The big man therefore was a regulator of regional political organization.

The Kapauku Papuans live in Irian Jaya, Indonesia (which is on the island of New Guinea) (Figure 17.2). Anthropologist Leopold Pospisil (1963) studied the Kapauku (45,000 people), who grow crops (with the sweet potato as their staple) and raise pigs. Their economy is too complex to be described as simple horticulture. The only political figure among the Kapauku was the big man, known as a *tonowi*. A tonowi achieved his status through hard work, amassing wealth in the form of pigs and other native riches. Characteristics that distinguished a big man from his fellows included wealth, generosity, eloquence, physical fitness, bravery, and supernatural powers. Men became big men because they had certain personalities. They had to amass

resources during their own lifetimes, as they did not inherit their wealth or position.

A man who was determined enough could become a big man, creating wealth through hard work and good judgment. Wealth resulted from successful pig breeding and trading. As a man's pig herd and prestige grew, he attracted supporters. He sponsored ceremonial pig feasts in which pigs were slaughtered and their meat distributed to guests.

Unlike the Yanomami village head, a big man's wealth exceeded that of his fellows. His supporters, recognizing his past favors and anticipating future rewards, recognized him as a leader and accepted his decisions as binding. The big man was an important regulator of regional events in Kapauku life. He helped determine the dates for feasts and markets. He persuaded people to sponsor feasts, which distributed pork and wealth. He initiated economic projects requiring the cooperation of a regional community.

The Kapauku big man again exemplifies a generalization about leadership in tribal societies: If someone achieves wealth and widespread respect and support, he or she must be generous. The big man worked hard not to hoard wealth but to be able to give away the fruits of his labor, to convert wealth into prestige and gratitude. A stingy big man would lose his support, his reputation plummeting. The Kapauku might take even more extreme measures against big men who hoarded wealth. Selfish and greedy men sometimes were murdered by their fellows.

Kapauku cultivation has used varied techniques for specific kinds of land. Labor-intensive cultivation in valleys involves mutual aid in turning the soil before planting. The digging of long drainage ditches, which a big man often helped organize, is even more complex. Kapauku plant cultivation supports a larger and denser population than does the simpler horticulture of the Yanomami. Kapauku society could not survive in its current form without collective cultivation and political regulation of the more complex economic tasks.

Pantribal Sodalities and Age Grades

Big men could forge regional political organization—albeit temporarily—by mobilizing people from different villages. Other social and political mechanisms in tribal societies, such as a belief in common ancestry, kinship, or descent, could be used to link local groups within a region. The same descent group, for example, might span several villages, and its dispersed members might follow a descent-group leader.

Principles other than kinship also can link local groups. In a modern nation, a labor union, national sorority or fraternity, political party, or religious denomination may provide such a nonkin-based link. In tribes, nonkin groups called

big man
Generous tribal entrepreneur with multivillage support.

The "big man" persuades people to organize feasts, which distribute pork and wealth. Shown here is such a regional event, drawing on several villages, in Papua New Guinea. Big men owe their status to their individual personalities rather than to inherited wealth or position. Does our society have equivalents of big men?

associations or sodalities may serve the same linking function. Often, sodalities are based on common age or gender, with all-male sodalities more common than all-female ones.

Pantribal sodalities (those that extend across the whole tribe, spanning several villages) sometimes arose in areas where two or more different cultures came into regular contact. Such sodalities were especially likely to develop in the presence of warfare between tribes. Drawing their membership from different villages of the same tribe, pantribal sodalities could mobilize men in many local groups for attack or retaliation against another tribe.

In the cross-cultural study of nonkin groups, we must distinguish between those that are confined to a single village and those that span several local groups. Only the latter, the pantribal groups, are important in general military mobilization and regional political organization. Localized men's houses and clubs, limited to particular villages, are found in many horticultural societies in tropical South America, Melanesia, and Papua New Guinea. These groups may organize village activities and even intervillage raiding, but their leaders are similar to village heads and their political scope is mainly local. The following discussion concerns pantribal groups.

The best examples of pantribal sodalities come from the Central Plains of North America and from tropical Africa. During the 18th and 19th centuries, native populations of the Great Plains of the United States and Canada experienced a rapid growth of pantribal sodalities. This development reflected an economic change that followed the spread of horses, which had been reintroduced to the Americas by the Spanish, to the states between the Rocky Mountains and the Mississippi River. Many Plains Indian societies changed their adaptive strategies because of the horse. At first, they had been foragers who hunted bison (buffalo) on foot. Later, they adopted a mixed economy based on hunting, gathering, and horticulture. Finally, they changed to a much more specialized economy based on horseback hunting of bison (eventually with rifles).

As the Plains tribes were undergoing these changes, other Indians also adopted horseback hunting and moved into the Plains. Attempting to occupy the same area, groups came into conflict. A pattern of warfare developed in which the members of one tribe raided another, usually for horses. The new economy demanded that people follow the movement of the bison herds. During the winter, when the bison dispersed, a tribe fragmented into small bands and families. In the summer, as huge herds assembled on the Plains, members of the tribe reunited. They camped together for social, political, and religious activities, but mainly for communal bison hunting.

Only two activities in the new adaptive strategy demanded strong leadership: organizing and

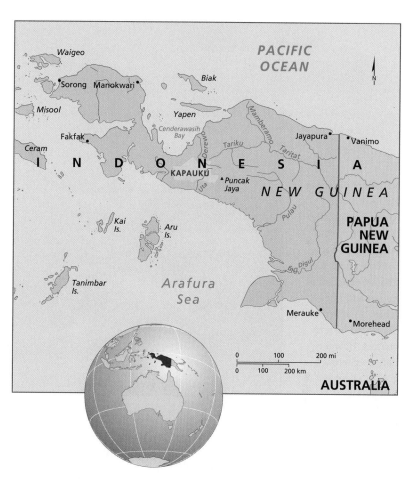

FIGURE 17.2 Location of the Kapauku.

carrying out raids on enemy camps (to capture horses) and managing the summer bison hunt. All the Plains cultures developed pantribal sodalities, and leadership roles within them, to police the summer hunt. Leaders coordinated hunting efforts, making sure that people did not cause a stampede with an early shot or an ill-advised action. Leaders imposed severe penalties, including seizure of a culprit's wealth, for disobedience.

Some of the Plains sodalities were **age sets** of increasing rank. Each set included all the men—from that tribe's component bands—born during a certain time span. Each set had its distinctive dance, songs, possessions, and privileges. Members of each set had to pool their wealth to buy admission to the next higher level as they moved up the age hierarchy. Most Plains societies had pantribal warrior associations whose rituals celebrated militarism. As noted previously, the leaders of these associations organized bison hunting and raiding. They also arbitrated disputes during the summer, when large numbers of people came together.

Many of the tribes that adopted this Plains strategy of adaptation had once been foragers for whom hunting and gathering had been individual or small-group affairs. They never had come together previously as a single social unit. Age

sodality, pantribal
Nonkin-based group with regional political significance.

age set
Unisex (usually male) political group; includes everyone born within a certain time span.

Natives of the Great Plains of North America originally hunted bison (buffalo) on foot, using the bow and arrow. The introduction of horses and rifles fueled a pattern of horse raiding and warfare. How far had the change gone, as depicted in this painting?

and gender were available as social principles that could quickly and efficiently forge unrelated people into pantribal groups.

Raiding of one tribe by another, this time for cattle rather than horses, also was common in eastern and southeastern Africa, where pantribal sodalities, including age sets, also developed. Among the pastoral Masai of Kenya and Tanzania (Figure 17.3), men born during the same four-year period were circumcised together and belonged to the same named group, an age set, throughout their lives. The sets moved through grades, the most important of which was the warrior grade. Members of the set who wished to enter the warrior grade were at first discouraged by its current occupants, who eventually vacated the warrior grade and married. Members of a set felt a strong allegiance to one another and eventually had sexual rights to each other's wives. Masai women lacked comparable set organization, but they also passed through culturally recognized age grades: the initiate, the married woman, and the postmenopausal woman.

To understand the difference between an age set and an age grade, think of a college class, the Class of 2012, for example, and its progress through the university. The age set would be the group of people constituting the Class of 2012, while the first ("freshman"), sophomore, junior, and senior years would represent the age grades.

Not all cultures with age grades also have age sets. When there are no sets, men can enter or leave a particular grade individually or collectively, often by going through a predetermined ritual. The grades most commonly recognized in Africa are these:

1. Recently initiated youths.

2. Warriors.

3. One or more grades of mature men who play important roles in pantribal government.

4. Elders, who may have special ritual responsibilities.

In certain parts of West Africa and Central Africa, the pantribal sodalities are *secret societies*, made up exclusively of men or women. Like our college fraternities and sororities, these associations have secret initiation ceremonies. Among the Mende of Sierra Leone, men's and women's secret societies are very influential. The men's group, the Poro, trains boys in social conduct, ethics, and religion and supervises political and economic activities. Leadership roles in the Poro often overshadow village headship and play an important part in social control, dispute management, and tribal political regulation. Like descent, then, age, gender, and ritual can link members of different local groups into a single social collectivity in tribal society and thus create a sense of ethnic identity, of belonging to the same cultural tradition.

Nomadic Politics

Although many pastoralists, such as the Masai, had tribal sociopolitical organization, a range of demographic and sociopolitical diversity occurs with pastoralism. A comparison of pastoralists shows that as regulatory problems increase, political hierarchies become more complex. Political organization becomes less personal, more formal, and less kinship-oriented. The pastoral strategy of adaptation does not dictate any particular political organization. A range of authority structures manage regulatory problems associated with specific environments. Some pastoralists have traditionally existed as well-defined ethnic groups in nation-states. This reflects pastoralists' need to interact with other populations—a need that is less characteristic of the other adaptive strategies.

The scope of political authority among pastoralists expands considerably as regulatory problems increase in densely populated regions. Consider two Iranian pastoral nomadic tribes: the Basseri and the Qashqai (Salzman 1974). Starting each year from a plateau near the coast, these groups took their animals to grazing land 17,000 feet (5,400 meters) above sea level. The Basseri and the Qashqai shared this route with one another and with several other ethnic groups (Figure 17.4).

Use of the same pasture land at different times was carefully scheduled. Ethnic-group movements were tightly coordinated. Expressing this schedule is *il-rah,* a concept common to all Iranian nomads. A group's *il-rah* is its customary path in time and space. It is the schedule, different for each group, of when specific areas can be used in the annual trek.

Each tribe had its own leader, known as the *khan* or *il-khan.* The Basseri *khan,* because he dealt with a smaller population, faced fewer problems in coordinating its movements than did the leaders of the Qashqai. Correspondingly, his rights, privileges, duties, and authority were weaker. Nevertheless, his authority exceeded that of any political figure we have discussed so far. However, the *khan*'s authority still came from his personal traits rather than from his office. That is, the Basseri followed a particular *khan* not because of a political position he happened to fill but because of their personal allegiance and loyalty to him as a man. The *khan* relied on the support of the heads of the descent groups into which Basseri society was divided.

In Qashqai society, however, allegiance shifts from the person to the office. The Qashqai had multiple levels of authority and more powerful chiefs or *khans.* Managing 400,000 people required a complex hierarchy. Heading it was the *il-khan,* helped by a deputy, under whom were the heads of constituent tribes, under each of whom were descent-group heads.

A case illustrates just how developed the Qashqai authority structure was. A hailstorm prevented some nomads from joining the annual migration at the appointed time. Although everyone

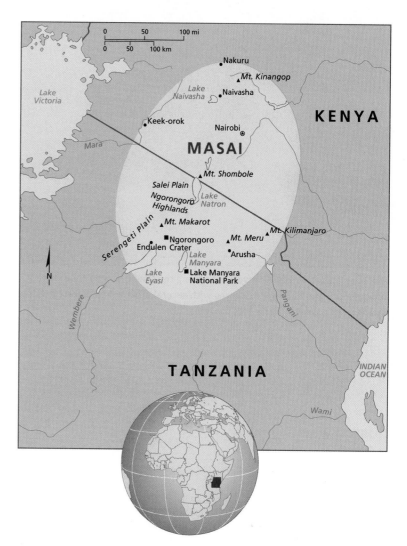

FIGURE 17.3 Location of the Masai.

Among the Masai of Kenya and Tanzania, men born during the same four-year period were circumcised together. They belonged to the same named group, an age set, throughout their lives. The sets moved through grades, of which the most important was the warrior grade. Here we see the warrior (*ilmurran*) age grade dancing with a group of girls of a lower age grade (*intoyie*). Do we have any equivalents of age sets or grades in our own society?

Political organization is well developed among the Qashqai, who share their nomadic route and strategic resources with several other tribes. Here, Qashqai nomads cross a river in Iran's Fars province.

recognized that they were not responsible for their delay, the *il-khan* assigned them less favorable grazing land, for that year only, in place of their usual pasture. The tardy herders and other Qashqai considered the judgment fair and didn't question it. Thus, Qashqai authorities regulated the annual migration. They also adjudicated disputes between people, tribes, and descent groups.

These Iranian cases illustrate the fact that pastoralism is often just one among many specialized economic activities within complex nation-states and regional systems. As part of a larger whole, pastoral tribes are constantly pitted against other ethnic groups. In these nations, the state becomes a final authority, a higher-level regulator that attempts to limit conflict between ethnic groups. State organization arose not just to manage agricultural economies but also to regulate the activities of ethnic groups within expanding social and economic systems.

CHIEFDOMS

Having looked at bands and tribes, we turn to more complex forms of sociopolitical organization: chiefdoms and states. The first states emerged in the Old World about 5,500 years ago. The first chiefdoms developed perhaps a thousand years earlier, but few survive today. In many parts of the world the chiefdom was a transitional form of organization that emerged during the evolution of tribes into states. State formation began in Mesopotamia (currently Iran and Iraq). It next occurred in Egypt, the Indus Valley of Pakistan and India, and northern China. A few thousand years later, states also arose in two parts of the Western Hemisphere: Mesoamerica (Mexico, Guatemala, Belize) and the central Andes (Peru and Bolivia). Early states are known as *archaic states*, or nonindustrial states, in contrast to modern industrial nation-states. Robert Carneiro defines the state as "an autonomous political unit encompassing many communities within its territory, having a centralized government with the power to collect taxes, draft men for work or war, and decree and enforce laws" (Carneiro 1970, p. 733).

The chiefdom and the state, like many categories used by social scientists, are *ideal types*. That is, they are labels that make social contrasts seem sharper than they really are. In reality, there is a continuum from tribe to chiefdom to state. Some societies have many attributes of chiefdoms but retain tribal features. Some advanced chiefdoms have many attributes of archaic states and thus are difficult to assign to either category. Recognizing this "continuous change" (Johnson and Earle, eds. 2000), some anthropologists speak of "complex chiefdoms" (Earle 1987), which are almost states.

FIGURE 17.4 Location of the Basseri and Qashqai.

Political and Economic Systems in Chiefdoms

Areas with chiefdoms included the circum-Caribbean (e.g., Caribbean islands, Panama, Colombia), lowland Amazonia, what is now the southeastern United States, and Polynesia. Between the emergence and spread of food production and the expansion of the Roman empire, much of Europe was organized at the chiefdom level, to which it reverted for centuries after the fall of Rome in the fifth century A.D. Chiefdoms created the megalithic cultures of Europe, such as the one that built Stonehenge. Bear in mind that chiefdoms and states can fall (disintegrate) as well as rise.

Much of our ethnographic knowledge about chiefdoms comes from Polynesia (Kirch 2000), where they were common at the time of European exploration. In chiefdoms, social relations are mainly based on kinship, marriage, descent, age, generation, and gender—as they are in bands and tribes. This is a basic difference between chiefdoms and states. States bring nonrelatives together and oblige them to pledge allegiance to a government.

Unlike bands and tribes, however, chiefdoms are characterized by *permanent political regulation* of the territory they administer. Chiefdoms might include thousands of people living in many villages and/or hamlets. Regulation was carried out by the chief and his or her assistants, who occupied political offices. An **office** is a permanent position, which must be refilled when it is vacated by death or retirement. Because offices were systematically refilled, the structure of a chiefdom endured across the generations, ensuring permanent political regulation.

In the Polynesian chiefdoms, the chiefs were full-time political specialists in charge of regulating the economy—production, distribution, and consumption. Polynesian chiefs relied on religion to buttress their authority. They regulated production by commanding or prohibiting (using religious taboos) the cultivation of certain lands and crops. Chiefs also regulated distribution and consumption. At certain seasons—often on a ritual occasion such as a first-fruit ceremony—people would offer part of their harvest to the chief through his or her representatives. Products moved up the hierarchy, eventually reaching the chief. Conversely, illustrating obligatory sharing with kin, chiefs sponsored feasts at which they gave back much of what they had received.

Such a flow of resources to and then from a central office is known as *chiefly redistribution*. Redistribution offers economic advantages. If the different areas specialized in particular crops, goods, or services, chiefly redistribution made those products available to the whole society. Chiefly redistribution also played a role in risk management. It stimulated production beyond

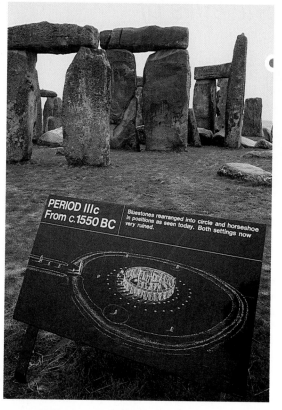

Stonehenge, England, and an educational display designed for tourists and visitors. Chiefdoms created the megalithic cultures of Europe, such as the one that built Stonehenge over 5,000 years ago. Between the emergence and spread of food production and the expansion of the Roman empire, much of Europe was organized at the chiefdom level, to which it reverted after the fall of Rome.

the immediate subsistence level and provided a central storehouse for goods that might become scarce at times of famine (Earle 1987, 1991). Chiefdoms and archaic states had similar economies, often based on intensive cultivation, and both administered systems of regional trade or exchange.

office
Permanent political position.

Social Status in Chiefdoms

Social status in chiefdoms was based on seniority of descent. Because rank, power, prestige, and resources came through kinship and descent, Polynesian chiefs kept extremely long genealogies. Some chiefs (without writing) managed to trace their ancestry back 50 generations. All the people in the chiefdom were thought to be related to each other. Presumably, all were descended from a group of founding ancestors.

The status of chief was ascribed, based on seniority of descent. The chief would

This photo, taken in 1981 in Neiafu, Savaii, Western Samoa, shows an orator chief, or *tula-fale*. His speaking staff and the fly whisk over his shoulder symbolize his status as a tula-fale. Traditional amoa provides one example of a Polynesian chiefdom. How do chiefs differ from ordinary people?

through the eyes of OTHERS

NAME: Jose Nicolas Cabrera-Schneider, M.S., M.A. Candidate

COUNTRY OF ORIGIN: **Guatemala**

SUPERVISING PROFESSOR: Carleen Sanchez

SCHOOL: University of Nebraska

Comparing Political Parties in Guatemala and the United States

My home country of Guatemala suffered 36 years of civil war starting in the 1960s. During the war, military and paramilitary forces implemented a policy of oppression and persecution toward anyone who did not share the ideology held by the military leaders of the moment. One result of this policy of oppression and persecution was the elimination of institutions, such as political parties, that promoted the formation of political leaders. In 1986 Guatemala returned to the democratic path, and in 1996 Guatemalan factions signed peace accords that allowed and promoted the formation of political parties. By 2003 the stage was set for the participation of many candidates, who attempted to convince Guatemalan voters that they were the best choice for president.

I arrived in the United States at the end of 2003, having left Guatemala just before an election took place—the fourth election since Guatemala returned to democratic government. During that 2003 election, there were about 10 political groups, each supporting its own candidate for president. The year after my arrival in Ann Arbor, Michigan, national elections were held in the United States. I was surprised that there were only two major parties presenting candidates for president. This observation made me wonder why Guatemala has so many political parties compared to the United States. After comparing the two election processes, I came up with some answers.

In effect, the presence of so many political parties in Guatemala is an attempt by the candidates to fill the vacuum of leader-generating institutions created by the civil war. In Guatemala, political parties are formed to express and enact the ideas of a small number of individuals, not the ideologies of a structured organization. This allows the governing group to rule in favor of a few, benefiting the group in the short run. However without a vision for the governing of the entire nation, the various political parties have little opportunity to remain in power. One result of this lack of structural organization in political parties is that a party dissolves if its candidates don't win an election, and the parties with few offices still have to survive power struggles within. This affects the chances for an individual to climb the political ladder. Most American presidential candidates, however, have climbed the political ladder; for example, they move from local elected positions to governor, member of the House, or senator, positions in which they share ideas for governing with members of the same large political group. Either major party can call on a number of people to lead it.

in turn would rank below the first. The children of an eldest brother, however, would all rank above the children of the next brother, whose children would in turn outrank those of younger brothers. However, even the lowest-ranking person in a chiefdom was still the chief's relative. In such a kin-based context, everyone, even a chief, had to share with his or her relatives.

Because everyone had a slightly different status, it was difficult to draw a line between elites and common people. Although other chiefdoms calculated seniority differently and had shorter genealogies than did those in Polynesia, the concern for genealogy and seniority and the absence of sharp gaps between elites and commoners were features of all chiefdoms.

Status Systems in Chiefdoms and States

The status systems of chiefdoms and states are similar in that both are based on **differential access** to resources. This means that some men and women had privileged access to power, prestige, and wealth. They controlled strategic resources such as land and water. Earle characterizes chiefs as "an incipient aristocracy with advantages in wealth and lifestyle" (1987, p. 290). Nevertheless, differential access in chiefdoms was still very much tied to kinship. The people with privileged access were generally chiefs and their nearest relatives and assistants.

Compared with chiefdoms, archaic states drew a much firmer line between elites and masses, distinguishing at least between nobles and commoners. Kinship ties did not extend from the nobles to the commoners because of *stratum endogamy*—marriage within one's own group. Commoners married commoners; elites married elites.

Such a division of society into socioeconomic strata contrasts strongly with bands and tribes, whose status systems are based on prestige, rather than on differential access to resources. The prestige differentials that do exist in bands reflect special qualities and abilities. Good hunters get respect from their fellows as long as they are generous. So does a skilled curer, dancer, storyteller—or anyone else with a talent or skill that others appreciate.

In tribes, some prestige goes to descent-group leaders, to village heads, and especially to the big man, a regional figure who commands the loyalty and labor of others. However, all these figures must be generous. If they accumulate more resources—that is, property or food—than others in the village, they must share them with the others. Since strategic resources are available to everyone, social classes based on the possession of unequal amounts of resources can never exist.

In many tribes, particularly those with patrilineal descent, men have much greater prestige

---

differential access
Favored access to resources by superordinates over subordinates.

be the oldest child (usually son) of the oldest child of the oldest child, and so on. Degrees of seniority were calculated so intricately on some islands that there were as many ranks as people. For example, the third son would rank below the second, who

SOCIOPOLITICAL TYPE	ECONOMIC TYPE	EXAMPLES	TYPE OF REGULATION
Band	Foraging	Inuit, San	Local
Tribe	Horticulture, pastoralism	Yanomami, Kapauku, Masai	Local, temporary regional
Chiefdom	Productive horticulture, pastoral nomadism, agriculture	Qashqai, Polynesia, Cherokee	Permanent regional
State	Agriculture, industrialism	Ancient Mesopotamia, contemporary United States and Canada	Permanent regional

and power than women do. The gender contrast in rights could diminish in chiefdoms, where prestige and access to resources were based on seniority of descent, so that some women were senior to some men. Unlike big men, chiefs were exempt from ordinary work and had rights and privileges that were unavailable to the masses. However, like big men, they still gave back much of the wealth they took in.

Stratification

The status system in chiefdoms, although based on differential access, differed from the status system in states because the privileged few were always relatives and assistants of the chief. However, this type of status system didn't last very long. Chiefs would start acting like kings and try to erode the kinship basis of the chiefdom. In Madagascar, they would do this by demoting their more distant relatives to commoner status and banning marriage between nobles and commoners (Kottak 1980). Such moves, *if accepted by the society,* created separate social strata—*unrelated* groups that differ in their access to wealth, prestige, and power. (A *stratum* is one of two or more groups that contrast in regard to social status and access to strategic resources. Each stratum includes people of both sexes and all ages.) The creation of separate social strata is called *stratification,* and its emergence signified the transition from chiefdom to state. *The presence and acceptance of stratification is one of the key distinguishing features of a state.*

The influential sociologist Max Weber (1922/ 1968) defined three related dimensions of social stratification: (1) Economic status, or **wealth,** encompasses all a person's material assets, including income, land, and other types of property. (2) **Power,** the ability to exercise one's will over others—to do what one wants—is the basis of political status. (3) **Prestige**—the basis of social status—refers to esteem, respect, or approval for acts, deeds, or qualities considered exemplary. Prestige, or "cultural capital" (Bourdieu 1984),

TABLE 17.1 Max Weber's Three Dimensions of Stratification

wealth	=>	economic status
power	=>	political status
prestige	=>	social status

provides people with a sense of worth and respect, which they may often convert into economic and political advantage (Table 17.1).

In archaic states—for the first time in human evolution—there were contrasts in wealth, power, and prestige between entire groups (social strata) of men and women. Each stratum included people of both sexes and all ages. The **superordinate** (the higher or elite) stratum had privileged access to wealth, power, and other valued resources. Access to resources by members of the **subordinate** (lower or underprivileged) stratum was limited by the privileged group.

Socioeconomic stratification continues as a defining feature of all states, archaic or industrial. The elites control a significant part of the means of production, for example, land, herds, water, capital, farms, or factories. Those born at the bottom of the hierarchy have reduced chances of social mobility. Because of elite ownership rights, ordinary people lack free access to resources. Only in states do the elites get to keep their differential wealth. Unlike big men and chiefs, they don't have to give it back to the people whose labor has built and increased it.

STATES

Recap 17.1 summarizes the information presented so far on bands, tribes, chiefdoms, and states. States, remember, are autonomous political units with social classes and a formal government, based on law. States tend to be large and populous, compared to bands, tribes, and chiefdoms. Certain statuses, systems, and subsystems with

superordinate
Upper, privileged, group in a stratified society.

subordinate
Lower, underprivileged, group in a stratified society.

wealth
All a person's material assets; basis of economic status.

power
Ability to control others; basis of political status.

prestige
Esteem, respect, or approval.

Lottery winners pose for photographs at a grocery store in Fond du Lac, Wisconsin. Are these new millionaires likely to gain prestige, or just money, from their luck?

anthropology **ATLAS**

Map 13 shows the global distribution of organized states and chiefdoms on the eve of European colonization.

specialized functions are found in all states. They include the following:

1. *Population control:* fixing of boundaries, establishment of citizenship categories, and the taking of a census.

2. *Judiciary:* laws, legal procedure, and judges.

3. *Enforcement:* permanent military and police forces.

4. *Fiscal:* taxation.

In archaic states, these subsystems were integrated by a ruling system or government composed of civil, military, and religious officials (Fried 1960).

Population Control

To know whom they govern, all states conduct censuses. States demarcate boundaries that separate them from other societies. Customs agents, immigration officers, navies, and coast guards patrol frontiers. Even nonindustrial states have boundary-maintenance forces. In Buganda, an archaic state on the shores of Lake Victoria in Uganda, the king rewarded military officers with estates in outlying provinces. They became his guardians against foreign intrusion.

States also control population through administrative subdivision: provinces, districts, "states," counties, subcounties, and parishes. Lower-level officials manage the populations and territories of the subdivisions.

In nonstates, people work and relax with their relatives, in-laws, fictive kin, and agemates—people with whom they have a personal relationship. Such a personal social life existed throughout most of human history, but food production spelled its eventual decline. After millions of years of human evolution, it took a mere 4,000 years for the population increase and regulatory problems spawned by food production to lead from tribe to chiefdom to state. With state organization, kinship's pervasive role diminished. Descent groups may continue as kin groups within states, but their importance in political organization declines.

States foster geographic mobility and resettlement, severing long-standing ties among people, land, and kin. Population displacements have increased in the modern world. War, famine, and job seeking across national boundaries churn up migratory currents. People in states come to identify themselves by new statuses, both ascribed and achieved, including ethnic background, place of birth or residence, occupation, party, religion, and team or club affiliation, rather than only as members of a descent group or extended family.

States also manage their populations by granting different rights and obligations to citizens and noncitizens. Status distinctions among citizens are also common. Many archaic states granted different rights to nobles, commoners, and slaves. Unequal rights within state-organized societies persist in today's world. In recent American history, before the Emancipation Proclamation, there were different laws for slaves and free people. In

European colonies, separate courts judged cases involving only natives and those that involved Europeans. In contemporary America, a military code of justice and court system continue to coexist alongside the civil judiciary.

Judiciary

States have laws, enforced legal codes, based on precedent and legislative proclamations. Without writing, laws may be preserved in oral tradition, with justices, elders, and other specialists responsible for remembering them. Oral traditions as repositories of legal wisdom have continued in some nations with writing, such as Great Britain. Laws regulate relations between individuals and groups.

Crimes are violations of the legal code, with specified types of punishment. However, a given act, such as killing someone, may be legally defined in different ways (e.g., as manslaughter, justifiable homicide, or first-degree murder). Furthermore, even in contemporary North America, where justice is supposed to be "blind" to social distinctions, the poor are prosecuted more often and more severely than are the rich.

To handle disputes and crimes, all states have courts and judges. Precolonial African states had subcounty, county, and district courts, plus a high court formed by the king or queen and his or her advisers. Most states allow appeals to higher courts, although people are encouraged to solve problems locally.

A striking contrast between states and nonstates is intervention in family affairs. In states, aspects of parenting and marriage enter the domain of public law. Governments step in to halt blood feuds and regulate previously private disputes. States attempt to curb *internal* conflict, but they aren't always successful. About 85 percent of the world's armed conflicts since 1945 have begun within states—in efforts to overthrow a ruling regime or as disputes over tribal, religious, and ethnic minority issues. Only 15 percent have been fights across national borders (Barnaby 1984). Rebellion, resistance, repression, terrorism, and warfare continue. Indeed, recent states have perpetrated some of history's bloodiest deeds.

Enforcement

All states have agents to enforce judicial decisions. Confinement requires jailers, and a death penalty calls for executioners. Agents of the state collect fines and confiscate property. These officials wield real power.

As a relatively new form of sociopolitical organization, states have competed successfully with less-complex societies throughout the world. Military organization helps states subdue neighboring nonstates, but this is not the only reason for the spread of state organization. Although states impose hard-

To handle disputes and crimes, all states, including Bermuda, shown here, have courts and judges. Does this photo say anything about cultural diffusion and/or colonialism?

ships, they also offer advantages. More obviously, they provide protection from outsiders and preserve internal order. By promoting internal peace, states enhance production. Their economies support massive, dense populations, which supply armies and colonists to promote expansion.

Fiscal Systems

A financial or **fiscal** system is needed in states to support rulers, nobles, officials, judges, military personnel, and thousands of other specialists. As in the chiefdom, the state intervenes in production, distribution, and consumption. The state may decree that a certain area will produce certain things or forbid certain activities in particular places. Although, like chiefdoms, states also have redistribution (through taxation), generosity and sharing are played down. A smaller proportion of what comes in flows back to the people.

In nonstates, people customarily share with relatives, but residents of states face added obligations to bureaucrats and officials. Citizens must turn over a substantial portion of what they produce to the state. Of the resources that the state collects, it reallocates part for the general good and uses another part (often larger) for the elite.

The state does not bring more freedom or leisure to the common people, who usually work harder than do the people in nonstates. They may be called on to build monumental public works. Some of these projects, such as dams and irrigation systems, may be economically necessary. However, people also build temples, palaces, and tombs for the elites.

Markets and trade are usually under at least some state control, with officials overseeing

fiscal
Pertaining to finances and taxation.

distribution and exchange, standardizing weights and measures, and collecting taxes on goods passing into or through the state. Taxes support government and the ruling class, which is clearly separated from the common people in regard to activities, privileges, rights, and obligations. Taxes also support the many specialists: administrators, tax collectors, judges, lawmakers, generals, scholars, and priests. As the state matures, the segment of the population freed from direct concern with subsistence grows.

The elites of archaic states reveled in the consumption of *sumptuary goods:* jewelry, exotic food and drink, and stylish clothing reserved for, or affordable only by, the rich. Peasants' diets suffered as they struggled to meet government demands. Commoners might perish in territorial wars that had little relevance to their own needs. Are any of these observations true of contemporary states?

SOCIAL CONTROL

Previous sections of this chapter have focused more on formal political organization than on political process. We've considered political regulation in various types of societies, using such convenient labels as *bands, tribes, chiefdoms,* and *states.* We've seen how the scale and strength of political systems have expanded over time and in relation to major economic changes, such as the origin and spread of food production. We've examined reasons why disputes arise and how they are settled in various types of society. We've looked at political decision making, including leaders and their limits. We've also recognized that all contemporary humans have been affected by states, colonialism, and the spread of the modern world system. In this section we'll see that political systems have their informal, social, and subtle aspects along with their formal, governmental, and public dimensions. When we think of politics, we tend to think of government, of federal and state institutions, of Washington, Ottawa, or perhaps our state capital, city hall, or courthouse. Or maybe today we think of talk radio, TV screamers, or incessant commentary, polling, and campaigns. Informal political institutions can substantially influence government and politics.

Consider the diwaniyas of Kuwait—neighborhood male-only meeting places where informal discussions have formal consequences (Prusher 2000). Much of Kuwait's political deliberation, decision making, networking, and influence peddling takes place in diwaniyas. Like a town hall meeting in the United States, the diwaniya also provides a forum where constituents can meet and consult with their parliamentary representatives. Kuwaiti political candidates don't go door to door, but diwaniya to diwaniya. Some neighborhoods have a common diwaniya, much like a

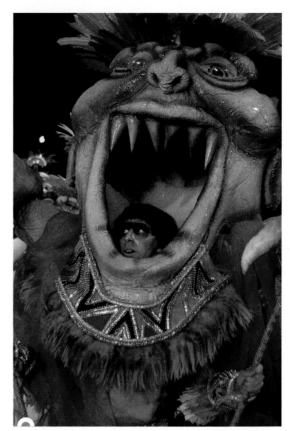

Because of its costumed anonymity, Carnaval is an excellent arena for expressing normally suppressed speech. Here a man peeks out of the mouth of a giant mask during the parade of the São Clemente Samba school in Rio de Janeiro, Brazil, on March 1, 2003. Is there anything like Carnaval in your society?

community center. At a typical diwaniya, men sit on a very long couch that follows the contours of the room in a giant U. Typically they meet once a week, from 8 P.M. to midnight or later.

The fact that mixed-gender or all-female diwaniyas are rare tends to limit women's participation in politics. The diwaniya system encourages democracy, as men regularly meet, talk, and vent for a few hours. On the other hand, this system tends to exclude women from debate, influence, and decision making. Functioning as an informal but influential "old boy's network," the diwaniya also takes men away from their homes, wives, and families.

In studying systems of domination—whether political, economic, religious, or cultural—we must pay attention not only to the formal institutions but to other forms of social control as well. Broader than the political is the concept of **social control,** which refers to "those fields of the social system (beliefs, practices, and institutions) that are most actively involved in the maintenance of any norms and the regulation of any conflict" (N. Kottak 2002, p. 290).

social control
Maintaining social norms and regulating conflict.

Hegemony

Antonio Gramsci (1971) developed the concept of **hegemony** for a stratified social order in which subordinates comply with domination by internalizing their rulers' values and accepting the "naturalness" of domination (this is the way things were meant to be). According to Pierre Bourdieu (1977, p. 164), every social order tries to make its own arbitrariness (including its mechanisms of control and oppression) seem natural. All hegemonic ideologies offer explanations about why the existing order is in everyone's interest. Often promises are made (things will get better if you're patient). Gramsci and others use the idea of hegemony to explain why people conform even when they are not forced to do so.

Both Bourdieu (1977) and Michel Foucault (1979) argue that it is easier and more effective to dominate people in their minds than to try to control their bodies. Besides, and often replacing, gross physical violence, industrial societies have devised more insidious forms of social control. These include various techniques of persuading and managing people and of monitoring and recording their beliefs, activities, and contacts. Can you think of some contemporary examples?

Hegemony, the internalization of a dominant ideology, is one way in which elites curb resistance and maintain power. Another way is to make subordinates believe they eventually will gain power—as young people usually foresee when they let their elders dominate them. Another way of curbing resistance is to separate or isolate people while supervising them closely, as is done in prisons. According to Foucault (1979), describing control over prisoners, solitary confinement is one effective way to get them to submit to authority.

Weapons of the Weak

The analysis of political systems also should consider the behavior that lies beneath the surface of evident, public behavior. In public, the oppressed may seem to accept their own domination, even as they question it offstage in private. James Scott (1990) uses **"public transcript"** to describe the open, public interactions between superordinates and subordinates—the outer shell of power relations. He uses **"hidden transcript"** to describe the critique of power that goes on offstage, where the power holders can't see it. In public, the elites and the oppressed observe the etiquette of power relations. The dominants act like haughty masters while their subordinates show humility and defer.

Often, situations that seem to be hegemonic do have active resistance, but it is individual and disguised rather than collective and defiant. James Scott (1985) uses Malay peasants, among whom he did field work, to illustrate small-scale acts of resistance—which he calls "weapons of the weak." The Malay peasants used an indirect strategy to resist an Islamic tithe (religious tax). Peasants were expected to pay the tithe, usually in the form of rice, which was sent to the provincial capital. In theory, the tithe would come back as charity, but it never did. Peasants didn't resist the tithe by rioting, demonstrating, or protesting. Instead they used a "nibbling" strategy, based on small acts of resistance. For example, they failed to declare their land or lied about the amount they farmed. They underpaid or delivered rice contaminated with water, rocks, or mud, to add weight. Because of this resistance, only 15 percent of what was due actually was paid (Scott 1990, p. 89).

Subordinates also use various strategies to resist *publicly*, but, again, usually in disguised form. Discontent may be expressed in public rituals and language, including metaphors, euphemisms, and folk tales. For example, trickster tales (like the Brer Rabbit stories told by slaves in the southern United States) celebrate the wiles of the weak as they triumph over the strong.

Resistance is most likely to be expressed openly when people are allowed to assemble. The hidden transcript may be publicly revealed on such occasions. People see their dreams and anger shared by others with whom they haven't been in direct contact. The oppressed may draw courage from the crowd, from its visual and emotional impact and its anonymity. Sensing danger, the elites discourage such public gatherings. They try to limit and control holidays, funerals, dances, festivals, and other occasions that might unite the oppressed. Thus, in the pre–Civil War era southern United States, gatherings of five or more slaves were forbidden unless a white person was present.

Factors that interfere with community formation—such as geographic, linguistic, and ethnic separation—also work to curb resistance. Consequently, southern U.S. plantation owners sought slaves with diverse cultural and linguistic backgrounds. Despite the measures used to divide them, the slaves resisted, developing their own popular culture, linguistic codes, and religious vision. The masters taught portions of the Bible that stressed compliance, but the slaves seized on the story of Moses, the promised land, and deliverance. The cornerstone of slave religion became the idea of a reversal in the conditions of whites and blacks. Slaves also resisted directly, through sabotage and flight. In many New World areas, slaves managed to establish free communities in the hills and other isolated areas (Price 1973).

Hidden transcripts tend to be expressed publicly at certain times (festivals and *Carnavals*) and in certain places (for example, markets). Because of its costumed anonymity, Carnaval is an excellent arena for expressing normally suppressed speech and aggression—antihegemonic discourse. (*Discourse* includes talk, speeches, gestures, and actions.) Carnavals celebrate freedom through immodesty, dancing, gluttony, and sexuality

hegemony
Subordinates accept hierarchy as "natural."

public transcript
Open, public interactions between dominators and oppressed.

hidden transcript
Hidden resistance to dominance, by the oppressed.

(DaMatta 1991). Carnaval may begin as a playful outlet for frustrations built up during the year. Over time, it may evolve into a powerful annual critique of stratification and domination and thus a threat to the established order (Gilmore 1987). (Recognizing that ceremonial license could turn into political defiance, the Spanish dictator Francisco Franco outlawed Carnaval.)

Politics, Shame, and Sorcery

We turn now to a case study of sociopolitical process, viewing it as part of a larger system of social control experienced by individuals in their everyday lives. No one today lives in an isolated band, tribe, chiefdom, or state. All groups studied by ethnographers, like the Makua to be discussed below, live in nation-states, where individuals have to deal with various levels and types of political authority, and experience other forms of social control.

Nicholas Kottak (2002) did an ethnographic field study of political systems, and social control more generally, among the rural Makua of northern Mozambique (Figure 17.5). He focused on three fields of social control: political, religious, and reputational systems. (Reputational systems have to do with the way various people are considered in the community—their reputations.) The significance of these fields emerged through conversations about social norms and crimes. Makua revealed their own ideas about social control most clearly in a discussion about stealing a neighbor's chicken.

Most Makua villagers have a makeshift chicken coop in a corner of the home. Chickens leave the coop before sunrise each day and wander in the surrounding area in search of scraps. Chickens usually return to their coop at dusk, but sometimes the chickens, often recently purchased ones, settle in another villager's coop. Villagers worry about their chickens as mobile assets. Owners can't always be sure where their birds are roaming. Villagers may be tempted to steal a neighbor's chicken when its owner seems oblivious to its whereabouts.

The Makua have few material possessions and a meat-poor diet, making wandering chickens a temptation. As the Makua identified chicken wandering and the occasional chicken theft as community problems, Kottak began to draw out their ideas about social control—about why people did *not* steal their neighbor's chickens. The Makua responses coalesced around three main disincentives or sanctions: *ehaya* (shame), *enretthe* (sorcery attack), and *cadeia* (jail). (As used here, a *sanction* refers to a kind of punishment that follows a norm violation.)

According to Kottak (2002), each of these terms (*jail, sorcery,* and *shame*) refers to an imagined "social script," culminating in an undesirable consequence. *Cadeia* (jail), for instance, represents the potential last phase of an extended political and legal process (most violations are resolved before this point). When the Makua responded *enretthe* (sorcery), they were referring to another sequence that might follow the chicken theft. They believed that once the neighbor discovered his chicken had been stolen, he would go to a traditional healer, who would direct a sorcery attack on his behalf. The Makua believed that such a punitive sorcery attack would either kill the thief or make him extremely ill.

The third and most popular answer to the chicken theft question was *ehaya* (shame). In the *ehaya* social script, the chicken thief, having been discovered, would have to attend a formal, publicly organized village meeting, where political authorities would meet to determine the appropriate punishment and compensation. Makua were concerned not so much with the fine as with the intense shame or embarrassment they would feel as a confirmed chicken thief in the village spotlight. The chicken thief also would experience an extended feeling of disgrace, also described as *ehaya*, from his or her knowledge of his or her now spoiled social identity or community reputation.

Living in a nation-state, the Makua have access to several types and levels of potential conflict

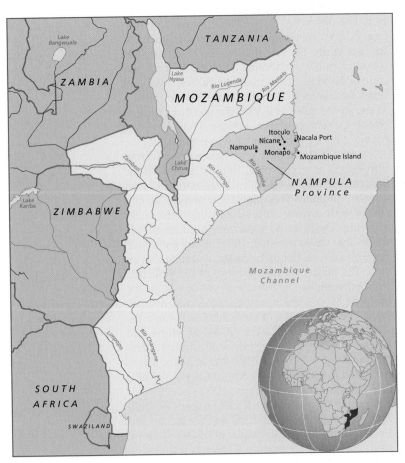

FIGURE 17.5 Location of the Makua and the village of Nicane in northern Mozambique. The province of Nampula shown here is Makua territory.

resolution. A dispute between two people can quickly become a broader conflict between their respective matrilineal descent groups. (In a matrilineal descent group, kinship is calculated through females only—see the next chapter.) The heads of the disputing descent groups meet to resolve the matter. If they can't settle it (e.g., through financial compensation), the conflict moves to a state political authority. Intervention by this official can prevent the individual dispute from escalating into ongoing conflict between the descent groups (e.g., a blood feud, as described earlier in this chapter).

A combination of newer and more traditional offices constitutes the Makua's formal political system. This system includes legitimate positions and officials and represents formal social control. This "political" part of the Makua social system has been explicitly or "formally" designated to handle conflict and crime. As has been discussed in previous sections of this chapter, anthropologists have tended to focus on the formal aspects of social control (i.e., the political field). But, like the Makua, anthropologists also recognize the importance of other fields of social control. When Nicholas Kottak asked Makua in one rural community about deterrents to theft, only 10 percent mentioned jail (the formal system), compared with the 73 percent who listed *ehaya* (shame) as the reason not to steal a neighbor's chicken.

Shame can be a powerful social sanction. Bronislaw Malinowski (1927) described how Trobriand Islanders might climb to the top of a palm tree and dive to their deaths because they couldn't tolerate the shame associated with public knowledge of some stigmatizing action, especially incest. Makua tell the story of a man rumored to have fathered a child with his stepdaughter. The political authorities imposed no formal sanctions (e.g., a fine or jail time) on this man, but gossip about the affair circulated widely. The gossip crystallized in the lyrics of a song that

groups of young women would perform. When the man heard his name and alleged incestuous behavior mentioned in that song, he told a few people he was going to take a trip to the district capital. He was found a few hours later hanging by the neck from a mango tree on the village periphery. The reason for the man's suicide was self-evident to the Makua—he felt too much *ehaya* (shame). (Previously we saw the role of song in the social control system of the Inuit.)

Many anthropologists cite the importance of "informal" processes of social control, which include gossip, stigma, and shame, especially in small-scale societies such as the Makua (see Freilich, Raybeck, and Savishinsky 1991). Gossip, which can lead to shame, sometimes is used when a direct or formal sanction is risky or impossible (Herskovits 1937). Margaret Mead (1937) and Ruth Benedict (1946) distinguished between *shame* as an external sanction (i.e., forces set in motion by others) and *guilt* as an internal sanction, psychologically generated by the individual. They regarded shame as a more prominent form of social control in non-Western societies and guilt as a dominant emotional sanction in Western societies.

Of course, to be effective as a sanction, the prospect of being shamed or of shaming oneself must be internalized by the individual. For the Makua, potential shame is a powerful deterrent. Rural Makua tend to remain in or around one community for their entire lives. Such communities usually have fewer than a thousand people, so that residents can keep track of most community members' identities and reputations. According to Kottak (2002), the rural Makua monitor, transmit, and memorize the details of each other's identities with remarkable precision. Tight clustering of homes, markets, and schools facilitates the monitoring process. In this social environment, people try to avoid behavior that might spoil their reputations and alienate them from their native community.

Nicholas Kottak (back center) attends a village meeting among the Makua of northern Mozambique. Two chiefs have called the meeting to renegotiate the boundaries of their political jurisdictions.

Beliefs in sorcery also facilitate social control. (Religion as social control is discussed further in the chapter on religion.) Although the Makua constantly discuss the existence of sorcerers and sorcery, they aren't explicit about who the sorcerers are. This identity ambiguity is coupled with a local theory of sorcery that strongly implicates malice, which everyone feels at some point. Having felt malice themselves, individual Makua probably experience moments of self-doubt about their own potential status as a sorcerer. And they recognize that others have similar feelings.

Beliefs in sorcery trigger anxieties about death, since the Makua think that a chicken thief will be the inevitable target of a vengeance sorcery attack. Local theories presume that sickness, social misfortune, and death are directly caused by malicious sorcery. Life expectancy is relatively short and infant mortality very high in a Makua village. Relatives drop dead suddenly from infectious diseases. Health, life, and existence are far more problematic than they are for most Westerners. Such uncertainty heightens the dramatic stakes associated with sorcery. Not just theft, but any conflict, is inherently dangerous because it could trigger a sorcery attack.

The following dialogue reported by Kottak (2002, p. 312) highlights the Makua's recognition of sorcery as a social control process.

Ethnographer: Why don't you steal your neighbor's chicken?

Informant: Huh? My neighbor's not short a chicken.

Ethnographer: No. I know. Your neighbor has a chicken. That chicken is always walking on your land. Sometimes it sleeps in your coop at night. Why don't you just take that chicken? What do you think is stopping you?

Informant: *Enretthe. Akwa.* (Sorcery. Death.)

The efficacy of social control depends on how clearly people envision the sanctions that an antisocial act might trigger. The Makua are well informed about norm violations, conflicts, and the sanctions that follow them. As we have seen, jail (*cadeia*), shame (*ehaya*), and sorcery (*enretthe*) are the main sanctions anticipated by the rural Makua.

This chapter began by quoting Fried's definition of political organization as comprising "those portions of social organization that specifically relate to the individuals or groups that manage the affairs of public policy" (Fried 1967, pp. 20–21). As I noted there, Fried's definition works nicely for nation-states but not so well for nonstate societies, where "public policy" is much harder to detect. For this reason, I claimed it was better to focus on sociopolitical organization in discussing the regulation of interrelations among individuals, groups, and their representatives. (Regulation, remember, is the process that corrects deviations from the norm and thus maintains a system's integrity.) Such regulation, we have learned, is a process that extends beyond the political to other fields of social control, including religion and reputational systems, which involve an interplay of public opinion with social norms and sanctions internalized by the individual.

Acing the COURSE

Summary

1. One sociopolitical typology classifies societies as bands, tribes, chiefdoms, and states. Foragers tended to live in egalitarian band-organized societies. Personal networks linked individuals, families, and bands. Band leaders were first among equals, with no sure way to enforce decisions. Disputes rarely arose over strategic resources, which were open to all. Political authority and power tend to increase along with population and the scale of regulatory problems. More people mean more relations among individuals and groups to regulate. Increasingly complex economies pose further regulatory problems.

2. Heads of horticultural villages are local leaders with limited authority. They lead by example and persuasion. Big men have support and authority beyond a single village. They are regional regulators, but temporary ones. In organizing a feast, they mobilize labor from several villages. Sponsoring such events leaves them with little wealth but with prestige and a reputation for generosity.

3. Age and gender also can be used for regional political integration. Among North America's Plains Indians, men's associations (pantribal sodalities) organized raiding and buffalo hunting. Such men's associations tend to emphasize the warrior grade. They serve for offense and defense when there is intertribal raiding for animals. Among pastoralists, the degree of authority and political

organization reflects population size and density, interethnic relations, and pressure on resources.

4. The state is an autonomous political unit that encompasses many communities. Its government collects taxes, drafts people for work and war, and decrees and enforces laws. The state is defined as a form of sociopolitical organization based on central government and social stratification—a division of society into classes. Early states are known as archaic, or nonindustrial, states, in contrast to modern industrial nation-states.

5. Unlike tribes, but like states, chiefdoms had permanent regional regulation and differential access to resources. But chiefdoms lacked stratification. Unlike states, but like bands and tribes, chiefdoms were organized by kinship, descent, and marriage. State formation did not occur, and only chiefdoms emerged in several areas, including the circum-Caribbean, lowland Amazonia, the southeastern United States, and Polynesia.

6. Weber's three dimensions of stratification are wealth, power, and prestige. In early states—for the first time in human history—contrasts in wealth, power, and prestige between entire groups of men and women came into being. A socioeconomic stratum includes people of both sexes and all ages. The superordinate—higher or elite—stratum enjoys privileged access to resources.

7. Certain systems are found in all states: population control, judiciary, enforcement, and fiscal. These are integrated by a ruling system or government composed of civil, military, and religious officials.

States conduct censuses and demarcate boundaries. Laws are based on precedent and legislative proclamations. Courts and judges handle disputes and crimes. A police force maintains internal order, and a military defends against external threats. A financial or fiscal system supports rulers, officials, judges, and other specialists.

8. *Hegemony* describes a stratified social order in which subordinates comply with domination by internalizing its values and accepting its "naturalness." Often, situations that appear hegemonic have resistance that is individual and disguised rather than collective and defiant. "Public transcript" refers to the open, public interactions between the dominators and the oppressed. "Hidden transcript" describes the critique of power that goes on offstage, where the power holders can't see it. Discontent also may be expressed in public rituals and language.

9. Broader than the political is the concept of social control—those fields of the social system most actively involved in the maintenance of norms and the regulation of conflict. Among the Makua of northern Mozambique, three such fields stand out: the political system (formal authority), religion (mainly involving fear of sorcery), and the reputational system (mainly involving avoidance of shame). Social control works best when people can clearly envision the sanctions that an antisocial act might trigger. The Makua are well informed about norm violations, conflicts, and the sanctions that follow them. Jail, shame, and sorcery attacks are the main sanctions anticipated by the rural Makua.

Key Terms

age set 399
big man 398
conflict resolution 393
differential access 404
fiscal 407
head, village 395
hegemony 409
hidden transcript 409
law 393
office 403

power 403
prestige 394
public transcript 409
social control 408
sodality, pantribal 399
subordinate 405
superordinate 405
tribe 392
wealth 405

Test Yourself!

MULTIPLE CHOICE

1. The anthropological approach to the study of political systems and organization is global and comparative,
   a. but it focuses exclusively on nonstates, leaving the study of states and nation-states to political scientists.
   b. and it includes nonstates as well as the states and nation-states traditionally studied by political scientists.
   c. although this sometimes leads to disciplinary turf wars with other disciplines such as political science and sociology.
   d. but it focuses on people's experiences and leaves the study of institutions of political power to other scholars.
   e. although this area is becoming less and less interesting to study because there are very few new nation-states.

2. Why is the term *sociopolitical organization* preferred over Morton Fried's term *political organization* in discussing the regulation or management of interrelations among groups and their representatives?
   a. The term *sociopolitical* is more politically correct.

b. Anthropologists and political scientists have an interest in political systems and organization, but they cannot agree on the same terminology.

c. Fried's definition is much less applicable to nonstates where it is often difficult to detect any "public policy."

d. *Sociopolitical* is the term that the founders of anthropology used to refer to the regulation or management of interrelations among groups and their representatives.

e. The term *political* only refers to contemporary Western states.

3. Which of the following statements about the Inuit song battle is true?
   a. It is sometimes the occasion for a "treacherous feast."
   b. It is a widespread feature of tribal society.
   c. It is a ritualized means of designating hunting lands.
   d. It is a means of resolving disputes so as to forestall open conflict.
   e. It is used to initiate colonial strategies.

4. A band refers to a small kin-based group found among foragers. In this type of political system,
   a. misbehavior was punished by a group of men who had more possessions than anyone else.
   b. band leaders were leaders in name only; sometimes they gave advice or made decisions, but they had no way to enforce their will on others.
   c. there is no way of settling disputes since everybody gets along among equals.
   d. laws dictating proper social norms are passed on through songs from generation to generation.
   e. there is no division of labor based on age and gender.

5. Which of the following factors is responsible for the recent changes in Yanomami tribal society?
   a. They are being overrun by the more expansion-minded Nilotic peoples.
   b. "Big Men" have amassed so much wealth that people have begun to regard them as chiefs.
   c. village raiding among tribal groups
   d. sexual dimorphism
   e. the encroachment by gold miners and cattle ranchers

6. Why are pantribal sodalities and age grades described in a chapter on political systems?
   a. They are organizing principles other than those based on kinship that are used to mobilize and link local groups to form alliances.

b. They are at the core of hegemonic power in nation-states.
c. They are organizing principles that stress the importance of kinship ties.
d. They illustrate the importance of knowing one's genealogy.
e. They are principles that precede the Western, modern concept of friendship.

7. The comparison between the Basseri and the Qashqai, two Iranian nomadic tribes, illustrates that
   a. among tribal sociopolitical organizations, pastoralists are the least likely to interact with other populations in the same space and time.
   b. as regulatory problems increase, political hierarchies become more complex.
   c. as regulatory problems decrease, political hierarchies become more complex.
   d. not all cultures with age grades have age sets.
   e. only those groups that have assimilated the Kuwaiti model of the diwaniyas are able to successfully resolve political feuds.

8. In foraging and tribal societies, what is the basis for the amount of respect or status attached to an individual?
   a. personal attributes, such as wisdom, leadership skills, and generosity
   b. prestige inherited from your parents
   c. the amount of possessions one owns and the ability to convert them into cash
   d. the amount of territory a person owns
   e. rank ascribed at birth, wives, and children

9. In what kind of society does differential access to strategic resources based on social stratification occur?
   a. chiefdoms
   b. bands
   c. states
   d. clans
   e. tribes

10. Antonio Gramsci developed the concept of hegemony to describe
    a. a stratified social order in which subordinates comply with domination by internalizing their rulers' values and accepting the "naturalness" of domination.
    b. overt sociopolitical strategies.
    c. social controls that induce guilt and shame in the population.
    d. the critique of power by the oppressed that goes on offstage—in private—where the power holders can't see it.
    e. the open, public interactions between dominators and oppressed—the outer shell of power relations.

FILL IN THE BLANK

1. _____ refers to a group uniting all men or women born during a certain span of time.

2. Among the different types of sociopolitical systems, _____ lack socioeconomic stratification and stratum endogamy although they do exhibit inequality and a permanent political structure.

3. The influential sociologist Max Weber defined three related dimensions of social stratification. They are _____, _____, and _____.

4. _____ is esteem, respect, or approval for culturally valued acts or qualities.

5. Broader than political control, the concept of _____ refers to those fields of the social system (beliefs, practices, and institutions) that are most actively involved in the maintenance of any norms and the regulation of any conflict.

CRITICAL THINKING

1. This chapter notes that Elman Service's typology of political organization is too simple to account for the full range of political diversity and complexity known to archaeologists and ethnographers. Why not get rid of this typology altogether if it does not accurately describe reality? What is the value, if any, of researchers retaining the use of ideal types to study society?

2. Why shouldn't modern hunter-gatherers be seen as representative of Stone Age peoples? What are some of the stereotypes associated with foragers?

3. What are sodalities? Does your society have them? Do you belong to any? Why or why not?

4. What conclusions do you draw from this chapter about the relationship between population density and political hierarchy?

5. This chapter describes population control as one of the specialized functions found in all states. What are examples of population control? Have you had direct experiences with these controls? (Think of the last time you traveled abroad, registered to vote, paid taxes, or applied for a driver's license.) Do you think these controls are good or bad for society?

Multiple Choice: 1. (B); 2. (C); 3. (D); 4. (B); 5. (E); 6. (A); 7. (B); 8. (A); 9. (C); 10. (A); **Fill in the Blank:** 1. Age set; 2. chiefdoms; 3. wealth, power, prestige; 4. Prestige; 5. social controls

Chagnon, N. A.
1997 *Yanomamö*, 5th ed. Fort Worth: Harcourt Brace. Most recent revision of a well-known account of the Yanomami, including their social organization, politics, warfare, and cultural change, and the crises they have confronted.

Cheater, A. P., ed.
1999 *The Anthropology of Power: Empowerment and Disempowerment in Changing Structures.* New York: Routledge. Overcoming social marginality through participation and political mobilization in today's world.

Ferguson, R. B.
2003 *State, Identity, and Violence: Political Disintegration in the Post–Cold War Era.* New York: Routledge. Political relations, the state, ethnic relations, and violence.

Gledhill, J.
2000 *Power and Its Disguises: Anthropological Perspectives on Politics.* Sterling, VA: Pluto Press. The anthropology of power.

Kurtz, D. V.
2001 *Political Anthropology: Power and Paradigms.* Boulder, CO: Westview. Up-to-date treatment of the field of political anthropology.

Otterbein, K.
2004 *How War Began.* College Station: Texas A&M University Press. The origins of war discussed in terms of human evolution, prehistory, and cross-cultural comparison.

Suggested Additional Readings

Go to our Online Learning Center website at **www.mhhe.com/kottak** for Internet exercises directly related to the content of this chapter.

Internet Exercises

How are biology and culture expressed in human sex/gender systems?

How do gender, gender roles, and gender stratification correlate with other social, economic, and political variables?

What is sexual orientation, and how do sexual practices vary cross-culturally?

Women today work increasingly outside the home in varied positions, including soldier. This photo, taken in Deu, Germany in 2001, shows one of the first women recruited into the German army–along with her male counterparts.

understanding OURSELVES

A table (18.1) in this chapter lists activities that are generally done by the men in a society, generally done by the women in a society, or done by either men or women (swing). In this table, you will see some "male" activities familiar to our own culture, such as hunting, butchering, and building houses, along with activities that we consider typically female, such as doing the laundry and cooking. This list may bring to mind as many exceptions as followers of these "rules." Although it is not typical, it certainly is not unheard of for an American woman to hunt large game (think of Sarah Palin) or an American man to cook (think of Emeril Lagasse or other male celebrity chefs). Celebrities aside, women in our culture increasingly work outside the home in a wide variety of jobs—doctor, lawyer, accountant, professor—traditionally considered men's work. It is not true, however, that women have achieved equity in all types of employment. As of this writing, only 17 out of 100 United States senators are women. Only three women have ever served on the United States Supreme Court.

Ideas about proper gender behavior are changing just as inconsistently as are the employment patterns of men and women. Popular shows like *Sex and the City* feature characters who display nontraditional gender behavior and sexual behavior, while old beliefs, cultural

expectations, and gender stereotypes linger. The American expectation that proper female behavior should be polite, restrained, or meek poses a challenge for women, because American culture also values decisiveness and "standing up for your beliefs." When American men and women display similar behavior— speaking their minds, for example—they are judged differently. A man's assertive behavior may be admired and rewarded, but similar behavior by a woman may be labeled "aggressive"—or worse.

Both men and women are constrained by their cultural training, stereotypes, and expectations. For example, American culture stigmatizes male crying. It's okay for little boys to cry, but becoming a man often means giving up this natural expression of joy and sadness. Why shouldn't "big lugs" cry when they feel emotions? American men are trained as well to make decisions and stick to them. In our stereotypes, changing one's mind is more associated with women than men and may be perceived as a sign of weakness. Men who do it may be seen as "girly." Politicians routinely criticize their opponents for being indecisive, for waffling or "flip-flopping" on issues. What a strange idea—that people shouldn't change their positions if they've discovered there's a better way. Males, females, and humanity may be equally victimized by aspects of cultural training.

SEX AND GENDER

Because anthropologists study biology, society, and culture, they are in a unique position to comment on nature (biological predispositions) and nurture (environment)

as determinants of human behavior. Human attitudes, values, and behavior are limited not only by our genetic predispositions— which are often difficult to identify—but also by our experiences during enculturation.

Our attributes as adults are determined both by our genes and by our environment during growth and development.

Questions about nature and nurture emerge in the discussion of human sex-gender roles and sexuality. Men and women differ genetically. Women have two X chromosomes, and men have an X and a Y. The father determines a baby's sex because only he has the Y chromosome to transmit. The mother always provides an X chromosome.

The chromosomal difference is expressed in hormonal and physiological contrasts. Humans are sexually dimorphic, more so than some primates, such as gibbons (small tree-living Asiatic apes), and less so than others, such as gorillas and orangutans. **Sexual dimorphism** refers to differences in male and female biology besides the contrasts in breasts and genitals. Women and men differ not just in primary (genitalia and reproductive organs) and secondary (breasts, voice, hair distribution) sexual characteristics but in average weight, height, strength, and longevity. Women tend to live longer than men and have excellent endurance capabilities. In a given population, men tend to be taller and to weigh more than women do. Of course, there is a considerable overlap between the sexes in terms of height, weight, and physical strength, and there has been a pronounced reduction in sexual dimorphism during human biological evolution.

Just how far, however, do such genetically and physiologically determined differences go? What effects do they have on the way men and women act and are treated in different societies? Anthropologists have discovered both similarities and differences in the roles of men and women in different cultures. The predominant anthropological position on sex-gender roles and biology may be stated as follows:

> The biological nature of men and women [should be seen] not as a narrow enclosure limiting the human organism, but rather as a broad base upon which a variety of structures can be built. (Friedl 1975, p. 6)

Although in most societies men tend to be somewhat more aggressive than women are, many of the behavioral and attitudinal differences between the sexes emerge from culture rather than biology. Sex differences are biological, but gender encompasses all the traits that a culture assigns to and inculcates in males and females. "Gender," in other words, refers to the cultural construction of whether one is female, male, or something else.

Given the "rich and various constructions of gender" within the realm of cultural diversity, Susan Bourque and Kay Warren (1987) note that the same images of masculinity and femininity do not always apply. Anthropologists have gathered systematic ethnographic data about similarities and differences involving gender in many cultural settings (Bonvillain 2007; Brettell and Sargent 2009;

The realm of cultural diversity contains richly different social constructions and expressions of gender roles, as is illustrated by these Wodaabe male celebrants in Niger. (Look closely for suggestions of diffusion.) For what reasons do men decorate their bodies in our society?

Gilmore 2001; Mascia-Lees and Black 2000; Nanda 2000; Ward and Edelstein 2009). Anthropologists can detect recurrent themes and patterns involving gender differences. They also can observe that gender roles vary with environment, economy, adaptive strategy, and type of political system. Before we examine the cross-cultural data, some definitions are in order.

Gender roles are the tasks and activities a culture assigns to the sexes. Related to gender roles are **gender stereotypes,** which are oversimplified but strongly held ideas about the characteristics of males and females. **Gender stratification** describes an unequal distribution of rewards (socially valued resources, power, prestige, human rights, and personal freedom) between men and women, reflecting their different positions in a social hierarchy. According to Ann Stoler (1977), the "economic determinants of gender status" include freedom or autonomy (in disposing of one's labor and its fruits) and social power (control over the lives, labor, and produce of others).

sexual dimorphism
Marked differences in male and female biology, beyond breasts and genitals.

gender roles
The tasks and activities that a culture assigns to each sex.

gender stereotypes
Oversimplified, strongly held views about males and females.

gender stratification
Unequal distribution of social resources between men and women.

 living anthropology **VIDEOS**

Marginalization of Women, www.mhhe.com/kottak
Despite declarations of equality, half the world's population suffers discrimination. Many cultures favor sons, reinforcing a mind-set that women are less than equal. This clip examines the economic, political, social, and cultural devaluation of women. Based on the discussion in this text chapter, is gender discrimination inevitable?

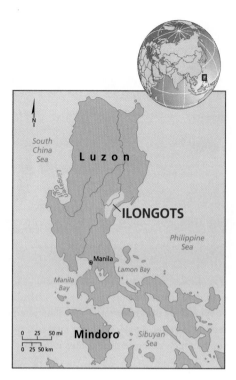

FIGURE 18.1 Location of Ilongots in the Philippines.

In stateless societies, gender stratification is often more obvious in regard to prestige than it is in regard to wealth. In her study of the Ilongots of northern Luzon in the Philippines (Figure 18.1), Michelle Rosaldo (1980*a*) described gender differences related to the positive cultural value placed on adventure, travel, and knowledge of the external world. More often than women, Ilongot men, as head-hunters, visited distant places. They acquired knowledge of the external world, amassed experiences there, and returned to express their knowledge, adventures, and feelings in public oratory. They received acclaim as a result. Ilongot women had inferior prestige because they lacked external experiences on which to base knowledge and dramatic expression. On the basis of Rosaldo's study and findings in other stateless societies, Ong (1989) argues that we must distinguish between prestige systems and actual power in a given society. High male prestige may not entail economic or political power held by men over their families.

RECURRENT GENDER PATTERNS

Remember from previous chapters that ethnologists compare ethnographic data from several cultures (i.e., cross-cultural data) to discover and explain differences and similarities. Data relevant to the cross-cultural study of gender can be drawn from the domains of economics, politics, domestic activity, kinship, and marriage. Table 18.1 shows cross-cultural data from 185 randomly selected societies on the division of labor by gender.

Remembering the discussion, in the chapter on culture, of universals, generalities, and particularities, the findings in Table 18.1 about the division of labor by gender illustrate generalities rather than universals. That is, among the societies known to ethnography, there is a very strong tendency for men to build boats, but there are exceptions. One was the Hidatsa, a Native American group in which the women made the boats used to cross the Missouri River. (Traditionally, the Hidatsa were village farmers and bison hunters on the North American Plains; they now live in North Dakota.) Another exception: Pawnee women worked wood; this is the only Native American group that assigned this activity to women. (The Pawnee, also traditionally Plains farmers and bison hunters, originally lived in what is now central Nebraska and central Kansas; they now live on a reservation in north central Oklahoma.) Among the Mbuti "pygmies" of Africa's Ituri forest, women hunt by catching small, slow animals, using their hands or a net (Murdock and Provost 1973).

Exceptions to cross-cultural generalizations may involve societies or individuals. That is, a society like the Hidatsa can contradict the cross-cultural generalization that men build boats by assigning that task to women. Or, in a society where the cultural expectation is that only men build boats, a particular woman or women can contradict that expectation by doing the male activity. Table 18.1 shows that in a sample of 185 societies, certain activities ("swing activities") are assigned to either or both men and women. Among the most important of such activities are planting, tending, and harvesting crops. We'll see below that some societies customarily assign more farming chores to women, whereas others call on men to be the main farm laborers. Among the tasks almost always assigned to men (Table 18.1), some (e.g., hunting large animals on land and sea) seem clearly related to the greater average size and strength of males. Others, such as working wood and making musical instruments, seem more culturally arbitrary. And women, of course, are not exempt from arduous and time-consuming physical labor, such as gathering firewood and fetching water. In Arembepe, Bahia, Brazil, women routinely transport water in five-gallon tins, balanced on their heads, from wells and lagoons located at long distances from their homes.

Notice that Table 18.1 includes no mention of trade and market activity, in which either or both men and women are active. Is Table 18.1 somewhat

TABLE 18.1 Generalities in the Division of Labor by Gender, Based on Data from 185 Societies

GENERALLY MALE ACTIVITIES	SWING (MALE OR FEMALE) ACTIVITIES	GENERALLY FEMALE ACTIVITIES
Hunting large aquatic animals (e.g., whales, walrus)	Making fire	Gathering fuel (e.g., firewood)
Smelting ores	Body mutilation	Making drinks
Metalworking	Preparing skins	Gathering wild vegetal foods
Lumbering	Gathering small land animals	Dairy production (e.g., churning)
Hunting large land animals	Planting crops	Spinning
Working wood	Making leather products	Doing the laundry
Hunting fowl	Harvesting	Fetching water
Making musical instruments	Tending crops	Cooking
Trapping	Milking	Preparing vegetal food (e.g., processing cereal grains)
Building boats	Making baskets	
Working stone	Carrying burdens	
Working bone, horn, and shell	Making mats	
Mining and quarrying	Caring for small animals	
Setting bones	Preserving meat and fish	
Butchering*	Loom weaving	
Collecting wild honey	Gathering small aquatic animals	
Clearing land	Clothing manufacture	
Fishing	Making pottery	
Tending large herd animals		
Building houses		
Preparing the soil		
Making nets		
Making rope		

*All the activities above "butchering" are almost always done by men; those from "butchering" through "making rope" usually are done by men.

SOURCE: Adapted from G. P. Murdock and C. Provost, "Factors in the Division of Labor by Sex: A Cross-Cultural Analysis," *Ethnology* 12(2) April 1973: 202–225. Copyright 1973 by University of Pittsburgh. Reprinted by permission.

androcentric in detailing more tasks for men than for women? More than men, women do child care, but the study on which Table 18.1 is based does not break down domestic activities to the same extent that it details extradomestic ones. Think about Table 18.1 in terms of today's home and job roles and with respect to the activities done by contemporary women and men. Men still do most of the hunting; either gender can collect the honey from a supermarket, even as most baby-bottom wiping (part of child care and not included in Table 18.1) continues to be in female hands.

Cross-culturally the subsistence contributions of men and women are roughly equal (Table 18.2). But in domestic activities and child care, female labor predominates, as we see in Tables 18.3 and 18.4. Table 18.3 shows that in about half the societies studied, men did virtually no domestic work.

TABLE 18.2 Time and Effort Expended on Subsistence Activities by Men and Women*

More by men	16
Roughly equal	61
More by women	23

*Percentage of 88 randomly selected societies for which information was available on this variable.

SOURCE: M. F. Whyte, "Cross-Cultural Codes Dealing with the Relative Status of Women," *Ethnology* 17(2):211–239.

Even in societies where men did some domestic chores, the bulk of such work was done by women. Adding together their subsistence activities and their domestic work, women tend to work more hours than men do. Has this changed in the contemporary world?

TABLE 18.3 Who Does the Domestic Work?*

Males do virtually none	51
Males do some, but mostly done by females	49

*Percentage of 92 randomly selected societies for which information was available on this variable.

SOURCE: M. F. Whyte, "Cross-Cultural Codes Dealing with the Relative Status of Women," *Ethnology* 17(2):211–239.

TABLE 18.4 Who Has Final Authority over the Care, Handling, and Discipline of Infant Children (under Four Years Old)?*

Males have more say	18
Roughly equal	16
Females have more say	66

*Percentage of 67 randomly selected societies for which information was available on this variable.

SOURCE: M. F. Whyte, "Cross-Cultural Codes Dealing with the Relative Status of Women," *Ethnology* 17(2):211–239.

TABLE 18.5 Does the Society Allow Multiple Spouses?*

Only for males	77
For both, but more commonly for males	4
For neither	16
For both, but more commonly for females	2

*Percentage of 92 randomly selected societies.

SOURCE: M. F. Whyte, "Cross-Cultural Codes Dealing with the Relative Status of Women," *Ethnology* 17(2):211–239.

TABLE 18.6 Is There a Double Standard with Respect to PREMARITAL Sex*

Yes—females are more restricted	44
No—equal restrictions on males and females	56

*Percentage of 73 randomly selected societies for which information was available on this variable.

SOURCE: M. F. Whyte, "Cross-Cultural Codes Dealing with the Relative Status of Women," *Ethnology* 17(2):211–239.

TABLE 18.7 Is There a Double Standard with Respect to EXTRAMARITAL Sex*

Yes—females are more restricted	43
Equal restrictions on males and females	55
Males punished more severely for transgression	3

*Percentage of 73 randomly selected societies for which information was available on this variable.

SOURCE: M. F. Whyte, "Cross-Cultural Codes Dealing with the Relative Status of Women," *Ethnology* 17(2):211–239.

What about child care? Women tend to be the main caregivers in most societies, but men often play a role. Again there are exceptions, both within and between societies. Table 18.4 uses cross-cultural data to answer the question "Who—men or women—has final authority over the care, handling, and discipline of children younger than four years?" Although women have primary authority over infants in two-thirds of the societies, there are still societies (18 percent of the total) in which men have the major say. In the United States and Canada today, some men are primary caregivers despite the cultural fact that the female role in child care remains more prominent in both countries. Given the critical role of breast-feeding in ensuring infant survival, it makes sense, for infants especially, for the mother to be the primary caregiver.

There are differences in male and female reproductive strategies. Women give birth, breast-feed, and assume primary responsibility for infant care. Women ensure that their progeny will survive by establishing a close bond with each baby. It's also advantageous for a woman to have a reliable mate to ease the child-rearing process and ensure the survival of her children. (Again, there are exceptions, for example, the Nayars discussed in the chapter "Families, Kinship, and Descent.") Women can have only so many babies during the course of their reproductive years, which begin after menarche (the advent of menstruation) and end with menopause (cessation of menstruation). Men, in contrast, have a longer reproductive period, which can last into the elder years. If they

choose to do so, men can enhance their reproductive success by impregnating several women over a longer time period. Although men do not always have multiple mates, they do have a greater tendency to do so than women do (see Tables 18.5, 18.6, and 18.7). Among the societies known to ethnography, polygyny is much more common than polyandry is (see Table 18.5).

Men mate, within and outside marriage, more than women do. Table 18.6 shows cross-cultural data on premarital sex, and Table 18.7 summarizes the data on extramarital sex. In both cases men are less restricted than women are, although the restrictions are equal in about half the societies studied.

Double standards that restrict women more than men illustrate gender stratification. This chapter's "Appreciating Diversity" shows how India, while formally offering equal rights to women, still denies them the privilege of moving untroubled through public space. Women routinely are harassed when they move from private (domestic) to public space. "Appreciating Diversity" describes an attempt to offer women relief from male indignities as they commute to work.

Several studies have shown that economic roles affect gender stratification. In one cross-cultural study, Sanday (1974) found that gender stratification decreased when men and women made roughly equal contributions to subsistence. She found that gender stratification was greatest when the women contributed either much more or much less than the men did.

GENDER AMONG FORAGERS

In foraging societies, gender stratification was most marked when men contributed much more to the diet than women did. This was true among the Inuit and other northern hunters and fishers. Among tropical and semitropical foragers, by contrast, gathering usually supplies more food than hunting and fishing do. Gathering is generally women's work. Men usually hunt and fish, but women also do some fishing and may hunt small animals. When gathering is prominent, gender status tends to be more equal than it is when hunting and fishing are the main subsistence activities.

Gender status is also more equal when the domestic and public spheres aren't sharply separated. (*Domestic* means within or pertaining to the home.) Strong differentiation between the home and the outside world is called the **domestic public dichotomy** or the *private–public contrast*. The outside world can include politics, trade, warfare, or work. Often when domestic and public spheres are clearly separated, public activities have greater prestige than domestic ones do. This can promote gender stratification, because men are more likely to be active in the public domain than women are (see "Appreciating Diversity"). Cross-culturally, women's activities tend to be closer to home than men's are. Thus, another reason hunter-gatherers have less gender stratification than food producers do is that the domestic–public dichotomy is less developed among foragers.

We've seen that certain gender roles are more sex-linked than others. Men are the usual hunters and warriors. Given such tools and weapons as spears, knives, and bows, men make better hunters and fighters because they are bigger and stronger on the average than are women in the same population (Divale and Harris 1976). The male hunter-fighter role also reflects a tendency toward greater male mobility.

In foraging societies, women are either pregnant or lactating during most of their childbear-

In many societies women routinely do hard physical labor, as is illustrated by these women working together to move logs at a sawmill in Langxiang, China. Anthropologists have described both commonalities and differences in gender roles and activities among the world's societies.

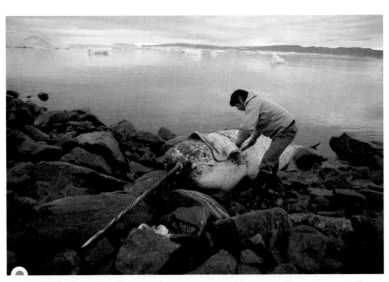

Among foragers, gender stratification tends to increase when men contribute much more to the diet than women do—as has been true among the Inuit and other northern hunters and fishers. Shown here, Mikile, an Inuit hunter, opens up a narwhal he hunted and killed near Qeqertat in northwestern Greenland.

ing period. Late in pregnancy and after childbirth, carrying a baby limits a woman's movements, even her gathering. However, among the Agta of the Philippines (Griffin and Estioko-Griffin, eds. 1985) women not only gather; they also hunt with dogs while carrying their babies with them. Still, given the effects of pregnancy and breast-feeding on mobility, it is rarely feasible for women to be the primary hunters (Friedl 1975). Warfare, which

domestic–public dichotomy
Work at home versus more valued work outside.

appreciating DIVERSITY

A Women's Train for India

Human diversity is expressed in varied gender roles in different societies. Such roles, however, are changing with globalization. India is experiencing significant changes in work patterns and gender roles. Like women in the United States, although still to a lesser degree, more and more Indian women are entering the workforce, many in jobs that are part of a global economy based on services and information.

How should we evaluate the status of women in a society, such as India? India's constitution guarantees equal rights for women. India has several prominent female political leaders. Indian law mandates equal pay for equal work, and there are laws against sexual harassment. Yet India still may be described as a patriarchal culture, where women are harassed routinely when they move from private (domestic) to public space. Described below is an attempt to offer women relief from the indignity of "eve teasing" as they commute by train to and from work.

PALWAL, India—As the morning commuter train rattled down the track, Chinu Sharma, an office worker, enjoyed the absence of men. Some of them pinch and grope women on trains, or shout insults and catcalls. . . .

Up and down the jostling train, women repeated the same theme: As millions of women have poured into the Indian work force over the last decade, they have met with different obstacles in a tradition-bound, patriarchal culture, but few are more annoying than the basic task of getting to work.

The problems of taunting and harassment, known as eve teasing, are so persistent that in recent months the government has decided to simply remove men altogether. In a pilot program, eight new commuter trains exclusively for female passengers have been introduced in India's four largest cities: New Delhi, Mumbai, Chennai and Calcutta.

The trains are known as Ladies Specials, and on one recent round trip in which a male reporter got permission to board, the women commuting between the industrial town of Palwal and New Delhi were very pleased.

"It's so nice here," said a teacher, Kiran Khas, who has commuted by train for 17 years. Ms. Khas said the regular trains were thronged with vegetable sellers, pickpockets, beggars and lots of men. "Here on this train," she said, as if describing a miracle, "you can board anywhere and sit freely."

India would seem to be a country where women have shattered the glass ceiling. The country's most powerful politician, Sonia Gandhi, president of the Congress Party, is a woman. The country's current president, a somewhat ceremonial position, is a woman. So are the foreign secretary and the chief minister of the country's most populous state, Uttar Pradesh, and the new minister of railways. India's Constitution guarantees equal rights for women, while Indian law stipulates equal pay and punishment for sexual harassment.

But the reality is very different for the average working woman, many analysts say.

Since India began economic reforms in the early 1990s, women have entered the urban work force, initially as government office workers, but now increasingly as employees in the booming services sector or in professional jobs. Overall, the number of working women has roughly doubled in 15 years.

But violence against women has also increased, according to national statistics. Between 2003 and 2007, rape cases rose by more than 30 percent, kidnapping or abduction cases rose by more than 50 percent, while torture and molestation also jumped sharply.

Mala Bhandari, who runs an organization focused on women and children, said the influx of women into the workplace had eroded the traditional separation between public space (the workplace) and private space (the home). "Now that women have started occupying public spaces, issues will always arise," she said. "And the first issue is security." India's newspapers are filled with accounts of the frictions wrought by so much social change.

Last week, a husband in Noida was brought in by the police and accused of beating his wife because she had cut her hair in a Western style. In June, four colleges in Kanpur tried to bar female students from wearing blue jeans, saying that they were "indecent" and that they contributed to rising cases of sexual harassment. After protests from female students, state officials ordered the colleges to drop the restriction.

For many years, women traveling by train sat with men, until crowding and security concerns prompted the railroad to reserve two compartments per train for women. But with trains badly overcrowded, men would break into cars for women and claim seats. Mumbai started operating two women-only trains in 1992, yet the program was never expanded. Then, with complaints rising from female passengers, Mamata Banerjee, the new minister of railways, announced the eight new Ladies Specials trains.

"It speaks of their coming of age and assertiveness," said Mukesh Nigam, a high-ranking railway official.

Many men are not thrilled. Several female passengers said eve teasing was worse here in

424   PART 3   Appreciating Cultural Diversity

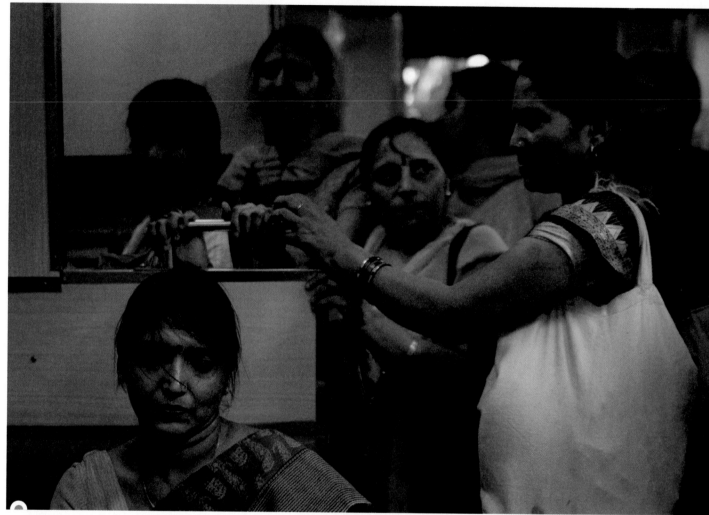

India has been described as a patriarchal culture, in which women routinely are harassed when they move from private (domestic) to public space. The women shown here enjoy their ride, unmolested, on the "Ladies Special" train from Palwal to Delhi, on September 10, 2009.

northern India than elsewhere in the country. As the Ladies Special idled on Track 7 at the station in Palwal, a few men glared from the platform. The Ladies Special was far less crowded, with clean, padded benches and electric fans, compared with the dirty, darkened train on Track 6 filled with sullen men. Vandals sometimes write profanities on the Ladies Special, or worse. . . .

As the train began moving, one woman sat meditating. Nearby, an accountant read a Hindu prayer book, while college students gossiped a few rows away. "If you go to work, then you are independent, you earn some money and can help the family," said Archana Gahlot, 25. "And if something happens to the marriage, you have something." . . .

SOURCE: Jim Yardley, "Indian Women Find New Peace in Rail Commute." From *The New York Times,* September 16, 2009. © The New York Times. All rights reserved. Used by permission and protected by the Copyright Laws of the United States. The printing, copying, redistribution, or retransmission of the Material without express written permission is prohibited. www.nytimes.com

also requires mobility, is not found in most foraging societies, nor is interregional trade well developed. Warfare and trade are two public arenas that can contribute to status inequality of males and females among food producers.

The Ju/'hoansi San illustrate the extent to which the activities and spheres of influence of men and women may overlap among foragers (Draper 1975). Traditional Ju/'hoansi gender roles were interdependent. During gathering, women discovered information about game animals, which they passed on to the men. Men and women spent about the same amount of time away from the camp, but neither worked more than three days a week. Between one-third and one-half of the band stayed home while the others worked.

The Ju/'hoansi saw nothing wrong in doing the work of the other gender. Men often gathered food and collected water. A general sharing ethos dictated that men distribute meat and that women share the fruits of gathering. Boys and girls of all ages played together. Fathers took an active role in raising children. Resources were adequate, and competition and aggression were discouraged. Exchangeability and interdependence of roles are adaptive in small groups.

Patricia Draper's field work among the Ju/'hoansi is especially useful in showing the relationships between economy, gender roles, and stratification because she studied both foragers and a group of former foragers who had become

sedentary. Most Ju/'hoansi are now sedentary, living near food producers or ranchers (see Kent 1992; Solway and Lee 1990; Wilmsen 1989).

Draper studied sedentary Ju/'hoansi at Mahopa, a village where they herded, grew crops, worked for wages, and did a small amount of gathering. Their gender roles were becoming more rigidly defined. A domestic–public dichotomy was developing as men traveled farther than women did. With less gathering, women were confined more to the home. Boys could gain mobility through herding, but girls' movements were more limited. The equal and communal world of the bush was yielding to the social features of sedentary life. A differential ranking of men according to their herds, houses, and sons began to replace sharing. Males came to be seen as more valuable producers.

If there is some degree of male dominance in virtually every contemporary society, it may be because of changes such as those that have drawn the Ju/'hoansi into wage work, market sales, and thus the world capitalist economy. A historic interplay between local, national, and international forces influences systems of gender stratification (Ong 1989). In traditional foraging cultures, however, egalitarianism extended to the relations between the sexes. The social spheres, activities, rights, and obligations of men and women overlapped. Foragers' kinship systems tend to be bilateral (calculated equally through males and females) rather than favoring either the mother's side or the father's side. Foragers may live with either the husband's or the wife's kin and often shift between one group and the other.

One last observation about foragers: It is among them that the public and private spheres are least separate, hierarchy is least marked, aggression and competition are most discouraged, and the rights, activities, and spheres of influence of men and women overlap the most. Our ancestors lived entirely by foraging until 10,000 years ago. If there is any most "natural" form of human society, it is best, although imperfectly, represented by foragers. Despite the popular stereotype of the club-wielding caveman dragging his mate by the hair, relative gender equality is a much more likely ancestral pattern.

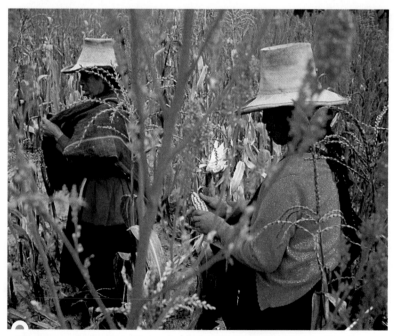

Women are the main producers in horticultural societies. Women like these South American corn farmers do most of the cultivating in such societies. What kinds of roles do women play in contemporary North American farming?

GENDER AMONG HORTICULTURALISTS

Gender roles and stratification among cultivators vary widely, depending on specific features of the economy and social structure. Demonstrating this, Martin and Voorhies (1975) studied a sample of 515 horticultural societies, representing all parts of the world. They looked at several variables, including descent and postmarital residence, the percentage of the diet derived from cultivation, and the productivity of men and women.

A descent group is one whose social unity and solidarity are based on a belief in common ancestry. Cross-culturally, two common rules serve to admit certain people as descent-group members while excluding others. With a rule of **matrilineal descent,** people join the mother's group automatically at birth (as an ascribed status) and stay members throughout life. Matrilineal descent groups therefore include only the children of the group's women. With **patrilineal descent,** people automatically have lifetime membership in the father's group. The children of all the group's men belong to the group. The children of the group's women are excluded; they belong to their father's group. Patrilineal descent is much more common than matrilineal descent. In a sample of 564 societies (Murdock 1957), about three times as many were found to be patrilineal (247 to 84) as matrilineal.

Societies with descent groups not only have membership rules; they also have rules about where members should live once they marry. With **patrilocality,** which is associated with patrilineal descent, the couple lives in the husband's (father's) community, so that related males stay put, as wives move to their husband's village. A less common residence rule, associated with matrilineal descent, is **matrilocality:** Married couples live in the wife's (mother's) community, and their children grow up in their mother's village. This rule keeps related women together.

Martin and Voorhies (1975) found women to be the main producers in horticultural societies. In 50 percent of those societies, women did most of the cultivating. In 33 percent, contributions to cultivation by men and women were equal. In only 17 percent did men do most of the work (Table 18.8). Women tended to do a bit more cultivating in matrilineal compared with patrilineal societies. They dominated horticulture in 64 percent of the matrilineal societies versus 50 percent of the patrilineal ones.

Reduced Gender Stratification— Matrilineal, Matrilocal Societies

Cross-cultural variation in gender status is related to rules of descent and postmarital residence (Friedl 1975; Martin and Voorhies 1975). Among horticulturalists with matrilineal descent and matrilocality, female status tends to be high (see Blackwood 2000). Matriliny and matrilocality disperse related males, rather than consolidating them. By contrast, patriliny and patrilocality keep male relatives together, an advantage given warfare. Matrilineal-matrilocal systems tend to occur in societies where population pressure on strategic resources is minimal and warfare is infrequent.

Women tend to have high status in matrilineal, matrilocal societies for several reasons. Descent-group membership, succession to political positions, allocation of land, and overall social identity all come through female links. In Negeri Sembilan, Malaysia (Peletz 1988), matriliny gave women sole inheritance of ancestral rice fields. Matrilocality created solidary clusters of female kin. Women had considerable influence beyond the household (Swift 1963). In such matrilineal contexts, women are the basis of the entire social structure. Although public authority may be (or may appear to be) assigned to the men, much of the power and decision making may actually belong to the senior women. Some matrilineal societies, including the *Iroquois* (Brown 1975), a confederation of tribes in aboriginal New York, show that women's economic, political, and ritual influence can rival that of men (Figure 18.2).

Iroquois women played a major subsistence role, while men left home for long periods to wage war. As is usual in matrilineal societies, *internal* warfare was uncommon. Iroquois men waged war only on distant groups; this could keep them away for years.

Iroquois men hunted and fished, but women controlled the local economy. Women did some fishing and occasional hunting, but their major productive role was in horticulture. Women owned the land, which they inherited from matrilocal

matrilineal descent
Descent traced through women only.

patrilineal descent
Descent traced through men only.

patrilocality
Married couple resides in husband's (father's) community.

matrilocality
Married couple resides in wife's (mother's) community.

TABLE 18.8 Male and Female Contributions to Production in Cultivating Societies

	HORTICULTURE (PERCENTAGE OF 104 SOCIETIES)	AGRICULTURE (PERCENTAGE OF 93 SOCIETIES)
Women are primary cultivators	50	15
Men are primary cultivators	17	81
Equal contributions to cultivation	33	3

SOURCE: K. Martin and B. Voorhies, *Female of the Species* (New York: Columbia University Press, 1975), p. 283.

FIGURE 18.2 Historic Territory of the Iroquois.

Many jobs that men do in some societies are done by women in others, and vice versa. In West Africa, women play a prominent role in trade and marketing. In Togo, shown here, women dominate textile sales. Is there a textile shop near you? Who runs it?

kinswomen. Women controlled the production and distribution of food.

Iroquois women lived with their husbands and children in the family compartments of a communal longhouse. Women born in a longhouse remained there for life. Senior women, or *matrons,* decided which men could join the longhouse as husbands, and they could evict incompatible men. Women therefore controlled alliances between descent groups, an important political job in tribal society.

Iroquois women thus managed production and distribution. Social identity, succession to office and titles, and property all came through the female line, and women were prominent in ritual and politics. Related tribes made up a confederacy, the League of the Iroquois, with chiefs and councils.

A council of male chiefs managed military operations, but chiefly succession was matrilineal. That is, succession went from a man to his brother, his sister's son, or another matrilineal relative. The matrons of each longhouse nominated a man as their representative. If the council rejected their first nominee, the women proposed others until one was accepted. Matrons constantly monitored the chiefs and could impeach them. Women could veto war declarations, withhold provisions for war, and initiate peace efforts. In religion, too, women shared power. Half the tribe's religious practitioners were women, and the matrons helped select the others.

Reduced Gender Stratification— Matrifocal Societies

Nancy Tanner (1974) also found that the combination of male travel and a prominent female economic role reduced gender stratification and promoted high female status. She based this finding on a survey of the **matrifocal** (mother-centered, often with no resident husband-father) organization of certain societies in Indonesia, West Africa, and the Caribbean. Matrifocal societies are not necessarily matrilineal. A few are even patrilineal.

For example, Tanner (1974) found matrifocality among the Igbo of eastern Nigeria, who are patrilineal, patrilocal, and polygynous (men have multiple wives). Each wife had her own house, where she lived with her children. Women planted crops next to their houses and traded surpluses. Women's associations ran the local markets, while men did the long-distance trading.

In a case study of the Igbo, Ifi Amadiume (1987) noted that either sex could fill male gender roles. Before Christian influence, successful Igbo women used wealth to take titles and acquire wives. Wives freed husbands (male and female) from domestic work and helped them accumulate wealth. Female husbands were not considered masculine but preserved their femininity. Igbo women asserted themselves in women's groups, including those of lineage daughters, lineage wives, and a community-wide women's council led by titled women. The high status and influence of Igbo women rested on the separation of males from local subsistence and on a marketing system that encouraged women to leave home and gain prominence in distribution and—through these accomplishments—in politics.

Matriarchy

Cross-culturally, anthropologists have described tremendous variation in the roles of men and women, and the power differentials between them. If a patriarchy is a political system ruled by men, what would a matriarchy be? Would a matriarchy be a political system ruled by women, or a political system in which women play a much more prominent role than men do in social and political organization? Anthropologist Peggy Sanday (2002) has concluded that matriarchies exist, but not as mirror images of patriarchies. The superior power that men typically have in a patriarchy isn't matched by women's equally disproportionate power in a matriarchy. Many societies, including the Minangkabau of West Sumatra, Indonesia, whom Sanday has studied for decades, lack the substantial power

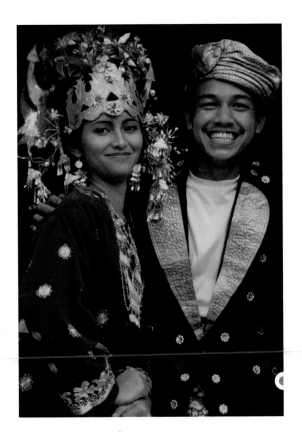

A Minangkabau bride and groom in West Sumatra, Indonesia, where anthropologist Peggy Reeves Sanday has conducted several years of ethnographic field work.

STUDENT: **Masha Sukovic, Ph.D. Candidate**
COUNTRY OF ORIGIN: **Serbia**
SUPERVISING PROFESSOR: **Thomas A. Green**
SCHOOL: **Texas A&M University**

Motherhood as the Key Component of Female Identity in Serbia

Being a mother represents an ultimate task in the life of a typical Serbian woman, and mothers in Serbia are oftentimes surrounded by a semisacred aura, which has historically provided otherwise oppressed and undermined females with a plane in which to exercise some sort of power. While they may be subjugated in other spheres of life, Serbian women are celebrated as mothers by their husbands, in-laws, parents, and others, especially if they bear sons. One of the major reasons for this attitude is the unusually large number of wars fought on Serbian territory, which influenced the idea that women are responsible for prolonging the life of the nation by bearing children. As social scientists have noted, Serbian families are *mother centered* in the sense that members of a family depend on women to satisfy essential nutritional and hygienic needs; that there is an inclination toward matricentric kinship; and that women actually achieve their domination, concentrating and even expanding their power, through self-sacrifice. Women in Serbia see self-sacrifice as a strategy to improve their individual position, to strengthen their confidence, and to help them reconstruct their identity in a period of social and political transition. Serbian women typically tend not to spend money on themselves and often feel guilty if they are spending too much time with their friends or engaging in leisure activities instead of taking care of their children.

Conversely, the concept of motherhood in the United States does not rely heavily on self-sacrifice as it does in Serbia. American women do not necessarily define themselves through motherhood and are not considered "selfish" if they choose not to have children. Women's power in the United States stems from their career status; the money they earn; their self-identification as a scholar, athlete, business owner, or successful, independent person. Whereas Serbian mothers seek to influence their children for as long as possible, American mothers expect that their college-aged children will live away from home, get jobs, and take care of themselves.

In Serbia, motherhood represents the key element of womanhood; indeed, in many ways women seem compelled to become mothers. Moreover, the ethics of self-sacrificial motherhood are deeply entrenched in the consciousness of Serbian women, as is confirmed by the high level of acceptance of the maxim, "Every normal woman should sacrifice for her children." In contrast, women in the United States have children if they wish, but their children do not necessarily define or limit their lives. Because the culture encourages them to shape their identities beyond motherhood, they do not typically see themselves as sacrificing the quality of their lives for their children.

differentials that typify patriarchal systems. Minangkabau women play a central role in social, economic, and ceremonial life and as key symbols. The primacy of matriliny and matriarchy is evident at the village level, as well as regionally, where seniority of matrilineal descent serves as a way to rank villages.

The four million Minangkabau constitute one of Indonesia's largest ethnic groups. Located in the highlands of West Sumatra, their culture is based on the coexistence of matrilineal custom and a nature-based philosophy called adat, complemented by Islam, a more recent (16th-century) arrival. The Minangkabau view men and women as cooperative partners for the common good rather than competitors ruled by self-interest. People gain prestige when they promote social harmony rather than by vying for power.

Sanday considers the Minangkabau a matriarchy because women are the center, origin, and foundation of the social order. Senior women are associated with the central pillar of the traditional house, the oldest one in the village. The oldest village in a cluster is called the "mother village." In ceremonies, women are addressed by the term

used for their mythical Queen Mother. Women control land inheritance, and couples reside matrilocally. In the wedding ceremony, the wife collects her husband from his household and, with her female kin, escorts him to hers. If there is a divorce, the husband simply takes his things and leaves. Yet despite the special position of women, the Minangkabau matriarchy is not the equivalent of female rule, given the Minangkabau belief that all decision making should be by consensus.

Increased Gender Stratification— Patrilineal-Patrilocal Societies

The Igbo are unusual among patrilineal-patrilocal societies, many of which have marked gender stratification. Martin and Voorhies (1975) link the decline of matriliny and the spread of the **patrilineal-patrilocal complex** (consisting of patrilineality, patrilocality, warfare, and male supremacy) to pressure on resources. Faced with scarce resources, patrilineal-patrilocal cultivators such as the Yanomami often wage warfare against other villages. This favors patrilocality and patriliny, customs that keep related men together in the same village, where they make strong allies in battle. Such societies tend to have a sharp domestic–public dichotomy, and men tend to dominate the prestige hierarchy. Men may use their public roles in warfare and trade and their greater prestige to symbolize and reinforce the devaluation or oppression of women.

The patrilineal-patrilocal complex characterizes many societies in highland Papua New Guinea. Women work hard growing and processing subsistence crops, raising and tending pigs (the main domesticated animal and a favorite food), and doing domestic cooking, but they are isolated from the public domain, which men control. Men grow and distribute prestige crops, prepare food for feasts, and arrange marriages. The men even get to trade the pigs and control their use in ritual.

In densely populated areas of the Papua New Guinea highlands, male–female avoidance is associated with strong pressure on resources (Lindenbaum 1972). Men fear all female contacts, including sex. They think that sexual contact with women will weaken them. Indeed, men see everything female as dangerous and polluting. They segregate themselves in men's houses and hide their precious ritual objects from women. They delay marriage, and some never marry.

By contrast, the sparsely populated areas of Papua New Guinea, such as recently settled areas, lack taboos on male–female contacts. The image of woman as polluter fades, heterosexual intercourse is valued, men and women live together, and reproductive rates are high.

In some parts of Papua New Guinea, the patrilineal-patrilocal complex has extreme social repercussions. Regarding females as dangerous and polluting, men may segregate themselves in men's houses (such as this one, located near the Sepik River), where they hide their precious ritual objects from women. Are there places like this in your society?

GENDER AMONG AGRICULTURALISTS

When the economy is based on agriculture, women typically lose their role as primary cultivators. Certain agricultural techniques, particularly plowing, have been assigned to men because of their greater average size and strength (Martin and Voorhies 1975). Except when irrigation is used, plowing eliminates the need for constant weeding, an activity usually done by women.

Cross-cultural data illustrate these contrasts in productive roles. Women were the main workers in 50 percent of the horticultural societies surveyed but in only 15 percent of the agricultural groups. Male subsistence labor dominated 81 percent of the agricultural societies but only 17 percent of the horticultural ones (Martin and Voorhies 1975) (see Table 18.8).

With the advent of agriculture, women were cut off from production for the first time in human history. Perhaps this reflected the need for women to stay closer to home to care for the larger numbers of children that typify agriculture, compared with less labor-intensive economies. Belief systems started contrasting men's valuable extradomestic labor with women's domestic role, now viewed as inferior. (**Extradomestic** means outside the home, within or pertaining to the public domain.) Changes in kinship and postmarital residence patterns also hurt women. Descent groups and polygyny declined with agriculture, and the nuclear family became more common. Living with her husband and children, a woman was isolated from her kinswomen and cowives. Female sexuality is carefully supervised in agricultural economies; men have easier access to divorce and extramarital sex, reflecting a "double standard."

Still, female status in agricultural societies is not inevitably bleak. Gender stratification is associated with plow agriculture rather than with intensive cultivation per se. Studies of peasant gender roles and stratification in France and Spain (Harding 1975; Reiter 1975), which have plow agriculture, show that people think of the house as the female sphere and the fields as the male domain. However, such a dichotomy is not inevitable, as my own research among Betsileo agriculturalists in Madagascar shows.

Betsileo women play a prominent role in agriculture, contributing a third of the hours invested in rice production. They have their customary tasks in the division of labor, but their work is more seasonal than men's is. No one has much to do during the ceremonial season, between mid-June and mid-September. Men work in the rice fields almost daily the rest of the year. Women's cooperative work occurs during transplanting (mid-September through November) and harvesting (mid-March through early May). Along

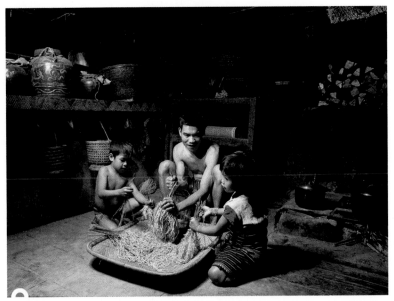

Bilateral kinship systems, combined with subsistence economies in which the sexes have complementary roles in food production and distribution, have reduced gender stratification. Such features are common among Asian rice cultivators, such as the Ifugao of the Philippines (shown here).

with other members of the household, women do daily weeding in December and January. After the harvest, all family members work together winnowing the rice and then transporting it to the granary.

If we consider the strenuous daily task of husking rice by pounding (a part of food preparation rather than production per se), women actually contribute slightly more than 50 percent of the labor devoted to producing and preparing rice before cooking.

Not just women's prominent economic role but traditional social organization enhances female status among the Betsileo. Although postmarital residence is mainly patrilocal, descent rules permit married women to keep membership in and a strong allegiance to their own descent groups. Kinship is broadly and bilaterally calculated (on both sides—as in contemporary North America). The Betsileo exemplify Aihwa Ong's (1989) generalization that bilateral (and matrilineal) kinship systems, combined with subsistence economies in which the sexes have complementary roles in food production and distribution, are characterized by reduced gender stratification. Such societies are common among South Asian peasants (Ong 1989).

Traditionally, Betsileo men participate more in politics, but the women also hold political office. Women sell their produce and products in markets, invest in cattle, sponsor ceremonials, and are mentioned during offerings to ancestors. Arranging marriages, an important extradomestic activity, is more women's concern than men's.

extradomestic
Outside the home; public.

Sometimes Betsileo women seek their own kinswomen as wives for their sons, reinforcing their own prominence in village life and continuing kin-based female solidarity in the village.

The Betsileo illustrate the idea that intensive cultivation does not necessarily entail sharp gender stratification. We can see that gender roles and stratification reflect not just the type of adaptive strategy but also specific cultural attributes. Betsileo women continue to play a significant role in their society's major economic activity, rice production.

PATRIARCHY AND VIOLENCE

Patriarchy describes a political system ruled by men in which women have inferior social and political status, including basic human rights. Barbara Miller (1997), in a study of systematic neglect of females, describes women in rural northern India as "the endangered sex." Societies that feature a full-fledged patrilineal-patrilocal complex, replete with warfare and intervillage raiding, also typify patriarchy. Such practices as dowry murders, female infanticide, and clitoridectomy exemplify patriarchy, which extends from tribal societies such as the Yanomami to state societies such as India and Pakistan.

Although more prevalent in certain social settings than in others, family violence and domestic abuse of women are worldwide problems. Domestic violence certainly occurs in nuclear family settings, such as Canada and the United States. Cities, with their impersonality and isolation from extended kin networks, are breeding grounds for domestic violence.

We've seen that gender stratification is typically reduced in matrilineal, matrifocal, and bilateral societies in which women have prominent roles in the economy and social life. When a woman lives in her own village, she has kin nearby to look after and protect her interests. Even in patrilocal polygynous settings, women often count on the support of their cowives and sons in disputes with potentially abusive husbands. Such settings, which tend to provide a safe haven for women, are retracting rather than expanding in today's world, however. Isolated families and patrilineal social forms have spread at the expense of matrilineality. Many nations have declared polygyny illegal. More and more women, and men, find themselves cut off from extended kin and families of orientation.

With the spread of the women's rights movement and the human rights movement, attention to domestic violence and abuse of women has increased. Laws have been passed, and mediating institutions established. Brazil's female-run police stations for battered women provide an example, as do shelters for victims of domestic abuse in the United States and Canada. But patriarchal institutions do persist in what should be a more enlightened world.

GENDER AND INDUSTRIALISM

The domestic–public dichotomy, which is developed most fully among patrilineal-patrilocal food producers and plow agriculturalists, also has affected gender stratification in industrial societies, including the United States and Canada. However, gender roles have been changing rapidly in North America. The "traditional" idea that "a woman's place is in the home" developed among middle- and upper-class Americans as industrialism spread after 1900. Earlier, pioneer women in the Midwest and West had been recognized as fully productive workers in farming and home industry. Under industrialism, attitudes about gendered work came to vary with class and region. In early industrial Europe, men, women, and children had flocked to factories as wage laborers. Enslaved Americans of both sexes had done grueling work in cotton fields. After abolition, southern African American women continued working as field hands and domestics. Poor white women labored in the South's early cotton mills. In the 1890s, more than one million American women held menial, repetitive, and unskilled factory positions (Margolis 1984, 2000; Martin and Voorhies 1975). Poor, immigrant, and African American women continued to work throughout the 20th century.

After 1900, European immigration produced a male labor force willing to work for wages lower than those of American-born men. Those immigrant men moved into factory jobs that previously had gone to women. As machine tools and mass production further reduced the need for female labor, the notion that women were biologically unfit for factory work began to gain ground (Martin and Voorhies 1975).

Maxine Margolis (1984, 2000) has shown how gendered work, attitudes, and beliefs have varied in response to American economic needs. For example, wartime shortages of men have promoted the idea that work outside the home is women's patriotic duty. During the world wars, the notion that women are biologically unfit for hard physical labor faded. Inflation and the culture of consumption have also spurred female employment. When prices and/or demand rises, multiple paychecks help maintain family living standards.

The steady increase in female paid employment since World War II also reflects the baby boom and industrial expansion. American culture has traditionally defined clerical work, teaching, and nursing as female occupations. With rapid population growth and business expansion after World War II, the demand for women to fill such jobs grew steadily. Employers also found that they could increase their profits by paying women lower wages than they would have to pay returning male war veterans.

Woman's role in the home has been stressed during periods of high unemployment, although when wages fall or inflation occurs simultaneously, female employment may still be accepted. Margolis (1984, 2000) contends that changes in the economy lead to changes in attitudes toward and about women. Economic changes paved the way for the contemporary women's movement, which also was spurred by the publication of Betty Friedan's book *The Feminine Mystique* in 1963 and the founding of NOW, the National Organization for Women, in 1966. The movement in turn promoted expanded work opportunities for women, including the goal of equal pay for equal work. Between 1970 and 2006, the female percentage of the American workforce rose from 38 to 47 percent. In other words, almost half of all Americans who work outside the home are women. Over 73 million women now have paid jobs, compared with 84 million men. Women now fill more than half (57 percent) of all professional jobs (*Statistical Abstract of the United States 2009*, p. 412). And it's not mainly single women working, as once was the case. Table 18.9 presents figures on the ever-increasing cash employment of American wives and mothers.

Note in Table 18.9 that the cash employment of American married men has been falling while that of American married women has been rising. There has been a dramatic change in behavior and attitudes since 1960, when 89 percent of all married men worked, compared with just 32 percent of married women. The comparable figures in 2007 were 77 percent and 62 percent. Ideas about the gender roles of males and females have changed. Compare your grandparents and your parents. Chances are you have a working mother, but your grandmother was more likely a stay-at-home mom. Your grandfather is more likely than your father to have worked in manufacturing and to have belonged to a union. Your father is more likely than your grandfather to have shared child care and domestic responsibilities. Age at marriage has been delayed for both men and women. College educations and professional degrees have increased. What other changes do you associate with the increase in female employment outside the home?

Table 18.10 details employment in the United States in 2006 by gender, income, and job type for year-round full-time workers. Overall, the ratio of female to male income rose from 68 percent in 1989 to 77 percent in 2006.

Today's jobs aren't especially demanding in terms of physical labor. With machines to do the heavy work, the smaller average body size and lesser average strength of women are no longer impediments to blue-collar employment. The main reason we don't see more modern-day Rosies working alongside male riveters is that the U.S. workforce itself is abandoning heavy-goods manufacture. In the 1950s, two-thirds of American jobs were blue-collar, compared with less than 15 percent today. The location of those jobs has shifted within the world capitalist economy. Third World countries with cheaper labor produce steel, automobiles, and other heavy goods less expensively than the United States can, but the United States excels at services. The American

TABLE 18.9 Cash Employment of American Mothers, Wives, and Husbands, 1960–2007*

YEAR	PERCENTAGE OF MARRIED WOMEN, HUSBAND PRESENT WITH CHILDREN UNDER SIX	PERCENTAGE OF ALL MARRIED WOMEN†	PERCENTAGE OF ALL MARRIED MEN‡
1960	19	32	89
1970	30	40	86
1980	45	50	81
1990	59	58	79
2007	62	62	77

*Civilian population 16 years of age and older.

†Husband present.

‡Wife present.

SOURCE: *Statistical Abstract of the United States 2009*, Table 576, p. 375; Table 579, p. 376. http://www.census.gov/compendia/statab/2009edition.html.

TABLE 18.10 Earnings in the United States by Gender and Job Type for Year-Round Full-Time Workers, 2006*

	MEDIAN ANNUAL SALARY		RATIO OF EARNINGS FEMALE/MALE	
	WOMEN	MEN	2006	1989
Median earnings	$32,515	$42,261	77	68
By Job Type				
Management/business/financial	$50,278	$65,777	76	61
Professional	43,005	61,950	69	71
Sales and office	30,365	41,244	74	54
Service	21,202	29,452	72	62

*By occupation of job held longest.

SOURCE: Based on data in *Statistical Abstract of the United States 2009*, Table 627, p. 412. http://www.census.gov/prod/www/statistical_abstract.html.

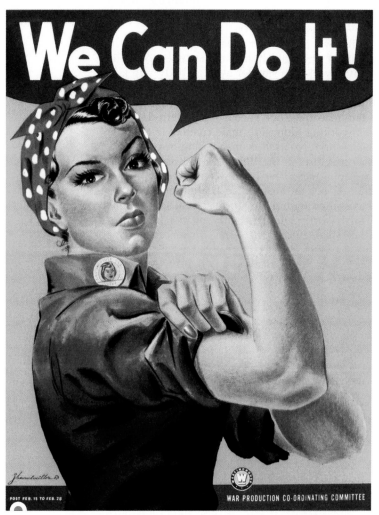

During the world wars, the notion that women were biologically unfit for hard physical labor faded. World War II's Rosie the Riveter—a strong, competent woman dressed in overalls and a bandanna—was introduced as a symbol of patriotic womanhood. Is there a comparable poster woman today? What does her image say about modern gender roles?

mass education system has many inadequacies, but it does train millions of people for service- and information-oriented jobs, from salesclerks to computer operators.

The Feminization of Poverty

Alongside the economic gains of many American women stands an opposite extreme: the feminization of poverty. This refers to the increasing representation of women (and their children) among America's poorest people. Women head over half of U.S. households with incomes below the poverty line. Feminine poverty has been a trend in the United States since World War II, but it has accelerated recently. In 1959, female-headed households accounted for just one-fourth of the American poor. Since then, that figure has more than doubled. About half the female poor are "in transition." These are women who are confronting a temporary economic crisis caused by the departure, disability, or death of a husband. The other half are more permanently dependent on the welfare system or on friends or relatives who live nearby. The feminization of poverty and its consequences in regard to living standards and health are widespread even among wage earners. Many American women continue to work part-time for low wages and meager benefits.

Married couples are much more secure economically than single mothers are. The data in Table 18.11 demonstrate that the average income for married-couple families is more than twice that of families maintained by a woman. The average one-earner family maintained by a woman had an annual income of $31,808 in 2006. This was less than one-half the mean income ($69,716) of a married-couple household.

TABLE 18.11 Median Annual Income of U.S. Households, by Household Type, 2006

	NUMBER OF HOUSEHOLDS (1,000s)	MEDIAN ANNUAL INCOME (DOLLARS)	PERCENTAGE OF MEDIAN EARNINGS COMPARED WITH MARRIED-COUPLE HOUSEHOLDS
All households	116,011	48,201	69
Family households	78,425	59,894	86
Married-couple households	58,945	69,716	100
Male earner, no wife	5,063	47,048	67
Female earner, no husband	14,416	31,808	46
Nonfamily households	37,587	29,083	42
Single male	17,338	35,614	51
Single female	20,249	23,876	34

SOURCE: *Statistical Abstract of the United States 2009*, Table 670, p. 443. http://www.census.gov/prod/www/statistical_abstract.html.

The feminization of poverty isn't just a North American trend. The percentage of female-headed households has been increasing worldwide. In Western Europe, for example, it rose from 24 percent in 1980 to 30 percent in 2000. The figure ranges from below 20 percent in certain South Asian and Southeast Asian countries to almost 50 percent in certain African countries and the Caribbean (Buvinic 1995).

Why must so many women be solo household heads? Where are the men going, and why are they leaving? Among the causes are male migration, civil strife (men off fighting), divorce, abandonment, widowhood, unwed adolescent parenthood, and, more generally, the idea that children are women's responsibility.

Globally, households headed by women tend to be poorer than are those headed by men. In one study, the percentage of single-parent families considered poor was 18 percent in Britain, 20 percent in Italy, 25 percent in Switzerland, 40 percent in Ireland, 52 percent in Canada, and 63 percent in the United States. Poverty, of course, has health consequences. Studies in Brazil, Zambia, and the Philippines show the survival rates of children from female-headed households to be inferior to those of other children (Buvinic 1995).

In the United States, the feminization of poverty is a concern of the National Organization for Women. NOW still exists, alongside many newer women's organizations. The women's movement has become international in scope and membership. And its priorities have shifted from mainly job-oriented to more broadly social issues. These include poverty, homelessness, women's health care, day care, domestic violence, sexual assault, and reproductive rights (Calhoun, Light, and Keller 1997). These issues and others that particularly affect women in the developing countries were addressed at the United Nations' Fourth World Conference on Women held in 1995 in Beijing. In attendance were women's groups from all over the world. Many of these were national and international NGOs (nongovernmental organizations), which work with women at the local level to augment productivity and improve access to credit.

It is widely believed that one way to improve the situation of poor women is to encourage them to organize. New women's groups can in some cases revive or replace traditional forms of social organization that have been disrupted. Membership in a group can help women to mobilize resources, to rationalize production, and to reduce the risks and costs associated with credit. Organization also allows women to develop self-confidence and to decrease dependence on others. Through such organization, poor women throughout the world are working to determine their own needs and priorities, and to change things so as to improve their social and economic situation (Buvinic 1995).

SEXUAL ORIENTATION

Sexual orientation refers to a person's habitual sexual attraction to, and sexual activities with, persons of the opposite sex, *heterosexuality*; the same sex, *homosexuality*; or both sexes, *bisexuality*. *Asexuality*, indifference toward or lack of attraction to either sex, is also a sexual orientation. All four of these forms are found in contemporary North America and throughout the world. But each type of desire and experience holds different meanings for individuals and groups. For example, an asexual disposition may be

anthropology **ATLAS**

Map 14 shows gender-based inequalities in cash employment and secondary education among countries of the world.

sexual orientation
Sexual attraction to persons of the opposite sex, same sex, or either sex.

appreciating ANTHROPOLOGY

Hidden Women, Public Men–Public Women, Hidden Men

Generations of anthropologists have applied their field's comparative, cross-cultural, and biocultural approaches to the study of sex and gender. To some extent at least, gender, sexual preferences, and even sexual orientation are culturally constructed. Here I describe a case in which popular culture and comments by ordinary Brazilians about beauty and sex led me to an analysis of some striking gender differences between Brazil and the United States.

For several years, one of Brazil's top sex symbols was Roberta Close, whom I first saw in a furniture commercial. Roberta ended her pitch with an admonition to prospective furniture buyers to accept no substitute for the advertised product. "Things," she warned, "are not always what they seem."

Nor was Roberta. This petite and incredibly feminine creature was actually a man. Nevertheless, despite the fact that he—or she (speaking as Brazilians do)—is a man posing as a woman, Roberta won a secure place in Brazilian mass culture. Her photos decorated magazines. She was a panelist on a TV variety show and starred in a stage play in Rio with an actor known for his supermacho image. Roberta even inspired a well-known, and apparently heterosexual, pop singer to make a video honoring her. In it, she pranced around Rio's Ipanema Beach in a bikini, showing off her ample hips and buttocks.

The video depicted the widespread male appreciation of Roberta's beauty. As confirmation, one heterosexual man told me he had recently been on the same plane as Roberta and had been struck by her looks. Another man said he wanted to have sex with her. These comments, it seemed to me, illustrated striking cultural contrasts about gender and sexuality. In Brazil, a Latin American country noted for its machismo, heterosexual men did not feel that attraction toward a transvestite blemished their masculine identities.

Roberta Close can be understood in relation to a gender-identity scale that jumps from extreme femininity to extreme masculinity, with little in between. Masculinity is stereotyped as active and public, femininity as passive and domestic. The male–female contrast in rights and behavior is much stronger in Brazil than it is in North America. Brazilians confront a more rigidly defined masculine role than North Americans do.

The active–passive dichotomy also provides a stereotypical model for male–male sexual relations. One man is supposed to be the active, masculine (inserting) partner, whereas the other is the passive, effeminate one. The latter man is derided as a *bicha* (intestinal worm), but little stigma attaches to the inserter. Indeed, many "active" (and married) Brazilian men like to have sex with transvestite prostitutes, who are biological males.

If a Brazilian man is unhappy pursuing either active masculinity or passive effeminacy, there is one other choice—active femininity. For Roberta Close and others like her, the

acceptable in some places but may be perceived as a character flaw in others. Male–male sexual activity may be a private affair in Mexico, rather than public, socially sanctioned, and encouraged as it was among the Etoro (see on pp. 438–439) of Papua New Guinea (see also Blackwood and Wieringa, eds. 1999; Herdt 1981; Kottak and Kozaitis 2008; Lancaster and Di Leonardo, eds. 1997; Nanda 2000).

Recently in the United States there has been a tendency to see sexual orientation as fixed and biologically based. There is not enough information at this time to determine the exact extent to which sexual orientation is based on biology. What we can say is that all human activities and preferences, including erotic expression, are at least partially culturally constructed.

In any society, individuals will differ in the nature, range, and intensity of their sexual interests and urges. No one knows for sure why such individual sexual differences exist. Part of the answer appears to be biological, reflecting genes or hormones. Another part may have to do with experiences during growth and development. But whatever the reasons for individual variation, culture always plays a role in molding individual sexual urges toward a collective norm. And such sexual norms vary from culture to culture.

What do we know about variation in sexual norms from society to society, and over time? A classic cross-cultural study (Ford and Beach 1951) found wide variation in attitudes about masturbation, bestiality (sex with animals), and homosexuality. Even in a single society, such as the United States, attitudes about sex differ over time and with socioeconomic status, region, and rural versus urban residence. However, even in the 1950s, prior to the "age of sexual permissiveness" (the pre-HIV period from the mid-1960s through the 1970s), research showed that almost all American men (92 percent) and more than half cultural demand of ultramasculinity has yielded to a performance of ultrafemininity. These men-women form a third gender in relation to Brazil's polarized male–female identity scale.

Transvestites like Roberta are particularly prominent in Rio de Janeiro's annual Carnaval, when an ambience of inversion rules the city. In the culturally accurate words of the American popular novelist Gregory McDonald, who sets one of his books in Brazil at Carnaval time:

Everything goes topsy-turvy . . . Men become women; women become men; grown-ups become children; rich people pretend they're poor; poor people, rich; sober people become drunkards; thieves become generous. Very topsy-turvy. (McDonald 1984, p. 154)

Most notable in this costumed inversion (DaMatta 1991), men dress as women. Carnaval reveals and expresses normally hidden tensions and conflicts as social life is turned upside down. Reality is illuminated through a dramatic presentation of its opposite.

Roberta Close, in her prime.

This is the final key to Roberta's cultural meaning. She emerged in a setting in which male–female inversion is part of the year's most popular festival. Transvestites are the pièces de résistance at Rio's Carnaval balls, where they dress as scantily as the real women do. They wear postage-stamp bikinis, sometimes with no tops. Photos of real women and transformed ones vie for space in the magazines. It is often impossible to tell the born women from the hidden men. Roberta Close is a permanent incarnation of Carnaval—a year-round reminder of the spirit of Carnavals past, present, and yet to come.

Roberta emerged from a Latin culture whose gender roles contrast strongly with those of the United States. From small village to massive city, Brazilian males are public and Brazilian females are private creatures. Streets, beaches, and bars belong to the men. Although bikinis adorn Rio's beaches on weekends and holidays, there are many more men than women there on weekdays. The men revel in their ostentatiously sexual displays. As they sun themselves and play soccer and volleyball, they regularly stroke their genitals to keep them firm. They are living publicly, assertively, and sexually in a world of men.

Brazilian men must work hard at this public image, constantly acting out their culture's definition of masculine behavior. Public life is a play whose strong roles go to men. Roberta Close, of course, was a public figure. Given that Brazilian culture defines the public world as male, we can perhaps better understand now why the nation's number one sex symbol has been a man who excels at performing in public as a woman.

of American women (54 percent) admitted to masturbation. In the famous Kinsey report (Kinsey, Pomeroy, and Martin 1948), 37 percent of the men surveyed admitted having had at least one sexual experience leading to orgasm with another male. In a later study of 1,200 unmarried women, 26 percent reported same-sex sexual activities. (Because Kinsey's research relied on nonrandom samples, it should be considered merely illustrative, rather than a statistically accurate representation, of sexual behavior at the time.)

Sex acts involving people of the same sex were absent, rare, or secret in only 37 percent of 76 societies for which data were available in the Ford and Beach study (1951). In the others, various forms of same-sex sexual activity were considered normal and acceptable. Sometimes sexual relations between people of the same sex involved transvestism on the part of one of the partners. This chapter's "Appreciating Anthropology" describes how *transvestites* (men dressing as women) form a third gender in relation to Brazil's polarized male–female identity scale. Transvestites, not uncommon in Brazil, are members of one gender (usually males) who dress as another (female). At the time of the case described in "Appreciating Anthropology," a Brazilian man who wished to be changed surgically into a woman (transgendered) could not obtain the necessary operation in Brazil. Some men, including Roberta Close, as described in "Appreciating Anthropology," traveled to Europe for the procedure. Today transgendered Brazilians are well known in Europe. In France, transvestites regardless of nationality commonly are referred to as "Brésiliennes" (the feminine form of the French word for *Brazilian*), so common are Brazilians among the transvestites in Europe. In Brazil many men do have sexual relations with transvestites, with little stigma attached, as described in "Appreciating Anthropology."

Transvestism is perhaps the most common way of forming genders alternative to male and female.

FIGURE 18.3 The Location of the Etoro, Kaluli, and Sambia in Papua New Guinea.

The western part of the island of New Guinea is part of Indonesia. The eastern part of the island is the independent nation of Papua New Guinea, home of the Etoro, Kaluli, and Sambia.

Among the Chukchee of Siberia certain men (usually shamans or religious specialists) copied female dress, speech, and hairstyles and took other men as husbands and sex partners. Female shamans could join a fourth gender, copying men and taking wives. Among the Crow Indians, certain ritual duties were reserved for *berdaches,* men who rejected the male role of bison hunter, raider, and warrior and formed a third gender (Lowie 1935).

Transvestism did not characterize male–male sex among the Sudanese Azande, who valued the warrior role (Evans-Pritchard 1970). Prospective warriors—young men aged 12 to 20—left their families and shared quarters with adult fighting men, who paid bridewealth for, and had sex with, them. During this apprenticeship, the young men did the domestic duties of women. Upon reaching warrior status, these young men took their own younger male brides. Later, retiring from the warrior role, Azande men married women. Flexible in

their sexual expression, Azande males had no difficulty shifting from sex with older men (as male brides), to sex with younger men (as warriors), to sex with women (as husbands) (see Murray and Roscoe, eds. 1998).

An extreme example of tension involving male–female sexual relations in Papua New Guinea is provided by the Etoro (Kelly 1976), a group of 400 people who subsist by hunting and horticulture in the Trans-Fly region (Figure 18.3). The Etoro illustrate the power of culture in molding human sexuality. The following account, based on ethnographic field work by Raymond C. Kelly in the late 1960s, applies only to Etoro males and their beliefs. Etoro cultural norms prevented the male anthropologist who studied them from gathering comparable information about female attitudes. Note, also, that the activities described have been discouraged by missionaries. Since there has been no restudy of the Etoro specifically focusing on these activities, the extent to which these practices continue today is unknown. For this reason, I'll use the past tense in describing them.

Etoro opinions about sexuality were linked to their beliefs about the cycle of birth, physical growth, maturity, old age, and death. Etoro men believed that semen was necessary to give life force to a fetus, which was, they believed, implanted in a woman by an ancestral spirit. Sexual intercourse during pregnancy nourished the growing fetus. The Etoro believed that men had a limited lifetime supply of semen. Any sex act leading to ejaculation was seen as draining that supply, and as sapping a man's virility and vitality. The birth of children, nurtured by semen, symbolized a necessary sacrifice that would lead to the husband's eventual death. Heterosexual intercourse, required only for reproduction, was discouraged. Women who wanted too much sex were viewed as witches, hazardous to their husbands' health. Etoro culture allowed heterosexual intercourse only about 100 days a year. The rest of the time it was tabooed. Seasonal birth clustering shows the taboo was respected.

So objectionable was male–female sex that it was removed from community life. It could occur neither in sleeping quarters nor in the fields. Coitus could happen only in the woods, where it was risky because poisonous snakes, the Etoro claimed, were attracted by the sounds and smells of male–female sex.

Although coitus was discouraged, sex acts between men were viewed as essential. Etoro believed that boys could not produce semen on their own. To grow into men and eventually give life force to their children, boys had to acquire semen orally from older men. From the age of 10 until adulthood, boys were inseminated by older men. No taboos were attached to this. Such oral insemination could proceed in the sleeping area or garden. Every three years, a group of boys around the age of 20 was formally initiated into manhood. They went to a secluded mountain lodge, where they were visited and inseminated by several older men.

Male–male sex among the Etoro was governed by a code of propriety. Although sexual relations between older and younger males were considered culturally essential, those between boys of the same age were discouraged. A boy who took semen from other youths was believed to be sapping their life force and stunting their growth. A boy's rapid physical development might suggest that he was getting semen from other boys. Like a sex-hungry wife, he might be shunned as a witch.

These sexual practices among the Etoro rested not on hormones or genes but on cultural beliefs and traditions. The Etoro were an extreme example of a male–female avoidance pattern that has been widespread in Papua New Guinea and in patrilineal-patrilocal societies. The Etoro shared a cultural pattern, which Gilbert Herdt (1984) calls "ritualized homosexuality," with some 50 other tribes in Papua New Guinea, especially in that country's Trans-Fly region. These societies illustrate one extreme of a male–female avoidance pattern that is widespread in Papua New Guinea and indeed in many patrilineal-patrilocal societies.

Flexibility in sexual expression seems to be an aspect of our primate heritage. Both masturbation and same-sex sexual activity exist among chimpanzees and other primates. Male bonobos (pygmy chimps) regularly engage in a form of mutual masturbation known as "penis fencing." Females get sexual pleasure from rubbing their genitals against those of other females (de Waal 1997). Our primate sexual potential is molded by culture, the environment, and reproductive necessity. Heterosexual coitus is practiced in all human societies—which, after all, must reproduce themselves—but alternatives are also widespread (Rathus, Nevid, and Fichner-Rathus 2010). Like gender roles and attitudes more generally, the sexual component of human personality and identity—just how we express our "natural" sexual urges—is a matter that culture and environment direct and limit.

Acing the COURSE

Summary

1. *Gender roles* are the tasks and activities that a culture assigns to each sex. *Gender stereotypes* are oversimplified ideas about attributes of males and females. *Gender stratification* describes an unequal distribution of rewards by gender, reflecting different positions in a social hierarchy. Cross-cultural comparison reveals some recurrent patterns involving the division of labor by

gender and gender-based differences in reproductive strategies. Gender roles and gender stratification also vary with environment, economy, adaptive strategy, level of social complexity, and degree of participation in the world economy.

2. When gathering is prominent, gender status is more equal than it is when hunting or fishing dominates the foraging economy. Gender status is more equal when the domestic and public spheres aren't sharply separated. Foragers lack two public arenas that contribute to higher male status among food producers: warfare and organized interregional trade.

3. Gender stratification also is linked to descent and residence. Women's status in matrilineal societies tends to be high because descent-group membership, political succession, land allocation, and overall social identity come through female links. Women in many societies wield power and make decisions, or are central to social organization. Scarcity of resources promotes intervillage warfare, patriliny, and patrilocality. The localization of related males is adaptive for military solidarity. Men may use their warrior role to symbolize and reinforce the social devaluation and oppression of women.

4. With the advent of plow agriculture, women were removed from production. The distinction between women's domestic work and men's "productive" labor reinforced the contrast between men as public and valuable and women as homebound and inferior. Patriarchy describes a political system ruled by men in which women have inferior social and political status, including basic human rights. Some expressions of patriarchy include female infanticide, dowry murders, domestic abuse, and forced genital operations.

5. Americans' attitudes toward gender vary with class and region. When the need for female labor declines, the idea that women are unfit for many jobs increases, and vice versa. Factors such as war, falling wages, and inflation help explain female cash employment and Americans' attitudes toward it. Countering the economic gains of many American women is the feminization of poverty. This has become a global phenomenon, as impoverished female-headed households have increased worldwide.

6. There has been a recent tendency to see sexual orientation as fixed and biologically based. But to some extent, at least, all human activities and preferences, including erotic expression, are influenced by culture. Sexual orientation stands for a person's habitual sexual attraction to, and activities with, persons of the opposite sex, *heterosexuality*; the same sex, *homosexuality*; or both sexes, *bisexuality*. Sexual norms vary widely from culture to culture.

Key Terms

domestic–public dichotomy 423
extradomestic 431
gender roles 419
gender stereotypes 419
gender stratification 419
matrifocal 430
matrilineal descent 427

matrilocality 427
patriarchy 432
patrilineal descent 427
patrilineal-patrilocal complex 430
patrilocality 427
sexual dimorphism 419
sexual orientation 435

Test Yourself!

MULTIPLE CHOICE

1. "The biological nature of men and women [should be seen] not as a narrow enclosure limiting the human organism, but rather as a broad base upon which a variety of structures can be built."
   a. This statement reflects an idea that is a cultural generality, but not a cultural universal.
   b. This passage reflects the predominant anthropological position on sex-gender roles and biology.
   c. The basic assumptions in this passage are threatened by new medical technologies.
   d. This passage is culturally ethnocentric.
   e. This statement reflects ideas on gender and sex that ignore over 50 years of ethnographic evidence.

2. Traditionally among the Hidatsa, women made boats. Pawnee women worked wood. Among the Mbuti "pygmies," women hunt. Cases such as these suggest that
   a. swing activities usually are done by women.
   b. biology has nothing to do with gender roles.
   c. anthropologists are overly optimistic about finding a society with perfect gender equality.

d. patterns of division of labor by gender are culturally general—not universal.

e. exceptions to cross-cultural generalization are actually the rule.

3. Among foragers
   a. men excel in the harsh life and therefore accrue vastly more prestige than women.
   b. warfare makes men dominant over women.
   c. the status of women falls when they provide most of the food.
   d. the lack of a clear public-domestic dichotomy is related to relatively mild gender inequality.
   e. men and women are completely equal; there is no gender inequality.

4. Which of the following statements about the domestic-public dichotomy is true?
   a. It is stronger among foragers than among peasants.
   b. It is not significant in urban industrial societies.
   c. It is stronger among peasants than among foragers.
   d. It is reinforced in American society by women working both inside and outside the home.
   e. It is not present in the modern industrial states of the Western world.

5. Which of the following is *not* part of the patrilineal-patrilocal complex?
   a. patrilineality
   b. patrilocality
   c. warfare
   d. male supremacy
   e. reduced gender stratification

6. In what kind of society do anthropologists most typically find forced female genital operations, intervillage raiding, female infanticide, and dowry?
   a. patrilineal-patrilocal
   b. matrilineal-patrilocal
   c. matrilineal-matrilocal
   d. patrilineal-matrilocal
   e. patrilineal-neolocal

7. The "traditional" idea that "a woman's place is in the home"
   a. developed among middle- and upper-class Americans as industrialism spread after 1900.
   b. is actually a cultural universal.
   c. accurately reflects the worldwide sexual division of labor.
   d. is based in the preindustrial era and began to disappear as women moved into the factories in the 1900s.
   e. was part of the Pledge of Allegiance until it was challenged in the early 1800s.

8. In comparing gender roles in different societies, which of the following is true?
   a. Equality between the genders is common among horticulturalists.
   b. There are many societies in which women control all the strategic resources and carry out the most prestigious activities.
   c. The more women contribute to the domestic sphere, the more publicly recognized power they achieve.
   d. The less women contribute to the public sphere, the more publicly recognized power they achieve.
   e. Patriarchies are strongest in societies in which men control significant goods that are exchanged with people outside the family.

9. What have recent cross-cultural studies of gender roles demonstrated?
   a. The gender roles of men and women are largely determined by their biological capabilities—such as relative strength, endurance, and intelligence.
   b. Women are subservient in nearly all societies because their subsistence activities contribute much less to the total diet than do those of men.
   c. Foraging, horticultural, pastoral, and industrial societies all have similar attitudes toward gender roles.
   d. The relative status of women is variable, depending on factors such as subsistence strategy, the importance of warfare, and the prevalence of a domestic-public dichotomy.
   e. Changes in the gender roles of men and women usually are associated with social decay and anarchy.

10. All of the following are key ideas to take away from this chapter's discussion of sexual orientation *except*:
    a. Different types of sexual desires and experiences hold different meanings for individuals and groups.
    b. In a society, individuals will differ in the nature, range, and intensity of sexual interests and urges.
    c. Culture always plays a role in molding individual sexual urges toward a collective norm and these norms vary from culture to culture.
    d. Asexuality, indifference toward, or lack of attraction to either sex, is also a sexual orientation.
    e. There is conclusive scientific evidence that sexual orientation is genetically determined.

FILL IN THE BLANK

1. Sex differences are biological, while _____ refers to the cultural construction of whether one is female, male, or something else.

2. _____ refer to the tasks and activities that a culture assigns to the sexes.

3. In general, the status of women is higher in societies with _____ descent than in those with _____ descent.

4. _____ refers to an unequal distribution of socially valued resources, power, prestige, and personal freedom between men and women.

5. Americans' attitudes towards gender vary with class and region. When the need for female labor declines, the idea that women are unfit for many jobs _____, and vice versa.

CRITICAL THINKING

1. How are sexuality, sex, and gender related to each other? What are the differences between these three concepts? Provide an argument about why anthropologists are uniquely positioned to study the relationship between sexuality, sex, and gender in society.

2. Using your own society, give an example of a gender role, a gender stereotype, and gender stratification.

3. Patricia Draper's research among the Ju/'hoansi is especially useful in showing the relationships between economics, gender roles, and stratification because she studied both foragers and a group of former foragers who had become sedentary. What did she find? How does this case illustrate the historical interplay between local, national, and international forces?

4. What is the feminization of poverty? Where is this trend occurring, and what are some of its causes?

5. This chapter describes Raymond Kelly's research among the Etoro of Papua New Guinea during the 1960s. What were his findings regarding Etoro male-female sexual relations? How did Kelly's own gender affect some of the content and extent of his study? Can you think of other research projects where the ethnographer's gender would have an impact?

Blackwood, E., and S. Wieringa, eds.

1999 *Female Desires: Same-Sex Relations and Transgender Practices across Cultures.* New York: Columbia University Press. Lesbianism and male homosexuality in cross-cultural perspective.

Bonvillain, N.

2007 *Women and Men: Cultural Constructions of Gender,* 4th ed. Upper Saddle River, NJ: Prentice Hall. A cross-cultural study of gender roles and relationships, from bands to industrial societies.

Brettell, C. B., and C. F. Sargent, eds.

2009 *Gender in Cross-Cultural Perspective,* 5th ed. Upper Saddle River, NJ: Pearson/Prentice Hall. Articles on variation in gender systems across cultures.

M. S., and M. A. Messner, eds.

2010 *Men's Lives,* 8th ed. Boston: Pearson/Allyn & Bacon. The study of men in society and concepts of masculinity in the United States.

Rathus, S. A., J. S. Nevid, and J. Fichner-Rathus

2010 *Human Sexuality in a World of Diversity,* 8th ed. Boston: Pearson/Allyn & Bacon. Multicultural and ethnic perspectives.

Ward, M. C., and M. Edelstein

2009 *A World Full of Women,* 5th ed. Boston: Allyn & Bacon. A global and comparative approach to the study of women.

Go to our Online Learning Center website at **www.mhhe.com/kottak** for Internet exercises directly related to the content of this chapter.

Why and how do anthropologists study kinship?

How do families and descent groups differ, and what are their social correlates?

How is kinship calculated, and how are relatives classified, in various societies?

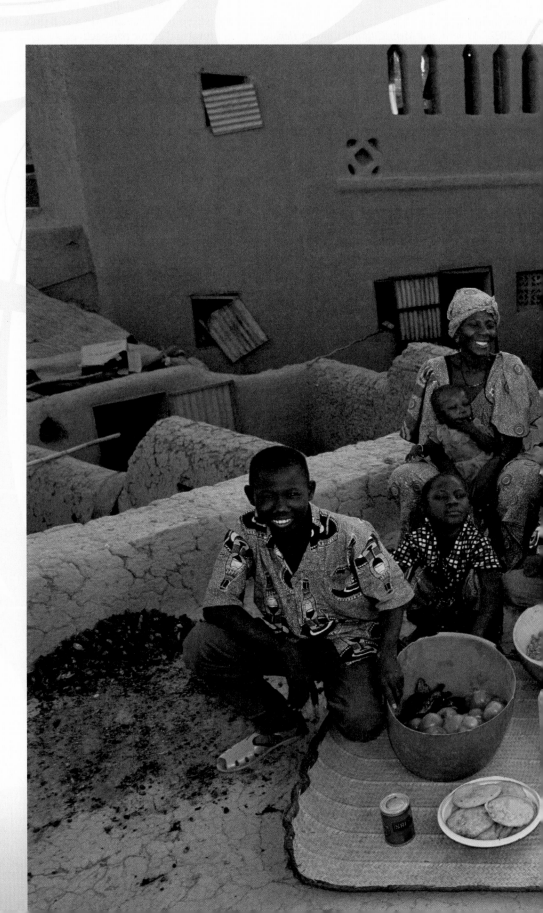

This polygynous family (a man with multiple wives) in Mali, West Africa, displays their normal weekly diet on the roof of their mud-brick home. Ethnographers have studied many family types besides the nuclear family–the traditional American ideal.

Families, Kinship, and Descent

understanding OURSELVES

Although it still is something of an ideal in our culture, the nuclear family (mother, father, and biological children) now accounts for fewer than one-fourth of all American households. Such phrases as "love and marriage," "marriage and the family," and "mom and pop" no longer apply to a majority of American households. What kind of family raised you? Perhaps it was a nuclear family. Or maybe you were raised by a single parent, with or without the help of extended kin. Perhaps your extended kin acted as your parents. Or maybe you had a stepparent and/or step- or half-siblings in a blended family. Maybe your family matches none of these descriptions, or fits different descriptions at different times.

Although contemporary American families may seem amazingly diverse, other cultures offer family alternatives that Americans might have trouble understanding. Imagine a society in which someone doesn't know for sure, and doesn't care much about, who his actual mother was. Consider Joseph Rabe, a Betsileo man who was my field assistant in Madagascar. Rabe, who had been raised by his aunt—his father's sister—told me about two sisters, one of whom was his mother and the other his mother's sister. He knew their names, but he didn't know which was which. Illustrating an adoptive pattern common among the Betsileo, Rabe was given as a toddler to his childless aunt. His mother and her sister lived far away and died in his childhood (as did his father), and so he didn't really know them. But he was very close to his father's sister, for whom he used the term for mother. Indeed, he had to call her that because the Betsileo have only one kin term, *reny*, for mother, mother's sister, and father's sister. (They also use a single term, *ray*, for father and all uncles.) The difference between "real" (biologically based) and socially constructed kinship didn't matter to Rabe.

Contrast the Betsileo case with Americans' attitudes about kinship and adoption. On family-oriented radio talk shows, I've heard hosts distinguish between "birth mothers" and adoptive mothers, and between "sperm daddies" and "daddies of the heart." The latter may be adoptive fathers, or stepfathers who have "been like fathers" to someone. American culture tends to promote the idea that kinship is, and should be, biological. It's increasingly common for adopted children to seek out their birth parents (which used to be discouraged as disruptive), even after a perfectly satisfactory upbringing in an adoptive family. The American emphasis on biology for kinship is seen also in the recent proliferation of DNA testing. Viewing our beliefs through the lens of cross-cultural comparison helps us appreciate that kinship and biology don't always converge, nor do they need to.

FAMILIES

The kinds of societies anthropologists have studied traditionally, including many examples considered in this chapter, have stimulated a strong interest in families, along with larger systems of kinship, descent, and marriage. Cross-culturally, the social construction of kinship illustrates considerable diversity. Understanding kinship systems has become an essential part of anthropology because of the importance of those systems to the people we study.

We are ready to take a closer look at the systems of kinship and descent that have organized human life during much of our history.

Ethnographers quickly recognize social divisions—groups—within any society they study. During field work, they learn about significant groups by observing their activities and composition. People often live in the same village or neighborhood or work, pray, or celebrate together because they are related in some way. To understand the social structure, an ethnographer must investigate such kin ties. For example, the most significant local groups may consist of descendants of the same grandfather. These people may live in neighboring houses, farm adjoining fields, and help each other in everyday tasks. Other sorts of groups, based on different or more distant kin links, get together less often.

The nuclear family is one kind of kin group that is widespread in human societies. The nuclear family consists of parents and children, normally living together in the same household. Other kin groups include extended families (families consisting of three or more generations) and descent groups—lineages and clans. Such groups are not usually residentially based as the nuclear family is. Extended family members get together from time to time, but they don't necessarily live together. Branches of a given descent group may reside in several villages and rarely assemble for common activity. **Descent groups,** which are composed of people claiming common ancestry, are basic units in the social organization of nonindustrial food producers.

Nuclear and Extended Families

A nuclear family lasts only as long as the parents and children remain together. Most people belong to at least two nuclear families at different times in their lives. They are born into a family consisting of their parents and siblings. When they reach adulthood, they may marry and establish a nuclear family that includes the spouse and eventually the children. Since most societies permit divorce, some people establish more than one family through marriage.

Anthropologists distinguish between the **family of orientation** (the family in which one is born and grows up) and the **family of procreation** (formed when one marries and has children). From the individual's point of view, the critical relationships are with parents and siblings in the family of orientation and with spouse and children in the family of procreation.

In most societies, relations with nuclear family members (parents, siblings, and children) take precedence over relations with other kin. Nuclear family organization is very widespread but not universal, and its significance in society differs greatly from one place to another. In a

Siblings play a prominent role in child rearing in many societies. Here, in China's Yunnan province, two sisters give their younger brother a drink of water from a folded leaf. Do your siblings belong to your family of orientation or your family of procreation?

descent group
Group based on belief in shared ancestry.

few societies, such as the classic Nayar case described below, nuclear families are rare or nonexistent. In others, the nuclear family plays no special role in social life. The nuclear family is not always the basis of residence or authority organization. Other social units—most notably descent groups and extended families—can assume many of the functions otherwise associated with the nuclear family.

Consider an example from the former Yugoslavia. Traditionally, among the Muslims of western Bosnia (Lockwood 1975), nuclear families lacked autonomy. Several such families were embedded in an extended family household called a *zadruga*. The *zadruga* was headed by a male household head and his wife, the senior woman. It also included married sons and their wives and children, and unmarried sons and daughters. Each nuclear family had a sleeping room, decorated and partly furnished from the bride's trousseau. However, possessions—even clothing items—were freely shared by *zadruga* members. Even trousseau items were appropriated for use elsewhere. Such a residential unit is known as a *patrilocal* extended family, because each couple resides in the husband's father's household after marriage.

The *zadruga* took precedence over its component units. Social interaction was more usual among women, men, or children than between spouses or between parents and children. Larger

family of orientation
Nuclear family in which one is born and grows up.

family of procreation
Nuclear family established when one marries and has children.

households ate at three successive settings: for men, women, and children. Traditionally, all children over 12 slept together in boys' or girls' rooms. When a woman wished to visit another village, she sought the permission of the male *zadruga* head. Although men usually felt closer to their own children than to those of their brothers, they were obliged to treat them equally. Children were disciplined by any adult in the household. When a nuclear family broke up, children under seven went with the mother. Older children could choose between their parents. Children were considered part of the household where they were born even if their mother left. One widow who remarried had to leave her five children, all over seven, in their father's *zadruga*, headed by his brother.

Another example of an alternative to the nuclear family is provided by the Nayars (or Nair), a large and powerful caste on the Malabar Coast of southern India (Figure 19.1). Their traditional kinship system was matrilineal (descent traced only through females). Nayar lived in matrilineal extended family compounds called *tarawads*. The *tarawad* was a residential complex with several buildings, its own temple, granary, water well, orchards, gardens, and land holdings. Headed by a senior woman, assisted by her brother, the *tarawad* housed her siblings, sisters' children, and other matrikin—matrilineal relatives (Gough 1959; Shivaram 1996).

FIGURE 19.1 Location of the Nayars in India's Kerala province.

This just-married Khasi couple poses (in 1997) in India's northeastern city of Shillong. The Khasis are matrilineal, tracing descent through women and taking their maternal ancestors' surnames. Women choose their husbands, family incomes are pooled, and extended family households are managed by older women.

Traditional Nayar marriage seems to have been hardly more than a formality—a kind of coming-of-age ritual. A young woman would go through a marriage ceremony with a man, after which they might spend a few days together at her *tarawad*. Then the man would return to his own *tarawad*, where he lived with his sisters, aunts, and other matrikin. Nayar men belonged to a warrior class, who left home regularly for military expeditions, returning permanently to their *tarawad* on retirement. Nayar women could have multiple sexual partners. Children became members of the mother's *tarawad*; they were not considered to be relatives of their biological father. Indeed, many Nayar children didn't even know who their genitor was. Child care was the responsibility of the *tarawad*. Nayar society therefore reproduced itself biologically without the nuclear family.

Industrialism and Family Organization

For many Americans and Canadians, the nuclear family is the only well-defined kin group. Family isolation arises from geographic mobility, which is associated with industrialism, so that a nuclear family focus is characteristic of many modern nations. Born into a family of orientation, North Americans leave home for work or college, and the break with parents is under way. Eventually most North Americans marry and start a family of procreation. Because less than 3 percent of the U.S. population now farms, most people aren't tied to the land. Selling our labor on the market, we often move to places where jobs are available.

Many married couples live hundreds of miles from their parents. Their jobs have determined where they live. Such a postmarital residence pattern is called **neolocality:** Married couples are expected to establish a new place of residence—a "home of their own." Among middle-class North Americans, neolocal residence is both a cultural preference and a statistical norm. Most middle-class Americans eventually establish households and nuclear families of their own.

Within stratified nations, value systems vary to some extent from class to class, and so does kinship. There are significant differences between middle-class and poorer North Americans. For example, in the lower class the incidence of *expanded family households* (those that include nonnuclear relatives) is greater than it is in the middle class. When an expanded family household includes three or more generations, it is an **extended family household,** such as the *zadruga*. Another type of expanded family is the *collateral household*, which includes siblings and their spouses and children.

The higher proportion of expanded family households among poorer Americans has been

Unable to survive economically as nuclear family units, relatives may band together in an expanded family household and pool their resources. This photo, taken in 2002 in Munich, Germany, shows German Roma, or Gypsies. Together with her children and grandchildren, this grandmother resides in an expanded family household.

In contemporary North America, single-parent families are increasing at a rapid rate. In 1960, 88 percent of American children lived with both parents, compared with 68 percent today. Shown here, a single mom helps her young son brush his teeth. What do you see as the main differences between nuclear families and single-parent families?

explained as an adaptation to poverty (Stack 1975). Unable to survive economically as nuclear family units, relatives band together in an expanded household and pool their resources. Adaptation to poverty causes kinship values and attitudes to diverge from middle-class norms. Thus, when North Americans raised in poverty achieve financial success, they often feel obligated

neolocality
Couple establishes new residence.

extended family household
Household with three or more generations.

appreciating DIVERSITY

Social Security, Kinship Style

In all societies people care for others. Sometimes, as in our own state-organized society, social security is a function of government as well as of the individual and the family. In other societies, such as Arembepe, as described here, social security is part of systems of kinship, marriage, and fictive kinship.

My book *Assault on Paradise,* 4th edition (Kottak 2006), describes social relations in Arembepe, the Brazilian fishing community I've studied since the 1960s. When I first studied Arembepe, I was struck by how similar its social relations were to those in the egalitarian, kin-based societies anthropologists have studied traditionally. The twin assertions "We're all equal here" and "We're all relatives here" were offered repeatedly as Arembepeiros' summaries of the nature and basis of local life. Like members of a clan (who claim to share common ancestry, but who can't say exactly how they are related), most villagers couldn't trace precise genealogical links to their distant kin.

"What difference does it make, as long as we know we're relatives?"

As in most nonindustrial societies, close personal relations were either based or modeled on kinship. A degree of community solidarity was promoted, for example, by the myth that everyone was kin. However, social solidarity was actually much *less* developed in Arembepe than in societies with clans and lineages—which use genealogy to include some people, and *exclude* others from membership, in a given descent group. Intense social solidarity demands that some people be excluded. By asserting they all were related—that is, by excluding no one—Arembepeiros were actually weakening kinship's potential strength in creating and maintaining group solidarity.

Rights and obligations always are associated with kinship and marriage. In Arembepe, the closer the kin connection and the more formal the marital tie, the greater the rights and obligations. Couples could be married formally

or informally. The most common union was a stable common-law marriage. Less common, but with more prestige, was legal (civil) marriage, performed by a justice of the peace and conferring inheritance rights. The union with the most prestige combined legal validity with a church ceremony.

The rights and obligations associated with kinship and marriage constituted the local social security system, but people had to weigh the benefits of the system against its costs. The most obvious cost was this: Villagers had to share in proportion to their success. As ambitious men climbed the local ladder of success, they got more dependents. To maintain their standing in public opinion, and to guarantee that they could depend on others in old age, they had to share. However, sharing was a powerful leveling mechanism. It drained surplus wealth and restricted upward mobility.

How, specifically, did this leveling work? As is often true in stratified nations, Brazilian national cultural norms are set by the upper classes. Middle- and upper-class Brazilians usually marry legally and in church. Even Arembepeiros knew this was the only "proper" way

to provide financial help to a wide circle of less fortunate relatives. This chapter's "Appreciating Diversity" shows how poor Brazilians use kinship, marriage, and fictive kinship as a form of social security.

Changes in North American Kinship

Although the nuclear family remains a cultural ideal for many Americans, Table 19.1 and Figure 19.2 show that nuclear families accounted for only about 23 percent of American households in 2007. Other domestic arrangements now outnumber the "traditional" American household more than four to one. There are several reasons for this changing household composition. Women increasingly are joining men in the cash workforce. This often removes them from their family of orientation while making it economically feasible to delay marriage.

Furthermore, job demands compete with romantic attachments. The median age at first marriage for American women rose from 21 years in 1970 to 26 in 2008. For men the comparable ages were 23 and 27 (U.S. Census Bureau 2009).

Also, the U.S. divorce rate has risen, making divorced Americans much more common today than they were in 1970. Between 1970 and 2007 the number of divorced Americans quintupled— some 23 million in 2007 versus 4.3 million in 1970. (Note, however, that each divorce creates two divorced people.) Table 19.2 shows the ratio of divorces to marriages in the United States for selected years between 1950 and 2006. The major jump in the American divorce rate took place between 1960 and 1980. During that period the ratio of divorces to marriage doubled. Since 1980 the ratio has stayed the same, slightly below 50 percent. That is, each year there are about half as many new divorces as there are new marriages.

to marry. The most successful and ambitious local men copied the behavior of elite Brazilians. By doing so, they hoped to acquire some of their prestige.

However, legal marriage drained individual wealth, for example, by creating a responsibility to help one's in-laws financially. Such obligations could be regular and costly. Obligations to kids also increased with income, because successful people tended to have more living children. Children were valued as companions and as an eventual economic benefit to their parents. Boys especially were prized because their economic prospects were so much brighter than those of girls.

Children's chances of survival surged dramatically in wealthier households with better diets. The normal household diet included fish—usually in a stew with tomatoes, onions, palm oil, vinegar, and lemon. Dried beef replaced fish once a week. Roasted manioc flour was the main source of calories and was eaten at all meals. Other daily staples included coffee, sugar, and salt. Fruits and vegetables were eaten in season. Diet was one of the main contrasts between households. The poorest people didn't eat fish regularly; often they subsisted on manioc flour, coffee, and sugar. Better-off households supplemented the staples with milk, butter, eggs, rice, beans, and more ample portions of fresh fish, fruits, and vegetables.

Adequate incomes bought improved diets and provided the means and confidence to seek out better medical attention than was locally available. Most of the children born in the wealthier households survived. But this meant more mouths to feed, and (since the heads of such households usually wanted a better education for their children) it meant increased expenditures on schooling. The correlation between economic success and large families was a siphoner of wealth that restricted individual economic advance. Tomé, a fishing entrepreneur, envisioned a life of constant hard work if he was to feed, clothe, and educate his growing family. Tomé and his wife had never lost a child. But he recognized that his growing family would, in the short run, be a drain on his resources. "But in the end, I'll have successful sons to help their mother and me, if we need it, in our old age."

Arembepeiros knew who could afford to share with others; success can't be concealed in a small community. Villagers based their expectations of others on this knowledge. Successful people had to share with more kin and in-laws, and with more distant kin, than did poorer people. Successful captains and boat owners were expected to buy beer for ordinary fishermen; store owners had to sell on credit. As in bands and tribes, any well-off person was expected to exhibit a corresponding generosity. With increasing wealth, people were also asked more frequently to enter ritual kin relationships. Through baptism—which took place twice a year when a priest visited, or which could be done outside—a child acquired two godparents. These people became the coparents (*compadres*) of the baby's parents. The fact that ritual kinship obligations increased with wealth was another factor limiting individual economic advance.

We see that kinship, marriage, and ritual kinship in Arembepe had costs and benefits. The costs were limits on the economic advance of individuals. The primary benefit was social security—guaranteed help from kin, in-laws, and ritual kin in times of need. Benefits, however, came only after costs had been paid—that is, only to those who had lived "proper" lives, not deviating too noticeably from local norms, especially those about sharing.

The rate of growth in single-parent families also has outstripped population growth, quintupling from fewer than 4 million in 1970 to 19 million in 2007. (The overall American population in 2007 was 1.5 times its size in 1970.) The percentage (23 percent) of children living in fatherless (mother-headed, no resident dad) households in 2007 was more than twice the 1970 rate, while the percentage (3 percent) in motherless (father-headed, no resident mom) homes increased fourfold. About 56 percent of American women and 60 percent of American men were currently married in 2006, versus 60 and 65 percent, respectively, in 1970 (Fields 2004; Fields and Casper 2001; *Statistical Abstract of the United States 2009*). Recent census data also reveal that more American women are now living without a husband than with one. In 2005, 51 percent of women said they were living without a spouse, compared with 35 percent in 1950 and 49 percent in 2000 (Roberts et al. 2007). To be sure, contemporary Americans maintain social lives through work, friendship, sports, clubs, religion, and organized social activities. However, the growing isolation from kin that these figures suggest may well be unprecedented in human history.

Table 19.3 documents similar changes in family and household size in the United States and Canada between 1980 and 2007. Those figures confirm a general trend toward smaller families and living units in North America. This trend is also detectable in Western Europe and other industrial nations.

The entire range of kin attachments is narrower for North Americans, particularly those in the middle class, than it is for nonindustrial peoples. Although we recognize ties to grandparents, uncles, aunts, and cousins, we have less contact with, and depend less on, those relatives than people in other cultures do. We see this when we

TABLE 19.1 Changes in Family and Household Organization in the United States, 1970 versus 2007

	1970	2007
Numbers:		
Total number of households	63 million	116 million
Number of people per household	3.1	2.6
Percentages:		
Married couples living with children	40%	23%
Family households	81%	68%
Households with five or more people	21%	10%
People living alone	17%	27%
Percentage of single-mother families	5%	12%
Percentage of single-father families	0%	4%
Households with own children under 18	45%	32%

SOURCES: From U.S. Census data in J. M. Fields, "America's Families and Living Arrangements: 2003," *Current Population Reports*, P20-553, November 2004, http://www.census.gov/prod/2004pubs/p20-553.pdf, p. 4; J. M. Fields and L. M. Casper, "America's Families and Living Arrangements: Population Characteristics, 2000," *Current Population Reports*, P20-537, June 2001, http://www.census.gov/prod/2001pubs/p20-537.pdf; U.S. Census Bureau, *Statistical Abstract of the United States 2009*, Tables 58, 60, 63, http://www.census.gov/compendia/statab/2009edition.html.

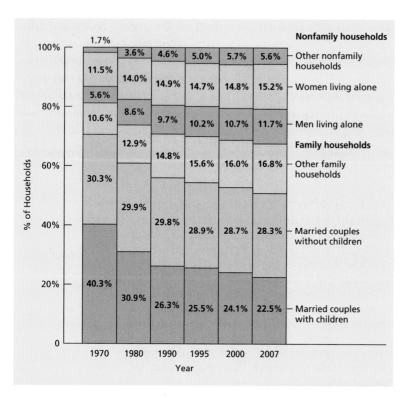

FIGURE 19.2 Households by Type: Selected Years, 1970 to 2007 (Percent Distribution).

SOURCES: J. M. Fields, "America's Families and Living Arrangements: 2003," *Current Population Reports*, P20-553, November 2004, http://www.census.gov/prod/2004pubs/p20-553.pdf, p. 4; *Statistical Abstract of the United States 2009*, Table 58, p. 52, and Table 60, p. 53, http://www.census.gov/compendia/statab/2009edition.html.

answer a few questions: Do we know exactly how we are related to all our cousins? How much do we know about our ancestors, such as their full names and where they lived? How many of the people with whom we associate regularly are our relatives?

Differences in the answers to these questions by people from industrial and those from nonindustrial societies confirm the declining importance of kinship in contemporary nations. Immigrants are often shocked by what they perceive as weak kinship bonds and lack of proper respect for family in contemporary North America. In fact, most of the people whom middle-class North Americans see every day are either nonrelatives or members of the nuclear family. On the other hand, Stack's (1975) study of welfare-dependent families in a ghetto area of a midwestern city showed that sharing with nonnuclear relatives is an important strategy that the urban poor use to adapt to poverty.

One of the most striking contrasts between the United States and Brazil, the two most populous nations of the Western Hemisphere, is in the meaning and role of the family. Contemporary North American adults usually define their families as consisting of their husbands or wives and their children. However, when middle-class Brazilians talk about their families, they mean their parents, siblings, aunts, uncles, grandparents, and cousins. Later they add their children, but rarely the husband or wife, who has his or her own family. The children are shared by the two families. Because middle-class Americans lack an extended family support system, marriage assumes

TABLE 19.2 Ratio of Divorces to Marriages per 1,000 U.S. Population, Selected Years, 1950–2006

1950	1960	1970	1980	1990	2000	2006
23%	26%	33%	50%	48%	49%	48%

SOURCE: *Statistical Abstract of the United States 2009*, Table 77, p. 63, http://www.census.gov/compendia/statab/2009edition.html.

TABLE 19.3 Household and Family Size in the United States and Canada, 1980 versus 2007

	1980	2007
Average family size:		
United States	3.3	3.1
Canada	3.4	3.0
Average household size:		
United States	2.9	2.6
Canada	2.9	2.6

SOURCES: J. M. Fields, "America's Families and Living Arrangements: 2003," *Current Population Reports*, P20-553, November 2004, http://www.census.gov/prod/2004pubs/p20-553.pdf, pp. 3–4; U.S. Census Bureau, *Statistical Abstract of the United States*, 2009, Table 58, p. 52; Statistics Canada, 2006 Census, http://www12.statcan.ca/english/census06/data/topics/, http://www40.statcan.ca/101/cst01/famil532.

FIGURE 19.3 Location of the Shoshoni.

more importance. The husband–wife relationship is supposed to take precedence over either spouse's relationship with his or her own parents. This places a significant strain on North American marriages.

Living in a less mobile society, Brazilians stay in closer contact with their relatives, including members of the extended family, than North Americans do. Residents of Rio de Janeiro and São Paulo, two of South America's largest cities, are reluctant to leave those urban centers to live away from family and friends. Brazilians find it hard to imagine, and unpleasant to live in, social worlds without relatives. Contrast this with a characteristic American theme: learning to live with strangers.

The Family among Foragers

Populations with foraging economies are far removed from industrial societies in terms of social complexity, but they do feature geographic mobility, which is associated with nomadic or seminomadic hunting and gathering. Here again the nuclear family is often the most significant kin group, although in no foraging society is the nuclear family the only group based on kinship. The two basic social units of traditional foraging societies are the nuclear family and the band.

Unlike middle-class couples in industrial nations, foragers don't usually reside neolocally. Instead, they join a band in which either the husband or the wife has relatives. However, couples and families may move from one band to another several times. Although nuclear families are ultimately as impermanent among foragers as they are in any other society, they are usually more stable than bands are.

Many foraging societies lacked year-round band organization. The Native American Shoshoni of the Great Basin in Utah and Nevada (Figure 19.3)

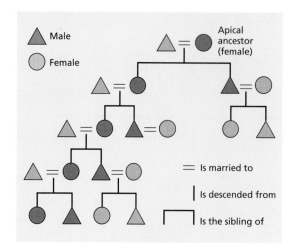

FIGURE 19.4 A Matrilineage Five Generations Deep.

Matrilineages are based on demonstrated descent from a female ancestor. Only the children of the group's women (blue) belong to the matrilineage. The children of the group's men are excluded; they belong to their mother's matrilineage.

In the figure legend:
Male
Female
Apical ancestor (female)
= Is married to
| Is descended from
⌐ Is the sibling of

provide an example. The resources available to the Shoshoni were so meager that for most of the year families traveled alone through the countryside hunting and gathering. In certain seasons families assembled to hunt cooperatively as a band; after just a few months together they dispersed.

In neither industrial nor foraging societies are people tied permanently to the land. The mobility and the emphasis on small, economically self-sufficient family units promote the nuclear family as a basic kin group in both types of societies.

DESCENT

We've seen that the nuclear family is important in industrial nations and among foragers. The analogous group among nonindustrial food producers is the descent group, a permanent social unit whose members say they have ancestors in common. Descent-group members believe they share, and descend from, those common ancestors. The group endures even though its membership changes, as members are born and die, move in and move out. Often, descent-group membership is determined at birth and is lifelong. In this case, it is an ascribed status.

Descent Groups

Descent groups frequently are exogamous (members must seek their mates from other descent groups). Two common rules serve to admit certain people as descent-group members while excluding others. With a rule of *matrilineal descent,* people join the mother's group automatically at birth and stay members throughout life. With *patrilineal descent,* people automatically have lifetime membership in the father's group. (In Figures 19.4 and 19.5, which show matrilineal and patrilineal descent groups, respectively, the triangles stand for males and the circles for females.) Matrilineal and patrilineal descent are types of **unilineal descent.** This means the descent rule uses one line only, either the male or the female line.

Descent groups may be **lineages** or **clans.** Common to both is the belief that members descend from the same *apical ancestor.* That person stands at the apex, or top, of the common genealogy. For example, Adam and Eve, according to the Bible, are the apical ancestors of all humanity. Since Eve is said to have come from Adam's rib, Adam stands as the original apical ancestor for the patrilineal genealogies laid out in the Bible.

How do lineages and clans differ? A lineage uses *demonstrated descent.* Members can recite the names of their forebears in each generation from the apical ancestor through the present. (This doesn't mean their recitations are accurate, only that lineage members think they are.) In the Bible the litany of men who "begat" other men is a demonstration of genealogical descent for a large patrilineage that ultimately includes Jews and Arabs (who share Abraham as their last common apical ancestor).

Unlike lineages, clans use *stipulated descent.* Clan members merely say they descend from the apical ancestor. They don't try to trace the actual genealogical links between themselves and that ancestor. The Betsileo of Madagascar have both clans and lineages. Descent may be demonstrated for the most recent 8 to 10 generations, then stipulated for the more remote past—sometimes with mermaids and vaguely defined foreign royalty mentioned among the founders (Kottak 1980). Like the Betsileo, many societies have both lineages and clans. In such a case, clans have more members and cover a larger geographic area than lineages do. Sometimes a clan's apical ancestor is not a human at all but an animal or plant (called a *totem*). Whether human or not, the ancestor symbolizes the social unity and identity of the members, distinguishing them from other groups.

The economic types that usually have descent-group organization are horticulture, pastoralism, and agriculture, as discussed in the chapter "Making a Living." Such societies tend to have several descent groups. Any one of them may be confined to a single village, but they usually span more than one village. Any branch of a descent group that lives in one place is a *local descent group.* Two or more local branches of different descent groups may live in the same village. Descent groups in the same village or different villages may establish alliances through frequent intermarriage.

Lineages, Clans, and Residence Rules

As we've seen, descent groups, unlike nuclear families, are permanent and enduring units, with new members added in every generation. Members have access to the lineage estate, where some of them must live, in order to benefit from and manage that estate across the generations. To endure, descent groups need to keep at least some of their members at home, on the ancestral estate. An easy way to do this is to have a rule about who belongs to the descent group and where they should live after they get married. Patrilineal and matrilineal descent, and the postmarital residence rules that usually accompany them, ensure that about half the people born in each generation will live out their lives on the ancestral estate. Neolocal residence, which is the rule for most middle-class Americans, isn't very common outside modern North America, Western Europe, and the European-derived cultures of Latin America.

Much more common is *patrilocality:* A married couple moves to the husband's father's community, so that the children will grow up in their father's village. Patrilocality is associated with patrilineal descent. This makes sense. If the group's male members are expected to exercise their rights in the ancestral estate, it's a good idea to raise them on that estate and to keep them there after they marry.

A less common postmarital residence rule, associated with matrilineal descent, is *matrilocality:* Married couples live in the wife's mother's community, and their children grow up in their mother's village. Together, patrilocality and matrilocality are known as *unilocal* rules of postmarital residence.

Ambilineal Descent

The descent rules examined so far admit certain people as members while excluding others. A unilineal rule uses one line only, either the female or the male. Besides the unilineal rules, there is another descent rule called nonunilineal or **ambilineal** descent. As in any descent group, membership comes through descent from a common ancestor. However, ambilineal groups differ from unilineal groups in that they do not *automatically* exclude either the children of sons or those of daughters. People can choose the descent group they join (for example, that of their father's father, father's mother, mother's father, or mother's mother). People also can change their descent-group membership, or belong to two or more groups at the same time.

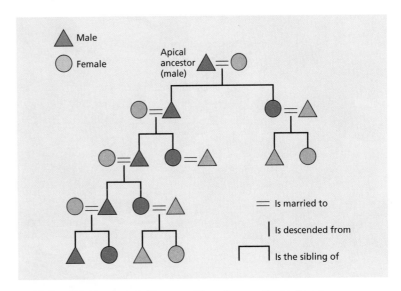

FIGURE 19.5 A Patrilineage Five Generations Deep.

Lineages are based on demonstrated descent from a common ancestor. With patrilineal descent, children of the group's men (blue) are included as descent-group members. Children of the group's female members are excluded; they belong to their father's patrilineage. Also notice lineage exogamy.

Unilineal descent is a matter of ascribed status; ambilineal descent illustrates achieved status. With unilineal descent, membership is automatic; no choice is permitted. People are born members of their father's group in a patrilineal society or of their mother's group in a matrilineal society. They are members of that group for life. Ambilineal descent permits more flexibility in descent-group affiliation.

Before 1950, descent groups were generally described simply as patrilineal or matrilineal. If the society tended toward patrilineality, the anthropologist classified it as a patrilineal rather than an ambilineal group. The treatment of ambilineal descent as a separate category was a formal recognition that many descent systems are flexible—some more so than others.

Family versus Descent

There are rights, duties, and obligations associated with kinship and descent. Many societies have both families and descent groups. Obligations to one may conflict with obligations to the other—more so in matrilineal than in patrilineal societies. In the latter, a woman typically leaves home when she marries and raises her children in her husband's community. After leaving home, she has no primary or substantial obligations to her own descent group. She can invest fully in her children, who will become members of her husband's group. In a matrilineal society things are different. A man has strong obligations both to his family of procreation (his wife and children) and to his closest matrikin (his sisters and

ambilineal
Flexible descent rule, neither patrilineal nor matrilineal.

Most societies have a prevailing opinion about where couples should live after they marry; this is called a postmarital residence rule. A common rule is patrilocality: the couple lives with the husband's relatives, so that children grow up in their father's community. The top image, taken in 2001, shows a 13-year-old Muslim bride (veiled in pink) in the West African country of Guinea Bissau. On the last day of her threeday wedding ceremony, she will collect laundry from her husband's family, wash it with her friends, and be taken to his village on a bicycle. In the bottom image, in Lendak, Slovakia, women transport part of the bride's dowry to the groom's house.

Compared with patrilineal systems, matrilineal societies tend to have higher divorce rates and greater female promiscuity (Schneider and Gough, eds. 1961). According to Nicholas Kottak (2002), among the matrilineal Makua of northern Mozambique, a husband is concerned about his wife's potential promiscuity. A man's sister also takes an interest in her brother's wife's fidelity; she doesn't want her brother wasting time on children who may not be his, thus diminishing his investment as an uncle (mother's brother) in her children. A confessional ritual that is part of the Makua birthing process demonstrates the sister's allegiance to her brother. When a wife is deep in labor, the husband's sister, who attends her, must ask, "Who is the real father of this child?" If the wife lies, the Makua believe the birth will be difficult, often ending in the death of the woman and/or the baby. This ritual serves as an important social paternity test. It is in both the husband's and his sister's interest to ensure that his wife's children are indeed his own.

KINSHIP CALCULATION

In addition to studying kin groups, anthropologists are interested in **kinship calculation**: the system by which people in a society reckon kin relationships. To study kinship calculation, an ethnographer must first determine the word or words for different types of "relatives" used in a particular language and then ask questions such as, "Who are your relatives?" Like race and gender (discussed in other chapters), kinship is culturally constructed. This means that some genealogical kin are considered to be relatives whereas others are not. It also means that even people who aren't genealogical relatives can be constructed socially as kin. Read this chapter's "Appreciating Anthropology," which describes ethnographic findings about the Barí of Venezuela. The Barí recognize multiple fathers, even though biologically there can be only one actual genitor. Cultures develop their own explanations for biological processes, including the role of insemination in the creation and growth of a human embryo.

Through questioning, the ethnographer discovers the specific genealogical relationships between "relatives" and the person who has named them—the **ego**. *Ego* means *I* (or *me*) in Latin. It's who you, the reader, are in the kin charts that follow. It's your perspective looking out on your kin. By posing the same questions to several local people, the ethnographer learns about the extent and direction of kinship calculation in that society. The ethnographer also begins to understand the relationship between kinship calculation and kin groups: how people use kinship to create and maintain personal ties and to join social groups.

kinship calculation
How people in a particular society reckon kin relations.

ego
Position from which one views an egocentric genealogy.

their children). The continuity of his descent group depends on his sisters and their children, since descent is carried by females, and he has descent-based obligations to look out for their welfare. He also has obligations to his wife and children. If a man is sure his wife's children are his own, he has more incentive to invest in them than is the case if he has doubts.

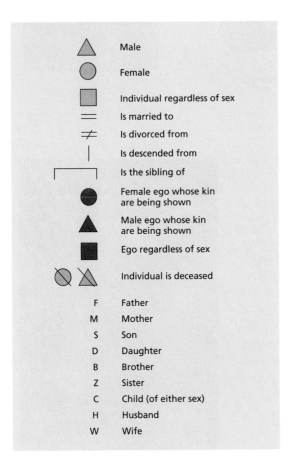

△	Male
○	Female
▢	Individual regardless of sex
=	Is married to
≠	Is divorced from
|	Is descended from
└─┘	Is the sibling of
⬤	Female ego whose kin are being shown
▲	Male ego whose kin are being shown
■	Ego regardless of sex
⊘ ◺	Individual is deceased
F	Father
M	Mother
S	Son
D	Daughter
B	Brother
Z	Sister
C	Child (of either sex)
H	Husband
W	Wife

FIGURE 19.6 Kinship Symbols and Genealogical Kin Type Notation.

In the kinship charts that follow, the gray square labeled "ego" identifies the person whose kinship calculation is being examined.

Genealogical Kin Types and Kin Terms

At this point, we may distinguish between *kin terms* (the words used for different relatives in a particular language) and *genealogical kin types.* We designate genealogical kin types with the letters and symbols shown in Figure 19.6. *Genealogical kin type* refers to an actual genealogical relationship (e.g., father's brother) as opposed to a kin term (e.g., *uncle*).

Kin terms reflect the social construction of kinship in a given culture. A kin term may (and usually does) lump together several genealogical relationships. In English, for instance, we use *father* primarily for one kin type: the genealogical father. However, *father* can be extended to an adoptive father or stepfather—and even to a priest. *Grandfather* includes mother's father and father's father. The term *cousin* lumps together several kin types. Even the more specific *first cousin* includes mother's brother's son (MBS), mother's brother's daughter (MBD), mother's

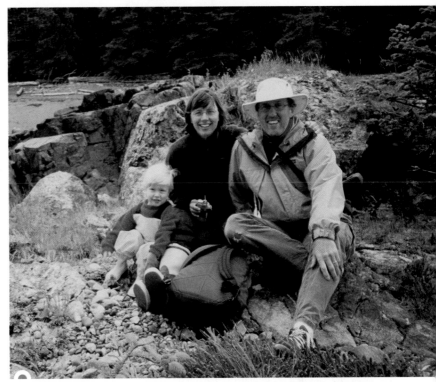

A nuclear family lunches in Bull Harbour, British Columbia, Canada. The nuclear family's relative isolation from other kin groups in modern nations reflects geographic mobility within an industrial economy with sale of labor for cash.

sister's son (MZS), mother's sister's daughter (MZD), father's brother's son (FBS), father's brother's daughter (FBD), father's sister's son (FZS), and father's sister's daughter (FZD). *First cousin* thus lumps together at least eight genealogical kin types.

Uncle encompasses mother's and father's brothers, and *aunt* includes mother's and father's sisters. We also use *uncle* and *aunt* for the spouses of our "blood" aunts and uncles. We use the same term for mother's brother and father's brother because we perceive them as being the same sort of relative. Calling them *uncles,* we distinguish between them and another kin type, F, whom we call *Father, Dad,* or *Pop.* In many societies, however, it is common to call a father and a father's brother by the same term. Later we'll see why.

In the United States and Canada, the nuclear family continues to be the most important group based on kinship. This is true despite an increased incidence of single parenthood, divorce, and remarriage. The nuclear family's relative isolation from other kin groups in modern nations reflects geographic mobility within an industrial economy with sale of labor for cash.

It's reasonable for North Americans to distinguish between relatives who belong to their nuclear families and those who don't. We are more likely to grow up with our parents than with our

When Are Two Dads Better than One?— When the Women Are in Charge

Like race, kinship is socially constructed. Cultures develop their own explanations for biological processes, including the role of insemination in the creation and growth of a human embryo. Scientifically informed people know that fertilization of an ovum by a single sperm is responsible for conception. But other cultures, including the Barí and their neighbors, hold different views about procreation. In some societies it is believed that spirits, rather than men, place babies in women's wombs. In others it is believed that a fetus must be nourished by continuing insemination during pregnancy.

There are cultures, including the Barí and others described here, in which people believe that multiple men can create the same fetus. When a baby is born, the Barí mother names the men she recognizes as fathers, and they help her raise the child. In the United States, having two dads may be the result of divorce, remarriage, stepparenthood, or a same-sex union. In the societies discussed here, multiple

(partible) paternity is a common and beneficial social fact.

[Among] the Barí people of Venezuela, . . . multiple paternity is the norm . . . In such societies, children with more than one official father are more likely to survive to adulthood than those with just one Dad . . . The findings have . . . been published in a book, *Cultures of Multiple Fathers: The Theory and Practice of Partible Paternity in Lowland South America* [Beckerman and Valentine 2002], that questions accepted theories about social organization, the balance of power between the sexes and human evolution.

[The book] . . . draws on more than two decades of fieldwork among South American tribal peoples. The central theme . . . is the concept of partible paternity—the widespread belief that fertilization is not a one-time event and

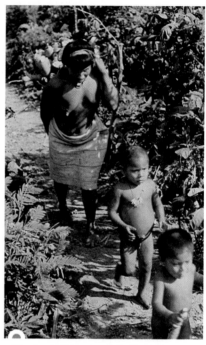

The Barí of Venezuela believe that a child can have multiple fathers.

aunts and uncles. We tend to see our parents more often than we see our uncles and aunts, who may live in different towns and cities. We often inherit from our parents, but our cousins have first claim to inherit from our aunts and uncles. If our marriage is stable, we see our children daily as long as they remain at home. They are our heirs. We feel closer to them than to our nieces and nephews.

American kinship calculation and kin terminology reflect these social features. Thus, the term *uncle* distinguishes between the kin types MB and FB on the one hand and the kin type F on the other. However, this term also lumps kin types together. We use the same term for MB and FB, two different kin types. We do this because American kinship calculation is **bilateral**—traced equally through males and females, for example, father and mother. Both kinds of uncle are brothers of one of our parents. We think of both as roughly the same kind of relative.

"No," you may object, "I'm closer to my mother's brother than to my father's brother." That

may be. However, in a representative sample of American students, we would find a split, with some favoring one side and some favoring the other. We'd actually expect a bit of *matrilateral skewing*—a preference for relatives on the mother's side. This occurs for many reasons. When contemporary children are raised by just one parent, it's much more likely to be the mother than the father. Also, even with intact marriages, the wife tends to play a more active role in managing family affairs, including family visits, reunions, holidays, and extended family relations, than the husband does. This would tend to reinforce her kin network over his and thus favor matrilateral skewing.

Bilateral kinship means that people tend to perceive kin links through males and females as being similar or equivalent. This bilaterality is expressed in interaction with, living with or near, and rights to inherit from relatives. We don't usually inherit from uncles, but if we do, there's about as much chance that we'll inherit from the father's

bilateral kinship calculation
Kin ties calculated equally through men and women.

that more than one father can contribute to the developing embryo. . . .

The authors have discovered a strong correlation between the status of women in the society and the benefits of multiple paternity . . . Among the Barí, 80% of children with two or more official dads survive to adulthood, compared with 64% with one father. This contrasts with male-dominated cultures such as the neighboring Curripaco, where children of doubtful parentage are outcast and frequently die young.

Explaining the significance of this discovery, Paul Valentine said: "The conventional view of the male-female bargain is that a man will provide food and shelter for a woman and her children if he can be assured that the children are biologically his. Our research turns this idea on its head . . . In societies where women control marriages and other aspects of social life, both men and women have multiple partners and spread the responsibilities of child rearing." It is of course scientifically impossible to have more than one biological father, but aboriginal peoples in South America, Africa and Australasia

[Australia and Asia] believe that it takes more than one act of intercourse to make a baby. In some of these societies, nearly all children have multiple fathers. In others, while partible paternity is accepted, socially the child has only one father. However, in the middle are groups where some children do have multiple fathers and some do not. In this case, the children can be compared to see how having more than one father benefits the children—and generational studies show that the children do benefit from the extra care.

When a child is born among the Barí, the mother publicly announces the names of the one or more men she believes to be the fathers, who, if they accept paternity, are expected to provide care for the mother and child . . . "In small egalitarian societies, women's interests are best served if mate choice is a non-binding, female decision; if a network of multiple females to aid or substitute for a woman in her mothering responsibilities exists; if multiple men support a woman and her children; and if a woman is shielded from the effects of male sexual jealousy." . . .

In cultures where women choose their mates, women have broad sexual freedom and partible paternity is accepted, women clearly have the upper hand. In Victorian-style societies where women's sexual activity is controlled by men, marriage is exclusive and male sexual jealousy is a constant threat, men have the upper hand. In between is a full range of combinations and options, all represented in the varying South American cultures. . . .

Robert Carneiro, curator at the American Museum of Natural History, said: "Rarely does a book thrust open a door, giving us a striking new view. It has long been known that . . . peoples around the world believe that one act of sexual intercourse is not enough for a child to be born. Now for the first time we have a volume that deals with the consequences and ramifications of this belief, and it does so in exhaustive and fascinating detail." . . .

SOURCE: Patrick Wilson, "When Are Two Dads Better Than One? When the Women Are in Charge," http://alphagalileo.org (June 12, 2002). Reprinted by permission of the University of East London, UK.

brother as from the mother's brother. We don't usually live with either aunt, but if we do, the chances are about the same that it will be the father's sister as the mother's sister.

KINSHIP TERMINOLOGY

People perceive and define kin relations differently in different cultures. In any culture, kinship terminology is a classification system, a taxonomy or typology. It is a *native taxonomy,* developed over generations by the people who live in a particular society. A native classification system is based on how people perceive similarities and differences in the things being classified.

However, anthropologists have discovered that there are a limited number of patterns in which people classify their kin. People who speak very different languages may use exactly the same system of kinship terminology. This section examines the four main ways of classifying

kin on the parental generation: lineal, bifurcate merging, generational, and bifurcate collateral. We also consider the social correlates of these classification systems. (Note that each of the systems described here applies to the parental generation. There are also differences in kin terminology on ego's generation. These systems involve the classification of siblings and cousins. There are six such systems, called Eskimo, Iroquois, Hawaiian, Crow, Omaha, and Sudanese cousin terminology, after societies that traditionally used them. You can see them diagrammed and discussed at the following websites: http://anthro.palomar.edu/kinship/kinship_5.htm; http://anthro.palomar.edu/kinship/kinship_6.htm; http://www.umanitoba.ca/faculties/arts/anthropology/tutor/kinterms/termsys.html.)

A **functional explanation** will be offered for each system of kinship terminology, such as lineal, bifurcate merging, and generational terminology. Functional explanations attempt to relate particular customs (such as the use of kin terms)

functional explanation
One based on correlation or co-occurrence of social variables.

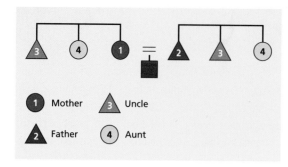

FIGURE 19.7 Lineal Kinship Terminology.

Kinship terms provide useful information about social patterns. If two relatives are designated by the same term, we can assume that they are perceived as sharing socially significant attributes. Several factors influence the way people interact with, perceive, and classify relatives. For instance, do certain kinds of relatives customarily live together or apart? How far apart? What benefits do they derive from each other, and what are their obligations? Are they members of the same descent group or of different descent groups? With these questions in mind, let's examine systems of kinship terminology.

Lineal Terminology

Our own system of kinship classification is called the *lineal system* (Figure 19.7). The number 3 and the color light blue stand for the term *uncle*, which we apply both to FB and to MB. **Lineal kinship terminology** is found in societies such as the United States and Canada in which the nuclear family is the most important group based on kinship.

Lineal kinship terminology has absolutely nothing to do with lineages, which are found in very different social contexts. (What contexts are those?) Lineal kinship terminology gets its name from the fact that it distinguishes lineal relatives from collateral relatives. What does that mean? A **lineal relative** is an ancestor or descendant, anyone on the direct line of descent that leads to and from ego (Figure 19.8). Thus, lineal relatives are one's parents, grandparents, great-grandparents, and other direct forebears. Lineal relatives also include children, grandchildren, and great-grandchildren. **Collateral relatives** are all other kin. They include siblings, nieces and nephews, aunts and uncles, and cousins (Figure 19.8). **Affinals** are relatives by marriage, whether of lineals (e.g., son's wife) or of collaterals (sister's husband).

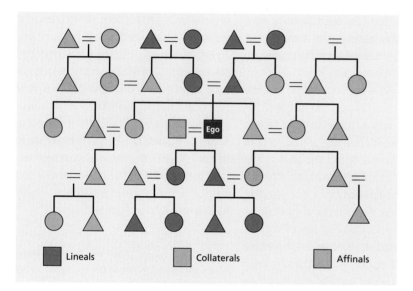

FIGURE 19.8 The Distinctions among Lineals, Collaterals, and Affinals as Perceived by Ego.

Bifurcate Merging Terminology

Bifurcate merging kinship terminology (Figure 19.9) *bifurcates,* or splits, the mother's side and the father's side. But it also *merges* same-sex siblings of each parent. Thus, mother and mother's sister are merged under the same term (1), while father and father's brother also get a common term (2). There are different terms for mother's brother (3) and father's sister (4).

People use this system in societies with unilineal (patrilineal and matrilineal) descent rules and unilocal (patrilocal and matrilocal) postmarital residence rules. When the society is unilineal and unilocal, the logic of bifurcate merging terminology is fairly clear. In a patrilineal society, for example, father and father's brother belong to the same descent group, gender, and generation. Since patrilineal societies usually have patrilocal

lineal kinship terminology
Four parental kin terms: M, F, FB = MB, and MZ = FZ.

lineal relative
Ego's direct ancestors and descendants.

collateral relative
Relative outside ego's direct line, e.g., B, Z, FB, MZ.

affinals
Relatives by marriage.

bifurcate merging kinship terminology
Four parental kin terms: M = MZ; F = FB; MB and FZ each stands alone.

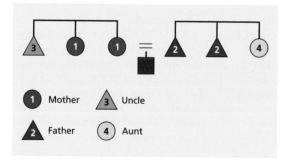

FIGURE 19.9 Bifurcate Merging Kinship Terminology.

to other features of a society, such as rules of descent and postmarital residence. Certain aspects of a culture are *functions* of others. That is, they are correlated variables, so that when one of them changes, the others inevitably change too. For certain terminologies, the social correlates are very clear.

residence, the father and his brother live in the same local group. Because they share so many attributes that are socially relevant, ego regards them as social equivalents and calls them by the same kinship term—2. However, the mother's brother belongs to a different descent group, lives elsewhere, and has a different kin term—3.

What about mother and mother's sister in a patrilineal society? They belong to the same descent group, the same gender, and the same generation. Often they marry men from the same village and go to live there. These social similarities help explain the use of the same term—1—for both.

Similar observations apply to matrilineal societies. Consider a society with two matrilineal clans, the Ravens and the Wolves. Ego is a member of his mother's clan, the Raven clan. Ego's father is a member of the Wolf clan. His mother and her sister are female Ravens of the same generation. If there is matrilocal residence, as there often is in matrilineal societies, they will live in the same village. Because they are so similar socially, ego calls them by the same kin term—1.

The father's sister, however, belongs to a different group, the Wolves; lives elsewhere; and has a different kin term—4. Ego's father and father's brother are male Wolves of the same generation. If they marry women of the same clan and live in the same village, this creates additional social similarities that reinforce this usage.

Generational Terminology

Like bifurcate merging kinship terminology, **generational kinship terminology** uses the same term for parents and their siblings, but the lumping is more complete (Figure 19.10). With generational terminology, there are only two terms for the parental *generation.* We may translate them as "father" and "mother," but more accurate translations would be "male member of the parental generation" and "female member of the parental generation."

Generational kinship terminology does not distinguish between the mother's and father's sides. It does not bifurcate, but it certainly does merge. It uses just one term for father, father's brother, and mother's brother. In a unilineal society, these three kin types would never belong to the same descent group. Generational kinship terminology also uses a single term for mother, mother's sister, and father's sister. Nor, in a unilineal society, would these three ever be members of the same group.

Nevertheless, generational terminology suggests closeness between ego and his or her aunts and uncles—much more closeness than exists between Americans and these kin types. How likely would you be to call your uncle "Dad" or your aunt "Mom"? We'd expect to find generational terminology in cultures in which kinship is much more important than it is in our own but in which there is no rigid distinction between the father's side and the mother's side.

It's logical, then, that generational kin terminology is typical of societies with ambilineal descent. In such contexts, descent-group membership is not automatic. People may choose the group they join, change their descent-group membership, or belong to two or more descent groups simultaneously. Generational terminology fits these conditions. The use of intimate kin terms signals that people have close personal relations with all their relatives of the parental generation. People exhibit similar behavior toward their aunts, uncles, and parents. Someday they'll have to choose a descent group to join. Furthermore, in ambilineal societies, postmarital residence is usually ambilocal. This means that the married couple can live with either the husband's or the wife's group.

Significantly, generational terminology also characterizes certain foraging bands, including Kalahari San groups and several native societies of North America. Use of this terminology reflects certain similarities between foraging bands and ambilineal descent groups. In both societies, people have a choice about their kin-group affiliation. Foragers always live with kin, but they often shift band affiliation and so may be members of several different bands during their lifetimes. Just as in food-producing societies with ambilineal descent, generational terminology among foragers helps maintain close personal relationships with several parental-generation relatives whom ego may eventually use as a point of entry into different groups. Recap 19.1 lists the types of kin group, the postmarital residence rule, and the economy associated with the four types of kinship terminology.

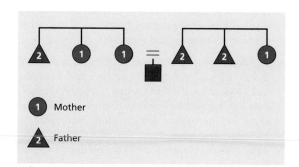

FIGURE 19.10 Generational Kinship Terminology.

Mother

Father

Bifurcate Collateral Terminology

Of the four kin classification systems, **bifurcate collateral kinship terminology** is the most specific. It has separate terms for each of the six kin

generational kinship terminology
Just two parental kin terms: M = MZ = FZ and F = FB = MB.

bifurcate collateral kinship terminology
Six separate parental kin terms: M, F, MB, MZ, FB, and FZ.

KINSHIP TERMINOLOGY	KIN GROUP	RESIDENCE RULE	ECONOMY
Lineal	Nuclear family	Neolocal	Industrialism, foraging
Bifurcate merging	Unilineal descent group—patrilineal or matrilineal	Unilocal—patrilocal or matrilocal	Horticulture, pastoralism, agriculture
Generational	Ambilineal descent group, band	Ambilocal	Agriculture, horticulture, foraging
Bifurcate collateral	Varies	Varies	Varies

types of the parental generation (Figure 19.11). Bifurcate collateral terminology isn't as common as the other types. Many of the societies that use it are in North Africa and the Middle East, and many of them are offshoots of the same ancestral group.

Bifurcate collateral terminology also may be used when a child has parents of different ethnic backgrounds and uses terms for aunts and uncles derived from different languages. Thus, if you have a mother who is Latina and a father who is Anglo, you may call your aunts and

FIGURE 19.11 Bifurcate Collateral Kinship Terminology.

uncles on your mother's side "tia" and "tio," while calling those on your father's side "aunt" and "uncle." And your mother and father may be "Mom" and "Pop." That's a modern form of bifurcate collateral kinship terminology.

Acing the COURSE

Summary

1. In nonindustrial societies, kinship, descent, and marriage organize social and political life. In studying kinship, we must distinguish between kin groups, whose composition and activities can be observed, and kinship calculation—how people identify and designate their relatives.

2. One widespread kin group is the nuclear family, consisting of a married couple and their children. There are functional alternatives to the nuclear family. That is, other groups may assume functions usually associated with the nuclear family. Nuclear families tend to be especially important in foraging and industrial societies. Among farmers and herders, other kinds of kin groups often overshadow the nuclear family.

3. In contemporary North America, the nuclear family is the characteristic kin group for the middle class. Expanded households and sharing with extended family kin occur more frequently among the poor, who may pool their resources in dealing with poverty. Today, however, even in the American middle class, nuclear family households are declining as single-person households and other domestic arrangements increase.

4. The descent group is a basic kin group among nonindustrial food producers (farmers and herders). Unlike families, descent groups have perpetuity—they last for generations. Descent-group members share and manage a common estate: land, animals, and other resources. There are several kinds of descent groups. Lineages are based on demonstrated descent; clans, on stipulated descent. Descent rules may be unilineal or ambilineal. Unilineal (patrilineal and matrilineal) descent is associated with

unilocal (respectively, patrilocal and matrilocal) postmarital residence. Obligations to one's descent group and to one's family of procreation may conflict, especially in matrilineal societies.

5. A kinship terminology is a classification of relatives based on perceived differences and similarities. Comparative research has revealed a limited number of ways of classifying kin. Because there are correlations between kinship terminology and other social practices, we often can predict kinship terminology from other aspects of culture. The four basic kinship terminologies for the parental generation are lineal, bifurcate merging, generational, and bifurcate collateral. Many foraging and industrial societies use lineal terminology, which is associated with nuclear family organization. Cultures with unilocal residence and unilineal descent tend to have bifurcate merging terminology. Generational terminology correlates with ambilineal descent and ambilocal residence.

Key Terms

MULTIPLE CHOICE

1. Why is a focus on the nuclear family characteristic of many modern nations? Because
   a. the nuclear family is the most common family arrangement in industrialized societies.
   b. isolation from the extended family arises from geographic mobility that is characteristic of many industrialized societies.
   c. modernity is associated with smaller and more exclusive households, especially among the urban poor.
   d. higher incomes have made it possible for most adults to achieve the American cultural ideal of a nuclear family.
   e. the nuclear family is the most developed form of domestic arrangement.

2. The nuclear family is the most common kin group in what kinds of societies?
   a. tribal societies and chiefdoms
   b. ambilineal and collateral
   c. lineages and clans
   d. industrial middle class and foraging bands
   e. patrilocal and matrilocal

3. Which of the following statements about the nuclear family is *not* true?
   a. The nuclear family is a cultural universal.
   b. In the United States, nuclear families accounted for just 22.5 percent of households in 2007.
   c. A family of orientation may be a nuclear family.
   d. A family of procreation may be a nuclear family.
   e. Most people belong to at least two nuclear families during their lives.

Test Yourself!

4. In kinship analysis, what does the classification of descent group as either lineages or clans indicate?
   a. A lineage uses demonstrated descent while clans use stipulated descent.
   b. Descent is always achieved.
   c. How individuals define and think about relationships of descent is culturally universal.
   d. Only in lineages do members descend from an apical ancestor.
   e. Members of lineages do not like to rely on their memory to know who their ancestors are.

5. Like race, kinship is culturally constructed. This means that
   a. the educational system is failing to educate people about real, biologically based human relations.
   b. like race, kinship is a fiction, with no real social consequence.
   c. it is a phenomenon separated from other real aspects of society, such as economics and politics.
   d. studies of kinship tell us little about people's actual experiences.
   e. people perceive and define kin relations differently in different cultures, although anthropologists have discovered a limited number of patterns in which people classify their kin.

6. Anthropologists are interested in kinship calculation,
   a. but only if it has any consequence in changing demographics over a 10-year period.
   b. the ways people evaluate the worth of the work of anthropologists.

c. and then they do their best to impose their etic perspective on people's emic views.

d. the ways people apply mathematical principles to determine degrees of relatedness with the ancestors of anatomically modern humans.

e. the system by which people in a society reckon kin relationships.

7. In any culture, kinship terminology is a classification system, a taxonomy or typology. More generally, a taxonomic system
   a. is only accurate when based on Western science.
   b. is based on how people perceive similarities and differences in the things being classified.
   c. only makes any sense to those who study it for years.
   d. usually changes with every generation.
   e. applies best to nonliving things.

8. What is another name for a person's "in-laws"?
   a. family of orientation
   b. merging relatives
   c. affinals
   d. collaterals
   e. lineals

9. In this chapter, a functional explanation is offered for various systems of kinship terminology. What does a functional explanation suggest about a system of kinship terminology?
   a. Kinship terminology only becomes a system when it *functions* properly.
   b. Certain kinship terms are what *cause* certain patterns of behavior.
   c. A functional explanation accurately *predicts* what types of kinship terminology will develop in future generations if enough data about the system are collected.
   d. A functional explanation attempts to *correlate* particular customs (in this case kinship terms) to other features of society.
   e. A functional explanation *distinguishes* genealogical kin types from kin terms.

10. In a bifurcate merging kinship terminology, which of the following pairs would be called by the same term?
    a. MZ and MB
    b. M and MZ
    c. MF and FF
    d. M and F
    e. MB and FB

FILL IN THE BLANK

1. The family of _____ is the name of the family in which a child is raised, while the family of _____ is the name of the family established when one marries and has children.

2. _____ refers to the postmarital residence pattern in which the married couple is expected to establish its own home.

3. A _____ refers to a unilineal descent group whose members demonstrate their common descent from an apical ancestor.

4. In _____ kinship calculation, kin ties are traced equally through males and females.

5. In a bifurcate merging kinship terminology, _____ and _____ relatives are merged.

CRITICAL THINKING

1. Why is kinship so important to anthropologists? How might the study of kinship be useful for research in fields of anthropology other than cultural anthropology?

2. What are some examples of alternatives to nuclear family arrangements considered in this chapter? What may be the impact of new (and increasingly accessible) reproductive technologies on domestic arrangements?

3. Although the nuclear family remains the cultural ideal for many Americans, other domestic arrangements now outnumber the "traditional" American household more than four to one. What are some reasons for this? Do you think this trend is good or bad? Why?

4. To what sorts of family or families do you belong? Have you belonged to other kinds of families? How do the kin terms you use compare with the four classification systems discussed in this chapter?

5. Cultures with unilocal residence and unilineal descent tend to have bifurcate merging terminology, while ambilineal descent and ambilocal residence correlate with generational terminology. Why does this make sense? What are some examples of each case?

Carsten, J.
  2004   *After Kinship.* New York: Cambridge University Press. Rethinking anthropological approaches to kinship for the modern world.

Hansen, K. V.
  2005   *Not-So-Nuclear Families: Class, Gender, and Networks of Care.* New Brunswick, NJ: Rutgers University Press. Support networks based in class, gender, and kinship.

Parkin, R., and L. Stone, eds.
  2004   *Kinship and Family: An Anthropological Reader.* Malden, MA: Blackwell. Up-to-date reader.

Stacey, J.
  1998   *Brave New Families: Stories of Domestic Upheaval in Late Twentieth Century America.* Berkeley: University of California Press. Contemporary family life in the United States, based on field work in California's Silicon Valley.

Stone, L.
  2001   *New Directions in Anthropological Kinship.* Lanham, MD: Rowman and Littlefield. How contemporary anthropologists think about kinship.

Willie, C. V., and R. J. Reddick
  2009   *A New Look at Black Families,* 6th ed. Lanham, MA: Rowman and Littlefield. Family experience in relation to socioeconomic status, presented through case studies.

Suggested Additional Readings

Go to our Online Learning Center website at **www.mhhe.com/kottak** for Internet exercises directly related to the content of this chapter.

Internet Exercises

How is marriage defined and regulated, and what rights does it convey?

What role does marriage play in creating and maintaining group alliances?

What forms of marriage exist cross-culturally, and what are their social correlates?

Part of a wedding ceremony in Khartoum, Sudan. On women's night, friends gather, and an older woman anoints the bride with oil.

Marriage

understanding OURSELVES

Accroding to the radio talk show psychologist (and undergraduate anthropology major) Dr. Joy Browne, parents' job is to give their kids "roots and wings." Roots, she says, are the easier part. In other words, it's easier to raise children than to let them go. Has that been true of your parents with respect to you? I've heard comments about today's "helicopter parents" hovering over even their college-aged kids, using cell phones, e-mail, and texting to follow their progeny more closely than in prior generations. Do you have any experience with such a pattern?

It can be difficult to make the transition between the family that raised us (our family of orientation) and the family we form if we marry and have children (our family of procreation). In contemporary America, we usually get a head start by "leaving home" long before we marry. We go off to college or find a job that enables us to support ourselves so that we can live independently, or with roommates. In nonindustrial societies people, especially women, may leave home abruptly when they marry. Often a woman must leave her home village and her own kin and move in with her husband and his relatives. This can be an unpleasant and alienating transition. Many women complain about feeling isolated in their husband's village, where they may be mistreated by their husband or in-laws, including the mother-in-law.

In contemporary North America, although neither women nor men typically have to adjust to in-laws living nearby full-time, conflicts with in-laws aren't at all uncommon. Just read "Dear Abby" or listen to Dr. Joy Browne (cited previously) for a week. Even more of a challenge is learning to live with our spouse. Marriage always raises issues of accommodation and adjustment. Initially the married couple is just that, unless there are children from a previous marriage. If there are, adjustment issues will involve stepparenthood—and a prior spouse—as well as the new marital relationship. Once a couple has its own child, the family-of-procreation mentality takes over. In the United States family loyalty shifts, but not completely, from the family of orientation to the family that includes spouse and child(ren). Given our bilateral kinship system, we maintain relations with our sons and daughters after they marry, and grandchildren theoretically are as close to one set of grandparents as to the other set. In practice, grandchildren tend to be a bit closer to their mother's than to their father's families. Can you speculate about why that might be? How is it for you? Are you closer to your paternal or maternal grandparents? How about your uncles and aunts on one side or the other? Why is that?

WHAT IS MARRIAGE?

"Love and marriage," "marriage and the family": These familiar phrases show how we link the romantic love of two individuals to marriage and how we link marriage to reproduction and family creation. But marriage is an institution with significant roles and functions in addition to reproduction. What is marriage, anyway?

No definition of marriage is broad enough to apply easily to all societies and situations. A commonly quoted definition comes from *Notes and Queries on Anthropology*:

> Marriage is a union between a man and a woman such that the children born to the woman are recognized as legitimate offspring of both partners. (Royal Anthropological Institute 1951, p. 111)

This definition isn't universally valid for several reasons. In many societies, marriages unite more than two spouses. Here we speak of *plural marriages,* as when a man weds two (or more) women, or a woman weds a group of brothers—an arrangement called *fraternal polyandry* that is characteristic of certain Himalayan cultures. In the Brazilian community of Arembepe, people can choose among various forms of marital union. Most people live in long-term "common-law" domestic partnerships that are not legally sanctioned. Some have civil marriages, which are licensed and legalized by a justice of the peace. Still others go through religious ceremonies, so that they are united in "holy matrimony," although not legally. And some have both civil and religious ties. The different forms of union permit someone to have multiple spouses (e.g., one common-law, one civil, one religious) without ever getting divorced.

Some societies recognize various kinds of same-sex marriages. In Sudan, a Nuer woman can marry a woman if her father has only daughters but no male heirs, who are necessary if his patrilineage is to survive. He may ask his daughter to stand as a son in order to take a bride. This daughter will become the socially recognized husband of another woman (the wife). This is a symbolic and social relationship rather than a sexual one. The "wife" has sex with a man or men (whom her female "husband" must approve) until she gets pregnant. The children born to the wife are accepted as the offspring of both the female husband and the wife. Although the female husband is not the actual **genitor,** the biological father, of the children, she is their **pater,** or socially recognized father. What's important in this Nuer case is *social* rather than *biological paternity.* We see again how kinship is socially constructed. The bride's children are considered the legitimate offspring of her female "husband," who is biologically a woman but socially a man, and the descent line continues.

INCEST AND EXOGAMY

In many nonindustrial societies, a person's social world includes two main categories: kin and strangers. Strangers are potential or actual enemies. Marriage is one of the primary ways of converting strangers into kin, of creating and maintaining personal and political alliances, relationships of affinity (*affinal* relationships). **Exogamy,** the practice of seeking a husband or wife outside one's own group, has adaptive value because it links people into a wider social network that nurtures, helps, and protects them in times of need.

Incest refers to sexual relations with someone considered to be a close relative. All cultures have taboos against it. However, although the taboo is a cultural universal, cultures define incest differently. As an illustration, consider some implications of the distinction between two kinds of first cousins: cross cousins and parallel cousins (see Ottenheimer 1996).

The children of two brothers or two sisters are **parallel cousins.** The children of a brother and a sister are **cross cousins.** Your mother's sister's children and your father's brother's children are your parallel cousins. Your father's sister's children and your mother's brother's children are your cross cousins.

The American kin term *cousin* doesn't distinguish between cross and parallel cousins, but in many societies, especially those with unilineal descent, the distinction is essential. As an example, consider a community with only two descent groups. This exemplifies what is known as *moiety* organization—from the French *moitié,* which means "half." Descent bifurcates the community so that everyone belongs to one half or the other. Some societies have patrilineal moieties; others have matrilineal moieties.

In Figures 20.1 and 20.2, notice that cross cousins are always members of the opposite moiety

genitor
A child's biological father.

pater
One's socially recognized father; not necessarily the genitor.

exogamy
Marriage outside a given group.

incest
Forbidden sexual relations with a close relative.

parallel cousins
Children of two brothers or two sisters.

cross cousins
Children of a brother and a sister.

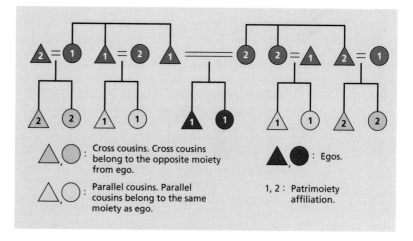

FIGURE 20.1 Parallel and Cross Cousins and Patrilineal Moiety Organization.

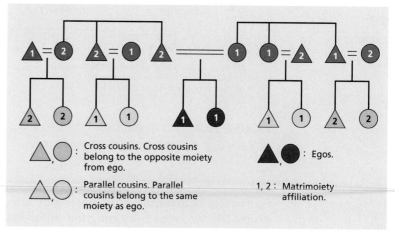

FIGURE 20.2 Matrilineal Moiety Organization.

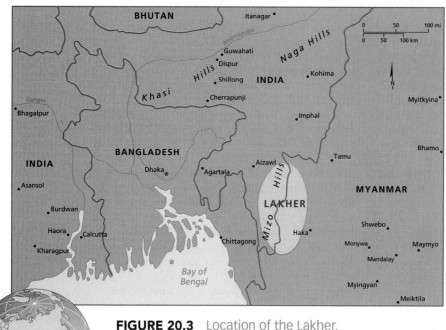

FIGURE 20.3 Location of the Lakher.

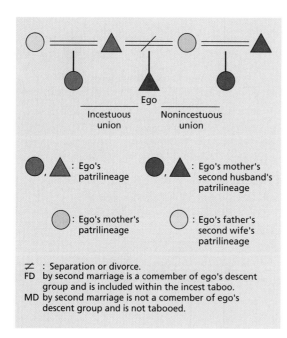

Ego

Incestuous union — Nonincestuous union

● , ▲ : Ego's patrilineage

● , ▲ : Ego's mother's second husband's patrilineage

○ : Ego's mother's patrilineage

○ : Ego's father's second wife's patrilineage

≠ : Separation or divorce.
FD by second marriage is a comember of ego's descent group and is included within the incest taboo.
MD by second marriage is not a comember of ego's descent group and is not tabooed.

FIGURE 20.4 Patrilineal Descent-Group Identity and Incest among the Lakher.

grams that your mother's sister's children (MZC) and your father's brother's children (FBC) always belong to your group. Your cross cousins—that is, FZC and MBC—belong to the other moiety.

Parallel cousins belong to the same generation and the same descent group as ego does, and they are like ego's brothers and sisters. They are called by the same kin terms as brothers and sisters are. Defined as close relatives, parallel cousins are tabooed as sex or marriage partners. They fall within the incest taboo, but cross cousins don't.

In societies with unilineal moieties, cross cousins always belong to the opposite group. Sex with cross cousins isn't incestuous, because they aren't considered relatives. In fact, in many unilineal societies, people must marry either a cross cousin or someone from the same descent group as a cross cousin. A unilineal descent rule ensures that the cross cousin's descent group is never one's own. With moiety exogamy, spouses must belong to different moieties.

Among the Yanomami of Venezuela and Brazil (Chagnon 1997), boys anticipate eventual marriage to a cross cousin by calling her "wife." They call their male cross cousins "brother-in-law." Yanomami girls call their male cross cousins "husband" and their female cross cousins "sister-in-law." Among the Yanomami, as in many societies with unilineal descent, sex with cross cousins is proper but sex with parallel cousins is considered incestuous.

A custom that is much rarer than cross-cousin marriage also illustrates that people define their kin, and thus incest, differently in different societies. When unilineal descent is very strongly developed, the parent who does not belong to one's own descent group isn't considered a relative. Thus, with strict patrilineality, the mother is not a relative but a kind of in-law who has married a member of ego's group—ego's father. With strict matrilineality, the father isn't a relative, because he belongs to a different descent group.

The Lakher of Southeast Asia (Figure 20.3) are strictly patrilineal (Leach 1961). Using the male ego in Figure 20.4, let's suppose that ego's father and mother get divorced. Each remarries and has a daughter by a second marriage. A Lakher always belongs to his or her father's group, all the members of which (one's *agnates,* or patrikin) are considered too closely related to marry because they are members of the same patrilineal descent group. Therefore, ego can't marry his father's daughter by the second marriage, just as in

and parallel cousins always belong to your (ego's) own moiety. With patrilineal descent (Figure 20.1), people take the father's descent-group affiliation; in a matrilineal society (Figure 20.2), they take the mother's affiliation. You can see from these dia-contemporary North America it's illegal for half-siblings to marry.

However, in contrast to our society, where all half-siblings are tabooed, the Lakher permit ego to marry his mother's daughter by a different father. She is not a forbidden relative because she belongs to her own father's descent group rather than ego's. The Lakher illustrate clearly that definitions of forbidden relatives, and therefore of incest, vary from culture to culture.

We can extend these observations to strict matrilineal societies. If a man's parents divorce and his father remarries, ego may marry his paternal half-sister. By contrast, if his mother remarries and has a daughter, the daughter is considered ego's sister, and sex between them is taboo. Cultures therefore have different definitions and expectations of relationships that are biologically or genetically equivalent.

EXPLAINING THE TABOO

Although Tabooed, Incest Does Happen

There is no simple or universally accepted explanation for the fact that all cultures ban incest. Do primate studies offer any clues? Research with primates does show that adolescent males (among monkeys) or females (among apes) often move away from the group in which they were born (Rodseth et al. 1991). This emigration reduces the frequency of incestuous unions, but it doesn't eliminate them. DNA testing of wild chimps has confirmed incestuous unions between adult sons and their mothers, who reside in the same group. Human behavior with respect to mating with close relatives may express a generalized primate tendency, in which we see both urges and avoidance.

A crosscultural study of 87 societies (Meigs and Barlow 2002) revealed that incest did occur in several of them. For example, among the Yanomami, Chagnon reported that "incest, far from being feared, is widely practiced" (1967, p. 66). Meyer Fortes observed about the Ashanti: "In the old days it [incest] was punished by death. Nowadays the culprits are heavily fined" (Fortes 1950, p. 257). Among 24 Ojibwa individuals from whom he obtained information about incest, A. Irving Hallowell found 8 cases of parent–child incest and 10 cases of brother–sister incest (Hallowell 1955, pp. 294–295).

In ancient Egypt, sibling marriage apparently was allowed not just for royalty (see below) but for commoners as well, in at least some districts. Based on official census records from Roman Egypt (first to third centuries A.D.) preserved on papyrus, 24 percent of all documented marriages in the Arsinoites district were between brothers and sisters. In the second century A.D., the rates

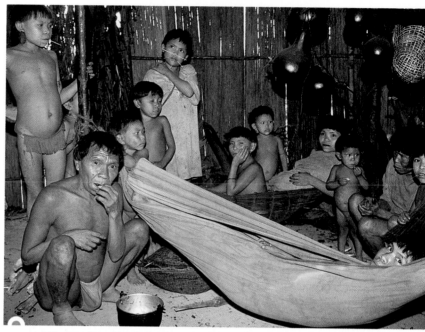

Among the Yanomami of Brazil and Venezuela (shown here), sex with (and marriage to) cross cousins is proper, but sex with parallel cousins is considered incestuous. With unilineal descent, sex with cross cousins isn't incestuous because cross cousins never belong to ego's descent group.

Discovered in Egypt's Valley of the Kings, a gold and silver inlaid throne from the tomb of Tutankhamun is now on display in Cairo's Egyptian Museum. Sibling marriage was allowed not only for ancient Egyptian royalty but also for commoners in some regions.

were 37 percent for the city of Arsinoe and 19 percent for the surrounding villages. These figures are much higher than any other documented levels of inbreeding among humans (Scheidel 1997).

According to Anna Meigs and Kathleen Barlow (2002), for Western societies with nuclear family organization, statistics show a significant risk of father–daughter incest under certain conditions (Russell 1986). Father–daughter incest is most common with stepfathers and nonbiological male household members, but it also happens with biological fathers, especially those who were absent or did little caretaking of their daughters in childhood (Williams and Finkelhor 1995). In a carefully designed study, Linda M. Williams and David Finkelhor (1995) found father–daughter incest to be least likely when there was substantial paternal parenting of daughters who were four to five years old. This experience enhanced the father's parenting skills and his feelings of nurturance, protectiveness, and identification with his daughter, thus reducing the risk of incest.

Crosscultural findings show that incest and its avoidance are shaped by kinship structures. Meigs and Barlow (2002) suggest that a cultural focus on risks and avoidance of father–daughter incest correlates with a patriarchal nuclear family structure, whereas the cultural focus is on avoiding brother–sister incest in societies that have such nonnuclear structures as lineages and clans.

Instinctive Horror

It has been argued (Hobhouse 1915; Lowie 1920/1961) that the incest taboo is universal because incest horror is instinctive: Humans have a genetically programmed disgust toward incest. Because of this feeling, early humans banned it. However, cultural universality doesn't necessarily entail an instinctual basis. Fire making, for example, is a cultural universal, but it certainly isn't an ability transmitted by the genes. Furthermore, if people really did have an instinctive horror of mating with blood relatives, a formal incest taboo would be unnecessary. No one would do it. However, as we have just seen, and as social workers, judges, psychiatrists, and psychologists know, incest is more common than we might suppose.

A final objection to the instinctive horror theory is that it can't explain why in some societies people can marry their cross cousins but not their parallel cousins. Nor does it tell us why the Lakher can marry their maternal, but not their paternal, half-siblings. No known instinct can distinguish between parallel and cross cousins.

The specific kin types included within the incest taboo—and the taboo itself—have a cultural rather than a biological basis. Even among nonhuman primates, there is no definite evidence for an instinct against incest. Adolescent dispersal does not prevent—but merely limits the frequency of—incestuous unions. Among humans, cultural traditions determine the specific relatives with whom sex is considered incestuous. They also deal with the people who violate prohibited relationships in different ways. Banishment, imprisonment, death, and threats of supernatural retaliation are some of the punishments imposed.

Biological Degeneration

Another theory is that the taboo emerged because early *Homo* noticed that abnormal offspring were born from incestuous unions (Morgan 1877/1963). To prevent this, our ancestors banned incest. The human stock produced after the taboo originated was so successful that it spread everywhere.

What is the evidence for this theory? Laboratory experiments with animals that reproduce faster than humans do (such as mice and fruit flies) have been used to investigate the effects of inbreeding: A decline in survival and fertility does accompany brother–sister mating across several generations. However, despite the potentially harmful biological results of systematic inbreeding, human marriage patterns are based on specific cultural beliefs rather than universal concerns about biological degeneration several generations in the future. Neither instinctive horror nor fear of biological degeneration explains the very widespread custom of marrying cross cousins. Nor can fears about degeneration explain why breeding with parallel cousins but not cross cousins is so often tabooed.

Attempt and Contempt

Sigmund Freud is the most famous advocate of the theory that children have sexual feelings toward their parents, which they eventually repress or resolve. Other scholars have looked to the dynamics of growing up for an explanation of the incest taboo. Bronislaw Malinowski believed that children would naturally seek to express their sexual feelings, particularly as they increased in adolescence, with members of their nuclear family, because of preexisting intimacy and affection. Yet, he thought, sex was too powerful a force to unleash in the family. It would threaten existing family roles and ties; it could destroy the family. Malinowski proposed that the incest taboo originated to direct sexual feeling outside—to avoid disruption of—existing family structure and relations.

The opposite theory is that children are not likely to be sexually attracted to those with whom they have grown up (Westermarck 1894). This is related to the idea of instinctive horror, but without assuming a biological (instinctual) basis. The notion here is that a lifetime of living together in particular, nonsexual relationships would make the idea of sex with a family member less desirable. The two opposed theories are sometimes characterized as "familiarity breeds attempt" versus "familiarity breeds contempt." One bit of evidence to support the contempt theory comes from Joseph Shepher's (1983) study of Israeli *kibbutzim*. He found that unrelated people who had been raised in the same *kibbutz* (domestic community) avoided intermarriage. They tended to choose their mates from outside—not because

This view emphasizes the role of marriage in creating and maintaining alliances. By forcing members to marry out, a group increases its allies. Marriage within the group, by contrast, would isolate that group from its neighbors and their resources and social networks, and might ultimately lead to the group's extinction. Exogamy and the incest taboo that propels it help explain human adaptive success. Besides the sociopolitical function, exogamy ensures genetic mixture between groups and thus maintains a successful human species.

ENDOGAMY

The practice of exogamy pushes social organization outward, establishing and preserving alliances among groups. In contrast, rules of **endogamy** dictate mating or marriage within a group to which one belongs. Formal endogamic rules are less common but are still familiar to anthropologists. Indeed, most societies *are* endogamous units, although they usually do not need a formal rule requiring people to marry someone from their own society. In our own society, classes and ethnic groups are quasi-endogamous groups. Members of an ethnic or religious group often want their children to marry within that group, although many of them do not do so. The outmarriage rate varies among such groups, with some more committed to endogamy than others are.

Homogamy means to marry someone similar, as when members of the same social class intermarry. There's a correlation between socioeconomic status (SES) and education. People with similar SES tend to have similar educational aspirations, to attend similar schools, and to aim at similar careers. For example, people who meet at an elite private university are likely to have similar backgrounds and career prospects. Homogamous marriage may work to concentrate wealth in social classes and to reinforce the system of social stratification. In the United States, for example, the rise in female employment, especially in professional careers, when coupled with homogamy, has dramatically increased household incomes in the upper classes. This pattern has been one factor in sharpening the contrast in household income between the richest and poorest quintiles (top and bottom 20 percent) of Americans.

endogamy
Marriage of people from the same group.

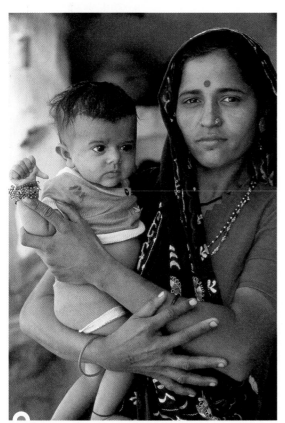

How many fingers do this Indian woman and her child have? Such genetically determined traits as polydactylism (extra fingers) may show up when there is a high incidence of endogamy. Despite the biological effects of inbreeding, marriage preferences and prohibitions are based on specific cultural beliefs rather than universal concerns about future biological degeneration.

they were related, but because their prior residential histories and roles made sex and marriage unappealing. Again, there is no final answer to the question of whether people who grow up together, related or unrelated, are likely to be sexually attracted to one another. Usually they aren't; sometimes they are. Incest is universally tabooed, but it does happen.

Marry Out or Die Out

One of the most accepted explanations for the incest taboo is that it arose in order to ensure exogamy, to force people to marry outside their kin groups (Lévi-Strauss 1949/1969; Tylor 1889; White 1959). In this view, the taboo originated early in human evolution because it was adaptively advantageous. Marrying a close relative, with whom one is already on peaceful terms, would be counterproductive. There is more to gain by extending peaceful relations to a wider network of groups.

Caste

An extreme example of endogamy is India's caste system, which was formally abolished in 1949, although its structure and effects linger. Castes are stratified groups in which membership is ascribed at birth and is lifelong. Indian castes are grouped

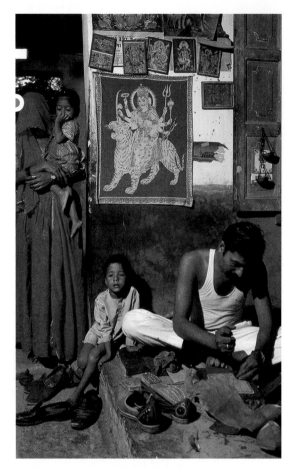

An extreme example of endogamy is India's caste system, which was formally abolished in 1949, although its structure and effects linger. In Gadwada village, cobblers still make shoes in a traditional style. Here, Devi-Lal sits with his child as his wife looks on. In the traditional caste system, such cobblers had a higher status than did sweepers and tanners, whose work is considered so smelly and dirty that they live at the far end of the village.

anthropology **ATLAS**

Map 13 shows organized states and chiefdoms around c.e. 1500. Royal endogamy was practiced in state-level societies, including Inca, ancient Egypt, and traditional Hawaii.

into five major categories, or *varna.* Each is ranked relative to the other four, and these categories extend throughout India. Each *varna* includes a large number of subcastes (*jati*), each of which includes people within a region who may intermarry. All the *jati* in a single *varna* in a given region are ranked, just as the *varna* themselves are ranked.

Occupational specialization often sets off one caste from another. A community may include castes of agricultural workers, merchants, artisans, priests, and sweepers. The untouchable *varna,* found throughout India, includes subcastes whose ancestry, ritual status, and occupations are considered so impure that higher-caste people consider even casual contact with untouchables to be defiling.

The belief that intercaste sexual unions lead to ritual impurity for the higher-caste partner has been important in maintaining endogamy. A man who has sex with a lower-caste woman can restore his purity with a bath and a prayer. However, a woman who has intercourse with a man of a lower caste has no such recourse. Her defilement cannot be undone. Because the women have the babies, these differences protect the purity of the caste line, ensuring the pure ancestry of high-caste

children. Although Indian castes are endogamous groups, many of them are internally subdivided into exogamous lineages. Traditionally this meant that Indians had to marry a member of another descent group from the same caste.

Royal Endogamy

Royal endogamy, based in a few societies on brother–sister marriage, is similar to caste endogamy. Inca Peru, ancient Egypt, and traditional Hawaii all allowed royal brother–sister marriages. In ancient Peru and Hawaii, such marriages were permitted despite the sibling incest taboo that applied to commoners in those societies.

Manifest and Latent Functions

To understand royal brother–sister marriage, it is useful to distinguish between the manifest and latent functions of customs and behavior. The *manifest function* of a custom refers to the reasons people in that society give for it. Its *latent function* is an effect the custom has on the society that its members don't mention or may not even recognize.

Royal endogamy illustrates this distinction. Hawaiians and other Polynesians believed in an impersonal force called *mana.* Mana could exist in things or people, in the latter case marking them off from other people and making them sacred. The Hawaiians believed that no one had as much mana as the ruler. Mana depended on genealogy. The person whose own mana was exceeded only by the king's was his sibling. The most appropriate wife for a king was his own full sister. Notice that the brother–sister marriage also meant that royal heirs would be as manaful, or sacred, as possible. The manifest function of royal endogamy in ancient Hawaii was part of that culture's beliefs about mana and sacredness.

Royal endogamy also had latent functions— political repercussions. The ruler and his wife had the same parents. Since mana was believed to be inherited, they were almost equally sacred. When the king and his sister married, their children indisputably had the most mana in the land. No one could question their right to rule. But if the king had taken as a wife someone with less mana than his sister, his sister's children eventually could cause problems. Both sets of children could assert their sacredness and right to rule. Royal sibling marriage therefore limited conflicts about succession by reducing the number of people with claims to rule. The same result would be true in ancient Egypt and Peru.

Other kingdoms, including European royalty, also have practiced endogamy, but based on cousin marriage rather than sibling marriage. In many cases, as in Great Britain, it is specified that the eldest child (usually the son) of the reigning monarch can succeed. This custom is called *primogeniture*. Commonly, rulers have banished or killed claimants who rival the chosen heir.

Royal endogamy also had a latent economic function. If the king and his sister had rights to inherit the ancestral estate, their marriage to each other, again by limiting the number of heirs, kept it intact. Power often rests on wealth, and royal endogamy tended to ensure that royal wealth remained concentrated in the same line.

MARITAL RIGHTS AND SAME-SEX MARRIAGE

The British anthropologist Edmund Leach (1955) observed that, depending on the society, several different kinds of rights are allocated by marriage. According to Leach, marriage can, but doesn't always, accomplish the following:

1. Establish the legal father of a woman's children and the legal mother of a man's.

2. Give either or both spouses a monopoly on the sexuality of the other.

3. Give either or both spouses rights to the labor of the other.

4. Give either or both spouses rights over the other's property.

STUDENT: **Murad Kakajykov, M.A.**
COUNTRY OF ORIGIN: Turkmenistan
SUPERVISING PROFESSOR: Dr. Patricia Owens, Wabash Valley College
SCHOOL: University of Kentucky, Patterson School of Diplomacy and International Commerce

Families, Kinship, and Descent (a Turkmen Student Writes)

In Turkmenistan, life revolves around family and friends. Traditionally, Turkmen families are composed of five to six members; and by custom, the youngest son and his family live with his parents and inherit their belongings. This is not to say that elder sons are relieved from family responsibilities or that daughters are forgotten: All family members have a responsibility to take care of their parents and show them respect. In fact, it is not uncommon for members of an ordinary Turkmen family to know all of their ancestors from the preceding seven generations. This family tree is known as *"yedi arka"* in the local language, or "seven ancestors" in English. In a culture with such customs and traditions, nursing homes are almost unheard of. Families remain close: Turkmen prefer to see each other, perhaps over green tea, rather than just talk on the telephone. And Turkmen people view their neighbors the same way as they do family. Whenever Turkmen families move into a new neighborhood, they always check on the neighbors first.

In contrast, most Americans have very little knowledge of their ancestors beyond the last generation or two. As a nine-year-old, I felt the same way many Americans do. I would have rather played with my friends than go through the list of my family tree. And few American couples would be happy living with the husband's parents for the rest of their lives. Another main difference between these cultures is how often American families move. It is very unusual for ordinary Turkmen families to move from place to place, but it's hard to find any American family that has not moved at least once. Thanks to communication technologies, American families can easily stay in contact despite the distance, although not face to face, as Turkmen prefer. And finally, Americans rarely see their neighbors as part of their family.

As part of their cultural concept of family, Turkmen believe it is especially important to have good kinship and clear descent in marriages. Whether a marriage is arranged or a matter of love, both the groom's and bride's family will learn about each other's families, kinship, and descent. Further marriage arrangements will be made only if the findings are satisfactory. Americans might consider this practice prejudicial or unfair. However, as modernization spreads, cultural attitudes toward family, kinship, and descent may change; and the American family may not seem so alien to Turkmen.

This lesbian family is participating in a Gay Pride Parade to commemorate the Stonewall uprising of 1968 (Greenwich Village, New York City), when gay patrons fought back against a police raid on the Stonewall Inn. Despite recent advances in gay rights, same-sex marriage remains illegal in most of the United States.

5. Establish a joint fund of property—a partnership—for the benefit of the children.

6. Establish a socially significant "relationship of affinity" between spouses and their relatives.

The discussion of same-sex marriage that follows will serve to illustrate the six rights just listed by seeing what happens in their absence. What if same-sex marriages, which by and large are illegal in the United States, were legal? Could a same-sex marriage establish legal parentage of children born to one or both partners after the partnership is formed? In the case of a different-sex marriage, children born to the wife after the marriage takes place usually are legally defined as her husband's regardless of whether he is the genitor.

Nowadays, of course, DNA testing makes it possible to establish paternity, just as modern reproductive technology makes it possible for a lesbian couple to have one or both partners artificially inseminated. If same-sex marriages were legal, the social construction of kinship could easily make both partners parents. If a Nuer woman married to a woman can be the pater of a child she did not father, why can't two lesbians be the **maters** (socially recognized mothers) of a child to whom only one of them gave birth? And if a married different-sex couple can adopt a child who becomes theirs through the social and legal con-

struction of kinship, the same logic could be applied to a gay male or lesbian couple.

Continuing with Leach's list of the rights transmitted by marriage, same-sex marriage could certainly give each spouse rights to the sexuality of the other. Unable to marry legally, gay men and lesbians have used various devices, such as mock weddings, to declare their commitment and desire for a monogamous sexual relationship. In April 2000, Vermont passed a bill allowing same-sex couples to unite legally, with virtually all the benefits of marriage. In June 2003, a court ruling established same-sex marriages as legal in the province of Ontario, Canada. On June 28, 2005, Canada's House of Commons voted to guarantee full marriage rights to same-sex couples throughout that nation. In the United States five states—Massachusetts, Connecticut, Iowa, Vermont, and New Hampshire—allowed same-sex marriage as of 2010. Civil unions for same-sex couples are legal in New Jersey. In reaction to same-sex marriage, voters in at least 19 U.S. states have approved measures in their state constitutions defining marriage as an exclusively heterosexual union. On November 4, 2008, Californians voted 52 percent to 48 percent to override the right to same-sex marriage, which the courts had approved earlier that year.

Legal same-sex marriages could easily give each spouse rights to the other spouse's labor and its products. Some societies have allowed marriage between members of the same biological

mater
Socially recognized mother of a child.

In Lagos, Nigeria, women work with green vegetables in a bayside market. In parts of Nigeria, prominent market women may take a wife. Such marriage allows wealthy women to strengthen their social status and the economic importance of their households.

sex, who may, however, be considered to belong to a different, socially constructed, gender. Several Native American groups had figures known as *berdaches*, representing a third gender (Murray and Roscoe 1998). These were biological men who assumed many of the mannerisms, behavior patterns, and tasks of women. Sometimes *berdaches* married men, who shared the products of their labor from hunting and filled traditional male roles, as the *berdache* fulfilled the traditional wifely role. Also, in some Native American cultures, a marriage of a "manly-hearted woman" (a third or fourth gender) to another woman brought the traditional male–female division of labor to their household. The manly woman hunted and did other male tasks, while the wife played the traditional female role.

There's no logical reason why same-sex marriage could not give spouses rights over the other's property. But in the United States, the same inheritance rights that apply to male–female couples do not apply to same-sex couples. For instance, even in the absence of a will, property can pass to a widow or a widower without going through probate. The wife or husband pays no inheritance tax. This benefit is not available to gay men and lesbians.

What about Leach's fifth right—to establish a joint fund of property—to benefit the children? Here again, gay and lesbian couples are at a disadvantage. If there are children, property is separately, rather than jointly, transmitted. Some organizations do make staff benefits, such as health and dental insurance, available to same-sex domestic partners.

Finally, there is the matter of establishing a socially significant "relationship of affinity" between spouses and their relatives. In many societies, one of the main roles of marriage is to establish an alliance between groups, in addition to the individual bond. Affinals are relatives through marriage, such as a brother-in-law or mother-in-law. For same-sex couples in contemporary North America, affinal relations are problematic. In an unofficial union, terms like "daughter-in-law" and "mother-in-law" may sound strange. Many parents are suspicious of their children's sexuality and lifestyle choices and may not recognize a relationship of affinity with a child's partner of the same sex.

This discussion of same-sex marriage has been intended to illustrate the different kinds of rights that typically accompany marriage by seeing what may happen when there is a permanent pair-bond without legal sanction. In just five of the United States are such unions fully legal. As we have seen, same-sex marriages have been recognized in different historical and cultural settings. In certain African cultures, including the Igbo of Nigeria and the Lovedu of South Africa, women may marry other women. In situations in which women, such as prominent market women in West Africa, are able to amass property and

other forms of wealth, they may take a wife. Such marriage allows the prominent woman to strengthen her social status and the economic importance of her household (Amadiume 1987).

MARRIAGE AS GROUP ALLIANCE

Outside industrial societies, marriage is often more a relationship between groups than one between individuals. We think of marriage as an individual matter. Although the bride and groom usually seek their parents' approval, the final choice (to live together, to marry, to divorce) lies with the couple. The idea of romantic love symbolizes this individual relationship.

Contemporary Western societies stress the notion that romantic love is necessary for a good marriage. Increasingly this idea characterizes other cultures as well. Described in this chapter's "Appreciating Anthropology" is a cross-cultural study that found romantic ardor to be widespread. The mass media and migration increasingly spread Western ideas about the importance of love for marriage to other societies. However, marriages in the nonWestern societies where anthropology grew up, even when cemented by passion, remain the concern of social groups rather than mere individuals. The scope of marriage extends from the social to the political. Strategic marriages are tried and true ways of establishing alliances between groups.

People don't just take a spouse; they assume obligations to a group of in-laws. When residence is patrilocal, for example, a woman often must leave the community where she was born. She faces the prospect of spending the rest of her life in her husband's village, with his relatives. She may even have to transfer her major allegiance from her own group to her husband's.

Bridewealth and Dowry

In societies with descent groups, people enter marriage not alone but with the help of the descent group. Descent-group members often have to contribute to the **bridewealth**, a customary gift before, at, or after the marriage from the husband and his kin to the wife and her kin. Another word for bridewealth is *brideprice*, but this term is inaccurate because people with the custom don't usually regard the exchange as a sale. They don't think of marriage as a commercial relationship between a man and an object that can be bought and sold.

Bridewealth compensates the bride's group for the loss of her companionship and labor. More important, it makes the children born to the woman full members of her husband's descent group. For this reason, the institution is also

bridewealth
Marital gift by husband's group to wife's group.

Love and Marriage

Love and marriage, the song says, go together like a horse and carriage. But does marriage always imply love? The link between love and marriage, may or may not be a cultural universal. Described here is a cross-cultural survey, published in the anthropological journal Ethnology, *which found romantic ardor to be widespread, perhaps universal. Previously, anthropologists had tended to ignore evidence for romantic love in other cultures, probably because arranged marriages were so common. Today, diffusion, mainly via the mass media, of Western ideas about the importance of love for marriage appears to be influencing marital decisions in other cultures.*

Some influential Western social historians have argued that romance was a product of European medieval culture that spread only recently to other cultures. They dismissed romantic tales from other cultures as representing the behavior of just the elites. Under the sway of this view, Western anthropologists did not even look for romantic love among the peoples they studied. But they are now beginning to think that romantic love is universal . . .

"For decades anthropologists and other scholars have assumed romantic love was unique to the modern West," said Dr. Leonard Plotnicov, an anthropologist at the University of Pittsburgh and editor of the journal *Ethnology*. "Anthropologists came across it in their field work, but they rarely mentioned it because it wasn't supposed to happen."

"Why has something so central to our culture been so ignored by anthropology?" asked Dr. William Jankowiak, an anthropologist at the University of Nevada.

The reason, in the view of Dr. Jankowiak and others, is a scholarly bias throughout the social sciences that viewed romantic love as a luxury in human life, one that could be indulged only by people in Westernized cultures or among the educated elites of other societies. For example, it was assumed in societies where life is hard that romantic love has less chance to blossom, because higher economic standards and more leisure time create more opportunity for dalliance. That also contributed to the belief that romance was for the ruling class, not the peasants.

But, said Dr. Jankowiak, "There is romantic love in cultures around the world." [In 1991] Dr. Jankowiak, with Dr. Edward Fischer, an anthropologist at Tulane University, published in *Ethnology* the first cross-cultural study, systematically comparing romantic love in many cultures.

In the survey of ethnographies from 166 cultures, they found what they considered clear evidence that romantic love was known in 147 of them—89 percent. And in the other 19 cultures, Dr. Jankowiak said, the absence of conclusive evidence seemed due more to anthropologists' oversight than to a lack of romance.

Some of the evidence came from tales about lovers, or folklore that offered love potions or other advice on making someone fall in love.

Another source was accounts by informants to anthropologists. For example, Nisa, a !Kung woman among the Bushmen of the Kalahari, made a clear distinction between the affection she felt for her husband, and that she felt for her lovers, which was "passionate and exciting," though fleeting. Of these extramarital affairs, she said: "When two people come together their hearts are on fire and their passion is very great. After a while the fire cools and that's how it stays." . . .

While finding that romantic love appears to be a human universal, Dr. Jankowiak allows that it is still an alien idea in many cultures that such infatuation has anything to do with the choice of a spouse.

"What's new in many cultures is the idea that romantic love should be the reason to marry someone," said Dr. Jankowiak. "Some cultures see being in love as a state to be pitied. One tribe in the mountains of Iran ridicules people who marry for love."

Of course, even in arranged marriages, partners may grow to feel romantic love for each other. For example, among villagers in the Kangra valley of northern India, "people's romantic longings and yearnings ideally would become focused on the person they're matched with by their families," said Dr. Kirin Narayan, an anthropologist at the University of Wisconsin.

But that has begun to change, Dr. Narayan is finding, under the influence of popular songs and movies. "In these villages the elders are worried that the younger men and women are getting a different idea of romantic love, one where you choose a partner yourself," said Dr. Narayan. "There are starting to be elopements, which are absolutely scandalous."

The same trend toward love matches, rather than arranged marriages, is being noted by anthropologists in many other cultures. Among aborigines in Australia's Outback, for example, marriages had for centuries been arranged when children were very young.

That pattern was disrupted earlier in the last century by missionaries, who urged that marriage not occur until children reached adolescence. Dr. Victoria Burbank, an anthropologist at the University of California at Davis, said that in pre-missionary days, the average age of a girl at marriage was always before menarche, sometimes as young as 9 years. Today the

The importance of love to marriage may be worldwide in scope, but marriage always unites more than just the bride and groom. This Indian wedding took place during the country's marriage season, from November to March.

average age at marriage is 17; girls are more independent by the time their parents try to arrange a marriage for them.

"More and more adolescent girls are breaking away from arranged marriages," said Dr. Burbank. "They prefer to go off into the bush for a 'date' with someone they like, get pregnant, and use that pregnancy to get parental approval for the match."

Even so, parents sometimes are adamant that the young people should not get married. They prefer, instead, that the girls follow the traditional pattern of having their mothers choose a husband for them.

"Traditionally among these people, you can't choose just any son-in-law," said Dr. Burbank. "Ideally, the mother wants to find a boy who is her maternal grandmother's brother's son, a pattern that insures partners are in the proper kin group."

Dr. Burbank added: "These groups have critical ritual functions. A marriage based on romantic love, which ignores what's a proper partner, undermines the system of kinship, ritual, and obligation."

Nevertheless, the rules for marriage are weakening. "In the grandmothers' generation, all marriages were arranged. Romantic love

had no place, though there were a few stories of a young man and woman in love running off together. But in the group I studied, in only one recent case did the girl marry the man selected for her. All the rest are love matches." . . .

Gift-giving customs are associated with marriage throughout the world. In this photo, guests bring presents in baskets to a wedding in Wenjiang, China.

called **progeny price.** Rather than the woman herself, it is her children, or progeny, who are permanently transferred to the husband's group. Whatever we call it, such a transfer of wealth at marriage is common in patrilineal groups. In matrilineal societies, children are members of the mother's group, and there is no reason to pay a progeny price.

Dowry is a marital exchange in which the bride's family or kin group provides substantial gifts when their daughter marries. For rural Greece, Ernestine Friedl (1962) has described a form of dowry in which the bride gets a wealth transfer from her mother, to serve as a kind of trust fund during her marriage. Usually, however, the dowry goes to the husband's family, and the custom is correlated with low female status. In this form of dowry, best known from India, women are perceived as burdens. When a man and his family take a wife, they expect to be compensated for the added responsibility.

Although India passed a law in 1961 against compulsory dowry, the practice continues. When the dowry is considered insufficient, the bride may be harassed and abused. Domestic violence can escalate to the point where the husband or his family burn the bride, often by pouring kerosene on her and lighting it, usually killing her. It should be pointed out that dowry doesn't necessarily lead to domestic abuse. In fact, Indian dowry murders seem to be a fairly recent phenomenon. It also has been estimated that the rate of spousal

murders in the contemporary United States may rival the incidence of India's dowry murders (Narayan 1997).

Sati was the very rare practice through which widows were burned alive, voluntarily or forcibly, on the husband's funeral pyre (Hawley 1994). Although it has become well known, *sati* was mainly practiced in a particular area of northern India by a few small castes. It was banned in 1829. Dowry murders and *sati* are flagrant examples of *patriarchy,* a political system ruled by men in which women have inferior social and political status, including basic human rights.

Bridewealth exists in many more cultures than dowry does, but the nature and quantity of transferred items differ. In many African societies, cattle constitute bridewealth, but the number of cattle given varies from society to society. *As the value of bridewealth increases, marriages become more stable.* Bridewealth is insurance against divorce.

Imagine a patrilineal society in which a marriage requires the transfer of about 25 cattle from the groom's descent group to the bride's. Michael, a member of descent group A, marries Sarah from group B. His relatives help him assemble the bridewealth. He gets the most help from his close agnates (patrilineal relatives): his older brother, father, father's brother, and closest patrilineal cousins.

The distribution of the cattle once they reach Sarah's group mirrors the manner in which they were assembled. Sarah's father, or her oldest brother if the father is dead, receives her bride-wealth. He keeps most of the cattle to use as bridewealth for his sons' marriages. However, a share also goes to everyone who will be expected to help when Sarah's brothers marry.

When Sarah's brother David gets married, many of the cattle go to a third group: C, which is David's wife's group. Thereafter, they may serve as bridewealth to still other groups. Men constantly use their sisters' bridewealth cattle to acquire their own wives. In a decade, the cattle given when Michael married Sarah will have been exchanged widely.

In such societies, marriage entails an agreement between descent groups. If Sarah and Michael try to make their marriage succeed but fail to do so, both groups may conclude that the marriage can't last. Here it becomes especially obvious that such marriages are relationships between groups as well as between individuals. If Sarah has a younger sister or niece (her older brother's daughter, for example), the concerned parties may agree to Sarah's replacement by a kinswoman.

However, incompatibility isn't the main problem that threatens marriage in societies with bridewealth. Infertility is a more important concern. If Sarah has no children, she and her group have not fulfilled their part of the marriage agreement. If the relationship is to endure, Sarah's group must furnish another woman, perhaps her younger sister, who can have children. If this happens, Sarah may choose to stay with her husband. Perhaps she will someday have a child. If she does stay on, her husband will have established a plural marriage.

Most nonindustrial food-producing societies, unlike most foraging societies and industrial nations, allow **plural marriages,** or *polygamy.* There are two varieties; one is common, and the other is very rare. The more common variant is **polygyny,** in which a man has more than one wife. The rare variant is **polyandry,** in which a woman has more than one husband. If the infertile wife remains married to her husband after he has taken a substitute wife provided by her descent group, this is polygyny. Reasons for polygyny other than infertility will be discussed shortly.

Durable Alliances

It is possible to exemplify the group-alliance nature of marriage by examining still another common practice: continuation of marital alliances when one spouse dies.

Sororate

What happens if Sarah dies young? Michael's group will ask Sarah's group for a substitute, often her sister. This custom is known as the **sororate** (Figure 20.5). If Sarah has no sister or if

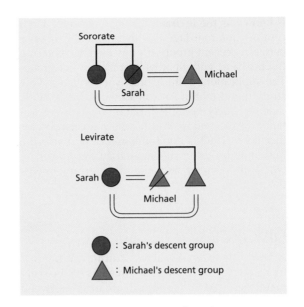

FIGURE 20.5 Sororate and Levirate.

all her sisters are already married, another woman from her group may be available. Michael marries her, there is no need to return the bridewealth, and the alliance continues. The sororate exists in both matrilineal and patrilineal societies. In a matrilineal society with matrilocal postmarital residence, a widower may remain with his wife's group by marrying her sister or another female member of her matrilineage **sororate** Widower marries sister of his deceased wife.

Levirate

What happens if the husband dies? In many societies, the widow may marry his brother. This custom

plural marriage
More than two spouses simultaneously, aka polygamy.

polygyny
Man has more than one wife at the same time.

polyandry
Woman has more than one husband at the same time.

sororate
Widower marries sister of his deceased wife.

 living anthropology **VIDEOS**

Courtship among the Dinka, www.mhhe.com/kottak

This clip shows courtship practices among the Dinka, pastoralists of southern Sudan. It describes the importance of brideprice or bridewealth, customarily given by the family of the groom to the family of the bride. We also see why bridewealth is sometimes called progeny price. According to the Dinka, why are cattle and children (progeny) similar? The narrator claims there is no room for romance in Dinka courtship. Based on the "Appreciating anthropology" box titled "Love and Marriage" and on what you see in this clip, do you believe this claim to be true? The clip also illustrates the text's point that marriage in such societies is as much a relation between groups as one between individuals. The Dinka have descent groups. Do you think they are patrilineal or matrilineal? Why? Among the Dinka, what are the barriers to marriage—and to polygyny?

levirate
Widow marries brother of her deceased husband.

is known as the **levirate.** Like the sororate, it is a continuation marriage that maintains the alliance between descent groups, in this case by replacing the husband with another member of his group. The implications of the levirate vary with age. One study found that in African societies, the levirate, though widely permitted, rarely involves cohabitation of the widow and her new husband. Furthermore, widows don't automatically marry the husband's brother just because they are allowed to. Often, they prefer to make other arrangements (Potash 1986).

DIVORCE

Ease of divorce varies across cultures. What factors work for and against divorce? As we've seen, marriages that are political alliances between groups are more difficult to dissolve than are marriages that are more individual affairs, of concern mainly to the married couple and their children. We've seen that substantial bridewealth may decrease the divorce rate for individuals and that replacement marriages (levirate and sororate) also work to preserve group alliances. Divorce tends to be more common in matrilineal than in patrilineal societies. When residence is matrilocal (in the wife's place), the wife may simply send off a man with whom she's incompatible.

Among the Hopi of the American Southwest, houses were owned by matrilineal clans, with matrilocal postmarital residence. The household head was the senior woman of that household,

which also included her daughters and their husbands and children. A son-in-law had no important role there; he returned to his own mother's home for his clan's social and religious activities. In this matrilineal society, women were socially and economically secure, and the divorce rate was high. Consider the Hopi of Oraibi (Orayvi) pueblo, northeastern Arizona (Levy with Pepper 1992; Titiev 1992). In a study of the marital histories of 423 Oraibi women, Mischa Titiev found that 35 percent had been divorced at least once. Jerome Levy found that 31 percent of 147 adult women had been divorced and remarried at least once. For comparison, of all ever-married women in the United States, only 4 percent had been divorced in 1960, 10.7 percent in 1980, and 11.5 percent in 2007. Titiev characterizes Hopi marriages as unstable. Part of this brittleness was due to conflicting loyalties to matrikin versus spouse. Most Hopi divorces appear to have been matters of personal choice. Levy generalizes that, crossculturally, high divorce rates are correlated with a secure female economic position. In Hopi society women were secure in their home and land ownership and in the custody of their children. In addition, there were no formal barriers to divorce.

Divorce is harder in a patrilineal society, especially when substantial bridewealth would have to be reassembled and repaid if the marriage failed. A woman residing patrilocally (in her husband's household and community) might be reluctant to leave him. Unlike the Hopi, who let the kids stay with the mother, in patrilineal, patrilocal societies, the children of divorce would be expected to remain with their father, as members of his patrilineage. From the women's perspective this is a strong impediment to divorce.

Political and economic factors complicate the divorce process. Among foragers, different factors tend to favor and oppose divorce. What factors work against durable marriages? Since foragers tend to lack descent groups, the political alliance functions of marriage are less important to them than they are to food producers. Foragers also tend to have minimal material possessions. The process of dissolving a joint fund of property is less complicated when spouses do not hold substantial resources in common. What factors favor marital stability among foragers? In societies where the family is an important year-round unit with a gender-based division of labor, ties between spouses tend to be durable. Also, sparse populations mean few alternative spouses if a marriage doesn't work out. But in band-organized societies, foragers can always find a band to join or rejoin if a marriage doesn't work. And food producers can always draw on their descent-group estate if a marriage fails. With patriliny, a woman often can return home, albeit without her children, and with matriliny, a man can do the

A Hopi woman outside her home near Monument Valley, Arizona. Among the Hopi, houses traditionally were owned by matrilineal clans, with matrilocal postmarital residence. Hopi women were socially and economically secure, and the divorce rate was high.

TABLE 20.1 Changing Divorce Rates (Number per Year) in the United States, 1940 through 2006

YEAR	DIVORCE RATE PER 1,000 POPULATION	DIVORCE RATE PER 1,000 WOMEN AGED 15 AND OLDER
1940	2.0	8.8
1950	2.6	10.3
1960	2.2	9.2
1970	3.5	14.9
1980	5.2	22.6
1990	4.7	20.9
2000	4.2	19.5
2006	3.6	NA

SOURCE: S. C. Clarke, "Advance Report of Final Divorce Statistics, 1989 and 1990," *Monthly Vital Statistics Report* 43(8, 9), Hyattsville, MD: National Center for Health Statistics; R. Hughes, Jr., "Demographics of Divorce," 1996, http://www.hec.ohiostate.edu/famlife/divorce/demo.htm; *National Vital Statistics Reports* 54(12), 2006, http://www.cdc.gov/nchs/data/nvsr/nvsr54/nvsr54_12.pdf; *Statistical Abstract of the United States* 2009, Table 77, p. 63.

same. Descent-group estates are not transferred through marriages, although movable resources such as bridewealth cattle certainly are.

In contemporary Western societies, when romance fails, so may the marriage. Or it may not fail, if the other rights associated with marriage, as discussed previously in this chapter, are compelling. Economic ties and obligations to kids, along with other factors, such as concern about public opinion, or simple inertia, may keep marriages intact after sex, romance, and/or companionship fade. Also, even in modern societies, royalty, leaders, and other elites may have political marriages similar to the arranged marriages of nonindustrial societies.

In the United States, divorce figures have been kept since 1860. Divorces tend to increase after wars and to decrease when times are bad economically. But with more women working outside the home, economic dependence on the husband as breadwinner is weaker, which no doubt facilitates a decision to divorce when a marriage has major problems.

Table 20.1 is based on two measures of the divorce rate. The left column shows the rate per 1,000 people per year in the overall population. The right column shows the annual rate per 1,000 married women over the age of 15, which is the best measure of divorce. In either case, comparing 2000 with 1960, the divorce rate more than doubled. Note that the rate rose slightly after World War II (1950), then declined a decade later (1960). The most notable rate rise occurred between 1960 and 1980. The

rate actually has been falling since 1980, and continued to fall between 2000 and 2005.

Among nations, the United States has one of the world's highest divorce rates. There are several probable causes: economic, cultural, and religious among them. Economically, the United States has a larger percentage of gainfully employed women than most nations have. Work outside the home provides a cash basis for independence, as it also places strains on marriage and social life for both partners. Culturally, Americans tend to value independence and its modern form, self-actualization. Also, Protestantism (in its various guises) is the most common form of religion in the United States. Of the two major religions in the United States and Canada (where Catholicism predominates), Protestantism has been less stringent in denouncing divorce than has Catholicism.

PLURAL MARRIAGES

In contemporary North America, where divorce is fairly easy and common, polygamy (marriage to more than one spouse at the same time) is against the law. Marriage in industrial nations joins individuals, and relationships between individuals can be severed more easily than can those between groups. As divorce grows more common, North Americans practice *serial monogamy:* Individuals have more than one spouse but never, legally, more than one at the same time. As stated earlier, the two forms of polygamy are polygyny and polyandry. Polyandry is practiced in only a few cultures, notably among certain groups in Tibet, Nepal, and India. Polygyny is much more common.

Polygyny

We must distinguish between the social approval of plural marriage and its actual frequency in a particular society. Many cultures approve of a man having more than one wife. However, even when polygyny is encouraged, most men are monogamous, and polygyny characterizes only a fraction of the marriages. Why is this true?

One reason is equal sex ratios. In the United States, about 105 males are born for every 100 females. In adulthood, the ratio of men to women equalizes, and eventually it reverses. The average North American woman outlives the average man. In many nonindustrial societies as well, the male-biased sex ratio among children reverses in adulthood.

The custom of men marrying later than women promotes polygyny. Among the Kanuri people of Bornu, Nigeria, men got married between the ages of 18 and 30; women, between 12 and 14 (Cohen 1967). The age difference between spouses meant

appreciating DIVERSITY

Five Wives and 55 Children

Diversity in marriage customs has been a prominent topic in anthropology since its origin. Many societies, including Turkey, that once allowed plural marriage have banned it. Polygyny is the form of polygamy (plural marriage) in which a man has more than one wife. Marriage usually is a domestic partnership, but under polygyny secondary wives may or may not reside near the first wife. In this Turkish case the five wives have their own homes. Polygamy, although formally outlawed, has survived in Turkey since the Ottoman period, when having several wives was viewed as a symbol of power, wealth, and sexual prowess. Unlike the past, when the practice was customary (for men who could afford it) and not illegal, polygamy can put contemporary women at risk. Because their marriages have no official status, secondary wives who are abused or mistreated have no legal recourse. Like all institutions studied by anthropologists, customs involving plural marriage are changing in the contemporary world and in the context of nation-states and globalization.

ISIKLAR, Turkey, July 6—With his 5 wives, 55 children and 80 grandchildren, 400 sheep, 1,200 acres of land and a small army of servants, Aga Mehmet Arslan would seem an unlikely defender of monogamy.

Though banned, polygamy is widespread in the Isiklar region. Yet if he were young again, said Mr. Arslan, a sprightly, potbellied, 64-year-old Kurdish village chieftain, he would happily trade in his five wives for one.

"Marrying five wives is not sinful, and I did so because to have many wives is a sign of power," he said, perched on a divan in a large cushion-filled room at his house, where a portrait of Turkey's first president, Mustafa Kemal Ataturk, who outlawed polygamy in 1926, is prominently displayed.

"But I wouldn't do it again," he added, listing the challenges of having so many kin—like the need to build each wife a house away from the others to prevent friction and his struggle to remember all of his children's names. "I was uneducated back then, and God commands us to be fruitful and multiply."

Though banned by Ataturk as part of an effort to modernize the Turkish republic and empower women, polygamy remains widespread

Many societies, including Turkey (as described here), that once permitted plural marriage have outlawed it. The Turkish bride shown here—Kubra Gul, the daughter of Turkey's president Abdullah Gul—will not have to share her bridegroom, Mehmet Sarimermer. The photo shows the couple on their wedding day (October 14, 2007) in Istanbul.

in this deeply religious and rural Kurdish region of southeastern Anatolia, home to one-third of Turkey's 71 million people. The practice is generally accepted under the Koran.

Polygamy is creating cultural clashes in a country struggling to reconcile the secularism

that there were more widows than widowers. Most of the widows remarried, some in polygynous unions. Among the Kanuri of Bornu and in other polygynous societies, widows made up a large number of the women involved in plural marriages (Hart, Pilling, and Goodale 1988). In many societies, including the Kanuri, the number of wives is an indicator of a man's household productivity, prestige, and social position (see "Appreciating Diversity"). The more wives, the more workers. Increased productivity means more wealth. This wealth in turn attracts additional wives to the household. Wealth and wives bring greater prestige to the household and its head.

If a plural marriage is to work, there needs to be some agreement among the existing spouses when another one is to be added, especially if they are to share the same household. In certain societies, the first wife requests a second wife to help with household chores. The second wife's status is lower than that of the first; they are senior and junior wives. The senior wife sometimes chooses the junior one from among her close kinswomen. Among the Betsileo of Madagascar, the different wives always lived in different villages. A man's first and senior wife, called "Big Wife," lived in the village where he cultivated his best rice field and spent most of his time. High-status men with several rice fields and multiple wives had households near each field. They spent most of their time with the senior wife but visited the others throughout the year.

of the republic with its Muslim traditions. It also risks undermining Turkey's drive to gain entry into the European Union.

"The E.U. is looking for any excuse not to let Turkey in, and polygamy reinforces the stereotype of Turkey as a backward country," said Handan Coskun, director of a women's center.

Because polygamous marriages are not recognized by the state—imams who conduct them are subject to punishment—the wives have no legal status, making them vulnerable when marriages turn violent. Yet the local authorities here typically turn a blind eye because the practice is viewed as a tradition. . . .

In Turkey, polygamy experts explain the practice as a hangover from the Ottoman period, when harem culture abounded and having several wives was viewed as a symbol of influence, sexual prowess and wealth.

Remzi Otto, a sociology professor at Dicle University in Diyarbakir, who conducted a survey of 50 polygamous families, said some men took second wives if their first wives could not conceive sons. Some also take widowed women and orphan girls as second wives to give them a social safety net. Love, he added, can also play a role.

"Many men in this region are forced into marriages when they are as young as 13, so finding their own wife is a way to rebel and express their independence," he said.

Isiklar, the remote village where Mr. Arslan is the aga, or chief, can be found at the end of a long dirt road, surrounded by sweeping verdant fields. Most of the local residents share the surname Arslan, which means lion in Turkish and connotes virility.

Mr. Arslan said he regretted his multiple marriages and had forbidden his sons to take more than one wife. He is also educating his daughters. "I have done nothing shameful," he said. "I don't drink. I treat everyone with respect. But having so many wives can create problems."

His biggest headache, he said, stems from jealousy among the wives, the first of whom he married out of love. "My rule is to behave equally toward all of my wives," he said. "But the first wife was very, very jealous when the second wife came. When the third arrived, the first two created an alliance against her. So I have to be a good diplomat."

Mr. Arslan, who owns land, real estate and shops throughout the region, said the financial burden of so many offspring could be overwhelming. "When I go to the shoe shop, I buy 100 pairs of shoes at a time," he said. "The clerk at the store thinks I'm a shoe salesman and tells me to go visit a wholesaler."

He also has trouble keeping track of his children. He recently saw two boys fighting in the street and told them they would bring shame on their families. "Do you not recognize me?" one replied. "I am your son." . . .

Women's groups say polygamy is putting women at risk. "These women can be abused, raped, mistreated, and because their marriages are not legal, they have nowhere to turn," said Ms. Coskun, the director of the women's center, which has opened breadmaking factories in poor rural areas where women can work and take classes on women's rights. . . .

Back in Isiklar, Mr. Arslan acknowledged that polygamy was an outmoded practice. "God has been giving to me because I am giving to my family," he said. "But if you want to be happy, marry one wife."

SOURCE: Dan Bilefsky, "Polygamy Fosters Culture Clashes (and Regrets) in Turkey." From *The New York Times*, July 10, 2006. © 2006 The New York Times. All rights reserved. Used by permission and protected by the Copyright Laws of the United States. The printing, copying, redistribution, or retransmission of the Material without express written permission is prohibited. www.nytimes.com

Plural wives can play important political roles in nonindustrial states. The king of the Merina, a society with more than one million people in the highlands of Madagascar, had palaces for each of his 12 wives in different provinces. He stayed with them when he traveled through the kingdom. They were his local agents, overseeing and reporting on provincial matters. The king of Buganda, the major precolonial state of Uganda, took hundreds of wives, representing all the clans in his nation. Everyone in the kingdom became the king's in-law, and all the clans had a chance to provide the next ruler. This was a way of giving the common people a stake in the government.

These examples show that there is no single explanation for polygyny. Its context and function vary from society to society and even within the same society. Some men are polygynous because they have inherited a widow from a brother (the levirate). Others have plural wives because they seek prestige or want to increase household productivity. Still others use marriage as a political tool or a means of economic advancement. Men and women with political and economic ambitions cultivate marital alliances that serve their aims. In many societies, including the Betsileo of Madagascar and the Igbo of Nigeria, women arrange the marriages.

Like all institutions studied by anthropologists, customs involving plural marriage are changing in the contemporary world and in the context of nation-states and globalization. This

This polygynous family includes two wives, six children, and one husband, all members of the Uighur ethnic group. They sit in front of their house at the Buzak Commune, near Khotan, Xinjiang Province, People's Republic of China. Would you expect most marriages to be polygynous in a society that allows polygyny?

chapter's "Appreciating Diversity" focuses on changing marriage customs in Turkey. Traditionally, polygyny has been allowed there for men who could afford multiple wives and many children. Polygyny now is outlawed, but it still is practiced. Because polygynous unions now lack legal status, secondary wives are at risk if their husband mistreats, neglects, or leaves them.

Polyandry

Polyandry is rare and is practiced under very specific conditions. Most of the world's polyandrous peoples live in South Asia—Tibet, Nepal, India, and Sri Lanka. In some of these areas, polyandry seems to be a cultural adaptation to mobility associated with customary male travel for trade, commerce, and military operations. Polyandry ensures there will be at least one man at home to accomplish male activities within a gender-based division of labor. Fraternal polyandry is also an effective strategy when resources are scarce. Brothers with limited resources (in land) pool their resources in expanded (polyandrous) households. They take just one wife. Polyandry restricts the number of wives and heirs. Less competition among heirs means that land can be transmitted with minimal fragmentation.

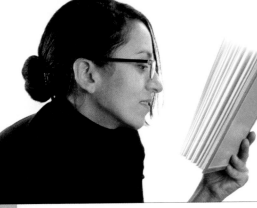

Acing the
COURSE

Summary

1. Marriage, which is usually a form of domestic partnership, is hard to define. All societies have some kind of incest taboo. Human behavior with respect to mating with close relatives may express a generalized primate tendency, illustrating both urges and avoidance. But types, risks, and avoidance of incest also reflect specific kinship structures. A cultural focus on father–daughter incest may correlate with a patriarchal nuclear family structure, whereas the cultural focus is on avoiding brother–sister incest in societies with lineages and clans.

2. The following are some of the explanations that have been offered for the incest taboo: (1) It codifies instinctive horror of incest, (2) it expresses concern about the biological effects of incestuous unions, (3) it reflects feelings of attraction or aversion that develop as one grows up in a household, and (4) it has an adaptive advantage because it promotes exogamy, thereby increasing networks of friends and allies.

3. Exogamy extends social and political ties outward. This is confirmed by a consideration of endogamy—marriage within the group. Endogamic rules are common in stratified societies. One extreme example is India, where castes are the endogamous units. Castes are subdivided into exogamous descent groups. The same culture can therefore have both endogamic and exogamic rules. Certain ancient kingdoms encouraged royal incest while condemning incest by commoners.

4. The discussion of same-sex marriage, which, by and large, is illegal in contemporary North America, illustrates the various rights that go along with different-sex marriages. Marriage establishes the legal parents of children. It gives each spouse rights to the sexuality, labor, and property of the other. And it establishes a socially significant "relationship of affinity" between each spouse and the other spouse's relatives. Some of these rights may be established by same-sex domestic partnerships.

5. In societies with descent groups, marriages are relationships between groups as well as between spouses. With the custom of bridewealth, the groom and his relatives transfer wealth to the bride and her relatives. As the bridewealth's value increases, the divorce rate declines. Bridewealth customs show that marriages among nonindustrial food producers create and maintain group alliances. So do the sororate, by which a man marries the sister of his deceased wife, and the levirate, by which a woman marries the brother of her deceased husband.

6. The ease and frequency of divorce vary across cultures. Political, economic, social, cultural, and religious factors affect the divorce rate. When marriage is a matter of intergroup alliance, as is typically true in societies with descent groups, divorce is less common. A large fund of joint property also complicates divorce.

7. Many societies permit plural marriages. The two kinds of polygamy are polygyny and polyandry. The former involves multiple wives; the latter, multiple husbands. Polygyny is much more common than is polyandry.

Key Terms

bridewealth 477
cross cousins 469
dowry 480
endogamy 473
exogamy 469
genitor 469
incest 469
levirate 482

mater 475
parallel cousins 469
pater 469
plural marriage 481
polyandry 481
polygyny 481
progeny price 480
sororate 481

Test Yourself!

MULTIPLE CHOICE

1. This chapter on marriage describes the example of marital unions between women in the Nuer community of Sudan. These unions are symbolic and social relationships rather than sexual ones, as in the case of a woman who marries another woman if her father has only daughters but no male heirs, who are necessary if his patrilineage is to survive. The "wife" can then have sex with another man until she gets pregnant. The resulting children are accepted as the offspring of both the female husband and the wife. Examples like this one highlight
   a. how some societies need a better educational system to teach people about proper kinship relationships.
   b. how some societies suffer from the lack of male fathers.
   c. how despite appearances, marriage has little to do with wealth and it is really all about sex.
   d. how kinship relationships take different meanings in different social contexts; they are socially constructed.
   e. how some societies could benefit from exposure to modernity.

2. How is exogamy adaptive?
   a. It increases the likelihood that disadvantageous alleles will find phenotypic expression and thus be eliminated from the population.
   b. It impedes peaceful relations among social groups and therefore promotes population expansion.
   c. It was an important causal factor in the origin of the state.

d. It is not adaptive; it is just a culture construction.
e. It increases the number of individuals on whom one can rely in time of need.

3. Who are your cross cousins?
   a. the children of your mother's brother or your father's sister
   b. the children of your mother's sister or your father's brother
   c. your father's cousins' children
   d. your mother's cousins' children
   e. your cousins of the opposite sex

4. Among the Yanomami, as in many societies with unilineal descent, sex with cross cousins is proper but sex with parallel cousins is considered incestuous. Why?
   a. The Yanomami consider parallel cousins to be relatives, whereas cross cousins are actual or potential affinals.
   b. Among the Yanomami, the cross cousins are actually the parallel cousins.
   c. The Yanomami, as well as members of other societies with unilineal descent, share a gene that impedes them from having sex with parallel cousins.
   d. This behavior is a human universal explained by Freud's theory of attempt and contempt.
   e. The Yanomami consider cross cousins closer relatives than all other kin.

5. Among social scientists, which is the most accepted explanation for the incest taboo?
   a. instinctive horror caused by genes
   b. marry out or die out
   c. the widespread fear of biological degeneration
   d. attempt or contempt
   e. genetically determined attraction for those most different from ourselves

6. Some Polynesian communities believe in the impersonal force called *mana* and that having high levels of mana marks people as sacred. The practice of royal endogamy was one way of making sure that this impersonal force remained within the ruling class. What type of explanation is this?
   a. a latent function, the explanation investigators give for people's customs
   b. an affinal function that encourages the extension of affinal bonds to an ever-widening circle of people
   c. a genetic explanation
   d. a manifest function, the explanations people give for their customs
   e. an etic explanation

7. Among some Native American groups, figures known as *berdaches* were biological men who assumed the behavior and tasks of women. Sometimes they married men and together they would share the products of each other's labor in the same way that different-sex marriages do. This example illustrates
   a. how Arizona is one of many states that recognize same-sex marriages in the United States.
   b. how, if legal, same-sex marriages could easily give each spouse rights to the other spouse's labor and its products.
   c. the rare social phenomenon of polyandry.
   d. how same-sex marriages make good economic sense.
   e. how Edmund Leach was wrong to suggest that all societies define marriage similarly.

8. Which of the following statements about divorce is *not* true?
   a. Divorce is more common now than it was a century ago.
   b. The more substantial the joint property, the more complicated the divorce.
   c. Divorce is unique to industrialized nation-states.
   d. Divorce is harder in a patrilineal society.
   e. Substantial bridewealth may decrease the divorce rate.

9. Which of the following is *not* a form of polygamy?
   a. a man who has three wives
   b. a woman who has three husbands, all of whom are brothers
   c. a man who marries, then divorces, then marries again, then divorces again, then marries again, each time to a different woman
   d. a man who has three wives, all of whom are sisters
   e. a man who has two wives, one of whom is biologically female, while the other is biologically male, but is regarded as having the spirit of a woman

10. Which of the following statements about marriage is true?
    a. It must involve at least one biological male and at least one biological female.
    b. It involves a woman and the genitor of her children.
    c. It always involves a priest.
    d. Rings must be exchanged.
    e. It is a cultural universal.

FILL IN THE BLANK

1. The term _____ refers to the biological father of a child, while _____ is the term anthropologists use to identify ego's socially recognized father.

2. _____ refers to the culturally sanctioned practice of marrying someone within a group to which one belongs.

3. _____ is a marital exchange in which the bride's family or kin group provides substantial gifts when their daughter marries. This custom is correlated with _____ female status.

4. When a widower marries a sister of his deceased wife, this is called a _____.

5. The custom called _____ occurs when a widow marries a brother of her deceased husband.

CRITICAL THINKING

1. What is homogamy? In countries such as the United States, what are the social and economic implications of homogamy (especially when coupled with other trends such as the rise of female employment)?

2. What is bridewealth? What else is it called and why? Do you have anything like it in your society? Why or why not?

3. According to Edmund Leach (1955), depending on the society, several different kinds of rights are allocated by marriage. What are these rights? Which among these rights do you consider more fundamental than others in your definition of marriage? Which ones can you do without? Why?

4. Outside industrial societies, marriage is often more a relationship between groups than one between individuals. What does this mean? What are some examples of this?

5. Divorce tends to be more common in matrilineal than in patrilineal societies. Why?

Multiple Choice: 1. (D); 2. (E); 3. (A); 4. (A); 5. (B); 6. (D); 7. (B); 8. (C); 9. (C); 10. (E); **Fill in the Blank:** 1. genitor, pater; 2. Endogamy; 3. Dowry, low; 4. sororate; 5. evirate

Collier, J. F., ed.
  1988 *Marriage and Inequality in Classless Societies.* Stanford, CA: Stanford University Press. Marriage and issues of gender stratification in bands and tribes.

Hart, C. W. M., A. R. Pilling, and J. C. Goodale
  1988 *The Tiwi of North Australia,* 3rd ed. Fort Worth: Harcourt Brace. Latest edition of classic case study of Tiwi marriage arrangements, including polygyny, and social change over 60 years of anthropological study.

Ingraham, C.
  2008 *White Weddings: Romancing Heterosexuality in Popular Culture,* 2nd ed. New York: Routledge. Love and marriage, including the ceremony, in today's United States.

Levine, N. E.
  1988 *The Dynamics of Polyandry: Kinship, Domesticity, and Population in the Tibetan Border.* Chicago: University of Chicago Press. Case study of fraternal polyandry and household organization in northwestern Nepal.

Malinowski, B.
  2001 (orig. 1927) *Sex and Repression in Savage Society.* New York: Routledge. Classic study of sex, marriage, and kinship among the matrilineal Trobrianders.

Simpson, B.
  1998 *Changing Families: An Ethnographic Approach to Divorce and Separation.* New York: Berg. Current marriage and divorce trends in Great Britain.

Go to our Online Learning Center website at **www.mhhe.com/kottak** for Internet exercises directly related to the content of this chapter.

What is religion, and what are its various forms, social correlates, and functions?

What is ritual, and what are its various forms and expressions?

What role does religion play in maintaining and changing societies?

A softball game featuring monks from the Gampo Abbey, Cape Breton Island, Nova Scotia, Canada. Magic and religion can blend into sports.

understanding OURSELVES

Have you ever noticed how much baseball players spit? Outside baseball—even among other male sports figures—spitting is considered impolite. Football players, with their customary headgear, don't spit, nor do basketball players, who might slip on the court. No spitting by Roger Federer, Tiger Woods, Paul or Morgan Hamm, or Michael Phelps. Not even Mark Spitz (a swimmer turned dentist). But watch any baseball game for a few innings and you'll see spitting galore. Since pitchers appear to be the spitting champions, the custom likely originated on the mound. It continues today as a carryover from the days when pitchers routinely chewed tobacco, believing that nicotine enhanced their concentration and effectiveness. The spitting custom spread to other players, who unabashedly spew saliva from the outfield to the dugout steps.

For the student of custom, ritual, and magic, baseball is an especially interesting game, to which lessons from anthropology are easily applied. The pioneering anthropologist Bronislaw Malinowski, writing about Pacific Islanders rather than baseball players, noted they had developed all sorts of magic to use in sailing, a hazardous activity. He proposed that when people face conditions they can't control (e.g., wind and weather), they turn to magic. Magic, in the form of rituals, taboos, and sacred objects, is particularly evident in baseball. Like

sailing magic, baseball magic serves to reduce psychological stress, creating an illusion of control when real control is lacking.

In several publications about baseball, the anthropologist George Gmelch makes use of Malinowski's observation that magic is most common in situations dominated by chance and uncertainty. All sorts of magical behaviors surround pitching and batting, which are full of uncertainty. There are fewer rituals for fielding, over which players have more control. (Batting averages of .350 or higher are very rare after a full season, but a fielding percentage below .900 is a disgrace.) Especially obvious are the rituals (like the spitting) of pitchers, who may: tug their cap between pitches, spit in a particular direction, magically manipulate the resin bag, talk to the ball, or wash their hands after giving up a run. Batters have their rituals, too. It isn't uncommon to see Minnesota Twins outfielder Carlos Gomez kiss his bat, which he likes to talk to, smell, threaten—and reward when he gets a hit. Another batter routinely would spit, then ritually touch his gob with his bat, to enhance his success at the plate.

Humans use tools to accomplish a lot, but technology still doesn't let us "have it all." To keep hope alive in situations of uncertainty, and for outcomes we can't control, all societies draw on magic and religion as sources of nonmaterial comfort, explanation, and control. What are your rituals?

WHAT IS RELIGION?

The anthropologist Anthony F. C. Wallace defined **religion** as "belief and ritual concerned with supernatural beings, powers, and forces" (1966, p. 5). The supernatural is the extraordinary realm outside (but be-

lieved to impinge on) the observable world. It is nonempirical and inexplicable in ordinary terms. It must be accepted "on faith." Supernatural beings—gods and goddesses, ghosts, and souls—are not of the material world. Nor are supernatural forces, some of which may be wielded by beings. Other sacred forces are impersonal; they simply exist. In many societies, however, people believe they can benefit from, become imbued with, or manipulate supernatural forces (see Bowie 2006; Crapo 2003).

Another definition of religion (Reese 1999) focuses on bodies of people who gather together regularly for worship. These congregants or adherents subscribe to and internalize a common system of meaning. They accept (adhere to or believe in) a set of doctrines involving the relationship between the individual and divinity, the supernatural, or whatever is taken to be the ultimate nature of reality. Anthropologists have stressed the collective, shared, and enacted nature of religion, the emotions it generates, and the meanings it embodies. Émile Durkheim (1912/2001), an early scholar of religion, stressed religious *effervescence*, the bubbling up of collective emotional intensity generated by worship. Victor Turner (1969/1995) updated Durkheim's notion, using the term **communitas,** an intense community spirit, a feeling of great social solidarity, equality, and togetherness. The word *religion* derives from the Latin *religare*, "to tie, to bind," but it is not necessary for all the members of a given religion to meet together as a common body. Subgroups meet regularly at local congregation sites. They may attend occasional meetings with adherents representing a wider region. And they may form an imagined community with people of similar faith throughout the world.

Like ethnicity and language, religion also is associated with social divisions within and between societies and nations. Religion both unites and divides. Participation in common rites may affirm, and thus maintain, the social solidarity of one religion's adherents. However, as we know from daily headlines, religious difference also may be associated with bitter enmity.

In studying religion crossculturally, anthropologists pay attention to the social nature and roles of religion as well as to the nature, content, and meaning to people of religious doctrines, acts, events, settings, practitioners, and organizations. We also consider such verbal manifestations of religious beliefs as prayers, chants, myths, texts, and statements about ethics and morality. Religion, by either definition offered here, exists in all human societies. It is a cultural universal. However, we'll see that it isn't always easy to distinguish the supernatural from the natural and that different societies conceptualize divinity, supernatural entities, and ultimate realities very differently.

ORIGINS, FUNCTIONS, AND EXPRESSIONS OF RELIGION

When did religion begin? No one knows for sure. There are suggestions of religion in Neandertal burials and on European cave walls, where painted stick figures may represent shamans, early religious specialists. Nevertheless, any statement about when, where, why, and how religion arose, or any description of its original nature, can only be speculative. However, although such speculations are inconclusive, many have revealed important functions and effects of religious behavior. Several theories will be examined now.

Animism

The founder of the anthropology of religion was the Englishman Sir Edward Burnett Tylor (1871/1958). Religion was born, Tylor thought, as people tried to understand conditions and events they could not explain by reference to daily experience. Tylor believed that our ancestors—and contemporary nonindustrial peoples—were particularly intrigued with death, dreaming, and trance. In dreams and trances, people see images they may remember when they wake up or come out of the trance state.

Tylor concluded that attempts to explain dreams and trances led early humans to believe that two entities inhabit the body: one active during the day and the other—a double or soul—active during sleep and trance states. Although they never meet, they are vital to each other. When the double permanently leaves the body, the person dies. Death is departure of the soul. From the Latin for soul, *anima*, Tylor named this belief animism. The soul was one sort of spiritual entity; people remembered various images from their dreams and trances—other spirits. For Tylor, **animism,** the earliest form of religion, was a belief in spiritual beings.

Tylor proposed that religion evolved through stages, beginning with animism. *Polytheism* (the belief in multiple gods) and then *monotheism* (the belief in a single, all-powerful deity) developed later. Because religion originated to explain things people didn't understand, Tylor thought it would decline as science offered better explanations. To an extent, he was right. We now have scientific explanations for many things that religion once elucidated. Nevertheless, because religion persists, it must do something more than explain the mysterious. It must, and does, have other functions and meanings.

Mana and Taboo

Besides animism—and sometimes coexisting with it in the same society—is a view of the supernatural as a domain of raw impersonal power, or *force*, that people can control under certain conditions. (You'd be right to think of *Star Wars*.) Such a conception of the supernatural is particularly prominent in Melanesia, the area of the South Pacific that includes Papua New Guinea and adjacent islands. Melanesians believed in **mana,** a sacred

religion
Belief and ritual concerned with supernatural beings, powers, and forces.

communitas
Intense feeling of social solidarity.

animism
Belief in souls or doubles.

mana
Impersonal sacred force, so named in Melanesia and Polynesia.

taboo
Sacred and forbidden; prohibition backed by supernatural sanctions.

impersonal force existing in the universe. Mana can reside in people, animals, plants, and objects.

Melanesian mana was similar to our notion of efficacy or luck. Melanesians attributed success to mana, which people could acquire or manipulate in different ways, such as through magic. Objects with mana could change someone's luck. For example, a charm or

amulet belonging to a successful hunter might transmit the hunter's mana to the next person who held or wore it. A woman might put a rock in her garden, see her yields improve dramatically, and attribute the change to the force contained in the rock.

Beliefs in manalike forces are widespread, although the specifics of the religious doctrines vary. Consider the contrast between mana in Melanesia and Polynesia (the islands included in a triangular area marked by Hawaii to the north, Easter Island to the east, and New Zealand to the southwest). In Melanesia, one could acquire mana by chance or by working hard to get it. In Polynesia, however, mana wasn't potentially available to everyone but was attached to political offices. Chiefs and nobles had more mana than ordinary people did.

So charged with mana were the highest chiefs that contact with them was dangerous to the commoners. The mana of chiefs flowed out of their bodies wherever they went. It could infect the ground, making it dangerous for others to walk in the chief's footsteps. It could permeate the containers and utensils chiefs used in eating. Contact between chief and commoners was dangerous because mana could have an effect like an electric shock. Because high chiefs had so much mana, their bodies and possessions were **taboo** (set apart as sacred and off-limits to ordinary people). Contact between a high chief and commoners was forbidden. Because ordinary people couldn't bear as much sacred current as royalty could, when commoners were accidentally exposed, purification rites were necessary.

One role of religion is to explain (see Horton 1993). A belief in souls explains what happens in sleep, trance, and death. Melanesian mana explains differential success that people can't understand in ordinary, natural terms. People fail at hunting, war, or gardening not because they are lazy, stupid, or inept but because success comes—or doesn't come—from the supernatural world.

The beliefs in spiritual beings (e.g., animism) and supernatural forces (e.g., mana) fit within the definition of religion given at the beginning of this chapter. Most religions include both spirits and impersonal forces. Likewise, the supernatural beliefs of contemporary North Americans include beings (gods, saints, souls, demons) and forces (charms, talismans, crystals, and sacred objects).

Ancient Greek polytheism is illustrated by this image of Apollo, with a lyre, and Artemis, sacrificing over an altar fire. The red-figured terra-cotta vessel dates to 490–480 B.C.E.

Illustrating baseball magic, Minnesota Twins outfielder Carlos Gomez kisses his bat, which he likes to talk to, smell, threaten–and reward when he gets a hit.

Magic and Religion

Magic refers to supernatural techniques intended to accomplish specific aims. These techniques include spells, formulas, and incantations used with deities or with impersonal forces. Magicians use *imitative magic* to produce a desired effect by imitating it. If magicians wish to injure or kill someone, they may imitate that effect on an image of the victim. Sticking pins in "voodoo dolls" is an example. With *contagious magic*, whatever is done to an object is believed to affect a person who once had contact with it. Sometimes practitioners of contagious magic use body products from prospective victims—their nails or hair, for example. The spell performed on the body product is believed to reach the person eventually and work the desired result. We find magic in cultures with diverse religious beliefs. It can be associated with animism, mana, polytheism, or monotheism. Magic is neither simpler nor more primitive than animism or the belief in mana.

Trobriand Islanders prepare a traditional trading canoe for use in the Kula, which is a regional exchange system. The woman brings trade goods in a basket, while the men prepare the long canoe to set sail. Magic is often associated with uncertainty, such as sailing in unpredictable waters.

Anxiety, Control, Solace

Religion and magic don't just explain things and help people accomplish goals. They also enter the realm of human feelings. In other words, they serve emotional needs as well as cognitive (e.g., explanatory) ones. For example, supernatural beliefs and practices can help reduce anxiety. Magical techniques can dispel doubts that arise when outcomes are beyond human control. Similarly, religion helps people face death and endure life crises.

Although all societies have techniques to deal with everyday matters, there are certain aspects of people's lives over which they lack control. When people face uncertainty and danger, according to Malinowski, they turn to magic.

> [H]owever much knowledge and science help man in allowing him to obtain what he wants, they are unable completely to control chance, to eliminate accidents, to foresee the unexpected turn of natural events, or to make human handiwork reliable and adequate to all practical requirements. (Malinowski 1931/ 1978, p. 39)

As was discussed in this chapter's "Understanding Ourselves," Malinowski found that the Trobriand Islanders used a variety of magical practices when they went on sailing expeditions, a hazardous activity. He proposed that because people can't control matters such as wind, weather,

and the fish supply, they turn to magic. People may call on magic when they come to a gap in their knowledge or powers of practical control yet have to continue in a pursuit (Malinowski 1931/1978).

Malinowski noted that it was only when confronted by situations they could not control that Trobrianders, out of psychological stress, turned from technology to magic. Despite our improving technical skills, we can't control every outcome, and magic persists in contemporary societies. As was discussed in "Understanding Ourselves," magic is particularly evident in baseball, where George Gmelch (1978, 2001) describes a series of rituals, taboos, and sacred objects. Like Trobriand sailing magic, these behaviors serve to reduce psychological stress, creating an illusion of magical control when real control is lacking. Even the best pitchers have off days and bad luck. Gmelch's conclusions confirm Malinowski's that magic is most prevalent in situations of chance and uncertainty, especially pitching and batting.

According to Malinowski, magic is used to establish control, but religion "is born out of . . . the real tragedies of human life" (1931/1978, p. 45). Religion offers emotional comfort, particularly when people face a crisis. Malinowski saw tribal religions as concerned mainly with organizing, commemorating, and helping people get through such life events as birth, puberty, marriage, and death.

magic
Using supernatural techniques to accomplish specific aims.

Rituals

Several features distinguish rituals from other kinds of behavior (Rappaport 1974). **Rituals** are formal—stylized, repetitive, and stereotyped. People perform them in special (sacred) places and at set times. Rituals include *liturgical orders*—sequences of words and actions invented prior to the current performance of the ritual in which they occur.

These features link rituals to plays, but there are important differences. Plays have audiences rather than participants. Actors merely *portray*

something, but ritual performers—who make up congregations—are in earnest. Rituals convey information about the participants and their traditions. Repeated year after year, generation after generation, rituals translate enduring messages, values, and sentiments into action.

Rituals are *social* acts. Inevitably, some participants are more committed than others are to the beliefs that lie behind the rites. However, just by taking part in a joint public act, the performers signal that they accept a common social and moral order, one that transcends their status as individuals.

Rites of Passage

Magic and religion, as Malinowski noted, can reduce anxiety and allay fears. Ironically, beliefs and rituals also can *create* anxiety and a sense of insecurity and danger (Radcliffe-Brown 1962/1965). Anxiety may arise *because* a rite exists. Indeed, participation in a collective ritual may build up stress, whose common reduction, through the completion of the ritual, enhances the solidarity of the participants.

Rites of passage, for example, the collective circumcision of teenagers, can be very stressful (Gennep 1960). The traditional vision quests of Native Americans, particularly the Plains Indians, illustrate **rites of passage** (customs associated with the transition from one place or stage of life to another), which are found throughout the world. Among the Plains Indians, to move from boyhood to manhood, a youth temporarily separated from his community. After a period of isolation in the wilderness, often featuring fasting and drug consumption, the young man would see a vision, which would become his guardian spirit. He would then return to his community as an adult.

The rites of passage of contemporary cultures include confirmations, baptisms, bar and bat mitzvahs, and fraternity hazing. Passage rites involve changes in social status, such as from boyhood to manhood and from nonmember to sorority sister. There are also rites and rituals in our business and corporate lives. Examples include promotion and retirement parties. More generally, a rite of passage may mark any change in place, condition, social position, or age.

All rites of passage have three phases: separation, liminality, and incorporation. In the first phase, people withdraw from the group and begin moving from one place or status to another. In the third phase, they reenter society, having completed the rite. The *liminal* phase is the most interesting. It is the period between states, the limbo during which people have left one place or state but haven't yet entered or joined the next (Turner 1969/1995).

Liminality always has certain characteristics. Liminal people occupy ambiguous social positions. They exist apart from ordinary distinctions

Passage rites are often collective. A group—such as these initiates in Togo or these Navy trainees in San Diego—passes through the rites as a unit. Such liminal people experience the same treatment and conditions and must act alike. They share communitas, an intense community spirit, a feeling of great social solidarity or togetherness.

LIMINALITY	NORMAL SOCIAL STRUCTURE
Transition	State
Homogeneity	Heterogeneity
Communitas	Structure
Equality	Inequality
Anonymity	Names
Absence of property	Property
Absence of status	Status
Nakedness or uniform dress	Dress distinctions
Sexual continence or excess	Sexuality
Minimization of sex distinctions	Maximization of sex distinctions
Absence of rank	Rank
Humility	Pride
Disregard of personal appearance	Care for personal appearance
Unselfishness	Selfishness
Total obedience	Obedience only to superior rank
Sacredness	Secularity
Sacred instruction	Technical knowledge
Silence	Speech
Simplicity	Complexity
Acceptance of pain and suffering	Avoidance of pain and suffering

SOURCE: Reprinted with permission from Victor W. Turner, *The Ritual Process: Structure and Anti-Structure* (New York: Aldine de Gruyter). Copyright © 1995 by Walter de Gruyter, Inc.

and expectations, living in a time out of time. They are cut off from normal social contacts. A variety of contrasts may demarcate liminality from regular social life. For example, among the Ndembu of Zambia, a chief underwent a rite of passage before taking office. During the liminal period, his past and future positions in society were ignored, even reversed. He was subjected to a variety of insults, orders, and humiliations.

Passage rites are often collective. Several individuals—boys being circumcised, fraternity or sorority initiates, men at military boot camps, football players in summer training camps, women becoming nuns—pass through the rites together as a group. Recap 21.1 lists the contrasts or oppositions between liminality and normal social life. Most notable is a social aspect of *collective liminality* called communitas (Turner 1967), an intense community spirit, a feeling of great social solidarity, equality, and togetherness. People experiencing liminality together form a community of equals. The social distinctions that have existed before or will exist afterward are temporarily forgotten. Liminal people experience the same treatment and conditions and must act alike. Liminality may be marked ritually and symbolically by reversals of ordinary behavior. For example, sexual taboos may be intensified, or, conversely, sexual excess may be encouraged.

Liminality is a basic part of every passage rite. Furthermore, in certain societies, including our own, liminal symbols may be used to set off one (religious) group from another, and from society as a whole. Such "permanent liminal groups" (e.g., sects, brotherhoods, and cults) are found most characteristically in complex societies—nation-states. Liminal features such as humility, poverty, equality, obedience, sexual abstinence, and silence may be required for all sect or cult members. Those who join such a group agree to abide by its rules. As if they were undergoing a passage rite—but in this case a never-ending one—they may rid themselves of their possessions and cut off former social links, including those with family members.

Totemism

Rituals serve the social function of creating temporary or permanent solidarity among people—forming a social community. We see this also in practices known as totemism. Totemism has been important in the religions of Native Australians. *Totems* can be animals, plants, or geographic

appreciating ANTHROPOLOGY

A Parisian Celebration and a Key Tourist Destination

During the last week of November 2008, France (along with several other countries) celebrated the 100th birthday of Claude Lévi-Strauss. Father of a school known as structural anthropology and a key figure in the anthropology of religion (especially myth and folklore), Lévi-Strauss (who died less than one year later—on October 30, 2009) is known for his theoretical books and his studies of Native Americans in lowland South America. Described here, too, is the Musée du Quai Branly, site of events honoring the French master, which he inspired and helped establish. That museum, which has become one of Paris's key tourist destinations, is a tribute to the arts, beliefs, and cosmology of non–Western peoples. This account suggests a more prominent public appreciation of anthropology in France than in the United States. Undoubtedly this prominence reflects France's colonial history, to be examined in the next chapter.

PARIS—Claude Lévi-Strauss, who altered the way Westerners look at other civilizations, turned 100 on Friday [November 28, 2008]. France celebrated with films, lectures and free admission to the museum he inspired, the Musée du Quai Branly. Mr. Lévi-Strauss is cherished in France. . . .

At the Quai Branly, 100 scholars and writers read from or lectured on the work of Mr. Lévi-Strauss, while documentaries about him were screened, and guided visits were provided to the collections, which include some of his own favorite artifacts.

Stéphane Martin, the president of the museum, . . . along with the French culture minister, Christine Albanel, and the minister of higher education and research, Valérie Pécresse, presided over the unveiling of a plaque outside the museum's theater, which is already named for Mr. Lévi-Strauss, who did not attend the festivities. Ms. Pécresse announced a new annual 100,000 euro prize (about $127,000) in his name for a researcher in "human sciences" working in France. President Nicolas Sarkozy visited Mr. Lévi-Strauss on Friday evening at his home. . . .

The museum was the grand project of former president Jacques Chirac, who loved anthropology and embraced the idea of a colloquy of civilizations, as opposed to the academic quality of the old Musée de l'Homme, which Philippe Descola, the chairman of the anthro-

pology department at the Collège de France, described as "an empty shell—full of artifacts but dead to themselves."

The new museum, which has 1.3 million visitors a year, was a sort of homage to Mr. Lévi-Strauss, who "blessed it from the beginning," Mr. Descola said . . .

In 1996, when asked his opinion of the project, Mr. Lévi-Strauss said in a handwritten letter to Mr. Chirac: "It takes into account the evolution of the world since the Musée de l'Homme was created. An ethnographic museum can no longer, as at that time, offer an authentic vision of life in these societies so different from ours. With perhaps a few exceptions that will not last, these societies are progressively integrated into world politics and economy. When I see the objects that I collected in the field between 1935 and 1938 again—and it's also true of others—I know that their relevance has become either documentary or, mostly, aesthetic."

The building is striking and controversial, imposing the ideas of the star architect Jean Nouvel on the organization of the spaces. But Mr. Martin says it is working well for the museum, whose marvelous objects—"fragile flowers of difference," as Mr. Lévi-Strauss once called them—can be seen on varying levels of aesthetics and serious study. They are presented as artifacts of great beauty but also

features. In each tribe, groups of people have particular totems. Members of each totemic group believe themselves to be descendants of their totem. Traditionally they customarily neither killed nor ate a totemic animal, but this taboo was lifted once a year, when people assembled for ceremonies dedicated to the totem. These annual rites were believed to be necessary for the totem's survival and reproduction.

Totemism uses nature as a model for society. The totems are usually animals and plants, which are part of nature. People relate to nature through their totemic association with natural species. Because each group has a different totem, social differences mirror natural contrasts. Diversity in the

natural order becomes a model for diversity in the social order. However, although totemic plants and animals occupy different niches in nature, on another level they are united because they all are part of nature. The unity of the human social order is enhanced by symbolic association with and imitation of the natural order (Durkheim 1912/2001; Lévi-Strauss 1963; Radcliffe-Brown 1962/1965).

Totemism is one form of **cosmology**—a system, in this case a religious one, for imagining and understanding the universe. In the Australian totemic cosmology just discussed, diversity in nature becomes a model for diversity in society. This chapter's "Appreciating Anthropology" focuses on the work and life of a key figure in the anthro-

cosmology
A system, often religious, for imagining and understanding the universe.

The French structural anthropologist Claude Lévi-Strauss helped inspire Paris's Musée du Quai Branly, where these totemic figures from Oceania are on display. The museum is devoted to non–Western art.

with defining context, telling visitors not only what they are, but also what they were meant to be when they were created . . .

On Tuesday there was a day-long colloquium at the Collège de France, where Mr. Lévi-Strauss once taught. Mr. Descola said that centenary celebrations were being held in at least 25 countries.

"People realize he is one of the great intellectual heroes of the 20th century," he said in an interview. "His thought is among the most complex of the 20th century, and it's hard to convey his prose and his thinking in English. But he gave a proper object to anthropology: not simply as a study of human nature, but a systematic study of how cultural practices vary, how cultural differences are systematically organized."

Mr. Levi-Strauss took difference as the basis for his study, not the search for commonality, which defined 19th-century anthropology, Mr. Descola said. In other words, he took cultures on their own terms rather than try to relate everything to the West . . .

One of the most remarkable aspects of the Quai Branly is its landscaping, designed by Gilles Clément to reflect the questing spirit of Mr. Lévi-Strauss. Mr. Clément tried to create a "non–Western garden," he said in an interview, "with more the spirit of the savannah," where most of the animist civilizations live whose artifacts fill the museum itself.

He tried to think through the symbols of the cosmology of these civilizations, their systems of gods and beliefs, which also animate their agriculture and their gardens. The garden here uses the symbol of the tortoise, not reflected literally, "but in an oval form that recurs," Mr. Clément said.

"We find the tortoise everywhere," he continued. "It's an animal that lives a long time, so it represents a sort of reassurance, or the eternal, perhaps."

Mr. Lévi-Strauss "is very important to me," Mr. Clément said, adding: "He represents an extremely subversive vision with his interest in populations that were disdained. He paid careful attention, not touristically but profoundly, to the human beings on the earth who think differently from us. It's a respect for others, which is very strong and very moving. He knew that cultural diversity is necessary for cultural creativity, for the future."

pology of religion (especially myth, folklore, totemism, and cosmology), Claude Lévi-Strauss. Described, too, in "Appreciating Anthropology," is the Musée du Quai Branly, now a key Paris tourist destination, which is a tribute to the arts, beliefs, and cosmology of non–Western peoples.

Along with most anthropologists, Lévi-Strauss would agree that one role of religious rites and beliefs is to affirm, and thus maintain, the solidarity of a religion's adherents. Totems are sacred emblems symbolizing common identity. This is true not just among Native Australians but also among Native American groups of the North Pacific coast of North America, whose totem poles are well known. Their totemic carvings, which commemorate, and tell visual stories about, ancestors, animals, and spirits, also are associated with ceremonies. In totemic rites, people gather together to honor their totem. In so doing, they use ritual to maintain the social oneness that the totem symbolizes.

In contemporary nations, too, totems continue to mark groups, such as states and universities (e.g., Badgers, Buckeyes, and Wolverines), professional teams (Lions, Tigers, and Bears), and political parties (donkeys and elephants). Although the modern context is more secular, one can still witness, in intense college football rivalries, some of the effervescence Durkheim noted in Australian totemic religion.

NAME: Saba Ghanem

COUNTRY OF ORIGIN: Yemen

SUPERVISING PROFESSOR: Robert Anderson

SCHOOL: Mills College

Driven by Religion or by Popular Culture

In my country, Yemen, Islam is the official religion and it plays a crucial role in one's everyday life and in society as a whole. In the villages where I grew up, where people work and live as a collaborative unit, the practice of Islam serves every child and elder as a manual for how to conduct one's life. The five pillars of Islam hold that it is an annual obligation for the rich to give charity or alms to the poor, and so the work and wealth of fields and farming are shared between rich and poor. Another pillar of Islam, congregational prayer, advocates stability. In every Yemeni village there is a *masjid* (mosque), which calls everyone to come together to pray five times a day. Another pillar is fasting during the month of Ramadhan. In the villages, this is a very spiritual time of sharing, motivation, and seeking forgiveness from God and from each other. Many other village practices can be related to the teachings of Islam. Children are taught basic skills such as washing hands or playing with other children. Teenagers grow up abiding by the rules of respecting elders and caring for parents, and the elders use Islam to guide them to reach consensus in everyday decisions. Religion is always in a person's conscious thought and influences almost all individual acts, dialogues, and decisions.

In the United States, religion appears to be less of a priority than it is in the villages of Yemen. In the United States, multiple religions are practiced, and the level of belief varies from individual to individual, which was a surprise to me. Secular culture dominates social life, and everyone leads an individual and unique life. I have observed that many people pray only when faced with hardships, that religious places often are sparsely attended, and that young people tend to be careless about religion. In the United States, one often learns not from religion or elders but from experience. The work world is competitive rather than collaborative, and good deeds come when there is a reward attached rather than from good will.

However, on my last visit to Yemen, I began to see secular culture taking prominence over religion. For example, today it is more common to see relatives fighting over ownership of houses and land. More villagers seem to be seeking materialistic power rather than focusing on their spirituality. These situations have led to instability and practices that undermine religion in some modern villages of Yemen, making them more like the West. In a traditional Yemeni village, a day's goal is to be able to work to feed, move to pray, and smile to live. In the United States, by contrast, it's work to save, move to work, and smile to be liked.

RELIGION AND CULTURAL ECOLOGY

Another domain in which religion plays a prominent role is cultural ecology. Behavior motivated by beliefs in supernatural beings, powers, and forces may help people survive in their material environment. In this section, we will see how beliefs and rituals may function as part of a group's cultural adaptation to its environment.

Sacred Cattle in India

The people of India revere zebu cattle, which are protected by the Hindu doctrine of *ahimsa,* a principle of nonviolence that forbids the killing of animals generally. Western economic development experts occasionally (and erroneously) cite the Hindu cattle taboo to illustrate the idea that religious beliefs can stand in the way of rational economic decisions. Hindus might seem to be irrationally ignoring a valuable food (beef) because of their cultural or religious traditions. The economic developers also comment that Indians don't know how to raise proper cattle. They point to the scraggly zebus that wander about town and country. Western techniques of animal husbandry grow bigger cattle that produce more beef and milk. Western planners lament that Hindus are set in their ways. Bound by culture and tradition, they refuse to develop rationally.

However, these assumptions are both ethnocentric and wrong. Sacred cattle actually play an important adaptive role in an Indian ecosystem that has evolved over thousands of years (Harris 1974, 1978). Peasants' use of cattle to pull plows and carts is part of the technology of Indian agriculture. Indian peasants have no need for large, hungry cattle of the sort that economic developers, beef marketers, and North American cattle ranchers prefer. Scrawny animals pull plows and carts well enough but don't eat their owners out of house and home. How could peasants with limited land and marginal diets feed supersteers without taking food away from themselves?

Indians use cattle manure to fertilize their fields. Not all the manure is collected, because peasants don't spend much time watching their cattle, which wander and graze at will during certain seasons. In the rainy season, some of the manure that cattle deposit on the hillsides washes down to the fields. In this way, cattle also fertilize the fields indirectly. Furthermore, in a country where fossil fuels are scarce, dry cattle dung, which burns slowly and evenly, is a basic cooking fuel.

Far from being useless, as the development experts contend, sacred cattle are essential to Indian cultural adaptation. Biologically adapted to poor pasture land and a marginal environment, the scraggly zebu provides fertilizer and fuel, is indispensable in farming, and is affordable for peasants. The Hindu doctrine of *ahimsa* puts the full power of organized religion behind the command not to destroy a valuable resource even in times of extreme need.

SOCIAL CONTROL

Religion has meaning for people. It helps men and women cope with adversity and tragedy. It offers hope that things will get better. Lives can be transformed through spiritual healing or rebirth. Sinners can repent and be saved—or they can go on sinning and be damned. If the faithful truly internalize a system of religious rewards and punishments, their religion becomes a powerful means of controlling their beliefs, their behavior, and what they teach their children.

Many people engage in religious activity because it seems to work. Prayers get answered. Faith healers heal. Sometimes it doesn't take much to convince the faithful that religious actions are efficacious. Many American Indian people in southwestern Oklahoma use faith healers at high monetary costs, not just because it makes them feel better about the uncertain but because it works (Lassiter 1998). Each year legions of Brazilians visit a church, Nosso Senhor do Bomfim, in the city of Salvador, Bahia. They vow to repay "Our Lord" (Nosso Senhor) if healing happens. Showing that the vows work, and are repaid, are the thousands of ex votos, plastic impressions of every conceivable body part, that adorn the church, along with photos of people who have been cured.

Religion can work by getting inside people and mobilizing their emotions—their joy, their wrath, their righteousness. We've seen how Émile Durkheim (1912/2001), a prominent French social theorist and scholar of religion, described the collective "effervescence" that can develop in religious contexts. Intense emotion bubbles up. People feel a deep sense of shared joy, meaning, experience, communion, belonging, and commitment to their religion.

The power of religion affects action. When religions meet, they can coexist peacefully, or their differences can be a basis for enmity and disharmony, even battle. Religious fervor has inspired Christians on crusades against the infidel and has led Muslims to wage holy wars against non-Islamic peoples. Throughout history, political leaders have used religion to promote and justify their views and policies.

By late September 1996, the Taliban movement had firmly imposed an extreme form of social control in the name of religion on Afghanistan (Figure 21.1) and its people. Led by Muslim clerics, the Taliban attempted to create their version of an Islamic society modeled on the teachings of

A wandering cow does not perturb these shoppers in Udaipur, Rajasthan. India's zebu cattle are protected by the doctrine of *ahimsa*, a principle of nonviolence that forbids the killing of animals generally. This Hindu doctrine puts the full power of organized religion behind the command not to destroy a valuable resource even in times of extreme need.

the Koran (Burns 1997). Various repressive measures were instituted. The Taliban barred women from work and girls from school. Females past puberty were prohibited from talking to unrelated men. Women needed an approved reason, such as shopping for food, to leave their homes. Men, who were required to grow bushy beards, also faced an array of bans—against playing cards, listening to music, keeping pigeons, and flying kites.

To enforce their decrees, the Taliban sent armed enforcers throughout the country. Those agents took charge of "beard checks" and other forms of scrutiny on behalf of a religious police force known as the General Department for the Preservation of Virtue and the Elimination of Vice (Burns 1997). By late fall 2001 the Taliban had been overthrown, with a new interim government established in Kabul, the Afghani capital, on December 22. The collapse of the Taliban followed American bombing of Afghanistan in response to the September 11, 2001, attacks on New York's World Trade Center and Washington's Pentagon. As the Taliban yielded Kabul to victorious Northern Alliance forces, local men flocked to barbershops to have their beards trimmed or shaved. They were using a key Taliban symbol to celebrate the end of religious repression.

Note that in the case of the Taliban, forms of social control were used to support a strict religious orthodoxy. This wasn't repression in religion's name, but repressive religion. In other countries, secular leaders use religion to justify

Near a royal tomb in Kabul, on January 30, 2004, a young boy prepares to launch a kite, illustrating Afghanistan's national (amateur) sport for boys. Banned by the Taliban, kite flying is once again popular.

leveling mechanism
Custom that brings standouts back in line with community norms.

FIGURE 21.1 Location of Afghanistan.

social control. Seeking power, they use religious rhetoric to get it. The Saudi Arabian government, for example, can be seen as using religion to divert attention from a repressive social policy.

How may leaders mobilize communities and, in so doing, gain support for their own policies? One way is by persuasion; another is by instilling hatred or fear. As we saw in the chapter "Political Systems," fears about and accusations of witchcraft and sorcery can be powerful means of social control by creating a climate of danger and insecurity that affects everyone.

Witchcraft accusations often are directed at socially marginal or anomalous individuals. Among the Betsileo of Madagascar, for example, who prefer patrilocal postmarital residence, men living in the wife's or the mother's village violate a cultural norm. Linked to their anomalous social position, just a bit of unusual behavior (e.g., staying up late at night) on their part is sufficient for them to be called witches and avoided as a result. In tribes and peasant communities, people who stand out economically, especially if they seem to be benefiting at the expense of others, often face accusations of witchcraft, leading to social ostracism or punishment. In this case witchcraft accusation becomes a **leveling mechanism,** a custom or social action that operates to reduce differences in wealth and thus to bring standouts in line with community norms—another form of social control.

To ensure proper behavior, religions offer rewards, such as the fellowship of the religious community, and punishments, such as the threat of being cast out or excommunicated. Many religions promise rewards for the good life and punishment for the bad. Your physical, mental, moral, and spiritual health, now and forever, may depend on your beliefs and behavior. For example, if you don't pay enough attention to the ancestors, they may snatch your kids from you.

Religions, especially the formal organized ones typically found in state societies, often prescribe a code of ethics and morality to guide behavior. The Judaic Ten Commandments lay down a set of prohibitions against killing, stealing, adultery, and other misdeeds. Crimes are breaches of secular laws, just as sins are breaches of religious strictures. Some rules (e.g., the Ten Commandments) proscribe or prohibit behavior; others prescribe behavior. The Golden Rule, for instance, is a religious guide to do unto others as you would have them do unto you. Moral codes are ways of maintaining order and stability. Codes of morality and ethics are repeated constantly in religious sermons, catechisms, and the like. They become internalized psychologically. They guide behavior and produce regret, guilt, shame, and the need for forgiveness, expiation, and absolution when they are not followed.

Religions also maintain social control by stressing the temporary and fleeting nature of this life. They promise rewards (and/or punishment) in an afterlife (Christianity) or reincarnation (Hinduism and Buddhism). Such beliefs serve to reinforce the status quo. People accept what they have now, knowing they can expect something better in the afterlife or the next life if they follow religious guidelines. Under slavery in the American South, the masters taught portions of the Bible, such as the story of Job, that stressed compliance. The slaves, however, seized on the story of Moses, the promised land, and deliverance.

KINDS OF RELIGION

Religion is a cultural universal. But religions are parts of particular cultures, and cultural differences show up systematically in religious beliefs and practices. For example, the religions of stratified, state societies differ from those of cultures with less marked social contrasts and power differentials.

Considering several cultures, Wallace (1966) identified four types of religion: shamanic, communal, Olympian, and monotheistic. Unlike priests, the **shamans** of a shamanic religion aren't full-time religious officials but part-time religious figures who mediate between people and supernatural beings and forces. All cultures have

medico-magico-religious specialists. *Shaman* is the general term encompassing curers ("witch doctors"), mediums, spiritualists, astrologers, palm readers, and other diviners. Wallace found shamanic religions to be most characteristic of foraging societies, particularly those found in the northern latitudes, such as the Inuit and the native peoples of Siberia.

Although they are only part-time specialists, shamans often set themselves off symbolically from ordinary people by assuming a different or ambiguous sex or gender role. (In nation-states, priests, nuns, and vestal virgins do something similar by taking vows of celibacy and chastity.) As was discussed in the chapter "Gender," among the Chukchee of Siberia (Figure 21.2), where coastal populations fished and interior groups hunted, male shamans copied the behavior and lifestyles of women (Bogoras 1904) and received respect for their supernatural and curative expertise. Female shamans could join a fourth gender and marry other women. Among the Crow Indians, certain ritual duties were reserved for *berdaches*, who rejected the traditional male role and thus formed a third gender. The fact that certain key rituals could be conducted only by *berdaches* indicates their regular and normal place in Crow social life (Lowie 1935).

Communal religions have, in addition to shamans, community rituals such as harvest

shaman
A part-time magico-religious practitioner.

communal religions
Based on community rituals, e.g., harvest ceremonies, passage rites.

FIGURE 21.2 Location of Chukchee in Siberia.

TYPE OF RELIGION (WALLACE)	TYPE OF PRACTITIONER	CONCEPTION OF SUPERNATURAL	TYPE OF SOCIETY
Monotheistic	Priests, ministers, etc.	Supreme being	States
Olympian	Priesthood	Hierarchical pantheon with powerful deities	Chiefdoms and archaic states
Communal	Part-time specialists; occasional community-sponsored events, including rites of passage	Several deities with some control over nature	Food-producing tribes
Shamanic	Shaman = part-time	Zoomorphic practitioner	Foraging band (plants and animals)

polytheism
Belief that multiple deities control aspects of nature.

Olympian religions
State religions with professional priesthoods.

monotheism
Worship of a single supreme being.

ceremonies and rites of passage. Although communal religions lack *full-time* religious specialists, they believe in several deities (**polytheism**) who control aspects of nature. Although some hunter-gatherers, including Australian totemites, have communal religions, these religions are more typical of farming societies.

Olympian religions, which arose with state organization and marked social stratification, add full-time religious specialists—professional *priesthoods*. Like the state itself, the priesthood is hierarchically and bureaucratically organized. The term *Olympian* comes from Mount Olympus, home of the classical Greek gods. Olympian religions are polytheistic. They include powerful anthropomorphic gods with specialized functions, for example, gods of love, war, the sea, and death. Olympian *pantheons* (collections of supernatural beings) were prominent in the religions of many nonindustrial nation-states, including the Aztecs of Mexico, several African and Asian kingdoms, and classical Greece and Rome. Wallace's fourth type—**monotheism**—also has priesthoods and notions of divine power, but it views the supernatural differently. In monotheism, all supernatural phenomena are manifestations of, or are under the control of, a single eternal, omniscient, omnipotent, and omnipresent supreme being. Recap 21.2 summarizes the four types and their features.

RELIGION IN STATES

Robert Bellah (1978) coined the term "world-rejecting religion" to describe most forms of Christianity, including Protestantism. World-rejecting religions arose in ancient civilizations, along with literacy and a specialized priesthood. These religions are so named because of their tendency to reject the natural (mundane, ordinary, material, secular) world and to focus instead on a higher (sacred, transcendent) realm of reality. The divine is a domain of exalted morality to which humans can only aspire. Salvation through fusion with the supernatural is the main goal of such religions.

Protestant Values and the Rise of Capitalism

Notions of salvation and the afterlife dominate Christian ideologies. However, most varieties of Protestantism lack the hierarchical structure of earlier monotheistic religions, including Roman Catholicism. With a diminished role for the priest (minister), salvation is directly available to individuals. Regardless of their social status, Protestants have unmediated access to the supernatural. The

We'wha, a Zuni *berdache*, in 1885. In some Native American societies, certain ritual duties were reserved for *berdaches*, men who rejected the male role and joined a third gender.

individualistic focus of Protestantism offers a close fit with capitalism and with American culture.

In his influential book *The Protestant Ethic and the Spirit of Capitalism* (1904/1958), the social theorist Max Weber linked the spread of capitalism to the values preached by early Protestant leaders. Weber saw European Protestants (and eventually their American descendants) as more successful financially than Catholics. He attributed this difference to the values stressed by their religions. Weber saw Catholics as more concerned with immediate happiness and security. Protestants were more ascetic, entrepreneurial, and future-oriented, he thought.

Capitalism, said Weber, required that the traditional attitudes of Catholic peasants be replaced by values befitting an industrial economy based on capital accumulation. Protestantism placed a premium on hard work, an ascetic life, and profit seeking. Early Protestants saw success on earth as a sign of divine favor and probable salvation. According to some Protestant credos, individuals could gain favor with God through good works. Other sects stressed predestination, the idea that only a few mortals have been selected for eternal life and that people cannot change their fates. However, material success, achieved through hard work, could be a strong clue that someone was predestined to be saved.

Weber also argued that rational business organization required the removal of industrial production from the home, its setting in peasant societies. Protestantism made such a separation possible by emphasizing individualism: individuals, not families or households, would be saved or not. Interestingly, given the connection that is usually made with morality and religion in contemporary American discourse about family values, the family was a secondary matter for Weber's early Protestants. God and the individual reigned supreme.

 living anthropology **VIDEOS**

Ritual Possession, www.mhhe.com/kottak

The central figure in this clip is Nana Kofi Owusu, a senior priest-healer among Ghana's Bono people. The Bono believe in a hierarchy of deities and spirits. The highest god is linked to ordinary people through lower-level deities and spirits and the priest-healers and others who receive spirits. Nana Owusu serves as the guardian of various shrines, including one principal one, which he keeps and honors in a separate room of his house and wears on his head during ceremonies. Among the Bono is it only men who receive spirits, or can women receive them, too? How is succession established for the position of priest-healer—how did Nana Owusu achieve this status? According to the professor shown in the clip, do people usually know it when they are possessed?

Today, of course, in North America as throughout the world, people of many religions and with diverse worldviews are successful capitalists. Furthermore, traditional Protestant values often have little to do with today's economic maneuvering. Still, there is no denying that the individualistic focus of Protestantism was compatible with the severance of ties to land and kin that industrialism demanded. These values remain prominent in the religious background of many of the people of the United States.

WORLD RELIGIONS

Information on the world's major religions is provided in Table 21.1 (number of adherents) and Figure 21.3 (percentage of world population). Based on people's claimed religions, Christianity is the world's largest, with some 2.1 billion adherents. Islam, with some 1.3 billion practitioners, is next, followed by Hinduism, then Chinese traditional religion (also known as Chinese folk religion or

TABLE 21.1   Religions of the World, by Estimated Number of Adherents, 2005

Christianity	2.1 billion
Islam	1.3 billion
Secular/Nonreligious/Agnostic/ Atheist	1.1 billion
Hinduism	900 million
Chinese traditional religion	394 million
Buddhism	376 million
Primal-indigenous	300 million
African traditional and diasporic	100 million
Sikhism	23 million
Juche	19 million
Spiritism	15 million
Judaism	14 million
Baha'i	7 million
Jainism	4.2 million
Shinto	4 million
Cao Dai	4 million
Zoroastrianism	2.6 million
Tenrikyo	2 million
Neo-Paganism	1 million
Unitarian-Universalism	800 thousand
Rastafarianism	600 thousand
Scientology	500 thousand

SOURCE: Adherents.com. 2005. http//www.adherents.com/ Religions_By_Adherents.html. Reprinted by permission of Preston Hunter, adherents.com.

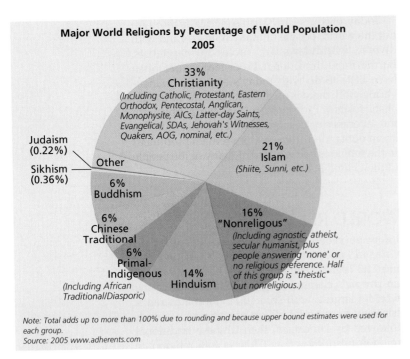

Major World Religions by Percentage of World Population 2005

- 33% Christianity *(Including Catholic, Protestant, Eastern Orthodox, Pentecostal, Anglican, Monophysite, AICs, Latter-day Saints, Evangelical, SDAs, Jehovah's Witnesses, Quakers, AOG, nominal, etc.)*
- 21% Islam *(Shiite, Sunni, etc.)*
- 16% "Nonreligous" *(Including agnostic, atheist, secular humanist, plus people answering 'none' or no religious preference. Half of this group is "theistic" but nonreligual.)*
- 14% Hinduism
- 6% Primal-Indigenous *(Including African Traditional/Diasporic)*
- 6% Chinese Traditional
- 6% Buddhism
- Other
- Sikhism (0.36%)
- Judaism (0.22%)

Note: Total adds up to more than 100% due to rounding and because upper bound estimates were used for each group.
Source: 2005 www.adherents.com

FIGURE 21.3 Major World Religions by Percentage of World Population, 2005.

SOURCE: Adherents.com. 2005. http//www.adherents.com/Religions_By_Adherents.html. Reprinted by permission of Preston Hunter, adherents.com.

Confucianism), and Buddhism. More than a billion people claim no official religion, but only about a fifth of them are self-proclaimed atheists. Worldwide, Christianity's growth rate of 2.3 percent just matches the rate of world population increase (Adherents.com 2002; Ontario Consultants 2001). Islam is growing at a faster pace, about 2.9 percent annually. This chapter's "Appreciating Diversity" examines how Islam has spread by adapting successfully to many national and cultural differences, including the presence of other religions that were already established in the areas to which Islam has spread.

Within Christianity, there is variation in the growth rate. There were an estimated 680 million "born-again" Christians (i.e., Pentecostals and Evangelicals) in the world in 2001, with an annual worldwide growth rate of 7 percent, versus just 2.3 percent for Christianity overall. (This would translate into 1.17 billion Pentecostals and Evangelicals in 2009.) The global growth rate of Roman Catholics has been estimated at only 1.3 percent, compared with a Protestant growth rate of 3.3 percent per year (Winter 2001). Much of this explosive growth, especially in Africa, is of a type of Protestantism that would be scarcely recognizable to most Americans, given its incorporation of many animistic elements.

Table 21.2 classifies 11 world religions according to their degree of internal unity and diversity.

anthropology **ATLAS**

Map 15 shows the distribution of the world's major religions, also summarized in Table 21.3.

TABLE 21.2 Classical World Religions Ranked by Internal Religious Similarity

MOST UNIFIED
Baha'i
Zoroastrianism
Sikhism
Islam
Jainism
Judaism
Taoism
Shinto
Christianity
Buddhism
Hinduism
MOST DIVERSE

SOURCE: Adherents.com. 2001. http//www.adherents.com/Religions_By_Adherents.html. Reprinted by permission of Preston Hunter, adherents.com.

Listed first are the most cohesive/unified groups. Listed last are the religions with the most internal diversity. The list is based mainly on the degree of doctrinal similarity among the various subgroups. To a lesser extent it reflects diversity in practice, ritual, and organization. (The list includes the majority manifestations of each religion, as well as subgroups that the larger branches may label "heterodox.") How would you decide whether a value judgment is implied by this list? Is it better for a religion to be highly unified, cohesive, monolithic, and lacking in internal diversity, or to be fragmented, schismatic, multifaceted, and abounding in variations on the same theme? Over time such diversity can give birth to new religions; for example, Christianity arose from Judaism, Buddhism from Hinduism, Baha'i from Islam, and Sikhism from Hinduism. Within Christianity, Protestantism developed out of Roman Catholicism.

RELIGION AND CHANGE

Fundamentalists seek order based on strict adherence to purportedly traditional standards, beliefs, rules, and customs. Christian and Islamic fundamentalists recognize, decry, and attempt to redress change, yet they also contribute to change. In a worldwide process, new religions challenge established churches. In the United States, conservative Christian TV hosts have become influential broadcasters and opinion shapers. In Latin America, evangelical Protestantism is winning millions of converts from Roman Catholicism.

Like political organization, religion helps maintain social order. And, like political mobilization, religious energy can be harnessed not just for change but also for revolution. Reacting to conquest or to actual or perceived foreign domination, for instance, religious leaders may seek to alter or revitalize their society. In an "Islamic Revolution," for example, Iranian ayatollahs marshaled religious fervor to create national solidarity and radical change. We call such movements nativistic movements (Linton 1943) or revitalization movements (Wallace 1956).

Revitalization Movements

Revitalization movements are social movements that occur in times of change, in which religious leaders emerge and undertake to alter or revitalize a society. Christianity originated as a revitalization movement. Jesus was one of several prophets who preached new religious doctrines while the Middle East was under Roman rule. It was a time of social unrest, when a foreign power ruled the land. Jesus inspired a new, enduring, and major religion. His contemporaries were not so successful.

The Handsome Lake religion arose around 1800 among the Iroquois of New York State (Wallace 1970). Handsome Lake, the founder of this revitalization movement, was a leader of one of the Iroquois tribes. The Iroquois had suffered because of their support of the British against the American colonials (and for other reasons). After the colonial victory and a wave of immigration to their homeland, the Iroquois were dispersed on small reservations. Unable to pursue traditional horticulture and hunting in their homeland, they became heavy drinkers and quarreled among themselves.

Handsome Lake was a heavy drinker who started having visions from heavenly messengers. The spirits warned him that unless the Iroquois changed their ways, they would be destroyed. His visions offered a plan for coping with the new order. Witchcraft, quarreling, and drinking would end. The Iroquois would copy European farming techniques, which, unlike traditional Iroquois horticulture, stressed male rather than female labor. Handsome Lake preached that the Iroquois should also abandon their communal longhouses and matrilineal descent groups for more permanent marriages and individual family households. The teachings of Handsome Lake produced a new church and religion, one that still has members in New York and Ontario. This revitalization movement helped the Iroquois adapt to and survive in a modified environment. They eventually gained a reputation among their non-Indian neighbors as sober family farmers.

Syncretisms

Especially in today's world, religious expressions emerge from the interplay of local, regional, national, and international cultural forces. **Syncretisms** are cultural mixes, including religious blends, that emerge from acculturation—the exchange of cultural features when cultures come into continuous firsthand contact. One example of religious syncretism is the mixture of African, Native American, and Roman Catholic saints and deities in Caribbean *vodun*, or "voodoo," cults. This blend also is present in Cuban *santeria* and in *candomblé*, an "Afro-Brazilian" cult. Another syncretism is the blend of Melanesian and Christian beliefs in cargo cults.

Like the Handsome Lake religion just discussed, cargo cults are revitalization movements. Such movements may emerge when natives have regular contact with industrial societies but lack their wealth, technology, and living standards. Some such movements attempt to explain European domination and wealth and to achieve similar success magically by mimicking European behavior and manipulating symbols of the desired lifestyle. The syncretic **cargo cults** of Melanesia and Papua New Guinea weave Christian doctrine with aboriginal beliefs (Figure 21.4). They take their name from their focus on cargo: European goods of the sort natives have seen unloaded from the cargo holds of ships and airplanes.

In one early cult, members believed that the spirits of the dead would arrive in a ship. These ghosts would bring manufactured goods for the natives and would kill all the whites. More recent cults replaced ships with airplanes (Worsley 1959/1985). Many cults have used elements of European culture as sacred objects. The rationale is that Europeans use these objects, have wealth, and therefore must know the "secret of cargo." By mimicking how Europeans use or treat objects, natives hope also to come upon the secret knowledge needed to gain cargo.

For example, having seen Europeans' reverent treatment of flags and flagpoles, the members of one cult began to worship flagpoles. They believed the flagpoles were sacred towers that could transmit messages between the living and the dead. Other natives built airstrips to entice planes bearing canned goods, portable radios, clothing, wristwatches, and motorcycles. Near the airstrips they made effigies of towers, airplanes, and radios. They talked into the cans in a magical attempt to establish radio contact with the gods.

Some cargo cult prophets proclaimed that success would come through a reversal of European domination and native subjugation. The day was near, they preached, when natives, aided by God, Jesus, or native ancestors, would turn the tables. Native skins would turn white, and those of Europeans would turn brown; Europeans would die or be killed.

syncretisms
Cultural, especially religious, mixes, emerging from acculturation.

revitalization movements
Movements aimed at altering or revitalizing a society.

cargo cults
Postcolonial, acculturative religious movements in Melanesia.

anthropology **ATLAS**

Map 10 shows the Iroquois in North America where the Handsome Lake revitalization movement began.

Islam Expanding Globally, Adapting Locally

Religious diversity has been a key interest of anthropology since the 19th century. One well-known anthropological definition of religion stresses beliefs and behavior concerned with supernatural beings, powers, and forces. Another definition focuses on congregants—a body of people who gather together regularly for worship, and who accept a set of doctrines involving the relationship between the individual and divinity. Some religions, and the beliefs, affirmations, and forms of worship they promote, have spread widely. We learn here how Islam, the world's fastest-growing religion, has adapted locally to various nations and cultures. In this process, although certain fundamentals endure, there is also room for considerable diversity. Local people always assign their own meanings to the messages and social forms, including religion, they receive from outside. Such meanings reflect their cultural backgrounds and experiences. Islam has adapted successfully to many cultural differences, including linguistic practices, building styles, and the presence of other religions, such as Hinduism, already established in that area.

One in every five people worldwide is a Muslim, some 1.3 billion believers. Islam is the world's fastest growing religion and it has spread across the globe.

Muslims everywhere agree on the Shahadah, the profession of faith: "There is no God but Allah; Mohammed is the prophet of Allah." But Islam is far from homogeneous—the faith reflects the increasingly diverse areas in which it is practiced.

"Islam is a world religion," said Ali Asani, a Harvard professor of Indo-Muslim Languages and Culture. "If you think about doctrine and theology, when these sets of religious ideas and concepts are transferred to different parts of the world—and Muslims live in many cultures and speak many different languages—the expressions of those doctrines and theology will necessarily be influenced by local culture."

Sometimes such regional distinctions are obvious to even casual observers. Mosques, for example, all share common features—they face Mecca and have a mihrab, or niche, that indicates that direction. Yet they also boast unique architectural elements and decor that suggest whether their location is Iran, Africa, or China. The houses of worship provide what Asani calls "a visual reminder of cultural diversity." Other easily grasped regional distinctions have their origins at the level of language. While Arabic is Islam's liturgical language, used for prayer, most Muslims' understanding of their faith occurs in their local language.

"Languages are really windows into culture," Asani explains. "So very often what you find is that theological Islamic concepts get translated into local idioms." . . .

Some Islamic fundamentalists might frown upon the diversity caused by local characteristics, but such are the predominant forms of Islam. "Rather than discussing Islam, we might more accurately talk about 'Islams' in different cultural contexts," Asani said. "We have Muslim literature from China, for example, where Islamic concepts are understood within a Confucian framework."

In the region of Bengal, now part of the nation of Bangladesh and the Indian state of West Bengal, a popular literary tradition created a context for the arrival of Islam. The concept of the avatar is important to the Hindu tradition, in which these deities become incarnate and descend to Earth to guide the righteous and fight evil.

"What you find in 16th century Bengal is the development of what you might call 'folk literature' where the Islamic idea of the prophet becomes understood within the framework of the avatar," Asani said. "So you have bridges being built between religious traditions as concepts resonate against each other."

This example is quite different from conditions in pre-Islam Arabia, at the time of Mohammed, where the poet held a special place in society. "If you consider the Koran, the word means 'recitation' in Arabic, and it's primarily an oral scripture, intended to be recited aloud and heard; to be performed," Asani said. "Viewed from a literary perspective, its form and structure relate very well to the poetic traditions of pre-Islamic Arabia. It's an example where the format of revelation was determined

---

As syncretisms, cargo cults blend aboriginal and Christian beliefs. Melanesian myths told of ancestors shedding their skins and changing into powerful beings and of dead people returning to life. Christian missionaries, who had been in Melanesia since the late 19th century, also spoke of resurrection. The cults' preoccupation with cargo is related to traditional Melanesian big-man systems. In the chapter "Political Systems," we saw that a Melanesian big man had to be generous. People worked for the big man, helping him amass wealth, but eventually he had to give a feast and give away all that wealth.

Because of their experience with big-man systems, Melanesians believed that all wealthy people eventually had to give their wealth away. For decades, they had attended Christian missions and worked on plantations. All the while they expected Europeans to return the fruits of their labor by the culture. In pre-Islamic Arabia the poet was often considered to be inspired in his poetic compositions by jinn from another world. So when the Prophet Muhammed began receiving revelations which were eventually compiled into the Koran, he was accused of being a poet, to which he responded 'I'm not a poet but a prophet.'" . . .

Islam came to Indonesia with merchants who were not theologians but simply practicing Muslims who people looked to as an example. There were also Sufi teachers who were quite willing to create devotional exercises that fit the way people in Sumatra or Java already practiced their faith. The two largest Muslim groups in Indonesia today, and perhaps in the world, are Muhammadyya and Nahdlatul Ulama. Each of them has over 30 million members, and each began as a local reform movement rooted in the promotion of a more modern education within the framework of Islam. . . .

A large number of Muslims, of course, don't live in Islamic nations at all but as minorities in other countries. The emergence of some minority Muslim communities has been an interesting and important development of the last 25 to 30 years.

Some relatively small communities can have a large impact. The European Muslim populations, for example, have a high component of refugee intellectuals. They've had an effect on their adopted countries, and also on the rest of the Islamic world. . . .

In South Africa the Muslim community is less than three percent of the population—but

Muslims before an Islamic mosque in Kano, northern Nigeria.

it's highly visible and highly educated. In the days of apartheid they had the advantage of being an intermediary, a community that was neither black nor white. By the 1980s the younger Muslim leadership became very opposed to apartheid on Islamic grounds and on basic human rights grounds. Muslims became quite active in the African National Congress (ANC). Though they were only a small minority when apartheid was destroyed, a number of Muslims became quite visible in the new South African regime—and throughout the larger Muslim world. Encompassing both Islamic states and minority communities,

Islam is the world's fastest growing religion and an increasingly common topic of global conversation. Yet much of the discourse paints the faith with a single brush. As more people become familiar with Islam around the world it may be well for them to first ask, as Professor Asani suggests: "Whose Islam? Which Islam?"

SOURCE: Brian Handwerk, "Islam Expanding Globally, Adapting Locally," *National Geographic News*, October 24, 2003. http://news.nationalgeographic.com. © 2003 National Geographic Society. Reprinted with permission.

as their own big men did. When the Europeans refused to distribute the wealth or even to let natives know the secret of its production and distribution, cargo cults developed.

Like arrogant big men, Europeans would be leveled, by death if necessary. However, natives lacked the physical means of doing what their traditions said they should do. Thwarted by well-armed colonial forces, natives resorted to magical leveling. They called on supernatural beings to

intercede, to kill or otherwise deflate the European big men and redistribute their wealth.

Cargo cults are religious responses to the expansion of the world capitalist economy. However, this religious mobilization had political and economic results. Cult participation gave Melanesians a basis for common interests and activities and thus helped pave the way for political parties and economic interest organizations. Previously separated by geography, language, and customs,

FIGURE 21.4 Location of Melanesia.

A cargo cult in Vanuatu. Boys and men march with spears, imitating British colonial soldiers. Does anything in your own society remind you of a cargo cult?

Melanesians started forming larger groups as members of the same cults and followers of the same prophets. The cargo cults paved the way for political action through which the indigenous peoples eventually regained their autonomy.

Antimodernism and Fundamentalism

Antimodernism describes the rejection of the modern in favor of what is perceived as an earlier, purer, and better way of life. This viewpoint grew out of disillusionment with Europe's Industrial Revolution and subsequent developments in science, technology, and consumption patterns. Antimodernists typically consider technology's use today to be misguided, or think technology should have a lower priority than religious and cultural values.

Religious fundamentalism, a form of contemporary antimodernism, can be compared to the revitalization movements discussed previously. **Fundamentalism** describes antimodernist movements in various religions. Ironically, religious fundamentalism is itself a modern phenomenon, based on a strong feeling among its adherents of alienation from the perceived secularism of the surrounding (modern) culture. Fundamentalists assert an identity separate from the larger religious group from which they arose. Their separation reflects their belief that the founding principles on which the larger religion is based have been corrupted, neglected, compromised, forgotten, or replaced with other principles. Fundamentalists advocate strict fidelity to the "true" religious principles of the larger religion.

Fundamentalists also seek to rescue religion from absorption into modern, Western culture, which they see as already having corrupted the mainstream version of their religion—and others. Fundamentalists establish a "wall of virtue" against alien religions as well as against the modernized, compromised version of their own religion. In Christianity, fundamentalists are "born again," as opposed to "mainline," "liberal," or "modernist" Protestants. In Islam they are *jama'at* (in Arabic, enclaves based on close fellowship) engaged in *jihad* (struggle) against a Western culture hostile to Islam and the God-given (*shariah*) way of life. In Judaism they are *Haredi,* "Torah-true" Jews. All such groups see a sharp divide between themselves and other religions, and between a "sacred" view of life and the "secular" world and "nominal religion" (see Antoun 2001).

Fundamentalists strive to protect a distinctive doctrine and way of life and of salvation. A strong sense of community is created, focused on a clearly defined religious way of life. The prospect of joining such a community may appeal to people who find little that is distinctive or vital in their previous religious identity. Fundamentalists get their converts, mainly from their larger religion, by convincing them of its inauthenticity. Many fundamentalists are politically aware citizens of nation-states. Often they believe that government processes and policies must recognize the way of life set forth in scripture. In their eyes, the state should be subservient to God.

A New Age

Fundamentalists may or may not be correct in seeing a rise in secularism in contemporary North America. Between 1990 and 2007, the number of Americans giving no religious preference grew from 7 to 16 percent. In Canada the comparable figure rose from 12 to 17 percent between 1991 and 2001 (Table 21.3). Of course, people who lack a religious preference aren't necessarily atheists. Many of them are believers who don't belong to a church. According to U.S. Census Bureau figures

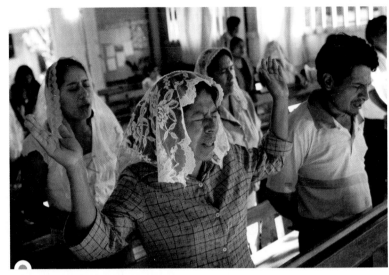

A Pentecostal church service in Oaxaca, Mexico, in 2003. There were an estimated 680 million "born-again" Christians (i.e., Pentecostals and Evangelicals) in the world in 2001, with an annual worldwide growth rate of 7 percent, versus just 2.3 percent for Christianity overall. (This would translate into more than one billion Pentecostals and Evangelicals today.)

for 2001, about two million Americans (just 1 percent of the population) self-identified as atheists or agnostics. Even fewer (less than 100,000 in 2001) called themselves "secular" or "humanists." Still, atheists and secular humanists do exist, and they, too, are organized.

Like members of religious groups, they use varied media, including print and the Internet, to communicate among themselves. Just as Buddhists can peruse *Tricycle: The Buddhist Review,* secular humanists can find their views validated in *Free Inquiry,* a quarterly identifying itself as "the international secular humanist magazine." Secular humanists speak out against organized religion and its "dogmatic pronouncements" and "supernatural or spiritual agendas" and the "obscurantist views" of religious leaders who presume "to inform us of God's views" by appealing to sacred texts (Steinfels 1997).

TABLE 21.3 Religious Composition of the Populations of the United States, 1990 and 2001, and Canada, 1991 and 2007

| | UNITED STATES | | CANADA | |
	1990	2007	1991	2001
Protestant	60%	51%	36%	29%
Catholic	26	24	46	44
Jewish	2	2	1	1
Other	5	7	4	9
None given	7	16	12	17

SOURCE: *Statistical Abstract of the United States 2009*, Table 74, p. 59, http://www.census.gov/statab/www/; *Census of Canada*, 2001. http://www40.statcan.ca/101/cst01/demo30a.htm?sdi=religion.

Is American society really growing more secular? A considerable body of sociological research suggests that levels of American religiosity haven't changed much over the past century (see Finke and Stark 2005). To be sure, there are new religious trends and forms of spiritualism. Some Americans have turned to charismatic Christianity. In the United States and Australia, respectively, some people who are not Native Americans or Native Australians have appropriated the symbols, settings, and purported religious practices of Native Americans and Native Australians, for New Age religions. Many natives have strongly protested the use of their sacred symbols and places by such groups.

New religious movements have varied origins. Some have been influenced by Christianity, others by Eastern (Asian) religions, still others by mysticism and spiritualism. Religion also evolves in tandem with science and technology. For example, the Raelian Movement, a religious group centered in Switzerland and Montreal, promotes cloning as a way of achieving "eternal life." Raelians believe that extraterrestrials called "Elohim" artificially created all life on earth. The group has established a company called Valiant Venture Ltd., which offers infertile and homosexual couples the opportunity to have a child cloned from one of the spouses (Ontario Consultants 1996).

In the United States, the official recognition of a religion entitles it to a modicum of respect, and certain benefits, such as exemption from taxation on its income and property (as long as it does not engage in political activity). Not all would-be religions receive official recognition. For example, Scientology is recognized as a church in the United States but not in Germany.

SECULAR RITUALS

In concluding this discussion of religion, we may recognize some problems with the definition of religion given at the beginning of this chapter. The first problem: If we define religion with reference to supernatural beings, powers, and forces, how do we classify ritual-like behavior that occurs in secular contexts? Some anthropologists believe there are both sacred and secular rituals. Secular rituals include formal, invariant, stereotyped, earnest, repetitive behavior and rites of passage that take place in nonreligious settings.

A second problem: If the distinction between the supernatural and the natural is not consistently made in a society, how can we tell what is religion and what isn't? The Betsileo of Madagascar, for example, view witches and dead ancestors as real people who play roles in ordinary life. However, their occult powers are not empirically demonstrable.

A third problem: The behavior considered appropriate for religious occasions varies tremendously from culture to culture. One society may consider drunken frenzy the surest sign of faith, whereas another may inculcate quiet reverence. Who is to say which is "more religious"?

Many Americans believe that recreation and religion are separate domains. From my field work in Brazil and Madagascar and my reading about other societies, I believe that this separation is both ethnocentric and false. Madagascar's tomb-centered ceremonies are times when the living and the dead are joyously reunited, when people get drunk, gorge themselves, and enjoy sexual license. Perhaps the gray, sober, ascetic, and moralistic aspects of many religious events in the United States, in taking the "fun" out of religion, force us to find our religion in fun. Many Americans seek in such apparently secular contexts as amusement parks, rock concerts, and sporting events what other people find in religious rites, beliefs, and ceremonies.

Acing the
COURSE

Summary

1. Religion, a cultural universal, consists of belief and behavior concerned with supernatural beings, powers, and forces. Religion also encompasses the feelings, meanings, and congregations associated with such beliefs and behavior. Anthropological studies have revealed many aspects and functions of religion.

2. Tylor considered animism—the belief in spirits or souls—to be religion's earliest and most basic form. He focused on religion's explanatory role, arguing that religion would eventually disappear as science provided better explanations. Besides animism, yet another view of the supernatural also occurs in nonindustrial societies. This sees

the supernatural as a domain of raw, impersonal power or force (called mana in Polynesia and Melanesia). People can manipulate and control mana under certain conditions.

3. When ordinary technical and rational means of doing things fail, people may turn to magic. Often they use magic when they lack control over outcomes. Religion offers comfort and psychological security at times of crisis. However, rites also can create anxiety. Rituals are formal, invariant, stylized, earnest acts in which people subordinate their particular beliefs to a social collectivity. Rites of passage have three stages: separation, liminality, and incorporation. Such rites can mark any change in social status, age, place, or social condition. Collective rites often are cemented by communitas, a feeling of intense solidarity.

4. Besides their psychological and social functions, religious beliefs and practices play a role in the adaptation of human populations to their environments. The Hindu doctrine of *ahimsa*, which prohibits harm to living things, makes cattle sacred and beef a tabooed food. The taboo's force stops peasants from killing their draft cattle even in times of extreme need.

5. Religion establishes and maintains social control through a series of moral and ethical beliefs, and real and imagined rewards and punishments, internalized in individuals. Religion also achieves social control by mobilizing its members for collective action.

6. Wallace defines four types of religion: shamanic, communal, Olympian, and monotheistic. Each has its characteristic ceremonies and practitioners. Religion helps maintain social order, but it also can promote change. Revitalization movements blend old and new beliefs and have helped people adapt to changing conditions.

7. Protestant values have been important in the United States, as they were in the rise and spread of capitalism in Europe. The world's major religions vary in their growth rates, with Islam expanding more rapidly than Christianity. There is growing religious diversity in the United States and Canada. Fundamentalists are antimodernists who claim an identity separate from the larger religious group from which they arose; they advocate strict fidelity to the "true" religious principles on which the larger religion was founded. Religious trends in contemporary North America include rising secularism and new religions, some inspired by science and technology, some by spiritism. There are secular as well as religious rituals.

Key Terms

animism 493
antimodernism 510
cargo cults 507
communal religions 503
communitas 493
cosmology 498
fundamentalism 510
leveling mechanism 502
liminality 496
magic 495
mana 493

monotheism 504
Olympian religions 504
polytheism 493
religion 493
revitalization movements 507
rites of passage 496
ritual 496
shaman 503
syncretisms 507
taboo 494

Test Yourself!

MULTIPLE CHOICE

1. According to Sir Edward Tylor, the founder of the anthropology of religion, what is the sequence through which religion evolved?
   a. animism, polytheism, monotheism
   b. Olympianism, polytheism, monotheism
   c. mana, polytheism, monotheism
   d. animism, cargo cults, monotheism
   e. polytheism, animism, monotheism

2. Which of the following describes the concept of mana, a sacred impersonal force existing in the universe, as was used in Polynesia and Melanesia?
   a. In Polynesia and Melanesia, mana was taboo.
   b. The concept of mana was absent in societies with differential access to strategic resources.
   c. In Melanesia, where mana was similar to the notion of luck, anyone could get it; but in Polynesia, mana was attached to political elites.
   d. Most anthropologists agree that mana was the most primitive religious doctrine in Polynesia and Melanesia.
   e. In both cases mana was concerned with supernatural beings rather than with powers or forces.

3. What is the irony that this chapter highlights when describing rites of passage?
   a. Despite their prevalence during the time that Victor Turner did his research, rites of passage have disappeared with the advent of modern life.
   b. Participants in rites of passage are tricked into believing that there was a big change in their lives.
   c. Rites of passage only make worse the anxieties caused by other aspects of religion.
   d. Beliefs and rituals can both diminish and create anxiety and a sense of insecurity and danger.
   e. Rites of passage would be effective in diminishing anxiety and fear if they did not involve the liminal phase.

4. What is typically observed during the liminal phase of a rite of passage?
   a. intensification of social hierarchy
   b. symbolic reversals of ordinary behavior
   c. formation of a ranking system
   d. use of secular language
   e. no change in the social norms

5. What does the anthropological analysis of the Hindu practice of *ahimsa* suggest?
   a. Religion is a realm of behavior in which people do *not* try to behave rationally (i.e., maximize profit and minimize loss).
   b. generalized reciprocity
   c. Beliefs about the supernatural can function as part of a group's adaptation to the environment.
   d. Religious beliefs often impede evolutionary progress by encouraging wasteful energy expenditure.
   e. Antagonism between the sexes characterizes primitive religious practice.

6. This chapter describes how the Taliban movement in Afghanistan imposed an extreme form of social control in the name of religion. However,
   a. political leaders also use religion to justify social control.
   b. religion is used this way only by Muslim clerics who want to control the politics of their society.
   c. this movement had no interest in women's lives; it just focused on men.
   d. using other leveling mechanisms, such as witchcraft accusations, would have been a more effective means of social control.
   e. the Taliban's extreme forms of social control did not succeed in determining people's actions.

7. In his influential book *The Protestant Ethic and the Spirit of Capitalism* (1904/1958), Max Weber argues that

a. communal religion was the perfect breeding ground for elements of capitalism.
b. the spirit of capitalism was a result of the rise of the concept of the modern antireligious self.
c. the rise of capitalism required the spread of the shamanistic ethic of individualism.
d. the rise of capitalism required overcoming idiosyncratic belief systems and placing Catholic values in their place.
e. the rise of capitalism required that the traditional attitudes of Catholic peasants be replaced by values fitting an industrial economy based on capital accumulation.

8. The syncretic religions that mix Melanesian and Christian beliefs known as cargo cults are
   a. a religious response to the expansion of the world capitalist economy, often with political and economic consequences.
   b. culturally defined activities associated with the transition from one place or stage of life to another.
   c. cultural acts that mock the widespread but erroneous belief of European cultural supremacy.
   d. just like religious fundamentalisms in that they are ancient cultural phenomena enjoying a rebirth in current world affairs.
   e. antimodernist movements that reject anything Western.

9. All of the following are true about religious fundamentalism *except*:
   a. It seeks to rescue religion from absorption into modern Western culture.
   b. It is a very modern phenomenon.
   c. It is a form of animism.
   d. It is based on a strong feeling among adherents of alienation from the perceived secularism of the surrounding (modern) culture.
   e. It is a form of antimodernism.

10. Is American society really growing more secular? On this question, a considerable body of sociological research suggests that
    a. it is becoming more secular because scientific education in schools is improving.
    b. this question cannot be answered accurately because people typically lie about their religious affiliations in surveys.
    c. is becoming more religious because more and more people feel their national identity threatened due to rising levels of migration from non-Christian countries.
    d. levels of American religiosity haven't changed much over the past century.
    e. it is becoming more secular because less people go to church.

FILL IN THE BLANK

1. According to Tylor, _____, a belief in spiritual beings, was the earliest form of religion.

2. _____ magic is based on the belief that whatever is done to an object will affect a person who once had contact with it.

3. The term _____ refers to an intense feeling of solidarity that characterizes collective liminality.

4. A _____ refers to a custom or social action that operates to reduce differences in wealth and bring standouts in line with community norms.

5. A _____ is a cultural, especially a religious, mix, emerging from acculturation.

CRITICAL THINKING

1. How did anthropologist Anthony Wallace define religion? After reading this chapter, what problems do you think there are with his definition?

2. Describe a rite of passage you or a friend have been through. How did it fit the three-stage model given in the text?

3. From the news or your own knowledge, can you provide additional examples of revitalization movements, new religions, or liminal cults?

4. Religion is a cultural universal. But religions are parts of particular cultures, and cultural differences show up systematically in religious beliefs and practices. How so?

5. This chapter notes that many Americans see recreation and religion as separate domains. Based on my field work in Brazil and Madagascar and my reading about other societies, I believe that this separation is both ethnocentric and false. Do you agree with this? What has been your own experience?

Bowie, F.
2006 *The Anthropology of Religion: An Introduction.* Malden, MA: Blackwell. Surveys classic and recent work in the anthropology of religion, including the politics of religious identity.

Crapo, R. H.
2003 *Anthropology of Religion: The Unity and Diversity of Religions.* Boston: McGraw-Hill. Examines religious universals and variation.

Cunningham, G.
1999 *Religion and Magic: Approaches and Theories.* New York: New York University Press. A survey of approaches to magic and religion, ancient and modern.

Hicks, D., ed.
2010 *Ritual and Belief: Readings in the Anthropology of Religion*, 3rd ed. Lanham, MD: AtlaMira. Up-to-date reader, with useful annotation.

Moro, P. A., and J. E. Meyers, eds.
2010 *Magic, Witchcraft, and Religion: An Anthropological Study of the Supernatural*, 8th ed. Boston: McGraw-Hill. A comparative reader covering Western and non-Western cultures.

Stein, R. L., and P. L. Stein
2008 *The Anthropology of Religion, Magic, and Witchcraft*, 2nd ed. Boston: Pearson. Religion and culture.

Suggested Additional Readings

Go to our Online Learning Center website at **www.mhhe.com/kottak** for Internet exercises directly related to the content of this chapter.

Internet Exercises

What are the arts,
and how have they
varied historically
and crossculturally?

How does culture
influence the media,
and vice versa?

How are culture and
cultural contrasts
expressed in
sports?

Fireworks at the dress
rehearsal for the 2008
opening of the Olympic
games in Beijing, China. The
Olympics unite arts, media,
and sports.

Arts, Media, and Sports

understanding OURSELVES

Imagine a TV broadcast attracting over 70 percent of a nation's viewers. That has happened repeatedly in Brazil as a popular *telenovela* draws to a close. (*Telenovelas* are prime-time serial melodramas that run for about 150 episodes, then end.) It happened in the United States in 1953, when 72 percent of all sets were tuned to *I Love Lucy* as Lucy Ricardo went to the hospital to give birth to Little Ricky. It happened even more impressively in 1956, when 83 percent of all sets tuned to *The Ed Sullivan Show* to watch Elvis Presley in his TV debut. A single broadcast's largest audience share in more recent years occurred in 1983 when 77 percent of all sets tuned to the final episode of *M*A*S*H*. In the 21st century, two Super Bowls (2008—Giants vs. Patriots, and 2009—Steelers vs. Cardinals) have attracted almost as many viewers as did the *M*A*S*H* finale, but within a significantly larger U.S. population. Neither managed an audience share exceeding 43 percent.

One notable development in the United States over the past few decades has been a shift from mass culture to segmented cultures. An increasingly differentiated nation recognizes, even celebrates, diversity. The mass media join—and intensify—this trend, measuring and catering to various "demographics." Products and messages are aimed less at the masses than at particular segments—*target audiences.*

As one example, consider the evolution of sports coverage. From 1961 to 1998 ABC offered a weekly sports anthology titled *Wide World of Sports*. On a given Saturday afternoon Americans might see bowling, track and field, skating, college wrestling, gymnastics, curling, swimming, diving, or another of many sports. It was like having a mini-Olympics running throughout the year. Today, dozens of specialized sports channels cater to every taste. Think of the myriad choices now available though cable and satellite, websites, the iPhone, Netflix, DVDs, DVRs, and the remote control. Target audiences now have access to a multiplicity of channels, featuring all kinds of music, sports, games, news, comedy, science fiction, soaps, movies, cartoons, old TV sitcoms, Spanish language programs, nature shows, travel shows, adventure shows, histories, biographies, and home shopping. News channels (e.g., Fox News or MSNBC) even cater to particular political interests. Although exciting Super Bowl matches still generate large audience shares, I doubt that if Elvis Presley and Michael Jackson returned from the dead for a sing-off on broadcast TV, it would get half the available audience. It seems likely there is a connection between these media developments and the "special interests" about which politicians perpetually complain. Do you think people might agree more—and Americans be less polarized—if everyone still watched the same TV programs? After all, who didn't love Lucy?

WHAT IS ART?

The **arts** include music, performance arts, visual arts, and storytelling and literature (oral and written). These manifestations of human creativity sometimes are called **expressive culture.** People express themselves in dance, music, song, painting, sculpture, pottery, cloth, storytelling, verse, prose, drama, and comedy. Many cultures lack terms that can be translated easily as "art" or "the arts." Yet even without a word for art, people everywhere do associate an aesthetic experience—a sense of beauty, appreciation, harmony, pleasure—with sounds, patterns, objects, and events that have certain qualities. The Bamana people of Mali have a word (like "art") for something that attracts your attention and directs your thoughts (Ezra 1986). Among the Yoruba of Nigeria, the word for art, *ona,* encompasses the designs made on objects, the art objects themselves, and the profession of the creators of such patterns and works. For two Yoruba lineages of leather workers, Otunisona and Osiisona, the suffix *-ona* in their names denotes art (Adepegba 1991).

A dictionary defines **art** as "the quality, production, expression, or realm of what is beautiful or of more than ordinary significance; the class of objects subject to aesthetic criteria" (*The Random House College Dictionary* 1982, p. 76). According to the same dictionary, **aesthetics** involves "the qualities perceived in works of art . . .; the . . . mind and emotions in relation to the sense of beauty" (p. 22). However, it is possible for a work of art to attract our attention, direct our thoughts, and have more than ordinary significance without being judged as beautiful by most people who experience that work. Pablo Picasso's *Guernica,* a famous painting of the Spanish Civil War, comes to mind as a scene that, while not beautiful, is indisputably moving and thus is a work of art.

George Mills (1971) notes that in many cultures, the role of art lover lacks definition because art isn't viewed as a separate activity. But this doesn't stop individuals from being moved by sounds, patterns, objects, and events in a way that we would call aesthetic. Our own society does provide a fairly well-defined role for the connoisseur of the arts, as well as sanctuaries—concert halls, theaters, museums—where people can retreat to be aesthetically pleased and emotionally moved by objects and performances.

Western culture tends to compartmentalize art as something apart from everyday life and ordinary culture. This reflects a more general modern separation of institutions like government and the economy from the rest of society. All these fields are considered distinct domains and have their own academic specialists. In non–Western societies the production and appreciation of art are part of everyday life, as popular culture is in our own society. When featured in Western museums, non–Western art often is treated in the same way as "fine art"—that is, separated from its living sociocultural context.

This chapter will not attempt to do a systematic survey of all the arts, or even their major subdivisions. Rather, the general approach will be to examine topics and issues that apply to expressive culture generally. "Art" will be used to encompass all the arts, including print and film

Many of the high points of Western art had religious inspiration, or were done in the service of religion. Consider *The Creation of Adam* (and other frescoes painted from 1508 to 1512) by Michelangelo on the ceiling of the Sistine Chapel in Vatican City, Rome, Italy.

narratives, not just the visual ones. In other words, the observations to be made about "art" are intended to apply to music, theater, film, television, books, stories, and lore, as well as to painting and sculpture. In this chapter, some arts and media inevitably receive more attention than others do. Bear in mind, however, that expressive culture encompasses far more than the visual arts. Also included are jokes, storytelling, theater, dance, children's play, games, and festivals, and anthropologists have written about all of these.

That which is aesthetically pleasing is perceived with the senses. Usually, when we think of art, we have in mind something that can be seen or heard. But others might define art more broadly to include things that can be smelled (scents, fragrances), tasted (recipes), or touched (cloth textures). How enduring must art be? Visual works and written works, including musical compositions, may last for centuries. Can a single noteworthy event, such as a feast, which is not in the least eternal, except in memory, be a work of art?

Art and Religion

Some of the issues raised in the discussion of religion also apply to art. Definitions of both art and religion mention the "more than ordinary" or the "extraordinary." Religious scholars may distinguish between the sacred (religious) and the profane (secular). Similarly, art scholars may distinguish between the artistic and the ordinary.

arts
Include visual arts, literature (written and oral), music, and performance arts.

expressive culture
Dance, music, painting, sculpture, pottery, cloth, stories, drama, comedy, etc.

art
Object, event, or other expressive form that evokes an aesthetic reaction.

aesthetics
The appreciation of qualities perceived in art.

Space transformed into art. "The Gates," by the experimental artist Christo and his wife, Jeanne-Claude, was unveiled in 2005 in New York City's Central Park. Long, billowy saffron ribbons meandered through the park. An army of paid helpers gradually released the panels of colored fabric from atop 7,500 gates standing 16 feet tall.

If we adopt a special attitude or demeanor when confronting a sacred object, do we display something similar when experiencing a work of art? According to the anthropologist Jacques Maquet (1986), an artwork is something that stimulates and sustains contemplation. It compels attention and reflection. Maquet stresses the importance of the object's form in producing such artistic contemplation. But other scholars stress feeling and meaning in addition to form. The experience of art involves feeling, such as being moved, as well as appreciation of form, such as balance or harmony.

Such an artistic attitude can be combined with and used to bolster a religious attitude. Much art has been done in association with religion. Many of the high points of Western art and music had religious inspiration, or were done in the service of religion, as a visit to a church or a large museum will surely illustrate. Bach and Handel are as well known for their church music as Michelangelo is for his religious painting and sculpture. The buildings (churches and cathedrals) in which religious music is played and in which visual art is displayed may themselves be works of art. Some of the major architectural achievements of Western art are religious structures.

Art may be created, performed, or displayed outdoors in public or in special indoor settings, such as a theater, concert hall, or museum. Just as churches demarcate religion, museums and theaters set art off from the ordinary world, making it special, while inviting spectators in. Buildings dedicated to the arts help create the artistic atmosphere. Architecture may accentuate the setting as a place for works of art to be presented.

The settings of rites and ceremonies, and of art, may be temporary or permanent. State societies have permanent religious structures: churches and temples. So, too, may state societies have buildings and structures dedicated to the arts. Nonstate societies tend to lack such permanently demarcated settings. Both art and religion are more "out there" in society. Still, in bands and tribes, religious settings can be created without churches. Similarly, an artistic atmosphere can be created without museums. At particular times of the year, ordinary space can be set aside for a visual art display or a musical performance. Such special occasions parallel the times set aside for religious ceremonies. In fact, in tribal performances, the arts and religion often mix. For example, masked and costumed performers may imitate spirits. Rites of passage often feature special music, dance, song, bodily adornment, and other manifestations of expressive culture.

In the chapter "Making a Living," we looked at the potlatching tribes of the North Pacific Coast of North America. Erna Gunther (1971) shows how various art forms combined among those tribes to create the visual aspects of ceremonialism. During the winter, spirits were believed to pervade the atmosphere. Masked and costumed dancers represented the spirits. They dramatically reenacted spirit encounters with human beings, which are part of the origin myths of villages, clans, and lineages. In some areas, dancers devised intricate patterns of choreography. Their esteem was measured by the number of people who followed them when they danced.

In any society, art is produced for its aesthetic value as well as for religious purposes. According to Schildkrout and Keim (1990), non-Western art is usually, but wrongly, assumed to have some kind of connection to ritual. Non-Western art may be, but isn't always, linked with religion. Westerners have trouble accepting the idea that non-Western societies have art for art's sake just as Western societies do. There has been a tendency for Westerners to ignore the individuality of non-Western artists and their interest in creative expression. According to Isidore Okpewho (1977), an oral literature specialist, scholars have tended to see religion in all traditional African arts. Even when acting in the service of religion, there is room for individual creative expression. In the oral arts, for example, the audience is much more interested in the delivery and performance of the artist than in the particular god for whom the performer may be speaking.

Locating Art

Aesthetic value is one way of distinguishing art. Another way is to consider placement. If something is displayed in a museum, or in another socially accepted artistic setting, someone at least must think it's art. Although tribal societies typically lack museums, they may maintain special areas where artistic expression takes place. One example, discussed below, is the separate space in which ornamental burial poles are manufactured among the Tiwi of North Australia.

Will we know art if we see it? Art has been defined as involving that which is beautiful and of more than ordinary significance. But isn't beauty in the eye of the beholder? Don't reactions to art differ among spectators? And, if there can be secular ritual, can there also be ordinary art? The boundary between what's art and what's not is blurred. The American artist Andy Warhol is famous for transforming Campbell's soup cans, Brillo pads, and images of Marilyn Monroe into art. Many recent artists, such as Christo (see the photo above), have tried to erase the distinction between art and ordinary life by converting the everyday into a work of art.

If something is mass produced or industrially modified, can it be art? Prints made as part of a series certainly may be considered art. Sculptures that are created in clay, then fired with molten metal, such as bronze, at a foundry also are art. But how does one know if a film is art? Is *Star Wars* art? How about *Citizen Kane*? When a book wins a National Book Award, is it immediately elevated to the status of art? What kinds of prizes make art? Objects never intended as art, such as an Olivetti typewriter, may be transformed into art by being placed in a museum, such as New York's Museum of Modern Art. Jacques Maquet (1986) distinguishes such "art by transformation" from art created and intended to be art, which he calls "art by destination."

In state societies, we have come to rely on critics, judges, and experts to tell us what's art and what isn't. A play titled *Art* is about conflict that arises among three friends when one of them buys an all-white painting. They disagree, as people often do, about the definition and value of a work of art. Such variation in art appreciation is especially common in contemporary society, with its professional artists and critics and great cultural diversity. We'd expect more uniform standards and agreement in less diverse, less stratified societies.

To be culturally relativistic, we need to avoid applying our own standards about what art is to the products of other cultures. Sculpture is art, right? Not necessarily. Previously, we challenged the view that non-Western art always has some kind of connection to religion. The Kalabari case to be discussed now makes the opposite point: that religious sculpture is not always art.

Among the Kalabari of southern Nigeria (Figure 22.1), wooden sculptures are carved not for aesthetic reasons but to serve as "houses" for spirits (Horton 1963). These sculptures are used to control the spirits of Kalabari religion. The Kalabari place such a carving, and thus localize a spirit, in a cult house into which the spirit is invited. Here, sculpture is done not for art's sake but as a means of manipulating spiritual forces.

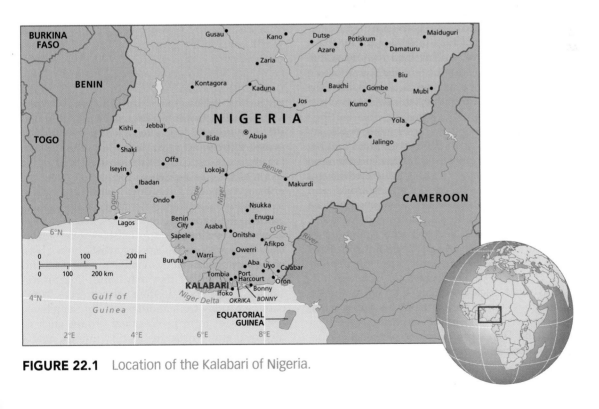

FIGURE 22.1 Location of the Kalabari of Nigeria.

The Kalabari do have standards for the carvings, but beauty isn't one of them. A sculpture must be sufficiently complete to represent its spirit. Carvings judged too crude are rejected by cult members. Also, carvers must base their work on past models. Particular spirits have particular images associated with them. It's considered dangerous to produce a carving that deviates too much from a previous image of the spirit or that resembles another spirit. Offended spirits may retaliate. As long as they observe these standards of completeness and established images, carvers are free to express themselves. But these images are considered repulsive rather than beautiful. And they are not manufactured for artistic but for religious reasons.

Art and Individuality

Those who work with non-Western art have been criticized for ignoring the individual and focusing too much on the social nature and context of art. When art objects from Africa or Papua New Guinea are displayed in museums, generally only the name of the tribe and of the Western donor are given, rather than that of the individual artist. It's as though skilled individuals don't exist in non-Western societies. The impression is that art is collectively produced. Sometimes it is; sometimes it isn't.

To some extent, there *is* more collective production of art in non-Western societies than in the United States and Canada. According to Hackett (1996), African artworks (sculpted figures, textiles, paintings, or pots) generally are enjoyed, critiqued, and used by communities or groups, rather than being the prerogative of the individual alone. The artist may receive more feedback during the creative process than the individual artist typically encounters in our own society. Here, the feedback often comes too late, after the product is complete, rather than during production, when it can still be changed.

During his field work among Nigeria's Tiv people, Paul Bohannan (1971) concluded that the proper study of art there should pay less attention to artists and more attention to art critics and products. There were few skilled Tiv artists, and such people avoided doing their art publicly. However, mediocre artists would work in public, where they routinely got comments from onlookers (critics). Based on critical suggestions, an artist often changed a design, such as a carving, in progress. There was yet another way in which Tiv artists worked socially rather than individually. Sometimes, when an artist put his work aside, someone else would pick it up and start working on it. The Tiv clearly didn't recognize the same kind of connection between individuals and their art that we do. According to Bohannan, every Tiv was free to know what he liked and to try to make

it if he could. If not, one or more of his fellows might help him out.

In Western societies, artists of many sorts (e.g., writers, painters, sculptors, actors, classical and rock musicians) have reputations for being iconoclastic and antisocial. Social acceptance may be more important in the societies anthropologists have traditionally studied. Still, there are well-known individual artists in non-Western societies. They are recognized as such by other community members and perhaps by outsiders as well. Their artistic labor may even be conscripted for special displays and performances, including ceremonies, or palace arts and events.

To what extent can a work of art stand apart from its artist? Philosophers of art commonly regard works of art as autonomous entities, independent of their creators (Haapala 1998). Haapala argues the contrary, that artists and their works are inseparable. "By creating works of art a person creates an artistic identity for himself. He creates himself quite literally into the pieces he puts into his art. He exists in the works he has created." In this view, Picasso created many Picassos, and exists in and through those works of art.

Sometimes little is known or recognized about the individual artist responsible for an enduring artwork. We are more likely to know the name of the recording artist than that of the writer of the songs we most commonly remember and perhaps sing. Sometimes we fail to acknowledge art individually because the artwork was collectively created. To whom should we attribute a pyramid or a cathedral? Should it be the architect, the ruler or leader who commissioned the work, or the master builder who implemented the design? A thing of beauty may be a joy forever even if and when we do not credit its creator(s).

The Work of Art

Some may see art as a form of expressive freedom, as giving free rein to the imagination and the human need to create or to be playful. But consider the word *opera*. It is the plural of *opus*, which means a work. For the artist, at least, art is work, albeit creative work. In nonstate societies, artists may have to hunt, gather, herd, fish, or farm in order to eat, but they still manage to find time to work on their art. In state societies, at least, artists have been defined as specialists—professionals who have chosen careers as artists, musicians, writers, or actors. If they manage to support themselves from their art, they may be full-time professionals. If not, they do their art part-time, while earning a living from another activity. Sometimes artists associate in professional groups such as medieval guilds or contemporary unions. Actors Equity in New York, a labor union, is a modern guild, designed to protect the interests of its artist members.

Just how much work is needed to make a work of art? In the early days of French impressionism, many experts viewed the paintings of Claude Monet and his colleagues as too sketchy and spontaneous to be true art. Established artists and critics were accustomed to more formal and classic studio styles. The French impressionists got their name from their sketches—*impressions* in French—of natural and social settings. They took advantage of technological innovations, particularly the availability of oil paints in tubes, to take their palettes, easels, and canvases into the field. There they captured the images of changing light and color that hang today in so many museums, where they are now fully recognized as art. But before impressionism became an officially recognized "school" of art, its works were perceived by its critics as crude and unfinished. In terms of community standards, the first impressionist paintings were evaluated as harshly as were the overly crude and incomplete Kalabari wood carvings of spirits, as discussed previously.

To what extent does the artist—or society—make the decision about completeness? For familiar genres, such as painting or music, societies tend to have standards by which they judge whether an artwork is complete or fully realized. Most people would doubt, for instance, that an all-white painting could be a work of art. Standards may be maintained informally in society, or by specialists, such as art critics. It may be difficult for unorthodox or renegade artists to innovate. But, like the impressionists, they may eventually succeed. Some societies tend to reward conformity, an artist's skill with traditional models and techniques. Others encourage breaks with the past, innovation.

ART, SOCIETY, AND CULTURE

More than 70,000 years ago, some of the world's first artists occupied Blombos Cave, located in a high cliff facing the Indian Ocean at the tip of what is now South Africa. They hunted game and ate fish from the waters below them. In terms of body and brain size, these ancient Africans were anatomically modern humans. They also were turning animal bones into finely worked tools and weapon points. Furthermore, they were engraving artifacts with symbolic marks—manifestations of abstract and creative thought and, presumably, communication through language (Wilford 2002b).

A group led by Christopher Henshilwood of South Africa has analyzed 28 bone tools and other artifacts from Blombos Cave, along with the mineral ochre, which may have been used for body painting. The most impressive bone tools are three sharp instruments. The bone appears first to have been shaped with a stone blade, then finished into

This musician living in the Central African Republic carved this instrument himself.

a symmetrical shape and polished for hours. According to Henshilwood (quoted in Wilford 2002b), "It's actually unnecessary for projectile points to be so carefully made. It suggests to us that this is an expression of symbolic thinking. The people said, 'Let's make a really beautiful object . . . ' Symbolic thinking means that people are using something to mean something else. The tools do not have to have only a practical purpose. And the ocher might be used to decorate their equipment, perhaps themselves."

In Europe, art goes back more than 30,000 years, to the Upper Paleolithic period in Western Europe (see Conkey et al. 1997). Cave paintings, the best-known examples of Upper Paleolithic art, were separated from ordinary life and social space. Those images were painted in true caves, located deep in the bowels of the earth. They may have been painted as part of some kind of rite of passage involving retreat from society. Portable art objects carved in bone and ivory, along with musical whistles and flutes, also confirm artistic expression throughout the Upper Paleolithic. Art usually is more public than the cave paintings. Typically, it is exhibited, evaluated, performed, and appreciated in society. It has spectators or audiences. It isn't just for the artist.

Ethnomusicology

Ethnomusicology is the comparative study of the musics of the world and of music as an aspect of culture and society. The field of ethnomusicology thus unites music and anthropology. The music side involves the study and analysis of the music itself and the instruments used to create it. The anthropology side views music as a way to explore a culture, to determine the

ethnomusicology
Comparative study of music as an aspect of culture and society.

role—historic and contemporary—that music plays in that society, and the specific social and cultural features that influence how music is created and performed.

Ethnomusicology studies non-Western music, traditional and folk music, even contemporary popular music from a cultural perspective. To do this there has to be field work—firsthand study of particular forms of music, their social functions and cultural meanings, within particular societies. Ethnomusicologists talk with local musicians, make recordings in the field, and learn about the place of musical instruments, performances, and performers in a given society (Kirman 1997). Nowadays, given globalization, diverse cultures and musical styles easily meet and mix. Music that draws on a wide range of cultural instruments and styles is called World Fusion, World Beat, or World Music—another topic within contemporary ethnomusicology.

Because music is a cultural universal, and because musical abilities seem to run in families, it has been suggested that a predisposition for music may have a genetic basis (Crenson 2000). Could a "music gene" that arose tens, or hundreds, of thousands of years ago have conferred an evolutionary advantage on those early humans who possessed it? The fact that music has existed in all known cultures suggests that it arose early in human history. Providing direct evidence for music's antiquity is an ancient carved bone flute from a cave in Slovenia. This "Divje babe flute," the world's oldest known musical instrument, dates back more than 43,000 years.

Exploring the possible biological roots of music, Sandra Trehub (2001) notes striking similarities in the way mothers worldwide sing to their children—with a high pitch, a slow tempo, and a distinctive tone. All cultures have lullabies, which sound so much alike they cannot be mistaken for anything else (Crenson 2000). Trehub speculates that music might have been adaptive in human evolution because musically talented mothers had an easier time calming their babies. Calm babies who fell asleep easily and rarely made a fuss might well have been more likely to survive to adulthood. Their cries would not attract predators; they and their mothers would get more rest; and they would be less likely to be mistreated. If a gene conferring musical ability appeared early in human evolution, given a selective advantage, musical adults would pass their genes to their children.

Music would seem to be among the most social of the arts. Usually it unites people in groups. Indeed, music is all about groups—choirs, symphonies, ensembles, and bands. Could it be that early humans with a biological penchant for music were able to live more effectively in social groups—another possible adaptive advantage? Even master pianists and violinists are frequently accompanied

by orchestras or singers. Alan Merriam (1971) describes how the Basongye people of the Kasai province of the Democratic Republic of the Congo (Figure 22.2) use three features to distinguish between music and other sounds, which are classified as "noise." First, music always involves humans. Sounds emanating from nonhuman creatures, such as birds and animals, are not music. Second, musical sounds must be organized. A single tap on the drum isn't music, but drummers playing together in a pattern is. Third, music must continue. Even if several drums are struck together simultaneously, it isn't music. They must go on playing to establish some kind of sound pattern. For the Basongye, then, music is inherently cultural (distinctly human) and social (dependent on cooperation).

Originally coined for European peasants, **folk** art, music, and lore refer to the expressive culture of ordinary people, as contrasted with the "high" art or "classic" art of the European elites. When European folk music is performed (see photo below), the combination of costumes, music, and often song and dance is supposed to say something about local culture and about tradition. Tourists and other outsiders often perceive rural and folk life mainly in terms of such performances. Community residents themselves often use such performances to display and enact their local culture and traditions for outsiders.

In Planinica, a Muslim village in (prewar) Bosnia, Yvonne Lockwood (1983) studied folksong, which could be heard there day or night. The most active singers were unmarried females age 16 to 26 (maidens). Lead singers, those who customarily began and led songs, had strong, full, clear voices with a high range. Like some of their counterparts in contemporary North America (but in a much milder fashion), some lead singers acted unconventionally. One was regarded as immodest because of her risqué lyrics. Another smoked (usually a man's habit) and liked to wear men's trousers. Local criticism aside, she was thought to be witty and to improvise songs better than others did.

The social transition from girl to maiden (marriageable female) was signaled by active participation in public song and dance. Adolescent girls were urged to join in by women and performing maidens. This was part of a rite of passage by which a little girl (*dite*) became a maiden (*cura*). Marriage, in contrast, moved most women from the public to the private sphere; public singing generally stopped. Married women sang in their own homes or among other women. Only occasionally would they join maidens in public song, but they never called attention to themselves by taking the lead. After age 50 wives tended to stop singing, even in private.

For women, singing thus signaled a series of transitions between age grades: girl to maiden

folk
Of the people; e.g., the art, music, and lore of ordinary people.

(public singing), maiden to wife (private singing), and wife to elder (no more singing). Lockwood describes how one recently married woman made her ritual first visit after marriage to her family of origin. (Postmarital residence was patrilocal.) Then, as she was leaving to return to her husband's village, for "old times' sake" she led the village maidens in song. She used her native daughter status to behave like a maiden this one last time. Lockwood calls it a nostalgic and emotional performance for all who attended.

Singing and dancing were common at *prelos* attended by males and females. In Planinica the Serbo-Croatian word *prelo*, usually defined as "spinning bee," meant any occasion for visiting. *Prelos* were especially common in winter. During the summer, villagers worked long hours, and *prelos* were few. The *prelo* offered a context for play, relaxation, song, and dance. All gatherings of maidens, especially *prelos*, were occasions for song. Married women encouraged them to sing, often suggesting specific songs. If males were also present, a singing duel might occur, in which maidens and young men teased each other. A successful *prelo* was well attended, with much singing and dancing.

Public singing was traditional in many other contexts among prewar Bosnian Muslims. After a day of cutting hay on mountain slopes, parties of village men would congregate at a specific place on the trail above the village. They formed lines according to their singing ability, with the best singers in front and the less talented ones behind. They proceeded to stroll down to the village together, singing as they went, until they reached the village center, where they dispersed.

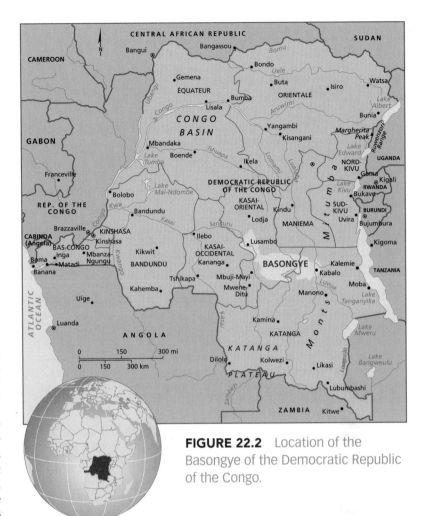

FIGURE 22.2 Location of the Basongye of the Democratic Republic of the Congo.

Musicians playing alpenhorns in a ceremony at Munster, Alsace, France. For whose pleasure do you suppose this performance is being given? Nowadays, such performances attract tourists as well as local people.

through the eyes of OTHERS

STUDENT: erica Tso

COUNTRY OF ORIGIN: China (Hong Kong)

SUPERVISING PROFESSOR: Elliot Fratkin

SCHOOL: Smith College

Visual Arts in Hong Kong and the United States

A rt preserves culture and memories. An American artist asked me what was special about art in Hong Kong. I replied without hesitation, "We have a bit of everything." Hong Kong is a dynamic city where East meets West. Art in Hong Kong helps preserve the 3,000-year history of Chinese and Hong Kong culture, but it also looks to the new. Some artists create traditional Chinese ink paintings, calligraphy, and seal-character engravings, while others work with more Western-oriented media like oil, watercolor, and acrylic paints. The most prominent feature of art in Hong Kong is its fusion of Eastern and Western themes and techniques. More and more artists fuse the two traditions—putting Japanese origami into oil paintings, writing Chinese calligraphy in colorful acrylic paints, for example—to create groundbreaking work unique to Hong Kong.

I have seen a diversity of artwork in the United States; to me, these pieces of art feel like totally individual works, in contrast to the deep connection I see between art and the artists who make it in Hong Kong. For example, the works of famous American artists like Andy Warhol, Chuck Close, and Leonard Baskin are all very different in their compositions, colors, meanings, and mediums. Not knowing the artists, it is probably harder to determine whether a piece of their work is "American Art." In Hong Kong, although all of the artwork is unique in its own way, the common incorporation of Chinese elements along with Chinese themes makes these works more easily identifiable as "Hong Kong Art." The amount of support for art in the United States was another difference that struck me when I first came to Massachusetts. In Hong Kong, a student would be considered odd and incapable if he or she chose to study geography, history, or art. Public opinion in the United States supports a person's choice to pursue life as an artist; people are not disparaged for what they choose to study. In this aspect of culture, I think Americans are more liberal than the Chinese. Most students and young adults in Hong Kong would be forced to follow the forces of a market economy.

Although Hong Kong was a British colony until 1997, the people of Hong Kong feel strongly a part of Chinese culture. We love our traditional culture, and many artists are working hard to preserve it. In the United States, however, art is in flux and does not show a strong sense of unique culture; brand-new ideas and media emerge every day—this constant change is perhaps in itself the distinctive quality of American art.

According to Lockwood, whenever an activity of work or leisure brought together a group of maidens or young men, it rarely ended without public song. It would not be wrong to trace the inspiration for parts of *Snow White* and *Shrek* (the movies) back to the European countryside.

Representations of Art and Culture

Art can stand for tradition, even when traditional art is removed from its original (rural) context. The creative products and images of folk, rural, and non-Western cultures are increasingly spread—and commercialized—by the media and tourism. A result is that many Westerners have come to think of "culture" in terms of colorful customs, music, dancing, and adornments: clothing, jewelry, and hairstyles.

A bias toward the arts and religion, rather than more mundane, less photogenic, economic and social tasks, shows up on TV's Discovery Channel, and even in many anthropological films. Many ethnographic films start off with music, often drumbeats: "Bonga, bonga, bonga, bonga. Here in (supply place name), the people are very religious." We see in such presentations the previously critiqued assumption that the arts of nonindustrial societies usually have a link with religion. The (usually unintended) message is that non-Western peoples spend much of their time wearing colorful clothes, singing, dancing, and practicing religious rituals. Taken to an extreme, such images portray culture as recreational and ultimately not serious, rather than as something that ordinary people live every day of their lives—not just when they have festivals.

Art and Communication

Art also functions in society as a form of communication between artist and community or audience. Sometimes, however, there are intermediaries between the artist and the audience. Actors, for example, are artists who translate the works and ideas of other artists (writers and directors) into the performances that audiences see and appreciate. Musicians play and sing compositions of other people along with music they themselves have composed. Using music written by others, choreographers plan and direct patterns of dance, which dancers then execute for audiences.

How does art communicate? We need to know what the artist intends to communicate and how the audience reacts. Often, the audience communicates right back to the artist. Live performers, for instance, get immediate feedback, as may writers and directors by viewing a performance of their own work. Artists expect at least some variation in reception. In contemporary societies, with increasing diversity in the audience, uniform reactions are rare. Contemporary artists, like businesspeople, are well aware that they have target audiences. Certain segments of the population are more likely to appreciate certain forms of art than other segments are.

Art can transmit several kinds of messages. It can convey a moral lesson or tell a cautionary tale. It can teach lessons the artist, or society, wants told. Like the rites that induce, then dispel, anxiety, the tension and resolution of drama can lead to **catharsis,** intense emotional release, in the audience. Art can move emotions, make us laugh, cry, feel up or down. Art appeals to the intellect as well as to the emotions. We may delight in a well-constructed, nicely balanced, well-realized work of art.

Often, art is meant to commemorate and to last, to carry an enduring message. Like a ceremony, art may serve a mnemonic function, making people remember. Art may be designed to make people remember either individuals or events, such as the AIDS epidemic that has proved so lethal in many world areas, or the cataclysmic events of September 11, 2001.

Art and Politics

What is art's social role? To what extent should art serve society? Art can be self-consciously prosocial. It can be used to either express or challenge community sentiment and standards. Art enters the political arena. Decisions about what counts as a work of art, or about how to display art, may be political and controversial. Museums have to balance concern over community standards with a wish to be as creative and innovative as the artists and works they display.

Much art that is valued today was received with revulsion in its own time. New York's Brooklyn Museum of Art has documented how art that shocks or offends when it is new becomes accepted and valued over time. Children were prohibited from seeing paintings by Matisse, Braque, and Picasso when those works first were displayed in New York in the Armory Show of 1913. The *New York Times* called that Armory Show "pathological." Almost a century later, the City of New York and then mayor Rudolph Giuliani took the Brooklyn Museum to court over its 1999–2000 "Sensation" show. After religious groups protested Chris Ofili's *Holy Virgin Mary*, a collage that included elephant dung, Giuliani deemed the work sacrilegious. The ensuing court trial prompted anticensorship groups and art advocates to speak out against the mayor's actions. The museum won the case, but Ofili's work again came under attack when a man smuggled paint inside the Brooklyn exhibition and tried to smear it on the *Virgin* (University of Virginia, n.d.). According to art professor Michael Davis, Ofili's collage is "shocking" because it deliberately provokes and intends to jolt viewers into an expanded frame of reference. The mayor's reactions may have been based on the narrow definition that art must be beautiful and an equally limited vision of a Virgin Mary as depicted in Italian Renaissance paintings (Mount Holyoke College 1999).

Appreciation for the arts must be learned. Here, three American boys seem intrigued by the painting *Paris on a Rainy Day* at the Chicago Art Institute. How does the placement of art in museums affect art appreciation?

Today, no museum director can mount an exhibit without worrying that it will offend some politically organized segment of society. In the United States there has been an ongoing battle between liberals and conservatives involving the National Endowment for the Arts. Artists have been criticized as aloof from society, as creating only for themselves and for elites, as out of touch with conventional and traditional aesthetic values, even as mocking the values of ordinary people.

catharsis
Intense emotional release.

The Cultural Transmission of the Arts

Because art is part of culture, appreciation of the arts depends on cultural background. Watch Japanese tourists in a Western art museum trying to interpret what they are seeing. Conversely, the form and meaning of a Japanese tea ceremony, or a demonstration of origami (Japanese paper folding), will be alien to a foreign observer. Appreciation for the arts must be learned. It is part of enculturation, as well as of more formal education. Robert Layton (1991) suggests that whatever universal principles of artistic expression may exist, they have been put into effect in a diversity of ways in different cultures.

What is aesthetically pleasing depends to some extent on culture. Based on familiarity, music with certain tonalities and rhythm patterns will please some people and alienate others. In a study of Navajo music, McAllester (1954) found that it reflected the overall culture

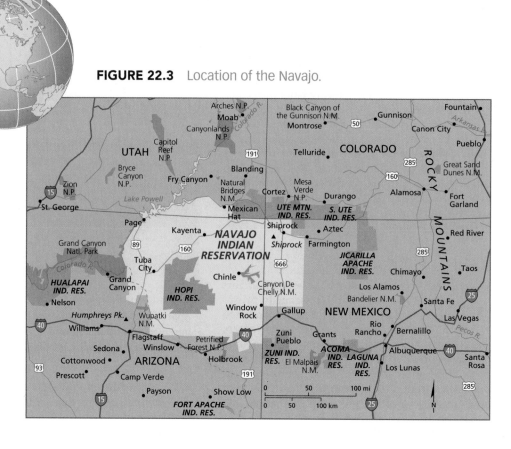

FIGURE 22.3 Location of the Navajo.

of that time in three main ways: First, individualism was a key Navajo cultural value. Thus, it was up to the individual to decide what to do with his or her physical property, knowledge, ideas, or songs. Second, McAllester found that a general Navajo conservatism also extended to music. The Navajo saw foreign music as dangerous and rejected it. (This second point is no longer true; there are now Navajo rock bands.) Third, a general stress on proper form applied to music. There was, in Navajo belief, a right way to sing every kind of song (see Figure 22.3 for the location of the Navajo).

People learn to listen to certain kinds of music and to appreciate particular art forms, just as they learn to hear and decipher a foreign language. Unlike Londoners and New Yorkers, Parisians don't flock to musicals. Despite its multiple French origins, even the musical *Les Miserables,* a huge hit in London, New York, and dozens of cities worldwide, bombed in Paris. Humor, too, a form of verbal art, depends on cultural background and setting. What's funny in one culture may not translate as funny in another. When a joke doesn't work, an American may say, "Well, you had to be there at the time." Jokes, like aesthetic judgments, depend on context.

At a smaller level of culture, certain artistic traditions may be transmitted in families. In Bali, for

living anthropology **VIDEOS**

Art of the Aborigines, www.mhhe.com/kottak

This clip focuses on an aboriginal artist in the community of Galiwinku in northern Australia. The clip provides an excellent illustration of how aspects of culture (art, religion, kinship, economics, law) that stand apart in our own society are so closely related as to be inseparable in others. The artist makes a string bag, based on a pattern her father originated. She uses knowledge taught to her by her mother, grandmother, and grandfather. According to the narrator, the artist weaves a story of the dreamtime—the mythical past when the world as we know it was created—into the bag, which thus has spiritual as well as artistic and functional significance. How widespread is this art in the community shown here? How was the bag used during gathering? How does the creative act here depict enculturation?

example, there are families of carvers, musicians, dancers, and mask makers. Among the Yoruba of Nigeria, two lineages of leather workers are entrusted with important bead embroidery works, such as for the king's crown and the bags and bracelets of priests. The arts, like other professions, often "run" in families. The Bachs, for example, produced not only Johann Sebastian but several other noted composers and musicians.

In Chapter 1, anthropology's approach to the arts was contrasted with a traditional humanities focus on "fine arts," as in art history, "Great Books," and classical music. Anthropology has extended the definition of "cultured" well beyond the elitist meaning of "high" art and culture. For anthropologists, everyone acquires culture through enculturation. In academia today, growing acceptance of the anthropological definition of culture has helped broaden the study of the humanities from fine art and elite art to "folk" and nonwestern arts, and the creative expressions of popular culture.

This chapter's "Appreciating Anthropology" shows that techniques that anthropologists have used to analyze myths and folktales can be extended to two fantasy films that most of you have seen: *The Wizard of Oz* and *Star Wars*. "Appreciating Anthropology" again highlights the contributions of the French anthropologist Claude Lévi-Strauss (1967) along with the neo-Freudian psychoanalyst Bruno Bettelheim (1975). Both have made important contributions to the study of myths and fairy tales.

In many societies, myths, legends, tales, and the art of storytelling play important roles in the transmission of culture and the preservation of tradition. In the absence of writing, oral traditions may preserve details of history and genealogy, as in many parts of West Africa. Art forms often go together. For example, music and storytelling may be combined for drama and emphasis (see the lower photo), much as they are in films and theater.

At what age do children start learning the arts? In some cultures, they start early. Contrast the photo of the Korean violin class (above left) with the photo of the Aleut gathering (below). The Korean scene shows formal instruction. The teachers take the lead in showing the kids how to play the violin. The Aleut photo shows a more informal local scene in which children are learning about the arts as part of their overall enculturation. Presumably, the Korean children are learning the arts because their parents want them to, not necessarily because they have an artistic temperament that they need or wish to express. Sometimes children's participation in arts or performance, including sports, exemplifies forced enculturation. It may be pushed by parents rather than by kids themselves. In the United States, performance, usually associated with schools, has a strong social, and usually competitive, component. Kids perform with their peers. In the process, they learn to compete, whether for a first-place finish in a sports event or a first chair in the school orchestra or band.

A violin class for a large group of four-year-old children at a Korean music school.

This photo was taken on St. Paul Island, on the Bering Sea coast of Alaska. A traditional Aleut storyteller uses a drum to tell his tale to young Aleut people. Who are the storytellers of your society? How do their narrative techniques and styles differ from the one shown here?

The Artistic Career

In nonindustrial societies, artists tend to be part-time specialists. In states, there are more ways for artists to practice their craft full-time. The number of positions in "arts and leisure" has mushroomed in contemporary societies, especially in North America. Many non-Western societies also offer career tracks in the arts: For example, a child born into a particular family or lineage may discover that he or she is destined for a career in leather working or weaving. Some societies are noted for particular arts, such as dance, wood carving, or weaving.

An artistic career also may involve some kind of a calling. Individuals may discover they have a

appreciating ANTHROPOLOGY

I'll Get You, My Pretty, and Your Little R2

Techniques that anthropologists have used to analyze myths and folktales can be extended to two fantasy films that most of you have seen. *The Wizard of Oz* has been telecast annually for decades. The original *Star Wars* remains one of the most popular films of all time. Both are familiar and significant cultural products with obvious mythic qualities. The contributions of the French structuralist anthropologist Claude Lévi-Strauss (1967) and the neo-Freudian psychoanalyst Bruno Bettelheim (1975) to the study of myths and fairy tales permit the following analysis of visual fairy tales that contemporary Americans know well.

Examining the myths and tales of different cultures, Lévi-Strauss determined that one tale could be converted into another through a series of simple operations, for example, by doing the following:

1. Converting the positive element of a myth into its negative.

2. Reversing the order of the elements.

3. Replacing a male hero with a female hero.

4. Preserving or repeating certain key elements.

Through such operations, two apparently dissimilar myths can be shown to be variations on a common structure, that is, to be transformations of each other.

We'll see now that *Star Wars* is a systematic structural transformation of *The Wizard of Oz*. We may speculate about how many of the resemblances were conscious and how many simply reflect a process of enculturation that *Star Wars* writer and director George Lucas shares with other Americans.

The Wizard of Oz and *Star Wars* both begin in arid country, the first in Kansas and the second on the desert planet Tatooine. (Recap 22.1 lists the similarities discussed here.) *Star Wars* converts *The Wizard*'s female hero into a boy, Luke Skywalker. Fairy-tale heroes usually have short, common first names and second names that describe their origin or

activity. Thus Luke, who travels aboard spaceships, is a Skywalker, while Dorothy Gale is swept off to Oz by a cyclone (a gale of wind). Dorothy leaves home with her dog, Toto, who is pursued by and has managed to escape from a woman who in Oz becomes the Wicked Witch of the West. Luke follows his "Two-Two" (R2D2), who is fleeing Darth Vader, the witch's structural equivalent.

Dorothy and Luke each start out living with an uncle and an aunt. However, because of the gender change of the hero, the primary relationship is reversed and inverted. Thus Dorothy's relationship with her aunt is primary, warm, and loving, whereas Luke's relationship with his uncle, though primary, is strained and distant. Aunt and uncle are in the tales for the same reason. They represent home (the nuclear family of orientation), which children (according to American culture norms) must eventually leave to make it on their own. As Bettelheim (1975) points out, fairy tales often disguise parents as uncle and aunt, and this establishes social distance. The child can deal with the hero's separation (in *The Wizard of Oz*) or the aunt's and uncle's deaths (in *Star Wars*) more easily than with

---

anthropology **ATLAS**

Locate the ethnographic site for the Tiwi of North Australia on Map 10.

particular talent and find an environment in which that talent is nourished. Separate career paths for artists usually involve special training and apprenticeship. Such paths are more likely in a complex society, where there are many separate career tracks, than in band or tribal societies, where expressive culture is less formally separated from daily life.

Artists need support if they are to devote full time to creative activity. They find support in their families or lineages if there is specialization in the arts involving kin groups. State societies often have patrons of the arts. Usually members of the elite class, patrons offer various kinds of support to aspiring and talented artists, such as court and palace painters, musicians, or sculptors. In some cases, an artistic career may entail a lifetime of dedication to religious art.

Goodale and Koss (1971) describe the manufacture of ornamental burial poles among the Tiwi of North Australia. Temporary separation and detachment from other social roles allowed burial pole artists to devote themselves to their work. The pole artists were ceremonially commissioned as such after a death. They were granted temporary freedom from the daily food quest. Other community members agreed to serve as their patrons. They supplied the artists with hard-to-get materials needed for their work. The burial pole artists were sequestered in a work area near the grave. That area was taboo to everyone else.

The arts usually are defined as neither practical nor ordinary. They rely on talent, which is individual, but which must be channeled and shaped in socially approved directions. Inevitably, artistic talent and production pull the artist away from the practical need to make a living. The issue of

---

the death of or separation from real parents. Furthermore, this permits the child's strong feelings toward his or her real parents to be represented in different, more central characters, such as the Wicked Witch of the West and Darth Vader.

Both films focus on the child's relationship with the parent of the same sex, dividing that parent into three parts. In *The Wizard*, the mother is split into two parts bad and one part good. They are the Wicked Witch of the East, dead at the beginning of the movie; the Wicked Witch of the West, dead at the end; and Glinda, the good mother, who survives. The original *Star Wars* reversed the proportion of good and bad, giving Luke a good father (his own), the Jedi knight who is proclaimed dead at the film's beginning. There is another good father, Ben Kenobi, who is ambiguously dead when the movie ends. Third is the evil father figure, Darth Vader. As the good-mother third survives *The Wizard of Oz*, the bad-father third lives on after *Star Wars*, to strike back in the sequel.

The child's relationship with the parent of the opposite sex also is represented in the two films. Dorothy's father figure is the Wizard of Oz, an initially terrifying figure who later is proved to be a fake. Bettelheim notes that the typical fairy-tale father is disguised as a monster or giant. Or else, when preserved as a human, he is weak, distant, or ineffective. Dorothy counts on the wizard to save her but finds that he makes seemingly impossible demands and in the end is just an ordinary man. She succeeds on her own, no longer relying on a father who offers no more than she herself possesses.

In *Star Wars* (although emphatically not in the later films), Luke's mother figure is Princess Leia. Bettelheim notes that boys commonly fantasize their mothers to be unwilling captives of their fathers. Fairy tales often disguise mothers as princesses whose freedom the boy-hero must obtain. In graphic Freudian imagery, Darth Vader threatens Princess Leia with a needle the size of the witch's broomstick. By the end of the film, Luke has freed Leia and defeated Vader.

There are other striking parallels in the structure of the two films. Fairy-tale heroes often are accompanied on their adventures by secondary characters who personify the virtues needed in a successful quest. Such characters often come in threes. Dorothy takes along wisdom (the Scarecrow), love (the Tin Woodman), and courage (the Lion). *Star Wars* includes a structurally equivalent trio—Han Solo, C3PO, and Chewbacca—but their association with particular qualities isn't as precise. The minor characters are also structurally parallel: Munchkins and Jawas, Apple Trees and Sand People, Flying Monkeys and Stormtroopers. And compare settings—the witch's castle and the Death Star, the Emerald City and the rebel base. The endings are also parallel. Luke accomplishes his objective on his own, using the Force (mana, magical power). Dorothy's goal is to return to Kansas. She does that by tapping her shoes together and drawing on the Force in her ruby slippers.

All successful cultural products blend old and new, drawing on familiar themes. They may rearrange them in novel ways and thus win a lasting place in the imaginations of the culture that creates or accepts them. *Star Wars* successfully used old cultural themes in novel ways. It did that by drawing on *the* American fairy tale, one that had been available in book form since the turn of the 20th century.

how to support artists and the arts arises again and again. We've all heard the phrase "struggling artist." But how should society support the arts? If there is state or religious support, something is typically expected in return. There is inevitably some limitation of the artist's "free" expression. Patronage and sponsorship also may result in the creation of art-works that are removed from public display. Art commissioned for elites often is displayed only in their homes, perhaps finding its way into museums after their deaths. Church-commissioned art may be closer to the people.

Continuity and Change

The arts go on changing, although certain art forms have survived for thousands of years. The Upper Paleolithic cave art that has survived for more than 30,000 years was itself a highly developed manifestation of human creativity and symbolism, with an undoubtedly long evolutionary history. Monumental architecture, along with sculpture, reliefs, ornamental pottery, and written music, literature, and drama, have survived from early civilizations.

Countries and cultures are known for particular contributions, including art. The Balinese are known for dance; the Navajo for sand paintings, jewelry, and weaving; and the French for making cuisine an art form. We still read Greek tragedies and comedies in college, as we also read Shakespeare and Milton, and view the works of Michelangelo. Greek theater is among the most enduring of the arts. The words of Aeschylus, Sophocles, Euripides, and Aristophanes have been captured in writing and live on. Who knows how many great preliterate creations and performances have been lost?

STAR WARS	THE WIZARD OF OZ
Male hero (Luke Skywalker)	Female hero (Dorothy Gale)
Arid Tatooine	Arid Kansas

Luke follows R2D2:
  R2D2 flees Vader
	Dorothy follows Toto:
	  Toto flees witch

Luke lives with uncle and aunt:
  Primary relationship with uncle
    (same sex as hero)
  Strained, distant relationship with uncle
	Dorothy lives with uncle and aunt:
	  Primary relationship with aunt
	    (same sex as hero)
	  Warm, close relationship with aunt

Tripartite division of same-sex parent:
  2 parts good, 1 part bad father
  Good father dead at beginning
  Good father dead (?) at end
  Bad father survives
	Tripartite division of same-sex parent:
	  2 parts bad, 1 part good mother
	  Bad mother dead at beginning
	  Bad mother dead at end
	  Good mother survives

Relationship with parent of opposite sex
    (Princess Leia Organa):
  Princess is unwilling captive
  Needle
  Princess is freed
	Relationship with parent of opposite sex
	    (Wizard of Oz):
	  Wizard makes impossible demands
	  Broomstick
	  Wizard turns out to be sham

Trio of companions:
  Han Solo, C3PO, Chewbacca
	Trio of companions:
	  Scarecrow, Tin Woodman, Cowardly Lion

Minor characters:
  Jawas
  Sand People
  Stormtroopers
	Minor characters:
	  Munchkins
	  Apple Trees
	  Flying Monkeys

Settings:
  Death Star
  Verdant Tikal (rebel base)
	Settings:
	  Witch's castle
	  Emerald City

Conclusion:
  Luke uses magic to accomplish goal
    (destroy Death Star)
	Conclusion:
	  Dorothy uses magic to accomplish goal
	    (return to Kansas)

Classic Greek theater survives throughout the world. It is read in college courses, seen in the movies, and performed live on stages from Athens to New York. In today's world, the dramatic arts are part of a huge "arts and leisure" industry, which links Western and non-Western art forms in an international network that has both aesthetic and commercial dimensions (see Marcus and Myers, eds. 1995; Root 1996). For example, non-Western musical traditions and instruments have joined the modern world system. We've seen that local musicians perform for outsiders, including tourists who increasingly visit their villages. And "tribal" instruments such as the Native Australian didgeridoo, a very long wooden wind instrument, are now exported worldwide. At least one store in Amsterdam, the Netherlands, specializes in didgeridoos, the only item it carries. Dozens of stores in any world capital hawk "traditional" arts, including musical instruments, from a hundred Third World countries.

American culture values change, experimentation, innovation, and novelty. But creativity also may be based on tradition. The Navajo, for example, can be at once individualistic, conservative, and attentive to traditional form. In some cases and cultures, as with the Navajo, it's not necessary for artists to be innovative as they are being creative. Creativity can be expressed in variations on a traditional form. We see an example of this in this chapter's "Appreciating Anthropology" above, in which *Star Wars*, despite its specific story and innovative special effects, is shown to share its narrative structure with a previous film and fairy tale. Often, artists show fealty to the past, associating with and building on, rather than rejecting, the work of their predecessors.

As ingredients and flavors from all over the world are combined in modern cuisine, so too are elements from many cultures and epochs woven into contemporary art and performance. We've seen that the arts typically draw in multiple media. Given the richness of today's media world, multimedia are even more marked.

MEDIA AND CULTURE

Today's mass culture, aka popular culture, features cultural forms that have appeared and spread rapidly because of major changes in the material conditions of contemporary life—particularly work organization, transportation, and communication, including the media. Sports, movies, TV shows, amusement parks, and fast-food restaurants have become powerful elements of national (and international) culture. They provide a framework of common expectations, experiences, and behavior overriding differences in region, class, formal religious affiliation, political sentiments, gender, ethnic group, and place of residence.

Using the Media

Any media-borne image or message can be analyzed in terms of its nature, including its symbolism, and its effects. It also can be analyzed as a text. We usually think of a text as a textbook, like this one, but the term has a more general meaning. **Text** can refer to anything that can be "read"—that is, processed, interpreted, and assigned meaning by anyone exposed to it. In this sense, a text doesn't have to be written. The term may refer to a film, an image, or an event. "Readers"—users of the text—make their own interpretations and derive their own feelings from it. "Readers" of media messages constantly produce their own meanings.

In his book *Understanding Popular Culture* (1989), John Fiske views each individual's use of popular culture as a creative act (an original "reading" of a text). For example, a particular rock star or movie means something different to each fan as well as each person who really hates that star or film. As Fiske puts it, "the meanings I make from a text are pleasurable when I feel that they are my meanings and that they relate to my everyday life in a practical, direct way" (1989, p. 57). All of us can creatively "read" print media, along with music, television, films, celebrities, and other popular culture products (see Fiske and Hartley 2003).

Media consumers actively select, evaluate, and interpret media in ways that make sense to them. People use media for all sorts of reasons: to validate beliefs, to indulge fantasies, to find messages

In Athens, Greece, ancient Greek theater is being staged for a contemporary audience. Theater is typically a multimedia experience, with visual, aural, and often musical attributes.

A synthesis of new and old theater techniques, including puppetry, is used in the Broadway production of Disney's *The Lion King*. What artistic influences have inspired the images shown in this photo?

unavailable in the local setting, to locate information, to make social comparisons, to relieve frustrations, to chart social courses, and to formulate life plans. Through popular culture, including various media, people may symbolically resist the unequal power relations they face each day in the family, at work, and in the classroom. Popular culture (from hip-hop to comedy) can be used to express discontent and resistance by groups that are or feel powerless or oppressed.

text
Cultural product that is processed and assigned meaning by anyone exposed to it.

For years, India's Bollywood film and TV industry has been an important non–Western center of cultural production. Shown here, an Indian cinema worker mounts a poster for the Oscar winning movie *Slumdog Millionaire* which was inspired in part by the Bollywood tradition.

In one town in southern Brazil, Alberto Costa found that women and young adults of both sexes were particularly attracted to *telenovelas,* melodramatic nightly programs often compared to American soap operas, usually featuring sophisticated urban settings (see Kottak 1990*a*). In the small community that Costa studied (as part of a larger study of TV in Brazil in which I participated), young people and women used the more liberal content of *telenovelas* to challenge conservative local norms. In Brazil, traditional information brokers and moral guardians (e.g., older men, elites, intellectuals, educators, and the clergy) tended to be more suspicious and dismissive of the media than were less powerful people—probably because media messages often clashed with their own.

In a more recent study in Michigan, focusing on media use in the context of work and family decisions, Lara Descartes and I (2009) found that parents selected media messages that supported and reinforced their own opinions and life choices. Varied media images of work and family allowed parents to get a sense of what others were thinking and doing, and to identify or contrast themselves with media figures. Our informants compared themselves with people and situations from the media as well as with people in their own lives. We also found, as in Brazil, that some people (traditionalists) were much more dismissive of, distrustful of, or hostile to media than others were.

When people seek certain messages and cannot easily find them in their home communities, they are likely to look somewhere else. The media offer a rich web of external connections (through cable, satellite, the Internet, television, movies, radio, telephones, print, and other sources) that can provide contact, information, entertainment, and potential social validation. In Brazil, greater use of all media (e.g., TV and print) was part of an external orientation, a general wish for information, contacts, models, and support beyond those that were locally and routinely available. This linking role of media probably is less important for people who feel most comfortable in and with their local setting. For some of our informants in Michigan, media offered a welcome gateway to a wider world, while others were comfortable with, and even sought to enhance, their isolation, limiting both media exposure and the outside social contacts of themselves and their children.

Connection to a wider world, real or imagined, is a way to move beyond local standards and expectations, even if the escape is only temporary and vicarious. David Ignatius (2007) describes the escapist value of 19th-century English novels, expressed particularly through their heroines—women who were "passionate seekers," pursuing "free thought and personal freedom," rejecting the "easy comforts and arranged marriages of their class" in their quest for something more. Despite (and/or because of) their independent or rebellious temperaments, characters such as Elizabeth Bennett in Jane Austen's *Pride and Prejudice* almost always found a happy ending. Sympathetic 19th-century readers found such a heroine's success "deeply satisfying" because there were so few opportunities in real life (the local community) to see such behavior and choices (all quotes from Ignatius 2007:A21).

The arts allow us to imagine possibilities beyond our own circumstances and experience. The mass media are an important source for such imagining. In this chapter's "Appreciating Diversity" we see how contemporary American popular culture creates idealized social worlds. As the media celebrate the rich and the famous, media portrayals often present a homogenized upper middle-class lifestyle in which social diversity is minimized. This contrasts with the class diversity that typifies Brazilian television, which is discussed later in this chapter. An anthropological approach to the arts recognizes that they must be understood in relation to sociocultural diversity in time and space.

Another role of the media is to provide social cement—a basis for sharing—as families or friends watch favorite programs or attend such events as games and performances together. The media can provide common ground for much larger groups, nationally and internationally. Brazilians and Italians can be just as excited, at the same moment but with radically different emotions, by a soccer goal scored in a World Cup match. And they can remember the same winning goal or head butt for decades. The common information and knowledge that people acquire through exposure to the same media illustrate *culture* in the anthropological sense. (For other media roles, functions, and effects, see Askew and Wilk, eds. 2002, and Ginsburg, Abu-Lughod, and Larkin, eds. 2002).

Assessing the Effects of Television

In the Brazilian study mentioned in the last section, and described more fully in Chapter 1, my associates and I studied how TV influences behavior, attitudes, and values. That research is the basis of my book *Prime-Time Society: An Anthropological Analysis of Television and Culture* (expanded ed. 2010)—a comparative study of television in Brazil and the United States. One possible effect of television on reproductive behavior was suggested by an account in the popular press. I first considered the possibility that TV might be influencing Brazilian family planning when I read an intriguing article in *the New York Times*. Based on interviews with Brazilians, that report suggested that TV (along with other factors) was influencing Brazilians to limit family size. Fortunately, we had the quantitative data to test that hypothesis.

Our findings in Brazil confirmed many other studies conducted throughout the world in showing that the strongest predictor of (smaller) family size is a woman's educational level. However, two television variables—current viewing level, and especially the number of years of TV presence in the home—were better predictors of (smaller) family size than were many other potential predictors, including income, class, and religiosity. Furthermore, the contraceptive effects of TV exposure had been totally unplanned.

In the four towns in our study with the longest exposure to television, the average woman had a

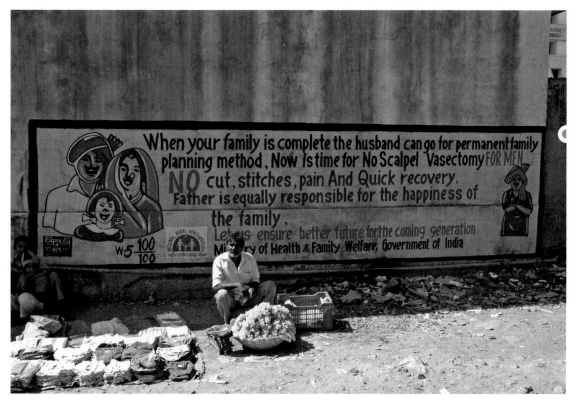

Popular demand for birth control often must be created, for example, through multimedia campaigns, illustrated by the poster shown in this photo from India. In Brazil, however, there has been little direct use of TV to get people to limit their offspring. How then has television influenced Brazilians to plan smaller families?

appreciating

DIVERSITY

What Ever Happened to Class?

All cultures express imagination—in dreams, fantasies, songs, myths, and stories. The arts allow us to imagine a set of possible lives beyond our own. One very important source for this imagining has been the mass media, including television, movies, and the popular press. Here we see how American popular culture has moved from a preoccupation with class differences to a tendency to deny or ignore their existence. Although the media continue to appreciate the lifestyles of the rich and famous, what is gone is the preoccupation with difference. The narratives we see on screen and in print today often present a homogenized upper middle-class lifestyle in which social diversity is minimized and the economic underpinnings of class are ignored.

On television and in the movies now, and even in the pages of novels, people tend to dwell in a classless, homogenized American Never-Never Land. This place is an upgrade, but not a drastic one, from the old neighborhood where Beaver, Ozzie and Harriet, and Donna Reed used to live; it's those yuppified city blocks where the friends on "Friends" and the "Seinfeld" gang had their apartments, or in the now more fashionable version, it's part of the same exurb as One Tree Hill and Wisteria Lane—those airbrushed suburbs where all the cool young people hang out and where the pecking order of sex and looks has replaced the old hierarchy of jobs and money. . . .

In the years before World War II, you couldn't go to the movies or get very far in a novel without being reminded that ours was a society where some were much better off than others,

and where the class divide—especially the gap separating middle from upper—was an inescapable fact of life. The yearning to bridge this gap is most persistently and most romantically evoked in [F. Scott] Fitzgerald, of course, in characters like the former Jay Gatz of Nowhere, N.D. (*The Great Gatsby*), staring across Long Island Sound at that distant green light, and all those moony young men standing in the stag line at the country club, hoping to be noticed by the rich girls.

But there is also a darker version, the one that turns up in Dreiser's "American Tragedy" (1925), for example, where class envy. . . . causes Clyde Griffiths to drown his hopelessly proletarian sweetheart, and where the impossibility of transcending his lot leads him inevitably to the electric chair. (In the upstate New York town of Lycurgus, where the story takes place, Dreiser reminds us that "the line of demarcation and stratification between the rich and the poor was as sharp as though cut by a knife or divided by a high wall.")

Some novels trade on class anxiety to evoke not the dream of betterment but the great American nightmare: the dread of waking up one day and finding yourself at the bottom. Frank Norris's "McTeague" is about a San Francisco dentist who, unmasked as a fraud, sinks to a life of crime and degradation . . . These books . . . suggested that the worst thing that could possibly happen to an American was to topple from his perch on the class ladder. . . .

The poor are noticeably absent, however, in the great artistic flowering of the American novel at the turn of the 19th century, in the work of writers like Henry James, William Dean Howells and Edith Wharton, who are almost exclusively concerned with the rich or the aspiring middle classes: their marriages, their houses, their money and their stuff. Not accidentally, these novels coincided with America's Gilded Age, the era of overnight fortunes and conspicuous spending that followed in the wake of the Civil War . . .

One of the messages of the novel is that in America new money very quickly, in a generation or less, takes on the patina of old; another is that the class structure is necessarily propped up by deceit and double standards . . .

What was the appeal? Vouyerism, in part . . . Fiction back then had a kind of documentary function; it was one of the places Americans went to learn about how other Americans lived. In time novels ceased to be so reportorial. . . .

Novels these days take place in a kind of all-purpose middle-class America, in neighborhoods that could be almost anyplace, and where the burdens are more psychic than economic, with people too busy tending to their faltering relationships to pay much attention to keeping up with the neighbors.

It's a place where everyone fits in, more or less, but where, if you look hard enough, nobody feels really at home.

Novel reading is a middle-class pastime, which is another reason that novels have so often focused on the middle and upper classes. Mass entertainment is another matter, and when Hollywood took up the class theme, which it did in the 1930's, it made a crucial adjustment. During the Depression, the studios,

TV set in her home for 15 years and had 2.3 pregnancies. In the three communities where TV had arrived most recently, the average woman had a home set for four years and had five pregnancies. Thus, length of site exposure was a useful predictor

of reproductive histories. Of course, television exposure at a site is an aspect of that site's increasing overall access to external systems and resources, which usually include improved methods of contraception. But the impact of longer home TV expo-

What's the class status of these "Desperate Housewives," who reside on TV's Wisteria Lane? From what do they derive this class status?

reality television, when Paris Hilton and Nicole Richie drop in on rubes in "The Simple Life," or when upper- and middle-class families trade moms on "Wife Swap" and experience a week of culture shock.

But most reality television trades in a fantasy of sorts, based on the old game-show formula: the idea that you can be plucked out of ordinary life and anointed the new supermodel, the new diva, the new survivor, the new assistant to Donald Trump. You get an instant infusion of wealth and are simultaneously vested with something far more valuable: celebrity, which has become a kind of super-class in America, and one that renders all the old categories irrelevant. Celebrities, in fact, have inherited much of the glamour and sexiness that used to attach itself to the aristocracy . . .

But if the margins have shifted, and if fame, for example, now counts for more than breeding, what persists is the great American theme of longing, of wanting something more, or other, than what you were born with—the wish not to rise in class so much as merely to become classy. If you believe the novels of Dickens or Thackeray, say, the people who feel most at home in Britain are those who know their place, and that has seldom been the case in this country, where the boundaries of class seem just elusive and permeable enough to sustain both the fear of falling and the dream of escape.

which were mostly run by immigrant Jews, turned out a string of formulaic fantasies about life among the Gentile upper crust.

These movies were essentially twin variations on a single theme: either a rich young man falls for a working girl . . . or an heiress takes up with a young man who has to work for a living. . . .

The upper-class person is thawed and humanized by the poorer one, but in every case the exchange is seen as fair and equitable, with the lower-class character giving as much as he or she gets in return. Unlike the novels of class, with their anxieties and sense of unbridgeable

gaps, these are stories of harmony and inclusion, and they added what proved to be an enduring twist on the American view of class: the notion that wealth and privilege are somewhat crippling conditions. . . .

Television used to be fascinated with blue-collar life, in shows like "The Honeymooners," "All in the Family," "Sanford and Son" and "Roseanne," but lately it too has turned its attention elsewhere. The only people who work on televison now are cops, doctors and lawyers, and they're so busy they seldom get to go home. The one vestige of the old curiosity about how other people live is in so-called

sure showed up not only when we compared sites but also within age cohorts, within sites, and among individual women in our total sample.

What social mechanisms were behind these correlations? Family planning opportunities (including contraception) are greater in Brazil now than they used to be. But, as Manoff (1994) notes, based on experience in Africa, Asia, and Latin America, family planning is not assured by the availability of contraceptives. Popular demand for contraception has to be created—often through "social marketing"—that is, planned multimedia campaigns such as that illustrated by the photo above showing an advertisement for vasectomies in India (see also Manoff 1994). In Brazil, however, there has been little direct use of TV to get people to limit their offspring. How then has television influenced Brazilians to plan smaller families?

We noticed that Brazilian TV families tend to have fewer children than traditional small-town Brazilians do. Narrative form and production costs limit the number of players in each *telenovela* (nightly soap opera) to about 50 characters. *Telenovelas* usually are gender-balanced and include three-generation extended families of different social classes, so that some of the main characters can "rise in life" by marrying up. (Notice how the Brazilian portrayal of class diversity contrasts with the current American tendency to overlook class differences, as described in "Appreciating Anthropology" on pp. 536–537.) These narrative conventions limit the number of young children per TV family. We concluded that people's ideas about proper family size are influenced as they see, day after day, nuclear families smaller than the traditional ones in their towns. Furthermore, the aim of commercial television is to sell products and lifestyles. Brazilian TV families routinely are shown enjoying consumer goods and lives of leisure, to which viewers learn to aspire. *Telenovelas* may convey the idea that viewers can achieve such lifestyles by emulating the apparent family planning of TV characters. The effect of Brazilian television on family planning seems to be a corollary of a more general, TV-influenced shift from traditional toward more liberal social attitudes, described in Chapter 1. Anthropologist Janet Dunn's (2000) further field work in Brazil has demonstrated how TV exposure actually works to influence reproductive choice and family planning.

SPORTS AND CULTURE

We now turn to the cultural context of sports and the cultural values expressed in them. Because so much of what we know about sports comes from the media, we also are extending our consideration in this section to the pervasive role of the mass media in contemporary life. This section mainly describes how sports and the media *reflect* culture. Sports and the media *influence* culture as well, as we just saw in the discussion of how Brazilian television modifies social attitudes and family planning. Thus, the influence of media (and sports) on culture and vice versa is reciprocal. Chapter 1 discussed how sports participation can modify body types, and how cultural values (about body proportions) causes sports participation by men and women to vary in different cultures.

Football

Football, we say, is only a game, yet it has become a hugely popular spectator sport. On fall Saturdays, millions of people travel to and from college football games. Smaller congregations meet in high school stadiums. Millions of Americans watch televised football. Indeed, nearly half the adult population of the United States watches the Super Bowl, which attracts fans of diverse ages, ethnic backgrounds, regions, religions, political parties, jobs, social statuses, levels of wealth, and genders.

The popularity of football, particularly professional football, depends directly on the mass media, especially television. Is football, with its territorial incursion, hard hitting, and violence, occasionally resulting in injury, popular because Americans are violent people? Are football spectators vicariously realizing their own hostile and aggressive tendencies? The anthropologist W. Arens (1981) discounts this interpretation. He points out that football is a peculiarly American pastime. Although a similar game is played in Canada, it is less popular there. Baseball has become a popular sport in the Caribbean, parts of Latin America, and Japan. Basketball and volleyball also are spreading. However, throughout most of the world, soccer is the most popular sport. Arens argues that if football were a particularly effective channel for expressing aggression, it would have spread (like soccer and baseball) to many other countries, where people have as many aggressive tendencies and hostile feelings as Americans do. Furthermore, he suggests that if a sport's popularity rested simply on a bloodthirsty temperament, boxing, a far bloodier sport, would be America's national pastime. He concludes reasonably that the explanation for football's popularity lies elsewhere.

Arens contends that football is popular because it symbolizes certain key aspects of American life. In particular, it features teamwork based on specialization and division of labor, which are pervasive features of contemporary life. Susan Montague and Robert Morais (1981) take the analysis a step further. They argue that Americans appreciate football because it presents a miniaturized and simplified version of modern organizations. People have trouble understanding organizational bureaucracies, whether in business, universities, or government. Football, the anthropologists argue, helps us understand how decisions are made and rewards are allocated in organizations.

Montague and Morais link football's values, particularly teamwork, to those associated with business. Like corporate workers, the ideal players are diligent and dedicated to the team. Within corporations, however, decision making is complicated, and workers aren't always rewarded for their dedication and good job performance. Decisions are simpler and rewards are more consistent in football, these anthropologists contend, and this helps explain its popularity. Even if we can't figure out how ExxonMobil or Microsoft run, any fan can become an expert on football's rules, teams, scores, statistics, and patterns of play. Even more important, football suggests that the values stressed by business really do pay off. Teams whose members work the hardest, show the most spirit, and best develop and coordinate their talents can be expected to win more often than other teams do.

Illustrating the values of hard work and teamwork, consider some quotes from a story about the selection of New England Patriots quarterback Tom Brady as 2007 Associated Press Male Athlete of the Year. On the value of hard work: "Tom Brady arrives at Gillette Stadium before the sun comes up. As always, there is work to be done, and no time to waste." "You see him here at 6:15 in the morning, lifting weights, watching film and working out." On the value of teamwork: "I play in a team sport," Brady said. "Everybody I play with is responsible for what each of us accomplishes as individuals and for what we all accomplish as a team." (All quotes from Ulman 2007).

What Determines International Sports Success?

Why do countries excel at particular sports? Why do certain nations pile up dozens of Olympic medals while others win only a handful, or none at all? It isn't simply a matter of rich and poor, developed and underdeveloped, or even of governmental or other institutional support of promising athletes. It isn't even a question of a "national will to win," for although certain nations stress winning even more than Americans do, a cultural focus on winning doesn't necessarily lead to the desired result.

Cultural values, social forces, and the media influence international sports success. We can see this by contrasting the United States and Brazil, two countries with continental proportions and large, physically and ethnically diverse populations. Although each is its continent's major economic power, they offer revealing contrasts in Olympic success: In the 2008 Summer Olympics the United States won 110 medals, while Brazil managed only 15.

Through visual demonstration, commentary, and explanation of rules and training, the media can heighten interest in all kinds of sports—amateur and professional, team and individual, spectator and participatory. Americans' interest in sports has been honed over the years by an ever-growing media establishment, which provides a steady stream of matches, games, playoffs, championships, and analyses. Cable and satellite TV offer almost constant sports coverage, including packages for every sport and season. The Super Bowl is a national event. The Olympic games get extensive coverage and attract significant audi-

ences. Brazilian television, by contrast, has much less sports coverage, with no nationally televised annual event comparable to the Superbowl or the World Series. The World (soccer) Cup, held every four years, is the only sports event that consistently draws huge national audiences.

In international competition, outstanding Brazilian athletes, such as 1984 Olympic silver medalist swimmer Ricardo Prado—or any soccer player in the Olympics or World Cup—represent Brazilians, almost in the same way as Congress is said to represent the people of the United States. A win by a Brazilian team or the occasional nationally known individual athlete is felt to bring respect to the entire nation, but the Brazilian media are strikingly intolerant of losers. When Prado swam for his medal in the finals of the 400 Individual Medley (IM), during prime time on national TV, one newsmagazine observed that "it was as though he was the country with a swimsuit on, jumping in the pool in a collective search for success" (*Isto É* 1984). Prado's own feelings confirmed the magazine, "When I was on the stands, I thought of just one thing: what they'll think of the result in Brazil." After beating his old world record by 1.33 seconds, in a second-place finish, Prado told a fellow team member, "I think I did everything right. I feel like a winner, but will they think I'm a loser in Brazil?" Prado realized as he swam that he was performing in prime time and that "all of Brazil would be watching" (*Veja* 1984a). He complained about having the expectations of an entire country focused on him. He contrasted the situations of Brazilian and American athletes. The United States has, he said, so many athletes that no single one has to summarize the country's hopes (*Veja* 1984a).

Fortunately, Brazil did seem to value Prado's performance, which was responsible for "Brazil's best result ever in Olympic swimming" (*Veja* 1984a). Previously the country had won a total of three bronze medals. Labeling Prado "the man of silver," the media never tired of characterizing his main event, the 400 IM, in which he once had held the world record, as the most challenging event in swimming. However, the kind words for Ricardo Prado did not extend to the rest of the Brazilian team. The press lamented their "succession of failures . . . accumulated in the first days of competition" (*Veja* 1984a). (Brazil finally got swimming gold at the 2008 games in

New England Patriots quarterback Tom Brady (12) calls a play during an NFL football game against the Denver Broncos on Sunday, Oct. 11, 2009, in Denver. Brady exemplifies the values of hard work and teamwork considered to be important in football.

Swimmers take off in a heat of the Men's 50m Butterfly at the World Swimming Championships in Rome, Italy, on July 26, 2009. Such sports as swimming, diving, and track give special value not only to winning but also to "personal bests" and "comebacks."

Beijing, with Cesar Cielo Filho winning the 50 meter freestyle race.)

Because Brazilian athletes are expected almost to be their country, and because team sports are emphasized, the Brazilian media focus too exclusively on winning. Winning, of course, is also an American cultural value, particularly for team sports, as in Brazil. American football coaches are famous for comments such as "Winning isn't everything; it's the only thing" and "Show me a good loser and I'll show you a loser." However, and particularly for sports such as running, swimming, diving, gymnastics, and skating, which focus on the individual, and in which American athletes usually do well, American culture also admires "moral victories," "personal bests," "comeback athletes," and "Special Olympics," and commends those who run good races without finishing first. In amateur and individual sports, American culture tells us that hard work and personal improvement can be as important as winning.

Americans are so accustomed to being told that their culture overemphasizes winning that they may find it hard to believe that other cultures value it even more. Brazil certainly does. Brazilian sports enthusiasts are preoccupied with world records, probably because only a win (as in soccer) or a best time (as in swimming) can make Brazil indisputably, even if temporarily, the best in the world at something. Prado's former world record in the 400 IM was mentioned constantly in the press prior to his Olympic swim. Such a best-time standard also provides Brazilians with a ready basis to fault a swimmer or runner for not going

fast enough, when they don't make previous times. One might predict, accurately, that sports with more subjective standards would not be very popular in Brazil. Brazilians like to assign blame to athletes who fail them, and negative comments about gymnasts or divers are more difficult because grace and execution can't be quantified as easily as time can.

Brazilians, I think, value winning so much because it is so rare. In the United States, resources are more abundant, social classes less marked, opportunities for achievement more numerous, poverty less pervasive, and individual social mobility easier. American society has room for many winners. Brazilian society is more stratified; a much smaller middle class and elite group comprise perhaps a third of the population. Brazilian sports echo lessons from the larger society: victories are scarce and reserved for the privileged few.

Being versus Doing

The factors believed to contribute to sports success belong to a larger context of cultural values. Particularly relevant is the contrast between ascribed and achieved status. Individuals have little control over their ascribed statuses (e.g., age, gender); these depend on what one *is* rather than what one *does*. On the other hand, people have more control over their achieved statuses (e.g., student, golfer, tennis player). Because we start out the same (at least in the eyes of American law), American culture emphasizes achieved over ascribed status: We are supposed to make of our lives what we will and can. Success comes through achievement. An American's identity emerges as a result of what he or she does.

In Brazil, on the other hand, identity rests on being rather than doing, on what one is from the start—a strand in a web of personal connections, originating in social class and the extended family. Parents, in-laws, and extended kin routinely are tapped for entries to desired settings and positions. Family position and network membership contribute substantially to individual fortune, and all social life is hierarchical. High-status Brazilians don't stand patiently in line as Americans do. Important people expect their business to be attended to immediately, and social inferiors readily yield. Rules don't apply uniformly, but differentially, according to social class. The final resort in any conversation is "Do you know who you're talking to?" The American opposite, reflecting our democratic and egalitarian ethos, is "Who do you think you are?" (DaMatta 1991).

The following description of a Brazilian judo medalist (as reported by *Veja* magazine) illustrates the importance of ascribed status and the fact that in Brazilian life victories are regarded as scarce and reserved for the privileged few.

> Middle-weight Olympic bronze medalist Walter Carmona began judo at age six and became a São Paulo champion at twelve . . . Carmona lives in São Paulo with his family (father, mother, siblings) . . . He is fully supported by his father, a factory owner. Walter Carmona's life has been comfortable—he has been able to study and dedicate himself to judo without worries (Veja 1984*b*, p. 61).

Faced with an athlete from a well-off family, American reporters, by contrast, rarely conclude that privilege is the main reason for success.

American media almost always focus on some aspect of doing, some special personal triumph or achievement. Often this involves the athlete's struggle with adversity (illness, injury, pain, the death of a parent, sibling, friend, or coach). The featured athlete is presented as not only successful but noble and self-sacrificing as well.

Given the Brazilian focus on ascribed status, the guiding assumption is that one can't do more than what one is. One year the Brazilian Olympic Committee sent no female swimmers to the Summer Olympics because none had made arbitrarily established cutoff times. This excluded a South American record holder, while swimmers with no better times were attending from other countries. No one seemed to imagine that Olympic excitement might spur swimmers to extraordinary efforts.

Achievement-oriented American sports coverage, in stark contrast, feasts on unexpected results, illustrating adherence to the American sports credo originally enunciated by the New York Yankee legend Yogi Berra: "It's not over till it's over." American culture, supposedly so practical and realistic, has a remarkable faith in coming from behind—in unexpected and miraculous achievements.

These values are those of an achievement-oriented society where (ideally) "anything is possible" compared with an ascribed-status society in which it's ended before it's begun. In American sports coverage, underdogs and unexpected results, virtually ignored by the Brazilian media, provide some of the "brightest" moments. Brazilian culture has little interest in the unexpected. Athletes internalize these values. Brazilians assume that if you go into an event with a top seed time, as Ricardo Prado did, you've got a chance to win a medal. Prado's second-place finish made perfect

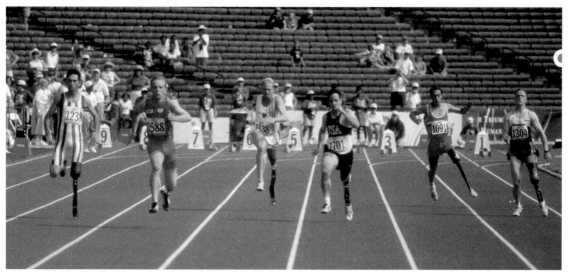

Reflecting larger cultural values, Americans usually do well in sports that emphasize individual achievement. "Special Olympics," such as the one shown here in Atlanta, Georgia, commend people who run good races without being the best in the world.

Chemically achieved success violates the American work ethic. The success of an artificially modified being is illegitimate compared with the achievements of a self-made champion. Anabolic (protein-building) steroids speed up muscle recovery after exercise, increasing muscle bulk and allowing a more intensive training schedule. Side effects include aggressiveness, liver damage, edema (fluid retention), impotence, acne, priapism (persistent painful erection), and virilization in women.

that by the time athletes actually enter Olympic competition all are so similar (the American value of equality) that only mysterious and chance factors can explain variable success. The American focus on the unexpected applies to losses as well as wins. Such concepts as chance, fate, mystery, and uncertainty are viewed as legitimate reasons for defeat. Runners and skaters fall; ligaments tear; a gymnast "inexplicably" falls off the pommel horse.

Americans thus recognize chance disaster as companion to unexpected success, but Brazilians place more responsibility on the individual, assigning personal fault. Less is attributed to factors beyond human control. When individuals who should have performed well don't, they are blamed for their failures. It is culturally appropriate in Brazil to use poor health as an excuse for losing. Brazilian athletes routinely mention colds or diarrhea as a reason for a poor performance, or even for withdrawing from a race at the last minute (*Veja* 1984c). Brazilians use health problems as an excuse, whereas Americans use poor health as a challenge that often can be met and bested.

Despite its characteristic focus on doing, American culture does not insist that individuals can fully control outcomes, and it's not as necessary as it is in Brazil for athletes to explain their own failures. The Brazilian media, by contrast, feel it necessary to assign fault for failure—and this usually means blaming the athlete(s). Characteristically, the American media talk much more about the injuries and illnesses of the victors and finishers than those of the losers and quitters. Recently, in the baseball steroid scandal, Americans have faulted athletes for chemically achieved success, certainly a violation of the American work ethic. Even if one is *doing* drugs, steroid use alters what one *is*. The success of a modified being is illegitimate compared with the achievements of an independently self-made champion.

sense back home because his former world record had been bettered before the race began.

Given the overwhelming value American culture places on work, it might seem surprising that our media devote so much attention to unforeseen results and so little to the years of training, preparation, and competition that underlie Olympic performance. It probably is assumed that hard work is so obvious and fundamental that it goes without saying. Or perhaps the assumption is

Acing the
COURSE

Summary

1. Even if they lack a word for "art," people everywhere do associate an aesthetic experience with objects and events having certain qualities. The arts, sometimes called "expressive culture," include the visual arts, literature (written and oral), music, and theater arts. Some issues raised about religion also apply to art. If we adopt a special attitude or demeanor when confronting a sacred object, do we display something similar with art? Much art has been done in association with religion. In tribal performances, the arts and religion often mix. But non-Western art isn't always linked to religion.

2. The special places where we find art include museums, concert halls, opera houses, and theaters. However, the boundary between what's art and what's not may be blurred. Variation in

art appreciation is especially common in contemporary society, with its professional artists and critics and great cultural diversity.

3. Those who work with non-Western art have been criticized for ignoring individual artists and for focusing too much on the social context and collective artistic production. Art is work, albeit creative work. In state societies, some people manage to support themselves as full-time artists. In nonstates artists are normally part-time. Community standards judge the mastery and completion displayed in a work of art. Typically, the arts are exhibited, evaluated, performed, and appreciated in society. Music, which is often performed in groups, is among the most social of the arts. Folk art, music, and lore refer to the expressive culture of ordinary, usually rural, people.

4. Art can stand for tradition, even when traditional art is removed from its original context. Art can express community sentiment, with political goals, used to call attention to social issues. Often, art is meant to commemorate and to last. Growing acceptance of the anthropological definition of culture has guided the humanities beyond fine art, elite art, and Western art to the creative expressions of the masses and of many cultures. Myths, legends, tales, and the art of storytelling often play important roles in the transmission of culture. Many societies offer career tracks in the arts; a child born into a particular family or lineage may discover that he or she is destined for a career in leather working or weaving.

5. The arts go on changing, although certain art forms have survived for thousands of years. Countries and cultures are known for particular contributions. Today, a huge "arts and leisure" industry links Western and non-Western art forms in an international network with both aesthetic and commercial dimensions.

6. Any media-borne message can be analyzed as a text, something that can be "read"—that is, processed, interpreted, and assigned meaning by anyone exposed to it. People use media to validate beliefs, indulge fantasies, seek out messages, make social comparisons, relieve frustrations, chart social courses, and resist unequal power relations. The media can provide common ground for social groups. Length of home TV exposure is a useful measure of the impact of television on values, attitudes, and beliefs. The effect of Brazilian television on family planning seems to be a corollary of a more general TV-influenced shift from traditional toward more liberal social attitudes.

7. Much of what we know about sports comes from the media. Sports and the media both reflect and influence culture. Football symbolizes and simplifies certain key aspects of American life and values (e.g., hard work and teamwork). Cultural values, social forces, and the media influence international sports success. In amateur and individual sports, American culture tells us that hard work and personal improvement can be as important as winning. Other cultures, such as Brazil, may value winning even more than Americans do. The factors believed to contribute to sports success belong to a larger context of cultural values. Particularly relevant is the contrast between ascribed and achieved status: being versus doing. An American's identity emerges as a result of what he or she does. In Brazil, by contrast, identity rests on being: what one is from the start—a strand in a web of personal connections, originating in social class and the extended family.

Key Terms

aesthetics 519
art 519
arts 519
catharsis 527

ethnomusicology 523
expressive culture 518
folk 524
text 533

MULTIPLE CHOICE

Test Yourself!

1. Which of the following statements about the relationship between art and religion is true?
   a. All non-Western art is produced for religious purposes.
   b. All the greatest accomplishments in Western art have been commissioned by formal religions.
   c. Since nonstate societies lack permanent buildings dedicated to art (museums) or religion (temples, churches), there is no link between art and religion in these societies.
   d. Western art today is completely divorced from religion.
   e. Most or all societies use creative expression for both religious and secular purposes.

2. How do most Western societies view, erroneously, non-Western art?
   a. as always linked to religion
   b. as purely secular
   c. as purely profane
   d. as the product of individuals
   e. as unimportant

3. The example of the Kalabari wooden sculpture that serves as "house" for spirits makes the point that
   a. sculpture is always art.
   b. religious sculpture is not always art.

c. the Kalabari do not have standards for carving.

d. non-Westerners have no concept of completeness.

e. non-Western art always has some kind of connection to religion.

4. To emphasize the dynamic nature of aesthetic values and tastes, this chapter describes how French impressionism was initially

a. heralded as one of the great innovations of 19th century painting.

b. based on abstract sand paintings from French colonies in West Africa.

c. a throwback to "old school" painting styles.

d. criticized for being too sketchy and spontaneous to be considered art.

e. lauded for being at the forefront of high society.

5. Symbolic thinking in art is an important aspect of appreciating the novelty of the emergence of culture in human history. Symbolic thinking means that

a. other forms of thinking, such as analytical skills, are sacrificed for the sake of aesthetic pleasure.

b. scientific thought becomes less important in society.

c. human groups stop making and using tools for practical ends and instead use them for ritual.

d. people use one thing to mean something else.

e. some cultural skills are more adaptive than others.

6. Exploring the possible biological roots of music, researchers have speculated that music might have been adaptive in human evolution because

a. musically talented mothers had an easier time calming their babies (calmer babies attract fewer predators, grant more rest to their moms, and are less likely to be mistreated).

b. music promotes competition.

c. music may have made the activities of hunting and gathering more productive.

d. singing and dancing are correlated with higher rates of pregnancy.

e. musically talented mothers increased their chances of attracting physically fit and caring male partners.

7. Alberto Costa's findings of what attracted young people and women in Brazil to *telenovelas* is an example of how

a. American soap operas are more popular in rural Brazil.

b. popular culture can be used to express discontent, in this case with conservative local norms.

c. people identify less and less with national TV programs.

d. cultural norms have not changed during the last 50 years in Brazil.

e. there has been a rise in conservative attitudes among the younger generation of Brazilians.

8. Brazilians and Italians being just as excited, at the same moment but with radically different emotions, by a soccer goal scored in a World Cup match is an example of

a. art's ability to provoke catharsis.

b. how people can find in messages in international that are unavailable in the local setting.

c. how much is lost in translation.

d. media's role as a social cement by providing a common ground for people, nationally and internationally.

e. how much more competitive Brazilians and Italians are in sports compared to everyone else.

9. A study assessing how TV influences behavior, attitudes, and values in Brazil found that smaller family size correlated with the number of years of TV presence in the home. What probable reason did researchers put forth to explain this correlation?

a. There is no social mechanism that can explain this correlation.

b. *Telenovelas* may convey the idea that viewers can achieve a different lifestyle (i.e. having fewer children) by emulating the apparent family planning of TV characters.

c. Greater exposure to TV was correlated to less time engaged in sexual activity.

d. Women with longer exposures to the moral code of TV characters rejected their extreme liberal ways.

e. More TV time correlated with higher divorce rates.

10. Cultural values, social forces, and the media influence international sports success. When comparing the United States and Brazil, which of the following is true?

a. Brazil has much more television sports coverage than the United States.

b. Americans' interest in sports has been honed much more over the years by an ever-growing media establishment.

c. The popularity of football among Americans proves that Americans are more violent than Brazilians.

d. Researchers have found that the increasing popularity of soccer correlates with less interest in teamwork.

e. Americans are more focused on winning than Brazilians are.

FILL IN THE BLANK

1. The term _____ *culture* is synonymous with the arts.

2. _____ is the study of the musics of the world and of music as an aspect of culture.

3. _____ refers to an intense emotional release.

4. Around _____ years ago, some of the world's first artists occupied Blombos Cave in what is now South Africa. In Europe, evidence of art goes back to about _____ years.

5. _____ can refer to anything that can be "read"—that is, processed, interpreted, and assigned meaning, by anyone exposed to it.

CRITICAL THINKING

1. Recall the last time you were in an art museum. What did you like, and why? How much of your aesthetic tastes can you attribute to your education, to your culture? How much do you think responds to your own individual tastes? How can you make the distinction?

2. Think of a musical composition or performance you consider to be art, but whose status as such is debatable. How would you convince someone else that it is art? What kinds of arguments against your position would you expect to hear?

3. Can you think of a political dispute involving art or the arts? What were the different positions being debated?

4. Media consumers actively select, evaluate, and interpret media in ways that make sense to them. People use media for all sorts of reasons. What are some examples? Which are most relevant to the way you consume, and maybe even creatively alter and produce, media?

5. This chapter describes how sports and the media *reflect* culture. Can you come up with examples of how sports and media *influence* culture?

Anderson, R. L.
   2004 *Calliope's Sisters: A Comparative Study of Philosophies of Art*, 2nd ed. Upper Saddle River, NJ: Prentice Hall. A comparative study of aesthetics in 10 cultures.

Askew, K. M., and R. R. Wilk, eds.
   2002 *The Anthropology of Media: A Reader.* Malden, MA: Oxford, Blackwell. Useful anthology, with numerous case studies involving media, society, and culture.

Blanchard, K.
   1995 *The Anthropology of Sport: An Introduction*, rev. ed. Westport, CT: Bergin and Garvey. Sports and games in crosscultural perspective.

Hatcher, E. P.
   1999 *Art as Culture: An Introduction to the Anthropology of Art*, 2nd ed. Westport, CT: Bergin & Garvey. Up-to-date introduction.

Morphy, H., and M. Perkins, eds.
   2006 *The Anthropology of Art: A Reader.* Malden, MA: Oxford/Blackwell. Survey of the major issues, with a focus on visual art.

Myers, F. R.
   2002 *Painting Culture: The Making of an Aboriginal High Art.* Durham, NC: Duke University Press. Artistic transformation in Australia's western desert.

Suggested Additional Readings

Internet Exercises

Go to our Online Learning Center website at **www.mhhe.com/kottak** for Internet exercises directly related to the content of this chapter.

When and why did the world system develop, and what is it like today?

When and how did European colonialism develop and how is its legacy expressed in postcolonial studies?

How do colonialism, Communism, neoliberalism, development, and industrialization exemplify intervention philosophies?

In Kebili, Tunisia, two Bedouin men use a laptop in the desert. Might they be uploading a photo of their camel to Facebook?

The World System and Colonialism

understanding OURSELVES

In our 21st century world system, people are linked as never before by modern means of transportation and communication. Descendants of villages that hosted ethnographers a generation ago now live transnational lives. For me, some of the most vivid illustrations of this new transnationalism come from Madagascar. They begin in Ambalavao, a town in southern Betsileo country, where I rented a small house in 1966–1967.

By 1966, Madagascar had gained independence from France, but its towns still had foreigners to remind them of colonialism. Besides my wife and me, Ambalavao had at least a dozen world-system agents, including an Indian cloth merchant, Chinese grocers, and a few French people. Two young men in the French equivalent of the Peace Corps were there teaching school. One of them, Noel, lived across the street from a prominent local family. Since Noel often spoke disparagingly of the Malagasy, I was surprised to see him courting a young woman from this family. She was Lenore, the sister of Leon, a schoolteacher who became my good friend.

My next trip to Madagascar was a brief visit in February 1981. I had to spend a few days in Antananarivo, the capital. There I was confined each evening to the newly built Hilton hotel by a curfew imposed after a civil insurrection. I shared the hotel with a group of Russian military pilots, there to teach the Malagasy to defend their island, strategically placed in the Indian Ocean, against imagined enemies. Later, I went down to Betsileo country to visit Leon, my schoolteacher friend from Ambalavao, who had become a prominent politician. Unfortunately for me, he was in Moscow, participating in a three-month exchange program.

During my next visit to Madagascar, in summer 1990, I met Emily, the 22-year-old daughter of Noel and Lenore, whose courtship I had witnessed in 1967. One of her aunts brought Emily to meet me at my hotel in Antananarivo. Emily was about to visit several cities in the United States, where she planned to study marketing. I met her again just a few months later in Gainesville, Florida. She asked me about her father, whom she had never met. She had sent several letters to France, but Noel had never responded.

Descendants of Ambalavao now live all over the world. Emily, a child of colonialism, has two aunts in France (Malagasy women married to French men) and another in Germany (working as a diplomat). Members of her family, which is not especially wealthy, have traveled to Russia, Canada, the United States, France, Germany, and West Africa. How many of your classmates, including perhaps you, yourself, have recent transnational roots? A descendant of a rural Kenyan village has even been elected president of the United States. How about that.

Although field work in small communities is anthropology's hallmark, isolated groups are impossible to find today. Truly isolated societies probably never have existed. For thousands of years, human groups have been in contact with one another. Local societies always have participated in a larger system, which today has global dimensions—we call it the *modern world system,* by which we mean a world in which nations are economically and politically interdependent.

THE WORLD SYSTEM

The world system and the relations among the countries within it are shaped by the capitalist world economy. A huge increase in international trade during and after the 15th century led to the **capitalist world economy** (Wallerstein 1982, 2004b), a single world system committed to production for sale or exchange, with the object of maximizing profits rather than supplying domestic needs. **Capital** refers to wealth or resources invested in business, with the intent of using the means of production to make a profit.

World-system theory can be traced to the French social historian Fernand Braudel. In his three-volume work *Civilization and Capitalism, 15th–18th Century* (1981, 1982, 1992), Braudel argued that society consists of interrelated parts assembled into a system. Societies are subsystems of larger systems, with the world system the largest. The key claim of **world-system theory** is that an identifiable social system, based on wealth and power differentials, extends beyond individual countries. That system is formed by a set of economic and political relations that has characterized much of the globe since the 16th century, when the Old World established regular contact with the New World (see Bodley 2003).

According to Wallerstein (1982, 2004b), countries within the world system occupy three different positions of economic and political power: core, periphery, and semiperiphery. The geographic center, or **core,** the dominant position in the world system, includes the strongest and most powerful nations. In core nations, "the complexity of economic activities and the level of capital accumulation is the greatest" (Thompson 1983, p. 12). With its sophisticated technologies and mechanized production, the core churns out products that flow mainly to other core countries. Some also go to the periphery and semiperiphery. According to Arrighi (1994), the core monopolizes the most profitable activities, especially the control of world finance.

Semiperiphery and periphery countries have less power, wealth, and influence than the core does. The **semiperiphery** is intermediate between the core and the periphery. Contemporary nations of the semiperiphery are industrialized. Like core nations, they export both industrial goods and commodities, but they lack the power and economic dominance of core nations. Thus Brazil, a semiperiphery nation, exports automobiles to Nigeria (a periphery nation) and auto engines, orange juice extract, coffee, and shrimp to the United States (a core nation). The **periphery** includes the world's least privileged and powerful countries. Economic activities there are less mechanized than are those in the semiperiphery, although some degree of industrialization has reached even periphery nations. The periphery produces raw materials, agricultural commodities, and, increasingly, human labor for export to the core and the semiperiphery (Shannon 1996).

In the United States and Western Europe today, immigration—legal and illegal—from the periphery and semiperiphery supplies cheap labor for agriculture in core countries. U.S. states as distant as California, Michigan, and South Carolina make significant use of farm labor from Mexico. The availability of relatively cheap workers from noncore nations such as Mexico (in the United States) and Turkey (in Germany) benefits farmers and business owners in core countries, while also supplying remittances to families in the semiperiphery and periphery. As a result of 21st-century telecommunications technology, cheap labor doesn't even need to migrate to the United States. Thousands of families in India are being supported as American companies "outsource" jobs—from telephone assistance to software engineering—to nations outside the core.

Consider recent moves by IBM, the world's largest information technology company. On June 24, 2005, the *New York Times* reported that IBM was planning to hire more than 14,000 additional workers in India, while laying off some 13,000 workers in Europe and the United States (Lohr 2005). These figures illustrate the ongoing globalization of work and the migration of even skilled jobs to low-wage countries. Its critics accuse IBM of shopping the globe for the cheapest labor, to enhance corporate profits at the expense of wages, benefits, and job security in the United States and other developed countries. In explaining the hiring in India, an IBM senior vice president (quoted in Lohr 2005) cited a surging demand for technology services in India's thriving economy and the opportunity to tap the many skilled Indian software engineers to work on projects around the world. Skilled Western workers must compete now against well-educated workers in such low-wage countries as India, where an experienced software programmer earns one-fifth the average salary of a comparable American worker—$15,000 versus $75,000 (Lohr 2005).

The Emergence of the World System

By the 15th century Europeans were profiting from a transoceanic trade-oriented economy, and people worldwide entered Europe's sphere of influence. What was new was the transatlantic component of a long history of Old World sailing and commerce. As early as 600 B.C.E., the Phoenicians/Carthaginians sailed around Britain on regular trade routes and circumnavigated Africa. Likewise, Indonesia and Africa have been linked in Indian Ocean trade for at least 2000 years. In the 15th century Europe established regular contact with Asia, Africa, and

capitalist world economy
Profit-oriented global economy based on production for sale.

capital
Wealth invested with the intent of producing profit.

world-system theory
Idea that a discernible social system, based on wealth and power differentials, transcends individual countries.

core
Dominant position in the world system; nations with advanced systems of production.

semiperiphery
Position in the world system intermediate between core and periphery.

periphery
Weakest structural and economic position in the world system.

appreciating DIVERSITY

Bones Reveal Some Truth in "Noble Savage" Myth

Conflict and violence are variable aspects of human diversity. Here we examine an anthropological debate about the origin and nature of warfare and the role of European contact in fostering conflicts among indigenous peoples in the Americas. Violence among Native Americans did increase after contact. As the article begins, it suggests, mistakenly, that Native Americans lived in prehistory and lacked "civilization." In fact, Native Americans developed states and "civilizations" (e.g., Aztec, Maya, Inca) comparable to those of the Old World (e.g., ancient Mesopotamia and Egypt). Native Americans, most notably the Maya, also developed writing, which they used to record their history—rendering the label prehistory inaccurate. As you read, to understand why violence increased after contact, pay attention to the role of trade, disease, and slave raiding.

A romantic-sounding notion dating back more than 200 years has it that people in prehistory, such as Native Americans, lived in peace and harmony.

Then "civilization" showed up, sowing violence and discord. Some see this claim as naive. It even has a derisive nickname, the "noble savage myth." But new research seems to suggest the "myth" contains at least some truth. Researchers examined thousands of Native American skeletons and found that those from after Christopher Columbus landed in the New World showed a rate of traumatic injuries more than 50 percent higher than those from before the Europeans arrived.

"Traumatic injuries do increase really significantly," said Philip L. Walker, an anthropology professor at the University of California at Santa Barbara, who conducted the study with Richard H. Steckel of Ohio State University.

The findings suggest "Native Americans were involved in more violence after the Europeans arrived than before," Walker said. But he emphasized there was also widespread violence before the Europeans came. Nevertheless, he said, "probably we're just seeing the tip of the iceberg" as far as the difference between violence levels before and after. That's because as many as half of bullet wounds miss the skeleton. Thus, the study couldn't detect much firearm violence, though some tribes wiped each other out using European-supplied guns.

The findings shed light on a controversy that has stirred not only living room discussions, but also an intense, sometimes ugly debate among anthropologists.

It involves two opposing views of human nature: Are we hard-wired for violence, or pushed into it?

Anthropologists who believe the latter seized on the findings as evidence for their view. "What it all says to me is that humans aren't demonic. Human males don't have an

The encounter between Hernán Cortés (1485–1547) and Montezuma II (1466–1520) is the subject of this 1820 painting by Gallo Gallina of Milan, Italy. Cortés went on to conquer Montezuma's Aztec empire.

eventually the New World (the Caribbean and the Americas). Christopher Columbus's first voyage from Spain to the Bahamas and the Caribbean in 1492 was soon followed by additional voyages. These journeys opened the way for a major exchange of people, resources, products, ideas, and diseases, as the Old and New Worlds were forever linked (Crosby 2003; Diamond 1997; Fagan 1998; Viola and Margolis 1991). Led by Spain and Portugal, Europeans extracted silver and gold, conquered the natives (taking some as slaves), and colonized their lands.

The frequency and nature of conflict, violence, and warfare vary among the world's cultures. This chapter's "Appreciating Diversity" examines a debate about the origin and characteristics of warfare among Native Americans. Did European contact play a role in fostering increased violence? The *Columbian exchange* is the term for the spread of people, resources, products, ideas, and diseases ingrained propensity for war . . . They can learn to be very peaceful, or terribly violent," said R. Brian Ferguson, a professor of anthropology at Rutgers University in Newark. Ferguson contends that before about 10,000 years ago, war was virtually nonexistent. But experts on the opposing side also said the findings fit their views.

"A 50 percent increase is the equivalent of moving from a suburb to the city, in terms of violence," said Charles Stanish, a professor of anthropology at the University of California at Los Angeles. "This shows the Native Americans were like us. Under stress, they fought more." Both sides called the study, which was presented Friday at the annual meeting of the American Association of Physical Anthropologists in Buffalo, a valuable contribution . . .

Walker and colleagues examined the skeletons of 3,375 pre-Columbian and 1,165 post-Columbian Native Americans, from archaeological sites throughout North and Central America.

The North Americans came mostly from the coasts and the Great Lakes region, Walker said.

Pre-Columbian skeletons showed an 11 percent incidence of traumatic injuries, he said, compared with almost 17 percent for the post-Columbians.

Walker said his findings surprised him. "I wasn't really expecting it," he said. Yet it undeniably suggests violence, he added. Most of the increase consisted of head injuries in young males, "which conforms pretty closely to the pattern you see today in homicides."

The researchers defined "traumatic injury" as anything leaving a mark on the skeleton, such as a skull fracture, a healed broken arm, or an embedded arrow point or bullet.

Walker said that although part of the increased injury rate doubtless stems from violence by whites themselves, it probably reflects mostly native-on-native violence. "In a lot of cases, such as in California, there weren't that many Europeans around—just a few priests, and thousands of Indians," he said.

Walker said the higher injury rate could have many explanations. Increased violence is normally associated with more densely populated, settled life, which Native Americans experienced in modernity, he said. Disease could also touch off war, he said.

"Here in California, there was a lot of inter-village warfare associated with the introduction of European diseases. People would attribute the disease to evil shamanic activity in another village," he said. Ferguson cited other factors. The Europeans often drew natives into their imperial wars, he said.

"Sometimes, the Europeans would enable someone to pursue a preexisting fight more aggressively, by backing one side," he added. Other times, he said, Europeans got natives to conduct slave raids on one another. Natives also fought over control of areas around trading outposts, to become middlemen, he said. "Sometimes that was a life-or-death matter, since it meant the difference between who would get guns or not." Stanish agreed. "Obviously, having an expanding imperial power coming at you is going to exacerbate tensions," he said . . . They're going to push you somewhere—into other groups."

"You're also going to get competition over access to the Europeans, who are a form of wealth," he added. Native Americans fought over areas rich in fur, which the whites would buy.

Yet Native American warfare was widespread long before that, Stanish said. . . .

Keith F. Otterbein, an anthropology professor at the State University of New York at Buffalo, said the skeleton findings contribute to a balanced, middle-of-the-road view.

"The folks who are saying there was no early warfare—they're wrong, too. There is, in fact, a myth of the peaceful savage," he said. Otterbein said the controversy won't end here; both sides are too ideologically entrenched.

"Underlying the 'noble savage' myth," Stanish said, "is a political agenda by both the far right and far left. The right tries to turn the 'savages' into our little brown brothers, who need to be pulled up . . . On the left, they have another agenda, that the Western world is bad."

SOURCE: Jack Lucentini, "Bones Reveal Some Truth in 'Noble Savage Myth'," *Washington Post*, April 15, 2002. Reprinted by permission of Jack Lucentini.

between eastern and western hemispheres after contact. As you read "Appreciating Diversity," consider the role of trade, disease, and slave raiding on Native Americans, including conflict and warfare.

Previously in Europe as throughout the world, rural people had produced mainly for their own needs, growing their own food and making clothing, furniture, and tools from local products. Production beyond immediate needs was undertaken to pay taxes and to purchase trade items such as salt and iron. As late as 1650 the English diet, like diets in most of the world today, was based on locally grown starches (Mintz 1985). In the 200 years that followed, however, the English became extraordinary consumers of imported goods. One of the earliest and most popular of those goods was sugar (Mintz 1985).

Sugarcane originally was domesticated in Papua New Guinea, and sugar was first processed in India. Reaching Europe via the Middle

East and the eastern Mediterranean, it was carried to the New World by Columbus (Mintz 1985). The climate of Brazil and the Caribbean proved ideal for growing sugarcane, and Europeans built plantations there to supply the growing demand for sugar. This led to the development in the 17th century of a plantation economy based on a single cash crop—a system known as *monocrop* production.

The demand for sugar in a growing international market spurred the development of the transatlantic slave trade and New World plantation economies based on slave labor. By the 18th century, an increased English demand for raw cotton led to rapid settlement of what is now the

Industrial Revolution (In Europe, after 1750), socioeconomic transformation through industrialization.

From producer to consumer, in the modern world system. The top photo, taken in the Caribbean nation of Dominica, shows the hard labor required to extract sugar using a manual press. In the bottom photo, an English middle-class family enjoys afternoon tea, sweetened with imported sugar. Which of the ingredients in your breakfast today were imported?

southeastern United States and the emergence there of another slave-based monocrop production system. Like sugar, cotton was a key trade item that fueled the growth of the world system.

INDUSTRIALIZATION

By the 18th century the stage had been set for the **Industrial Revolution**—the historical transformation (in Europe, after 1750) of "traditional" into "modern" societies through industrialization of the economy. The seeds of industrial society were planted well before the 18th century (Gimpel 1988). For example, a knitting machine invented in England in 1589 was so far ahead of its time that it played a profitable role in factories two and three centuries later. The appearance of cloth mills late in the Middle Ages foreshadowed the search for new sources of wind and water power that characterized the Industrial Revolution. Industrialization required capital for investment. The established system of transoceanic trade and commerce supplied this capital from the enormous profits it generated. Wealthy people sought investment opportunities and eventually found them in machines and engines to drive machines. Industrialization increased production in both farming and manufacturing. Capital and scientific innovation fueled invention.

European industrialization developed from (and eventually replaced) the *domestic system* of manufacture (or home-handicraft system). In this system, an organizer-entrepreneur supplied the raw materials to workers in their homes and collected the finished products from them. The entrepreneur, whose sphere of operations might span several villages, owned the materials, paid for the work, and arranged the marketing.

Causes of the Industrial Revolution

The Industrial Revolution began with cotton products, iron, and pottery. These were widely used goods whose manufacture could be broken down into simple routine motions that machines could perform. When manufacturing moved from homes to factories, where machinery replaced handwork, agrarian societies evolved into industrial ones. As factories produced cheap staple goods, the Industrial Revolution led to a dramatic increase in production. Industrialization fueled urban growth and created a new kind of city, with factories crowded together in places where coal and labor were cheap.

The Industrial Revolution began in England rather than in France (Figure 23.1). Why? Unlike the English, the French didn't have to transform their domestic manufacturing system by industrializing. Faced with an increased need for products, with a late 18th-century population at least

FIGURE 23.1 Location of England (United Kingdom) and France.

twice that of Great Britain, France could simply augment its domestic system of production by drawing in new homes. Thus, the French were able to increase production *without innovating*—they could enlarge the existing system rather than adopt a new one. To meet mounting demand for staples—at home and in the colonies—England had to industrialize.

As its industrialization proceeded, Britain's population began to increase dramatically. It doubled during the 18th century (especially after 1750) and did so again between 1800 and 1850. This demographic explosion fueled consumption, but British entrepreneurs couldn't meet the increased demand with the traditional production methods. This spurred experimentation, innovation, and rapid technological change.

English industrialization drew on national advantages in natural resources. Britain was rich in coal and iron ore, and had navigable waterways and easily negotiated coasts. It was a seafaring island-nation located at the crossroads of international trade. These features gave Britain a favored position for importing raw materials and exporting manufactured goods. Another factor in England's industrial growth was the fact that much of its 18th-century colonial empire was occupied by English settler families who looked to the mother country as they tried to replicate European civilization in the New World. These colonies bought large quantities of English staples.

It also has been argued that particular cultural values and religion contributed to industrialization. Many members of the emerging English middle class were Protestant nonconformists. Their beliefs and values encouraged industry, thrift, the dissemination of new knowledge, inventiveness, and willingness to accept change (Weber 1904/1958).

SOCIOECONOMIC EFFECTS OF INDUSTRIALIZATION

The socioeconomic effects of industrialization were mixed. English national income tripled between 1700 and 1815 and increased 30 times more by 1939. Standards of comfort rose, but prosperity was uneven. At first, factory workers got wages higher than those available in the domestic system. Later, owners started recruiting labor in places where living standards were low and labor (including that of women and children) was cheap.

Social ills worsened with the growth of factory towns and industrial cities, amid conditions like those Charles Dickens described in *Hard Times.* Filth and smoke polluted the 19th-century cities. Housing was crowded and unsanitary, with insufficient water and sewage disposal facilities. People experienced rampant disease and rising death rates. This was the world of Ebenezer Scrooge, Bob Cratchit, Tiny Tim—and Karl Marx.

Industrial Stratification

The social theorists Karl Marx and Max Weber focused on the stratification systems associated with industrialization. From his observations in

bourgeoisie
Owners of the means of production.

working class, or proletariat
People who must sell their labor to survive.

England and his analysis of 19th-century industrial capitalism, Marx (Marx and Engels 1848/1976) saw socioeconomic stratification as a sharp and simple division between two opposed classes: the bourgeoisie (capitalists) and the proletariat (propertyless workers). The bourgeoisie traced its origins to overseas ventures and the world capitalist economy, which had transformed the social structure of northwestern Europe, creating a wealthy commercial class.

Industrialization shifted production from farms and cottages to mills and factories, where mechanical power was available and where workers could be assembled to operate heavy machinery. The **bourgeoisie** were the owners of the factories, mines, large farms, and other means of production. The **working class,** or proletariat, was made up of people who had to sell their labor to survive. With the decline of subsistence production and with the rise of urban migration and the possibility of unemployment, the bourgeoisie came to stand between workers and the means of production.

Industrialization hastened the process of *proletarianization*—the separation of workers from the means of production. The bourgeoisie also came to dominate the means of communication, the schools, and other key institutions. *Class consciousness* (recognition of collective interests and personal identification with one's economic group) was a vital part of Marx's view of class. He saw bourgeoisie and proletariat as socioeconomic divisions with radically opposed interests. Marx viewed classes as powerful collective forces that could mobilize human energies to influence the course of history. On the basis of their common experience, workers would develop class consciousness, which could lead to revolutionary change. Although no proletarian revolution was to occur in England, workers did develop organizations to protect their interests and increase their share of industrial profits. During the 19th century, trade unions and socialist parties emerged to express a rising anticapitalist spirit. The concerns of the English labor movement were to remove young children from factories and limit the hours during which women and children could work. The profile of stratification in industrial core nations gradually took shape. Capitalists controlled production, but labor was organizing for better wages and working conditions. By 1900 many governments had factory legislation and social-welfare programs. Mass living standards in core nations rose as population grew.

In today's capitalist world system the class division between owners and workers is now worldwide. However, publicly traded companies complicate the division between capitalists and workers in industrial nations. Through pension plans and personal investments, many American workers now have some proprietary interest in the means of production. They are part-owners

The Art of STOCKING-FRAME-WORK-KNITTING.

Engrav'd for the Universal Magazine 1750 for J. Hinton at the Kings Arms in St Pauls Church Yard LONDON.

In the home-handicraft, or domestic, system of production, an organizer supplied raw materials to workers in their homes and collected their products. Family life and work were intertwined, as in this English scene. Is there a modern equivalent to the domestic system of production?

Large paintings of Karl Marx (1818–1883) on display in Tiananmen Square, Beijing, China.

rather than propertyless workers. The key difference is that the wealthy have *control* over these means. The key capitalist now is not the factory owner, who may have been replaced by thousands of stockholders, but the CEO or the chair of the board of directors, neither of whom may actually own the corporation.

Modern stratification systems aren't simple and dichotomous. They include (particularly in core and semiperiphery nations) a middle class of skilled and professional workers. Gerhard Lenski (1966) argues that social equality tends to increase in advanced industrial societies. The masses improve their access to economic benefits and political power. In Lenski's scheme, the shift of political power to the masses reflects the growth of the middle class, which reduces the polarization between owning and working classes. The proliferation of middle-class occupations creates opportunities for social mobility. The stratification system grows more complex (Giddens 1973).

Weber faulted Marx for an overly simple and exclusively economic view of stratification. As we saw in the chapter "Political Systems," Weber (1922/1968) defined three dimensions of social stratification: wealth, power, and prestige. Although, as Weber showed, wealth, power, and prestige are separate components of social ranking, they tend to be correlated. Weber also believed that social identities based on ethnicity, religion, race, nationality, and other attributes could take priority over class (social identity based on economic status). In addition to class contrasts, the

Max Weber (1864–1920). Did Weber improve on Marx's view of stratification?

modern world system *is* cross-cut by collective identities based on ethnicity, religion, and nationality (Shannon 1996). Class conflicts tend to occur within nations, and nationalism has prevented global class solidarity, particularly of proletarians.

Although the capitalist class dominates politically in most countries, growing wealth has made it easier for core nations to grant higher wages (Hopkins and Wallerstein 1982). However, the improvement in core workers' living standards wouldn't have occurred without the world system. The added surplus that comes from the periphery

NAME: Tim Ormsby

COUNTRY OF ORIGIN: Australia

SUPERVISING PROFESSOR: Claire Smith (Flinders University), Joe Watkins (University of New Mexico)

SCHOOL: Flinders University, Adelaide, Australia

Education and Colonialism

When studying at the University of New Mexico in Albuquerque, I took classes in Native American studies and anthropology. In my Native American studies classes, I was often the only white student in a class of approximately 20. All of my classmates were Native Americans. In addition, all my lecturers were also Native American. This situation stands in stark contrast to the archaeological and Aboriginal studies classes here in Australia, where almost all the students are white, with only one or two Indigenous Australians. While the Australian situation might be reflected in other universities in the United States, no university in Australia has an Indigenous enrollment similar to that at UNM. A chief factor in this difference seems to be ease of access. Albuquerque is situated very close to numerous pueblos, making it much easier for young Native Americans to access higher education. In Australia, all major higher education facilities are located in large cities, chiefly on the coasts, thousands of miles away from the remote areas of Australia where a high proportion of Indigenous Australians live. Distance, as well as socioeconomic problems, mean that many young Indigenous people miss out on higher education.

In New Mexico, opportunities for Native Americans to attend university were definitely greater than they are for Indigenous peoples in Australia. For me, being in a class where everyone else was Native American opened up a new dimension: I was able to get a much more comprehensive, personal, and humanized view of important issues (e.g., repatriation, research ethics, treaty law) because my classmates could discuss personal experiences they had with the issues being examined. This enriched the education I received while I was in Albuquerque. One of my classmates even invited me to his home at Jemez Pueblo for the San Diego feast day celebrations, an experience I will remember for the rest of my life. Learning about a culture in a classroom is one thing. Being able to experience it personally adds a new dimension.

My experience in Albuquerque led me to understand that centralization, which hinders educational opportunities, is a major component of the ongoing colonial nature of Australian society. It puts Indigenous Australians at a great disadvantage. Non-Indigenous Australians take for granted the concentration of basic facilities and services in and around service centers. Comparable access to education, health care and employment opportunities is not available in remote Indigenous communities. Australian governments have largely ignored the problems that centralization creates.

imperialism
Policy aimed at seizing and ruling foreign territory and peoples.

allows core capitalists to maintain their profits while satisfying the demands of core workers. In the periphery, wages and living standards are much lower. The current *world stratification system* features a substantial contrast between both capitalists and workers in the core nations and workers on the periphery.

COLONIALISM

World-system theory stresses the existence of a global culture. It emphasizes historical contacts, linkages, and power differentials between local people and international forces. The major forces influencing cultural interaction during the past 500 years have been commercial expansion, industrial capitalism, and the dominance of colonial and core nations (Wallerstein 1982, 2004b; Wolf 1982). As state formation had done previously, industrialization accelerated local participation in larger networks. According to Bodley (1985), perpetual expansion is a distinguishing feature of industrial economic systems. Bands and tribes were small, self-sufficient, subsistence-based systems. Industrial economies, by contrast, are large, highly specialized systems in which market exchanges occur with profit as the primary motive (Bodley 1985).

During the 19th century European business interests initiated a concerted search for markets. This process led to European imperialism in Africa, Asia, and Oceania. **Imperialism** refers to a policy of extending the rule of a country or empire over foreign nations and of taking and holding foreign colonies. Imperialism goes back to early states, including Egypt in the Old World and the Incas in the New. A Greek empire was forged by Alexander the Great, and Julius Caesar and his successors spread the Roman empire. More recent examples include the British, French, and Soviet empires (Scheinman 1980).

During the second half of the 19th century, European imperial expansion was aided by improved transportation, which facilitated the colonization of vast areas of sparsely settled lands in the interior of North and South America and Australia. The new colonies purchased masses of goods from the industrial centers and shipped back wheat, cotton, wool, mutton, beef, and leather. The first phase of European colonialism had been the exploration and exploitation of the Americas and the Caribbean after Columbus. A new second phase began as European nations competed for colonies between 1875 and 1914, setting the stage for World War I.

Colonialism is the political, social, economic, and cultural domination of a territory and its people by a foreign power for an extended time (see Bremen and Shimizu, eds. 1999; Cooper and Stoler, eds. 1997). If imperialism is almost as old as the state, colonialism can be traced back to the Phoenicians, who established colonies along the eastern Mediterranean 3,000 years ago. The ancient Greeks and Romans were avid colonizers as well as empire builders.

The first phase of modern colonialism began with the European "Age of Discovery"—of the Americas and of a sea route to the Far East. After 1492, the Spanish, the original conquerors of the

Aztecs and the Incas, explored and colonized widely in the New World—the Caribbean, Mexico, the southern portions of what was to become the United States, and Central and South America. In South America, Portugal ruled over Brazil. Rebellions and wars aimed at independence ended the first phase of European colonialism by the early 19th century. Brazil declared independence from Portugal in 1822. By 1825 most of Spain's colonies were politically independent. Spain held onto Cuba and the Philippines until 1898, but otherwise withdrew from the colonial field. During the first phase of colonialism, Spain and Portugal, along with Britain and France, were major colonizing nations. The latter two (Britain and France) dominated the second phase.

British Colonialism

At its peak about 1914, the British empire covered a fifth of the world's land surface and ruled a fourth of its population (see Figure 23.2). Like several other European nations, Britain had two stages of colonialism. The first began with the Elizabethan voyages of the 16th century. During the 17th century, Britain acquired most of the eastern coast of North America, Canada's St. Lawrence basin, islands in the Caribbean, slave stations in Africa, and interests in India.

The British shared the exploration of the New World with the Spanish, Portuguese, French, and Dutch. The British by and large left Mexico, along with Central and South America, to the Spanish and the Portuguese. The end of the Seven Years'

War in 1763 forced a French retreat from most of Canada and India, where France previously had competed with Britain (Cody 1998; Farr 1980).

The American revolution ended the first stage of British colonialism. A second colonial empire, on which the "sun never set," rose from the ashes of the first. Beginning in 1788, but intensifying after 1815, the British settled Australia. Britain had acquired Dutch South Africa by 1815. The establishment of Singapore in 1819 provided a base for a British trade network that extended to much of South Asia and along the coast of China. By this time, the empires of Britain's traditional rivals, particularly Spain, had been severely diminished in scope. Britain's position as imperial power and the world's leading industrial nation was unchallenged (Cody 1998; Farr 1980).

During the Victorian Era (1837–1901), as Britain's acquisition of territory and of further trading concessions continued, Prime Minister Benjamin Disraeli implemented a foreign policy justified by a view of imperialism as shouldering "the white man's burden"—a phrase coined by the poet Rudyard Kipling. People in the empire were seen as unable to govern themselves, so that British guidance was needed to civilize and Christianize them. This paternalistic and racist doctrine served to legitimize Britain's acquisition and control of parts of central Africa and Asia (Cody 1998).

After World War II, the British empire began to fall apart, with nationalist movements for independence. India became independent in 1947, as did Ireland in 1949. Decolonization in Africa and Asia accelerated during the late 1950s. Today, the

colonialism
Long-term foreign control of a territory and its people.

FIGURE 23.2 Map of British Empire in 1765 and 1914.

SOURCE: From the *Academic American Encyclopedia*, Vol. 3, p. 496. 1998 Edition. Copyright © 1998 by Grolier Incorporated. Reprinted with permission.

On January 1, 1900, a British officer in India receives a pedicure from a servant. What does this photo say to you about colonialism? Who gives pedicures in your society?

lost along with Canada to Great Britain in 1763 (Harvey 1980).

The foundations of the second French empire were established between 1830 and 1870. In Great Britain the sheer drive for profit led expansion, but French colonialism was spurred more by the state, church, and armed forces than by pure business interests. France acquired Algeria and part of what eventually became Indochina (Cambodia, Laos, and Vietnam). By 1914 the French empire covered 4 million square miles and included some 60 million people (see Figure 23.3). By 1893 French rule had been fully established in Indochina. Tunisia and Morocco became French protectorates in 1883 and 1912, respectively (Harvey 1980).

To be sure, the French, like the British, had substantial business interests in their colonies, but they also sought, again like the British, international glory and prestige. The French promulgated a *mission civilisatrice*, their equivalent of Britain's "white man's burden." The goal was to implant French culture, language, and religion, Roman Catholicism, throughout the colonies (Harvey 1980).

The French used two forms of colonial rule: *indirect rule*, governing through native leaders and established political structures, in areas with long histories of state organization, such as Morocco and Tunisia; and *direct rule* by French officials in many areas of Africa, where the French imposed new government structures to control diverse societies, many of them previously stateless. Like the British empire, the French empire began to disintegrate after World War II. France fought long—and ultimately futile—wars to keep its empire intact in Indochina and Algeria (Harvey 1980).

ties that remain between Britain and its former colonies are mainly linguistic or cultural rather than political (Cody 1998).

French Colonialism

French colonialism also had two phases. The first began with the explorations of the early 1600s. Prior to the French revolution in 1789, missionaries, explorers, and traders carved out niches for France in Canada, the Louisiana Territory, several Caribbean islands, and parts of India, which were

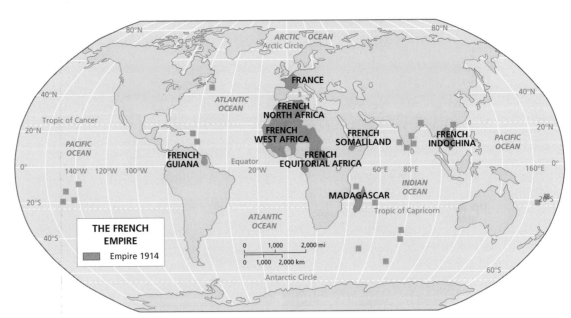

FIGURE 23.3   Map of the French Empire at Its Height around 1914.

SOURCE: From the *Academic American Encyclopedia*, Vol. 8, p. 309. 1998 Edition. Copyright © 1998 by Grolier Incorporated. Reprinted with permission.

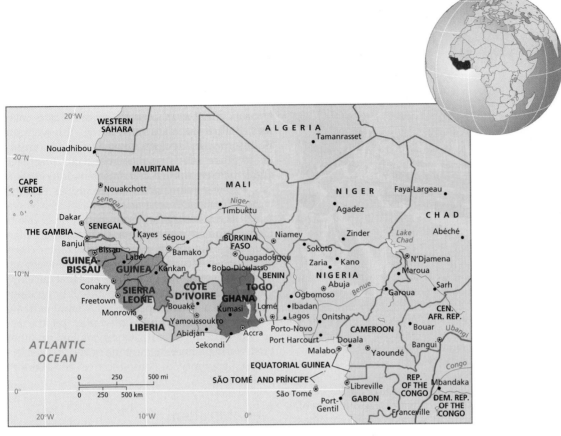

FIGURE 23.4 Small West African Nations Created by Colonialism.

Colonialism and Identity

Many geopolitical labels in the news today had no equivalent meaning before colonialism. Whole countries, along with social groups and divisions within them, were colonial inventions. In West Africa, for example, by geographic logic, several adjacent countries could be one (Togo, Ghana, Ivory Coast [Côte d'Ivoire], Guinea, Guinea-Bissau, Sierra Leone, Liberia). Instead, they are separated by linguistic, political, and economic contrasts promoted under colonialism (Figure 23.4).

Hundreds of ethnic groups and "tribes" are colonial constructions (see Ranger 1996). The Sukuma of Tanzania, for instance, were first registered as a single tribe by the colonial administration. Then missionaries standardized a series of dialects into a single Sukuma language into which they translated the Bible and other religious texts. Thereafter, those texts were taught in missionary schools and to European foreigners and other non-Sukuma speakers. Over time this standardized the Sukuma language and ethnicity (Finnstrom 1997).

As in most of East Africa, in Rwanda and Burundi farmers and herders live in the same areas and speak the same language. Historically they have shared the same social world, although their social organization is "extremely hierarchical," almost "castelike" (Malkki 1995, p. 24). There has been a tendency to see the pastoral Tutsis as superior to the agricultural Hutus. Tutsis have been presented as nobles, Hutus as commoners. Yet when distributing identity cards in Rwanda, the Belgian colonizers simply identified all people with more than 10 head of cattle as Tutsi. Owners of fewer cattle were registered as Hutus (Bjuremalm 1997). Years later, these arbitrary colonial registers were used systematically for "ethnic" identification during the mass killings (genocide) that took place in Rwanda in 1994 (as portrayed vividly in the film *Hotel Rwanda*).

Postcolonial Studies

In anthropology, history, and literature, the field of postcolonial studies has gained prominence since the 1970s (see Ashcroft, Griffiths, and Tiffin 1989; Cooper and Stoler, eds. 1997). **Postcolonial** refers to the study of the interactions between European nations and the societies they colonized (mainly after 1800). In 1914, European empires, which broke up after World War II, ruled more than 85 percent of the world (Petraglia-Bahri 1996). The term *postcolonial* also has been used to

postcolonial
Relations between European nations and areas they colonized and once ruled.

Black workers wash the hair of white customers at a hair salon in Johannesburg's (South Africa) exclusive Hyde Park shopping center. What story does the photo tell you?

intervention philosophy
Ideological justification for outsiders to guide or rule native peoples.

neoliberalism
Governments shouldn't regulate private enterprise; free market forces should rule.

describe the second half of the 20th century in general, the period succeeding colonialism. Even more generically, "postcolonial" may be used to signify a position against imperialism and Eurocentrism (Petraglia-Bahri 1996).

The former colonies (*postcolonies*) can be divided into settler, nonsettler, and mixed (Petraglia-Bahri 1996). The settler countries, with large numbers of European colonists and sparser native populations, include Australia and Canada. Examples of nonsettler countries include India, Pakistan, Bangladesh, Sri Lanka, Malaysia, Indonesia, Nigeria, Senegal, Madagascar, and Jamaica. All these had substantial native populations and relatively few European settlers. Mixed countries include South Africa, Zimbabwe, Kenya, and Algeria. Such countries had significant European settlement despite having sizable native populations.

Given the varied experiences of such countries, "postcolonial" has to be a loose term. The United States, for instance, was colonized by Europeans and fought a war for independence from Britain. Is the United States a postcolony? It usually isn't perceived as such, given its current world power position, its treatment of Native Americans (sometimes called internal colonization), and its annexation of other parts of the world (Petraglia-Bahri 1996). Research in postcolonial studies is growing, permitting a wide-ranging investigation of power relations in varied contexts. Broad topics in the field include the formation of an empire, the impact of colonization, and the state of the postcolony today (Petraglia-Bahri 1996).

DEVELOPMENT

During the Industrial Revolution, a strong current of thought viewed industrialization as a beneficial process of organic development and progress. Many economists still assume that industrialization increases production and income. They seek to create in Third World ("developing") countries a process like the one that first occurred spontaneously in 18th-century Great Britain.

We have seen that Britain used the notion of a white man's burden to justify its imperialist expansion and that France claimed to be engaged in a *mission civilisatrice*, a civilizing mission, in its colonies. Both these ideas illustrate an **intervention philosophy,** an ideological justification for outsiders to guide native peoples in specific directions. Economic development plans also have intervention philosophies. John Bodley (1988) argues that the basic belief behind interventions—whether by colonialists, missionaries, governments, or development planners—has been the same for more than 100 years. This belief is that industrialization, modernization, Westernization, and individualism are desirable evolutionary advances and that development schemes that promote them will bring long-term benefits to local people. In a more extreme form, intervention philosophy may pit the assumed wisdom of enlightened colonial or other First World planners against the purported conservatism, ignorance, or "obsolescence" of "inferior" local people.

Neoliberalism

One currently influential intervention philosophy is neoliberalism. This term encompasses a set of assumptions that have become widespread during the last 25–30 years. Neoliberal policies are being implemented in developing nations, including postsocialist societies (e.g., those of the former Soviet Union). **Neoliberalism** is the current form of the classic economic liberalism laid out in Adam Smith's famous capitalist manifesto *The Wealth of Nations*, published in 1776, soon after the Industrial Revolution. Smith advocated laissez-faire (hands-off) economics as the basis of capitalism: The government should stay out of its

The face of the Scottish economist Adam Smith aptly appears on this English twenty pound banknote. In his famed capitalist manifesto, *The Wealth of Nations*, published in 1776, Smith advocated "free" enterprise and competition, with the goal of generating profits.

nation's economic affairs. Free trade, Smith thought, was the best way for a nation's economy to develop. There should be no restrictions on manufacturing, no barriers to commerce, and no tariffs. This philosophy is called "liberalism" because it aimed at liberating or freeing the economy from government controls. Economic liberalism encouraged "free" enterprise and competition, with the goal of generating profits. (Note the difference between this meaning of *liberal* and the one that has been popularized on American talk radio, in which "liberal" is used—usually as a derogatory term—as the opposite of "conservative." Ironically, Adam Smith's liberalism is today's capitalist "conservatism.")

living anthropology VIDEOS

Globalization, www.mhhe.com/kottak

This clip draws parallels between the 1890s and today, mentioning advances in technology that took place through the discoveries and efforts of Bell, Edison, Carnegie, and Morgan. A century ago, laissez-faire economic policies allowed the barons of industry to increase profits and grow wealthy. The United States moved from semiperiphery to core. The clip mentions sweatshops, child labor, and low wages as the downside of capitalism. Today, transnational corporations increasingly operate internationally, beyond the boundaries of uniform national laws. This creates new business opportunities but also new legal, ethical, and moral challenges. What's the technological basis of the global village described in the clip? The clip suggests that because the world is so tightly integrated, events in Asia can have immediate ripple effects in the West. Can you think of any examples?

Economic liberalism prevailed in the United States until President Franklin Roosevelt's New Deal during the 1930s. The Great Depression produced a turn to Keynesian economics, which challenged liberalism. John Maynard Keynes (1927, 1936) insisted that full employment was necessary for capitalism to grow, that governments and central banks should intervene to increase employment, and that government should promote the common good.

Especially since the fall of Communism (1989–1991), there has been a revival of economic liberalism, now known as neoliberalism, which has been spreading globally. Around the world, neoliberal policies have been imposed by powerful financial institutions such as the International Monetary Fund (IMF), the World Bank, and the Inter-American Development Bank (see Edelman and Haugerud 2004). Neoliberalism entails open (tariff- and barrier-free) international trade and

investment. Profits are sought through lowering of costs, whether through improving productivity, laying off workers, or seeking workers who accept lower wages. In exchange for loans, the governments of postsocialist and developing nations have been required to accept the neoliberal premise that deregulation leads to economic growth, which will eventually benefit everyone through a process sometimes called "trickle down." Accompanying the belief in free markets and the idea of cutting costs is a tendency to impose austerity measures that cut government expenses. This can entail reduced public spending on education, health care, and other social services (Martinez and Garcia 2000).

THE SECOND WORLD

The labels "First World," "Second World," and "Third World" represent a common, although ethnocentric, way of categorizing nations. The *First World* refers to the "democratic West"—traditionally conceived in opposition to a "Second World" ruled by "Communism." The *Second World* refers to the former Soviet Union and the socialist and once-socialist countries of Eastern Europe and Asia. Proceeding with this classification, the "less-developed countries" or "developing nations" make up the *Third World*.

Communism

The two meanings of communism involve how it is written, whether with a lowercase (small) or an uppercase (large) *c*. Small-*c* **communism** describes a social system in which property is owned by the community and in which people work for the common good. Large-C **Communism** was a political movement and doctrine seeking to overthrow capitalism and to establish a form of communism such as that which prevailed in the Soviet Union (USSR) from 1917 to 1991. The heyday of Communism was a 40-year period from 1949 to 1989, when more Communist regimes existed than at any time before or after. Today only five Communist states remain—China, Cuba, Laos, North Korea, and Vietnam, compared with 23 in 1985.

Communism, which originated with Russia's Bolshevik Revolution in 1917, and took its inspiration from Karl Marx and Friedrich Engels, was not uniform over time or among countries. All Communist systems were *authoritarian* (promoting obedience to authority rather than individual freedom). Many were *totalitarian* (banning rival parties and demanding total submission of the individual to the state). Several features distinguished Communist societies from other authoritarian regimes (e.g., Spain under Franco) and from socialism of a social democratic type. First,

communism
Property owned by the community; people working for the common good.

Communism
Political movement aimed at replacing capitalism with Soviet-style communism.

anthropology **ATLAS**

Map 17 represents
an attempt to assess
and display the
quality of life by
country, based on
economic, social, and
demographic data.

the Communist Party monopolized power in every Communist state. Second, relations within the party were highly centralized and strictly disciplined. Third, Communist nations had state ownership, rather than private ownership, of the means of production. Finally, all Communist regimes, with the goal of advancing communism, cultivated a sense of belonging to an international movement (Brown 2001).

Social scientists have tended to refer to such societies as socialist rather than Communist. Today research by anthropologists is thriving in *postsocialist* societies—those that once

emphasized bureaucratic redistribution of wealth according to a central plan (Verdery 2001). In the postsocialist period, states that once had planned economies have been following the neoliberal agenda, by divesting themselves of state-owned resources in favor of privatization. These societies in transition are undergoing democratization and marketization. Some of them have moved toward formal liberal democracy, with political parties, elections, and a balance of powers (Grekova 2001).

Postsocialist Transitions

Neoliberal economists assumed that dismantling the Soviet Union's planned economy would raise gross domestic product (GDP) and living standards. The goal was to enhance production by substituting a decentralized market system and providing incentives through privatization. In October 1991, Boris Yeltsin, who had been elected president of Russia that June, announced a program of radical market-oriented reform, pursuing a changeover to capitalism. Yeltsin's program of "shock therapy" cut subsidies to farms and industries and ended price controls. Since then, postsocialist Russia has faced many problems. The anticipated gains in productivity did not materialize. After the fall of the Soviet Union, Russia's GDP fell by half. Poverty increased, with a quarter of the population sinking below the poverty line. Life expectancy and the birth rate declined. Another problem to emerge in the postsocialist transition is corruption. Since 1996, the World Bank and other international organizations have launched anticorruption programs worldwide. *Corruption* is defined as the abuse of public office for private gain.

The World Bank's approach to corruption assumes a clear and sharp distinction between the state (the public or official domain) and the private sphere, and that the two should be kept separate. The idea that the public sphere can be separated neatly from the private sphere is ethnocentric. According to Janine Wedel (2002), postsocialist states provide rich contexts in which to explore variability in relations between public and private domains. Alexei Yurchak (2002, 2005) describes two spheres that operate in Russia today; these spheres do not mesh neatly with the assumption of a public–private split. He calls them the official–public sphere and the personal–public sphere, referring to domains that coexist and sometimes overlap. State officials may respect the law (official–public), while also working with informal or even criminal groups

Before and after Communism. Above: on May Day (May 1, 1975), large photos of Politburo members (Communist Party leaders) adorn buildings in Moscow. Below: on January 31, 2006, in a Moscow electronics store, a potential customer considers a display of TV sets, broadcasting live the annual press conference of Russian prime minister Vladimir Putin.

PERIPHERY TO SEMIPERIPHERY	SEMIPERIPHERY TO CORE	CORE TO SEMIPERIPHERY
United States (1800–1860)	United States (1860–1900)	Spain (1620–1700)
Japan (1868–1900)	Japan (1945–1970)	
Taiwan (1949–1980)	Germany (1870–1900)	
S. Korea (1953–1980)		

SOURCE: Thomas R. Shannon, *An Introduction to the World-System Perspective*, 2nd ed., p. 147. Copyright © 1989, 1996 by Westview Press, Inc. Reprinted by permission of Westview Press, a member of the Perseus Books Group.

(personal–public). Officials switch from official–public to personal–public behavior all the time in order to accomplish specific tasks.

In an illustrative case from Poland, a man selling an apartment he had inherited was to pay a huge sum in taxes. He visited the state tax office, where a bureaucrat informed him of how much he was being assessed (official–public). She also told him how to avoid paying it (personal–public). He followed her advice and saved a lot of money. The man didn't know the bureaucrat personally. She didn't expect anything in return, and he didn't offer anything. She said she routinely offers such help.

In postsocialist societies, what is legal (official–public) and what is considered morally correct don't necessarily correspond. The bureaucrat just described seemed still to be operating under the old communist notion that state property (tax dollars in this case) belongs both to everyone and to no one. For further illustration of this view of state property, imagine two people working in the same state-owned construction enterprise. To take home for private use materials belonging to the enterprise (that is, to everyone and no one) is morally

acceptable. No one will fault you for it because "everyone does it." However, if a fellow worker comes along and takes materials someone else had planned to take home, that would be stealing and morally wrong (Wedel 2002). In evaluating charges of corruption, anthropologists point out that property notions and spheres of official action in postsocialist societies are in transition.

THE WORLD SYSTEM TODAY

The process of industrialization continues today, although nations have shifted their positions within the world system. Recap 23.1 summarizes those shifts. By 1900, the United States had become a core nation within the world system and had overtaken Great Britain in iron, coal, and cotton production. In a few decades (1868–1900), Japan had changed from a medieval handicraft economy to an industrial one, joining the semiperiphery by 1900 and moving to the core between 1945 and 1970. Figure 23.5 is a map showing the modern world system.

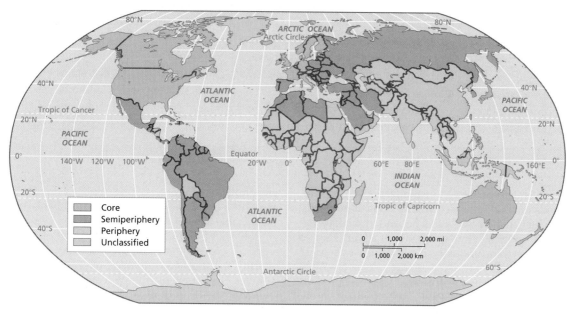

FIGURE 23.5 The World System in 2000.

appreciating ANTHROPOLOGY

Is Mining Sustainable?

How can anthropologists help the people they study? The spread of industrialization, illustrated by the mining described here, has contributed to the destruction of indigenous economies, ecologies, and populations. Today, multinational conglomerates, along with nations such as Papua New Guinea, are repeating—at an accelerated rate—the process of resource depletion that started in Europe and the United States during the Industrial Revolution. Fortunately, however, today's world has some environmental watchdogs, including anthropologists, that did not exist during the first centuries of the Industrial Revolution. Described here is a conundrum confronting a major university. Is a firm whose operations have destroyed the landscapes and livelihoods of indigenous peoples a proper advisor for an institute devoted to ecological sustainability?

In the 1990s, the giant mining company now known as BHP Billiton drew worldwide condemnation for the environmental damage caused by its copper and gold mine in Papua New Guinea. Its mining practices destroyed the way of life of thousands of farming and fishing families who lived along and subsisted on the rivers polluted by the mine, and it was only after being sued in a landmark class-action case that the company agreed to compensate them.

Today several activists and academics who work on behalf of indigenous people around the world say the company continues to dodge responsibility for the problems its mines create for communities in undeveloped parts of the world.

Yet at the University of Michigan at Ann Arbor, BHP Billiton enjoys a loftier reputation: It is one of 14 corporate members of an External Advisory Board for the university's new Graham Environmental Sustainability Institute.

Critics at and outside the university contend that Michigan's decision to enlist BHP Billiton as an adviser to an institute devoted to sustainability reflects badly on the institution and allows the company to claim a mantle of environmental and social responsibility that it does not deserve.

The institute's director says he is satisfied that the company is serious about operating in a more sustainable way. . . .

The arguments echo the discussions about corporate "greenwashing" that have arisen at Stanford University and the University of California at Berkeley over major research grants from ExxonMobil and BP, respectively, and more recently, the debate at the Smithsonian Institution among its trustees over whether to accept a gift from the American Petroleum Institute for a museum exhibition about oceans. (The gift was withdrawn in November.)

For one BHP Billiton critic at Michigan, the issue is personal. Stuart Kirsch, an associate professor of anthropology, has spent most of his academic career documenting the damage caused by BHP Billiton's Ok Tedi mine in Papua New Guinea. . . .

Mr. Kirsch, who first visited some of the affected communities as a young ethnographer in 1987, became involved in the class-action lawsuit brought against the company and helped villagers participate in the 1996 legal settlement. "I put my career on hold while being an activist," he says.

He subsequently published several papers related to his work with the Yonggom people as they fought for recognition and compensation from mine operators—scholarship that helped him win tenure this year—and he remains involved with the network of activists and academics who follow mining and its impact on undeveloped communities around the world. . . .

The company's practices polluted the Ok Tedi and Fly Rivers and caused thousands of people to leave their homes because the mining-induced flooding made it impossible for them to grow food to feed themselves, says Mr. Kirsch.

BHP Billiton, based in Australia, later acknowledged that the mine was "not compatible with our environmental values," and spun it off to an independent company that pays all of its mining royalties to the government of Papua New Guinea.

But Mr. Kirsch says that in doing so, the company skirted responsibility for ameliorating the damage it caused. BHP Billiton says it would have preferred to close the mine, but

---

Twentieth-century industrialization added hundreds of new industries and millions of new jobs. Production increased, often beyond immediate demand, spurring strategies, such as advertising, to sell everything industry could churn out. Mass production gave rise to a culture of consumption, which valued acquisitiveness and conspicuous consumption (Veblen 1934). Industrialization entailed a shift from reliance on renewable resources to the use of fossil fuels. Fossil fuel energy, stored over millions of years, is being depleted rapidly to support a previously unknown and probably unsustainable level of consumption (Bodley 1985).

Table 23.1 compares energy consumption in various types of cultures. Americans are the world's foremost consumers of nonrenewable resources. In terms of energy consumption, the average American is about 35 times more expensive than the average forager or tribesperson. Since 1900, the United States has tripled its per the Papua New Guinea government, in need of the mine revenues, pressed to keep it open. The deal freed BHP Billiton from any future liabilities for environmental damage.

"They didn't clean it up; they didn't take responsibility for the damage they had done," Mr. Kirsch says of the company. With that record, "it's supposed to provide education to the University of Michigan?" . . .

Illtud Harri, a BHP Billiton spokesman, says the company regrets its past with Ok Tedi but considers its pullout from the mine "a responsible exit" that left in place a system that supports educational, agricultural, and social programs for the people of the community.

He says the company also aims for the most ethical standards in its projects. The company mines only when it can fully comply with the host country's environmental laws. In places where those regulatory requirements fall below the company's, "we will always be guided by our higher standards," he says.

Mr. Talbot, the interim director of the two-year-old sustainability institute, says . . . "We intentionally selected a cross-sector group of organizations" for the advisory board from a list of about 140 nominees, . . . and several companies that "weren't making any serious efforts" toward sustainability were rejected. . . .

BHP Billiton, a company formed from the 2001 merger of the Australian mining enterprise Broken Hill Proprietary Company with London-based Billiton, is now the world's

This photo of the Ok Tedi copper mine, taken February 10, 2002, shows the ecological devastation of the native landscape.

largest mining company, with more than 100 operations in 25 countries. . . .

The BHP Billiton charter includes a statement that the company has "an overriding commitment to health, safety, environmental responsibility, and sustainable development." But its critics say the company continues to play a key role in mining projects with questionable records on environmental and human rights, even though in many of those cases, it is not directly responsible. . . .

Mr. Kirsch, who is now on leave from Michigan to write a book, says he is planning to press for an open forum at the university that includes environmental scientists, indigenous people affected by the Ok Tedi mine, and company officials themselves.

BHP Billiton has the resources to present itself as the "golden boy," but, says Mr. Kirsch, "it's much harder to see the people on the Ok Tedi and Fly rivers."

A forum could help to right that imbalance, he says. "Let the students and faculty decide whether this is an appropriate company to advise the University of Michigan," says Mr. Kirsch. "It would be an educational process for everyone involved."

SOURCE: Goldie Blumenstyk, "Mining Company Involved in Environmental Disaster Now Advises Sustainability Institute at U. of Michigan," *Chronicle of Higher Education*, Vol. 54, Issue 15 (December 7, 2007), p. A22. Copyright 2007, The Chronicle of Higher Education. Reprinted with permission.

capita energy use. It also has increased its total energy consumption thirtyfold.

Table 23.2 compares energy consumption, per capita and total, in the United States and selected other countries. The United States represents 21.8 percent of the world's annual energy consumption, compared with China's 14.5 percent, but the average American consumes 6.6 times the energy used by the average Chinese, and 23 times the energy used by the average inhabitant of India.

Industrial Degradation

Industrialization and factory labor now characterize many societies in Latin America, Africa, the Pacific, and Asia. One effect of the spread of industrialization has been the destruction of indigenous economies, ecologies, and populations, as we see in this chapter's "Appreciating Anthropology." Two centuries ago, as industrialization was developing, 50 million people still lived

TABLE 23.1 Energy Consumption in Various Contexts

TYPE OF SOCIETY	DAILY KILOCALORIES PER PERSON
Bands and tribes	4,000–12,000
Preindustrial states	26,000 (maximum)
Early industrial states	70,000
Americans in 1970	230,000
Americans in 1990	275,000

SOURCE: John H. Bodley, *Anthropology and Contemporary Human Problems* (Mountain View, CA: Mayfield Publishing, 1985). Reprinted by permission of the author.

TABLE 23.2 Energy Consumption in Selected Countries, 2005

	TOTAL	PER CAPITA
World	462.8*	72[†]
United States	100.7	340
China	67.1	51
Russia	30.3	212
India	16.2	15
Germany	14.5	176
Canada	14.3	436
France	11.4	182
United Kingdom	10.0	166

*462.8 quadrillion (462,800,000,000,000,000) Btu.

[†]70 million Btu.

SOURCE: Based on data in *Statistical Abstract of the United States, 2009* (Table 1355), p. 841.

in politically independent bands, tribes, and chiefdoms. Occupying vast areas, those nonstate societies, although not totally isolated, were only marginally affected by nation-states and the world capitalist economy. In 1800 bands, tribes, and chiefdoms controlled half the globe and 20 percent of its population (Bodley, ed. 1988). Industrialization tipped the balance in favor of states.

As industrial states have conquered, annexed, and "developed" nonstates, there has been genocide on a grand scale. *Genocide* refers to a deliberate policy of exterminating a group through warfare or murder. Examples include the Holocaust, Rwanda in 1994, and Bosnia in the early 1990s. Bodley (1988) estimates that an average of 250,000 indigenous people perished annually between 1800 and 1950. Besides war-

indigenous peoples Original inhabitants of particular areas.

fare, the causes included foreign diseases (to which natives lacked resistance), slavery, land grabbing, and other forms of dispossession and impoverishment.

Many native groups have been incorporated within nation-states, in which they have become ethnic minorities. Some such groups have been able to recoup their population. Many indigenous peoples survive and maintain their ethnic identity despite having lost their ancestral cultures to varying degrees (partial ethnocide). And many descendants of tribespeople live on as culturally distinct and self-conscious colonized peoples, many of whom aspire to autonomy. As the original inhabitants of their territories, they are called **indigenous peoples** (see Maybury-Lewis 2002).

Around the world many contemporary nations are repeating—at an accelerated rate—the process of resource depletion that started in Europe and the United States during the Industrial Revolution. Fortunately, however, today's world has some environmental watchdogs that did not exist during the first centuries of the Industrial Revolution. Given national and international cooperation and sanctions, the modern world may benefit from the lessons of the past. This chapter's "Appreciating Anthropology" shows how anthropologists can help local people fight the environmental degradation, in this case from mining, that often accompanies the spread of industrialization. Also raised in "Appreciating Anthropology" is the question of whether a corporation whose operations endanger indigenous peoples is a proper advisor for an institute devoted to ecological sustainability.

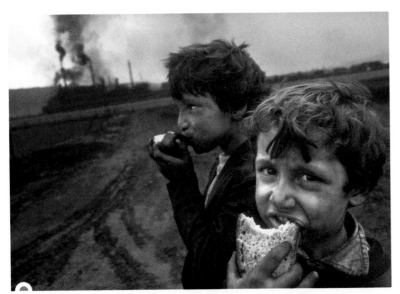

Copsa Mica, Romania, may well be the world's most polluted city. A factory belches out smoke that leaves its mark on these boys' faces, food, and lungs. What's the term for such environmental devastation?

Acing the COURSE

Summary

1. Local societies increasingly participate in wider systems—regional, national, and global. The capitalist world economy depends on production for sale, with the goal of maximizing profits. The key claim of world-system theory is that an identifiable social system, based on wealth and power differentials, extends beyond individual countries. That system is formed by a set of economic and political relations that has characterized much of the globe since the 16th century. World capitalism has political and economic specialization at the core, semiperiphery, and periphery.

2. Columbus's voyages opened the way for a major exchange between the Old and New Worlds. Seventeenth-century plantation economies in the Caribbean and Brazil were based on sugar. In the 18th century, plantation economies based on cotton arose in the southeastern United States.

3. The Industrial Revolution began in England around 1750. Transoceanic commerce supplied capital for industrial investment. Industrialization hastened the separation of workers from the means of production. Marx saw a sharp division between the bourgeoisie and the proletariat. Class consciousness was a key feature of Marx's view of this stratification. Weber believed that social solidarity based on ethnicity, religion, race, or nationality could take priority over class. Today's capitalist world economy maintains the contrast between those who own the means of production and those who don't, but the division is now worldwide. There is a substantial contrast between not only capitalists but workers in the core nations and workers on the periphery.

4. Imperialism is the policy of extending the rule of a nation or empire over other nations and of taking and holding foreign colonies. Colonialism is the domination of a territory and its people by a foreign power for an extended time. European colonialism had two main phases. The first started in 1492 and lasted through 1825. For Britain this phase ended with the American Revolution. For France it ended when Britain won the Seven Years' War, forcing the French to abandon Canada and India. For Spain it ended with Latin American independence. The second phase of European colonialism extended approximately from 1850 to 1950. The British and French empires were at their height around 1914, when European empires controlled 85 percent of the world. Britain and France had colonies in Africa, Asia, Oceania, and the New World.

5. Many geopolitical labels and identities were created under colonialism that had little or nothing to do with existing social demarcations. The new ethnic or national divisions were colonial inventions, sometimes aggravating conflicts.

6. Like colonialism, economic development has an intervention philosophy that provides a justification for outsiders to guide native peoples toward particular goals. Development usually is justified by the idea that industrialization and modernization are desirable evolutionary advances. Neoliberalism revives and extends classic economic liberalism: the idea that governments should not regulate private enterprise and that free market forces should rule. This intervention philosophy currently dominates aid agreements with postsocialist and developing nations.

7. Spelled with a lowercase c, communism describes a social system in which property is owned by the community and in which people work for the common good. Spelled with an uppercase C, Communism indicates a political movement and doctrine seeking to overthrow capitalism and to establish a form of communism such as that which prevailed in the Soviet Union from 1917 to 1991. The heyday of Communism was between 1949 and 1989. The fall of Communism can be traced to 1989–1990 in eastern Europe and 1991 in the Soviet Union. Postsocialist states have followed the neoliberal agenda, through privatization, deregulation, and democratization.

8. By 1900 the United States had become a core nation. Mass production gave rise to a culture that valued acquisitiveness and conspicuous consumption. One effect of industrialization has been the destruction of indigenous economies, ecologies, and populations. Another has been the accelerated rate of resource depletion.

Key Terms

bourgeoisie 554
capital 549
capitalist world economy 549
colonialism 557
communism 561
Communism 561
core 549
imperialism 556
indigenous peoples 556

Industrial Revolution 552
intervention philosophy 560
neoliberalism 560
periphery 549
postcolonial 559
semiperiphery 549
working class, or proletariat 554
world-system theory 549

Test Yourself!

MULTIPLE CHOICE

1. The modern world system is
   a. a system in which ethnic groups are increasingly isolated from the economic and political influence of nation-states.
   b. a theory that was popular in the 1980s but has since been replaced with the capitalist world economy.
   c. Karl Marx's theory of social stratification.
   d. a system of global dimensions in which nations are economically and politically interdependent.
   e. Max Weber's theory of the emergence of capitalism.

2. Which of the following statements about world system theory is *not* true?
   a. According to Wallerstein, countries within the world system occupy three different positions of economic and political power: core, periphery, and semiperiphery.
   b. It sees society as consisting of parts assembled into an interrelated system.
   c. It applies mainly to non-Western societies.
   d. It claims that a set of economic and political interconnections has characterized much of the globe since the 16th century.
   e. It is based political and economic specialization and interdependence.

3. The increasing dominance of world trade has led to
   a. diminishing rates of poverty, social stratification, and environmental degradation.
   b. the disintegration of national boundaries and the free and fair flow of people and resources all around the globe.
   c. the capitalist world economy, a single world system committed to production for sale or exchange, with the object of maximizing profits rather than supplying domestic needs.
   d. a growing concern by all nations-states for ensuring the livelihood of indigenous peoples living within their borders.

   e. the socialist welfare state, a system that attends to the needs of people who have been displaced by the capitalist world economy.

4. What fueled the European "Age of Discovery"?
   a. a desire to save the souls of the natives
   b. pilgrims fleeing persecution in their European homelands
   c. the feudal kingdoms of East Asia reaching out to establish trade links with Europe, mainly through such Middle Eastern countries as Arabia
   d. European commercial interest in exotic raw materials, such as spices and tropical hardwoods
   e. a seven-year drought in Europe that forced governments to look outside their borders to support their populations

5. Which of the following resulted in the growth of a market for sugar in Europe?
   a. the development of the trans-Atlantic slave trade
   b. the strengthening of independent indigenous nations of Mexico and South America
   c. the movement of sugar-producing nations from the periphery to the core of the world system
   d. capitalism, once a cultural trait specific to Papua New Guinea (where sugar was first domesticated), spread to the rest of the world
   e. a long-term improvement in the distribution of wealth among the rural peasantry of England

6. From his observations in England and his analysis of 19th-century industrial capitalism, Karl Marx saw socioeconomic stratification as a sharp division between two classes: the bourgeoisie and the proletariat. He also argued that class consciousness comes about as a result of
   a. the continuation of ethnic identities even though ethnic "markers" (distinct clothing styles, etc.) have more or less disappeared.

b. people recognizing they have a common economic interest and identifying themselves as part of the group that shares that interest.

c. a growing distinction among religious beliefs in complex industrialized societies.

d. people extending notions of kinship beyond the boundaries of actual biological relations.

e. the gradual elaboration of gendered differences first established during the period of peasant subsistence farming.

7. This chapter defines imperialism as the policy of extending the rule of a nation or empire, such as the British empire, over foreign nations and of taking and holding foreign colonies, while *colonialism* refers specifically to

a. the political, social, economic, and cultural domination of a territory and its people by a foreign power for an extended period of time.

b. imperial influence that disappears once formal independence is granted to former colonies.

c. the political, social, economic, and cultural domination of a territory and its people by Europe.

d. the informal and often benevolent approach to enlightening the non-Western world with Western values.

e. the same as imperialism, but the modern form of imperialism that was created with the rise of the Industrial Revolution.

8. The Sukuma of Tanzania were first registered as a single tribe by colonial administrators. In Rwanda and Burundi, the distribution of colonial identity cards created arbitrary ethnic divisions. These two cases

a. suggest that strong ethnic identities are a key ingredient of development.

b. illustrate that many ethnic groups and tribes are colonial constructions, sometimes inciting and aggravating conflict.

c. are evidence that colonial administrators were informed about the cultures of their colonial subjects.

d. show how tribal distinctions are better than ethnic ones because the latter always leads to civil violence.

e. are examples of the Spanish intervention philosophy that eventually all colonial administrations adopted because of its success in Latin America.

9. Since the fall of Communism (1989–1991), neoliberalism, a revival of the older economic liberalism of Adam Smith,

a. has emphasized "the common good" over "individual responsibility."

b. has rejected the imposition of austerity measures on governments, a policy more associated with John Maynard Keynes.

c. has promoted the involvement of the United Nations to ensure it reaches the social groups most in need.

d. has been an influential intervention philosophy that has become a popular doctrine of powerful financial institutions.

e. has rarely been favored as a viable policy by powerful financial institutions and states alike.

10. Industrialization and factory labor now characterize many societies in Latin America, Africa, the Pacific, and Asia. One effect of the spread of industrialization has been

a. a worldwide decrease in energy consumption because of the use of renewable resources.

b. the increasing overlap of the official-public and the personal-public spheres.

c. the destruction of indigenous economies, ecologies, and populations.

d. the rise of corruption, defined as the abuse of public office for private gain.

e. the increasing confusion of what is public or private property.

FILL IN THE BLANK

1. _____ refers to wealth or resources invested in business with the intent of producing a profit.

2. Weber faulted Marx for an overly simple and exclusively economic view of stratification. According to Weber, there are three dimensions of social stratification. They are _____, _____, and _____.

3. Britain used the notion of a white man's burden to justify its imperialist expansion. France claimed to be engaged in a civilizing mission in its colonies. These, together with some forms of economic development plans, illustrate an _____, an ideological justification for outsiders to guide native peoples in specific directions.

4. The term _____ is used to describe the relations between European countries and their former colonies in the second half of the 20th century.

5. Spelled with an uppercase C, _____ indicates a political movement and doctrine seeking to overthrow capitalism that originated with Russia's Bolshevik Revolution in 1917. Spelled with a lowercase c, _____ describes a social system in which property is owned by the community and in which people work for the common good.

CRITICAL THINKING

1. According to world-system theory, societies are subsystems of bigger systems, with the world system as the largest. What are the various systems, at different levels, in which you participate?

2. How does world-system theory help explain the pressures that lead companies such as IBM, the world's largest information technology company, to hire more than 14,000 additional workers in India, while laying off 13,000 workers in Europe and the United States?

3. What were the causes of the Industrial Revolution? Why did it begin in England rather than France? Why do you think that this knowledge is relevant for an anthropologist interested in investigating the dynamics of industrialization today?

4. Think of a recent case in which a core nation has intervened in the affairs of another nation. What was the intervention philosophy used to justify the action?

5. This chapter describes the labels "First World," "Second World," and "Third World" as a common, although ethnocentric, way of categorizing nations. Why is it ethnocentric? Do you think there is any reason to keep using these labels, despite their problems? Why or why not?

Suggested Additional Readings

Bodley, J.H.
2008 *Anthropology and Contemporary Human Problems*, 5th ed. Lanham, MD: AltaMira. Overview of major problems of today's industrial world: overconsumption, the environment, resource depletion, hunger, overpopulation, violence, and war.

Crosby, A.W., Jr.
2003 *The Columbian Exchange: Biological and Cultural Consequences of 1492.* Westport, CT: Praeger. Describes how Columbus's voyages opened the way for a major exchange of people, resources, and ideas as the Old and New Worlds were forever joined together.

Diamond, J.M.
2005 *Guns, Germs, and Steel: The Fates of Human Societies.* New York: W. W. Norton. An ecological approach to expansion and conquest in world history.

Edelman, M., and A. Haugerud
2004 *The Anthropology of Development and Globalization: From Classical Political Economy to Contemporary Neoliberalism.* Malden, MA: Blackwell. Surveys theories and approaches to development and the global.

Wallerstein, I. M.
2004b *World-Systems Analysis: An Introduction.* Durham, NC: Duke University Press. Basics of world-system theory from the master of that approach.

Wolf, E. R.
1982 *Europe and the People without History.* Berkeley: University of California Press. An anthropologist examines the effects of European expansion on tribal peoples and sets forth a world-system approach to anthropology.

Go to our Online Learning Center website at **www.mhhe.com/kottak** for Internet exercises directly related to the content of this chapter.

Internet
Exercises

What is global climate change, and how can anthropologists study it, along with other environmental threats?

What is cultural imperialism, and what forces work to favor and oppose it?

What are indigenous peoples, and how and why has their importance increased in recent years?

Perito Moreno glacier, in Patagonia, Argentina. In 2009, for the first time ever in winter, part of this glacier collapsed, possibly due to global warming.

understanding OURSELVES

What's your favorite science-fiction movie or TV show? What imagined images of other planets stand out in your memory? Can you visualize *Star Wars'* Death Star, poor old Alderan, Luke's encounter with Yoda on a misty world in the Dagoba system, the two suns of Tatooine. Such images may be as familiar to you as those of real planets. Think, too, about how extraterrestrials have been portrayed in movies–from *ET'*s harmless plant collectors to the would-be conquerors of *Independence Day*, *Starship Troopers*, and a hundred others, to the all-powerful guardians of interplanetary affairs in *The Day the Earth Stood Still* (either the 1951 or the 2008 version). Does "Klaatu barada nikto" mean anything to you?

If some of our most vivid perceptions of other planets are based in fiction, modern technology makes it easier than ever for us to perceive the Earth as both a planet and our world. Each time I start my iPhone a famous image of Earth taken from space appears. Anthropologists can use Google Earth to locate communities they have studied in remote corners of the world. My colleagues and I have even used space images to choose communities to study on Earth. Interested in the causes of deforestation in Madagascar, we examined a series of satellite images taken in successive years to determine areas where the forest cover had diminished significantly. Then we traveled to Madagascar to study those areas on the ground.

It's interesting to imagine what an alien might "see" in similar images. If these aliens were (as the more benevolent science-fiction movies imagine) interested in studying life on Earth, rather than conquering or controlling its inhabitants, they would have a lot to interpret. In my work abroad (and on the ground) I've been impressed by two major global trends: population increase and the shift from subsistence to cash economies. These trends have led to agricultural intensification, resource depletion (including deforestation), and emigration, and have made it increasingly harder to *not* think globally when asking ourselves who we are.

I'm struck by the growing number of young people who have abandoned traditional subsistence pursuits. They seek jobs for cash, but work is scarce, spurring migration within and across national boundaries. They enter the informal economy—often illegally. In turn, transnational migration increases cultural diversity in the United States, Canada, and western European countries. Even small towns in the South and Midwest have Chinese restaurants. Pizza and tacos are as American as apple pie. Every day we encounter people whose ancestral countries and cultures have been studied by anthropologists for generations—making cultural anthropology all the more relevant to our daily lives in an increasingly interconnected world.

This chapter applies an anthropological perspective to contemporary global issues, beginning with a discussion of climate change, aka global warming. Next, we return to issues of development, this time alongside an intervention philosophy that seeks to impose global ecological morality without due attention to cultural variation and autonomy. Also considered is the threat that deforestation poses to global biodiversity. The second half of this chapter turns from ecology to the contemporary flows of people, technology, finance, information, images, and ideology that contribute to a global culture of consumption. Globalization promotes intercultural communication, through the media, travel, and migration, which bring people from different societies into direct contact. Finally, we'll consider how such contacts and external linkages influence indigenous peoples, and how those groups have organized to confront and deal with national and global issues, including human, cultural, and political rights.

Note that it would be impossible for me in a single chapter to discuss all or even most global issues that are salient today and that anthropologists have studied. Some such issues (e.g., war, displacement, terrorism, NGOs, the media) have been considered in previous chapters. For timely anthropological analysis of a range of global issues, see recent books by John H. Bodley (2008a, 2008b) and Richard H. Robbins (2008). The current global issues these anthropologists consider include, but are not limited to, hunger, international interventions, peacekeeping, global health, and sanitation.

GLOBAL CLIMATE CHANGE

The Earth's surface temperatures have risen about 1.4°F (0.7°C) since the early 20th century. (This chapter's "Appreciating Diversity" discusses how this rise has affected an indigenous group in Alaska.) About two-thirds of this increase has been since 1978 (Figure 24.1). Along with rising temperatures, shrinking glaciers and melting polar ice provide additional evidence for global warming. Scientific measurements confirm that global warming is not due to increased solar radiation. The causes are mainly anthropogenic—caused by humans and their activities.

Because our planet's climate is always changing, the key question becomes: How much global warming is due to human activities versus natural climate variability. Most scientists agree that human activities play a major role in global climate change. How can the human factor not be significant given population growth and rapidly increasing use of fossil fuels, which produce greenhouse gases in the atmosphere?

The role of one such gas—carbon dioxide (CO_2)—in warming the Earth's surface has been known for over a century. For hundreds of thousands of years, world temperatures have varied depending on the amount of CO_2 in the atmosphere. The burning of fossil fuels (oil, natural gas, and coal) releases substantial amounts of carbon dioxide. The recent rapid rise in both CO_2 and the Earth's surface temperature is one of the proofs that humans are fueling global warming.

The **greenhouse effect** is a natural phenomenon that keeps the Earth's surface warm. Without greenhouse gases—water vapor (H_2O), carbon dioxide (CO_2), methane (CH_4), nitrous oxide (N_2O), halocarbons, and ozone (O_3)—life as we know it wouldn't exist. Like a greenhouse window, such gases allow sunlight to enter and then prevent heat from escaping the atmosphere. All those gases have increased since the Industrial Revolution. Today, the atmospheric concentration of greenhouse gases has reached its highest level in 400,000 years. It will continue to rise—as will global temperatures—without actions to slow it down (National Academies 2006).

Scientists prefer the term **climate change** to global warming. The former term points out that, beyond rising temperatures, there have been changes in sea levels, precipitation, storms, and ecosystem effects. Along with many ordinary people, some scientists see recent weather events as reflecting climate change. Such events include Florida's 2007 worst-in-a-century drought, the 2005 hurricane season featuring Katrina, the first-ever hurricane in the South Atlantic in 2004, and the severe European heat wave of 2003. Although it is difficult to link any one event to climate change, the conjunction of several events may indicate climate change is playing a role.

The precise effects of climate change on regional weather patterns have yet to be determined. Land areas are expected to warm more than oceans, with the greatest warming in higher latitudes, such as Canada, the northern United States, and northern Europe. Global warming may benefit these areas, offering milder winters and extended growing seasons. However, many more people worldwide probably will be harmed. Already we know that in the Arctic,

anthropology **ATLAS**

Map 18 shows the impact of global warming on ocean temperatures.

greenhouse effect Warming from trapped atmospheric gases.

climate change Global warming plus changing sea levels, precipitation, storms, and ecosystem effects.

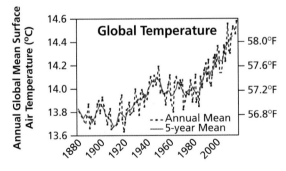

FIGURE 24.1 Global Temperature Change.

Global annual-mean surface air temperature derived from measurements at meteorological stations has increased by 1.4°F (0.7°C) since the early 20th century, with about 0.9°F (0.5°C) of the increase occurring since 1978.

SOURCE: Goddard Institute for Space Studies, from "Understanding and Responding to Climate Change: Highlights of National Academies Reports," http://dels.nas.edu/basc/Climate-HIGH.pdf.

appreciating DIVERSITY

The Plight of Climate Refugees

Human diversity is under attack from climate change. Human beings, their cultures, and their habitats are threatened. Globally, climate change (aka global warming) is raising questions about how to deal with hurricanes, drought, and other threats that affect millions of people and involve huge sums of money. The people described here are among the first climate change refugees in the United States. Residents of Newtok, Alaska, belong to a federally recognized American Indian tribe. Decades ago, the U.S. government mandated that they and other Alaskan natives abandon a nomadic life based on hunting and fishing for sedentism. They now reside in what used to be a winter camp. What obligations does government have to local people whose lives have been disrupted not only by government decree but also by evident global warming?

NEWTOK, Alaska . . . The earth beneath much of Alaska is not what it used to be. The permanently frozen subsoil, known as permafrost, upon which Newtok and so many other Native Alaskan villages rest is melting, yielding to warming air temperatures and a warming ocean. Sea ice that would normally protect coastal villages is forming later in the year, allowing fall storms to pound away at the shoreline.

Erosion has made Newtok an island, caught between the ever widening Ninglick River and a slough to the north. The village is below sea level, and sinking. Boardwalks squish into the spring muck. Human waste, collected in "honey buckets" that many residents use for toilets, is often dumped within eyeshot in a village where no point is more than a five-minute walk from any other. The ragged wooden houses have to be adjusted regularly to level them on the shifting soil.

Studies say Newtok could be washed away within a decade. Along with the villages of Shishmaref and Kivalina farther to the north, it has been the hardest hit of about 180 Alaska villages that suffer some degree of erosion. Some villages plan to hunker down behind sea walls built or planned by the Army Corps of Engineers, at least for now. Others, like Newtok, have no choice but to abandon their patch of tundra. The corps has estimated that to move Newtok could cost $130 million because of its remoteness, climate and topography. That comes to almost $413,000 for each of the 315 residents. . . .

Newtok's leaders say the corps' relocation estimates are inflated, that they intend to move piecemeal rather than in one collective migration, which they say will save money. But they say government should pay, no matter the cost—if only there were a government agency charged with doing so. There is not a formal process by which a village can apply to the government to relocate.

"They grossly overestimate it, and that's why federal and state agencies are afraid to step in," said Stanley Tom, the current tribal administrator . . . "They don't want to spend that much money." Still, Newtok has made far more progress toward moving than other villages, piecing together its move grant by grant.

Through a land swap with the United States Fish and Wildlife Service, it has secured a new site, on Nelson Island, nine miles south. It is safe from the waves on a windy rise above the Ninglick River. They call it Mertarvik, which means "getting water from the spring." They tell their children they will grow up in a place where E. coli does not thrive in every puddle, the way it does here.

With the help of state agencies, it won a grant of about $1 million to build a barge landing at the new site. Bids go out this summer, and construction could be complete next year, providing a platform to unload equipment for building roads, water and sewer systems, houses and a new landing strip. . . .

Senator Ted Stevens, the lion of Alaska politics, is now the ranking minority member on the Senate's new Disaster Recovery subcommittee. His aides say that, while he has yet to push for money to move specific villages, he was instrumental in passing legisla-

temperatures have risen almost twice as much as the global average. Arctic landscapes and ecosystems are changing rapidly and perceptibly, as "Appreciating Diversity" illustrates.

The Intergovernmental Panel on Climate Change (IPCC) is composed of hundreds of scientists from the United States and other countries. In 2001 the IPCC predicted that by 2100 average global surface temperatures will rise 2.5 to 10.4°F (1.4 to 5.8°C) above 1990 levels. The IPCC also forecast ocean warming trends—the combined effects of melting glaciers, melting ice caps, and seawater expansion. The global average sea level is projected to rise 4 to 35 inches (0.1 to 0.9 meters) between 1990 and 2100.

Coastal communities can anticipate increased flooding and more severe storms and surges. At risk are people, animals, plants, freshwater supplies, and such industries as tourism and farming. Along with many island nations, Bangladesh, one of the world's poorest countries, is projected to lose a significant portion (17.5 percent) of its land, displacing millions of people (National Academies 2006). Given the political will, developed countries tion in 2005 that gave the corps broader authority to help. . . .

The administrative leaders of Newtok are mostly men in their 40s, nearly all of them related. They are widely praised by outsiders for their initiative and determination to relocate.

Yet nearly any place would seem an improvement over Newtok as it exists today, and not all of its problems are rooted in climate change. Some are almost universal to Alaskan villages, which have struggled for decades to reconcile their culture of subsistence hunting and fishing with the expectations and temptations of the world outside.

Excrement dumped from honey buckets is piled on the banks of the slow-flowing Newtok River, not far from wooden shacks where residents take nightly steam baths. An elderly man drains kerosene into a puddle of snowmelt. Children pedal past a walrus skull left to rot, tusks intact, in the mud beside a boardwalk that serves as a main thoroughfare. There are no cars here, just snow machines, boats and all-terrain vehicles that tear up the tundra. Village elders speak their native Yupik more often than they speak English. They remember when the village was a collection of families who moved with the seasons, making houses from sod, fishing from Nelson Island in the summer, hunting caribou far away in the winter.

Many men still travel with the seasons to hunt and fish. Some will take boats into Bristol Bay this summer to catch salmon alongside commercial fishermen from out of state. But the waterproof jacket sewn from seal gut that Stanley Tom once wore is now stuffed inside a display case at Newtok School next to other relics.

Now Mr. Tom puts on a puffy parka to walk the few hundred feet he travels to work. He checks his e-mail messages to see if there is news from the corps or from Senator Stevens while his brother, Nick, sketches out a budget proposal for a nonprofit corporation to help manage the relocation, presuming the money arrives.

Thousands of indigenous people living on the Alaskan tundra derive 90 percent or more of what they eat annually from the land, the rivers, and the Bering Sea. Among them are Stanley and Elizabeth Tom and their children, shown here standing beside the Niutaq River in Newtok, Alaska. The local and regional effects of global warming have made the Toms and their fellow villagers climate change refugees.

might use science and technology to anticipate and deal with climate impacts and to help less developed countries adapt to climate change.

The U.S. National Academy of Sciences and other national academies have issued several reports on climate change. Citations and highlights of these reports can be found in a brochure titled "Understanding and Responding to Climate Change: Highlights of National Academies Reports" (http://dels.nas.edu/basc/Climate-HIGH.pdf), on which some of this discussion has been based.

Several factors, known as *radiative forcings*, work to warm and cool the Earth. (Recap 24.1 summarizes them.). Positive forcings, including those due to greenhouse gases, tend to warm the Earth. Negative forcings, such as certain aerosols from industrial processes or volcanic eruptions, tend to cool it. If positive and negative forcings remained in balance, there would be no warming or cooling, but this is not the case today.

Greenhouse gases can remain in the atmosphere for decades, centuries, or longer. Failure to regulate emissions now will make the job

Methane (CH$_4$) is a greenhouse gas whose atmospheric concentration has risen due to an increase in various human activities, including livestock raising. Shown here, cattle wait to be fed at Lubbock Feeders in Lubbock, Texas. How do cattle produce methane?

Many scientists see recent weather catastrophes as reflecting climate change. Such events include the 2005 hurricane season featuring Katrina and fires that devastated southern California in late October 2007. The upper image shows Hurricane Katrina, with sustained winds of 140 mph, in the Gulf of Mexico. Katrina made landfall in southeastern Louisiana on August 29, 2005. The lower photo shows one of dozens of epic fires that swept southern California. One fire was the size of a small European nation. Shown here, on October 23, 2007, firefighters watch as a San Diego Fire Department helicopter drops water on a fire on Via Conejo, between Lake Hodges and Escondido.

anthropology **ATLAS**

Map 16 shows annual energy consumption around the world.

harder in the future. As of this writing, the United States, China, and India—three of the world's major producers of greenhouse gases—have yet to endorse the 1997 Kyoto Protocol. That agreement, signed by 170 countries and in effect through 2012, imposes mandatory caps on greenhouse gases. Political will is needed to curb emissions substantially. In the past, governments have worked together to reduce, and even reverse, human damage to nature. Consider the successful international effort to end the use of chlorofluorocarbons (CFCs) in aerosol sprays and refrigerants. CFCs were destroying the Earth's protective ozone layer.

Meeting energy needs is the single greatest obstacle to slowing climate change. In the United States, about 80 percent of all energy used comes from fossil fuels. Worldwide, energy use continues to grow with economic and population expansion. China and India in particular are rapidly increasing their use of energy, mainly from fossil fuels, and consequently their emissions of CO$_2$ (Figure 24.2). These emissions could be reduced by using energy more efficiently or by using renewable sources. One alternative is ethanol, of which the United States is a limited producer. American policy makers give lip service to the value of ethanol, while restricting its inflow from nations, such as Brazil, that produce it most effectively.

Among the alternatives to fossil fuels are nuclear power and such renewable energy technologies as solar, wind, and biomass generators. Replacing coal-fired electric power plants with more efficient natural-gas-fired turbines would

WARMING:

Carbon dioxide (CO_2)	Has natural and human sources; levels increasing due to burning of fossil fuels.
Methane (CH_4)	Has risen due to an increase in human activities, including livestock raising, rice growing, landfill use, and the extraction, handling, and transport of natural gas.
Ozone (O_3)	Has natural sources, especially in the stratosphere, where chemicals have depleted the ozone layer; ozone also produced in the troposphere (lower part of the atmosphere) when hydrocarbons and nitrogen oxide pollutants react.
Nitrous oxide (N_2O)	Has been rising from agricultural and industrial sources.
Halocarbons	Include chlorofluorocarbons (CFCs), which remain from refrigerants in appliances made before CFC ban.
Aerosols	Some airborne particles and droplets warm the planet; black carbon particles (soot) produced when fossil fuels or vegetation are burned; generally have a warming effect by absorbing solar radiation.

COOLING:

Aerosols	Some cool the planet; sulfate (SO_4) aerosols from burning fossil fuels reflect sunlight back to space.
Volcanic eruptions	Emit gaseous SO_2, which, once in the atmosphere, forms sulfate aerosol and ash. Both reflect sunlight back to space.
Sea ice	Reflects sunlight back to space.
Tundra	Reflects sunlight back to space.

WARMING/COOLING:

Forests	Deforestation creates land areas that reflect more sunlight back to space (cooling); it also removes trees that absorb CO_2 (warming).

reduce carbon emissions. In the United States, these technologies currently are too expensive, or, in the case of nuclear power, they raise environmental or other concerns. This could change with the development and increasing use of new technologies and as the cost of fossil fuels rises.

ENVIRONMENTAL ANTHROPOLOGY

Anthropology always has been concerned with how Environmental forces influence humans and how human activities affect the biosphere and the Earth itself. The 1950s–1970s witnessed the emergence of an area of study known as *cultural ecology* or **ecological anthropology.** That field focused on how cultural beliefs and practices helped human populations adapt to their environments, and how people used elements of their culture to maintain their ecosystems.

Early ecological anthropologists showed that many indigenous groups did a reasonable job of managing their resources and preserving their ecosystems. Such groups had traditional ways of categorizing resources, regulating their use, and preserving the environment. An **ethnoecology** is any society's set of environmental practices and perceptions—that is, its cultural model of the environment and its relation to people and society. Indigenous ethnoecologies increasingly are being challenged, as migration, media, and commerce spread people, institutions, information, and technology. In the face of national and international incentives to exploit and degrade, ethnoecological systems that once preserved local and regional environments increasingly are ineffective or irrelevant.

Anthropologists routinely witness threats to the people they study and their environments. Among such threats are commercial logging, industrial pollution (see last chapter's "Appreciating Anthropology"), and the imposition of external management systems on local ecosystems (see this chapter's "Appreciating Diversity"). Today's ecological anthropology, aka *environmental anthropology,* attempts not only to understand but also to find solutions to environmental problems. Such problems must be tackled at the national and international levels (e.g., global warming). Even in remote places, ecosystem management now involves multiple levels. For example, among the Antankarana of northern Madagascar

ethnoecology
A culture's set of environmental practices and perceptions.

ecological anthropology
Study of cultural adaptations to environments.

FIGURE 24.2

The panels compare CO_2 emissions per nation in 2000 (top) and projections for 2025 (bottom). In 2000, the largest emitter of CO_2 was the United States, which was responsible for 25 percent of global emissions. In 2025, China and the developing world may significantly increase their CO_2 emissions relative to the United States.

SOURCE: Images courtesy of the Marian Koshland Science Museum of the National Academy of Sciences.

The world's most populous nations, China and India, are rapidly increasing their use of energy, mainly from fossil fuels, and consequently their emissions of CO_2. Pictured here are crowds of cars and buses moving slowly during a serious Beijing traffic jam on December 31, 2005.

(Gezon 2006), several levels of authority claim the right to use and regulate natural resources and local ecosystems. Actual or would-be regulators there include local communities, traditional leaders (the regional king or chief), provincial and national governments, and the WWF, the Worldwide Fund for Nature (formerly the World Wildlife Fund), an international NGO. Local people, their landscapes, their ideas, their values, and their traditional management systems face attacks from all sides. Outsiders attempt to remake native landscapes and cultures in their own image. The aim of many agricultural development projects, for example, seems to be to make the world as much like a Midwestern American agricultural state as possible. Often there is an attempt to impose mechanized farming and nuclear family ownership, even though these institutions may be inappropriate in areas far removed from the Midwestern United States. Development projects usually fail when they try to replace indigenous institutions with culturally alien concepts (Kottak 1990*b*).

Global Assaults on Local Autonomy

A clash of cultures related to environmental change may occur when development threatens indigenous peoples and their environments (as we saw in the last chapter's "Appreciating Anthropology"). A second clash of cultures related to environmental change may occur when external regulation aimed at conservation confronts indigenous peoples and their ethnoecologies. Like development projects, conservation schemes may ask people to change their ways in order to satisfy planners' goals rather than local goals. In places as different as Madagascar, Brazil, and the Pacific Northwest of the United States, people have been asked, told, or forced to abandon basic economic activities because to do so is good for "nature" or "the globe." "Good for the globe" doesn't play very well in Brazil, whose Amazon is a focus of international environmentalist attention. Brazilians complain that outsiders (e.g., Europeans and North Americans) promote "global needs" and "saving the Amazon" after having destroyed their own forests for economic growth. Well-intentioned conservation plans can be as insensitive as development schemes that promote radical changes without involving local people in planning and carrying out the policies that affect them. When people are asked to give up the basis of their livelihood, they usually resist.

Consider the case of a Tanosy man living on the edge of the Andohahela reserve of southeastern Madagascar. For years he has relied on rice fields and grazing land inside that reserve. Now external agencies are telling him to abandon this land

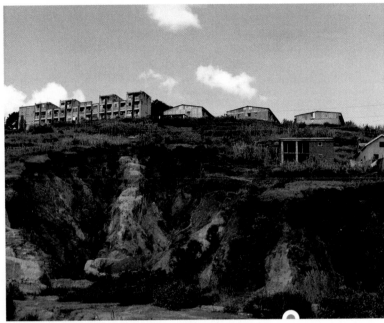

A scene from the "great red island" of Madagascar. On that island, the effects of deforestation, water runoff, and soil erosion are visible to the naked eye.

for the sake of conservation. This man is a wealthy *ombiasa* (traditional sorcerer-healer). With four wives, a dozen children, and 20 head of cattle, he is an ambitious, hardworking, and productive peasant. With money, social support, and supernatural authority, he has mounted effective resistance against the park ranger who has been trying to get him to abandon his fields. The *ombiasa* claims he has already relinquished some of his fields, but he is waiting for compensatory land. His most effective resistance has been supernatural. The death of the ranger's young son was attributed to the *ombiasa*'s magic. After that, the ranger became less vigilant in his enforcement efforts.

The spread of environmentalism may expose radically different notions about the "rights" and value of plants and animals versus humans. In Madagascar, many intellectuals and officials complain that foreigners seem more concerned about lemurs and other endangered species than about the people of Madagascar (the Malagasy). As a geographer there remarked to me, "The next time you come to Madagascar, there'll be no more Malagasy. All the people will have starved to death, and a lemur will have to meet you at the airport." Most Malagasy perceive human poverty as a more pressing problem than animal and plant survival.

Still, who can doubt that conservation, including the preservation of biodiversity, is a worthy goal? The challenge for applied ecological anthropology is to devise culturally appropriate strategies for achieving biodiversity conservation in the face of unrelenting population growth and commercial expansion. How does one get people to support conservation measures that may, in the short run at least, diminish their access to

Applied anthropology uses anthropological perspectives to identify and solve contemporary problems that affect humans. Deforestation is one such problem. Here women take part in a reforestation project in coastal Tanzania near Dar es Salaam.

resources? Like development plans in general, the most effective conservation strategies pay attention to the needs and wishes of the local people.

Deforestation

Deforestation is a global concern. Forest loss can lead to increased greenhouse gas (CO_2) production, which contributes to global warming. The destruction of tropical forests also is a major factor in the loss of global biodiversity, since many species, often of limited distribution and including many primates, live in forests. Tropical forests contain at least half of Earth's species while covering just 6 percent of the planet's land surface. Yet tropical forests are disappearing at the rate of 10 million to 20 million hectares per year (the size of New York State).

Generations of anthropologists have studied how human economic activities (ancient and modern) affect the environment. Anthropologists know that food producers (farmers and herders) typically do more to degrade the environment than foragers do. Population increase and the need to expand farming caused deforestation in many parts of the ancient Middle East and Mesoamerica. Even today, many farmers think of trees as giant weeds to be removed and replaced with productive fields.

Often, deforestation is demographically driven—caused by population pressure. For example, Madagascar's population is growing at a rate of 3 percent annually, doubling every generation. Population pressure leads to migration, including rural–urban migration. Madagascar's capital, Antananarivo, had just 100,000 people in 1967. The population had risen to about 2 million by 2007. Urban growth promotes deforestation if city dwellers rely on fuel wood from the countryside, as is true in Madagascar. As forested watersheds disappear, crop productivity declines. Madagascar is known as the "great red island," after the color of its soil. On that island, the effects of soil erosion and water runoff are visible to the naked eye. From the look of its rivers, Madagascar appears to be bleeding to death. Increasing runoff of water no longer trapped by trees causes erosion of low-lying rice fields near swollen rivers as well as siltation in irrigation canals (Kottak 2007).

Besides population pressure, another prominent cause of deforestation is commercial logging, which can degrade forests in several ways. Obviously, logging deforests because it removes trees. Less evident are the destructive effects of road building, tree dragging, and other features of commercial logging. A logging road may cut a swath for erosion. Loggers may kill a dozen trees for every log they drag out (Kottak, Gezon, and Green 1994).

The global scenarios of deforestation include demographic pressure (from births or immigration) on subsistence economies, commercial logging, road building, cash cropping, fuel wood needs associated with urban expansion, and clearing and burning associated with livestock and grazing. The fact that forest loss has several causes has a policy implication: Different deforestation scenarios require different conservation strategies.

What can be done? On this question applied anthropology weighs in, spurring policy makers to think about new conservation strategies. The traditional approach has been to restrict access to forested areas designated as parks, then employ park guards and punish violators. Modern strategies are more likely to consider the needs, wishes, and abilities of the people (often impoverished) living in and near the forest. Since effective conservation depends on the cooperation of the local people, their concerns must be addressed in devising conservation strategies.

Typically, forests have substantial economic and cultural utility for the communities in and near them. Forests supply firewood and wood for house and granary construction, fences, and technology (e.g., oxcarts and mortars and pestles—for pounding grain). Some forests are used for food production, including slash-and-burn or shifting cultivation. Tree crops such as bananas, fruits, and coffee do well in the forest, where foraging for wild products and medicinal plants also proceeds. Forests also contain vital cultural products. In Madagascar, for example, these products include medicinal plants and pastes considered essential for the proper growth of children. In one ethnic group, rice from a forest field is part of the ceremony used to ensure a successful and fertile marriage. Another ethnic group has its most sacred tombs in the forests. Traditionally, these culturally vital areas of the forest have been tabooed for burning and wood cutting. They are part of an indigenous ethnoecology and a local conservation system that has been in place for generations.

What happens when activities are banned not by the traditional culture but by an external agency? Government-imposed conservation policies may require people to change the way they have been doing things for generations to meet the goals of outside planners rather than those of local people. When communities are asked to give up traditional activities on which they depend for their livelihood, they usually resist, as in the Tanosy case discussed previously.

Reasons to change behavior must make sense to local people. In Madagascar, the economic value of the forest for agriculture (as an anti-erosion mechanism and reservoir of potential irrigation water) provides a much more powerful incentive against forest degradation than do such global goals as "preserving biodiversity." Most Malagasy have no idea that lemurs and other endemic species exist only in Madagascar. Nor would such knowledge provide much of an incentive for them to conserve the forests if doing so jeopardized their livelihoods.

To curb the global deforestation threat, we need conservation strategies that work. Laws and enforcement may help reduce commercially driven deforestation caused by burning and clear-cutting. But local people also use and abuse forested lands. A challenge for the environmentally oriented applied anthropologist is to find ways to make forest preservation attractive to local people and ensure their cooperation. Successful conservation must be based on culturally appropriate policies, which applied anthropologists can help devise for specific places. To provide locally meaningful incentives, we need good anthropological knowledge of each affected area. Applied anthropologists work to make "good for the globe" good for the people.

Risk Perception

Contemporary (applied) ecological anthropologists work to plan and implement policies aimed at environmental preservation. They also advocate for people who are at risk, actually or potentially. One role for today's environmental anthropologist is to assess the extent and nature of risk perception in various groups and to harness that awareness to combat environmental degradation.

anthropology **ATLAS**

Map 1 shows annual percent of world forest loss. Deforestation is associated with a loss of biodiversity, especially in tropical forests.

Seeking audience-grabbing stories, news agencies focus on every conceivable risk—from anthrax to contaminated spinach to the latest tropical depression or suspected terrorist plot. The media underplay long-term hazards, such as obesity and global warming. Shown here, Seattle firefighters hold a suspicious vial found by a mail carrier in downtown Seattle on Thursday, October 11, 2001.

Paradoxically, risk perception may be *more* developed in groups that are *less* endangered objectively. (Compare a fitness-obsessed member of the North American upper middle class with an impoverished peasant in North Korea.) In Brazil, environmental awareness is most developed in places and groups that are most directly influenced by the media and by environmentalism, rather among those who are most endangered.

The mass media hone risk perception. Seeking audience-grabbing stories, news agencies focus on every conceivable "risk"—from anthrax to bird flu to the latest tropical depression or suspected terrorist plot. A world filled with ubiquitous "risks," many unseen and of unmeasured magnitude, is a rich domain for magical thought, which diverts attention from more serious problems. While heightening fears about risks that might kill a dozen rats in 100 years, the media tend to underplay more significant proven hazards, such as obesity or global warming.

The rise of the Internet and cable/satellite TV, with its 24-hour newscasting, has blurred the distinction between the global, the national, and the local. All threats appear closer to home. Constant rebroadcasting magnifies risk perception. Geographical distance is obscured by the national media and their barrage of information; a threat in Buffalo or Sacramento is perceived as one nearby, even if one lives in Atlanta. Globalization has spawned threats that are increasingly magnified by governments, the media, interest groups, and litigation. With so much to worry about, how can we be rationally selective? Brazil has many more unregulated ecological hazards than the United States does, but Brazilians worry much less about them. To be sure, Brazilians are also selective in their risk perception. For years, crime, violence, and lack of jobs have been their main worries.

How is risk *perception* related to *actions* that can reduce threats to the environment? In the United States, politicians tapped fears raised by the attacks of September 11, 2001, to gain support for a "war on terror" and an invasion of Iraq. It may be possible to tap concerns raised by Katrinalike weather events (which many Americans perceive, whether accurately or not, as related to global warming) to spur actions to combat destructive climate change. Once they have perceived the risk, people also need concrete incentives to take action against it (e.g., the need to maintain the water supply for irrigation, to save money, to obtain insurance for a beach house).

INTERETHNIC CONTACT

Since at least the 1920s anthropologists have investigated the changes—on both sides—that arise from contact between industrial and nonindustrial societies. Studies of "social change" and "acculturation" are abundant. British and American ethnographers, respectively, have used these terms to describe the same process. As mentioned, *acculturation* refers to changes that result when groups come into continuous firsthand contact—changes in the cultural patterns of either or both groups (Redfield, Linton, and Herskovits 1936, p. 149).

Acculturation differs from diffusion, or cultural borrowing, which can occur without firsthand contact. For example, most North Americans who eat hot dogs ("frankfurters") have never been to Frankfurt, Germany, nor have most North American Toyota owners or sushi eaters ever visited Japan. Although *acculturation* can be applied to any case of cultural contact and change, the term most often has described **westernization**—the influence of Western expansion on indigenous peoples and their cultures. Thus, local people who wear store-bought clothes, learn Indo-European languages, and otherwise adopt Western customs are called acculturated. Acculturation may be voluntary or forced, and there may be considerable resistance to the process.

Different degrees of destruction, domination, resistance, survival, adaptation, and modification of native cultures may follow interethnic contact. In the most destructive encounters, native and subordinate cultures face obliteration. In cases where contact between the indigenous societies and more powerful outsiders leads to destruction—a situation that is particularly characteristic of colonialist and expansionist eras—a "shock phase" often follows the initial encounter (Bodley, ed. 1988). Outsiders may attack or exploit the native people. Such exploitation may increase mortality, disrupt subsistence, fragment kin groups, damage social support systems, and inspire new religious movements, such as the cargo cults examined in the chapter "Religion" (Bodley, ed. 1988). During the shock phase, there may be civil repression backed by military force. Such factors may lead to the group's cultural collapse (*ethnocide*) or physical extinction (*genocide*).

Religious Change

Religious proselytizing can promote ethnocide, as native beliefs and practices are replaced by Western ones. Sometimes a religion and associated customs are replaced by ideology and behavior more compatible with Western culture. One example is the Handsome Lake religion (as described in the chapter on religion), which led the Iroquois to copy European farming techniques, stressing male rather than female labor. The Iroquois also gave up their communal longhouses and matrilineal descent groups for nuclear family households. The teachings of Handsome Lake led to a new church and religion. This revitalization movement helped the Iroquois survive in a drastically modified environment, but much ethnocide was involved.

westernization
The acculturative influence of Western expansion on local cultures worldwide.

Handsome Lake was a native who created a new religion, drawing on Western models. More commonly, missionaries and proselytizers representing the major world religions, especially Christianity and Islam, are the proponents of religious change. Protestant and Catholic missionization continues even in remote corners of the world. Evangelical Protestantism, for example, is advancing today in Peru, Brazil, and other parts of Latin America. It challenges an often jaded Catholicism that has too few priests and that is sometimes seen mainly as women's religion.

Sometimes the political ideology of a nation-state is pitted against traditional religion. Officials of the former Soviet empire discouraged Catholicism, Judaism, and Islam. In Central Asia, Soviet dominators destroyed Muslim mosques and discouraged religious practice. On the other hand, governments often use their power to advance a religion, such as Islam in Iran or Sudan (see Figure 24.3).

A military government seized power in Sudan in 1989. It immediately launched a campaign to change that country of more than 35 million people, where one-quarter were not Muslims, into an Islamic nation. Sudan adopted a policy of religious, linguistic, and cultural imperialism. The government sought to extend Islam and the Arabic language to the non-Muslim south. This was an area of Christianity and tribal religions that had resisted the central government for a decade (Hedges 1992a).

This resistance continues and has spilled over into Sudan's drought-stricken and impoverished western province of Darfur. As of this writing, more than 2 million Sudanese are living in camps, having fled years of fighting in the region. Sudan's government and pro-government Arab militias have been accused of war crimes against the region's black African population. The Darfur conflict began early in 2003 as non–Islamic rebels waged attacks against government targets, claiming the government was oppressing black Africans in favor of Arabs. Darfur has faced many years of tension over land and grazing rights between nomadic Arabs and black African farmers. One of the two main rebel groups, the Sudan Liberation Army (SLA), includes Nuer and other Nilotic populations.

Cultural Imperialism

Cultural imperialism refers to the spread or advance of one culture at the expense of others, or its imposition on other cultures, which it modifies, replaces, or destroys—usually because of differential economic or political influence. Thus, children in the French colonial empire learned French history, language, and culture from standard textbooks also used in France. Tahitians, Malagasy, Vietnamese, and Senegalese learned

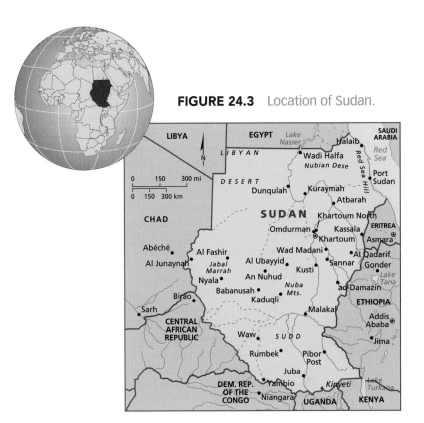

FIGURE 24.3 Location of Sudan.

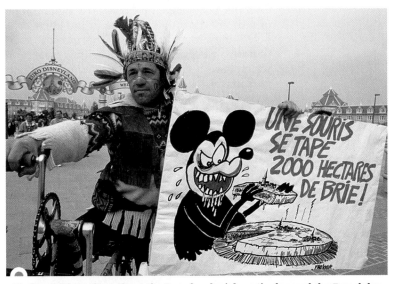

Native children throughout the French colonial empire learned the French language by reciting from books about "our ancestors the Gauls." More recently, French citizens have criticized or resisted what they see as American "cultural imperialism"—one prominent symbol of which has been Euro Disneyland. Has there also been resistance to the expansion of Disney enterprises in the United States?

the French language by reciting from books about "our ancestors the Gauls."

To what extent is modern technology, especially the mass media, an agent of cultural imperialism? Some commentators see modern technology as erasing cultural differences, as

cultural imperialism
Spread of one (dominant) culture at the expense of others.

homogeneous products reach more people worldwide. But others see a role for modern technology in allowing social groups (local cultures) to express themselves and to survive (Marcus and Fischer 1999). Modern radio and TV, for example, constantly bring local happenings (for example, a "chicken festival" in Iowa) to the attention of a larger public. The North American media play a role in stimulating local activities of many sorts. Similarly, in Brazil, local practices, celebrations, and performances are changing in the context of outside forces, including the mass media and tourism.

In the town of Arembepe, Brazil (Kottak 1999a), TV coverage has stimulated participation in a traditional annual performance, the *Chegança*. This is a fishermen's danceplay that reenacts the Portuguese discovery of Brazil. Arembepeiros have traveled to the state capital to perform the *Chegança* before television cameras, for a TV program featuring traditional performances from many rural communities.

One national Brazilian Sunday-night variety program (*Fantástico*) is especially popular in rural areas because it shows such local events. In several towns along the Amazon River, annual folk ceremonies are now staged more lavishly for TV cameras. In the Amazon town of Parantíns, for example, boatloads of tourists arriving any time of year are shown a videotape of the town's annual Bumba Meu Boi festival. This is a costumed performance mimicking bullfighting, parts of which have been shown on *Fantástico*. This pattern, in which local communities preserve, revive, and intensify the scale of traditional ceremonies to perform for TV and tourists, is expanding.

living anthropology **VIDEOS**

Cultural Survival through History, www.mhhe.com/kottak

In this clip, a genial host tours the village museum built by the local community of San José Magote in Oaxaca, Mexico. The narrator highlights artifacts and exhibits commemorating the site's 3,500-year history, including pottery from an ancient chiefly center, a scale model of a Spanish hacienda, and a portrayal of villagers' successful efforts to return land seized by the Spaniards to community ownership. The clip shows one path to cultural survival. The idea that they are the rightful heirs to the cultural traditions of ancient Mexico is an important part of the identity of the local Zapotec people. How are genealogies used to portray local history? How does the clip link those genealogies to the present? Based on the clip, what roles have women played in Zapotec history?

Brazilian television also has played a "top-down" role, by spreading the popularity of holidays like Carnaval and Christmas (Kottak 1990a). TV has aided the national spread of Carnaval beyond its traditional urban centers. Still, local reactions to the nationwide broadcasting of Carnaval and its trappings (elaborate parades, costumes, and frenzied dancing) are not simple or uniform responses to external stimuli.

Rather than direct adoption of Carnaval, local Brazilians respond in various ways. Often they don't take up Carnaval itself but modify their local festivities to fit Carnaval images. Others actively spurn Carnaval. One example is Arembepe,

In San Gimignano, Italy, boys and young men don Medieval costumes and beat drums in a parade through the streets during one of the town's many pageants. Increasingly, local communities perform "traditional" ceremonies for TV and tourists.

where Carnaval has never been important, probably because of its calendrical closeness to the main local festival, which is held in February to honor Saint Francis of Assisi. In the past, villagers couldn't afford to celebrate both occasions. Now, not only do the people of Arembepe reject Carnaval; they are also increasingly hostile to their own main festival. Arembepeiros resent the fact that the Saint Francis festival has become "an outsiders' event," because it draws thousands of tourists to Arembepe each February. The villagers think that commercial interests and outsiders have appropriated Saint Francis.

In opposition to these trends, many Arembepeiros now say they like and participate more in the traditional June festivals honoring Saint John, Saint Peter, and Saint Anthony. In the past, these were observed on a much smaller scale than was the festival honoring Saint Francis. Arembepeiros celebrate them now with a new vigor and enthusiasm, as they react to outsiders and their celebrations, real and televised.

MAKING AND REMAKING CULTURE

To understand culture change, it is important to recognize that meaning may be locally manufactured. People assign their own meanings and value to the texts, messages, and products they receive. Those meanings reflect their cultural backgrounds and experiences.

Indigenizing Popular Culture

When forces from world centers enter new societies, they are **indigenized**—modified to fit the local culture. This is true of cultural forces as different as fast food, music, housing styles, science, terrorism, celebrations, and political ideas and institutions (Appadurai 1990). Consider the reception of the movie *Rambo* in Australia as an example of how popular culture may be indigenized. Michaels (1986) found *Rambo* to be very popular among aborigines in the deserts of central Australia, who had manufactured their own meanings from the film. Their "reading" was very different from the one imagined by the movie's creators and by most North Americans. The Native Australians saw Rambo as a representative of the Third World who was engaged in a battle with the white officer class. This reading expressed their negative feelings about white paternalism and about existing race relations. The Native Australians also imagined that there were tribal ties and kin links between Rambo and the prisoners he was rescuing. All this made sense, based on their experience. Native Australians are disproportionately represented in Australian jails. Their most likely liberator would be someone with a

When products and images enter new settings, they are typically indigenized—modified to fit the local culture. Jeans Street, in Bandung, Indonesia, is a strip of stores, vendors, and restaurants catering to young people interested in Western pop culture. How is the poster of *Batman and Robin* indigenized?

personal link to them. These readings of *Rambo* were relevant meanings produced *from* the text, not *by* it (Fiske 1989).

A Global System of Images

All cultures express imagination—in dreams, fantasies, songs, myths, and stories. Today, however, more people in many more places imagine "a wider set of 'possible' lives than they ever did before. One important source of this change is the mass media, which present a rich, ever-changing store of possible lives" (Appadurai 1991, p. 197). The United States as a media center has been joined by Canada, Japan, Western Europe, Brazil, Mexico, Nigeria, Egypt, India, and Hong Kong.

As print has done for centuries (Anderson 1991), the electronic mass media also can spread, even help create, national and ethnic identities. Like print, television and radio can diffuse the cultures of different countries within their own boundaries, thus enhancing national cultural identity. For example, millions of Brazilians who were formerly cut off (by geographic isolation or illiteracy) from urban and national events and information now participate in a national communication system, through TV networks (Kottak 1990*a*).

Crosscultural studies of television contradict a belief Americans ethnocentrically hold about televiewing in other countries. This misconception is that American programs inevitably triumph over local products. This doesn't happen when there is appealing local competition. In Brazil, for example, the most popular network (TV Globo) relies heavily on native productions, especially *telenovelas*.

indigenized
Modified to fit the local culture.

Globo plays each night to the world's largest and most devoted audience (perhaps 80 million viewers throughout the nation). The programs that attract this horde are made by Brazilians, for Brazilians. Thus, it is not North American culture but a new pan-Brazilian national culture that Brazilian TV is propagating. Brazilian productions also compete internationally. They are exported to over 100 countries, spanning Latin America, Europe, Asia, and Africa.

We may generalize that programming that is culturally alien won't do very well anywhere when a quality local choice is available. Confirmation comes from many countries. National productions are highly popular in Japan, Mexico, India, Egypt, and Nigeria. In a survey during the mid-1980s, 75 percent of Nigerian viewers preferred local productions. Only 10 percent favored imports, and the remaining 15 percent liked the two options equally. Local productions are successful in Nigeria because "they are filled with everyday moments that audiences can identify with. These shows are locally produced by Nigerians" (Gray 1986). Thirty million people watched one of the most popular series, *The Village Headmaster*, each week. That program brought rural values to the screens of urbanites who had lost touch with their rural roots (Gray 1986).

The mass media also can play a role in maintaining ethnic and national identities among people who lead transnational lives. Arabic-speaking Muslims, including migrants, in several countries follow the TV network Al Jazeera, based in Qatar, which helps reinforce ethnic and religious identities. As groups move, they can stay linked to each other and to their homeland through the media. Diasporas (people who have spread out from an original, ancestral homeland) have enlarged the markets for media, communication, and travel services targeted at specific ethnic, national, or religious audiences. For a fee, a PBS station in Fairfax, Virginia, offers more than 30 hours a week to immigrant groups in the D.C. area, to make programs in their own languages.

A Global Culture of Consumption

Besides the electronic media, another key transnational force is finance. Multinational corporations and other business interests look beyond national boundaries for places to invest and draw profits. As Arjun Appadurai (1991, p. 194) puts it, "money, commodities, and persons unendingly chase each other around the world." Residents of many Latin American communities now depend on outside cash, remitted from international labor migration. Also, the economy of the United States is increasingly influenced by foreign investment, especially from Britain, Canada, Germany, the Netherlands, and Japan (Rouse 1991). The American economy also has increased its dependence

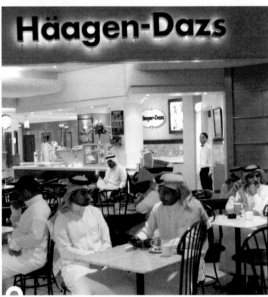

Business and the media have increased the craving for products throughout the world. Barbie dolls and Pocahontas videos are sold in China, as is Häagen-Dazs ice cream in the Middle East.

on foreign labor—through both the immigration of laborers and the export of jobs.

Contemporary global culture is driven by flows of people, technology, finance, information, images, and ideology (Appadurai 1990, 2001). Business, technology, and the media have increased the craving for commodities and images throughout the world (Gottdiener 2000). This has forced nation-states to open to a global culture of consumption. Almost everyone today participates in this culture. Few people have never seen a T-shirt advertising a Western product. American and English rock stars' recordings blast through the streets of Rio de Janeiro, while taxi drivers from Toronto to Madagascar play Brazilian music tapes. Peasants and tribal people participate in the modern world system not only because they have been hooked on cash, but also because their products and images are appropriated by world capitalism (Root 1996). They are commercialized by others (like the San in the movie *The Gods Must Be Crazy*). Furthermore, indigenous peoples also market their own images and products, through outlets like Cultural Survival (see Mathews 2000).

PEOPLE IN MOTION

The linkages in the modern world system have both enlarged and erased old boundaries and distinctions. Arjun Appadurai (1990, p. 1) characterizes today's world as a "translocal" "interactive system" that is "strikingly new." Whether as refugees, migrants, tourists, pilgrims, proselytizers, laborers, businesspeople, development workers, employees of nongovernmental organizations, politicians, terrorists, soldiers, sports figures, or media-borne images, people appear to travel more than ever.

In previous chapters, we saw that foragers and herders are typically seminomadic or nomadic. Today, however, the scale of human movement has expanded dramatically. So important is transnational migration that many Mexican villagers find "their most important kin and friends are as likely to be living hundreds or thousands of miles away as immediately around them" (Rouse 1991). Most migrants maintain their ties with their native land (phoning, e-mailing, visiting, sending money, watching "ethnic TV"). In a sense, they live multilocally—in different places at once. Dominicans in New York City, for example, have been characterized as living "between two islands": Manhattan and the Dominican Republic (Grasmuck and Pessar 1991). Many Dominicans—like migrants from other countries—migrate to the United States temporarily, seeking cash to transform their lifestyles when they return to the Caribbean.

Decisions about whether to risk migration, perhaps illegal, across national boundaries are based on social reasons, such as whether kin already live in the host nation, and economic reasons, in response to ebbs and flows in the global economy. This chapter's "Appreciating Anthropology" discusses how large numbers of Brazilians, and by extension other recent migrants to the United States, are returning home because of the recent economic downturn here, as well as more restrictive immigration laws and enforcement policies.

With so many people "in motion," the unit of anthropological study expands from the local

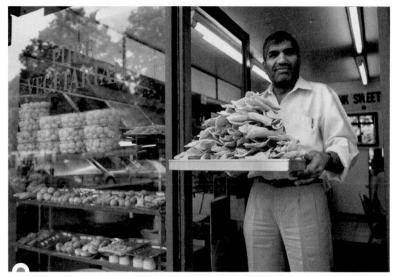

With so many people on the move, the unit of anthropological study has expanded from the local community to the diaspora. This refers to the offspring of an area (e.g., South Asia) who have spread to many lands, such as this Indian sweets shop owner on Ealing Road in London, UK.

community to the **diaspora**—the offspring of an area who have spread to many lands. Anthropologists increasingly follow descendants of the villages we have studied as they move from rural to urban areas and across national boundaries. For the 1991 annual meeting of the American Anthropological Association in Chicago, the anthropologist Robert Kemper organized a session of presentations about long-term ethnographic field work. Kemper's own longtime research focus has been the Mexican village of Tzintzuntzan, which, with his mentor George Foster, he has studied for decades. However, their database now includes not just Tzintzuntzan but its descendants all over the world. Given the Tzintzuntzan diaspora, Kemper was even able to use some of his time in Chicago to visit people from Tzintzuntzan who had established a colony there. In today's world, as people move, they take their traditions and their anthropologists along with them.

Postmodernity describes our time and situation: today's world in flux, these people on the move who have learned to manage multiple identities depending on place and context. In its most general sense, **postmodern** refers to the blurring and breakdown of established canons (rules or standards), categories, distinctions, and boundaries. The word is taken from **postmodernism**—a style and movement in architecture that succeeded modernism, beginning in the 1970s. Postmodern architecture rejected the rules, geometric order, and austerity of modernism. Modernist buildings were expected to have a clear and functional design. Postmodern design is "messier" and more playful. It draws on a diversity of styles from different times and places—including popular,

diaspora
Offspring of an area who have spread to many lands.

postmodernity
Time of questioning of established canons, identities, and standards.

postmodern
Breakdown of established canons, categories, distinctions, and boundaries.

postmodernism
Movement after modernism in architecture; now much wider.

appreciating ANTHROPOLOGY

Giving up the American Dream

Migration studies are common in contemporary anthropology, reflecting the interconnectedness of the world today. Among the migrants studied by anthropologists are descendants of our field sites, who now move not only from rural to urban areas but also across national boundaries. The anthropologist Robert Kemper, for example, follows the worldwide diaspora of a Mexican village, Tzintzuntzan, which he has studied for decades. In today's world, as people move, they take their traditions and their anthropologists along with them. The anthropologist Maxine Margolis, described here for her studies of Brazilians in the United States, originally did field work in Brazil. Later she became interested in Brazilian migration to Paraguay, then the United States. She tracks the fortunes and movements of Brazilians as they respond to events in Brazil, the United States, and the global economy. Described here is a return movement to Brazil spurred by the declining U.S. economy, particularly in construction, a rise in anti-immigrant sentiment, and the rising value of the Brazilian currency relative to the U.S. dollar.

Like hundreds of thousands of middle-class Brazilians who moved to the United States over the last two decades, Jose Osvandir Borges and his wife, Elisabeth, came on tourist visas and stayed as illegal immigrants, putting down roots in ways they never expected.

After packing up their plasma-screen TV, scholastic trophies and other fruits of 12 prosperous years in the Ironbound in Newark, the couple and their American-born daughter, Marianna, 10, were scheduled to fly back to Brazil for good this morning. . . .

"You can't spend your entire life waiting to be legal," said Mr. Borges, 42, reflecting on a hard decision born of lost hopes, new fears and changing economies in both countries since he arrived in 1996. By law, the couple faces a 10-year bar on re-entering the United States, even as visitors.

That decision—to give up on life in the United States—is being made by more and more Brazilians across the country, according to consular officials, travel agencies swamped by one-way ticket bookings, and community leaders in the neighborhoods that Brazilian immigrants have transformed, from Boston to Pompano Beach, Fla. . . .

In the last half year, the reverse migration has become unmistakable among Brazilians in the United States, a population estimated at 1.1 million by Brazil's government—four to five times the official census figures. . . .

Homeward-bound Brazilians point to a rising fear of deportation and a slumping American economy. Many cite the expiration of

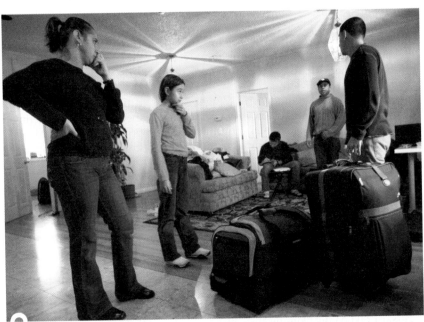

Many Brazilian migrants to the United States, including the ones shown here, are giving up their "American Dream" and returning to Brazil. The photo includes Elisabeth Borges (left), her daughter, Marianna, her husband, Jose Osvandir Borges (seated), and their son, Thiago (right), with Jose Silva, a family friend, in their Newark home on Monday, December 3, 2007.

ethnic, and non-Western cultures. Postmodernism extends "value" well beyond classic, elite, and Western cultural forms. *Postmodern* is now used to describe comparable developments in music, literature, and visual art. From this origin, *postmodernity* describes a world in which traditional standards, contrasts, groups, boundaries, and

identities are opening up, reaching out, and breaking down.

Globalization promotes intercultural communication, including travel and migration, which bring people from different societies into direct contact. The world is more integrated than ever. Yet *disintegration* also surrounds us. Nations dissolve driver's licenses that can no longer be renewed under tougher rules, coupled with the steep drop in the value of the dollar against the currency of Brazil, where the economy has improved . . .

In Massachusetts, says Fausto da Rocha, the founder of the Boston-area Brazilian Immigrant Center, his compatriots—many here illegally—are leaving by the thousands, some after losing homes in the subprime mortgage crisis. . . .

And at Brazil's consulate in Miami, which serves Brazilians in five Southeastern states, officials said a recent survey of moving companies and travel agencies confirmed what they had already surmised from their foot traffic: More Brazilians are leaving the region than arriving—the reversal of an upward curve that seemed unstoppable as recently as 2005, when Brazilians unable to meet tightened visa requirements were sneaking across the United States–Mexico border in record numbers.

It is too soon to say whether the reverse migration of Brazilians puts them in the vanguard of a larger trend among immigrants, or underscores their distinctiveness . . . They generally come from more urban and educated classes than other major groups of illegal immigrants from Latin America, studies show. Many returning now have been investing their American earnings in Brazilian property.

But their own explanation for the surge back to Brazil contradicts conventional wisdom on both sides of the immigration debate.

For years, advocates of giving people like the Borgeses a chance to earn legal status have argued that illegal immigrants will only be driven further underground by enforcement measures like raids or denying them driver's licenses. Advocates of harsher restrictions and penalties have argued that illegal immigration is now growing independently of the ebb and flow of the American economy. Returning Brazilians defy both contentions.

Faced with diminishing rewards and rising expenses in the United States, long separated from aging relatives in Brazil, "people say, 'Is this worth it, being illegal, being scared?'" said Maxine L. Margolis, a professor of anthropology at the University of Florida in Gainesville who has written extensively on Brazilians in the United States.

There are regional variations, but the pattern is consistent. In South Florida, the expiration of a driver's license is often a turning point for families already caught short by the slump in housing construction . . . Until seven years ago, Brazilians with tourist visas could get Florida licenses valid for eight years, but they are all expiring now and cannot be renewed . . .

In Massachusetts, where there is more public transportation, a spate of high-profile immigration raids, coupled with home foreclosures, have played a key role in the exodus . . .

While Brazil does not yet offer the job opportunities of Ireland, which has drawn back emigrants in droves, neither is it an economically bleak or war-torn country. And like Italian immigrants early in the 20th century, who typically planned to return to Italy—half of them eventually doing so—many Brazilians arrived with the intention of going back as soon as they met their financial goals.

But like the Borges family, they soon changed their timetable.

"We came here to save enough money to buy a house" in Brazil, Mr. Borges said, recalling the early weeks when the family slept in a friend's basement and he worked in construction for the first time. They expected to return to Brazil after two years.

Instead, he found his inner entrepreneur. He started a plumbing and construction business that soon employed upward of seven compatriots, paid taxes and helped build name-brand hotels in three states.

But in 2005, as the construction boom began to go bust, larger companies, prompted by labor unions, started to demand working papers, he said. And when his crew could not produce them, they were let go.

As the housing market faltered, weekly earnings in his business shrank from a high of $6,000 to barely $2,000, he said. Expenses like gas and rent rose, making it harder for him and Ms. Borges, who cleaned houses in New York, to pay off loans for the farm they were buying in Brazil.

The dollar, which once bought four Brazilian reals, dropped to a historic low of 1.7 reals in May. Then in June came their personal tipping point: the collapse of the bipartisan bill in Congress that would have offered them, and millions of other illegal residents, a path to legal status.

"After the law didn't pass, it was like all the hope went away at once," said Mr. Borges.

(Yugoslavia, the Soviet Union), as do political blocs (the Warsaw Pact nations) and ideologies ("Communism"). The notion of a "Free World" collapses because it existed mainly in opposition to a group of "Captive Nations"—a label once applied by the United States and its allies to the former Soviet empire that has lost much of its meaning today.

Simultaneously, new kinds of political and ethnic units are emerging. In some cases, cultures and ethnic groups have banded together in larger associations. There is a growing pan-Indian identity (Nagel 1996) and an international pantribal movement as well. Thus, in June 1992, the World Conference of Indigenous Peoples met in Rio de

Janeiro concurrently with UNCED (the United Nations Conference on the Environment and Development). Along with diplomats, journalists, and environmentalists came 300 representatives of the tribal diversity that survives in the modern world—from Lapland to Mali (Brooke 1992; see also Maybury-Lewis 2002).

INDIGENOUS PEOPLES

The term and concept *indigenous people* gained legitimacy within international law with the creation in 1982 of the United Nations Working Group on Indigenous Populations (WGIP). This group, which meets annually, has representation from all six continents. The draft of the Declaration of Indigenous Rights, produced by the WGIP in 1989, was accepted by the UN for discussion in 1993. Convention 169, an ILO (International Labor Organization) document that supports cultural diversity and indigenous empowerment, was approved in 1989. Such declarations and documents, along with the work of the WGIP, have influenced governments, NGOs, and international agencies, including the World Bank, to express greater concern for, and to adopt policies designed to benefit, indigenous peoples. Social movements worldwide have adopted the term *indigenous people* as a self-identifying and political label based on past oppression but now legitimizing a search for social, cultural, and political rights (de la Peña 2005).

In Spanish-speaking Latin America, social scientists and politicians favor the term *indígena* (indigenous person) over *indio* (Indian)—the colonial term that the Spanish and Portuguese conquerors used to refer to the native inhabitants of the Americas. With the national independence movements that ended Latin American colonialism, the situation of indigenous peoples did not necessarily improve. For the white and *mestizo* (mixed) elites of the new nations, *indios* and their lifestyle were perceived as alien to (European) civilization. But Indians also were seen as redeemable by intellectuals, who argued for social policies to improve their welfare (de la Peña 2005).

Until the mid- to late 1980s, Latin American public discourse and state policies emphasized assimilation and discouraged indigenous identification and mobilization. Indians were associated with a romanticized past but marginalized in the present, except for museums, tourism, and folkloric events. Argentina's Indians were all but invisible. Indigenous Bolivians and Peruvians were encouraged to self-identify as *campesinos* (peasants). The past 30 years have seen a dramatic shift. The emphasis has shifted from biological and cultural assimilation—*mestizaje*—to identities that value difference, especially Indianness. In Ecuador groups seen previously as Quichua-speaking peasants are classified now as indigenous communities with assigned territories. Other Andean "peasants" have experienced reindigenization as well. Brazil has recognized 30 new indigenous communities in the northeast, a region previously seen as having lost its indigenous population (see "Beyond the Classroom"). In Guatemala, Nicaragua, Brazil, Colombia, Mexico, Paraguay, Ecuador, Argentina, Bolivia, Peru, and Venezuela, constitutional reforms have recognized those nations as

Working to promote cultural survival is a growing international pantribal movement. In June 1992, the World Conference of Indigenous Peoples met in Rio de Janeiro. Along with diplomats, journalists, and environmentalists came 300 representatives of the tribal diversity that survives in the modern world.

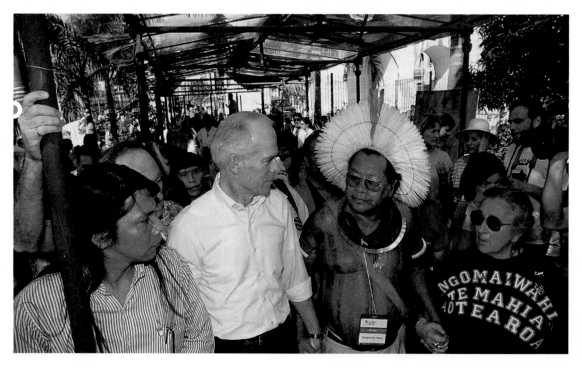

multicultural (Jackson and Warren 2005). Several national constitutions now recognize the rights of indigenous peoples to cultural distinctiveness, sustainable development, political representation, and limited self-government. In Colombia, for example, indigenous communities have been confirmed as rightful owners of large territories. Their leaders and councils have the same benefits as any local government. Two seats in the Colombian senate are reserved for Indian representatives (de la Peña 2005).

In Latin America, the drive by indigenous peoples for self-determination has emphasized (1) their cultural distinctiveness; (2) political reforms involving a restructuring of the state; (3) territorial rights and access to natural resources, including control over economic development; and (4) reforms of military and police powers over indigenous peoples (Jackson and Warren 2005).

The indigenous rights movement, and government responses to it, take place in the context of globalization, including transnational social movements focusing on such issues as human rights, women's rights, and environmentalism. Transnational organizations have helped indigenous peoples influence national legislative agendas. NGOs specializing in development and human rights have come to see indigenous peoples as clients. Many Latin American countries have signed international human rights treaties and covenants.

Although Latin America has experienced a general shift from authoritarian to democratic rule since the 1980s, ethnic and racial discrimination and inequality haven't disappeared. We should recognize as well that indigenous organizing has a high toll, including assassinations of indigenous leaders and their supporters. Especially in Guatemala, Peru, and Colombia there has been severe political repression, along with thousands of indigenous deaths, indigenous refugees, and internally displaced persons (Jackson and Warren 2005).

Ceuppens and Geschiere (2005) explore a recent upsurge of the notion of *autochthony* (being native to, or formed in, the place where found)—with an implicit call for excluding strangers—in different parts of the world. The terms *autochthony* and *indigenous* both go back to classical Greek history, with similar implications. *Autochthony* refers to self and soil. *Indigenous* literally means born inside, with the connotation in classical Greek of being born "inside the house." Both notions stress the need to safeguard ancestral lands (patrimony) from strangers, along with the rights of first-comers to special privileges and protection versus later immigrants—legal or illegal (Ceuppens and Geschiere 2005).

During the 1990s, autochthony became an issue in many parts of Africa, inspiring violent efforts to exclude "strangers"—especially in Francophone (French-speaking) areas, but spilling over into Anglophone (English-speaking) countries as well.

La Paz, Bolivia, May 23, 2005: Bolivians claiming an Indian (indigenous) identity rally for indigenous rights and the nationalization of that country's gas resources. In December 2005, Bolivians elected as their president Evo Morales, the candidate of the Indigenous Movement toward Socialism party. The party made further gains in 2006 parliamentary elections.

Simultaneously, autochthony became a key notion in debates about immigration and multiculturalism in Europe. Unlike "indigenous peoples," the label *autochthon* has been claimed by majority groups in Europe. This term highlights the prominence that the exclusion of strangers has assumed in day-to-day politics worldwide (Ceuppens and Geschiere 2005). One familiar example is the United States, as represented in the congressional debate that broke out, beginning in spring 2006, over illegal immigration.

Identity in Indigenous Politics

Essentialism describes the process of viewing an identity as established, real, and frozen, to hide the historical processes and politics within which that identity developed. One example would be the ethnic labels "Hutu" and "Tutsi" in Rwanda, as discussed in the chapter "The World System and Colonialism." Those labels actually had nothing to do with ethnicity when they were created. Nation-states have used essentializing strategies (e.g., the Tutsi–Hutu distinction) to perpetuate hierarchies and to justify violence against categories seen as less than fully human.

Identities, emphatically, are not fixed. We saw in the chapter "Ethnicity and Race" that identities are fluid and multiple. People seize on particular, sometimes competing, self-labels and identities. Some Peruvian groups, for instance, self-identify as *mestizos* but still see themselves as indigenous. Identity is a fluid, dynamic process, and there are

essentialism
Viewing identities that have developed historically as innate and unchanging.

multiple ways of being indigenous. Neither speaking an indigenous language nor wearing "native" clothing is required. Identities are asserted at particular times and places by particular individuals and groups, and after various kinds of negotiations. Indigenous identity coexists with, and must be managed in the context of, other identity components, including religion, race, and gender. Identities always must be seen as (1) potentially plural, (2) emerging through a specific process, and (3) ways of being someone or something in particular times and places (Jackson and Warren 2005).

No social movement exists apart from the nation that includes it. Nor is any contemporary nation isolated from the world system, globalization, and transnational organization.

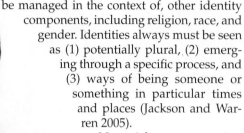

THE CONTINUANCE OF DIVERSITY

Anthropology has a crucial role to play in promoting a more humanistic vision of social change, one that respects the value of human biological and cultural diversity. The existence of anthropology is itself a tribute to the continuing need to understand similarities and differences among human beings throughout the world. Anthropology teaches us that the adaptive responses of humans can be more flexible than those of other species because our main adaptive means are sociocultural. However, the cultural forms, institutions, values, and customs of the past always influence subsequent adaptation, producing continued diversity and giving a certain uniqueness to the actions and reactions of different groups. With our knowledge and our awareness of our professional responsibilities, let us work to keep anthropology, the study of humankind, the most humanistic of all the sciences.

Acing the
COURSE

Summary

1. Fueling global warming are human population growth and use of fossil fuels, which produce greenhouse gases. The atmospheric concentration of those gases has increased since the Industrial Revolution, and especially since 1978. Climate change encompasses global warming along with changing sea levels, precipitation, storms, and ecosystem effects. Coastal communities can anticipate increased flooding and more severe storms and surges. Greenhouse gases can remain in the atmosphere for centuries. Political will is needed to curb emissions now.

2. Anthropology always has been concerned with how environmental forces influence humans and how human activities affect the biosphere. Many indigenous groups did a reasonable job of preserving their ecosystems. An ethnoecology is any society's set of environmental practices and perceptions—that is, its cultural model of the environment in relation to people and society. Indigenous ethnoecologies increasingly are being challenged by global forces that work to exploit and degrade—and that sometimes aim to protect—the environment. The challenge for applied ecological anthropology is to devise culturally appropriate strategies for conservation in the face of unrelenting population growth and commercial expansion.

3. Deforestation is a major factor in the loss of global biodiversity. The global scenarios of deforestation include demographic pressure (from births or immigration) on subsistence economies, commercial logging, road building, cash cropping, fuel wood needs associated with urban expansion, and clearing and burning associated with livestock and grazing. The fact that forest loss has several causes has a policy implication: Different deforestation scenarios require different conservation strategies. Applied anthropologists must work to make "good for the globe" good for the people.

4. One role for today's environmental anthropologist is to assess the extent and nature of risk perception in various groups and to harness that awareness to combat environmental degradation. Risk perception tends to be greatest in places and among groups that are most directly influenced by the media and by environmentalism, rather than among those who are most endangered. It may be possible to tap concerns raised by recent weather events to spur actions to combat destructive climate change.

5. Different degrees of destruction, domination, resistance, survival, and modification of native cultures may follow interethnic contact. This may lead to a tribe's cultural collapse (ethnocide) or its

physical extinction (genocide). *Cultural imperialism* refers to the spread of one culture and its imposition on other cultures, which it modifies, replaces, or destroys—usually because of differential economic or political influence. Some worry that modern technology, including the mass media, is destroying traditional cultures. But others see an important role for new technology in allowing local cultures to express themselves.

6. When forces from global centers enter new societies, they are *indigenized*. Like print, the electronic mass media can help diffuse a national culture within its own boundaries. The media also play a role in preserving ethnic and national identities among people who lead transnational lives. Business, technology, and the media have increased the craving for commodities and images throughout the world, creating a global culture of consumption.

7. People travel more than ever. But migrants also maintain ties with home, so they live multilocally. With so many people "in motion," the unit of anthropological study expands from the local community to the diaspora. *Postmodernity* describes this world in flux, such people on the move who manage multiple social identities depending on place and context. New kinds of political and ethnic units are emerging as others break down or disappear.

8. The term and concept *indigenous people* has gained legitimacy within international law. Governments, NGOs, and international agencies have adopted policies designed to recognize and benefit indigenous peoples. Social movements worldwide have adopted this term as a self-identifying and political label based on past oppression but now signaling a search for social, cultural, and political rights.

9. In Latin America, emphasis has shifted from biological and cultural assimilation to identities that value difference. Several national constitutions now recognize the rights of indigenous peoples. Transnational organizations have helped indigenous peoples influence national legislative agendas. Recent use of the notion of *autochthony* (being native to, or formed in, the place where found) includes a call to exclude strangers, such as recent and illegal immigrants. Identity is a fluid, dynamic process, and there are multiple ways of being indigenous. No social movement exists apart from the nation and world that include it.

Key Terms

Test Yourself!

MULTIPLE CHOICE

1. Scientific measurements confirm that global warming is not due to increased solar radiation. The causes are mainly anthropogenic. This means that
   a. they are caused by humans and their activities.
   b. they are indigenized.
   c. they affect the lives of humans but are caused by normal climate fluctuations.
   d. they are social constructions that politicians and scientists produce to create fear among the general public and justify their salaries.
   e. they are a natural result of 5 million years of human evolution.

2. All of the following are true about the greenhouse effect *except*:
   a. Without greenhouse gases—water vapor, carbon dioxide, methane, nitrous oxide, halocarbons, and ozone—life as we know it wouldn't exist.
   b. It is a natural phenomenon that keeps the Earth's surface warm.
   c. Greenhouse gases can remain in the atmosphere for decades, centuries, or longer.
   d. Because it is a natural phenomenon, any increase in the production of greenhouse gases will be solved by nature's own balancing mechanisms, always preserving life on Earth.
   e. Today, the atmospheric concentration of greenhouse gases has reached its highest level in 400,000 years.

3. Environmental anthropology
   a. is concerned with ethnoecology—that is, an indigenous society's set of environmental practices and perceptions and how they deviate from the truth that only scientists have discovered about nature.
   b. focuses on how indigenous ecologies are increasingly incorporated into the environmental policies of nation-states.
   c. attempts not only to understand but also to find solutions to environmental problems.
   d. supports agricultural development projects that help educate people on how to increase mechanized farming and nuclear family ownership.

e. emerged in the 1950s but since the 1970s its popularity has waned because environmental problems have become too complex to study from an anthropological perspective.

4. One role for today's environmental anthropologists is to assess the extent and nature of risk perception in various groups and to harness that awareness to combat environmental degradation. Paradoxically,
   a. risk perception may be *more* developed in groups that are *less* endangered objectively.
   b. the mass media have little to do with risk perception.
   c. risk perception has no effect on actions that can reduce threats to the environment.
   d. the rise of the Internet and cable/satellite TV has accentuated the distinction between the global, the national, and the local, making it easier for environmental anthropologists to study risk perception.
   e. risk perception translates directly into concrete actions to help reduce this source of risk.

5. Which of the following statements about environmentalism is *not* true?
   a. Brazilians complain that First World moralists preach about global needs and saving the Amazon after having destroyed their own forests for First World economic growth.
   b. It began in the Third World in response to the destruction of tropical forests.
   c. Much of the non-Western world sees Western ecological morality as yet another imperialist message.
   d. Often it is an intervention philosophy.
   e. Its advocates can be as ethnocentric as are advocates of development.

6. When forces from world centers enter new societies, they are often modified to fit the local culture. Which of the following terms refers to this process?
   a. texting
   b. forced acculturation
   c. essentialization
   d. selective modification
   e. indigenization

7. Which of the following statements about television is true?
   a. Studies show that people reject its messages without much processing or reinterpretation.
   b. It is especially favored by the French because of its role in promoting and exposing the French to other cultures.
   c. It plays a role in allowing people to express themselves and in disseminating local cultures.
   d. It is more popular in urban than in rural areas.
   e. It plays no "top-down" role.

8. What term does Arjun Appadurai (1990) use to describe the linkages in the modern world that have both enlarged and erased old boundaries and distinctions?
   a. postmodern
   b. ethnocentric
   c. translocal
   d. essentialized
   e. diasporic

9. What is the term for our contemporary world in flux, with people on the move, in which established groups, boundaries, identities, contrasts, and standards are reaching out and breaking down?
   a. postmodernism
   b. diaspora
   c. hegemony
   d. postmodernity
   e. globalization

10. In Latin America, the drive by indigenous peoples for self-identification has emphasized all of the following *except*
   a. their cultural distinctiveness.
   b. political reforms involving a restructuring of the state.
   c. territorial rights and access to natural resources, including control over economic development.
   d. reforms of military and police powers over indigenous peoples.
   e. their autochthony, with an implicit call for excluding strangers from their communities.

FILL IN THE BLANK

1. Scientists prefer the term _____ to *global warming*. The former term points out that, beyond rising temperature, there have been changes in sea levels, precipitation, storms, and ecosystem effects.

2. An _____ is any society's set of environmental practices and perceptions—that is, its cultural model of the environment and its relation to people and society.

3. _____ refers to changes that result when groups come into continuous firsthand contact. _____, however, can occur without firsthand contact.

4. _____ refers to the rapid spread or advance of one culture at the expense of others, or its imposition on other cultures.

5. With so many people "in motion," in today's world, the unit of anthropological study expands from the local community to the _____—the offspring of an area who have spread to many lands.

CRITICAL THINKING

1. What does it mean to apply an anthropological perspective to contemporary global issues? Can you come up with an anthropological research question that investigates such issues? Imagine you had a year (and the money!) to carry out this project. How would you spend your time and your resources?

2. The topic of global climate change has been hotly debated during the last few years. Why is there so much debate? Are you concerned with global climate change? Do you think everyone on the planet should be equally concerned and share the responsibility of doing something about it? Why or why not?

3. Consider majority and minority rights in the context of contemporary events involving religion, politics, and law. Should religion be an ascribed or an achieved status? Should someone in a Muslim nation be allowed to convert to a different religion? Why? In your country, how much influence should majority and minority religions be allowed to have on politics and the law?

4. Do you now live, or have you ever lived, multilocally? How so?

5. What term do anthropologists use to describe the view that identities have developed historically as innate and unchanging? We know, however, that identities are not fixed; they are fluid and multiple. What does this mean? What implications does this have for understanding indigenous political movements?

Multiple Choice: 1. (A); 2. (D); 3. (C); 4. (A); 5. (B); 6. (E); 7. (C); 8. (C); 9. (D); 10. (E); **Fill in the Blank:** 1. *climate change*; 2. ethnoecology; 3. Acculturation, Diffusion; 4. Cultural imperialism; 5. diaspora.

Ahmed, A. S.
2004 *Postmodernism and Islam: Predicament and Promise*, rev. ed. New York: Routledge. Clear presentation of postmodernism in relation to the media and to images of Islam.

Appadurai, A., ed.
2001 *Globalization*. Durham, NC: Duke University Press. The flows that create today's world system.

Bodley, J. H.
2008 *Victims of Progress*, 5th ed. Lanham, MD: AltaMira. Social change, acculturation, and culture conflict involving indigenous peoples.

Johansen, B. E.
2003 *Indigenous Peoples and Environmental Issues: An Encyclopedia*. Westport, CT: Greenwood.

A compendium of knowledge about environmental issues as they affect and reflect local communities.

Maybury-Lewis, D.
2002 *Indigenous Peoples, Ethnic Groups, and the State*, 2nd ed. Boston: Allyn & Bacon. Indigenous peoples and ethnicity in the contemporary world.

Robbins, R. H.
2008 *Global Problems and the Culture of Capitalism*, 4th ed. Boston: Pearson/Allyn & Bacon. Examines issues of domination, resistance, and social and economic problems in today's world.

Suggested
Additional
Readings

Go to our Online Learning Center website at **www.mhhe.com/kottak** for Internet exercises directly related to the content of this chapter.

Internet
Exercises

GLOSSARY

Audible pronunciations for many of the following terms are provided in the electronic Glossary on the Online Learning Center at **www.mhhe.com/kottak.**

A. afarensis Early forms of *Australopithecus*, known from Hadar in Ethiopia ("Lucy") and Laetoli in Tanzania; the Hadar remains date to 3.3–3.0 m.y.a.; the Laetoli remains are older, dating to 3.8–3.6 m.y.a.; despite its many apelike features, *A. afarensis* was an upright biped.

A. (Australopithecus) africanus Gracile *Australopithecus* species (3.0?–2.0? m.y.a.), South Africa; first australopithecine ever discovered.

A. anamensis Earliest known *Australopithecus* species (4.2–3.9 m.y.a.), from Kenya.

A. boisei Late, hyperrobust *Australopithecus* species (2.6?–1.2 m.y.a.), East Africa; coexisted with early *Homo*.

absolute dating Dating techniques that establish dates in numbers or ranges of numbers; examples include the radiometric methods of ^{14}C, K/A, ^{238}U, TL, and ESR dating.

acculturation The exchange of cultural features that results when groups come into continuous firsthand contact; the cultural patterns of either or both groups may be changed, but the groups remain distinct.

Acheulian Derived from the French village of St. Acheul, where these tools were first identified; Lower Paleolithic tool tradition associated with *H. erectus*.

achieved status Social status that comes through talents, choices, actions, and accomplishments, rather than ascription.

adaptive Favored by natural selection in a particular environment.

adaptive strategy Means of making a living; productive system.

aesthetics Appreciation of the qualities perceived in works of art; the mind and emotions in relation to a sense of beauty.

affinals Relatives by marriage, whether of lineals (e.g., son's wife) or collaterals (e.g., sister's husband).

A. garhi Tool-making *Australopithecus* species (2.5 m.y.a..); discovered in Ethiopia.

agency The actions of individuals, alone and in groups, that create and transform culture.

age set Group uniting all men or women born during a certain time span; this group controls property and often has political and military functions.

agriculture Nonindustrial systems of plant cultivation characterized by continuous and intensive use of land and labor.

allele A biochemical variant of a particular gene.

Allen's rule Rule stating that the relative size of protruding body parts (such as ears, tails, bills, fingers, toes, and limbs) tends to increase in warmer climates.

ambilineal Principle of descent that does not automatically exclude the children of either sons or daughters.

AMHs See *anatomically modern humans.*

analogies Similarities arising as a result of similar selective forces; traits produced by convergent evolution.

anatomically modern humans (AMHs) Including the Cro-Magnons of Europe (31,000 B.P.) and the older fossils from Skhūl (100,000), Qafzeh (92,000), Herto, and other sites; continue through the present; also known as *H. sapiens sapiens.*

animism Belief in souls or doubles.

anthropoids Members of Anthropoidea, one of the two suborders of primates; monkeys, apes, and humans are anthropoids.

anthropology The study of the human species and its immediate ancestors.

anthropology and education Anthropological research in classrooms, homes, and neighborhoods, viewing students as total cultural creatures whose enculturation and attitudes toward education belong to a larger context that includes family, peers, and society.

anthropometry The measurement of human body parts and dimensions, including skeletal parts (*osteometry*).

antimodernism The rejection of the modern in favor of what is perceived as an earlier, purer, and better way of life.

applied anthropology The application of anthropological data, perspectives, theory, and methods to identify, assess, and solve contemporary social problems.

arboreal Tree-dwelling; arboreal primates include gibbons, New World monkeys, and many Old World monkeys.

archaeological anthropology The study of human behavior and cultural patterns and processes through the culture's material remains.

archaic H. sapiens Early *H. sapiens*, consisting of the Neandertals of Europe and the Middle East, the Neandertal-like hominids of Africa and Asia, and the immediate ancestors of all these hominids; lived from about 300,000 to 28,000 B.P.

Ardipithecus Earliest recognized hominin genus (5.8–4.4 m.y.a), Ethiopia; species are kadabba (earlier) and ramidus (later).

A. robustus aka *Paranthropus*; robust *Australopithecus* species (2.0?–1.0? m.y.a.), South Africa.

art An object or event that evokes an aesthetic reaction—a sense of beauty, appreciation, harmony, and/or pleasure; the quality, production, expression, or realm of what is beautiful or of more than ordinary significance; the class of objects subject to aesthetic criteria.

arts The arts include the visual arts, literature (written and oral), music, and theater arts.

ascribed status Social status (e.g., race or gender) that people have little or no choice about occupying.

assimilation The process of change that a minority group may experience when it moves to a country where another culture dominates; the minority is incorporated into the dominant culture to the point that it no longer exists as a separate cultural unit.

association An observed relationship between two or more variables.

australopithecines Varied group of Pliocene–Pleistocene hominids. The term is derived from their former classification as members of a distinct subfamily, the Australopithecinae; now they are distinguished from *Homo* only at the genus level.

Aztec Last independent state in the Valley of Mexico; capital was Tenochtitlan. Thrived between 1325 and the Spanish Conquest in 1520.

balanced polymorphism Two or more forms, such as alleles of the same gene, that maintain a constant frequency in a population from generation to generation.

balanced reciprocity See *generalized reciprocity*.

band Basic unit of social organization among foragers. A band includes fewer than 100 people; it often splits up seasonally.

behavioral ecology Study of the evolutionary basis of social behavior.

behavioral modernity Fully human behavior based on symbolic thought and cultural creativity.

Bergmann's rule Rule stating that the smaller of two bodies similar in shape has more surface area per unit of weight and therefore can dissipate heat more efficiently; hence, large bodies tend to be found in colder areas and small bodies in warmer ones.

bifurcate collateral kinship terminology Kinship terminology employing separate terms for M, F, MB, MZ, FB, and FZ.

bifurcate merging kinship terminology Kinship terminology in which M and MZ are called by the same term, F and FB are called by the same term, and MB and FZ are called by different terms.

big man Regional figure found among tribal horticulturalists and pastoralists. The big man occupies no office but creates his reputation through entrepreneurship and generosity to others. Neither his wealth nor his position passes to his heirs.

bilateral kinship calculation A system in which kinship ties are calculated equally through both sexes: mother and father, sister and brother, daughter and son, and so on.

biocultural Referring to the inclusion and combination (to solve a common problem) of both biological and cultural approaches—one of anthropology's hallmarks.

biological anthropology The study of human biological variation in time and space; includes evolution, genetics, growth and development, and primatology.

bipedal Upright two-legged locomotion, the key feature distinguishing early hominins from the apes.

Black English Vernacular (BEV) A rule-governed dialect of American English with roots in Southern English. BEV is spoken by African American youth and by many adults in their casual, intimate speech—sometimes called "ebonics."

blade tool The basic Upper Paleolithic tool type, hammered off a prepared core.

bone biology The study of bone as a biological tissue, including its genetics; cell structure; growth, development, and decay; and patterns of movement (*biomechanics*).

bourgeoisie One of Marx's opposed classes; owners of the means of production (factories, mines, large farms, and other sources of subsistence).

brachiation Under-the-branch swinging; characteristic of gibbons, siamangs, and some New World monkeys.

bridewealth See *progeny price*.

broad-spectrum revolution Period beginning around 15,000 B.P. in the Middle East and 12,000 B.P. in Europe, during which a wider range, or broader spectrum, of plant and animal life was hunted, gathered, collected, caught, and fished; revolutionary because it led to food production.

bronze An alloy of arsenic and copper or tin and copper.

call systems Systems of communication among nonhuman primates, composed of a limited number of sounds that vary in intensity and duration. Tied to environmental stimuli.

capital Wealth or resources invested in business, with the intent of producing a profit.

capitalist world economy The single world system, which emerged in the 16th century, committed to production for sale, with the object of maximizing profits rather than supplying domestic needs.

cargo cults Postcolonial, acculturative religious movements, common in Melanesia, that attempt to explain European domination and wealth and to achieve similar success magically by mimicking European behavior.

catastrophism View that extinct species were destroyed by fires, floods, and other catastrophes. After each destructive event, God created again, leading to contemporary species.

catharsis Intense emotional release.

chiefdom A ranked society in which relations among villages as well as among individuals are unequal, with smaller villages under the authority of leaders in larger villages; has a two-level settlement hierarchy.

chiefdom Form of sociopolitical organization intermediate between the tribe and the state; kin-based with differential access to resources and a permanent political structure.

chromosomes Basic genetic units, occurring in matching (homologous) pairs; lengths of DNA made up of multiple genes.

clan Unilineal descent group based on stipulated descent.

climate change Global warming plus changing sea levels, precipitation, storms, and ecosystem effects.

cline A gradual shift in gene frequencies between neighboring populations.

Clovis Stone technology based on a projectile point that was fastened to the end of a hunting spear; it flourished between 12,000 and 11,000 B.P. in North America.

collateral relative A genealogical relative who is not in ego's direct line, such as B, Z, FB, or MZ.

colonialism The political, social, economic, and cultural domination of a territory and its people by a foreign power for an extended time.

communal religions In Wallace's typology, these religions have, in addition to shamanic cults, communal cults in which people organize community rituals such as harvest ceremonies and rites of passage.

Communism Spelled with an uppercase C, a political movement and doctrine seeking to overthrow capitalism and to establish a form of communism such as that which prevailed in the Soviet Union from 1917 to 1991.

communism Spelled with a lowercase c, describes a social system in which property is owned by the community and in which people work for the common good.

communitas Intense community spirit, a feeling of great social solidarity, equality, and togetherness; characteristic of people experiencing liminality together.

complex societies Nations; large and populous, with social stratification and central governments.

configurationalism View of culture as integrated and patterned.

conflict resolution Means of settling disputes.

convergent evolution Independent operation of similar selective forces; the process by which analogies are produced.

core Dominant structural position in the world system; consists of the strongest and most powerful states with advanced systems of production.

core values Key, basic, or central values that integrate a culture and help distinguish it from others.

correlation An association between two or more variables such that when one changes (varies), the other(s) also change(s) (covaries); for example, temperature and sweating.

cosmology A system, often religious, for imagining and understanding the universe.

Cro Magnon The first fossil find (1868) of an AMH, from France's Dorlogne Valley.

cross cousins Children of a brother and a sister.

crossing over During meiosis, the process by which homologous chromosomes intertwine and exchange segments of their DNA.

cultivation continuum A continuum based on the comparative study of nonindustrial cultivating societies in which labor intensity increases and fallowing decreases.

cultural anthropology The study of human society and culture; describes, analyzes, interprets, and explains social and cultural similarities and differences.

cultural colonialism Internal domination by one group and its culture or ideology over others.

cultural consultants Subjects in ethnographic research; people the ethnographer gets to know in the field, who teach him or her about their culture.

cultural imperialism The rapid spread or advance of one culture at the expense of others, or its imposition on other cultures, which it modifies, replaces, or destroys—usually because of differential economic or political influence.

cultural materialism Idea (Harris) that cultural infrastructure determines structure and superstructure.

cultural relativism The position that the values and standards of cultures differ and deserve respect. Anthropology is characterized by methodological rather than moral relativism: In order to understand another culture fully, anthropologists try to understand its members' beliefs and motivations. Methodological relativism does not preclude making moral judgments or taking action.

cultural resource management (CRM) The branch of applied archaeology aimed at preserving sites threatened by dams, highways, and other projects.

cultural rights Doctrine that certain rights are vested in identifiable groups, such as religious and ethnic minorities and indigenous societies. Cultural rights include a group's ability to preserve its culture, to raise its children in the ways of its forebears, to continue its language, and not to be deprived of its economic base by the nation-state in which it is located.

cultural transmission A basic feature of language; transmission through learning.

culture Distinctly human; transmitted through learning; traditions and customs that govern behavior and beliefs.

cuneiform Early Mesopotamian writing that used a stylus (writing implement) to write wedge-shaped impressions on raw clay; from the Latin word for "wedge."

curer Specialized role acquired through a culturally appropriate process of selection, training, certification, and acquisition of a professional image; the curer is consulted by patients, who believe in his or her special powers, and receives some form of special consideration; a cultural universal.

daughter languages Languages developing out of the same parent language; for example, French and Spanish are daughter languages of Latin.

dendrochronology Or tree-ring dating: a method of absolute dating based on the study and comparison of patterns of tree-ring growth.

descent Rule assigning social identity on the basis of some aspect of one's ancestry.

descent group A permanent social unit whose members claim common ancestry; fundamental to tribal society.

development anthropology The branch of applied anthropology that focuses on social issues in—and the cultural dimension of—economic development.

diachronic (Studying societies) across time.

diaspora The offspring of an area who have spread to many lands.

differential access Unequal access to resources; basic attribute of chiefdoms and states. Superordinates have favored access to such resources, while the access of subordinates is limited by superordinates.

diffusion Borrowing of cultural traits between societies, either directly or through intermediaries.

diglossia The existence of "high" (formal) and "low" (informal, familial) dialects of a single language, such as German.

discrimination Policies and practices that harm a group and its members.

disease A scientifically identified health threat caused by a bacterium, virus, fungus, parasite, or other pathogen.

displacement A basic feature of language; the ability to speak of things and events that are not present.

domestic–public dichotomy Contrast between women's role in the home and men's role in public life, with a corresponding social devaluation of women's work and worth.

dominant Allele that masks another allele in a heterozygote.

dowry A marital exchange in which the wife's group provides substantial gifts to the husband's family.

ecological anthropology Study of cultural adaptations to environments.

economizing The rational allocation of scarce means (or resources) to alternative ends (or uses); often considered the subject matter of economics.

economy A population's system of production, distribution, and consumption of resources.

egalitarian society A type of society, most typically found among hunter-gatherers, that lacks status distinctions except for those based on age, gender, and individual qualities, talents, and achievements.

ego Latin for *I*. In kinship charts, the point from which one views an egocentric genealogy.

emic The research strategy that focuses on local explanations and criteria of significance.

empire A mature, territorially large, and expansive, state; empires are typically multiethnic, multilinguistic, and more militaristic, with a better developed bureaucracy than earlier states.

enculturation The social process by which culture is learned and transmitted across the generations.

endogamy Rule or practice of marriage between people of the same social group.

equity, increased A reduction in absolute poverty and a fairer (more even) distribution of wealth.

essentialism The process of viewing an identity as established, real, and frozen to hide the historical processes and politics within which that identity developed.

ethnic group Group distinguished by cultural similarities (shared among members of that group) and differences (between that group and others); ethnic-group members share beliefs, customs, and norms and, often, a common language, religion, history, geography, and kinship.

ethnicity Identification with, and feeling part of, an ethnic group and exclusion from certain other groups because of this affiliation.

ethnocentrism The tendency to view one's own culture as best and to judge the behavior and beliefs of culturally different people by one's own standards.

ethnocide Destruction of cultures of certain ethnic groups.

ethnoecology Any society's set of environmental practices and perceptions; its cultural model of the environment and its relation to people and society.

ethnography Field work in a particular culture.

ethnology Crosscultural comparison; the comparative study of ethnographic data, society, and culture.

ethnomusicology The comparative study of the musics of the world and of music as an aspect of culture and society.

ethnosemantics The study of lexical (vocabulary) contrasts and classifications in various languages.

etic The research strategy that emphasizes the ethnographer's rather than the locals' explanations, categories, and criteria of significance.

evolution Belief that species arose from others through a long and gradual process of transformation, or descent with modification.

excavation Digging through the layers of deposits that make up an archaeological or fossil site.

exogamy Rule requiring people to marry outside their own group.

expressive culture The arts; people express themselves creatively in dance, music, song, painting, sculpture, pottery, cloth, storytelling, verse, prose, drama, and comedy.

extended family household Expanded household including three or more generations.

extradomestic Outside the home; within or pertaining to the public domain.

family of orientation Nuclear family in which one is born and grows up.

family of procreation Nuclear family established when one marries and has children.

fiscal Pertaining to finances and taxation.

focal vocabulary A set of words and distinctions that are particularly important to certain groups (those with particular foci of experience or activity), such as types of snow to Eskimos or skiers.

folk Of the people; originally coined for European peasants; refers to the art, music, and lore of ordinary people, as contrasted with the "high" art or "classic" art of the European elites.

food production Cultivation of plants and domestication (stockbreeding) of animals; first developed 10,000 to 12,000 years ago.

fossils Remains (e.g., bones), traces, or impressions (e.g., footprints) of ancient life.

functional explanation Explanation that establishes a correlation or interrelationship between social customs. When customs are functionally interrelated, if one changes, the others also change.

functionalism Approach focusing on the role (function) of sociocultural practices in social systems.

fundamentalism Describes antimodernist movements in various religions. Fundamentalists assert an identity separate from the larger religious group from which they arose; they advocate strict fidelity to the "true" religious principles on which the larger religion was founded.

gender roles The tasks and activities that a culture assigns to each sex.

gender stereotypes Oversimplified but strongly held ideas about the characteristics of males and females.

gender stratification Unequal distribution of rewards (socially valued resources, power, prestige, and personal freedom) between men and women, reflecting their different positions in a social hierarchy.

gene Area in a chromosome pair that determines, wholly or partially, a particular biological trait, such as whether one's blood type is A, B, or O.

gene flow Exchange of genetic material between populations of the same species through direct or indirect interbreeding.

gene pool All the alleles, genes, chromosomes, and genotypes within a breeding population—the "pool" of genetic material available.

genealogical method Procedures by which ethnographers discover and record connections of kinship, descent, and marriage, using diagrams and symbols.

general anthropology The field of anthropology as a whole, consisting of cultural, archaeological, biological, and linguistic anthropology.

generality Culture pattern or trait that exists in some but not all societies.

generalized reciprocity Principle that characterizes exchanges between closely related individuals. As social distance increases, reciprocity becomes balanced and finally negative.

generational kinship terminology Kinship terminology with only two terms for the parental generation, one designating M, MZ, and FZ and the other designating F, FB, and MB.

genetic evolution Change in gene frequency within a breeding population.

genitor Biological father of a child.

genocide Deliberate elimination of a group through mass murder.

genotype An organism's hereditary makeup.

gibbons The smallest apes, natives of Asia; arboreal.

glacials The four or five major advances of continental ice sheets in northern Europe and North America.

globalization The accelerating interdependence of nations in a world system linked economically and through mass media and modern transportation systems.

gracile Opposite of robust; "gracile" indicates that members of *A. africanus* were a bit smaller and slighter, less robust, than members of *A. robustus*.

greenhouse effect Warming from trapped atmospheric gases.

Halafian An early (7500–6500 B.P.) and widespread pottery style, first found in northern Syria; refers to a delicate ceramic style and to the period when the first chiefdoms emerged.

haplogroup A lineage marked by one or more specific genetic mutations.

head, village A local leader in a tribal society who has limited authority, leads by example and persuasion, and must be generous.

health-care systems Beliefs, customs, and specialists concerned with ensuring health and preventing and curing illness; a cultural universal.

hegemony As used by Antonio Gramsci, a stratified social order in which subordinates comply with domination by internalizing its values and accepting its "naturalness."

Herto Very early (160,000–154,000 B.P.) AMHs found in Ethiopia.

heterozygous Having dissimilar alleles of a given gene.

hidden transcript As used by James Scott, the critique of power by the oppressed that goes on offstage—in private—where the power holders can't see it.

Hilly Flanks Woodland zone that flanks the Tigris and Euphrates rivers to the north; zone of wild wheat and barley and of sedentism (settled, nonmigratory life) preceding food production.

historical linguistics Subdivision of linguistics that studies languages over time.

Historical particularism Idea (Boas) that histories are not comparable; diverse paths can lead to the same cultural result.

holistic Interested in the whole of the human condition: past, present, and future; biology, society, language, and culture.

hominid A member of the taxonomic family that includes humans and the African apes and their immediate ancestors.

hominin A member of the human lineage after its split from ancestral chimps; the term *hominin* is used to describe all the human species that ever have existed, including the extinct ones, and excluding chimps and gorillas.

hominoids Members of the superfamily including humans and all the apes.

Homo habilis Term coined by L. S. B. and Mary Leakey; immediate ancestor of *H. erectus*; lived from about 2.4 to 1.4 m.y.a.

homologies Traits that organisms have jointly inherited from a common ancestor.

homozygous Possessing identical alleles of a particular gene.

honorific A term, such as "Mr." or "Lord," used with people, often by being added to their names, to "honor" them.

horticulture Nonindustrial system of plant cultivation in which plots lie fallow for varying lengths of time.

human rights Doctrine that invokes a realm of justice and morality beyond and superior to particular countries, cultures, and religions. Human rights, usually seen as vested in individuals, would include the right to speak freely, to hold religious beliefs without persecution, and not to be murdered, injured, enslaved, or imprisoned without charge.

hypodescent Rule that automatically places the children of a union or mating between members of different socioeconomic groups in the less privileged group.

hypothesis A suggested but as yet unverified explanation.

illness A condition of poor health perceived or felt by an individual.

imperialism A policy of extending the rule of a nation or empire over foreign nations or of taking and holding foreign colonies.

incest Forbidden sexual relations with a close relative.

independent assortment Mendel's law of; chromosomes are inherited independently of one another.

independent invention Development of the same cultural trait or pattern in separate cultures as a result of comparable needs, circumstances, and solutions.

indigenized Modified to fit the local culture.

indigenous peoples The original inhabitants of particular territories; often descendants of tribespeople who live on as culturally distinct colonized peoples, many of whom aspire to autonomy.

Industrial Revolution The historic transformation (in Europe, after 1750) of "traditional" into "modern" societies through industrialization of the economy.

informed consent Agreement to take part in research, after the people being studied have been told about that research's purpose, nature, procedures, and potential impact on them.

interglacials Extended warm periods between such major glacials as Riss and Würm.

international culture Cultural traditions that extend beyond national boundaries.

interpretive anthropology (Geertz) The study of a culture as a system of meaning.

intervention philosophy Guiding principle of colonialism, conquest, missionization, or development; an ideological justification for outsiders to guide native peoples in specific directions.

interview schedule Ethnographic tool for structuring a formal interview. A prepared form (usually printed or mimeographed) that guides interviews with households or individuals being compared systematically. Contrasts with a *questionnaire* because the researcher has personal contact with the local people and records their answers.

IPR Intellectual property rights, consisting of each society's cultural base—its core beliefs and principles. IPR are claimed as a group right—a cultural right—allowing indigenous groups to control who may know and use their collective knowledge and its applications.

key cultural consultant Person who is an expert on a particular aspect of local life.

kinesics The study of communication through body movements, stances, gestures, and facial expressions.

kinship calculation The system by which people in a particular society reckon kin relationships.

language Human beings' primary means of communication; may be spoken or written; features productivity and displacement and is culturally transmitted.

law A legal code, including trial and enforcement; characteristic of state-organized societies.

leveling mechanism A custom or social action that operates to reduce differences in wealth and thus to bring standouts in line with community norms.

levirate Custom by which a widow marries the brother of her deceased husband.

lexicon Vocabulary; a dictionary containing all the morphemes in a language and their meanings.

life history Of a key consultant or narrator; provides a personal cultural portrait of existence or change in a culture.

liminality The critically important marginal or in between phase of a rite of passage.

lineage Unilineal descent group based on demonstrated descent.

lineal kinship terminology Parental generation kin terminology with four terms: one for M, one for F, one for FB and MB, and one for MZ and FZ.

lineal relative Any of ego's ancestors or descendants (e.g., parents, grandparents, children, grandchildren) on the direct line of descent that leads to and from ego.

linguistic anthropology The descriptive, comparative, and historical study of language and of linguistic similarities and differences in time, space, and society.

longitudinal research Long-term study of a community, region, society, culture, or other unit, usually based on repeated visits.

magic Use of supernatural techniques to accomplish specific aims.

maize Corn; domesticated in highland Mexico.

mana Sacred impersonal force in Melanesian and Polynesian religions.

manioc Cassava; a tuber domesticated in the South American lowlands.

market principle Profit-oriented principle of exchange that dominates in states, particularly industrial states. Goods and services are bought and sold, and values are determined by supply and demand.

mater Socially recognized mother of a child.

matrifocal Mother-centered; often refers to a household with no resident husband-father.

matrilineal descent Unilineal descent rule in which people join the mother's group automatically at birth and stay members throughout life.

matrilocality Customary residence with the wife's relatives after marriage, so that children grow up in their mother's community.

means (or factors) of production Land, labor, technology, and capital—major productive resources.

medical anthropology Unites biological and cultural anthropologists in the study of disease, health problems, health-care systems, and theories about illness in different cultures and ethnic groups.

meiosis Special process by which sex cells are produced; four cells are produced from one, each with half the genetic material of the original cell.

melanin Substance manufactured in specialized cells in the lower layers of the epidermis (outer skin layer);

melanin cells in dark skin produce more melanin than do those in light skin.

Mesoamerica Middle America, including Mexico, Guatemala, and Belize.

Mesolithic Middle Stone Age, whose characteristic tool type was the microlith; broad-spectrum economy.

Mesopotamia The area between the Tigris and Euphrates rivers in what is now southern Iraq and southwestern Iran; location of the first cities and states.

metallurgy Knowledge of the properties of metals, including their extraction and processing and the manufacture of metal tools.

mitosis Ordinary cell division; DNA molecules copy themselves, creating two identical cells out of one.

mode of production Way of organizing production—a set of social relations through which labor is deployed to wrest energy from nature by means of tools, skills, and knowledge.

molecular anthropology Genetic analysis, involving comparison of DNA sequences, to determine evolutionary links and distances among species and among ancient and modern populations.

monotheism Worship of an eternal, omniscient, omnipotent, and omnipresent supreme being.

morphology The study of form; used in linguistics (the study of morphemes and word construction) and for form in general—for example, biomorphology relates to physical form.

Mousterian Middle Paleolithic tool-making tradition associated with Neandertals.

multiculturalism The view of cultural diversity in a country as something good and desirable; a multicultural society socializes individuals not only into the dominant (national) culture but also into an ethnic culture.

multivariate Involving multiple factors, causes, or variables.

mutation Change in the DNA molecules of which genes and chromosomes are built.

m.y.a. Million years ago.

nation Once a synonym for "ethnic group," designating a single culture sharing a language, religion, history, territory, ancestry, and kinship; now usually a synonym for state or *nation-state*.

national culture Cultural experiences, beliefs, learned behavior patterns, and values shared by citizens of the same nation.

nationalities Ethnic groups that once had, or wish to have or regain, autonomous political status (their own country).

nation-state An autonomous political entity; a country like the United States or Canada.

Natufians Widespread Middle Eastern culture, dated to between 12,500 and 10,500 B.P.; subsisted on intensive wild cereal collecting and gazelle hunting and had year-round villages.

natural selection The process by which the forms most fit to survive and reproduce in a given environment do so in greater numbers than others in the same population; more

than survival of the fittest, natural selection is differential reproductive success.

Neandertals *H. sapiens neanderthalensis*, representing an archaic *H. sapiens* subspecies, lived in Europe and the Middle East between 130,000 and 28,000 B.P.

negative reciprocity See *generalized reciprocity*.

neoliberalism Revival of Adam Smith's classic economic liberalism, the idea that governments should not regulate private enterprise and that free-market forces should rule; a currently dominant intervention philosophy.

Neolithic New Stone Age, coined to describe techniques of grinding and polishing stone tools; the first cultural period in a region in which the first signs of domestication are present.

neolocality Postmarital residence pattern in which a couple establishes a new place of residence rather than living with or near either set of parents.

nomadism, pastoral Movement throughout the year by the whole pastoral group (men, women, and children) with their animals; more generally, such constant movement in pursuit of strategic resources.

office Permanent political position.

Oldowan Earliest (2.5 to 1.2 m.y.a.) stone tools; sharp flakes struck from cores (choppers).

Olympian religions In Wallace's typology, develop with state organization; have full-time religious specialists—professional priesthoods.

opposable thumb A thumb that can touch all the other fingers.

out of Africa theory Theory that a small group of anatomically modern people arose recently, probably in Africa, from which they spread and replaced the native and more archaic populations of other inhabited areas.

overinnovation Characteristic of projects that require major changes in natives' daily lives, especially ones that interfere with customary subsistence pursuits.

paleoanthropology Study of hominid and human life through the fossil record.

Paleolithic Old Stone Age (from Greek roots meaning "old" and "stone"); divided into Lower (early), Middle, and Upper (late).

paleontology Study of ancient life through the fossil record.

paleopathology Study of disease and injury in skeletons from archaeological sites.

palynology Study of ancient plants through pollen samples from archaeological or fossil sites in order to determine a site's environment at the time of occupation.

parallel cousins Children of two brothers or two sisters.

particularity Distinctive or unique culture trait, pattern, or integration.

pastoralists People who use a food-producing strategy of adaptation based on care of herds of domesticated animals.

pater Socially recognized father of a child; not necessarily the genitor.

patriarchy Political system ruled by men in which women have inferior social and political status, including basic human rights.

patrilineal descent Unilineal descent rule in which people join the father's group automatically at birth and stay members throughout life.

patrilineal-patrilocal complex An interrelated constellation of patrilineality, patrilocality, warfare, and male supremacy.

patrilocality Customary residence with the husband's relatives after marriage, so that children grow up in their father's community.

peasant Small-scale agriculturalist living in a state with rent fund obligations.

periphery Weakest structural position in the world system.

phenotype An organism's evident traits, its "manifest biology"—anatomy and physiology.

phenotypical adaptation Adaptive biological changes that occur during the individual's lifetime, made possible by biological plasticity.

phoneme Significant sound contrast in a language that serves to distinguish meaning, as in minimal pairs.

phonemics The study of the sound contrasts (phonemes) of a particular language.

phonetics The study of speech sounds in general; what people actually say in various languages.

phonology The study of sounds used in speech.

physical anthropology See *biological anthropology*.

Pleistocene Epoch of *Homo*'s appearance and evolution; began 1.8 million years ago; divided into Lower, Middle, and Upper.

plural marriage Any marriage with more than two spouses, aka polygamy.

plural society A society that combines ethnic contrasts and economic interdependence of the ethnic groups.

political economy The web of interrelated economic and power relations in society.

polyandry Variety of plural marriage in which a woman has more than one husband.

polygyny Variety of plural marriage in which a man has more than one wife.

polytheism Belief in several deities who control aspects of nature.

population genetics Field that studies causes of genetic variation, maintenance, and change in breeding populations.

postcolonial Referring to interactions between European nations and the societies they colonized (mainly after 1800); more generally, "postcolonial" may be used to signify a position against imperialism and Eurocentrism.

postmodern In its most general sense, describes the blurring and breakdown of established canons (rules, standards), categories, distinctions, and boundaries.

postmodernism A style and movement in architecture that succeeded modernism. Compared with modernism, postmodernism is less geometric, less functional, less austere, more playful, and more willing to include elements from diverse times and cultures; postmodern now describes comparable developments in music, literature, visual art, and anthropology.

postmodernity Condition of a world in flux, with people on the move, in which established groups, boundaries, identities, contrasts, and standards are reaching out and breaking down.

potlatch Competitive feast among Indians on the North Pacific Coast of North America.

power The ability to exercise one's will over others—to do what one wants; the basis of political status.

prejudice Devaluing (looking down on) a group because of its assumed behavior, values, capabilities, attitudes, or other attributes.

prestige Esteem, respect, or approval for acts, deeds, or qualities considered exemplary.

primary states States that arise on their own (through competition among chiefdoms), not through contact with other state societies.

primatology The study of fossil and living apes, monkeys, and prosimians, including their behavior and social life.

productivity A basic feature of language; the ability to use the rules of one's language to create new expressions comprehensible to other speakers.

progeny price A gift from the husband and his kin to the wife and her kin before, at, or after marriage; legitimizes children born to the woman as members of the husband's descent group.

prosimians The primate suborder that includes lemurs, lorises, and tarsiers.

protolanguage Language ancestral to several daughter languages.

public transcript As used by James Scott, the open, public interactions between dominators and oppressed—the outer shell of power relations.

punctuated equilibrium Evolutionary theory that long periods of stasis (stability), during which species change little, are interrupted (punctuated) by evolutionary leaps.

questionnaire Form (usually printed) used by sociologists to obtain comparable information from respondents. Often mailed to and filled in by research subjects rather than by the researcher.

race An ethnic group assumed to have a biological basis.

racial classification The attempt to assign humans to discrete categories (purportedly) based on common ancestry.

racism Discrimination against an ethnic group assumed to have a biological basis.

random genetic drift Change in gene frequency that results not from natural selection but from chance; most evident in small populations.

random sample A sample in which all members of the population have an equal statistical chance of being included.

ranked society A type of society with hereditary inequality but not social stratification; individuals are ranked in terms of their genealogical closeness to the chief, but there is a continuum of status, with many individuals and kin groups ranked about equally.

recessive Genetic trait masked by a dominant trait.

reciprocity One of the three principles of exchange; governs exchange between social equals; major exchange mode in band and tribal societies.

reciprocity continuum Runs from generalized (closely related/deferred return) to negative (strangers/immediate return) reciprocity.

redistribution Major exchange mode of chiefdoms, many archaic states, and some states with managed economies.

refugees People who have been forced (involuntary refugees) or who have chosen (voluntary refugees) to flee a country, to escape persecution or war.

relative dating Dating technique, for example, stratigraphy, that establishes a time frame in relation to other strata or materials, rather than absolute dates in numbers.

religion Belief and ritual concerned with supernatural beings, powers, and forces.

remote sensing Use of aerial photos and satellite images to locate sites on the ground.

revitalization movements Movements that occur in times of change, in which religious leaders emerge and undertake to alter or revitalize a society.

rickets Nutritional disease caused by a shortage of vitamin D; interferes with the absorption of calcium and causes softening and deformation of the bones.

rites of passage Culturally defined activities associated with the transition from one place or stage of life to another.

ritual Behavior that is formal, stylized, repetitive, and stereotyped, performed earnestly as a social act; rituals are held at set times and places and have liturgical orders.

robust Large, strong, sturdy; said of skull, skeleton, muscle, and teeth; opposite of gracile.

sample A smaller study group chosen to represent a larger population.

Sapir-Whorf hypothesis Theory that different languages produce different ways of thinking.

science A systematic field of study or body of knowledge that aims, through experiment, observation, and deduction, to produce reliable explanations of phenomena, with reference to the material and physical world.

scientific medicine As distinguished from Western medicine, a health-care system based on scientific knowledge and procedures, encompassing such fields as pathology, microbiology, biochemistry, surgery, diagnostic technology, and applications.

sedentism Settled (sedentary) life; preceded food production in the Old World and followed it in the New World.

semantics A language's meaning system.

semiperiphery Structural position in the world system intermediate between core and periphery.

settlement hierarchy A ranked series of communities differing in size, function, and type of building; a three-level settlement hierarchy indicates state organization.

sexual dimorphism Marked differences in male and female biology besides the contrasts in breasts and genitals.

sexual orientation A person's habitual sexual attraction to, and activities with, persons of the opposite sex, heterosexuality; the same sex, homosexuality; or both sexes, bisexuality.

sexual selection Based on differential success in mating, the process in which certain traits of one sex (e.g., color in male birds) are selected because of advantages they confer in winning mates.

shaman A part-time religious practitioner who mediates between ordinary people and supernatural beings and forces.

smelting The high-temperature process by which pure metal is produced from an ore.

social control Those fields of the social system (beliefs, practices, and institutions) that are most actively involved in the maintenance of norms and the regulation of conflict.

sociolinguistics Investigates relationships between social and linguistic variations.

sodality, pantribal A nonkin-based group that exists throughout a tribe, spanning several villages.

sororate Custom by which a widower marries the sister of his deceased wife.

speciation Formation of new species; occurs when subgroups of the same species are separated for a sufficient length of time.

species Population whose members can interbreed to produce offspring that can live and reproduce.

state Sociopolitical organization based on central government and socioeconomic stratification—a division of society into classes.

state (nation-state) Complex sociopolitical system that administers a territory and populace with substantial contrasts in occupation, wealth, prestige, and power. An independent, centrally organized political unit; a government. A form of social and political organization with a formal, central government and a division of society into classes.

status Any position that determines where someone fits in society; may be ascribed or achieved.

stereotypes Fixed ideas—often unfavorable—about what the members of a group are like.

stratification A stratified society has sharp social divisions—*strata*—based on unequal access to wealth and power (e.g., into noble and commoner classes).

stratification Characteristic of a system with socioeconomic strata—groups that contrast in regard to social status and access to strategic resources. Each stratum includes people of both sexes and all ages.

stratified Class-structured; stratified societies have marked differences in wealth, prestige, and power between social classes.

stratigraphy Science that examines the ways in which earth sediments are deposited in demarcated layers known as *strata* (singular, *stratum*).

style shifts Variations in speech in different contexts.

subcultures Different cultural traditions associated with subgroups in the same complex society.

subgroups Languages within a taxonomy of related languages that are most closely related.

subordinate The lower, or underprivileged, group in a stratified system.

superordinate The upper, or privileged, group in a stratified system.

superorganic (Kroeber) The special domain of culture, beyond the organic and inorganic realms.

survey research Characteristic research procedure among social scientists other than anthropologists. Studies society through sampling, statistical analysis, and impersonal data collection.

symbol Something, verbal or nonverbal, that arbitrarily and by convention stands for something else, with which it has no necessary or natural connection.

symbolic anthropology The study of society through sampling, statistical analysis, and impersonal data collection.

synchronic (Studying societies) at one time.

syncretisms Cultural mixes, including religious blends, that emerge from acculturation—the exchange of cultural features when cultures come into continuous firsthand contact.

syntax The arrangement and order of words in phrases and sentences.

systematic survey Information gathered on patterns of settlement over a large area; provides a regional perspective on the archaeological record.

taboo Set apart as sacred and off-limits to ordinary people; prohibition backed by supernatural sanctions.

taphonomy The study of the processes that affect the remains of dead animals, such as their scattering by carnivores and scavengers, their distortion by various forces, and their possible fossilization.

taxonomy Classification scheme; assignment to categories (*taxa*; singular, *taxon*).

teosinte Or teocentli, a wild grass; apparent ancestor of maize.

Teotihuacan A.D. 100 to 700; first state in the Valley of Mexico and earliest major Mesoamerican empire.

terrestrial Ground-dwelling; baboons, macaques, and humans are terrestrial primates; gorillas spend most of their time on the ground.

text Any cultural product that can be "read"—that is, processed, interpreted, and assigned meaning by anyone (any "reader") exposed to it.

theory A set of ideas formulated (by reasoning from known facts) to explain something. The main value of a theory is to promote new understanding. A theory suggests patterns, connections, and relationships that may be confirmed by new research.

Thomson's nose rule Rule stating that the average nose tends to be longer in areas with lower mean annual temperatures; based on the geographic distribution of nose length among human populations.

transhumance One of two variants of pastoralism; part of the population moves seasonally with the herds while the other part remains in home villages.

tribe Form of sociopolitical organization usually based on horticulture or pastoralism. Socioeconomic stratification and centralized rule are absent in tribes, and there is no means of enforcing political decisions.

tropics Geographic belt extending about 23 degrees north and south of the equator, between the Tropic of Cancer (north) and the Tropic of Capricorn (south).

underdifferentiation Planning fallacy of viewing less developed countries as an undifferentiated group; ignoring cultural diversity and adopting a uniform approach (often ethnocentric) for very different types of project beneficiaries.

uniformitarianism Belief that explanations for past events should be sought in ordinary forces that continue to work today.

unilineal descent Matrilineal or patrilineal descent.

unilinear evolutionism Idea (19th century) of a single line or path of cultural development—a series of stages through which all societies must evolve.

universal Something that exists in every culture.

Upper Paleolithic Blade-tool-making traditions associated with early *H. sapiens sapiens*; named from their location in upper, or more recent, layers of sedimentary deposits.

urban anthropology Anthropological study of cities and urban life.

variables Attributes (e.g., sex, age, height, weight) that differ from one person or case to the next.

wealth All a person's material assets, including income, land, and other types of property; the basis of economic status.

westernization The acculturative influence of Western expansion on native cultures.

working class, or proletariat Those who must sell their labor to survive; the antithesis of the bourgeoisie in Marx's class analysis.

world-system theory Idea that a discernible social system, based on wealth and power differentials, transcends individual countries.

Zapotec state First Mesoamerican state, in the Valley of Oaxaca.

BIBLIOGRAPHY

Abelmann, N., and J. Lie. 1995. *Blue Dreams: Korean Americans and the Los Angeles Riots.* Cambridge, MA: Harvard University Press.

Abiodun, R. 1996 Foreword. In *Art and Religion in Africa,* by R. I. J. Hackett, pp. viii–ix. London: Cassell.

Abu-Lughod, J. L. 1989 *Before European Hegemony: The World System A.D. 1250–1350.* New York: Oxford University Press.

Adams, R. M. 1981 *Heartland of Cities.* Chicago: Aldine.

Adepegba, C. O. 1991 The Yoruba Concept of Art and Its Significance in the Holistic View of Art as Applied to African Art. *African Notes* 15: 1–6.

Adherents.com 2002 Major Religions of the World Ranked by Number of Adherents. http://www.adherents.com/Religions_By_Adherents.html.

Agar, M. H. 1980 *The Professional Stranger: An Informal Introduction to Ethnography.* New York: Academic Press.

Ahmed, A. S. 1992 *Postmodernism and Islam: Predicament and Promise.* New York: Routledge.
2004 *Postmodernism and Islam: Predicament and Promise,* rev. ed. New York: Routledge.

Aiello, L., and M. Collard 2001 Our Newest Oldest Ancestor? *Nature* 410: 526–527.

Akazawa, T. 1980 *The Japanese Paleolithic: A Techno-Typological Study.* Tokyo: Rippo Shobo.

Akazawa, T., and C. M. Aikens, eds. 1986 *Prehistoric Hunter-Gatherers in Japan: New Research Methods.* Tokyo: University of Tokyo Press.

Albert, B. 1989 Yanomami "Violence": Inclusive Fitness or Ethnographer's Representation? *Current Anthropology* 30: 637–640.

Altman, D. 2001 *Global Sex.* Chicago: University of Chicago Press.

Amadiume, I. 1987 *Male Daughters, Female Husbands.* Atlantic Highlands, NJ: Zed.
1997 *Reinventing Africa: Matriarchy, Religion, and Culture.* New York: Zed.

American Almanac 1994–1995 1994 *Statistical Abstract of the United States,* 114th ed. Austin, TX: Reference Press.

American Almanac 1996–1997 1996 *Statistical Abstract of the United States,* 116th ed. Austin, TX: Reference Press.

American Anthropological Association *AAA Guide: A Guide to Departments, a Directory of Members.* (Formerly *Guide to Departments of Anthropology.*) Published annually by the American Anthropological Association, Washington, DC. *Anthropology Newsletter.* Published nine times annually by the American Anthropological Association, Washington, DC. *General Anthropology: Bulletin of the Council for General Anthropology.*

Amick III, B., S. Levine, A. R. Tarlov, and D. C. Walsh, eds. 1995 *Society and Health.* New York: Oxford University Press.

Anderson, B. 1991 *Imagined Communities: Reflections on the Origin and Spread of Nationalism,* rev. ed. London: Verso.
1998 *The Spectre of Comparisons: Nationalism, Southeast Asia, and the World.* New York: Verso.

Anderson, R. L. 1989 *Art in Small Scale Societies.* Upper Saddle River, NJ: Prentice Hall.
1996 *Magic, Science, and Health: The Aims and Achievements of Medical Anthropology.* Fort Worth: Harcourt Brace.
2000 *American Muse: Anthropological Excursions into Art and Aesthetics.* Upper Saddle River, NJ: Prentice Hall.
2004 *Calliope's Sisters: A Comparative Study of Philosophy of Art,* 2nd ed. Upper Saddle River, NJ: Prentice Hall.

Anderson, R., and K. Field, eds. 1993 *Art in Small-Scale Societies: Contemporary Readings.* Upper Saddle River, NJ: Prentice Hall.

Angier, N. 1998 When Nature Discovers the Same Design Over and Over, Lookalike Creatures Spark Evolutionary Debate. *New York Times,* December 15, pp. D1, D6.

2002 Why We're So Nice: We're Wired to Cooperate. *New York Times,* July 23. http://www.nytimes.com/2002/07/23/health/psychology/23COOP.html.

Annenberg/CPB Exhibits 2000 "Collapse, Why Do Civilizations Fall?" http://www.learner.org/exhibits/collapse/.

Antoun, R. T. 2001 *Understanding Fundamentalism: Christian, Islamic, and Jewish Movements.* Walnut Creek, CA: AltaMira.

Aoki, M. Y., and M. B. Dardess, eds. 1981 *As the Japanese See It: Past and Present.* Honolulu: University Press of Hawaii.

Aoyagi, K., P. J. M. Nas, and J. Traphagan, eds. 1998 *Toward Sustainable Cities: Readings in the Anthropology of Urban Environments.* Leiden, Netherlands: Leiden Development Studies, Institute of Cultural and Social Studies, University of Leiden.

Apostolopoulos, Y., S. Sönmez, and D. J. Timothy 2001 *Women as Producers and Consumers of Tourism in Developing Regions.* Westport, CT: Praeger.

Appadurai, A. 1990 Disjuncture and Difference in the Global Cultural Economy. *Public Culture* 2(2): 1–24.
1991 Global Ethnoscapes: Notes and Queries for a Transnational Anthropology. In *Recapturing Anthropology: Working in the Present,* ed. R. G. Fox, pp. 191–210. Santa Fe: School of American Research Advanced Seminar Series.

Appadurai, A., ed. 2001 *Globalization.* Durham, NC: Duke University Press.

Appel, R., and P. Muysken 1987 *Language Contact and Bilingualism.* London: Edward Arnold.

Appell, G. N. 1978 *Ethical Dilemmas in Anthropological Inquiry: A Case Book.* Waltham, MA: Crossroads Press.

Appiah, K. A. 1990 Racisms. In *Anatomy of Racism,* ed. David Theo Goldberg, pp. 3–17. Minneapolis: University of Minnesota Press.

Applebome, P. 1996 English Unique to Blacks Is Officially Recognized. *New York Times,* December 20. http://www.nytimes.com.
1997 Dispute over Ebonics Reflects a Volatile Mix. *New York Times,* March 1. http://www.nytimes.com.

Arce, A., and N. Long, eds. 2000 *Anthropology, Development, and Modernities: Exploring Discourses, Counter-Tendencies, and Violence.* New York: Routledge.

Archer, M. S. 1996 *Culture and Agency: The Place of Culture in Social Theory,* rev ed. Cambridge, UK: Cambridge University Press.

Arens, W. 1981 Professional Football: An American Symbol and Ritual. In *The American Dimension: Cultural Myths and Social Realities,* ed. W. Arens and S. P. Montague, pp. 1–10. Sherman Oaks, CA: Alfred.

Arens, W., and S. P. Montague 1981 *The American Dimension: Cultural Myths and Social Realities,* 2nd ed. Sherman Oaks, CA: Alfred.

Arensberg, C. 1987 Theoretical Contributions of Industrial and Development Studies. In *Applied Anthropology in America,* ed. E. M. Eddy and W. L. Partridge. New York: Columbia University Press.

Arnold, B., and B. Gibson, eds. 1995 *Celtic Chiefdom, Celtic State.* New York: Cambridge University Press.

Arrighi, G. 1994 *The Long Twentieth Century: Money, Power, and the Origins of Our Times.* New York: Verso.

Asfaw, B., T. White, and O. Lovejoy 1999 *Australopithecus garhi:* A New Species of Early Hominid from Ethiopia. *Science* 284: 629.

Ashcroft, B., G. Griffiths, and H. Tiffin 1989 *The Empire Writes Back: Theory and Practice in Post-Colonial Literatures.* New York: Routledge.

Ashmore, W., and R. Sharer 2000 *Discovering Our Past: A Brief Introduction to Archaeology,* 3rd ed. Boston: McGraw-Hill.

Askew, K. M. 2001 *Performing the Nation: Swahili Music and Cultural Politics in Tanzania.* Chicago: University of Chicago Press.

Askew, K. M., and R. R. Wilk, eds. 2002 *The Anthropology of Media: A Reader.* Malden, MA: Oxford, Blackwell.

Auman-Bauer, K. 2006 Penn State Part of International Malaria Research, Education Partnership, February 9. http://live.psu.edu/story/16002.

Baer, H. A., M. Singer, and I. Susser 2003 *Medical Anthropology and the World System.* Westport, CT: Praeger.

Bailey, E. J. 2000 *Medical Anthropology and African American Health.* Westport, CT: Bergin and Garvey.

Bailey, R. C. 1990 *The Behavioral Ecology of Efe Pygmy Men in the Ituri Forest, Zaire.* Ann Arbor: Anthropological Papers, Museum of Anthropology, University of Michigan, no. 86.

Bailey, R. C., G. Head, M. Jenike, B. Owen, R. Rechtman, and E. Zechenter 1989 Hunting and Gathering in Tropical Rain Forests: Is It Possible? *American Anthropologist* 91: 59–82.

Baker, P. T. 1978 *The Biology of High Altitude Peoples.* New York: Cambridge University Press.

Baker, P. T., and J. S. Weiner, eds. 1966 *The Biology of Human Adaptability.* Oxford: Oxford University Press.

Bakhtin, M. 1984 *Rabelais and His World.* Translated by Helen Iswolksy. Bloomington: Indiana University Press.

Balick, M. J., and P. A. Cox 1996 *Plants, People, and Culture: The Science of Ethnobotany.* New York: Scientific American Library.

Balick, M. J., E. Elisabetsky, and S. A. Laird 1995 *Medicinal Resources of the Tropical Forest: Biodiversity and Its Importance to Human Health.* New York: Columbia University Press.

Banton, M. 1957 *West African City: A Study in Tribal Life in Freetown.* London: Oxford University Press.

Barash, D. P. 1982 *Sociobiology and Behavior,* 2nd ed. Amsterdam: Elsevier.

Barber, B. R. 1992 Jihad vs. McWorld. *Atlantic Monthly* 269(3): 53–65, March 1992.
1995 *Jihad vs. McWorld.* New York: Times Books.

Barlett, P. F., ed. 1980 *Agricultural Decision Making: Anthropological Contribution to Rural Development.* New York: Academic Press.

Barnaby, F., ed. 1984 *Future War: Armed Conflict in the Next Decade.* London: M. Joseph.

Barnard, A. 1979 Kalahari Settlement Patterns. In *Social and Ecological Systems,* ed. P. Burnham and R. Ellen, pp. 131–144. New York: Academic Press.

Barnes, E. 2005 *Diseases and Human Evolution.* Albuquerque: University of New Mexico Press.

Barnouw, V. 1985 *Culture and Personality,* 4th ed. Belmont, CA: Wadsworth.

Baro, M., and T. F. Deubel 2006 Persistent Hunger: Perspectives on Vulnerability, Famine, and Food Security in Sub-Saharan Africa. *Annual Review of Anthropology* 35: 521–538.

Baron, D. 1986 *Grammar and Gender.* New Haven, CT: Yale University Press.

Barringer, F. 1989 32 Million Lived in Poverty in '88, a Figure Unchanged. *New York Times,* October 19, p. 18.
1992 New Census Data Show More Children Living in Poverty. *New York Times,* May 29, pp. A1, A12, A13.

Barry, H., M. K. Bacon, and I. L. Child 1959 Relation of Child Training to Subsistence Economy. *American Anthropologist* 61: 51–63.

Barth, F. 1964 *Nomads of South Persia: The Basseri Tribe of the Khamseh Confederacy.* London: Allen and Unwin.
1968 (orig. 1958). Ecologic Relations of Ethnic Groups in Swat, North Pakistan. In *Man in*

Adaptation: The Cultural Present, ed. Yehudi Cohen, pp. 324–331. Chicago: Aldine.
1969 Ethnic Groups and Boundaries: The Social Organization of Cultural Difference. London: Allen and Unwin.

Bar-Yosef, O. 1987 Pleistocene Connections between Africa and Southwest Asia: An Archaeological Perspective. African Archaeological Review 5: 29–38.

Bar-Yosef, O., and D. Pilbeam, eds. 2000 The Geopraphy of Neandertals and Modern Humans in Europe and the Greater Mediterranean. Cambridge, MA: Peabody Museum of Archaeology and Ethnology, Harvard University.

Batalla, G. B. 1966 Conservative Thought in Applied Anthropology: A Critique. Human Organization 25: 89–92.

Bates, D. G. 2005 Human Adaptive Strategies: Ecology, Culture, and Politics, 3rd ed. Boston: Allyn & Bacon.

Bateson, M. C. 1984 With a Daughter's Eye: A Memoir of Margaret Mead and Gregory Bateson. New York: William Morrow.

BBC News 2006 Neanderthal Yields Nuclear DNA, May 16.http://news.bbc.co.uk/go/pr/fr/-/2/hi/science/nature/4986668.stm.

Beall, C. M. 2001 Tibetan and Andean Patterns of Adaptation to High-Altitude Hypoxia. Human Biology 72: 201–228.

Beckerman, S., and P. Valentine 2002 Cultures of Multiple Fathers: The Theory and Practice of Partible Paternity in Lowland South America. Gainesville: University of Florida Press.

Beeman, W. 1986 Language, Status, and Power in Iran. Bloomington: Indiana University Press.

Begun, D. R. 2003 Planet of the Apes. Scientific American 289(2): 74–83.

Begun, D. R., C. V. Ward, and M. D. Rose 1997 Description: Function, Phylogeny, and Fossils: Miocene Hominoid Evolution and Adaptations. New York: Plenum Press.

Behar, R. 1993 Translated Woman: Crossing the Border with Esperanza's Story. Boston: Beacon Press.

Behar, R., and D. A. Gordon, eds. 1995 Women Writing Culture. Berkeley: University of California Press.

Bell, W. 1981 Neocolonialism. In Encyclopedia of Sociology, p. 193. Guilford, CT: DPG Publishing.

Bellah, R. N. 1978 Religious Evolution. In Reader in Comparative Religion: An Anthropological Approach, 4th ed., ed. W. A. Lessa and E. Z. Vogt, pp. 36–50. New York: Harper & Row.

Bellwood, P. S. 2004 The First Farmers: Origins of Agricultural Societies. Malden, MA: Blackwell.

Benedict, B. 1970 Pluralism and Stratification. In Essays in Comparative Social Stratification, ed. L. Plotnicov and A. Tuden, pp. 29–41. Pittsburgh: University of Pittsburgh Press.

Benedict, R. 1940 Race, Science and Politics. New York: Modern Age Books.
1946 The Chrysanthemum and the Sword. Boston: Houghton Mifflin.
1959 (orig. 1934). Patterns of Culture. New York: New American Library.

Bennett, J. W. 1969 Northern Plainsmen: Adaptive Strategy and Agrarian Life. Chicago: Aldine.

Bennett, J. W., and J. R. Bowen, eds. 1988 Production and Autonomy: Anthropological Studies and Critiques of Development. Monographs in Economic Anthropology, no. 5, Society for Economic Anthropology. New York: University Press of America.

Berg, B. L. 2004 Qualitative Research Methods for the Social Sciences, 5th ed. Boston: Pearson.

Berkeleyan 1999 Berkeley Researchers Head Team That Discovers New Species of Human Ancestor: Earliest Evidence of Meat-Eating, Early Beings Has Been Unearthed in Ethiopia. April 28–May 4, pp. 27, 32. http://www.berkeley.edu/news/berkeleyan/1999/0428/species.html.

Berlin, B. D., E. Breedlove, and P. H. Raven 1974 Principles of Tzeltal Plant Classification: An Introduction to the Botanical Ethnography of a Mayan-Speaking People of Highland Chiapas. New York: Academic Press.

Berlin, B. D., and P. Kay 1969 Basic Color Terms: Their Universality and Evolution. Berkeley: University of California Press.
1991 Basic Color Terms: Their Universality and Evolution, 2nd ed. Berkeley: University of California Press.
1999 Basic Color Terms: Their Universality and Evolution. Stanford, CA: Center for the Study of Language and Information.

Bernard, H. R. 1994 Research Methods in Cultural Anthropology, 2nd ed. Thousand Oaks, CA: Sage.
2006 Research Methods in Anthropology: Qualitative and Quantitative Methods, 4th ed. Walnut Creek, CA: AltaMira.

Bernard, H. R., ed. 1998 Handbook of Methods in Cultural Anthropology. Walnut Creek, CA: AltaMira.

Berndt, R. M. 1969 The Concept of Protest within an Australian Aboriginal Context. In A Question of Choice: An Australian Aboriginal Dilemma, ed. R. M. Berndt, pp. 25–43. Nedlands: University of West Australia Press.

Berreman, G. D. 1962 Pahari Polyandry: A Comparison. American Anthropologist 64: 60–75.
1975 Himalayan Polyandry and the Domestic Cycle. American Ethnologist 2: 127–138.

Besteman, C. L., and H. Gusterson 2005 Why America's Top Pundits Are Wrong: Anthropologists Talk Back. Berkeley: University of California Press.

Bettelheim, B. 1975 The Uses of Enchantment: The Meaning and Importance of Fairy Tales. New York: Vintage.

Bicker, A., P. Sillitoe, and J. Pottier, eds. 2004 Investigating Local Knowledge: New Directions, New Approaches. Burlington, VT: Ashgate.

Binford, L. R. 1968 Post-Pleistocene Adaptations. In New Perspectives in Archeology, ed. S. R. Binford and L. R. Binford, pp. 313–341. Chicago: Aldine.
1981 Bones: Ancient Men and Modern Myths. New York: Academic Press.

Binford, L. R., and S. R. Binford 1979 Stone Tools and Human Behavior. In Human Ancestors, Readings from Scientific American, ed. G. L. Isaac and R. E. F. Leakey, pp. 92–101. San Francisco: W. H. Freeman.

Biology-Online.org 2005 Natural Selection in Action: Industrial Melanism. http://www.biology-online.org/2/11_natural_selection.htm.

Bird-David, N. 1992 Beyond "The Original Affluent Society": A Culturalist Reformulation. Current Anthropology 33(1): 25–47.

Birdsell, J. B. 1981 Human Evolution: An Introduction to the New Physical Anthropology, 3rd ed. Boston: Houghton Mifflin.

Bjuremalm, H. 1997 Rättvisa kan skipas i Rwanda: Folkmordet 1994 går att förklara och analysera på samma sätt som förintelsen av judarna. Dagens Nyheter [06-03-1997, p. B3].

Blackwood, E. 2000 Webs of Power: Women, Kin, and Community in a Sumatran Village. Lanham, MD: Rowman and Littlefield.

Blackwood, E., and S. Wieringa, eds. 1999 Female Desires: Same-Sex Relations and Transgender Practices across Cultures. New York: Columbia University Press.

Blanchard, K. 1995 The Anthropology of Sport: An Introduction, rev. ed. Westport, CT: Bergin and Garvey.

Blanton, R. E. 1999 Ancient Oaxaca: The Monte Alban State. New York: Cambridge University Press.

Blanton, R. E., S. A. Kowalewski, G. M. Feinman, and L. M. Finsten, eds. 1993 Ancient Mesoamerica: A Comparison of Change in Three Regions, 2nd ed. New York: Cambridge University Press.

Bloch, M., ed. 1975 Political Language and Oratory in Traditional Societies. London: Academic.

Blum, H. F. 1961 Does the Melanin Pigment of Human Skin Have Adaptive Value? Quarterly Review of Biology 36: 50–63.

Boas, F. 1966 (orig. 1940). Race, Language, and Culture. New York: Free Press.

Boaz, N. T. 1993 Quarry: Closing in on the Missing Link. New York: Free Press.
1997 Eco Homo: How the Human Being Emerged from the Cataclysmic History of the Earth. New York: Basic Books.
1999 Essentials of Biological Anthropology. Upper Saddle River, NJ: Prentice Hall.

Boaz, N. T., and A. J. Almquist 2002 Biological Anthropology: A Synthetic Approach to Human Evolution, 2nd ed. Upper Saddle River, NJ: Prentice Hall.

Boaz, N. T., and R. L. Ciochon 2004 Headstrong Hominids. Natural History 113(1): 28–34.

Bock, P. K. 1980 Continuities in Psychological Anthropology. San Francisco: W. H. Freeman.

Bodley, J. H. 1985 Anthropology and Contemporary Human Problems, 2nd ed. Mountain View, CA: Mayfield.
1995 Anthropology and Contemporary Human Problems, 3rd ed. Mountain View, CA: Mayfield.
2003 The Power of Scale: A Global History Approach. Armonk, NY: M. E. Sharpe.
2008a Anthropology and Contemporary Human Problems, 5th ed. Lanham, MD: AltaMira.
2008b Victims of Progress, 5th ed. Lanham, MD: AltaMira.

Bodley, J. H., ed. 1988 Tribal Peoples and Development Issues: A Global Overview. Mountain View, CA: Mayfield.

Bogaard, A. 2004 Neolithic Farming in Central Europe: An Archaeobotanical Study of Crop Husbandry Practices. New York: Routledge.

Bogin, B. 1999 Patterns of Human Growth, 2nd ed. New York: Cambridge University Press.
2001 The Growth of Humanity. New York: Wiley-Liss.

Bogoras, W. 1904 The Chukchee. In The Jesup North Pacific Expedition, ed. F. Boas. New York: Memoir of the American Museum of Natural History.

Bogucki, P. I. 1988 Forest Farmers and Stockherders: Early Agriculture and Its Consequences in North-Central Europe. New York: Cambridge University Press.

Bohannan, P. 1955 Some Principles of Exchange and Investment among the Tiv. American Anthropologist 57: 60–70.
1971 Artist and Critic in an African Society. In Anthropology and Art: Readings in Cross-Cultural Aesthetics, ed. C. Otten, pp. 172–181. Austin: University of Texas Press.
1995 How Culture Works. New York: Free Press.

Bohannan, P., and J. Middleton, eds. 1968 Marriage, Family, and Residence. Garden City, NY: Natural History Press.

Bolton, R. 1981 Susto, Hostility, and Hypoglycemia. Ethnology 20(4): 227–258.

Bond, G. C., J. Kreniske, I. Susser, and J. Vincent, eds. 1996 AIDS in Africa and the Caribbean. Boulder, CO: Westview Press.

Bonnichsen, R., and A. L. Schneider 2000 Battle of the Bones. New York Academy of Sciences, The Sciences, July/August. http://www.friendsofpast.org/forum/battle.html.

Bonvillain, N. 2006 Women and Men: Cultural Constructions of Gender, 4th ed. Upper Saddle River, NJ: Prentice Hall.
2008 Language, Culture, and Communication: The Meaning of Messages, 5th ed. Upper Saddle River, NJ: Prentice Hall.

Borneman, J. 1998 Subversions of International Order: Studies in the Political Anthropology of Culture. Albany: State University of New York Press.

Boserup, E. 1965 The Conditions of Agricultural Growth. Chicago: Aldine.
1970 Women's Role in Economic Development. London: Allen and Unwin.

Bourdieu, P. 1977 Outline of a Theory of Practice. Translated by Richard Nice. Cambridge, UK: Cambridge University Press.
1982 Ce Que Parler Veut Dire. Paris: Fayard.
1984 Distinction: A Social Critique of the Judgment of Taste. Translated by R. Nice. Cambridge, MA: Harvard University Press.

Bourguignon, E. 1979 Psychological Anthropology: An Introduction to Human Nature and Cultural Differences. New York: Harcourt Brace Jovanovich.

Bourque, S. C., and K. B. Warren 1981 Women of the Andes: Patriarchy and Social Change in Two Peruvian Villages. Ann Arbor: University of Michigan Press.
1987 Technology, Gender and Development. Daedalus 116(4): 173–197.

Bower, B. 2000 Inside Violent Worlds—Social Scientists Study Social Consequences of Violent Conflicts.

Science News Online, August 5. http://www
.sciencenews.org/articles/20000805/bob8ref.asp.

Bower, J., and D. Lubell, eds. 1988 *Prehistoric Cultures and Environments in the Late Quaternary of Africa.* Cambridge Monographs in African Archaeology, 26. Oxford, UK: B.A.R.

Bowie, F. 2006 *The Anthropology of Religion: An Introduction.* Malden, MA: Blackwell.

Bowler, J. M., H. Johnston, J. M. Olley, J. R. Prescott, R. G. Roberts, W. Shawcross, and N. A. Spooner. 2003 New Ages for Human Occupation and Climatic Change at Lake Mungo, Australia. *Nature* 421:837–840.

Brace, C. L. 1964 A Nonracial Approach towards the Understanding of Human Diversity. In *The Concept of Race,* ed. A. Montagu, pp. 103–152. New York: Free Press.
   1995 *The Stages of Human Evolution,* 5th ed. Englewood Cliffs, NJ: Prentice Hall.
   2000 *Evolution in an Anthropological View.* Walnut Creek, CA: AltaMira.

Brace, C. L., and F. B. Livingstone 1971 On Creeping Jensenism. In *Race and Intelligence,* ed. C. L. Brace, G. R. Gamble, and J. T. Bond, pp. 64–75. Anthropological Studies, no. 8. Washington, DC: American Anthropological Association.

Bradley, B. J., D. M. Doran-Sheehy, D. Lukas, C. Boesch, and L. Vigilant 2004 Dispersed Male Networks in Western Gorillas. *Current Biology* 14: 510–513.

Bradley, C., C. Moore, M. Burton, and D. White 1990 A Cross-Cultural Historical Analysis of Subsistence Change. *American Anthropologist* 92(2): 447–457.

Brady, I., ed. 1983 Special Section: Speaking in the Name of the Real: Freeman and Mead on Samoa. *American Anthropologist* 85: 908–947.

Braidwood, R. J. 1975 *Prehistoric Men,* 8th ed. Glenview, IL: Scott Foresman.

Bramwell, A. 1989 *Ecology in the Twentieth Century: A History.* New Haven: Yale University Press.

Braudel, F. 1973 *Capitalism and Material Life: 1400–1800.* Translated by M. Kochan. London: Weidenfeld and Nicolson.
   1981 *Civilization and Capitalism, 15th–18th Century.* Volume I: *The Structure of Everyday Life: The Limits.* Translated by S. Reynolds. New York: Harper & Row.
   1982 *Civilization and Capitalism, 15th–18th Century.* Volume II: *The Wheels of Commerce.* New York: HarperCollins.
   1984 *Civilization and Capitalism, 15th–18th Century.* Volume III: *The Perspective of the World.* New York: HarperCollins.
   1992 *Civilization and Capitalism, 15th–18th Century.* Volume III: *The Perspective of the World.* Berkeley: University of California Press.

Bremen, J. V., and A. Shimizu, eds. 1999 *Anthropology and Colonialism in Asia and Oceania.* London: Curzon.

Brenneis, D. 1988 Language and Disputing. *Annual Review of Anthropology* 17: 221–237.

Brettell, C. B., and C. F. Sargent, eds. 2005 *Gender in Cross-Cultural Perspective.* Upper Saddle River, NJ: Pearson/Prentice Hall.

Briggs, C. L. 2005 Communicability, Racial Discourse, and Disease. *Annual Review of Anthropology* 34: 269–291.

Brim, J. A., and D. H. Spain 1974 *Research Design in Anthropology.* New York: Harcourt Brace Jovanovich.

Bringa, T. 1995 *Being Muslim the Bosnian Way: Identity and Community in a Central Bosnian Village.* Princeton, NJ: Princeton University Press.

Brogger, J. 1992 *Nazaré: Women and Men in a Prebureaucratic Portuguese Fishing Village.* Fort Worth: Harcourt Brace.

Bronfenbrenner, U. 1975 Nature with Nurture: A Reinterpretation of the Evidence. In *Race and IQ,* ed. A. Montagu, pp. 114–144. New York: Oxford University Press.

Brooke, J. 1992 Rio's New Day in Sun Leaves Laplander Limp. *New York Times,* June 1, p. A7.
   2000 A Commercial Makes Canadian Self-Esteem Bubble to the Surface. *New York Times,* May 29, late edition, final, section A, p. 6, column 1.

Brown, A. 2001 Communism. *International Encyclopedia of the Social & Behavioral Sciences,* pp. 2323–2326. New York: Elsevier.

Brown, D. 1991 *Human Universals.* New York: McGraw-Hill.

Brown, J. K. 1975 Iroquois Women: An Ethnohistoric Note. In *Toward an Anthropology of Women,* ed. R. Reiter, pp. 235–251. New York: Monthly Review Press.

Brown, K. M. 2001 *Mama Lola: A Vodou Priestess in Brooklyn,* rev. ed. Berkeley: University of California Press.

Brown, M. F. 2003 *Who Owns Native Culture?* Cambridge, MA: Harvard University Press.

Brown, P. J. 1998 *Understanding and Applying Medical Anthropology.* Boston: McGraw-Hill.

Brown, P. J., and V. Bentley-Condit 1996 Culture, Evolution, and Obesity. In *Obesity: Its Causes and Management,* ed. A. J. Stunkard and T. Wadden. New York: Raven Press.

Brown, P. J., and S. V. Krick 2001 Culture and Economy in the Etiology of Obesity: Diet, Television and the Illusions of Personal Choice. Atlanta, GA: Emory University MARIAL Center, Working Paper 003-01.

Brown, R. W. 1958 *Words and Things.* Glencoe, IL: Free Press.

Brumfiel, E. M. 1980 Specialization, Market Exchange, and the Aztec State: A View from Huexotla. *Current Anthropology* 21(4): 459–478.

Bryant, B., and P. Mohai 1991 Race, Class, and Environmental Quality in the Detroit Area. In *Environmental Racism: Issues and Dilemmas,* ed. B. P. Bryant and P. Mohai. Ann Arbor: University of Michigan Office of Minority Affairs.

Bryant, V. M. 1999 Review of Piperno, D. R., and D. M. Pearsall, *The Origins of Agriculture in the Lowland Neotropics* (1998), *North American Archaeologist* (26): 245–246.
   2003 Invisible Clues to New World Domestication. *Science* February 14, 299 (5609): 1029–1030.
   2007a Artifact: Maize Pollen. *Archaeology* 60(4). www.archaeology.org/0707/etc/artifact.html.
   2007b Little Things Mean a Lot: The Search for Starch Grains at Archaeological Sites. *Mammoth Trumpet* 22(4): 3-4, 16.

Bryson, K. 1996 Household and Family Characteristics: March 1995, P20-488, November 26. United States Department of Commerce, Bureau of Census, Public Information Office, CB96-195.

Buchler, I. R., and H. A. Selby 1968 *Kinship and Social Organization: An Introduction to Theory and Method.* New York: Macmillan.

Burke, P., and R. Porter 1987 *The Social History of Language.* Cambridge, UK: Cambridge University Press.

Burley, D. V., and W. R. Dickinson 2001 Origin and Significance of a Founding Settlement in Polynesia. *Proceedings of the National Academy of Sciences* 98: 11829–11831.

Burling, R. 1970 *Man's Many Voices: Language in Its Cultural Context.* New York: Harcourt Brace Jovanovich.

Burns, J. F. 1992a Bosnian Strife Cuts Old Bridges of Trust. *New York Times,* May 22, pp. A1, A6.
   1992b A Serb, Fighting Serbs, Defends Sarajevo. *New York Times,* July 12, section 4, p. E3.
   1997 A Year of Harsh Islamic Rule Weighs Heavily for Afghans. *New York Times,* September 24, late edition, final, section A, p. 6, column 1.

Burton, F. D., and M. Eaton 1995a *The Multimedia Guide to Non-Human Primates.* Upper Saddle River, NJ: Prentice Hall. 1995b *The Guide to Non-Human Primates.* Englewood Cliffs, NJ: Prentice Hall. The print version of the above.

Butler, R. 2005 World's Largest Cities: [Ranked by City Population]. http://www.mongabay.com/cities_pop_01.htm.

Buvinic, M. 1995 The Feminization of Poverty? Research and Policy Needs. In *Reducing Poverty through Labour Market Policies.* Geneva: International Institute for Labour Studies.

Cachel, S. 2006 *Primate and Human Evolution.* New York: Cambridge University Press.

Calcagno, J. M., ed. 2003 *Biological Anthropology: Historical Perspectives on Current Issues, Disciplinary Connections, and Future Directions.* Special issue of the *American Anthropologist* 101(1).

Caldeira, T. P. R. 1996 Fortified Enclaves: The New Urban Segregation. *Public Culture* 8(2): 303–328.

Calhoun, C., D. Light, and S. Keller 1997 *Sociology,* 7th ed. New York: McGraw-Hill.

Campbell, B. G. 1998 *Human Evolution: An Introduction to Man's Adaptations,* 4th ed. New York: Aldine.

Campbell, B. G., J. D. Loy, and K. Cruz-Uribe, eds. 2006 *Humankind Emerging,* 9th ed. Boston: Pearson Allyn & Bacon.

Cann, R. L., M. Stoneking, and A. C. Wilson 1987 Mitochondrial DNA and Human Evolution. *Nature* 325: 31–36.

Carey, B. 2007 Washoe, a Chimp of Many Words Dies at 42. *New York Times,* November 1. http://www.nytimes.com.

Carlson, T. J. S., and L. Maffi 2004 *Ethnobotany and Conservation of Biocultural Diversity.* Bronx: New York Botanical Garden Press.

Carneiro, R. L. 1956 Slash-and-Burn Agriculture: A Closer Look at Its Implications for Settlement Patterns. In *Men and Cultures,* Selected Papers of the Fifth International Congress of Anthropological and Ethnological Sciences, pp. 229–234. Philadelphia: University of Pennsylvania Press.
   1968 (orig. 1961). Slash-and-Burn Cultivation among the Kuikuru and Its Implications for Cultural Development in the Amazon Basin. In *Man in Adaptation: The Cultural Present,* ed. Y. A. Cohen, pp. 131–145. Chicago: Aldine.
   1970 A Theory of the Origin of the State. *Science* 69: 733–738.
   1990 Chiefdom-Level Warfare as Exemplified in Fiji and the Cauca Valley. In *The Anthropology of War,* ed. J. Haas, pp. 190–211. Cambridge, UK: Cambridge University Press.
   1991 The Nature of the Chiefdom as Revealed by Evidence from the Cauca Valley of Colombia. In *Profiles in Cultural Evolution,* ed. A. T. Rambo and K. Gillogly, *Anthropological Papers* 85, pp. 167–190. Ann Arbor: University of Michigan Museum of Anthropology.

Carrier, J. 1995 *De Los Otros: Intimacy and Homosexuality among Mexican Men: Hidden in the Blood.* New York: Columbia University Press.

Carsten, J. 2004 *After Kinship.* New York: Cambridge University Press.

Carter, J. 1988 Freed from Keepers and Cages, Chimps Come of Age on Baboon Island. *Smithsonian,* June, pp. 36–48.

Cartmill, M. 1974 Rethinking Primate Origins. *Science* (April 26): 436–437.
   1992 New Views on Primate Origins. *Evolutionary Anthropology* 1: 105–111.

Carver, T. 1996 *Gender Is Not a Synonym for Women.* Boulder, CO: Lynne Rienner.

Casper, L., and K. Bryson 1998 Growth in Single Fathers Outpaces Growth in Single Mothers, Census Bureau Reports. http://www.census.gov/Press-Release/cb98-228.html.

Casson, R. 1983 Schemata in Cognitive Anthropology. *Annual Review of Anthropology* 12: 429–462.

Cavalli-Sforza, L. L. 1977 *Elements of Human Genetics,* 2nd ed. Menlo Park, CA: W. A. Benjamin.
   2000 *Genes, Peoples, and Languages.* Translated by M. Seielstad. New York: North Point.

Cavalli-Sforza, L. L., and W. F. Bodmer 1994 *The History and Geography of Human Genes.* Princeton, NJ: Princeton University Press.
   1999 *The Genetics of Human Populations.* Mineola, NY: Dover.

Cavalli-Sforza, L. L., P. Menozzi, and A. Piazza 1994 *The History and Geography of Human Genes.* Princeton, NJ: Princeton University Press.

Centers for Disease Control and Prevention (CDC) 2006 *National Vital Statistics Report,* v. 54, no. 12, March 3. http://www.cdc.gov/nchs/products/pubs/pubd/nvsr/54/54-pre.htm.

Cernea, M. M., ed. 1991 *Putting People First: Sociological Variables in Rural Development,* 2nd ed. New York: Oxford University Press (published for the World Bank).

Cernea, M. M., and C. McDowell, eds. 2000 *Risks and Reconstruction: Experiences of Resettlers and Refugees.* Washington, DC: World Bank.

Ceuppens, B., and P. Geschiere 2005 Autocthony: Local or Global? New Modes in the Struggle over Citizenship and Belonging in Africa and Europe. *Annual Review of Anthropology* 34: 385–407.

Chagnon, N. A. 1967 *Yanomamo Warfare: Social Organization and Marriage Alliances.* Ann Arbor, MI: University Microfilms.
1968 *Yanomamo: The Fierce People.* New York: Holt, Rinehart and Winston.
1997 *Yanomamö,* 5th ed. Fort Worth: Harcourt Brace.

Chagnon, N. A., and W. Irons, eds. 1979 *Evolutionary Biology and Human Social Behavior: An Anthropological Perspective.* North Scituate, MA: Duxbury.

Chambers, E. 1985 *Applied Anthropology: A Practical Guide.* Englewood Cliffs, NJ: Prentice Hall.
1987 Applied Anthropology in the Post-Vietnam Era: Anticipations and Ironies. *Annual Review of Anthropology* 16: 309–337.
2000 *Native Tours: The Anthropology of Travel and Tourism.* Prospect Heights, IL: Waveland.

Chambers, E., ed. 1997 *Tourism and Culture: An Applied Perspective.* Albany: State University of New York Press.

Champion, T., and C. Gamble, eds. 1984 *Prehistoric Europe.* New York: Academic Press.

Chang, K. C. 1977 *The Archaeology of Ancient China.* New Haven, CT: Yale University Press.

Chatty, D. 1996 *Mobile Pastoralists: Development Planning and Social Change in Oman.* New York: Columbia University Press.

Cheater, A. P., ed. 1999 *The Anthropology of Power: Empowerment and Disempowerment in Changing Structures.* New York: Routledge.

Cheney, D. L., and R. M. Seyfarth 1990 In the Minds of Monkeys: What Do They Know and How Do They Know It? *Natural History,* September, pp. 38–46.

Cheney, D. L., R. M. Seyfarth, B. B. Smuts, and R. W. Wrangham 1987 The Study of Primate Societies. In *Primate Societies,* ed. B. B. Smuts, D. L. Cheney, R. M. Seyfarth, R. W. Wrangham, and T. T. Struhsaker, pp. 1–8. Chicago: University of Chicago Press.

Cherlin, A. J. 1992 *Marriage, Divorce, Remarriage.* Cambridge, MA: Harvard University Press.

Child, A. B., and I. L. Child 1993 *Religion and Magic in the Life of Traditional Peoples.* Englewood Cliffs, NJ: Prentice Hall.

Childe, V. G. 1951 *Man Makes Himself.* New York: New American Library.

Chiseri-Strater, E., and B. S. Sunstein 2002 *Fieldworking: Reading and Writing Research,* 2nd ed. Upper Saddle River, NJ: Prentice Hall.

Chomsky, N. 1955 *Syntactic Structures.* The Hague: Mouton.

Cigno, A. 1994 *Economics of the Family.* New York: Oxford University Press.

Ciochon, R. L. 1983 Hominoid Cladistics and the Ancestry of Modern Apes and Humans. In *New Interpretations of Ape and Human Ancestry,* ed. R. L. Ciochon and R. S. Corruccini, pp. 783–843. New York: Plenum Press.

Ciochon, R. L., J. Olsen, and J. James 1990 *Other Origins: The Search for the Giant Ape in Human Prehistory.* New York: Bantam Books.

Clammer, J., ed. 1976 *The New Economic Anthropology.* New York: St. Martin's Press.

Clark, J. D., and S. A. Brandt 1984 *From Hunters to Farmers: The Causes and Consequences of Food Production in Africa.* Berkeley: University of California Press.

Clarke, S. C. 1995 Advance Report of Final Divorce Statistics, 1989 and 1990. *Monthly Vital Statistics Report,* v. 43, nos. 8, 9. Hyattsville, MD: National Center for Health Statistics.

Clifford, J. 1982 *Person and Myth: Maurice Leenhardt in the Melanesian World.* Berkeley: University of California Press.
1988 *The Predicament of Culture: Twentieth-Century Ethnography, Literature, and Art.* Cambridge, MA: Harvard University Press.

Clifton, J. A., ed. 1970 *Applied Anthropology: Readings in the Uses of the Science of Man.* Boston: Houghton Mifflin.

Coates, J. 1986 *Women, Men, and Language.* London: Longman.

Cody, D. 1998 British Empire. http://www.victorianweb.org/.

Coe, M. D., and K. Flannery 1964 Microenvironments and Mesoamerican Prehistory. *Science* 143: 650–654.

Cohen, M. 1998 *Culture of Intolerance: Chauvinism, Class, and Racism.* New Haven, CT: Yale University Press.

Cohen, M. N., and G. J. Armelagos, eds. 1984 *Paleopathology at the Origins of Agriculture.* New York: Academic Press.

Cohen, Roger 1995 Serbs' Shift Opens a Chance for Peace, a U.S. Envoy Says. *New York Times,* September 1, pp. A1, A6.

Cohen, Ronald 1967 *The Kanuri of Bornu.* New York: Harcourt Brace Jovanovich.

Cohen, Ronald, and E. R. Service, eds. 1978 *Origins of the State: The Anthropology of Political Evolution.* Philadelphia: Institute for the Study of Human Issues.

Cohen, Y. A. 1974a *Man in Adaptation: The Cultural Present,* 2nd ed. Chicago: Aldine.
1974b Culture as Adaptation. In *Man in Adaptation: The Cultural Present,* 2nd ed., ed. Y. A. Cohen, pp. 45–68. Chicago: Aldine.

Cole, S. 1975 *Leakey's Luck: The Life of Louis Bazett Leakey, 1903–1972.* New York: Harcourt Brace Jovanovich.

Collier, J. F. 1997 *From Duty to Desire: Remaking Families in a Spanish Village.* Princeton, NJ: Princeton University Press.

Collier, J. F., ed. 1988 *Marriage and Inequality in Classless Societies.* Stanford, CA: Stanford University Press.

Collier, J. F., and S. J. Yanagisako, eds. 1987 *Gender and Kinship: Essays toward a Unified Analysis.* Stanford, CA: Stanford University Press.

Collins, T. W. 1989 Rural Economic Development in Two Tennessee Counties: A Racial Dimension. Paper presented at the annual meetings of the American Anthropological Association, Washington, DC.

Colson, E. 1971 *The Social Consequences of Resettlement: The Impact of the Kariba Resettlement on the Gwembe Tonga.* Manchester, UK: Manchester University Press.

Colson, E., and T. Scudder 1975 New Economic Relationships between the Gwembe Valley and the Line of Rail. In *Town and Country in Central and Eastern Africa,* ed. David Parkin, pp. 190–210. London: Oxford University Press.
1988 *For Prayer and Profit: The Ritual, Economic, and Social Importance of Beer in Gwembe District, Zambia, 1950–1982.* Stanford, CA: Stanford University Press.

Comaroff, J. 1982 Dialectical Systems, History and Anthropology: Units of Study and Questions of Theory. *Journal of Southern African Studies* 8: 143–172.

Combs-Schilling, E. 1989 *Sacred Performances: Islam, Sexuality, and Sacrifice.* New York: Columbia University Press.

Conkey, M., O. Soffer, D. Stratmann, and N. Jablonski 1997 *Beyond Art: Pleistocene Image and Symbol.* San Francisco: Memoirs of the California Academy of Sciences, no. 23.

Conklin, H. C. 1954 *The Relation of Hanunóo Culture to the Plant World.* Unpublished Ph.D. dissertation, Yale University.

Connah, G. 1987 *African Civilizations.* New York: Cambridge University Press.
2004 *Forgotten Africa: An Introduction to Its Archaeology.* New York: Routledge.

Connell, R. W. 1995 *Masculinities.* Berkeley: University of California Press.
2002 *Gender.* Malden, MA: Blackwell.

Conner, J. K., and D. L. Hartl 2004 *A Primer of Population Genetics.* Sunderland, MA: Sinauer.

Connor, W. 1972 Nation-Building or Nation Destroying. *World Politics* 24(3): 319–355.

Cook-Gumperz, J. 1986 *The Social Construction of Literacy.* Cambridge, UK: Cambridge University Press.

Cooper, F., and A. L. Stoler 1989 Introduction, Tensions of Empire: Colonial Control and Visions of Rule. *American Ethnologist* 16: 609–621.

Cooper, F., and A. L. Stoler, eds. 1997 *Tensions of Empire: Colonial Cultures in a Bourgeois World.* Berkeley: University of California Press.

Coote, J., and A. Shelton, eds. 1992 *Anthropology, Art, and Aesthetics.* New York: Oxford University Press.

Crane, J. G., and M. V. Angrosino 1992 *Field Projects in Anthropology: A Student Handbook,* 3rd ed. Prospect Heights, IL: Waveland.

Crapo, R. H. 2006 *Anthropology of Religion: The Unity and Diversity of Religions.* Boston: McGraw-Hill.

Crenson, M. 2000 Music—From the Heart or from the Genes. http://www.cis.vt.edu/modernworld/d/musicgenes.html.

Cresswell, T. 2006 *On the Move: Mobility in the Modern West.* New York: Routledge.

Crick, F. H. C. 1968 (orig. 1962). The Genetic Code. In *The Molecular Basis of Life: An Introduction to Molecular Biology, Readings from Scientific American,* pp. 198–205. San Francisco: W. H. Freeman.

Critser, G. 2003 *Fat Land: How Americans Became the Fattest People in the World.* Boston: Houghton Mifflin.

Crosby, A. W., Jr. 1986 *Ecological Imperialism: The Biological Expansion of Europe, 900–1900.* New York: Cambridge University Press.
1994 *Germs, Seeds & Animals: Studies in Ecological History.* Armonk, NY: M. E. Sharpe.
2003 *The Columbian Exchange: Biological and Cultural Consequences of 1492.* Westport, CT: Praeger.

Cueppens, B., and P. Geschiere 2005 Autochthony: Local or Global? New Modes in the Struggle over Citizenship and Belonging in Africa and Europe. *Annual Review of Anthropology* 34: 385–407.

Cultural Survival Inc. 1992 *At the Threshold.* Cambridge, MA: Cultural Survival. Originally published as the Spring 1992 issue of *Cultural Survival Quarterly.*

Cultural Survival Quarterly 1989 Quarterly journal. Cambridge, MA: Cultural Survival.

Cunningham, G. 1999 *Religion and Magic: Approaches and Theories.* New York: New York University Press.

Dahlberg, F., ed. 1981 *Woman the Gatherer.* New Haven, CT: Yale University Press.

Dalton, G., ed. 1967 *Tribal and Peasant Economies.* Garden City, NY: Natural History Press.

Dalton, R. 2006 Ethiopia: Awash with Fossils. http://www.nature.com/news/2006/060102/full/439014a.html.

DaMatta, R. 1991 *Carnivals, Rogues, and Heroes: An Interpretation of the Brazilian Dilemma.* Translated from the Portuguese by John Drury. Notre Dame, IN: University of Notre Dame Press.

D'Andrade, R. 1984 Cultural Meaning Systems. In *Culture Theory: Essays on Mind, Self, and Emotion,* ed. R. A. Shweder and R. A. Levine, pp. 88–119. Cambridge, UK: Cambridge University Press.
1995 *The Development of Cognitive Anthropology.* New York: Cambridge University Press.

Darwin, C. 1958 (orig. 1859). *On the Origin of Species.* New York: Dutton.

Darwin, E. 1796 (orig. 1794). *Zoonomia, Or the Laws of Organic Life,* 2nd ed. London: J. Johnson.

Das, V. 1995 *Critical Events: An Anthropological Perspective on Contemporary India.* New York: Oxford University Press.

Davies, C. A. 1999 *Reflexive Ethnography: Guide to Researching Selves and Others.* New York: Routledge.

Davis, D. L., and R. G. Whitten 1987 The Cross-Cultural Study of Human Sexuality. *Annual Review of Anthropology* 16: 69–98.

Degler, C. 1970 *Neither Black nor White: Slavery and Race Relations in Brazil and the United States.* New York: Macmillan.

Delamont, S. 1995 *Appetites and Identities: An Introduction to the Social Anthropology of Western Europe.* London: Routledge.

de la Peña, G. 2005 Social and Cultural Policies toward Indigenous Peoples: Perspectives from Latin America. *Annual Review of Anthropology* 34: 717–739.

Delson, E., ed. 1985 *Ancestors: The Hard Evidence*. New York: Alan R. Liss.

DeLumley, H. 1976 (orig. 1969). A Paleolithic Camp at Nice. In *Avenues to Antiquity, Readings from Scientific American*, ed. B. M. Fagan, pp. 36–44. San Francisco: W. H. Freeman.

DeMarco, E. 1997 New Dig at 9,000-Year-Old City Is Changing Views on Ancient Life. *New York Times*, November 11. http://www.nytimes.com.

Dembski, W. A. 2004 *The Design Revolution: Answering the Toughest Questions about Intelligent Design*. Downers Grove, IL: InterVarsity Press.

Dentan, R. K. 1979 *The Semai: A Nonviolent People of Malaya*, fieldwork edition. New York: Harcourt Brace.

Descartes, L., and C. P. Kottak 2009 *Media and Middle-Class Moms*. New York: Routledge.

Desjarlais, R., L. Eisenberg, B. Good, and A. Kleinman, eds. 1995 *World Mental Health: Problems and Priorities in Low-Income Countries*. New York: Oxford University Press.

Despres, L., ed. 1975 *Ethnicity and Resource Competition*. The Hague: Mouton.

DeVita, P. R. 1992 *The Naked Anthropologist: Tales from around the World*. Belmont, CA: Wadsworth.

DeVita, P. R., and J. D. Armstrong, eds. 2002 *Distant Mirrors: America as a Foreign Culture*, 3rd ed. Belmont, CA: Wadsworth.

De Vos, G. A. 1971 *Japan's Outcastes: The Problem of the Burakumin*. London: Minority Rights Group.

De Vos, G. A., and H. Wagatsuma 1966 *Japan's Invisible Race: Caste in Culture and Personality*. Berkeley: University of California Press.

De Vos, G. A., W. O. Wetherall, and K. Stearman 1983 *Japan's Minorities: Burakumin, Koreans, Ainu and Okinawans*. Report no. 3. London: Minority Rights Group.

De Waal, F. B. M. 1995 Bonobo Sex and Society: The Behavior of a Close Relative Challenges Assumptions about Male Supremacy in Human Evolution. *Scientific American*, March, pp. 82–88.
1997 *Bonobo: The Forgotten Ape*. Berkeley: University of California Press.
2000 *Chimpanzee Politics: Power and Sex among Apes*, rev. ed. Baltimore: Johns Hopkins University Press.
2001 *The Ape and the Sushi Master: Cultural Reflections by a Primatologist*. New York: Basic Books.

Diamond, J. M. 1989 Blood, Genes, and Malaria. *Natural History*, February, pp. 8–18.
1990 A Pox upon Our Genes. *Natural History*, February, pp. 26–30.
2005 *Guns, Germs, and Steel: The Fates of Human Societies*. New York: W. W. Norton.

Dibble, H. L., S. P. McPherron, and B. J. Roth 2003 *Virtual Dig: A Simulated Archaeological Excavation of a Middle Paleolithic Site in France*, 2nd ed. Boston: McGraw-Hill.

Dickau, R, A. J. Ranere, and R. G. Cooke 2007 Starch Grain Evidence for the Preceramic Dispersals of Maize and Root Crops into Tropical Dry and Humid Forests of Panama. *Proceedings of the National Academy of Sciences of the United States of America*. 104(9): 3651–3656. http://www.pnas.org/cgi/content/full/104/9/3651.

Di Leonardo, M., ed. 1991 *Gender at the Crossroads of Knowledge: Feminist Anthropology in the Postmodern Era*. Berkeley: University of California Press.

Divale, W. T., and M. Harris 1976 Population, Warfare, and the Male Supremacist Complex. *American Anthropologist* 78: 521–538.

Dobzhansky, T., F. J. Ayala, G. L. Stebbins, and J. W. Valentine 1977 *Evolution*. San Francisco: W. H. Freeman.

Dolhinow, P., and A. Fuentes, eds. 1999 *The Nonhuman Primates*. Mountain View, CA: Mayfield.

Douglas, M., and A. Wildavsky 1982 *Risk and Culture: An Essay on the Selection of Technical and Environmental Dangers*. Berkeley: University of California Press.

Douglass, W. A. 1969 *Death in Murelaga: Funerary Ritual in a Spanish Basque Village*. Seattle: University of Washington Press.
1975 *Echalar and Murelaga: Opportunity and Rural Exodus in Two Spanish Basque Villages*. London: C. Hurst 1992 Basques. *Encyclopedia of World Cultures*, ed. L. Bennett, vol. 4. Boston: GK Hall.

http://ets.umdl.umich.edu/cgi/e/ehraf/ehraf-idx?c=ehrafe&view=owc&owc=EX08.

Downes, W. 1998 *Language and Society*, 2nd ed. New York: Cambridge University Press.

Draper, P. 1975 !Kung Women: Contrasts in Sexual Egalitarianism in Foraging and Sedentary Contexts. In *Toward an Anthropology of Women*, ed. R. Reiter, pp. 77–109. New York: Monthly Review Press.

Dreifus, C. 2000 Saving the Orangutan: Preserving Paradise. *New York Times*, March 21. http://www.nytimes.com/library/national/science/032100sci-animal-orangutan.html.

Drennan, R. D., and C. A. Uribe, eds. 1987 *Chiefdoms in the Americas*. Landon, MD: University Press of America.

Dressler, W. W., K. S. Oths, and C. C. Gravlee 2005 Race and Ethnicity in Public Health Research. *Annual Review of Anthropology* 34: 231–252.

Dublin, M. 2001 *Native America Collected: The Culture of an Art World*. Albuquerque: University of New Mexico Press.

Dunn, J. S. 2000 *The Impact of Media on Reproductive Behavior in Northeastern Brazil*. Ph.D. dissertation, Department of Anthropology, University of Michigan, Ann Arbor.

Durkheim, E. 1951 (orig. 1897). *Suicide: A Study in Sociology*. Glencoe, IL: Free Press.
2001 (orig. 1912). *The Elementary Forms of the Religious Life*. Translated by Carol Cosman. Abridged with an introduction and notes by Mark S. Cladis. New York: Oxford University Press.

Durrenberger, E. P., and T. D. King, eds. 2000 *State and Community in Fisheries Management: Power, Policy, and Practice*. Westport, CT: Bergin and Garvey.

Dwyer, K. 1982 *Moroccan Dialogues: Anthropology in Question*. Baltimore: Johns Hopkins University Press.

Eagleton, T. 1983 *Literary Theory: An Introduction*. Minneapolis: University of Minnesota Press.

Earle, T. K. 1987 Chiefdoms in Archaeological and Ethnohistorical Perspective. *Annual Review of Anthropology* 16: 279–308.
1991 *Chiefdoms: Power, Economy, and Ideology*. New York: Cambridge University Press.
1997 *How Chiefs Come to Power: The Political Economy in Prehistory*. Stanford, CA: Stanford University Press.

Eastman, C. M. 1975 *Aspects of Language and Culture*. San Francisco: Chandler and Sharp.

Echeverria, J. 1999 *Home away from Home: A History of Basque Boardinghouses*. Reno: University of Nevada Press.

Eckert, P. 1989 *Jocks and Burnouts: Social Categories and Identity in the High School*. New York: Teachers College Press, Columbia University.
2000 *Linguistic Variation as Social Practice: The Linguistic Construction of Identity in Belten High*. Malden, MA: Blackwell.

Eckert, P., and S. McConnell-Ginet 2003 *Language and Gender*. New York: Cambridge University Press.

Eckert, P., and J. R. Rickford, eds. 2001 *Style and Sociolinguistic Variation*. New York: Cambridge University Press.

Eddy, E. M., and W. L. Partridge, eds. 1987 *Applied Anthropology in America*, 2nd ed. New York: Columbia University Press.

Edelman, M., and A. Haugerud 2004 *The Anthropology of Development and Globalization: From Classical Political Economy to Contemporary Neoliberalism*. Malden, MA: Blackwell.

Eder, J. 1987 *On the Road to Tribal Extinction: Depopulation, Deculturation, and Adaptive Well-Being among the Batak of the Philippines*. Berkeley: University of California Press.

Edgerton, R. 1965 "Cultural" versus "Ecological" Factors in the Expression of Values, Attitudes and Personality Characteristics. *American Anthropologist* 67: 442–447.

Edwards, D. N. 2004 *The Nubian Past: An Archaeology of Sudan*. New York: Routledge.

Eggert, K. 1988 Malafaly as Misnomer. In *Madagascar: Society and History*, ed. C. P. Kottak, J. A. Rakotoarisoa, A. Southall, and P. Verin,

pp. 321–336. Durham, NC: Carolina Academic Press.

Eiseley, L. 1961 *Darwin's Century*. Garden City, NY: Doubleday, Anchor Books.

Eldredge, N. 1985 *Time Frames: The Rethinking of Darwinian Evolution and the Theory of Punctuated Equilibria*. New York: Simon & Schuster.
1997 *Fossils: The Evolution and Extinction of Species*. Princeton, NJ: Princeton University Press.

Ellen, R., P. Parkes, and A. Bicker, eds. 2000 *Indigenous Environmental Knowledge and Its Transformations*. Amsterdam: Harwood Academic.

Elson, C. 2007 *Excavations at Cerro Tilcajete: A Monte Alban II Administrative Center in the Valley of Oaxaca*. Memoir 42 of the Museum of Anthropology, University of Michigan, Ann Arbor.

Ember, C., and Ember, M. 2001 *Cross-Cultural Research Methods*. Walnut Creek, CA: AltaMira.

Ember, M., and C. R. Ember 1997 Science in Anthropology. In *The Teaching of Anthropology: Problems, Issues, and Decisions*, ed. C. P. Kottak, J. J. White, R. H. Furlow, and P. C. Rice, pp. 29–33. Mountain View, CA: Mayfield.

Endicott, K. M., and R. Welsch 2001 *Taking Sides: Clashing Views on Controversial Issues in Anthropology*. Guilford, CT: McGraw-Hill/Dushkin.

Erickson, P., H. Ward, and K. Wachendorf 2002 *Voices of a Thousand People: The Makah Cultural and Research Center*. Lincoln/London: University of Nebraska Press.

Erlanger, S. 1992 An Islamic Awakening in Central Asian Lands. *New York Times*, June 9, pp. A1, A7.

Errington, F., and D. Gewertz 1987 *Cultural Alternatives and a Feminist Anthropology: An Analysis of Culturally Constructed Gender Interests in Papua New Guinea*. New York: Cambridge University Press.

Ervin, A. M. 2005 *Applied Anthropology: Tools and Perspectives for Contemporary Practice*. 2nd ed. Boston: Pearson/Allyn & Bacon.

Escobar, A. 1991 Anthropology and the Development Encounter: The Making and Marketing of Development Anthropology. *American Ethnologist* 18: 658–682.
1994 Welcome to Cyberia: Notes on the Anthropology of Cyberculture. *Current Anthropology* 35(3): 211–231.
1995 *Encountering Development: The Making and Unmaking of the Third World*. Princeton, NJ: Princeton University Press.

Eskridge, W. N., Jr. 1996 *The Case for Same-Sex Marriage: From Sexual Liberty to Civilized Commitment*. New York: Free Press.

Evans-Pritchard, E. E. 1940 *The Nuer: A Description of the Modes of Livelihood and Political Institutions of a Nilotic People*. Oxford: Clarendon Press.
1970 Sexual Inversion among the Azande. *American Anthropologist* 72: 1428–1433.

Ezra, K. 1986 *A Human Ideal in African Art: Bamana Figurative Sculpture*. Washington, DC: Smithsonian Institution Press for the National Museum of African Art.

Fagan, B. M. 1987 *The Great Journey: The Peopling of Ancient America*. London: Thames and Hudson.
1996 *World Prehistory: A Brief Introduction*. New York: HarperCollins.
1998 *Clash of Cultures*, 2nd ed. Walnut Creek, CA: AltaMira.
2006a *Ancient Lives: An Introduction to Method and Theory in Archaeology*, 3rd ed. Upper Saddle River, NJ: Prentice Hall. 2006b *Archaeology: A Brief Introduction*, 9th ed. Upper Saddle River, NJ: Prentice Hall.
2007 *People of the Earth: A Brief Introduction to World Prehistory*, 12th ed. Upper Saddle River, NJ: Prentice Hall.
2008 *World Prehistory: A Brief Introduction*, 7th ed. Upper Saddle River, NJ: Prentice Hall.

Falk, D. 2000 *Primate Diversity*. New York: W. W. Norton.

Farb, P., and G. Armelagos 1980 *Consuming Passions: The Anthropology of Eating*. Boston: Literary Guild.

Farner, R. F., ed. 2004 *Nationalism, Ethnicity, and Identity: Cross-National and Comparative Perspectives*. New Brunswick, NJ: Transaction.

Farnsworth, C. H. 1992 Canada to Divide Its Northern Land. *New York Times,* May 6, p. A7.

Farooq, M. 1966 Importance of Determining Transmission Sites in Planning Bilharziasis Control: Field Observations from the Egypt-49 Project Area. *American Journal of Epidemiology* 83: 603–612.

Farr, D. M. L. 1980 British Empire. *Academic American Encyclopedia,* vol. 3, pp. 495–496. Princeton, NJ: Arete.

Fasold, R. W. 1990 *The Sociolinguistics of Language.* Oxford: Blackwell.

Feder, K. L. 2004 *Linking to the Past: A Brief Introduction to Archaeology.* New York: Oxford University Press.

Fedigan, L. M. 1992 *Primate Paradigms: Sex Roles and Social Bonds.* Chicago: University of Chicago Press.

Feinman, G. M., and J. Marcus, eds. 1998 *Archaic States.* Santa Fe, NM: School of American Research Press.

Feinman, G. M., and T. D. Price 2001 *Archaeology at the Millennium: A Sourcebook.* New York: Kluwer Academic/Plenum Press.

Feld, S. 1990 *Sound and Sentiment: Birds, Weeping, Poetics, and Song in Kaluli Expression,* 2nd ed. Philadelphia: University of Pennsylvania Press.
1991 Voices of the Rainforest. *Public Culture* 4(1): 131–140.

Fenlason, L. 1990 Wolpoff Questions "Eve's" Origin Date, Says It Ignores Contradictory Fossil Data. *University Record* (University of Michigan, Ann Arbor) 45(21): 12.

Ferguson, J. 1994 *The Anti-Politics Machine: "Development," Depoliticization, and Bureaucratic Power in Lesotho.* Minneapolis: University of Minnesota Press.

Ferguson, R. B. 1995 *Yanomami Warfare: A Political History.* Santa Fe, NM: School of American Research Press. 2003 *The State, Identity, and Violence: Political Disintegration in the Post–Cold War Era.* New York: Routledge.

Ferguson, R. B., and N. L. Whitehead 1991 *War in the Tribal Zone: Expanding States and Indigenous Warfare.* Santa Fe, NM: School of American Research Press.

Ferraro, G. P. 2006 *The Cultural Dimension of International Business,* 5th ed. Upper Saddle River, NJ: Prentice Hall.

Fields, J. M. 2004 America's Families and Living Arrangements: 2003. U.S. Census Bureau. *Current Population Reports,* P20–553, November. http://www.census.gov.

Fields, J. M., and L. M. Casper 2001 America's Families and Living Arrangements: Population Characteristics, 2000. U.S. Census Bureau. *Current Population Reports,* P20-537, June 2001. http://www.census.gov/prod/2001pubs/p20-537.pdf.

Finke, R., and R. Stark 2005 *The Churching of America, 1776–2005: Winners and Losers in Our Religious Economy.* New Brunswick, NJ: Rutgers University Press.

Finkler, K. 1985 *Spiritualist Healers in Mexico: Successes and Failures of Alternative Therapeutics.* South Hadley, MA: Bergin and Garvey.
2000 *Experiencing the New Genetics: Family and Kinship on the Medical Frontier.* Philadelphia: University of Pennsylvania Press.

Finnstrom, S. 1997 Postcoloniality and the Postcolony: Theories of the Global and the Local. http://www.postcolonialweb.org/.

Fisher, A. 1988*a* The More Things Change. *MOSAIC* 19(1): 22–33.
1988*b* On the Emergence of Humanness. *MOSAIC* 19(1): 34–45.

Fiske, J. 1989 *Understanding Popular Culture.* Boston: Unwin Hyman.

Fiske, J., and J. Hartley 2003 *Reading Television,* 2nd ed. New York: Routledge.

Flannery, K. V. 1969 Origins and Ecological Effects of Early Domestication in Iran and the Near East. In *The Domestication and Exploitation of Plants and Animals,* ed. P. J. Ucko and G. W. Dimbleby, pp. 73–100. Chicago: Aldine.
1972 The Cultural Evolution of Civilizations. *Annual Review of Ecology and Systematics* 3: 399–426.
1973 The Origins of Agriculture. *Annual Review of Anthropology* 2: 271–310.

1995 Prehistoric Social Evolution. In *Research Frontiers in Anthropology,* ed. C. R. Ember and M. Ember, pp. 1–26. Englewood Cliffs, NJ: Prentice Hall.
1999 Chiefdoms in the Early Near East: Why It's So Hard to Identify Them. In *The Iranian World: Essays on Iranian Art and Archaeology,* ed. A. Alizadeh, Y. Majidzadeh, and S. M. Shahmirzadi. Tehran: Iran University Press.

Flannery, K. V., ed. 1986 *Guila Naquitz: Archaic Foraging and Early Agriculture in Oaxaca, Mexico.* Orlando, FL: Academic Press.

Flannery, K. V., and J. Marcus 2000 Formative Mexican Chiefdoms and the Myth of the "Mother Culture." *Journal of Anthropological Archaeology* 19: 1–37.
2003*a The Cloud People: Divergent Evolution of the Zapotec and Mixtec Civilizations.* Clinton Corners, NY: Percheron Press.
2003*b* The Origin of War: New 14C Dates from Ancient Mexico. *Proceedings of the National Academy of Sciences of the United States of America,* 100(20): 11801–11805.

Flannery, K. V., J. Marcus, and R. G. Reynolds 1989 *The Flocks of the Wamani: A Study of Llama Herders on the Punas of Ayacucho, Peru.* San Diego: Academic Press.

Fleagle, J. G. 1999 *Primate Adaptation and Evolution,* 2nd ed. San Diego: Academic Press.

Fleagle, J. G., C. H. Janson, and K. E. Reed, eds. 1999 *Primate Communities.* New York: Cambridge University Press.

Fleisher, M. L. 1998 Cattle Raiding and Its Correlates: The Cultural-Ecological Consequences of Market-Oriented Cattle Raiding among the Kuria of Tanzania. *Human Ecology* 26(4): 547–572.
2000 *Kuria Cattle Raiders: Violence and Vigilantism on the Tanzania/Kenya Frontier.* Ann Arbor: University of Michigan Press.

Fluehr-Lobban, C. 2005 *Race and Racism: An Introduction.* Lanham, MD: AltaMira.

Foley, W. A. 1997 *Anthropological Linguistics: An Introduction.* Cambridge, MA: Blackwell.

Ford, C. S., and F. A. Beach 1951 *Patterns of Sexual Behavior.* New York: Harper Torchbooks.

Forman, S., ed. 1994 *Diagnosing America: Anthropology and Public Engagement.* Ann Arbor: University of Michigan Press.

Fortes, M. 1950 Kinship and Marriage among the Ashanti. In *African Systems of Kinship and Marriage,* ed. A. R. Radcliffe-Brown and D. Forde, pp. 252–284. London: Oxford University Press.

Fossey, D. 1981 The Imperiled Mountain Gorilla. *National Geographic* 159: 501–523.
1983 *Gorillas in the Mist.* Boston: Houghton Mifflin.

Foster, G. M. 1965 Peasant Society and the Image of Limited Good. *American Anthropologist* 67: 293–315.

Foster, G. M., and B. G. Anderson 1978 *Medical Anthropology.* New York: McGraw-Hill.

Foucault, M. 1979 *Discipline and Punish: The Birth of the Prison.* Translated by Alan Sheridan. New York: Vintage Books, University Press.
1990 *The History of Sexuality,* vol. 2, *The Use of Pleasure.* Translated by R. Hurley. New York: Vintage.

Fountain, H. 2002 Iceman's Last Meal. *New York Times,* September 17. http://www.nytimes.com/2002/09/17/science/17OBSE.html.

Fouts, R. 1997 *Next of Kin: What Chimpanzees Have Taught Me about Who We Are.* New York: William Morrow.

Fouts, R. S., D. H. Fouts, and T. E. Van Cantfort 1989 The Infant Loulis Learns Signs from Cross-Fostered Chimpanzees. In *Teaching Sign Language to Chimpanzees,* ed. R. A. Gardner, B. T. Gardner, and T. E. Van Cantfort, pp. 280–292. Albany: State University of New York Press.

Fox, J. W. 1987 *Maya Postclassic State Formation.* Cambridge, UK: Cambridge University Press.

Fox, Richard G., ed. 1990 Nationalist Ideologies and the Production of National Cultures. American Ethnological Society Monograph Series, no. 2. Washington, DC: American Anthropological Association.

Fox, Robin 1985 *Kinship and Marriage.* New York: Viking Penguin.

Frake, C. O. 1961 The Diagnosis of Disease among the Subanun of Mindanao. *American Anthropologist* 63: 113–132.

Franke, R. 1977 Miracle Seeds and Shattered Dreams in Java. In *Readings in Anthropology,* pp. 197–201. Guilford, CT: Dushkin.

Free Dictionary 2004 Honorific. http://encyclopedia.thefreedictionary.com/Honorific.

Freeman, D. 1983 *Margaret Mead and Samoa: The Making and Unmaking of an Anthropological Myth.* Cambridge, MA: Harvard University Press.

Freilich, M., D. Raybeck, and J. Savishinsky 1991 *Deviance: Anthropological Perspectives.* Westport, CT: Bergin and Garvey.

French, H. W. 1992 Unending Exodus from the Caribbean, with the U.S. a Constant Magnet. *New York Times,* May 6, pp. A1, A8.
2002 Whistling Past the Global Graveyard. *New York Times,* July 14. http://www.nytimes.com/2002/07/14/weekinreview/14FREN.html.

Freud, S. 1950 (orig. 1918). *Totem and Taboo.* Translated by J. Strachey. New York: W. W. Norton.

Fricke, T. 1994 *Himalayan Households: Tamang Demography and Domestic Processes,* 2nd ed. New York: Columbia University Press.

Fried, M. H. 1960 On the Evolution of Social Stratification and the State. In *Culture in History,* ed. S. Diamond, pp. 713–731. New York: Columbia University Press.
1967 *The Evolution of Political Society: An Essay in Political Anthropology.* New York: McGraw-Hill.

Friedan, B. 1963 *The Feminine Mystique.* New York: W. W. Norton.

Friedl, E. 1962 *Vasilika: A Village in Modern Greece.* New York: Holt, Rinehart, and Winston.
1975 *Women and Men: An Anthropologist's View.* New York: Harcourt Brace Jovanovich.

Friedman, J. 1994 *Cultural Identity and Global Process.* Thousand Oaks, CA: Sage.

Friedman, J., ed. 2003 *Globalization, the State, and Violence.* Walnut Creek, CA: AltaMira.

Friedman, J., and M. J. Rowlands, eds. 1978 *The Evolution of Social Systems.* Pittsburgh: University of Pittsburgh Press.

Frisancho, A. R. 1975 Functional Adaptation to High Altitude Hypoxia. *Science* 187: 313–319.
1990 *Anthropometric Standards for the Evaluation of Growth and Nutritional Status.* Ann Arbor: University of Michigan Press.
1993 *Human Adaptation and Accommodation.* Ann Arbor: University of Michigan Press.

Fry, D. P. 2006 *The Human Potential for Peace: An Anthropological Challenge to Assumptions about War and Violence.* New York: Oxford University Press.

Fry, D. P., and K. Bjorkqvist, eds. 1997 *Cultural Variation in Conflict Resolution: Alternatives to Violence.* Mahwah, NJ: Lawrence Erlbaum.

Futuyma, D. J. 1995 *Science on Trial,* updated ed. New York: Pantheon.
1998 *Evolutionary Biology.* Sunderland, MA: Sinauer Associates.

Gal, S. 1989 Language and Political Economy. *Annual Review of Anthropology* 18: 345–367.

Gamble, C. 1999 *The Palaeolithic Societies of Europe.* New York: Cambridge University Press.
2004 *Archaeology, the Basics.* New York: Routledge.

Garbarino, M. S., and R. F. Sasso 1994 *Native American Heritage,* 3rd ed. Prospect Heights, IL: Waveland.

Gardner, R. A., B. T. Gardner, and T. E. Van Cantfort, eds. 1989 *Teaching Sign Language to Chimpanzees.* Albany: State University of New York Press.

Gargan, E. A. 1992 A Single-Minded Man Battles to Free Slaves. *New York Times,* June 4, p. A7.

Gates, C. 2003 *Ancient Cities: The Archaeology of Urban Life in the Ancient Near East and Egypt, Greece, and Rome.* New York: Routledge.

Geertz, C. 1973 *The Interpretation of Cultures.* New York: Basic Books.
1980 Blurred Genres: The Refiguration of Social Thought. *American Scholar* 29(2): 165–179.
1983 *Local Knowledge.* New York: Basic Books.
1995 *After the Fact: Two Countries, Four Decades, One Anthropologist.* Cambridge, MA: Harvard University Press.

Geis, M. L. 1987 *The Language of Politics.* New York: Springer-Verlag.

Gellner, E. 1983 *Nations and Nationalism.* Ithaca, NY: Cornell University Press.
1997 *Nationalism.* New York: New York University Press.
General Anthropology: Bulletin of the Council for General Anthropology.
Gennep, A. Van 1960 *The Rites of Passage,* translated by M. B. Vizedom and G. L. Caffe. London: Routledge.
Gezon, L. L. 1997 Political Ecology and Conflict in Ankarana, Madagascar. *Ethnology* 36:85–100.
Gibbons, A. 2001 The Peopling of the Pacific. *Science* 291: 1735. http://www.familytreedna.com/pdf/Gibbons_Science2001.pdf.
Gibbs, N. 1989 How America Has Run Out of Time. *Time,* April 24, pp. 59–67.
Giddens, A. 1973 *The Class Structure of the Advanced Societies.* New York: Cambridge University Press.
Gilad, Y., V. Wiebe, M. Przeworski, D. Lancet, and S. Pääbo 2004 Loss of Olfactory Receptor Genes Coincides with the Acquisition of Full Trichomatic Vision in Primates. http://www.pubmedcentral.nih.gov/articlerender.fcgi?artid=314465.
Gilchrist, R. 1999 *Gender and Archaeology: Contesting the Past.* New York: Routledge.
Gillespie, J. H. 2004 *Population Genetics: A Concise Guide,* 2nd ed. Baltimore: Johns Hopkins University Press.
Gilmore, D. D. 1987 *Aggression and Community: Paradoxes of Andalusian Culture.* New Haven, CT: Yale University Press.
1991 *Manhood in the Making: Cultural Concepts of Masculinity.* New Haven, CT: Yale University Press.
2001 *Misogyny: The Male Malady.* Philadelphia: University of Pennsylvania Press.
Gilmore-Lehne, W. J. 2000 Pre-Sumerian Cultures: Natufian through Ubaid Eras: 10,500–3500 B.C.E. http://loki.stockton.edu/~gilmorew/consorti/1bnear.htm.
Gimpel, J. 1988 *The Medieval Machine: The Industrial Revolution of the Middle Ages,* 2nd ed. Aldershot, Hants, England: Wildwood House.
Ginsburg, F. D., L. Abu-Lughod, and B. Larkin, eds. 2002 *Media Worlds: Anthropology on New Terrain.* Berkeley: University of California Press.
Gledhill, J. 2000 *Power and Its Disguises: Anthropological Perspectives on Politics.* Sterling, VA: Pluto Press.
Glick-Schiller, N., and G. Fouron 1990 "Everywhere We Go, We Are in Danger": Ti Manno and the Emergence of Haitian Transnational Identity. *American Ethnologist* 17(2): 327–347.
Gmelch, G. 1978 Baseball Magic. *Human Nature* 1(8): 32–40.
2001 *Inside Pitch: Life in Professional Baseball.* Washington, DC: Smithsonian Institution Press.
Gmelch, G., and W. Zenner, eds. 2002 *Urban Life: Readings in the Anthropology of the City.* Prospect Heights, IL: Waveland.
Goldberg, D. T. 1997 *Racial Subjects: Writing on Race in America.* New York: Routledge.
Goldberg, D. T., ed. 1990 *Anatomy of Racism.* Minneapolis: University of Minnesota Press.
Goldberg, P., V. T. Holliday, and C. R. Ferring 2000 *Earth Sciences and Archaeology.* New York: Kluwer Academic/Plenum Press.
Golden, T. 1997 Oakland Revamps Plan to Teach Black English. *New York Times,* January 14. http://www.nytimes.com.
Goldschmidt, W. 1965 Theory and Strategy in the Study of Cultural Adaptability. *American Anthropologist* 67: 402–407.
Goodale, J., and J. D. Koss 1971 The Cultural Context of Creativity among Tiwi. In *Anthropology and Art: Readings in Cross-Cultural Aesthetics,* ed. C. Otten, pp. 182–203. Austin: University of Texas Press.
Goodall, J. 1968 A Preliminary Report on Expressive Movements and Communication in Gombe Stream Chimpanzees. In *Primates: Studies in Adaptation and Variability,* ed. P. C. Jay, pp. 313–374. New York: Harcourt Brace Jovanovich.
1986 *The Chimpanzees of Gombe: Patterns of Behavior.* Cambridge, MA: Belknap Press of Harvard University Press.

1988 *In the Shadow of Man,* rev. ed. Boston: Houghton Mifflin.
1996 *My Life with the Chimpanzees.* New York: Pocket Books.
Goodenough, W. H. 1953 *Native Astronomy in the Central Carolines.* Philadelphia: University of Pennsylvania Press.
Goodman, J., P. E. Lovejoy, and A. Sherratt 1995 *Consuming Habits: Drugs in History and Anthropology.* London: Routledge.
Goodman, M., M. L. Baba, and L. L. Darga 1983 The Bearings of Molecular Data on the Cladograms and Times of Divergence of Hominoid Lineages. In *New Interpretations of Ape and Human Ancestry,* ed. R. L. Ciochon and R. S. Corruccini, pp. 67–87. New York: Plenum Press.
Goody, J. 1977 *Production and Reproduction: A Comparative Study of the Domestic Domain.* New York: Cambridge University Press.
Goody, J., and S. T. Tambiah 1973 *Bridewealth and Dowry.* Cambridge, UK: Cambridge University Press.
Gordon, A. A. 1996 *Transforming Capitalism and Patriarchy: Gender and Development in Africa.* Boulder, CO: Lynne Rienner.
Gorer, G. 1943 Themes in Japanese Culture. *Transactions of the New York Academy of Sciences* (Series II) 5: 106–124.
Gorman, C. F. 1969 Hoabinhian: A Pebble-Tool Complex with Early Plant Associations in Southeast Asia. *Science* 163: 671–673.
Gottdiener, M., ed. 2000 *New Forms of Consumption: Consumers, Culture, and Commodification.* Lanham, MD: Rowman and Littlefield.
Gough, E. K. 1959 The Nayars and the Definition of Marriage. *Journal of Royal Anthropological Institute* 89: 23–34.
Gould, S. J. 1996 *The Mismeasure of Man.* New York: W. W. Norton.
1999 *Rock of Ages: Science and Religion in the Fullness of Life.* New York: Ballantine Books.
2002 *The Structure of Evolutionary Theory.* Cambridge, MA: Belknap Press of Harvard University Press.
Gowlett, J. A. J. 1993 *Ascent to Civilization: The Archaeology of Early Humans.* New York: McGraw-Hill.
Graburn, N. 1976 *Ethnic and Tourist Arts: Cultural Expressions from the Fourth World.* Berkeley: University of California Press.
Graburn, N., ed. 1971 *Readings in Kinship and Social Structure.* New York: Harper & Row.
Gramsci, A. 1971 *Selections from the Prison Notebooks.* Edited and translated by Quenten Hoare and Geoffrey Nowell Smith. London: Wishart.
Grasmuck, S., and P. Pessar 1991 *Between Two Islands: Dominican International Migration.* Berkeley: University of California Press.
Grassmuck, K. 1985 Local Educators Join Push for "A Computer in Every Classroom." *Ann Arbor News,* February 19, p. A11. (Quotes testimony of Linda Tarr-Whelan of the National Education Association to the House Committee on Science, Research and Technology.)
Gray, J. 1986 With a Few Exceptions, Television in Africa Fails to Educate and Enlighten. *Ann Arbor News,* December 8.
Gray, J. P. 1985 *Primate Sociobiology.* New Haven, CT: HRAF Press.
Greaves, T. C. 1995 Problems Facing Anthropologists: Cultural Rights and Ethnography. *General Anthropology* 1(2): 1, 3–6.
Green, E. C. 1992 (orig. 1987). The Integration of Modern and Traditional Health Sectors in Swaziland. In *Applying Anthropology,* ed. A. Podolefsky and P. J. Brown, pp. 246–251. Mountain View, CA: Mayfield.
Green, G. M., and R. W. Sussman 1990 Deforestation History of the Eastern Rain Forests of Madagascar from Satellite Images. *Science* 248: 212–215.
Green, R. E., J. Krause, S. E. Ptak, A. W. Briggs, M. T. Ronan, J. F. Simons, L. Du, M. Egholm, J. M. Rothberg, M. Paunovic, and S. Pääbo 2006 Analysis of one million base pairs of Neanderthal DNA. *Nature* 444: (November 16):

330–336. http://www.nature.com/nature/journal/v444/n7117/full/nature05336.html.
Green, T. 2006 Archaeologist Makes the Case for Burying Dominant Theory of First Americans. Austin: University of Texas Research. http://www.utexas.edu/research/impact/collins.html.
Greenwood, Davydd J. 1976 *Unrewarding Wealth: The Commercialization and Collapse of Agriculture in a Spanish Basque Town.* Cambridge, UK: Cambridge University Press.
Greiner, T. M. 2003 What Is the Difference between Hominin and Hominid When Classifying Humans? MadSci Network: Evolution. http://www.madsci.org/posts/archives/Apr2003/1050350684.Ev.r.html.
Grekova, M. 2001 Postsocialist Societies. *International Encyclopedia of the Social and Behavioral Sciences,* pp. 11877–11881. New York: Elsevier.
Griffin, P. B., and A. Estioko-Griffin, eds. 1985 *The Agta of Northeastern Luzon: Recent Studies.* Cebu City, Philippines: University of San Carlos.
Gross, D. 1971 The Great Sisal Scheme. *Natural History,* March, pp. 49–55.
Gross, D., and B. Underwood 1971 Technological Change and Caloric Costs: Sisal Agriculture in Northeastern Brazil. *American Anthropologist* 73: 725–740.
Gudeman, S. 2001 *The Anthropology of Economy: Community, Market, and Culture.* Malden, MA: Blackwell.
Gudeman, S., ed. 1998 *Economic Anthropology.* Northhampton, MA: E. Elgar.
Gugliotta, G. 2002 Earliest Human Ancestor? Skull Dates to When Apes, Humans Split. *Washington Post,* July 11, p. A01.
2004 New Evidence of Controlled Fire Is Unearthed: Israeli Team's Finds at Ancient Campsite Near Jordan River Suggest Humans Harnessed Blazes 790,000 Years Ago. *Washington Post,* May 10, p. A-10.
2005a More Fossil Evidence from "Hobbit" Island. *Washington Post,* October 12, p. A-03.
2005b Tools Found in Britain Show Much Earlier Human Existence. *Washington Post,* December 15, p. A-24.
Gulliver, P. H. 1974 (orig. 1965). The Jie of Uganda. In *Man in Adaptation: The Cultural Present,* 2nd ed., ed. Y. A. Cohen, pp. 323–345. Chicago: Aldine.
Gumperz, J. J. 1982 *Language and Social Identity.* Cambridge, UK: Cambridge University Press.
Gumperz, J. J., and S. C. Levinson, eds. 1996 *Rethinking Linguistic Relativity.* New York: Cambridge University Press.
Gunther, E. 1971 Northwest Coast Indian Art. In *Anthropology and Art: Readings in Cross-Cultural Aesthetics,* ed. C. Otten, pp. 318–340. Austin: University of Texas Press.
Gupta, A., and J. Ferguson 1997a Culture, Power, Place: Ethnography at the End of an Era. In *Culture, Power, Place: Explorations in Critical Anthropology,* ed. A. Gupta and J. Ferguson, pp. 1–29. Durham, NC: Duke University Press.
1997b Beyond "Culture": Space, Identity, and the Politics of Difference. In *Culture, Power, Place: Explorations in Critical Anthropology,* ed. A. Gupta and J. Ferguson, pp. 33–51. Durham, NC: Duke University Press.
Gupta, A., and J. Ferguson, eds. 1997a *Anthropological Locations: Boundaries and Grounds of a Field Science.* Berkeley: University of California Press.
1997b *Culture, Power, Place: Explorations in Critical Anthropology.* Durham, NC: Duke University Press.
Guthrie, S. 1995 *Faces in the Clouds: A New Theory of Religion.* New York: Oxford University Press.
Guyot, J., and C. Hughes 2007 Researches Find Earliest Evidence for Modern Human Behavior. *Arizona State University Research Magazine.* http://researchmag.asu.edu/2008/02researchers_find_earliest_evid.html.
Gwynne, M. A. 2003 *Applied Anthropology: A Career-Oriented Approach.* Boston: Allyn & Bacon.
Haapala, A. 1998 Literature: Invention of the Self. *Canadian Aesthetics Journal* 2. http://www.uqtr.ca/AE/vol_2/haapala.html.

Hackett, R. I. J. 1996 *Art and Religion in Africa*. London: Cassell.

Hall, E. T. 1990 *Understanding Cultural Differences*. Yarmouth, ME: Intercultural Press. 1992 *An Anthropology of Everyday Life: An Autobiography*. New York: Doubleday.

Hall, T. D., ed. 1999 *A World-System Reader: New Perspectives on Gender, Urbanism, Cultures, Indigenous Peoples, and Ecology*. Lanham, MD: Rowman and Littlefield.

Hallowell, A. I. 1955 *Culture and Experience*. Philadelphia: University of Pennsylvania Press.

Hamburg, D. A., and E. R. McCown, eds. 1979 *The Great Apes*. Menlo Park, CA: Benjamin Cummings.

Hamilton, M. B. 1995 *The Sociology of Religion: Theoretical and Comparative Perspectives*. London: Routledge.

Hanks, W. F. 1995 *Language and Communicative Practices*. Boulder, CO: Westview Press.

Hansen, K. V. 2004 *Not-So-Nuclear Families: Class, Gender, and Networks of Care*. New Brunswick, NJ: Rutgers University Press.

Hansen, K. V., and A. I. Garey, eds. 1998 *Families in the U.S.: Kinship and Domestic Politics*. Philadelphia: Temple University Press.

Harcourt, A. H., D. Fossey, and J. Sabater-Pi 1981 Demography of *Gorilla gorilla*. *Journal of Zoology* 195: 215–233.

Harding, S. 1975 Women and Words in a Spanish Village. In *Toward an Anthropology of Women*, ed. R. Reiter, pp. 283–308. New York: Monthly Review Press.

Hargrove, E. C. 1986 *Religion and Environmental Crisis*. Athens: University of Georgia Press.

Harlan, J. R., and D. Zohary 1966 Distribution of Wild Wheats and Barley. *Science* 153: 1074–1080.

Harlow, H. 1966 Development of Patterns of Affection in Macaques. *Yearbook of Physical Anthropology* 14: 1–7.

Harris, M. 1964 *Patterns of Race in the Americas*. New York: Walker. 1970 Referential Ambiguity in the Calculus of Brazilian Racial Identity. *Southwestern Journal of Anthropology* 26(1): 1–14. 1974 *Cows, Pigs, Wars, and Witches: The Riddles of Culture*. New York: Random House. 1978 *Cannibals and Kings*. New York: Vintage. 1989 *Our Kind: Who We Are, Where We Came from, Where We Are Going*. New York: Harper & Row. 2001a (orig. 1979). *Cultural Materialism: The Struggle for a Science of Culture*. Walnut Creek, CA: AltaMira. 2001b (orig. 1968). *The Rise of Anthropological Theory*. Walnut Creek, CA: AltaMira.

Harris, M., and C. P. Kottak 1963 The Structural Significance of Brazilian Racial Categories. *Sociologia* 25: 203–209.

Harris, N. M., and G. Hillman 1989 *Foraging and Farming: The Evolution of Plant Exploitation*. London: Unwin Hyman.

Harrison, G. G., W. L. Rathje, and W. W. Hughes 1994 Food Waste Behavior in an Urban Population. In *Applying Anthropology: An Introductory Reader*, 3rd ed., ed. A. Podolefsky and P. J. Brown, pp. 107–112. Mountain View, CA: Mayfield.

Harrison, K. D. 2007 *When Languages Die: The Extinction of the World's Languages and the Erosion of Human Knowledge*. New York: Oxford University Press.

Hart, C. W. M., A. R. Pilling, and J. C. Goodale 1988 *The Tiwi of North Australia*, 3rd ed. Fort Worth: Harcourt Brace.

Hart, D., and R. W. Sussman 2005 *Man the Hunted: Primates, Predators, and Human Evolution*. Boulder, CO: Westview Press.

Hartl, D. L. 1997 *Principles of Population Genetics*, 3rd ed. Sunderland, MA: Sinauer. 2000 *A Primer of Population Genetics*, 3rd ed. Sunderland, MA: Sinauer Associates.

Hartl, D. L., and E. W. Jones 2006 *Essential Genetics*, 4th ed. Boston: Jones and Bartlett.

Harvey, D. J. 1980 French Empire. *Academic American Encyclopedia*, vol. 8, pp. 309–310. Princeton, NJ: Arete.

Harvey, K. 1996 Online for the Ancestors: The Importance of Anthropological Sensibility in Information Superhighway Design. *Social Science Computing Review* 14(1): 65–68.

Hassig, R. 1985 *Trade, Tribute, and Transportation: The Sixteenth-Century Political Economy of the Valley of Mexico*. Norman: University of Oklahoma Press.

Hastings, A. 1997 *The Construction of Nationhood: Ethnicity, Religion, and Nationalism*. New York: Cambridge University Press.

Hatcher, E. P. 1999 *Art as Culture: An Introduction to the Anthropology of Art*, 2nd ed. Westport, CT: Bergin & Garvey.

Hatfield, E., and R. L. Rapson 1996 *Love and Sex: Cross-Cultural Perspectives*. Needham Heights, MA: Allyn & Bacon.

Hausfater, G., and S. Hrdy, eds. 1984 *Infanticide: Comparative and Evolutionary Perspectives*. Hawthorne, NY: Aldine.

Hawkes, K., J. O'Connell, and K. Hill 1982 Why Hunters Gather: Optimal Foraging and the Aché of Eastern Paraguay. *American Ethnologist* 9: 379–398.

Hawks, J., and M. Wolpoff 2003 Sixty Years of Modern Human Origins in the American Anthropological Association. *American Anthropologist* 105(1): 89–100.

Hawley, J. S., ed. 1994 *Sati, the Blessing and the Curse: The Burning of Wives in India*. New York: Oxford University Press.

Hayden, B. 1981 Subsistence and Ecological Adaptations of Modern Hunter/Gatherers. In *Omnivorous Primates: Gathering and Hunting in Human Evolution*, ed. R. S. Harding and G. Teleki, pp. 344–421. New York: Columbia University Press.

Headland, T. N., ed. 1992 *The Tasaday Controversy: Assessing the Evidence*. Washington, DC: American Anthropological Association.

Headland, T. N., and L. A. Reid 1989 Hunter-Gatherers and Their Neighbors from Prehistory to the Present. *Current Anthropology* 30: 43–66.

Heath, D. B., ed. 1995 *International Handbook on Alcohol and Culture*. Westport, CT: Greenwood Press.

Hedges, C. 1992a Sudan Presses Its Campaign to Impose Islamic Law on Non-Muslims. *New York Times*, June 1, p. A7. 1992b Sudan Gives Its Refugees a Desert to Contemplate. *New York Times*, June 3, p. A4.

Heider, K. G. 1988 The Rashomon Effect: When Ethnographers Disagree. *American Anthropologist* 90: 73–81. 1997 *Grand Valley Dani: Peaceful Warriors*, 3rd ed. Fort Worth: Harcourt Brace.

Heller, M. 1988 *Codeswitching: Anthropological and Sociolinguistic Perspectives*. Berlin: Mouton de Gruyter.

Helman, C. 2001 *Culture, Health, and Illness: An Introduction for Health Professionals*, 4th ed. Boston: Butterworth-Heinemann.

Henry, D. O. 1989 *From Foraging to Agriculture: The Levant at the End of the Ice Age*. Philadelphia: University of Pennsylvania Press. 1995 *Prehistoric Cultural Ecology and Evolution: Insights from Southern Jordan*. New York: Plenum Press.

Henry, J. 1955 Docility, or Giving Teacher What She Wants. *Journal of Social Issues* 2: 33–41.

Herdt, G. 1981 *Guardians of the Flutes*. New York: McGraw-Hill. 1986 *The Sambia: Ritual and Gender in New Guinea*. Fort Worth: Harcourt Brace.

Herdt, G. H., ed. 1984 *Ritualized Homosexuality in Melanesia*. Berkeley: University of California Press.

Herrnstein, R. J. 1971 I.Q. *Atlantic* 228(3): 43–64.

Herrnstein, R. J., and C. Murray 1994 *The Bell Curve: Intelligence and Class Structure in American Life*. New York: Free Press.

Herskovits, M. 1937 *Life in a Haitian Valley*. New York: Knopf.

Hess, D. J. 1995 A Democratic Research Agenda in the Social Studies of the National Information Infrastructure. Paper prepared for the National Science Foundation Workshop on Culture, Society, and Advanced Information Technology. Washington, DC: May 31–June 1, 1995.

Hess, D. J., and R. A. DaMatta, eds. 1995 *The Brazilian Puzzle: Culture on the Borderlands of the Western World*. New York: Columbia University Press.

Hewitt, R. 1986 *White Talk, Black Talk*. Cambridge, UK: Cambridge University Press.

Heyerdahl, T. 1971 *The Ra Expeditions*. Translated by P. Crampton. Garden City, NY: Doubleday.

Heyneman, D. 1984 Development and Disease: A Dual Dilemma. *Journal of Parasitology* 70: 3–17.

Hicks, D., ed. 2001 *Ritual and Belief: Readings in the Anthropology of Religion*, 2nd ed. Boston: McGraw-Hill.

Hill, C. E., ed. 1986 Current Health Policy Issues and Alternatives: An Applied Social Science Perspective. *Southern Anthropological Society Proceedings*. Athens: University of Georgia Press.

Hill, J. H. 1978 Apes and Language. *Annual Review of Anthropology* 7: 89–112.

Hill, K., H. Kaplan, K. Hawkes, and A. Hurtado 1987 Foraging Decisions among Aché Hunter-Gatherers: New Data and Implications for Optimal Foraging Models. *Ethology and Sociobiology* 8: 1–36.

Hill-Burnett, J. 1978 Developing Anthropological Knowledge through Application. In *Applied Anthropology in America*, ed. E. M. Eddy and W. L. Partridge, pp. 112–128. New York: Columbia University Press.

Hinde, R. A., ed. 1983 *Primate Social Relationships: An Integrated Approach*. Sunderland, MA: Sinauer.

Hobhouse, L. T. 1915 *Morals in Evolution*, rev. ed. New York: Holt.

Hobsbawm, E. J. 1992 *Nations and Nationalism since 1780: Programme, Myth, Reality*, 2nd ed. New York: Cambridge University Press.

Hoebel, E. A. 1954 *The Law of Primitive Man*. Cambridge, MA: Harvard University Press. 1968 (orig. 1954). The Eskimo: Rudimentary Law in a Primitive Anarchy. In *Studies in Social and Cultural Anthropology*, ed. J. Middleton, pp. 93–127. New York: Crowell.

Holden, A. 2005 *Tourism Studies and the Social Sciences*. New York: Routledge.

Hole, F., K. V. Flannery, and J. A. Neely 1969 *The Prehistory and Human Ecology of the Deh Luran Plain*. Memoir no. 1. Ann Arbor: University of Michigan Museum of Anthropology.

Holland, D., and N. Quinn, eds. 1987 *Cultural Models in Language and Thought*. Cambridge, UK: Cambridge University Press.

Holloway, R. L. 1975 (orig. 1974). The Casts of Fossil Hominid Brains. In *Biological Anthropology, Readings from Scientific American*, ed. S. H. Katz, pp. 69–78. San Francisco: W. H. Freeman.

Holmes, L. D. 1987 *Quest for the Real Samoa: The Mead/Freeman Controversy and Beyond*. South Hadley, MA: Bergin and Garvey.

Holst, I., J. E. Moreno, and D. R. Piperno 2007 The Identification of Teosinte, Maize, and *Tripsacum* in Mesoamerica by Using Pollen, Starch Grains, and Phytoliths. *Proceedings of the National Academy of Sciences USA* 104: 17608–17613.

Holtzman, J. 2000 *Nuer Journeys, Nuer Lives*. Boston: Allyn & Bacon.

Hooker, R. 1996 Civilizations in Africa. http://www.wsu.edu:8080/~dee/civafrca/contents.htm.

Hopkin, M. 2007 Twin Fossil Find Adds Twist to Human Evolution. http://www.nature.com/news/2007/070806/full/070806-5.html

Hopkins, T., and I. Wallerstein 1982 Patterns of Development of the Modern World System. In *World System Analysis: Theory and Methodology*, by T. Hopkins, I. Wallerstein, R. Bach, C. Chase-Dunn, and R. Mukherjee, pp. 121–141. Thousand Oaks, CA: Sage.

Hopkins, T. K. 1996 *The Age of Transition: Trajectory of the World-System 1945–2025*. Atlantic Highlands, NJ: Zed.

Horton, R. 1963 The Kalabari Ekine Society: A Borderland of Religion and Art. *Africa* 33: 94–113. 1993 *Patterns of Thought in Africa and the West: Essays on Magic, Religion, and Science*. New York: Cambridge University Press.

Hostetler, J., and G. E. Huntington 1992 *Amish Children: Education in the Family*, 2nd ed. Fort Worth: Harcourt Brace. 1996 *The Hutterites in North America*, 3rd ed. Fort Worth: Harcourt Brace.

Howells, W. W. 1976 Explaining Modern Man: Evolutionists versus Migrationists. *Journal of Human Evolution* 5: 477–496.

Hrdy, S. B. 1999 *The Woman That Never Evolved*, rev. ed. Cambridge, MA: Harvard University Press.

Hudjashov, G., T. Kivisilda, P. A. Underhill, P. Endicott, J. J. Sanchez, A. A. Lin, P. Shen, P. Oefner, C. Renfrew, R. Villems, and P. Forster. 2007 Revealing the Prehistoric Settlement of Australia by Y Chromosome and mtDNA Analysis. *Proceedings of the National Academy of Sciences* 104(21): 8726–8730.

Hughes, R., Jr. 1996 Demographics of Divorce. http://missourifamilies.org/features/divorcearticles/divorcefeature17.htm.

Human Organization Quarterly journal. Oklahoma City: Society for Applied Anthropology.

Hunter, M. L. 2005 *Race, Gender, and the Politics of Skin Tone*. New York: Routledge.

Hurtado. A. M., C. A. Lambourne, P. James, K. Hill, K. Cheman, and K. Baca 2005 Human Rights, Biomedical Science, and Infections Diseases among South American Indigenous Groups. *Annual Review of Anthropology* 34: 639–665.

Hutchinson, S. E. 1996 *Nuer Dilemmas: Coping with Money, War, and the State*. Berkeley: University of California Press.

Ignatius, D. 2007 Summer's Escape Artists. *Washington Post*, July 26. http://www.washingtonpost.com/wp-dyn/content/article/2007/07/25/AR2007072501879.html.

Ingold, T., D. Riches, and J. Woodburn 1991 *Hunters and Gatherers*. New York: Berg (St. Martin's Press).

Ingraham, C. 1999 *White Weddings: Romancing Heterosexuality in Popular Culture*. New York: Routledge.

Inhorn, M. C., and P. J. Brown 1990 The Anthropology of Infectious Disease. *Annual Review of Anthropology* 19: 89–117.

Iqbal, S. 2002 A New Light on Skin Color. *National Geographic Online Extra*. http://magma.nationalgeographic.com/ngm/0211/feature2/online_extra.html.

Irving, W. N. 1985 Context and Chronology of Early Man in the Americas. *Annual Review of Anthropology* 14: 529–555.

Isaac, G. L. 1972 Early Phases of Human Behavior: Models in Lower Paleolithic Archaeology. In *Models in Archaeology*, ed. D. L. Clarke, pp. 167–199. London: Methuen.
1978 Food Sharing and Human Evolution: Archaeological Evidence from the Plio-Pleistocene of East Africa. *Journal of Anthropological Research* 34: 311–325.

Isto É 1984 *Olimpíadas*, August 8.

Ives, E. D. 1995 *The Tape-Recorded Interview: A Manual for Fieldworkers in Folklore and Oral History*, 2nd ed. Knoxville: University of Tennessee Press.

Jablonski, N. G., and Chaplin, G. 2000 The Evolution of Human Skin Coloration. *Journal of Human Evolution* (39): 57–106.

Jackson, B. 1987 *Fieldwork*. Champaign–Urbana: University of Illinois Press.

Jackson, J., and K. B. Warren 2005 Indigenous Movements in Latin America, 1992–2004: Controversies, Ironies, New Directions. *Annual Review of Anthropology* 34: 549–573.

Jacoby, R., and N. Glauberman, eds. 1995 *The Bell Curve Debate: History, Documents, Opinions*. New York: Free Press. New York: Random House/Times Books.

Jameson, F. 1984 Postmodernism, or the Cultural Logic of Late Capitalism. *New Left Review* 146: 53–93.
1988 *The Ideologies of Theory: Essays 1971–1986*. Minneapolis: University of Minnesota Press.

Jankowiak, W. R., and E. F. Fischer 1992 A Cross-Cultural Perspective on Romantic Love. *Ethnology* 31(2): 149–156.

Janson, C. H. 1986 Capuchin Counterpoint: Divergent Mating and Feeding Habits Distinguish Two Closely Related Monkey Species in the Peruvian Forest. *Natural History* 95: 44–52.

Jasim, S. A. 1985 The Ubaid Period in Iraq: Recent Excavations in the Hamrin Region. *BAR International Series* 267 (Oxford).

Jenks, C. 2004 *Culture*, 2nd ed. New York: Routledge.

Jensen, A. 1969 How Much Can We Boost I.Q. and Scholastic Achievement? *Harvard Educational Review* 29: 1–123.

Jodelet, D. 1991 *Madness and Social Representations: Living with the Mad in One French Community*. Translated from the French by Gerard Duveen. Berkeley: University of California Press.

Johansen, B. E. 2003 *Indigenous Peoples and Environmental Issues: An Encyclopedia*. Westport, CT: Greenwood Press.

Johanson, D. C., and M. Edey 1981 *Lucy: The Origins of Humankind*. New York: Simon & Schuster.

Johanson, D. C., and B. Edgar 1996 *From Lucy to Language*. New York: Simon & Schuster.

Johanson, D. C., and T. D. White 1979 A Systematic Assessment of Early African Hominids. *Science* 203: 321–330.

Johnson, A. W. 1978 *Quantification in Cultural Anthropology: An Introduction to Research Design*. Stanford, CA: Stanford University Press.

Johnson, A. W., and T. Earle, eds. 1987 *The Evolution of Human Societies: From Foraging Group to Agrarian State*. Stanford, CA: Stanford University Press.
2000 *The Evolution of Human Societies: From Foraging Group to Agrarian State*, 2nd ed. Stanford, CA: Stanford University Press.

Johnson, G. A. 1987 The Changing Organization of Uruk Administration in the Susiana Plain. In *The Archaeology of Western Iran*, ed. F. Hole, pp. 107–139. Washington, DC: Smithsonian Institution Press.

Johnson, T. J., and C. F. Sargent, eds. 1990 *Medical Anthropology: A Handbook of Theory and Method*. New York: Greenwood Press.

Johnston, F. E., and S. Low 1994 *Children of the Urban Poor: The Sociocultural Environment of Growth, Development, and Malnutrition in Guatemala City*. Boulder, CO: Westview Press.

Jolly, A. 1985 *The Evolution of Primate Behavior*, 2nd ed. New York: Macmillan.

Jolly, C. J., and F. Plog 1986 *Physical Anthropology and Archaeology*, 4th ed. New York: McGraw-Hill.

Jolly, C. J., and R. White 1995 *Physical Anthropology and Archaeology*, 5th ed. New York: McGraw-Hill.

Jones, D. 1999 Hot Asset in Corporate: Anthropology Degrees. *USA Today*, February 18, p. B1.

Jones, G., and R. Krautz 1981 *The Transition to Statehood in the New World*. Cambridge, UK: Cambridge University Press.

Joralemon, D. 2006 *Exploring Medical Anthropology*, 2nd ed. Boston: Pearson.

Jordan, A. 2003 *Business Anthropology*. Prospect Heights, IL: Waveland.

Joyce, R. A. 2000 *Gender and Power in Prehispanic Mesoamerica*. Austin: University of Texas Press.

Jurmain, R. 1997 *Introduction to Physical Anthropology*, 7th ed. Belmont, CA: Wadsworth.

Kan, S. 1986 The 19th-Century Tlingit Potlatch: A New Perspective. *American Ethnologist* 13: 191–212.
1989 *Symbolic Immortality: The Tlingit Potlatch of the Nineteenth Century*. Washington, DC: Smithsonian Institution Press.

Kantor, P. 1996 Domestic Violence against Women: A Global Issue. http://www.ucis.unc.edu/resources/pubs/carolina/Abuse/Abuse.html.

Kaplan, R. D. 1994 The Coming Anarchy: How Scarcity, Crime, Overpopulation, and Disease Are Rapidly Destroying the Social Fabric of Our Planet. *Atlantic Monthly*, February, pp. 44–76.

Kardiner, A., ed. 1939 *The Individual and His Society*. New York: Columbia University Press.

Kardulias, P. N. 1999 *World-Systems Theory in Practice: Leadership, Production, and Exchange*. Lanham, MD: Rowman and Littlefield.

Katzenberg, M.A., and S. R. Saunders, eds. 2000 *Biological Anthropology of the Human Skeleton*. New York: Wiley.

Kaufman, S. R., and L. M. Morgan 2005 The Anthropology of the Beginnings and Ends of Life. *Annual Review of Anthropology*, 34: 317–341.

Kearney, M. 1996 *Reconceptualizing the Peasantry: Anthropology in Global Perspective*. Boulder, CO: Westview Press.
2004 *Changing Fields of Anthropology: From Local to Global*. Lanham, MD: Rowman and Littlefield.

Kehoe, A. B. 1989 *The Ghost Dance Religion: Ethnohistory and Revitalization*. Fort Worth: Harcourt Brace.

Keiser, L. 1991 *Friend by Day, Enemy by Night: Organized Vengeance in a Kohistani Community*. Fort Worth: Harcourt Brace.

Kelly, R. C. 1976 Witchcraft and Sexual Relations: An Exploration in the Social and Semantic Implications of the Structure of Belief. In *Man and Woman in the New Guinea Highlands*, ed. P. Brown and G. Buchbinder, pp. 36–53. Special Publication, no. 8. Washington, DC: American Anthropological Association.
1985 *The Nuer Conquest: The Structure and Development of an Expansionist System*. Ann Arbor: University of Michigan Press.
2000 *Warless Societies and the Origin of War*. Ann Arbor: University of Michigan Press.

Kelly, R. L. 1995 *The Foraging Spectrum: Diversity in Hunter-Gatherer Lifeways*. Washington, DC: Smithsonian Institution Press.

Kemp, T. S. 1999 *Fossils and Evolution*. New York: Oxford University Press.

Kennedy, R. G. 1994 *Hidden Cities: The Discovery and Loss of Ancient North American Civilization*. New York: Free Press.

Kent, S. 1992 The Current Forager Controversy: Real versus Ideal Views of Hunter-Gatherers. *Man* 27: 45–70.
1996 *Cultural Diversity among Twentieth-Century Foragers: An African Perspective*. New York: Cambridge University Press.
1998 *Gender in African Prehistory*. Walnut Creek, CA: AltaMira.

Kent, S., and H. Vierich 1989 The Myth of Ecological Determinism: Anticipated Mobility and Site Organization of Space. In *Farmers as Hunters: The Implications of Sedentism*, ed. S. Kent, pp. 96–130. New York: Cambridge University Press.

Keppel, K. G., J. N. Pearch, and D. K. Wagener 2002 Trends in Racial and Ethnic-Specific Rates for the Health Status Indicators: United States, 1990–98. *Healthy People Statistical Notes* 23. Hyattsville, MD: National Center for Health Statistics.

Kerr, R. A. 1998 Sea-Floor Dust Shows Drought Felled Akkadian Empire. *Science* 279 (5349—January 16): 325–326.

Keynes, J. M. 1927 *The End of Laissez-Faire*. London: L. and Virginia Woolf. 1936 *General Theory of Employment, Interest, and Money*. New York: Harcourt Brace.

Kimbel, W. H., and L. B. Martin, eds. 1993 *Species, Species Concepts, and Primate Evolution*. New York: Plenum Press.

Kimmel, M. S. 2004 *The Gendered Society*, 2nd ed. New York: Oxford University Press.

Kimmel, M. S., J. Hearn, and R. W. Connell 2005 *Handbook of Studies on Men and Masculinities*. Thousand Oaks, CA: Sage.

Kimmel, M. S., and M. A. Messner, eds. 2007 *Men's Lives*, 7th ed. Boston: Allyn & Bacon.

Kimmel, M. S., and R. Plante 2004 *Sexualities: Identities, Behaviors, and Society*. New York: Oxford University Press.

King, B. J., ed. 1994 *The Information Continuum: Evolution of Social Information Transfer in Monkeys, Apes, and Hominids*. Santa Fe: School of American Research Press.

Kinsey, A. C., W. B. Pomeroy, and C. E. Martin 1948 *Sexual Behavior in the Human Male*. Philadelphia: W. B. Saunders.

Kirch, P. V. 1984 *The Evolution of the Polynesian Chiefdoms*. Cambridge, UK: Cambridge University Press.
2000 *On the Road of the Winds: An Archaeological History of the Pacific Islands before European Contact*. Berkeley: University of California Press.

Kirman, P. 1997 An Introduction to Ethnomusicology. http://www.insideworldmusic.com/library/weekly/aa101797.htm.

Klass, M. 1995 *Ordered Universes: Approaches to the Anthropology of Religion*. Boulder, CO: Westview Press.
2003 *Mind over Mind: The Anthropology and Psychology of Spirit Possession*. Lanham, MD: Rowman and Littlefield.

Klass, M., and M. Weisgrau, eds. 1999 *Across the Boundaries of Belief: Contemporary Issues in the Anthropology of Religion.* Boulder, CO: Westview Press.

Klein, R. G. 1999 *The Human Career: Human Biological and Cultural Origins,* 2nd ed. Chicago: University of Chicago Press.

Klein, R. G., with B. Edgar 2002 *The Dawn of Human Culture.* New York: Wiley.

Kleinfeld, J. 1975 Positive Stereotyping: The Cultural Relativist in the Classroom. *Human Organization* 34: 269–274.

Kleymeyer, C. D., ed. 1994 *Cultural Expression and Grassroots Development: Cases from Latin America and the Caribbean.* Boulder, CO: Lynne Rienner.

Klineberg, O. 1951 Race and Psychology. In *The Race Question in Modern Science.* Paris: UNESCO.

Kling, R. 1996 Synergies and Competition between Life in Cyberspace and Face-to-Face Communities. *Social Science Computing Review* 14(1): 50–54.

Kluckhohn, C. 1944 *Mirror for Man: A Survey of Human Behavior and Social Attitudes.* Greenwich, CT: Fawcett.

Kluge, A. G. 1983 Cladistics and the Classification of the Great Apes. In *New Interpretations of Ape and Human Ancestry,* ed. R. L. Ciochon and R. S. Corruccini, pp. 151–177. New York: Plenum Press.

Knauft, B. 2005 *The Gebusi: Life Transformed in a Rainforest World.* Boston: McGraw-Hill.

Knecht, H., A. Pike-Tay, and R. White, eds. 1993 *Before Lascaux: The Complex Record of the Early Upper Paleolithic.* Boca Raton, FL: CRC Press.

Kohler, M., and S. Moyá-Solá 1997 Ape-Like or Hominid-Like? The Positional Behavior of *Oreopithecus bambolii* Reconsidered. *Proceedings of the National Academy of Sciences* 94 (October 14):11, 747.

Kolata, G. 1997 On Cloning Humans, "Never" Turns Swiftly into "Why Not?" *New York Times,* December 2, late edition, final, section A, p. 1.

Kopytoff, V. G. 1995 Meat Viewed as Staple of Chimp Diet and Mores. *New York Times,* June 27, pp. B5–B6.

Korten, D. C. 1980 Community Organization and Rural Development: A Learning Process Approach. *Public Administration Review,* September–October, pp. 480–512.

Kosty, P. 2002 Indonesia's Matriarchal Minangkabau Offer an Alternative Social System, EurekAlert. org, May 9. http://www.eurekalert.org/pub_releases/2002-05/uop-imm050902.php.

Kottak, C. P. 1980 *The Past in the Present: History, Ecology, and Social Organization in Highland Madagascar.* Ann Arbor: University of Michigan Press.
1990a *Prime-Time Society: An Anthropological Analysis of Television and Culture.* Belmont, CA: Wadsworth.
1990b Culture and Economic Development. *American Anthropologist* 92(3): 723–731. 1991 When People Don't Come First: Some Lessons from Completed Projects. In *Putting People First: Sociological Variables in Rural Development,* 2nd ed., ed. M. Cernea, pp. 429–464. New York: Oxford University Press.
1999a *Assault on Paradise: Social Change in a Brazilian Village,* 3rd ed. New York: McGraw-Hill.
1999b The New Ecological Anthropology. *American Anthropologist* 101(1): 23–35.
2004 An Anthropological Take on Sustainable Development: A Comparative Study of Change. *Human Organization* 63(4): 501–510. 2006 *Assault on Paradise: The Globalization of a Little Community in Brazil,* 4th ed. New York: McGraw-Hill.
2007 Return to Madagascar: A Forty Year Retrospective. *General Anthropology: Bulletin of the General Anthropology Division of the American Anthropological Association* 14(2): 1–10.

Kottak, C. P., ed. 1982 *Researching American Culture: A Guide for Student Anthropologists.* Ann Arbor: University of Michigan Press.

Kottak, C. P., and A. C. G. Costa 1993 Ecological Awareness, Environmentalist Action, and International Conservation Strategy. *Human Organization* 52(4): 335–343.

Kottak, C. P., L. L. Gezon, and G. Green 1994 Deforestation and Biodiversity Preservation in Madagascar: The View from Above and Below.

CIESIN Human Dimensions Kiosk. http://www.ciesin.com.

Kottak, C. P., and K. A. Kozaitis 2008 *On Being Different: Diversity and Multiculturalism in the North American Mainstream,* 3rd ed. Boston: McGraw-Hill.

Kottak, N. C. 2002 *Stealing the Neighbor's Chicken: Social Control in Northern Mozambique.* Ph.D. dissertation. Department of Anthropology, Emory University, Atlanta, GA.

Kramarae, R., M. Shulz, and M. O'Barr, eds. 1984 *Language and Power.* Thousand Oaks, CA: Sage.

Kreider, R. M., and J. M. Fields 2002 Number, Timing and Duration of Marriages and Divorces: 1996. U.S. Census Bureau. *Current Population Reports,* P70–80, February, 2002. http://www.census.gov/prod/2002pubs/p70-80.pdf.

Kretchmer, N. 1975 (orig. 1972). Lactose and Lactase. In *Biological Anthropology, Readings from Scientific American,* ed. S. H. Katz, pp. 310–318. San Francisco: W. H. Freeman.

Kristof, N. D. 1995 Japan's Feminine Falsetto Falls Right Out of Favor. *New York Times,* December 13, pp. A1, A4.

Kroeber, A. L. 1923 *Anthropology.* New York: Harcourt, Brace.
1944 *Configurations of Cultural Growth.* Berkeley: University of California Press.
1987 (orig. 1952). *The Nature of Culture.* Chicago: University of Chicago Press.

Kroeber, A. L., and C. Kluckhohn 1963 *Culture: A Critical Review of Concepts and Definitions.* New York: Vintage.

Kryshtanovskaya, O. 1997 Illegal Structures in Russia. *Trends in Organized Crime* 3(1): 14–17.

Kuhn, S. L., M. C. Stiner, and D. S. Reese 2001 Ornaments of the Earliest Upper Paleolithic: New Insights from the Levant. *Proceedings of the National Academy of Sciences of the United States of America* 98(13): 7641–7646.

Kulick, D. 1998 *Travesti: Sex, Gender, and Culture among Brazilian Transgendered Prostitutes.* Chicago: University of Chicago Press.

Kuniholm, P. I. 1995 Dendrochronology, in Science in Archaeology: A Review. *American Journal of Archaeology* 99: 79–142.
2004 Home page of the Malcolm and Carolyn Wiener Laboratory for Aegean and Near Eastern Dendrochronology at Cornell University. http://www.arts.cornell.edu/dendro/.

Kunitz, S. J. 1994 *Disease and Social Diversity: The European Impact on the Health of Non-Europeans.* New York: Oxford University Press.

Kuper, L. 2006 *Race, Class, and Power: Ideology and Revolutionary Change in Plural Societies.* New Brunswick, NJ: Transaction.

Kurtz, D. V. 2001 *Political Anthropology: Power and Paradigms.* Boulder, CO: Westview Press.

Kutsche, P. 1998 *Field Ethnography: A Manual for Doing Cultural Anthropology.* Upper Saddle River, NJ: Prentice Hall.

LaBarre, W. 1945 Some Observations of Character Structure in the Orient: The Japanese. *Psychiatry* 8: 326–342.

Labov, W. 1972a *Language in the Inner City: Studies in the Black English Vernacular.* Philadelphia: University of Pennsylvania Press.
1972b *Sociolinguistic Patterns.* Philadelphia: University of Pennsylvania Press.

La Fraugh, R. J. n.d. Euskara: The History, a True Mystery. The La Fraugh Name History. http://planetrjl.tripod.com/LaFraughName/id5.html.

Laguerre, M. S. 1984 *American Odyssey: Haitians in New York.* Ithaca, NY: Cornell University Press.
1998 *Diasporic Citizenship: Haitian Americans in Transnational America.* New York: St. Martin's Press.
1999 *The Global Ethnopolis: Chinatown, Japantown, and Manilatown in American Society.* New York: St. Martin's Press.
2001 *Urban Multiculturalism and Globalization in New York City.* New York: Palgrave Macmillan.

Laird, S. A. 2002 *Biodiversity and Traditional Knowledge: Equitable Partnerships in Practice.* Sterling, VA: Earthscan.

Lakoff, R. T. 2000 *Language War.* Berkeley: University of California Press.
2004 *Language and Woman's Place.* New York: Harper & Row.

Lamberg-Karlovsky, C. C., and J. A. Sabloff 1995 *Ancient Civilizations: The Near East and Mesoamerica.* Prospect Heights, IL: Waveland.

Lamphere, L., H. Ragone, and P. Zavella, eds. 1997 *Situated Lives: Gender and Culture in Everyday Life.* New York: Routledge.

Lancaster, R. N., and M. Di Leonardo, eds. 1997 *The Gender/Sexuality Reader: Culture, History, Political Economy.* New York: Routledge.

Lance, L. M., and E. E. McKenna 1975 Analysis of Cases Pertaining to the Impact of Western Technology on the Non-Western World. *Human Organization* 34: 87–94.

Lansing, J. S. 1991 *Priests and Programmers: Technologies of Power in the Engineered Landscape of Bali.* Princeton, NJ: Princeton University Press.

Largent, F. 2007a Clovis Dethroned: A New Perspective on the First Americans, Part 1. *Mammoth Trumpet* 22(3): 1–3, 20.
2007b Clovis Dethroned: A New Perspective on the First Americans, Part 2. *Mammoth Trumpet* 22(4): 1–2, 13.

Larsen, C. S. 2000 *Skeletons in Our Closet: Revealing Our Past through Bioarchaeology.* Princeton, NJ: Princeton University Press.

Larson, A. 1989 Social Context of Human Immunodeficiency Virus Transmission in Africa: Historical and Cultural Bases of East and Central African Sexual Relations. *Review of Infectious Diseases* 11: 716–731.

Lassiter, L. E. 1998 *The Power of Kiowa Song: A Collaborative Ethnography.* Tucson: University of Arizona Press.

Laughlin, J. C. H. 2003 *Fifty Major Cities of the Bible.* New York: Routledge.

Layton, R. 1991 *The Anthropology of Art,* 2nd ed. New York: Cambridge University Press.

Leach, E. R. 1955 Polyandry, Inheritance and the Definition of Marriage. *Man* 55: 182–186.
1961 *Rethinking Anthropology.* London: Athlone Press. 1970 (orig. 1954). *Political Systems of Highland Burma: A Study of Kachin Social Structure.* London: Athlone Press.
1985 *Social Anthropology.* New York: Oxford University Press.

Leakey, M. G., C. S. Feibel, I. McDougall, and A. Walker 1995 New Four-Million-Year-Old Hominid Species from Kanapoi and Allia Bay, Kenya. *Nature* 376: 565–571.

Leakey, R. E., M. G. Leakey, and A. C. Walker 1988 Morphology of *Afropithecus turkanensis* from Kenya. *American Journal of Physical Anthropology* 76: 289–307.

LeClair, E. E., and H. K. Schneider, eds. 1968 (orig. 1961). *Economic Anthropology: Readings in Theory and Analysis.* New York: Holt, Rinehart and Winston.

Lee, R. B. 1974 (orig. 1968). What Hunters Do for a Living, or, How to Make Out on Scarce Resources. In *Man in Adaptation: The Cultural Present,* 2nd ed., ed. Y. A. Cohen, pp. 87–100. Chicago: Aldine.
1979 *The !Kung San: Men, Women, and Work in a Foraging Society.* New York: Cambridge University Press.
1984 *The Dobe !Kung.* New York: Holt, Rinehart and Winston. 2003 *The Dobe Ju/'hoansi,* 3rd ed. Belmont, CA: Wadsworth.

Lee, R. B., and R. H. Daly 1999 *The Cambridge Encyclopedia of Hunters and Gatherers.* New York: Cambridge University Press.

Lee, R. B., and I. DeVore, eds. 1977 *Kalahari Hunter-Gatherers: Studies of the !Kung San and Their Neighbors.* Cambridge, MA: Harvard University Press.

Lehmann, A. C., J. E. Meyers, and P. A. Moro, eds. 2005 *Magic, Witchcraft, and Religion: An Anthropological Study of the Supernatural,* 6th ed. Mountain View, CA: Mayfield.

Leman, J. 2001 *The Dynamics of Emerging Ethnicities: Immigrant and Indigenous Ethnogenesis in Confrontation.* New York: Peter Lang.

Lemonick, M. D., and A. Dorfman 1999 Up from the Apes: Remarkable New Evidence Is Filling In the Story of How We Became Human. *Time* 154(8): 5–58.

Lenski, G. 1966 *Power and Privilege: A Theory of Social Stratification.* New York: McGraw-Hill.

Lessa, W. A., and E. Z. Vogt, eds. 1979 *Reader in Comparative Religion: An Anthropological Approach,* 4th ed. New York: Harper & Row.

Lévi-Strauss, C. 1963 *Totemism.* Translated by R. Needham. Boston: Beacon Press.
1967 *Structural Anthropology.* New York: Doubleday.
1969 (orig. 1949). *The Elementary Structures of Kinship.* Boston: Beacon Press.

Levine, L., ed. 1995 *Genetics of Natural Populations: The Continuing Importance of Theodosius Dobzhansky.* New York: Columbia University Press.

Levine, N. E. 1988 *The Dynamics of Polyandry: Kinship, Domesticity, and Population on the Tibetan Border.* Chicago: University of Chicago Press.

Levine, R. A. 1982 *Culture, Behavior, and Personality: An Introduction to the Comparative Study of Psychosocial Adaptation,* 2nd ed. Chicago: Aldine.

Levine, R. A., ed. 1974 *Culture and Personality: Contemporary Readings.* Chicago: Aldine.

Levy, J. E., with B. Pepper 1992 *Orayvi Revisited: Social Stratification in an "Egalitarian" Society.* Santa Fe, NM: School of American Research Press; Seattle: University of Washington Press.

Lewin, R. 1998 *Principles of Human Evolution: A Core Textbook.* Malden, MA: Blackwell Science.
2005 *Human Evolution: An Illustrated Introduction,* 5th ed. Malden, MA: Blackwell.

Lewis, H. S. 1989 *After the Eagles Landed: The Yemenites of Israel.* Boulder, CO: Westview Press.

Lewis, O. 1959 *Five Families.* New York: Basic Books.

Lewis, P. 1992 U.N. Sees a Crisis in Overpopulation. *New York Times,* April 30, p. A6.

Lewontin, R. 2000 *It Ain't Necessarily So: The Dream of the Human Genome and Other Illusions.* New York: New York Review of Books.

Lie, J. 2001 *Multiethnic Japan.* Cambridge, MA: Harvard University Press.

Lieban, R. W. 1977 The Field of Medical Anthropology. In *Culture, Disease, and Healing: Studies in Medical Anthropology,* ed. D. Landy, pp. 13–31. New York: Macmillan.

Lieberman, P. 1998 *Eve Spoke: Human Language and Human Evolution.* New York: W. W. Norton.

Light, D., S. Keller, and C. Calhoun 1994 *Sociology,* 6th ed. New York: McGraw-Hill.

Linden, E. 1986 *Silent Partners: The Legacy of the Ape Language Experiments.* New York: Times Books.

Lindenbaum, S. 1972 Sorcerers, Ghosts, and Polluting Women: An Analysis of Religious Belief and Population Control. *Ethnology* 11: 241–253.

Lindholm, C. 2001 *Culture and Identity: The History, Theory, and Practice of Psychological Anthropology.* Boston: McGraw-Hill.

Linton, R. 1927 Report on Work of Field Museum Expedition in Madagascar. *American Anthropologist* 29: 292–307.
1943 Nativistic Movements. *American Anthropologist* 45: 230–240.

Lipke, D. J. 2000 Dead End Ahead? Income May Be the Real Barrier to the Internet On-Ramp. *American Demographics,* August. http://www.demographics.com/publications/ad/00_ad/ad000805c.htm.

Little, K. 1965 *West African Urbanization: A Study of Voluntary Associations in Social Change.* Cambridge, UK: Cambridge University Press.
1971 *Some Aspects of African Urbanization South of the Sahara. McCaleb Modules in Anthropology.* Reading, MA: Addison-Wesley.

Livingstone, F. B. 1958 Anthropological Implications of Sickle Cell Gene Distribution in West Africa. *American Anthropologist* 60: 533–562.
1969 Gene Frequency Clines of the *b* Hemoglobin Locus in Various Human Populations and Their Similarities by Models Involving Differential Selection. *Human Biology* 41: 223–236.

Lizot, J. 1985 *Tales of the Yanomami: Daily Life in the Venezuelan Forest.* New York: Cambridge University Press.

Lockwood, W. G. 1975 *European Moslems: Economy and Ethnicity in Western Bosnia.* New York: Academic Press.

Lockwood, Y. R. 1983 *Text and Context: Folksong in a Bosnian Muslim Village.* Columbus, OH: Slavica.

Lohr, S. 2005 Cutting Here, but Hiring Over There. *New York Times,* June 24. http://www.nytimes.com/2005/06/24/technology/24blue.html?pagewanted=print.

London School of Economics 2004 Definition of Civil Society. LSE Centre for Civil Society, March 22. http://www.lse.ac.uk/collections/CCS/introduction.htm.

Loomis, W. F. 1967 Skin-Pigmented Regulation of Vitamin-D Biosynthesis in Man. *Science* 157: 501–506.

Lordkipanidze, D., et al. 2005 The Earliest Toothless Hominin Skull. *Nature* 434: 717–718.

Loveday, L. 1986 Japanese Sociolinguistics: An Introductory Survey. *Journal of Pragmatics* 10: 287–326.
2001 *Explorations in Japanese Sociolinguistics.* Philadelphia: J. Benjamins.

Lowie, R. H. 1935 *The Crow Indians.* New York: Farrar and Rinehart.
1961 (orig. 1920). *Primitive Society.* New York: Harper & Brothers.

Lugaila, T. 1998*a* Numbers of Divorced and Never-Married Adults Increasing, Says Census Bureau Report. http://www.census.gov/Press-Release/cb98-56.html. 1998*b* Marital Status and Living Arrangements, March 1998 (Update). http://www.census.gov/prod/99pubs/p20-514.pdf.
1999 Married Adults Still in the Majority, Census Bureau Reports. http://www.census.gov/Press-Release/www/1999/cb99-03.html.

Lutz, C., and J. L. Collins 1993 *Reading National Geographic.* Chicago: University of Chicago Press.

Lyell, C. 1969 (orig. 1830–37). *Principles of Geology.* New York: Johnson.

Lyotard, J. F. 1993 *The Postmodern Explained.* Translated by J. Pefanis, M. Thomas, and D. Barry. Minneapolis: University of Minnesota Press.

MacKinnon, J. 1974 *In Search of the Red Ape.* New York: Ballantine.

Madra, Y. M. 2004 Karl Polanyi: Freedom in a Complex Society. *Econ-Atrocity Bulletin: In the History of Thought.* http://www.fguide.org/Bulletin/polanyi.htm.

Maher, J. C., and G. MacDonald, eds. 1995 *Diversity and Language in Japanese Culture.* New York: Columbia University Press.

Mair, L. 1969 *Witchcraft.* New York: McGraw-Hill.

Malinowski, B. 1926 *Crime and Custom in Savage Society.* London: Routledge and Kegan Paul.
1927 *Sex and Repression in Savage Society.* London and New York: International Library of Psychology, Philosophy and Scientific Method.
1929*a* Practical Anthropology. *Africa* 2: 23–38.
1929*b* *The Sexual Life of Savages in North-Western Melanesia.* New York: Harcourt, Brace, and World.
1944 *A Scientific Theory of Culture, and Other Essays.* Chapel Hill: University of North Carolina Press. 1961 (orig. 1922), *Argonauts of the Western Pacific.* New York: Dutton.
1978 (orig. 1931). The Role of Magic and Religion. In *Reader in Comparative Religion: An Anthropological Approach,* 4th ed., ed. W. A. Lessa and E. Z. Vogt, pp. 37–46. New York: Harper & Row.
2001 (orig. 1927). *Sex and Repression in Savage Society.* Chicago: University of Chicago Press.

Malkin, C. 2004 Earliest Primate Discovered in China. *Science Now,* January 5. American Association for the Advancement of Science. http://cmbi.bjmu.edu.cn/news/0401/13.htm.

Malkki, L. H. 1995 *Purity and Exile: Violence, Memory, and National Cosmology among Hutu Refugees in Tanzania.* Chicago: University of Chicago Press.

Mann, A. 1975 *Paleodemographic Aspects of the South African Australopithecines.* Publications in Anthropology, no. 1. Philadelphia: University of Pennsylvania.

Manners, R. 1973 (orig. 1956). Functionalism, Realpolitik and Anthropology in Underdeveloped Areas. *America Indigena* 16. Also in *To See Ourselves: Anthropology and Modern Social Issues,* gen. ed. T. Weaver, pp. 113–126. Glenview, IL: Scott, Foresman.

Manoff, Richard K. 1994 How Family Planning Came to Bangladesh. Letter to the Editor. *New York Times,* Sunday, January 16, pp. 4–16.

Maquet, J. 1964 Objectivity in Anthropology. *Current Anthropology* 5: 47–55 (also in Clifton, ed., 1970).
1986 *The Aesthetic Experience: An Anthropologist Looks at the Visual Arts.* New Haven, CT: Yale University Press.

Mar, M. E. 1997 Secondary Colors: The Multiracial Option. *Harvard Magazine,* May–June 1997, pp. 19–20.

Marcus, G. E., and D. Cushman 1982 Ethnographies as Texts. *Annual Review of Anthropology* 11: 25–69.

Marcus, G. E., and M. M. J. Fischer 1986 *Anthropology as Cultural Critique: An Experimental Moment in the Human Sciences.* Chicago: University of Chicago Press.
1999 *Anthropology as Cultural Critique: An Experimental Moment in the Human Sciences,* 2nd ed. Chicago: University of Chicago Press.

Marcus, G. E., and F. R. Myers, eds. 1995 *The Traffic in Culture: Refiguring Art and Anthropology.* Berkeley: University of California Press.

Marcus, J. 1989 From Centralized Systems to City-States: Possible Models for the Epiclassic. In *Mesoamerica After the Decline of Teotihuacan: A.D. 700–900,* ed. R. A. Diehl and J. C. Berlo, pp. 201–208. Dumbarton Oaks: Washington, D.C.
1992 *Mesoamerican Writing Systems: Propaganda, Myth, and History in Four Ancient Civilizations.* Princeton, NJ: Princeton University Press.

Marcus, J., and K. V. Flannery 1996 *Zapotec Civilization: How Urban Society Evolved in Mexico's Oaxaca Valley.* New York: Thames and Hudson.

Margolis, M. 1984 *Mothers and Such: American Views of Women and How They Changed.* Berkeley: University of California Press.
1994 *Little Brazil: An Ethnography of Brazilian Immigrants in New York City.* Princeton, NJ: Princeton University Press. 2000 *True to Her Nature: Changing Advice to American Women.* Prospect Heights, IL: Waveland.

Marks, J. M. 1995 *Human Biodiversity: Genes, Race, and History.* New York: Aldine de Gruyter.

Marshack, A. 1972 *Roots of Civilization.* New York: McGraw-Hill.

Martin, E. 1987 *The Woman in the Body: A Cultural Analysis of Reproduction.* Boston: Beacon Press.

Martin, J. 1992 *Cultures in Organizations: Three Perspectives.* New York: Oxford University Press.

Martin, K., and B. Voorhies 1975 *Female of the Species.* New York: Columbia University Press.

Martin, P., and E. Midgley 1994 Immigration to the United States: Journey to an Uncertain Destination. *Population Bulletin* 49(3): 1–47.

Martinez, E., and A. Garcia 2000 What Is Neo-Liberalism: A Brief Definition. Updated February 26, 2000. http://www.globalexchange.org/campaigns/econ101/neoliberalDefined.html.

Marx, K., and F. Engels 1976 (orig. 1848). *Communist Manifesto.* New York: Pantheon.

Mascia-Lees, F., and N. J. Black 2000 *Gender and Anthropology.* Prospect Heights, IL: Waveland.

Mathews, G. 2000 *Global Culture/Individual Identity: Searching for Home in the Cultural Supermarket.* New York: Routledge.

Maugh, T. H., III 2007 One Language Disappears Every 14 Days; about Half of the World's Distinct Tongues Could Vanish This Century, Researchers Say. *Los Angeles Times,* September 19.

Maybury-Lewis, D. 2002 *Indigenous Peoples, Ethnic Groups, and the State,* 2nd ed. Boston: Allyn & Bacon.

Mayell, H. 2003 Orangutans Show Signs of Culture, Study Says. *National Geographic News,* January 3. http://news.nationalgeographic.com/news/2002/12/1220_021226_orangutan.html.
2004*a* Wild Orangs, Extinct by 2023? *National Geographic News,* March 9. http://news.nationalgeographic.com/news/2003/09/0930_030930_orangutanthreat.html.
2004*b* Is Bead Find Proof Modern Thought Began in Africa? *National Geographic News,* March 31. http://news.nationalgeographic.com/news/2004/03/0331_040331_ostrichman.html.

Mayr, E. 1970 *Population, Species, and Evolution.* Cambridge, MA: Harvard University Press. 2001 *What Evolution Is.* New York: Basic Books.

McAllester, D. P. 1954 *Enemy Way Music: A Study of Social and Esthetic Values as Seen in Navaho Music.* Cambridge, MA: Peabody Museum of American Archaeology and Ethnology, Papers 41(3).

McBrearty, S., and A. S. Brooks 2000 The Revolution That Wasn't: A New Interpretation of the Origin of Modern Human Behavior. *Journal of Human Evolution* 39: 453–563.

McBrearty, S., and N. G. Jablonski 2005 First Fossil Chimpanzee. *Nature* 437: 105–108.

McCaskie, T. C. 1995 *State and Society in Pre-Colonial Asante.* New York: Cambridge University Press.

McDonald, G. 1984 *Carioca Fletch.* New York: Warner Books.

McDonald, J. H., ed. 2002 *The Applied Anthropology Reader.* Boston: Allyn & Bacon.

McDougall, I., F. H. Brown, and J. G. Fleagle 2005 Stratigraphic Placement and Age of Modern Humans from Kibish, Ethiopia. *Nature* 433: 733–736.

McElroy, A., and P. K. Townsend 1996 *Medical Anthropology in Ecological Perspective*, 3rd ed. Boulder, CO: Westview Press. 2003 *Medical Anthropology in Ecological Perspective*, 4th ed. Boulder, CO: Westview Press.

McGraw, T. K., ed. 1986 *America versus Japan.* Boston: Harvard Business School Press.

McGrew, W. C. 1979 Evolutionary Implications of Sex Differences in Chimpanzee Predation and Tool Use. In *The Great Apes*, ed. D. A. Hamburg and E. R. McCown, pp. 441–463. Menlo Park, CA: Benjamin Cummings.

McGrew, W., L. Marchant, and T. Nishida 1996 *Great Ape Societies.* Cambridge, UK: Cambridge University Press.

McKee, J. K., F. E. Poirier, and W. S. McGraw 2005 *Understanding Human Evolution*, 5th ed. Upper Saddle River, NJ: Prentice Hall.

McKinley, J. 1996 Board's Decision on Black English Stirs Debate. *New York Times*, December 21. http://www.nytimes.com.

McKusick, V. 1966 *Mendelian Inheritance in Man.* Baltimore: Johns Hopkins University Press. 1990 *Mendelian Inheritance in Man: Catalogs of Autosomal Dominant, Autosomal Recessive, and X-Linked Phenotypes*, 9th ed. Baltimore: Johns Hopkins University Press.

Mead, M. 1930 *Growing Up in New Guinea.* New York: Blue Ribbon. 1937 *Cooperation and Competition among Primitive Peoples.* New York: McGraw-Hill. 1950 (orig. 1935). *Sex and Temperament in Three Primitive Societies.* New York: New American Library. 1961 (orig. 1928). *Coming of Age in Samoa.* New York: Morrow Quill. 1972 *Blackberry Winter: My Earlier Years.* New York: Simon & Schuster.

Meadow, R., ed. 1991 *Harappa Excavations 1986–1990: A Multidisciplinary Approach to Third Millennium Urbanism.* Monographs in World Archeology, no. 3. Madison, WI: Prehistory Press.

Meadow, R. H., and J. M. Kenoyer 2000 The Indus Valley Mystery: One of the World's First Great Civilizations Is Still a Puzzle. *Discovering Archaeology*, April, pp. 38–43.

Meigs, A., and K. Barlow 2002 Beyond the Taboo: Imagining Incest. *American Anthropologist* 104(1): 38–49.

Mercader, J., M. Panger, and C. Boesch 2002 Excavation of a Chimpanzee Stone Tool Site in the African Rainforest. *Science* 296: 1452–1455.

Merlan, F. 2005 Indigenous Movements in Australia. *Annual Review of Anthropology* 34: 473–494.

Merriam, A. 1971 The Arts and Anthropology. In *Anthropology and Art: Readings in Cross-Cultural Aesthetics*, ed. C. Otten, pp. 93–105. Austin: University of Texas Press.

Michaels, E. 1986 Aboriginal Content. Paper presented at the meeting of the Australian Screen Studies Association, December, Sydney.

Michaelson, K. 1996 Information, Community, and Access. *Social Science Computing Review* 14(1): 57–59.

Michrina, B. P., and C. Richards 1996 *Person to Person: Fieldwork, Dialogue, and the Hermeneutic Method.* Albany: State University of New York Press.

Middleton, J. 1967 Introduction. In *Myth and Cosmos: Readings in Mythology and Symbolism*, ed. John Middleton, pp. ix–xi. Garden City, NY: Natural History Press. 1993 *The Lugbara of Uganda*, 2nd ed. Fort Worth: Harcourt Brace.

Middleton, J., ed. 1967 *Gods and Rituals.* Garden City, NY: Natural History Press.

Miles, H. L. 1983 Apes and Language: The Search for Communicative Competence. In *Language in Primates*, ed. J. de Luce and H. T. Wilder, pp. 43–62. New York: Springer-Verlag.

Miller, B. D. 1997 *The Endangered Sex: Neglect of Female Children in Rural North India.* New York: Oxford University Press.

Miller, B. D., ed. 1993 *Sex and Gender Hierarchies.* New York: Cambridge University Press.

Miller, J. n.d. Alaskan Tlingit and Tsimtsian. Seattle: University of Washington Libraries, Digital Collections. http://content.lib.washington.edu/aipnw/miller1.html.

Miller, L. 2004 The Ancient Bristlecone Pine, Dendrochronology. http://www.sonic.net/bristlecone/dendro.html.

Miller, N., and R. C. Rockwell, eds. 1988 *AIDS in Africa: The Social and Policy Impact.* Lewiston, ME: Edwin Mellen.

Mills, G. 1971 Art: An Introduction to Qualitative Anthropology. In *Anthropology and Art: Readings in Cross-Cultural Aesthetics*, ed. C. Otten, pp. 66–92. Austin: University of Texas Press.

Mintz, S. W. 1985 *Sweetness and Power: The Place of Sugar in Modern History.* New York: Viking Penguin.

Mirzoeff, N. 1999 *An Introduction to Visual Culture.* New York: Routledge.

Mishler, E. G. 1991 *Research Interviewing: Context and Narrative.* Cambridge, MA: Harvard University Press.

Mitani, J. C., and D. P. Watts 1999 Demographic Influences on the Hunting Behavior of Chimpanzees. *American Journal of Physical Anthropology* 109: 439–454.

Mitchell, J. C. 1966 Theoretical Orientations in African Urban Studies. In *The Social Anthropology of Complex Societies*, ed. M. Banton, pp. 37–68. London: Tavistock.

Moerman, M. 1965 Ethnic Identification in a Complex Civilization: Who Are the Lue? *American Anthropologist* 67(5, Part I): 1215–1230.

Moisala, P., and B. Diamond, eds. 2000 *Music and Gender.* Champaign–Urbana: University of Illinois Press.

Molnar, S. 2006 *Human Variation: Races, Types, and Ethnic Groups*, 6th ed. Upper Saddle River, NJ: Prentice Hall.

Moncure, S. 1998 Anthropologist Assists in Police Investigations. *University of Delaware Update* 17, no. 39, August 20. http://www.udel.edu/PR/UpDate/98/39/anthrop.html.

Montagu, A. 1975 *The Nature of Human Aggression.* New York: Oxford University Press. 1981 *Statement on Race: An Annotated Elaboration and Exposition of the Four Statements on Race Issued by the United Nations Educational, Scientific, and Cultural Organization.* Westport, CT: Greenwood Press.

Montagu, A., ed. 1996 *Race and IQ*, expanded ed. New York: Oxford University Press. 1997 *Man's Most Dangerous Myth: The Fallacy of Race*, 6th ed. Walnut Creek, CA: AltaMira. 1999 *Race and IQ*, expanded ed. New York: Oxford University Press.

Montague, S., and R. Morais 1981 Football Games and Rock Concerts: The Ritual Enactment. In *The American Dimension: Cultural Myths and Social Realities*, 2nd ed., ed. W. Arens and S. B. Montague, pp. 33–52. Sherman Oaks, CA: Alfred.

Montgomery, S. 1991 *Walking with the Great Apes: Jane Goodall, Dian Fossey, Biruté Galdikas.* Boston: Houghton Mifflin.

Moore, A. D. 1985 The Development of Neolithic Societies in the Near East. *Advances in World Archaeology* 4:1–69.

Moore, S. F. 1986 *Social Facts and Fabrications.* Cambridge, UK: Cambridge University Press.

Moran, E. F. 1982 *Human Adaptability: An Introduction to Ecological Anthropology.* Boulder, CO: Westview Press.

Moran, L. 1993 Evolution Is a Fact and a Theory. The Talk Origins Archive. http://www.talkorigins.org/faqs/evolution-fact.html.

Morbeck, M. E., A. Galloway, and A. L. Zihlman, eds. 1997 *The Evolving Female: A Life-History Perspective.* Princeton, NJ: Princeton University Press.

Morgan, L. H. 1963 (orig. 1877). *Ancient Society.* Cleveland: World Publishing. 1966 (orig. 1851). *League of the Ho-dé-no-sau-nee or Iroquois.* New York: B. Franklin. 1997 (orig. 1870). *Systems of Consanguinity and Affinity of the Human Family.* Lincoln: University of Nebraska Press.

Morgen, S., ed. 1989 *Gender and Anthropology: Critical Reviews for Research and Teaching.* Washington, DC: American Anthropological Association.

Morkot, R. 2005 *The Egyptians: An Introduction.* New York: Routledge.

Morphy, H., and M. Perkins, eds. 2006 *The Anthropology of Art: A Reader.* Malden, MA: Oxford, Blackwell.

Morris, B. 1987 *Anthropological Studies of Religion: An Introductory Text.* New York: Cambridge University Press.

Motseta, S. 2006 Botswana Gives Bushmen Tough Conditions. *Washington Post*, December 14. http://www.washingtonpost.com/wp-dyn/content/article/2006/12/14/AR2006121401008.html.

Mount Holyoke College 1999 Dung-Covered Madonna Sparks Controversy; Art Professor Michael Davis Takes a Look. *College Street Journal* 13(6), October 8. http://www.mtholyoke.edu/offices/comm/csj/991008/madonna.html.

Mowat, F. 1987 *Woman in the Mists: The Story of Dian Fossey and the Mountain Gorillas of Africa.* New York: Warner Books.

Moyá-Solá, S., et al. 2004 *Pierolapithecus catalaunicus:* A New Middle Miocene Great Ape from Spain. *Science* 306(5700): 1339–1344.

Muhlhausler, P. 1986 *Pidgin and Creole Linguistics.* London: Blackwell.

Mukhopadhyay, C. C., R. Henze, and Y. T. Moses 2007 *How Real Is Race? A Sourcebook on Race, Culture, and Biology.* Lanham, MD: AltaMira.

Mukhopadhyay, C., and P. Higgins 1988 Anthropological Studies of Women's Status Revisited: 1977–1987. *Annual Review of Anthropology* 17: 461–495.

Mullings, L., ed. 1987 *Cities of the United States: Studies in Urban Anthropology.* New York: Columbia University Press.

Murdock, G. P. 1934 *Our Primitive Contemporaries.* New York: Macmillan. 1957 World Ethnographic Sample. *American Anthropologist* 59: 664–687.

Murdock, G. P., and C. Provost 1973 Factors in the Division of Labor by Sex: A Cross-Cultural Analysis. *Ethnology* 12(2): 203–225.

Murphy, R. F. 1990 *The Body Silent.* New York: W. W. Norton.

Murphy, R. F., and L. Kasdan 1959 The Structure of Parallel Cousin Marriage. *American Anthropologist* 61: 17–29.

Murray, S. O., and W. Roscoe, eds. 1998 *Boy-Wives and Female Husbands: Studies in African Homosexualities.* New York: St. Martin's Press.

Mydans, S. 1992a Criticism Grows over Aliens Seized during Riots. *New York Times*, May 29, p. A8. 1992b Judge Dismisses Case in Shooting by Officer. *New York Times*, June 4, p. A8.

Myers, F. R. 2002 *Painting Culture: The Making of an Aboriginal High Art.* Durham, NC: Duke University Press.

Nafte, M. 2000 *Flesh and Bone: An Introduction to Forensic Anthropology.* Durham, NC: Carolina Academic Press.

Nagel, J. 1996 *American Indian Ethnic Renewal: Red Power and the Resurgence of Identity and Culture.* New York: Oxford University Press.

Nanda, S. 2000 *Gender Diversity: Crosscultural Variations.* Prospect Heights, IL: Waveland.

Napier, A. D. 1992 *Foreign Bodies: Performance, Art, and Symbolic Anthropology.* Berkeley: University of California Press.

Narayan, U. 1997 *Dislocating Cultures: Identities, Traditions, and Third World Feminisms.* New York: Routledge.

Nash, D. 1999 *A Little Anthropology,* 3rd ed. Upper Saddle River, NJ: Prentice Hall.

Nash, J., and H. Safa, eds. 1986 *Women and Change in Latin America.* South Hadley, MA: Bergin and Garvey.

National Academies 2007 Understanding and Responding to Climate Change: Highlights of National Academies Reports. http://dels.nas.edu/basc/Climate-HIGH.pdf.

National Academy of Sciences 2008 Understanding and Responding to Climate Change: Highlights of National Academies Reports. http://dels.nas.edu/dels/rpt_briefs/climate_change_2008_final.pdf.

National Association for the Practice of Anthropology 1991 *NAPA Directory of Practicing Anthropologists.* Washington, DC: American Anthropological Association.

National Vital Statistics Reports 2000 Births, Marriages, Divorces, and Deaths: Provisional Data for November 1999. October 31. Hyattsville, MD: U.S. Department of Health and Human Services, Centers for Disease Control and Prevention, National Center for Health Statistics. 2001 *National Vital Statistics Reports,* vol. 46, no. 6. http://www.cdc.gov/nchs/data/nvsr/nvsr49/nvsr49_06.pdf.

Naylor, L. L. 1996 *Culture and Change: An Introduction.* Westport, CT: Bergin and Garvey.

Nelson, H., and R. Jurmain 1991 *Introduction to Physical Anthropology,* 5th ed. St. Paul, MN: West.

Nelson, S. N., and M. Rosen-Ayalon, eds. 2002 *In Pursuit of Gender: Worldwide Archaeological Approaches.* Walnut Creek, CA: AltaMira.

Netting, R. M. C., R. R. Wilk, and E. J. Arnould, eds. 1984 *Households: Comparative and Historical Studies of the Domestic Group.* Berkeley: University of California Press.

Nevid, J. S., and Rathus, S. A. 1995 *Human Sexuality in a World of Diversity,* 2nd ed. Needham Heights, MA: Allyn & Bacon.

New York Times 1990 Tropical Diseases on March, Hitting 1 in 10. March 28, p. A3.
1992*a* Alexandria Journal: TV Program for Somalis Is a Rare Unifying Force. December 18.
1992*b* Married with Children: The Waning Icon. August 23, p. E2.
2005 Intelligent Design Derailed. Editorial Desk, December 22. http://www.nytimes.com/2005/12/22/opinion/22thur1.html?ex=1292907600&en=af56b21719a9dd8f&ei=5090&partner=rssuserl and&emc=rss.

Newman, M. 1992 Riots Bring Attention to Growing Hispanic Presence in South-Central Area. *New York Times,* May 11, p. A10.

Ni, X., W. Wang, Y. Hu, and C. Li 2004 A Euprimate Skull from the Early Eocene of China. *Nature* 427: 65–68.

Nielsson, G. P. 1985 States and Nation-Groups: A Global Taxonomy. In *New Nationalisms of the Developed World,* ed. E. A. Tiryakian and R. Rogowski, pp. 27–56. Boston: Allen and Unwin.

Nolan, R. W. 2002 *Development Anthropology: Encounters in the Real World.* Boulder, CO: Westview Press.
2003 *Anthropology in Practice.* Boulder, CO: Lynne Rienner.

Nowak, R. M. 1999 *Walker's Primates of the World.* Baltimore: Johns Hopkins University Press.

Nussbaum, M., and J. Glover, eds. 1995 *Women, Culture, and Development: A Study of Human Capabilities.* New York: Oxford University Press.

Nussbaum, M. C. 2000 *Women and Human Development: The Capabilities Approach.* New York: Cambridge University Press.

Oakley, K. P. 1976 *Man the Tool-Maker,* 6th ed. Chicago: University of Chicago Press.

O'Connell, J. F. and J. Allen 2004 Dating the colonization of Sahul (Pleistocene Australia–New Guinea): A review of recent research. *Journal of Archaeological Science* 31: 835–853.

O'Dougherty, M. 2002 *Consumption Intensified: The Politics of Middle-Class Daily Life in Brazil.* Durham, NC: Duke University Press.

Ohlmacher, S. 2006 2006: The Year of the 300M Mark: Face of America Changes as Country Grows. *Charleston Post and Courier,* June 26, pp. 1A, 11A.

Okpewho, I. 1977 Principles of Traditional African Art. *Journal of Aesthetics and Art Criticism* 35(3): 301–314.

O'Leary, C. M. 2002 *Class Formation, Diet and Economic Transformation in Two Brazilian Fishing Communities.* Ph.D. dissertation, Department of Anthropology, University of Michigan, Ann Arbor.

Omohundro, J. T. 2001 *Careers in Anthropology,* 2nd ed. Boston: McGraw-Hill.

Ong, A. 1987 *Spirits of Resistance and Capitalist Discipline: Factory Women in Malaysia.* Albany: State University of New York Press.
1989 Center, Periphery, and Hierarchy: Gender in Southeast Asia. In *Gender and Anthropology: Critical Reviews for Research and Teaching,* ed. S. Morgen, pp. 294–312. Washington, DC: American Anthropological Association.
2006 *Neoliberalism as Exception: Mutations in Citizenship and Sovereignty.* Durham, NC: Duke University Press.

Ong, A., and S. J. Collier, eds. 2005 *Global Assemblages: Technology, Politics, and Ethics as Anthropological Problems.* Malden, MA: Blackwell.

Ong, A., and M. G. Peletz, eds. 1995 *Bewitching Women, Pious Men: Gender and Body Politics in Southeast Asia.* Berkeley: University of California Press.

Ontario Consultants on Religious Tolerance 1996 Religious Access Dispute Resolved. Internet Mailing List, April 12. 1997 Swiss Cult Promotes Cloning. 2001 Religions of the World: Number of Adherents; Rates of growth. http://www.religioustolerance.org/worldrel.htm.

O'Reilly, K. 2004 *Ethnographic Methods.* New York: Routledge.

O'Rourke, D. H. 2003 Anthropological Genetics in the Genomic Era: A Look Back and Ahead. *American Anthropologist* 105(1): 101–109.

Ortner, S. B. 1984 Theory of Anthropology Since the Sixties. *Comparative Studies in Society and History* 126(1): 126–166.

Ott, S. 1981 *The Circle of Mountains: A Basque Shepherding Community.* Oxford, UK: Clarendon Press.

Otten, C. M., ed. 1971 *Anthropology and Art: Readings in Cross-Cultural Aesthetics.* Garden City, NY: American Museum of Natural History.

Ottenheimer, M. 1996 *Forbidden Relatives: The American Myth of Cousin Marriage.* Champaign–Urbana: University of Illinois Press.

Otterbein, K. F. 1968 (orig. 1963). Marquesan Polyandry. In *Marriage, Family and Residence,* ed. P. Bohannan and J. Middleton, pp. 287–296. Garden City, NY: Natural History Press.
2004 *How War Began.* College Station: Texas A&M University Press.

Owen, J. 2006 "Lucy's Baby"–World's Oldest Child–Found by Fossil Hunters. *National Geographic News,* September 20. http://news.nationalgeographic.com/news/2006/09/060920-lucys-baby.html.

Palmer, S. 2001 The Rael Deal. *Religion in the News* 4:2. Hartford, CT: Trinity College, The Leonard E. Greenberg Center for the Study of Religion in Public Life. http://www.trincoll.edu/depts/csrpl/RINVol4No2/Rael.htm.

Park, M. A. 2005 *Biological Anthropology,* 4th ed. Boston: McGraw-Hill.

Parker, S., and R. Kleiner 1970 The Culture of Poverty: An Adjustive Dimension. *American Anthropologist* 72: 516–527.

Parkin, R. 1997 *Kinship: An Introduction to Basic Concepts.* Cambridge, MA: Blackwell.

Parkin, R., and L. Stone, eds. 2004 *Kinship and Family: An Anthropological Reader.* Malden, MA: Blackwell.

Parsons, J. R. 1974 The Development of a Prehistoric Complex Society: A Regional Perspective from the Valley of Mexico. *Journal of Field Archaeology* 1: 81–108.

1976 The Role of Chinampa Agriculture in the Food Supply of Aztec Tenochtitlan. In *Cultural Change and Continuity: Essays in Honor of James Bennett Griffin,* ed. C. E. Cleland, pp. 233–262. New York: Academic Press.

Pasternak, B., C. R. Ember, and M. Ember 1997 *Sex, Gender, and Kinship: A Cross-Cultural Perspective.* Upper Saddle River, NJ: Prentice Hall.

Patterson, F. 1978 Conversations with a Gorilla. *National Geographic,* October, pp. 438–465.

Patterson, T. C. 1993 *Archaeology: The Historical Development of Civilizations,* 2nd ed. Englewood Cliffs, NJ: Prentice Hall.

Paul, R. 1989 Psychoanalytic Anthropology. *Annual Review of Anthropology* 18: 177–202.

Paulson, T. E. 2005 Chimp, Human DNA Comparison Finds Vast Similarities, Key Differences. *Seattle Post-Intelligencer Reporter,* September 1, 2005. http://seattlepi.nwsource.com/local/238852_chimp01.html.

Pear, R. 1992 Ranks of U.S. Poor Reach 35.7 Million, the Most Since '64. *New York Times,* September 3, pp. A1, A12.

Peletz, M. 1988 *A Share of the Harvest: Kinship, Property, and Social History among the Malays of Rembau.* Berkeley: University of California Press.

Pelto, P. 1973 *The Snowmobile Revolution: Technology and Social Change in the Arctic.* Menlo Park, CA: Cummings.

Pelto, P. J., and G. H. Pelto 1978 *Anthropological Research: The Structure of Inquiry,* 2nd ed. New York: Cambridge University Press.

Peplau, L. A., ed. 1999 *Gender, Culture, and Ethnicity: Current Research about Women and Men.* Mountain View, CA: Mayfield.

Perlman, D. 2004 Fossil Find May Be the Father of Us All: It's Hailed as Last Common Kin of the Great Apes and Humans. *San Francisco Chronicle,* November 22, p. A-4.

Perry, Linda, et al. 2007 Starch Fossils and the Domestication and Dispersal of Chili Peppers (Capsicum spp. L.) in the Americas. *Science* 315: 986–988.

Peters, J. D. 1997 Seeing Bifocally: Media, Place, Culture. In *Culture, Power, Place: Explorations in Critical Anthropology,* ed. A. Gupta and J. Ferguson, pp. 75–92. Durham, NC: Duke University Press.

Peters-Golden, H. 2006 *Culture Sketches,* 5th ed. Boston: McGraw-Hill.

Petraglia-Bahri, D. 1996 Introduction to Postcolonial Studies. http://www.emory.edu/ENGLISH/Bahri/.

Pettifor, E. 1995 From the Teeth of the Dragon—*Gigantopithecus blacki.* http://www.wynja.com/arch/gigantopithecus.html.

Pfeiffer, J. 1985 *The Emergence of Humankind,* 4th ed. New York: HarperCollins.

Phillipson, D. W. 1993 *African Archaeology,* 2nd ed. New York: Cambridge University Press.

Pickrell, J. 2004 Gorilla Mafia? Groups Ruled by Related Males, Study Says. *National Geographic News,* March 31. http://news.nationalgeographic.com/news/2004/03/0331_040331_westerngorillas.html.

Piddington, R. 1970 Action Anthropology. In *Applied Anthropology: Readings in the Uses of the Science of Man,* ed. James Clifton, pp. 127–143. Boston: Houghton Mifflin.

Piddocke, S. 1969 The Potlatch System of the Southern Kwakiutl: A New Perspective. In *Environment and Cultural Behavior,* ed. A. P. Vayda, pp. 130–156. Garden City, NY: Natural History Press.

Piperno, D. R. 2001 On Maize and the Sunflower. *Science* 292(5525): 2260–2261.

Piperno, D. R., and D. M. Pearsall 1998 *The Origins of Agriculture in the Lowland Neotropics.* San Diego: Academic Press.

Piperno, D. R., and K. E. Stothert 2003 Phytolith Evidence for Early Holocene *Cucurbita* Domestication in Southwest Ecuador. *Science,* February 14, 299 (5609): 1054–1057.

Plattner, S., ed. 1989 *Economic Anthropology.* Stanford, CA: Stanford University Press.

Podolefsky, A. 1992 *Simbu Law: Conflict Management in the New Guinea Highlands.* Fort Worth: Harcourt Brace.

Podolefsky, A., and P. J. Brown, eds. 1992 *Applying Anthropology: An Introductory Reader,* 2nd ed. Mountain View, CA: Mayfield. 2007 *Applying Anthropology: An Introductory Reader,* 8th ed. Boston: McGraw-Hill.

Pohl, M. E. D, D. R., Piperno, K. O. Pope, and J. G. Jones 2007 Microfossil Evidence for Pre-Columbian Maize Dispersals in the Neotropics from San Andrés, Tabasco, Mexico. *Proceedings of the National Academy of Sciences of the United States of America* 104(29):11874–11881. April 10. 10.1073/pnas.0701425104.

Polanyi, K. 1968 *Primitive, Archaic and Modern Economies: Essays of Karl Polanyi.* Edited by G. Dalton. Garden City, NY: Anchor Books.

Pollan, M. 2003 You Want Fries with That? *New York Times Book Review,* January 12, p. 6.

Pollard, T. M., and S. B. Hyatt 1999 *Sex, Gender, and Health.* New York: Cambridge University Press.

Pollock, S. 1999 *Ancient Mesopotamia: The Eden That Never Was.* Cambridge, UK: Cambridge University Press.

Pospisil, L. 1963 *The Kapauku Papuans of West New Guinea.* New York: Harcourt Brace Jovanovich.

Potash, B., ed. 1986 *Widows in African Societies: Choices and Constraints.* Stanford, CA: Stanford University Press.

Potts, D. T. 1997 *Mesopotamian Civilization: The Material Foundations.* Ithaca, NY: Cornell University Press.

Prag, J., and R. Neave 1997 *Making Faces: Using Forensic and Archaeological Evidence.* College Station: Texas A&M University Press.

Price, R., ed. 1973 *Maroon Societies.* New York: Anchor Books, Doubleday.

Price, T. D., ed. 2000 *Europe's First Farmers.* New York: Cambridge University Press.

Price, T. D., and G. M. Feinman 2005 *Images of the Past,* 4th ed. Boston: McGraw-Hill.

Price, T. D., and A. B. Gebauer, eds. 1995 *Last Hunters, First Farmers: New Perspectives on the Prehistoric Transition to Agriculture.* Santa Fe, NM: School of American Research Press.

Public Culture Journal published by the University of Chicago.

Punch, M. 1985 *The Politics and Ethics of Fieldwork.* Beverly Hills, CA: Sage.

Quiatt, D., and V. Reynolds 1995 *Primate Behavior: Information, Social Knowledge, and the Evolution of Culture.* New York: Cambridge University Press.

Quinn, N., and C. Strauss 1989 A Cognitive Cultural Anthropology. Paper presented at the Invited Session "Assessing Developments in Anthropology," American Anthropological Association 88th Annual Meeting, November 15–19, 1989, Washington, DC.
1994 A Cognitive Cultural Anthropology. *In Assessing Cultural Anthropology,* ed. R. Borofsky. New York: McGraw-Hill.

Radcliffe-Brown, A. R. 1965 (orig. 1962). *Structure and Function in Primitive Society.* New York: Free Press.

Radcliffe-Brown, A. R., and D. Forde, eds. 1994 *African Systems of Kinship and Marriage.* New York: Columbia University Press.

Rak, Y. 1986 The Neandertal: A New Look at an Old Face. *Journal of Human Evolution* 15(3): 151–164.

Random House College Dictionary 1982 Revised ed. New York: Random House.

Ranger, T. O. 1996 Postscript. In *Postcolonial Identities,* ed. R. Werbner and T. O. Ranger. London: Zed.

Rappaport, R. A., 1966 *Pigs for the Ancestors: Ritual in the Ecology of a New Guinea People.* New Haven, CT: Yale University Press.
1971 Nature, Culture, and Ecological Anthropology. In *Man, Culture, and Society,* ed. H. Shapiro, pp. 237–268. New York: Oxford University Prees.
1974 Obvious Aspects of Ritual. *Cambridge Anthropology* 2: 2–60.
1979 *Ecology, Meaning, and Religion.* Richmond, CA: North Atlantic Books.
1999 *Holiness and Humanity: Ritual in the Making of Religious Life.* Cambridge: Cambridge University Press.

Rathje, W. L., and C. Murphy 2001 *Rubbish!: The Archaeology of Garbage.* Tucson: University of Arizona Press.

Rathus, S. A., J. S. Nevid, and J. Fichner-Rathus 1997 *Human Sexuality in a World of Diversity,* 3rd ed. Boston: Allyn & Bacon.
2008 *Human Sexuality in a World of Diversity,* 7th ed. Boston: Allyn & Bacon.

Read-Martin, C. E., and D. W. Read 1975 Australopithecine Scavenging and Human Evolution: An Approach from Faunal Analysis. *Current Anthropology* 16: 359–368.

Reade, J. 1991 *Mesopotamia.* Cambridge, MA: Harvard University Press.

Redfield, R. 1941 *The Folk Culture of Yucatan.* Chicago: University of Chicago Press.

Redfield, R., R. Linton, and M. Herskovits 1936 Memorandum on the Study of Acculturation. *American Anthropologist* 38: 149–152.

Redmond, E. M. 1994 Tribal and Chiefly Warfare in South America. *Museum of Anthropology Memoir* 28, University of Michigan (Ann Arbor).

Redmond, E. M., ed. 1998 *Chiefdoms and Chieftaincy in the Americas.* Gainesville: University of Florida Press.

Reed, R. 1997 *Forest Dwellers, Forest Protectors: Indigenous Models for International Development.* Boston: Allyn & Bacon.

Reese, W. L. 1999 *Dictionary of Philosophy and Religion: Eastern and Western Thought.* Amherst, NY: Humanities Books.

Reiter, R. 1975 Men and Women in the South of France: Public and Private Domains. In *Toward an Anthropology of Women,* ed. R. Reiter, pp. 252–282. New York: Monthly Review Press.

Reiter, R., ed. 1975 *Toward an Anthropology of Women.* New York: Monthly Review Press.

Relethford, J. H. 2005 *The Human Species: An Introduction to Biological Anthropology,* 6th ed. Boston: McGraw-Hill.

Renfrew, C., and P. Bahn 1996 *Archaeology: Theories, Methods, and Practice,* 2nd ed. London: Thames and Hudson. 2004 *Archaeology: Theories, Methods, and Practice,* 4th ed. London: Thames and Hudson. 2005 *Archaeology: The Key Concepts,* New York: Routledge.

Reynolds, V. 1971 *The Apes.* New York: Harper Colophon.

Rice, P. 2002 Paleoanthropology 2001—Part II. *General Anthropology* 8(2): 11–14.

Richards, D. 1994 *Masks of Difference: Cultural Representations in Literature, Anthropology, and Art.* New York: Cambridge University Press.

Richards, P. 1973 The Tropical Rain Forest. *Scientific American* 229(6): 58–67.

Rickford, J. R. 1997 Suite for Ebony and Phonics. http://www.stanford.edu/~rickford/papers/SuiteForEbonyandPhonics.html (also published in *Discover,* December 1997).
1999 *African American Vernacular English: Features, Evolution, Educational Implications.* Malden, MA: Blackwell.

Rickford, J. R., and Rickford, R. J. 2000 *Spoken Soul: The Story of Black English.* New York: Wiley.

Ricoeur, P. 1971 The Model of the Text: Meaningful Action Considered as a Text. *Social Research* 38: 529–562.

Rightmire, G. P. 1990 *The Evolution of* Homo erectus: *Comparative Anatomical Studies of an Extinct Human Species.* New York: Cambridge University Press.

Rilling, J. K., D. A. Gutman, T. R. Zeh, G. Pagnoni, G. S. Berns, and C. D. Kilts 2002 A Neural Basis for Social Cooperation. *Neuron* 35: 395–405.

Rindos, D. 1984 *The Origins of Agriculture: An Evolutionary Perspective.* New York: Academic Press.

Roach, J. 2007 "Hobbit" Human Was Unique Species, Wrist Bones Suggest. *National Geographic News,* September 20. http://news.nationalgeographic.com/news/pf/65255655.html.

Robbins, R. 2008 *Global Problems and the Culture of Capitalism,* 4th ed. Boston: Pearson/Allyn & Bacon.

Roberts, D. F. 1953 Body Weight, Race and Climate. *American Journal of Physical Anthropology* 11: 533–558.
1986 *Genetic Variation and Its Maintenance: With Particular Reference to Tropical Populations.* New York: Cambridge University Press.

Roberts, J. 1995 *Dian Fossey.* San Diego: Lucent Books.

Roberts, S. 1979 *Order and Dispute: An Introduction to Legal Anthropology.* New York: Penguin.

Roberts, S., A. Sabar, B. Goodman, and M. Balleza 2007 51% of Women Are Now Living without Spouse. *New York Times,* January 16. http://www.nytimes.com.

Robertson, A. F. 1995 *The Big Catch: A Practical Introduction to Development.* Boulder, CO: Westview Press.

Robertson, J. 1992 Koreans in Japan. Paper presented at the University of Michigan Department of Anthropology, Martin Luther King Jr. Day Panel, January. Ann Arbor: University of Michigan Department of Anthropology (unpublished).

Rodseth, L., R. W. Wrangham, A. M. Harrigan, and B. Smuts 1991 The Human Community as a Primate Society. *Current Anthropology* 32: 221–254.

Rogers, C. 2005 A Conversation with Carel van Schaik; Revealing Behavior in "Orangutan Heaven and Human Hell." *New York Times,* November 15, late edition, final, p. F2.

Romaine, S. 2000 *Language in Society: An Introduction to Sociolinguistics,* 2nd ed. New York: Oxford University Press.
1999 *Communicating Gender.* Mahwah, NJ: Erlbaum.

Romer, A. S. 1960 *Man and the Vertebrates,* 3rd ed., vol. 1. Harmondsworth, UK: Penguin.

Root, D. 1996 *Cannibal Culture: Art, Appropriation, and the Commodification of Difference.* Boulder, CO: Westview Press.

Rosaldo, M. Z. 1980a *Knowledge and Passion: Notions of Self and Social Life.* Stanford, CA: Stanford University Press.
1980b The Use and Abuse of Anthropology: Reflections on Feminism and Cross-Cultural Understanding. *Signs* 5(3): 389–417.

Rosaldo, M. Z., and L. Lamphere, eds. 1974 *Woman, Culture, and Society.* Stanford, CA: Stanford University Press.

Rose, M. 1997 Neandertal DNA. Newsbriefs. *Archaeology* 50 (September/October): 5. http://www.archaeology.org/9709/newsbriefs/dna.html.

Roseberry, W. 1988 Political Economy. *Annual Review of Anthropology* 17: 161–185.

Rosenberg, K.R., and W.R. Trevathan 2001 The Evolution of Human Birth. *Scientific American* 285(5): 60–65.

Rothstein, E. 2006 Protection for Indian Patrimony That Leads to a Paradox. *New York Times,* March 29.

Rouse, R. 1991 Mexican Migration and the Social Space of Postmodernism. *Diaspora* 1(1): 8–23.

Royal Anthropological Institute 1951 *Notes and Queries on Anthropology,* 6th ed. London: Routledge and Kegan Paul.

Rushing, W. A. 1995 *The AIDS Epidemic: Social Dimension of an Infectious Disease.* Boulder, CO: Westview Press.

Rushing, W. Jackson, ed. 1999 *Native American Art in the Twentieth Century.* New York: Routledge.

Russell, D. 1986 *The Secret Trauma: Incest in the Lives of Girls and Women.* New York: Basic Books.

Russon, A. E., K. A. Bard, and S. Taylor Parker, eds. 1996 *Reaching into Thought: The Minds of the Great Apes.* New York: Cambridge University Press.

Ryan, S. 1990 *Ethnic Conflict and International Relations.* Brookfield, MA: Dartmouth.
1995 *Ethnic Conflict and International Relations,* 2nd ed. Brookfield, MA: Dartmouth.

Sachs, C. E. 1996 *Gendered Fields: Rural Women, Agriculture, and Environment.* Boulder, CO: Westview Press.

Sade, D. 1972 A Longitudinal Study of Social Behavior of Rhesus Monkeys. In *The Functional and Evolutionary Biology of Primates,* ed. R. Tuttle, pp. 378–398. Chicago: University of Chicago Press.

Saggs, H. 1989 *Civilization before Greece and Rome.* New Haven, CT: Yale University Press.

Sahlins, M. D. 1961 The Segmentary Lineage: An Organization of Predatory Expansion. *American Anthropologist* 63: 322–345.
1968 *Tribesmen.* Englewood Cliffs, NJ: Prentice Hall.

1981 *Historical Metaphors and Mythical Realities: Structure in the Early History of the Sandwich Islands Kingdom.* Ann Arbor: University of Michigan Press.

2004 (orig. 1972) *Stone Age Economics.* New York: Routledge.

Saitoti, T. O. 1988 *The Worlds of a Maasai Warrior: An Autobiography.* Berkeley: University of California Press.

Saluter, A. 1995 Household and Family Characteristics: March 1994, P20-483, Press release, October 16, CB95-186, Single-Parent Growth Rate Stabilized; 2-parent Family Growth Renewed, Census Bureau Reports. United States Department of Commerce, Bureau of Census, Public Information Office.

1996 Marital Status and Living Arrangements: March 1994, P20-484, U.S. Census Bureau, Press release, March 13, 1996, CB96-33. United States Department of Commerce, Bureau of Census, Public Information Office. http://www.census.gov/prod/www/titles.html#popspec.

Salzman, P. C. 1974 Political Organization among Nomadic Peoples. In *Man in Adaptation: The Cultural Present,* 2nd ed., ed. Y. A. Cohen, pp. 267–284. Chicago: Aldine.

2004 *Pastoralists: Equality, Hierarchy, and the State.* Boulder, CO: Westview Press.

Salzman, P. C., and J. G. Galaty, eds. 1990 *Nomads in a Changing World.* Naples: Istituto Universitario Orientale.

Salzmann, Z. 2007 *Language, Culture, and Society: An Introduction to Linguistic Anthropology,* 4th ed. Boulder, CO: Westview Press.

Sanday, P. R. 1974 Female Status in the Public Domain. In *Woman, Culture, and Society,* ed. M. Z. Rosaldo and L. Lamphere, pp. 189–206. Stanford, CA: Stanford University Press.

2002 *Women at the Center: Life in a Modern Matriarchy.* Ithaca, NY: Cornell University Press.

Sanders, W. T. 1972 Population, Agricultural History, and Societal Evolution in Mesoamerica. In *Population Growth: Anthropological Implications,* ed. B. Spooner, pp. 101–153. Cambridge, MA: MIT Press.

1973 The Cultural Ecology of the Lowland Maya: A Reevaluation. In *The Classic Maya Collapse,* ed. T. P. Culbert, pp. 325–366. Albuquerque: University of New Mexico Press.

Sanders, W. T., J. R. Parsons, and R. S. Santley 1979 *The Basin of Mexico: Ecological Processes in the Evolution of a Civilization.* New York: Academic Press.

Sankoff, G. 1980 *The Social Life of Language.* Philadelphia: University of Pennsylvania Press.

Santino, J. 1983 Night of the Wandering Souls. *Natural History* 92(10): 42.

Santley, R. S. 1984 Obsidian Exchange, Economic Stratification, and the Evolution of Complex Society in the Basin of Mexico. In *Trade and Exchange in Early Mesoamerica,* ed. K. G. Hirth, pp. 43–86. Albuquerque: University of New Mexico Press.

1985 The Political Economy of the Aztec Empire. *Journal of Anthropological Research* 41(3): 327–337.

Sapir, E. 1931 Conceptual Categories in Primitive Languages. *Science* 74: 578–584.

Sargent, C. F., and C. B. Brettell 1996 *Gender and Health: An International Perspective.* Upper Saddle River, NJ: Prentice Hall.

Schaefer, R. 1989 *Sociology,* 3rd ed. New York: McGraw-Hill.

Schaik, C. V. 2004 *Among Orangutans: Red Apes and the Rise of Human Culture.* Tucson: University of Arizona Press.

Schaller, G. 1963 *The Mountain Gorilla: Ecology and Behavior.* Chicago: University of Chicago Press.

Scheffler, H. W. 2001 *Filiation and Affiliation.* Boulder, CO: Westview Press.

Scheidel, W. 1997 Brother-Sister Marriage in Roman Egypt. *Journal of Biosocial Science* 29(3): 361–371.

Scheinman, M. 1980 Imperialism. *Academic American Encyclopedia,* vol. 11, pp. 61–62. Princeton, NJ: Arete.

Scheper-Hughes, N. 1987 Culture, Scarcity, and Maternal Thinking: Mother Love and Child Death in Northeast Brazil. In *Child Survival,* ed. N. Scheper-Hughes, pp. 187–208. Boston: D. Reidel.

1992 *Death without Weeping: The Violence of Everyday Life in Brazil.* Berkeley: University of California Press.

Schick, K. D., and N. Toth 1993 *Making Silent Stones Speak: Human Evolution and the Dawn of Technology.* New York: Simon & Schuster.

Schieffelin, E. 1976 *The Sorrow of the Lonely and the Burning of the Dancers.* New York: St. Martin's Press.

Schildkrout, E., and C. A. Keim 1990 *African Reflections: Art from Northeastern Zaire.* Seattle: University of Washington Press.

Schlee, G., ed. 2002 *Imagined Differences: Hatred and the Construction of Identity.* New York: Palgrave.

Schneider, D. M. 1968 *American Kinship: A Cultural Account.* Englewood Cliffs, NJ: Prentice Hall.

Schneider, D. M., and K. Gough, eds. 1961 *Matrilineal Kinship.* Berkeley: University of California Press.

Scholte, J. A. 2000 *Globalization: A Critical Introduction.* New York: St. Martin's Press.

Schweingruber, F. H. 1988 *Tree Rings: Basics and Applications of Dendrochronology.* Hingham, MA: Kluwer Academic.

Scott, J. 2002 Prehistoric Human Footpaths Lure Archaeologists Back to Costa Rica. University of Colorado Press Release, May 20. http://www.eurekalert.org/ pub_releases/2002-05/uoca-phf052002.php.

Scott, J. C. 1985 *Weapons of the Weak.* New Haven, CT: Yale University Press.

1990 *Domination and the Arts of Resistance.* New Haven, CT: Yale University Press.

1998 *Seeing Like a State: How Certain Schemes to Improve the Human Condition Have Failed.* New Haven, CT: Yale University Press.

Scudder, T. 1982 The Impact of Big Dam-building on the Zambezi River Basin. In *The Careless Technology: Ecology and International Development,* ed. M. T. Farvar and J. P. Milton, pp. 206–235. New York: Natural History Press.

Scudder, T., and E. Colson 1980 *Secondary Education and the Formation of an Elite: The Impact of Education on Gwembe District, Zambia.* London: Academic Press.

Scudder, T., and J. Habarad 1991 Local Responses to Involuntary Relocation and Development in the Zambian Portion of the Middle Zambezi Valley. In *Migrants in Agricultural Development,* ed. J. A. Mollett, pp. 178–205. New York: New York University Press.

Scupin, R. 2003 *Race and Ethnicity: An Anthropological Focus on the United States and the World.* Upper Saddle River, NJ: Prentice Hall.

Sebeok, T. A., and J. Umiker-Sebeok, eds. 1980 *Speaking of Apes: A Critical Anthropology of Two-Way Communication with Man.* New York: Plenum Press.

Seligson, M. A. 1984 *The Gap between Rich and Poor: Contending Perspectives on the Political Economy of Development.* Boulder, CO: Westview Press.

Sengupta, S. 2004 Kinshasa Journal: The Gentlest of Beasts, Making Love, Ravaged by War. *New York Times,* May 3, late edition, final, section A, p. 4, column 3.

Senut, B., M. Pickford, D. Gommery, P. Mein, K. Cheboi, and Y. Coppens 2001 First Hominid from the Miocene (Lukeino Formation, Kenya). *Comptes Rendus de l'Academie des Sciences, Series IIA—Earth and Planetary Science* 332. 2(30): 137–144.

Sered, S. S. 1996 *Priestess, Mother, Sacred Sister: Religions Dominated by Women.* New York: Oxford University Press.

Service, E. R. 1962 *Primitive Social Organization: An Evolutionary Perspective.* New York: McGraw-Hill.

1966 *The Hunters.* Englewood Cliffs, NJ: Prentice Hall.

1975 *Origins of the State and Civilization: The Process of Cultural Evolution.* New York: W. W. Norton.

Shabecoff, P. 1989a Ivory Imports Banned to Aid Elephant. *New York Times,* June 7, p. 15.

1989b New Lobby Is Helping Wildlife of Africa. *New York Times,* June 9, p. 14.

Shanklin, E. 1994 *Anthropology and Race.* Belmont, CA: Wadsworth.

Shannon, T. R. 1989 *An Introduction to the World-System Perspective.* Boulder, CO: Westview Press.

1996 *An Introduction to the World-System Perspective,* 2nd ed. Boulder, CO: Westview Press.

Sharer, R., and W. Ashmore 2006 *Discovering Our Past: The Process of Archaeological Research.* 4th ed. Boston: McGraw-Hill.

Shepher, J. 1983 *Incest, a Biosocial View.* New York: Academic Press.

Shermer, M. 2002 *In Darwin's Shadow: The Life and Science of Alfred Russel Wallace.* New York: Oxford University Press.

Sherwood, R. J., Ward, S. C., and A. Hill 2002 The Taxonomic Status of the Chemeron Temporal (KNM-BCI). *Science Direct,* February 27. http://www.sciencedirect.com.

Shigeru, K. 1994 *Our Land Was a Forest: An Ainu Memoir.* Boulder, CO: Westview Press.

Shipman, P. 2001 *The Man Who Found the Missing Link.* New York: Simon & Schuster.

Shivaram, C. 1996 Where Women Wore the Crown: Kerala's Dissolving Matriarchies Leave a Rich Legacy of Compassionate Family Culture. *Hinduism Today* 96(02). http://www.hinduism-today.com/archives/1996/2/1996-2-03.shtml.

Shore, B. 1996 *Culture in Mind: Meaning, Construction, and Cultural Cognition.* New York: Oxford University Press.

Shostak, M. 1981 *Nisa, the Life and Words of a !Kung Woman.* New York: Vintage Books.

2000 *Return to Nisa.* Cambridge, MA: Harvard University Press.

Shreeve, J. 1992 The Dating Game: How Old Is the Human Race? *Discover* 13(9): 76–83.

Shweder, R., and H. Levine, eds. 1984 *Culture Theory: Essays on Mind, Self, and Emotion.* Cambridge, UK: Cambridge University Press.

Sibley, C. G., and J. E. Ahlquist 1984 The Phylogeny of the Hominoid Primates, as Indicated by DNA-DNA Hybridization. *Journal of Molecular Evolution* 20: 2–15.

Signo, A. 1994 *Economics of the Family.* New York: Oxford University Press.

Silberbauer, G. 1981 *Hunter and Habitat in the Central Kalahari Desert.* New York: Cambridge University Press.

Silverberg, J., and J. P. Gray, eds. 1992 *Aggression and Peacefulness in Humans and Other Primates.* New York: Oxford University Press.

Simons, A. 1995 *Networks of Dissolution: Somalia Undone.* Boulder, CO: Westview Press.

Simons, E. L., and P. C. Ettel 1970 *Gigantopithecus. Scientific American,* January, pp. 77–85.

Simpson, B. 1998 *Changing Families: An Ethnographic Approach to Divorce and Separation.* New York: Berg.

Singer, M., and H. Baer 2007 *Introducing Medical Anthropology: A Discipline in Action.* Lanham, MD: AltaMira.

Sinnott, M. J. 2004 *Toms and Dees: Transgender Identity and Female Same-Sex Relationships in Thailand.* Honolulu: University of Hawaii Press.

Slade, M. F. 1984 Displaying Affection in Public. *New York Times,* December 17, p. B14.

Small, M. F. 1993 *Female Choices: Sexual Behavior of Female Primates.* Ithaca, NY: Cornell University Press.

Smart, A., and J. Smart 2003 Urbanization and the Global Perspective. *Annual Review of Anthropology* 32: 263–285.

Smith, B. D. 1995 *The Emergence of Agriculture.* New York: Scientific American Library, W. H. Freeman.

Smith, C. A. 1990 The Militarization of Civil Society in Guatemala: Economic Reorganization as a Continuation of War. *Latin American Perspectives* 17: 8–41.

Smith, M. E., and M. A. Masson, eds. 2000 *The Ancient Civilizations of Mesoamerica: A Reader.* Malpen, MA: Blackwell.

Smith, M. G. 1965 *The Plural Society in the British West Indies.* Berkeley: University of California Press.

Smitherman, G. 1986 *Talkin and Testifyin: The Language of Black America.* Detroit: Wayne State University Press.

Smuts, B. B. 1999 (orig. 1985) *Sex and Friendship in Baboons.* Cambridge, MA: Harvard University Press.

Solheim, W. G., II 1976 (orig. 1972). An Earlier Agricultural Revolution. In *Avenues to Antiquity:*

Readings from Scientific American, ed. B. M. Fagan, pp. 160–168. San Francisco: W. H. Freeman.

Solway, J., and R. Lee 1990 Foragers, Genuine and Spurious: Situating the Kalahari San in History (with CA treatment). *Current Anthropology* 31(2): 109–146.

Sonneville-Bordes, D. de 1963 Upper Paleolithic Cultures in Western Europe. *Science* 142: 347–355.

Sotomayor, S. 2009 A Latina Judge's Voice. The Judge Mario G. Olmos Memorial Lecture, delivered at the University of California, Berkeley, School of Law in 2001; published in the spring 2002 issue of the *Berkeley La Raza Law Journal*, republished by the *New York Times* on May 14, 2009.

Spencer, C. S. 2003 War and Early State Formation in Oaxaca, Mexico. *Proceedings of the National Academy of Sciences of the United States of America.* 100(20): 11185–11187. http://www.pnas.org/cgi/doi/10.1073/pnas.2034992100.

Spickard, P., ed. 2004 *Race and Nation: Ethnic Systems in the Modern World.* New York: Routledge.

Spindler, G. D., ed. 1978 *The Making of Psychological Anthropology.* Berkeley: University of California Press. 1982 *Doing the Ethnography of Schooling: Educational Anthropology in Action.* New York: Holt, Rinehart and Winston.
2000 *Fifty Years of Anthropology and Education, 1950–2000: A Spindler Anthology.* Mahwah, NJ: Erlbaum.
2005 *New Horizons in the Anthropology of Education.* Mahwah, NJ: Erlbaum.

Spiro, M. E. 1993 *Oedipus in the Trobriands.* New Brunswick, NJ: Transaction.

Sponsel, L. E., and T. Gregor, eds. 1994 *The Anthropology of Peace and Nonviolence.* Boulder, CO: Lynne Rienner.

Spoor, F., M. G. Leakey, P. N. Gathongo, F. H. Brown, S. C. Anton, I. McDougall, C. Kiarie, F. K. Manthi, and L. N. Leakey. 2007 Implications of New Early Homo Fossils from Ileret, East of Lake Turkana, Kenya. *Nature* 448 (7154): 688–691. http://news.nature.com//news/2007/070806/070806-5.html.

Spradley, J. P. 1979 *The Ethnographic Interview.* New York: Harcourt Brace Jovanovich.

Srivastava, J., N. J. H. Smith, and D. A. Forno 1999 *Integrating Biodiversity in Agricultural Intensification: Toward Sound Practices.* Washington, DC: World Bank.

Stacey, J. 1996 *In the Name of the Family: Rethinking Family Values in the Postmodern Age.* Boston: Beacon Press.
1998 *Brave New Families: Stories of Domestic Upheaval in Late Twentieth Century America.* Berkeley: University of California Press.

Stack, C. B. 1975 *All Our Kin: Strategies for Survival in a Black Community.* New York: Harper Torchbooks.

Staeck, J. 2002 *Back to the Earth: An Introduction to Archaeology.* Boston: McGraw-Hill.

Stanford, C. B. 1999 *The Hunting Apes: Meat Eating and the Origins of Human Behavior.* Princeton, NJ: Princeton University Press.

Stanford, C. B., and H. T. Bunn, eds. 2001 *Meat-Eating and Human Evolution.* New York: Oxford University Press.

Statistical Abstract of the United States 1991 111th ed. Washington, DC: U.S. Bureau of the Census, U.S. Government Printing Office.
1996 116th ed. Washington, DC: U.S. Bureau of the Census, U.S. Government Printing Office.
2003 *Statistical Abstract of the United States,* 2003. http://www.census.gov/statab/www/.
2006 *Statistical Abstract of the United States,* 2006. http://www.census.gov/prod/www/statistical-abstract.html.
2007 *Statistical Abstract of the United States,* 2007. http://www.census.gov/prod/www/statistical-abstract.html.
2008 *Statistical Abstract of the United States,* 2008. http://www.census.gov/prod/www/statistical-abstract.html, 2009 *Statistical Abstract of the United States,* 2009. http://www.census.gov/prod/www/statistical-abstract.html.

Statistics Canada 1998 1996 Census: Ethnic Origin, Visible Minorities. *The Daily,* February 17.

http://www.statcan.ca/Daily/English/980217/d980217.htm.
2001a 1996 Census. Nation Tables. http://www.statcan.ca/english/census96/nation.htm.
2001b Selected Religions, Provinces and Territories. http://www40.statcan.ca/101/cst01/demo30a.htm.

Staub, S. 1989 *Yemenis in New York City: The Folklore of Ethnicity.* Philadelphia: Balch Institute Press.

Steegman, A. T., Jr. 1975 Human Adaptation to Cold. *In Physiological Anthropology,* ed. A. Damon, pp. 130–166. New York: Oxford University Press.

Stein, R. L., and P. L. Stein 2005 *The Anthropology of Religion, Magic, and Witchcraft.* Boston: Pearson/Allyn & Bacon.

Steinfels, P. 1997 Beliefs: Cloning, as Seen by Buddhists and Humanists. *New York Times,* July 12. http://www.nytimes.com.

Stephens, S., ed. 1996 *Children and the Politics of Culture.* Princeton, NJ: Princeton University Press.

Stephens, W. R. 2002 *Careers in Anthropology: What an Anthropology Degree Can Do for You.* Boston: Allyn & Bacon.

Steponaitis, V. 1986 Prehistoric Archaeology in the Southeastern United States. *Annual Review of Anthropology* 15: 363–404.

Stern, A. 2000 Experts Say 138 World Primate Species Endangered. Reuters. http://www.forests.org/archive/general/exsay138.htm.

Stevens, W. K. 1992 Humanity Confronts Its Handiwork: An Altered Planet. *New York Times,* May 5, pp. B5–B7.

Stevenson, D. 2003 *Cities and Urban Cultures.* Philadelphia: Open University Press.

Stevenson, R. F. 1968 *Population and Political Systems in Tropical Africa.* New York: Columbia University Press.

Steward, J. H. 1955 *Theory of Culture Change.* Urbana: University of Illinois Press.
1956 *The People of Puerto Rico: A Study in Social Anthropology.* Urbana: University of Illinois Press.

Stocking, G. W., ed. 1986 *Malinowski, Rivers, Benedict and Others: Essays on Culture and Personality.* Madison: University of Wisconsin Press.

Stoler, A. 1977 Class Structure and Female Autonomy in Rural Java. *Signs* 3: 74–89.

Stoler, A. L. 1995 *Race and the Education of Desire: Foucault's History of Sexuality and the Colonial Order of Things.* Durham, NC: Duke University Press.
2002 *Carnal Knowledge and Imperial Power: Race and the Intimate in Colonial Rule.* Berkeley: University of California Press.

Stone, L. 2000 *Kinship and Gender: An Introduction,* 2nd ed. Boulder, CO: Westview.
2001 *New Directions in Anthropological Kinship.* Lanham, MD: Rowman and Littlefield.

Stoneman, B. 1997 Income Is Rising, So Is Poverty. *American Demographics,* Forecast, November. http://www.demographics.com/publications/fc/97_fc/9711_fc/fc97111.htm.

Stout, D., and B. Knowlton 2007 Bush Calls for Global Goals for Emissions. *New York Times,* May 31. www.nytimes.com.

Strachan, T., and A. P. Read 2004 *Human Molecular Genetics,* 3rd ed. New York: Garland Science.

Strathern, A., and P. J. Stewart 1999 *Curing and Healing: Medical Anthropology in Global Perspective.* Durham, NC: Carolina Academic Press.

Strathern, M. 1988 *The Gender of the Gift: Problems with Women and Problems with Society in Melanesia.* Berkeley: University of California Press.

Strier, K. B. 2003 Primate Behavioral Ecology: From Ethnography to Ethology and Back. *American Anthropologist* 105(1): 16–27.2007 *Primate Behavioral Ecology,* 3rd ed. Boston: Allyn & Bacon.

Strong, P. T. 2005 Recent Ethnographic Research on North American Indigenous Peoples. *Annual Review of Anthropology* 34: 253–268.

Strum, S. C., and L. M. Fedigan, eds. 2000 *Primate Encounters: Models of Science, Gender, and Society.* Chicago: University of Chicago Press.

Suarez-Orozco, M. M., G. Spindler, and L. Spindler, eds. 1994 *The Making of Psychological Anthropology II.* Fort Worth: Harcourt Brace.

Susman, R. L. 1987 Pygmy Chimpanzees and Common Chimpanzees: Models for the Behavioral Ecology of the Earliest Hominids. In *The Evolution of Human Behavior: Primate Models,* ed. W. G. Kinzey, pp. 72–86. Albany: State University of New York Press.

Susser, I., and T. C. Patterson, eds. 2000 *Cultural Diversity in the United States: A Critical Reader.* Malden, MA: Blackwell.

Sussman, R. W. 2004 Flowering Plants and the Origins of Primates: A New Theory. In *Encyclopedia of Animal Behavior,* ed. M. Bekoff, pp. 967–969. Portsmouth, NH: Greenwood Press.

Sussman, R. W., G. M. Green, and L. K. Sussman 1994 Satellite Imagery, Human Ecology, Anthropology, and Deforestation in Madagascar. *Human Ecology* 22: 333–54.

Suttles, W. 1960 Affinal Ties, Subsistence, and Prestige among the Coast Salish. *American Anthropologist* 62: 296–395.

Swift, M. 1963 Men and Women in Malay Society. In *Women in the New Asia,* ed. B. Ward, pp. 268–286. Paris: UNESCO.

Swindler, D. R. 1998 *Introduction to the Primates.* Seattle: University of Washington Press.

Tague, R. G., and C. O. Lovejoy 1986 The Obstetric Pelvis of A. L. 288-1 (Lucy). *Journal of Human Evolution* 15: 237–255.

Tainter, J. 1987 *The Collapse of Complex Societies.* New York: Cambridge University Press.

Tanaka, J. 1980 *The San Hunter-Gatherers of the Kalahari.* Tokyo: University of Tokyo Press.

Tannen, D. 1990 *You Just Don't Understand: Women and Men in Conversation.* New York: Ballantine.

Tannen, D., ed. 1993 *Gender and Conversational Interaction.* New York: Oxford University Press.

Tanner, N. 1974 Matrifocality in Indonesia and Africa and among Black Americans. In *Women, Culture, and Society,* ed. M. Z. Rosaldo and L. Lamphere, pp. 127–156. Stanford, CA: Stanford University Press.

Tattersall, I. 1995a *The Fossil Trail: How We Know What We Think We Know about Human Evolution.* New York: Oxford University Press.
1995b *The Last Neanderthal: The Rise, Success, and Mysterious Extinction of Our Closest Human Relatives.* New York: Macmillan.
1998 *Becoming Human: Evolution and Human Uniqueness.* New York: Harcourt Brace.

Taylor, A. 1993 *Women Drug Users: An Ethnography of a Female Injecting Community.* New York: Oxford University Press.

Taylor, C. 1987 Anthropologist-in-Residence. In *Applied Anthropology in America,* 2nd ed., ed. E. M. Eddy and W. L. Partridge. New York: Columbia University Press. 1996 *The Black Churches of Brooklyn.* New York: Columbia University Press.

Teleki, G. 1973 *The Predatory Behavior of Wild Chimpanzees.* Lewisburg, PA: Bucknell University Press.

Terrace, H. S. 1979 *Nim.* New York: Knopf.

Terrell, J. E. 1998 The Prehistoric Pacific. *Archaeology,* vol. 51, no. 6. Archaeological Institute of America. http://www.archaeology.org/9811/abstracts/pacific.html.

Thomas, D. H. 2003 *Skull Wars: Kennewick Man, Archaeology, and the Battle for Native American Identity.* New York: Basic Books.

Thomas, L., and S. Wareing, eds. 2004 *Language, Society and Power.* New York: Routledge.

Thomason, S. G., and T. Kaufman 1988 *Language Contact, Creolization and Genetic Linguistics.* Berkeley: University of California Press.

Thompson, W. 1983 Introduction: World System with and without the Hyphen. In *Contending Approaches to World System Analysis,* ed. W. Thompson, pp. 7–26. Thousand Oaks, CA: Sage.

Thomson, A., and L. H. D. Buxton 1923 Man's Nasal Index in Relation to Certain Climatic Conditions. *Journal of the Royal Anthropological Institute* 53: 92–112.

Tice, K. 1997 Reflections on Teaching Anthropology for Use in the Public and Private Sector. In *The Teaching of Anthropology: Problems, Issues, and Decisions,* ed. C. P. Kottak, J. J. White, R. H. Furlow, and P. C. Rice, pp. 273–284. Mountain View, CA: Mayfield.

Titiev, M. 1992 *Old Oraibi: A Study of the Hopi Indians of Third Mesa.* Albuquerque: University of New Mexico Press.

Tobler, A. J. 1950 *Excavations at Tepe Gawra,* vol. 2. Philadelphia: University of Pennsylvania Museum.

Todt, R. 2000 Western Hemisphere Inhabited at Least 15,000 Years Ago. ABCNews.Go.com News Briefs, April 7. http://abcnews.go.com/sections/science/DailyNews/first_americans000407.html.

Toner, R. 1992 Los Angeles Riots Are a Warning, Americans Fear. *New York Times,* May 11, pp. A1, A11.

Toth, N. 1985 The Oldowan Reassessed: A Close Look at Early Stone Artifacts. *Journal of Archaeological Science* 2: 101–120.

Toth, N., and Schick, K. 1986 The First Million Years: The Archaeology of Protohuman Culture. *Advances in Archaeological Method and Theory,* pp. 1–96.

Trask, L. 1996 FAQs about Basque and the Basques. http://www.cogs.susx.ac.uk/users/larryt/basque.faqs.html.

Trehub, S. E. 2001 Musical Predispositions in Infancy. *Annals of the New York Academy of Sciences* 930(1): 1–16.

Trigger, B. G. 1993 *Early Civilizations: Ancient Egypt in Context.* New York: Columbia University Press.
2003 *Understanding Early Civilizations: A Comparative Study.* Cambridge, UK: Cambridge University Press.

Trivedi, B. P. 2001 Scientists Identify a Language Gene. *National Geographic News,* October 4. http://news.nationalgeographic.com/news/2001/10/1004_TVlanguagegene.html.

Trudgill, P. 1983 *Sociolinguistics: An Introduction to Language and Society,* rev. ed. Baltimore: Penguin.
2000 *Sociolinguistics: An Introduction to Language and Society,* 4th ed. New York: Penguin.

Turnbaugh, W. A., R. Jurmain, L. Kilgore, and H. Nelson 2002 *Understanding Physical Anthropology and Archaeology,* 8th ed. Belmont, CA: Wadsworth.

Turnbull, C. 1965 *Wayward Servants: The Two Worlds of the African Pygmies.* Garden City, NY: Natural History Press.

Turner, B. S. 1998 *Readings in the Anthropology and Sociology of Family and Kinship.* London: Routledge/Thoemmes.

Turner, T. 1993 The Role of Indigenous Peoples in the Environmental Crisis: The Example of the Kayapo of the Brazilian Amazon. *Perspectives in Biology and Medicine* 36: 526–545.

Turner, V. W. 1967 *The Forest of Symbols: Aspects of Ndembu Ritual.* Ithaca, NY: Cornell University Press.
1995 (orig. 1969) *The Ritual Process.* Hawthorne, NY: Aldine.1996 (orig. 1957) *Schism and Continuity in an African Society: A Study of Ndembu Village Life.* Washington, DC: Berg.

Tylor, E. B. 1889 On a Method of Investigating the Development of Institutions: Applied to Laws of Marriage and Descent. *Journal of the Royal Anthropological Institute* 18: 245–269. 1958 (orig. 1871) *Primitive Culture.* New York: Harper Torchbooks.

Ucko, P., and A. Rosenfeld 1967 *Paleolithic Cave Art.* London: Weidenfeld and Nicolson.

Ucko, P. J., and G. W. Dimbleby, eds. 1969 *The Domestication and Exploitation of Plants and Animals.* Chicago: Aldine.

Ulman, H. 2007 Brady an Easy Winner of AP Male Athlete. *Associated Press,* December 22. http://abcnws.go.com/sports/wireStory?id=4042479.

University of Virginia n.d. American Studies Program, Armory Show of 1913. http://xroads.virginia.edu/~MUSEUM/Armory/ofili.html.

Urban, Greg 2001 *Metaculture: How Culture Moves through the World.* Minneapolis: University of Minnesota Press.

U.S. Census Bureau 1998 Unpublished Tables—Marital Status and Living Arrangements, March 1998 (Update). http://www.census.gov/prod/99pubs/p20-514u.pdf.
1999 *Statistical Abstract of the United States.* http://www.census.gov/prod/99pubs/99statab/sec01.

pdf and http://www.census.gov/prod/99pubs/99statab/sec02.pdf. 2004 *Statistical Abstract of the United States, 2003.* Table 688, p. 459. http://www.census.gov/prod/2004pubs/03statab/income.pdf.
2005 *Statistical Abstract of the United States, 2004.* http://www.census.gov/prod/2004pubs/04statab/labor.pdf.
2006a *Statistical Abstract of the United States, 2006.* http://www.census.gov/prod/www/statistical-abstract.html.
2006b *Historical Income Tables—Households.* http://www.census.gov/hhes/www/income/histinc/h03ar.html.

Valentine, C. 1968 *Culture and Poverty.* Chicago: University of Chicago Press.

Valladas, H., J. L. Reyss, J. L. Joron, G. Valladas, O. Bar-Joseph, and B. Vandermeersch 1988 Thermoluminescence Dating of Mousterian "Proto-Cro-Magnon" Remains from Israel and the Origin of Modern Man. *Nature* 331: 614–616.

Van Cantfort, T. E., and J. B. Rimpau 1982 Sign Language Studies with Children and Chimpanzees. *Sign Language Studies* 34: 15–72.

Van der Elst, D., and P. Bohannan 2003 *Culture as Given, Culture as Choice.* 2nd ed. Prospect Heights, IL: Waveland.

Van Schaik, C. P., and J. A. R. A. M. van Hooff 1983 On the Ultimate Causes of Primate Social Systems. *Behaviour* 85: 91–117.

Van Willingen, J. 1987 *Becoming a Practicing Anthropologist: A Guide to Careers and Training Programs in Applied Anthropology.* NAPA Bulletin 3. Washington, DC: American Anthropological Association/National Association for the Practice of Anthropology.
2002 *Applied Anthropology: An Introduction,* 3rd ed. Westport CT: Bergin and Garvey.

Vayda, A. P. 1968 (orig. 1961) Economic Systems in Ecological Perspective: The Case of the Northwest Coast. In *Readings in Anthropology,* 2nd ed., vol. 2, ed. M. H. Fried, pp. 172–178. New York: Crowell.

Veblen, T. 1934 *The Theory of the Leisure Class: An Economic Study of Institutions.* New York: The Modern Library.

Veja 1984a *Olimpíadas,* August 8, pp. 36–50.
1984b *Vitórias no Tatame.* August 15, p. 61. 1984c *Brasil de Ouro e de Prata.* August 15, p. 48. BBC News.

Vekua, A., D. Lordkipanidze, and G. P. Rightmire 2002 A Skull of Early Homo from Dmanisi, Georgia. *Science,* July 5, pp. 85–89.

Verdery, K. 2001 Socialist Societies: Anthropological Aspects. *International Encyclopedia of the Social & Behavioral Sciences,* pp. 14496–14500. New York: Elsevier.

Verlinden, C. 1980 Colonialism. *Academic American Encyclopedia,* vol. 5, pp. 111–112. Princeton, NJ: Arete.

Vidal, J. 2003 Every Third Person Will Be a Slum Dweller within 30 Years, UN Agency Warns: Biggest Study of World's Cities Finds 940 Million Already Living in Squalor. *The Guardian,* October 4. http://www.guardian.co.uk/international/story/0,3604,1055785,00.html.

Viegas, J. 2000 Planet of the Dying Apes: Conference Reveals Steep Decline in Primate Populations. http://abcnews.go.com/sections/science/DailyNews/apeconference000512.html.

Vietnam Labor Watch 1997 Nike Labor Practices in Vietnam, March 20. http://www.saigon.com/~nike/reports/report1.html.

Vigil, J. D. 2003 Urban Violence and Street Gangs. *Annual Review of Anthropology* 32: 225–242.

Vincent, J. 1990 *Anthropology and Politics: Visions, Traditions, and Trends.* Tucson: University of Arizona Press.

Vincent, J., ed. 2002 *The Anthropology of Politics: A Reader in Ethnography, Theory, and Critique.* Malden, MA: Blackwell.

Viola, H. J., and C. Margolis 1991 *Seeds of Change: Five Hundred Years since Columbus, a Quincentennial Commemoration.* Washington, DC: Smithsonian Institution Press.

Von Daniken, E. 1971 *Chariots of the Gods: Unsolved Mysteries of the Past.* New York: Bantam.

Wade, N. 1997 Testing Genes to Save a Life without Costing You a Job. *New York Times.* September 14. http://www.nytimes.com.
2001 Gene Study Shows Ties Long Veiled in Europe. *New York Times,* April 10. http://www.angelfire.com/nt/dragon9/BASQUES2.html.
2003 A Course in Evolution, Taught by Chimps. *New York Times,* November 25, late edition, final, section F, p. 1, column 1.
2004 New Species Revealed: Tiny Cousins of Humans. *New York Times,* October 28, national edition, pp. A1, A6.
2007 Fossil DNA Expands Neanderthal Range. *New York Times,* October 2. www.nytimes.com.

Wade, N., ed. 2001 *The New York Times Book of Fossils and Evolution,* rev. ed. New York: Lyons Press.

Wade, P. 2002 *Race, Nature, and Culture: An Anthropological Perspective.* Sterling, VA: Pluto Press.

Wagley, C. W. 1968 (orig. 1959) The Concept of Social Race in the Americas. In *The Latin American Tradition,* ed. C. Wagley, pp. 155–174. New York: Columbia University Press.

Wagner, R. 1981 *The Invention of Culture,* rev. ed. Chicago: University of Chicago Press.

Wallace, A. F. C. 1956 Revitalization Movements. *American Anthropologist* 58: 264–281.
1966 *Religion: An Anthropological View.* New York: McGraw-Hill.
1970 *The Death and Rebirth of the Seneca.* New York: Knopf.

Wallerstein, I. M. 1974 *The Modern World-System: Capitalist Agriculture and the Origins of the European World-Economy in the Sixteenth Century.* New York: Academic Press. 1980 *The Modern World System II: Mercantilism and the Consolidation of the European World-Economy, 1600–1750.* New York: Academic Press.
1982 The Rise and Future Demise of the World Capitalist System: Concepts for Comparative Analysis. In *Introduction to the Sociology of "Developing Societies,"* ed. H. Alavi and T. Shanin, pp. 29–53. New York: Monthly Review Press.
2000 *The Essential Wallerstein.* New York: New Press, W. W. Norton.
2004a *The Decline of American Power: The U.S. in a Chaotic World.* New York: New Press.
2004b *World-Systems Analysis: An Introduction.* Durham, NC: Duke University Press.

Wallman, S., ed. 1977 *Perceptions of Development.* New York: Cambridge University Press.

Ward, C. 2003 The Evolution of Human Origins. *American Anthropologist* 105(1): 77–88.

Ward, C. V., M. G. Leakey, and A. Walker 2001 Morphology of Australopithecus anamensis from Kanapoi and Allia Bay, Kenya. *Journal of Human Evolution* 40–41: 253–368.

Ward, M. C., and M. Edelstein 2008 *A World Full of Women,* 5th ed. Needham Heights, MA: Allyn & Bacon.

Ward, S., B. Brown, A. Hill, J. Kelley, and W. Downs 1999 Equatorius: A New Hominoid Genus from the Middle Miocene of Kenya. *Science EurekAlert!* August 27. http://www.eurekalert.org.

Warren, K. B. 1998 *Indigenous Movements and Their Critics: Pan-Maya Activism in Guatemala.* Princeton, NJ: Princeton University Press.

Washburn, S. L., and R. Moore 1980 *Ape into Human: A Study of Human Evolution,* 2nd ed. Boston: Little, Brown.

Waters, M. R., and T. W. Stafford, Jr. 2007 Redefining the Age of Clovis: Implications for the Peopling of the Americas. *Science,* February 23, 315: 1122–1126. 10.1126/science.1137166.

Watson, J. D. 1970 *Molecular Biology of the Gene.* New York: Benjamin.

Watson, P. 1972 *Can Racial Discrimination Affect IQ? In Race and Intelligence; The Fallacies behind the Race-IQ Controversy,* ed. K. Richardson and D. Spears, pp. 56–67. Baltimore: Penguin.

Watson, P. J. 1983 The Halafian Culture: A Review and Synthesis. In *The Hilly Flanks and Beyond: Essays on the Prehistory of Southwestern Asia,* ed. T. C. Young, P. E. L. Smith, and P. Mortensen. *Studies in Ancient Oriental Civilization* 36: 231–250. Oriental Institute, University of Chicago.

Watzman, H. 2006 The Echoes of Ancient Humans. *Chronicle of Higher Education*, January 27. http://chronicle.com/weekly/v52/i21/21a01601.htm.

Weaver, T., gen. ed. 1973 *To See Ourselves: Anthropology and Modern Social Issues*. Glenview, IL: Scott, Foresman.

Weber, M. 1958 (orig. 1904) *The Protestant Ethic and the Spirit of Capitalism*. New York: Scribner. 1968 (orig. 1922) *Economy and Society*. Translated by E. Fischoff et al. New York: Bedminster Press.

Webster's New World Encyclopedia 1993 College Edition. Englewood Cliffs, NJ: Prentice Hall.

Wedel, J. 2002 Blurring the Boundaries of the State-Private Divide: Implications for Corruption. Paper presented at the European Association of Social Anthropologists (EASA) Conference in Copenhagen, August 14–17. http://www.anthrobase.com/Txt/W/Wedel_J_01.htm.

Weiner, A. 1988 *The Trobrianders of Papua New Guinea*. New York: Holt, Rinehart and Winston.

Weiner, J. 1994 *The Beak of the Finch: A Story of Evolution in Our Time*. New York: Knopf.

Weiner, J. S. 1954 Nose Shape and Climate. *American Journal of Physical Anthropology* 12: 1–4.

Weise, E. 1999 Anthropologists Adapt Technology to World's Cultures. *USA Today*, May 26. http://eclectic.ss.uci.edu/~drwhite/center/news/USAToday5-25-99.htm.

Weiss, H. 2005 *Collapse*. New York: Routledge.

Weiss, K. M. 1993 *Genetic Variation and Human Disease: Principles and Evolutionary Approaches*. New York: Cambridge University Press.

Weiss, K. M., and A. Buchanan 2004 *Genetics and the Logic of Evolution*. Hoboken, NJ: Wiley-Liss.

Weiss, M. L., and A. E. Mann 1990 *Human Biology and Behavior: An Anthropological Perspective*, 5th ed. Glenview, IL: Scott, Foresman.

Wendorf, F., and R. Schild 2000 Late Neolithic Megalithic Structures at Nabta Playa (Sahara), Southwestern Egypt. http://www.comp-archaeology.org/WendorfSAA98.html.

Wenke, R. J. 1996 *Patterns in Prehistory: Mankind's First Three Million Years*, 4th ed. New York: Oxford University Press.

Wenke, R. J., and D. I. Olszewski 2007 *Patterns in Prehistory: Mankind's First Three Million Years*, 5th ed. New York: Oxford University Press.

Werner, O., and G. M. Shoepfle 1987 *Systematic Fieldwork*. Newbury Park, CA: Sage.

Westermarck, E. 1894 *The History of Human Marriage*. London: Macmillan.

Weston, K. 1991 *Families We Choose: Lesbians, Gays, Kinship*. New York: Columbia University Press.

White, L. A. 1949 *The Science of Culture: A Study of Man and Civilization*. New York: Farrar, Strauss. 1959 *The Evolution of Culture: The Development of Civilization to the Fall of Rome*. New York: McGraw-Hill.

White, T. D., and P. A. Folkens 2000 *Human Osteology*, 2nd ed. San Diego: Academic Press.

Whiting, B. E., ed. 1963 *Six Cultures: Studies of Child Rearing*. New York: Wiley.

Whiting, J. M. 1964 Effects of Climate on Certain Cultural Practices. In *Explorations in Cultural Anthropology: Essays in Honor of George Peter Murdock*, ed. W. H. Goodenough, pp. 511–544. New York: McGraw-Hill.

Whorf, B. L. 1956 A Linguistic Consideration of Thinking in Primitive Communities. In *Language, Thought, and Reality: Selected Writings of Benjamin Lee Whorf*, ed. J. B. Carroll, pp. 65–86. Cambridge, MA: MIT Press.

Whyte, M. F. 1978 Cross-Cultural Codes Dealing with the Relative Status of Women. *Ethnology* 17(2): 211–239.

Wikipedia 2004 Fundamentalism, in *Wikipedia, the Free Encyclopedia*. http://en.wikipedia.org/wiki/Fundamentalism.

Wilford, J. N. 1995 The Transforming Leap, from 4 Legs to 2. *New York Times*, September 5, pp. B5(N), C1(L). 2000 Ruins Alter Ideas of How Civilization Spread. *New York Times*, May 23. http://www.nytimes.com. 2001a Skull May Alter Experts' View of Human Descent's Branches. *New York Times*, March 22, late edition, final, section A, p. 1, column 1. http://www.nytimes.com. 2001b African Artifacts Suggest an Earlier Modern Human. *New York Times*, December 2, late edition, final, section 1A, p. 1, column 5. http://www.nytimes.com. 2002a Seeking Polynesia's Beginnings in an Archipelago of Shards. *New York Times*, January 8, Science Desk. 2002b When Humans Became Human. *New York Times*, February 26, late edition, final, section F, p. 1, column 1. http://www.nytimes.com. 2003 Big Teeth in Ancient Jaw Offer Clues about Our Ancestors. *New York Times*, September 30, late edition, final, section F, p. 4, column 2. 2005a For Neandertals and *Homo Sapiens*, Was It De-Lovely? *New York Times*, February 15. http://www.nytimes.com/2005/02/15/science/15nean.html?ex=1147492800&en=7d5fadb91364f1d5&ei=5070. 2005b Fossils of Apelike Creature Still Stir Lineage Debate. *New York Times*, April 12, late edition, final, p. F4.

Wilford, J. N. 2007a Fossils in Kenya Challenge Linear Evolution, *New York Times*, August 9, p. A6. 2007b Fossils Reveal Clues on Human Ancestors. *New York Times*, September 20. www.nytimes.com.

Wilford, J. N. 2009 Fossil Skeleton From Africa Predates Lucy. *New York Times*, October 2, pp. A1, A6.

Wilford, J. N. 2009 Feet Offer Clue about Tiny Hominid. *New York Times*, May 9. http://www.nytimes.com.

Wilk, R. R. 1996 *Economies and Cultures: An Introduction to Economic Anthropology*. Boulder, CO: Westview Press.

Williams, B. 1989 A Class Act: Anthropology and the Race to Nation across Ethnic Terrain. *Annual Review of Anthropology* 18: 401–444.

Williams, L. M., and D. Finkelhor 1995 Paternal Caregiving and Incest: Test of a Biosocial Model. *American Journal of Orthopsychiatry* 65(1): 101–113.

Willie, C. V. 2003 *A New Look at Black Families*. Walnut Creek, CA: AltaMira.

Wilmsen, E. N. 1989 *Land Filled with Flies: A Political Economy of the Kalahari*. Chicago: University of Chicago Press.

Wilmsen, E. N., and P. McAllister, eds. 1996 *The Politics of Difference: Ethnic Premises in a World of Power*. Chicago: University of Chicago Press.

Wilson, C. 1995 *Hidden in the Blood: A Personal Investigation of AIDS in the Yucatan*. New York: Columbia University Press.

Wilson, D. S. 2002 *Darwin's Cathedral: Evolution, Religion, and the Nature of Society*. Chicago: University of Chicago Press.

Wilson, M. L., and R. W. Wrangham 2003 Intergroup Relations in Chimpanzees. *Annual Review of Anthropology* 32: 363–392.

Wilson, R., ed. 1996 *Human Rights: Culture and Context: Anthropological Perspectives*. Chicago: Pluto Press.

Winslow, J. H., and A. Meyer 1983 The Perpetrator at Piltdown. *Science* 83 (September): 33–43.

Winter, R. 2001 Religions of the World: Number of Adherents; Names of Houses of Worship; Names of Leaders; Rates of Growth. http://www.religioustolerance.org/worldrel.htm.

Winzeler, R. L. 1995 *Latah in Southeast Asia: The Ethnography and History of a Culture-Bound Syndrome*. New York: Cambridge University Press.

Wittfogel, K. A. 1957 *Oriental Despotism: A Comparative Study of Total Power*. New Haven, CT: Yale University Press.

Wolf, E. R. 1966 *Peasants*. Englewood Cliffs, NJ: Prentice Hall. 1982 *Europe and the People without History*. Berkeley: University of California Press. 1999 *Envisioning Power: Ideologies of Dominance and Crisis*. Berkeley: University of California Press.

Wolf, E. R., with S. Silverman 2001 *Pathways of Power: Building an Anthropology of the Modern World*. Berkeley: University of California Press.

Wolpoff, M., B. Senut, M. Pickford, and J. Hawks 2002 Sahelanthropus or "Sahelpithecus"? *Nature* 419: 581–582.

Wolpoff, M. H. 1980a *Paleoanthropology*. Boston: McGraw-Hill. 1980b Cranial Remains of Middle Pleistocene Hominids. *Journal of Human Evolution* 9: 339–358. 1999 *Paleoanthropology*, 2nd ed. New York: McGraw-Hill.

Wolpoff, M. H., and R. Caspari 1997 *Race and Human Evolution*. New York: Simon & Schuster.

Woolard, K. A. 1989 *Double Talk: Bilingualism and the Politics of Ethnicity in Catalonia*. Stanford, CA: Stanford University Press.

World Almanac & Book of Facts Published annually. New York: Newspaper Enterprise Association.

World Health Organization 1997 *World Health Report*. Geneva: World Health Organization.

World Malaria Report 2005 2005 Roll Back Malaria. World Health Organization, UNICEF. http://rbm.who.int/wmr2005/pdf/WMReport_lr.pdf.

Worsley, P. 1984 *The Three Worlds: Culture and World Development*. Chicago: University of Chicago Press. 1985 (orig. 1959) Cargo Cults. In *Readings in Anthropology 85/86*. Guilford, CT: Dushkin.

Wrangham, R. W. 1980 An Ecological Model of Female-Bonded Primate Groups. *Behavior* 75: 262–300. 1987 The Significance of African Apes for Reconstructing Human Social Evolution. In *The Evolution of Human Behavior: Primate Models*, ed. W. G. Kinzey, pp. 51–71. Albany: State University of New York Press.

Wrangham, R. W., ed. 1994 *Chimpanzee Cultures*. Cambridge, MA: Harvard University Press.

Wrangham, R., W. McGrew, F. de Waal, and P. Heltne, eds. 1994 *Chimpanzee Cultures*. Cambridge, MA: Harvard University Press.

Wrangham, R. W., and D. Peterson 1996 *Demonic Males: Apes and the Origins of Human Violence*. Boston: Houghton Mifflin.

Wright, H. T. 1977 Recent Research on the Origin of the State. *Annual Review of Anthropology* 6: 379–397.

Wright, H. T., and G. A. Johnson 1975 Population, Exchange, and Early State Formation in Southwestern Iran. *American Anthropologist* 77: 267–289. 1994 Prestate Political Formations. In *Chiefdoms and Early States in the Near East: The Organizational Dynamics of Complexity*, ed. G. Stein and M. S. Rothman, *Monographs in World Archaeology* 18: 67–84. Madison, WI: Prehistory Press.

Wright, S., ed. 1994 *Anthropology of Organizations*. London: Routledge.

Wulff, R. M., and S. J. Fiske, eds. 1987 *Anthropological Praxis: Translating Knowledge into Action*. Boulder, CO: Westview Press.

Yanagisako, S. J. 2002 *Producing Culture and Capital: Family Firms in Italy*. Princeton, NJ: Princeton University Press.

Yellen, J. E., A. S. Brooks, and E. Cornelissen. 1995 A Middle Stone Age Worked Bone Industry from Katanda, Upper Semliki Valley, Zaire. *Science* 268: 553–556.

Yetman, N., ed. 1991 *Majority and Minority: The Dynamics of Race and Ethnicity in American Life*, 5th ed. Boston: Allyn & Bacon. 1999 *Majority and Minority: The Dynamics of Race and Ethnicity in American Life*, 6th ed. Boston: Allyn & Bacon.

Young, W. C. 1996 *The Rashaayada Bedouin: Arab Pastoralists of Eastern Sudan*. Fort Worth: Harcourt Brace.

Yurchak, A. 2002 Entrepreneurial Governmentality in Postsocialist Russia. In *The New Entrepreneurs of Europe and Asia*, ed. V. Bonnell and T. Gold, p. 301. Armonk, NY: M. E. Sharpe. 2005 *Everything Was Forever Until It Was No More: The Last Soviet Generation*. Princeton, NJ: Princeton University Press.

Zeder, Melinda A. 1997 The American Archaeologist: Results of the 1994 SAA Census. *SAA Bulletin* 15(2): 12–17.

Zou, Y., and E. T. Trueba 2002 *Ethnography and Schools: Qualitative Approaches to the Study of Education*. Lanham, MD: Rowman and Littlefield.

Zulaika, J. 1988 *Basque Violence: Metaphor and Sacrament*. Reno: University of Nevada Press.

CREDITS

Photo Credits

FRONT MATTER
Page xxxi: (top) Nicolas Monu/iStockphoto, (bottom) Sean Locke/iStockphoto

CHAPTER 1
Page 3: Steve McCurry/Magnum Photos; p. 6 (bottom): Fred R. Conrad/The New York Times/Redux; p. 8: ©National Anthropological Archives. Neg.#906-B; p. 9: ©Vincent Laforet/Redux Pictures; p. 11: ©Peter Bennett/Eyevine; p. 14: Courtesy Maria Alejandra Perez; p. 15: ©Bruce Avera Hunter/National Geographic Image Collection; p. 17 (bottom): AP Images/Obama Presidential Campaign; p. 18: Ton Koene/Peter Arnold; p. 20 (top): ©Ricardo Funari/Brazil Photos/Alamy

CHAPTER 2
p. 25: Gregory Adam/Lonely Planet Images; p. 28: Bill Bachmann/PhotoEdit, Inc.; p. 29 (left): ©William Gottlieb/Corbis; p. 29 (right): ©Jamie Rose/Aurora Photos; p. 30: ©Francesco Broli/The New York Times/Redux Pictures; p. 33: Courtesy Pavlina Lobb; p. 34: ©Kenneth Garrett/National Geographic Image Collection; p. 35: ©OSF/Clive Bromhall/Animals, Animals; p. 36 (top): ©Hideo Haga/Image Works; p. 36 (bottom): ©Carl D. Walsh/Aurora Photos; p. 37: ©Sean Sprague/Image Works; p. 39: ©Joao Silva/Picturenet Africa; p. 41 (both): ©Dan Levine/AFP/Getty Images; p. 43: ©Joerg Mueller/Visum/Image Works

CHAPTER 3
p. 49: Mark Edwards/Peter Arnold; p. 51: ©Will & Deni McIntyre/Corbis; p. 52: ©Charles Harbutt/Actuality, Inc.; p. 53: ©Mike Yamashita/Woodfin Camp & Associates; p. 54: ©Ozier Muhammad/The New York Times/Redux Pictures; p. 56: ©J.L. Dugast/Lineair/Peter Arnold; p. 57: ©Betty Press/Woodfin Camp & Associates; p. 58: Christina Kennedy/Photo Edit, Inc.; p. 60 ©Eros Hoagland/Zuma Press; p. 61: ©Carl D. Walsh/Aurora Photos; p. 62: ©UNEP/Peter Arnold; p. 63: Courtesy Professor Marietta Baba, Michigan State University

CHAPTER 4
p. 71: Javier Trueba/Madrid Scientific Films/Photo Researchers, Inc.; p. 75 (both): ©Harley Soltes/The New York Times/Redux Pictures; p. 76 (all): Courtesy of Dolores R. Piperno, National Museum of Natural History, Smithsonian Institution; p. 77: Melissa Farlow/Aurora Photos; p. 78: ©Richard T. Nowitz/Corbis; p. 79: ©Dr. Jerome Rose, University of Arkansas; p. 82 (top): Georg Gerster/Photo Researchers, Inc.; p. 82 (bottom): ©Kenneth Garrett/National Geographic Image Collection; p. 83: ©Jonathan Blair/Corbis; p. 84: ©Mary Rhodes/Earth Scenes/Animals Animals; p. 86 (left): Nigel Pavitt/John Warburton-Lee Photography Ltd/Aurora; p. 86 (right): Charles V. Angelo/Photo Researchers, Inc.; p. 87: ©Jim Sugar/Corbis

CHAPTER 5
p. 93: Bob Sacha; p. 94: ©Michael Newman/PhotoEdit; p. 95: ©Noah's Ark by Edward Hicks, 1846, 261/2 × 301/2, Oil on canvas, Philadelphia Museum of Art, Bequest of Lisa Norris Elkins [1950-92-7]; p. 97 (top): ©English Heritage/Topham-HIP/Image Works; p. 97 (bottom): ©Michael Tweedie/Photo Researchers; p. 99: ©National Library of Medicine; p. 102: ©Dr. Gopal Mujrti/PhotoTake; p. 104: ©Ethel Wolvovitz/Image Works; p. 105: ©Cathy & Gordon ILLG/Animals Animals; p. 106: Holly Wilmeth/Aurora Photos; p. 108: ©Alfred Pasieka/Peter Arnold; p. 109: Courtesy Maryna Yevhenivna Bazylevych

CHAPTER 6
p. 115: Gary Houlder/Getty Images; p. 117: ©Paul Grebliunas/Getty Images; p. 119: ©Werner Forman/Corbis; p. 120 (top): ©Sabine Vielmo/Argus Fotoarchiv/Peter Arnold; p. 120 (center): ©Darrell Gulin/Corbis; p. 120 (bottom): ©Medford Taylor/National Geographic Image Collection; p. 121: ©Steve McCurry/Magnum Photos; p. 122: Courtesy Natasha Musalem-Perez; p. 124: Richard Lord/PhotoEdit, Inc.; p. 125 (top): ©Jan Spieczny/Peter Arnold; p. 125 (bottom): ©Nancy Brown/Getty Images; p. 126 (top): AP Images/Tony Camerano; p. 126 (bottom): ©National Library of Medicine; p. 127 (top): ©Robert Caputo/Stock Boston; p. 127 (bottom): ©Bryan & Cherry Alexander/Arctic Photo; p. 129: ©Phil Schermeister/Corbis

CHAPTER 7
p. 135: Paul Souders/Getty Images; p. 141: Front cover from AMONG ORANGUTANS: RED APES AND THE RISE OF HUMAN CULTURE by Carel van Schaik, reprinted by permission of the publisher, The Belknap Press of Harvard University Press, Cambridge, Mass. Copyright @ 2004 by the President and Fellows of Harvard College.; p. 142 (top): ©All rights reserved, Image Archives, Denver Museum of Nature and Science; p. 142 (center left): ©Tom McHugh/Photo Researchers; p. 143 (top): ©Frans Lanting/Corbis; p. 143 (bottom): ©Karen Kasmauski/National Geographic Image Collection; p. 145 (top): ©Mack Henley/Visuals Unlimited; p. 145 (bottom): Fotograf/Peter Arnold; p. 146: AP Images; p. 147: Michael Nichols/National Geographic/Getty Images; p. 149: ©Gallo Images/Corbis; p. 153 (left): ©Tom McHugh/Photo Researchers; p. 153 (right): ©Roland Seitre/Peter Arnold; p. 155 (left): ©Russell L. Ciochon, University of Iowa; p. 155 (right): ©Luis Gene/AFP/Getty Images

CHAPTER 8
p. 161: Kenneth Garrett; p. 163: ©Natural History Museum, London; p. 164: ©Lealisa Westerhoff/AFP/Getty Images; p. 166: ©AFP/Getty Images; p. 168 (left): Tim White; p. 168 (right): David Brill; p. 169: Tim White; p. 170: ©Kenneth Garrett; p. 171: ©John Reader/SPL/Photo Researchers; p. 172: ©Kenneth Garrett/National Geographic Image Collection; p. 173: ©Lionel Bret/Photo Researchers; p. 177 (both): ©Natural History Museum, London; p. 178 (top): ©Luba Dmytryk Gudz/National Geographic Image Collection; p. 178 (center): ©Des Bartlett/Photo Researchers; p. 179 (both): ©Peter Bostrom

CHAPTER 9
p. 185: Kenneth Garrett; p. 187: ©Kenneth Garrett; p. 188: ©Natural History Museum, London; p. 189: ©Kenneth Garrett/National Geographic Image Collection; p. 191 (left): ©David Brill; p. 191 (center): ©John Reader/Photo Researchers; p. 191 (right): ©Natural History Museum, London; p. 192: ©Kenneth Garrett; p. 194 (all): Courtesy of H. Baba, National Science Museum, Tokyo; p. 197: Patrick Kovarik/AFP/Getty Images; p. 198: ©Conrad P. Kottak; p. 199 (top): AP Images/Frank Franklin II; p. 199 (bottom): ©Natural History Museum, London; p. 201 (top): ©Natural History Museum, London; p. 201 (bottom): ©Philippe Plailly/Photo Researchers; p. 202 (top): ©Dr. Peter Brown

CHAPTER 10
p. 207: Sisse Brimberg/National Geographic Society; p. 209 (all): ©Luba Dmytryk Gudz/National Geographic Image Collection; p. 210 (top): ©Natural History Museum, London; p. 210 (bottom): Courtesy Professor William Calvin, University of Washington School of Medicine; p. 214: Courtesy Dr. Curtis W. Marean, Arizona State University; p. 215 (top left): ©Lindsay Hebberd/Woodfin Camp; p. 215 (top right): ©Toby Canham/Pressnet/Topham/Image Works; p. 215 (bottom): ©Visual Arts Library of London/Alamy; p. 217: JM Labat/Photo Researchers; p. 218: Courtesy Dr. Curtis W. Marean, Arizona State University; p. 221: Published by Permission of Traditional Owners, photo Prof. J.M. Bowler; p. 223 (top): ©Robert Frerck/Odyssey Productions; p. 223 (bottom): ©Roger Green, Anthropology Photographic Archive, University of Auckland; p. 225: ©Gianni Dagli Orti/Corbis; p. 226 (top left): ©Gonzalez/laif/Aurora Photos; p. 226 (top right): ©©Albrecht G. Schaefer/Corbis

CHAPTER 11
p. 231: Steve McCurry/Magnum Photos; p. 233: ©Gustavo Tomsich/Corbis; p. 234: ©Erich Lessing/Art Resource NY; p. 236: ©Will Yurman/Image Works; p. 238: ©A Tovy/Robertstock/IPNstock; p. 240: ©Michael Andrews/Earth Scenes/Animals Animals; p. 242 (top): ©Craig Lovell/Corbis; p. 242 (bottom): ©Ron Giling/Lineair/Peter Arnold; p. 243: AP Images/Marco Ugarte; p. 245: ©Mariana Bazo/Reuters/Corbis; p. 246: ©2006 Banco de Mexico Diego Rivera & Frida Kahlo Museums Trust. Av. Cinco de Mayo No. 2, Col. Centro, Del. Cuauhtemoc 06059, Mexico, D.F. Photo: Schalkwijk/Art Resource NY; p. 249: ©John Isaac/Still Pictures/Peter Arnold

CHAPTER 12
p. 255: Jeffrey Becom/Peter Arnold, Inc.; p. 259: ©Roger Wood/Corbis; p. 261: ©David James/Entertainment Pictures; p. 263: ©Ancient Art and Architecture Collection Ltd./Bridgeman Art Library; p. 264: ©Robert Grossman; p. 265 (top): ©Heinz Plenge/Peter Arnold;

NAME INDEX

Page references followed by italicized "*f*" or "*t*" refer to figures or tables, respectively.

A

Abelmann, N., 354
Abu-Lughod, L., 535
Academic American Encyclopedia,
 557*f*, 558*f*
Adams, R. M., 268
Adepegba, C. O., 519
Adherents.com, 506*f*
Ahmed, A. S., 350
Aiello, L., 167
Aikens, C. M., 233
Akazawa, T., 233
Albanel, C., 498
Aldenderfer, M., 128, 129
Alemseged, Z., 164, 164*f*
Alfred, M., 296
Allen, J. A., 130, 220, 221
Amadiume, I., 428, 477
American Anthropological Association
 (AAA), 340, 341
Amoa-Mensah, P., 119
Anderson, B. G., 62, 63, 347, 587
Anderson, R. L., 61
Angier, N., 80, 81, 138
Annenberg/CPB Exhibits, 276
Anton, S. C., 178, 188
Antoun, R. T., 511
Aoki, M. Y., 344
Aoyagi, K., 59
Appadurai, A., 43, 59, 587, 588, 589
Appiah, K. A., 344
Arens, W., 538
Arensberg, C., 64
Armelagos, G. J., 62, 107, 249
Arrighi, G., 549
Arsian, A. M., 484
Arsuaga, J. L., 195, 196
Asani, A., 508
Asfaw, B., 167, 168*f*, 179, 180, 209
Ashcroft, B., 559
Askew, K. M., 535
Ataturk, M. K., 484
Austen, J., 534

B

Baca, K., 61
Baer, H. A., 61, 62
Bailey, E. J., 63, 288
Bailey, R. C., 363
Balleza, M., 451
Banerjee, M., 424
Banton, M., 60
Barlow, K., 471, 472
Barnaby, F., 407
Barnard, A., 366
Barnes, E., 61
Baro, M., 62
Baron, D., 323
Barringer, F., 339
Barth, F., 337, 348
Bar-Yosef, O., 210
Bazylevych, M. Y., 109
Beach, F. A., 436, 437
Beall, C., 128
Beckerman, S., 458
Beeman, W., 326
Bellah, R. N., 504
Benedict, R., 8, 295, 298*f*, 411

Bennett, J. W., 11
Berdahl, R. M., 293
Bergmann, K. C., 130
Berkleyan, 179, 180
Berlin, B. D., 320, 321
Bernard, H. R., 18, 283, 294, 330
Berns, G. S., 80
Bernstein, N., 591
Berra, Y., 541
Berryman, H., 74
Best, A. L., 7
Bettelheim, B., 529, 530
Bhandari, M., 424
Bicker, A., 320
Bilefsky, D., 485
Binford, L. R., 193, 200, 235, 236
Binford, S. R., 200
Bingham, H., 73
Bird-David, N., 381
Birdsell, J. B., 105*f*
Bjuremalm, H., 559
Black, N. J., 419
Blackwood, E., 427, 436
Blanton, R. E., 273
Bloch, M., 326
Blumenstyk, G., 565
Boas, F., 10, 42, 121, 294, 295, 296,
 304, 305*t*
Boaz, N. T., 142, 190, 191
Bodley, J. H., 55, 549, 556, 560, 564, 566,
 566*t*, 575, 584
Boesch, C., 33, 144
Bogaard, A., 239
Bogin, B., 104, 130
Bogoras, W., 503
Bohannan, P., 522
Bolton, R., 62
Bonnichsen, R., 223
Bonvillain, N., 419
Borges, E., 590, 590*f*
Borges, J. O., 590, 590*f*, 591
Borges, M., 590, 590*f*
Borges, T., 590*f*
Botto, C., 397
Boule, M., 201
Bourdieu, P., 303, 304, 305*t*, 326,
 405, 409
Bourque, S. C., 419
Bowie, F., 493
Brace, C. L., 127, 199
Bradley, B. J., 144
Brady, T., 539, 539*f*
Braidwood, R. J., 235
Braudel, F., 549
Breedlove, E., 320
Bremen, J. V., 556
Brenneis, D., 326
Brettell, C. B., 419
Briggs, C. L., 61, 63
Brooke, J., 592
Brooks, A. S., 214
Broom, R., 177*f*
Brown, A., 562
Brown, D., 35
Brown, F. H., 178, 188, 209
Brown, J. K., 427
Brown, M. F., 73
Brown, P. J., 12, 61, 62, 63
Browne, J., 468
Brunet, M., 166*f*
Bryant, V., 77, 243, 244, 245
Burbank, V., 478, 479

Burley, D., 224, 225
Burling, R., 319
Burns, J. F., 501
Bush, G. W., 98, 292
Buvinic, M., 435
Buxton, L. H. D., 127

C

Cabrera-Schneider, J. N., 404
Calhoun, C., 435
Campbell, B. C., 30, 31
Cann, R. L., 87, 121, 211
Carey, B., 313
Carlson, T. J. S., 320
Carneiro, R. L., 257, 258, 263, 368,
 402, 459
Carsten, J., 286
Carter, J., 314
Casper, L. M., 451, 452*t*
Cernea, M. M., 56
Ceuppens, B., 593
Chagnon, N. A., 376, 395, 396, 397,
 470, 471
Chakravartti, M. R., 126
Chambers, E., 15
Champion, T., 233
Chang, K. C., 240
Chaplin, G., 124
Chavez, H., 396
Cheater, A. P., 391
Cheboi, K., 167
Cheman, K., 61
Cheney, D. L., 144
Childe, V. G., 234
Chirac, J., 498
Chiseri-Strater, E., 288
Chomsky, N., 318
Christo, 520*f*, 521
Ciochon, R. L., 138, 155, 155*f*,
 190, 191
Clarke, S. C., 483*t*
Clément, G., 499
Clinton, W. J., 326
Close, R., 436, 437, 437*f*
Coates, J., 324
Cody, D., 557, 558
Cohen, M., 62, 249, 338
Cohen, P., 293
Cohen, R., 483
Cohen, Y. A., 363
Collard, M., 167
Collier, S. J., 44
Colson, E., 288, 289
Columbus, C., 106, 550
Conkey, M., 523
Conklin, H. C., 320
Connah, G., 269
Connor, W., 347
Cook, J., 225
Cooke, R. G., 244
Cooper, F., 305*t*, 556, 559
Coppens, Y., 167
Cornelissen, E., 214
Coskun, H., 485
Costa, A., 534
Crapo, R. H., 493
Crenson, M., 524
Cresswell, T., 43
Crick, F. H. C., 101
Crocker, W., 395
Crosby, A. W., Jr., 550
Cultural Survival Quarterly, 397

Solheim, W. G., II, 240
Solway, J., 364, 426
Sorid, D., 323
Sotomayor, S., 339, 340, 341
Spanier, G., 293
Spencer, C. S., 274
Spickard, P., 337
Spindler, G. D., 58
Spiro, M. E., 15
Spoor, F., 165, 178, 188
Squier, E. G., 271
Srivastava, J., 370
Stafford, T. W., Jr., 222
Stanish, C., 551
Stark, R., 512
Statistical Abstract of the United States, 337t, 433, 433t, 434t, 435t, 451, 453t, 511t, 566
Statistics Canada, 343, 344f
Stearman, K., 344, 345
Steckel, R. H., 550
Steegman, A. T., Jr., 130
Steinfels, P., 511
Stern, A., 149
Stevens, T., 577
Stevenson, D., 59
Stevenson, R. F., 258
Steward, J. H., 299, 303, 305t
Stewart, P. J., 63
Stiner, M. C., 214
Stoler, A. L., 304, 305t, 419, 556, 559
Stone, A., 211
Stoneking, M., 87, 121, 211
Stothert, K. E., 243
Strachan, T., 103
Strathern, A., 63
Stratmann, D., 523
Stringer, C., 84, 197
Sukovic, M., 429
Sunstein, B. S., 288
Susman, R. L., 147
Susser, I., 61, 62
Sussman, R. W., 78
Suttles, W., 383
Suwa, G., 167
Sweatnam, T., 87, 87f
Swift, M., 427

T
Tacuma, 370
Tague, R. G., 175
Taieb, M., 170
Tanaka, J., 393
Tannen, D., 13, 316, 321, 323, 324
Tanner, N., 428
Taylor, C., 64
Terrace, H. S., 315
Terrell, J. E., 223, 224, 226
Thomas, D. H., 73
Thomas, L., 326
Thompson, W., 549
Thomson, A., 127
Tice, K., 53
Tiffin, H., 559
Titiev, M., 482
Tiwari, S., 323
Tom, E., 576f

Tom, S., 576f, 577
Toner, R., 354
Toth, N., 179
Townsend, P. K., 63
Traphagan, J., 59
Trask, L., 352
Trehub, S. E., 524
Trivedi, B. P., 315
Trudgill, P., 321, 324t
Tso, E., 526
Turnbull, C., 363
Turner, V. W., 298, 301, 302f, 305t, 493, 496, 497, 497t
Tylor, E. B., 27, 294, 295, 305t, 473, 493

U
Ulman, H., 539
Umiker-Sebeok, J., 315
Underhill, P. A., 220
U. S. Census Bureau, 343f, 349, 349f, 450, 452t
Ussher, J., 95

V
Valentine, P., 458, 459
Van Cantfort, T. E., 313, 314, 315
Vayda, A. P., 383, 384
Veblen, T., 564
Veja, 539, 541, 542
Vekua, A., 193
Verano, J. W., 107
Verdery, K., 562
Vidal, J., 59
Viegas, J., 149
Vierich, H., 393
Vigil, J. D., 59, 60, 61
Vigilant, L., 144
Villems, R., 220
Vincent, J., 303
Viola, H. J., 550
Vogel, F., 126
Von Daniken, E., 260, 261
Voorhies, B., 426, 427, 427t, 430, 431, 432
Voth, H. R., 73

W
Wade, N., 199, 201
Wade, P., 193
Wagatsuma, H., 344
Wagener, D. K., 61
Wagley-Kottak, I., 289
Walker, A., 170, 176
Walker, P. L., 550, 551
Wallace, A. F. C., 492, 503, 507
Wallace, A. R., 96, 300
Wallerstein, I. M., 549, 555, 556
Ward, M. C., 419
Ward, S. C., 177
Wardley, J., 425
Wareing, S., 326
Warhol, A., 521
Warren, K. B., 419, 593, 594
Waters, M. R., 222
Watson, J. D., 101
Watson, P., 41f
Watson, P. J., 265

Watts, D. P., 34
Watzman, H., 79
Weber, M., 300, 405, 505, 554, 555, 555f
Wedel, J., 562, 563
Weiner, A., 15
Weiner, J. S., 96, 127
Weiss, H., 166, 277
Weiss, K. M., 127
Wendorf, F., 239
Wenke, R. J., 235
Westermarck, E., 472
Wetherall, W. O., 344, 345
We'wha, 504f
White, L. A., 27, 299, 300, 305t, 473
White, R., 176, 192f, 193f, 195, 214, 236, 240, 248
White, T., 78, 166, 167, 168f, 178, 179, 180, 188, 209
Whiting, J. M., 18
Whitten, N., 330
Whorf, B. L., 318
Whyte, M. F., 421t, 422t
Wieringa, S., 436
Wiesnner, P., 381
Wilder, T., 270
Wilford, J. N., 107, 169, 188, 194, 202, 209, 213, 214, 224, 225, 226, 245, 266, 330, 523
Wilk, R. R., 374, 535
Williams, B., 342, 350
Williams, L. M., 472
Williamson, B., 77
Wilmsen, E. N., 393, 426
Wilson, A. C., 87, 121, 211
Wilson, D. S., 96
Wilson, M. L., 144, 148
Winslow, J. H., 85
Winter, R., 506
Wissler, C., 296
Wittfogel, K. A., 257
Wolf, E. R., 10, 303, 304, 305t, 369, 374, 377, 391, 556
Wolpoff, M. H., 165, 173, 176, 201
Wood, B., 166
Woods, T., 342f
World Malaria Report, 125
Worsley, P., 507
Wrangham, R. W., 144, 148, 471
Wright, H. T., 274, 275
Wright, R., 51
Wright, S., 265

Y
Yardley, W., 577
Yellen, J. E., 214
Yeltsin, B., 562
Yetman, N., 342
Yurchak, A., 356, 562

Z
Zechenter, E., 363
Zeder, M., 84
Zeh, T. R., 80
Zenner, W., 59
Zias, J., 78f
Zohary, D., 236
Zulaika, J., 352, 353

SUBJECT INDEX

Page references followed by italicized "*f*" or "*t*" refer to figures or tables, respectively.

A

AAA. *See* American Anthropological Association
ABO blood groups, 100, 101*f*, 125–127
Aboriginal people (Australia)
  ceremonies of increase, 217
  educational opportunities for, 556
  as foragers, 363
  Intellectual Property Rights of, 73
  Rambo popularity among, 587
absolute dating, 85–87, 86*f*
Abu Hureyra (Syria), 236
academic/theoretical anthropology, 51, 52
accelerator mass spectrometry, 245
acculturation, 43, 584
Aché people, 363–364
Acheulian tools, 190–192, 191*f*, 192*f*
achieved statuses, 337, 540–542
action theory, 303
adaptation. *See also* natural selection
  to altitude, 5–6, 7*t*, 128–129, 129*f*
  body build and, 127, 127*f*, 130
  cold-adapted Neandertals, 199–200
  cultural, 6–7
  definition of, 5
  disease susceptibility and, 125–127, 126*f*
  for economic production, 362–363, 373*t*
  facial features, 127
  by *Homo erectus*, 192–193
  phenotypical, 130–131
  sickle-cell anemia and, 105–108, 105*f*, 124–125, 249
adaptive strategies, 362–363, 373*t*. *See also* economic production
adaptive traits, 104
adat, 430
adoption, cultural attitudes towards, 109, 446
aerial photos, 77, 77*f*
aerosols, 579*t*
aesthetics, 519. *See also* arts
affinals, 460, 460*f*
affinity, relationships of, 477
Afghanistan, Taliban in, 501–502, 502*f*
Africa. *See also specific countries*
  Bantu migrations, 269
  foraging in, 363
  Great Rift Valley, 85–86, 86*f*, 164–165, 173*f*
  HIV/AIDS in, 62
  "practical anthropology" in colonies, 52
  rise of states in, 269–272
  slavery diaspora from, 118–119
African Americans
  Black English Vernacular, 326–328, 327*f*
  gender roles of, 432
  in Ghana, 118–119
  hypodescent rule and, 342
  in Los Angeles riots, 354
  négritude and, 347
  population in the United States, 349, 349*f*
  slavery of, 118–119, 340

agency, 38, 303, 304
"Age of Discovery," 556–557
age sets, 399–400
agnates, 470
agriculture. *See also* farming (ancient); horticulture; irrigation systems
  Basque, 353
  costs and benefits of, 369–372
  in the cultivation continuum, 369
  development projects in, 581
  domesticated animals, 237–238, 240, 246–247, 368
  gender and, 431–432, 431*f*
  intensification of, 369–372
  monocrop production, 552
  overfarming, 276
  peasants in, 379–380
  rise of cities and, 268
  state formation and, 257, 372
  terracing, 368–369, 369*f*
ahimsa, 500, 501*f*
AIDs, 62
Ainu people, 75
Alaska. *See also* Inuit people; Pacific Northwest peoples
  Aleuts, 529, 529*f*
  climate change and, 576–577, 576*f*
Aleuts, 529, 529*f*
alienation in industrial economies, 376, 377*f*
alleles, 99–100, 109
Allen's rule, 130
alluvial desert, 235, 237
alpaca, 242
alpenhorns, 525*f*
altitude, adaptation to, 5–6, 7*t*, 128–129, 129*f*
ambilineal descent, 455
American Anthropological Association (AAA)
  Code of Ethics, 53, 73, 76, 292
  on collaboration with host country, 73, 76
  on race, 339, 340–341
  on study of terrorism, 292–293, 292*f*
  subgroups of, 305
American Indians. *See* Native North Americans
American Kinship: A Cultural Account (Schneider), 302
American Sign Language (ASL), 313–315, 314*f*
"American Tragedy" (Dreiser), 536
Americas. *See also* Native North Americans; Pacific Northwest peoples; *specific country*
  first farmers in, 241–246, 241*f*, 242*f*, 243*f*, 245*f*, 246*f*
  herding in, 241–242, 242*f*
  New World monkeys, 142, 143
  settling of, 221–223, 222*f*, 223*f*
AMHs. *See* anatomically modern humans
Among Orangutans (van Schaik), 140–141
anabolic steroids, 542, 542*f*
analogies, 138
anatomically modern humans (AMHs)
  art by, 523
  behavioral modernity in, 212–214, 214*f*, 215*f*
  Cro Magnons, 200, 210, 210*f*

  evidence for migration from Africa, 208–211, 209*f*, 210*f*
  evolution of, 200
  glacial retreat and, 216–217
  Neandertals and, 210, 211, 212–213
  settling of Australia by, 219–221, 220*f*
  settling of the Pacific islands by, 223–226, 223*f*, 224*f*, 225*f*, 226*f*
  settling the Americas by, 221–223, 222*f*, 223*f*
  summary of data on, 195*t*
  technological advances, 215–216, 216*f*
ancestry, knowledge of, 475
Ancient Society (Morgan), 294
Andes
  adaptation to altitude in, 5–6, 7*t*, 128–129, 129*f*
  causes of state formation in, 257–258, 258*f*
  Inca suspension bridges in, 268–269, 270–271, 270*f*
  invention of farming in, 241–242, 241*f*
  Moche people, 265*f*
  Ñanchoc Valley, 244–245
  plant domestication in, 244–245, 245*f*
anemia, 276
animal domestication, 237–238, 240, 246–247, 368
animism, 493
Anopheles mosquito, 108*f*
anthropoids, 139, 153–154
anthropological theory, 294–304
  Boasians, 295–297, 296*f*
  configurationalism, 298–299, 298*f*
  contemporary, 304–306
  cultural materialism, 300, 300*f*
  culturology, 300–301
  determinism and science in, 300
  evolutionism, 294–295
  functionalism, 297–298, 297*f*, 298*f*
  hegemony, 304, 409
  neoevolutionism, 299–300
  processual approaches, 303
  structuralism, 302–303
  symbolic and interpretive anthropology, 301–302
  timeline and key works in, 305*t*
  world-system theory and political economy, 303–304
anthropology. *See also* applied anthropology
  academic/theoretical, 51, 52
  archaeological, 8, 10–12, 50, 51*t*
  biocultural perspective, 9, 9*f*
  biological, 8, 12, 50–51, 51*t*, 73–79
  business and, 64–65
  careers in, 65–66
  cultural, 8–10, 10*t*, 14, 15, 51*t*
  definition of, 5
  development, 54–56
  ecological, 299, 579–584
  economic, 374, 377
  education and, 58–59
  environmental, 579–584, 580*f*, 581*f*, 582*f*
  forensic, 51, 51*f*, 78
  four-field, 295, 304
  general, 8–9
  historical, 303–304
  humanities and, 13–14
  linguistic, 8, 12–13, 51*t*

medical, 61–64
molecular, 78–79
paleoanthropology, 12, 73, 79–83, 82f, 85
psychological, 14–15
sociology and, 14
symbolic and interpretive, 301–302
urban, 59–61
anthropology and education, 58–59
anthropometry, 78, 78f
antibodies, 126
antimodernism, 510
anxiety, religion and, 495
apartheid, 351
apes, 144–149
bonobos, 147–149
chimpanzees (*See* chimpanzees)
communication in, 313
endangered, 148
evolution of, 154–156, 154f, 155f
gibbons, 144, 145, 145f, 150
Gigantopithecus, 154–155, 155f
gorillas, 140, 146–148, 146f, 177, 314–315
orangutans, 139, 140–141, 145–146, 145f, 148
sign language in, 313–315, 314f
social groups of, 144
taxonomy of, 137
tool use by, 34
traits of, 144, 144f
apical ancestor, 454
applied anthropology, 49–66
academic anthropology and, 51, 52
business and, 64–65
careers in, 65–66
definition of, 15, 50
development anthropology, 54–58
early applications, 52
education and, 58–59
ethnographic method in, 51
increased equity and, 55–56
indigenous models, 57–58
innovation strategies, 56–58
medical anthropology, 61–64
in New Orleans, 54–55
overview of, 50–51, 51t
roles of, 52–53
urban anthropology, 59–61
arboreal, 139, 143
arboreal theory, 151
archaeological anthropology, 8, 10–12, 50, 51t
archaeology
applied, 15
bioarchaeology, 76
excavation in, 81–83, 82f
kinds of, 83–84
public, 15, 54–55, 55f
systematic survey in, 80–81
tool use evidence in, 79
underwater, 11–12, 83f, 84
visible remains in, 76–77
archaic *Homo sapiens*, 194–198, 195t
archaic states, 402, 404. *See also* states
Ardi, 168–169, 168f
Ardipithecus, bipedalism in, 163
Ardipithecus kadabba, 167–168
Ardipithecus ramidus, 167–168, 168f
Arembepe, Brazil
first impressions of, 284–285, 284f, 285f
kinship in, 450
media coverage of events in, 586
racial classification in, 346
team research in, 289, 289f
Arenal volcano, 77
Ariaal people, 30–31, 30f
Armory Show of 1913, 527

artistic careers, 529–531
arts, 518–533
artistic careers, 529–531
arts and leisure industry, 532
cave paintings, 212–213, 217–219, 217f, 523
communication and, 526–527
continuity and change, 531–533
cultural transmission of, 527–529, 527f
definitions of, 518–519
ethnomusicology, 523–528, 523f, 525f
in Hong Kong, 526
individuality and, 522
locating, 520–522
politics and, 527
religion and, 519–520, 519f
representations of culture and, 526
Western *vs.* non-Western, 520
works of art, 522–523
ascribed status, 337, 345, 540–541
asexuality, 435–436
ASL (American Sign Language), 313–315, 314f
asphalt, 235f, 237
Assault on Paradise (Kottak), 450
assimilation, 347–348, 348f, 355, 356t, 592
associations, in science, 15–18
Atapuerca site (Spain), 196–197
attractiveness, cultural standards of, 9, 9f
Australia. *See also* Aboriginal people (Australia)
Austronesians, 223–224
foraging in, 363
indigenous education in, 556
Lake Mungo site, 221, 221f
settling of, 219–221, 220f
Tiwi people, 521, 530
australopithecines. *See also specific species*
chimps and *Homo* compared with, 173t
cranial capacity in, 173t, 176–177
diet of, 176
gracile, 175, 177, 177f, 178f
hyperrobust, 176, 177–178, 177f
robust, 175–177, 178f
sexual dimorphism in, 176
skulls of, 177f, 178f
species chronology, 170, 173t
split with *Homo*, 178
Australopithecus aethiopicus, 176
Australopithecus afarensis
cranial capacity of, 163, 172
dentition of, 171–172, 172f
fossils of, 164–165, 164f, 170–171
Lucy's baby, 164–165, 164f
mixture of apelike and hominin features in, 173–174
relationship to *Australopithecus robustus*, 176
sexual dimorphism in, 172–173
skull of, 178f
Australopithecus africanus, 175, 177, 177f, 178f
Australopithecus anamensis, 170, 172, 172f
Australopithecus boisei
classification of, 176
dentition of, 178f
ecological niche of, 177–178
extinction of, 180, 187
Homo habilis and, 187
skull of, 177f, 178f
Australopithecus garhi, 179–180
Australopithecus robustus, 175–177, 178f
Austronesians, 223–224
authoritarian systems, 561
authority, definition of, 391
autochthon, 593
autochthony, 593
awls, 216

Azande people, 438
Aztecs, 275, 275f

B
baboons, 143, 144
balanced polymorphism, 105–108
balanced reciprocity, 380–381
Bamana people, 519
bands
energy consumption in, 566t
gender in, 367, 393–394, 423, 423f, 426, 426f
old people in, 367
political organization of, 366–367, 392–395, 392f, 405t
theft in, 394
Bangladesh, rising sea levels and, 576
Bantu migrations, 269
baptism, 451
bargaining, 380
Barí people, 456, 458–459, 458f
barley, 235, 237, 237f
Basarwa San, 364–365, 366f, 393
baseball, magic in, 492, 495
base substitution mutation, 103
Basongye people, 524, 525f
Basques, 352–353, 352f, 355
Basseri people, 373, 401, 402f
Batak people, 10
beans, 242
behavioral ecology, 150
behavioral modernity, 212–214, 214f, 215f
bejel, 107
Benin (Nigeria), 271–272
berdaches, 477, 503, 504f
Bergmann's rule, 130
Beringia, 221, 222f, 223f
Betsileo people
descent groups among, 454
funerals of, 37
gender roles among, 431–432
polygyny in, 484
rice cultivation by, 374–375
scarcity and, 378–379, 379f
witchcraft accusations among, 502
world system and, 548
BEV (Black English Vernacular), 326–328, 327f
Bhasha Project, 323
BHP Billiton, 564–565
bifurcate collateral kinship terminology, 461–462, 462t
bifurcate merging kinship terminology, 460–461, 460f
bigfoot, 154
"big man," 398
bilateral kinship, 426, 431, 431f, 458–459
bioarchaeology, 76
biocultural perspective, 9, 9f
biological anthropology
applications of, 50–51, 51t
bone biology, 78
interests within, 8, 12
Kennewick Man, 73, 74–75
molecular anthropology, 78–79
multidisciplinary methods, 76–78
biomechanics, 78
biomedicine, 62–63
bipedalism
childhood dependency and, 163
evolution of, 163, 172f
grasping and, 139
importance of, 162
tool use and, 163–164
birth canal expansion, 175
birth control, 535–538, 535f
bisexuality, 435
bison, 399, 400f

complex societies, 291
computers, 322–323, 330
configurationalism, 298–299, 298f
conflict
  ethnic, 350–356, 352f, 354f, 355f, 356t
  Inuit on resolution of, 393–394
  role of, 298
  village head and, 395
Congo
  Basongye people, 524, 525f
  Katanda region, 214
  Mbuti people (pygmies), 382, 392, 420
conjectural history, 297
conscience collectif, 301
conservation schemes, 581–582, 581f, 582f
contagious magic, 495
continental drift, 151, 152f
continental shelf, 216
continental slope, 216
contract archaeologists, 84
control, religion and, 495
Convention on International Trade in Endangered Species, 148
convergent evolution, 138
cooperation, 34, 80–81
cooperatives, 57
Copán (Maya), 276, 276f
copper, 267
copula deletion, 327
core, in world-system theory, 549
cores, tool, 179, 179f
core values, 32
correlation, 19–20, 366–367
corruption, 562–563
cosmology, 498–499
cotton, 245
cranial capacity
  in archaic Homo sapiens, 195
  in australopithecines, 173t, 176–177
  in Australopithecus afarensis, 163, 172
  of Australopithecus boisei, 187
  in chimpanzees, 177
  in gorillas, 177
  of Homo erectus, 188, 192
  of Homo habilis, 187
  of Homo rudolfensis, 187
  hunting and, 189
  in Neandertals, 186, 200
creationism, 95, 95f, 98–99, 110
The Creation of Adam (Michelangelo), 519f
creativity, 532
creole languages, 318, 326
CRM. See cultural resource management
Cro Magnons, 200, 210, 210f
cross cousins, 469–470, 469f
cross-cultural perspective, 4, 5
crossdating, 86
crossing over, in genetics, 102–103
cultivation. See also agriculture
  cultivation continuum, 369
  horticulture, 367–368, 367f, 369
  intensification, 369–372
cultivation continuum, 369
cultural anthropology
  applications of, 51t
  ethnography (See ethnography)
  ethnology, 10, 10t, 15
  overview of, 8, 9–10, 10t
  sociology and, 14
cultural borrowing, 36
cultural colonialism, 355–356
cultural consultants, 287
cultural diversity. See diversity
cultural ecology. See ecological anthropology
cultural generalities, 296
cultural imperialism, 585–587, 585f

cultural materialism, 300, 300f
Cultural Materialism: The Struggle for a Science of Culture (Harris), 300
cultural relativism, 39, 521
cultural resource management (CRM)
  definition of, 15
  ethical ambiguities in, 52–53
  impact studies, 81
  restoration in, 53f
cultural rights, 39
cultural transmission, 314
culture, 26–44
  acculturation, 43, 584
  as adaptive or maladaptive, 32
  as all-encompassing, 29
  arts transmission through, 527–529, 527f
  assimilation, 347–348, 348f, 355, 356t, 592
  bifocality in, 290
  change mechanisms in, 42–43
  of consumption, 588–589, 588f
  cultural imperialism, 585–587, 585f
  definitions of, 5, 27, 29
  diffusion and, 42–43, 296–297
  evolutionary basis of, 32–35
  generality in, 35–36
  global system of images, 587–588
  hospitality and, 33
  ideal vs. real, 37
  indigenizing popular, 587, 587f
  individuals and, 37–38, 300–301
  as integrated, 29, 32
  as learned, 27
  levels of, 38, 38t
  mass vs. segmented, 518
  media and, 533–538, 533f, 534f, 535f
  nature and, 28–29
  nonverbal communication and, 316
  particularity in, 36–37
  practice theory and, 38
  primate society and, 33–34
  role of, 4
  as shared, 28
  sports in, 538–542, 539f, 540f, 541f, 542f
  as symbolic, 27–28
  universality in, 35
culture core, 299–300
culture shock, by ethnographers, 283, 284–285
Cultures of Multiple Fathers (Beckerman and Valentine), 458
culturology, 300–301
cuneiform writing, 266, 267f
curers, 63
cytoplasm, 101

D
Darfur region of Sudan, 354f, 585, 585f
dating methods, 84–88
  dendrochronology, 86–87, 87f
  fluorine absorption analysis, 85
  molecular dating, 87–88
  radiometric, 85–86, 86f, 212–213, 245
  relative dating, 85
  summary of, 87t
daughter languages, 328
de facto discrimination, 351, 356t
deforestation
  endangered primates in, 148–149
  global climate change and, 579t
  intensive agriculture and, 370
  motivations for behavior change, 582f, 583
  pressures for, 582–583
de jure discrimination, 351, 356t
demonstrated descent, 454

dendrochronology, 86–87, 87f
dentition
  of Ardipithecus, 164–165
  of Australopithecus afarensis, 171–172, 172f, 176
  of chimpanzees, 172f, 175f
  of hominins, 164–165
  of Homo, 175f
  of Homo erectus, 192
  of Homo rudolfensis, 187
  of Homo sapiens, 178f
  of humans, 172f
  hunting and, 189
  of Neandertals, 199
dependent variables, 17
descent. See also kinship
  ambilineal, 455
  demonstrated, 454
  descent groups, 57–58, 395, 427, 454–455
  families vs. descent groups, 455–456
  hypodescent rule, 342, 343, 344
  kinship calculation, 456–459
  local descent group, 454–455
  matrilineal, 14, 411, 427–428, 448–449, 454
  moiety organization, 469–470, 469f
  patrilineal, 427, 454, 455f
  residence rules, 455, 456f
  stipulated, 454
  unilineal, 454, 460–461
descent groups, 57–58, 395, 427, 454–455
descent rule, 342
descriptive linguistics, 317
determinism, 300
development anthropology, 54–58
development projects
  cultural compatibility of, 56–57
  equity and, 55–56
  impact studies for, 81
  innovation strategies, 56–58
  underdifferentiation fallacy, 57
diabetes, Type I, 125
diachronic science, 297
dialects, 322–323, 323f, 326, 328
diaries, of ethnographers, 283
diaspora, 118–119, 119f, 589, 589f
diet
  of archaic Homo sapiens, 198
  of australopithecines, 176
  of Australopithecus afarensis, 171–172
  of Australopithecus garhi, 179–180
  of Brazilians, 451
  postpartum sexual taboo and, 18, 18f
  in sedentary communities, 249
differential access, 404–405
diffusion
  cultural change through, 42–43
  Heyerdahl on, 260
  independent invention vs., 296–297
  of romantic love concept, 478–479, 479f
digging, 82–83
digital divide, 323
diglossia, 322, 328
directional selection, 104–105
direct rule, 558
Disaster Mortuary Operational Response Teams (Dmort), 55
discourse, 409
discrimination
  against Basque Americans, 353
  definition of, 351, 356t
  against Haitians in the United States, 350
  against Japanese burakumin, 344–345, 345f
  segregation, 351
  slavery as, 118–119, 340

diseases
  blood type and, 125–127, 126*f*
  bubonic plague, 126
  cervical cancer, 126
  colonialism and, 62
  cultural factors in spread of, 62
  definition of, 61
  disease-theory systems, 62
  food production and, 249
  genes and susceptibility to, 125–127, 126*f*
  H1N1 virus, 106, 106*f*
  HIV/AIDS, 62, 127
  introduction of European, 551
  kwashiorkor, 18, 18*f*
  malaria, 106–108, 125, 249
  rickets, 123–124
  schistosomiasis, 61*f*, 62, 125
  sickle-cell anemia, 105–108, 105*f*, 249
  smallpox, 116, 125–126, 126*f*
  stomach cancer, 126
  syphilis, 106–107
  violence and, 551
disease-theory systems, 62
displacement, linguistic, 315
distribution, 380–382, 381*f*, 403
diversity
  adaptation and, 4–5
  in business, 65
  changing places and identities, 13
  continuance of, 594
  ethnocentrism and, 26, 39, 42
  among foragers, 393
  within Islam, 508–509
  linguistic, 321–323, 330
  in matrilineal and patrilineal clans, 482, 482*f*
  in public displays of affection, 6–7
  underdifferentiation of, 57
Divje babe flute, 524
divorce
  dowry and, 480–481
  in matrilineal societies, 456
  rates of, 450, 453*t*, 482–483, 483*f*
diwaniyas, 408
Djurab Desert, 166
Dmanisi site (Georgia), 193
Dmort (Disaster Mortuary Operational Response Teams), 55
DNA. *See also* genetics; mitochondrial DNA
  dating through, 87–88
  mutations in, 103
  natural selection and mutations in, 98
  Neandertal, 78–79
  structure and functions of, 101–102, 101*f*
dogs, 233, 240, 242
domains, ethnosemantic, 320
domesticated animals, 237–238, 240, 246–247, 368
domestic–public dichotomy, 423, 426, 430, 432
domestic violence, 424, 432, 480
dominant traits, 99
double negatives, 324, 324*t*
dowry, 480–481
dry farming, 234
dugout canoes, 233
Dunham, Ann (Stanley Ann Dunham Soetoro), 16–17

E
ecological anthropology, 579–584. *See also* cultural anthropology
  climate change, 575–579, 575*f*, 576*f*, 578*f*, 579*t*, 580*f*
  deforestation, 148–149, 370, 579*t*, 582–583, 582*f*

environmental threats and, 579–581
  ethnoecology in, 579
  global assaults on local autonomy, 581–582, 581*f*, 582*f*
  neoevolutionism and, 299
  potlatch and, 383
  religion and, 500–501, 501*f*
  risk perception in, 583–584, 583*f*
ecological niches, in a plural society, 348
ecology, definition of, 11
economic anthropology, 374, 377
economic production, 362–384. *See also* agriculture
  adaptive strategies, 362–363, 373*t*
  agriculture as adaptive strategy, 368–369, 369*f*
  alienation in industrial economies, 376, 377*f*
  caste system and, 474
  children and, 372
  cultivation continuum, 369
  distribution and exchange, 380–382, 381*f*
  economizing and maximization, 377–380
  energy consumption and, 564–565, 565*t*
  foraging, 363–367, 364*f*, 365*t*, 366*f*
  generosity and, 395–396
  horticulture, 367–368, 367*f*, 369
  Industrial Revolution, 552–554, 554*f*
  intensification, 369–372
  means of production, 375–376
  modes of production, 374–375
  in nonindustrial societies, 374–375
  pastoralism, 372–373, 373*f*, 401–402
  potlatching, 382–384, 383*f*, 384*f*
  specialization in, 375–376
economizing, 377
economy, definition of, 374
Ecuador, Quechua people in, 330
education, 58–59, 556
effervescence, religious, 493, 501
egalitarian societies, 263, 264*t*, 426
ego, in kinship calculation, 456–457
Egypt, ancient
  early state in, 269
  Nabta Playa, 239
  sibling marriage among royalty, 471, 471*f*
electron spin resonance (ESR) dating, 86, 87*f*
elephantiasis, 125
El Palenque (Mesoamerica), 274
emic approach, 287
emotionalistic disease theories, 62
empires, formation of, 258
enculturation, 27, 65
endangered primates, 148–149
endogamy, 473–475, 473*f*
Enduring Voices Project, 329
energy consumption
  climate change and, 578–579, 580*f*
  social organization and, 564–565, 565*t*
England
  British colonialism, 557–558, 557*f*, 558*f*
  hominin fossils in, 196–197
  Industrial Revolution in, 552–553, 553*f*, 554*f*
  industrial stratification in, 554
  Stonehenge, 403, 403*f*
environmental anthropology, 579–584, 581*f*, 582*f*. *See also* ecological anthropology
environmental degradation
  deforestation, 148–149, 370, 579*t*, 582–583, 582*f*
  food production and, 249, 370–371

industrialization and, 565–566
  mining, 564–565
  resource depletion, 564–565
  state collapse and, 276–277
Eocene epoch, 151, 151*f*, 152*f*, 153
equity, increased, 55–56
ESR (electron spin resonance) dating, 86, 87*f*
essentialism, 593
ETA (*Euskadi Ta Azkatasuna*), 352–353
ethanol, 578
ethical issues
  Code of Ethics, 53, 73, 76
  in cultural resource management, 52–53
  in development anthropology, 54–55
  ethnographic authority, 305
  informed consent in research, 73, 76
  intellectual property rights, 39, 42, 42*f*, 73
  Kennewick Man and, 73, 74–75
Ethiopia
  Gona, 179–180
  Hadar, 170
  Herto site, 209
  high-altitude adaptations in, 128
  Omo Kibish site, 209
ethnic cleansing, 354*f*
ethnic expulsion, 355, 356*f*
ethnic identity, 337*t*, 349, 350, 593–594
ethnicity, 335–356
  American Hispanics and, 338–339, 338*t*, 339*f*
  assimilation and, 347–348, 348*f*, 356*t*
  Basques, 352–353, 352*f*, 355
  in Brazil, 345–347, 346*f*
  definition of, 337
  ethnic conflict and violence, 350–356, 352*f*, 354*f*, 355*f*, 356*t*
  ethnic groups, 337
  ethnic identity, 337*t*, 349–350, 349*f*, 593–594
  hypodescent rule, 342, 343, 344
  in Japan, 343–345, 345*f*
  migration and, 350
  multiculturalism, 349–350, 349*f*, 356*t*
  nationalities and, 347
  in a plural society, 348, 356*t*
  race and, 338–341
  status shifting, 337–338, 338*f*
  types of ethnic interaction, 356*t*
ethnocentrism, 26, 39, 42, 53
ethnocide, 355, 584
ethnoecology, 579
ethnographic authority, 305
ethnographic method, 51
ethnographic techniques, 283–290
  conversation and interviewing, 284–286
  etic *vs.* emic approaches, 287
  flows and linkages in communities, 289–290
  genealogical method, 286
  key cultural consultants, 286–287
  life histories, 287
  longitudinal research, 288–289, 288*f*
  observation and participant observation, 283–284
  problem-oriented, 288
  team research, 289
ethnography. *See also* ethnographic techniques
  contemporary, 304–305
  definition of, 9–10, 10*t*
  problem-oriented, 288
  as research strategy, 283
  sociology and, 14
  survey research *vs.*, 281*t*

San people *(Cont.)*
  kinship calculation of, 461
  !Kung, 478
  land for, 375
  location of, 382*f*
  modern, 364–365, 366*f*
  political organization of, 393
  skin color of, 120
santeria, 507
Sapir-Whorf hypothesis, 318–319
satellite imagery, 77–78
sati, 480
scarcity, 378–379
Schism and Continuity in an African Society (Turner), 301
schistosomiasis, 61*f*, 62, 125
science, definition of, 13
The Science of Culture (White), 300
scientific medicine, 63
scientific method, 15–20, 18*f*, 19*t*
scientific theory, 15, 96
A Scientific Theory of Culture, and Other Essays (Malinowski), 300
scrapers, 200, 200*f*, 216
sea level rise, 576
seals, social ranking and, 266
secret societies, 400
sectorial fallowing, 369
secular humanists, 511
secular rituals, 512
sedentism, 235, 246
self-determination, 593
Semai people, 381
semantics, 320
semiperiphery, 549
Serbia, motherhood in, 429
settlement hierarchy, 275
settlement patterns, 80
sex, gender and, 418–420
Sex and Temperament in Three Primitive Societies (Mead), 299
sexual behavior
  in agricultural societies, 431
  conflict avoidance by, 148–149
  diet and, 18, 18*f*
  gender differences in, 422–423, 422*t*
  incest taboo, 35, 469–471, 469*f*, 470*f*
  in the Inuit, 394
  Kinsey report on, 437
  mating in humans *vs.* other primates, 34–35
  in matrilineal societies, 456
  in Papua New Guinea, 438–439, 438*f*
  sexual orientation, 435–439
sexual dimorphism
  in australopithecines, 176
  in *Australopithecus afarensis*, 172–173
  in *Homo erectus*, 188–189
  in modern humans, 419
  in primates, 143
sexually transmitted diseases (STDs), 62, 106
sexual selection, 105, 105*f*
shamans, 63, 438, 503, 504*f*
shame, in social control, 410–411
Shan, 303
Shang dynasty (China), 268, 269*f*
sharing, 450
Shasavan people, 373*f*
sheep, domestication of, 237–238
shifting cultivation, 368
Shoshoni people, 453–454, 453*f*
siamangs, 145
Siberia, Chukchee people in, 503, 503*f*
sickle-cell anemia, 105–108, 105*f*, 124–125, 249
Sierra Leone, Mende in, 400
sign language, 313–315, 314*f*

silent trade, 382
silverbacks, 147
Sima dos Huesos (Spain), 195–196
singing, 524–526
situational negotiation of social identity, 336, 337–338
Skhūl site (Israel), 210, 210*f*
skin color, 121–124, 123*t*, 340
skulls
  of archaic *Homo sapiens*, 209*f*
  childhood dependency and size of, 163
  of *Homo erectus*, 190–191, 191*f*, 192, 192*f*, 209*f*
  of *Homo sapiens*, 192*f*, 209*f*
  of *Homo vs.* chimpanzee, 175*f*
  of Neandertals, 209*f*
  of robust and gracile australopithecines, 177*f*
slash-and-burn horticulture, 243, 367–368, 367*f*
slavery, 118–119, 340
Slumdog Millionaire, 534*f*
smallpox, 116, 125–126, 126*f*
smell to sight, 139–140
smelting, 267–268
Smilodectes, 153*f*
social anthropology. *See* cultural anthropology
social classes
  burials and, 259*f*, 263, 265*f*
  class consciousness, 554
  industrialization and, 554–556
  marriage within, 473–474, 474*f*
  Marx on, 554–555, 555*f*
  mass media and, 536–538
  in states, 259, 263–265
  Weber on, 555, 555*f*
social control, 408–412
  definition of, 408
  hegemony and, 304
  Kuwaiti diwaniyas and, 408
  politics, shame, and sorcery and, 410–412, 410*f*, 411*f*
  religion and, 501–503, 502*f*
  weapons of the weak in, 409–410
social facts, 301
social fund, 378
social indicators, 294
socialism, 554, 562
social marketing, 538
social status, in chiefdoms and states, 403–405, 403*f*
sociocultural anthropology. *See* cultural anthropology
sociolinguistics, 321–328. *See also* language
  Black English Vernacular, 326–328, 327*f*
  field of, 12–13, 321
  gender speech contrasts, 323–324, 324*t*
  Internet and, 322–323
  language and status position, 324–325, 324*t*
  linguistic diversity, 321–323, 330
  stratification and, 325–326, 325*f*
sociology, cultural anthropology and, 14
sociopolitical organization, 391. *See also* political organization
sociopolitical typology, 391–392
solace, religion and, 495
solar radiation, bipedalism and, 163
Solomon Islands, 223, 223*f*, 224*f*
sorcery, in social control, 410, 412
sororate, 481, 481*f*
South Africa
  apartheid in, 351
  australopithecines from, 175–177, 177*f*

  behavioral modernity evidence in, 214, 218–219, 218*f*
  Blombos Cave, 523
  Homo sapiens skulls from, 209–210
  Klasies River Mouth cave sites, 215
  Pinnacle Point cave site, 214, 218–219, 218*f*
  Rose Cottage cave site, 77
  Taung quarry, 175
  Upper Paleolithic blade tools at, 215
South America, foragers in, 363
Soviet Union, ethnic conflict in former, 355, 355*f*
Spain
  Atapuerca site, 196–197
  Basques in, 352–353, 352*f*, 355
  Sima dos Huesos, 195–196
spear points, 222, 222*f*
specialization, craft, 375–376
Special Olympics, 541*f*
speciation, 109
species, definition of, 109
spermatogenesis, folate and, 124
spina bifida, 124, 124*f*
spirit possession, factory work and, 376
sports
  achieved *vs.* ascribed status and, 540–542, 541*f*, 542*f*
  anabolic steroids in, 542, 542*f*
  football, 538–539, 539*f*
  international success in, 539–542, 540*f*, 541*f*, 542*f*
  Iroquois and, 275*f*
  media coverage of, 518, 535
  Mesoamerican, 275*f*
squash, 242, 243, 244
stabilizing selection, 105–108
Standard (American) English (SE), 317, 317*f*, 326–327
starch grains, 77
Star Wars (film), 530–531, 532*t*
states. *See also* political organization
  in Africa, 269–272
  archaic, 402, 404
  attributes of, 259
  causes of formation of, 257–259, 258*f*, 273
  collapse of, 276–277
  definition of, 256, 347, 402
  earliest, 256–257
  enforcement in, 407
  fiscal systems in, 407–408
  functions of, 405–406
  judiciary in, 407, 407*f*
  in Mesoamerica, 272–276, 272*f*, 273*f*, 275*f*
  in Mesopotamia, 266–268, 267*t*, 268*f*
  population control in, 406–407
  primary, 265
  pseudo-archaeology concerning, 260–261
  religion in, 504–505, 504*t*
  rights in, 406–407
  river valley states, 269*f*
  social ranking and chiefdoms, 263–265
  urban life, 260–263
  warfare and, 257, 258*f*, 273–274, 273*f*
status
  achieved status, 337, 540–542
  ascribed status, 337, 345
  in chiefdoms and states, 403–405
  concept of race and, 340
  definition of, 337
  language and, 324–325, 324*t*
  in matrilineal, matrilocal societies, 427
  status shifting, 337–338, 338*f*

STDs (sexually transmitted diseases), 62, 106
stereoscopic vision, 140
stereotypes, 351
stipulated descent, 454
stomach cancer, 126
Stonehenge, England, 403, 403f
stone picks, 191
storytelling, 529, 529f
stratification, social
    in archaic states, 405
    characteristics of, 263, 264t
    in chiefdoms, 405
    gender and, 419, 423, 423f, 431
    hegemony and, 304
    industrialization and, 554–556, 555f
    in Japan, 345
    language and, 325–326, 325f, 326f
    in Mesopotamia, 268
    ranked societies and, 263
stratigraphy, 81, 82f, 83, 85
stratum endogamy, 404
structural functionalism, 297, 303
structuralism, 302–303
style shifts, in speech, 322
subcultures, 38, 38t
subgroups, language, 328
subordinate stratum, 405
subsistence fund, 377–378
subspecies, 117
Sudan
    ancient Egypt and, 269
    Azande people, 438
    Darfur region, 354f, 585, 585f
    Nuer people, 297, 469, 585
sugar, 551–552, 552f
Sumatra, endangered apes in, 148
Sumerian script, 265f, 266
sumptuary goods, 408
sunflowers, 243
supernatural, 492–493. *See also* religion
superordinate stratum, 405
superorganic, 301
superposition, principle of, 81
superstructure, 300
supply and demand, 380
survey research, 290–291, 291t, 294
survivals, 295
suspension bridges, 268–271, 270f
susto, 62
Sweetness and Power (Mintz), 304
symbiosis, 372
symbolic anthropology, 301–302
symbolic capital, 326, 328
symbols, 27–28
synchronic science, 297
syncretisms, 507–510, 510f
syntax, 317
syphilis, 106–107
systematic survey, 80–81
Systems of Consanguinity and Affinity of the Human Family (Morgan), 294

T

taboo, 494, 494f
tactile organs, 140
Taliban movement, 501–502, 502f
Tanzania
    Laetoli, 170, 171f, 172
    Masai people, 400, 401f
    Olduvai Gorge, 86f, 179, 187–188, 194
taphonomy, 84
tarawads, 448–449
target audiences, 518
tarsiers, 142, 142f
Tasmania, settling of, 219–220, 220f
Taung quarry (South Africa), 175
taxation and tribute, 258, 259, 274, 407–408

taxonomy
    of humans, 137–138, 137f, 137t
    of *Kenyanthropus platyops*, 169
    Linnaeus on, 95
    of primates, 138t
teeth. *See* dentition
Teilhardina asiatica, 152
telenovelas, 518, 534, 538, 587–588
television viewing
    global system of images, 587–588
    studying effects of, 18–20, 535–538, 586
    telenovelas, 518, 534, 538, 587–588
Tell es-Sawwan, 265
Tell Hamoukar, 266
Ten Commandments, 503
Tenochtitlán, 275–276
teosinte, 243–244
Teotihuacán, 274–275, 275f
terming, 33–34
Terra Amata site (France), 197, 198f
terracing, 368–369, 369f
terrestrial monkeys and apes, 136, 143
terrorism, anthropological studies of, 290, 292–293, 292f
Tertiary period, 151, 151f, 152f
test pits, 82
text, media as, 533
Thailand, Nok Nok Tha in, 240, 268
theft, 394, 410–412
theoretical anthropology, 51, 52
theory, definition of, 15, 95, 96
Theory of Culture Change (Steward), 299
The Theory of the Leisure Class (Veblen), 383
thermoluminescence (TL) dating, 86, 87t
third gender, 477, 503, 504f
Thomson's nose rule, 127, 199
Tibetans, high-altitude adaptations of, 128, 129, 130
Tiv people, 522
Tiwi people, 521, 530
TL (thermoluminescence) dating, 86, 87t
Toltec culture, 275
Tonga, settling of, 224–225
tongue rolling, 94f
tonowi, 398
tools
    Acheulian tools, 190–192, 191f, 192f
    by *Australopithecus garhi*, 179–180
    bone, 216
    chimp use of, 33–34, 150
    Clovis tradition, 222, 222f
    data from, 77
    early hominin use of, 34, 79
    by *Homo habilis*, 179
    hunting and, 189
    microlith, 233
    Mousterian tools, 200, 200f, 201f
    Neolithic, 234f
    Oldowan pebble tools, 179, 179f
    orangutan use of, 140–141
    Upper Paleolithic blade tools, 215–216, 216f, 219
    upright bipedalism and, 163–164
top-down change, 50
topography, adaptation to, 5
totalitarian systems, 561
totemism, 296, 454, 497–499
trade
    globalization and, 43
    in Mesoamerica, 272, 275–276
    state formation and, 257
    trans-Saharan, 271
trade unions, 554
transformism, 96. *See also* evolution
transgendered people, 437
transhumance, 373
transvestism, 436–438, 437f

tree-ring dating, 86–87, 87f
tribal cultivators, 395
tribes
    definition of, 392
    as descent groups, 57–58, 395
    energy consumption in, 566t
    pantribal sodalities, 398–400
    status systems in, 404–405
"trickle down" economics, 561
trickster tales, 409
Tricycle: The Buddhist Review, 511
tripartite scheme of racial classification, 117, 120
triplets, of RNA bases, 102
Trobriand Islands
    magic and, 495, 495f
    Malinowski's work in, 14–15, 14f, 15f, 297, 297f
tropics, 122
tulafale, 403f
tundra, 195
Turkey
    Çatal Hüyük site, 87, 262, 262f
    polygamy in, 484–485, 484f
turkeys, domestication of, 242
Turkmen families, 475
Tutankhamun, 259f
Tutsis, 559, 593
TV Globo, 587–588
two-tier settlement hierarchy, 265
Tzintzuntzan diaspora, 589, 590–591

U

Ubaid culture, 263, 265, 266, 267t
Uganda, polygamy in, 485
Uighurs, 486f
Umatilla Indians, 73, 74
UNCED (United Nations Conference on the Environment and Development), 592
underdifferentiation, 57
Understanding Popular Culture (Fiske), 533
underwater archaeology, 11–12, 83f, 84
uniformitarianism, 96
unilineal descent, 454, 460–461. *See also* matrilineal descent; patrilineal descent
unilinear evolutionism, 295
unilocal societies, 460
United Kingdom. *See* England
United Nations Conference on the Environment and Development (UNCED), 592
United Nations Fourth World Conference on Women, 435
United Nations Working Group on Indigenous Populations (WGIP), 592
United States
    achieved *vs.* ascribed status in, 540–542, 541f, 542f
    African Americans (*See* African Americans)
    Basque Americans, 353
    bilateral kinship in, 458–459
    Brazilians leaving, 590–591, 590f
    cash employment of women in, 432–434, 433t, 434t
    as a core nation, 563, 563f, 563t
    divorce rates in, 483, 483f
    energy consumption in, 564–565, 566t, 578
    ethnic composition of, 349, 349f
    feminization of poverty, 434–435, 435t
    Hispanic Americans (*See* Hispanics)
    importance of race in, 122
    invention of farming in, 241f
    kinship changes in, 450–453, 452t, 453t
    New Orleans, 54–55, 54f, 351f, 578f

MAP ATLAS

CONTENTS

MAP 1

Annual Percent
of World Forest Loss,
1990–2000

Deforestation is a major environmental problem. In the tropics, large corporations clear forests seeking hardwoods for the global market in furniture and fine woods. As well, the agriculturally driven clearing of the great rain forests of the Amazon Basin, west and central Africa, Middle America, and Southeast Asia has drawn public attention. Reduced forest cover means the world's vegetation system will absorb less carbon dioxide, resulting in global warming. Of concern, too, is the loss of biodiversity (large numbers of plants and animals), the destruction of soil systems, and disruptions in water supply that accompany clearing.

QUESTIONS

Look at Map 1, "Annual Percent of World Forest Loss, 1990–2000."

1. On what continents do you find stable or increased forest cover?

2. Are there areas of Africa with stable or increased forest cover? Where are they? What might the reasons be for this lack of deforestation?

3. How does deforestation in India compare with the area to its east, which includes mainland and insular Southeast Asia?

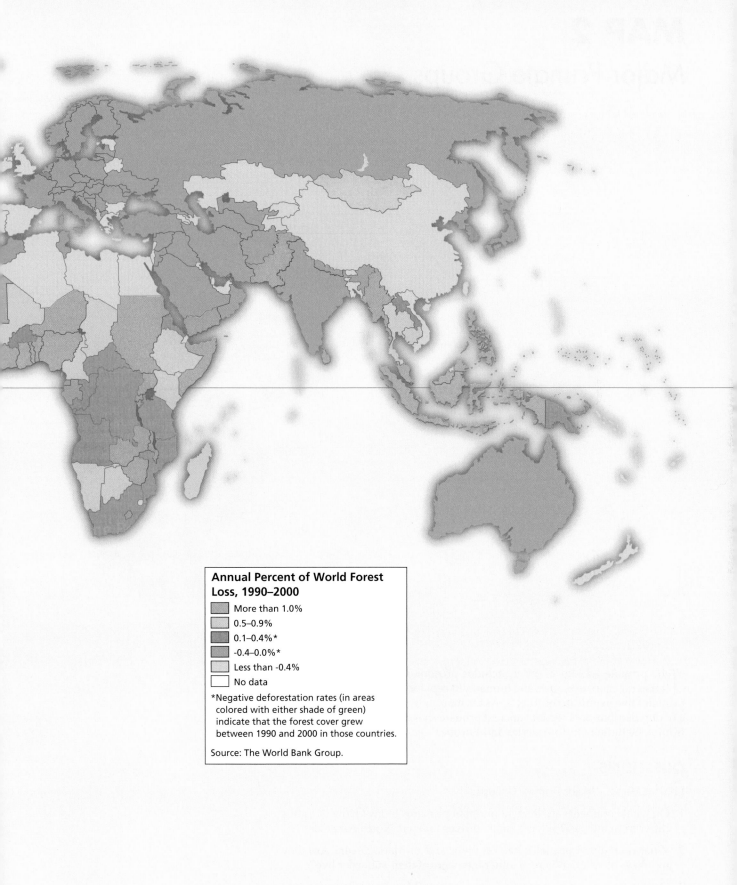

Annual Percent of World Forest Loss, 1990–2000

More than 1.0%

0.5–0.9%

0.1–0.4%*

-0.4–0.0%*

Less than -0.4

No data

*Negative deforestation rates (in areas colored with either shade of green) indicate that the forest cover grew between 1990 and 2000 in those countries.

Source: The World Bank Group.

MAP 2
Major Primate Groups

The primate zoological order includes prosimians (lemurs, lorises, and tarsiers), monkeys, apes, and humans. Except for humans, contemporary primates live mainly in the tropics. As the map shows, primates used to have a wider distribution. Fossils of ancient primates have been found outside the tropics, including North America and Europe.

QUESTIONS

Look at Map 2, "Major Primate Groups."

1. On what continents are there nonhuman primates today? How does this differ from the past? What primate thrives today in North America?

2. What nonhuman primates live on the island of Madagascar? Are they monkeys or what? Where do other members of their suborder live?

3. On what continents can you find apes in the wild today? What continent that used to have apes lacks them today (except, of course, in zoos).

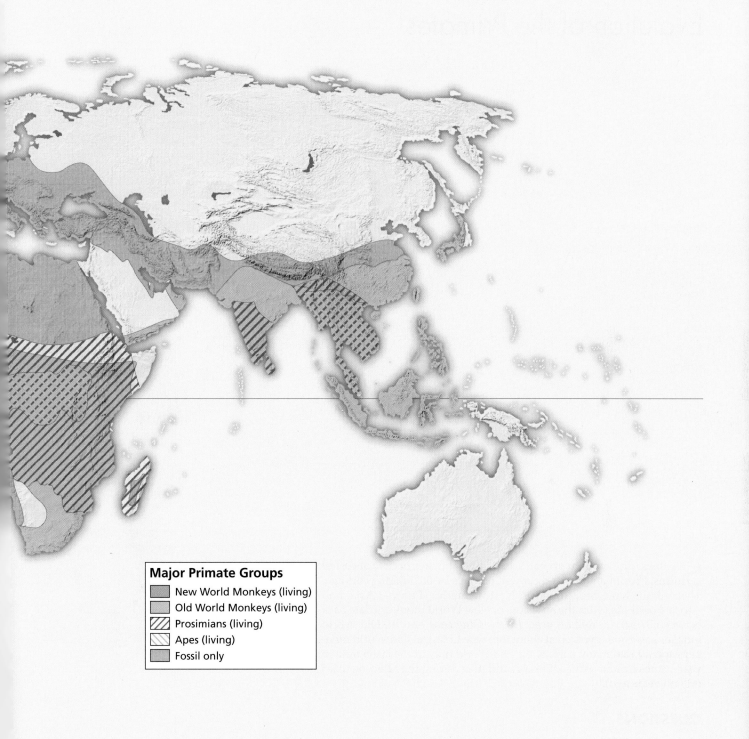

Major Primate Groups

- New World Monkeys (living)
- Old World Monkeys (living)
- Prosimians (living)
- Apes (living)
- Fossil only

MAP 3
Evolution of the Primates

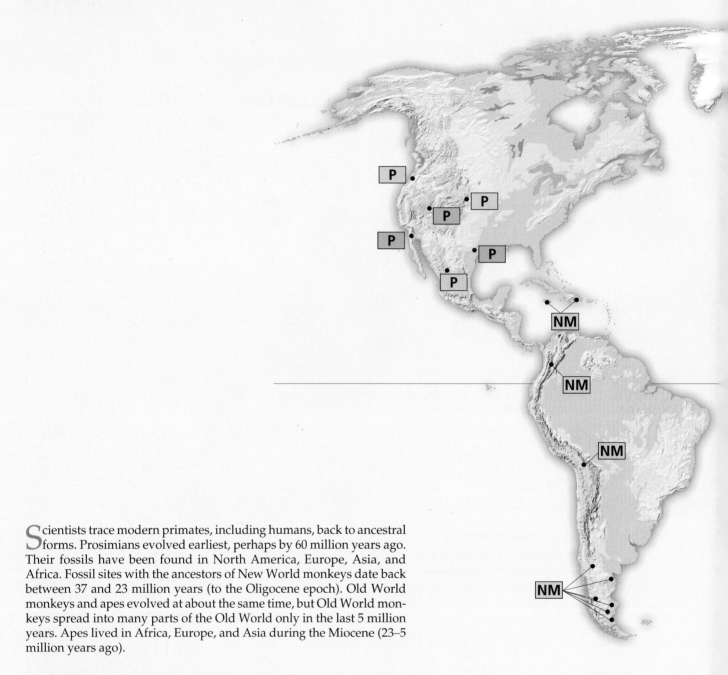

Scientists trace modern primates, including humans, back to ancestral forms. Prosimians evolved earliest, perhaps by 60 million years ago. Their fossils have been found in North America, Europe, Asia, and Africa. Fossil sites with the ancestors of New World monkeys date back between 37 and 23 million years (to the Oligocene epoch). Old World monkeys and apes evolved at about the same time, but Old World monkeys spread into many parts of the Old World only in the last 5 million years. Apes lived in Africa, Europe, and Asia during the Miocene (23–5 million years ago).

QUESTIONS

Look at Map 3, "Evolution of the Primates."

1. What continent(s) had the first primates? What kinds of primates were those?

2. On what continent has the evolution of primates been most continuous? Does this have implications for human evolution?

3. Which continent with several of the earliest primates has the fewest nonhuman primates today?

Evolution of the Primates

- Eocene: 57–37 million years ago
- Oligocene: 37–23 million years ago
- Miocene: 23–5 million years ago

OM Old World monkeys
NM New World monkeys
P Prosimians
A Apes

Map inset labels:

ETHIOPIA
UGANDA
Lake Turkana
Lake Baringo
Lake Victoria
KENYA
TANZANIA

0 100 200 Miles
0 100 200 Kilometers

See Inset

MAP 4
Early Hominins (and Hominids): Origins and Diffusion

The earliest hominins, including the ancestors of modern humans, evolved in Africa around 6 million years ago. Many sites date to the late Miocene (8–5 million years ago) when the lines leading to modern humans, chimps, and gorillas may have separated. Some sites dating to the end of the Pliocene epoch (5–1.8 million years ago) contain fossil remains of human ancestors, *Homo*. During the Pleistocene Era(1.8 million–11,000 years ago), humans spread all over the world. Scholars don't always agree on the evolutionary connections between the different fossils, as indicated in the question marks and broken lines on the time line.

QUESTIONS

Look at Map 4, "Early Hominins (and Hominids): Origins and Diffusion."

1. How many African countries have early hominin or hominid sites? Which countries contain sites of hominids that may not have been hominins? Name those two sites. How many African countries have sites from the Miocene? From the Pliocene? And from the Pleistocene?

2. Compare the African distribution of nonhuman primate fossils in Map 3 with the distribution of early hominins in Map 4. Which fossil record is better—the one for nonhuman primates or the one for hominins?

3. Compare the distribution of contemporary African apes, as shown in Map 2, with the distribution of early hominin sites in Map 4. Also look at the distribution of extinct African apes in Map 3. What patterns do you notice? Where did early hominins overlap with the African apes (extinct and contemporary)? Where were there apes but no known early hominins, and vice versa?

**Early Hominins (and Hominids):
Origins and Diffusion**

- ◻ Late Miocene localities
- ◼ Pliocene localities
- △ Early and Middle Pleistocene localities

Pierolapithecus catalaunicus

40°N
10°W
30°N

−20°N

Bahr el Ghazal
Toumai

CHAD

• N'Djamena

−10°N

Middle Awash *Dikika*

Hadar

W. Turkana *Omo* **ETHIOPIA**

Fejej
Lothagam *Koobi Fora*
Black Skull
Kanapoi *Tugen Hills*
Lukeino *Chesawanja*
Kanam *Chemeron*

Peninj

KENYA

TANZANIA

*ATLANTIC
OCEAN*

*INDIAN
OCEAN*

10°S

Gladysvale
Sterkfontein *Makapansgat*
Swartkrans • Pretoria
Kromdraai • Johannesburg
Taung *Drimolen*
Kimberley •

**SOUTH
AFRICA**

△ *Pinnacle Point*

20°S

0°
10°E
0°
10°W

10°S
20°S
30°S
40°E
30°E
20°E

MAP 5
The Emergence of Modern Humans

Early forms of *Homo (H.) erectus*, sometimes called *H. ergaster*, have been found in East Africa and the former Soviet Georgia. By 1.7 million years ago, *H. erectus* had spread from Africa into Asia, including Indonesia, and eventually Europe. The *H. erectus* period may have lasted until 300,000 years ago. Other archaic forms of *Homo*, including fossils sometimes called *H. antecessor* and *H. heidelbergensis*, have been found in various parts of the Old World.

QUESTIONS

Look at Map 5, "The Emergence of Modern Humans."

1. Locate the site of Dmanisi (Georgia). Locate the site of Nariokotome (East Turkana, Kenya). These are sites where similarly dated early remains of *Homo erectus* (or *Homo ergaster*) have been found. Find two additional sites where hominins with similar dates (1.8–1.6 m.y.a.) have been found.

2. Considering Africa and Asia, name five sites (other than Dmanisi and Nariokotome) where *Homo erectus* fossils have been found.

3. Locate Heidelberg (Mauer) and Ceprano. What kinds of hominin fossils have been found there?

Okladnikov
Cave

Dmanisi (1.7–1.8 m.y.a.)

*CAUCASUS
MTS.*

Black Sea

ASIA

*Caspian
Sea*

Shanidar

Teshik Tash

Zhoukoudian, "Peking man"
(450,000 years ago)

a

Skhul
Tabun
ara Cave
Zuttiyen

Amud

Lantian

Langtandong

Qafzeh

Yunxian

Hominid
migration

Maba

Nazlet Khatir

Red Sea

Yuanmou
(Earliest evidence of
hominids in East Asia,
1.7 million years ago)

Tham Khuyen

Buia

Herto
Hadar

RICA

Bouri

Omo
Jariokotome
Koobi Fora
Ileret
Lake Turkana,
"Nariokotome boy" (1.6 m.y.a.)

INDIAN OCEAN

Sangiran, Java (1.6–1.8 m.y.a)

Kedungbrubus

Trinil, "Java man"
(700,000 years ago)

Flores

Konso-Gardula

Olduvai Gorge

of Hearths

fontein (2 m.y.a.)

Border Cave
wartkrans (1.5 m.y.a.)

AUSTRALIA

ARCHAEOLOGICAL SITE

- *Homo habilis*
- *Homo erectus*
- Archaic *Homo sapiens*
- Neandertals
- *Homo sapiens*
- *Homo floresiensis*

Mouth
e of the earliest
omically modern
00,000 years ago)

MAP 6
Origins and Distribution of Modern Humans

EUROPE
Settled c. 35,000 B.P.
Mladeč
Cro-Magnon
Last Neandertals die out at c. 28,000 B.P.
First evidence of human burials
c.100,000–90,000 B.P.
Black Sea
Volga R.
First settled c. 45,000 B.P.
Aral Sea
Caspian Sea
Shanidar
Euphrates R.
Tigris R.
ARABIAN PENINSULA
INDIA
HIMALAYAS
ASIA
SIBERIA
GOBI
Yellow R.
Zhoukoudian
JAPAN
First settled c. 40,000 B.P.
Yangtze R.
Maba
East Asia: Earliest evidence of hominid colonizatio[n] dates to c. 1.7 million B.P.
SAHARA
AFRICA
Niger R.
SAHEL
Herto (c. 160,000–154,000 B.P.)
Omo
ATLANTIC OCEAN
Congo R.
L. Victoria
GREAT RIFT VALLEY
Radiation of *Homo sapiens* began from here c. 130,000 B.P.?
Olduvai Gorge
Zambezi R.
KALAHARI DESERT
Madagascar
INDIAN OCEAN
Klasies River Mouth
Settled c. 100,000–90,000 B.P.
Mekong R.
Philippine Islands
Niah Cave
Sunda
Borneo
Sumatra
Java
Earliest evidence of use of boats
Flores
H. floresiensis (c. 95,000–13,000 B.P.)
New Guinea
AUSTRALIA
Lake Mungo
Keilor
Tasmania

Anatomically modern humans (AMHs), appeared earliest in Africa (at Herto?) and migrated into the rest of the Old World, perhaps around 130,000 years ago. Whether these early modern humans interbred with archaic humans, such as Neandertals, outside of Africa is still debated. Sometime between 25,000 and 9,000 years ago, humans colonized the New World.

QUESTIONS

Look at Map 6, "Origins and Distribution of Modern Humans."

1. When and from where was Australia first settled?

2. When and from where was North America first settled? How many migrations are shown as figuring in the settlement of North America? How were these migrations related to the glacial ice cover? Did they all follow the same route?

3. Locate three sites providing early evidence of AMHs in Africa. How do their dates compare with those of AMHs in Europe?

LAURENTIDE ICE SHEET
St. Lawrence R.
Great Lakes

NORTH AMERICA

Corridor
opened
from
11,300 B.P.

BERINGIA
(c. 80,000 to 7,000 B.P.)

ROCKY MTS.
GREAT PLAINS
Meadowcroft
APPALACHIAN MTS.

ATLANTIC OCEAN

Clovis
Rio Grande
Mississippi R.

West Indies

AN

Orinoco R.
GUIANA HIGHLANDS

Nanchoc Valley
A
N
D
E
S
AMAZON BASIN

Pedra
Furada

Monte
Verde

PATAGONIA

and

**Origins and Distribution
of Modern Humans**

↖ Possible settlement direction

▲ Archaic *Homo sapiens* (c. 650,000–28,000 B.P.)

△ Neandertals (c. 130,000–28,000? B.P.)

■ Modern *Homo sapiens* (c. 130,000 B.P.–present)

☐ Areas covered by ice in late
Pleistocene era (18,000 B.P.)

▨ Beringia

MAP 7
The Distribution
of Human Skin Color
(Before C.E. 1400)

Human skin color varies. The pigmentation is caused by the presence of melanin in the skin, which protects the skin from damage due to ultra-violet radiation. In areas with much UV radiation, people biologically adapted to their environments by increased melanin production.

QUESTIONS

Look at Map 7, "The Distribution of Human Skin Color (Before C.E. 1400)."

1. Where are the Native Americans with the darkest skin color located? What factors help explain this distribution?

2. In both western and eastern hemispheres, is the lightest skin color found in the north or the south? Outside Asia, where do you find skin color closest to northern Asian skin color? Is this surprising given what you have read about migrations and settlement history?

3. Where are skin colors darkest? How might you explain this distribution?

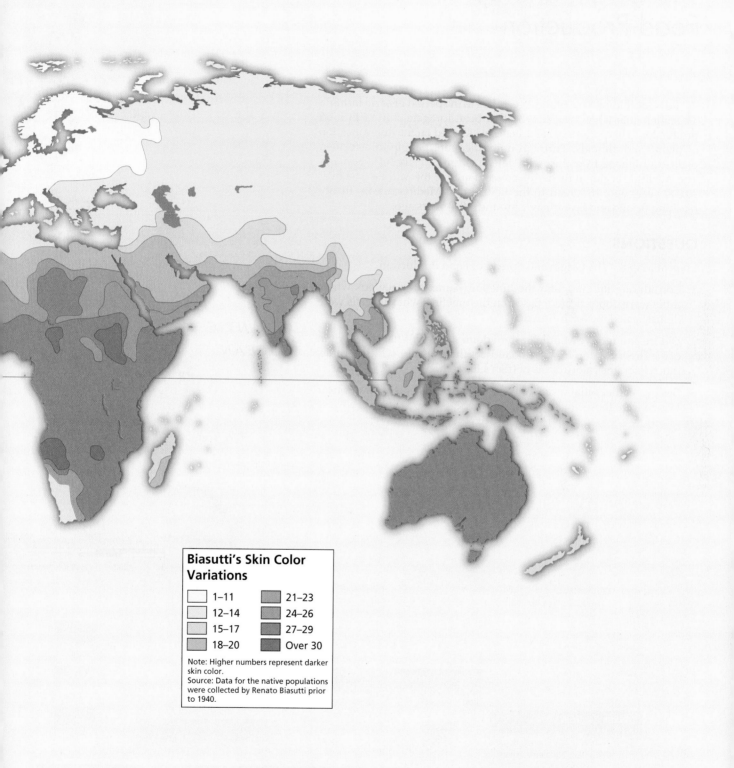

Biasutti's Skin Color Variations

☐ 1–11	▨ 21–23
☐ 12–14	▨ 24–26
▨ 15–17	▨ 27–29
▨ 18–20	▨ Over 30

Note: Higher numbers represent darker skin color.
Source: Data for the native populations were collected by Renato Biasutti prior to 1940.

MAP 8
The Origin and Spread of Food Production

The Neolithic, or New Stone Age, refers to the period of early farming settlements when people who had been foragers shifted to food production. This pattern of subsistence was based on the domestication of plants and animals. Through domestication, people transformed plants and animals from their wild state to a form more useful to humans. The Neolithic began in the fertile crescent area of the Middle East over 10,000 years ago. It spread to the Levant and Mediterranean, finally reaching Britain and Scandinavia around 5,000 years ago.

QUESTIONS

Look at Map 8, "The Origin and Spread of Food Production."

1. Considering the map and the timeline, name three regions where cattle were domesticated. Based on the timeline, what animals were domesticated in North America?

2. Did Ireland receive Middle Eastern domesticates? What is the origin of the "Irish potato," or white potato (see the timeline), which became, much later, the caloric basis of Irish subsistence?

3. Besides cattle, what animals were domesticated more than once? Where were those areas of domestication?

Early Neolithic Sites of the Middle East and Europe

Settlement region and date
Settlement sites
Possible migration routes
Areas of domestication

Lake Ladoga
Lake Peipus
Aral Sea
Baltic Sea
Elbe R.
ose
Oder R.
Bug R.
Vistula R.
Dniester R.
Dnieper R.
Horse
Volga R.
Ural R.
Caspian Sea
Danube R.
Sea of Azov
Sava R.
7,500
Black Sea
7,700
7,700
Danube R.
7,800
Adriatic Sea
7,800
9,000
Cattle
Pig
10,300
Sheep
8,000
Cattle
9,800
Tigris R.
Goat
8,400
9,600
Euphrates R.
Goat
Persian Gulf
9,000
9,400?
8,900
Po R.
Mediterranean Sea
10,300
Dromedary
Ass
Honey Bee
Cat

Mediterranean Domestication

Barley	Dates	Grapes
Cattle	Garlic	Lentils
Celery	Goat	Lettuce
		Olives

Southwest Asia Domestication

Barley	Duck	Melons
Beans	Fruits (seed	Oats
Beets	and stone)	Oil seeds
Camel (Bactrian)	Goat	Onions
Carrots	Grapes	Rye
Cattle	Hemp	Sheep
Dog	Horse	Wheat

Yam, oil palm
Cat (Egypt)
Chickens (south-central Asia)

4000	3000	2000	1000 Years Ago

Marsh elder
Sunflower
Squash

Lamb's quarters

Maize

North America

White potato

MAP 9
Ancient Civilizations of the Old World

Archaic states developed in many parts of the Old World at different periods. The earliest civilizations, such as Mesopotamia, Egypt, and the Indus Valley, are generally placed at about 5500 B.P. States developed later in Asia, Africa, and the Americas (see Map 13).

QUESTIONS

Look at Map 9, "Ancient Civilizations of the Old World."

1. What contemporary nations would you have to visit if you wanted to see all the places where ancient civilizations developed in the Old World? Would some countries be off limits for political reasons? How do you think such limitations have affected the archaeological record?

2. Of the ancient states shown on Map 9, which developed latest? Why do you think the first states developed when and where they did?

3. In which of the ancient states shown on Map 9 were Middle Eastern domesticates basic to the economy? In which states shown on Map 9 were other domesticates basic to the economy?

Mycenaean
0 B.P.
Çatal Hüyük

Tigris-Euphrates
(Mesopotamia and
Babylonia)
5500 B.P.–4000 B.P.

Harappa

Jericho

Nile
(Ancient Egypt)
4920 B.P.–3100 B.P.

Tell el-Ubaid

Mohenjo-daro

Indus-Ganges
(Harappan and Vedic Civilizations)
5000 B.P.–2150 B.P.

Nok Nok Tha

Khmer
A.D. 802–1218

e (Nubia)
2591 B.P.–
(A.D. 325)

Aksum/Axum
?2200 B.P.–1300 B.P. (A.D. 700)

Funan
A.D. 100–546

Chenla
A.D. 611–802

Yellow River (Shang)
4000 B.P.–3027 B.P.

Caspian Sea

Red Sea

Arabian
Sea

Bay of Bengal

South
China
Sea

East
China
Sea

Sea
of
Japan

Sea
of
Okhotsk

Lake
Baikal

PACIFIC
OCEAN

INDIAN OCEAN

babwe
1000–1450

Ancient Civilizations of the Old World

	Before 5500 B.P.
	5500–3000 B.P.
	4100–3000 B.P.
	After 2600 B.P.

Funan
Meroe (Nubia)
Aksum/Axum
Chenia
Jenne-jeno
Ghana
Khmer
Rome
Zimbabwe
Mali
Songhay/Songhai

2500   2000   1500   1000   500
        (500 A.D)   (1000 A.D)   (1500 A.D)

Years (B.P.)

MAP 10
Ethnographic Study Sites Prior to 1950

The development of anthropology as a scientific discipline can be traced to the middle to late part of the 19th century. In cultural anthropology, ethnographic field work became usual and common during the early 20th century. American ethnographers turned to the study of Native Americans, while European anthropologists often studied people living in world areas, such as Africa, which had been conquered and/or colonized by the anthropologist's nation of origin.

QUESTIONS

Look at Map 10, "Ethnographic Study Sites Prior to 1950."

1. Anthropology originated as the scientific study of nonwestern peoples and cultures. Yet Map 10 shows that many anthropological studies conducted prior to 1950 were done in North America. What societies were being studied in North America? Were they considered western or nonwestern? What does this tell us about the concept of "western"?

2. How would you describe the range of ethnographic sites prior to 1950? Were some world areas being neglected, such as the Middle East or mainland Asia? What might be the reasons for such omissions?

3. Think about how changes in transportation and communication have affected the way anthropologists do their research. How might a list of contemporary ethnographic sites contrast with the distribution shown in Map 10. How has longitudinal research been affected by changes in transportation and communication?

Ethnographic Study Sites Prior to 1950

North America
1. Eastern Eskimo
2. Central Eskimo
3. Naskapi
4. Iroquois
5. Delaware
6. Natchez
7. Shawnee
8. Kickapoo
9. Sioux
10. Crow
11. Nez Percé
12. Shoshone
13. Paviotso
14. Kwakiutl
15. Tsimshian
16. Haida
17. Tlingit
18. Navajo
19. Hopi
20. Zuñi
21. Aztec
22. Tzintzuntzan and Cuanajo
23. Maya
24. Cherokee
25. San Pedro

South America
Ecuador
26. Jívaro
Peru
27. Inca
28. Machiguenga
29. Achuara
30. Campa
Bolivia
31. Aymara
Chile
32. Yahgan
Venezuela
33. Yanomamö
Brazil
34. Tapirapé
35. Mundurucu
36. Mehinacu
37. Kuikuru
38. Caingang

Africa
Ghana
39. Ashanti
Nigeria
40. Kadar

Sudan
41. Fur
42. Dinka
43. Nuer
44. Azande
Uganda
45. Bunyoro
46. Ganda
Dem. Rep. of Congo
47. Mbuti
Rwanda
48. Watusi
Kenya
49. Masai
Tanzania
50. Nyakyusa
51. Lovedu
Zambia
52. Ndembu
53. Barotse
Mozambique
54. Bathonga
South Africa
55. !Kung Bushmen
56. Zulu

Asia
Sri Lanka
57. Vedda
58. Sinhalese
India
59. Andaman
60. Nayar
61. Tamil
62. Rajput
Siberia
63. Tungus
Japan
64. Ainu
China
65. Luts'un village
Taiwan
66. Taiwan Chinese
Vietnam
67. Mnong-Gar
Malaya
68. Semai

Pacific
Philippines
69. Tasaday
Indonesia Area
70. Dyaks
71. Alorese
72. Tetum
Australia
73. Tiwi
74. Arunta
75. Murngin
76. Saibai Islanders
New Guinea
77. Arapesh
78. Dani
79. Gururumba
80. Kai
81. Kapauku
82. Mae Enga
83. Kuma
84. Mundugumor
85. Tchambuli
86. Tsembaga Maring
87. Tavade
88. Foré
89. Etoro

Melanesian Islands
90. Manus Islanders
91. New Hanover Islanders
92. Trobriand Islanders
93. Dobuans
94. Rossel Islanders
95. Kaoka
96. Malaita Islanders
97. Espiritu Santo Islanders
98. Tana Islanders
99. Tikopia
100. Sivai

Polynesian Islands
101. Maori
102. Tongans
103. Samoans
104. Mangians
105. Tahitians
106. Hawaiians

Micronesian Islands
107. Truk

MAP 11
Major Families of World Languages

Language, like religion, is an important identifying and distinguishing characteristic of culture. Knowing the distribution of the major world languages and language families helps us understand some of the reasons behind important current events. In areas that have emerged from recent colonial rule, for example, the participants in conflicts over territory and power are often defined in terms of linguistic groups. Language distributions also help us understand our past by providing clues that enable us to chart the course of human migrations, as is suggested by the distribution of Indo-European, Austronesian, and Hamito-Semitic languages.

QUESTIONS

Look at Map 11, "Major Families of World Languages."

1. Name three language families or subfamilies that are spoken on more than one continent. How do you explain this distribution?

2. Where are the Austronesian languages spoken? How might one explain this distribution?

3. What language families are spoken on the African continent? Locate the Niger-Congo language family, of which the Bantu languages comprise a subfamily.

Major Families of World Languages

Indo-European
- 1 Germanic
- 2 Romance
- 3 Slavic
- 4 Baltic
- 5 Iranian
- 6 Indo-Aryan
- 7 Celtic
- 8 Greek
- 9 Armenian

- Eskimo-Aleut
- Native American
- Hamito-Semitic
- Niger-Congo
- Nilo-Saharan
- Austronesian
- Australian
- Samoyed
- Finno-Ugric
- Basque
- Khosian
- Ural-Altaic
- Caucasian
- Sino-Tibetan
- Paleo-Siberian
- Korean
- Japanese
- Burushaski
- Austro-Asiatic
- Vietnamese
- Thai-Kadai
- Papuan
- Dravidian
- Unpopulated Regions

MAP 12
World Land Use,
C.E. 1500

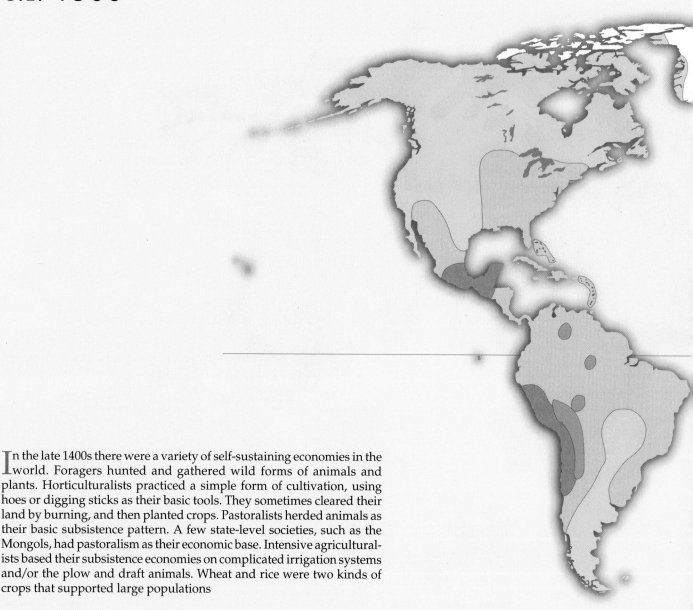

In the late 1400s there were a variety of self-sustaining economies in the world. Foragers hunted and gathered wild forms of animals and plants. Horticulturalists practiced a simple form of cultivation, using hoes or digging sticks as their basic tools. They sometimes cleared their land by burning, and then planted crops. Pastoralists herded animals as their basic subsistence pattern. A few state-level societies, such as the Mongols, had pastoralism as their economic base. Intensive agriculturalists based their subsistence economies on complicated irrigation systems and/or the plow and draft animals. Wheat and rice were two kinds of crops that supported large populations

QUESTIONS

Look at Map 12, "World Land Use, C.E. 1500."

1. Name three continents with significant herding economies. On which continents was pastoralism absent?

2. How do the various types of agriculture vary among the continents? Which continent had the largest area under intensive cultivation? Which continent or continents had the least amount of intensive cultivation?

3. What were the main uses of land in Europe when the European age of discovery and conquest began?

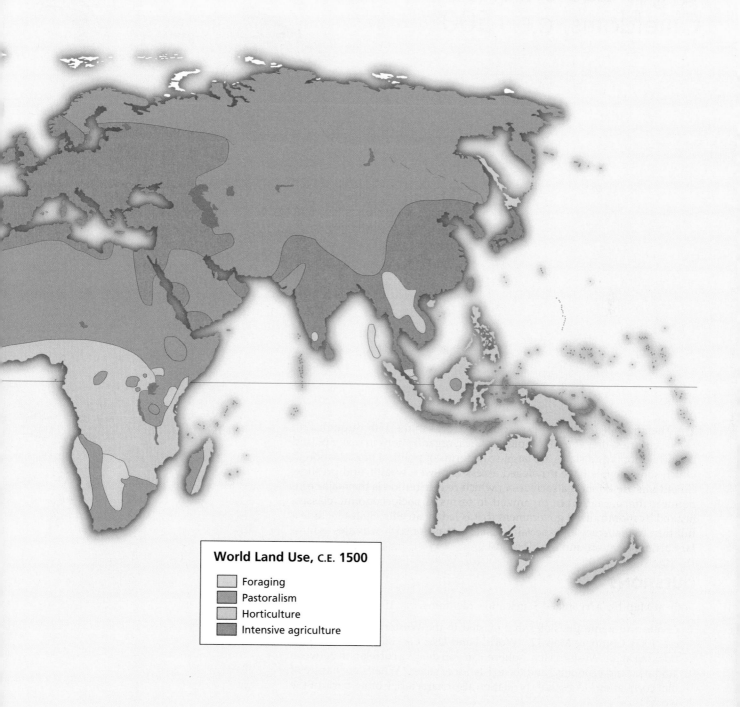

World Land Use, C.E. 1500

- Foraging
- Pastoralism
- Horticulture
- Intensive agriculture

MAP 13
Organized States and Chiefdoms, C.E. 1500

TARASCA

AZTEC STATE

OTHER MEXICAN STATES

CHIBCHA

INCA STATE

PACIFIC OCEAN

ATLANTIC OCEAN

When Europeans started exploring the world in the 15th through 17th centuries, they found complex political organizations in many places. Both chiefdoms and states are large-scale forms of political organization in which some people have privileged access to power, wealth, and prestige. Chiefdoms are kin-based societies in which redistribution is the major economic pattern. States are organized in terms of socioeconomic classes, headed by a centralized government that is led by an elite. States include a full-time bureaucracy and specialized subsystems for such activities as military action, taxation, and social control.

QUESTIONS

Look at Map 13, "Organized States and Chiefdoms, C.E. 1500."

1. Locate and name the states that existed in the Western Hemisphere in C.E. 1500. Compare Map 12, "World Land Use: C.E. 1500," with Map13. Looking at the Western Hemisphere, can you detect a correlation between land use (and economy) and the existence of states? What's the nature of that correlation? Does that correlation also characterize other parts of the world?

2. Locate three regions of the world where chiefdoms existed in C.E. 1500. Compare Map 12, "World Land Use: C.E. 1500," with Map 13. Can you detect a correlation between land use (and economy) and the existence of chiefdoms? What's the nature of that correlation?

3. Some parts of the world lacked either chiefdoms or states in C.E. 1500. What are some of those areas? What kinds of political systems did they probably have?

SONGHAI

KANEM-
BORNU

ETHIOPIA

OYO
ENIN

KONGO

LUBA

Zanzibar

• Kilwa

• Sofala

MONOMATAPA

INDIAN
OCEAN

EUROPEAN
STATES

ISLAMIC STATES

SEMI NOMADIC
STATES

INDIAN
STATES

CHINA

JAPAN

PACIFIC
OCEAN

PHILIPPINES

HINDU/
MUSLIM
STATES

NEW
GUINEA

Ceylon

Strait
of Malacca

Malaya

Moluccas

Sumatra

THE
EAST INDIES

Java

AUSTRALIA

Organized States and
Chiefdoms, C.E. 1500

No chiefdoms or states

Chiefdoms

States

MAP 14
Female/Male Inequality in Education and Employment

Inuit

Hidatsa

Iroquois

Pawnee

Arembepe

Women in developed countries have made significant advances in socio-economic status in recent years. In most of the world, however, females suffer from significant inequality when compared with their male counterparts. Although women can vote in most countries, in over 90 percent of those countries that right was granted only during the last 50 years. In most regions, literacy rates for women still fall far short of those for men. In Africa and Asia, for example, only about half as many women are as literate as men. Inequalities in education and employment are perhaps the most telling indicators of the unequal status of women in most of the world. Even where women are employed in positions similar to those held by men, they tend to receive less compensation. The gap between rich and poor involves not only a clear geographic differentiation, but a clear gender differentiation as well.

QUESTIONS

Look at Map 14 "Female/Male Inequality in Education and Employment."

1. Locate and name three Third World countries with the same degree of gender-based inequality as the United States and Canada.

2. Two of the world's largest developing nations are coded as having "less inequality." What are they?

3. Most European countries are coded as having "least inequality." Which western European countries are exceptions?

Female/Male Inequality in Education and Employment

- Least inequality
- Less inequality
- Average inequality
- More inequality
- Most inequality
- No data

MAP 15
World Religions

Because religion is a fundamental characteristic of human culture, a depiction of the spatial distribution of religions comes close to a map of cultural patterns. More than just a set of behavior patterns having to do with worship and ceremony, religion influences the ways in which people deal with one another, with their institutions, and with their environments. An examination of this map in the context of conflict within and among nations also shows that the tension between countries and the internal stability of states are also functions of the spatial distribution of religion.

QUESTIONS

Look at Map 15, "World Religions."

1. Which continent has the most diversity with respect to the major religions?

2. Which continent is most Protestant? Why do you think that is the case?

3. Where in the world are "tribal" religions still practiced?

Predominant Religions

Christianity (C)*
- Roman Catholic
- Protestant
- Mormon (LDS)
- Eastern Churches
- Mixed

Islam (M)
- Sunni
- Shi'a

Buddhism (B)
- Hinayanistic
- Lamaistic

Hinduism (H)

Judaism (J)

- Sikhism
- **Animism (Tribal)**
- **Chinese Complex**
  (Confucianism, Taoism, and Buddhism)
- **Korean Complex**
  (Buddhism, Confucianism, Christianity, and Chondogyo)
- **Japanese Complex**
  (Shinto and Buddhism)
- **Vietnamese Complex**
  (Buddhism, Taoism, Confucianism, and Cao Dai)
- **Unpopulated Regions**

*Capital letters indicate the presence of locally important minority adherents of nonpredominant faiths.

MAP 16
Total Annual Energy Consumption by Country

All of the countries defined by the World Bank as having high incomes consume at least 100 gigajoules of commercial energy (the equivalent of more than 10 metric tons of coal) per person per year. With the exception of the oil-rich Persian Gulf states, where consumption figures include the costly "burning off" of excess energy in the form of natural gas flares at wellheads, most of the highest-consuming countries are concentrated in North America and Western Europe. At the other end of the scale are low-income countries, whose consumption rates are often less than 1 percent of those of the United States and other high consumers. These figures don't include the consumption of noncommercial energy—the traditional fuels of firewood, animal dung, and other organic matter—widely used in the less developed parts of the world.

QUESTIONS

Look at Map 16, " Total Annual Energy Consumption by Country." What five countries are the world's foremost energy consumers? Does this mean that the average person in each of these countries consumes more energy than the average European? Why or why not?

1. Compare energy consumption in Europe and North America. Do all European countries consume energy at the same rate as the United States and Canada?

2. What are some exceptions to the generalization that the highest rates of energy consumption are in core countries, with the lowest rates on the periphery?

3. How is energy consumption related to measures of the quality of life, as shown in Map 17?

**Total Annual Energy
Consumption by Country**

In million tonnes of oil equivalent

- 1–100
- 101–250
- 251–1,000
- 1,001–2,500
- No data

MAP 17

The Quality of Life: The Index of Human Development, 2007

This map is based on a development index that considers a wide variety of demographic, health, and educational data, including population growth, per capita gross domestic income, longevity, literacy, and years of schooling. Compared with earlier years, there has been substantial improvement in the quality of life in Middle and South America. Africa and South Asia, however, face the challenge of providing basic access to health care, education, and jobs for rapidly increasing populations. This map illustrates an enduring difference in quality of life between those who inhabit the world's equatorial and tropical regions and those fortunate enough to live in the temperate zones, where the quality of life is significantly higher.

QUESTIONS

Look at Map 17, "The Quality of Life: The Index of Human Development, 2007."

1. What countries in central and South America have Human Development Index (HDI) scores comparable to those of some European nations? Does this surprise you?

2. Given that Brazil has one of the world's top 10 economies, does its HDI score surprise you? How do Brazil, Mexico, and Venezuela compare in terms of the HDI?

3. Do you notice a correlation between deforestation (Map 1) and quality of life? Does India fit this correlation?

Levels of Human Development, 2007

- 9 and above
- 8–8.99
- 7–7.99
- 6–6.99
- 5–5.99
- 4–4.99
- 3–3.99
- Under 2.99
- No data

MAP 18
Global Warming

Since the early 20th century, the Earth's surface temperatures have risen about 1.4° F (0.7° C). Rising temperatures, shrinking glaciers, and melting polar ice provide additional evidence for global warming. Scientists prefer the term climate change to *global warming*. Scientific measurements confirm that global warming is not due to increased solar radiation, but rather are mainly *anthropogenic*—caused by humans and their activities. Because our planet's climate is always changing, the key question becomes: How much global warming is due to human activities versus natural climate variability. Most scientists agree that human activities play a major role in global climate change. Given population growth and rapidly increasing use of fossil fuels, the human factor is significant. The map represents the relative impact of global warming in different regions of the world.

QUESTIONS

Look at Map 18, "Global Warming."

1. Which geographical regions of the world show noticeable effects of global warming? Which show the least? What about the polar regions? Why are certain major sections of the oceans affected?

2. Widespread and long-term trends toward warmer global temperatures and a changing climate are referred to as "fingerprints." Researchers look for them to detect and confirm that climate change. What are some of the recent fingerprints that have been covered in the media?

3. "Harbingers" refer to such events as fires, exceptional droughts, and downpours. They can also include the spread of disease-bearing insects and widespread bleaching of coral reefs. Any and all may be directly or partly caused by a warmer climate. Have you noticed any recent harbingers in the U.S. in the past year? Have they been confined to any specific geographical regions?

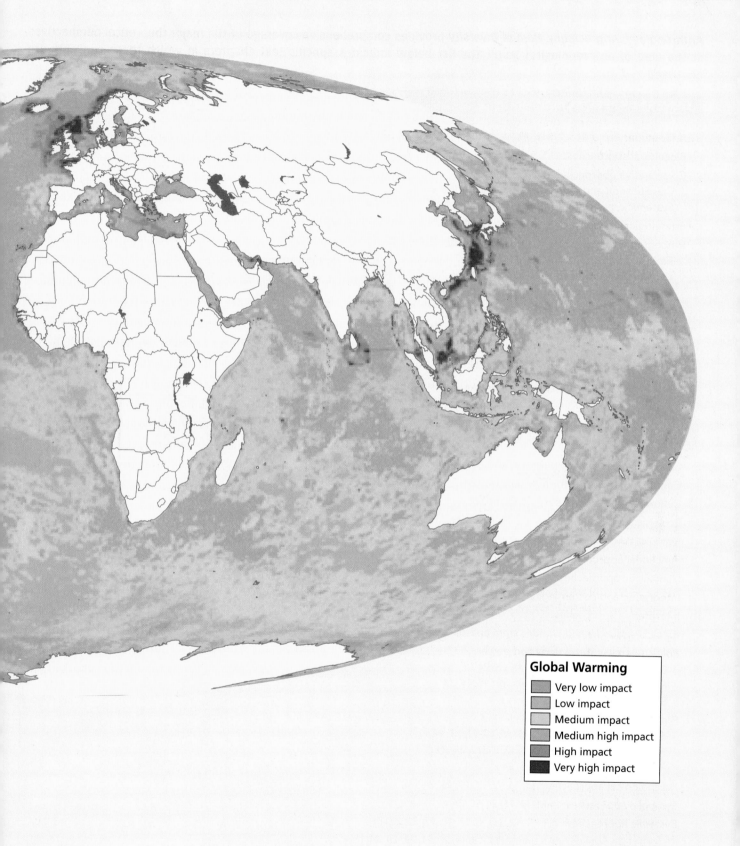

Global Warming
- Very low impact
- Low impact
- Medium impact
- Medium high impact
- High impact
- Very high impact

Important Theories

Anthropology: Appreciating Human Diversity provides comprehensive coverage of the major theoretical perspectives at the core of anthropological study. The list below indicates specific text chapters in which these concepts are discussed.

GENERAL APPROACHES

Adaptation: *1, 2, 3, 5, 6, 7, 8, 9, 10, 15, 16, 17, 18, 19, 20, 21, 22, 23, 24*

Biocultural approaches: *1, 3, 5, 6, 7, 8, 9, 10, 16, 20, 21, 22, 23*

Comparative approaches: *1, 2, 6, 7, 11, 12, 13, 15, 16, 17, 18, 19, 20, 21, 22, 23, 24*
  Classification and typologies: *2, 6, 7, 8, 9, 10, 11, 12, 13, 16, 17, 18, 19, 20, 21, 22, 23, 24*
  Systemic cross-cultural comparison: *2, 13, 18, 21, 22, 23*

Ethnological theory: *1, 2, 3, 13, 15, 18, 19, 20, 21, 22, 23, 24*

Ethnography: *1, 2, 3, 13, 16, 17, 18, 19, 20, 21, 22, 23, 24*
  Emic and etic approaches: *2, 3, 13, 16, 19, 21, 22, 23, 24*
  Longitudinal and multi-sited approaches: *2, 13, 17, 18, 24*
  Quantitative and qualitative approaches: *2, 13, 18, 21, 22*

Evolutionary theory: *5, 6, 7, 8, 9, 10, 11, 12, 13, 16, 17, 21, 22, 23*

Explanation: *1, 2, 3, 5, 6, 7, 8, 9, 10, 11, 12, 13, 15, 16, 17, 18, 19, 20, 21, 22, 23, 24*

Holism: *1, 3, 16, 22*

Scientific theory: *1, 2, 3, 5, 7, 8, 9, 10, 11, 12, 13, 16, 17, 18, 20, 21, 22, 23, 24*

Social theory: *1, 2, 3, 13, 21, 22, 23, 24*

SPECIFIC APPROACHES

Colonialism and postcolonial studies: *2, 13, 15, 17, 21, 23, 24*

Configurationalism/cultural patterning: *2, 13, 16, 17, 21, 22, 23, 24*

Cultural studies and postmodernism: *24*

Ecological anthropology: *16, 17, 18, 21, 22, 23*

Feminist theory: *3, 13, 18, 23*

Functional approaches: *13, 16, 17, 18, 19, 20, 21, 22, 23, 24*

Humanistic approaches: *1, 2, 13, 21, 22, 23, 24*

Integration and patterning: *2, 3, 13, 15, 17, 21, 22, 23, 24*

Interpretive approaches: *2, 13, 17, 21, 22, 24*

Political-economy and world-system approaches: *2, 3, 13, 15, 16, 17, 18, 21, 23, 24*

Political/legal anthropology and power: *2, 3, 12, 13, 15, 17, 18, 20, 21, 22, 23, 24*
  Conflict: *3, 13, 15, 16, 17, 18, 21, 23, 24*
  Rise and fall of state, theories for: *12, 16, 23*
  Social control: *17, 21, 23, 24*

Practice theory: *2, 8, 13, 23, 24*
  Culture as contested: *2, 3, 13, 15, 18, 21, 23, 24*
  Public and private culture: *2, 17, 21, 22, 23, 24*
  Resistance: *2, 3, 15, 17, 21, 23, 24*

Psychological approaches: *13, 16, 17, 21, 22, 23, 24*

Symbolic approaches: *2, 12, 13, 18, 21, 22, 24*

Systemic approaches: *2, 3, 11, 12, 13, 16, 17, 18, 19, 21, 23, 24*

Theories of social construction: *2, 15, 18, 19, 20, 21, 22, 23, 24*
  Identities: *15, 17, 18, 19, 20, 21, 22, 23, 24*
  Native theories (folk classification): *2, 3, 13, 15, 17, 18, 19, 20, 21, 22*
  Race and ethnicity: *2, 15, 17, 19, 21, 22, 23, 24*
  Social status: *2, 15, 16, 17, 18, 19, 20, 21, 22, 23*